African Statistical Yearbook

Annuaire Statistique pour l'Afrique

2018

Economic Commission for Africa

P.O. Box 3001
Addis Ababa, Ethiopia
Tel: +251 11 551 7200
Fax: +251 11 551 0365
Email: ecainfo@un.org
www.uneca.org

African Development Bank Group

Avenue Joseph Anoma
01 BP 1387
Abidjan 01, Côte d'Ivoire
Tél. (Standard) : +225 20 26 10 20
Email: Statistics@afdb.org
www.afdb.org

African Union Commission

P.O. Box 3243
Roosevelt Street (Old Airport Area)
W21K19 Addis Ababa, Ethiopia
Tel: (251) 11 518 26 74
Fax:(251) 11 551 78 44
Email: austatdivision@africa-union.org
www.au.int

Commission économique pour l'Afrique

P.O. Box 3001 Addis Abeba,
Ethiopie
Tel: +251 11 551 7200
Fax:+251 11 551 0365
Email: ecainfo@un.org
www.uneca.org

Groupe de la Banque africaine de développement

Avenue Joseph Anoma
01 BP 1387
Abidjan 01, Côte d'Ivoire
Tél. (Standard) : +225 20 26 10 20
Email: Statistics@afdb.org
www.afdb.org

Commission de l'Union africaine

P.O. Box 3243
Roosevelt Street (Old Airport Area)
W21K19 Addis Abeba,
Ethiopie
Tel: (251) 11 518 26 74
Fax:(251) 11 551 78 44
Email: austatdivision@africa-union.org
www.au.int

Design/layout by ECA's African Centre for Statistics
Printed in Addis Ababa, Ethiopia by the ECA Printing and Publishing Unit. ISO 14001:2004 certified.
Printed on chlorine free paper.

Print ISSN: 0252-5488
Online ISSN: 2411-9822

ISBN: 978-92-1-025176-1
eISBN: 978-92-1-045179-6
Print ISSN: 0252-5488
Online ISSN: 2411-9822

The African Statistical Yearbook 2018 was prepared under the aegis of the African Statistical Coordination Committee (ASCC) set up by major continental organizations dealing with statistical development, namely: the African Development Bank (AfDB), the African Union Commission (AUC), and the United Nations Economic Commission for Africa (ECA) within the framework of the implementation of the Reference Regional Strategic Framework for Statistical Capacity Building in Africa (RRSF).

It was prepared under the overall guidance of Mr. Oliver J.M. Chinganya, Director, African Centre for Statistics (ACS) of ECA, Dr. Charles Leyeka Lufumpa, Director, the Statistics Department of the AfDB, Dr. René N'Guettia Kouassi, Director, Economic Affairs Department (AUC), and the leadership of Mr. Louis Koua Kouakou, Division Manager at the AfDB, Dr. Leila Ben Ali, Head of Statistics Division at AUC, and Mr. Molla Hunegnaw, Officer-in-Charge, Data Technology Section at ECA.

The joint AfDB-AUC-ECA Technical Team comprised the following personnel. From the AfDB: Mr. Slaheddine Saidi, Mr. Chaouch Anouar, Mr. Christophe Baradandikanya, Mr. Mohamed Ben M'Barek, Mr. Kadisha Mbiya Hilaire, Mr. Maurice Mubila, Ms Amel Kchouk, and Mr. Jerbi Slim. From the ECA: Mr. Negussie Gorfe, Mr. David Boko, Mr. Yared Bekele, Ms. Meaza Bekele, Mr. Tesfaye Belay, Mr. Elias Fisseha, Mr. Gulilat Tesfaye, Mr. Haile Mulualem, Mr. Thomas Sinmegn and Mr. Yonathan Tadesse. From the AUC: Mr. Jose Awong Alene, Mr. Nougbodohoue Samson Bel-Aube, Mr. Yeo Dossina, Mrs Tanteliniana Nomenjanahary, Ms. Selamawit Mussie, Mr. Gildas C. Nzingoula and Mr. Musaemura Guest Charumbira.

The following National Data Focal persons: provided useful data for their respective countries: Benin: Akohonwe D. Marcel, Botswana: Ruth K. Mothibi, Burkina Faso: Nakelse Pascal, Burundi: Nizigiyimana Venerand, Cabo Verde: Danilton Tavares, Chad: Mbaiogoum Tinro, Comoros: Achirafi Youssouf Mbechezi, Cote d'Ivoire: Katchire Serena Michelle, DR Congo: Ntambwe Mpungwe Dieudonne,

L'annuaire statistique pour l'Afrique 2018 a été élaboré sous l'égide du Comité africain de coordination de la statistique (CACS) adopté par les principales organisations du continent en charge du développement de la statistique, à savoir, la Banque africaine de développement (BAD), la Commission de l'union africaine (CUA), et la Commission économique pour l'Afrique des Nations Unies (ECA) dans le cadre de la mise en œuvre du Cadre Stratégique Régional de Référence pour le renforcement des capacités statistiques en Afrique (CSRR).

Il a été conçu sous la direction générale de M. Oliver J.M. Chinganya, Directeur, Centre Africain pour les Statistiques (CAS) de la CEA, de Dr. Charles Leyeka Lufumpa, Directeur du Département des statistiques de la BAD, de Dr. René N'Guettia Kouassi, Directeur du Département des affaires économiques de la CUA et sous la conduite de M. Louis Koua Kouakou, Chef de Division à la BAD, Dr. Leila Ben Ali, Chef de la Division Statistique de la CUA et M. Molla Hunegnaw à la CEA.

L'équipe technique conjointe BAD, CUA, CEA a été composée du personnel suivant. Pour la BAD : M. Slaheddine Saidi , M. Chaouch Anouar , M. Christophe Baradandikanya, M. Mohamed Ben M'Barek, M. Kadisha Mbiya Hilaire, M. Maurice Mubila, Mme Amel Kchouk, et M. Jerbi Slim. Pour la CEA : M. Negussie Gorfe, M. David Boko, M. Yared Bekele , Mme. Meaza Bekele , M. Tesfaye Belay , M. Elias Fisseha, M. Gulilat Tesfaye , M. Haile Mulualem, M. Thomas Sinmegn et M.Yonathan Tadesse. Pour la CUA : M. Jose Awong Alene, M. Nougbodohoue Samson Bel-Aube, M. Yeo Dossina, Mlle Tanteliniana Nomenjanahary, Mme Selamawit Mussie, M. Gildas C. Nzingoula et M. Musaemura Guest Charumbira.

Les Correspondants Nationaux des Données (CND) suivants ont fourni des données pour leur pays : Benin: Akohonwe D. Marcel, Botswana : Ruth K. Mothibi, Burkina Faso: Nakelse Pascal, Burundi: Nizigiyimana Venerand, Cabo Verde: Danilton Tavares, Tchad : Mbaiogoum Tinro, Comoros : Achirafi Youssouf Mbechezi, Cote d'Ivoire : Katchire Serena Michelle, Congo, Rep. Dem : Ntambwe Mpungwe Dieudonne,

Egypt: Ihab Gad, Equatorial Guinea: Ciriaco Edjang Esono, Ethiopia: Dawit Berhanu Mamo, Gabon: Nze Claudia Emeline, Ghana: Edward Asuo Afram, Guinea-Bissau: Mendis Osvaldo Cristo, Guinee: Sayon Oulaye, Kenya: Benjamin Muchiri, Madagascar: Ando Rahasimbelonirina, Maroc: Kada Sakina, Malawi: Lameck Biziweck Million, Mauritania: Mohamed Essaleck, Mauritius: Ramlukon Heemandanee Devi, Mozambique: Felicidade Pires, Namibia: Aloysius Tshechama, Niger: Daouda Baoua Ahamed, Nigeria: Elisha Ajebiyi Fafunmi, Sao Tome et Principe: Fernandes De Freitas Adelino, Senegal: Jean Paul Diagne, Seychelles : Laura Ahtime, Somalia: Abdinasir Roble Abukar, South Sudan: David Chan Thiang, Sudan: Eltuhami Mohamed Ahmed, Swaziland: Hanson Dlamini, Tanzania: Gregory Luxford Elias Millinga, Togo: Telou Tchilabalo, Tunisia: Ouechtali Fethia, Uganda: James Ambayo, Zambia: Joseph Tembo, Zimbabwe: Godfrey Makware.

Egypte : Ihab Gad, Guinée Equatoriale : Ciriaco Edjang Esono, Ethiopie: Dawit Berhanu Mamo, Gabon : Nze Claudi Emeline, Ghana : Edward Asuo Afram, Guinée Bissau : Mendis Osvaldo Cristo, Guinee : Savon Oulaye, Kenya : Benjamin Muchiri, Madagascar : Ando Rahasimbelonirina, Maroc: Kada Sakina, Malawi : Lameck Biziweck Million, Mauritanie : Mohamed Essaleck, Maurice : Ramlukon Heemandanee Devi, Mozambique : Felicidade Pires, Namibie : Aloysius Tshechama, Niger : Daouda Baoua Ahamed, Nigéria : Elisha Ajebiyi Fafunmi, Sao Tome et Principe : Fernandes De Freitas Adelino, Sénégal : Jean Paul Diagne, Seychelles : Laura Ahtime, Somalie: Addinasir Roble Abukar, Soudan du Sud : David Chan Thiang, Soudan : Eltuhami Mohamed Ahmed, Swaziland : Hanson Dlamini, Tanzanie : Gregory Luxford Elias Millinga, Togo : Telou Tchilabalo, Tunisie : Ouechtali Fethia, Ouganda : James Ambayo, Zambia : Joseph Tembo, Zimbabwe : Godfrey Makware.

Table of Contents
Table des matières

Table of Contents
Table des matières
2018

Table of Contents
Table des matières 2018

2018

Foreword
Avant-propos

The African Statistical Yearbook (ASYB) 2018 is the tenth edition jointly produced by the African Development Bank (AfDB), the African Union Commission (AUC) and the United Nations Economic Commission for Africa (ECA). It is a result of the fruitful collaboration that exists among the three pan-African organizations within the field of statistics. This synergistic collaboration has two principal benefits: (1) it minimizes the risk of inconsistent information being produced by the three organizations, and (2) it reduces the reporting burden on member states, who might otherwise be obliged to submit data separately to each institution.

As with the previous eight editions, this 2018 edition presents a time series showing how African countries performed on several economic and social indicators over the period 2009–2017.

As our collective efforts to build the capacity of national statistical systems bear fruit, we are able to use more national data for the country tables, in some cases even to source data directly from online dissemination facilities of national statistical offices (NSOs) – as the custodians of countries' official statistics and coordinators of the National Statistical Systems.

Invariably, there are some data sets that have to be sourced from international organizations that have been designated to compile comparable statistics on specific themes for the whole world, including Africa. Still it is important that such series are confirmed by the countries so that any variations resulting, for instance from methodological differences, are reconciled before compiling the final figures in the ASYB. We have therefore continued to emphasize the importance of involving our member states in the validation process. In that regard, each country received a draft of the country tables to review and correct as necessary. Thereafter, representatives of selected NSOs were convened in a validation workshop for further discussion and clarification of outstanding issues.

Users of this publication may observe differences between figures published here and those published elsewhere. These are unavoidable as a result, for instance, of different release dates and associated stages of the datasets in the compilation process

L'édition 2018 de l'Annuaire Statistique pour l'Afrique (ASA) est la dixième produite conjointement par la Banque Africaine de Développement (BAD), la Commission de l'Union Africaine (CUA) et la Commission Économique des Nations Unies pour l'Afrique (CEA). C'est le fruit du renforcement continu de la collaboration qui existe entre ces trois institutions panafricaines dans le domaine statistique. La production conjointe à travers un mécanisme panafricain donne à cette publication un sceau continental. Cette collaboration permet aux trois institutions de réduire : (1) le risque de publier des données incohérentes sur l'Afrique, et (2) le fardeau sur nos États membres qui, autrement, auraient à soumettre les mêmes données à trois reprises.

Comme les huit éditions précédentes, cette édition 2018 présente des séries temporelles montrant les performances des pays africains dans plusieurs domaines économiques et sociaux sur la période 2009–2017.

Nos efforts collectifs pour renforcer les capacités des systèmes statistiques africains ayant commencé à porter des fruits, nous sommes maintenant en mesure d'utiliser plus de données de sources nationales pour les profils statistiques des pays ; dans certains cas, nous sommes même en mesure de collecter des données directement à partir des systèmes de diffusion en ligne des Instituts Nationaux de la Statistique (INS) – en tant que dépositaires des statistiques officielles des pays et coordinateurs des Systèmes Statistiques Nationaux.

Inévitablement, certaines données doivent être collectées à partir de sources internationales qui ont été mandatées pour produire des statistiques comparables dans des domaines spécifiques pour le monde entier, y compris l'Afrique. Néanmoins, il est important que de telles séries soient confirmées par les pays de telle sorte que toutes les divergences, résultant par exemple de l'application de méthodologies différentes, soient réconciliées avant la diffusion des données définitives dans l'annuaire statistique. Nous avons par conséquent continué à souligner l'importance d'impliquer nos états membres dans le processus de validation. Dans cette optique, chaque pays a reçu une copie de la version initiale de son profil statistique afin d'en faire la revue et de réaliser des corrections le cas échéant. Ensuite, des représentants d'instituts nationaux de la statistique choisis ont été

at the time of the respective releases. As a result of these differences, one may observe apparent discrepancies between values published in the 2017 edition of the ASYB, as member states or international data providers recompute data series based on improved or otherwise revised data points and/or models. Differences may also be observed between data from national sources and those published and disseminated by international organizations due to the fact that the latter may have been adjusted for comparability among countries.

The yearbook continues to serve the intended purpose of bringing together, in one volume, data on African countries for policy-makers, researchers and other users. We are therefore committed to continue producing, jointly, the African Statistical Yearbook on an annual basis. And bearing in mind that the original collection of the statistics takes place at the national level, we shall continue in our efforts, again jointly, to continuously reinforce the capacities of the national structures to produce quality and credible statistics, first for their development needs, and then to feed into appropriate continental and global databases and repositories.

invités à un atelier de validation pour continuer la discussion et apporter des éclaircissements sur des questions en suspens.

Les utilisateurs de cette publication ne manqueront pas d'observer des différences entre les données publiées ici et celles fournies par d'autres sources. Ceci est inévitable en raison, entre autres, des différentes mises à jour des données, tout au long du processus de compilation. Comme résultats de ces différences, l'on peut avoir l'impression qu'il y a des divergences entre les données publiées dans l'édition 2017 de l'annuaire statistique et celles publiées dans la présente édition. Ceci est dû au fait que les pays membres et les fournisseurs internationaux de données recalculent les séries en tenant compte de nouvelles informations et/ou de modèles plus récents. Des différences peuvent aussi apparaître entre les données issues de sources nationales et celles issues de sources internationales car ces dernières ajustent dans certains cas les données pour les rendre comparables sur le plan international.

L'annuaire statistique africain continue de servir sa mission qui est de regrouper en un seul volume des données sur les pays africains à l'usage des décideurs politiques, des chercheurs ainsi que d'autres catégories d'utilisateurs. Nous réaffirmons notre engagement à produire conjointement cette publication sur une base annuelle. Compte tenu du fait que la production de statistiques a lieu essentiellement au niveau national, nous continuerons nos efforts conjoints pour renforcer les capacités des structures nationales afin qu'elles soient en mesure de produire des statistiques fiables et de qualité, d'abord pour leurs propres besoins de développement, ensuite pour alimenter les bases de données continentales et mondiales.

Mr. Oliver J. M. Chinganya
Director
African Centre for Statistics
United Nations Economic
Commission for Africa

Dr. Charles Leyeka Lufumpa
Director
Statistics Department
African Development Bank

Dr. René N'Guettia Kouassi
Director
Economic Affairs Department
African Union Commission

The Yearbook series is a result of joint efforts by major African regional organizations to set up a joint data collection mechanism of socioeconomic data on African countries as well as the development of a common harmonized database. The Joint African Statistical Yearbook is meant to break with the practices of the past where each regional/sub-regional organization was publishing statistical data on African countries of the continent in an inefficient way, leading to duplication of efforts, inefficient use of scarce resources, increased burden on countries and sending different signals to users involved in tracking development efforts on the continent. It is expected that the joint collection and sharing of data between regional institutions will promote wider use of country data, reduce costs and significantly improve the quality of the data and lead to better monitoring of development initiatives on the continent.

The data in this issue of the Yearbook are arranged generally for the years 2009 to 2017 or for the last ten years for which data are available.

The Yearbook is published in one volume consisting of two parts: a set of summary tables followed by country tables.

La série de publication de l'annuaire, est le résultat des efforts conjoints des principales organisations régionales africaines pour disposer d'un mécanisme commun de collecte des données socio-économiques et d'une base de données commune et harmonisée sur les pays africains. L'annuaire statistique commun marque le début d'une rupture avec les pratiques du passé où chaque organisation régionale/sous régionale éditait des données statistiques sur les pays africains d'une manière inefficace. En effet, ces anciennes pratiques conduisaient à la duplication des efforts, à une mauvaise utilisation des ressources rares et à l'accroissement des fardeaux sur les pays. En même temps, elles envoyaient des messages differents aux utilisateurs impliqués dans les efforts de suivi du développement du continent. On s'attend à ce que la collecte et le partage communs des données entre les institutions régionales favorisent une utilisation plus large des données des pays, réduisent leurs coûts d'accès, améliorent de manière significative leur qualité et conduit à un meilleur suivi des initiatives de développement du continent.

Le présent annuaire présente généralement les données sur la période allant de 2009 à 2017 ou sur les dix dernières années pour lesquelles des données sont disponibles.

L'annuaire est édité en un volume composé de deux parties : un ensemble de tableaux synoptiques et un ensemble de profils-pays.

2018

Abbreviations and symbols used
Abréviations et sigles utilisés

Abbreviations and symbols used
Abréviations et sigles utilisés
2018

...	Data not available / Données non disponibles
–	Magnitude zero or less than half of the unit used / Résultats rigoureusement nuls ou inférieurs à la moitié de l'unité utilisée
ACBF	African Capacity Building Foundation / Fondation pour le renforcement des capacités en Afrique
AEO/PEA	African Economic Outlook / Perspectives de l'Économie Africaine
AfDB/BAD	African Development Bank / Banque Africaine de Développement
AfDF/FAD	African Development Fund / Fonds Africain de Développement
AFREC	African Energy Commission / Commission africaine sur l'énergie
ACS/CAS	African Centre for Statistics / Centre Africain pour la Statistique
AUC/CUA	African Union Commission / Commission de l'Union Africaine
ADEA/ADEA	Association for the Development of Education in Africa / Association pour le Développent de l'Education en Afrique
C.I.F./ c.a.f.	Cost, Insurance and Freight / cout, assurance, fret
CPC/CCP	Central Product Classification / Classification Centrale des Produits des Nations Unies
CPI/IPC	Consumer Price Index / Indice des Prix à la Consommation
COMTRADE	United Nations Commodity Trade Statistics Database / Base de données des statistiques du commerce des Nations Unies
ECA/CEA	Economic Commission for Africa / Commission Économique pour l'Afrique
FAO	Food and Agriculture Organisation / Organisation des Nations Unies pour l'Alimentation et l'Agriculture
F. O.B/FAB	Free On Board / Franco à bord
IDA	International Development Association / Association Internationale de Développement
ILO/BIT	International Labor Organization / Bureau International du Travail
IMF/FMI	International Monetary Fund / Fonds Monétaire International
ISIC/CITI	International Standard Industrial Classification / Classification Internationale Type par Industrie
ITU/UIT	International Telecommunication Union / Union Internationale des Télécommunications
M1	Broad Money / Masse monétaire
M2	M1 + quasi money / M1+ «quasi monnaie»
SDGs/ODDs	Sustainable Development Goals / Objectifs de développement durable
ODA/APD	Official Development Assistance / Aide Publique au Développement
SDR/DTS	Special Drawing Rights / Droits de Tirage Spéciaux
SHaSA	Strategy for the Harmonization of Statistics in Africa / Stratégie pour l'Harmonisation des Statistiques en Afrique
SNA/SCN	System of National Accounts / Système de Comptabilité Nationale
UN/ONU	United Nations / Organisation des Nations Unies
UNCTAD/ CNUCED	United Nations Conference on Trade and Development / Conférence des Nations Unies sur le Commerce et le Développement
UNDATA	United Nations Statistical Databases / Bases des données statistiques des Nations Unies
UNESCO	United Nations Educational, Scientific and Cultural Organization / Organisation des Nations Unies pour l'Education, la Science et la Culture
UNPD	United Nations Population Division / Division de la Population des Nations Unies
US/EU	United States / Etats-Unis d'Amérique
WTO/OMC	World Trade Organization / Organisation Mondiale du Commerce

2018

General notes
Notes générales

The Statistics presented in the yearbook are, as possible in accordance with international recommendations and definitions. Where important deviations are known to exist, they are indicated in footnotes at the end of each country's table. Owing to the rounding of figures, the totals shown in tables do not always correspond exactly to the sum of their component items.

The sources of the data reported in this publication, consist of filled questionnaires from national data focal persons, national publications, national websites, national databases. International sources have been used to supplement missing data as well as for those variables solely produced by none national sources. Owing to variations in definition for some indicators, data presented in summary pages may be cited from international sources when comparing the data across countries.

I. SOCIAL AND DEMOGRAPHIC INDICATORS

Population

Mid-year population
Unless otherwise stated, the figures shown relate to de facto population. Population (Urban) refers to the number of persons living in areas defined as urban according to national definitions of this concept. Since national definitions differ, cross-country comparisons should be made with care.

Migration
The data component of the Joint Labour Migration Programme (JLMP) seeks to enhance collection, exchange, and utilization of gender and age disaggregated data on migrants' economic activity, employment skills, education, working conditions and social protection. The data collected in this section are coming from National Statistics Offices of the AU Member States.

Average annual growth rate
The number of people added to (or subtracted from) a population in a year due to natural increase and net migration expressed as a percentage of the population at the beginning of the time period.
Average annual population growth is the exponential rate of growth of midyear population from year t-1 to t, expressed as a percentage.

Crude birth rate
Number of births over a given period divided by the person-years lived by the population over that period. It is expressed as number of births per 1,000 population.

Crude death rate
Number of deaths over a given period divided by the person-years lived by the population over that period. It is expressed as number of deaths per 1,000 population.

Population by age groups
Three age groups are used in order to highlight the proportion of active population vis-à-vis the dependant population. Population aged 15-64 is the number of people who could potentially be economically active, excluding children.

Economically active population
The economically active population comprises all employed and unemployed persons (including those seeking jobs for the first time). It covers employers, persons working on their own account, salaried employees, wage earners, unpaid family workers, and members of producers' co-operatives and members of the armed forces.

Life expectancy
Life expectancy at birth is the average number of years a new-born infant would live if prevailing patterns of mortality of the total population at the time of his/her birth were to stay the same throughout his/her life.

Net reproduction rate
The net reproduction rate is the average number of daughters that would be born to a woman if she passed through her lifetime conforming to the age -specific fertility and mortality rates of a given year. This rate is similar to the gross reproduction rate but takes into account that some women will die before completing their childbearing years.

Total fertility rate

The total fertility rate is the average number of children that would be born per woman if she experiences no mortality and were subject to a given set of age-specific fertility throughout her lifetime.

Health

Percentage of mothers provided at least one antenatal care

Antenatal care coverage (at least one visit) is the percentage of women aged 15–49 with a live birth in a given time period that received antenatal care provided by skilled health personnel at least once during their pregnancy.

Percentage of deliveries attended by skilled health personnel

Percentage of births attended by skilled health personnel (doctors, nurses or midwives) is the percentage of deliveries attended by health personnel trained in providing lifesaving obstetric care, including giving the necessary supervision, care and advice to women during pregnancy, labour and the post-partum period; conducting deliveries on their own; and caring for new-borns. Traditional birth attendants, even if they receive a short training course, are not included.

Births registered (%)

The percent of births registered during a specified time period for a country or designated region.

Deaths registered (%)

The percent of deaths registered during a specified time period for a country.

Physicians (per 10 000 population)

Practising physicians, practising general practitioners, practising specialists refers to the number of physicians, general practitioners and specialists (including self-employed) who are actively practicing medicine in public and private institutions. The data should exclude dentists, stomatologists, qualified physicians who are working abroad, working in administration, research and industry positions. Data should include foreign physicians licensed to practice and actively practicing medicine in the country. Data should be calculated to represent full-time equivalents.

Nurses (per 10 000 population)

Nurses refers to the total number of nurses certified or registered and who actively practicing in public and private hospitals, clinics and other health facilities, including self-employed. Nursing assistants and midwives should be included. Data should exclude nurses who are working abroad, working in administrative, research and industry positions.
The figures for physicians and nurses relate to those registered at the government offices.

Hospital beds - Total (per 10 000 population)

The number of hospital beds is calculated for public and private hospitals.

Percentage of children provided the vaccines (BCG, DPT3, Polio, Measles)

Child immunization measures the percentage of children ages 12-23 months who received specific vaccinations before 12 months or at any time. A child is considered adequately immunized against measles after receiving one dose of vaccine.
A child is considered adequately immunized against:

- diphtheria, pertussis (or whooping cough), and tetanus (DPT) after receiving three doses of vaccine;
- measles after receiving one dose of measles vaccine;
- tuberculosis after receiving Bacille Calmette-Guérin vaccine (BCG);
- Polio after receiving the three doses of polio vaccine.

Access to safe water

It is measured by the number of people who have a reasonable means of getting an adequate amount of clean water, expressed as a percentage of the total population.

Education

Student enrolment at specific level

First level student enrolment is the number of pupils enrolled at the primary level of education, regardless of age. Second level student Enrolment is the total number of students enrolled at the secondary level of education, regardless of age.

Adult illiteracy rate
Percentage of persons aged 15 and over who cannot read and write.

Pupil-teacher ratio
Pupil-teacher ratio is the average number of pupils (students) per teacher at a specific level of education in a given school-year.

Gender parity index
Gross rate of Registration on the Girls Boys, expressed as having a value of one when there is gender parity. Parity index between gender (PIG) measures progress in achieving gender parity in education participation and / or learning opportunities available to women compared to those available to men. This is a comparison of values assigned to women and men for a given indicator in a given year. It also reflects the level of development of women in society.
This indicator should be disaggregated by level of education (pre-primary, primary and secondary).

II. NATIONAL ACCOUNTS

This section provides information on national accounts. National accounts data provide essential information on the economic performance of African countries in terms of growth and structure of output, capital information, consumption and savings. National accounts data are obtained from various national sources and supplemented with data from international sources such as the UN Yearbook of National accounts, estimated data from AfDB and ECA African Centre for Statistics estimates and AUC Database as well. Where necessary, official figures have been adjusted to conform to the System of National Accounts (SNA). Many countries continue to compile their national accounts in accordance with the 1993 SNA, but more and more are adopting the 2008 SNA. A few countries still use concepts and classifications from older SNA guidelines, including valuations at factor cost and outdated industrial classifications, in

describing major economic aggregates. Therefore, the tables presented in the yearbook are the result of compromising with these circumstances.

Gross Domestic Product (GDP)
Gross Domestic Product is an aggregate measure of production equal to the sum of the gross values added of all resident institutional units engaged in production (plus any taxes, and minus any subsidies, on products not included in the value of their outputs).

GDP by kind of economic activity
GDP by kind of economic activity gives value-added by the broad categories of the ISIC classification. Value added is evaluated at basic prices or factor costor at producer prices depending on the current practice in the country. Data is provided at current prices and in terms of growth rates over the previous year based on data at constant prices.

Expenditure on GDP

General Government final consumption
General Government final consumption expenditure comprises all current expenditure for purchases of goods and services by all levels of government, as well as capital expenditure on national defence and security.

Private final consumption
Household final consumption expenditure represents the final consumption of households and non-profit institutions. It includes imputed rent for owner-occupied dwellings but excludes purchases of dwellings and it also includes any statistical discrepancy.

Gross capital formation
Gross capital formation consists of gross domestic fixed capital formation plus net changes in the level of inventories.

Exports and imports of goods and services
Exports and imports of goods and services refer to the value of goods and non-factor services provided to or from the rest of the world. They do not include receipts and payments for factor services such as

investment income, interest and labour income. The data are generally estimated on the basis of foreign trade statistics and are not directly comparable with those from the balance of payments.

III. INFLATION

Inflation is commonly measured by the annual percent changes in Consumer price index. Consumer price index (CPI) shows the cost of acquisition of a basket of goods and services purchased by the average consumer. Weights for the computation of the index numbers are obtained from household budget surveys. CPI data are provided by the national statistical systems, mainly by the national bureau of statistics or Central banks.

IV. AGRICULTURAL PRODUCTION

Agricultural production
The data on major crops produced is obtained from the National Statistical Offices of the following countries; Burkina Faso, Burundi, Cameroon, Congo, Côte d'Ivoire, Democratic Republic of Congo, Gabon, Gambia, Guinea-Bissau, Kenya, Lesotho, Madagascar, Malawi, Mali, Mauritania, Mauritius, Morocco, Mozambique, Nigeria, Senegal, Sudan, Swaziland, Zambia, and Zimbabwe. For the remaining countries the data is obtained from the online database of the Food and Agricultural Organization (FAO). For those countries, the five major crops per country are obtained by calculating the average yearly production of each crop produced by a given country (considering only years when the crop is produced); and ranking it in descending order.

Agricultural and food production index
The various indices of agricultural production illustrate the relative level of the aggregate volume of agricultural production for each year, in comparison with the base period 2004-2006. These indices of agricultural production obtained from the FAO online database are computed using the Laspeyres formula, using the price weighted sum of the production of various commodities less seed and feed. The price used for weighting the production quantity of each commodity is the average price during the years indicated as the base year.

V. MINING PRODUCTION

The sources of the data reported are national statistical offices (for those countries for which the AfDB, AUC and ECA questionnaire was sent), the United Nations Industrial Commodity Database accessed through UNDATA (at http://data.un.org/) and the United Nations Industrial Commodity Yearbook. Data for some of the minerals were also obtained from British Geological Survey, and the United States Geological Survey website.

Mining production
For a details description of the minerals included in this publication, the user may refer to the Central Product Classification (CPC) Ver.1.1, Statistical Papers, Series M, No.77, Ver.1.1 (United Nations publication, Sales No. E.03.XVII.3). It was difficult to identify the three major commodities for each country because of the reference period being too narrow and commodities varying from one country to another. First, we obtained the export values of minerals for the years 2005 through 2013. We then considered the average value (considering only years when the commodity is available) to help us decide which commodity to include in the publication. In addition, we decided to choose strategic commodities (such as oil, gas and diamonds) when the country is produces them.

VI. ENERGY

The data provided for this section are mainly from the African Energy Commission (AFREC) based in Algers and missing data are supplemented from United Nations Energy Statistical Yearbook and the Energy Database which could be accessed through UNDATA (at http://data.un.org/),.

Electricity production
The figures reported for production refer to gross generation of electricity, which include the consumption by station auxiliaries and any losses in transformers as well as electricity generated by pumping stations without deducting the electric energy consumed by the pumps. The production of electricity could fall into public utilities, whose primary purpose is to generate and transmit electric energy for

use by the public, and self-producers, undertakings which produce electric energy intended, in whole or in part, for their own uses.

VII. TOURISM AND INFRASTRUCTURE

Tourism

Data on Tourism have been primarily collected from National sources, and where national sources are not available, from the online databases UNWTO and Tourism Decision Metrics of Tourism Economics.

The indicators published are the number of arrivals in the country, the number of hotel rooms, overnight stays, tourism receipts, Tourism total contribution to GDP and Tourism total contribution to employment. The number of tourists to a country, unless otherwise stated, refers to all persons (checked at the frontier) travelling for pleasure, health, business, meetings or studies and stopping in that country for twenty-four hours or more. The figures exclude immigrants and residents in a frontier zone.

Infrastructure

Paved road (% of total)

Paved roads are those surfaced with crushed stone (macadam) and hydrocarbon binder or bituminized agents, with concrete, or with cobblestones, as a percentage of all the country's roads, measured in length.

Total network (Railways-km)

Rail lines are the length of railway route available for train service, irrespective of the number of parallel tracks.

Main telephone Lines

Telephone lines are fixed telephone lines that connect a subscriber's terminal equipment to the public switched telephone network and that have a port on a telephone exchange. Integrated services digital network channels and fixed wireless subscribers are included.

Mobile cellular subscribers

Mobile cellular telephone subscriptions are subscriptions to a public mobile telephone service using cellular technology, which provide access to the public switched telephone network. Post-paid and prepaid subscriptions are included.

VIII. FINANCIAL AND MONETARY STATISTICS

Monetary statistics

Data for this section are essentially obtained from the IMF International Financial Statistics Database and National Central Banks.

Money supply (M1)

Money supply comprises transferable deposits and currency outside deposit money banks.

Quasi money

Quasi money comprises time, savings and foreign currency deposits.

Net foreign assets

Net foreign assets equal the sum of foreign assets, less the sum of foreign liabilities of monetary authorities and deposit money banks.

Domestic credit

Domestic credit includes all domestic assets of the banking system. It is the sum of claims on the central government (net), on official entities and the private sector. Credit to the private sector is shown separately but as a subset of domestic credit.

International reserves

International reserves consist of the country's holding of monetary gold, Special Drawing Rights (SDRs) and foreign exchange, as well as its reserve position in the International Monetary Fund (IMF).

Exchange rates

Exchange rates expressed in national currency unit per US dollar unit are reported as end period and period averages of market exchange rates and official rates. The market rate is defined as the rate determined largely by market forces; and the official rate is that determined by the authorities.

Public Finance

Data for this section have been primarily collected from National Authorities such as National Statistics Offices, Ministries of Finance and Central Banks; and where national sources are not available; data from IMF publications (Country Reports) are used.

For countries: Botswana, Egypt, Ethiopia, Kenya, Malawi, Mauritius, Namibia, South Africa and Swaziland, the data were compiled following their respective fiscal period as annual data. Therefore, the years 2006 – 2014 represent the ending calendar year according to the fiscal period of each country.

Revenue and grants

It includes all non-repayable receipts, requited and unrequited, current and capital, and non-compulsory, non-repayable, unrequited receipts from other governments (domestic or foreign) and international institutions.

Tax revenue

It includes compulsory, unrequited, non-repayable contributions exacted by a government for public purposes.

Non-tax revenue

It includes requited receipts from property incomes, fees and charges, non-industrial and incidental sales, the cash operating surpluses of departmental enterprises and unrequited receipts such as fines, forfeits and current private donations.

Grants

Unrequited, non-repayable, non-compulsory government receipts from other governments or international institutions.

Expenditure and net lending

IIt includes all non-repayable payments by government, whether requited or unrequited and whether current or capital, as well as government transactions in debt and equity claims upon others acquired for purposes of public policy.

Current expenditure

It includes all non-repayable payments by government, whether requited or unrequited, other than capital expenditure or grants.

Capital expenditure

Expenditure for acquisition of fixed capital assets, stocks, land or intangible assets plus unrequited transfers for the purpose of permitting the recipient to acquire such assets. In order to be classified as a capital asset, an asset acquired must exceed a minimum value and be intended for use for more than one year in the process of production.

Net lending

Net lending (lending minus repayments) comprises government transactions in claims upon others acquired for purposes of public policy rather than for management of government liquidity or earning a return. It covers both debt and equities and both payments and receipts.

Fiscal Balance

Fiscal balance or Government overall surplus/deficit is defined as total revenue and grants received less total expenditure and net lending.

Balance of Payments

The Balance of payments is a statistical statement that summarizes, for a specific period, the economic transactions of an economy with the rest of the world. Transactions for the most part between residents and non-residents consist of those involving goods, services, and income; those involving financial claims on, and liabilities to, the rest of the world; and those classified as transfers which involve offsetting entries to balance, in an accounting sense, one-sided transactions. Data in this section are obtained from African Central Banks and where data are not available from national sources or if country data do not meet the required quality, IMF Country Reports are also used. Data from international sources relate to the following countries: Equatorial Guinea, Liberia, Lesotho, Sierra Leone, and Libya.

Trade balance
Trade balance is equal to exports less imports of goods, both measured on the « free-on-board » (f.o.b.) basis that is, by the value of the goods at the border of the exporting country. Goods cover general merchandise, goods for processing, repairs on goods, goods procured in ports by carriers, and non-monetary gold.

Services balance
Services include transportation (freight and passenger transportation); travel; communication services; construction services; insurance services; financial services; computer and information services; royalties and license fees; personal, cultural, and recreational services; government services. Service Balance is defined as exports minus imports of services.

Net income
Income includes compensation of employees which covers wages, salaries, and other benefits; investment income which consist of direct investment income, portfolio investment income and other investment income. Net income is income received from investments abroad less income paid to foreigners investing in the country.

Compensation of employees
Compensation of employee's includes salaries, wages, salaries paid by non-resident employers to their resident employees and vice versa.

Investment Income
Investment income covers direct investment income, portfolio investment income (equity and debt) and other investment income (interest from other financial transactions).

Current transfers
Current transfers consist of all transfers that do not involve: (i) transfers of ownership of fixed asset s; (ii) transfers of funds linked to acquisition or disposal of fixed assets; (iii) forgiveness, without any counterparts being received in return, of liabilities by creditors.

Net official transfers
It comprises net transfer payment between governments of the reporting country and the rest of the world

Workers' remittances
Workers' remittances return amounts transferred abroad by resident workers and vice versa.

Other private transfers
Other private transfers comprise net transfer payments between private persons and non-official organizations of the reporting country and the rest of the world that carry no provisions for repayments.

Current account balance
Current account balance is the sum of net exports of goods and services, net income, and net current transfers.

Capital account
The capital account covers international capital transfers (e.g. debt forgiveness) and the acquisition/disposal of non-produced, nonfinancial assets (such as patents).

Financial account
The financial account deals with transactions involving financial claims on, or liabilities to, the rest of the world, including international purchases of securities, such as stocks and bonds.

Errors & omissions
Net Errors & omissions are derived residually as the difference between total of receipts and payments (both current and capital together with the financial account)

Overall balance
The balance of payments is a record of a country's

international transactions with the rest of the world. Transactions are organized in two different accounts, the current account and the capital and financial account.

External debt and Financial Flows

Data in this section are mainly obtained from the following international sources: IMF World Economic Outlook database, OECD Online Database and UNCTAD online database. However, few countries have submitted their data and they are published in this edition of the Year book. The purpose of the yearbook is to include data from national sources to the extent possible when the data quality is acceptable. Data from national sources relate to the following countries: Benin, Burkina Faso, Cameroon, Equatorial Guinea, Lesotho, and Niger.

External debt

External Debt (total outstanding debt) is the amount, at any given time, of disbursed and outstanding contractual liabilities of residents of a country to non-residents to repay principal, with or without interest, or to pay interest with or without principal. It is the sum of public and publicly-guaranteed short and long-term debt, private non-guaranteed short and long-term debt and the use of IMF credit.

External debt service

Total External Debt service is the sum of principal repayments and interest actually made. It is debt service payment on short and long term debt (public and publicly-guaranteed and private non-guaranteed) and the use of IMF credit.

Present value of external debt

Present value of debt is the sum of short-term external debt plus the discounted sum of total debt service payments due on public, publicly guaranteed, and private nonguaranteed long-term external debt over the life of existing loans.

Total government Domestic debt

The Total Government Domestic debt consists of liabilities that owed by a country's citizens and government.

Foreign direct investment

Foreign direct investment refers to investment made to acquire or add to a lasting management interest (usually 10 percent of voting stock) enterprise operating in a country other than that of the investor. It is the sum of equity capital, reinvestment of earnings and other shorthand long-term capital as shown in the balance of payments.

Official development assistance

ODA relates to grants or concessional loans (i.e. with a grant element of at least 25 percent), undertaken by the official sector, whose main objective is the promotion of economic development and welfare. Data in this section are net disbursements of ODA.

IX. EXTERNAL TRADE

Data for this section are mainly obtained from national sources. This is the case for the following countries: Algeria, Benin, Burkina Faso, Burundi, Cameroon, Côte d'Ivoire, Egypt, Ethiopia, The Gambia, Guinea-Bissau, Kenya, Malawi, Mali, Morocco, Mozambique, Namibia, Niger, Nigeria, Rwanda, Sudan, Swaziland, Tanzania, Togo, Zambia and Zimbabwe. Where national data were not available, we have used the United Nations UNCTAD online database. The major Export and Import commodities have been selected by the reporting countries themselves. For the data obtained from UNCTAD the harmonized system (rev1) classification is used to determine the list of main exports and imports commodities. Unless otherwise indicated the import statistics are reported on CIF valuation base while exports are reported on FOB.

Les statistiques présentées dans cet Annuaire sont, autant que possible, conformes aux recommandations et définitions internationales. Lorsque des divergences importantes sont connues, elles sont indiquées dans les notes figurant à la fin du tableau de chaque pays concerné. A cause des chiffres arrondis, les totaux indiqués dans certains tableaux ne correspondent pas toujours exactement à la somme de leurs composantes.

I. INDICATEURS SOCIAUX ET DÉMOGRAPHIQUES

Population

Les données présentées dans cette section sont tirées principalement des publications: «Perspectives d'avenir de la population mondiale, estimations et projections», «Perspectives d'Urbanisation Mondiale» de la Division de la Population du Secrétariat de l'ONU, «Estimations et Projections de la Main d'Œuvre, 1980-2020» du Bureau International du Travail (BIT). Les sources nationales ont été utilisées pour compléter les données non disponibles, dans la mesure où elles étaient comparables aux séries de l'ONU.

Population en milieu d'année

Sauf indication contraire, les chiffres indiqués se rapportent à la population de fait. La population urbaine est le nombre des personnes vivant dans les zones considérées comme urbaines selon les définitions de ce concept dans chaque pays. Etant donné que cette définition varie quelque peu d'un pays à un autre, la prudence s'impose lorsqu'on procède à des comparaisons entre pays.

Migration

La composante données du Programme conjoint sur les migrations de main-d'œuvre vise à améliorer la collecte, l'échange et l'utilisation de données ventilées par sexe et par âge sur l'activité économique des migrants, leurs compétences professionnelles, leur éducation, leurs conditions de travail et leur protection sociale. Les données collectées dans cette section proviennent des bureaux nationaux de statistiques des États membres de l'UA.

Taux de croissance annuel moyen

Le nombre de personnes ajouté (ou soustrait) à une population en un an en raison de l'accroissement naturel et la migration nette exprimé en pourcentage de la population au début de la période de référence. La croissance annuelle moyenne de la population est le taux de croissance exponentielle de la population en milieu d'année de l'année t-1 à t, exprimée en pourcentage.

Taux brut de natalité

Nombre de naissances sur une période donnée divisé par la population totale moyenne au cours de cette période. Il est exprimé en nombre de naissances pour 1000 habitants.

Taux brut de mortalité

Nombre de décès sur une période donnée divisé par la population totale moyenne au cours de cette période. Il est exprimé en nombre de décès pour 1000 habitants.

Groupes d'âges

Trois groupes d'âge sont utilisés dans le but de mettre en lumière la proportion du groupe d'âge actif par rapport aux dépendants. La population âgée de 15-64 ans est le nombre de personnes qui peuvent potentiellement être économiquement actives, et exclut les enfants.

Population économiquement active

La population active comprend toutes les personnes employées ou non (y compris celles qui sont à la recherche de leur premier emploi). Elle comprend les employeurs, les travailleurs indépendants, les salariés, les rentiers, les travailleurs familiaux non rémunérés, les membres des coopératives de producteurs et ceux des forces armées.

Espérance de vie, taux bruts de natalité et de mortalité

L'espérance de vie à la naissance indique le nombre moyen d'années que vivrait un nouveau-né si les tendances de la mortalité observées pour l'ensemble de la population au moment de sa naissance restaient inchangées tout au long de sa vie. Les taux bruts de natalité et de mortalité représentent respectivement le nombre annuel moyen de naissances et de décès pour 1000 habitants. La mortalité est le fait d'une disparition permanente de toute évidence de vie, à tout moment, après que la naissance ait eu lieu. Cette définition exclut les morts nés.

Taux net de reproduction

Le taux net de reproduction est le nombre moyen de filles qui seraient nés d'une femme si elle a traversé sa vie conformément à la fécondité spécifique par âge et au taux de mortalité pour une année donnée.

Ce taux est similaire au taux brut de reproduction, mais prend en compte le fait que certaines femmes mourront avant d'avoir terminé leurs années de procréation.

Indice synthétique de fécondité

L'indice synthétique de fécondité est le nombre moyen de naissances qu'une femme soumise à un ensemble de fécondités spécifiques par âge, pourrait avoir au cours de sa période de procréation.

Santé

Pourcentage de mères ayant reçu au moins un soin prénatal

La couverture des soins prénataux (au moins une visite) est le pourcentage de femmes de 15-49 ans, avec une naissance vivante dans une période de temps donnée, qui a reçu des soins prénataux dispensés par un personnel de santé qualifié au moins une fois pendant leur grossesse.

Pourcentage d'accouchements assistés par du personnel de santé qualifié

Pourcentage d'accouchements assistés par un personnel de santé qualifié (médecins, infirmiers ou sages-femmes) est le pourcentage d'accouchements assistés par du personnel de santé qualifié dans la pratique des soins obstétricaux vitaux (y compris les contrôles nécessaires, les soins et les conseils aux femmes pendant la grossesse, le travail et la période post partum), des accouchements; et des soins aux nouveau-nés. Les accoucheuses traditionnelles, même si elles reçoivent une formation de courte durée, ne sont pas incluses.

Naissances enregistrées (%)

C'est le pourcentage des naissances enregistrées au cours d'une période de temps spécifiée pour un pays ou une région désignée.

Décès enregistrés (%)

C'est le pourcentage des décès enregistrés pendant une période de temps spécifiée pour un pays.

Les médecins (pour 10 000 habitants)

Les médecins (pour 10 000 habitants), se réfèrent se réfèrent au nombre de médecins, généralistes et spécialistes (y compris les travailleurs indépendants) qui pratiquent activement la médecine dans les établissements publics ou privés. Les données devraient exclure les dentistes, les stomatologues, les médecins qualifiés qui travaillent à l'étranger, ou qui occupent des postes dans l'administration, dans l'industrie ou dans recherche. Les données devraient inclure des médecins étrangers autorisés à exercer et à pratiquer activement la médecine dans le pays. Les données doivent être calculées pour représenter l'équivalent du temps plein de travail.

Les infirmiers (pour 10 000 habitants)

Les infirmières se réfère au nombre total d'infirmiers certifiés ou enregistrés et qui exercent activement dans les hôpitaux publics et privés, les cliniques et autres établissements de santé, y compris les travailleurs indépendants. Les infirmiers auxiliaires et sages-femmes devraient être inclus. Les données devraient exclure les infirmiers qui travaillent à l'étranger, qui travaillent dans des postes administratifs, la recherche et dans l'industrie.

Les chiffres pour les médecins et les infirmiers se rapportent à ceux enregistrés dans les bureaux du gouvernement.

Les lits d'hôpitaux - total (pour 10 000 habitants)

Le nombre de lits d'hôpitaux se calcule pour les hôpitaux publics et privés.

Pourcentage d'enfants ayant reçu les vaccins (BCG, DTC3, polio, rougeole)

La vaccination des enfants mesure le pourcentage des enfants âgés de 12 à 23 mois qui ont reçu certains vaccins spécifiques avant 12 mois après. Un enfant est considéré suffisamment immunisé contre la rougeole après avoir reçu une dose de vaccin.

Un enfant est considéré suffisamment immunisé contre :

- la diphtérie, la coqueluche et le tétanos (DCT) après avoir reçu trois doses de vaccin;
- la rougeole après avoir reçu une dose de vaccin contre la rougeole ;
- la tuberculose après avoir reçu le Bacille Calmette-Guérin (BCG);
- la poliomyélite après la troisième dose du vaccin de la polio.

Accès à l'eau potable

Elle est mesurée par le nombre de personnes qui ont un moyen raisonnable d'obtenir une quantité suffisante d'eau potable, exprimée en pourcentage de la population totale.

Education

Les sources des données sur l'éducation présentées dans cette publication sont les publications nationales et l'Annuaire statistique de l'UNESCO. Les données présentées portent en général sur les écoles de l'Etat (publiques) et les écoles indépendantes (privées). Les années indiquées se rapportent au commencement de l'année scolaire. Sont exclus la formation des adultes, les stages d'apprentissage et les cours par correspondance. Compte tenu des différences des systèmes scolaires, la comparaison des données présentées est sujette à caution.

Elèves inscrits selon le degré

La scolarisation dans le premier degré est le nombre d'enfants de tous âges inscrits à l'école primaire. La scolarisation dans le second degré est le nombre d'élèves de tous âges inscrits dans le cycle d'enseignement secondaire.

Taux d'analphabétisme des adultes

C'est le pourcentage des adultes âgés de plus de 15 ans qui ne savent ni lire ni écrire.

Ratio élèves-enseignants

Le rapport elèves-enseignants est le nombre moyen d'élèves (étudiants) par enseignant dans un degré d'enseignement déterminé dans une année scolaire donnée.

Indice de Parité de Genre

Le taux Brut d'Inscription des Filles relatif à celui des Garçons, prend la valeur un quand il y a parité entre les genres. L'indice de parité entre les genres (GPI) mesure les progrès effectués dans la réalisation de la parité de genre dans la participation à l'éducation et/ou aux opportunités d'apprentissage offertes aux femmes par rapport à celles offertes aux hommes. Il s'agit d'une comparaison entre des valeurs attribuées aux femmes et aux hommes pour un indicateur donné au cours d'une année donnée. Il reflète aussi le niveau d'épanouissement des femmes dans la société. Cet indicateur doit être désagrégé par niveau d'enseignement (enseignement pré-primaire, primaire et secondaire).

II. COMPTES NATIONAUX

Cette section présente des informations sur la comptabilité nationale. Les données de la comptabilité nationale fournissent des indications essentielles sur la performance économique des pays africains en termes de croissance et de structure de production, d'investissement et d'épargne. Les données de la comptabilité nationale proviennent de diverses sources nationales et sont complétées par d'autres sources internationales telles que l'Annuaire de Comptabilité nationale de l'ONU , les estimations de la BAD et du Centre africain pour la statistique de la CEA et la Base de données de la CUA. Les chiffres officiels ont été ajustés en fonction du Système de Comptabilité Nationale (SCN) quand cela s'est avéré nécessaire. De nombreux pays continuent d'élaborer La majorité des pays membres régionaux élaborent leur comptes nationaux selon les recommandations du SCN 1993. Ceci étant, certains pays sont en train de migrer vers le SCN 2008. Concepts provenant des anciennes recommandations du SCN incluant la comptabilisation des agrégats économiques aux coûts des facteurs.

Produit intérieur brut (PIB)

Le produit intérieur brut est une mesure globale de la production qui est égale à la somme des valeurs ajoutées brutes de toutes les unités institutionnelles résidentes engagées dans le processus de production (plus les taxes indirects/impôt sur les produit et moins les subventions).

Le PIB par branche d'activité

Le PIB par secteur donne la valeur ajoutée pour les grandes catégories de la classification CITC. La valeur ajoutée est évaluée aux prix de base ou aux coûts des facteurs ou encore au prix du producteur selon la pratique en vigueur du pays. Les données nominales sur les valeurs ajoutées sont fournies aux prix courants et les taux de croissance annuels pour chaque catégorie sont calculés à partir des données à prix constants.

Emplois du PIB

La consommation finale des administrations publiques

La consommation finale des administrations publiques comprend toutes les dépenses courantes consacrées à l'achat de biens et de services par les administrations de tous les niveaux, ainsi que les dépenses en capital au titre de la défense et de la sécurité nationale.

La consommation finale privée

La consommation finale privée représente la consommation finale des ménages et des institutions à but non lucratif. Elle ne comprend pas les achats de logement mais elle inclut le loyer imputé des logements occupés par leur propriétaire. Elle comprend aussi tout écart statistique.

La formation brute de capital

La formation brute de capital comprend les dépenses consacrées à l'accroissement du capital fixe de l'économie, majorées des variations nettes du niveau des stocks.

Les exportations et importations de biens et services

Les exportations et importations de biens et services représentent la valeur des biens et services non facteurs fournis au reste du monde ou reçus de celui-ci. La valeur des revenus et des paiements des services facteurs comme le produit des placements, les intérêts et le revenu du travail, en est exclue. Les données sont généralement estimées sur la base des statistiques du commerce extérieur et ne sont pas directement comparables à celles de la balance des paiements.

III. INFLATION

L'inflation est mesurée par la variation moyenne annuelle de l'Indice des Prix à la Consommation (IPC). L'IPC montre le coût d'acquisition par un consommateur moyen d'un panier de biens et services. Les coefficients de pondération pour le calcul des indices sont obtenus à partir d'enquêtes sur les dépenses des ménages. Les données de l'IPC proviennent des systèmes statistiques nationaux, et essentiellement des Instituts nationaux de statistique ou des Banques centrales.

IV. PRODUCTION AGRICOLE

Production agricole

Les données sur les principales productions agricoles sont obtenues via les instituts nationaux de statistiques des pays suivants : Burkina Faso, Burundi, Cameroun, Congo, Côte d'Ivoire, République démocratique du Congo, Gabon, Gambie, Guinée-Bissau, Kenya, Lesotho, Madagascar, Malawi, Mali, Mauritanie, île Maurice, Maroc, Mozambique, Nigeria, Sénégal, Soudan, Swaziland, Zambie, et Zimbabwe. Pour les autres mettre une virgule données sont tirées de la base de données en ligne de l'Organisation pour l'Alimentation et l'Agriculture (FAO). Pour ces pays, les cinq principales productions agricoles sont obtenues en calculant la production annuelle moyenne de chaque produit du pays (seules les années où le produit est récolté sont retenues) et en rangeant ces productions par ordre décroissant

Indices de la production agricole et alimentaire

Les différents indices de la production agricole illustrent le niveau du volume global de production agricole chaque année, relativement à la période de base 2004-2006. Ces indices sont obtenus à partir de la base de données en ligne de la FAO et calculés en utilisant la formule de la formule de Laspeyres, en utilisant la somme pondérée pondérée par les prix des productions des différents produits hors semences et graines d'alimentation. Le prix utilisés pour pondérer la quantité de chaque produit est le prix moyen au cours des années de référence.

V. PRODUCTION MINIERE

Les sources des données présentées sont soit : les instituts nationaux de statistiques, pour les pays auxquels le questionnaire conjoint BAD - CUA – CEA a été envoyé, soit : la base des données sur les produits industriels des Nations Unies, accessible via UNDATA (à http://data.un.org/) ou l'annuaire des produits industriels des Nations Unies. Pour certains minerais, les données ont également été obtenues à partir de l'enquête géologique britannique et sur le site internet de l'enquête géologique des Etats-Unis.

Production minière

Pour les descriptions détaillées des produits miniers inclus dans cette publication, le lecteur peut se référer à la Classification Centrale des Produits (CCP), Papiers statistiques, Séries M, N077, Ver 1.1 (Publication des Nations Unies, Ventes N0. E.03.XVII.3). Il était difficile d'identifier les trois principaux produits puisque la période de référence était très variable et courte pour plusieurs produits et aussi les produits varient d'un pays à un autre. Dans un premier temps, nous avons obtenu les valeurs des exportations des produits miniers pour les années 2005 à 2013. Nous avons ensuite calculé la valeur moyenne (en ne considerant que les années où le produit est disponible), afin de choisir les produits à inclure dans cette publication. Finalement, nous avons décidé de choisir les produits stratégiques (tels que le pétrole, le gaz et le diamant) lorsque le pays continue de les produire.

VI. ENERGIE

Les sources des données publiées proviennent de l'Annuaire statistique sur l'énergie des Nations Unies et de la base de données sur l'énergie accessible à travers UNDATA (http://data.un.org) et aussi de la Commission africaine sur l'Energie (AFREC).

Production d'électricité

Les chiffres publiés pour la production sont relatifs à la production brute d'électricité, qui inclut la consommation des stations auxiliaires et toutes pertes dans la transformation et aussi l'électricité produite par les stations de pompage sans déduction de l'énergie consommée par ces mêmes pompes. La production d'électricité comprend, d'une part, les installations publiques, dont le but primaire est la génération et la transmission de l'énergie électrique pour la consommation publique, et d'autre part, les producteurs privés qui produisent l'énergie électrique, totalement ou en partie, pour leur propre consommation.

VII. TOURISME ET INFRASTRUCTURE

Tourisme

Les données sur le tourisme ont été principalement collectées auprès de sources nationales ; quand les sources nationales ne sont pas disponibles, les données sont tirées des bases des données en ligne UNWTO et Tourism Decision Metrics (TDM) de Tourism Economics.

Les indicateurs publiés sont : le nombre d'arrivées dans le pays le nombre de chambres d'hôtel, le nombre de nuitées, les recettes touristiques, la contribution totale du tourisme au PIB et la contribution totale du tourisme à l'emploi. Le nombre de touristes d'un pays se rapporte, sauf indication contraire, à toutes les personnes contrôlées à la frontière et voyageant pour le plaisir, la santé, les affaires, les réunions ou les études, s'arrêtant dans le pays pour vingt-quatre heures ou plus. Les données excluent les immigrés et résidants frontaliers.

Infrastructure

Routes asphaltées (% du total)

Les routes pavées sont celles dont la surface est construite avec de la pierre concassée (macadam) et de liant hydrocarboné ou d'agents bitumineux, du béton ou de pavés. Le dénominateur est l'ensemble des routes du pays, mesurées en longueur.

Réseaux total (Railways-km)
Il s'agit de la longueur la longueur de l'itinéraire disponible pour le service de train , quel que soit le nombre de pistes parallèles.

Lignes téléphoniques principales
Les lignes téléphoniques sont les lignes téléphoniques fixes qui relient l'équipement terminal d'un abonné au réseau public commuté téléphonique et qui ont un port sur un central téléphonique. Les réseaux de canaux de service numérique intégrés et les abonnés fixes sans fil sont inclus.

Les abonnés au réseau cellulaire mobile
Les abonnements téléphoniques mobiles sont les abonnements à un service de téléphonie public mobile utilisant la technologie cellulaire, qui fournissent un accès au réseau téléphonique public commuté. Les abonnés Post-payés et prépayés sont inclus.

VIII. FINANCES ET STATISTIQUES MONETAIRES

Statistiques monétaires
Les données de cette section proviennent essentiellement des banques centrales africaines et de la base de données sur les Statistiques financières internationales du FMI.

Monnaie (M1)
La masse monétaire au sens strict (M1) comprend les dépôts transférables et la circulation fiduciaire hors banques.

Quasi-monnaie
La quasi-monnaie englobe les dépôts à terme, les dépôts d'épargne et les dépôts en devises.

Avoirs extérieurs nets
Les avoirs extérieurs nets sont égaux à la somme des avoirs extérieurs moins la somme des engagements extérieurs des autorités monétaires et des banques créatrices de monnaie.

Crédits intérieurs
Le crédit intérieur est égal à la somme des créances nettes sur l'Etat, sur les entreprises publiques et le secteur privé. Le crédit au secteur privé est présenté séparément mais en tant que sous-groupe du crédit intérieur.

Réserves internationales
Les réserves internationales comprennent les avoirs du pays en or monétaire, droits de tirage spéciaux (DTS) et devises, ainsi que ses réserves auprès du Fonds monétaire international (FMI).

Taux de change
Les taux de change, exprimés en unité de monnaie nationale par rapport au dollar EU, sont indiqués comme des taux de fin de période et des moyennes sur la période des taux de change du marché et des taux officiels. Le taux du marché est défini comme le taux déterminé à enlever par les forces du marché; et le taux officiel est celui fixé par les autorités.

Finances publiques
Les données de cette section sont principalement collectées par les autorités nationales, telles que les instituts nationaux de statistiques, les ministères des finances et les banques centrales ; quand les sources nationales ne sont pas disponibles, les données des publications du FMI (rapports des pays) sont utilisées.

Pour le Botswana, l'Egypte, l'Ethiopie, le Kenya, le Malawi, les îles Maurice, la Namibie, l'Afrique du Sud et le Swaziland, les données ont été compilées selon l'année fiscale, comme données annuelles. Ainsi, les années 2006 à 2014 représentent bien l'année civile selon la période fiscale de chaque pays.

Recettes totales et dons
Les recettes publiques incluent toutes les recettes non remboursables de l'Etat, avec ou sans contrepartie, provenant d'autres administrations (locales ou étrangères) et des institutions internationales.

Recettes fiscales
Les recettes fiscales regroupent les impôts, taxes, droits et autres transferts obligatoires autres que les cotisations de sécurité sociale. Elles sont la principale source de revenu de la plupart des administrations publiques et constituent des transferts obligatoires vers ce secteur.

Recettes non fiscales

Elles regroupent les impôts sur les revenus de la propriété, les droits et taxes non industrielles et les ventes de biens existants, les amendes, les pénalités, les confiscations, les indemnisations accordées par un tribunal, et les transferts volontaires autres que les dons.

Dons

Les dons sont des transferts non obligatoires courants ou en capital qu'une administration publique peut recevoir d'une autre administration publique ou d'une organisation internationale.

Dépenses et prêts nets

Ils comprennent tous les paiements non remboursables effectués par l'Administration publique, avec ou sans contrepartie, y compris les dépenses courantes et en capital, les transactions au titre de la dette publique et les participations au capital pour des raisons de politique publique.

Dépenses courantes

Elles comprennent tous les paiements non remboursables effectués par l'Administration publique, avec ou sans contrepartie, autres que les dépenses en capital ou les subventions.

Dépenses en capital

Il s'agit des dépenses pour l'acquisition d'immobilisations, des stocks, des terrains ou des actifs incorporels ainsi que les transferts sans contrepartie dans le but de permettre au bénéficiaire d'acquérir ces actifs. Pour être classé comme un capital, un bien acquis doit dépasser une valeur minimale et être destiné à plus d'un an d'utilisation dans le processus de production.

Prêts nets

Les prêts nets (total des prêts moins les remboursements) comprennent les transactions de l'Etat relatives aux créances sur des tiers obtenues à des fins de politique publique plutôt que d'en tirer profit. Ce chiffre porte à la fois sur les paiements et les recettes.

Déficit fiscal

L'excédent/déficit global des finances publiques est la différence entre, d'une part, les recettes courantes, les recettes en capital et les dons publics reçus et, d'autre part, les dépenses totales et les prêts moins les remboursements.

Balance des paiements

La balance des paiements est un état statistique où sont résumées, pour une période donnée, les transactions d'une économie avec le reste du monde. Les transactions, pour la plupart entre résidents et non-résidents, sont celles qui portent sur les biens, services et revenus; celles qui font naître des créances financières sur le reste du monde ou des engagements financiers envers celui-ci et celles qui sont considérées comme des transferts, pour lesquels il y a lieu de passer des contre-écritures de manière à solder les transactions à sens unique. Les données de cette section proviennent des Banques centrales africaines. Lorsque ces données ne sont pas disponibles ou de mauvaise qualité, les Rapports pays du FMI ont été utilisés en remplacement. Les données provenant de sources internationales portent sur les pays suivants : Guinée Equatoriale, Liberia, Lesotho, Sierra Leone et Libye.

Balance commerciale

Elle est égale à la différence entre les exportations et les importations de biens, évalués sur la base FAB (franco à bord) c'est-à-dire à la frontière du pays exportateur. Le poste des biens englobe les marchandises générales, les biens importés ou exportés pour subir une transformation, la valeur des réparations de biens, les biens achetés dans les ports par les transporteurs non-résidents, et l'or non monétaire.

Balance des services

Les services recouvrent les transports (Fret et transport international des passagers), la rubrique des voyages, les services de communication, les services des bâtiments et travaux publics, les services d'assurance, les services d'informatique et d'information; les redevances et droits de licence: les services personnels, culturels et relatifs aux loisirs; les services fournis ou reçus par les administrations publiques. La balance des services est définie par les revenus moins les paiements au titre des services.

Revenus nets
Le poste revenus enregistre deux types de flux: ceux qui relèvent de la rémunération des salariés qui comprend les salaires, traitements et autres prestations; et ceux qui correspondent au revenu des investissements qui comprend les revenus des investissements directs, des investissements de portefeuille et d'autres investissements.

Rémunération des salariés
Les rémunérations des salariés comprennent les salaires, gages, traitements versés par des employeurs non-résidents à leurs salariés résidents et inversement.

Revenus des investissements
Les revenus des investissements couvrent les revenus des investissements directs, les revenus des investissements de portefeuille (participation au capital et titres de créance) ainsi que les autres revenus d'investissement (intérêts provenant d'autres opérations financières).

Transferts courants
Les transferts courants sont tous ceux qui ne font pas intervenir : i) le transfert de propriété d'un actif fixe, ii) le transfert de fonds lié ou subordonné à l'acquisition ou à la cession d'un actif fixe, iii) la remise, sans contrepartie, d'une dette par un créancier.

Transferts officiels nets
Transferts officiels nets comprennent les paiements de transfert net entre les gouvernements du pays déclarant et le reste du monde

Envois de fonds des travailleurs
Les envois de fonds des travailleurs reprennent les montants transférés à l'étranger par des travailleurs résidents et vice-versa

Autres transferts privés
Autres transferts privés comprennent les paiements de transfert net entre personnes privées et des organisations non officielles du pays déclarant et le reste du monde qui ne transportent aucune provision pour les remboursements.

Solde du compte courant
La balance des comptes des opérations courantes est la somme des exportations nettes des biens et services, du revenu net et des transferts courants nets.

Compte de capital
Le compte de capital couvre les transferts internationaux de capitaux (ex. annulation de dette) et l'acquisition/ la cession d'actifs non produits et non financiers

Compte financier
Le compte financier couvre les opérations impliquant un transfert de propriété de parties de l'actif et du passif d'une économie par rapport au reste du monde, dont les achats internationaux de titres tels que des actions ou des obligations.

Erreurs et omissions
Erreurs et omissions nettes sont calculées de façon résiduelle comme la différence entre le total des recettes et des dépenses (courantes et en capital ainsi que le compte financier).

Balance générale
La balance des paiements est un registre des transactions internationales d'un pays avec le reste du monde. Les opérations sont organisées dans deux comptes différents, le compte courant et le compte capital et financier.

Dette extérieure et flux financiers
Les données de cette section proviennent essentiellement des sources internationales suivantes : la base de données sur les «Perspectives de l'économie mondiale » du FMI, les bases de données en ligne de l'OCDE et de la CNUCED. Cependant, quelques pays ont fourni leurs données pour cette édition de l'annuaire. L'objectif de l'annuaire est d'inclure les données fournies par les pays eux-mêmes dans la mesure du possible pourvu que la qualité des données le permette. Les données nationales proviennent des pays suivants : Bénin, Burkina Faso, Cameroun, Guinée Equatoriale, Lesotho et Niger.

Dette extérieure totale

La dette extérieure totale est le montant dû mais non remboursé, à un moment donné, par les résidents d'un pays à des non-résidents, et qui se sont engagés à rembourser le principal, avec ou sans intérêt, ou à payer les intérêts avec ou sans le principal. Elle est la somme de la dette publique, de la dette garantie publique, de la dette privée non garantie à long terme, du recours au crédit du FMI et de la dette à court terme.

Service de la dette extérieure

Le service total de la dette (extérieure) est la somme des remboursements du principal et des paiements des intérêts. Il s'agit du service de la dette à court terme et de la dette à long terme (dette publique, dette privée à garantie publique et dette non garantie privée) et du recours au crédit du FMI.

Valeur actuelle de la dette extérieure

La valeur actualisée de la dette est la somme de la dette extérieure à court terme plus la valeur actualisée du total des paiements du service de la dette dus sur la dette extérieure à long terme publique et garantie par l'État et la dette extérieure à long terme privée non garantie au cours de la vie des prêts existants.

Dette publique intérieure

La dette publique intérieure : détenue par les agents économiques résidents de l'État émetteur et libellée en monnaie nationale.

Investissements directs étrangers

L'investissement direct étranger représente l'investissement effectué pour acquérir ou accroître une participation durable au capital d'une entreprise (généralement 10 pourcent du pouvoir de vote) opérant dans un pays autre que celui de l'investisseur. C'est la somme du capital social, du réinvestissement des bénéfices et d'autres capitaux à court et à long termes comme il est indiqué dans la section traitant de la balance des paiements.

Aide publique au développement

L'APD représente les dons et les prêts accordés à des conditions financières privilégiées (c'est-à-dire avec un élément de libéralité d'au moins 25 pour cent) au secteur public dans le but principal de promouvoir le développement économique et le bien-être social. Il s'agit des décaissements nets d'APD.

IX. COMMERCE EXTERIEUR

Les données pour cette section proviennent majoritairement des sources nationales. C'est le cas des pays suivant s : Algérie, Bénin, Burkina Faso, Burundi, Cameroun, Côte d'Ivoire, Egypte, Ethiopie, Gambie, Guinée Bissau, Kenya, Malawi, Mali, Maroc, Mozambique, Namibie, Niger, Nigeria, Rwanda, Soudan, Swaziland, Tanzanie, Togo, Zambie et Zimbabwé. Dans le cas où des données nationales n'ont pu être trouvées, nous avons eu recours à la base de données en ligne de la CNUCED. Les principaux produits d'exportation et d'importation ont été choisis par les pays eux-mêmes. Pour les données obtenues de la CNUCED la nomenclature du système harmonisé (rev1) a été employée pour déterminer la liste des produits principaux d'exportations et d'importation. Sauf indication contraire, les statistiques d'importation sont valorisées sur la base CAF tandis que les exportations sont valorisées FOB.

1. Overview of data issues in Africa

The Sustainable Development Goals have rekindled interest in the quality and availability of statistics for management, programme design and the monitoring and evaluation of performance. It is estimated that some $1 billion annually is required to enable 77 of the world's lower-income countries to establish statistical systems capable of supporting and measuring the Goals. Existing mechanisms, such as multilateral lending, bilateral grants and technical assistance, ought to be used to support statistics. Equally, multilateral trust funds and special development grants ought to cover the financial gap in developing statistics for the Goals.

African development statistics are asvaried as the conti- nent itself and the herculean task has always been to bring all actors into a continental framework for statis- tical development. In October 2014, the Independent Expert Advisory Group on Data Revolution for Sustainable Development underscored the opportunities and challenges confronting statistical production for sustainable development. It was clearly stated that investment is required to improve statistics for the effective measurement of sustainable development indicators. Equally, the monitoring and evaluation of the Goals will require additional investment in order to consolidate gains made during the Millennium Development Goal period, enabling the development of reliable, high-quality data on a range of subjects, including but not limited to climate change and inequalities. As a result, the African national statistical system and subregional and regional organizations dealing with statistics and statistical development have been not only challenged, but also given the opportunity, among other things, to raise public awareness of the importance of statistics in the development of the continent and in harnessing national, subregional, regional and international resources in building the capacities of African countries to meet the increased demand in quality statistics emanating from their development agendas.

The recent upsurge in the demand for statistics in Africa is driven, among other factors, by the global recession of 2008 and the search for data for invest-ment opportunities in the continent. The emerging capital markets and stock exchanges require quality data on inflation, gross domestic product (GDP) and other economic data for appropriate investment decisions, to some extent explaining the pressure exerted on national statistical offices. Domestic requirements for good governance and accountability as a tool for evaluating government performance has increased demand for data. Donors also exert demand for data, especially on social trends to enable them to be held accountable to their constituents, leading to donor- driven data generation that is sometimes irrelevant to Africa's development (Kiregyera, 2015). The problem is aggravated by the underfunding of national statis- tical offices and a reliance on donors, in particular for household surveys and censuses. This calls for increased investment in both economic and social data.

1.1 Situation of data and statistics in Africa

It is noted by development practitioners and other actors that deficiencies in statistical information hamper Africa's development and transformation processes. Although some progress had been made in statistical development, this progress is uneven and the national statistical systems still face a number of challenges. In response to concerns raised by stake- holders in the national statistical systems in various forums, a number of initiatives, frameworks and strategies have been developed in the past decades to improve statistics in support of Africa's development agenda (Economic Commission for Africa, 2008; 2013). *Figure 1. highlights the key milestones in the development of statistics in Africa.*

Figure 1. MILESTONES IN THE DEVELOPMENT OF

STATISTICS IN AFRICA

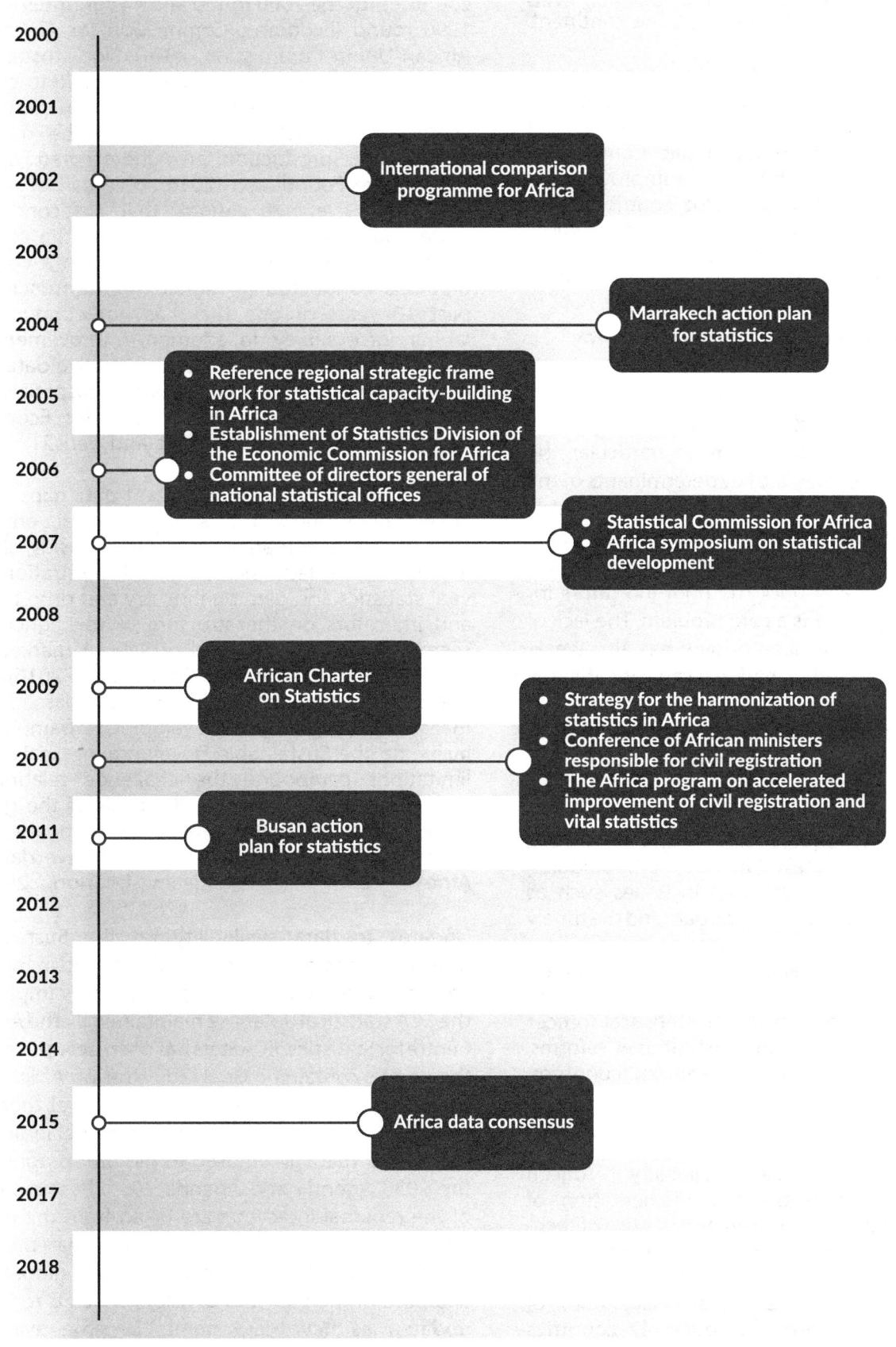

2000

2001

2002 — International comparison programme for Africa

2003

2004 — Marrakech action plan for statistics

2005

2006
- Reference regional strategic frame work for statistical capacity-building in Africa
- Establishment of Statistics Division of the Economic Commission for Africa
- Committee of directors general of national statistical offices

2007
- Statistical Commission for Africa
- Africa symposium on statistical development

2008

2009 — African Charter on Statistics

2010
- Strategy for the harmonization of statistics in Africa
- Conference of African ministers responsible for civil registration
- The Africa program on accelerated improvement of civil registration and vital statistics

2011 — Busan action plan for statistics

2012

2013

2014

2015 — Africa data consensus

2017

2018

These deliberate efforts need to be put into concrete action at the country and regional levels in order to develop data systems on the continent.

Those initiatives, together with the efforts to measure progress on achieving the Millennium Development Goals, led to increased investment in a number of national statistics systems (Economic Commission for Africa, 2016) and contributed to improvements in data availability. They have also contributed to significant capacity development in the region. The main challenges to statistical development in Africa are discussed in the paragraphs that follow.

i. Inadequate funding and limited autonomy of the national statistical offices

Adequate and sustained resourcing and autonomy of the national statistics system, in particular the national statistical offices, are key determinants of the production of accurate, credible, timely and neutral data. African developmental statistics is under transformation and inadequate funding to sustain statistical development and track the right indicators for decision-making remains a core problem. The lack of institutional and political autonomy has also weakened the technical and managerial capacity of many offices to deliver effectively. Of the 54 African countries, only 12 are considered to have autonomous offices (Economic Commission for Africa, 2010).

These shortfalls contribute to capacity limits that have resulted in inadequate access to and use of data, an inability to use the latest statistical methodologies, and a statistical knowledge gap in issues such as metadata flow, updating statistical data and the timely production of quality data to monitor and evaluate national continental and global development agendas. Several countries in Africa are working towards granting their national statistical offices autonomy through legal and institutional reforms. However, progress is uneven among countries.

ii. Data availability

There is improvement in data availability in African countries following increased implementation of censuses and household surveys and the use of technology in these processes. The unprecedented participation of African countries in the 2010 round of the population and housing census is an illustration of this improvement. During that round, 47 countries conducted population censuses, compared with 38 countries for the 2000 round and 44 countries for the 1990 round (Economic Commission for Africa and African Union Commission, 2014). Notwithstanding this progress, most countries are not able to collect data in a regular and timely manner, in particular conflict and post-conflict countries. The gaps in regular data production are underscored by the Mo Ibrahim Foundation (2016): only half of Africa's population live in a country that has conducted more than two comparable surveys in the past 10 years and a little more than half live in a country that has conducted an agriculture census in the past 10 years or one that has not conducted a labour force survey. In addition, improvements in other data sources such as administrative data, civil registration and vital statistics and geospatial data, have been very slow (Organization for Economic Cooperation and Development and Paris21, 2013).

These limitations lead to persistent data gaps in key development indicators, such as social, environmental and governance indicators (Cassidy, 2014), administrative data (including civil registration and vital statistics and data on industry and drug usage) and indicators on the structure of the agriculture sector and landholders and on labour market and employment (Mo Ibrahim Foundation, 2016). The data gaps impede the establishment of baselines for measuring progress on development frameworks, including the Sustainable Development Goals. Data limitations compound the challenge relating to moni- toring the Goals. On the basis of the global database on the Goals, updated on 4 January 2017, only 37.8 per cent of the indicators have data on African coun- tries (Statistics Division, 2017b).

Updates to data availability on the Sustainable Development Goals in Africa will be found in the ECA database, called ECAStats, following the revamping of the ECA statistical database maintained by the African Centre for Statistics. ECAStats has been set up as one of the portals containing Goal indicators on Africa, with accompanying metadata. At the Africa level, there are ongoing initiatives to develop a regional indicators framework that will be used to monitor progress on the 2030 Agenda and Agenda 2063. Because most of the regional indicators are taken from the global list of Goal indicators, it is essential that the ECA portal mirror African data available in the global Goal database of the Statistics Division, which is regularly updated as new data points become available.

iii. Data quality

Data quality is another area of concern in Africa's statistical development. Efforts to improve data availability have not resulted in corresponding improvements in quality data production. Many African countries still face challenges in producing systematic, accurate, relevant, comparable and timely data. Key drivers of these shortcomings are differences in methodology, concepts and definitions used, a lack of coordination within the national statistics system, inadequate financial and human resources and weak infrastructure and data technology. These have contributed to significant discrepancies between data from various national sources and between national and regional and international sources. The Center for Global Development (2014) highlighted discrep- ancies between administrative data and household survey estimates in Africa with regard to education, agriculture, health and poverty. The use of various methodologies, concepts and definitions makes data comparability difficult.

iV. Data accessibility and use

Data accessibility and use are a challenge in many countries owing to political issues, weak infrastructure and data technology, as well as inadequate capacity and funding. For example, data generated from censuses and surveys are often published late. There are efforts to use technology, including mobile devices and geospatial information, in censuses and surveys in a number of countries, which is helping to fill these gaps. The use of various formats by various data producers also limits data accessibility. Combined with the non-integration of user needs in data dissemination and publication policy, inadequate information on available data and how to access them create further uncertainties about the usability of data and actual usage (Kiregyera, 2015).

V. Use of geospatial data

As the geospatial community works through the Sustainable Development Goals and their indicators, it is realizing that, among the existing data sets, there are a number of data gaps. Some of them are significant, not so much in their spatial resolution but in their temporal resolution. For example, a few of the indicators require more current data, while the data currently available to measure these indicators is three-to-four years out of date. Data production therefore needs to be more agile and adaptable to user requirements. This is a challenge for the professional community and requires partnerships with other organizations and the private sector, who often have a greater ability to generate data faster.

The United Nations Initiative on Global Geospatial Information Management is working closely with the statistical community at the national, regional and global levels to develop the global indicator framework with the inter-agency and expert group on the Sustainable Development Goal indicators. Bearing in mind that the accessibility of fundamental geospatial data is a prerequisite for calculating the indicators, there is need to build consensus on the need to integrate national spatial data infrastructure into national development plans. A strategy on such infrastructure that is aligned with sustainable development as an all-encompassing theme will provide the essential data and information for monitoring the indicators. It will also bring the analysis and evidence-base to the process and, therefore, a consistent monitoring and reporting framework to benefit all areas of government.

The Addis Ababa Action Agenda of the Third International Conference on Financing for Development provided a comprehensive framework for the international community to finance sustainable development. Financing the Sustainable Development Goals will require at least $1.5 trillion annually over what was required for the Millennium Development Goals ($120 billion annually). With respect to satellite-based Earth observation imagery, one estimate puts the investment required at $150 million for start-up costs and $5 million in annual costs covering all 77 countries receiving support from the International Development Association (IDA)[1] of the World Bank. (Digital Globe, 2015).

[1] IDA is a multi-issue institution that provides loans and grants for development activities to poor countries at highly concessional rates. Eligibility for IDA support depends first and foremost on a country's relative poverty, defined as gross national income per capita below an established threshold ($1,215 in 2016). IDA also supports some countries, including small island economies that are above the per capita income threshold, but lack the creditworthiness required to borrow at non-concessional rates.

2. Statistics for progress reporting on the 2030 Agenda and Agenda 2063

2.1 Indicators for the 2030 Agenda and Agenda 2063:Africa's contribution

African countries are required to report progress on the implementation of 2030 Agenda and Agenda 2063, which requires large amounts of data. The 2030 Agenda has 17 Goals and 169 targets. In 2015, the Statistical Commission established the inter-agency and expert group on Sustainable Development Goal indicators to develop the monitoring and reporting framework for the 2030 Agenda. In March 2016, the Commission agreed on a set of 230 global indicators, subject to future technical refinement. The global list of indicators will be complemented by indicators at the continental and national levels. At the global level, the follow-up and review at the high-level political forum will be informed by the annual progress report on the Goals to be prepared by the Secretary-General in cooperation with the United Nations system, on the basis of the global indicator framework and data produced by national statistical systems and informa- tion collected at the regional level.

Agenda 2063 has 20 goals and 174 targets. Its results framework represents a logical relationship between the African Union vision, the seven African aspira- tions, the goal/priority areas under each aspiration and the associated targets. Following the adoption of Agenda 2063 by the heads of State and Governments of the African Union in January 2015, the African Union Commission prepared the first 10-year imple- mentation plan, for the period 2014-2023. It contains 63 core indicators for monitoring and reporting on Agenda 2063, of which 40 are identical to the Sustainable Development Goal indicators.

In 2016, the Conference of African Ministers of Finance, Planning and Economic Development encouraged pan-African institutions to adopt a coherent strategy for the effective and coordinated implementation of Agenda 2063 and the 2030 Agenda. The ministers agreed to a single monitoring and evaluation framework, accommodating both Agendas, and a common reporting architecture that will produce a single periodic performance report. They also acknowledged that the implementation of, reporting on and follow-up to both Agendas require a coherent strategy and an integrated set of goals, targets and indicators, along with a harmonized review and reporting platform.

Many African countries are in the process of aligning the global and continental development goals with their national development priorities, which entails efforts to harmonize, coordinate or integrate data requirements. The pan-African institutions are currently working on an integrated monitoring and evaluation framework that will be used to monitor and report on Agenda 2063 and the 2030 Agenda at the continent level. This requires large amounts of data to be produced and disseminated by countries.

2.2 Data availability and opportunities for reporting on Agenda 2063 and the 2030 Agenda

The Statistics Division led the development of the global Sustainable Development Goal database dissemination platform, which currently has a reasonable amount of data on the indicators (Statistics Division, 2017b). Of the 230 indicators, the portal has 91 on African countries, or 37.8 per cent of the total. Table 1 . provides a summary of the sources of the data points in the database. Some of the indica- tors are disaggregated by sex, age group and location. There are also data for 33 additional indicators, which could help to measure the targets. In addition to data at the country level, aggregates are provided for Africa (excluding North Africa) and Northern Africa. The data are for the years 1990-2016. Globally, there are 139 indicators that require data in order to monitor and report on the relevant Goals and targets.

Some of the Sustainable Development Goals have data for more than half the indicators, such as Goal 3 (69.2 per cent), Goal 7 (66.7 per cent), Goal 9 (66.7 per cent), Goal 8 (58.8 per cent), Goal 2 (57.1 per cent) and Goal 4 (54.5 per cent). On the other hand, there are no data for all the indicators under Goal 13.

Table 1. SUSTAINABLE DEVELOPMENT GOAL DATA AVAILABILITY ON AFRICAN COUNTRIES

| SUSTAINABLE DEVELOPMENT GOAL | DATA AVAILABILITY BY INDICATOR TYPE | | | TOTAL NUMBER OF INDICATORS * | PERCENTAGE OF INDICATORS WITH DATA |
	SUSTAINABLE DEVELOPMENT	ADDITIONAL	TOTAL		
1	3	3	6	12	25.0
2	8	4	12	14	57.1
3	18	7	25	26	69.2
4	6	3	9	11	54.5
5	3	1	5	14	21.4
6	2	4	6	11	18.2
7	4	0	4	6	66.7
8	10	1	11	17	58.8
9	8	1	9	12	66.7
10	5	0	5	11	45.5
11	1	1	2	15	6.7
12	2	1	3	14	14.3
13	0	0	0	9	0.0
14	1	0	1	7	14.3
15	6	0	6	14	42.9
16	6	5	11	23	26.1
17	8	3	11	25	32.0
Total	**91**	**33**	**124**	**241**	**37.8**

*A total of 11 indicators are repeated.

Table 1 highlights the need for strong efforts by African countries to align national development plans with the Sustainable Development Goals (Economic Commission for Africa et al., 2016). Efforts to this effect have begun in Côte d'Ivoire, Kenya, Nigeria, Senegal, South Africa and the United Republic of Tanzania (Economic Commission for Africa, 2016)

Building on investments in data production to monitor progress towards the Millennium Development Goals, a number of national statistical systems have some capacity to produce data to measure progress, especially in the social and economic dimensions of the Goals (i.e., Goals 1-4 and 6-10). With the exception of South Africa, which has the strongest national statistical capacity on the continent. Data production, dissemination and use with respect to Goals 11-15 remain relatively weak in many countries. In the United Republic of Tanzania, for example, most of the indicators in these areas are new to the national statistical system. A total of 27 indicators in these areas require new data collection systems, with 11 of them needing new systems with respect to Goal 15 alone.

2.3 Africa's contributions to informing the global database of Sustainable Development Goal indicators on Africa

The extent of indicators without data on Africa in the Global SDG database demonstrates the persistence of a data gap in national statistical systems (Statistics Division, 2017a). The sources of the data points in the global Sustainable Development Goal database are summarized in Table 2. It can be observed that esti- mation, global monitoring and modelled data provide some 54 per cent of the total data on the Goals regarding Africa. Although there have been improve- ments in the share of country and country-adjusted data, from 22.8 per cent during the period 1990- 2005 to 33.5 per cent during the period 2006-2016, the overall share for the whole duration was only 28.9 per cent.

During the period 2006-2016, the range of the country or country-adjusted data source lies between 16.6 per cent in Libya to 37.2 per cent in Mauritius. Countries with the share of country or country-adjusted data source below 20 per cent include Libya, Somalia (18.6 per cent) and South Sudan (18.8 per cent). On the other hand, more than one-third of data from South Africa (33.3 per cent), Ethiopia (33.7), Egypt (33.7 per cent), Cabo Verde (34.3 per cent), Niger (34.6 per cent), Ghana (35.9 per cent), Morocco (36.2 per cent) and Mauritius are country or country-adjusted. A total of 39 per cent of the indicators on Africa are estimated by international organizations.

This small share of data obtained from country sources stresses the need for further investment in the national statistical systems in order to develop capacity in a range of areas, such as administrative records and civil registration and vital statistics. This will help to improve the collection, analysis, dissemi- nation and availability of accurate, timely and compa- rable data. Investment in data is also needed to support effective decision-making and monitoring of progress on national development plans and the dissemination of data among subregional, regional and international organizations that monitor and report on Agenda 2063 and the 2030 Agenda. Moreover, national statistical authorities need to work with other stake- holders, such as the private sector and civil society organizations that are involved in data-production activities.

2.4 Advocacy for action

The Sustainable Development Goals require that all the actors, stakeholders and beneficiaries have access to relevant information to play their relevant roles in the development process, including implementing, monitoring and reporting on progress. The relevant information should always include official statistics.

Notwithstanding notable progress made by African countries in the production and dissemination of statistics during the past decade or so, official statis- tics produced by national statistical systems are not always available in forms that allow easy access. Therefore, monitoring the broad range of develop- ment issues covered by the Sustainable Development Goals

Table 2. DATA SOURCES OF SUSTAINABLE DEVELOPMENT GOAL INDICATORS ON AFRICA

DATA SOURCE TYPE	1990 - 2005		2006 - 2016		1990 - 2016	
	TOTAL DATA POINTS	SHARE (%)	TOTAL DATA POINTS	SHARE (%)	TOTAL DATA POINTS	SHARE (%)
Country or country-adjusted	7 948	22.8	15 443	33.5	23 391	28.9
Estimation	14 981	42.9	16 600	36.0	31 581	39.0
Global monitoring	2 672	7.7	4 867	10.6	7 539	9.3
Modelling	1 957	5.6	2 656	5.8	4 613	5.7
Others	7 336	21.0	6 493	14.1	13 829	17.1
Total	34 894	100	46 059	100	80 953	100

Source: Global Sustainable Development Goal database. Available from www.un.org/en/africa/osaa/peace/agenda2063.shtml.

and the need to fulfil the principle of disaggregation along dimensions of, among others, age, gender, income and geography constitute an additional challenge to the already weak statistical systems that lack adequate technological infrastructure and to finan- cial and human resource capacities.

The measurement of progress towards achieving the Sustainable Development Goals and those contained Agenda 2063 necessitates investing massively in statistics to fill the gaps that limit the generation of quality, relevant, timely and comparable data, including capacity gaps and technology (Economic Commission for Africa, 2016). Investing in statistics can provide excellent returns. It stands not only to benefit evidence-based decision-making and monitoring, but also to strengthen the overall statistical system by building capacity in a range of areas, such as the accuracy of administrative records and improved data analysis and dissemination.

The cost of these investments, however, in particular data collection for the 2030 Agenda, Agenda 2063 and national development priorities, will be very high if it is to be met by the official statistics community alone. Collaboration among various data communi- ties and the coordination, harmonization and integration of data from various sources within data ecosystems will therefore be helpful in filling in gaps in official statistics, reducing costs and enhancing data accessibility and use (Economic Commission for Africa, 2016). There are capacities and resources to be tapped within the national data ecosystems, such as the private sector, civil society, academia, citizenry and open data communities.

The need for collaboration among various data communities was also a key element of discussions concerning statistical capacity for the post-2015 development agenda that called for a wider range of actors to be involved in the development of statis- tical methods, such as data scientists and geospatial specialists from the private sector and research community, government officials and other data users. These requirements were echoed by the high-level panel of eminent persons that went further

and called for a "data revolution"[2] for development. The data revolution can be harnessed to catalyse positive social, economic and environmental trans- formation in Africa. The increasing demand for data and statistics under the 2030 Agenda and Agenda 2063 is an opportunity for Africa to embark on the data revolution in order to improve statistical capacity in all domains, given that their adoption coincides with unprecedented innovation in data technologies used to collect data and analyse and disseminate a huge volume and type of data, leading to the availability and use of bigger and more detailed data than before (Independent Expert Advisory Group on the Data Revolution for Sustainable Development, 2014). Considerable innovation and experimentation is currently under way within multiple data communities and ecosystems in African countries. For the most part, however, these are small-scale and often isolated initiatives. If Africa is to benefit from the full transformative potential of the data revolution, more systematic, large-scale, integrated and sustainable efforts are going to be needed (Economic Commission for Africa, 2015).

African Governments recognize the importance of the data revolution as embodied in the Africa data consensus (Economic Commission for Africa et al., 2015) and other statistical and development initiatives, including the African Charter on Statistics and the African Union's strategy for the harmonization of statistics in Africa. The consensus is a strategy for implementing the data revolution in Africa that was adopted at a high-level conference on the data revolution, held in March 2015, in response to calls for a framework on the data revolution in Africa and its implications for Agenda 2063 and the 2030 Agenda.

At the national level, this can be seen in long-term national development plans, and numerous changes, reforms and innovations are needed to enable member States to embark on a data revolution. In this regard, access to and the use of new sources of data, in particular big data, to complement official statis- tics is needed. This requires strategic

---

[2] The term "data revolution" refers to a "rapid increase in the volume of data, speed of data production, number of data producers, dissemination of data, and the range of things on which there is data, supported by new technologies e.g. mobile phones and the 'internet of things', and from other sources, such as qualitative data, citizen- generated data and perceptions data; and growing demand for data from all parts of society" (Independent Expert Advisory Group on the Data Revolution for Sustainable Development, 2014).

and innovative partnerships and collaboration between national statistical systems and other actors of various data communities. A challenge in this collaboration is that big data do not always follow statistical principles, making it difficult for the analysis and generation of results. In this respect, a lot of work in terms of, among other things, methodologies, definitions and classifications is required. Moreover, some issues, such as technical, legal, proprietary and privacy issues relating to big data, limit their effective access and use, notwithstanding their timeliness and cost-ef- fectiveness (Robin et al., 2016). Legal, legislative and policy reforms are required to address these issues. According to the guidelines of the national strategy for the development of statistics on the data revolution, "by providing a legal framework for countries to guide their own legislative processes, the Charter indeed provides leverage and guidelines that help in modifying the law accounting for new data developments, such as the use of Big Data".[3]

The adoption of open data principles for both national statistical systems and other national data ecosystems is one of the most effective approaches to making data available to a wide audience. Open data are online, free of cost and accessible, and can be used, reused and redistributed, subject only, at most, to the requirements to attribute and to share.

The improvement in existing data sources is also key to effective progress monitoring. Census survey and administrative data are the main sources of data used to inform the 2030 Agenda and Agenda 2063. This requires improvement in the coverage and frequency of censuses and surveys, and the modernization of administrative systems, including civil registration and vital statistics. It entails significant investment in data technologies, capacity, infrastructure and human and financial resources.

The development of the national spatial data infrastructure is needed for capacity-building, funding, coordination, fundamental data sets and reference systems. Capacity needs and data gap assessments will help to support efforts towards statistical development within the framework of the 2030 Agenda and Agenda 2063 at the national, regional and international levels.

[3] Available from www.paris21.org/nsdsguidelines.

3. Conclusion

Previous efforts to monitor and report progress of the Millennium Development Goals and other initiatives led to increased government and development partner investments to improve national statistical systems and data availability. Further work is needed to strengthen the capacities of member States in the production, analysis, storage, dissemination and use of statistical data. Additional funding, embracing new data sources and innovations and geospatial information are required. Initiatives on statistical development have to take into account challenges discussed above so that African countries can produce and disseminate adequate, high-quality and timely statistical data for monitoring the implementation of their national development plans and to report on the progress in achieving the Sustainable Development Goals and the goals contained in Agenda 2063.

In the Africa data consensus, the following key actions are underscored to support the data revolution for effective monitoring of the 2030 Agenda and Agenda 2063 in African countries:

- Create an inclusive data ecosystem involving Government, the private sector, academia, civil society, local communities and development part- ners that tackles the informational aspects of development decision-making in a coordinated way. Governments must play a proactive role in engaging this community, and other stakeholders should prioritize partnership with Government. This is linked to the strategy for statistical development. Existing national strategies for the development of statistics should be revised to make them more inclusive of all data communities

- As a critical first step towards strengthening the data ecosystem, review the capacity needs, legal and financial frameworks, participating institutions, data assets and gaps at the national, subnational and community levels to recognize the roles of the various stakeholders and create a workable road map with clear milestones

- Have Governments take the lead in ensuring that the recurrent costs of production and dissemination of all required data is financed from sustainable national resources. A resource mobilization strategy should be put in place

- Have Governments identify a body authorized to provide credentials to data communities providing open data on the basis of established criteria for quality, reliability, timeliness and relevance to statistical information needs

- Develop civil registration systems that produce credible vital statistics that are a cornerstone of the data revolution. Likewise, population, economic, labour, health, education, land and agri- cultural management information systems should be supported to ensure timely and accurate data to drive decision-making at the national and subnational levels

- Adopt, foster and strengthen public-private part- nerships as a strategy for knowledge and tech- nology transfer and to promote sustainable collaboration, funding and the sharing of experiences

- Extend, where applicable, all international norms and standards relating to official statistics to all data in order to improve their validity and credibility

- Promote innovative and integrated methodologies and technologies, including geospatial technology, to improve data collection, analysis and usage. It is important to integrate gender statistics and gender-specific indicators into monitoring and evaluation

- Have pan-African institutions, such as AfDB, the African Union Commission and ECA take the lead in the realization of the Africa data consensus, in partnership with other development partners.

La statistique en Afrique : principaux problèmes

1. Vue d'ensemble des problèmes liés aux données en Afrique

Les objectifs de développement durable ont ranimé l'intérêt porté à la qualité et à la disponibilité des statistiques pour la gestion, la conception de programmes et le suivi et l'évaluation des performances. On estime à quelque 1 milliard de dollars la somme annuelle nécessaire pour permettre à 77 pays à faible revenu d'établir des systèmes de statistiques en mesure de soutenir la mise en œuvre des objectifs et de mesurer l'avancée de celle-ci. Pour soutenir la statistique en Afrique, il convient d'employer les mécanismes existants, tels que les prêts multilatéraux, les subventions bilatérales et l'assistance technique. De même, les fonds multilatéraux d'affectation spéciale et les subventions spéciales au développement doivent compenser le manque de financement qui freine le développement de la statistique dans le cadre des objectifs.

En Afrique, les statistiques de développement sont aussi diversifiées que le continent lui-même et la réunion de tous les acteurs dans un cadre continental pour le développement de la statistique a toujours représenté une tâche herculéenne. En octobre 2014, les membres du Groupe consultatif d'experts indépendants sur la révolution des données au profit du développement durable ont souligné les opportunités et les défis de la production statistique au profit du développement durable. Ils ont affirmé qu'il était nécessaire d'investir pour améliorer la statistique et mesurer efficacement les indicateurs de développement durable. De même, le suivi et l'évaluation de la réalisation des objectifs nécessiteront un investissement supplémentaire en vue de consolider les progrès enregistrés au cours de la période des objectifs du Millénaire pour le développement, ce qui permettra d'obtenir des données fiables et de qualité sur une large gamme de sujets, notamment sur le changement climatique et les inégalités. En plus d'avoir été mis au défi, le système statistique national africain et les organisations infra-régionales et régionales chargées de la statistique et de son développement ont eu l'occasion de sensibi-liser les populations à l'importance que revêt la statistique, aussi bien pour le développement du continent que pour l'exploitation des ressources nationales, infrarégionales et régionales en vue de renforcer les capacités des pays africains à répondre à la demande accrue en statistiques de qualité dans le cadre de leurs programmes pour le développement.

La hausse récente de la demande en statistiques en Afrique est en partie motivée par la récession mondiale de 2008 et par la recherche de données sur les opportunités d'investissement sur le continent. Les marchés de capitaux et les marchés boursiers émergents ont besoin de données de qualité sur l'inflation, le produit intérieur brut (PIB) et d'autres paramètres économiques pour prendre les décisions d'investissement en connaissance de cause, ce qui dans une certaine mesure explique la pression subie par les bureaux de statistiques nationaux. Les donateurs sollicitent également des données, particulièrement sur les tendances sociales, de façon à pouvoir rendre des comptes à leurs soutiens électoraux, ce qui conduit au développement de données qui leur sont destinées alors qu'elles ne sont pas toujours pertinentes au regard du développe-ment de l'Afrique (Kiregyera, 2015). Ce problème est encore aggravé par le sous-financement des bureaux de statistiques nationaux et par la dépendance aux donateurs, en particulier pour les enquêtes sur les ménages et les recensements. Pour toutes ces raisons, une hausse des investissements en faveur des données économiques et sociales est nécessaire.

1.1 État des données et de la statistique en Afrique

Les acteurs, du développement en particulier, ont noté que les insuffisances en termes d'informations statistiques entravent les processus de développement et de transformation du continent africain. Quoique réels, les progrès réalisés dans le développement de la statistique sont irréguliers et les systèmes de statistiques nationaux font toujours face à plusieurs difficultés. En réponse aux problèmes soulevés par les parties prenantes aux systèmes de statistiques nationaux et à l'occasion de divers forums, un certain nombre d'initiatives, de cadres et de stratégies ont été mis au point au cours des dernières décennies afin d'améliorer la statistique et de soutenir le programme de dévelopement de l'Afrique (Commission économique pour l'Afrique, 2008-2013). La Figure 1 souligne les étapes clés du développement de la statistique en Afrique. Pour développer les systèmes de statistique sur le continent, il est nécessaire de transcrire ces efforts déterminés en mesures concrètes à the scale national comme à l'échelon régional.

Associées aux efforts d'évaluation de la mise en œuvre des objectifs du Millénaire pour le développement, ces initiatives ont débouché sur davantage d'investissements dans un certain nombre de systèmes de statistique nationaux (Commission économique pour l'Afrique, 2016) et ont contribué à améliorer la disponibilité des données. Elles ont également participé à un développement des capacités significatif dans la région. Les principales difficultés relatives au développement de la statistique en Afrique sont traitées dans les paragraphes ci-après.

i. Les bureaux de statistiques nationaux sont insuffisamment financés et manquent d'autonomie

L'octroi pérenne de financements adéquats et l'auto- nomie des systèmes de statistique nationaux, en particulier des bureaux de statistique nationaux, conditionnent la production en temps opportun de données précises, crédibles et objectives. Les statistiques sur le développement africain évoluent et le manque de financements visant à pérenniser le développement de la statistique et à suivre les indicateurs pertinents au regard des processus de décision reste un problème central. Le manque d'autonomie institutionnelle et politique a également affaibli les capacités techniques et de gestion de nombreux bureaux, compromettant ainsi leur efficacité. Sur les 54 pays d'Afrique, on consi- dère que seuls 12 possèdent des bureaux autonomes (Commission économique pour l'Afrique, 2010).

Ces insuffisances contribuent à réduire les capacités, ce qui entraîne une exploitation superficielle de données déjà limitées, l'incapacité de faire usage des dernières méthodologies statistiques et des lacunes sur des sujets tels que le flux de métadonnées, la mise à jour des données statistiques et la production rapide de données de qualité permettant de suivre et d'évaluer la mise en œuvre des programmes de développement nationaux, continentaux et mondiaux. Plusieurs pays d'Afrique réfléchissent actuellement à des réformes juridiques et institutionnelles devant garantir une plus grande autonomie à leurs bureaux. Tous les pays n'avancent cependant pas au même rythme.

ii. Disponibilité des données

On note une certaine amélioration dans la disponibi- lité des données dans les pays africains du fait d'une augmentation des recensements et des enquêtes sur les ménages et du recours à la technologie dans le cadre de ces processus. La participation sans précédent des pays africains au recensement de la population et de l'habitation en 2010 illustre cette amélioration. Au cours de cet événement, 47 pays ont conduit des recensements contre 38 en 2000 et 44 en 1990 (Commission économique pour l'Afrique et Commission de l'Union africaine, 2014). Malgré ces progrès, la plupart des pays ne sont pas en mesure de collecter des données de façon régulière et efficiente, en particulier les pays en situation de conflit ou de post-conflit. La fondation Mo Ibrahim souligne l'irré- gularité dans la production de données (2016) : seule la moitié de la population africaine vit dans un pays qui a mené plus de deux enquêtes comparables au cours des dix dernières années, et un peu plus de la moitié vit dans un pays qui a mené un recensement agricole au cours des dix dernières années ou qui n'a pas mené d'enquête sur les forces de travail. De plus, les progrès en matière de données administratives, notamment l'enregistrement des faits d'état civil, l'établissement des statistiques de l'état civil et les données géospatiales, sont particulièrement lents (Organisation de coopération et de développement économiques et PARIS21, 2013).

Ces contraintes sont à l'origine d'un manque de données constant sur les indicateurs clés du déve- loppement tels que les indicateurs sociaux, environ- nementaux et de gouvernance (Cassidy, 2014), les données administratives (y compris les données relatives à l'enregistrement des faits d'état civil et d'éta- blissement des statistiques de l'état civil et celles sur l'industrie et l'usage de stupéfiants), ou encore les indicateurs concernant la structure du secteur agricole, les propriétaires fonciers, le marché du travail et l'emploi (Fondation Mo Ibrahim, 2016). Ce manque de données fait obstacle à la mise en place de bases de référence permettant de mesurer les progrès réalisés par rapport aux cadres de développement, dont les objectifs de développement durable, et ajoute à la difficulté que représente le suivi de la mise en place de ces Objectifs. Selon la banque de données mondiale sur les objectifs, mise à jour le 4 janvier 2017, il n'existe des données pour les pays africains que pour 37,8 % des indicateurs (Division de statistique, 2017b).

FIGURE 1. ÉTAPES IMPORTANTES DU DÉVELOPPEMENT DE LA STATISTIQUE EN AFRIQUE

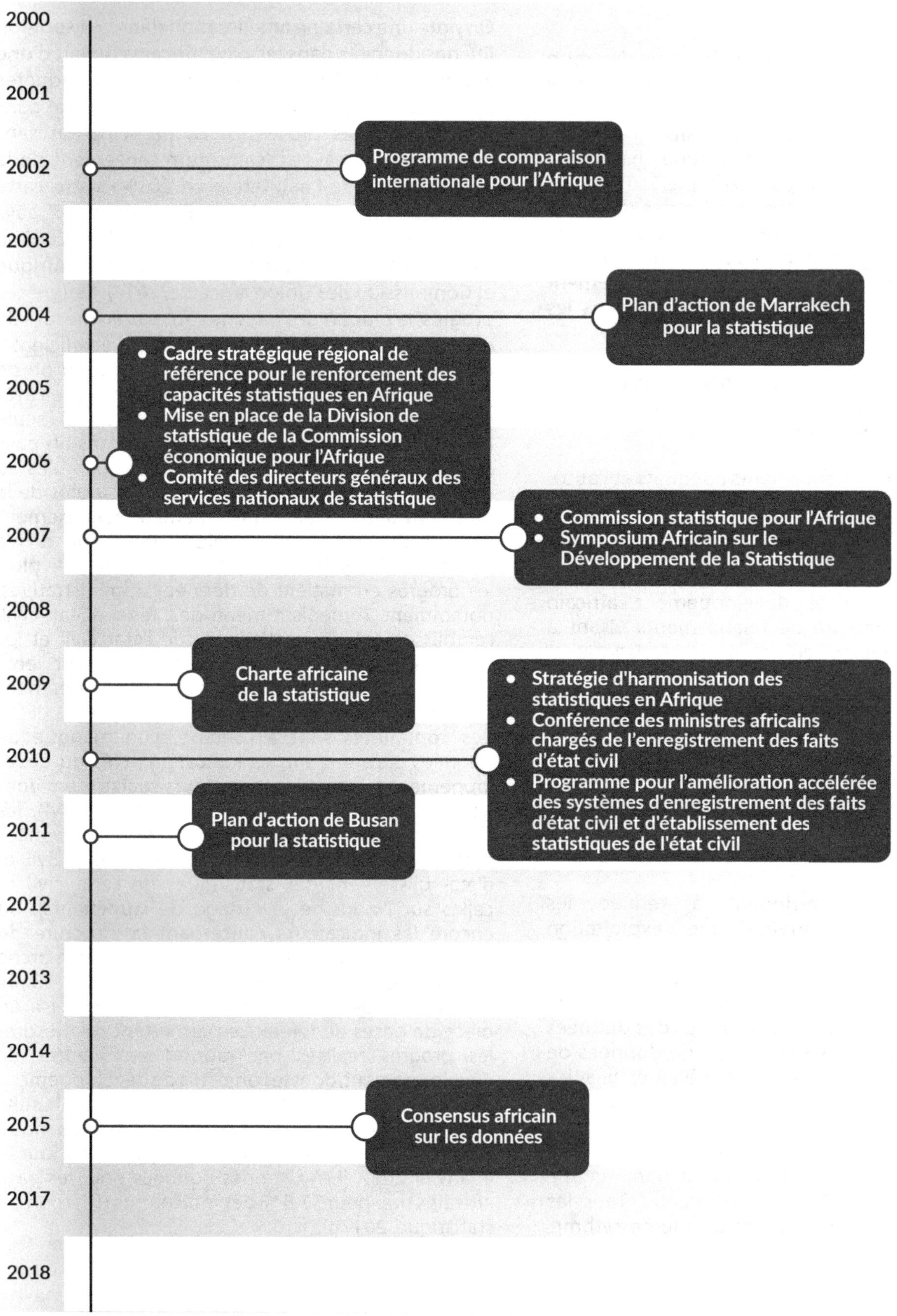

2000

2001

2002 — Programme de comparaison internationale pour l'Afrique

2003

2004 — Plan d'action de Marrakech pour la statistique

2005 – 2006
- Cadre stratégique régional de référence pour le renforcement des capacités statistiques en Afrique
- Mise en place de la Division de statistique de la Commission économique pour l'Afrique
- Comité des directeurs généraux des services nationaux de statistique

2007
- Commission statistique pour l'Afrique
- Symposium Africain sur le Développement de la Statistique

2008

2009 — Charte africaine de la statistique

2010
- Stratégie d'harmonisation des statistiques en Afrique
- Conférence des ministres africains chargés de l'enregistrement des faits d'état civil
- Programme pour l'amélioration accélérée des systèmes d'enregistrement des faits d'état civil et d'établissement des statistiques de l'état civil

2011 — Plan d'action de Busan pour la statistique

2012

2013

2014

2015 — Consensus africain sur les données

2017

2018

Des mises à jour quant à la disponibilité des données sur les objectifs de développement durable en Afrique seront disponibles sur la base de données de la CEA, ECAStats, après que le Centre africain pour la statistique aura réorganisé la base de données statistique de la CEA. La base ECAStats est l'un des portails donnant accès à certains indicateurs des objectifs pour l'Afrique ainsi qu'aux métadonnées correspondantes. En ce qui concerne l'Afrique, des initiatives sont actuellement prises en vue d'élaborer un cadre d'indicateurs régional qui permettra de suivre les progrès réalisés par rapport à la mise en œuvre du Programme 2030 et de l'Agenda 2063. Étant donné que la plupart des indicateurs régionaux sont tirés de la liste mondiale des indicateurs des objectifs, il est essentiel que le portail de la CEA reflète les données africaines disponibles dans la base de données mondiale de la Division de statistique sur les objectifs, laquelle est mise à jour régulièrement au fur et à mesure que de nouvelles données sont disponibles.

iii. Qualité des données

La qualité des données est un autre sujet d'inquiétude concernant le développement statistique de l'Afrique. Les efforts visant à améliorer la disponibilité des données n'ont pas permis d'en accroître la qualité. Pour de nombreux pays africains, il reste difficile de produire en temps opportun des données systématiques, précises, pertinentes et comparables. Ces difficultés s'expliquent principalement par les différences de méthodologies, conceptuelles et définitoires, par un manque de coordination au sein du système de statistique national, par la faiblesse des financements et des ressources humaines, par des infrastructures insuffisantes et par un certain retard au regard de la technologie des données. Ces éléments ont contribué à d'importants écarts entre les données provenant de diverses sources nationales et entre les sources nationales, régionales et internationales. Le Centre pour le développement mondial (2014) a souligné les écarts entre les données administratives et les estimations des enquêtes sur les ménages en Afrique concernant l'éducation, l'agriculture, la santé et la pauvreté. Le recours à des méthodologies, concepts et définitions différents complique la comparaison des données.

iv. Accessibilité et utilisation des données

L'accessibilité et l'utilisation des données sont un défi pour la plupart des pays en raison de problèmes d'ordre politique, d'infrastructures insuffisantes et d'un retard dans la technologie des données, ou encore par manque de capacités et de financements. Les données obtenues par le biais des opérations de recensements ou d'études, par exemple, sont souvent publiées tardivement. Pour les mener à bien, certains pays font l'effort d'utiliser les technologies, notamment les dispositifs mobiles et les systèmes d'informations géospatiales, ce qui contribue à réduire les écarts existants. Le fait que les différents producteurs de données n'utilisent pas les mêmes formats limite également l'accessibi- lité des données. Le manque d'informations sur les données disponibles et la façon d'y accéder, associé à la non-prise en compte des besoins des utilisateurs en termes de diffusion et de publication, rend l'usage potentiel et réel des données d'autant plus incertain (Kiregyera, 2015).

V. Utilisation des données géospatiales

À mesure que la communauté géospatiale se penche sur les objectifs de développement durable et leurs indicateurs, elle se rend compte qu'il existe des manques parmi les ensembles de données existants. Certains sont considérables, pas tant du point de vue spatial que chronologique. Par exemple, certains indicateurs nécessitent un plus grand nombre de données actuelles alors que les données disponibles pour les mesurer ont entre trois et quatre ans. Il est donc nécessaire que la production de données soit plus flexible et s'adapte plus facilement aux besoins des utilisateurs. Ce constat représente un défi pour la communauté professionnelle ; il met en lumière la nécessité de mettre en place des partenariats avec d'autres organi- sations ainsi qu'avec le secteur privé, qui sont souvent mieux à même de générer des données rapidement.

Les États membres de l'Initiative des Nations unies sur la gestion de l'information géospatiale à l'échelle mondiale travaillent en étroite collaboration avec la communauté statistique aux niveaux national, régional et mondial pour développer un cadre mondial d'indicateurs en association avec le Groupe d'experts des Nations unies et de l'extérieur chargé des indicateurs relatifs aux objectifs de développement durable. Tout en gardant à l'esprit que l'accessibilité des données géospatiales fondamentales est indispensable à l'évaluation des indicateurs, il est nécessaire de trouver un consensus sur le besoin d'intégrer les infrastructures de données spatiales nationales aux plans de développement nationaux. Une stratégie de mise en place de telles infrastructures en accord avec le thème global du développement durable permettra d'obtenir des données et des informations essentielles au suivi des indicateurs. Elle apportera également une dimension d'analyse et une base factuelle au processus et dessinera ainsi un cadre de suivi et de compte rendu cohérent dont bénéficiera l'ensemble des domaines publics.

Le Programme d'action d'Addis-Abeba, né de la troi- sième Conférence internationale sur le financement du développement, a posé le cadre du financement du développement durable par la communauté inter- nationale. Le financement des objectifs de développement requerra au moins 1 500 milliards de dollars par an de plus que les 120 milliards de dollars annuels qui ont été nécessaires aux objectifs du Millénaire pour le développement. En ce qui concerne l'observation de la Terre par images satellites, on estime à 150 millions de dollars les frais de lancement et à 5 millions de dollars annuels le coût du soutien aux 77 pays par l'Association internationale de développement (IDA)[1] de la Banque mondiale. (Digital Globe, 2015).

2. Statistiques permettant de rendre compte de l'avancée de la mise en œuvre du Programme 2030 et de l'Agenda 2063

2.1 Indicateurs du Programme 2030 et de l'Agenda 2063 : la contribution de l'Afrique

Il est demandé aux pays d'Afrique de rendre compte de l'avancée relative à la mise en œuvre du Programme 2030 et de l'Agenda 2063, ce qui requiert une grande quantité de données. Le Programme 2030 présente 17 objectifs et 169 cibles. En 2015, la Commission statistique a constitué le Groupe d'experts des Nations unies et de l'extérieur chargé des indicateurs relatifs aux objectifs de développement durable afin de définir le cadre de suivi et de compte rendu du Programme 2030. En mars 2016, la Commission a approuvé un ensemble de 230 indicateurs mondiaux qui feront l'objet de futures précisions techniques. Celui-ci sera complété par des indicateurs continentaux et nationaux. À l'échelle mondiale, les parties prenantes en charge du suivi et de l'examen assurés à l'occasion du Forum Politique de haut niveau tiendront compte du rapport annuel sur l'état d'avancement de la mise en œuvre des objectifs préparés par le Secrétaire général en collaboration avec le système des Nations unies sur la base du cadre mondial d'indicateurs, des données fournies par les systèmes de statistique nationaux et d'informations collectées à l'echelle régional.

L'Agenda 2063 présente 20 objectifs et 174 cibles. Son cadre de résultats illustre les liens qui unissent logiquement la vision de l'Union africaine, les sept aspirations de l'Afrique, les domaines dans lesquels s'inscrivent chaque objectif ou priorité et les cibles associées. Suite à l'adoption de l'Agenda 2063 par les chefs d'État ou de gouvernement de l'Union africaine en janvier 2015, la Commission africaine a élaboré le premier plan de mise en œuvre sur dix ans, lequel couvre la période 2014-2023. Celui-ci présente 63 indicateurs clés pour suivre la mise en œuvre de l'Agenda 2063 et en rendre compte, dont 40 sont identiques aux indicateurs relatifs aux objectifs de développement durable.

En 2016, la Conférence des ministres africains des Finances, de la planification et du développement économique ont encouragé les institutions panafricaines à adopter une stratégie cohérente pour une mise en œuvre efficace et coordonnée de l'Agenda 2063 et du Programme 2030. Les ministres ont convenu d'un cadre de suivi et d'évaluation unique adapté au programme et à l'agenda, ainsi que d'un mécanisme d'établissement de rapport commun qui permettra l'élaboration d'un rapport de performance périodique unique. Ils ont également reconnu que la mise en œuvre du Programme et de l'Agenda, son suivi et l'élaboration de comptes rendus nécessitent une stratégie cohérente et un ensemble coordonné d'objectifs, de cibles et d'indicateurs, ainsi qu'une plateforme de revue et de compte rendu harmonisée. De nombreux pays africains tentent actuellement d'aligner les objectifs de développement mondiaux et continentaux sur leurs propres priorités nationales de développement, ce qui implique d'harmoniser, de coordonner ou d'unifier les besoins en matière

---

[1] L'IDA est une institution présente dans plusieurs domaines qui accorde des prêts à taux très favorable ou des dons pour financer les activités de développement des pays pauvres. L'éligibilité à l'aide de l'IDA dépend avant tout de la pauvreté relative du pays. En l'occurrence le revenu national brut par habitant ne doit pas dépasser un certain plafond (1215 dollars en 2016). L'IDA soutient également des pays, notamment de petites économies insulaires, qui dépassent le seuil mais n'ont pas la solvabilité nécessaire pour emprunter à des taux non concessionnels.

de données. Les institutions panafricaines travaillent actuellement sur un cadre de suivi et d'évaluation cohérent qui servira à suivre la mise en œuvre de l'Agenda 2063 et du Programme 2030 à l'échelle du continent et à en rendre compte. Pour ce faire, les pays doivent produire et diffuser de grandes quantités de données.

2.2 Disponibilité des données et possibilités de rendre compte de l'Agenda 2063 et du Programme 2030

La Division de statistique a conduit à la création de la plateforme de diffusion de la base de données mondiale sur les objectifs de développement durable qui possède aujourd'hui une quantité honnête de données relatives aux indicateurs (Division de statistique, 2017b). Sur un total de 230 indicateurs, 91 portent sur les pays d'Afrique, soit 37,8 %. Le tableau 1.2 récapitule les sources des points de données présentes dans la base de données. Certains indicateurs sont ventilés par sexe, âge et localisation géographique. Le tableau présente également 33 indicateurs supplémentaires susceptibles de contribuer à mesurer les objectifs. En plus des données à l'echelle national sont fournis des totaux sur l'Afrique subsaharienne et l'Afrique du Nord. Ces données couvrent la période 1990-2016. À l'echelle mondial, 139 indicateurs n'ont pas les données nécessaires pour suivre la réalisation des objectifs et cibles afférentes et pour en rendre compte.

TABLEAU 1. ACCESSIBILITÉ DES DONNÉES RELATIVES AUX OBJECTIFS DE DÉVELOPPEMENT DURABLE DANS LES PAYS AFRICAINS

OBJECTIFS DE DÉVELOPPEMENT DURABLE	DONNÉES DISPONIBLES PAR TYPE D'INDICATEUR			NOMBRE TOTAL D'INDICATEURS*	POURCENTAGE D'INDICATEURS DISPOSANT DE DONNÉES
	DÉVELOPPEMENT DURABLE	SUPPLÉMENTAIRE	TOTAL		
1	3	3	6	12	25,0
2	8	4	12	14	57,1
3	18	7	25	26	69,2
4	6	3	9	11	54,5
5	3	1	5	14	21,4
6	2	4	6	11	18,2
7	4	0	4	6	66,7
8	10	1	11	17	58,8
9	8	1	9	12	66,7
10	5	0	5	11	45,5
11	1	1	2	15	6,7
12	2	1	3	14	14,3
13	0	0	0	9	0,0
14	1	0	1	7	14,3
15	6	0	6	14	42,9
16	6	5	11	23	26,1
17	8	3	11	25	32,0
Total	91	33	124	241	37,8

Au total, 11 indicateurs sont répétés.

Certains objectifs de développement durable disposent de suffisamment de données pour plus de la moitié des indicateurs, comme l'objectif 3 (69,2 %), l'objectif 7 (66,7 %), l'objectif 9 (66,7 %), l'objectif 8 (58,8 %), l'objectif 2 (57,1 %) et l'objectif 4 (54,5 %). Il n'existe en revanche pas de données pour les indicateurs de l'objectif 13.

Le tableau 2 souligne la nécessité pour les pays d'Afrique de déployer des efforts considérables en vue d'aligner les plans de développement nationaux sur les objectifs de développement durable (Commission pour l'Afrique et al., 2016). L'Afrique du Sud, la Côte d'Ivoire, le Kenya, le Nigéria, la République unie de Tanzanie, et le Sénégal agissent actuellement dans ce sens (Commission économique pour l'Afrique, 2016). Tirant profit des investissements consacrés à la production de données en vue de suivre l'avancée de la réalisation des objectifs du Millénaire pour le développement, un certain nombre de systèmes de statistique sont en mesure de produire des données permettant de mesurer les progrès accomplis, notamment en ce qui concerne les domaines sociaux-économiques des objectifs (c'est-à-dire les objectifs 1 à 4 et 6 à 10). À l'exception de l'Afrique du Sud, qui possède la capacité de production de statistiques la plus élevée du continent, la production, la diffusion et l'utilisation de données relatives aux objectifs 11 à 15 restent insuffisantes pour de nombreux pays. En République unie de Tanzanie, par exemple, la plupart des indicateurs dans ces deux domaines sont nouveaux pour le système de statistiques national. Au total, 27 indicateurs de ces domaines requièrent de nouveaux systèmes de collecte de données, dont 11 pour le seul objectif 15.

2.3 La contribution de l'Afrique à la base de données mondiale sur les objectifs de développement durable en Afrique

Le nombre d'indicateurs sans données sur l'Afrique dans la base de données mondiale des objectifs de développement durable montre la persistance des lacunes dans les systèmes de statistique nationaux (Division de statistique, 2017a). Les sources des points de données au sein de la base de données mondiale sur les objectifs de développement durable sont reportées dans le tableau 2. On notera que les estimations, le suivi mondial et dans le sens de modélisation fournissent 54 % des données totales relatives aux objectifs concernant l'Afrique. Malgré

une augmentation de la part de données nationales et de données ajustées à l'échelle nationale, passant de 22,8 % pour la période 1990-2005 à 33,5 % pour la période 2006-2016, leur part globale sur les deux périodes confondues n'atteignait que 28,9 %.

Au cours de la période 2006-2016, la proportion de sources de données nationales ou ajustées à l'échelle nationale variait entre 16,6 % en Libye et 37,2 % à Maurice. Les pays dont la part de données nationales ou ajustées à l'échelle nationale est inférieure à 20 % comprennent la Libye (18,6 %), la Somalie (18,6 %) et le Soudan du Sud (18,8 %). À l'inverse, plus d'un tiers des données en Afrique du Sud (33,3 %), en Éthiopie (33,7 %), en Égypte (33,7 %), à Cabo Verde (34,3 %), au Niger (34,6 %), au Ghana (35,9 %), au Maroc (36,2 %) et à Maurice sont nationales ou ajustées à l'échelle nationale. Au total, les estimations des organisations internationales concernent 39 % des indicateurs.

Cette proportion réduite de données de sources nationales souligne la nécessité d'investir davantage dans les systèmes de statistiques nationaux afin de développer leurs capacités dans différents domaines comme celui de l'administration, des enregistrements des faits d'état civil et de l'établissement des statistiques de l'état civil. Cela permettra d'améliorer la collecte, l'analyse, la diffusion et la disponibilité de données précises, opportunes et comparables. Il est également nécessaire d'investir dans les données afin de rendre plus efficaces les processus de décision et le suivi de la mise en œuvre des programmes de développement nationaux et d'encourager le partage des données avec les organisations infrarégionales, régionales et internationales qui suivent et rendent compte de l'Agenda 2063 et du Programme 2030. De plus, les autorités nationales de statistique se doivent de collaborer avec les autres parties prenantes, telles que les organisations du secteur privé et de la société civile impliquées dans des activités de production de données.

2.4 Un plaidoyer pour l'action

La réalisation des objectifs de développement durable requiert que tous les acteurs, parties prenantes et bénéficiaires aient accès aux informations pertinentes afin de pouvoir jouer leur rôle dans le processus de développement, et notamment dans la mise en œuvre des programmes, le suivi de celle-ci et l'élaboration de rapports sur les progrès réalisés. Ces informations devraient toujours inclure des statistiques officielles.

TABLEAU 2. ORIGINES DES DONNÉES DES INDICATEURS DES OBJECTIFS DE DÉVELOPPEMENT DURABLE EN AFRIQUE

TYPE DE SOURCE	1990 – 2005		2006 – 2016		1990 - 2016	
	TOTAL DES POINTS DE DONNÉES	PROPORTION (POURCENTAGE)	TOTAL DES POINTS DE DONNÉES	PROPORTION (POURCENTAGE)	TOTAL DES POINTS DE DONNÉES	PROPORTION (POURCENTAGE)
Nationale ou ajustée à l'échelle nationale	7 948	22,8	15 443	33,5	23 391	28,9
Estimation	14 981	42,9	16 600	36,0	31 581	39,0
Suivi mondial	2 672	7,7	4 867	10,6	7 539	9,3
Modélisation	1 957	5,6	2 656	5,8	4 613	5,7
Autres	7 336	21,0	6 493	14,1	13 829	17,1
Total	34 894	100	46 059	100	80 953	100

Source : Base de données mondiale sur les objectifs de développement durable. Disponible à l'adresse suivante : http://www.un.org/ fr/africa/osaa/peace/agenda2063.shtml.

Malgré les progrès significatifs réalisés ces dix dernières années en Afrique en matière de production et de diffusion de statistiques, les statistiques officielles produites par les systèmes de statistique nationaux ne sont pas toujours faciles d'accès en raison de leur format. Ainsi, le suivi de la large gamme de questions de développement couvertes par les objectifs de développement durable et la nécessité de respecter le principe de ventilation par âge, sexe, revenu ou situation géographique représentent un défi supplémentaire pour des systèmes de statistique déjà fragiles en raison du manque d'infrastructures technologiques et de ressources financières et humaines.

La mesure de la réalisation des objectifs de développement durable et des objectifs de l'Agenda 2063 implique d'investir de fortes sommes dans la statistique pour combler les lacunes qui freinent la produc- tion de données de qualité, pertinentes, opportunes et comparables, notamment dans les capacités et les moyens technologiques (Commission économique pour l'Afrique, 2016). Le retour sur investissement peut s'avérer très profitable et bénéficier non seulement aux processus de décision et de suivi fondés sur des données factuelles, mais également à l'ensemble du système statistique par l'ouverture d'une marge de progrès dans différents domaines, par exemple l'admi nistration ou l'analyse et de la diffusion de données.

Le coût de ces investissements sera cependant extrêmement élevé s'il doit être pris en charge par la seule communauté statistique officielle, tout particulièrement celui de la collecte de données dans le cadre du Programme 2030, de l'Agenda 2063 et des priorités nationales de développement. La collaboration des différentes communautés de données entre elles ainsi que la coordination, l'harmonisation et l'intégration des données de différentes sources au sein des écosystèmes de données seront donc utiles pour combler les manques dans les statistiques officielles, réduire les Ce besoin de collaboration entre les différentes communautés de données était déjà au centre des débats sur la question des capacités statistiques du programme de développement pour l'après-2015, lequel appelait à faire intervenir un plus grand éventail d'acteurs dans le développement des méthodes statistiques, notamment des scientifiques des données et des spécialistes du domaine géospatial issus du secteur privé et du milieu de la recherche, des représentants du gouvernement et d'autres utilisateurs de données. Ces besoins ont été rappelés par le Groupe de personnalités de haut niveau qui a même appelé à une « révolution des données »[2] en faveur du développement.

[2] *L'expression « révolution des données » fait référence à « une augmentation rapide du volume de données, de la vitesse de production de données, du nombre de producteurs de données, de la Diffusion des données et de pla gamme d'éléments qui disposent données grâce à l'appui des nouvelles technologies telles que les téléphones portables et « l'Internet des objets » ainsi que d'autres sources, comme les données qualitatives, les données générées par les citoyens et les données de perception ; de même qu'une demande grandissante de données de toutes les sphères de la société » (Groupe consultatif d'experts indépendants sur la révolution des données pour le développement durable, 2014).*

Cette révolution des données peut servir de catalyseur d'une transformation sociale, économique et environ- nementale en Afrique. La hausse de la demande en données et en statistiques dans le cadre du Programme 2030 et de l'Agenda 2063 représente pour l'Afrique une opportunité de s'engager dans une révolution des données et d'améliorer par là même ses capacités statistiques dans tous les domaines. Leur adoption coïncide en effet avec l'innovation sans précédent des technologies des données utilisées pour collecter, analyser et diffuser d'importants volumes de données de tous types, ce qui permettra d'améliorer l'accès et l'exploitation des données plus nombreuses et plus détaillées qu'auparavant (Groupe consultatif d'experts indépen- dants sur la révolution des données pour le dévelop- pement durable, 2014). Aujourd'hui, les communautés et écosystèmes de données africains osent innover et expérimenter, mais il s'agit dans la plupart des cas d'initiatives d'envergure modérée et souvent isolées. S'il doit exploiter tout le potentiel de transformation que lui offre la révolution des données, le continent africain devra consentir à des efforts plus réguliers, à grande échelle, coordonnés et durables (Commission économique pour l'Afrique, 2015).

Les gouvernements africains reconnaissent l'impor- tance d'une révolution des données telle qu'elle est incarnée par le Consensus africain sur les données (Commission économique pour l'Afrique et al., 2015) et les autres initiatives statistiques et de développe- ment, y compris la Charte africaine de la statistique et la Stratégie pour l'harmonisation des statistiques en Afrique mise en place par l'Union africaine. Le consensus est une stratégie de mise en œuvre de la révolution des données en Afrique adoptée à l'occasion d'une conférence de haut niveau sur la révolution des données, qui s'est déroulée en mars 2015 en réponse à la demande d'un cadre pour la révolution des données en Afrique et aux implications de celle-ci pour l'Agenda 2063 et pour le Programme 2030.

À l'échelle national, cela se traduit par des programmes de développement à long terme ; les changements, les réformes et les innovations nécessaires pour permettre aux États membres de s'engager sur la voie de la révolution des données sont nombreux. Il est donc nécessaire de pouvoir accéder à de nouvelles sources de données, et en particulier de mégadonnées, pour compléter les statistiques officielles, et de mettre en place des partenariats stratégiques innovants entre les systèmes de statistiques nationaux et d'autres acteurs des diverses communautés de données. Les mégadonnées ne respectent cependant pas toujours les principes statistiques, ce qui représente un défi de taille, car l'analyse et l'obtention de résultats s'en trouvent compliquées. Un travail important sur les méthodologies, les définitions ou encore les méthodes de classification est donc essentiel. En outre, des problèmes d'ordre technique, juridique, relatifs à la propriété et à la confidentialité soulevés par les mégadonnées entravent en effet l'accès à cellesci et leur exploitation malgré leur ponctualité et leur rentabilité (Robin et al., 2016). Ces problèmes appellent des réformes juridiques, législatives et politiques. Selon les lignes directrices de la stratégie nationale de développement de la statistique sur la révolution des données, « en fournissant un cadre juridique aux pays afin de guider leurs propres processus législatifs, la Charte fournit en effet une base et des lignes directrices qui soutiennent la modification des lois concernant les développements des nouvelles données tels que l'usage de mégadonnées »[3].

L'adoption de principes sur les données ouvertes pour les systèmes de statistique nationaux comme pour d'autres écosystèmes de données nationaux est l'une des approches les plus efficaces pour mettre les données à disposition d'un public large. Les données ouvertes sont accessibles gratuitement en ligne et peuvent être utilisées, réutilisées et redistribuées à la seule condition d'en citer la provenance et de les partager.

Ces avancées au regard des sources de données existantes sont également un élément clé d'un suivi efficace des progrès accomplis. Les enquêtes de recensement et les données administratives sont les principales sources de données utilisées dans le cadre de la mise en œuvre du Programme 2030 et de l'Agenda 2063. Il sera donc primordial d'étendre la portée des recensements et des enquêtes, d'augmenter leur fréquence et de moderniser les systèmes administratifs, y compris l'enregistrement des faits d'état civil et l'établissement des statistiques de l'état civil. Cela implique d'investir considérablement dans les technologies des données, les capacités, les infrastructures et les ressources humaines et financières.

---

[3] Disponible à l'adresse suivante : http://www.paris21.org/nsdsguidelines/fr

Le développement de l'infrastructure nationale de données spatiales est nécessaire au renforcement des capacités, au financement, à la coordination, aux ensembles de données fondamentales et aux systèmes de référence. L'évaluation des besoins en capacités et des lacunes permettra de soutenir les efforts de développement de la statistique dans le cadre du Programme 2030 et de l'Agenda 2063 aux niveaux national, régional et international.

3. Conclusion

Parmi les initiatives prises en faveur du développement, un processus de développement statistique continu a été mis en place pour aider les pays en développement à produire les données nécessaires au suivi de la réalisation des objectifs du Millénaire pour le développement et à l'élaboration de comptes rendus. Il est impératif de continuer à travailler au renforcement des capacités des États membres à produire, analyser, stocker, diffuser et exploiter leurs données statistiques. Il est nécessaire d'obtenir des financements supplémentaires et d'accepter les nouvelles sources de données, les innovations et les informations géospatiales. Les initiatives prises pour le développement statistique doivent prendre en compte les difficultés énumérées ci-dessus de façon à ce que les pays africains puissent produire et diffuser en temps opportun des données statistiques de haute qualité et pertinentes, ceci afin de suivre la mise en œuvre de leurs programmes de développement nationaux et de rendre compte des progrès réalisés par rapport à la réalisation des objectifs de développement durable et des objectifs de l'Agenda 2063.

Le Consensus africain sur les données préconise les actions suivantes pour accompagner la révolution des données et suivre efficacement la mise en œuvre du Programme 2030 et de l'Agenda 2063 dans les pays d'Afrique :

- Établir un écosystème de données inclusif, impliquant le gouvernement, le secteur privé, le milieu universitaire, la société civile, les communautés locales et les partenaires du développement capable d'appréhender les aspects informationnels de la prise de décision en matière de développement d'une manière coordonnée. Les gouvernements doivent jouer un rôle proactif pour impliquer cette communauté et les autres parties prenantes doivent mettre en avant le partenariat avec le gouvernement. Cet élément peut être rapproché de la stratégie de développement de la statistique. Les stratégies nationales existantes pour le déve-loppement de la statistique devraient être révisées afin de tendre vers l'inclusion de l'intégralité des communautés de données.

- Comme premier pas critique pour renforcer l'écosystème des données, évaluer les besoins en matière de capacités, les cadres juridiques et financiers, les institutions participantes, les atouts et lacunes en matière de données au niveau national, local et communautaire en vue de reconnaître les rôles des diverses parties prenantes et d'élaborer une feuille de route réalisable identifiant les étapes clés.

- Faire en sorte que les gouvernements mènent le processus pour s'assurer que les coûts de production et de vulgarisation de toute donnée requise soient financés par des ressources provenant de sources nationales et durables. Il convient de mettre en place une stratégie de mobilisation des ressources.

- Faire en sorte que les gouvernements identifient une structure autorisée à certifier les données ouvertes produites par les communautés de données, sur la base des critères reconnus de qualité, de fiabilité, d'opportunité et de pertinence par rapport aux besoins en informations statistiques.

- Élaborer des systèmes d'enregistrement d'état civil qui produisent des données essentielles et fiables doit constituer la pierre angulaire de la révolution des données. De la même façon, il faut appuyer les systèmes de données sur la population, l'économie, l'emploi, la santé, l'éducation, la gestion foncière et agricole pour assurer la production de données fiables et à temps en vue d'assister le processus de prise de décisions aux niveaux national et local.

- Adopter, encourager et renforcer les partenariats public-privé comme stratégie pour le transfert

des connaissances et des technologies et la promotion des collaborations, un financement et un partage d'expériences durables

- Étendre, tant que c'est possible, l'applicabilité des normes et standards relatifs aux données officielles à toutes les données pour améliorer leur validité et fiabilité.

- Encourager des méthodologies et technologies innovantes et intégrées, y compris les technologies géospatiales, dans l'objectif

d'améliorer la collecte, l'analyse et l'utilisation des données. Il est important d'intégrer des données statistiques des indicateurs spécifiques sensibles au genre dans le suivi et l'évaluation.

- Faire en sorte que les institutions panafricaines telles que la BAD, la Commission de l'Union africaine et la CEA s'approprient la mise en oeuvre du Consensus africain sur les données conjointement avec d'autres partenaires du développement.

Part 1
Partie 1

Summary Tables
Tableaux résumés

Section 1

Social and Demographic Indicators

Indicateurs démographiques et sociaux

1-1 Total mid-year population - Population totale au milieu de l'année

THOUSANDS										MILLIERS
Country	2009	2010	2011	2012	2013	2014	2015	2016	2017	Pays
Algeria	35 466	36 118	36 820	37 566	38 339	39 113	39 872	40 606	41 318	Algérie
Angola	22 550	23 369	24 219	25 096	25 998	26 920	27 859	28 813	29 784	Angola
Benin	8 945	9 199	9 461	9 729	10 004	10 287	10 576	10 872	11 176	Bénin
Botswana	1 980	2 015	2 051	2 089	2 129	2 169	2 209	2 250	2 292	Botswana
Burkina Faso	15 141	15 605	16 082	16 571	17 073	17 586	18 111	18 646	19 193	Burkina Faso
Burundi	8 489	8 767	9 043	9 320	9 600	9 892	10 199	10 524	10 864	Burundi
Cabo Verde	497	502	508	514	520	526	533	540	546	Cabo Verde
Cameroon	19 433	19 971	20 520	21 082	21 656	22 240	22 835	23 439	24 054	Cameroun
Central African Republic	4 404	4 449	4 476	4 490	4 500	4 515	4 546	4 595	4 659	République Centrafricaine
Chad	11 503	11 887	12 289	12 705	13 134	13 569	14 009	14 453	14 900	Tchad
Comoros	673	690	707	724	742	759	777	796	814	Comores
Congo	4 254	4 387	4 513	4 633	4 751	4 871	4 996	5 126	5 261	Congo
Côte d'Ivoire	19 936	20 401	20 895	21 419	21 966	22 531	23 108	23 696	24 295	Côte d'Ivoire
Democratic Republic of the Congo	62 409	64 523	66 714	68 979	71 316	73 723	76 197	78 736	81 340	Rép. Démocratique du Congo
Djibouti	837	851	866	881	897	912	927	942	957	Djibouti
Egypt	82 465	84 108	85 898	87 813	89 807	91 813	93 778	95 689	97 553	Egypte
Equatorial Guinea	909	951	994	1 039	1 084	1 129	1 175	1 221	1 268	Guinée Equatoriale
Eritrea	4 310	4 391	4 475	4 561	4 651	4 746	4 847	4 955	5 069	Erythrée
Ethiopia	85 416	87 703	90 047	92 444	94 888	97 367	99 873	102 403	104 957	Ethiopie
Gabon	1 587	1 640	1 697	1 757	1 817	1 876	1 930	1 980	2 025	Gabon
Gambia, the	1 640	1 692	1 746	1 802	1 859	1 918	1 978	2 039	2 101	Gambie
Ghana	23 904	24 512	25 122	25 733	26 346	26 963	27 583	28 207	28 834	Ghana
Guinea	10 557	10 794	11 035	11 281	11 537	11 806	12 092	12 396	12 717	Guinée
Guinea-Bissau	1 517	1 556	1 596	1 638	1 681	1 726	1 771	1 816	1 861	Guinée-Bissau
Kenya	40 237	41 350	42 487	43 647	44 827	46 024	47 236	48 462	49 700	Kenya
Lesotho	2 019	2 041	2 064	2 090	2 117	2 146	2 175	2 204	2 233	Lesotho
Liberia	3 812	3 948	4 070	4 182	4 286	4 391	4 500	4 614	4 732	Libéria
Libya	6 121	6 169	6 194	6 198	6 196	6 204	6 235	6 293	6 375	Libye
Madagascar	20 569	21 152	21 744	22 347	22 961	23 590	24 234	24 895	25 571	Madagascar
Malawi	14 715	15 167	15 628	16 097	16 577	17 069	17 574	18 092	18 622	Malawi
Mali	14 607	15 075	15 541	16 007	16 478	16 963	17 468	17 995	18 542	Mali
Mauritania	3 506	3 610	3 718	3 830	3 946	4 064	4 182	4 301	4 420	Mauritanie
Mauritius	1 244	1 248	1 251	1 253	1 255	1 257	1 259	1 262	1 265	Maurice
Morocco	31 990	32 410	32 859	33 334	33 825	34 318	34 803	35 277	35 740	Maroc
Mozambique	23 524	24 221	24 939	25 677	26 434	27 212	28 011	28 829	29 669	Mozambique
Namibia	2 137	2 173	2 216	2 264	2 317	2 371	2 426	2 480	2 534	Namibie
Niger	15 814	16 426	17 065	17 732	18 426	19 148	19 897	20 673	21 477	Niger
Nigeria	154 402	158 578	162 877	167 297	171 829	176 461	181 182	185 990	190 886	Nigéria
Rwanda	9 977	10 247	10 516	10 789	11 065	11 345	11 630	11 918	12 208	Rwanda
Sao Tome and Principe	171	175	179	183	187	191	196	200	204	Sao Tomé-et-Principe
Senegal	12 551	12 916	13 301	13 704	14 120	14 546	14 977	15 412	15 851	Sénégal
Seychelles	91	91	92	92	93	93	94	94	95	Seychelles
Sierra Leone	6 310	6 459	6 612	6 766	6 922	7 079	7 237	7 396	7 557	Sierra Leone
Somalia	11 708	12 053	12 405	12 764	13 132	13 513	13 908	14 318	14 743	Somalie
South Africa	50 971	51 585	52 264	52 998	53 767	54 540	55 291	56 015	56 717	Afrique du Sud
South Sudan	9 671	10 067	10 449	10 818	11 177	11 531	11 882	12 231	12 576	Soudan du Sud
Sudan	33 651	34 386	35 167	35 990	36 850	37 738	38 648	39 579	40 533	Soudan
Swaziland	1 181	1 203	1 225	1 248	1 271	1 295	1 319	1 343	1 367	Swaziland
Tanzania, United Republic of	44 664	46 099	47 571	49 083	50 637	52 235	53 880	55 572	57 310	Tanzanie, République Unie de
Togo	6 330	6 503	6 679	6 859	7 043	7 229	7 417	7 606	7 798	Togo
Tunisia	10 522	10 640	10 761	10 887	11 015	11 144	11 274	11 403	11 532	Tunisie
Uganda	32 772	33 915	35 094	36 307	37 554	38 833	40 145	41 488	42 863	Ouganda
Zambia	13 456	13 850	14 265	14 700	15 153	15 621	16 101	16 591	17 094	Zambie
Zimbabwe	13 811	14 086	14 387	14 711	15 055	15 412	15 777	16 150	16 530	Zimbabwe
Africa	**1 022 859**	**1 049 446**	**1 076 934**	**1 105 285**	**1 134 398**	**1 164 130**	**1 194 370**	**1 225 081**	**1 256 268**	**Afrique**

Source: UNPD

1-2. Urban and female population - Population urbaine et féminine

PERCENTAGE	Urban / Urbain				Female / Feminine				POURCENTAGE
Country	2000	2005	2010	2017	2000	2005	2010	2017	Pays
Algeria	59.9	63.8	67.5	71.9	49.3	49.5	49.5	49.5	Algérie
Angola	32.4	36.2	40.1	45.6	50.7	50.6	51.1	51.0	Angola
Benin	38.3	40.0	41.9	44.9	51.0	50.5	50.3	50.1	Bénin
Botswana	53.2	55.1	56.2	58.0	50.2	50.1	50.6	50.6	Botswana
Burkina Faso	17.8	21.5	25.7	31.5	50.9	50.7	50.4	50.1	Burkina Faso
Burundi	8.3	9.4	10.6	12.7	50.7	50.6	50.9	50.8	Burundi
Cameroon	45.5	48.5	51.5	66.8	50.2	50.1	50.3	50.2	Cameroun
Cabo Verde	53.4	57.7	61.8	55.5	51.7	51.1	50.0	50.0	Cabo Verde
Central African Republic	37.6	38.1	38.8	40.7	50.9	50.8	50.7	50.7	République Centrafricaine
Chad	21.6	21.8	22.0	22.8	50.2	50.1	50.0	49.9	Tchad
Comoros	28.1	27.9	27.9	28.5	49.7	49.6	49.6	49.6	Comores
Congo	58.7	61.0	63.2	66.2	50.1	50.0	50.0	50.0	Congo
Côte d'Ivoire	43.5	46.8	50.6	55.6	50.4	50.3	49.0	49.3	Côte d'Ivoire
Democratic Republic of the Congo	35.1	37.5	39.9	43.5	48.3	48.7	50.2	50.1	Rép. Démocratique du Congo
Djibouti	76.5	76.8	77.0	77.5	49.7	49.7	49.8	49.8	Djibouti
Egypt	42.8	43.0	43.0	43.3	49.7	49.6	49.5	49.4	Egypte
Equatorial Guinea	38.8	38.9	39.2	40.3	48.8	48.7	45.7	44.6	Guinée Equatoriale
Eritrea	17.6	18.9	20.6	23.6	50.3	50.1	50.0	49.9	Erythrée
Ethiopia	14.7	15.7	17.3	20.4	50.1	50.1	50.1	50.1	Ethiopie
Gabon	80.1	83.4	85.7	87.6	50.4	49.9	49.0	48.6	Gabon
Gambia	47.9	52.3	56.3	60.8	50.3	50.4	50.5	50.5	Gambie
Ghana	43.9	47.3	50.7	55.3	49.5	50.0	50.5	50.2	Ghana
Guinea	31.0	32.8	34.9	38.2	50.2	50.0	50.0	49.9	Guinée
Guinea-Bissau	36.7	40.9	45.2	50.8	50.6	50.4	51.0	50.8	Guinée-Bissau
Kenya	19.9	21.7	23.6	26.5	50.1	50.0	50.3	50.3	Kenya
Lesotho	19.6	22.3	24.8	28.4	51.5	51.2	51.6	51.5	Lesotho
Liberia	44.3	46.1	47.8	50.5	50.0	49.9	49.7	49.6	Libéria
Libya	76.4	76.9	77.6	79.0	47.8	48.3	49.0	49.6	Libye
Madagascar	27.1	28.8	31.9	36.4	50.2	50.2	50.2	50.1	Madagascar
Malawi	14.6	15.1	15.5	16.7	50.4	50.3	50.6	50.5	Malawi
Mali	28.4	32.1	36.0	41.4	50.1	49.8	50.0	50.0	Mali
Mauritania	49.2	53.1	56.7	61.0	49.9	49.8	49.8	49.6	Mauritanie
Mauritius	42.7	41.6	40.6	39.5	50.4	50.4	50.4	50.5	Maurice
Morocco	53.3	55.1	57.7	61.2	50.5	50.7	50.7	50.5	Maroc
Mozambique	29.1	30.0	31.0	32.8	52.0	51.7	51.4	51.2	Mozambique
Namibia	32.4	36.6	41.6	48.6	50.9	51.2	51.6	51.4	Namibie
Niger	16.2	16.7	17.6	19.3	50.0	49.8	50.0	49.9	Niger
Nigeria	34.8	39.1	43.5	49.4	49.4	49.3	49.4	49.3	Nigéria
Rwanda	14.9	19.3	24.0	30.7	52.0	52.3	51.0	51.0	Rwanda
Sao Tome and Principe	53.4	58.0	61.9	66.2	50.4	50.3	50.2	50.2	Sao Tomé-et-Principe
Senegal	40.4	41.1	42.2	44.4	50.8	51.0	51.0	50.9	Sénégal
Seychelles	50.1	51.1	52.3	54.5	50.2	50.0	48.4	50.7	Seychelles
Sierra Leone	35.6	36.8	38.2	40.7	50.6	50.7	50.6	50.5	Sierra Leone
Somalia	33.3	35.2	37.3	40.5	50.4	50.3	50.1	50.2	Somalie
South Africa	56.9	59.5	62.2	65.8	50.8	50.9	50.9	50.9	Afrique du Sud
South Sudan	16.5	17.2	17.9	19.3	50.2	50.1	50.0	49.9	Soudan du Sud
Sudan	32.5	32.8	33.1	34.2	49.8	49.8	50.1	50.0	Soudan
Swaziland	22.7	22.0	21.5	21.3	51.6	51.1	51.5	51.6	Swaziland
Tanzania, United Republic of	22.3	24.9	28.1	33.0	50.3	50.4	50.7	50.6	Tanzanie, République Unie de
Togo	32.9	35.2	37.5	41.0	51.1	50.9	50.2	50.2	Togo
Tunisia	63.4	65.1	65.9	67.3	49.8	50.2	50.4	50.6	Tunisie
Uganda	12.1	13.0	14.5	16.8	50.3	50.2	50.4	50.3	Ouganda
Zambia	34.8	36.6	38.7	41.8	50.3	50.2	50.4	50.4	Zambie
Zimbabwe	33.8	34.1	33.2	32.2	50.2	50.4	51.3	51.3	Zimbabwe
Africa	34.49	36.28	38.30	41.31	50.2	50.2	50.1	50.1	37.88

Source: UNPD

1-3 Economically active population - Population active

Country	Total ('000)						Female / Femmes (%)						Pays
	2012	2013	2014	2015	2016	2017	2012	2013	2014	2015	2016	2017	
Algeria	11 598	12 064	11 643	11 799	11 937	12 106	18.8	19.2	18.4	18.3	18.2	18.3	Algérie
Angola	10 292	10 671	11 063	11 464	11 871	12 299	50.0	50.0	50.0	50.1	50.1	50.1	Angola
Benin	3 888	4 008	4 134	4 265	4 397	4 542	49.1	49.1	49.1	49.1	49.1	49.2	Bénin
Botswana	962	1 028	1 052	1 077	1 102	1 130	45.7	46.2	46.4	46.4	46.5	46.5	Botswana
Burkina Faso	6 132	6 247	6 360	6 572	6 787	6 995	44.1	44.4	44.7	44.7	44.7	44.6	Burkina Faso
Burundi	4 081	4 181	4 283	4 424	4 572	4 713	52.2	52.3	52.4	52.4	52.3	52.4	Burundi
Cameroon	9 085	9 352	9 628	9 911	10 196	10 500	46.8	46.8	46.9	46.9	46.9	47.0	Cameroun
Cabo Verde	205	210	215	220	225	230	40.0	40.5	40.5	40.9	41.3	41.3	Cabo Verde
Central African Republic	1 832	1 831	1 829	1 833	1 856	1 892	45.6	45.2	45.2	45.2	45.3	45.2	République Centrafricaine
Chad	4 710	4 879	5 053	5 232	5 412	5 603	45.5	45.6	45.7	45.8	45.7	45.8	Tchad
Comoros	182	187	193	199	205	211	41.2	41.2	41.5	41.7	41.5	41.7	Comores
Congo	1 871	1 916	1 960	2 007	2 060	2 116	48.6	48.6	48.6	48.6	48.5	48.6	Congo
Côte d'Ivoire	7 218	7 361	7 511	7 664	7 806	8 016	49.8	49.8	49.8	49.9	49.8	49.8	Côte d'Ivoire
Democratic Republic of the Congo	26 835	27 725	28 650	29 613	30 595	31 644	39.2	39.7	40.1	40.5	41.0	41.1	Rép. Démocratique du Congo
Djibouti	346	354	363	372	380	389	40.8	41.0	41.3	41.7	41.8	41.9	Djibouti
Egypt	29 134	29 844	29 973	30 078	30 469	31 149	22.5	23.1	23.1	23.1	23.0	23.1	Egypte
Equatorial Guinea	376	395	416	438	455	472	40.7	40.5	40.1	39.7	39.3	39.2	Guinée Equatoriale
Eritrea	2 145	2 186	2 230	2 277	2 336	2 401	46.9	46.8	46.8	46.8	46.9	46.9	Erythrée
Ethiopia	43 679	45 197	46 668	48 172	49 662	51 450	46.9	46.9	47.0	47.2	47.3	47.3	Ethiopie
Gabon	556	581	606	631	650	668	39.6	39.8	39.9	39.9	40.0	40.1	Gabon
Gambia	577	596	616	637	657	681	43.8	44.0	44.0	44.1	44.3	44.3	Gambie
Ghana	11 956	12 307	12 626	12 951	13 273	13 637	49.8	49.6	49.6	49.6	49.6	49.5	Ghana
Guinea	4 137	4 238	4 347	4 464	4 582	4 716	48.9	48.9	48.9	48.9	49.1	49.1	Guinée
Guinea-Bissau	676	696	717	738	759	780	47.0	47.1	47.0	47.0	47.0	47.1	Guinée-Bissau
Kenya	16 513	17 056	17 610	18 172	18 748	19 352	47.7	47.9	48.1	48.3	48.5	48.5	Kenya
Lesotho	884	894	910	926	943	959	46.8	46.6	46.8	46.9	46.9	46.7	Lesotho
Liberia	1 337	1 371	1 408	1 447	1 488	1 533	47.9	48.2	48.3	48.4	48.5	48.4	Libéria
Libya	2 373	2 346	2 326	2 333	2 363	2 403	26.1	25.2	24.5	24.5	24.5	24.6	Libye
Madagascar	11 286	11 612	11 931	12 238	12 618	13 054	49.5	49.3	49.0	48.8	48.8	48.8	Madagascar
Malawi	6 767	7 021	7 255	7 495	7 746	8 030	48.1	47.9	48.0	48.0	48.1	48.1	Malawi
Mali	5 704	5 995	6 293	6 481	6 684	6 933	41.1	42.1	43.0	43.0	43.0	43.1	Mali
Mauritania	1 120	1 156	1 195	1 234	1 273	1 312	30.9	31.1	31.1	31.3	31.3	31.3	Mauritanie
Mauritius	576	586	596	606	603	606	37.7	38.2	38.8	39.3	39.0	39.1	Maurice
Morocco	11 796	12 003	12 198	12 357	12 542	12 714	25.9	26.1	26.1	26.1	26.1	26.1	Maroc
Mozambique	11 084	11 417	11 764	12 125	12 498	12 899	55.0	55.0	55.0	55.0	55.0	54.8	Mozambique
Namibia	843	874	906	932	959	990	49.1	49.2	49.3	49.5	49.5	49.5	Namibie
Niger	6 989	7 254	7 533	7 826	8 120	8 439	43.6	43.5	43.5	43.5	43.5	43.4	Niger
Nigeria	51 416	52 824	54 261	55 789	57 352	58 959	45.1	45.3	45.4	45.4	45.3	45.4	Nigéria
Rwanda	5 473	5 630	5 788	5 949	6 116	6 296	51.3	51.3	51.4	51.5	51.5	51.5	Rwanda
Sao Tome and Principe	59	61	63	64	66	68	35.6	36.1	34.9	35.9	36.4	35.3	Sao Tomé-et-Principe
Senegal	4 408	4 555	4 704	4 855	5 007	5 179	41.2	41.1	41.1	41.2	41.2	41.4	Sénégal
Seychelles	...	...	...	...	...	...	...	...	...	...	...	...	Seychelles
Sierra Leone	2 273	2 305	2 338	2 412	2 472	2 534	50.3	50.3	50.3	50.0	50.2	50.2	Sierra Leone
Somalia	3 082	3 188	3 299	3 415	3 528	3 641	19.6	19.8	20.1	20.3	20.4	20.5	Somalie
South Africa	19 543	20 097	20 527	21 349	21 702	22 041	44.4	44.8	44.9	45.0	44.9	45.0	Afrique du Sud
South Sudan	4 502	4 662	4 822	4 983	5 141	5 306	48.8	48.9	49.0	49.1	49.2	49.2	Soudan du Sud
Sudan	9 754	10 010	10 281	10 559	10 847	11 150	25.0	25.2	25.4	25.6	25.8	25.7	Soudan
Swaziland	406	418	430	442	454	466	40.6	40.9	41.2	41.2	41.4	41.4	Swaziland
Tanzania, United Republic of	22 389	23 118	23 845	24 618	25 424	26 306	50.1	49.5	48.9	48.9	48.9	48.9	Tanzanie, République Unie de
Togo	3 078	3 166	3 255	3 346	3 438	3 534	49.2	49.2	49.2	49.3	49.3	49.2	Togo
Tunisia	3 977	4 006	4 030	4 061	4 083	4 110	27.0	27.0	26.8	26.7	26.5	26.4	Tunisie
Uganda	13 173	13 664	14 172	14 698	15 233	15 840	47.6	47.6	47.7	47.8	47.9	47.9	Ouganda
Zambia	5 944	6 151	6 367	6 591	6 818	7 061	47.5	47.6	47.6	47.7	47.8	47.8	Zambie
Zimbabwe	7 132	7 311	7 496	7 687	7 887	8 123	49.1	49.1	49.2	49.2	49.2	49.2	Zimbabwe
Africa	404 056	415 897	428 092	440 601	453 381	466 428	43.1	43.2	43.3	43.4	43.5	43.6	Afrique

Source: ILO database

1.4 Total international migrants - Effectifs en milieu d'année de migrants internationaux

Country	By country of origin Par pays d'origine				By country of destination Par pays de destination				
	2000	2005	2010	2017	2000	2005	2010	2017	
Algeria	1 025 039	1 588 723	1 630 181	1 792 712	250 110	197 422	216 964	248 624	Algérie
Angola	870 514	680 405	624 284	632 699	46 108	61 329	76 549	638 499	Angola
Benin	319 432	490 875	528 120	627 997	133 730	171 499	209 267	253 284	Bénin
Botswana	26 393	30 883	47 041	80 103	57 064	88 829	120 912	166 430	Botswana
Burkina Faso	1 234 174	1 312 349	1 387 884	1 472 712	520 039	596 972	673 904	708 921	Burkina Faso
Burundi	738 397	616 738	281 111	435 630	125 628	172 874	235 259	299 569	Burundi
Cabo Verde	125 931	142 011	152 986	226 786	11 027	12 700	14 373	15 295	Cabo Verde
Cameroon	161 419	217 615	278 383	333 316	228 383	258 737	289 091	540 266	Cameroun
Central African Republic	55 328	131 192	238 620	724 669	123 529	94 449	93 466	88 774	République Centrafricaine
Chad	205 856	210 019	198 851	246 960	104 825	352 062	416 924	489 690	Tchad
Comoros	70 493	96 141	108 558	116 574	13 799	13 209	12 618	12 555	Comores
Congo	129 315	165 547	195 519	254 824	305 002	315 238	419 649	398 890	Congo
Côte d'Ivoire	540 996	695 065	782 050	832 581	1 994 135	2 010 824	2 095 185	2 197 152	Côte d'Ivoire
Democratic Republic of the Congo	831 305	1 079 545	1 226 680	1 661 988	744 387	622 869	588 950	879 223	Rép. Démocratique du Congo
Djibouti	9 039	12 207	13 531	15 823	100 507	92 091	101 575	116 089	Djibouti
Egypt	1 707 426	1 900 048	2 611 995	3 412 957	173 452	274 001	295 714	478 310	Egypte
Equatorial Guinea	55 319	67 673	78 268	95 714	4 517	6 588	8 658	221 865	Guinée Equatoriale
Eritrea	510 432	289 183	278 086	607 917	12 952	14 314	15 676	16 041	Erythrée
Ethiopia	443 926	521 088	623 562	800 879	611 384	514 242	567 720	1 227 143	Ethiopie
Gabon	17 885	41 038	59 450	66 898	195 571	214 123	243 992	280 197	Gabon
Gambia	39 718	57 473	79 505	87 532	182 514	181 905	185 763	205 063	Gambie
Ghana	468 279	616 174	716 044	857 603	191 601	304 436	337 017	417 642	Ghana
Guinea	350 522	370 909	401 766	426 010	560 075	229 611	177 998	122 796	Guinée
Guinea-Bissau	77 537	82 908	92 400	97 890	20 450	20 736	21 061	23 405	Guinée-Bissau
Kenya	308 199	344 121	407 446	501 204	699 139	756 894	926 959	1 078 572	Kenya
Lesotho	120 497	144 122	243 782	326 612	6 167	6 290	6 414	6 749	Lesotho
Liberia	263 082	368 417	264 173	260 155	151 868	87 188	99 129	98 630	Libéria
Libya	78 811	98 964	127 168	158 795	567 436	625 212	683 998	788 419	Libye
Madagascar	76 309	147 749	157 849	172 130	23 541	26 058	28 905	33 844	Madagascar
Malawi	184 770	224 606	275 237	342 826	232 620	221 661	217 722	237 104	Malawi
Mali	722 660	792 284	851 520	1 066 120	189 475	256 797	336 607	383 721	Mali
Mauritania	105 587	99 141	113 363	120 433	57 366	58 119	84 679	168 438	Mauritanie
Mauritius	115 984	127 711	153 279	167 121	15 543	19 647	24 836	28 713	Maurice
Morocco	1 948 424	2 376 184	2 766 342	2 898 721	53 034	54 379	70 909	95 835	Maroc
Mozambique	636 775	559 674	587 849	653 251	195 702	204 830	214 612	246 954	Mozambique
Namibia	48 723	59 385	99 897	190 132	134 403	106 274	102 405	95 067	Namibie
Niger	193 050	285 366	311 263	362 955	122 260	124 461	126 464	295 610	Niger
Nigeria	599 702	782 992	985 865	1 255 425	487 882	969 294	988 679	1 235 088	Nigéria
Rwanda	321 694	287 089	329 189	568 848	347 076	432 797	436 787	443 088	Rwanda
Sao Tome and Principe	24 829	29 430	30 810	82 358	4 365	3 433	2 700	2 293	Sao Tomé-et-Principe
Senegal	388 250	462 698	537 339	559 952	231 901	238 298	256 092	265 601	Sénégal
Seychelles	9 290	9 776	32 608	36 318	6 574	8 997	11 420	12 926	Seychelles
Sierra Leone	508 526	147 341	135 569	159 017	98 241	149 615	97 452	95 248	Sierra Leone
Somalia	1 004 443	1 150 483	1 578 233	1 988 458	20 087	20 670	23 995	44 868	Somalie
South Africa	512 309	618 026	740 273	898 407	1 001 825	1 210 936	2 096 886	4 036 696	Afrique du Sud
South Sudan	342 628	243 075	403 896	1 752 014	-	-	257 905	845 239	Soudan du Sud
Sudan	859 690	1 175 018	1 197 225	1 951 705	801 883	541 994	578 363	735 821	Soudan
Swaziland	33 647	40 531	68 700	91 621	22 855	27 097	30 476	33 263	Swaziland
Tanzania, United Republic of	220 108	238 881	267 834	324 394	928 180	770 846	308 600	492 574	Tanzanie, République Unie de
Togo	263 575	365 019	383 473	454 396	137 891	203 379	255 262	283 966	Togo
Tunisia	480 276	572 919	599 051	767 155	36 446	35 040	43 172	57 663	Tunisie
Uganda	552 835	557 486	702 606	739 667	634 703	652 968	529 160	1 692 120	Ouganda
Zambia	160 252	178 057	213 589	275 089	321 167	252 749	149 637	156 982	Zambie
Zimbabwe	310 753	478 835	813 942	1 025 204	410 041	392 693	397 891	403 866	Zimbabwe
Africa	**21 410 353**	**24 381 189**	**28 014 245**	**36 059 257**	**14 650 460**	**15 279 676**	**16 806 401**	**24 440 681**	**Afrique**

Source: UNPD, 2015 Revision

1-5. Adult illiteracy rate (%) - Taux d'analphabetisme des adultes (%)

PERCENTAGE | | | | | | | | | | POURCENTAGE

Country	2001-2007			2008-2014			2015-2017			Pays
	MF	M	F	MF	M	F	MF	M	F	
Algeria	27.4	18.72	36.1	24.9	17.38	32.45	...	...	...	Algérie
Angola	32.6	17.08	45.8	34.0	20.03	46.59	...	...	...	Angola
Benin	71.3	59.38	81.6	...	55.04	77.91	...	...	...	Bénin
Botswana	18.8	19.57	18.2	...	...	...	...	...	...	Botswana
Burkina Faso	71.3	63.32	78.4	65.4	55.62	73.78	...	...	...	Burkina Faso
Burundi	...	...	...	38.4	30.31	45.34	...	...	...	Burundi
Cameroon	29.3	...	...	28.7	9.53	19.50	...	8.31	17.96	Cameroun
Cabo Verde	...	21.05	37.0	...	21.67	35.20	...	...	...	Cabo Verde
Central African Republic	...	...	...	63.3	49.29	75.64	...	...	...	République Centrafricaine
Chad	71.6	60.63	82.0	...	...	...	77.7	68.67	86.04	Tchad
Comoros	...	...	...	...	43.52	57.36	...	...	...	Comores
Congo	...	...	...	20.7	13.57	27.12	...	...	...	Congo
Côte d'Ivoire	...	...	...	56.1	49.30	63.22	...	...	...	Côte d'Ivoire
Democratic Republic of the Congo	38.8	23.08	53.9	...	12.09	37.08	23.0	11.48	33.50	Rép. Démocratique du Congo
Djibouti	...	...	...	...	...	...	...	...	...	Djibouti
Egypt	33.6	25.38	42.2	24.9	17.37	32.82	...	...	...	Egypte
Equatorial Guinea	...	...	...	...	...	...	...	...	...	Guinée Equatoriale
Eritrea	47.5	34.61	59.8	35.3	24.93	45.20	...	...	...	Erythrée
Ethiopia	61.0	50.87	71.1	...	...	...	...	...	...	Ethiopie
Gabon	...	...	...	...	15.13	20.12	...	...	...	Gabon
Gambia	...	...	...	58.1	48.58	66.42	...	...	...	Gambie
Ghana	...	...	...	28.5	21.65	34.71	...	...	...	Ghana
Guinea	70.3	57.10	81.8	68.0	56.36	78.04	...	...	...	Guinée
Guinea-Bissau	...	...	...	54.4	37.84	69.23	...	...	...	Guinée-Bissau
Kenya	27.8	21.92	33.1	21.3	16.22	25.99	...	...	...	Kenya
Lesotho	...	...	...	23.4	32.25	15.07	...	...	...	Lesotho
Liberia	57.1	39.23	73.0	...	...	...	...	...	...	Libéria
Libya	...	...	...	...	...	...	...	...	...	Libye
Madagascar	...	...	...	35.5	24.97	31.72	...	...	...	Madagascar
Malawi	...	...	...	34.9	24.02	44.87	...	30.25	44.80	Malawi
Mali	73.8	65.14	81.8	66.4	56.73	75.36	...	54.93	77.80	Mali
Mauritania	54.5	42.60	64.7	...	...	...	...	...	...	Mauritanie
Mauritius	...	...	...	7.5	5.23	9.72	...	5.14	9.35	Maurice
Morocco	47.7	34.29	60.4	32.9	19.62	40.87	...	...	...	Maroc
Mozambique	51.8	34.42	66.8	49.4	32.65	63.55	...	...	...	Mozambique
Namibia	23.5	25.67	21.7	11.7	11.37	12.05	...	...	...	Namibie
Niger	85.6	80.36	90.6	...	76.75	91.06	...	...	...	Niger
Nigeria	45.2	33.23	56.7	48.9	38.75	58.61	...	...	...	Nigéria
Rwanda	...	...	...	34.2	27.55	35.34	...	...	...	Rwanda
Sao Tome and Principe	15.1	7.77	22.1	30.5	5.04	14.56	...	...	...	Sao Tomé-et-Principe
Senegal	58.1	47.74	67.0	57.2	47.20	66.40	...	...	...	Sénégal
Seychelles	8.2	8.59	7.7	6.1	6.54	5.55	...	...	...	Seychelles
Sierra Leone	65.2	53.35	75.8	67.6	58.67	75.14	...	...	...	Sierra Leone
Somalia	...	...	...	...	...	...	...	...	...	Somalie
South Africa	11.3	9.28	13.0	5.9	4.71	6.93	...	4.60	6.59	Afrique du Sud
South Sudan	...	...	...	73.2	65.16	80.81	...	...	...	Soudan du Sud
Sudan	...	...	...	46.5	40.20	53.30	...	...	...	Soudan
Swaziland	...	...	...	16.9	16.10	17.55	...	...	...	Swaziland
Tanzania, United Republic of	30.6	29.73	55.6	32.2	25.94	52.02	...	22.74	48.76	Tanzanie, République Unie de
Togo	43.1	13.95	31.5	39.6	13.94	27.78	...	...	...	Togo
Tunisia	22.8	18.61	37.9	21.0	20.88	38.03	...	...	...	Tunisie
Uganda	28.6	22.49	37.8	26.8	16.62	26.65	...	16.80	26.91	Ouganda
Zambia	38.6	28.05	48.2	17.0	11.32	22.25	...	...	...	Zambie
Zimbabwe	...	...	...	11.3	10.81	11.72	...	...	...	Zimbabwe
Africa	...	...	...	...	...	...	...	...	...	Afrique

Source: Computed from UNESCO, Institute for Statistics data

1-6. Gross enrolment ratio in primary - Taux brut de scolarisation au primaire

PERCENTAGE   POURCENTAGE

Country	2001-2007			2008-2014			2015-2017			Pays
	MF	M	F	MF	M	F	MF	M	F	
Algeria	106.8	110.9	102.6	118.34	121.30	115.26	113.65	116.56	110.61	Algérie
Angola	105.2	...	...	118.65	146.74	91.23	..	...	...	Angola
Benin	96.7	111.5	81.9	129.60	134.62	124.43	132.47	137.19	127.62	Bénin
Botswana	107.3	108.0	106.5	105.36	107.18	103.52	..	...	...	Botswana
Burkina Faso	55.0	61.5	48.2	87.34	88.45	86.18	91.11	92.09	90.09	Burkina Faso
Burundi	79.9	86.8	73.1	137.90	137.14	138.64	130.92	130.51	131.32	Burundi
Cameroon	99.6	107.5	91.6	116.24	122.86	109.53	119.16	125.33	112.89	Cameroun
Cabo Verde	112.4	114.3	110.4	100.15	103.87	96.38	96.69	99.94	93.39	Cabo Verde
Central African Republic	68.3	81.3	55.5	89.81	104.22	75.59	105.67	119.98	91.55	République Centrafricaine
Chad	71.0	85.1	56.8	102.75	116.40	88.87	88.10	99.02	77.00	Tchad
Comoros	107.7	115.9	99.3	104.97	108.62	101.20	..	...	...	Comores
Congo	108.2	111.9	104.4	106.89	110.04	103.70	..	...	...	Congo
Côte d'Ivoire	72.9	81.9	63.9	88.12	94.25	81.96	96.71	102.11	91.30	Côte d'Ivoire
Democratic Republic of the Congo	76.5	84.7	68.2	110.24	115.46	104.96	108.04	108.44	107.64	Rép. Démocratique du Congo
Djibouti	41.7	46.6	37.7	65.12	69.51	60.61	63.90	67.53	60.18	Djibouti
Egypt	99.6	101.9	97.1	101.13	101.27	100.97	103.62	103.59	103.67	Egypte
Equatorial Guinea	102.7	104.9	100.5	67.56	67.71	67.41	61.58	61.81	61.34	Guinée Equatoriale
Eritrea	64.9	71.0	58.6	55.71	60.05	51.20	54.08	58.04	49.95	Erythrée
Ethiopia	72.6	80.8	64.3	99.92	104.14	95.62	101.94	106.76	97.03	Ethiopie
Gabon	139.4	139.6	139.2	138.72	140.78	136.63	..	...	...	Gabon
Gambia	91.1	91.7	90.4	88.25	85.87	90.66	97.12	93.27	101.03	Gambie
Ghana	88.0	89.6	86.3	105.37	105.40	105.33	104.78	104.08	105.50	Ghana
Guinea	74.8	83.9	65.4	93.93	101.65	86.09	..	...	...	Guinée
Guinea-Bissau	104.1	...	...	118.08	122.12	114.05	..	...	...	Guinée-Bissau
Kenya	104.3	106.2	102.4	108.11	107.75	108.47	105.31	105.14	105.48	Kenya
Lesotho	117.5	116.7	118.2	106.32	107.84	104.79	103.90	105.65	102.13	Lesotho
Liberia	92.5	96.1	88.8	95.86	99.75	91.81	94.09	98.70	89.28	Libéria
Libya	110.2	111.0	109.4	...	...	...	..	...	...	Libye
Madagascar	124.3	126.8	121.8	145.25	145.45	145.05	143.82	143.70	143.95	Madagascar
Malawi	130.6	130.9	130.3	142.23	140.78	143.70	139.26	137.24	141.31	Malawi
Mali	70.4	78.5	62.0	76.98	81.51	72.32	77.08	81.80	72.21	Mali
Mauritania	88.4	88.1	88.7	97.15	94.54	99.83	93.86	91.02	96.79	Mauritanie
Mauritius	102.6	102.7	102.5	102.45	101.42	103.51	102.45	101.56	103.38	Maurice
Morocco	103.4	108.6	98.0	109.68	112.17	107.05	110.26	113.03	107.34	Maroc
Mozambique	91.4	100.0	82.9	105.47	109.95	100.96	106.32	110.92	101.68	Mozambique
Namibia	110.9	110.9	110.8	111.31	113.49	109.14	..	...	...	Namibie
Niger	45.3	52.7	37.5	69.79	75.25	64.11	73.69	79.08	68.08	Niger
Nigeria	98.2	106.0	90.2	94.07	95.25	92.84	..	...	...	Nigéria
Rwanda	129.4	129.1	129.6	136.44	134.91	137.97	137.02	137.27	136.78	Rwanda
Sao Tome and Principe	126.6	129.0	124.2	106.93	109.13	104.69	110.23	112.37	108.07	Sao Tomé-et-Principe
Senegal	76.1	78.2	73.9	84.15	79.41	89.00	83.09	78.36	87.92	Sénégal
Seychelles	106.1	106.1	106.0	115.43	116.52	114.33	112.83	113.22	112.43	Seychelles
Sierra Leone	83.3	98.3	68.6	114.87	115.11	114.64	114.84	114.45	115.22	Sierra Leone
Somalia	29.2	37.6	20.8	...	...	...	..	...	...	Somalie
South Africa	101.0	98.5	103.8	98.49	100.63	96.31	...	106.56	98.99	Afrique du Sud
South Sudan	...	...	...	84.76	101.76	67.40	66.59	77.80	55.10	Soudan du Sud
Sudan	61.6	66.4	56.7	72.39	76.14	68.52	73.59	76.74	70.35	Soudan
Swaziland	101.0	103.9	98.1	109.07	113.97	104.14	107.87	112.76	102.93	Swaziland
Tanzania, United Republic of	96.5	98.5	94.5	82.62	81.66	83.58	123.92	79.52	81.96	Tanzanie, République Unie de
Togo	114.3	124.7	103.9	123.01	126.64	119.36	114.71	126.98	120.84	Togo
Tunisia	111.9	114.4	109.4	113.16	114.77	111.48	99.75	116.17	113.18	Tunisie
Uganda	129.1	130.0	128.2	106.61	105.63	107.59	80.74	98.25	101.27	Ouganda
Zambia	98.8	100.9	96.6	102.33	102.02	102.65	..	...	...	Zambie
Zimbabwe	98.8	99.8	97.8	98.69	99.45	97.93	..	...	...	Zimbabwe
Africa	...	...	...	...	...	...	...	...	...	**Afrique**

Source: UNESCO, Institute for Statistics

1-7. Gross enrolment ratio in secondary - Taux brut de scolarisation au secondaire

PERCENTAGE | | | | | | | | | POURCENTAGE

Country	2001-2007			2008-2014			2015-2017			Pays
	MF	M	F	MF	M	F	MF	M	F	
Algeria	74.3	71.4	77.3	91.7	90.4	93.1	...	...	...	Algérie
Angola	16.2	18.0	14.4	26.6	31.1	22.1	...	...	...	Angola
Benin	25.9	35.6	16.3	52.1	63.1	41.0	...	...	...	Bénin
Botswana	77.9	76.0	79.8	...	...	...	...	...	...	Botswana
Burkina Faso	13.6	15.9	11.2	24.2	26.9	21.5	35.8	36.7	34.9	Burkina Faso
Burundi	11.9	14.7	10.7	27.7	31.7	23.9	48.4	49.2	47.6	Burundi
Cameroon	28.2	31.8	24.5	47.0	51.0	43.0	61.8	66.4	57.1	Cameroun
Cabo Verde	70.3	66.2	74.6	88.7	82.3	95.0	84.6	80.7	88.4	Cabo Verde
Central African Republic	11.8	15.6	8.1	16.3	21.2	11.4	15.4	18.8	12.0	République Centrafricaine
Chad	15.2	22.3	7.9	22.4	31.3	13.4	22.7	31.0	14.3	Tchad
Comoros	39.5	43.5	35.4	59.8	58.3	61.4	...	...	...	Comores
Congo	41.8	47.5	36.1	54.5	58.4	50.6	...	...	...	Congo
Côte d'Ivoire	...	...	...	40.1	47.0	33.2	46.1	53.3	38.8	Côte d'Ivoire
Democratic Republic of the Congo	35.1	45.6	24.4	40.6	51.0	30.0	...	...	...	Rép. Démocratique du Congo
Djibouti	20.6	24.6	16.5	39.7	44.8	34.4	44.1	48.1	40.1	Djibouti
Egypt	81.1	83.4	78.8	79.6	80.2	79.0	85.9	86.7	85.2	Egypte
Equatorial Guinea	27.0	32.8	21.2	...	...	...	...	...	...	Guinée Equatoriale
Eritrea	26.5	32.2	20.8	34.3	38.5	30.0	...	...	...	Erythrée
Ethiopia	23.1	28.4	17.8	35.1	38.3	31.7	...	...	...	Ethiopie
Gabon	52.9	...	...	...	...	...	...	...	...	Gabon
Gambia	...	...	...	58.0	59.7	56.4	...	...	...	Gambie
Ghana	45.3	49.1	41.5	59.6	62.6	56.5	60.4	61.2	59.6	Ghana
Guinea	24.5	33.5	15.4	37.0	45.3	28.2	...	...	...	Guinée
Guinea-Bissau	31.6	...	...	...	...	...	...	...	...	Guinée-Bissau
Kenya	46.0	47.4	44.7	62.5	65.2	59.8	...	...	...	Kenya
Lesotho	37.8	32.7	43.1	50.0	41.9	58.4	52.3	44.5	60.2	Lesotho
Liberia	...	...	...	41.5	46.0	36.9	...	...	...	Libéria
Libya	102.4	96.7	108.4	...	...	...	...	...	...	Libye
Madagascar	23.8	24.4	23.3	34.5	35.3	33.7	38.3	38.4	38.2	Madagascar
Malawi	28.9	32.2	25.7	34.5	36.7	32.4	37.4	39.5	35.3	Malawi
Mali	25.7	31.6	19.6	39.0	45.2	32.5	42.9	49.1	36.6	Mali
Mauritania	21.6	23.6	19.5	23.9	25.5	22.4	31.6	32.0	31.1	Mauritanie
Mauritius	85.0	85.1	84.9	91.5	89.8	93.3	93.4	90.8	96.0	Maurice
Morocco	47.7	51.7	43.5	63.1	67.6	58.4	...	...	...	Maroc
Mozambique	12.0	14.2	9.9	25.8	27.8	23.7	...	...	...	Mozambique
Namibia	63.9	60.1	67.8	...	...	...	...	...	...	Namibie
Niger	8.9	11.1	6.8	14.6	17.6	11.6	23.6	27.3	19.9	Niger
Nigeria	31.9	35.2	28.5	44.2	46.7	41.7	...	...	...	Nigéria
Rwanda	14.9	15.7	14.2	33.8	33.4	34.2	36.6	34.9	38.4	Rwanda
Sao Tome and Principe	42.4	40.8	44.0	57.8	52.2	57.1	89.7	83.5	96.0	Sao Tomé-et-Principe
Senegal	19.8	23.1	16.5	35.1	37.7	32.5	48.1	47.8	48.4	Sénégal
Seychelles	75.4	72.3	78.6	77.2	75.0	79.5	93.0	89.9	96.1	Seychelles
Sierra Leone	27.1	31.8	22.5	45.6	50.6	40.8	40.5	42.4	38.6	Sierra Leone
Somalia	7.4	10.1	4.6	...	...	...	...	...	...	Somalie
South Africa	88.8	85.0	92.8	90.6	84.7	97.1	...	...	...	Afrique du Sud
South Sudan	...	...	...	...	...	...	...	...	...	Soudan du Sud
Sudan	35.3	36.9	33.8	39.8	41.8	37.7	...	...	...	Soudan
Swaziland	45.9	46.0	45.8	60.3	60.5	60.0	...	...	...	Swaziland
Tanzania, United Republic of	...	...	...	32.5	35.1	30.0	...	...	...	Tanzanie, République Unie de
Togo	41.9	55.6	28.3	54.7	...	...	...	...	...	Togo
Tunisia	82.3	78.6	83.1	90.6	88.7	94.3	92.9	88.1	97.9	Tunisie
Uganda	20.1	22.2	17.9	26.5	28.5	24.5	...	...	...	Ouganda
Zambia	...	...	...	...	...	...	...	...	...	Zambie
Zimbabwe	40.7	43.2	38.3	47.1	47.7	46.5	...	...	...	Zimbabwe
Africa	...	...	...	...	...	...	...	...	...	Afrique

Source: UNESCO Institute for Statistics

1-8. Pupil teacher ratio - Ratio éleves enseignant

Country	Primary - Primaire			Secondary - Secondaire			Pays
PER TEACHER							**PAR ENSEIGNANT**
	2001-2007	2008-2014	2015-2017	2001-2007	2008-2014	2015-2017	
Algeria	26.2	23.7	24.2	...	...	...	Algérie
Angola	41.0	42.5	...	19.0	27.4	...	Angola
Benin	51.8	45.9	45.0	22.6	9.9	10.3	Bénin
Botswana	25.9	22.6	...	14.4	...	...	Botswana
Burkina Faso	46.7	44.5	41.5	29.7	27.1	23.4	Burkina Faso
Burundi	50.8	43.7	49.7	23.9	37.2	32.1	Burundi
Cameroon	53.1	44.2	42.7	18.1	20.4	19.3	Cameroun
Cabo Verde	26.9	22.6	21.5	23.3	16.0	16.0	Cabo Verde
Central African Republic	88.6	81.3	83.4	...	66.8	34.6	République Centrafricaine
Chad	66.6	56.2	56.9	34.3	36.6	27.1	Tchad
Comoros	36.7	27.8	...	12.7	8.6	...	Comores
Congo	62.8	47.1	...	31.2	...	...	Congo
Côte d'Ivoire	43.9	42.5	42.5	...	22.3	25.8	Côte d'Ivoire
Democratic Republic of the Congo	36.3	35.3	33.2	15.7	14.6	14.2	Rép. Démocratique du Congo
Djibouti	34.6	33.2	30.4	32.5	24.5	22.7	Djibouti
Egypt	23.9	27.7	23.1	17.2	12.1	14.8	Egypte
Equatorial Guinea	37.7	27.9	23.2	19.2	...	...	Guinée Equatoriale
Eritrea	46.4	42.5	43.3	51.2	40.6	38.9	Erythrée
Ethiopia	...	55.1	...	...	40.3	...	Ethiopie
Gabon	42.6	24.5	...	...	...	...	Gabon
Gambia	37.8	44.7	38.7	...	...	...	Gambie
Ghana	32.7	30.1	27.3	18.6	15.8	15.6	Ghana
Guinea	45.2	45.6	...	33.4	33.1	...	Guinée
Guinea-Bissau	62.2	51.9	...	37.3	...	...	Guinée-Bissau
Kenya	38.8	31.4	30.7	28.6	33.4	...	Kenya
Lesotho	43.3	32.8	33.8	24.7	23.5	23.2	Lesotho
Liberia	28.0	26.5	30.4	...	14.9	18.4	Libéria
Libya	...	...	...	...	...	...	Libye
Madagascar	49.8	41.7	40.6	23.2	23.1	...	Madagascar
Malawi	78.1	72.7	69.5	38.5	39.2	37.9	Malawi
Mali	55.5	42.5	39.1	24.0	18.9	19.5	Mali
Mauritania	41.0	34.4	36.4	27.4	33.1	26.4	Mauritanie
Mauritius	23.0	18.7	17.8	17.8	13.3	12.6	Maurice
Morocco	27.7	25.7	26.6	18.4	...	...	Maroc
Mozambique	66.1	54.8	54.7	34.9	40.0	39.7	Mozambique
Namibia	31.4	29.8	...	24.7	...	...	Namibie
Niger	41.7	35.8	36.3	27.8	25.1	26.7	Niger
Nigeria	39.8	37.6	...	34.2	23.2	...	Nigéria
Rwanda	62.4	58.2	58.5	26.3	21.7	18.6	Rwanda
Sao Tome and Principe	31.8	32.7	31.2	21.7	24.4	24.8	Sao Tomé-et-Principe
Senegal	43.3	32.2	31.7	26.2	25.1	19.7	Sénégal
Seychelles	13.6	13.3	14.0	14.0	13.2	11.6	Seychelles
Sierra Leone	37.3	34.8	37.3	26.6	20.7	22.0	Sierra Leone
Somalia	35.5	...	...	19.3	...	...	Somalie
South Africa	34.7	32.8	30.3	30.0	25.0	27.8	Afrique du Sud
South Sudan	...	49.9	46.8	...	...	27.5	Soudan du Sud
Sudan	...	...	...	...	...	...	Soudan
Swaziland	32.3	28.0	27.6	17.6	15.9	15.8	Swaziland
Tanzania, United Republic of	53.6	43.1	...	...	...	...	Tanzanie, République Unie de
Togo	36.3	41.1	41.4	34.5	26.2	...	Togo
Tunisia	20.6	16.5	16.2	17.8	13.6	...	Tunisie
Uganda	51.1	45.6	42.7	18.4	...	...	Ouganda
Zambia	53.1	47.9	...	...	...	...	Zambie
Zimbabwe	38.7	36.4	...	24.2	22.5	...	Zimbabwe
Africa	...	...	...	...	...	...	**Afrique**

Source: UNESCO, Institute for Statistics

1-9. Gender Parity Index, primary, total - Indice de parité de genre, primaire, total

Country	2009	2010	2011	2012	2013	2014	2015	2016	2017	Pays
Algeria	0.935	0.937	0.938	0.944	0.948	0.950	0.952	0.949	...	Algérie
Angola	0.824	0.789	0.622	...	...	...	...	...	...	Angola
Benin	0.876	0.892	0.895	0.907	0.915	0.924	0.930	...	...	Bénin
Botswana	0.964	...	...	0.973	0.967	0.966	...	...	...	Botswana
Burkina Faso	0.887	0.910	0.928	0.947	0.967	0.974	0.974	0.978	...	Burkina Faso
Burundi	0.947	0.966	0.982	0.991	0.996	1.011	1.010	1.006	...	Burundi
Cameroon	0.867	0.865	0.870	0.877	...	0.892	0.899	0.901	...	Cameroun
Cabo Verde	0.931	0.933	0.931	0.924	0.929	0.928	0.935	0.934	...	Cabo Verde
Central African Republic	0.709	0.711	0.725	0.743	...	...	...	0.763	...	République Centrafricaine
Chad	0.710	0.735	0.753	0.762	0.767	0.763	0.776	0.778	...	Tchad
Comoros	...	...	0.846	...	0.942	0.932	...	...	...	Comores
Congo	0.931	0.944	0.942	1.072	...	...	...	...	...	Congo
Côte d'Ivoire	0.817	...	0.838	0.849	0.863	0.870	0.880	0.894	...	Côte d'Ivoire
Democratic Republic of the Congo	0.858	0.870	0.870	0.882	0.906	0.909	0.993	...	...	Rép. Démocratique du Congo
Djibouti	0.899	...	0.909	0.901	0.883	0.872	0.888	0.887	0.891	Djibouti
Egypt	0.967	0.971	0.955	0.987	0.991	0.997	...	1.001	...	Egypte
Equatorial Guinea	0.972	0.986	0.996	0.994	...	...	0.992	...	...	Guinée Equatoriale
Eritrea	0.844	0.852	0.839	0.842	1.044	0.853	0.861	...	...	Erythrée
Ethiopia	0.926	0.924	0.920	0.928	...	0.918	0.909	...	...	Ethiopie
Gabon	...	...	0.971	...	...	...	...	...	...	Gabon
Gambia	1.044	1.027	1.039	1.046	1.044	1.056	1.068	1.076	1.083	Gambie
Ghana	0.982	...	0.991	0.997	0.998	0.999	1.001	1.015	1.014	Ghana
Guinea	0.841	0.824	0.852	0.843	0.844	0.847	...	...	...	Guinée
Guinea-Bissau	...	0.934	...	...	...	...	...	...	...	Guinée-Bissau
Kenya	0.980	...	...	1.008	...	1.007	0.999	1.003	...	Kenya
Lesotho	0.996	0.975	0.966	0.969	0.975	0.972	0.968	0.967	...	Lesotho
Liberia	0.896	...	0.916	...	...	0.920	0.905	...	...	Libéria
Libya	...	...	...	...	...	...	...	...	...	Libye
Madagascar	0.978	0.982	0.981	0.987	0.993	0.997	1.000	1.002	...	Madagascar
Malawi	1.016	1.023	1.026	1.023	1.020	1.021	1.023	1.030	...	Malawi
Mali	0.845	0.858	0.870	0.875	...	0.887	0.898	0.883	...	Mali
Mauritania	1.045	1.043	1.053	1.050	1.048	1.056	1.050	1.063	...	Mauritanie
Mauritius	1.003	1.005	1.008	1.007	1.017	1.021	1.018	1.018	...	Maurice
Morocco	0.932	0.941	0.949	0.953	0.955	0.954	0.947	0.950	...	Maroc
Mozambique	0.893	0.898	0.905	0.908	0.912	0.918	0.917	...	...	Mozambique
Namibia	0.971	0.968	...	0.963	0.962	...	...	...	...	Namibie
Niger	0.788	0.811	0.825	0.836	0.840	0.852	0.853	0.861	...	Niger
Nigeria	0.896	0.908	0.933	0.974	0.975	...	...	...	...	Nigéria
Rwanda	1.029	1.026	1.029	1.021	1.022	1.023	1.011	0.996	...	Rwanda
Sao Tome and Principe	1.002	0.990	0.968	0.967	0.974	0.959	0.956	0.952	0.962	Sao Tomé-et-Principe
Senegal	1.042	1.057	1.121	1.113	1.119	1.121	1.120	1.122	...	Sénégal
Seychelles	1.035	1.031	1.048	1.026	0.996	0.981	0.993	0.993	...	Seychelles
Sierra Leone	...	...	0.941	0.983	0.996	...	1.010	1.007	...	Sierra Leone
Somalia	...	...	...	...	...	...	...	...	...	Somalie
South Africa	0.964	0.959	0.957	0.955	0.954	0.957	0.929	...	...	Afrique du Sud
South Sudan	...	...	0.662	...	...	...	0.708	...	...	Soudan du Sud
Sudan	0.892	0.899	0.887	0.892	0.900	...	0.917	...	...	Soudan
Swaziland	0.915	0.912	0.893	0.912	0.911	0.914	0.913	...	...	Swaziland
Tanzania, United Republic of	0.995	1.007	1.015	1.010	1.015	1.024	1.031	...	...	Tanzanie, République Unie de
Togo	0.854	0.902	0.910	0.924	0.936	0.942	0.947	0.952	...	Togo
Tunisia	0.966	0.966	0.968	0.974	0.969	0.971	0.972	0.974	...	Tunisie
Uganda	1.010	1.015	1.017	1.016	1.019	...	1.019	1.031	...	Ouganda
Zambia	0.989	1.013	0.995	1.009	1.006	...	...	...	...	Zambie
Zimbabwe	...	...	...	0.987	0.985	...	...	...	...	Zimbabwe
Africa	**0.931**	**0.936**	**0.931**	**0.945**	**0.949**	**0.951**	**0.955**	**0.957**		**Afrique**

Source: UNESCO, Institute for Statistics

1-10. Gender Parity Index, secondary, total - Indice de parité de genre, secondaire, total

Country	2009	2010	2011	2012	2013	2014	2015	2016	2017	Pays
Algeria	1.010	1.035	1.038	...	...	...	...	...	...	Algérie
Angola	0.744	0.666	0.629	...	...	...	...	...	...	Angola
Benin	...	...	0.623	...	0.670	0.690	0.714	...	...	Bénin
Botswana	...	...	...	...	...	...	...	...	...	Botswana
Burkina Faso	0.745	0.764	0.780	0.811	0.846	0.873	0.922	0.951	...	Burkina Faso
Burundi	0.683	0.680	0.699	0.729	0.780	0.844	0.908	0.967	...	Burundi
Cameroon	0.837	...	0.848	0.858	0.858	0.853	0.857	0.860	...	Cameroun
Cabo Verde	1.193	1.189	1.169	1.176	1.143	1.125	1.104	1.096	...	Cabo Verde
Central African Republic	0.557	...	0.551	0.513	...	...	...	0.638	...	République Centrafricaine
Chad	0.413	0.423	0.438	0.457	0.460	0.452	0.451	0.462	...	Tchad
Comoros	...	...	...	...	1.038	1.068	...	...	...	Comores
Congo	...	...	...	0.866	...	...	...	...	...	Congo
Côte d'Ivoire	...	...	...	...	...	0.705	0.715	0.728	...	Côte d'Ivoire
Democratic Republic of the Congo	0.562	0.577	0.588	0.592	0.620	0.622	0.640	...	...	Rép. Démocratique du Congo
Djibouti	0.738	...	0.803	0.770	0.768	0.809	0.802	0.820	0.835	Djibouti
Egypt	0.991	0.973	0.989	0.984	0.979	0.995	...	0.983	...	Egypte
Equatorial Guinea	...	...	...	...	...	...	...	...	...	Guinée Equatoriale
Eritrea	0.716	0.766	0.788	0.793	0.799	0.816	0.850	...	...	Erythrée
Ethiopia	0.783	0.831	0.883	0.903	...	...	0.959	...	...	Ethiopie
Gabon	...	...	...	...	...	...	...	...	...	Gabon
Gambia	0.958	0.951	...	...	...	...	...	...	...	Gambie
Ghana	0.876	...	0.899	0.898	0.910	0.938	0.949	0.968	0.974	Ghana
Guinea	...	...	0.631	...	...	0.656	...	...	...	Guinée
Guinea-Bissau	...	...	...	...	...	...	...	...	...	Guinée-Bissau
Kenya	0.904	...	...	...	...	...	...	...	...	Kenya
Lesotho	1.402	1.409	1.397	1.384	1.347	1.355	1.344	1.351	...	Lesotho
Liberia	...	...	0.820	...	...	0.780	0.776	...	...	Libéria
Libya	...	...	...	...	...	...	...	...	...	Libye
Madagascar	0.939	...	0.950	0.954	...	0.981	0.989	0.995	...	Madagascar
Malawi	0.863	0.895	0.901	0.886	0.897	0.906	0.918	0.893	...	Malawi
Mali	0.656	0.687	0.699	...	0.783	0.741	0.793	0.744	...	Mali
Mauritania	0.836	0.851	0.844	0.845	0.936	0.914	0.929	0.971	...	Mauritanie
Mauritius	1.043	1.046	1.047	1.048	1.029	1.018	1.044	1.057	...	Maurice
Morocco	0.866	0.871	0.863	0.854	...	...	...	...	...	Maroc
Mozambique	0.785	0.815	0.863	0.888	0.900	0.906	0.919	...	...	Mozambique
Namibia	...	...	...	...	...	...	...	...	...	Namibie
Niger	0.594	0.664	0.635	0.661	0.672	0.697	0.704	0.726	...	Niger
Nigeria	0.869	0.874	0.853	0.911	0.910	...	...	...	...	Nigéria
Rwanda	0.928	0.991	1.033	1.071	1.074	1.095	1.085	1.098	...	Rwanda
Sao Tome and Principe	1.112	1.018	1.142	1.128	1.102	1.096	1.107	1.134	1.150	Sao Tomé-et-Principe
Senegal	...	0.872	0.917	0.942	0.970	0.998	0.979	1.011	...	Sénégal
Seychelles	1.114	1.063	1.055	0.997	1.085	1.032	1.045	1.069	...	Seychelles
Sierra Leone	...	...	0.732	0.839	0.854	...	0.863	0.909	...	Sierra Leone
Somalia	...	...	...	...	...	...	...	...	...	Somalie
South Africa	1.055	1.060	1.056	1.057	...	1.095	0.985	...	...	Afrique du Sud
South Sudan	...	...	0.512	...	...	...	0.537	...	...	Soudan du Sud
Sudan	0.868	0.867	0.916	0.913	0.945	...	0.987	...	...	Soudan
Swaziland	1.003	0.992	0.965	0.959	0.975	0.986	0.994	...	...	Swaziland
Tanzania, United Republic of	...	0.791	...	0.863	0.915	...	...	...	...	Tanzanie, République Unie de
Togo	...	...	...	...	...	...	...	...	...	Togo
Tunisia	1.069	1.067	1.046	...	...	...	...	1.111	...	Tunisie
Uganda	...	...	...	...	...	...	...	...	...	Ouganda
Zambia	...	...	...	...	...	...	...	...	...	Zambie
Zimbabwe	...	...	...	0.971	0.980	...	...	...	...	Zimbabwe
Africa	**0.892**	**0.897**	**0.904**	**0.912**	**0.920**	**0.927**	**0.926**	**0.926**	**...**	**Afrique**

Source: UNESCO Institute for Statistics

1-11. Primary health care - Soins de santé primaire

Immunization - Vaccination (5)

PERCENTAGE	Access to safe water Accès à l'eau potable		Tuberclosis Tuberculose		Diphtheria (DPT3) - Dipthérie		Measles Rougeole		POURCENTAGE
Country	2000	2015	1990	2016	1990	2016	1990	2016	Pays
Algeria	90	93	99	99	89	91	83	94	Algérie
Angola	38	41	48	58	24	64	38	49	Angola
Benin	60	67	92	96	74	82	79	74	Bénin
Botswana	77	79	93	98	92	95	87	97	Botswana
Burkina Faso	47	54	95	98	66	91	79	88	Burkina Faso
Burundi	52	56	97	93	86	94	74	93	Burundi
Cameroon	55	65	76	70	48	85	56	78	Cameroun
Cabo Verde	78	86	97	96	88	96	79	92	Cabo Verde
Central African Republic	52	54	96	74	82	47	82	49	République Centrafricaine
Chad	39	43	59	56	20	46	32	58	Tchad
Comoros	86	84	99	94	94	91	87	99	Comores
Congo	57	68	90	85	79	80	75	80	Congo
Côte d'Ivoire	72	73	62	95	54	85	56	77	Côte d'Ivoire
Democratic Republic of the Congo	34	42	65	80	35	79	38	77	Rép. Démocratique du Congo
Djibouti	75	77	81	90	85	84	85	75	Djibouti
Egypt	98	98	89	96	87	95	86	95	Egypte
Equatorial Guinea	49	50	94	48	77	19	88	30	Guinée Equatoriale
Eritrea	17	19	...	97	...	95	...	93	Erythrée
Ethiopia	17	39	64	75	49	77	38	70	Ethiopie
Gabon	79	88	96	94	78	75	76	64	Gabon
Gambia	74	80	98	98	92	95	86	97	Gambie
Ghana	64	78	71	94	58	93	61	89	Ghana
Guinea	54	67	50	72	17	57	35	54	Guinée
GuineaBissau	53	69	90	94	61	87	53	81	GuinéeBissau
Kenya	46	58	92	99	84	89	78	75	Kenya
Lesotho	66	72	89	98	82	93	80	90	Lesotho
Liberia	62	70	...	97	...	79	...	80	Libéria
Libya	-	97	90	99	84	97	89	97	Libye
Madagascar	37	51	67	70	46	77	47	58	Madagascar
Malawi	52	67	97	86	87	84	81	81	Malawi
Mali	49	74	82	92	42	68	43	75	Mali
Mauritania	54	70	79	85	33	73	38	70	Mauritanie
Mauritius	99	100	87	98	85	96	76	92	Maurice
Morocco	64	83	96	99	81	99	79	99	Maroc
Mozambique	22	47	59	95	46	80	59	91	Mozambique
Namibia	77	79	...	94	...	92	...	85	Namibie
Niger	38	46	50	77	22	67	25	74	Niger
Nigeria	46	67	80	64	56	49	54	51	Nigéria
Rwanda	47	57	92	99	84	98	83	95	Rwanda
Sao Tome and Principe	67	80	99	92	92	96	71	93	Sao ToméetPrincipe
Senegal	62	75	90	97	51	93	51	93	Sénégal
Seychelles	93	96	98	99	99	96	86	97	Seychelles
Sierra Leone	39	58	...	92	...	84	...	83	Sierra Leone
Somalia	21	40	31	37	19	42	30	46	Somalie
South Africa	77	85	57	74	72	66	79	75	Afrique du Sud
South Sudan	-	50	...	37	...	26	...	20	Soudan du Sud
Sudan	43	59	77	96	62	93	57	86	Soudan
Swaziland	52	68	96	97	89	90	85	89	Swaziland
Tanzania, United Republic of	32	50	85	99	78	97	80	90	Tanzanie, République Unie de
Togo	45	63	99	79	77	89	73	87	Togo
Tunisia	88	94	96	95	93	98	93	96	Tunisie
Uganda	30	39	75	93	45	78	52	82	Ouganda
Zambia	49	61	97	99	91	91	90	93	Zambie
Zimbabwe	70	67	91	95	88	90	87	95	Zimbabwe
Africa									**Afrique**

Source: UNICEF

Section 2

Economic Statistics

Statistiques économiques

Million US$										Million $ EU
Country	2009	2010	2011	2012	2013	2014	2015	2016	2017	Pays
Algeria	137 211	161 207	200 019	209 059	209 751	213 807	165 877	159 054	165 470	Algérie
Angola	69 962	83 799	111 790	128 053	136 707	145 716	115 144	101 829	119 914	Angola
Benin	7 097	6 970	7 814	8 117	9 113	9 590	8 462	8 572	9 237	Bénin
Botswana	10 267	12 787	15 352	14 420	14 900	16 244	14 419	15 650	17 402	Botswana
Burkina Faso	8 369	8 980	10 724	11 166	11 938	12 276	10 425	11 525	12 986	Burkina Faso
Burundi	1 781	2 032	2 236	2 333	2 452	2 706	2 814	2 874	2 991	Burundi
Cameroon	26 018	26 144	29 337	29 104	32 358	34 998	30 932	32 213	32 531	Cameroun
Cabo Verde	1 712	1 664	1 865	1 752	1 851	1 860	1 597	1 639	1 803	Cabo Verde
Central African Republic	1 982	1 986	2 213	2 184	1 495	1 694	1 504	1 590	1 719	République Centrafricaine
Chad	9 425	10 970	12 977	14 004	13 812	14 523	11 743	10 952	10 875	Tchad
Comoros	1 069	1 068	1 150	1 150	1 260	1 313	1 104	1 150	1 229	Comores
Congo	9 339	12 281	14 798	13 656	14 026	14 099	8 554	7 867	8 790	Congo
Côte d'Ivoire	24 277	24 885	25 670	26 787	31 281	35 373	33 148	36 493	39 567	Côte d'Ivoire
Democratic Republic of the Congo	18 648	21 566	25 840	29 306	32 680	35 909	37 587	36 308	37 642	Rép. Démocratique du Congo
Djibouti	1 049	1 129	1 239	1 354	1 455	1 589	1 737	1 892	2 010	Djibouti
Egypt	188 985	218 895	235 997	276 348	286 005	301 498	332 698	332 791	235 370	Egypte
Equatorial Guinea	15 028	16 299	21 329	22 390	21 949	21 771	13 187	11 253	12 582	Guinée Equatoriale
Eritrea	1 857	2 117	2 608	3 092	3 502	4 045	4 659	4 659	...	Erythrée
Ethiopia	28 476	26 605	30 479	42 210	46 534	54 151	63 069	70 865	78 726	Ethiopie
Gabon	12 065	14 359	18 187	17 171	17 596	18 209	14 347	13 721	14 623	Gabon
Gambia	901	952	904	913	904	849	939	986	1 047	Gambie
Ghana	25 978	32 174	39 565	40 647	47 906	39 084	37 318	42 801	47 337	Ghana
Guinea	6 717	6 853	6 785	7 638	8 377	8 778	8 794	8 694	9 111	Guinée
Guinea-Bissau	826	849	1 098	989	1 046	1 055	1 036	1 164	1 241	Guinée-Bissau
Kenya	37 023	40 017	41 970	50 413	55 099	61 447	63 767	70 529	81 877	Kenya
Lesotho	1 866	2 386	2 788	2 678	2 525	2 615	2 506	2 291	2 291	Lesotho
Liberia	1 155	1 292	1 538	2 359	2 497	2 447	3 097	2 919	2 653	Libéria
Libya	50 808	68 974	31 999	79 758	51 964	24 308	29 485	20 463	33 314	Libye
Madagascar	8 550	8 730	9 893	9 920	10 602	10 674	9 703	10 126	11 739	Madagascar
Malawi	6 191	6 960	8 004	5 721	5 290	5 965	6 472	5 309	6 404	Malawi
Mali	10 181	10 679	12 978	12 443	13 250	14 411	13 045	14 000	13 187	Mali
Mauritania	3 662	4 338	5 166	5 231	5 640	5 373	4 833	4 746	4 604	Mauritanie
Mauritius	9 129	10 004	11 518	11 669	12 130	12 804	11 691	12 221	13 367	Maurice
Morocco	92 897	93 217	101 371	98 266	106 768	110 033	101 232	103 580	117 155	Maroc
Mozambique	10 912	10 154	13 131	15 265	16 021	16 963	14 799	10 896	15 193	Mozambique
Namibia	8 876	11 282	12 410	13 016	12 711	12 789	11 768	11 308	13 247	Namibie
Niger	5 397	5 719	6 409	6 942	7 670	8 243	7 255	7 606	8 179	Niger
Nigeria	270 534	369 062	411 744	460 954	514 970	568 508	494 584	405 083	376 385	Nigéria
Rwanda	5 379	5 774	6 492	7 316	7 622	8 016	8 261	8 475	9 136	Rwanda
Sao Tome and Principe	188	197	233	253	303	349	318	349	344	Sao Tomé-et-Principe
Senegal	12 772	12 914	14 352	14 194	14 811	15 309	13 617	14 764	14 436	Sénégal
Seychelles	847	970	1 018	1 059	1 328	1 343	1 378	1 427	1 490	Seychelles
Sierra Leone	2 454	2 578	2 943	3 802	4 920	5 015	4 215	3 675	3 754	Sierra Leone
Somalia	2 012	1 071	1 067	1 306	1 399	1 375	1 332	1 318	-	Somalie
South Africa	295 936	375 349	416 624	396 289	366 645	350 638	317 509	295 739	348 971	Afrique du Sud
South Sudan	9 577	12 288	18 062	9 570	13 428	15 848	13 406	6 534	-	Soudan du Sud
Sudan	60 562	69 665	70 010	68 126	66 702	82 107	95 932	112 382	129 361	Soudan
Swaziland	3 632	4 499	4 872	4 755	4 416	4 299	3 927	3 721	3 921	Swaziland
Tanzania, United Republic of	28 574	31 105	33 562	38 809	44 413	48 220	45 628	47 653	53 748	Tanzanie, République Unie de
Togo	3 366	3 426	3 867	3 874	4 322	4 576	4 181	4 448	4 699	Togo
Tunisia	43 456	44 051	45 811	45 044	46 385	47 568	43 188	41 769	40 368	Tunisie
Uganda	19 057	19 683	21 483	24 446	25 713	27 829	25 066	25 366	28 101	Ouganda
Zambia	15 328	20 265	23 460	25 504	28 024	27 163	21 249	20 960	25 807	Zambie
Zimbabwe	8 622	10 142	12 098	14 242	15 452	15 891	16 305	16 620	18 243	Zimbabwe
Africa	1 637 983.5	1 953 363.2	2 166 848.6	2 337 068.3	2 411 920.5	2 503 262.8	2 310 840.0	2 202 823.5	2 246 177.0	Afrique

Source: National Statistics Offices

2-2. Real GDP growth rate - Taux de croissance réelle du PIB

Percentage / Pourcentage

Country	2009	2010	2011	2012	2013	2014	2015	2016	2017	Pays
Algeria	1.6	3.6	2.9	3.4	2.8	3.8	3.7	3.3	1.6	Algérie
Angola	3.4	5.4	3.5	8.5	5.0	4.1	0.9	0.1	1.1	Angola
Benin	2.3	2.1	3.0	4.8	7.2	6.4	2.1	4.0	5.6	Bénin
Botswana	-7.7	8.6	6.0	4.5	11.3	4.1	-1.7	4.3	2.4	Botswana
Burkina Faso	3.0	8.4	6.6	6.5	5.8	4.3	3.9	5.9	6.7	Burkina Faso
Burundi	3.8	5.1	4.0	4.4	4.9	4.2	-0.3	1.7	2.5	Burundi
Cameroon	2.2	3.4	4.1	4.5	5.4	5.9	5.7	4.5	3.1	Cameroun
Cabo Verde	-1.3	1.5	4.0	1.1	0.8	0.6	1.0	3.8	4.0	Cabo Verde
Central African Republic	1.7	3.0	3.3	4.0	-36.7	1.0	4.8	4.5	4.0	République Centrafricaine
Chad	-2.0	15.0	7.6	8.4	-4.6	3.4	3.8	-2.7	0.1	Tchad
Comoros	4.0	1.5	1.6	2.1	3.4	3.4	-0.2	2.2	2.5	Comores
Congo	7.5	8.7	3.4	3.8	3.3	6.8	2.6	-2.8	-3.4	Congo
Côte d'Ivoire	3.3	2.0	-4.2	10.1	9.3	8.8	8.8	8.2	7.6	Côte d'Ivoire
Democratic Republic of Congo	2.9	7.1	6.9	7.1	8.5	9.5	7.7	1.7	3.6	Rép. Démocratique du Congo
Djibouti	5.0	3.5	4.5	4.8	5.0	6.0	6.5	6.3	7.0	Djibouti
Egypt	4.9	4.8	1.8	2.2	2.2	2.9	4.4	4.3	4.2	Egypte
Equatorial Guinea	1.3	-8.9	6.5	8.3	-4.1	0.4	-9.1	-8.6	-2.5	Guinée équatoriale
Eritrea	3.9	2.2	8.7	7.0	3.1	5.0	4.8	3.7	...	Erythrée
Ethiopia	8.8	12.4	11.2	8.6	10.6	10.3	10.4	7.6	10.2	Ethiopie
Gabon	0.1	7.1	7.1	5.2	5.6	4.3	3.9	2.9	0.3	Gabon
Gambia	6.4	6.5	-4.3	5.9	4.8	0.9	4.3	2.2	3.5	Gambie
Ghana	4.8	7.9	14.0	9.3	7.3	4.0	3.8	3.7	8.5	Ghana
Guinea	-1.1	4.8	5.6	5.9	3.9	3.7	3.8	10.5	6.7	Guinée
Guinea-Bissau	3.3	4.7	8.1	-1.7	3.3	1.0	6.1	5.8	5.9	Guinée-Bissau
Kenya	3.3	8.4	6.1	4.5	5.9	5.4	5.7	5.8	4.8	Kenya
Lesotho	2.2	6.1	6.9	6.0	1.8	3.1	2.5	2.4	3.1	Lesotho
Liberia	7.8	7.3	8.2	11.3	4.6	5.2	9.3	-1.6	2.3	Libéria
Libya	-3.0	3.2	-66.7	124.7	-52.1	-67.2	...	-7.4	70.8	Libye
Madagascar	-4.0	0.3	1.5	3.0	2.3	3.3	3.1	4.0	3.9	Madagascar
Malawi	8.3	6.9	4.9	-0.6	6.3	6.2	3.3	2.7	6.2	Malawi
Mali	4.7	5.4	3.2	-0.8	2.3	7.0	6.0	5.4	5.4	Mali
Mauritania	-1.0	4.8	4.7	5.8	6.1	5.6	0.9	1.7	3.1	Mauritanie
Mauritius	3.3	4.4	4.1	3.5	3.4	3.7	3.6	3.8	3.9	Maurice
Morocco	4.2	3.8	5.2	3.0	4.5	2.7	4.5	1.2	4.1	Maroc
Mozambique	6.4	6.7	7.1	7.2	7.1	7.4	6.6	3.8	3.7	Mozambique
Namibia	0.3	6.0	5.1	5.1	5.6	6.4	6.1	0.7	-0.8	Namibie
Niger	-0.7	8.4	2.3	11.8	5.3	7.5	4.3	4.9	4.9	Niger
Nigeria	6.9	7.8	4.9	4.3	5.4	6.3	2.7	-1.5	0.7	Nigéria
Rwanda	6.3	7.3	7.8	8.8	4.7	7.6	8.9	6.0	6.1	Rwanda
Sao Tome and Principe	2.4	6.7	4.4	3.1	4.8	6.5	3.8	4.1	5.2	Sao Tomé-et-Principe
Senegal	2.4	4.2	1.8	4.4	3.5	4.3	6.5	6.6	6.8	Sénégal
Seychelles	-1.1	5.9	5.4	3.7	6.0	4.5	4.9	4.5	6.3	Seychelles
Sierra Leone	3.2	5.3	6.3	15.2	20.7	4.6	-20.6	6.1	5.8	Sierra Leone
Somalia	2.6	2.6	2.6	2.6	2.6	3.7	2.7	...	...	Somalie
South Africa	-1.5	3.0	3.3	2.2	2.5	1.8	1.3	0.6	1.3	Afrique du Sud
South Sudan	7.4	-1.8	1.9	-51.5	30.2	22.2	5.1	0.3	...	Soudan du Sud
Sudan	4.5	6.5	0.9	3.5	6.8	7.0	4.3	4.9	5.8	Soudan
Swaziland	4.5	3.5	2.0	3.5	4.8	3.6	1.1	0.7	2.3	Swaziland
Tanzania, United Republic of	5.4	6.4	7.9	5.1	7.3	7.0	7.0	7.0	6.7	Tanzanie, République Unie de
Togo	5.5	6.1	6.4	6.5	6.1	5.9	5.7	5.1	4.4	Togo
Tunisia	3.1	3.0	-1.9	3.9	2.3	2.4	1.2	1.0	1.9	Tunisie
Uganda	6.9	8.2	5.9	3.2	4.7	4.5	5.6	2.5	3.9	Ouganda
Zambia	9.2	10.3	5.6	7.6	5.1	4.7	2.9	3.8	4.1	Zambie
Zimbabwe	-	12.6	15.4	14.8	5.5	2.1	1.7	0.6	2.9	Zimbabwe
Africa	**3.3**	**5.8**	**2.9**	**7.3**	**3.6**	**3.7**	**3.4**	**2.3**	**3.7**	**Afrique**

Source: National Statistics Offices

2-3. GDP per capita - PIB par habitant

US Dollars Country	2009	2010	2011	2012	2013	2014	2015	2016	2017	Dollars EU Pays
Algeria	3 876	4 473	5 448	5 584	5 493	5 491	4 182	3 939	4 030	Algérie
Angola	3 409	3 949	5 095	5 645	5 830	6 014	4 602	3 942	4 499	Angola
Benin	768	733	799	808	883	905	778	768	806	Bénin
Botswana	5 115	6 244	7 346	6 761	6 846	7 317	6 373	6 793	7 424	Botswana
Burkina Faso	552	574	666	673	699	698	576	619	677	Burkina Faso
Burundi	195	215	228	230	234	250	252	249	251	Burundi
Cameroon	1 296	1 270	1 389	1 344	1 457	1 537	1 325	1 346	1 327	Cameroun
Cabo Verde	3 517	3 394	3 766	3 498	3 648	3 619	3 068	3 110	3 380	Cabo Verde
Central African Republic	454	447	488	473	317	353	307	318	337	République Centrafricaine
Chad	819	922	1 055	1 101	1 051	1 069	837	756	727	Tchad
Comoros	1 567	1 529	1 606	1 568	1 676	1 705	1 401	1 425	1 488	Comores
Congo	2 364	3 020	3 542	3 186	3 192	3 130	1 851	1 659	1 806	Congo
Côte d'Ivoire	1 233	1 236	1 246	1 269	1 447	1 596	1 460	1 569	1 661	Côte d'Ivoire
Democratic Republic of the Congo	292	327	380	417	450	480	486	455	458	Rép. Démocratique du Congo
Djibouti	1 279	1 358	1 472	1 587	1 683	1 814	1 956	2 103	2 205	Djibouti
Egypt	2 349	2 668	2 817	3 226	3 264	3 366	3 636	3 564	2 472	Egypte
Equatorial Guinea	21 251	22 366	28 404	28 937	27 537	26 521	15 605	12 941	14 067	Guinée Equatoriale
Eritrea	404	451	544	632	701	792	891	870	..	Erythrée
Ethiopia	334	304	339	458	492	558	635	696	754	Ethiopie
Gabon	8 004	9 312	11 530	10 642	10 662	10 789	8 316	7 782	8 119	Gabon
Gambia	550	563	517	505	484	440	472	480	494	Gambie
Ghana	1 096	1 323	1 587	1 591	1 831	1 459	1 361	1 527	1 652	Ghana
Guinea	627	622	600	657	701	715	697	672	685	Guinée
Guinea-Bissau	517	520	656	577	595	586	562	616	642	Guinée-Bissau
Kenya	943	992	1 013	1 185	1 261	1 370	1 385	1 493	1 689	Kenya
Lesotho	938	1 187	1 371	1 302	1 212	1 240	1 174	1 061	1 048	Lesotho
Liberia	302	326	377	563	582	557	688	633	561	Libéria
Libya	8 183	11 008	5 088	12 693	8 293	3 884	4 696	3 233	5 198	Libye
Madagascar	417	414	456	445	462	453	400	406	458	Madagascar
Malawi	432	471	526	364	327	357	376	299	350	Malawi
Mali	693	704	830	772	799	843	741	772	706	Mali
Mauritania	1 046	1 208	1 403	1 385	1 456	1 353	1 188	1 139	1 079	Mauritanie
Mauritius	7 344	8 016	9 192	9 273	9 600	10 093	9 182	9 567	10 432	Maurice
Morocco	2 929	2 903	3 116	2 979	3 192	3 244	2 945	2 975	3 324	Maroc
Mozambique	461	418	525	593	605	623	529	379	514	Mozambique
Namibia	4 124	5 143	5 540	5 680	5 417	5 323	4 786	4 498	5 158	Namibie
Niger	344	351	378	394	418	431	365	367	379	Niger
Nigeria	1 743	2 315	2 514	2 740	2 980	3 203	2 714	2 166	1 962	Nigéria
Rwanda	537	561	615	676	688	707	712	713	751	Rwanda
Sao Tome and Principe	1 123	1 156	1 335	1 415	1 661	1 872	1 669	1 798	1 735	Sao Tomé-et-Principe
Senegal	1 015	997	1 074	1 030	1 041	1 043	900	947	899	Sénégal
Seychelles	9 175	10 421	10 856	11 209	13 946	14 006	14 283	14 712	15 273	Seychelles
Sierra Leone	435	446	498	629	796	794	653	557	558	Sierra Leone
Somalia	215	112	109	130	136	131	124	119	...	Somalie
South Africa	5 804	7 271	7 976	7 500	6 864	6 497	5 827	5 379	6 295	Afrique du Sud
South Sudan	1 277	1 796	911	872	1 172	1 331	1 086	513	...	Soudan du Sud
Sudan	1 716	1 929	1 896	1 806	1 732	2 087	2 384	2 729	3 068	Soudan
Swaziland	3 095	3 770	4 019	3 860	3 531	3 388	3 051	2 853	2 970	Swaziland
Tanzania, United Republic of	646	681	712	798	884	930	853	864	945	Tanzanie, République Unie de
Togo	541	536	589	574	624	643	572	593	611	Togo
Tunisia	4 130	4 140	4 258	4 140	4 215	4 274	3 838	3 672	3 512	Tunisie
Uganda	594	594	627	691	703	737	642	629	675	Ouganda
Zambia	1 135	1 456	1 636	1 725	1 838	1 728	1 311	1 254	1 497	Zambie
Zimbabwe	628	726	849	978	1 037	1 042	1 045	1 041	1 117	Zimbabwe
Africa	**1 650**	**1 918**	**2 026**	**2 130**	**2 142**	**2 167**	**1 951**	**1 814**	**1 849**	**Afrique**

Source: Compiled by authors from national statistics offices data

2-4. Structure of GDP and Gross Value Added (at current market prices) - Structure du PIB (aux prix courants du marché)

Share of GDP (%) Country	Agriculture 2009	Agriculture 2016	Total Industry 2009	Total Industry 2016	Manufacturing 2009	Manufacturing 2016	Services 2009	Services 2016	Part du PIB (%) Pays
Algeria	10.1	13.3	51.6	37.8	5.0	4.8	38.3	48.9	Algérie
Angola	6.8	10.1	45.4	43.4	5.3	5.5	47.8	46.5	Angola
Benin	26.9	26.0	25.0	22.5	16.3	13.3	48.1	51.5	Bénin
Botswana	3.2	2.2	32.1	35.2	7.2	5.7	64.7	62.5	Botswana
Burkina Faso	35.6	31.0	19.3	24.0	9.2	8.8	45.1	45.1	Burkina Faso
Burundi	40.1	40.7	18.5	16.1	12.4	11.8	41.4	43.2	Burundi
Cameroon	14.6	16.7	29.0	26.6	16.3	15.9	56.4	56.7	Cameroun
Cabo Verde	9.5	9.7	21.9	20.0	5.6	8.1	68.6	70.2	Cabo Verde
Central African Republic	54.6	47.0	13.7	13.7	6.8	7.6	31.7	39.3	République Centrafricaine
Chad	29.4	33.1	30.0	25.7	7.1	10.2	40.5	41.2	Tchad
Comoros	38.3	42.2	11.5	11.8	6.8	9.1	50.2	45.9	Comores
Congo	4.6	7.7	72.3	56.1	4.6	7.8	23.0	36.2	Congo
Côte d'Ivoire	23.6	23.7	27.9	30.6	18.4	16.4	48.5	45.7	Côte d'Ivoire
Democratic Republic of the Congo	25.2	20.5	35.1	43.0	20.1	20.2	39.7	36.5	Rép. Démocratique du Congo
Djibouti*	3.9	3.3	19.5	22.1	3.5	2.5	76.6	74.6	Djibouti
Egypt	13.6	11.9	37.5	32.9	16.6	17.1	48.9	55.2	Egypte
Equatorial Guinea	1.1	2.4	75.9	52.8	18.2	18.8	23.0	44.8	Guinée Equatoriale
Eritrea	14.5	17.3	22.4	23.5	5.7	6.0	63.0	59.1	Erythrée
Ethiopia	50.8	37.7	10.4	24.0	3.7	6.0	38.8	38.3	Ethiopie
Gabon	5.5	5.5	54.7	46.2	5.0	7.9	39.9	48.2	Gabon
Gambia	29.3	22.1	14.0	14.9	5.6	5.2	56.7	63.0	Gambie
Ghana	32.9	19.7	19.7	25.4	7.2	4.9	47.4	54.9	Ghana
Guinea	17.6	19.7	34.7	34.4	13.5	12.7	47.7	45.9	Guinée
Guinea-Bissau	45.6	49.1	13.8	13.5	12.4	12.2	40.6	37.4	Guinée-Bissau
Kenya	26.1	35.6	21.0	19.0	13.4	10.0	52.9	45.4	Kenya
Lesotho	6.2	5.8	34.2	36.8	17.7	17.4	59.6	57.4	Lesotho
Liberia	68.1	70.3	11.6	9.0	5.5	5.2	20.3	20.7	Libéria
Libya	1.0	0.7	80.1	80.6	6.1	3.4	18.9	18.7	Libye
Madagascar	29.1	26.1	20.1	18.1	14.6	13.4	50.7	55.9	Madagascar
Malawi*	32.8	29.9	16.5	15.4	11.2	10.1	50.7	54.7	Malawi
Mali	34.6	40.3	27.5	19.4	18.1	13.4	37.9	40.3	Mali
Mauritania	25.8	26.3	35.3	30.8	8.6	8.6	38.9	42.9	Mauritanie
Mauritius	4.3	3.6	26.1	20.9	16.7	13.9	69.6	75.6	Maurice
Morocco	14.7	13.6	27.3	29.5	17.5	17.9	58.0	56.8	Maroc
Mozambique	30.1	24.9	19.0	21.8	11.9	9.6	50.9	53.3	Mozambique
Namibia	9.0	6.6	31.6	31.7	14.1	12.0	59.4	61.7	Namibie
Niger	42.3	41.7	16.2	17.8	5.4	6.0	41.5	40.5	Niger
Nigeria	37.1	21.2	34.2	18.5	2.5	8.8	28.7	60.4	Nigéria
Rwanda	31.3	31.5	15.1	17.6	6.4	6.3	53.5	50.9	Rwanda
Sao Tome and Principe	11.6	11.6	20.0	16.9	9.8	7.3	68.4	71.6	Sao Tomé-et-Principe
Senegal	17.3	18.0	23.3	24.0	13.9	13.5	59.4	58.0	Sénégal
Seychelles	2.7	2.4	16.6	13.7	9.2	7.0	80.8	83.8	Seychelles
Sierra Leone	58.2	60.9	6.9	5.9	2.2	1.9	34.9	33.2	Sierra Leone
Somalia	60.2	60.2	7.4	7.4	2.5	2.5	32.5	32.5	Somalie
South Africa	3.0	2.4	30.4	29.2	15.0	13.5	66.6	68.4	Afrique du Sud
South Sudan	...	...	...	...	...	...	...	...	Soudan du Sud
Sudan	32.6	32.7	25.0	20.4	8.5	10.5	42.4	46.9	Soudan
Swaziland	9.5	10.0	41.0	37.5	35.7	33.2	49.5	52.4	Swaziland
Tanzania, United Republic of	32.4	31.5	20.0	27.3	7.4	5.5	47.6	41.2	Tanzanie, République Unie de
Togo	36.2	29.0	16.9	18.6	9.2	8.1	46.9	52.4	Togo
Tunisia	9.3	10.3	30.7	26.2	18.6	16.3	60.0	63.5	Tunisie
Uganda	29.9	25.5	19.9	22.7	8.3	9.7	50.2	51.8	Ouganda
Zambia	12.4	6.5	32.4	36.6	9.3	8.1	55.2	56.9	Zambie
Zimbabwe	14.1	11.1	27.8	23.1	14.5	9.7	58.1	65.8	Zimbabwe
Africa	**18.1**	**17.3**	**34.7**	**28.3**	**10.7**	**11.1**	**47.2**	**54.4**	**Afrique**

* The data of 2016 correspond to those of year 2015

* Les données de 2016 correspondent à celles de l'année 2015

Source: Compiled from national statistics offices.

2-5. Structure of uses (at current market prices) - Structure de la demande (aux prix courants du marché)

Share of GDP (%) Country	Household Final Cons. Expenditure Dep. des menages en cons. finale		General Government Final Cons. Expenditure Dep. Generale du gouv. en cons. finale		Gross Capital Formation Formation brute de capital		Exports of Goods and Non Factor Services Exportations de biens et services non facteurs		less Imports of Goods and Non Factor Services moins Importations de biens et services non facteurs		Part du PIB (%) Pays
	2009	2016	2009	2016	2009	2016	2009	2016	2009	2016	
Algeria	37.6	42.8	16.1	20.8	46.9	50.7	35.4	21.0	36.0	35.3	Algérie
Angola*	41.9	52.3	20.0	16.6	43.0	34.5	59.0	30.0	64.0	33.4	Angola
Benin	73.2	67.6	16.9	16.9	21.9	26.8	20.4	24.8	32.3	36.1	Bénin
Botswana	60.8	44.1	21.1	18.2	35.2	31.1	34.8	49.7	51.9	43.2	Botswana
Burkina Faso	68.5	55.2	21.6	23.0	24.9	31.7	12.7	28.5	27.7	38.5	Burkina Faso
Burundi	87.0	82.9	19.4	27.0	16.1	9.6	6.6	6.3	29.2	25.8	Burundi
Cameroon	69.7	70.3	11.6	12.3	23.7	22.2	21.4	18.6	26.4	23.4	Cameroun
Cabo Verde	63.9	65.5	18.2	19.5	43.8	36.1	31.1	38.5	57.0	59.5	Cabo Verde
Central African Republic	92.2	94.9	8.4	14.8	11.3	13.0	9.5	14.6	21.4	37.2	République Centrafricaine
Chad	74.0	71.5	11.8	9.2	22.9	18.6	32.1	25.5	40.7	24.8	Tchad
Comoros	91.3	91.9	9.7	10.6	15.8	13.7	7.3	9.3	24.1	25.4	Comores
Congo*	30.6	52.4	10.6	14.1	42.2	46.2	78.0	58.8	61.4	71.5	Congo
Côte d'Ivoire	67.7	64.8	12.6	11.3	8.7	19.9	50.9	29.3	39.9	25.4	Côte d'Ivoire
Democratic Republic of the Congo	85.8	75.7	11.2	13.4	14.6	19.1	33.2	24.5	44.8	32.7	Rép. Démocratique du Congo
Djibouti*	62.0	84.8	21.8	22.9	33.3	30.7	38.1	34.4	55.1	72.8	Djibouti
Egypt	76.1	83.1	11.3	11.4	19.2	15.0	25.0	10.3	31.6	19.9	Egypte
Equatorial Guinea	23.0	47.7	11.1	25.6	39.4	16.6	74.3	51.3	47.9	41.2	Guinée Equatoriale
Eritrea	89.5	76.9	20.1	19.2	9.3	7.4	4.5	15.8	23.4	19.2	Erythrée
Ethiopia	86.6	70.3	8.9	11.3	22.7	38.0	10.5	8.0	28.7	27.6	Ethiopie
Gabon	35.1	43.0	16.1	15.2	28.0	28.5	52.2	42.6	31.3	29.4	Gabon
Gambia	84.0	92.6	10.5	10.8	26.8	18.8	7.7	11.3	28.9	33.5	Gambie
Ghana	89.0	83.6	7.6	9.1	16.4	14.5	29.3	41.0	42.3	48.2	Ghana
Guinea	93.5	83.9	10.0	16.4	21.3	51.8	22.5	29.4	47.3	81.5	Guinée
Guinea-Bissau	94.5	82.4	15.5	13.5	6.4	5.0	18.9	26.1	35.3	27.0	Guinée-Bissau
Kenya	76.3	77.9	15.2	13.6	19.3	17.2	20.0	14.6	30.8	23.4	Kenya
Lesotho	98.6	77.7	38.4	34.9	27.7	28.3	41.8	42.2	106.5	83.1	Lesotho
Liberia	99.3	61.7	19.2	23.8	18.0	40.2	13.2	29.1	49.7	54.9	Libéria
Libya*	23.6	19.5	35.2	17.1	34.5	46.5	82.7	34.1	76.1	17.2	Libye
Madagascar	85.0	76.0	9.5	8.8	34.8	19.2	22.4	35.2	51.6	39.1	Madagascar
Malawi	93.0	88.5	12.4	9.8	13.4	23.8	21.4	22.6	40.2	44.7	Malawi
Mali	70.5	72.8	14.6	16.5	22.0	17.4	21.7	20.4	28.8	27.1	Mali
Mauritania	59.4	55.7	21.6	21.6	34.9	40.2	40.9	35.1	56.8	52.7	Mauritanie
Mauritius	71.4	76.1	13.9	15.4	23.8	17.9	47.7	44.5	56.8	53.9	Maurice
Morocco	58.6	57.9	18.2	19.2	35.0	33.1	28.0	35.1	39.9	45.3	Maroc
Mozambique	78.5	71.1	18.1	28.3	14.7	38.1	30.0	36.8	41.3	74.4	Mozambique
Namibia	70.5	74.9	23.9	24.2	26.5	23.7	52.3	41.1	73.1	64.0	Namibie
Niger	75.6	67.6	16.2	15.5	34.7	34.2	20.3	16.2	46.9	33.5	Niger
Nigeria	75.2	81.6	13.0	5.4	12.1	15.3	30.8	9.2	31.0	11.5	Nigéria
Rwanda	80.8	77.2	13.8	15.1	23.4	25.9	11.7	14.9	29.7	33.1	Rwanda
Sao Tome and Principe	117.2	82.5	13.9	13.2	18.4	29.1	9.0	28.2	58.5	53.0	Sao Tomé-et-Principe
Senegal	80.6	74.8	14.3	15.9	22.1	25.8	24.4	28.7	41.3	45.2	Sénégal
Seychelles	62.6	55.8	28.7	20.2	25.4	36.4	100.3	80.5	117.0	92.9	Seychelles
Sierra Leone	93.8	102.2	10.5	10.4	10.1	17.7	13.5	23.5	27.9	53.9	Sierra Leone
Somalia	72.6	72.6	8.7	8.7	20.0	20.0	0.3	0.3	1.7	1.7	Somalie
South Africa	59.5	59.2	19.4	20.8	20.7	19.4	27.9	30.7	27.5	30.1	Afrique du Sud
South Sudan	46.0	75.5	15.5	9.6	13.7	6.0	60.5	28.4	35.7	19.5	Soudan du Sud
Sudan	75.9	74.6	8.4	9.1	20.5	20.1	13.7	2.7	18.6	6.4	Soudan
Swaziland	78.3	74.5	21.0	22.3	15.2	6.4	51.2	49.5	65.6	52.7	Swaziland
Tanzania, United Republic of	66.3	64.6	17.5	13.9	25.1	24.6	17.4	19.5	26.3	22.6	Tanzanie, République Unie de
Togo	82.1	80.8	11.5	14.1	21.1	26.1	35.6	41.6	50.2	62.7	Togo
Tunisia	62.0	71.8	16.6	20.5	24.3	18.4	45.0	40.0	48.0	50.7	Tunisie
Uganda	75.5	75.0	8.6	8.0	25.8	24.6	17.5	17.7	27.4	25.3	Ouganda
Zambia	52.1	52.5	16.7	14.8	31.3	42.8	29.2	37.1	29.3	47.2	Zambie
Zimbabwe	93.3	77.0	10.6	24.9	14.3	12.2	19.1	24.7	37.3	38.7	Zimbabwe
Africa	**64.2**	**68.6**	**15.6**	**14.0**	**24.2**	**23.9**	**32.0**	**21.0**	**36.0**	**27.6**	**Afrique**

* The data of 2016 correspond to those of year 2015

* Les données de 2016 correspondent à celles de l'année 2015

Source: Compiled from national statistics offices

2-6. Inflation (Average annual growth rates) (%) - Inflation (Taux de croissance moyenne annuel) (%)

Country	2009	2010	2011	2012	2013	2014	2015	2016	2017	Pays
Algeria	4.9	5.7	3.9	4.5	8.9	3.3	2.9	4.8	6.4	Algérie
Angola	12.4	13.7	14.5	13.5	10.3	8.8	7.3	12.2	33.0	Angola
Benin	7.9	0.4	2.1	2.7	6.7	1.0	-1.1	0.3	-0.9	Bénin
Botswana	12.6	8.1	6.9	8.5	7.5	5.9	4.4	3.1	2.8	Botswana
Burkina Faso	10.7	0.9	-0.6	2.8	3.8	0.5	-0.3	1.0	-0.4	Burkina Faso
Burundi	24.4	10.5	6.5	9.6	18.2	7.9	4.4	5.5	5.5	Burundi
Cameroon	5.7	3.0	1.3	2.9	2.4	2.1	1.9	2.7	0.9	Cameroun
Cabo Verde	6.8	1.0	2.1	4.5	2.5	1.5	-0.2	0.1	-1.4	Cabo Verde
Central African Republic	9.3	3.6	1.5	1.8	5.3	1.5	8.2	...	...	République Centrafricaine
Chad	8.3	10.1	-2.1	2.0	7.5	0.2	1.7	3.7	-3.1	Tchad
Comoros	4.9	-2.9	3.8	1.8	6.3	1.6	2.7	3.5	-2.0	Comores
Congo	4.5	5.8	0.3	2.1	6.1	6.0	-0.1	...	...	Congo
Côte d'Ivoire	...	0.2	2.0	4.9	1.3	2.6	0.4	1.2	0.7	Côte d'Ivoire
Democratic Republic of the Congo	44.7	29.0	17.2	12.6	3.7	1.3	1.3	1.3	...	Rép. Démocratique du Congo
Djibouti	12.0	1.7	4.0	5.1	3.7	3.2	-2.2	2.1	2.8	Djibouti
Egypt	18.3	11.5	11.5	10.1	7.1	9.5	10.0	10.4	13.8	Egypte
Equatorial Guinea	6.0	5.5	4.7	7.3	3.6	3.6	3.6	2.7	1.4	Guinée Equatoriale
Eritrea	19.9	34.7	20.5	13.3	12.3	12.3	11.4	...	...	Erythrée
Ethiopia	25.5	36.4	2.8	33.2	23.0	7.7	8.1	7.7	9.7	Ethiopie
Gabon	5.3	1.9	1.4	1.3	2.7	0.5	4.5	-0.3	...	Gabon
Gambia	4.4	4.6	5.0	4.8	4.3	5.7	5.7	7.2	...	Gambie
Ghana	16.5	19.2	10.7	8.7	9.2	11.8	15.5	17.1	17.5	Ghana
Guinea	23.1	4.7	15.5	21.4	15.2	11.9	6.2	11.8	8.7	Guinée
Guinea-Bissau	7.9	-2.8	2.2	4.8	2.3	1.2	-1.5	1.4	1.7	Guinée-Bissau
Kenya	16.2	9.5	4.1	14.0	9.4	5.7	6.9	6.6	6.3	Kenya
Lesotho	10.7	7.4	3.6	5.0	6.1	5.0	5.3	3.1	...	Lesotho
Liberia	17.5	7.4	7.3	8.5	6.8	7.6	9.3	7.7	8.8	Libéria
Libya	10.4	2.4	2.4	15.9	6.1	2.6	2.4	...	...	Libye
Madagascar	9.3	9.0	9.2	9.5	5.7	5.8	6.1	7.4	12.4	Madagascar
Malawi	8.7	8.4	7.4	7.6	21.3	27.3	23.8	21.9	21.7	Malawi
Mali	9.2	2.4	1.2	3.0	5.3	-0.6	0.9	1.4	-1.8	Mali
Mauritania	7.3	2.2	5.7	6.2	4.9	4.1	3.5	0.5	0.9	Mauritanie
Mauritius	9.8	2.5	2.9	6.5	3.9	2.9	3.0	1.3	1.0	Maurice
Morocco	3.7	1.0	0.9	0.9	1.3	1.9	0.4	1.6	1.6	Maroc
Mozambique	14.5	3.8	12.4	11.2	2.6	4.3	2.6	3.6	19.9	Mozambique
Namibia	9.1	9.5	4.9	5.0	6.7	5.6	5.4	3.4	6.7	Namibie
Niger	11.3	0.5	0.9	2.9	0.5	2.3	-0.9	1.0	0.2	Niger
Nigeria	11.6	12.5	13.7	10.8	12.2	8.5	8.0	9.0	15.7	Nigéria
Rwanda	15.4	10.3	-0.7	3.1	10.3	5.9	2.4	2.5	7.2	Rwanda
Sao Tome and Principe	24.8	16.1	12.9	11.9	10.4	7.1	6.4	4.0	5.1	Sao Tomé-et-Principe
Senegal	5.8	-2.2	1.2	3.4	1.4	0.7	-1.1	0.1	0.8	Sénégal
Seychelles	37.0	31.8	-2.4	2.6	7.1	4.3	1.4	3.9	-0.9	Seychelles
Sierra Leone	14.5	6.4	16.8	16.1	12.1	11.1	7.2	8.1	...	Sierra Leone
Somalia	...	...	...	...	...	...	...	...	...	Somalie
South Africa	10.1	-15.5	4.1	5.0	5.7	5.8	6.1	4.5	6.6	Afrique du Sud
South Sudan	19.2	5.0	1.2	47.3	45.1	0.0	1.7	52.8	165.0	Soudan du Sud
Sudan	14.3	11.3	13.0	18.0	35.6	36.4	36.9	16.9	11.8	Soudan
Swaziland	12.7	7.4	4.5	6.1	8.9	5.6	5.7	5.0	...	Swaziland
Tanzania, United Republic of	10.3	12.1	8.2	12.7	16.0	7.9	6.1	5.6	5.2	Tanzanie, République Unie de
Togo	8.7	3.7	1.5	3.6	2.6	1.8	0.2	1.8	0.9	Togo
Tunisia	4.9	3.5	4.2	3.5	5.1	5.8	4.9	4.9	3.7	Tunisie
Uganda	...	17.9	4.9	16.0	12.9	5.0	3.1	5.4	5.5	Ouganda
Zambia	12.4	13.4	8.5	6.4	6.6	7.0	7.8	10.0	18.2	Zambie
Zimbabwe	5	12	3.0	3.5	3.7	1.6	-0.2	-2.4	-1.6	Zimbabwe
Africa	**10.8**	**8.6**	**6.1**	**9.1**	**9.2**	**6.7**	**7.0**	**7.4**	**10.1**	**Afrique**

Source: National Statistics Offices

2-7. Agricultural and food production index – Indice de la production agricole et alimentaire

2004 - 2006 = 100	Agricultural production Procuction agricole				Food production Production alimentaire				2004 - 2006 = 100
Country	2011	2012	2013	2014	2011	2012	2013	2014	Pays
Algeria	134.6	148.4	164.3	160.2	134.8	148.6	164.7	160.6	Algérie
Angola	183.1	152.2	205.8	174.9	184.0	152.6	207.0	175.6	Angola
Benin	127.3	133.7	142.7	151.6	132.0	139.9	147.8	158.1	Bénin
Botswana	143.7	128.2	127.2	109.8	144.1	128.6	127.6	110.2	Botswana
Burkina Faso	106.9	124.6	125.5	130.5	115.1	131.8	126.9	134.1	Burkina Faso
Burundi	102.3	89.8	128.1	108.8	112.1	98.8	144.8	121.8	Burundi
Cameroon	91.5	94.9	98.7	98.2	91.3	94.7	98.5	98.1	Cameroun
Cabo Verde	144.0	152.0	155.6	155.0	149.1	156.6	160.6	160.0	Cabo Verde
Central African Republic	120.2	122.3	124.1	113.7	119.8	121.4	123.2	112.7	République Centrafricaine
Chad	110.0	163.3	145.9	145.9	115.4	171.0	152.7	151.4	Tchad
Comoros	106.2	102.2	107.1	107.0	106.2	102.2	107.1	106.9	Comores
Congo	126.9	130.7	133.1	106.3	127.2	131.0	133.3	106.0	Congo
Côte d'Ivoire	110.1	119.5	123.3	122.3	113.8	121.0	124.2	122.6	Côte d'Ivoire
Democratic Republic of the Congo	110.4	111.6	110.4	104.2	110.5	111.7	110.6	104.1	Rép. Démocratique du Congo
Djibouti	131.3	134.5	133.6	133.4	131.3	134.5	133.6	133.4	Djibouti
Egypt	113.4	119.3	116.3	120.3	114.1	120.5	117.6	121.5	Egypte
Equatorial Guinea	111.1	113.7	115.0	116.6	112.3	114.3	116.3	118.3	Guinée Equatoriale
Eritrea	109.0	109.3	112.0	109.2	109.0	109.3	112.0	109.1	Erythrée
Ethiopia	138.7	146.3	152.6	158.1	137.9	147.0	152.1	157.4	Ethiopie
Gabon	117.7	117.5	121.0	97.4	114.8	114.1	117.4	92.2	Gabon
Gambia	89.1	107.3	98.2	82.4	89.0	107.3	98.2	82.4	Gambie
Ghana	131.4	138.8	143.3	143.9	131.4	138.8	143.3	143.9	Ghana
Guinea	124.8	128.1	132.5	130.0	124.8	128.9	133.4	130.7	Guinée
Guinea-Bissau	126.9	133.9	139.8	137.5	127.3	134.5	140.4	138.0	Guinée-Bissau
Kenya	116.5	121.5	125.2	125.5	117.4	122.8	125.9	125.9	Kenya
Lesotho	110.4	98.7	110.8	100.8	110.4	98.0	110.8	100.2	Lesotho
Liberia	107.1	113.5	110.1	103.6	131.4	134.1	130.5	120.7	Libéria
Libya	113.3	115.5	114.7	113.3	113.6	115.8	115.0	113.6	Libye
Madagascar	122.6	128.1	117.2	119.2	123.5	129.1	117.9	119.9	Madagascar
Malawi	164.5	172.8	186.0	148.9	166.9	181.9	192.9	150.4	Malawi
Mali	144.0	143.6	139.5	153.7	152.9	151.1	147.5	157.0	Mali
Mauritania	110.8	119.5	120.6	125.3	110.8	119.5	120.6	125.3	Mauritanie
Mauritius	98.3	95.8	93.6	95.7	98.1	95.8	93.7	95.8	Maurice
Morocco	130.2	124.0	131.4	129.8	130.5	124.2	131.7	130.1	Maroc
Mozambique	161.3	128.7	129.6	136.6	166.5	130.1	128.5	136.9	Mozambique
Namibia	88.2	91.3	89.7	88.5	88.7	91.9	90.3	89.0	Namibie
Niger	128.9	139.5	144.2	148.4	128.9	139.5	144.3	148.4	Niger
Nigeria	98.3	108.6	106.0	116.2	98.7	109.1	106.6	116.8	Nigéria
Rwanda	151.8	161.7	166.1	138.7	152.5	163.0	167.7	139.3	Rwanda
Sao Tome and Principe	100.8	102.6	111.6	119.0	100.8	102.7	111.7	119.1	Sao Tomé-et-Principe
Senegal	108.8	125.1	121.2	126.2	109.4	125.7	121.9	127.2	Sénégal
Seychelles	102.2	103.0	104.9	104.7	106.1	107.2	109.4	108.9	Seychelles
Sierra Leone	156.0	160.9	169.2	168.4	156.3	160.7	169.1	168.3	Sierra Leone
Somalia	108.0	110.8	117.0	111.9	108.0	110.8	117.0	111.9	Somalie
South Africa	116.7	120.6	122.7	125.0	117.2	121.2	123.4	125.8	Afrique du Sud
South Sudan	...	...	...	...	...	...	...	...	Soudan du Sud
Sudan	...	...	...	...	...	...	...	...	Soudan
Swaziland	109.4	112.2	114.7	114.4	109.8	112.6	115.1	114.8	Swaziland
Tanzania, United Republic of	138.4	147.5	167.1	175.8	139.4	148.6	169.1	180.1	Tanzanie, République Unie de
Togo	137.2	134.9	125.0	140.3	141.2	138.6	128.2	142.8	Togo
Tunisia	105.6	118.1	117.5	108.0	105.7	118.3	117.6	108.1	Tunisie
Uganda	97.6	92.4	93.8	92.6	96.0	90.9	91.7	90.1	Ouganda
Zambia	179.5	187.8	185.8	179.5	182.3	184.5	187.9	180.5	Zambie
Zimbabwe	101.7	102.8	99.2	98.9	94.3	98.6	97.0	98.3	Zimbabwe

Source: FAO

2-8. Industrial, mining and manufacturing production index - Indice de la production industrielle, minière et manufacturière

Country	Base	Industrial production Production Industrielle				Mining production Production Minière				Manufacturing production Production Manufacturière				Pays
		2012	2013	2014	2015	2012	2013	2014	2015	2012	2013	2014	2015	
Algeria	2010=100	102.0	102.9	107.8	...	85.4	90.5	96.6	...	98.8	100.5	101.2	...	Algérie
Angola	2010=100	225.8	236.0	239.6	110.4	100.0	99.9	97.0	104.3	108.4	118.5	153.1	156.1	Angola
Benin	2010=100	109.9	114.2	112.5	...	...	...	...	...	...	...	...	...	Bénin
Botswana	2010=100	...	...	...	...	92.5	108.5	112.0	94.0	...	...	...	...	Botswana
Burkina Faso	2010=100	96.5	101.2	101.1	113.0	...	...	...	...	...	...	...	...	Burkina Faso
Burundi	2010=100	118.3	119.5	116.9	107.7	155.4	88.3	57.6	27.9	114.9	113.6	112.5	107.3	Burundi
Cameroon	2010=100	105.0	120.3	116.3	...	...	...	...	...	106.5	106.9	137.0	...	Cameroun
Cabo Verde	...	...	...	...	...	...	...	...	...	...	...	...	...	Cabo Verde
Central African Republic	2010=100	114.1	68.2	32.8	...	...	...	...	...	...	...	...	...	République Centrafricaine
Chad	2005=100	93.1	82.8	85.6	...	...	...	...	...	...	...	...	...	Tchad
Comoros	2011=100	91.3	116.0	...	...	...	...	...	...	...	...	...	...	Comores
Congo	...	...	...	...	...	...	...	...	...	...	...	...	...	Congo
Democratic Republic of the Congo	...	...	...	...	...	...	...	...	...	...	...	...	...	Rép. Démocratique du Congo
Côte d'Ivoire	2010=100	124.4	130.2	135.3	138.1	...	...	...	...	...	...	...	...	Côte d'Ivoire
Djibouti	...	...	...	...	...	...	...	...	...	...	...	...	...	Djibouti
Egypt	2010=100								...	96.9	96.8	100.2	100.4	Egypte
Equatorial Guinea	...	...	...	...	...	...	...	...	...	...	...	...	...	Guinée Equatoriale
Eritrea	...	...	...	...	...	...	...	...	...	...	...	...	...	Erythrée
Ethiopia	...	...	...	...	...	...	...	...	...	...	...	...	...	Ethiopie
Gabon	2005=100	...	...	...	...	...	...	...	...	...	...	...	...	Gabon
Gambia	...	...	...	...	...	...	...	...	...	...	...	...	...	Gambie
Ghana	2010=100	170.4	180.1	182.2	181.2	356.6	397.9	410.5	429.0	119.3	118.7	117.7	108.9	Ghana
Guinea		87.8	...	...	...	...	...	...	...	...	...	...	...	Guinée
Guinea-Bissau	...	...	...	...	...	...	...	...	...	...	...	...	...	Guinée-Bissau
Kenya	...	...	...	...	...	...	...	...	...	...	...	...	...	Kenya
Lesotho	...	...	...	...	...	...	...	...	...	...	...	...	...	Lesotho
Liberia	...	...	...	...	...	...	...	...	...	...	...	...	...	Libéria
Libya	...	...	...	...	...	...	...	...	...	...	...	...	...	Libye
Madagascar	...	...	...	...	...	...	...	...	...	...	...	...	...	Madagascar
Malawi	...	...	...	...	...	...	...	...	...	...	...	...	...	Malawi
Mali	2010=100	113.1	116.5	123.1	126.9	...	...	...	...	...	...	...	...	Mali
Mauritania	2010=100	103.5	113.7	113.7	106.1	100.6	112.0	114.3	...	126.9	132.6	117.5	...	Mauritanie
Mauritius	2010=100	103.3	107.3	109.5	109.4	74.3	70.9	69.1	66.8	103.3	107.4	109.4	109.5	Maurice
Morocco	2010=100	...	...	...	...	101.8	99.9	103.2	99.5	104.5	104.8	105.7	106.6	Maroc
Mozambique	...	...	...	...	...	...	...	...	...	...	...	...	...	Mozambique
Namibia	...	...	...	...	...	...	...	...	...	...	...	...	...	Namibie
Niger	2010=100	112.2	127.6	131.5	118.5	...	...	...	...	...	...	...	...	Niger
Nigeria	2010=100	109.0	109.4	115.7	111.7	97.5	85.0	84.1	79.6	133.7	162.8	186.8	184.1	Nigéria
Rwanda	...	...	...	...	...	...	...	...	...	...	...	...	...	Rwanda
Sao Tome and Principe	...	...	...	...	...	...	...	...	...	...	...	...	...	Sao Tomé-et-Principe
Senegal	2010=100	105.9	101.0	98.9	105.1	114.8	92.6	90.6	102.0	105.5	100.4	96.8	102.3	Sénégal
Seychelles	...	...	...	...	...	...	...	...	...	...	...	...	...	Seychelles
Sierra Leone	...	...	...	...	...	...	...	...	...	...	...	...	...	Sierra Leone
Somalia	...	...	...	...	...	...	...	...	...	...	...	...	...	Somalie
South Africa	2010=100				...	96.0	99.5	98.1	101.2	105.1	106.5	106.6	106.5	Afrique du Sud
South Sudan	...	...	...	...	...	...	...	...	...	...	...	...	...	Soudan du Sud
Sudan	...	...	...	...	...	...	...	...	...	...	...	...	...	Soudan
Swaziland	...	...	...	...	...	...	...	...	...	...	...	...	...	Swaziland
Tanzania, United Republic of	...	...	...	...	...	...	...	...	...	...	...	...	...	Tanzanie, République Unie de
Togo	2010=100	114.4	101.4	126.3	95.9	158.2	191.2	213.9	128.2	117.4	112.8	108.1	104.9	Togo
Tunisia	2010=100	96.8	97.8	96.9	95.2	81.3	77.8	71.7	67.0	101.6	104.2	104.7	103.9	Tunisie
Uganda	2010=100	...	...	...	...	...	...	...	...	...	...	...	...	Ouganda
Zambia	2010=100	107.1	112.6	113.9	114.2	99.0	102.4	99.1	99.3	117.3	123.1	128.0	131.8	Zambie
Zimbabwe	...	...	...	...	...	...	...	...	...	...	...	...	...	Zimbabwe

Source: UN Monthly Bulletin of Statistics Online Database

Source: NU, Bulletin mensuel des statistiques (base de données en ligne)

2-9. Electricity production by type - Production d'Electricité par catégorie

Country	Total electricity generation (GWh)			Total hydro production (GWh)			Total production from fuels (GWh)			Pays
	2015	2016	2017	2015	2016	2017	2015	2016	2017	
Algeria	66923	66287	69157	72	74	75	66553	65897	68741	Algérie
Angola	9695	9918	10157	5192	5341	5502	4498	4572	4650	Angola
Benin	345	352	359	14	14	15	323	330	337	Bénin
Botswana	2981	3017	3056	-	-	-	2966	3001	3040	Botswana
Burkina Faso	1804	1903	2022	93	102	112	1710	1801	1909	Burkina Faso
Burundi	186	189	192	181	184	186	4	4	4	Burundi
Cameroon	6829	7177	7561	5068	5261	5466	1614	1764	1937	Cameroun
Cabo Verde	360	368	376	-	-	-	322	330	338	Cabo Verde
Central African Republic	148	150	152	141	142	144	-	-	-	République Centrafricaine
Chad	290	294	299	-	-	-	290	294	299	Tchad
Comoros	68	70	74	5	5	6	62	65	68	Comores
Congo	1731	1800	1878	925	974	1028	806	826	850	Congo
Democratic Republic of the Congo	9485	10175	10933	9451	10141	10898	16	16	17	Rép. Démocratique du Congo
Côte d'Ivoire	8829	9196	9593	1352	1375	1399	7254	7581	7936	Côte d'Ivoire
Djibouti	364	373	383	-	-	-	361	370	380	Djibouti
Egypt	181977	184157	186440	13432	13615	13801	166947	168794	170718	Egypte
Equatorial Guinea	970	982	997	567	571	577	403	411	419	Guinée Equatoriale
Eritrea	413	426	439	-	-	-	404	416	429	Erythrée
Ethiopia	10437	10856	11330	9674	10082	10543	4	4	4	Ethiopie
Gabon	2130	2300	2489	918	999	1088	1196	1284	1382	Gabon
Gambia	316	322	329	-	-	-	310	316	322	Gambie
Ghana	11491	12012	12570	5845	6211	6600	5643	5798	5967	Ghana
Guinea	1240	1301	1366	688	725	764	544	569	595	Guinée
Guinea-Bissau	147	156	167	-	-	-	144	153	164	Guinée-Bissau
Kenya	9651	9861	10086	3787	3901	4020	1205	1229	1253	Kenya
Lesotho	402	420	438	402	420	438	-	-	-	Lesotho
Liberia	109	113	118	-	-	-	108	112	117	Libéria
Libya	37722	38718	39768	-	-	-	37713	38709	39758	Libye
Madagascar	2675	2765	2865	971	1047	1130	1678	1691	1704	Madagascar
Malawi	2681	2725	2771	2659	2702	2748	8	8	8	Malawi
Mali	2230	2396	2583	744	789	838	1425	1543	1677	Mali
Mauritania	709	745	786	184	199	217	498	519	540	Mauritanie
Mauritius	2998	3068	3141	122	123	124	2316	2356	2399	Maurice
Morocco	29911	30605	31361	2281	2320	2361	25108	25605	26121	Maroc
Mozambique	19105	19423	19790	16398	16633	16873	2706	2789	2916	Mozambique
Namibia	1555	1579	1603	1502	1524	1546	34	36	38	Namibie
Niger	531	552	575	-	-	-	527	548	571	Niger
Nigeria	31504	32304	33153	5718	6080	6464	25708	26139	26592	Nigéria
Rwanda	533	540	547	217	219	222	311	315	320	Rwanda
Sao Tome and Principe	30	31	32	11	12	13	18	19	19	Sao Tomé-et-Principe
Senegal	3907	3998	4095	342	350	358	3472	3551	3634	Sénégal
Seychelles	441	454	467	-	-	-	423	435	448	Seychelles
Sierra Leone	352	378	408	189	203	219	152	164	177	Sierra Leone
Somalia	394	406	418	11	12	12	383	394	406	Somalie
South Africa	249656	255512	261632	3720	3858	4002	228935	234176	239537	Afrique du Sud
South Sudan	352	357	362	22	23	25	328	331	335	Soudan du Sud
Sudan	13267	13724	14228	8420	8747	9112	4627	4748	4878	Soudan
Swaziland	886	904	923	216	221	225	322	331	340	Swaziland
Tanzania, United Republic of	6292	6424	6565	2108	2155	2204	4145	4228	4317	Tanzanie, République Unie de
Togo	104	111	120	56	61	66	20	21	23	Togo
Tunisia	19286	19568	19860	61	66	72	18719	18988	19267	Tunisie
Uganda	3283	3365	3454	2433	2475	2519	635	659	684	Ouganda
Zambia	13442	13582	13727	13035	13168	13305	404	411	419	Zambie
Zimbabwe	9585	10014	10466	4990	5240	5503	4590	4769	4958	Zimbabwe
Africa	782751	798423	818658	124217	128365	132819	628894	639420	653964	Afrique

Source: AFREC

Section **3**

Monetary and Financial Statistics

Statistiques monétaires et financières

3-1. Broad Money Supply / Masse monétaire

Country	Amount (billions nat. currency) Montant (milliards de mon. nat.)			Annual % Growth Acr. Annuel en %			Income Velocity of Money (GDP/M2) Vitesse de circ. de la monnaie (PIB/M2)			Pays
	2015	2016	2017	2015	2016	2017	2015	2016	2017	
Algeria	13 704.5	13 816.3	15 145.1	0.3	0.8	9.6	1.0	0.9	1.0	Algérie
Angola	5 711.9	6 519.8	7 602.5	11.8	14.1	16.6	2.0	1.7	1.8	Angola
Benin	2 540.4	2 473.6	2 661.6	7.9	- 2.6	7.6	1.6	1.5	1.5	Bénin
Botswana	40.7	46.5	49.1	2.0	14.3	5.6	1.8	1.6	1.7	Botswana
Burkina Faso	2 563.2	2 868.3	3 211.5	19.7	11.9	12.0	2.0	1.7	1.7	Burkina Faso
Burundi	1 061.3	1 129.7	1 218.4	1.5	6.4	7.9	3.1	3.1	3.3	Burundi
Cameroon	4 116.4	4 345.7	4 460.7	9.1	5.6	2.6	3.4	3.3	3.2	Cameroun
Cabo Verde	156.9	170.0	181.6	6.3	8.4	6.8	0.7	0.6	0.6	Cabo Verde
Central African Republic	257.8	272.6	296.4	5.3	5.8	8.7	2.9	2.8	2.8	République Centrafricaine
Chad	1 027.0	948.0	1 002.7	- 4.7	- 7.7	5.8	6.0	5.8	5.7	Tchad
Comoros	113.8	125.4	132.3	17.1	10.3	5.5	3.7	3.2	3.1	Comores
Congo	2 330.1	1 971.8	1 906.3	- 11.2	- 15.4	- 3.3	2.3	1.9	2.0	Congo
Democratic Republic of the Congo	3 060.5	3 274.9	3 654.8	17.0	7.0	11.6	3.9	3.8	3.9	Rép. Démocratique du Congo
Côte d'Ivoire	4 317.9	5 257.6	7 356.8	10.5	21.8	39.9	6.5	6.1	5.9	Côte d'Ivoire
Djibouti	279.4	303.9	328.3	19.0	8.7	8.0	0.9	0.8	0.9	Djibouti
Egypt	1 765.5	2 094.5	2 921.9	16.4	18.6	39.5	0.8	0.8	0.7	Egypte
Equatorial Guinea	1 386.8	1 160.0	1 389.9	- 10.9	- 16.4	19.8	6.0	4.8	4.7	Guinée Equatoriale
Eritrea	85.1	98.5	113.8	13.9	15.7	15.5	...	...	...	Erythrée
Ethiopia	369.7	445.0	527.6	24.2	20.4	18.5	...	...	...	Ethiopie
Gabon	2 180.0	2 026.4	2 201.8	- 0.5	- 7.0	8.7	3.0	2.9	3.0	Gabon
Gambia	20.2	23.3	25.9	- 0.9	15.3	11.4	1.2	...	...	Gambie
Ghana	45.4	56.7	69.6	23.3	24.8	22.7	2.3	2.2	2.2	Ghana
Guinea	17 644.3	19 394.6	21 638.7	20.3	9.9	11.6	3.4	3.0	3.1	Guinée
Guinea-Bissau	302.9	326.3	373.1	25.4	7.7	14.3	1.9	1.8	1.9	Guinée-Bissau
Kenya	2 658.2	2 753.5	3 119.6	14.1	3.6	13.3	1.5	1.5	1.8	Kenya
Lesotho	9.8	10.6	12.0	6.4	7.4	13.4	2.0	2.1	2.2	Lesotho
Liberia	0.7	0.7	0.7	1.7	- 4.5	- 1.8	0.1	0.1	0.1	Libéria
Libya	81.0	83.8	...	3.5	3.5	...	0.4	0.3	0.3	Libye
Madagascar	7 502.3	8 993.1	10 339.8	14.6	19.9	15.0	3.1	2.9	2.8	Madagascar
Malawi	778.8	897.3	1 052.1	23.7	15.2	17.3	2.6	2.6	2.7	Malawi
Mali	2 237.1	2 401.3	2 666.7	13.2	7.3	11.1	2.9	2.7	2.7	Mali
Mauritania	512.1	548.4	588.7	0.4	7.1	7.3	2.8	2.6	...	Mauritanie
Mauritius	438.0	477.8	501.4	10.2	9.1	4.9	0.6	0.6	0.5	Maurice
Morocco	1 148.0	1 205.8	1 278.1	5.7	5.0	6.0	0.6	0.6	0.6	Maroc
Mozambique	249.3	255.2	279.5	21.7	2.4	9.5	1.8	1.6	1.8	Mozambique
Namibia	81.9	85.9	93.0	10.2	4.9	8.2	1.2	1.2	1.3	Namibie
Niger	1 151.3	1 249.7	1 383.3	3.6	8.5	10.7	3.2	3.1	3.1	Niger
Nigeria	19 924.7	23 193.4	26 587.5	5.9	16.4	14.6	2.9	3.1	2.9	Nigéria
Rwanda	1 482.1	1 594.7	1 801.4	21.1	7.6	13.0	3.7	3.4	3.4	Rwanda
Sao Tome and Principe	2 828.2	2 691.2	2 664.0	13.1	- 4.8	- 1.0	2.0	2.0	2.3	Sao Tomé-et-Principe
Senegal	3 953.1	4 427.6	4 868.7	13.4	12.0	10.0	1.7	1.6	1.5	Sénégal
Seychelles	12.2	13.6	15.0	2.9	12.1	10.0	1.3	1.4	1.3	Seychelles
Sierra Leone	5 172.3	6 096.1	6 786.2	4.9	17.9	11.3	3.6	3.3	3.2	Sierra Leone
Somalia	0.0	0.0	...	...	...	...	...	...	...	Somalie
South Africa	2 975.3	3 156.2	3 355.6	10.3	6.1	6.3	0.9	0.8	0.9	Afrique du Sud
South Sudan	17.1	41.3	42.0	117.4	142.5	1.6	...	...	...	Soudan du Sud
Sudan	93.1	121.1	157.5	19.8	30.0	30.1	4.4	4.5	4.2	Soudan
Swaziland	13.2	16.7	17.9	13.6	26.4	7.2	2.6	2.6	2.0	Swaziland
Tanzania, United Republic of	22 115.3	23 642.3	26 621.2	18.8	6.9	12.6	3.0	2.9	3.2	Tanzanie, République Unie de
Togo	1 319.0	1 489.4	1 676.2	20.2	12.9	12.5	1.4	1.3	1.2	Togo
Tunisia	61.9	66.9	73.6	5.3	8.1	10.0	0.9	0.9	0.9	Tunisie
Uganda	17 069.6	18 971.9	21 699.3	11.7	11.1	14.4	3.4	3.4	3.3	Ouganda
Zambia	47.3	44.6	50.8	35.2	- 5.7	14.0	3.4	2.8	3.6	Zambie
Zimbabwe	4.7	5.6	6.2	8.2	19.0	10.5	...	...	...	Zimbabwe
Africa	...	...	...	...	...	...	...	...	...	Afrique

Source: IMF

3-2. Exchange Rate - Taux de change

Average exchange rate (National currency per US$)/Taux de change (moyen) (monnaie nationale par dollars)

Country	2009	2010	2011	2012	2013	2014	2015	2016	2017	Pays
Algeria	72.6	74.4	72.9	77.5	79.4	80.6	100.7	109.4	111.0	Algérie
Angola	79.3	91.9	93.9	95.5	96.5	98.3	120.1	163.7	165.9	Angola
Benin	472.2	495.3	471.9	510.5	493.9	493.6	591.2	593.1	582.1	Bénin
Botswana	7.2	6.8	6.8	7.6	8.4	9.0	10.1	10.9	10.4	Botswana
Burkina Faso	472.2	495.3	471.9	510.5	493.9	493.6	591.2	593.1	582.1	Burkina Faso
Burundi	1 230.2	1 230.7	1 261.1	1 442.5	1 555.1	1 546.7	1 571.9	1 654.6	1 735.2	Burundi
Cameroon	472.2	495.3	471.9	510.5	493.9	493.6	591.2	592.7	617.5	Cameroun
Cabo Verde	79.4	83.3	79.3	85.8	83.1	83.0	99.4	99.7	97.8	Cabo Verde
Central African Republic	472.2	495.3	471.9	510.5	493.9	493.6	591.2	593.1	582.1	République Centrafricaine
Chad	472.2	495.3	471.9	510.5	494.0	494.4	591.4	593.1	582.1	Tchad
Comoros	354.1	371.5	353.9	382.9	370.5	370.8	443.6	444.8	436.6	Comores
Congo	472.2	495.3	471.9	510.5	493.9	493.6	591.2	592.7	617.5	Congo
Democratic Republic of the Congo	809.8	905.9	919.5	919.8	919.6	925.2	926.0	1 010.3	1 294.2	Rép. Démocratique du Congo
Côte d'Ivoire	472.2	495.3	471.9	510.5	493.9	493.6	591.2	593.1	582.1	Côte d'Ivoire
Djibouti	177.7	177.7	177.7	177.7	177.7	177.7	177.7	177.7	177.7	Djibouti
Egypt	5.5	5.5	5.8	6.0	6.4	7.0	7.3	8.1	14.7	Egypte
Equatorial Guinea	472.2	495.3	471.9	510.5	493.9	493.6	591.2	593.1	582.1	Guinée Equatoriale
Eritrea	...	...	...	...	...	...	...	...	...	Erythrée
Ethiopia	11.8	14.4	16.9	17.7	18.6	19.6	20.6	21.7	22.9	Ethiopie
Gabon	472.2	495.3	471.9	510.5	493.9	493.6	591.2	592.7	617.5	Gabon
Gambia	26.6	28.0	29.5	32.1	36.0	41.7	42.5	43.9	46.0	Gambie
Ghana	1.4	1.4	1.5	1.9	2.0	2.9	3.7	3.9	4.4	Ghana
Guinea	4 801.1	5 726.1	6 658.0	6 986.1	6 907.9	7 014.1	7 485.5	8 959.7	9 117.6	Guinée
Guinea-Bissau	472.2	495.3	471.9	510.5	493.9	493.6	591.2	593.1	582.1	Guinée-Bissau
Kenya	77.4	79.2	88.8	84.5	86.1	87.9	98.2	101.5	103.4	Kenya
Lesotho	8.5	7.3	7.3	8.2	9.7	10.9	12.8	14.7	13.3	Lesotho
Liberia	1.0	1.0	1.0	1.0	1.0	1.0	1.0	1.0	1.0	Libéria
Libya	1.2	1.3	1.3	1.2	1.3	1.3	1.3	1.4	1.4	Libye
Madagascar	1 956.2	2 090.0	2 025.1	2 195.0	2 206.9	2 414.8	2 934.4	3 176.5	3 116.1	Madagascar
Malawi	141.2	150.5	156.5	249.1	364.4	424.9	496.4	718.0	730.3	Malawi
Mali	472.2	495.3	471.9	510.5	493.9	493.6	591.2	593.1	582.1	Mali
Mauritania	262.4	275.9	281.1	296.6	300.7	302.7	324.7	352.4	357.9	Mauritanie
Mauritius	32.0	30.8	28.7	30.0	30.7	30.6	35.1	35.5	34.5	Maurice
Morocco	8.1	8.4	8.1	8.6	8.4	8.4	9.8	9.8	9.7	Maroc
Mozambique	27 518.3	33 960.1	29 067.6	28 373.0	30 100.0	31 350.0	39 980.0	63 060.0	63 580.0	Mozambique
Namibia	8.5	7.3	7.3	8.2	9.7	10.9	12.8	14.7	13.3	Namibie
Niger	472.2	495.3	471.9	510.5	493.9	493.6	591.2	593.1	582.1	Niger
Nigeria	148.9	150.3	154.7	157.5	157.3	158.6	192.4	253.5	305.3	Nigéria
Rwanda	568.3	583.1	600.3	614.3	646.6	681.9	721.0	787.3	831.5	Rwanda
Sao Tome and Principe	16 208.5	18 498.6	17 622.9	19 068.4	18 450.0	18 466.4	22 090.6	22 148.9	23 234.0	Sao Tomé-et-Principe
Senegal	472.2	495.3	471.9	510.5	493.9	493.6	591.2	593.1	582.1	Sénégal
Seychelles	13.6	12.1	12.4	13.7	12.1	12.8	13.3	13.3	13.6	Seychelles
Sierra Leone	3 385.7	3 978.1	4 349.2	4 344.0	4 332.5	4 524.2	5 080.8	6 289.9	7 353.3	Sierra Leone
Somalia	...	...	...	...	...	...	...	...	...	Somalie
South Africa	8.5	7.3	7.3	8.2	9.7	10.9	12.8	14.7	13.3	Afrique du Sud
South Sudan	...	...	...	...	...	...	...	...	...	Soudan du Sud
Sudan	2.3	2.3	2.7	3.6	4.8	5.7	6.0	6.2	6.7	Soudan
Swaziland	8.5	7.3	7.3	8.2	9.7	10.9	12.8	14.7	13.3	Swaziland
Tanzania, United Republic of	1 320.3	1 409.3	1 572.1	1 583.0	1 597.6	1 653.2	1 991.4	2 177.1	2 228.0	Tanzanie, République Unie de
Togo	472.2	495.3	471.9	510.5	493.9	493.6	591.2	593.1	582.1	Togo
Tunisia	1.4	1.4	1.4	1.6	1.6	1.7	2.0	2.2	2.4	Tunisie
Uganda	2 030.5	2 177.6	2 522.7	2 504.6	2 586.9	2 599.8	3 240.7	3 420.1	3 611.2	Ouganda
Zambia	5.0	4.8	4.9	5.1	5.4	6.2	8.6	10.3	9.5	Zambie
Zimbabwe	1.0	1.0	1.0	1.0	1.0	1.0	1.0	1.0	1.0	Zimbabwe

Source: IMF

MONETARY STATISTICS - STATISTIQUES MONETAIRES

3-3. Government Finance - Finances Publiques

% of GDP Country	Revenue Recettes			Expenditure Dépenses			Fiscal balance Solde budgétaire			% du PIB Pays
	2015	2016	2017	2015	2016	2017	2015	2016	2017	
Algeria	30.6	29.4	32.0	45.8	41.9	36.8	- 15.3	- 12.6	- 4.7	Algérie
Angola	24.3	18.5	19.2	27.3	23.6	24.1	- 3.0	- 5.1	- 4.9	Angola
Benin	17.3	15.2	16.1	25.3	21.4	21.9	- 8.0	- 6.2	- 5.8	Bénin
Botswana	31.2	33.3	32.4	35.8	32.7	32.5	- 4.6	0.7	- 0.1	Botswana
Burkina Faso	20.9	20.8	21.3	22.9	24.6	28.8	- 2.0	- 3.8	- 7.5	Burkina Faso
Burundi	16.7	15.9	20.4	24.4	23.0	26.9	- 7.7	- 7.1	- 6.5	Burundi
Cameroon	16.2	14.6	15.9	19.0	20.4	19.0	- 2.7	- 5.8	- 3.1	Cameroun
Cabo Verde	26.2	26.5	27.9	30.9	30.0	30.9	- 4.6	- 3.5	- 3.0	Cabo Verde
Central African Republic	15.1	15.6	14.8	15.7	13.9	14.4	- 0.7	1.7	0.3	République Centrafricaine
Chad	12.2	12.5	12.8	17.1	14.5	14.4	- 4.9	- 2.0	- 1.5	Tchad
Comoros	16.8	12.5	15.4	14.5	16.4	16.3	2.3	- 3.9	- 0.9	Comores
Congo	30.4	32.3	31.7	72.1	45.2	36.8	- 41.7	- 12.9	- 5.1	Congo
Democratic Republic of the Congo	17.2	12.3	10.7	17.5	13.2	10.6	- 0.3	- 0.9	0.1	Rép. Démocratique du Congo
Côte d'Ivoire	20.0	19.3	19.8	22.8	23.1	24.3	- 2.8	- 3.9	- 4.6	Côte d'Ivoire
Djibouti	37.2	33.6	34.5	58.9	51.8	49.5	- 21.7	- 18.2	- 15.0	Djibouti
Egypt	22.0	21.5	21.3	33.4	32.7	30.9	- 11.4	- 11.2	- 9.5	Egypte
Equatorial Guinea	26.6	17.2	17.9	29.9	20.9	20.2	- 3.3	- 3.7	- 2.3	Guinée Equatoriale
Eritrea	14.5	14.3	14.4	28.0	28.5	28.3	- 13.6	- 14.2	- 13.9	Erythrée
Ethiopia	15.9	14.9	14.9	18.2	18.2	18.4	- 2.3	- 3.3	- 3.5	Ethiopie
Gabon	21.1	17.1	17.9	22.3	21.8	21.4	- 1.1	- 4.7	- 3.5	Gabon
Gambia	21.6	20.0	30.4	29.7	29.8	34.3	- 8.1	- 9.7	- 3.9	Gambie
Ghana	23.4	20.1	20.0	29.2	29.1	26.7	- 5.8	- 8.9	- 6.7	Ghana
Guinea	14.9	16.3	17.5	21.8	15.9	17.0	- 6.9	0.3	0.6	Guinée
Guinea-Bissau	20.2	16.5	17.0	22.8	20.5	19.8	- 2.6	- 4.0	- 2.8	Guinée-Bissau
Kenya	19.6	18.2	18.3	28.1	26.4	27.5	- 8.6	- 8.2	- 9.3	Kenya
Lesotho	49.8	47.2	40.9	49.5	48.2	47.3	0.3	- 1.0	- 6.3	Lesotho
Liberia	31.4	30.9	30.8	39.5	40.3	34.9	- 8.1	- 9.4	- 4.1	Libéria
Libya	21.5	21.3	22.7	148.1	124.0	65.6	- 126.6	- 102.7	- 43.0	Libye
Madagascar	11.8	15.4	15.2	15.1	17.5	18.1	- 3.3	- 2.1	- 2.9	Madagascar
Malawi	21.2	21.8	23.1	27.6	28.6	28.7	- 6.4	- 6.8	- 5.6	Malawi
Mali	19.2	19.2	19.7	21.0	22.2	23.0	- 1.8	- 3.1	- 3.3	Mali
Mauritania	29.3	27.6	27.7	32.7	28.1	27.8	- 3.4	- 0.5	- 0.1	Mauritanie
Mauritius	21.5	21.6	22.5	25.2	25.1	25.4	- 3.7	- 3.4	- 2.9	Maurice
Morocco	24.3	24.1	23.7	28.5	28.2	27.2	- 4.2	- 4.1	- 3.5	Maroc
Mozambique	28.8	26.2	25.0	33.2	32.5	29.4	- 4.4	- 6.2	- 4.4	Mozambique
Namibia	33.9	31.2	34.2	42.3	40.5	39.4	- 8.5	- 9.3	- 5.2	Namibie
Niger	23.2	20.1	19.7	32.3	26.3	25.4	- 9.1	- 6.3	- 5.7	Niger
Nigeria	7.6	5.6	5.7	11.1	9.5	10.8	- 3.5	- 3.9	- 5.1	Nigéria
Rwanda	25.3	25.0	23.6	30.6	28.5	28.4	- 5.3	- 3.5	- 4.8	Rwanda
Sao Tome and Principe	28.2	31.1	31.4	34.3	32.8	33.4	- 6.1	- 1.7	- 2.1	Sao Tomé-et-Principe
Senegal	25.1	26.8	27.1	29.9	31.1	30.9	- 4.8	- 4.2	- 3.8	Sénégal
Seychelles	34.2	38.1	39.1	31.2	37.9	39.6	3.0	0.2	- 0.5	Seychelles
Sierra Leone	15.6	15.3	15.4	20.7	21.0	22.2	- 5.2	- 5.7	- 6.8	Sierra Leone
Somalia	...	...	...	...	...	...	...	...	...	Somalie
South Africa	29.5	29.2	28.8	33.1	32.7	33.1	- 3.7	- 3.5	- 4.3	Afrique du Sud
South Sudan	29.1	25.0	35.6	37.5	50.2	57.4	- 8.5	- 25.2	-21.8	Soudan du Sud
Sudan	9.4	8.2	8.4	11.0	9.7	10.1	- 1.5	- 1.5	- 1.8	Soudan
Swaziland	29.5	26.4	24.7	30.3	30.7	35.1	- 0.8	- 4.2	- 10.4	Swaziland
Tanzania, United Republic of	14.6	15.4	15.9	17.9	19.1	17.3	- 3.3	- 3.7	- 1.4	Tanzanie, République Unie de
Togo	25.4	26.6	27.0	31.6	34.9	28.5	- 6.2	- 8.3	- 1.5	Togo
Tunisia	23.8	23.1	23.6	28.2	29.1	28.9	- 4.5	- 6.0	- 5.3	Tunisie
Uganda	14.1	14.3	15.6	18.2	18.4	18.9	- 4.1	- 4.0	- 3.3	Ouganda
Zambia	18.8	18.2	17.1	28.1	24.0	22.9	- 9.3	- 5.8	- 5.8	Zambie
Zimbabwe	23.9	21.1	20.1	24.9	29.3	29.1	- 1.0	- 8.2	- 9.0	Zimbabwe
Africa										**Afrique**

Source: IMF

Section 4

External Sector

Secteur Extérieur

4-1. External Debt - Dette extérieure

% of GDP	Debt outstanding (As % of GDP) / Encours de la dette (En % du PIB)						Debt service (As % of Exports) / Service de la dette (En % des exportations)						% du PIB
Country	2012	2013	2014	2015	2016	2017	2012	2013	2014	2015	2016	2017	Pays
Algeria	1.7	1.6	1.7	1.8	2.5	2.4	1.8	1.5	2.1	2.6	5.0	0.3	Algérie
Angola	18.8	23.6	27.4	35.8	44.7	35.4	2.7	3.0	3.5	6.1	10.6	14.0	Angola
Benin	15.7	17.3	18.4	20.9	21.4	24.8	3.3	3.5	3.1	2.3	3.2	3.5	Bénin
Botswana	28.9	28.1	22.8	27.8	31.1	28.9	15.3	15.9	12.8	10.0	10.7	13.9	Botswana
Burkina Faso	22.9	22.1	22.0	24.2	24.1	23.7	2.2	2.8	2.9	3.1	4.1	3.7	Burkina Faso
Burundi	22.6	21.0	18.9	18.2	16.7	27.4	2.2	6.4	14.8	14.9	19.6	19.9	Burundi
Cameroon	9.0	12.5	16.2	21.1	21.8	25.7	2.2	2.5	3.0	3.5	6.1	6.0	Cameroun
Cabo Verde	91.2	106.2	99.3	113.9	110.7	111.7	9.9	10.3	10.8	12.1	11.2	10.6	Cabo Verde
Central African Republic	9.9	15.0	21.4	20.1	17.9	17.1	3.7	9.1	9.1	7.5	9.0	9.5	République Centrafricaine
Chad	20.5	21.8	27.0	24.5	25.8	28.6	2.2	3.2	4.0	15.7	9.6	16.5	Tchad
Comoros	41.4	18.7	19.4	24.1	28.4	27.0	9.9	10.4	2.0	1.5	0.8	3.9	Comores
Congo	25.9	32.1	35.1	78.2	87.4	95.7	1.1	1.2	2.9	3.6	4.3	8.0	Congo
Democratic Republic of the Congo	21.4	19.5	18.9	23.0	25.2	28.8	1.4	1.8	1.3	1.4	2.1	2.6	Rép. Démocratique du Congo
Côte d'Ivoire	44.8	40.0	35.7	41.1	39.2	44.0	21.6	9.4	12.6	8.1	10.3	12.0	Côte d'Ivoire
Djibouti	49.2	46.2	49.9	69.3	85.3	87.4	7.9	8.5	8.2	34.7	31.8	37.5	Djibouti
Egypt	12.3	15.0	12.9	12.5	15.7	24.8	11.5	11.6	11.6	22.9	15.1	18.4	Egypte
Equatorial Guinea	7.5	6.4	4.8	8.5	10.1	15.4	0.1	0.6	2.5	2.2	2.3	3.4	Guinée Equatoriale
Eritrea	29.1	25.2	22.1	21.5	19.2	19.3	33.5	13.1	8.3	8.3	6.8	6.1	Erythrée
Ethiopia	20.6	23.5	25.2	34.9	35.1	34.2	3.3	6.0	7.3	10.9	16.5	21.3	Ethiopie
Gabon	16.6	24.2	25.3	33.3	35.6	45.1	3.9	4.8	11.7	5.8	10.1	10.3	Gabon
Gambia	45.6	47.9	56.9	60.0	56.1	53.0	33.8	30.5	31.5	39.4	43.9	46.6	Gambie
Ghana	25.2	29.3	40.1	46.8	42.5	40.0	3.2	3.9	4.7	7.0	8.7	18.7	Ghana
Guinea	17.9	18.8	20.8	21.4	22.8	24.2	7.4	98.4	2.8	3.1	5.2	4.9	Guinée
Guinea-Bissau	27.3	25.7	22.7	23.3	21.5	20.4	1.2	1.2	0.1	1.0	1.0	1.4	Guinée-Bissau
Kenya	30.2	29.3	35.9	40.1	41.3	43.7	50.3	43.3	55.1	63.4	21.1	28.0	Kenya
Lesotho	28.1	31.4	35.3	38.0	41.1	34.9	3.1	3.2	4.4	4.1	5.0	5.0	Lesotho
Liberia	10.3	11.7	17.9	25.9	32.3	38.3	7.3	8.3	3.5	5.1	4.6	3.4	Libéria
Libya	...	...	...	...	...	...	...	...	...	...	...	...	Libye
Madagascar	43.6	43.8	42.4	46.1	43.7	44.6	23.0	24.6	23.9	21.3	19.9	18.9	Madagascar
Malawi	23.9	30.6	33.6	31.3	36.7	34.3	1.3	1.8	3.8	4.2	10.5	9.2	Malawi
Mali	22.2	22.2	19.5	22.2	23.7	24.3	5.9	4.1	4.5	5.9	8.5	7.4	Mali
Mauritania	81.1	81.4	86.3	104.0	109.2	85.4	3.3	4.7	4.8	6.8	11.0	9.6	Mauritanie
Mauritius	87.9	104.0	105.1	92.1	88.1	98.9	3.5	3.6	3.9	4.7	4.1	4.4	Maurice
Morocco	29.1	30.2	31.0	33.4	33.6	34.1	6.7	7.3	8.1	7.7	7.8	7.2	Maroc
Mozambique	69.7	83.0	90.2	115.1	150.1	140.7	16.4	11.9	12.9	12.1	14.8	19.9	Mozambique
Namibia	35.5	39.1	43.0	50.5	59.3	55.8	30.2	39.2	31.6	40.6	41.8	43.0	Namibie
Niger	50.1	47.5	47.2	56.9	59.7	61.3	4.4	4.3	6.1	4.1	6.0	7.0	Niger
Nigeria	7.0	6.3	7.4	9.6	11.0	13.1	0.3	0.2	0.4	0.4	0.6	0.9	Nigéria
Rwanda	20.2	25.2	26.7	30.1	37.6	40.1	2.4	10.2	19.1	5.5	7.0	14.8	Rwanda
Sao Tome and Principe	81.0	71.1	69.6	86.0	79.6	74.2	8.0	7.3	8.6	3.7	4.3	4.5	Sao Tomé-et-Principe
Senegal	61.8	70.0	68.4	72.6	68.5	74.3	13.7	7.6	6.9	10.7	8.2	9.3	Sénégal
Seychelles	167.8	125.2	118.2	99.6	98.3	101.3	3.4	3.6	7.8	2.5	6.9	5.7	Seychelles
Sierra Leone	25.8	21.3	22.5	29.4	36.8	43.4	4.8	2.0	2.2	3.0	7.7	5.1	Sierra Leone
Somalia	...	...	...	...	...	...	...	...	...	...	...	...	Somalie
South Africa	35.8	37.2	41.3	39.1	48.4	46.0	27.3	31.5	37.4	42.3	46.9	46.0	Afrique du Sud
South Sudan	...	...	...	...	...	...	...	...	...	...	...	...	Soudan du Sud
Sudan	68.9	68.7	65.8	61.1	57.4	46.5	2.8	6.6	2.8	3.6	10.0	5.2	Soudan
Swaziland	12.1	13.8	12.0	14.3	13.8	15.8	19.5	7.3	9.3	12.0	10.7	9.3	Swaziland
Tanzania, United Republic of	25.3	26.1	27.3	31.9	32.9	33.1	3.5	2.8	3.5	3.9	5.2	5.7	Tanzanie, République Unie de
Togo	13.3	14.3	17.1	21.1	19.7	20.8	2.7	3.1	3.2	4.3	3.5	3.7	Togo
Tunisia	53.3	56.2	56.0	62.7	64.3	75.2	12.3	12.3	9.6	8.5	10.1	12.6	Tunisie
Uganda	28.2	30.8	29.7	36.3	38.4	41.8	4.2	4.9	5.6	6.9	9.0	10.2	Ouganda
Zambia	17.3	20.1	27.4	71.9	81.9	70.3	2.0	5.4	2.7	6.5	6.9	7.6	Zambie
Zimbabwe	58.5	60.6	64.1	67.9	66.7	55.3	12.2	17.9	17.3	21.7	26.0	27.0	Zimbabwe
Africa	**22.3**	**23.2**	**23.9**	**26.9**	**30.7**	**32.7**	**12.4**	**14.1**	**15.3**	**21.7**	**23.6**	**24.1**	**Afrique**

Source: IMF

EXTERNAL SECTOR - SECTEUR EXTERIEUR

4-2. Balance of payments - Balance des paiements

As % of GDP	Trade balance / Solde commercial					Current account balance / Solde du compte courant					En % du PIB
Country	2012	2013	2014	2015	2016	2012	2013	2014	2015	2016	Pays
Algeria	9.6	4.7	0.1	-10.8	-12.6	5.8	0.6	-4.4	-16.4	-16.5	Algérie
Angola	37.0	30.6	21.0	10.8	12.5	10.8	6.1	-2.6	-8.9	-6.3	Angola
Benin	-6.9	-6.7	-7.3	-6.1	-7.8	-7.1	-7.4	-9.1	-9.0	-9.4	Bénin
Botswana	-15.2	-1.9	3.2	-6.2	2.0	-1.2	9.3	15.2	8.3	11.7	Botswana
Burkina Faso	1.9	-5.6	-2.1	-2.3	-	-0.7	-11.4	-8.1	-8.6	-6.8	Burkina Faso
Burundi	-24.7	-23.7	-19.3	-17.2	-14.5	-10.9	-10.4	-14.5	-13.3	-12.3	Burundi
Cameroon	-0.9	-0.6	-1.3	-1.2	-0.7	-3.3	-3.6	-4.0	-3.8	-3.3	Cameroun
Cabo Verde	-37.5	-33.5	-32.6	-29.6	-32.6	-14.0	-5.8	-9.1	-3.2	-2.7	Cabo Verde
Central African Republic	-6.1	-7.5	-18.6	-17.2	-15.1	-4.6	-3.1	-5.6	-9.5	-10.0	République Centrafricaine
Chad	7.7	6.6	2.8	0.5	2.2	-8.7	-9.2	-9.0	-10.1	-8.6	Tchad
Comoros	-17.2	-16.4	-16.3	-15.2	-13.3	-3.6	-4.7	-3.3	-0.2	-3.9	Comores
Congo	43.1	34.5	23.9	-5.1	-18.2	17.7	1.7	-11.6	-42.9	-70.1	Congo
Democratic Republic of the Congo	11.4	9.6	11.0	9.6	8.4	-1.2	-1.4	1.4	-0.6	-1.2	Rép. Démocratique du Congo
Côte d'Ivoire	0.2	6.6	-1.1	-0.8	-0.6	-4.3	-5.2	-4.8	-3.9	-3.3	Côte d'Ivoire
Djibouti	-41.2	-41.2	-42.5	-54.6	-53.6	-18.8	-23.3	-25.1	-31.8	-30.4	Djibouti
Egypt	-12.4	-10.7	-11.2	-11.7	-11.6	-3.7	-2.2	-0.9	-3.6	-6.0	Egypte
Equatorial Guinea	47.5	37.8	32.9	16.4	24.2	-1.1	-2.5	-4.3	-16.3	-0.6	Guinée Equatoriale
Eritrea	...	...	...	...	...	...	...	...	...	...	Erythrée
Ethiopia	-17.1	-17.4	-21.0	-18.5	-15.5	-5.5	-6.3	-10.3	-8.9	-7.9	Ethiopie
Gabon	42.2	32.0	27.9	15.4	13.3	17.6	7.0	7.3	-5.7	-10.2	Gabon
Gambia	-22.0	-19.0	-25.7	-28.9	-22.9	-8.6	-10.1	-11.2	-14.7	-8.9	Gambie
Ghana	-10.4	-8.5	-3.5	-8.3	-4.1	-12.1	-12.6	-9.4	-7.5	-6.7	Ghana
Guinea	-4.6	-0.6	-3.5	-4.7	-23.8	-25.7	-16.9	-11.2	-11.6	-32.4	Guinée
Guinea-Bissau	-5.1	-2.9	-4.6	4.3	4.0	-8.4	-5.0	0.6	1.9	-2.5	Guinée-Bissau
Kenya	-15.4	-18.6	-17.4	-13.1	-11.2	-7.0	-8.8	-10.4	-6.7	-5.2	Kenya
Lesotho	-44.0	-38.8	-37.8	-34.5	-32.8	-8.1	-5.5	-5.2	-4.8	-6.3	Lesotho
Liberia	-19.9	-19.8	-26.1	-43.1	-32.0	-15.9	-23.6	-22.1	-33.8	-25.3	Libéria
Libya	44.0	16.8	-64.4	-36.6	-4.9	29.9	-	-78.4	-54.4	-24.7	Libye
Madagascar	-11.2	-8.0	-5.1	-3.4	-2.6	-6.9	-5.9	-0.3	-1.9	0.6	Madagascar
Malawi	-18.4	-26.8	-7.5	-7.5	-10.9	-13.7	-23.2	-8.5	-9.4	-13.5	Malawi
Mali	0.9	-1.9	-3.5	-3.6	-4.1	-2.2	-2.8	-4.7	-5.3	-6.6	Mali
Mauritania	-9.4	-6.9	-13.2	-11.5	-10.5	-23.4	-22.5	-27.3	-19.7	-14.9	Mauritanie
Mauritius	-21.1	-18.7	-17.7	-15.8	-16.8	-10.3	-6.2	-5.6	-4.8	-4.3	Maurice
Morocco	-20.4	-19.0	-18.6	-14.1	-17.1	-9.5	-7.4	-5.7	-1.9	-4.4	Maroc
Mozambique	-26.5	-31.1	-27.6	-28.1	-12.9	-44.5	-42.9	-37.9	-40.3	-40.6	Mozambique
Namibia	-22.2	-24.4	-30.2	-32.9	-25.4	-11.3	-13.7	-16.4	-20.5	-20.1	Namibie
Niger	-6.4	-5.6	-9.0	-12.3	-9.0	-14.5	-15.0	-15.9	-20.5	-15.5	Niger
Nigeria	8.5	8.2	3.8	-1.3	-0.1	3.8	3.7	0.2	-3.2	0.7	Nigéria
Rwanda	-17.4	-15.1	-15.8	-14.9	-15.3	-10.2	-7.3	-11.8	-13.4	-14.3	Rwanda
Sao Tome and Principe	-20.2	-20.1	-18.3	-15.8	-14.1	-20.3	-14.0	-21.6	-11.8	-5.8	Sao Tomé-et-Principe
Senegal	-37.2	-38.3	-36.6	-33.9	-30.8	-10.7	-10.4	-8.8	-6.9	-5.7	Sénégal
Seychelles	-44.3	-33.5	-40.4	-34.3	-37.3	-25.8	-10.1	-22.0	-17.9	-20.1	Seychelles
Sierra Leone	-24.0	-0.6	-6.8	-17.0	-6.9	-31.8	-17.5	-11.2	-14.4	-7.8	Sierra Leone
Somalia	...	...	...	...	...	...	...	...	...	...	Somalie
South Africa	-1.1	-2.1	-1.7	-0.9	0.3	-5.1	-5.9	-5.3	-4.4	-3.3	Afrique du Sud
South Sudan	...	...	...	...	...	...	...	...	...	...	Soudan du Sud
Sudan	-7.0	-5.7	-4.5	-5.4	-3.8	-10.3	-8.5	-6.1	-6.8	-4.6	Soudan
Swaziland	1.6	4.4	4.7	7.8	5.2	3.2	5.0	3.1	9.8	0.7	Swaziland
Tanzania, United Republic of	-11.4	-13.0	-11.6	-9.7	-5.8	-9.7	-11.2	-9.8	-7.9	-4.5	Tanzanie, République Unie de
Togo	-14.4	-20.1	-19.4	-24.7	-21.9	-7.6	-13.2	-10.0	-11.0	-9.9	Togo
Tunisia	-13.6	-12.8	-14.0	-11.7	-11.5	-8.3	-8.4	-9.1	-8.9	-8.9	Tunisie
Uganda	-10.0	-8.3	-8.5	-9.1	-5.9	-6.8	-7.2	-7.8	-6.8	-3.0	Ouganda
Zambia	6.3	5.9	6.0	-0.3	-0.1	5.4	-0.6	2.1	-3.9	-4.9	Zambie
Zimbabwe	-19.1	-19.2	-17.2	-15.0	-9.2	-12.8	-15.4	-15.1	-9.2	-4.0	Zimbabwe
Africa	**1.9**	**0.1**	**-3.0**	**-6.2**	**-5.3**	**-0.9**	**-2.7**	**-4.7**	**-6.9**	**-5.8**	**Afrique**

Source: IMF

4-3. Financial Flows - Flux financiers

US $ per Capita	Official development assistance (ODA) / Aide publique au développement (APD)					Foreign direct investment (FDI) inflows / Investissement direct étranger (IDE) entrant					$ EU par habitant
Country	2012	2013	2014	2015	2016	2012	2013	2014	2015	2016	Pays
Algeria	3.9	5.3	4.1	2.2	3.9	40.0	44.1	38.7	-14.7	38.3	Algérie
Angola	10.7	12.2	9.7	15.2	8.0	664.6	611.8	682.8	646.5	556.1	Angola
Benin	50.5	64.0	56.5	39.5	44.1	22.8	34.9	38.2	13.8	14.4	Bénin
Botswana	34.3	49.3	44.8	29.0	39.4	228.4	183.1	232.1	300.3	4.5	Botswana
Burkina Faso	69.5	61.2	63.9	55.1	54.9	19.8	28.7	20.2	12.8	16.6	Burkina Faso
Burundi	51.8	53.4	47.6	32.8	64.2	0.1	0.7	4.4	0.7	0.0	Burundi
Cameroon	27.6	33.9	37.6	28.4	31.6	34.1	25.5	31.9	26.9	5.4	Cameroun
Cabo Verde	490.4	483.3	450.3	293.6	215.1	250.7	137.1	350.8	222.4	226.6	Cabo Verde
Central African Republic	49.4	43.1	127.2	99.3	100.0	15.2	0.4	0.7	0.6	6.2	République Centrafricaine
Chad	37.4	34.9	28.8	43.2	43.1	45.6	39.6	-49.7	39.9	38.6	Tchad
Comoros	138.5	108.1	97.3	83.4	67.7	14.2	5.6	6.1	6.5	9.9	Comores
Congo	32.7	34.4	23.6	19.2	18.5	502.1	663.1	1221.4	403.9	423.1	Congo
Democratic Republic of the Congo	40.5	35.6	32.1	33.6	26.4	47.1	28.9	24.6	21.7	15.1	Rép. Démocratique du Congo
Côte d'Ivoire	137.8	58.9	41.7	28.8	28.3	15.7	18.8	19.8	21.8	20.7	Côte d'Ivoire
Djibouti	174.0	172.6	189.6	191.0	205.8	128.9	330.8	174.6	139.7	177.9	Djibouti
Egypt	21.2	62.9	39.5	27.3	22.8	70.4	48.6	51.5	75.7	86.8	Egypte
Equatorial Guinea	18.7	5.8	0.6	8.9	8.0	1273.4	731.4	204.5	276.1	62.1	Guinée Equatoriale
Eritrea	27.8	16.3	16.5	18.0	12.5	8.5	8.8	9.1	9.4	9.8	Erythrée
Ethiopia	35.2	41.1	37.0	32.5	40.0	3.0	14.2	19.1	22.1	31.4	Ethiopie
Gabon	42.7	52.8	65.9	57.3	23.5	515.9	467.3	599.2	361.6	398.8	Gabon
Gambia	76.9	60.2	52.0	54.1	44.6	22.6	13.3	18.2	5.3	-0.9	Gambie
Ghana	70.4	50.8	41.9	64.5	46.9	128.9	123.3	125.3	116.5	124.3	Ghana
Guinea	54.5	39.1	45.9	42.7	43.4	52.2	11.2	6.3	3.8	8.1	Guinée
Guinea-Bissau	46.8	60.1	61.2	51.5	105.4	3.9	11.2	16.0	10.1	10.4	Guinée-Bissau
Kenya	62.4	75.7	59.3	53.5	46.3	32.4	25.6	18.3	13.5	8.3	Kenya
Lesotho	134.3	153.9	50.8	38.9	52.2	67.5	59.2	76.6	79.1	61.2	Lesotho
Liberia	135.2	124.8	170.5	243.0	176.6	235.0	247.2	62.9	139.2	98.2	Libéria
Libya	13.9	20.6	33.6	25.1	28.4	226.8	112.0	8.0	115.6	77.8	Libye
Madagascar	16.5	21.8	25.0	27.9	25.0	36.4	24.7	14.9	18.2	21.7	Madagascar
Malawi	74.6	70.0	55.8	61.0	70.0	8.2	27.5	35.9	16.7	18.3	Malawi
Mali	61.8	84.2	72.3	68.4	66.7	24.7	18.6	8.4	15.6	6.9	Mali
Mauritania	108.5	76.1	65.7	78.2	69.8	367.6	290.7	126.2	123.4	65.2	Mauritanie
Mauritius	140.4	115.3	35.1	61.6	33.2	468.1	232.2	329.8	163.6	273.5	Maurice
Morocco	44.6	60.0	66.0	43.1	57.2	82.7	98.6	105.0	94.7	66.7	Maroc
Mozambique	80.5	87.4	77.4	64.9	53.3	218.8	233.3	180.1	138.2	107.6	Mozambique
Namibia	110.2	111.2	94.1	57.9	67.6	494.6	341.1	179.7	445.4	109.3	Namibie
Niger	50.5	43.4	48.0	43.6	45.9	47.7	39.2	43.0	26.6	14.1	Niger
Nigeria	11.4	14.6	14.0	13.3	13.4	42.4	32.5	26.4	16.8	23.8	Nigéria
Rwanda	81.2	98.1	91.3	93.5	96.6	23.6	23.3	40.5	32.7	34.5	Rwanda
Sao Tome and Principe	284.1	294.7	222.1	257.2	241.9	126.1	66.7	145.4	150.1	113.9	Sao Tomé-et-Principe
Senegal	78.1	69.9	75.6	58.1	47.2	20.0	21.9	27.4	27.0	25.2	Sénégal
Seychelles	367.6	288.0	125.2	70.3	58.9	2765.0	1788.1	2398.7	2016.6	1599.9	Seychelles
Sierra Leone	72.8	72.7	144.7	146.6	105.1	119.5	69.5	64.0	40.8	78.3	Sierra Leone
Somalia	98.7	102.7	105.5	116.2	105.6	10.7	25.1	26.9	28.4	30.6	Somalie
South Africa	20.2	24.2	20.0	26.1	21.5	86.3	155.4	106.9	31.7	41.3	Afrique du Sud
South Sudan	108.0	122.2	164.9	135.7	124.9	14.7	-69.2	3.7	-5.8	-1.3	Soudan du Sud
Sudan	36.3	39.1	22.2	22.4	19.7	61.3	43.8	31.8	43.0	25.8	Soudan
Swaziland	72.8	94.2	68.1	72.0	113.1	72.8	23.5	20.9	24.6	-8.1	Swaziland
Tanzania, United Republic of	58.0	68.4	51.1	48.3	42.0	37.0	41.6	32.3	30.0	24.8	Tanzanie, République Unie de
Togo	36.3	32.7	29.6	27.3	22.0	18.0	26.5	7.6	35.3	34.0	Togo
Tunisia	93.9	64.9	82.9	42.2	55.2	147.3	101.5	95.6	89.0	84.2	Tunisie
Uganda	46.4	46.4	43.2	41.7	43.6	34.0	30.0	28.0	13.8	13.4	Ouganda
Zambia	64.7	75.1	63.5	49.2	57.6	117.1	137.7	94.7	97.6	28.0	Zambie
Zimbabwe	68.8	55.5	49.9	50.5	41.0	27.4	26.8	35.7	27.0	20.0	Zimbabwe
Africa	41.3	45.0	40.4	37.0	35.5	68.8	64.5	60.2	50.6	47.7	Afrique

Source: OECD and UNCTAD

4-4 Intra-African Trade by Regional Economic Communities in 2016 - Commerce intra-africain par zone économique en 2016

Economic Grouping	AMU UMA	CEN-SAD	COMESA	EAC	ECCAS CEEAC	ECOWAS CEDEAO	IGAD	SADC	AFRICA AFRIQUE	World MONDE	Zone économique
Export to →					(millions of US $) / (Millions de $ EU)						**← Exportations vers**
AMU	3 057.7	4 567.3	2 061.1	80.6	315.6	1 123.0	336.9	224.7	6 161.8	73 824.5	UMA
CEN-SAD	3 533.2	13 979.7	5 217.2	1 740.2	2 182.5	9 202.4	2 367.5	5 870.1	24 035.2	152 329.2	CEN-SAD
COMESA	1 472.6	4 860.8	6 877.8	3 125.1	1 787.2	371.1	3 582.1	6 499.2	13 605.2	67 165.0	COMESA
EAC	33.1	1 550.4	3 685.5	2 745.6	1 512.3	64.5	1 940.5	2 022.2	5 014.8	13 517.3	EAC
ECCAS	70.7	649.0	424.6	131.9	977.6	208.1	95.1	1 579.8	2 688.3	53 793.0	CEEAC
ECOWAS	271.0	8 282.4	427.8	28.0	1 206.4	7 780.1	38.7	4 495.4	13 897.0	73 319.1	CEDEAO
IGAD	33.1	1 817.4	2 853.5	2 273.8	966.3	56.9	2 260.0	1 171.3	4 309.0	13 497.3	IGAD
SADC	269.4	3 056.5	11 268.8	1 929.3	2 575.0	1 372.0	1 335.8	29 438.8	33 199.0	143 146.2	SADC
Africa	5 042.5	20 404.9	18 470.3	4 803.1	6 195.7	10 818.0	5 121.0	36 060.2	62 192.8	350 421.0	AFRIQUE
World	115 470.4	273 423.5	155 317.1	35 128.3	33 878.8	99 126.7	50 561.6	148 014.0	501 643.1	15 940 045.8	MONDE
Export to →					(% of total exports) / (% des exportations totales)						**← Exportations vers**
AMU	4.1	6.2	2.8	0.1	0.4	1.5	0.5	0.3	8.3	100.0	UMA
CEN-SAD	2.3	9.2	3.4	1.1	1.4	6.0	1.6	3.9	15.8	100.0	CEN-SAD
COMESA	2.2	7.2	10.2	4.7	2.7	0.6	5.3	9.7	20.3	100.0	COMESA
EAC	0.2	11.5	27.3	20.3	11.2	0.5	14.4	15.0	37.1	100.0	EAC
ECCAS	0.1	1.2	0.8	0.2	1.8	0.4	0.2	2.9	5.0	100.0	CEEAC
ECOWAS	0.4	11.3	0.6	0.0	1.6	10.6	0.1	6.1	19.0	100.0	CEDEAO
IGAD	0.2	13.5	21.1	16.8	7.2	0.4	16.7	8.7	31.9	100.0	IGAD
SADC	0.2	2.1	7.9	1.3	1.8	1.0	0.9	20.6	23.2	100.0	SADC
Africa	1.4	5.8	5.3	1.4	1.8	3.1	1.5	10.3	17.7	100.0	AFRIQUE
World	0.7	1.7	1.0	0.2	0.2	0.6	0.3	0.9	3.1	100.0	MONDE
← Import from					(millions of US $) / (Millions de $ EU)						**Importations de →**
AMU	3 031.0	3 410.7	1 523.8	48.7	72.5	347.5	51.0	349.3	5 230.4	120 824.9	UMA
CEN-SAD	4 765.9	14 505.3	4 123.0	971.3	740.6	8 886.2	1 192.8	3 347.3	20 749.1	244 066.2	CEN-SAD
COMESA	1 829.6	5 030.1	7 581.5	3 125.3	1 371.6	491.3	2 477.4	13 241.8	19 738.2	143 836.8	COMESA
EAC	80.2	1 668.9	2 801.9	2 166.0	74.3	27.7	1 794.9	2 185.2	4 592.0	31 632.9	EAC
ECCAS	423.2	2 432.4	1 182.6	1 483.4	1 459.8	1 555.4	645.6	3 473.6	7 365.7	40 758.2	CEEAC
ECOWAS	1 335.6	9 880.5	485.4	90.2	250.3	8 225.9	130.7	1 718.5	11 880.5	87 078.6	CEDEAO
IGAD	274.8	2 059.3	2 636.4	1 269.2	37.0	32.6	1 352.3	1 537.1	4 163.7	44 619.9	IGAD
SADC	267.9	3 489.6	6 277.6	1 352.6	2 825.0	2 460.1	597.6	31 218.5	35 188.1	144 985.0	SADC
Africa	6 245.2	22 518.3	12 775.6	3 871.6	4 396.3	12 897.5	3 135.9	36 155.1	62 938.2	478 392.4	AFRIQUE
World	81 695.6	169 526.5	70 774.0	14 893.3	56 224.9	81 091.2	15 835.2	177 979.7	404 707.2	16 022 514.1	MONDE
← Import from					(% of total imports) / (% des importations totales)						**Importations de →**
AMU	2.5	2.8	1.3	0.0	0.1	0.3	0.0	0.3	4.3	100.0	UMA
CEN-SAD	2.0	5.9	1.7	0.4	0.3	3.6	0.5	1.4	8.5	100.0	CEN-SAD
COMESA	1.3	3.5	5.3	2.2	1.0	0.3	1.7	9.2	13.7	100.0	COMESA
EAC	0.3	5.3	8.9	6.8	0.2	0.1	5.7	6.9	14.5	100.0	EAC
ECCAS	1.0	6.0	2.9	3.6	3.6	3.8	1.6	8.5	18.1	100.0	CEEAC
ECOWAS	1.5	11.3	0.6	0.1	0.3	9.4	0.2	2.0	13.6	100.0	CEDEAO
IGAD	0.6	4.6	5.9	2.8	0.1	0.1	3.0	3.4	9.3	100.0	IGAD
SADC	0.2	2.4	4.3	0.9	1.9	1.7	0.4	21.5	24.3	100.0	SADC
Africa	1.3	4.7	2.7	0.8	0.9	2.7	0.7	7.6	13.2	100.0	AFRIQUE
World	0.5	1.1	0.4	0.1	0.4	0.5	0.1	1.1	2.5	100.0	MONDE

Source: UNCTAD

Section 5

Economic Infrastructure and Investment Climate

Infrastructures économiques et climat des affaires

5-1. Tourism and Infrastructure / Tourisme et Infrastructure

Country	Arrival of tourists (Thousands) / Arrivée des touristes (Milliers)		Rooms in hotels (Thousands) / Chambres d'hôtels (Milliers)		Paved roads (% of total) Routes asphaltées (% du total)		Total Network (Railways-km) / Réseau total voies ferrées (km)		Pays
	2015	2017	Year/Année		2009	2015	2008	2014	
Algeria	1 710	2 102	...	...	74.0	...	3 572.0	4 175.0	Algérie
Angola	592	457	2016	13.0		...	...	...	Angola
Benin	255	258	2016	14.8	35.0	...	758.0	...	Bénin
Botswana	1 528	1 797	2016	10.9	75.8	33.0	888.0	891.0	Botswana
Burkina Faso	163	159	2016	10.8	15.3	...	622.0	622.0	Burkina Faso
Burundi	120	117	2015	3.6	15.1	15.0	...	...	Burundi
Cabo Verde	520	717	2017	12.5	...	...	...	...	Cabo Verde
Cameroon	452	360	2017	36.0	...	...	977.0	976.0	Cameroun
Central African Republic	121	139	2015	1.1	6.8	...	...	...	République Centrafricaine
Chad	120	142	2015	1.8	...	...	...	...	Tchad
Comoros	24	27	2017	5.2	77.0	...	...	...	Comores
Congo	264	166	2016	15.6	7.1	...	795.0	...	Congo
Democratic Republic of the Congo	215	240	2013	3.1	...	...	4 007.0	3 641.0	Rép, Démocratique du Congo
Côte d'Ivoire	416	375	2016	38.0	7.9	...	639.0	639.0	Côte d'Ivoire
Djibouti	118		2016	1.2	...	...	...	...	Djibouti
Egypt	9 071	8 292	2016	202.1	89.4	...	5 063.0	5 195.0	Egypte
Equatorial Guinea	...	...	...	...	...	...	...	...	Guinée Equatoriale
Eritrea	...	...	2016	5.6	...	...	...	...	Erythrée
Ethiopia	864	1 013	2016	25.5	14.8	13.0	781.0	...	Ethiopie
Gabon	624	586	2007	4.2	...	...	810.0	810.0	Gabon
Gambia	135	159	2015	8.6	0.8	20.6	780.0	...	Gambie
Ghana	1 134	1 278	2017	47.0	12.6		953.0	...	Ghana
Guinea	35	63	2017	5.5	...	...	1 185.0	1 185.0	Guinée
Guinea-Bissau	...	...	2015	3.7	32.8	33.0	...	...	Guinée-Bissau
Kenya	1 114	1 428	2016	13.6	13.6	...	2 597.0	2 706.0	Kenya
Lesotho	800	1 001	2016	2.9	19.8	...	...	...	Lesotho
Liberia	...	...	2006	0.2	...	...	...	...	Libéria
Libya	...	...	2016	17.0	...	...	...	...	Libye
Madagascar	244	254	2016	25.3	15.9	...	854.0	...	Madagascar
Malawi	805	840	...	...	26.0	...	797.0	...	Malawi
Mali	168	...	2013	9.5	24.6	...	729.0	643.0	Mali
Mauritania	...	...	...	...	27.8	...	728.0	728.0	Mauritanie
Mauritius	1 151	1 342	2017	13.5	98.1	98.0	...	...	Maurice
Morocco	10 177	11 310	2016	112.4	70.3	...	1 989.0	2 109.0	Maroc
Mozambique	1 552	2 016	2017	32.2	24.3	25.4	3 116.0	3 116.0	Mozambique
Namibia	1 330	1 528	2017	18.7	14.1	...	2 409.0	2 466.9	Namibie
Niger	32	37	2017	3.2	20.9	...	...	...	Niger
Nigeria	1 255	1 530	2008	43.8	...	...	3 505.0	...	Nigéria
Rwanda	987	1 073	2016	8.4	...	...	...	...	Rwanda
Sao Tome and Principe	46	42	2005	0.4	...	...	...	...	Sao Tomé-et-Principe
Senegal	1 007	1 074	2015	18.3	32.0	35.3	...	...	Sénégal
Seychelles	276	350	2017	5.0	96.5	97.7	...	...	Seychelles
Sierra Leone	24	51	2016	2.3	...	...	...	...	Sierra Leone
Somalia			...	...	...	...	...	...	Somalie
South Africa	8 904	10 273	2016	79.8	...	...	24 487.0	20 500.0	Afrique du Sud
South Sudan			...	...	...	...	...	...	Soudan du Sud
Sudan	741	698	2009	4.6	32.0	...	4 578.0	4 313.0	Soudan
Swaziland	873	995	2017	601.3	37.6	45.6	300.0	300.0	Swaziland
Tanzania, United Republic of	1 104	1 236	2009	32.3	14.9	23.0	4 460.0	3 681.8	Tanzanie, République Unie de
Togo	273	345	2017	13.2	...	...	...	593.0	Togo
Tunisia	4 202	5 743	2017	117.2	75.2	...	2 218.0	3 835.0	Tunisie
Uganda	1 303	1 449	2014	328.9	...	...	...	...	Ouganda
Zambia	932	969	2016	32.3	...	...	...	...	Zambie
Zimbabwe	2 052	2 294	2016	6.2	...	...	2 583.0	...	Zimbabwe
Africa	**59 832**	**66 323**	...	...	...	...	...	...	

Source: TDM, Oxford Economics (for tourism figures)

ECONOMIC INFRASTRUCTURE AND INVESTMENT CLIMATE / INFRASTRUCTURE ECONOMIQUE ET CLIMAT DES AFFAIRES

5-2 Information and Communication Technology / Technologies de l'information et de la communication

Country	Main Telephone Lines per 100 inhabitants/ Lignes téléphoniques fixes pour 100 habitants		Mobile Cellular Subscribers per 100 inhabitants/ Abonnés aux téléphones mobiles pour 100 habitants		Percentage of Individuals using the Internet / Pourcentage de personnes utilisant l'Internet		Fixed -broadband subscriptions per 100 inhabitants /Abonnements à l'Internet fixe à large bande pour 100 habitants		Pays
	2009	2016	2009	2016	2009	2016	2009	2016	
Algeria	7.1	8.2	9-	117.0	11.2	42.9	2.2	6.9	Algérie
Angola	1.6	1.3	42.8	55.3	2.3	13.0	0.1	0.5	Angola
Benin	1.4	1.1	54.5	79.6	2.2	12.0	0.2	0.8	Bénin
Botswana	7.0	6.9	96.0	158.5	6.2	39.4	0.5	2.8	Botswana
Burkina Faso	1.0	0.3	25.3	83.6	1.1	14.0	0.1	-	Burkina Faso
Burundi	0.3	0.2	10.3	48.0	0.9	5.2	-	-	Burundi
Cabo Verde	14.8	11.6	59.8	122.0	21.0	50.3	2.3	3.0	Cabo Verde
Cameroon	2.2	4.4	39.8	68.1	3.8	25.0	-	0.2	Cameroun
Central African Republic	0.1	-	20.2	25.5	1.8	4.0	...	-	République Centrafricaine
Chad	0.5	0.1	20.1	44.5	1.5	5.0	-	0.1	Tchad
Comoros	4.6	1.7	18.4	57.7	3.5	7.9	-	0.4	Comores
Congo	0.3	0.4	73.8	113.3	4.5	8.1	-	...	Congo
Democratic Republic of the Congo	0.1	-	15.6	39.5	0.6	6.2	...	-	Rép, Démocratique du Congo
Côte d'Ivoire	1.5	1.3	70.9	126.0	2.0	26.5	0.1	0.6	Côte d'Ivoire
Djibouti	2.0	2.7	15.7	37.8	4.0	13.1	0.6	3.0	Djibouti
Egypt	13.4	7.1	72.1	113.7	2-	41.2	1.4	5.2	Egypte
Equatorial Guinea	1.5	1.2	29.5	65.9	2.1	23.8	-	0.5	Guinée Equatoriale
Eritrea	0.9	1.0	2.5	7.3	0.5	1.2	-	-	Erythrée
Ethiopia	1.1	1.1	4.8	50.5	0.5	15.4	-	0.6	Ethiopie
Gabon	2.4	1.1	95.4	144.2	9.5	48.1	0.2	0.7	Gabon
Gambia	3.0	1.9	80.6	139.6	7.6	18.5	-	0.2	Gambie
Ghana	1.1	0.9	63.8	139.1	5.4	34.7	0.1	0.3	Ghana
Guinea	0.2	-	32.9	85.3	0.9	9.8	...	-	Guinée
Guinea-Bissau	0.3	-	36.1	70.3	2.3	3.8	...	-	Guinée-Bissau
Kenya	1.7	0.2	48.6	81.3	6.1	26.0	-	0.3	Kenya
Lesotho	2.0	1.9	33.2	106.6	3.7	27.4	-	0.1	Lesotho
Liberia	0.1	0.2	28.4	83.1	2.0	7.3	-	0.2	Libéria
Libya	17.8	21.5	159.9	119.8	10.8	20.3	1.1	2.6	Libye
Madagascar	0.9	0.6	30.7	41.8	1.6	4.7	-	0.1	Madagascar
Malawi	0.8	0.1	17.1	40.3	1.1	9.6	-	-	Malawi
Mali	0.6	1.2	32.9	120.3	1.8	11.1	0.1	-	Mali
Mauritania	2.1	1.3	62.1	86.5	2.3	18.0	0.2	0.3	Mauritanie
Mauritius	30.6	30.7	88.6	144.2	22.5	52.2	5.9	16.9	Maurice
Morocco	11.2	6.0	80.9	120.7	41.3	58.3	1.5	3.7	Maroc
Mozambique	0.4	0.3	25.6	66.3	2.7	17.5	0.1	0.1	Mozambique
Namibia	6.9	7.7	76.1	109.2	6.5	31.0	-	2.2	Namibie
Niger	0.5	0.6	17.0	48.9	0.8	4.3	-	0.1	Niger
Nigeria	1.0	0.1	48.0	81.8	9.3	25.7	0.1	-	Nigéria
Rwanda	0.3	0.1	23.1	69.9	7.7	2-	-	0.2	Rwanda
Sao Tome and Principe	4.4	2.8	46.7	85.3	16.4	28.0	0.3	0.7	Sao Tomé-et-Principe
Senegal	2.2	1.9	54.8	98.7	7.5	25.7	0.5	0.6	Sénégal
Seychelles	28.8	22.1	122.2	161.2	...	56.5	5.0	14.9	Seychelles
Sierra Leone	0.6	0.3	20.6	97.6	0.3	11.8	...	...	Sierra Leone
Somalia	1.1	0.4	6.8	58.1	1.2	1.9	...	0.8	Somalie
South Africa	9.6	6.6	91.2	142.4	1-	54.0	0.9	2.8	Afrique du Sud
South Sudan		-	...	21.5	...	...	...	-	Soudan du Sud
Sudan	0.9	0.3	36.1	68.6	...	28.0	...	0.1	Soudan
Swaziland	3.8	3.2	56.6	76.4	8.9	28.6	0.1	0.5	Swaziland
Tanzania, United Republic of	0.4	0.2	4-	74.4	2.4	13.0	-	0.3	Tanzanie, République Unie de
Togo	2.9	0.5	35.6	74.9	2.6	11.3	0.1	0.6	Togo
Tunisia	12.2	8.6	93.2	125.8	34.1	49.6	3.5	5.6	Tunisie
Uganda	0.7	0.9	28.6	55.1	9.8	21.9	-	0.3	Ouganda
Zambia	0.7	0.6	34.4	74.9	6.3	25.5	0.1	0.2	Zambie
Zimbabwe	3.0	2.0	31.0	83.2	4.0	23.1	0.4	1.1	Zimbabwe
Africa	**3.3**	**2.1**	**45.2**	**81.5**	**7.7**	**23.9**	**0.4**	**1.2**	**Afrique**

Source: ADB Statistics Department based on data from ITU

5-3. Doing Business in 2016 (Rank over 185countries) / Climat des affaires en 2016 (Rang sur 185 pays)

Country	Ease of Doing Business / Facilité de faire des affaires	Dealing with Li- censes / Agréments	Enforcing Contracts / Exécution des con- trats	Registering Property / Enregis- trement de biens	Getting Credit / Obtention de crédits	Protecting Investors/ Protection des inves- tisseurs	Paying Taxes / Paiement des impôts	Trading Across Bor- ders / Commerce transfron- talier	Closing a Business / Fermeture d'une entreprise	Pays
Algeria	166	146	103	163	177	170	157	181	74	Algérie
Angola	175	80	186	172	183	81	103	180	169	Angola
Benin	151	46	170	127	142	146	174	136	115	Bénin
Botswana	81	59	133	81	77	76	47	50	64	Botswana
Burkina Faso	148	53	163	140	142	146	153	113	112	Burkina Faso
Burundi	164	168	150	95	177	132	138	164	141	Burundi
Cameroon	163	140	162	176	68	138	183	186	122	Cameroun
Cabo Verde	127	67	43	71	122	164	75	107	169	Cabo Verde
Central African Republic	184	180	182	169	142	146	187	145	146	République Centrafricaine
Chad	180	153	154	159	142	160	188	172	146	Tchad
Comoros	158	79	180	111	122	146	168	111	169	Comores
Congo	179	125	155	177	133	146	185	184	117	Congo
Democratic Republic of the Congo	182	121	172	158	142	164	181	188	169	Rép. Démocratique du Congo
Côte d'Ivoire	139	152	101	113	142	146	175	155	68	Côte d'Ivoire
Djibouti	154	84	175	168	183	96	108	159	71	Djibouti
Egypt	128	66	160	119	90	81	167	170	109	Egypte
Equatorial Guinea	173	160	104	162	122	146	177	174	169	Guinée Equatoriale
Eritrea	189	186	119	178	186	172	148	189	169	Erythrée
Ethiopia	161	169	68	139	173	176	133	167	120	Ethiopie
Gabon	167	149	178	173	122	160	165	169	123	Gabon
Gambia	146	118	107	129	122	164	169	105	117	Gambie
Ghana	120	131	116	119	55	96	116	158	155	Ghana
Guinea	153	75	117	143	142	146	182	165	113	Guinée
Guinea-Bissau	176	176	168	126	142	138	155	141	169	Guinée-Bissau
Kenya	80	124	90	125	29	62	92	106	92	Kenya
Lesotho	104	167	95	109	77	108	111	40	121	Lesotho
Liberia	172	184	174	183	105	177	69	177	168	Libéria
Libya	185	186	141	187	186	183	128	118	169	Libye
Madagascar	162	183	158	161	133	96	131	134	127	Madagascar
Malawi	110	144	151	96	6	96	134	117	162	Malawi
Mali	143	134	159	137	142	146	166	85	99	Mali
Mauritania	150	109	65	98	159	108	179	138	169	Mauritanie
Mauritius	25	9	27	35	55	33	10	70	39	Maurice
Morocco	69	17	57	86	105	62	25	65	131	Maroc
Mozambique	138	56	184	104	159	138	117	109	65	Mozambique
Namibia	106	107	59	175	68	89	79	132	97	Namibie
Niger	144	164	137	116	142	146	160	122	105	Niger
Nigeria	145	147	96	179	6	33	171	183	140	Nigéria
Rwanda	41	112	85	2	6	16	31	87	73	Rwanda
Sao Tome and Principe	169	103	185	171	159	187	135	114	158	Sao Tomé-et-Principe
Senegal	140	145	142	121	142	138	178	135	101	Sénégal
Seychelles	95	131	130	62	133	108	29	88	62	Seychelles
Sierra Leone	160	182	100	165	159	81	85	162	148	Sierra Leone
Somalia		...	...	...	...	...	...	...	...	Somalie
South Africa	74	99	113	105	62	22	51	139	50	Afrique du Sud
South Sudan	186	178	73	181	175	179	68	177	169	Soudan du Sud
Sudan	168	145	147	89	170	187	141	184	153	Soudan
Swaziland	111	91	175	117	82	132	76	31	95	Swaziland
Tanzania, United Republic of	132	136	59	132	44	145	154	180	100	Tanzanie, République Unie de
Togo	154	180	145	183	139	145	169	117	87	Togo
Tunisia	77	59	76	92	101	118	106	92	58	Tunisie
Uganda	115	151	64	116	44	106	75	136	111	Ouganda
Zambia	98	78	135	145	20	87	58	161	83	Zambie
Zimbabwe	161	181	165	111	82	102	164	148	145	Zimbabwe

Source: World Bank Group Doing Business

Section 6

Sustainable Development Goals / Agenda 2063

Objectifs de développement durable / Agenda 2063

1. End poverty in all its forms everywhere /
Éliminer la pauvreté sous toutes ses formes et partout dans le monde

Country	Population below $1.90 (PPP) per day, percentage / Proportion de la population disposant de moins de 1,90 $ par jour en parité du pouvoir d'achat		Proportion of population living below the national poverty line (%) / Proportion de la population vivant au dessous du seuil de pauvreté fixé au niveau national (%)				Proportion of employed population below the international poverty line of US$1.90 per day, by sex and by age (%), 2016 / Proportion de la population active vivant au-dessous du seuil de pauvreté international de 1,90 $ US par jour, selon le sexe et l'âge (%), 2016			Pays
	Year/ Année	%	Year/ Année	Total	Urban/ Urbain	Rural	Youth/ Jeunes	Men / Hommes	Women / Femmes	
Algeria	...	...	2011	5.5	5.8	4.8	2.0	2.3	1.8	Algérie
Angola	2008	30.1	2008	36.6	18.7	58.3	31.2	26.3	27.8	Angola
Benin	2011	53.1	2011	36.2	31.4	39.7	34.3	37.1	21.4	Bénin
Botswana	2009	18.2	2009	19.3	11.0	24.3	10.0	6.8	8.2	Botswana
Burkina Faso	2014	43.7	2014	40.1	13.7	47.5	37.6	34.8	38.6	Burkina Faso
Burundi	2006	77.7	2014	64.6	27.6	68.8	79.9	76.9	79.3	Burundi
Cabo Verde	2007	8.1	2007	26.6	13.2	44.3	14.1	10.2	10.4	Cabo Verde
Cameroon	2014	24.0	2014	37.5	8.9	56.8	15.6	13.9	17.3	Cameroun
Central African Republic	2008	66.3	2008	62.0	49.6	69.4	79.5	75.6	78.3	République Centrafricaine
Chad	2011	38.4	2011	46.7	20.9	52.5	22.4	18.9	19.9	Tchad
Comoros	2004	13.5	2004	44.8	34.5	48.7	10.4	6.9	8.3	Comores
Congo	2011	37.0	2011	46.5	43.3	74.8	21.1	15.5	18.0	Congo
Democratic Republic of the Congo	2012	77.1	2012	63.6	61.6	64.9	75.5	72.0	75.1	Rép, Démocratique du Congo
Côte d'Ivoire	2008	29.0	2015	46.3	35.9	56.8	20.3	16.0	19.1	Côte d'Ivoire
Djibouti	2013	22.5	...	...	...	...	...	...	...	Djibouti
Egypt	...	...	2010	25.2	15.3	32.3	11.6	8.7	9.3	Egypte
Equatorial Guinea	...	...	2006	76.8	31.5	79.9	6.4	4.9	5.5	Guinée Equatoriale
Eritrea	...	...	...	...	62.0	...	18.0	16.5	16.3	Erythrée
Ethiopia	2010	33.5	2010	29.6	25.7	30.4	5.9	5.7	5.3	Ethiopie
Gabon	2005	8.0	2005	32.7	29.8	44.6	6.3	3.4	6.7	Gabon
Gambia	2003	45.3	2010	48.4	32.7	73.9	46.4	39.8	42.5	Gambie
Ghana	2005	25.2	2012	24.2	10.6	37.9	11.5	8.3	9.4	Ghana
Guinea	2012	35.3	2012	55.2	35.4	64.7	28.0	23.6	25.4	Guinée
Guinea-Bissau	2010	67.1	2010	69.3	51.0	75.6	67.3	61.1	64.9	Guinée-Bissau
Kenya	2005	33.6	2005	45.9	33.7	49.1	8.6	5.9	6.8	Kenya
Lesotho	2010	59.7	2010	57.1	39.6	61.2	47.6	42.0	39.5	Lesotho
Liberia	2007	68.6	2007	63.8	55.1	67.7	71.7	65.0	69.4	Libéria
Libya	...	...	...	...	...	...	1.6	3.7	1.8	Libye
Madagascar	2012	77.8	2010	75.3	51.1	81.5	81.1	76.3	78.6	Madagascar
Malawi	2010	70.9	2010	50.7	17.3	56.6	64.6	61.6	69.1	Malawi
Mali	2009	49.3	2009	43.6	18.9	50.6	49.8	45.4	48.7	Mali
Mauritania	2014	5.9	2008	42.0	20.8	59.4	7.2	4.8	5.7	Mauritanie
Mauritius	2012	0.5	...	...	...	...	4.1	2.7	3.6	Maurice
Morocco	2006	3.1	2007	8.9	4.8	14.4	2.1	2.1	3.0	Maroc
Mozambique	2008	68.7	2008	54.7	49.6	56.9	54.4	51.0	55.5	Mozambique
Namibia	2009	22.6	2009	28.7	14.6	37.4	14.4	8.7	11.4	Namibie
Niger	2014	45.7	2011	48.9	18.6	55.2	34.9	31.7	33.1	Niger
Nigeria	2009	53.5	2009	46.0	34.1	52.8	54.9	44.3	42.0	Nigéria
Rwanda	2013	60.4	2010	44.9	22.1	48.7	44.6	40.8	42.4	Rwanda
Sao Tome and Principe	2010	32.3	2009	61.7	63.8	59.4	...	...	...	Sao Tomé-et-Principe
Senegal	2011	38.0	2010	46.7	33.1	57.1	33.9	25.5	29.3	Sénégal
Seychelles	2013	1.1	2013	39.3	39.0	37.2	...	...	...	Seychelles
Sierra Leone	2011	52.3	2011	52.9	31.2	66.1	53.4	44.2	49.4	Sierra Leone
Somalia	...	...	...	...	...	...	13.1	10.2	11.5	Somalie
South Africa	2011	16.6	2010	53.8	39.2	77.0	6.6	5.7	6.0	Afrique du Sud
South Sudan	2009	42.7	2009	50.6	24.4	55.4	...	...	...	Soudan du Sud
Sudan	2009	14.9	2009	46.5	26.5	57.6	2.5	5.3	2.3	Soudan
Swaziland	2009	42.0	2009	63.0	31.1	73.1	15.6	10.3	12.4	Swaziland
Tanzania, United Republic of	2011	46.6	2011	28.2	15.5	33.3	37.2	31.6	34.8	Tanzanie, République Unie de
Togo	2011	54.2	2015	55.1	35.9	68.7	36.9	33.6	32.1	Togo
Tunisia	2010	2.0	2010	15.5	...	...	1.2	1.0	1.3	Tunisie
Uganda	2012	34.6	2012	19.5	9.6	22.4	16.7	17.3	18.9	Ouganda
Zambia	2010	64.4	2010	60.5	27.5	77.9	57.3	50.3	54.3	Zambie
Zimbabwe	2011	21.4	2011	72.3	46.5	84.3	69.0	62.6	66.5	Zimbabwe
Africa	...	...	...	...	...	...	...	...	...	Afrique

Source: UNSD, SDG Indicators Global Database

2. End hunger, achieve food security and improved nutrition and promote sustainable agriculture / Éliminer la faim, assurer la sécurité alimentaire, améliorer la nutrition et promouvoir l'agriculture durable

Country	Prevalence of undernourishment (%) / Prévalence de la sous-alimentation (%)			Prevalence of stunting among children under 5 years of age / Prévalence du retard de croissance chez les enfants de moins de 5 ans		Agriculture orientation index for government expenditures (Unit) / Indice d'orientation agricole des dépenses publiques (Unité)		Total official flows (official development assistance plus other official flows) to the agriculture sector (Millions of constant 2014 $US) / Total des apports publics (aide publique au développement plus autres apports publics) alloués au secteur agricole (Millions de $ EU constants de 2014)			Pays
	2005	2010	2015	Year	(%)	Year	(%)	2000	2010	2015	
Algeria	7.0	5.1	<5,0	2012	11.7	2009	0.4	1.7	6.5	4.9	Algérie
Angola	34.2	20.7	14.2	2016	37.6	2015	0.1	7.8	31.9	13.6	Angola
Benin	15.9	12.1	7.5	2014	34.0	2010	0.1	47.7	52.4	56.7	Bénin
Botswana	32.8	30.4	24.1	2007	31.4	2015	1.9	4.0	1.8	9.0	Botswana
Burkina Faso	25.9	22.5	20.7	2012	32.9	2011	0.1	148.5	117.2	109.2	Burkina Faso
Burundi	...	...	...	2010	57.5	2013	0.1	11.4	42.3	49.7	Burundi
Cabo Verde	15.9	12.6	9.4	...	...	2012	0.7	4.4	12.0	4.2	Cabo Verde
Cameroon	23.1	13.4	9.9	2014	31.7	...	...	19.7	55.2	44.8	Cameroun
Central African Republic	41.8	34.1	47.7	2010	40.7	2009	0.1	6.7	3.9	6.5	République Centrafricaine
Chad	39.7	41.0	34.4	2015	39.9	...	...	31.4	26.6	37.5	Tchad
Comoros	...	...	...	2012	32.1	...	...	2.0	2.2	3.7	Comores
Congo	30.2	31.5	30.5	2015	21.2	2010	0.7	1.2	4.0	7.0	Congo
Democratic Republic of the Congo	...	...	...	2013	42.6	2015	0.2	4.0	74.7	80.5	Rép, Démocratique du Congo
Côte d'Ivoire	14.8	14.7	13.3	2012	29.6	2014	0.2	70.3	53.5	132.6	Côte d'Ivoire
Djibouti	37.2	23.1	15.9	2012	33.5	...	...	1.2	1.3	5.6	Djibouti
Egypt	<5,0	<5,0	<5,0	2014	22.3	2011	0.1	218.6	71.5	316.1	Egypte
Equatorial Guinea	...	...	...	2010	26.2	2009	0.8	1.6	0.3	0.0	Guinée Equatoriale
Eritrea	...	...	...	2010	50.3	...	...	40.0	7.3	10.3	Erythrée
Ethiopia	45.9	37.6	32.0	2016	38.4	2007	0.4	76.3	304.4	360.5	Ethiopie
Gabon	<5,0	<5,0	<5,0	2012	17.5	...	...	7.1	14.8	5.7	Gabon
Gambia	15.0	8.8	5.3	2013	25.0	...	...	5.5	8.1	7.5	Gambie
Ghana	11.6	6.5	<5,0	2014	18.7	2002	0.0	146.7	272.4	165.2	Ghana
Guinea	23.1	18.3	16.4	2012	31.3	...	...	17.9	17.4	11.8	Guinée
Guinea-Bissau	25.4	23.0	20.7	2014	27.6	2015	0.1	0.9	7.8	8.0	Guinée-Bissau
Kenya	31.8	24.8	21.2	2014	26.0	2014	0.1	91.8	127.5	186.2	Kenya
Lesotho	11.0	11.4	11.2	2014	33.2	2005	0.4	15.9	2.8	2.3	Lesotho
Liberia	39.7	34.9	31.9	2013	32.1	2006	0.0	4.3	13.5	39.3	Libéria
Libya	...	...	...	2007	21.0	...	...		0.4	0.6	Libye
Madagascar	37.4	31.6	33.0	2009	49.2	2008	0.3	83.2	52.5	56.2	Madagascar
Malawi	27.7	21.8	20.7	2014	42.4	2014	0.7	56.0	102.5	131.7	Malawi
Mali	10.1	<5,0	<5,0	2006	38.5	2011	0.4	159.1	209.9	127.9	Mali
Mauritania	11.4	7.9	5.6	2012	22.0	...	...	27.7	29.8	14.1	Mauritanie
Mauritius	5.6	<5,0	<5,0	...	...	2014	0.8	2.1	2.5	0.0	Maurice
Morocco	5.5	5.3	<5,0	2011	14.9	2012	0.0	48.4	98.7	164.1	Maroc
Mozambique	37.3	31.8	25.3	2011	43.1	2014	0.4	54.8	129.2	208.2	Mozambique
Namibia	25.4	37.6	42.3	2013	23.1	2011	0.8	17.6	15.8	16.0	Namibie
Niger	15.4	11.1	9.5	2012	43.0	...	...	109.9	65.0	60.5	Niger
Nigeria	7.2	6.1	7.0	2014	32.9	2013	0.1	27.9	106.0	152.7	Nigéria
Rwanda	46.7	37.3	31.6	2015	37.9	2012	0.1	72.2	136.3	207.4	Rwanda
Sao Tome and Principe	10.0	6.2	6.6	2014	17.2	2010	0.3	7.1	1.9	2.3	Sao Tomé-et-Principe
Senegal	22.9	13.6	10.0	2014	19.4	...	...	94.8	85.8	191.8	Sénégal
Seychelles	...	...	...	2012	7.9	2015	1.0	0.3	3.8	2.3	Seychelles
Sierra Leone	39.3	29.0	22.3	2013	37.9	...	...	15.0	42.9	6.7	Sierra Leone
Somalia	...	...	...	2009	25.3	...	...	0.2	14.3	20.3	Somalie
South Africa	<5,0	<5,0	<5,0	2008	23.9	2008	0.8	53.7	29.9	11.0	Afrique du Sud
South Sudan	...	...	...	2010	31.1	...	...			65.2	Soudan du Sud
Sudan	...	...	...	2014	38.2	...	...	24.9	77.2	134.9	Soudan
Swaziland	15.8	23.6	26.8	2014	25.5	2012	0.6	4.2	11.7	18.7	Swaziland
Tanzania, United Republic of	36.7	34.7	32.1	2015	34.4	2015	0.0	124.8	192.2	128.0	Tanzanie, République Unie de
Togo	25.3	20.5	11.4	2014	27.5	2010	0.0	5.9	22.3	15.2	Togo
Tunisia	<5,0	<5,0	<5,0	2012	10.2	2012	0.6	242.6	34.4	63.8	Tunisie
Uganda	21.9	25.1	25.5	2012	34.2	2003	0.2	124.9	79.5	154.3	Ouganda
Zambia	49.4	51.7	47.8	2013	40.0	2010	0.7	44.8	35.2	92.7	Zambie
Zimbabwe	41.6	34.7	33.4	2014	27.6	...	...	21.5	51.4	46.2	Zimbabwe
Africa	...	...	...	...		...		2411.94	2964.36	3770.69	Afrique

Source: UNSD, SDG Indicators Global Database

3. Ensure healthy lives and promote well-being for all at all ages /
Permettre à tous de vivre en bonne santé et promouvoir le bien-être de tous à tout âge

Country	Under-five mortality rate (per 1 000) / Taux de mortalité des enfants de moins de 5 ans (pour 1 000)			Maternal mortality ratio (per 100 000) / Taux de mortalité maternelle (pour 100 000)			Malaria incidence per 1 000 population / Incidence du paludisme pour 1 000 habitants			Total net official development assistance to medical research and basic health sectors (Millions of constant $US) / Montant total net de l'aide publique au développement consacrée à la recherche médicale et aux soins de santé de base (Millions de $ EU constants)			Pays
	2000	2010	2015	2000	2010	2015	2000	2010	2015	2000	2010	2015	
Algeria	40	27	26	170	147	140	-	-	-	0.6	1.5	0.3	Algérie
Angola	217	183	157	924	561	477	316	114	124	20.2	54.4	50.0	Angola
Benin	145	112	100	572	446	405	389	332	294	21.3	50.2	47.0	Bénin
Botswana	83	54	44	311	169	129	44	5	1	0.4	4.5	3.5	Botswana
Burkina Faso	186	114	89	547	417	371	622	601	389	5.1	94.4	108.0	Burkina Faso
Burundi	152	99	82	954	808	712	419	198	126	3.5	46.4	49.8	Burundi
Cabo Verde	36	28	25	83	51	42	9	2	0	0.2	1.4	2.5	Cabo Verde
Cameroon	150	105	88	750	676	596	461	322	264	21.8	23.4	95.3	Cameroun
Central African Republic	175	150	130	1200	909	882	438	365	290	1.2	9.1	23.2	République Centrafricaine
Chad	190	160	139	1370	1040	856	242	194	163	29.5	39.3	22.3	Tchad
Comoros	101	86	74	499	388	335	281	275	5	0.8	7.7	2.3	Comores
Congo	122	61	45	653	509	442	364	217	173	2.1	21.6	9.3	Congo
Democratic Republic of the Congo	161	116	98	874	794	693	509	427	246	31.3	261.7	518.3	Rép, Démocratique du Congo
Côte d'Ivoire	146	109	93	671	717	645	525	446	349	2.5	69.1	51.7	Côte d'Ivoire
Djibouti	101	76	65	401	275	229	57	8	25	0.2	3.7	6.2	Djibouti
Egypt	47	29	24	63	40	33	...	...	...	45.1	16.6	13.4	Egypte
Equatorial Guinea	152	111	94	702	379	342	365	200	215	5.0	6.7	0.9	Guinée Equatoriale
Eritrea	89	56	47	733	579	501	23	23	15	31.0	27.3	11.9	Erythrée
Ethiopia	145	76	59	897	523	353	662	106	59	19.1	193.5	392.1	Ethiopie
Gabon	85	63	51	405	322	291	359	152	232	...	2.1	3.3	Gabon
Gambia	119	81	69	887	753	706	337	244	209	0.5	15.2	21.3	Gambie
Ghana	101	75	62	467	325	319	488	396	266	16.1	125.9	148.2	Ghana
Guinea	170	112	94	976	720	679	472	410	368	4.7	23.6	139.8	Guinée
Guinea-Bissau	178	116	93	800	570	549	434	102	89	0.5	19.5	18.5	Guinée-Bissau
Kenya	108	62	49	759	605	510	274	95	166	58.0	182.2	192.2	Kenya
Lesotho	117	101	90	649	587	487	...	...	...	3.4	18.8	2.3	Lesotho
Liberia	182	89	70	1270	811	725	497	335	246	6.9	46.2	211.2	Libéria
Libya	28	17	13	17	9	9	...	...	...	...	0.5	0.0	Libye
Madagascar	109	60	50	536	436	353	115	33	104	6.2	104.1	112.4	Madagascar
Malawi	174	91	64	890	629	634	432	420	189	36.6	58.8	163.4	Malawi
Mali	220	137	115	834	630	587	477	365	449	27.6	98.2	132.9	Mali
Mauritania	114	98	85	813	723	602	110	80	74	4.1	7.4	13.3	Mauritanie
Mauritius	19	15	14	40	59	53	...	...	...	0.1	...	0.2	Maurice
Morocco	50	33	28	221	153	121	...	...	...	3.3	22.4	3.9	Maroc
Mozambique	171	103	79	915	619	489	516	383	298	128.8	113.2	239.2	Mozambique
Namibia	76	54	45	352	319	265	70	2	14	1.2	4.5	4.0	Namibie
Niger	227	124	96	794	657	553	444	500	356	2.0	61.9	67.0	Niger
Nigeria	187	130	109	1170	867	814	498	416	381	18.6	179.9	697.9	Nigéria
Rwanda	184	64	42	1020	381	290	426	106	301	13.1	69.4	83.1	Rwanda
Sao Tome and Principe	89	56	47	222	162	156	344	29	18	0.2	3.1	3.7	Sao Tomé-et-Principe
Senegal	135	65	47	488	375	315	234	141	98	5.2	52.8	83.5	Sénégal
Seychelles	14	14	14	...	...	...	...	...	...	...	...	0.2	Seychelles
Sierra Leone	236	160	120	2650	1630	1360	486	482	303	3.0	33.0	140.8	Sierra Leone
Somalia	174	160	137	1080	820	732	110	38	86	5.1	25.0	56.7	Somalie
South Africa	75	54	41	85	154	138	12	5	3	13.5	15.7	87.8	Afrique du Sud
South Sudan	182	111	93	1310	876	789	297	180	156	...	...	118.6	Soudan du Sud
Sudan	106	80	70	544	349	311	93	36	37	12.0	114.5	109.5	Soudan
Swaziland	128	88	61	586	436	389	13	3	1	0.1	4.0	5.8	Swaziland
Tanzania, United Republic of	131	63	49	842	514	398	407	176	114	21.3	212.9	315.5	Tanzanie, République Unie de
Togo	121	91	78	491	393	368	517	458	345	15.0	19.6	16.4	Togo
Tunisia	32	17	14	84	67	62	...	...	...	0.3	3.5	4.3	Tunisie
Uganda	148	75	55	620	420	343	517	429	218	52.6	90.8	203.9	Ouganda
Zambia	163	82	64	541	262	224	382	156	174	33.0	46.7	143.4	Zambie
Zimbabwe	106	90	71	590	446	443	143	130	114	2.7	89.9	117.8	Zimbabwe
Africa	**140**	**92**	**76**	**671**	**502**	**444**	**384**	**254**	**204**	**736.3**	**2797.8**	**5069.9**	**Afrique**

Source: UNSD, SDG Indicators Global Database

SUSTAINABLE DEVELOPMENT GOALS/ OBJECTIFS DE DÉVELOPPEMENT DURABLE

4. Ensure inclusive and equitable quality education and promote lifelong learning opportunities for all / Assurer l'accès de tous à une éducation de qualité, sur un pied d'égalité, et promouvoir les possibilités d'apprentissage tout au long de la vie

Country	Proportion of children and young people at the end of primary achieving at least a minimum proficiency level in: Proportion d'enfants et de jeunes en fin de cycle primaire qui maîtrisent au moins les normes d'aptitudes minimales en:								Gender parity index of teachers in primary education who are trained Indice de parité des enseignants formés au Primaire		Total official development assistance flows for scholarships (Constant US$ Millions) Aide publique totale au développement consacrée aux bourses d'études (Millions de $ EU constants)			Pays
	Reading/Lecture (%)			Maths (%)									
	Year	Total	Girls	Boys	Year	Total	Girls	Boys	Year	%	2006	2010	2015	
Algeria	...	...	...	...	...	...	...	...	2014	1.0	1.8	6.9	14.6	Algérie
Angola	...	...	...	...	...	...	...	...	2011	1.1	1.1	1.4	1.9	Angola
Benin	2014	52	...	52	2014	40	40	40	2014	0.9	1.0	1.2	1.9	Bénin
Botswana	2011	56	56	48	2011	61	65	56	2008	1.0	0.0	0.7	1.8	Botswana
Burkina Faso	2014	57	63	58	2014	59	56	62	2009	1.1	1.2	8.1	1.3	Burkina Faso
Burundi	2014	57	...	51	2014	87	92	82	2015	1.0	1.3	1.6	1.1	Burundi
Cabo Verde	...	...	53	...	...	...	...	...	2014	1.0	1.7	1.5	1.5	Cabo Verde
Cameroon	2014	49	...	45	2014	35	37	34	2015	2.6	0.8	3.2	8.3	Cameroun
Central African Republic	...	...	13	...	...	...	...	...	2012	1.7	0.5	1.0	1.1	République Centrafricaine
Chad	2014	16	...	17	2014	19	14	22	...	...	1.2	1.1	1.2	Tchad
Comoros	...	...	43	...	...	...	...	...	2013	1.1	0.1	0.3	4.8	Comores
Congo	2014	41	...	39	2010	77	27	31	2012	1.2	0.6	0.7	3.9	Congo
Democratic Republic of the Congo	...	...	49	...	...	...	...	...	2012	1.0	3.4	2.2	3.5	Rép, Démocratique du Congo
Côte d'Ivoire	2014	48	...	47	2010	89	24	30	2001	1.0	0.2	1.3	4.1	Côte d'Ivoire
Djibouti	...	...	...	...	...	...	...	...	2009	1.0	0.8	1.2	1.0	Djibouti
Egypt	...	...	...	...	...	...	...	...	2013	1.1	1.0	7.4	13.9	Egypte
Equatorial Guinea	...	...	...	...	...	...	...	...	2015	1.2	0.2	0.1	0.2	Guinée Equatoriale
Eritrea	...	...	...	...	...	...	...	...	2015	1.2	0.2	0.1	0.1	Erythrée
Ethiopia	...	...	...	...	...	...	...	...	2009	1.1	2.1	3.4	7.0	Ethiopie
Gabon	...	...	...	...	...	...	...	...	2003	1.0	0.9	0.9	1.6	Gabon
Gambia	...	...	...	...	...	...	...	...	2011	1.0	0.0	0.2	1.0	Gambie
Ghana	...	...	...	...	...	...	...	...	2016	1.3	0.4	1.9	6.4	Ghana
Guinea	...	...	...	...	...	...	...	...	2014	1.1	0.6	0.5	2.4	Guinée
Guinea-Bissau	...	...	91	...	...	...	...	...	2010	1.8	0.9	0.8	0.4	Guinée-Bissau
Kenya	2010	92	76	93	2010	89	90	88	2003	1.0	0.9	3.6	7.9	Kenya
Lesotho	2010	78	...	81	2010	58	57	59	2015	1.2		0.5	0.8	Lesotho
Liberia	...	...	...	...	...	...	...	...	2015	1.2		0.1	0.9	Libéria
Libya	...	...	...	...	...	...	...	...	...	...	0.0	0.2	1.2	Libye
Madagascar	...	...	68	...	...	...	...	...	2015	1.6	0.6	1.1	2.9	Madagascar
Malawi	2010	64	...	60	2010	40	44	36	2010	1.0	0.3	0.7	2.0	Malawi
Mali	...	...	...	...	...	...	...	...	2011	1.1	0.9	2.9	3.4	Mali
Mauritania	...	...	...	...	...	...	...	...	2014	1.0	0.7	1.0	1.3	Mauritanie
Mauritius	...	...	...	...	...	...	...	...	2000	1.0	0.1	1.5	2.0	Maurice
Morocco	...	...	79	...	...	...	...	...	2005	1.0	2.8	5.4	20.4	Maroc
Mozambique	2010	78	83	77	2010	67	70	63	2015	1.0	2.0	2.8	2.7	Mozambique
Namibia	2010	86	8	89	2010	52	52	52	2009	1.0	0.0	0.4	1.3	Namibie
Niger	2014	9	...	9	2010	58	6	9	2015	1.2	1.1	18.0	1.2	Niger
Nigeria	2014	61	...	...	...	...	...	...	2010	1.2	1.2	1.4	5.3	Nigéria
Rwanda	...	...	...	...	...	...	...	...	2002	1.0	0.8	19.5	3.9	Rwanda
Sao Tome and Principe	...	...	60	...	...	...	...	...	2016	1.4	0.8	1.0	0.5	Sao Tomé-et-Principe
Senegal	...	...	82	62	2010	40	57	61	2012	0.9	1.7	3.7	5.9	Sénégal
Seychelles	2010	88	...	95	2010	82	77	88	2015	1.1	0.1	0.3	0.9	Seychelles
Sierra Leone	...	...	...	...	...	...	...	...	2012	1.4	0.1	0.1	0.9	Sierra Leone
Somalia	...	...	68	...	...	...	...	...	...	...			0.3	Somalie
South Africa	2010	72	...	76	2010	59	57	61	2002	0.9	0.4	6.0	8.5	Afrique du Sud
South Sudan	...	...	...	...	...	...	...	...	...	...			0.5	Soudan du Sud
Sudan	...	...	98	...	...	...	...	...	...	...	1.6	1.4	2.5	Soudan
Swaziland	2010	99	97	99	2010	92	93	91	2010	1.0		0.1	1.1	Swaziland
Tanzania, United Republic of	2010	96	41	96	2010	87	90	85	2001	1.0	1.0	3.2	7.6	Tanzanie, République Unie de
Togo	2014	38	...	37	2010	67	46	49	2012	1.0	0.9	1.3	1.7	Togo
Tunisia	...	...	80	...	...	...	...	...	2012	1.0	1.3	4.9	14.3	Tunisie
Uganda	2010	79	59	78	2010	59	61	58	2011	0.9	0.7	2.0	5.6	Ouganda
Zambia	2010	56	76	53	2010	33	37	29	2012	1.1	0.6	1.5	2.7	Zambie
Zimbabwe	2010	81	78	84	2010	72	70	73	2013	1.1	0.1	0.9	3.3	Zimbabwe
Africa		...	...	...		...	...	...		...	42.24	133.04	198.24	Afrique

Source: UNSD, SDG Indicators Global Database

5. Achieve gender equality/ and empower all women and girls /
Parvenir à l'égalité des sexes et autonomiser toutes les femmes et les filles

Country	Proportion of women aged 20-24 years who were married or in a union before age: / Proportion de femmes âgées de 20 à 24 ans qui étaient mariées ou en couple avant l'âge de:			Proportion of girls and women aged 15-49 years who have undergone female genital mutilation/cutting / Proportion de filles et de femmes âgées de 15 à 49 ans ayant subi une mutilation ou une ablation génitale		Proportion of seats held by women in national parliaments (%) / Proportion de sièges occupés par des femmes dans les parlements nationaux (%)			Pays
	Year	(15) years	(18) years	Year	%	2000	2010	2017	
Algeria	2013	0.4	2.5	...	...	3.2	7.7	31.6	Algérie
Angola	...	...	...	...	...	15.5	38.6	38.2	Angola
Benin	2014	7.0	25.9	2014	9.2	6.0	10.8	7.2	Bénin
Botswana	...	...	...	...	...	17.0	7.9	9.5	Botswana
Burkina Faso	2010	10.2	51.6	2010	75.8	8.1	15.3	11.0	Burkina Faso
Burundi	2010	2.5	20.4	...	...	6.0	31.4	36.4	Burundi
Cabo Verde	2005	2.8	18.0	...	...	11.1	18.1	23.6	Cabo Verde
Cameroon	2014	10.2	31.0	2004	1.4	5.6	13.9	31.1	Cameroun
Central African Republic	2010	29.1	67.9	2010	24.2	7.3	9.6	8.6	République Centrafricaine
Chad	2015	29.7	66.9	2015	38.4	2.4	5.2	12.8	Tchad
Comoros	2012	10.0	31.6	...	...	...	3.0	6.1	Comores
Congo	2012	6.1	32.6	...	...	12.0	7.3	7.4	Congo
Democratic Republic of the Congo	2014	10.0	37.3	...	...	...	8.4	8.9	Rép, Démocratique du Congo
Côte d'Ivoire	2012	9.8	33.2	2012	38.2	8.5	8.9	11.5	Côte d'Ivoire
Djibouti	2006	1.8	5.4	2006	93.1	0.0	13.9	10.8	Djibouti
Egypt	2014	2.0	17.4	2015	87.2	2.0	1.8	14.9	Egypte
Equatorial Guinea	2011	8.6	29.5	...	...	5.0	10.0	24.0	Guinée Equatoriale
Eritrea	2010	12.9	40.7	2010	83.0	14.7	22.0	22.0	Erythrée
Ethiopia	2011	16.3	41.0	2016	65.2	2.0	21.9	38.8	Ethiopie
Gabon	2012	5.6	21.9	...	...	8.3	14.7	17.1	Gabon
Gambia	2013	9.3	30.4	2013	74.9	2.0	7.6	9.4	Gambie
Ghana	2014	4.9	20.7	2011	3.8	9.0	8.3	12.7	Ghana
Guinea	2012	21.3	51.7	2012	96.9	8.8	...	21.9	Guinée
Guinea-Bissau	2014	6.3	24.4	2014	44.9	7.8	10.0	13.7	Guinée-Bissau
Kenya	2014	4.4	22.9	2014	21.0	3.6	9.8	19.4	Kenya
Lesotho	2014	1.0	17.3	...	...	3.8	24.2	25.0	Lesotho
Liberia	2013	8.8	35.9	2013	49.8	7.8	12.5	12.3	Libéria
Libya	...	...	...	...	...	...	7.7	16.0	Libye
Madagascar	2013	12.4	41.2	...	...	8.0	...	19.2	Madagascar
Malawi	2014	8.9	46.3	...	...	8.3	20.8	16.7	Malawi
Mali	2010	14.5	55.0	2015	82.7	12.2	10.2	8.8	Mali
Mauritania	2011	14.2	34.3	2015	66.6	3.8	22.1	25.2	Mauritanie
Mauritius	...	...	...	...	...	7.6	17.1	11.6	Maurice
Morocco	2004	2.5	15.9	...	...	0.6	10.5	20.5	Maroc
Mozambique	2011	14.3	48.2	...	...	30.0	39.2	39.6	Mozambique
Namibia	2013	1.6	6.9	...	...	22.2	26.9	41.4	Namibie
Niger	2012	28.0	76.3	2012	2.0	1.2	9.7	17.0	Niger
Nigeria	2013	17.3	42.8	2013	24.8	...	7.0	5.6	Nigéria
Rwanda	2015	0.4	6.8	...	...	17.1	56.3	61.3	Rwanda
Sao Tome and Principe	2014	7.9	35.4	...	...	9.1	7.3	18.2	Sao Tomé-et-Principe
Senegal	2015	8.5	31.0	2015	24.2	12.1	22.7	42.7	Sénégal
Seychelles	...	...	...	...	...	23.5	23.5	21.2	Seychelles
Sierra Leone	2013	12.5	38.9	2013	89.6	8.8	13.2	12.4	Sierra Leone
Somalia	2006	8.4	45.3	2006	97.9	...	6.9	24.2	Somalie
South Africa	2003	0.8	5.6	...	...	30.0	44.5	42.2	Afrique du Sud
South Sudan	2010	8.9	51.5	...	...	...	...	28.5	Soudan du Sud
Sudan	2014	11.9	34.2	2014	86.6	...	...	30.5	Soudan
Swaziland	2014	0.8	5.3	...	...	3.1	13.6	6.2	Swaziland
Tanzania, United Republic of	2016	5.2	30.5	2016	10.0	22.2	30.7	36.4	Tanzanie, République Unie de
Togo	2014	5.5	21.8	2014	4.7	4.9	11.1	17.6	Togo
Tunisia	2012	0.0	1.6	...	...	11.5	27.6	31.3	Tunisie
Uganda	2011	9.9	39.7	2011	1.4	17.9	31.5	34.3	Ouganda
Zambia	2014	5.9	31.4	...	...	10.1	14.0	18.0	Zambie
Zimbabwe	2015	3.7	32.4	...	...	14.0	15.0	32.6	Zimbabwe
Africa		...	...	...	...	9.0	16.3	23.7	Afrique

Source: UNSD, SDG Indicators Global Database

6. Ensure availability and sustainable management of water and sanitation for all / Garantir l'accès de tous à l'eau et à l'assainissement et assurer une gestion durable des ressources en eau

Country	Proportion of population using safely managed drinking water services (%) / Proportion de la population utilisant des services d'alimentation en eau potable gérés en toute sécurité (%)			Proportion of population using safely managed sanitation services (%) / Proportion de la population utilisant des services d'assainissement gérés en toute sécurité (%)			Level of water stress: freshwater withdrawal as a proportion of available freshwater resources / Niveau de stress hydrique: prélèvements d'eau douce en proportion des ressources en eau douce disponibles	Total official flows for water supply and sanitation (Constant US$ Millions) / Montant total des ressources allouées à l'approvisionnement en eau et l'assainissement (Millions $ EU constants)			Pays
	2000	2010	2015	2000	2010	2015	2014	2000	2010	2015	
Algeria	...	...	...	21	20	19	88.0	0.6	11.9	5.4	Algérie
Angola	...	...	...	...	...	...	0.7	28.6	9.1	36.0	Angola
Benin	...	...	...	...	...	...	0.7	40.1	84.6	24.4	Bénin
Botswana	...	...	...	...	...	...	2.1	...	1.3	0.4	Botswana
Burkina Faso	...	...	...	...	...	...	9.5	70.5	88.1	106.8	Burkina Faso
Burundi	...	...	...	...	...	...	3.1	11.1	37.1	14.0	Burundi
Cabo Verde	...	...	...	...	...	...	9.0	1.0	13.2	30.3	Cabo Verde
Cameroon	...	...	...	...	...	...	0.5	6.2	19.6	109.3	Cameroun
Central African Republic	...	...	...	...	...	...	0.1	0.3	5.7	4.8	République Centrafricaine
Chad	...	...	...	...	...	...	2.4	40.0	36.0	42.1	Tchad
Comoros	...	...	...	...	...	...	1.2	...	0.8	7.2	Comores
Congo	30	35	37	...	...	...	0.01	0.7	2.1	4.5	Congo
Democratic Republic of the Congo	...	...	...	...	...	...	0.1	2.3	118.2	162.7	Rép, Démocratique du Congo
Côte d'Ivoire	36	43	46	...	...	...	2.7	18.8	38.9	27.8	Côte d'Ivoire
Djibouti	...	...	...	...	...	...	7.9	2.2	8.3	16.0	Djibouti
Egypt	...	...	...	53	58	61	159.9	118.7	148.1	236.3	Egypte
Equatorial Guinea	...	...	...	...	...	...	0.1	0.1	...	...	Guinée Equatoriale
Eritrea	...	...	...	...	...	...	10.1	0.6	7.6	0.6	Erythrée
Ethiopia	5	8	11	...	...	...	11.6	12.6	136.3	221.6	Ethiopie
Gabon	...	...	...	...	...	...	0.1	0.1	9.0	7.0	Gabon
Gambia	...	...	...	...	...	...	1.5	0.3	8.3	2.7	Gambie
Ghana	16	23	27	...	...	...	2.8	65.7	118.7	156.8	Ghana
Guinea	...	...	...	...	...	...	0.3	8.2	11.2	13.3	Guinée
Guinea-Bissau	...	...	...	...	...	...	0.7	0.5	2.2	3.9	Guinée-Bissau
Kenya	...	...	...	...	...	...	14.3	22.9	170.3	171.1	Kenya
Lesotho	...	...	...	...	...	...	2.1	5.0	38.7	18.2	Lesotho
Liberia	...	...	...	...	...	...	0.1	0.1	8.1	41.7	Libéria
Libya	...	...	...	29	27	26	1072.0	...	...	...	Libye
Madagascar	...	...	...	...	...	...	5.8	20.3	13.8	19.2	Madagascar
Malawi	...	...	...	...	...	...	11.1	28.0	31.0	69.4	Malawi
Mali	...	...	...	...	...	...	5.8	125.7	125.9	87.2	Mali
Mauritania	...	...	...	...	...	...	15.9	2.0	91.7	61.6	Mauritanie
Mauritius	...	...	...	...	...	...	26.4	7.3	0.5	3.7	Maurice
Morocco	55	64	69	31	36	38	49.0	246.9	170.9	404.0	Maroc
Mozambique	...	...	...	...	...	...	0.9	95.0	99.5	184.9	Mozambique
Namibia	...	...	...	...	...	...	0.9	3.0	14.7	2.8	Namibie
Niger	...	...	...	4	7	9	3.8	72.8	43.3	80.5	Niger
Nigeria	17	19	19	...	...	...	5.8	57.2	117.6	219.5	Nigéria
Rwanda	...	...	...	...	...	...	1.4	41.9	41.4	40.0	Rwanda
Sao Tome and Principe	...	...	...	...	...	...	0.5	5.4	3.2	6.9	Sao Tomé-et-Principe
Senegal	...	...	...	18	22	24	7.2	27.5	77.5	133.2	Sénégal
Seychelles	...	...	...	...	...	...		...	0.7	0.1	Seychelles
Sierra Leone	...	...	...	...	...	...	0.2	4.2	12.9	23.1	Sierra Leone
Somalia	...	...	...	20	16	14	30.3	3.2	3.5	23.7	Somalie
South Africa	...	...	...	...	...	...	42.9	12.2	51.0	3.7	Afrique du Sud
South Sudan	...	...	...	...	...	...	1.3	...	...	41.7	Soudan du Sud
Sudan	...	...	...	...	...	...	93.7	4.0	106.3	157.1	Soudan
Swaziland	...	...	...	...	...	...	32.4	0.1	4.5	12.0	Swaziland
Tanzania, United Republic of	...	...	...	...	...	...	7.5	58.9	227.9	146.9	Tanzanie, République Unie de
Togo	...	...	...	...	...	...	1.8	0.4	12.9	16.6	Togo
Tunisia	37	89	93	58	69	73	94.0	89.6	135.9	131.9	Tunisie
Uganda	4	6	6	...	...	...	1.3	51.1	162.8	138.4	Ouganda
Zambia	...	...	...	...	...	...	2.1	130.7	40.7	116.5	Zambie
Zimbabwe	...	...	...	...	...	...	24.3	4.0	18.3	27.6	Zimbabwe
Africa	...	...	...	...	...	...	...	**1548.5**	**2741.4**	**3616.6**	**Afrique**

Source: UNSD, SDG Indicators Global Database

7. Ensure access to affordable, reliable, sustainable and modern energy for all /
Garantir l'accès de tous à des services énergétiques fiables, durables et modernes à un coût abordable

Country	Proportion of population with access to electricity (%) / Proportion de la population ayant accès à l'électricité (%)			Proportion of population with primary reliance on clean fuels and technology (%) / Proportion de la population utilisant principalement des carburants et technologies propres (%)			Renewable energy share in the total final energy consumption (%) / Part de l'énergie renouvelable dans la consommation finale d'énergie (%)			Energy intensity measured in terms of primary energy and GDP (%) / Intensité énergétique [rapport entre énergie primaire et produit intérieur brut (PIB)] (%)			Pays
	2005	2010	2014	2005	2010	2014	2005	2010	2014	2005	2010	2014	
Algeria	98	100	100	>95.0	>95.0	>95.0	0.6	0.3	0.1	3.3	3.6	4.1	Algérie
Angola	38	35	32	29.0	39.4	47.6	71.0	54.2	50.8	4.6	3.7	3.7	Angola
Benin	27	34	34	<5.0	5.3	6.6	59.2	51.6	48.6	7.6	9.1	8.7	Bénin
Botswana	38	48	56	52.0	57.8	62.5	30.8	30.2	29.2	3.6	3.4	3.4	Botswana
Burkina Faso	12	13	19	<5,0	6.0	7.0	86.5	83.7	76.5	6.9	6.4	6.0	Burkina Faso
Burundi	5	5	7	<5.0	<5.0	<5.0	97.3	96.8	90.1	15.1	13.3	7.8	Burundi
Cabo Verde	47	53	57	62.8	67.3	70.9	26.6	21.7	26.2	6.4	5.5	4.9	Cabo Verde
Cameroon	67	81	90	15.4	16.6	17.6	85.8	78.6	77.4	3.5	3.2	2.7	Cameroun
Central African Republic	8	10	12	<5.0	<5.0	<5.0	85.7	79.8	77.2	6.5	5.7	8.9	République Centrafricaine
Chad	5	6	8	<5.0	<5.0	<5.0	91.7	90.8	89.2	3.7	3.2	2.8	Tchad
Comoros	52	64	74	<5.0	<5.0	7.0	44.3	46.4	46.5	4.7	4.9	4.7	Comores
Congo	34	39	43	13.3	15.7	17.6	63.5	55.2	62.4	2.6	3.1	4.1	Congo
Democratic Republic of the Congo	6	13	14	<5.0	<5.0	5.9	97.4	96.8	92.9	23.2	21.1	22.6	Rép, Démocratique du Congo
Côte d'Ivoire	59	58	62	18.7	18.6	18.5	78.1	75.5	70.8	8.2	7.8	8.4	Côte d'Ivoire
Djibouti	53	49	47	<5.0	6.9	10.2	33.1	34.4	34.2	5.0	4.8	4.1	Djibouti
Egypt	99	100	100	94.0	>95.0	>95.0	6.5	5.7	6.4	4.2	3.7	3.5	Egypte
Equatorial Guinea	63	65	68	16.7	19.4	21.5	7.9	5.9	6.4	2.4	2.5	2.6	Guinée Equatoriale
Eritrea	35	41	46	7.7	11.1	13.8	74.9	81.3	80.3	4.9	5.0	5.0	Erythrée
Ethiopia	14	22	27	<5.0	<5.0	<5.0	95.1	94.5	92.7	27.5	19.0	14.6	Ethiopie
Gabon	82	85	89	60.5	67.5	73.2	85.2	85.9	81.1	5.3	8.5	6.8	Gabon
Gambia	36	42	47	<5.0	<5.0	<5.0	60.0	50.2	48.1	4.5	4.4	4.6	Gambie
Ghana	55	65	78	11.5	16.7	20.8	61.4	49.9	45.2	4.5	4.1	3.6	Ghana
Guinea	20	24	28	<5.0	<5.0	5.6	82.6	79.1	80.0	11.6	11.4	10.2	Guinée
Guinea-Bissau	0	6	17	<5.0	<5.0	<5.0	88.5	87.8	87.1	13.9	12.9	12.4	Guinée-Bissau
Kenya	20	19	36	<5.0	5.4	6.2	81.2	76.3	75.5	8.4	8.0	7.8	Kenya
Lesotho	9	19	28	23.9	28.3	31.8	55.3	53.5	51.8	13.4	11.7	11.0	Lesotho
Liberia	0	5	9	<5.0	<5.0	<5.0	89.5	89.3	89.8	32.1	27.1	24.0	Libéria
Libya	99	99	98	0.0	0.0	0.0	1.8	1.6	1.8	4.9	4.8	8.0	Libye
Madagascar	15	16	17	<5.0	<5.0	<5.0	80.5	81.9	73.6	5.0	5.1	5.2	Madagascar
Malawi	7	9	12	<5.0	<5.0	<5.0	83.9	79.7	80.6	8.2	6.3	5.5	Malawi
Mali	16	22	27	<5.0	<5.0	<5.0	86.2	84.9	83.6	3.7	2.4	2.0	Mali
Mauritania	18	32	39	36.4	41.0	44.7	38.8	34.0	32.6	3.8	3.7	3.5	Mauritanie
Mauritius	99	99	99	93.7	>95.0	>95.0	17.7	13.7	10.6	3.1	2.8	2.6	Maurice
Morocco	76	86	92	93.9	>95.0	>95.0	20.8	14.5	11.8	3.7	3.4	3.2	Maroc
Mozambique	12	17	21	<5.0	<5.0	<5.0	93.6	91.3	88.9	22.9	18.8	16.6	Mozambique
Namibia	40	45	50	38.8	42.8	45.9	32.1	26.4	27.6	3.8	3.5	3.3	Namibie
Niger	7	12	14	<5.0	<5.0	<5.0	87.6	80.7	78.1	7.0	7.0	7.0	Niger
Nigeria	48	48	58	9.4	5.2	<5.0	84.1	86.8	87.3	7.7	6.2	5.6	Nigéria
Rwanda	5	10	20	<5.0	<5.0	<5.0	89.2	90.7	88.5	7.7	6.1	5.3	Rwanda
Sao Tome and Principe	56	60	69	22.4	26.9	30.4	48.0	43.8	41.6	5.7	5.1	4.6	Sao Tomé-et-Principe
Senegal	47	53	61	38.0	36.8	35.8	41.2	50.3	43.3	4.9	5.7	5.1	Sénégal
Seychelles	96	97	100	85.9	>95.0	>95.0	0.4	0.6	1.0	6.5	3.3	3.0	Seychelles
Sierra Leone	15	14	13	<5.0	<5.0	<5.0	87.3	84.2	73.1	9.5	7.6	5.7	Sierra Leone
Somalia	10	15	19	<5.0	6.3	9.1	93.3	93.6	93.9	41.9	43.4	40.1	Somalie
South Africa	81	83	86	65.6	74.6	81.8	16.3	17.1	16.6	10.2	9.7	9.2	Afrique du Sud
South Sudan	0	2	5	<5.0	<5.0	<5.0	...	...	29.8	...	...	1.3	Soudan du Sud
Sudan	36	37	45	12.4	18.2	22.8	72.4	61.4	62.4	5.9	4.7	4.1	Soudan
Swaziland	36	51	65	30.1	33.0	35.3	49.7	62.7	63.6	5.0	4.8	5.0	Swaziland
Tanzania, United Republic of	12	15	16	<5.0	<5.0	<5.0	91.0	90.3	86.7	10.4	9.2	8.5	Tanzanie, République Unie de
Togo	27	37	46	<5.0	<5.0	6.3	77.2	65.8	72.8	14.8	16.6	14.5	Togo
Tunisia	99	100	100	>95.0	>95.0	>95.0	14.2	12.7	12.9	3.9	3.9	3.7	Tunisie
Uganda	9	13	20	<5.0	<5.0	<5.0	93.3	92.0	89.2	10.8	8.3	7.0	Ouganda
Zambia	20	22	28	14.3	15.3	16.1	89.0	92.1	88.1	10.4	7.8	7.4	Zambie
Zimbabwe	34	36	32	29.5	30.5	31.3	80.2	82.9	81.1	18.8	20.7	17.8	Zimbabwe
Africa	**40**	**43**	**47**	**...**	**...**	**...**	**57.5**	**56.8**	**56.3**	**7.3**	**6.5**	**6.2**	**Afrique**

Source: UNSD, SDG Indicators Global Database

**8. Promote sustained, inclusive and sustainable economic growth, full and productive employment and decent work for all /
Promouvoir une croissance économique soutenue, partagée et durable, le plein emploi productif et un travail décent pour tous**

Country	Unemployment rate, by sex and by age (%) / Taux de chômage par sexe et par âge (%)				Proportion of children aged 5-17 years engaged in child labour / Proportion d'enfants âgés de 5 à 17 ans qui travaillent		Growth rate of real GDP per employed person (%) / Taux de croissance annuelle du PIB réel par personne pourvue d'un emploi (%)			Total official flows disbursed for Aid for Trades (Millions of constant US$) / Flux officiels totaux décaissés dans le cadre de l'initiative Aide pour le commerce (Millions de $ EU constants)			Pays
	Youth/Jeunes (15-24)		Adults/Adultes (15+)										
	Years	Total	Years	Female/Femmes	Years	2014	2005	2010	2016	2006	2010	2015	
Algeria	2014	25.2	2014	17.1	2012	4.7	0.7	0.9	2.2	120.5	38.1	15.4	Algérie
Angola	...	...	...	...	...	...	15.0	-0.4	-3.4	24.6	75.2	212.0	Angola
Benin	2010	2.4	2010	1.1	2011	15.2	-1.8	-1.1	1.4	67.7	189.2	167.1	Bénin
Botswana	2010	36.0	2010	21.4	...	...	-0.3	8.8	1.7	9.8	20.5	4.8	Botswana
Burkina Faso	2006	3.8	2007	3.9	2010	35.9	6.2	5.1	1.8	172.1	216.5	299.9	Burkina Faso
Burundi	...	...	2008	1.1	2010	19.6	-3.4	-0.2	-3.4	48.5	108.7	89.7	Burundi
Cabo Verde	2010	21.3	...	...	...	...	3.3	-1.5	1.6	41.6	145.6	52.1	Cabo Verde
Cameroon	2010	6.4	2010	4.9	2011	45.8	-2.2	0.2	2.0	115.0	142.5	196.9	Cameroun
Central African Republic	...	...	...	...	2010	24.8	-1.0	0.7	2.8	58.0	31.7	18.6	République Centrafricaine
Chad	...	...	2011	4.2	2010	22.0	12.7	9.6	-4.6	50.4	24.7	87.9	Tchad
Comoros	...	...	...	...	2012	18.6	-0.4	-1.1	-0.6	3.0	6.9	13.6	Comores
Congo	...	...	2012	10.8	2011	20.0	8.5	3.8	-0.3	11.8	16.9	27.6	Congo
Democratic Republic of the Congo	...	...	2005	2.9	2013	24.3	2.8	3.7	0.5	182.3	266.9	460.7	Rép, Démocratique du Congo
Côte d'Ivoire	...	...	2012	11.9	2011	24.6	-0.1	-0.5	5.1	17.1	169.4	218.2	Côte d'Ivoire
Djibouti	...	...	...	...	2006	7.7	-0.1	0.6	4.5	1.8	26.8	54.9	Djibouti
Egypt	2015	31.3	2013	24.2	2005	5.6	0.7	1.8	1.0	476.9	805.6	857.5	Egypte
Equatorial Guinea	...	...	...	...	...	...	11.7	-7.3	-12.1	0.0	0.3	0.1	Guinée Equatoriale
Eritrea	...	...	...	...	...	...	-1.8	0.1	0.9	20.8	22.7	10.6	Erythrée
Ethiopia	2013	7.3	2013	7.3	2011	18.7	7.8	9.0	3.4	455.5	508.6	763.6	Ethiopie
Gabon	2010	35.7	2010	28.5	2012	15.1	1.6	14.2	-0.8	15.7	45.3	65.5	Gabon
Gambia	2012	44.3	2012	38.3	2006	23.9	-4.6	3.0	-0.7	12.4	31.6	36.6	Gambie
Ghana	2013	10.9	2013	5.5	2012	18.6	3.9	-1.4	1.1	291.2	523.6	466.0	Ghana
Guinea	...	...	...	...	2012	25.4	0.1	-1.6	0.8	28.2	56.5	53.1	Guinée
Guinea-Bissau	...	...	...	...	2014	40.8	1.6	1.6	2.1	27.8	12.3	10.0	Guinée-Bissau
Kenya	...	...	2009	12.2	...	...	3.9	5.1	2.3	195.9	348.9	931.6	Kenya
Lesotho	2008	34.4	2013	27.2	2000	13.7	10.1	7.3	1.9	13.8	24.7	14.5	Lesotho
Liberia	2010	5.1	2010	4.1	2010	14.9	3.4	1.1	-0.9	1.6	100.7	172.3	Libéria
Libya	2012	48.7	2012	25.1	...	...	8.4	3.6	-4.3	0.6	27.2	1.4	Libye
Madagascar	2012	2.6	2012	1.6	...	...	0.0	-3.9	1.2	244.9	117.1	131.1	Madagascar
Malawi	2013	8.6	2013	6.8	2014	24.4	-0.8	3.4	-0.8	77.3	166.9	244.2	Malawi
Mali	2014	11.1	2010	10.1	2012	19.3	-1.0	-3.2	1.8	175.7	326.0	250.9	Mali
Mauritania	...	...	2012	12.6	2011	9.9	6.5	-1.0	0.8	42.8	110.1	102.1	Mauritanie
Mauritius	2015	26.3	2015	11.6	...	...	0.8	2.2	2.6	1.6	14.8	67.6	Maurice
Morocco	2014	20.0	2014	10.4	...	...	2.6	2.4	0.5	314.3	651.2	969.5	Maroc
Mozambique	2012	39.4	2014	26.8	2008	17.5	6.3	4.6	1.0	361.5	310.8	555.6	Mozambique
Namibia	2013	56.2	2013	33.2	...	...	1.2	-4.6	-0.7	21.1	52.1	51.0	Namibie
Niger	2007	2.3	2007	0.5	2009	41.8	1.1	4.5	1.3	66.6	117.9	106.7	Niger
Nigeria	2015	7.6	2015	5.1	2011	23.1	0.6	4.8	-3.8	167.9	412.8	594.2	Nigéria
Rwanda	2012	4.5	2012	4.0	2008	5.5	3.8	4.8	2.5	68.2	185.1	341.6	Rwanda
Sao Tome and Principe	2012	20.8	2006	24.5	2014	15.0	4.4	0.3	1.3	5.1	4.7	15.7	Sao Tomé-et-Principe
Senegal	2011	12.7	2011	13.4	2015	18.8	4.8	-1.8	2.8	180.7	226.2	416.9	Sénégal
Seychelles	2015	14.0	2015	5.2	...	...				5.6	3.9	2.9	Seychelles
Sierra Leone	2004	5.2	2014	2.4	2013	38.3	-0.4	2.5	1.5	36.2	103.9	65.4	Sierra Leone
Somalia	...	...	...	...	2006	39.2	0.5	-0.1	-0.3	6.5	21.7	70.5	Somalie
South Africa	2015	50.1	2015	27.5	...	...	-0.4	6.0	-0.6	82.4	123.7	594.1	Afrique du Sud
South Sudan	2008	18.5	2008	13.2	...	...						132.2	Soudan du Sud
Sudan	2009	20.0	2009	23.0	2014	18.0	4.9	0.5	0.2	14.8	246.5	265.2	Soudan
Swaziland	...	...	2007	31.2	2010	7.3	2.2	-1.7	-2.4	13.5	9.3	26.2	Swaziland
Tanzania, United Republic of	2013	5.8	2013	3.8	2014	24.2	5.3	5.2	4.1	352.2	685.9	852.7	Tanzanie, République Unie de
Togo	...	...	...	...	2010	26.4	-2.3	0.9	2.2	7.8	32.7	84.1	Togo
Tunisia	2012	37.6	2013	23.0	2012	2.1	1.2	1.4	0.1	145.8	427.4	388.7	Tunisie
Uganda	2013	2.6	2013	2.4	2012	18.1	3.7	0.7	1.2	230.2	387.8	432.4	Ouganda
Zambia	2012	15.2	2012	8.6	2008	15.5	4.9	9.6	-0.6	151.8	101.5	266.8	Zambie
Zimbabwe	2011	8.7	2011	6.0	...	...	-5.4	11.3	-2.8	6.5	74.5	59.7	Zimbabwe
Africa	...	...	...	...			...	...	...	5 245.3	8 901.8	12 390.1	**Afrique**

Source: UNSD, SDG Indicators Global Database

**9. Build resilient infrastructure, promote inclusive and sustainable industrialization and foster innovation /
Bâtir une infrastructure résiliente, promouvoir une industrialisation durable qui profite à tous et encourager l'innovation**

Country	Manufacturing value added per capita (Constant 2010 US $) / Valeur ajoutée dans l'industrie manufacturière par habitant (constants $ EU de 2010)			Manufacturing employment as a proportion of total employment (%) / Emploi dans l'industrie manufacturière, en proportion de l'emploi total (%)		Research and development expenditure as a proportion of GDP / Dépenses de recherche-développement en proportion du PIB		Total official international support to infrastructure (Millions of Constant US$) / Montant total de l'aide publique internationale allouée aux infrastructures (Millions de $ EU constants)			Pays
	2005	2010	2015	Year	%	Year	%	2005	2010	2015	
Algeria	158	182	207	2014	11.3	2005	0.1	76.2	25.0	40.7	Algérie
Angola	123	258	302	...	...	...	...	12.1	26.5	197.1	Angola
Benin	57	53	55	2010	7.6	...	...	40.9	143.4	120.4	Bénin
Botswana	271	415	487	2010	2.5	2012	0.3	1.8	19.9	0.0	Botswana
Burkina Faso	54	39	49	2006	3.7	2009	0.2	61.5	119.4	177.8	Burkina Faso
Burundi	15	23	26	2012	4.6	2011	0.1	8.6	75.0	41.9	Burundi
Cabo Verde	147	185	200	...	...	2011	0.1	39.3	134.4	62.8	Cabo Verde
Cameroon	186	172	186	...	...	...	...	79.4	126.9	154.0	Cameroun
Central African Republic	65	81	54	...	...	...	...	4.2	25.5	10.4	République Centrafricaine
Chad	41	42	47	...	...	...	...	63.5	5.9	58.4	Tchad
Comoros	34	42	40	...	...	...	...	4.6	4.7	10.0	Comores
Congo	87	106	129	...	...	...	...	9.8	11.7	18.8	Congo
Democratic Republic of the Congo	84	56	69	...	...	2009	0.1	154.7	194.5	366.8	Rép, Démocratique du Congo
Côte d'Ivoire	250	172	167	...	...	...	...	1.4	109.7	185.4	Côte d'Ivoire
Djibouti	24	30	35	...	...	...	...	2.7	40.0	49.2	Djibouti
Egypt	360	443	468	2015	11.2	2014	0.7	352.8	1 516.5	1 323.1	Egypte
Equatorial Guinea	17	32	42	...	...	...	...	0.2	0.0	0.0	Guinée Equatoriale
Eritrea	31	21	22	...	...	...	...	15.3	16.6	0.3	Erythrée
Ethiopia	8	12	18	2014	14.0	2013	0.6	271.4	339.0	400.6	Ethiopie
Gabon	357	397	485	...	...	2009	0.6	13.1	59.4	79.1	Gabon
Gambia	33	27	25	2012	8.3	2011	0.1	7.6	22.7	29.0	Gambie
Ghana	85	85	95	2010	10.7	2010	0.4	215.4	307.4	316.6	Ghana
Guinea	27	27	28	...	...	2010	0.8	8.4	45.4	38.3	Guinée
Guinea-Bissau	65	60	61	...	...	...	...	10.5	5.2	2.9	Guinée-Bissau
Kenya	108	110	118	...	...	...	...	90.7	237.9	1 087.0	Kenya
Lesotho	113	131	145	2008	18.0	2011	0.0	7.6	23.6	9.0	Lesotho
Liberia	10	14	17	2010	6.3	...	...	0.1	89.9	282.9	Libéria
Libya	706	759	256	...	...	...	...	...	26.4	0.8	Libye
Madagascar	60	55	56	2015	6.6	2014	0.0	139.9	58.7	72.0	Madagascar
Malawi	26	46	46	...	...	...	...	45.5	70.7	108.1	Malawi
Mali	50	33	38	2004	11.5	2010	0.7	104.2	125.3	122.5	Mali
Mauritania	108	86	97	...	...	...	...	17.2	82.1	109.6	Mauritanie
Mauritius	1 087	1 192	1 307	2015	14.3	2012	0.2	1.7	87.8	91.1	Maurice
Morocco	377	406	421	2013	10.9	2010	0.7	415.4	909.6	1 312.0	Maroc
Mozambique	47	50	62	...	...	2002	0.4	228.7	225.3	304.3	Mozambique
Namibia	580	648	644	2013	4.8	2010	0.1	34.0	33.3	101.2	Namibie
Niger	18	17	21	...	...	...	...	19.8	52.9	48.8	Niger
Nigeria	113	149	255	2010	11.0	2007	0.2	93.4	406.9	862.7	Nigéria
Rwanda	24	29	32	2012	2.7	...	...	59.2	80.3	136.5	Rwanda
Sao Tome and Principe	91	95	103	2006	6.4	...	...	6.0	1.9	13.7	Sao Tomé-et-Principe
Senegal	128	121	116	2011	13.1	2010	0.5	102.7	127.1	261.3	Sénégal
Seychelles	994	856	917	2015	7.4	2005	0.3	0.1	5.0	1.9	Seychelles
Sierra Leone	9	10	8	2004	0.5	...	...	21.6	57.8	56.2	Sierra Leone
Somalia	2	2		...	...	...	...	0.1	7.3	50.6	Somalie
South Africa	935	952	971	2015	11.2	2012	0.7	452.5	992.4	1 083.3	Afrique du Sud
South Sudan				...	...	...	...	...	...	59.2	Soudan du Sud
Sudan	123	148	143	...	...	2004	0.3	0.3	133.1	130.3	Soudan
Swaziland	1 168	1 073	1 041	...	...	...	...	40.6	0.8	12.4	Swaziland
Tanzania, United Republic of	37	48	56	2014	3.0	2013	0.5	188.6	469.2	696.2	Tanzanie, République Unie de
Togo	38	39	45	...	...	2014	0.3	6.2	7.2	83.0	Togo
Tunisia	624	685	703	2013	18.8	2014	0.6	158.9	852.9	832.5	Tunisie
Uganda	57	65	61	2013	4.4	2010	0.5	93.7	320.5	301.7	Ouganda
Zambia	104	107	120	2012	4.1	2008	0.3	84.3	64.1	237.0	Zambie
Zimbabwe	79	85	84	2014	4.0	...	...	1.2	21.8	6.8	Zimbabwe
Africa	174	187	206	...	...	...	...	3 869.1	8 946.5	12 157.7	Afrique

Source: UNSD, SDG Indicators Global Database

10. Reduce inequality within and among countries /
Réduire les inégalités dans les pays et d'un pays à l'autre

Country	Labour share of GDP, comprising wages and social protection transfers (%) Part du travail dans le PIB, y compris les salaires et les transferts sociaux (%)		Total resource flows for development (US $ Millions) Montant total des ressources allouées au développement (Millions $ EU)				Pays
	Year	%	2000	2005	2010	2015	
Algeria	...	...	-401.3	-1 390.4	1 300.7	2 811.4	Algérie
Angola	...	...	117.5	1 668.0	1 632.6	-1 652.9	Angola
Benin	...	...	232.9	379.9	689.2	372.2	Bénin
Botswana	...	...	83.3	81.8	231.1	-73.6	Botswana
Burkina Faso	...	...	187.3	726.4	1 072.6	1 016.4	Burkina Faso
Burundi	...	...	79.0	372.9	691.4	260.5	Burundi
Cabo Verde	...	...	119.8	261.1	322.0	215.3	Cabo Verde
Cameroon	...	...	218.4	242.7	231.2	1 328.5	Cameroun
Central African Republic	...	...	50.8	90.1	229.4	465.8	République Centrafricaine
Chad	...	...	-224.8	389.8	502.4	614.6	Tchad
Comoros	...	...	-1.4	41.4	71.3	54.3	Comores
Congo	...	...	87.3	1 301.4	286.6	2 456.2	Congo
Democratic Republic of the Congo	...	...	193.1	1 655.9	2 579.7	2 790.7	Rép Démocratique du Congo
Côte d'Ivoire	...	...	715.6	190.8	690.5	1 814.3	Côte d'Ivoire
Djibouti	...	...	92.3	95.9	108.2	65.1	Djibouti
Egypt	...	...	3 266.2	4 755.7	6 700.6	9 784.5	Egypte
Equatorial Guinea	...	...	21.9	471.3	91.1	-122.6	Guinée Equatoriale
Eritrea	...	...	185.6	348.7	160.9	85.4	Erythrée
Ethiopia	...	...	681.7	1 920.2	3 710.0	4 116.3	Ethiopie
Gabon	...	...	76.5	-78.4	503.6	-721.9	Gabon
Gambia	...	...	45.3	67.4	120.7	116.4	Gambie
Ghana	...	...	520.9	2 092.5	2 461.2	3 020.9	Ghana
Guinea	2010	14.9	329.9	155.6	205.9	580.3	Guinée
Guinea-Bissau	...	...	84.9	65.0	134.3	94.5	Guinée-Bissau
Kenya	...	...	863.4	1 070.4	1 514.1	2 539.5	Kenya
Lesotho	...	...	11.0	50.7	240.3	79.8	Lesotho
Liberia	...	...	631.6	-2 327.7	2 381.6	1 828.3	Libéria
Libya	...	...	-930.8	523.6	-293.1	423.0	Libye
Madagascar	...	...	320.9	723.3	996.9	647.8	Madagascar
Malawi	...	...	433.1	572.4	1 049.7	1 049.3	Malawi
Mali	...	...	313.6	770.7	1 119.3	1 271.1	Mali
Mauritania	...	...	222.8	190.6	373.2	358.9	Mauritanie
Mauritius	2015	40.5	410.3	147.0	4 390.5	-651.0	Maurice
Morocco	...	...	629.3	2 223.6	3 566.3	2 407.8	Maroc
Mozambique	...	...	1 177.1	1 281.5	2 899.8	2 217.5	Mozambique
Namibia	...	...	127.4	157.7	33.6	394.2	Namibie
Niger	...	...	183.8	397.4	674.3	949.9	Niger
Nigeria	...	...	-1 993.8	7 581.1	1 248.7	22 488.9	Nigéria
Rwanda	...	...	318.2	560.7	1 025.9	1 115.5	Rwanda
Sao Tome and Principe	...	...	36.3	32.1	46.4	44.4	Sao Tomé-et-Principe
Senegal	...	...	482.8	699.6	926.5	1 132.7	Sénégal
Seychelles	...	...	72.7	23.9	209.8	-109.2	Seychelles
Sierra Leone	...	...	185.1	339.1	444.9	869.7	Sierra Leone
Somalia	...	...	101.4	240.2	490.0	1 260.6	Somalie
South Africa	...	...	-490.6	14 784.0	4 870.0	6 316.1	Afrique du Sud
South Sudan	...	...				1 651.4	Soudan du Sud
Sudan	...	...	320.3	1 850.3	2 139.7	879.0	Soudan
Swaziland	...	...	35.5	51.0	64.4	125.1	Swaziland
Tanzania, United Republic of	...	...	1 229.3	1 669.0	3 047.2	2 776.5	Tanzanie, République Unie de
Togo	...	...	60.3	91.9	266.2	553.3	Togo
Tunisia	...	...	660.6	517.8	702.1	1 446.1	Tunisie
Uganda	...	...	830.6	1 258.0	1 857.5	2 985.0	Ouganda
Zambia	...	...	700.9	1 559.6	790.4	1 299.2	Zambie
Zimbabwe	2014	50.0	212.8	399.0	742.5	829.0	Zimbabwe
Africa	...	...	13 918.6	53 343.9	62 546.0	88 671.6	Afrique

Source: UNSD, SDG Indicators Global Database

**11. Make cities and human settlements inclusive, safe, resilient and sustainable /
Faire en sorte que les villes et les établissements humains soient ouverts à tous, sûrs, résilients et durables**

Country	Proportion of urban population living in slums (%) Proportion de la population urbaine vivant dans des taudis (%)				Annual mean levels of fine particulate matter (PM2.5) in cities, population weighted, 2012 (%) Niveau moyen annuel de particules fines (PM 2,5) dans les villes, pondéré en fonction du nombre d'habitants, 2012 (%)	Pays
	2000	2005	2009	2014	Total	
Algeria	...	...	...	...	25	Algérie
Angola	86.5	86.5	65.8	55.5	42	Angola
Benin	74.3	71.8	69.8	61.5	28	Bénin
Botswana	...	...	...	...	19	Botswana
Burkina Faso	66.0	59.5	...	65.8	37	Burkina Faso
Burundi	...	64.3	...	57.9	49	Burundi
Cabo Verde	...	...	...	...	...	Cabo Verde
Cameroon	48.4	47.4	46.1	37.8	64	Cameroun
Central African Republic	91.9	94.1	95.9	93.3	56	République Centrafricaine
Chad	93.9	91.4	89.3	88.2	61	Tchad
Comoros	65.4	69.0	...	69.6	16	Comores
Congo	...	53.4	49.9	46.9	57	Congo
Democratic Republic of the Congo	...	76.4	61.7	74.8	61	Rép Démocratique du Congo
Côte d'Ivoire	55.3	56.2	57.0	56.0	19	Côte d'Ivoire
Djibouti	...	...	...	65.6	46	Djibouti
Egypt	28.1	17.1	13.1	10.6	101	Egypte
Equatorial Guinea	...	66.3	...	66.2	32	Guinée Equatoriale
Eritrea	...	...	...	...	36	Erythrée
Ethiopia	88.6	81.8	76.4	73.9	36	Ethiopie
Gabon	...	38.7	...	37.0	36	Gabon
Gambia	...	45.4	...	34.8	43	Gambie
Ghana	52.1	45.4	40.1	37.9	22	Ghana
Guinea	57.3	45.7	...	43.3	19	Guinée
Guinea-Bissau	...	83.1	...	82.3	29	Guinée-Bissau
Kenya	54.8	54.8	54.7	56.0	17	Kenya
Lesotho	...	35.1	53.7	50.8	22	Lesotho
Liberia	...	...	68.3	65.7	6	Libéria
Libya	...	...	...	...	58	Libye
Madagascar	84.2	80.6	76.2	77.2	32	Madagascar
Malawi	66.4	66.4	69.0	66.7	26	Malawi
Mali	75.4	65.9	65.9	56.3	35	Mali
Mauritania	...	...	...	79.9	86	Mauritanie
Mauritius	...	...	...	...	14	Maurice
Morocco	24.2	13.1	13.1	13.1	19	Maroc
Mozambique	78.2	79.5	80.5	80.3	22	Mozambique
Namibia	33.9	33.9	33.5	33.2	18	Namibie
Niger	82.6	82.1	81.7	70.1	51	Niger
Nigeria	69.6	65.8	62.7	50.2	38	Nigéria
Rwanda	79.8	71.6	65.1	53.2	51	Rwanda
Sao Tome and Principe	...	...	...	86.6	...	Sao Tomé-et-Principe
Senegal	48.9	43.3	38.8	39.4	43	Sénégal
Seychelles	...	...	...	...	13	Seychelles
Sierra Leone	...	97.0	...	75.6	17	Sierra Leone
Somalia	...	73.5	73.6	73.6	17	Somalie
South Africa	33.2	28.7	23.0	23.0	31	Afrique du Sud
South Sudan	...	...	...	95.6	32	Soudan du Sud
Sudan	...	...	...	91.6	53	Soudan
Swaziland	...	...	...	32.7	20	Swaziland
Tanzania, United Republic of	70.1	66.4	63.5	50.7	24	Tanzanie, République Unie de
Togo	...	62.1	...	51.2	26	Togo
Tunisia	...	...	...	8.0	35	Tunisie
Uganda	75.0	66.7	60.1	53.6	80	Ouganda
Zambia	57.2	57.2	57.3	54.0	29	Zambie
Zimbabwe	3.3	17.9	24.1	25.1	24	Zimbabwe
Africa	**60.0**	**57.3**	**54.2**	**52.8**	**42**	**Afrique**

Source: UNSD, SDG Indicators Global Database

12. Ensure sustainable consumption and production patterns / Établir des modes de consommation et de production durables

Country	Total material footprint (Thousands of metrics tons) / Empreinte matérielle totale (Milliers de tonnes métriques)			Material footprint per capita (Tonnes per capita) / Empreinte matérielle totale par habitant (Tonnes par habitant)			Total domestic material consumption (Thousands of metrics tons) / Consommation matérielle nationale (Milliers de tonnes métriques)			Total domestic material consumption per capita (Tonnes per capita) / Consommation matérielle nationale par habitant (Tonnes par habitant)			Pays
	2000	2005	2010	2000	2005	2010	2000	2005	2010	2000	2005	2010	
Algeria	63 480	81 130	115 060	2.0	2.4	3.1	152 162	209 021	298 421	4.8	6.2	8.1	Algérie
Angola	23 490	39 670	62 130	1.7	2.4	3.2	20 684	38 261	54 202	1.5	2.3	2.8	Angola
Benin	16 057	19 889	33 997	2.3	2.4	3.6	22 798	24 572	38 813	3.3	3.0	4.1	Bénin
Botswana	24 600	28 490	34 310	14.0	15.2	17.4	17 950	20 868	25 303	10.2	11.1	12.9	Botswana
Burkina Faso	20 652	33 787	47 879	1.8	2.5	3.1	29 752	42 905	55 298	2.6	3.2	3.6	Burkina Faso
Burundi	10 005	14 489	15 440	1.5	1.9	1.7	11 253	15 682	15 952	1.7	2.0	1.7	Burundi
Cabo Verde	2 001	2 396	2 870	4.5	5.0	5.9	986	1 064	1 723	2.2	2.2	3.5	Cabo Verde
Cameroon	25 538	30 716	37 755	1.6	1.7	1.8	42 387	53 577	65 079	2.7	3.0	3.2	Cameroun
Central African Republic	6 697	9 067	11 280	1.8	2.3	2.6	11 267	11 791	13 359	3.1	3.0	3.1	République Centrafricaine
Chad	12 973	15 102	22 091	1.6	1.5	1.9	21 023	28 519	31 511	2.5	2.9	2.7	Tchad
Comoros	...	...	...	...	...	...	963	1 209	1 177	1.8	2.0	1.7	Comores
Congo	5 470	7 825	11 016	1.8	2.2	2.7	8 189	9 022	12 339	2.6	2.6	3.0	Congo
Democratic Republic of the Congo	83 320	94 210	112 790	1.8	1.7	1.8	87 294	96 016	109 059	1.9	1.8	1.8	Rép Démocratique du Congo
Côte d'Ivoire	21 220	20 365	19 240	1.3	1.2	1.0	45 195	43 772	48 731	2.8	2.5	2.6	Côte d'Ivoire
Djibouti	2 468	2 643	2 722	3.4	3.4	3.3	1 721	2 104	2 317	2.4	2.7	2.8	Djibouti
Egypt	342 160	350 700	485 100	5.2	4.9	6.2	447 126	479 339	694 027	6.8	6.7	8.9	Egypte
Equatorial Guinea	...	...	...	...	...	...	8 573	27 540	30 059	16.6	45.6	43.2	Guinée Equatoriale
Eritrea	4 577	4 941	3 263	1.2	1.0	0.6	4 734	4 629	2 748	1.2	1.0	0.5	Erythrée
Ethiopia	1 787	3 485	5 710	0.0	0.0	0.0	136 425	180 222	231 322	1.0	1.2	1.3	Ethiopie
Gabon	6 032	6 351	6 441	4.9	4.6	4.1	5 113	3 498	4 284	4.2	2.5	2.8	Gabon
Gambia	3 242	4 495	4 243	2.6	3.1	2.5	2 604	4 159	4 836	2.1	2.9	2.9	Gambie
Ghana	40 254	63 300	79 610	2.1	3.0	3.3	97 124	116 295	141 940	5.2	5.4	5.9	Ghana
Guinea	20 020	19 896	21 793	2.3	2.1	2.0	41 649	51 135	49 027	4.8	5.3	4.5	Guinée
Guinea-Bissau	...	...	...	...	...	...	2 418	2 769	4 600	1.9	2.0	2.9	Guinée-Bissau
Kenya	88 040	103 300	124 860	2.8	2.9	3.1	74 700	103 026	135 067	2.4	2.9	3.3	Kenya
Lesotho	5 558	6 336	9 860	3.0	3.3	4.9	6 763	4 764	5 465	3.6	2.5	2.7	Lesotho
Liberia	2 348	2 696	4 181	0.8	0.8	1.1	4 657	8 300	9 112	1.6	2.5	2.3	Libéria
Libya	22 572	17 902	23 950	4.4	3.2	4.0	50 172	57 697	83 192	9.7	10.3	13.8	Libye
Madagascar	8 778	11 317	18 568	0.6	0.6	0.9	33 242	38 453	48 412	2.1	2.1	2.3	Madagascar
Malawi	11 349	11 768	17 410	1.0	0.9	1.2	23 381	21 661	36 304	2.1	1.7	2.4	Malawi
Mali	25 751	44 648	59 769	2.5	3.7	4.3	38 918	56 099	76 274	3.8	4.7	5.5	Mali
Mauritania	7 592	9 091	8 786	2.8	2.9	2.4	15 258	13 693	32 686	5.6	4.4	9.1	Mauritanie
Mauritius	16 840	18 215	20 530	14.2	15.0	16.7	13 076	13 311	13 938	11.0	11.0	11.3	Maurice
Morocco	78 780	97 000	112 800	2.7	3.2	3.6	135 038	177 571	236 411	4.7	5.9	7.5	Maroc
Mozambique	27 113	31 768	37 030	1.5	1.5	1.6	34 630	43 015	49 848	1.9	2.1	2.1	Mozambique
Namibia	10 290	13 630	13 320	5.4	6.7	6.1	8 644	16 460	14 535	4.6	8.1	6.7	Namibie
Niger	22 385	36 583	52 965	2.0	2.8	3.3	37 041	45 215	57 723	3.4	3.4	3.6	Niger
Nigeria	189 850	255 730	299 890	1.6	1.8	1.9	316 532	386 263	421 069	2.6	2.8	2.6	Nigéria
Rwanda	13 843	17 799	25 795	1.7	1.9	2.4	13 734	16 918	21 749	1.6	1.8	2.0	Rwanda
Sao Tome and Principe	900	976	1 265	6.5	6.3	7.1	400	457	563	2.9	3.0	3.2	Sao Tomé-et-Principe
Senegal	20 191	30 612	37 634	2.1	2.7	2.9	29 946	42 010	51 610	3.0	3.7	4.0	Sénégal
Seychelles	2 099	2 334	2 246	26.2	26.8	24.7	620	992	750	7.8	11.4	8.2	Seychelles
Sierra Leone	6 065	8 318	13 233	1.5	1.6	2.3	7 659	9 513	14 502	1.9	1.9	2.5	Sierra Leone
Somalia	28 841	35 137	33 526	3.9	4.2	3.5	32 968	38 736	40 408	4.5	4.6	4.2	Somalie
South Africa	416 200	472 000	450 000	9.3	9.8	8.8	605 975	616 024	639 635	13.5	12.8	12.4	Afrique du Sud
South Sudan	...	...	...	...	...	...	...	...	...	...	...	...	Soudan du Sud
Sudan	...	...	...	...	...	...	146 302	193 407	200 896	4.3	4.9	4.4	Soudan
Swaziland	10 220	12 660	12 800	9.6	11.5	10.7	8 175	10 813	11 018	7.7	9.8	9.2	Swaziland
Tanzania, United Republic of	44 050	56 640	62 330	1.3	1.5	1.4	72 001	102 665	120 774	2.1	2.6	2.7	Tanzanie, République Unie de
Togo	11 339	10 697	13 226	2.3	1.9	2.1	16 925	11 947	18 295	3.5	2.2	2.9	Togo
Tunisia	60 770	60 140	64 050	6.4	6.0	6.0	80 402	86 634	97 789	8.4	8.6	9.2	Tunisie
Uganda	51 298	69 142	90 770	2.1	2.4	2.7	79 048	88 905	103 829	3.3	3.1	3.1	Ouganda
Zambia	23 684	38 550	42 710	2.3	3.4	3.2	46 402	71 226	111 165	4.6	6.2	8.4	Zambie
Zimbabwe	17 080	13 240	13 850	1.4	1.0	1.1	45 594	38 255	42 400	3.7	3.0	3.2	Zimbabwe
Africa	1 959 868	2 341 175	2 802 092	2.6	2.8	2.9	3 197 593	3 781 997	4 631 546	3.9	4.0	4.4	**Afrique**

Source: UNSD, SDG Indicators Global Database

13. Take urgent action to combat climate change and its impacts/
Prendre d'urgence des mesures pour lutter contre les changements climatiques et leurs répercussions

Country	Number of deaths, missing persons and directly affected persons attributed to disasters per 100,000 population / Nombre de personnes décédées, disparues ou directement touchées lors de catastrophes, pour 100 000 personnes		Number of countries that adopt and implement national disaster risk reduction strategies in line with the Sendai Framework for Disaster Risk Reduction 2015–2030 / Nombre de pays ayant adopté et mis en place des stratégies nationales de réduction des risques, conformément au Cadre de Sendai pour la réduction des risques de catastrophe (2015-2030)		Pays
	Year/ Année	Number/Nombre	Year/ Année	Number/Nombre	
Algeria	...	...	2013	1	Algérie
Angola	...	...	...	...	Angola
Benin	...	...	2015	1	Bénin
Botswana	...	...	...	...	Botswana
Burkina Faso	2016	2	2015	1	Burkina Faso
Burundi	...	...	2015	1	Burundi
Cabo Verde	...	...	2015	1	Cabo Verde
Cameroon	...	...	2015	1	Cameroun
Central African Republic	...	...	...	...	République Centrafricaine
Chad	...	...	...	...	Tchad
Comoros	2013	4	...	...	Comores
Congo	...	...	...	...	Congo
Democratic Republic of the Congo	...	...	2015	1	Rép Démocratique du Congo
Côte d'Ivoire	...	...	2013	1	Côte d'Ivoire
Djibouti	2012	28	2013	1	Djibouti
Egypt	2010	68	...	...	Egypte
Equatorial Guinea	...	...	...	...	Guinée Equatoriale
Eritrea	...	...	...	...	Erythrée
Ethiopia	2010	62	2013	1	Ethiopie
Gabon	...	...	2015	1	Gabon
Gambia	...	...	2015	1	Gambie
Ghana	...	...	2013	1	Ghana
Guinea	...	...	2015	1	Guinée
Guinea-Bissau	2016	32	...	...	Guinée-Bissau
Kenya	2016	582	2013	1	Kenya
Lesotho	...	...	2015	1	Lesotho
Liberia	2014	3	...	...	Libéria
Libya	...	...	...	...	Libye
Madagascar	2015	215	2015	1	Madagascar
Malawi	...	...	2013	1	Malawi
Mali	2014	7	2015	1	Mali
Mauritania	...	...	...	...	Mauritanie
Mauritius	2014	10	2015	1	Maurice
Morocco	2014	1	2015	1	Maroc
Mozambique	2012	28	2013	1	Mozambique
Namibia	...	...	...	...	Namibie
Niger	2013	426	2013	1	Niger
Nigeria	...	...	2015	1	Nigéria
Rwanda	2016	35	2013	1	Rwanda
Sao Tome and Principe	...	...	...	...	Sao Tomé-et-Principe
Senegal	2015	1	2015	1	Sénégal
Seychelles	2011	2	2015	1	Seychelles
Sierra Leone	2015	8	...	...	Sierra Leone
Somalia	...	...	...	...	Somalie
South Africa	...	...	2015	1	Afrique du Sud
South Sudan	...	...	...	...	Soudan du Sud
Sudan	...	...	...	...	Soudan
Swaziland	...	...	2015	1	Swaziland
Tanzania, United Republic of	...	...	2013	1	Tanzanie, République Unie de
Togo	2014	161	2015	1	Togo
Tunisia	2013	2	2013	1	Tunisie
Uganda	2014	6	...	...	Ouganda
Zambia	...	...	...	...	Zambie
Zimbabwe	...	...	2015	1	Zimbabwe
	...	...			
Africa		...		...	**Afrique**

Source: UNSD, SDG Indicators Global Database

**14. Conserve and sustainably use the oceans, seas and marine resources for sustainable development /
Conserver et exploiter de manière durable les océans, les mers et les ressources marines aux fins du développement durable**

Coverage of protected areas in relation to marine areas (%)

Proportion de la surface maritime couverte par des aires marines protégées (%)

Country	206	Pays
Algeria	0.1	Algérie
Angola	0.0	Angola
Benin	...	Bénin
Botswana	...	Botswana
Burkina Faso	...	Burkina Faso
Burundi	...	Burundi
Cabo Verde	...	Cabo Verde
Cameroon	3.4	Cameroun
Central African Republic	...	République Centrafricaine
Chad	...	Tchad
Comoros	0.0	Comores
Congo	3.2	Congo
Democratic Republic of the Congo	0.2	Rép Démocratique du Congo
Côte d'Ivoire	0.1	Côte d'Ivoire
Djibouti	0.5	Djibouti
Egypt	5.0	Egypte
Equatorial Guinea	0.2	Guinée Equatoriale
Eritrea	...	Erythrée
Ethiopia	...	Ethiopie
Gabon	1.0	Gabon
Gambia	0.1	Gambie
Ghana	0.1	Ghana
Guinea	0.5	Guinée
Guinea-Bissau	10.0	Guinée-Bissau
Kenya	0.8	Kenya
Lesotho	...	Lesotho
Liberia	0.1	Libéria
Libya	0.6	Libye
Madagascar	0.4	Madagascar
Malawi	...	Malawi
Mali	...	Mali
Mauritania	4.2	Mauritanie
Mauritius	0.0	Maurice
Morocco	0.5	Maroc
Mozambique	2.2	Mozambique
Namibia	1.7	Namibie
Niger	...	Niger
Nigeria	0.0	Nigéria
Rwanda	...	Rwanda
Sao Tome and Principe	0.0	Sao Tomé-et-Principe
Senegal	1.1	Sénégal
Seychelles	0.0	Seychelles
Sierra Leone	0.5	Sierra Leone
Somalia	...	Somalie
South Africa	12.1	Afrique du Sud
South Sudan	...	Soudan du Sud
Sudan	16.0	Soudan
Swaziland	...	Swaziland
Tanzania, United Republic of	2.5	Tanzanie, République Unie de
Togo	0.2	Togo
Tunisia	1.0	Tunisie
Uganda	...	Ouganda
Zambia	...	Zambie
Zimbabwe	...	Zimbabwe
Africa	...	**Afrique**

Source: UNSD, SDG Indicators Global Database

15. Protect, restore and promote sustainable use of terrestrial ecosystems, sustainably manage forests, combat desertification, and halt and reverse land degradation and halt biodiversity loss /
Préserver et restaurer les écosystèmes terrestres en veillant à les exploiter de façon durable, gérer durablement les forêts, lutter contre la désertification, enrayer et inverser le processus de dégradation des terres et mettre fin à l'appauvrissement de la biodiversité

Country	Forest area as a proportion of total land area (%) / Proportion de la surface émergée totale couverte par des zones forestières (%)			Proportion of important sites for terrestrial biodiversity that are covered by protected areas (%) / Proportion des sites importants pour la biodiversité terrestre qui sont couverts par des aires protégées (%)			Red List Index / Indice de la Liste rouge			Total official development assistance for biodiversity on conservation and sustainable use of biodiversity and ecosystems (US $ Millions) / Total de l'aide publique au développement consacrée à la conservation et à l'utilisation durable de la biodiversité et des écosystèmes (Millions $ EU)			Pays
	2000	2010	2015	2000	2010	2017	2000	2010	2017	2005	2010	2015	
Algeria	0.7	0.8	0.8	24.6	38.4	38.8	0.91	0.91	0.90	7.0	3.8	14.0	Algérie
Angola	47.9	46.9	46.4	28.4	28.4	28.4	0.94	0.94	0.94	2.5	8.8	6.4	Angola
Benin	45.8	41.2	39.0	77.4	77.4	77.4	0.91	0.91	0.91	35.4	3.3	70.0	Bénin
Botswana	22.1	20.0	19.1	47.1	47.1	47.1	0.98	0.98	0.98	...	0.2	2.6	Botswana
Burkina Faso	22.8	20.7	19.6	66.7	71.8	71.8	0.99	0.99	0.99	0.3	41.8	70.9	Burkina Faso
Burundi	7.7	9.9	10.8	43.2	45.5	51.2	0.92	0.92	0.92	...	4.6	12.7	Burundi
Cabo Verde	20.4	21.1	22.3	0.0	0.0	7.1	0.86	0.87	0.88	21.5	5.8	29.7	Cabo Verde
Cameroon	46.8	42.1	39.8	23.2	33.1	36.3	0.84	0.84	0.84	7.5	12.9	44.7	Cameroun
Central African Republic	36.0	35.7	35.6	74.2	74.4	74.4	0.94	0.94	0.94	9.4	0.1	5.9	République Centrafricaine
Chad	5.0	4.4	3.9	67.3	70.6	70.6	0.93	0.92	0.92	38.0	18.5	7.5	Tchad
Comoros	24.2	21.0	19.9	0.0	14.8	14.8	0.84	0.79	0.77	...	1.0	0.0	Comores
Congo	66.1	65.6	65.4	40.6	61.2	72.1	0.98	0.98	0.98	3.1	3.1	70.4	Congo
Democratic Republic of the Congo	69.4	68.0	67.3	34.7	36.7	36.7	0.89	0.89	0.89	11.5	28.8	255.3	Rép Démocratique du Congo
Côte d'Ivoire	32.5	32.7	32.7	72.3	77.7	77.7	0.89	0.89	0.89	0.8	14.2	30.2	Côte d'Ivoire
Djibouti	0.2	0.2	0.2	0.0	0.0	1.0	0.86	0.84	0.82	...	...	...	Djibouti
Egypt	0.1	0.1	0.1	32.6	39.6	39.6	0.96	0.93	0.91	3.9	56.7	0.3	Egypte
Equatorial Guinea	62.1	58.0	55.9	100.0	100.0	100.0	0.82	0.81	0.81	0.0	0.1	0.3	Guinée Equatoriale
Eritrea	15.6	15.2	15.0	13.3	13.3	13.3	0.95	0.93	0.91	...	1.8	0.1	Erythrée
Ethiopia	12.5	11.2	11.4	18.6	19.8	19.8	0.84	0.84	0.84	8.9	197.3	305.2	Ethiopie
Gabon	85.4	85.4	89.3	11.4	61.2	61.2	0.96	0.96	0.96	4.2	26.7	8.9	Gabon
Gambia	46.1	48.0	48.8	28.9	34.6	34.6	0.98	0.98	0.98	8.8	5.7	0.0	Gambie
Ghana	39.2	40.4	41.0	85.0	85.0	85.0	0.85	0.85	0.85	30.6	18.0	34.4	Ghana
Guinea	28.1	26.6	25.9	62.6	67.2	67.2	0.90	0.90	0.90	0.0	1.4	4.8	Guinée
Guinea-Bissau	75.4	71.9	70.1	52.2	52.2	52.6	0.96	0.96	0.96	0.5	1.2	5.2	Guinée-Bissau
Kenya	6.3	7.4	7.8	34.7	36.8	37.5	0.85	0.82	0.80	1.0	43.2	191.1	Kenya
Lesotho	1.4	1.5	1.6	15.0	15.3	15.3	0.97	0.97	0.97	...	0.3	...	Lesotho
Liberia	48.1	44.9	43.4	4.9	14.8	14.8	0.90	0.89	0.89	0.0	17.8	24.5	Libéria
Libya	0.1	0.1	0.1	4.6	4.6	4.6	0.97	0.97	0.97	0.0	0.0	1.2	Libye
Madagascar	22.4	21.6	21.5	37.2	40.1	40.8	0.85	0.82	0.79	49.1	3.4	61.6	Madagascar
Malawi	37.8	34.3	33.4	81.6	81.6	81.6	0.80	0.81	0.81	20.9	65.2	37.4	Malawi
Mali	4.8	4.2	3.9	5.8	33.8	33.8	0.99	0.98	0.98	38.6	47.7	85.6	Mali
Mauritania	0.3	0.2	0.2	14.6	14.6	14.6	0.98	0.98	0.98	1.3	12.1	14.2	Mauritanie
Mauritius	20.9	19.1	19.2	24.5	24.6	25.7	0.50	0.45	0.40	0.0	85.0	0.3	Maurice
Morocco	11.2	12.7	12.6	3.6	15.2	43.5	0.90	0.89	0.89	45.8	6.5	91.0	Maroc
Mozambique	52.4	49.6	48.3	21.9	22.2	36.5	0.87	0.85	0.83	13.4	85.9	85.1	Mozambique
Namibia	9.8	8.9	8.4	33.1	82.4	85.4	0.97	0.97	0.97	6.5	31.5	14.7	Namibie
Niger	1.1	1.0	0.9	13.2	40.7	42.8	0.96	0.95	0.94	2.0	10.7	49.8	Niger
Nigeria	14.4	9.9	7.7	76.0	79.6	79.6	0.88	0.87	0.87	0.4	2.7	174.5	Nigéria
Rwanda	13.9	18.1	19.5	41.0	45.7	45.7	0.85	0.85	0.85	0.3	15.8	71.2	Rwanda
Sao Tome and Principe	58.3	55.8	55.8	0.0	54.4	54.4	0.79	0.79	0.79	0.1	0.6	0.4	Sao Tomé-et-Principe
Senegal	46.2	44.0	43.0	39.2	41.1	41.2	0.96	0.95	0.94	91.9	66.5	173.7	Sénégal
Seychelles	88.4	88.4	88.4	21.9	21.9	21.9	0.72	0.69	0.67	0.6	0.4	0.2	Seychelles
Sierra Leone	40.8	38.1	42.5	54.6	69.0	80.3	0.92	0.91	0.91	...	5.1	15.3	Sierra Leone
Somalia	12.0	10.8	10.1	0.0	0.0	0.0	0.95	0.92	0.90	...	1.4	39.0	Somalie
South Africa	7.6	7.6	7.6	41.3	50.3	54.5	0.82	0.80	0.78	0.7	12.7	10.7	Afrique du Sud
South Sudan	11.3	11.3	11.3	30.3	33.6	33.6	0.94	0.93	0.93	...	...	18.4	Soudan du Sud
Sudan	11.7	10.8	10.3	9.1	18.6	25.0	0.98	0.95	0.94	0.1	24.9	7.3	Soudan
Swaziland	30.1	32.7	34.1	57.4	57.4	57.4	0.82	0.82	0.82	...	1.1	0.0	Swaziland
Tanzania, United Republic of	58.6	54.1	52.0	49.5	53.6	53.6	0.78	0.73	0.69	5.3	41.4	165.1	Tanzanie, République Unie de
Togo	8.9	5.3	3.5	75.0	97.0	97.0	0.85	0.85	0.85	0.0	5.8	0.9	Togo
Tunisia	5.4	6.4	6.7	14.8	27.2	40.9	0.97	0.97	0.97	31.3	6.3	4.6	Tunisie
Uganda	19.4	13.8	10.4	60.7	73.7	73.7	0.80	0.77	0.75	3.3	101.3	105.3	Ouganda
Zambia	68.8	66.5	65.4	44.9	48.3	48.3	0.88	0.88	0.88	35.2	25.8	51.3	Zambie
Zimbabwe	48.8	40.4	36.4	62.7	80.7	85.9	0.80	0.79	0.79	0.3	39.2	5.2	Zimbabwe
Africa	**22.7**	**21.6**	**22.1**	**31.3**	**39.9**	**43.5**	**...**	**...**	**...**	**541.9**	**1215.6**	**2478.6**	**Afrique**

Source: UNSD, SDG Indicators Global Database

16. Promote peaceful and inclusive societies for sustainable development, provide access to justice for all and build effective, accountable and inclusive institutions at all levels /
Promouvoir l'avènement de sociétés pacifiques et ouvertes à tous aux fins du développement durable, assurer l'accès de tous à la justice et mettre en place, à tous les niveaux, des institutions efficaces, responsables et ouvertes à tous

Country	Number of victims of intentional homicide per 100,000 population / Nombre de victimes d'homicide volontaire pour 100 000 habitants		Proportion of children under 5 years of age whose births have been registered with a civil authority / Proportion d'enfants de moins de 5 ans ayant été enregistrés par une autorité d'état civil		Unsentenced detainees as a proportion of overall prison population (%) / Proportion de la population carcérale en instance de jugement (%)		Proportion of firms experiencing at least one bribe payment request / Proportion d'entreprises ayant eu, au moins une fois, affaire à une demande de paiement de pot-de-vin		Pays
	Years	(%)	Years	(%)	2005	2014	Years	(%)	
Algeria	2015	1.4	2013	99.6	35.5	7.2	2007	18.8	Algérie
Angola	2015	9.7	2001	35.6	...	...	2010	51.3	Angola
Benin	2015	6.0	2014	84.8	...	...	2016	14.6	Bénin
Botswana	2011	10.5	2014	83.2	53.0	23.4	2010	8.4	Botswana
Burkina Faso	2012	0.7	2010	76.9	47.4	40.1	2009	9.8	Burkina Faso
Burundi	2014	4.0	2010	75.2	64.9	53.9	2014	30.3	Burundi
Cabo Verde	2015	8.8	2010	91.4	...	...	2009	2.0	Cabo Verde
Cameroon	2012	4.1	2014	66.1	76.2	60.2	2016	26.7	Cameroun
Central African Republic	2015	13.1	2010	61.0	...	...	2011	21.0	République Centrafricaine
Chad	2015	9.0	2015	12.0	...	...	2009	35.0	Tchad
Comoros	2015	7.6	2012	87.3	...	...	...	...	Comores
Congo	2015	10.1	2015	95.9	...	...	2009	37.5	Congo
Democratic Republic of the Congo	2015	13.4	2014	24.6	...	...	2013	56.5	Rép Démocratique du Congo
Côte d'Ivoire	2015	11.8	2012	65.0	...	...	2009	19.3	Côte d'Ivoire
Djibouti	2015	6.8	2006	91.7	...	...	2013	11.1	Djibouti
Egypt	2011	3.2	2014	99.4	...	...	2013	17.4	Egypte
Equatorial Guinea	2015	3.2	2011	53.5	...	...	...	...	Guinée Equatoriale
Eritrea	2015	7.5	...	...	...	...	2009	0.0	Erythrée
Ethiopia	2015	7.6	2005	6.6	...	...	2015	26.9	Ethiopie
Gabon	2015	9.0	2012	89.6	...	...	2009	23.2	Gabon
Gambia	2015	9.1	2013	72.0	...	...	2006	25.1	Gambie
Ghana	2011	1.7	2014	70.5	30.6	21.1	2013	18.7	Ghana
Guinea	2015	8.5	2012	57.9	...	...	2016	7.9	Guinée
Guinea-Bissau	2015	9.2	2014	23.7	...	...	2006	27.6	Guinée-Bissau
Kenya	2015	5.8	2014	66.9	49.9	39.9	2013	26.4	Kenya
Lesotho	2010	38.0	2014	43.3	19.0	21.2	2016	14.6	Lesotho
Liberia	2012	3.2	2013	24.6	...	...	2009	70.5	Libéria
Libya	2015	2.5	...	...	68.5	86.9	...	...	Libye
Madagascar	2010	0.6	2013	83.0	88.8	53.6	2013	32.9	Madagascar
Malawi	2012	1.8	2014	5.6	30.4	16.1	2014	24.2	Malawi
Mali	2015	10.8	2015	87.2	...	...	2016	33.7	Mali
Mauritania	2015	10.2	2015	65.6	...	...	2014	28.9	Mauritanie
Mauritius	2011	2.7	...	...	35.9	43.0	2009	3.9	Maurice
Morocco	2014	1.1	2011	94.0	51.8	43.0	2013	37.3	Maroc
Mozambique	2011	3.4	2011	47.9	75.3	32.5	2007	12.4	Mozambique
Namibia	2012	16.9	2013	87.1	...	...	2014	9.1	Namibie
Niger	2012	4.5	2012	63.9	...	...	2009	18.5	Niger
Nigeria	2015	9.8	2013	29.8	72.7	68.0	2014	28.9	Nigéria
Rwanda	2013	4.5	2015	56.0	...	...	2011	6.9	Rwanda
Sao Tome and Principe	2011	3.4	2014	95.2	46.5	8.2	...	...	Sao Tomé-et-Principe
Senegal	2015	7.3	2014	72.7	8.3	40.5	2014	11.1	Sénégal
Seychelles	2010	2.2	...	...	...	...	...	...	Seychelles
Sierra Leone	2015	1.9	2013	76.7	14.9	55.1	2009	18.1	Sierra Leone
Somalia	2015	5.6	2006	3.0	...	...	...	...	Somalie
South Africa	2015	34.3	2012	85.0	26.5	28.1	2007	4.2	Afrique du Sud
South Sudan	2012	13.7	2010	35.4	...	...	2014	48.0	Soudan du Sud
Sudan	2015	6.5	2014	67.3	12.7	20.4	2014	17.6	Soudan
Swaziland	2013	8.2	2014	53.5	48.0	17.7	2016	6.7	Swaziland
Tanzania, United Republic of	2015	7.0	2016	26.4	57.0	49.1	2013	20.8	Tanzanie, République Unie de
Togo	2015	9.1	2014	78.1	...	...	2016	7.0	Togo
Tunisia	2012	3.1	2012	99.2	...	...	2013	10.3	Tunisie
Uganda	2014	11.8	2011	29.9	60.7	54.6	2013	22.0	Ouganda
Zambia	2010	5.9	2014	11.3	44.6	22.5	2013	15.8	Zambie
Zimbabwe	2012	6.7	2014	32.3	30.2	18.2	2011	16.2	Zimbabwe
Africa		...		...	...	...		...	Afrique

Source: UNSD, SDG Indicators Global Database

**17. Strengthen the means of implementation and revitalize the Global Partnership for Sustainable Development /
Renforcer les moyens de mettre en oeuvre le Partenariat mondial pour le développement durable et le revitaliser**

Country	Financial and technical assistance disbursed to developing countries (Constant US$ Billions) / Engagements d'aide financière et technique contractés en faveur des pays en développement (Milliards de $EU constants)			Countries with a national statistical plan that is fully funded and under implementation / Pays ayant un plan statistique national intégralement financé et en cours de mise en oeuvre		Total amount of all resources made available to strengthen statistical capacity (Thousands of US$) / Montant total de l'ensemble des ressources allouées au renforcement des capacités statistiques (Milliers de $ EU)			Countries that have conducted at least one population and housing census in the last 10 years / Pays qui ont procédé à au moins un recensement de la population et de l'habitat au cours des 10 dernières années		Pays
	2000	2010	2014	Years	Number/ Nombre	2006	2010	2014	Years	Number/ Nombre	
Algeria	389.8	32.3	53.7	2015	0	207.0	203.5	1.6	2008	1	Algérie
Angola	59.0	27.0	30.4	2015	1	195.9	151.4		2014	1	Angola
Benin	79.0	97.5	89.9	2015	1	278.8	12.0	165.2	2013	1	Bénin
Botswana	25.0	46.2	48.1	...	1	47.6	441.6	54.7	2011	1	Botswana
Burkina Faso	239.6	160.3	93.9	2015	1	2 538.1	214.2	3 159.6	...	...	Burkina Faso
Burundi	15.0	77.6	100.3	2014	1	336.5	2 705.5	376.3	2008	1	Burundi
Cabo Verde	24.6	45.3	15.7	2015	1	1 697.7	162.3	881.5	2010	1	Cabo Verde
Cameroon	118.0	64.7	62.7	2015	1	752.6		1 281.8	...	...	Cameroun
Central African Republic	27.0	16.2	44.4	2015	1	220.4	22.0		...	...	République Centrafricaine
Chad	101.2	40.0	41.4	2015	0	120.9	32.9	368.4	2009	1	Tchad
Comoros	9.3	10.9	20.0	2014	1	421.1	362.6		...	...	Comores
Congo	21.3	12.6	19.3	2015	0	141.7	5 806.4	5 443.2	2007	1	Congo
Democratic Republic of the Congo	18.1	205.0	268.6	2015	1	1 470.4	350.1	24 917.2	...	...	Rép Démocratique du Congo
Côte d'Ivoire	55.8	93.9	164.3	2015	0	422.6	109.2	13 191.3	2014	1	Côte d'Ivoire
Djibouti	19.6	18.5	12.4	2015	0	302.5	411.9	652.2	2009	1	Djibouti
Egypt	256.6	678.4	240.9	2011	0	283.9	9.0	150.7	...	...	Egypte
Equatorial Guinea	2.7	11.6	2.5	2010	1	18.5	614.7	70.9	2015	1	Guinée Equatoriale
Eritrea	78.0	21.2	9.5	2014	0	191.1	121.1	174.1	...	...	Erythrée
Ethiopia	114.1	359.8	527.0	2015	1	4 375.2	1.2	30 438.0	2007	1	Ethiopie
Gabon	46.1	56.4	10.0	2015	0	79.7	21.0		2013	1	Gabon
Gambia	16.4	14.5	14.1	2012	0	704.0	3 166.0	164.1	2013	1	Gambie
Ghana	167.9	403.8	250.2	2014	1	793.6	234.4	865.2	2010	1	Ghana
Guinea	66.6	18.2	77.4	2015	0	100.1	63.1	1 500.0	2014	1	Guinée
Guinea-Bissau	22.7	22.1	16.2	2011	0	277.5	91.5	6 647.2	2009	1	Guinée-Bissau
Kenya	211.9	243.7	355.5	2015	1	7 270.5	392.6	105.0	2009	1	Kenya
Lesotho	28.1	27.9	14.2	2015	1	652.7	410.5	111.6	2016	1	Lesotho
Liberia	4.4	62.5	74.7	2014	0	82.5		1 326.8	2008	1	Libéria
Libya	...	1.8	22.6	2011	0	10.8	417.4		...	...	Libye
Madagascar	81.0	67.1	86.8	2015	1	360.9	2 089.4	7 960.7	...	...	Madagascar
Malawi	122.4	120.0	116.3	2015	1	3 915.4	2 430.1	2 480.7	2008	1	Malawi
Mali	137.7	196.2	111.6	2015	1	4 587.4	25.4	2 728.1	2009	1	Mali
Mauritania	60.5	44.6	50.6	2015	0	224.3	16.7	1 690.4	2013	1	Mauritanie
Mauritius	19.0	42.8	14.5	2012	0		2 014.7		2011	1	Maurice
Morocco	540.2	303.5	430.1	2012	0	567.0	1 389.5	7 426.8	2014	1	Maroc
Mozambique	324.9	383.7	349.3	2015	1	7 952.9	1 317.9	13 326.1	2007	1	Mozambique
Namibia	40.7	33.6	50.0	2015	1	206.0	1 078.1	31.5	2011	1	Namibie
Niger	49.9	69.9	93.7	2015	1	1 182.9	1 718.1	3 125.7	2012	1	Niger
Nigeria	209.3	412.3	421.8	2014	0	5 982.0	12 271.9	720.5	...	...	Nigéria
Rwanda	119.8	138.4	106.0	2014	1	442.8	69.4	40 042.2	2012	1	Rwanda
Sao Tome and Principe	14.5	6.2	6.7	2015	0	370.5	82.0		2012	1	Sao Tomé-et-Principe
Senegal	231.1	165.6	153.6	2015	0	343.6		2 360.0	2013	1	Sénégal
Seychelles	2.9	10.5	8.1	2011	1		184.2		2010	1	Seychelles
Sierra Leone	81.5	57.8	91.0	2012	0	2 019.2	99.3	1 600.0	2015	1	Sierra Leone
Somalia	1.9	22.5	108.6	...	0	314.6	284.0	827.0	...	...	Somalie
South Africa	205.3	93.4	251.0	2015	1	108.2			2011	1	Afrique du Sud
South Sudan	...	...	97.3	2015	1		1 432.8	10 782.4	2008	1	Soudan du Sud
Sudan	33.7	214.8	45.6	2015	1	4 811.4	15.7	355.1	2008	1	Soudan
Swaziland	4.6	8.7	5.8	2015	1	90.0	11 542.9		2007	1	Swaziland
Tanzania, United Republic of	296.4	546.9	452.4	2014	1	1 486.5	102.9	11 367.3	2012	1	Tanzanie, République Unie de
Togo	23.5	18.3	28.7	2015	0	265.7	34.5	3 075.3	2010	1	Togo
Tunisia	65.0	144.3	148.9	2012	0	272.3	3 638.9	1.2	2014	1	Tunisie
Uganda	342.2	189.0	203.7	2015	1	858.3	6 546.7	826.9	2014	1	Ouganda
Zambia	401.0	113.9	139.9	2015	1	672.0	604.3	3 808.2	2010	1	Zambie
Zimbabwe	75.0	31.7	52.7	2015	1	210.5	604.3	332.5	2012	1	Zimbabwe
Africa	**5 701.8**	**6 305.1**	**6 304.4**		**30**	**61 238.1**	**65 517.3**	**206 915.6**		**43**	**Afrique**

Source: UNSD, SDG Indicators Global Database

Part
Partie 2

Country Tables
Tableaux par pays

AREA (km2)		2381740	**SUPERFICIE (KM2)**
CAPITAL CITY	Algiers	Alger	**CAPITALE**
CURRENCY	Algerian Dinar	Dinar algérien	**MONNAIE**

I SOCIAL AND DEMOGRAPHIC INDICATORS — INDICATEURS DEMOGRAPHIQUES ET SOCIAUX

Population	Year Année	Value Valeur	Charts / Graphiques	Population
Population ('000)	2017	41 800.0		Population ('000)
Female (%)	...	...		Féminine (%)
Urban (%)	2008	65.9		Urbaine (%)
Average annual growth rate	2016	2.2		Taux de croissance annuel
Active population ('000)	2017	12 298.0		Population active ('000)
Population by age group ('000)				Population par groupe d'âge ('000)
0-14 years	2016	11 954.0		0-14 ans
15-64 years	2016	26 434.0		15-64 ans
65+ years	2016	2 448.0		65+ ans
Economically active population in agriculture (%)	2017	10.1		Participation de la population active agricole (%)
Crude birth rate	2016	26.1		Taux brut de natalité
Crude death rate	2016	4.4		Taux brut de mortalité
Total fertility rate	2016	3.1		Indice synthétique de fécondité
Life expectancy at birth - Total (years)	2016	77.6		Espérance de vie à la naissance - Totale (années)
Dependency ratio - Total (%)	2016	54.5		Taux de dépendance - Total (%)
Health				**Santé**
Percentage of children under-five and underweight	2005	3.7		% d'enfants de moins de cinq ans avec insuffisance pondérale
Prevalence of undernourishment	2006	6.8		Prévalence de la malnutrition
Under five mortality rate (per 1 000 live births)	2016	25.4		Taux de mortalité de moins de 5 ans (les deux sexes, pour 1000)
Infant mortality rate (per 1 000 live births)	2016	20.9		Taux de mortalité infantile (les deux sexes) par 1000
Neonatal mortality rate (per 1 000 live births)	2006	18.8		Le taux de mortalité néonatale (pour 1000 naissances vivantes)
Percentage of children provided the vaccines :				Pourcentage d'enfants vaccinés :
BCG	2006	99.0		BCG
DPT3	2006	95.0		DTC3
Polio	...	...		polio
Measles	2006	91.0		rougeole
Percentage of mothers provided at least one antenatal care (%)	2006	89.4		Pourcentage de mères ayant au moins reçu un soin prénatal (%)
Percentage of deliveries attended by skilled health personnel	2006	95.2		% d'accouchements assistés par un personnel de santé qualifié
Number of doctors (per 10,000 population)	2016	18.3		Nombre de médecins (pour 10.000 habitants)
Number of nurses (per 10,000 population)	2016	22.4		Nombre d'infirmiers (pour 10.000 habitants)
Hospital beds - Total (per 10,000 population)	2016	16.0		Nombre de lits d'hôpitaux - Total (pour 10 000)
Births registered (per 1,000)	2016	26.1		Naissances enregistrées (pour 1000)
Deaths registered (per 1,000)	2016	4.1		Décès enregistrés (pour 1000)
Budget allocation to health (%)	2006	7.8		Dépenses publiques consacrées à la santé (% du budget)
Education				**Education**
Enrolment in primary education (000)	2016	4 231.6		Scolarisation dans le primaire (000)
Female	2016	2 016.2		Féminine
Enrolment in secondary education (000)	2016	2 685.8		Scolarisation dans le secondaire (000)
Female	2016	1 289.2		Féminine
Enrolment in tertiary education (000)	2016	1 286.6		Scolarisation dans le tertiaire (000)
Female	2016	728.7		Féminine
Literacy rate	2008	77.4		Taux d'alphabétisation (deux sexes)
Male	2008	84.1		Masculin
Female	2008	70.6		Féminin
Pupil teacher ratio - primary	2016	19.0		Ratio élève-enseignant
Budget allocation to education (%)	...	...		Dépenses publiques consacrées à l'enseignement (% du budget)
Poverty				**Pauvreté**
GNI per capita, PPP (current int. $)	2016	14390.0		RNB par habitant, ($ PPA inter. courants)
Human Poverty Index (HPI-1) Value (%)	2007	17.5		Valeur de l'Indice de pauvreté (IPH-1) (%)
Population below Inter. poverty line ($2/day) (%)	...	...		Population sous le seuil inter. de pauvreté (2$/Jour) (%)
Share of income held by richest 10%	...	...		% de revenu des 10% plus riches
Share of income held by poorest 10%	...	...		% de revenu des 10% plus pauvres
GINI index	...	...		Indice de GINI

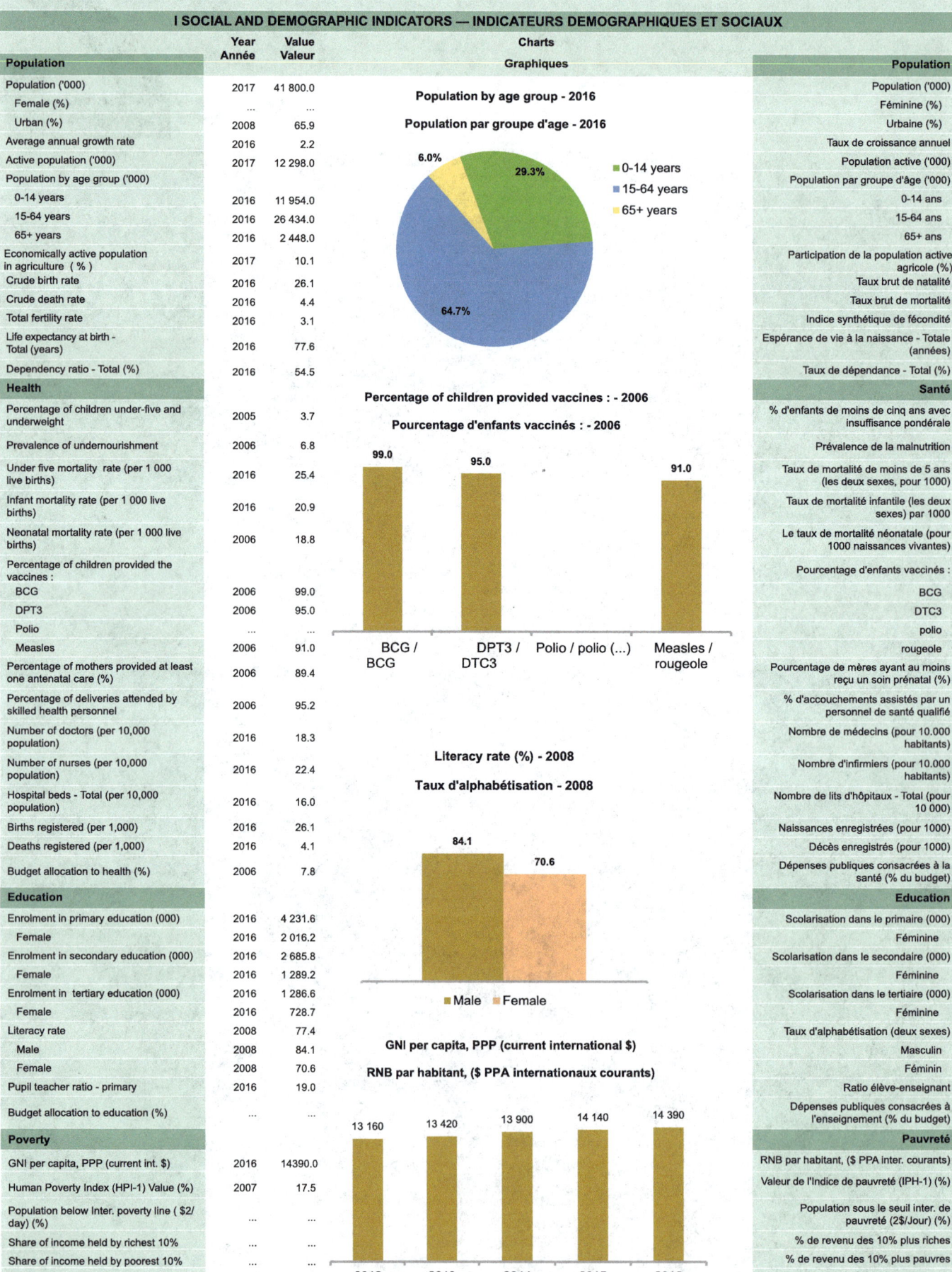

Population by age group - 2016 / Population par groupe d'age - 2016
6.0% / 29.3% / 64.7% — 0-14 years, 15-64 years, 65+ years

Percentage of children provided vaccines : - 2006 / Pourcentage d'enfants vaccinés : - 2006
BCG / BCG 99.0 — DPT3 / DTC3 95.0 — Polio / polio (...) — Measles / rougeole 91.0

Literacy rate (%) - 2008 / Taux d'alphabétisation - 2008
Male 84.1 — Female 70.6

GNI per capita, PPP (current international $) / RNB par habitant, ($ PPA internationaux courants)
2012: 13 160 — 2013: 13 420 — 2014: 13 900 — 2015: 14 140 — 2016: 14 390

II NATIONAL ACCOUNTS — COMPTES NATIONAUX

	2009	2010	2011	2012	2013	2014	2015	2016	2017	
GROSS DOMESTIC PRODUCT BY KIND OF ECONOMIC ACTIVITY AT CURRENT PRICES *ALGERIAN DINAR (MILLIONS)*										**PRODUIT INTÉRIEUR BRUT PAR BRANCHE D'ACTIVITÉ ÉCONOMIQUE AUX PRIX COURANTS** *DINAR ALGÉRIEN (MILLIONS)*
Agriculture, hunting , forestry and Fishing	931 341	1 015 258	1 183 216	1 421 693	1 640 006	1 772 202	1 935 113	2 140 305	2 318 870	Agriculture, chasse sylviculture et Pêche
Mining and quarrying	3 216 901	4 261 874	5 332 750	5 639 183	5 048 595	4 744 647	3 217 952	3 132 996	3 692 885	Industries extractives
Manufacturing	466 054	500 581	534 046	584 211	617 175	672 033	723 837	767 399	814 378	Industries manufacturières
Electricity, gas & water	91 211	98 622	110 602	122 553	132 169	142 640	154 447	180 182	195 413	Electricité, gaz et eau
Construction	1 000 055	1 194 113	1 262 567	1 411 160	1 569 314	1 730 198	1 859 785	1 990 038	2 129 483	Bâtiments et travaux publics
Wholesale & retail trade, restaurants, hotels	1 270 747	1 404 044	1 580 312	1 801 208	2 041 287	2 256 539	2 472 135	2 581 634	2 713 591	Commerce de gros et de détail, restaurants et hôtels
Finance, insurance, real estate, etc.	631 527	673 622	742 338	780 125	816 365	852 094	886 530	991 182	1 088 027	Banques, assurances, affaires immobilières
Transport and communications	865 215	933 707	1 074 148	1 194 842	1 463 055	1 550 497	1 658 814	1 796 979	1 939 949	Transport(s) et communications
Public administration and defense	1 180 794	1 569 007	2 368 273	2 634 958	2 538 308	2 722 276	2 893 473	2 990 442	3 082 927	Administrations publiques et défense
Education	...	...	...	...	...	...	...	...	...	Education
Health And Social Work	...	...	...	...	...	...	...	...	...	Santé et Actions Sociales
Other services	114 542	125 832	138 445	154 480	167 114	180 095	202 439	230 311	275 194	Autres services
Less Imputed Service Charges	- 516 523	- 532 785	- 592 364	- 612 321	- 625 119	- 636 719	- 656 142	- 733 782	- 743 100	Moins Services d'intermédiation financière
Gross domestic product at factor cost / basic prices	9 251 863	11 243 875	13 734 334	15 132 092	15 408 269	15 986 502	15 348 382	16 067 685	17 507 617	Produit intérieur brut aux couts des facteurs / prix de base
Plus: Indirect Taxes / taxes on products, less subsidies	716 162	747 689	854 636	1 077 506	1 239 650	1 242 096	1 353 736	1 339 141	1 398 943	Plus taxes indirectes/impôts sur les produits, moins les subventions
EXPENDITURE ON GROSS DOMESTIC PRODUCT AT CURRENT PURCHASER'S VALUES *ALGERIAN DINAR (MILLIONS)*										**EMPLOI DU PRODUIT INTÉRIEUR BRUT AUX PRIX COURANTS D'ACQUISION** *DINAR ALGÉRIEN (MILLIONS)*
Government final consumption	1 609 366	2 065 755	3 015 170	3 293 472	3 186 869	3 409 669	3 613 382	3 617 679	...	Consommation finale des administrations publiques
Private final consumption	3 743 918	4 115 566	4 548 234	5 210 992	5 769 783	6 264 725	6 853 952	7 446 007	...	Consommation finale privée
Gross fixed capital formation	3 811 419	4 350 922	4 620 307	4 992 412	5 690 894	6 446 692	7 041 677	7 467 342	...	Formation brute de capital fixe
Change in inventories	861 238	617 218	931 535	1 354 988	1 532 737	1 401 698	1 424 514	1 359 497	...	Variation des stocks
Exports of goods and services	3 525 855	4 610 103	5 658 617	5 979 809	5 528 757	5 206 330	3 872 627	3 655 740	...	Exportations de biens et services
Less imports of goods and services	3 583 772	3 768 000	4 184 893	4 622 075	5 061 122	5 500 516	6 104 033	6 139 437	...	Moins importations de biens et services
GDP at purchasers' values	9 968 025	11 991 564	14 588 970	16 209 598	16 647 919	17 228 598	16 702 119	17 406 826	18 906 560	PIB aux prix d'acquisition
GROSS DOMESTIC PRODUCT BY KIND OF ECONOMIC ACTIVITY AT CONSTANT PRICES *ANNUAL GROWTH RATES (%)*										**PRODUIT INTÉRIEUR BRUT PAR BRANCHE D'ACTIVITÉ ECONOMIQUE AUX PRIX CONSTANTS** *TAUX DE CROISSANCE ANNUEL (%)*
Agriculture, hunting , forestry and Fishing	21.1	4.9	11.6	7.2	8.2	2.5	6.0	1.8	1.2	Agriculture, chasse sylviculture et Pêche
Mining and quarrying	- 7.8	- 2.0	- 3.1	- 3.3	- 5.3	- 0.5	0.3	7.6	-3.0	Industries extractives
Manufacturing	9.7	2.7	3.6	3.8	3.6	2.9	3.0	2.8	3.5	Industries manufacturières
Electricity, gas & water	9.7	5.4	7.4	10.2	4.3	7.1	6.8	4.4	8.3	Electricité, gaz et eau
Construction	0.1	9.6	5.2	8.6	7.1	6.9	4.8	5.1	4.4	Bâtiments et travaux publics
Wholesale & retail trade, restaurants, hotels	10.5	7.6	7.9	5.4	9.1	9.7	4.7	...	2.8	Commerce de gros et de détail, restaurants et hôtels
Finance, insurance, real estate, etc.	8.9	10.6	16.5	6.1	4.8	6.5	4.7	4.1	4.8	Banques, assurances, affaires immobilières
Transport and communications	4.0	6.2	6.2	8.7	8.0	6.1	6.1	4.3	5.2	Transport(s) et communications
Public administration and defense	7.6	5.7	5.2	4.1	3.0	4.3	3.5	1.3	2.2	Administrations publiques et défense
Education	...	...	...	...	...	...	...	...	...	Education
Health And Social Work	...	...	...	...	...	...	...	...	...	Santé et Actions Sociales
Other services	3.3	4.1	5.3	2.4	4.8	4.7	7.3	6.9	2.2	Autres services
Less Imputed Service Charges	32.5	9.6	20.6	19.5	18.3	9.8	7.0	1.2	5.5	Moins Services d'intermédiation financière
Gross domestic product at factor cost / basic prices	1.0	3.6	3.2	1.8	1.6	3.7	3.4	4.0	1.8	Produit intérieur brut aux couts des facteurs / prix de base
Plus: Indirect Taxes / taxes on products, less subsidies	9.0	3.8	0.0	20.7	13.9	4.4	6.3	- 2.1	-4.0	Plus taxes indirectes/impôts sur les produits, moins les subventions
Gross domestic product at market prices	1.6	3.6	2.9	3.4	2.8	3.8	3.7	3.3	1.6	Produit intérieur brut aux prix du marché
EXPENDITURE ON GROSS DOMESTIC PRODUCT AT CONSTANT PURCHASERS' VALUES *ANNUAL GROWTH RATES (%)*										**EMPLOIS DU PRODUIT INTÉRIEUR BRUT AUX PRIX CONSTANTS D'ACQUISION** *TAUX DE CROISSANCE ANNUEL (%)*
Government final consumption	8.5	5.8	9.8	2.8	0.8	1.1	3.1	1.3	...	Consommation finale des administrations publiques
Private final consumption	6.1	5.6	6.0	4.9	4.9	4.3	6.0	- 2.1	...	Consommation finale privée
Gross fixed capital formation	8.8	7.0	2.9	7.2	8.6	6.4	5.7	3.5	...	Formation brute de capital fixe
Exports of goods and services	- 10.1	...	- 2.7	- 3.8	- 5.7	0.2	0.6	7.9	...	Exportations de biens et services
Less imports of goods and services	12.8	4.5	- 4.6	13.8	9.8	8.4	6.4	- 3.0	...	Moins importations de biens et services

III INFLATION

	2009	2010	2011	2012	2013	2014	2015	2016	2017	
Annual growth rates (%)										**Taux de croissance annuel (%)**
All item	5.7	3.9	4.5	8.9	3.3	2.9	4.8	6.4	5.6	Ensemble
of which:										dont:
Food and non-alcoholic beverages	8.2	4.2	4.2	12.2	3.2	3.9	4.7	3.4	5.0	Alimentation et boissons non alcoolisés
Alcoholic beverages, tobacco and narcotics	...	...	...	...	...	...	...	...	...	Boissons alcoolisées et tabacs
Clothing and footwear	0.4	2.7	3.7	5.8	7.8	7.1	8.7	13.7	8.9	Habillement et chaussures
Housing, water, electricity, gas and other fuels	2.7	1.9	1.4	4.5	1.6	1.3	1.3	6.4	2.3	Logement, eau, électricité, gaz et autres combustibles
Furnishings, household equipment and routine household maintenance	1.8	3.5	3.5	3.9	2.7	3.6	4.4	5.3	4.2	Meubles, articles de ménage et entretien courant
Health	3.4	2.8	4.4	4.3	4.1	4.4	6.1	6.6	5.7	Santé
Transport	3.6	2.5	3.0	4.5	5.6	- 1.1	3.7	11.7	4.7	Transport
Communication	...	...	...	...	...	...	...	...	...	Communication
Recreation and culture	6.0	- 0.1	0.6	2.9	- 2.9	8.9	4.9	- 1.4	2.9	Loisirs et culture
Education	...	...	...	...	...	...	...	...	...	Enseignement
Restaurants and hotels	7.9	11.0	14.9	13.4	0.8	0.6	6.8	10.8	11.1	Restaurants et hôtels
Miscellaneous goods and services	...	...	...	...	...	...	...	...	...	Biens et Services divers

ALGÉRIE

IV AGRICULTURAL PRODUCTION - PRODUCTION AGRICOLE

	2009	2010	2011	2012	2013	2014	2015	2016	2017	
TONNES (THOUSAND)										**Tonnes (milliers)**
Potatoes	2 636	3 300	3 862	4 219	4 887	4 674	4 540	4 783	...	Pommes de terre
Wheat	2 953	2 605	2 911	3 432	3 299	2 436	2 657	2 440	...	Blé
Dates	601	645	725	789	848	934	990	1 030	...	Dattes
Olives	475	311	611	394	579	483	654	697	...	Olives
Tomatoes	1 023	1 480	1 477	1 649	1 883	2 159	2 455	2 516	...	Tomates

V MINING PRODUCTION - PRODUCTION MINIERE

	2009	2010	2011	2012	2013	2014	2015	2016	2017	
	...		...	...	...	...	...	...		
	...	...	...	...	...	...	...	...		
Iron ores and concentrates - Production, metric tons (thousands)	1 307	1 474	1 718	1 784	1 067	911	944	608	...	"Minerais de fer et leurs concentrés

- Production, tonnes métriques (milliers)"

	2009	2010	2011	2012	2013	2014	2015	2016	2017	
Total electricity generation (GWh)	42 769	42 834	51 313	56 985	60 121	64 527	67 111	69 914	...	Production électrique totale (GWh)
of which										dont
Production of electricity from fossil fuels (GWh)	42 427	42 663	51 062	56 776	59 560	63 988	66 553	69 331	...	Production d'électricité à partir de combustibles fossiles (GWh)
Production of hydro electricity (GWh)	342	171	173	126	330	254	260	267	...	Production d'électricité d'origine hydraulique (GWh)
Production of electricity from solar, wind, tide, wave and other sources (GWh)	...	...	78	83	231	285	298	316	...	Production d'électricité d'origine solaire, éolienne, marée motrice et autres (GWh)

VII TOURISM AND INFRASTRUCTURE - TOURISME ET INFRASTUCTURE

	2009	2010	2011	2012	2013	2014	2015	2016	2017	
VII-1 Tourism										**VII-1 Tourisme**
International tourist arrivals (thousands)	1 912	2 070	2 395	2 634	2 733	2 301	1 710	2 039	2 102	Arrivées de touristes internationaux (milliers)
Rooms in hotels and similar establishments (thousands)	...	...	...	...	...	...	...	...	...	Chambres d'hôtels et établissements assimilés (milliers)
Overnight stays (thousands)	7 400	7 976	11 614	11 041	11 713	9 875	9 886	13 255	14 161	Nuitées (milliers)
Tourism receipts (US$ thousand)	246 000	219 800	209 100	217 000	249 400	257 800	307 500	203 200	207 295	Recettes touristiques (milliers de $ EU)
Total contribution to GDP (%)	7.7	6.9	6.4	6.8	7.2	6.8	7.1	6.9	6.8	Contribution totale au PIB (%)
Total contribution to Employment (%)	6.1	5.4	5.3	6.0	6.2	5.9	6.2	6.0	6.0	Contribution totale à l'emploi (%)
VII-2 Infrastructure										**VII-2 Infrastructure**
Paved road (% of total)	74.0	77.1	...	...	...	...	...	...	...	Routes asphaltées (% du total)
Total network (Railways-km)	...	...	4 691	4 691	4 691	4 175	...	...	...	Réseau total voies ferrées-Km
Main telephone lines (per 100 inhabitants)	7.1	7.9	8.1	8.5	8.0	7.8	8.0	8.2	...	Lignes téléphoniques fixes (pour 100 habitants)
Mobile cellular subscribers (per 100 inhabitants)	90.0	88.4	94.3	97.5	100.8	108.4	106.4	117.0	...	Abonnés aux téléphones mobiles (pour 100 habitants)
Internet users per 100 inhabitants	11.2	12.5	14.9	18.2	22.5	29.5	38.2	42.9	...	Utilisateurs Internet par 100 Habitants
Fixed (wired)-broadband subscriptions per 100 inhabitants	2.2	2.4	2.6	3.0	3.3	4.0	5.6	6.9	...	Abonnements à l'Internet fixe (filaire) à large bande pour 100 habitants, par débit

VIII EXTERNAL TRADE - COMMERCE EXTERIEUR

	2009	2010	2011	2012	2013	2014	2015	2016	2017	
US$ (MILLIONS) EXPORTS, FOB										**$ E.U (MILLIONS) EXPORTATIONS, FÀB**
Exports - Total	45 194	57 051	73 436	71 866	65 998	60 388	34 796	29 992	...	Exportations - Total
Exports to Africa	1 423	1 839	2 398	2 914	3 490	3 589	2 134	1 530	...	Exportations vers l'Afrique
Main products										**Principaux produits**
Liquefied propane and butane	3 329	5 071	5 503	4 784	5 055	5 540	2 804	2 318	...	Propane liquéfié et butane
Natural gas, whether or not liquefied	14 526	17 391	19 776	22 217	20 621	18 240	11 914	9 444	...	Gaz naturel, même liquéfié
Petroleum oils or bituminous minerals > 70 % oil	4 976	8 282	11 071	9 922	7 770	12 008	6 190	5 062	...	Huiles de pétrole ou de minéraux bitumineux> 70% d'huile
Petroleum oils, oils from bitumin. materials, crude	21 284	24 779	35 028	32 879	30 380	22 018	11 891	11 332	...	Huiles de pétrole, huiles de bitume. matériaux bruts
Residual petroleum products, n.e.s., related mater.	314	559	835	909	1 068	884	527	396	...	Produits pétroliers résiduels, n.d.a.
Main destinations										**Principales destinations**
France	4 424	3 776	6 534	6 124	6 786	6 456	4 578	3 424	...	France
Italy	5 702	8 779	10 441	11 513	9 017	8 190	5 264	5 208	...	Italie
Spain	5 402	5 909	7 186	7 809	10 344	9 253	6 164	3 879	...	Espagne
United Kingdom	1 142	1 290	2 855	3 668	7 202	5 073	2 430	1 061	...	Royaume-Uni
United States	10 365	13 827	15 127	10 778	5 341	4 779	2 211	3 866	...	États-Unis
IMPORTS, CIF										
Imports - Total	39 258	41 000	47 220	50 369	54 910	58 618	51 803	47 091	...	Importations - Total (millions)
Imports from Africa	1 332	1 298	1 721	1 932	2 108	1 759	1 539	1 422	...	Importations en provenance de l'Afrique
Main products										**Principaux produits**
Iron & steel bars, rods, angles, shapes & sections	1 960	1 492	2 447	2 746	2 559	2 701	2 063	1 513	...	Barres, tiges, cornières et profilés en fer et en acier
Motor vehic. for transport of goods, special purpo.	1 835	1 554	1 807	2 579	2 582	2 525	1 693	1 020	...	Véhicule à moteur pour le transport de marchandises, spécial.
Motor vehicles for the transport of persons	1 524	1 456	2 109	3 909	3 729	2 965	2 042	1 352	...	Véhicules à moteur pour le transport de personnes
Petroleum oils or bituminous minerals > 70 % oil	91	327	489	4 436	3 770	2 191	1 985	1 337	...	Huiles de pétrole ou de minéraux bitumineux> 70% d'huile
Wheat (including spelt) and meslin, unmilled	1 830	1 252	2 847	2 129	2 123	2 373	2 400	1 790	...	Blé (y compris l'épeautre) et méteil, non moulu
Main origin										**Principales provenances**
China	4 751	4 605	4 737	5 965	6 828	8 244	8 260	8 410	...	Chine
France	6 160	6 120	7 115	6 433	6 258	6 336	5 439	4 774	...	France
Germany	2 765	2 382	2 558	2 591	2 861	3 802	3 431	3 025	...	Allemagne
Italy	3 660	4 113	4 675	5 191	5 653	5 044	4 860	4 646	...	Italie
Spain	2 971	2 644	3 427	4 343	5 084	5 028	3 953	3 566	...	Espagne

	2009	2010	2011	2012	2013	2014	2015	2016	2017	
IX-1 MONETARY STATISTICS *ALGERIAN DINAR (MILLIONS)*										**IX-1 STATISTIQUES MONÉTAIRES** *DINAR ALGÉRIEN (MILLIONS)*
Money supply (M1)	7 292 695	8 280 740	9 929 188	11 015 135	11 941 508	13 663 912	13 704 511	13 816 309	15 145 065	Masse monétaire (M1)
Quasi-money	2 229 057	2 524 281	2 732 489	3 194 644	3 615 397	4 023 377	4 365 437	4 343 076	4 582 295	Quasi-monnaie
of which demand deposit	...	...	...	...	...	...	...	...	...	dont Monnaie scripturale
Net foreign assets	10 758 043	11 871 426	13 795 216	14 810 906	15 099 127	15 601 795	15 221 757	12 442 768	11 057 964	Avoirs extérieurs nets
Domestic credit	- 892 479	- 794 639	- 658 563	- 342 269	500 028	3 101 592	6 680 141	9 530 710	12 641 847	Crédit intérieur
of which claims on private sector	-4 079 485	-4 143 004	-4 458 146	-4 707 890	-4 741 928	-3 502 757	- 702 256	1 499 475	3 653 107	dont créances sur le secteur privé
of which claims on government sector, net	1 621 380	1 823 706	2 000 952	2 273 446	2 746 556	3 161 789	3 628 614	4 006 614	4 606 150	dont créances nettes sur le gouvernement
International reserves (millions US$)	148 910	162 220	182 224	190 661	192 357	177 400	142 644	112 930	93 046	Réserves internationales (millions $EU)
Average exchange rate (National currency per US$)	73	74	73	78	79	81	101	109	111	Taux de change (moyen) (monnaie nationale par $ EU)
IX-2 PUBLIC FINANCE *ALGERIAN DINAR (MILLIONS)*										**IX-2 FINANCES PUBLIQUES** *DINAR ALGÉRIEN (MILLIONS)*
Total Revenues and Grants	3 676 000	4 392 800	5 790 100	6 339 600	5 975 500	5 738 400	5 103 100	5 110 200	...	Recettes totales et dons
Direct taxes (on income, profits)	462 100	561 700	684 700	862 288	823 110	881 254	1 034 468	1 103 800	...	Taxes directes
Domestic indirect taxes revenues	478 500	514 700	572 600	652 000	741 600	768 500	824 300	857 200	...	Taxes Indirectes
Trade taxes	170 200	181 900	222 400	338 209	403 771	370 906	411 156	367 396	...	Taxes sur le commerce extérieur
Other taxes	2 448 500	2 944 600	4 027 100	4 240 689	3 758 623	3 459 178	2 458 222	1 942 973	...	Autres taxes
Other revenues	116 700	189 800	283 300	246 353	248 375	258 440	374 893	838 790	...	Autres recettes
Grants	...	100	...	61	21	122	61	41	...	Dons
Total Expenditures and Net Lending	4 389 100	4 571 100	5 958 900	7 058 300	6 024 200	6 995 700	7 656 300	7 297 600	...	Dépenses totales et prêts nets
Current expenditure	2 262 600	2 625 800	3 841 700	4 748 637	4 010 297	4 338 560	4 505 924	4 283 037	...	Dépenses courantes
Wages and Salaries	910 900	1 212 600	1 774 700	1 988 427	1 855 293	2 007 230	2 170 918	2 279 500	...	Rémunérations et salaires
Other purchases of goods and services	112 500	121 700	129 700	135 152	149 093	161 945	179 688	137 807	...	Achat de biens et services
Other current expenditure	130 700	151 300	163 200	185 328	226 475	218 358	223 042	198 000	...	Autres dépenses courantes
Current transfers	1 108 500	1 140 200	1 774 100	2 439 730	1 779 436	1 951 027	1 932 276	1 667 730	...	Transferts courants
Interest payments	37 400	33 200	37 700	42 024	44 208	37 798	42 554	46 833	...	Intérêts
Capital expenditure	1 946 300	1 807 900	1 974 400	2 275 539	1 892 595	2 501 442	3 039 322	2 921 930	...	Dépenses d'équipement
Net lending	142 800	104 200	105 100	- 7 900	77 100	117 900	68 500	45 800	...	Prêts nets
Fiscal balance	- 713 100	- 178 300	- 168 800	- 718 700	- 48 700	-1 257 300	-2 553 200	-2 187 400	...	Solde global y compris les dons
IX-3 BALANCE OF PAYMENTS *ALGERIAN DINAR (MILLIONS)*										**IX-3 BALANCE DES PAIEMENTS** *DINAR ALGÉRIEN (MILLIONS)*
Trade balance	565	1 355	1 890	1 550	784	19	- 1 809	- 2 197	...	Balance commerciale
Services Balance	- 630	- 619	- 639	- 550	- 552	- 656	- 755	- 802	...	Balance des services
Net primary income	- 95	- 26	- 154	- 300	- 359	- 388	- 434	- 173	...	Revenus primaires nets
Compensation of employees	...	...	...	...	...	...	...	...	...	Rémunération des salariés
Investment income	...	...	...	...	...	...	...	...	...	Revenus des investissements
Net secondary income	191	197	193	245	221	259	256	308	...	Revenus secondaires nets
Net official transfers	...	...	...	...	...	...	...	...	...	Transferts officiels nets
Workers' remittances	...	...	...	...	...	...	...	...	...	Envois de fonds des travailleurs
Other private transfers	...	...	...	...	...	...	...	...	...	Autres transferts privés
Current account balance	31	906	1 290	945	94	- 766	- 2 742	- 2 864	...	Solde du compte courant
Capital and financial account	281	291	70	72	72	165	- 96	236	...	Comptes de capital et financier
Capital account	...	-	-	- 1	...	...	...	...	...	Compte de capital
Financial account	281	291	70	73	72	165	- 96	236	...	Compte financier
Errors and omissions	- 31	- 48	113	- 83	- 158	123	74	- 196	...	Erreurs et omissions
Overall balance	281	1 150	1 473	934	9	- 479	- 2 763	- 2 824	...	Balance générale

ALGÉRIE

X DEBT AND FINANCIAL FLOWS - DETTE ET FLUX FINANCIERS

	2009	2010	2011	2012	2013	2014	2015	2016	2017	
X-1 DEBT *US $ (MILLIONS)*										**X-1 DETTE EXTÉRIEURE** *$ E.U (MILLIONS)*
Total external debt	5 587	5 458	4 310	3 592	3 296	3 635	3 020	3 925	4 265	Dette extérieure totale
Private	3 420	3 432	2 502	2 297	2 105	2 682	2 264	2 348	...	Privée
Public	2 167	2 026	1 808	1 295	1 191	953	756	1 576	...	Publique
Total external debt service	955	618	1 272	987	470	243	412	181	...	Service de la dette extérieure
Present value of external debt	...	...	...	...	...	...	...	955	...	Valeur actuelle de la dette extérieure
Total government domestic debt, National currency (millions)	...	1 107	1 215	1 312	1 173	1 239			...	Dette publique intérieure
X-2 FINANCIAL FLOWS *US $ (MILLIONS)*										**X-2 FLUX FINANCIERS** *$ E.U (MILLIONS)*
Net Foreign Direct Investment Inflows	2 754	2 301	2 580	1 499	1 684	1 507	- 584	1 546	...	Investissements étranger direct (flux nets entrants)
Main origin of FDI inflows										**Principales origines de l'IDE entrant:**
United States	476	618	582	- 753	...	...	...	...	...	États-Unis
Italy	116	189	1 646	1 685	...	...	...	...	...	Italie
France	308	196	361	266	...	...	...	...	...	France
Spain	198	91	...	78	...	...	...	...	...	Espagne
Germany	54	57	...	...	...	...	...	...	...	Allemagne
African countries	160	51	...	...	...	...	...	...	...	Pays africains
Net total official development assistance	302	201	193	147	203	161	87	157	...	Aide publique au développement (nette totale)
Main origin of net ODA										**Principales origines de l'APD nette**
France	94	70	73	58	72	61	53	...	...	France
Spain	54	10	- 1	2	- 16	1	- 27	...	...	Espagne
Italy	4	5	6	1	-	1	1	...	...	Italie
Belgium	11	10	7	7	8	7	-	...	...	Belgique
United Arab Emirates	11	- 3	...	- 5	...	...	...	...	...	Emirates Arabes

ALGERIA

SOURCES AND NOTES - SOURCES ET NOTES

External trade - Total exports, fob: UNCTAD	Commerce exterieur - Exportation, fab: CNUCED
External trade - Total import, cif: UNCTAD	Commerce exterieur - Imporations, caf: CNUCED
ODA: OECD	APD: OCDE
Monetary statistics: IMF	Statistiques monétaires: FMI
National Accounts: 2014 Semi-Final-2015-2016:provisional	Comptes nationaux: 2014 Semi-Définitive-2015-2016:provisoire
National Accounts : The annual data for 2017 are previsions based on the sum of four quarters of 2017.	Comptes Nationaux: Les données de L'année 2017 sont estimées à partir des comptes trimestriels
Poverty: World Bank	Pauvreté: Banque mondiale

AREA (km2)		1246700		**SUPERFICIE (KM2)**
CAPITAL CITY	Luanda		Luanda	**CAPITALE**
CURRENCY	Angolan Kwanza		Kwanza angolais	**MONNAIE**

I SOCIAL AND DEMOGRAPHIC INDICATORS — INDICATEURS DEMOGRAPHIQUES ET SOCIAUX

	Year Année	Value Valeur	Charts Graphiques	
Population				**Population**
Population ('000)	2015	25 022.0		Population ('000)
Female (%)	2015	50.4		Féminine (%)
Urban (%)	2015	40.2		Urbaine (%)
Average annual growth rate	2015	3.2		Taux de croissance annuel
Active population ('000)	2015	8 276.9		Population active ('000)
Population by age group ('000)				Population par groupe d'âge ('000)
0-14 years	2015	11 923.1		0-14 ans
15-64 years	2015	12 520.0		15-64 ans
65+ years	2015	578.9		65+ ans
Economically active population in agriculture (%)	2015	80.6		Participation de la population active agricole (%)
Crude birth rate	2015	45.0		Taux brut de natalité
Crude death rate	2015	13.4		Taux brut de mortalité
Total fertility rate	2015	6.0		Indice synthétique de fécondité
Life expectancy at birth - Total (years)	2015	52.7		Espérance de vie à la naissance - Totale (années)
Dependency ratio - Total (%)	2015	99.9		Taux de dépendance - Total (%)
Health				**Santé**
Percentage of children under-five and underweight	2007	15.6		% d'enfants de moins de cinq ans avec insuffisance pondérale
Prevalence of undernourishment	2015	14.2		Prévalence de la malnutrition
Under five mortality rate (per 1 000 live births)	2015	156.9		Taux de mortalité de moins de 5 ans (les deux sexes, pour 1000)
Infant mortality rate (per 1 000 live births)	2015	96.0		Taux de mortalité infantile (les deux sexes) par 1000
Neonatal mortality rate (per 1 000 live births)	2015	48.7		Le taux de mortalité néonatale (pour 1000 naissances vivantes)
Percentage of children provided the vaccines :				Pourcentage d'enfants vaccinés :
BCG	2014	81.0		BCG
DPT3	2014	80.0		DTC3
Polio	2012	88.0		polio
Measles	2014	85.0		rougeole
Percentage of mothers provided at least one antenatal care (%)	2009	67.6		Pourcentage de mères ayant au moins reçu un soin prénatal (%)
Percentage of deliveries attended by skilled health personnel	2007	47.3		% d'accouchements assistés par un personnel de santé qualifié
Number of doctors (per 10,000 population)	2009	1.7		Nombre de médecins (pour 10.000 habitants)
Number of nurses (per 10,000 population)	2009	16.6		Nombre d'infirmiers (pour 10.000 habitants)
Hospital beds - Total (per 10,000 population)	2005	8.0		Nombre de lits d'hôpitaux - Total (pour 10 000)
Births registered (per 1,000)	2015	45.0		Naissances enregistrées (pour 1000)
Deaths registered (per 1,000)	2015	13.4		Décès enregistrés (pour 1000)
Budget allocation to health (%)	2013	7.7		Dépenses publiques consacrées à la santé (% du budget)
Education				**Education**
Enrolment in primary education (000)	2011	5 026.8		Scolarisation dans le primaire (000)
Female	2011	1 956.0		Féminine
Enrolment in secondary education (000)	2011	885.0		Scolarisation dans le secondaire (000)
Female	2011	348.9		Féminine
Enrolment in tertiary education (000)	2013	218.7		Scolarisation dans le tertiaire (000)
Female	2013	98.1		Féminine
Literacy rate	2012	70.6		Taux d'alphabétisation (deux sexes)
Male	2012	82.5		Masculin
Female	2012	59.1		Féminin
Pupil teacher ratio - primary	...	...		Ratio élève-enseignant
Budget allocation to education (%)	2010	8.7		Dépenses publiques consacrées à l'enseignement (% du budget)
Poverty				**Pauvreté**
GNI per capita, PPP (current int. $)	2016	6090.0		RNB par habitant, ($ PPA inter. courants)
Human Poverty Index (HPI-1) Value (%)	2007	37.2		Valeur de l'Indice de pauvreté (IPH-1) (%)
Population below Inter. poverty line ($2/ day) (%)	2008	30.1		Population sous le seuil inter. de pauvreté (2$/Jour) (%)
Share of income held by richest 10%	2008	32.3		% de revenu des 10% plus riches
Share of income held by poorest 10%	2008	2.1		% de revenu des 10% plus pauvres
GINI index	2008	42.7		Indice GINI

Population by age group - 2015

Population par groupe d'age - 2015

- 0-14 years
- 15-64 years
- 65+ years

2.3%
47.7%
50.0%

Percentage of children provided vaccines : - 2014

Pourcentage d'enfants vaccinés : - 2014

81.0   80.0   88.0   85.0

BCG / BCG   DPT3 / DTC3   Polio / polio (2012)   Measles / rougeole

Literacy rate (%) - 2012

Taux d'alphabétisation - 2012

82.5   59.1

■ Male ■ Female

GNI per capita, PPP (current international $)

RNB par habitant, ($ PPA internationaux courants)

5 560   5 890   6 130   6 250   6 090

2012   2013   2014   2015   2016

II NATIONAL ACCOUNTS — COMPTES NATIONAUX

	2009	2010	2011	2012	2013	2014	2015	2016	2017	
GROSS DOMESTIC PRODUCT BY KIND OF ECONOMIC ACTIVITY AT CURRENT PRICES *ANGOLAN KWANZA (MILLIONS)*										**PRODUIT INTÉRIEUR BRUT PAR BRANCHE D'ACTIVITÉ ÉCONOMIQUE AUX PRIX COURANTS** *KWANZA ANGOLAIS (MILLIONS)*
Agriculture, hunting , forestry and Fishing	369 287	478 605	616 997	745 926	863 526	1 168 277	1 375 265	...	...	Agriculture, chasse sylviculture et Pêche
Mining and quarrying	1 569 632	2 961 791	4 578 228	5 102 377	4 806 461	4 109 104	3 260 081	...	...	Industries extractives
Manufacturing	284 970	351 717	439 901	541 142	640 575	714 222	739 635	...	...	Industries manufacturières
Electricity, gas & water	38 687	42 580	43 860	47 987	59 670	61 368	71 421	...	...	Electricité, gaz et eau
Construction	563 885	699 352	851 469	1 303 450	1 574 395	1 809 187	1 811 230	...	...	Bâtiments et travaux publics
Wholesale & retail trade, restaurants, hotels	671 633	852 803	1 087 419	1 308 265	1 519 704	1 889 578	2 175 547	...	...	Commerce de gros et de détail, restaurants et hôtels
Finance, insurance, real estate, etc.	429 403	500 325	559 737	685 002	739 875	752 098	858 072	...	...	Banques, assurances, affaires immobilières
Transport and communications	299 927	342 542	498 422	556 772	630 814	706 218	626 441	...	...	Transport(s) et communications
Public administration and defense	764 125	817 429	1 030 556	1 217 430	1 426 946	1 764 890	1 570 856	...	...	Administrations publiques et défense
Education	...	...	...	...	...	...	...	...	...	Education
Health And Social Work	...	...	...	...	...	...	...	...	...	Santé et Actions Sociales
Other services	533 737	688 252	894 412	1 035 241	1 285 385	1 430 269	1 295 640	...	...	Autres services
Less Imputed Service Charges	- 111 407	- 117 861	- 152 838	- 151 781	- 172 357	- 158 134	- 222 352	...	...	Moins Services d'intermédiation financière
Gross domestic product at factor cost / basic prices	5 413 879	7 617 535	10 448 164	12 391 810	13 374 992	14 247 078	13 561 836	...	...	Produit intérieur brut aux couts des facteurs / prix de base
Plus: Indirect Taxes / taxes on products, less subsidies	136 109	84 117	52 778	- 166 860	- 179 988	76 781	262 338	...	...	Plus taxes indirectes/impôts sur les produits, moins les subventions
EXPENDITURE ON GROSS DOMESTIC PRODUCT AT CURRENT PURCHASER'S VALUES *ANGOLAN KWANZA (MILLIONS)*										**EMPLOI DU PRODUIT INTÉRIEUR BRUT AUX PRIX COURANTS D'ACQUISITION** *KWANZA ANGOLAIS (MILLIONS)*
Government final consumption	1 110 006	1 312 361	1 915 372	2 180 931	2 852 760	2 575 430	2 292 048	...	...	Consommation finale des administrations publiques
Private final consumption	2 326 616	2 757 192	3 568 220	4 328 855	4 954 724	6 368 388	7 231 425	...	...	Consommation finale privée
Gross fixed capital formation	2 386 960	2 174 946	2 771 199	3 261 617	3 451 813	3 936 197	3 935 742	...	...	Formation brute de capital fixe
Change in inventories	1 675	- 3 081	3 150	- 1 222	- 2 639	2 865	836 363	...	...	Variation des stocks
Exports of goods and services	3 276 974	4 739 596	6 370 921	6 838 637	6 696 464	6 402 765	4 151 399	...	...	Exportations de biens et services
Less imports of goods and services	3 552 242	3 279 363	4 127 920	4 383 867	4 758 118	4 961 785	4 622 804	...	...	Moins importations de biens et services
GDP at purchasers' values	5 549 989	7 701 652	10 500 942	12 224 950	13 195 004	14 323 859	13 824 174	...	...	PIB aux prix d'acquisition
GROSS DOMESTIC PRODUCT BY KIND OF ECONOMIC ACTIVITY AT CONSTANT PRICES *ANNUAL GROWTH RATES (%)*										**PRODUIT INTÉRIEUR BRUT PAR BRANCHE D'ACTIVITÉ ECONOMIQUE AUX PRIX CONSTANTS** *TAUX DE CROISSANCE ANNUEL (%)*
Agriculture, hunting , forestry and Fishing	7.8	8.5	9.2	7.1	4.0	23.1	10.1	...	...	Agriculture, chasse sylviculture et Pêche
Mining and quarrying	- 4.2	- 2.5	- 5.1	8.3	- 0.8	- 2.4	11.2	...	...	Industries extractives
Manufacturing	8.9	9.6	9.1	9.6	7.7	2.3	- 1.1	...	...	Industries manufacturières
Electricity, gas & water	8.0	9.8	3.9	10.3	25.3	3.6	10.6	...	...	Electricité, gaz et eau
Construction	5.9	12.6	8.4	23.9	16.1	4.1	- 2.2	...	...	Bâtiments et travaux publics
Wholesale & retail trade, restaurants, hotels	5.1	8.5	8.8	7.0	5.6	13.3	4.0	...	...	Commerce de gros et de détail, restaurants et hôtels
Finance, insurance, real estate, etc.	8.5	4.9	4.8	13.8	1.0	- 5.9	9.4	...	...	Banques, assurances, affaires immobilières
Transport and communications	12.4	8.3	39.1	8.0	12.0	10.5	- 12.9	...	...	Transport(s) et communications
Public administration and defense	49.6	2.8	6.6	3.1	9.4	9.8	- 7.0	...	...	Administrations publiques et défense
Education	...	...	...	...	...	...	...	...	...	Education
Health And Social Work	...	...	...	...	...	...	...	...	...	Santé et Actions Sociales
Other services	10.0	10.0	7.4	0.5	10.8	- 2.2	- 18.9	...	...	Autres services
Less Imputed Service Charges	13.1	- 7.1	13.1	- 12.3	5.3	- 16.2	46.9	...	...	Moins Services d'intermédiation financière
Gross domestic product at factor cost / basic prices	5.7	5.2	4.1	8.8	5.0	3.9	0.9	...	...	Produit intérieur brut aux couts des facteurs / prix de base
Plus: Indirect Taxes / taxes on products, less subsidies	- 123.0	13.4	- 48.9	- 51.5	7.8	- 6.6	10.9	...	...	Plus taxes indirectes/impôts sur les produits, moins les subventions
Gross domestic product at market prices	3.4	5.4	3.5	8.5	5.0	4.1	0.9	...	...	Produit intérieur brut aux prix du marché
EXPENDITURE ON GROSS DOMESTIC PRODUCT AT CONSTANT PURCHASERS' VALUES *ANNUAL GROWTH RATES (%)*										**EMPLOIS DU PRODUIT INTÉRIEUR BRUT AUX PRIX CONSTANTS D'ACQUISITION** *TAUX DE CROISSANCE ANNUEL (%)*
Government final consumption	- 9.2	4.5	27.2	0.6	21.4	- 17.5	- 8.8	...	...	Consommation finale des administrations publiques
Private final consumption	19.1	5.4	10.2	9.8	8.3	12.7	3.0	...	...	Consommation finale privée
Gross fixed capital formation	9.2	- 8.9	10.3	7.3	1.7	3.3	- 2.3	...	...	Formation brute de capital fixe
Exports of goods and services	- 2.7	- 2.4	- 5.1	5.2	- 1.2	0.7	- 14.7	...	...	Exportations de biens et services
Less imports of goods and services	- 0.5	- 11.7	11.0	- 0.1	4.4	- 5.2	- 23.9	...	...	Moins importations de biens et services

III INFLATION

	2009	2010	2011	2012	2013	2014	2015	2016	2017	
Annual growth rates (%)										**Taux de croissance annuel (%)**
All item	13.7	14.5	13.5	10.3	8.8	7.3	9.2	30.7	29.8	Ensemble
of which:										dont:
Food and non-alcoholic beverages	...	...	...	...	...	...	...	...	...	Alimentation et boissons non alcoolisés
Alcoholic beverages, tobacco and narcotics	...	...	...	...	...	...	...	...	...	Boissons alcoolisées et tabacs
Clothing and footwear	...	...	...	...	...	...	...	...	...	Habillement et chaussures
Housing, water, electricity, gas and other fuels	...	...	...	...	...	...	...	...	...	Logement, eau, électricité, gaz et autres combustibles
Furnishings, household equipment and routine household maintenance	...	...	...	...	...	...	...	...	...	Meubles, articles de ménage et entretien courant
Health	...	...	...	...	...	...	...	...	...	Santé
Transport	...	...	...	...	...	...	...	...	...	Transport
Communication	...	...	...	...	...	...	...	...	...	Communication
Recreation and culture	...	...	...	...	...	...	...	...	...	Loisirs et culture
Education	...	...	...	...	...	...	...	...	...	Enseignement
Restaurants and hotels	...	...	...	...	...	...	...	...	...	Restaurants et hôtels
Miscellaneous goods and services	...	...	...	...	...	...	...	...	...	Biens et Services divers

IV AGRICULTURAL PRODUCTION - PRODUCTION AGRICOLE

TONNES (THOUSAND)	2009	2010	2011	2012	2013	2014	2015	2016	2017	Tonnes (milliers)
Cassava	12 828	13 859	14 334	10 636	16 412	7 639	7 727	9 981	...	Manioc
Bananas	1 985	2 048	2 646	2 991	3 095	3 483	3 595	3 858	...	Bananes
Maize	983	987	1 045	645	1 200	1 929	1 933	1 831	...	Maïs
Cabbages and other brassicas	970	1 073	1 262	454	1 549	1 687	1 878	1 500	...	Choux et autres brassicacée
Beans, dry	823	841	841	654	670	671	669	721	...	Haricots secs

V MINING PRODUCTION - PRODUCTION MINIERE

	2009	2010	2011	2012	2013	2014	2015	2016	2017	
	...	...	...	...	...	...	...	...	...	
	...	...	...	...	...	...	...	...	...	
	...	...	...	...	...	...	...	...	...	

VI ENERGY - ENERGIE

	2009	2010	2011	2012	2013	2014	2015	2016	2017	
Total electricity generation (GWh) of which	4 172	5 448	5 654	6 000	6 370	6 762	7 180	...	...	Production électrique totale (GWh) dont
Production of electricity from fossil fuels (GWh)	999	1 745	1 644	1 710	1 778	1 849	1 923	...	...	Production d'électricité à partir de combustibles fossiles (GWh)
Production of hydro electricity (GWh)	3 173	3 703	4 007	4 287	4 588	4 909	5 252	...	...	Production d'électricité d'origine hydraulique (GWh)
Production of electricity from solar, wind, tide, wave and other sources (GWh)	...	...	3	3	4	4	5	...	...	Production d'électricité d'origine solaire, éolienne, marée motrice et autres (GWh)

VII TOURISM AND INFRASTRUCTURE - TOURISME ET INFRASTUCTURE

	2009	2010	2011	2012	2013	2014	2015	2016	2017	
VII-1 Tourism										**VII-1 Tourisme**
International tourist arrivals (thousands)	366	425	481	528	650	595	592	397	457	Arrivées de touristes internationaux (milliers)
Rooms in hotels and similar establishments (thousands)	...	...	...	...	9	11	11	13	...	Chambres d'hôtels et établissements assimilés (milliers)
Overnight stays (thousands)	1 899	2 856	1 436	1 429	1 754	1 769	1 612	1 203	1 380	Nuitées (milliers)
Tourism receipts (US$ thousand)	517 116	702 116	629 516	689 516	1 216 720	1 572 020	1 145 720	613 702	794 325	Recettes touristiques (milliers de $ EU)
Total contribution to GDP (%)	4.6	3.9	3.3	4.0	4.4	4.3	4.2	3.7	3.8	Contribution totale au PIB (%)
Total contribution to Employment (%)	4.6	4.0	3.1	3.7	4.1	3.7	3.6	3.2	3.3	Contribution totale à l'emploi (%)
VII-2 Infrastructure										**VII-2 Infrastructure**
Paved road (% of total)	...	...	...	...	...	...	...	...	...	Routes asphaltées (% du total)
Total network (Railways-km)	...	...	...	...	...	...	...	...	...	Réseau total voies ferrées-Km
Main telephone lines (per 100 inhabitants)	1.6	1.4	0.8	1.0	1.0	1.3	1.2	1.3	...	Lignes téléphoniques fixes (pour 100 habitants)
Mobile cellular subscribers (per 100 inhabitants)	42.8	48.1	59.8	61.4	61.9	63.5	60.8	55.3	...	Abonnés aux téléphones mobiles (pour 100 habitants)
Internet users per 100 inhabitants	2.3	2.8	3.1	6.5	8.9	10.2	12.4	13.0	...	Utilisateurs Internet par 100 Habitants
Fixed (wired)-broadband subscriptions per 100 inhabitants	...	...	...	...	...	...	0.7	0.5	...	Abonnements à l'Internet fixe (filaire) à large bande pour 100 habitants, par débit

VIII EXTERNAL TRADE - COMMERCE EXTERIEUR

US$ (MILLIONS) EXPORTS, FOB	2009	2010	2011	2012	2013	2014	2015	2016	2017	$ E.U (MILLIONS) EXPORTATIONS, FÁB
Exports - Total	40 639	52 612	66 427	70 863	67 713	58 672	33 048	27 196	...	Exportations - Total
Exports to Africa	1 559	1 737	1 787	3 039	1 793	1 993	1 377	1 002	...	Exportations vers l'Afrique
Main products										**Principaux produits**
Fish, fresh (live or dead), chilled or frozen	32	28	25	44	49	49	46	55	...	Poissons frais (vivants ou morts), réfrigérés ou congelés
Natural abrasives, n.e.s. (incl. industri. diamonds)	814	1 072	1 209	1 110	1 156	1 274	1 088	628	...	Abrasifs naturels, n.e.s. (y compris les diamants industriels)
Petroleum oils, oils from bitumin. materials, crude	39 262	50 789	64 140	68 863	65 464	56 440	31 394	26 077	...	Huiles de pétrole, huiles de bitume. matériaux bruts
Residual petroleum products, n.e.s., related mater.	530	722	1 052	845	1 041	897	501	420	...	Produits pétroliers résiduels, n.d.a.
Stone, sand and gravel	...	...	...	...	...	7	9	11	...	Pierre, sable et gravier
Main destinations										**Principales destinations**
China	15 954	20 963	24 361	33 710	31 947	27 527	14 276	12 640	...	Chine
TAIWAN, PROVINCE OF CHINA	1 155	2 699	5 386	4 700	4 007	2 329	1 409	1 239	...	TAÏWAN, PROVINCE DE CHINE
India	3 660	5 118	6 842	6 932	6 764	4 507	2 676	2 306	...	Inde
Spain	740	974	650	1 628	2 482	3 726	2 241	1 689	...	Espagne
United States	7 708	9 966	16 475	6 595	5 018	2 549	1 210	1 281	...	États-Unis
IMPORTS, CIF										
Imports - Total	23 919	18 143	20 791	23 717	26 756	28 753	20 693	12 538	...	Importations - Total (millions)
Imports from Africa	3 075	2 110	2 362	2 115	2 201	1 952	1 550	1 090	...	Importations en provenance de l'Afrique
Main products										**Principaux produits**
Civil engineering & contractors' plant & equipment	1 057	618	537	772	651	708	779	367	...	Génie civil et installations et équipements des entrepreneurs
Motor vehicles for the transport of persons	901	501	598	932	865	1 375	408	257	...	Véhicules à moteur pour le transport de personnes
Petroleum oils or bituminous minerals > 70 % oil	2 190	1 974	1 763	1 086	1 549	1 250	641	515	...	Huiles de pétrole ou de minéraux bitumineux> 70 % d'huile
Ships, boats & floating structures	1 222	643	1 525	734	2 473	1 330	1 543	324	...	Navires, bateaux et structures flottantes
Tubes, pipes & hollow profiles, fittings, iron, steel	764	723	478	660	642	847	739	362	...	Tubes, tuyaux et profilés creux, raccords, fer, acier
Main origin										**Principales provenances**
Brazil	1 668	1 011	1 097	1 241	1 314	1 391	824	636	...	Brazil
China	2 631	2 054	2 602	3 712	3 742	5 076	4 042	1 696	...	Chine
Republic of Korea	428	185	1 095	449	2 514	1 354	2 030	453	...	Corée, République de
Portugal	3 866	2 710	3 561	4 285	4 467	4 477	2 841	1 892	...	Portugal
United States	1 875	1 525	1 711	1 782	1 624	2 159	1 425	1 476	...	États-Unis

ANGOLA

IX FINANCIAL AND MONETARY STATISTICS - FINANCES ET STATISTIQUES MONETAIRES										
	2009	2010	2011	2012	2013	2014	2015	2016	2017	
IX-1 MONETARY STATISTICS *ANGOLAN KWANZA (MILLIONS)*										**IX-1 STATISTIQUES MONÉTAIRES** *KWANZA ANGOLAIS (MILLIONS)*
Money supply (M1)	2 543 723	2 678 230	3 673 111	3 853 027	4 398 099	5 110 116	5 711 899	6 519 777	7 602 483	Masse monétaire (M1)
Quasi-money	736 250	964 612	1 409 778	1 620 181	1 809 217	2 006 708	2 284 003	2 671 044	2 785 604	Quasi-monnaie
of which demand deposit	...	...	...	...	...	...	...	...	...	dont Monnaie scripturale
Net foreign assets	1 181 572	1 731 026	2 927 440	3 165 722	3 115 369	3 097 464	3 570 441	3 861 278	2 697 537	Avoirs extérieurs nets
Domestic credit	1 747 767	1 460 323	1 627 397	1 705 104	2 261 543	3 015 869	3 821 200	4 486 385	6 074 975	Crédit intérieur
of which claims on private sector	397 233	- 222 513	- 446 380	- 942 291	- 665 549	69 166	351 751	1 101 344	2 707 999	dont créances sur le secteur privé
of which claims on government sector, net	1 285 702	1 532 272	1 973 568	2 451 384	2 819 717	2 852 043	3 354 423	3 295 599	3 254 033	dont créances nettes sur le gouvernement
International reserves (millions US$)	12 879	18 441	27 164	31 659	31 998	27 735	24 419	24 441	17 926	Réserves internationales (millions \$EU)
Average exchange rate (National currency per US$)	79	92	94	95	97	98	120	164	166	Taux de change (moyen) (monnaie nationale par \$ EU)
IX-2 PUBLIC FINANCE *ANGOLAN KWANZA (MILLIONS)*										**IX-2 FINANCES PUBLIQUES** *KWANZA ANGOLAIS (MILLIONS)*
Total Revenues and Grants	2 069 733	3 295 490	4 775 555	5 055 160	4 847 000	4 402 100	3 365 700	3 085 900	...	Recettes totales et dons
Direct taxes (on income, profits)	197 736	238 970	318 562	324 700	501 000	544 800	663 700	757 100	...	Taxes directes
Domestic indirect taxes revenues	147 721	160 890	169 126	165 000	201 000	228 900	176 600	332 600	...	Taxes Indirectes
Trade taxes	106 311	101 941	112 287	111 300	124 400	182 000	130 500	152 600	...	Taxes sur le commerce extérieur
Other taxes	1 536 454	2 592 670	3 927 770	4 231 560	3 895 600	3 229 200	2 221 900	1 602 700	...	Autres taxes
Other revenues	79 266	199 093	245 987	221 000	123 200	215 700	171 800	239 600	...	Autres recettes
Grants	2 246	1 927	1 823	1 600	1 800	1 500	1 200	1 300	...	Dons
Total Expenditures and Net Lending	2 510 282	3 034 517	3 927 632	4 548 500	4 816 300	5 221 300	3 773 800	3 939 500	...	Dépenses totales et prêts nets
Current expenditure	1 663 872	2 076 981	2 839 983	3 087 500	3 338 100	3 518 700	2 789 100	2 866 700	...	Dépenses courantes
Wages and Salaries	665 000	713 759	877 330	1 031 000	1 154 800	1 318 900	1 390 000	1 462 600	...	Rémunérations et salaires
Other purchases of goods and services	383 000	625 000	1 037 000	1 305 000	1 228 300	1 249 400	787 200	732 600	...	Achat de biens et services
Other current expenditure	...	...	...	...	...	...	...	...	...	Autres dépenses courantes
Current transfers	615 872	738 222	925 654	751 500	955 000	950 400	611 900	671 500	...	Transferts courants
Interest payments	103 136	89 536	94 648	105 000	99 100	147 200	248 500	271 700	...	Intérêts
Capital expenditure	743 275	868 000	993 000	1 356 000	1 379 100	1 555 400	736 200	801 100	...	Dépenses d'équipement
Net lending	...	...	...	...	...	...	...	...	...	Prêts nets
Fiscal balance	- 440 549	260 973	847 923	506 660	30 700	- 819 200	- 408 100	- 853 600	...	Solde global y compris les dons
IX-3 BALANCE OF PAYMENTS *ANGOLAN KWANZA (MILLIONS)*										**IX-3 BALANCE DES PAIEMENTS** *KWANZA ANGOLAIS (MILLIONS)*
Trade balance	18 168	33 928	47 082	47 376	41 903	30 583	12 489	...	...	Balance commerciale
Services Balance	- 18 546	- 17 897	- 22 938	- 21 339	- 21 531	- 23 246	- 16 020	...	...	Balance des services
Net primary income	- 6 823	- 8 087	- 9 697	- 10 422	- 9 900	- 8 850	- 5 908	...	...	Revenus primaires nets
Compensation of employees	...	...	...	...	...	...	...	...	...	Rémunération des salariés
Investment income	...	...	...	...	...	...	...	...	...	Revenus des investissements
Net secondary income	- 370	- 438	- 1 362	- 1 762	- 2 124	- 2 211	- 834	...	...	Revenus secondaires nets
Net official transfers	...	...	...	...	...	...	...	...	...	Transferts officiels nets
Workers' remittances	...	...	...	...	...	...	...	...	...	Envois de fonds des travailleurs
Other private transfers	...	...	...	...	...	...	...	...	...	Autres transferts privés
Current account balance	- 7 572	7 506	13 085	13 853	8 348	- 3 722	- 10 273	...	...	Solde du compte courant
Capital and financial account	2 498	- 1 137	- 3 979	- 8 884	- 8 209	- 985	6 927	...	...	Comptes de capital et financier
Capital account	4	1	2	...	...	...	6	...	...	Compte de capital
Financial account	2 494	- 1 137	- 3 982	- 8 884	- 8 209	- 985	6 921	...	...	Compte financier
Errors and omissions	457	240	- 17	- 326	- 55	290	310	...	...	Erreurs et omissions
Overall balance	- 4 616	6 609	9 088	4 643	84	- 4 417	- 3 036	...	...	Balance générale

X DEBT AND FINANCIAL FLOWS - DETTE ET FLUX FINANCIERS

	2009	2010	2011	2012	2013	2014	2015	2016	2017	
X-1 DEBT *US $ (MILLIONS)*										**X-1 DETTE EXTÉRIEURE** *$ E.U (MILLIONS)*
Total external debt	15 213	17 021	20 260	21 663	29 471	34 685	36 858	42 621	43 968	Dette extérieure totale
Private	...	...	...	...	...	...	...	...	...	Privée
Public	15 213	17 021	20 260	21 663	29 471	34 685	36 858	42 621	...	Publique
Total external debt service	3 734	2 183	1 849	2 121	2 454	3 713	3 328	3 100	...	Service de la dette extérieure
Present value of external debt	...	...	...	...	...	...	...	29 612	...	Valeur actuelle de la dette extérieure
Total government domestic debt, National currency (millions)	...	...	...	...	...	...	...	...	...	Dette publique intérieure
X-2 FINANCIAL FLOWS *US $ (MILLIONS)*										**X-2 FLUX FINANCIERS** *$ E.U (MILLIONS)*
Net Foreign Direct Investment Inflows	2 205	12 157	14 124	15 078	14 346	16 543	16 176	14 364	...	Investissements étranger direct (flux nets entrants)
Main origin of FDI inflows	...									**Principales origines de l'IDE entrant:**
France	- 478	1 511	979	953	...	...	...	...	...	France
Norway	2 282	908	...	...	...	...	...	...	...	Norvège
United States	77	1 968	707	...	...	...	...	...	...	États-Unis
...	...	...	...	...	...	...	...	...	...	...
...	...	...	...	...	...	...	...	...	...	...
African countries	...	...	...	...	...	...	...	...	...	Pays africains
Net total official development assistance	239	235	193	244	286	235	380	207	...	Aide publique au développement (nette totale)
Main origin of net ODA										**Principales origines de l'APD nette**
Global Fund	10	26	4	11	38	-	...	...	...	Fonds Mondial
United States	42	54	65	77	61	59	61	53	...	États-Unis
Japan	7	38	12	14	15	8	197	5	...	Japon
Norway	18	13	13	12	10	12	7	8	...	Norvège
International Development Association [IDA]	20	4	7	36	47	40	22	26	...	International Development Association

ANGOLA

SOURCES AND NOTES - SOURCES ET NOTES

External trade - Total exports, fob: UNCTAD

External trade - Total import, cif: UNCTAD

ODA: OECD

Monetary statistics: IMF

National Accounts: 2014: Provisional Data -2015 : Preliminairy Data

Poverty: World Bank

Commerce exterieur - Exportation, fab: CNUCED

Commerce exterieur - Imporations, caf: CNUCED

APD: OCDE

Statistiques monétaires: FMI

Comptes nationaux: 2014: Données provisoires - 2015: Données préliminaires

Pauvreté: Banque mondiale

AREA (km2)		114760		SUPERFICIE (KM2)
CAPITAL CITY	Porto-Novo		Porto-Novo	CAPITALE
CURRENCY	CFA Franc		Franc CFA	MONNAIE

I SOCIAL AND DEMOGRAPHIC INDICATORS — INDICATEURS DEMOGRAPHIQUES ET SOCIAUX

	Year Année	Value Valeur	Charts Graphiques	
Population				**Population**
Population ('000)	2017	11 231.5		Population ('000)
Female (%)	2017	50.9		Féminine (%)
Urban (%)	2017	47.4		Urbaine (%)
Average annual growth rate	2017	2.8		Taux de croissance annuel
Active population ('000)	2015	4 461.5		Population active ('000)
Population by age group ('000)				Population par groupe d'âge ('000)
0-14 years	2017	5 061.2		0-14 ans
15-64 years	2017	5 856.3		15-64 ans
65+ years	2017	314.0		65+ ans
Economically active population in agriculture (%)	2015	37.4		Participation de la population active agricole (%)
Crude birth rate	2017	35.0		Taux brut de natalité
Crude death rate	2017	6.9		Taux brut de mortalité
Total fertility rate	2017	4.6		Indice synthétique de fécondité
Life expectancy at birth - Total (years)	2015	59.8		Espérance de vie à la naissance - Totale (années)
Dependency ratio - Total (%)	2017	91.8		Taux de dépendance - Total (%)
Health				**Santé**
Percentage of children under-five and underweight	2006	20.2		% d'enfants de moins de cinq ans avec insuffisance pondérale
Prevalence of undernourishment	2015	7.5		Prévalence de la malnutrition
Under five mortality rate (per 1 000 live births)	2015	99.5		Taux de mortalité de moins de 5 ans (les deux sexes, pour 1000)
Infant mortality rate (per 1 000 live births)	2015	64.2		Taux de mortalité infantile (les deux sexes) par 1000
Neonatal mortality rate (per 1 000 live births)	2016	29.3		Le taux de mortalité néonatale (pour 1000 naissances vivantes)
Percentage of children provided the vaccines :				Pourcentage d'enfants vaccinés :
BCG	2016	113.8		BCG
DPT3	2014	70.0		DTC3
Polio	2011	56.2		polio
Measles	2014	63.0		rougeole
Percentage of mothers provided at least one antenatal care (%)	2011	85.8		Pourcentage de mères ayant au moins reçu un soin prénatal (%)
Percentage of deliveries attended by skilled health personnel	2016	80.5		% d'accouchements assistés par un personnel de santé qualifié
Number of doctors (per 10,000 population)	2016	1.4		Nombre de médecins (pour 10.000 habitants)
Number of nurses (per 10,000 population)	2008	7.7		Nombre d'infirmiers (pour 10.000 habitants)
Hospital beds - Total (per 10,000 population)	2016	4.4		Nombre de lits d'hôpitaux - Total (pour 10 000)
Births registered (per 1,000)	2015	35.6		Naissances enregistrées (pour 1000)
Deaths registered (per 1,000)	2015	9.2		Décès enregistrés (pour 1000)
Budget allocation to health (%)	2013	10.7		Dépenses publiques consacrées à la santé (% du budget)
Education				**Education**
Enrolment in primary education (000)	2016	2 268.0		Scolarisation dans le primaire (000)
Female	2015	1 063.1		Féminine
Enrolment in secondary education (000)	2017	874.6		Scolarisation dans le secondaire (000)
Female	2017	374.9		Féminine
Enrolment in tertiary education (000)	2015	125.6		Scolarisation dans le tertiaire (000)
Female	2015	35.4		Féminine
Literacy rate	2006	28.7		Taux d'alphabétisation (deux sexes)
Male	2006	40.6		Masculin
Female	2006	18.4		Féminin
Pupil teacher ratio - primary	2012	44.0		Ratio élève-enseignant
Budget allocation to education (%)	2014	22.2		Dépenses publiques consacrées à l'enseignement (% du budget)
Poverty				**Pauvreté**
GNI per capita, PPP (current int. $)	2016	2170.0		RNB par habitant, ($ PPA inter. courants)
Human Poverty Index (HPI-1) Value (%)	2007	43.2		Valeur de l'Indice de pauvreté (IPH-1) (%)
Population below Inter. poverty line ($2/day) (%)	2011	53.1		Population sous le seuil inter. de pauvreté (2$/Jour) (%)
Share of income held by richest 10%	2011	34.5		% de revenu des 10% plus riches
Share of income held by poorest 10%	2011	2.5		% de revenu des 10% plus pauvres
GINI index	2011	43.4		Indice de GINI

Population by age group - 2017

Population par groupe d'age - 2017

- 0-14 years
- 15-64 years
- 65+ years

2.8% / 45.1% / 52.1%

Percentage of children provided vaccines : - 2014

Pourcentage d'enfants vaccinés : - 2014

BCG / BCG	DPT3 / DTC3	Polio / polio (2011)	Measles / rougeole
	70.0	56.2	63.0

Literacy rate (%) - 2006

Taux d'alphabétisation - 2006

40.6   18.4

- Male
- Female

GNI per capita, PPP (current international $)

RNB par habitant, ($ PPA internationaux courants)

2012	2013	2014	2015	2016
1 870	1 990	2 090	2 110	2 170

BENIN

II NATIONAL ACCOUNTS — COMPTES NATIONAUX

	2009	2010	2011	2012	2013	2014	2015	2016	2017	
GROSS DOMESTIC PRODUCT BY KIND OF ECONOMIC ACTIVITY AT CURRENT PRICES *CFA FRANC (MILLIONS)*										**PRODUIT INTÉRIEUR BRUT PAR BRANCHE D'ACTIVITÉ ÉCONOMIQUE AUX PRIX COURANTS** *FRANC CFA (MILLIONS)*
Agriculture, hunting , forestry and Fishing	796 500	784 900	842 300	928 300	955 900	982 900	1 023 849	1 181 500	1 209 300	Agriculture, chasse sylviculture et Pêche
Mining and quarrying	23 400	24 100	20 300	23 800	22 400	21 000	23 723	29 100	33 600	Industries extractives
Manufacturing	483 900	477 100	490 800	523 400	579 500	603 200	694 002	603 700	653 000	Industries manufacturières
Electricity, gas & water	14 900	20 000	25 400	33 300	33 500	35 300	38 637	43 600	47 200	Electricité, gaz et eau
Construction	217 100	243 000	259 900	261 400	277 100	311 200	348 245	347 100	418 700	Bâtiments et travaux publics
Wholesale & retail trade, restaurants, hotels	387 200	382 000	481 900	531 800	613 100	690 000	686 553	599 500	607 900	Commerce de gros et de détail, restaurants et hôtels
Finance, insurance, real estate, etc.	371 900	374 300	377 900	395 500	446 500	475 600	507 317	125 800	141 300	Banques, assurances, affaires immobilières
Transport and communications	272 400	295 100	317 600	467 300	508 100	506 500	509 784	552 000	570 900	Transport(s) et communications
Public administration and defense	256 100	288 800	304 400	338 200	365 800	383 000	409 556	471 100	477 900	Administrations publiques et défense
Education	157 900	168 600	181 900	190 700	206 100	216 300	228 219	259 300	263 300	Education
Health And Social Work	29 000	33 200	34 800	38 100	42 900	45 800	48 206	56 900	58 100	Santé et Actions Sociales
Other services	...	...	...	...	...	...	...	354 700	393 600	Autres services
Less Imputed Service Charges	- 49 000	- 52 800	- 51 500	- 54 500	- 71 200	- 80 100	- 90 833	- 79 000	- 87 300	Moins Services d'intermédiation financière
Gross domestic product at factor cost / basic prices	2 961 300	3 038 300	3 285 700	3 677 300	3 979 700	4 190 700	4 427 258	4 545 300	4 787 500	Produit intérieur brut aux couts des facteurs / prix de base
Plus: Indirect Taxes / taxes on products, less subsidies	390 031	413 944	401 680	466 656	521 253	543 388	574 955	538 700	588 800	Plus taxes indirectes/impôts sur les produits, moins les subventions
EXPENDITURE ON GROSS DOMESTIC PRODUCT AT CURRENT PURCHASER'S VALUES *CFA FRANC (MILLIONS)*										**EMPLOI DU PRODUIT INTÉRIEUR BRUT AUX PRIX COURANTS D'ACQUISITION** *FRANC CFA (MILLIONS)*
Government final consumption	565 300	581 800	604 300	693 600	749 000	754 300	863 575	857 400	897 800	Consommation finale des administrations publiques
Private final consumption	2 452 700	2 535 100	2 665 600	2 966 100	3 115 800	3 221 400	3 351 670	3 437 500	3 545 400	Consommation finale privée
Gross fixed capital formation	728 431	804 244	877 380	886 856	1 261 553	1 156 688	1 098 854	1 291 900	1 576 600	Formation brute de capital fixe
Change in inventories	5 600	- 5 700	12 500	51 900	21 200	25 300	25 300	70 700	- 53 600	Variation des stocks
Exports of goods and services	682 700	821 200	788 400	1 023 600	1 231 200	1 711 200	1 448 447	1 262 200	1 505 300	Exportations de biens et services
Less imports of goods and services	1 083 400	1 284 400	1 260 800	1 478 100	1 877 800	2 134 800	1 785 632	1 833 700	2 095 500	Moins importations de biens et services
GDP at purchasers' values	3 351 331	3 452 244	3 687 380	4 143 956	4 500 953	4 734 088	5 002 214	5 084 000	5 376 300	PIB aux prix d'acquisition
GROSS DOMESTIC PRODUCT BY KIND OF ECONOMIC ACTIVITY AT CONSTANT PRICES *ANNUAL GROWTH RATES (%)*										**PRODUIT INTÉRIEUR BRUT PAR BRANCHE D'ACTIVITÉ ÉCONOMIQUE AUX PRIX CONSTANTS** *TAUX DE CROISSANCE ANNUEL (%)*
Agriculture, hunting , forestry and Fishing	4.7	- 1.9	2.0	3.1	4.8	5.4	- 7.2	10.7	5.6	Agriculture, chasse sylviculture et Pêche
Mining and quarrying	- 1.7	2.6	0.8	- 6.7	- 18.9	- 200.0	- 258.9	- 6.1	4.5	Industries extractives
Manufacturing	- 1.1	- 0.7	- 2.0	0.2	6.9	10.6	8.2	4.6	6.7	Industries manufacturières
Electricity, gas & water	- 21.3	45.8	29.1	98.2	- 5.0	11.5	- 13.7	0.8	7.4	Electricité, gaz et eau
Construction	4.9	9.0	- 3.9	- 2.6	16.7	7.4	8.6	- 0.5	10.9	Bâtiments et travaux publics
Wholesale & retail trade, restaurants, hotels	- 5.4	- 4.6	19.7	- 0.2	10.4	2.9	-	3.4	3.8	Commerce de gros et de détail, restaurants et hôtels
Finance, insurance, real estate, etc.	65.1	12.9	- 10.0	32.3	1.1	47.4	9.5	8.9	9.0	Banques, assurances, affaires immobilières
Transport and communications	- 11.1	4.2	3.0	10.5	11.2	0.2	4.0	2.7	5.0	Transport(s) et communications
Public administration and defense	8.9	12.3	2.5	- 1.8	4.4	5.1	13.0	3.8	3.2	Administrations publiques et défense
Education	13.5	5.7	5.4	6.6	7.4	5.9	11.2	3.8	3.0	Education
Health And Social Work	- 30.9	8.7	4.2	12.0	6.5	18.0	13.0	3.8	3.0	Santé et Actions Sociales
Other services	6.9	3.1	7.6	4.6	-0.4	3.8	-4.3	4.0	6.8	Autres services
Less Imputed Service Charges	9.8	19.2	8.3	21.5	15.8	25.4	9.9	8.9	9.0	Moins Services d'intermédiation financière
Gross domestic product at factor cost / basic prices	2.1	1.8	3.7	3.8	6.3	5.9	2.6	5.1	5.7	Produit intérieur brut aux couts des facteurs / prix de base
Plus: Indirect Taxes / taxes on products, less subsidies	4.3	4.2	- 1.8	12.4	12.8	9.0	- 1.2	- 3.0	5.0	Plus taxes indirectes/impôts sur les produits, moins les subventions
Gross domestic product at market prices	2.3	2.1	3.0	4.8	7.2	6.4	2.1	4.0	5.6	Produit intérieur brut aux prix du marché
EXPENDITURE ON GROSS DOMESTIC PRODUCT AT CONSTANT PURCHASERS' VALUES *ANNUAL GROWTH RATES (%)*										**EMPLOIS DU PRODUIT INTÉRIEUR BRUT AUX PRIX CONSTANTS D'ACQUISITION** *TAUX DE CROISSANCE ANNUEL (%)*
Government final consumption	9.3	0.9	1.9	5.6	7.3	- 1.1	12.4	- 0.1	- 0.1	Consommation finale des administrations publiques
Private final consumption	1.9	1.8	2.3	2.6	3.1	5.4	0.7	3.9	4.3	Consommation finale privée
Gross fixed capital formation	7.3	9.6	2.6	0.4	45.5	13.5	- 3.8	- 0.3	21.3	Formation brute de capital fixe
Exports of goods and services	- 6.0	5.6	- 9.7	24.1	20.7	24.8	- 10.1	14.7	14.6	Exportations de biens et services
Less imports of goods and services	4.2	7.0	- 5.8	12.3	30.0	16.1	- 8.4	5.9	18.4	Moins importations de biens et services

III INFLATION

	2009	2010	2011	2012	2013	2014	2015	2016	2017	
Annual growth rates (%)										**Taux de croissance annuel (%)**
All item	0.4	2.1	2.7	6.7	1.0	- 1.1	0.3	- 0.9	0.1	Ensemble
of which:										dont:
Food and non-alcoholic beverages	2.4	4.0	5.7	4.7	2.6	- 0.8	0.5	- 0.5	- 0.2	Alimentation et boissons non alcoolisés
Alcoholic beverages, tobacco and narcotics	5.4	- 0.1	1.2	2.5	0.8	1.0	2.4	0.3	- 0.1	Boissons alcoolisées et tabacs
Clothing and footwear	- 0.1	2.4	1.4	0.5	0.8	0.6	1.2	- 0.9	- 0.6	Habillement et chaussures
Housing, water, electricity, gas and other fuels	4.7	5.4	2.1	1.6	- 0.5	1.0	- 0.1	- 0.8	1.1	Logement, eau, électricité, gaz et autres combustibles
Furnishings, household equipment and routine household maintenance	0.5	- 0.1	1.1	1.6	1.2	- 0.1	0.5	- 0.1	0.4	Meubles, articles de ménage et entretien courant
Health	0.6	1.8	0.3	1.4	0.3	- 0.1	- 0.3	0.5	0.5	Santé
Transport	- 7.1	3.0	2.4	31.7	- 0.3	- 7.1	- 1.1	- 4.2	-	Transport
Communication	- 14.7	- 3.3	- 5.9	- 2.0	-	- 0.8	- 1.4	- 0.2	...	Communication
Recreation and culture	- 2.8	0.2	0.6	- 0.4	- 0.7	- 0.1	0.2	- 0.3	- 0.3	Loisirs et culture
Education	2.2	- 1.5	0.6	0.3	-	- 0.3	0.5	0.1	- 0.4	Enseignement
Restaurants and hotels	5.8	0.3	2.7	3.0	0.9	1.6	1.4	0.5	-	Restaurants et hôtels
Miscellaneous goods and services	5.7	- 3.5	2.2	9.5	0.8	0.4	1.6	- 0.1	0.2	Biens et Services divers

BÉNIN

IV AGRICULTURAL PRODUCTION - PRODUCTION AGRICOLE

TONNES (THOUSAND)	2009	2010	2011	2012	2013	2014	2015	2016	2017	Tonnes (milliers)
Cassava	3 996	3 445	3 915	3 296	3 696	4 067	3 421	3 892	...	Manioc
Yams	2 374	2 624	2 934	2 739	3 178	3 221	2 650	3 041	...	Ignames
Maize	1 205	1 013	1 437	1 175	1 346	1 354	1 286	1 377	...	Maïs
Cottonseed	166	137	174	240	306	393	267	451	...	Graines de coton
Sorghum	123	157	158	134	115	100	130	130	...	Sorgho

V MINING PRODUCTION - PRODUCTION MINIERE

	2009	2010	2011	2012	2013	2014	2015	2016	2017	
	...	...	...	...	...	...	...	...	...	
	...	...	...	...	...	...	...	...	...	
Gold ores and concentrates - Production (Kilograms)	20	20	20	...	...	...	...	...	...	Minerais d'or et leurs concentrés - Production (Kilogrammes)

VI ENERGY - ENERGIE

	2009	2010	2011	2012	2013	2014	2015	2016	2017	
Total electricity generation (GWh) of which	140	152	155	162	162	299	627	...	...	Production électrique totale (GWh) dont
Production of electricity from fossil fuels (GWh)	138	150	153	160	160	290	592	...	...	Production d'électricité à partir de combustibles fossiles (GWh)
Production of hydro electricity (GWh)	1	1	1	1	1	1	1	...	...	Production d'électricité d'origine hydraulique (GWh)
Production of electricity from solar, wind, tide, wave and other sources (GWh)	...	...	...	...	...	7	20	...	...	Production d'électricité d'origine solaire, éolienne, marée motrice et autres (GWh)

VII TOURISM AND INFRASTRUCTURE - TOURISME ET INFRASTUCTURE

	2009	2010	2011	2012	2013	2014	2015	2016	2017	
VII-1 Tourism										**VII-1 Tourisme**
International tourist arrivals (thousands)	190	199	209	220	231	242	255	267	258	Arrivées de touristes internationaux (milliers)
Rooms in hotels and similar establishments (thousands)	20	20	...	12	13	13	14	15	...	Chambres d'hôtels et établissements assimilés (milliers)
Overnight stays (thousands)	4 720	5 163	5 473	6 264	6 530	7 323	7 522	7 450	7 031	Nuitées (milliers)
Tourism receipts (US$ thousand)	131 000	148 900	177 000	169 600	188 900	150 800	140 600	152 118	161 056	Recettes touristiques (milliers de $ EU)
Total contribution to GDP (%)	6.1	6.2	6.7	6.5	6.4	5.3	5.9	5.7	5.7	Contribution totale au PIB (%)
Total contribution to Employment (%)	5.3	5.4	5.8	5.7	5.6	4.6	5.1	4.8	4.8	Contribution totale à l'emploi (%)
VII-2 Infrastructure										**VII-2 Infrastructure**
Paved road (% of total)	35.0	35.7	...	...	...	...	...	...	...	Routes asphaltées (% du total)
Total network (Railways-km)	...	...	...	...	...	...	...	...	...	Réseau total voies ferrées-Km
Main telephone lines (per 100 inhabitants)	1.4	1.4	1.6	1.6	1.5	1.8	1.8	1.1	...	Lignes téléphoniques fixes (pour 100 habitants)
Mobile cellular subscribers (per 100 inhabitants)	54.5	74.4	79.4	83.7	93.3	81.7	85.6	79.6	...	Abonnés aux téléphones mobiles (pour 100 habitants)
Internet users per 100 inhabitants	2.2	3.1	4.1	4.5	4.9	6.0	11.3	12.0	...	Utilisateurs Internet par 100 Habitants
Fixed (wired)-broadband subscriptions per 100 inhabitants	...	...	...	...	...	...	0.7	0.8	...	Abonnements à l'Internet fixe (filaire) à large bande pour 100 habitants, par débit

VIII EXTERNAL TRADE - COMMERCE EXTERIEUR

US$ (MILLIONS) EXPORTS, FOB	2009	2010	2011	2012	2013	2014	2015	2016	2017	$ E.U (MILLIONS) EXPORTATIONS, FÀB
Exports - Total	1 225	1 282	1 410	1 443	1 982	2 563	1 778	1 354	...	Exportations - Total
Exports to Africa	776	865	835	752	893	1 359	509	380	...	Exportations vers l'Afrique
Main products										**Principaux produits**
Cotton	215	106	124	162	334	366	456	290	...	Coton
Fruits and nuts (excluding oil nuts), fresh or dried	126	55	111	114	166	200	317	201	...	Fruits et noix (à l'exclusion des oléagineux), frais ou secs
Gold, non-monetary (excluding gold ores and concentrates)	9	155	133	259	361	311	261	297	...	Or, non monétaire (à l'exclusion des minerais d'or et des concentrés)
Liquefied propane and butane	18	175	214	454	4	58	5	2	...	Propane liquéfié et butane
Petroleum oils or bituminous minerals > 70 % oil	69	388	300	138	60	895	97	100	...	Huiles de pétrole ou de minéraux bitumineux> 70% d'huile
Main destinations										**Principales destinations**
China	158	82	111	182	260	262	103	64	...	Chine
India	139	76	151	146	197	215	334	210	...	Inde
Nigeria	311	208	124	40	217	149	194	152	...	Nigéria
Sierra Leone	251	170	381	452	424	531	48	-	...	Sierra Leone
United Arab Emirates	-	67	104	126	152	226	210	268	...	Emirates Arabes
IMPORTS, CIF										
Imports - Total	2 064	2 134	2 070	2 316	2 941	3 704	2 475	2 251	...	Importations - Total (millions)
Imports from Africa	234	203	189	303	321	403	261	258	...	Importations en provenance de l'Afrique
Main products										**Principaux produits**
Cotton fabrics, woven	266	233	175	195	289	313	192	130	...	Tissus de coton, tissés
Fixed vegetable fats & oils, crude, refined, fract.	110	144	84	104	146	193	119	118	...	Graisses et huiles végétales fixes, brutes, raffinées, fract.
Motor vehicles for the transport of persons	111	131	119	184	203	289	209	88	...	Véhicules à moteur pour le transport de personnes
Other meat and edible meat offal	89	88	77	141	143	176	121	81	...	Autres viandes et abats comestibles
Rice	160	147	60	201	465	536	260	441	...	Véhicules automobiles et autres véhicules automobiles
Main origin										**Principales provenances**
China	627	606	528	678	873	1 118	849	664	...	Chine
France	192	204	251	175	186	193	149	146	...	France
India	61	68	108	138	315	298	169	242	...	Inde
Thailand	116	108	38	84	184	283	131	228	...	Thaïlande
United States	127	124	114	160	204	299	186	85	...	États-Unis

	2009	2010	2011	2012	2013	2014	2015	2016	2017	
IX-1 MONETARY STATISTICS *CFA FRANC (MILLIONS)*										**IX-1 STATISTIQUES MONÉTAIRES** *FRANC CFA (MILLIONS)*
Money supply (M1)	1 295 917	1 446 120	1 578 412	1 719 978	2 017 150	2 353 511	2 540 422	2 473 595	2 661 641	Masse monétaire (M1)
Quasi-money	424 330	466 744	507 543	590 633	638 182	724 278	816 587	872 581	859 013	Quasi-monnaie
of which demand deposit	...	...	...	...	...	...	...	...	...	dont Monnaie scripturale
Net foreign assets	657 785	735 182	719 363	792 007	910 536	1 121 431	1 207 040	1 037 540	930 770	Avoirs extérieurs nets
Domestic credit	599 334	593 701	747 748	760 412	880 445	1 021 092	1 023 657	1 220 025	1 397 012	Crédit intérieur
of which claims on private sector	- 99 214	- 164 117	- 97 212	- 164 028	- 142 137	- 123 539	- 126 650	36 994	195 826	dont créances sur le secteur privé
of which claims on government sector, net	698 548	757 818	844 960	924 440	1 022 582	1 032 091	1 031 825	1 107 656	1 098 400	dont créances nettes sur le gouvernement
International reserves (millions US$)	10	82	86	81	83	84	723	708	245	Réserves internationales (millions $EU)
Average exchange rate (National currency per US$)	472	495	472	511	494	494	591	593	582	Taux de change (moyen) (monnaie nationale par $ EU)
IX-2 PUBLIC FINANCE *CFA FRANC (MILLIONS)*										**IX-2 FINANCES PUBLIQUES** *FRANC CFA (MILLIONS)(MILLIONS)*
Total Revenues and Grants	675 840	651 070	691 797	797 245	873 578	824 757	848 282	771 829	...	Recettes totales et dons
Direct taxes (on income, profits)	112 715	119 813	136 225	145 825	142 110	160 331	169 834	187 463	...	Taxes directes
Domestic indirect taxes revenues	128 465	127 687	136 372	155 051	154 368	178 770	197 556	165 166	...	Taxes Indirectes
Trade taxes	259 215	278 400	261 200	297 070	371 600	362 098	345 670	288 500	...	Taxes sur le commerce extérieur
Other taxes	...	...	...	...	...	...	...	...	...	Autres taxes
Other revenues	75 384	77 100	70 900	124 400	127 300	79 543	106 383	104 600	...	Autres recettes
Grants	100 060	48 070	87 100	74 900	78 200	44 015	28 840	26 100	...	Dons
Total Expenditures and Net Lending	809 006	702 170	754 740	815 760	952 000	916 550	1 242 345	1 086 282	...	Dépenses totales et prêts nets
Current expenditure	478 400	486 730	500 700	569 330	631 500	635 083	809 026	717 800	...	Dépenses courantes
Wages and Salaries	225 900	238 700	253 200	279 360	300 300	317 390	343 443	353 800	...	Rémunérations et salaires
Other purchases of goods and services	102 700	90 300	89 300	110 000	119 000	103 865	141 113	100 100	...	Achat de biens et services
Other current expenditure	39 800	43 630	48 700	55 500	61 200	67 466	74 967	78 400	...	Autres dépenses courantes
Current transfers	110 000	114 100	109 500	124 470	151 000	146 362	249 504	185 500	...	Transferts courants
Interest payments	15 606	17 700	14 960	23 100	19 900	18 325	36 289	63 342	...	Intérêts
Capital expenditure	302 300	177 140	226 580	217 300	288 100	249 630	376 863	299 600	...	Dépenses d'équipement
Net lending	12 700	20 600	12 500	6 030	12 500	13 511	20 167	5 540	...	Prêts nets
Fiscal balance	- 133 167	- 51 100	- 62 943	- 18 515	- 78 422	- 91 793	- 394 063	- 314 453	...	Solde global y compris les dons
IX-3 BALANCE OF PAYMENTS *CFA FRANC (MILLIONS)*										**IX-3 BALANCE DES PAIEMENTS** *FRANC CFA (MILLIONS)*
Trade balance	- 242 329	- 244 500	- 259 300	- 285 600	- 302 300	- 351 300	- 298 500	- 339 500	...	Balance commerciale
Services Balance	- 129 829	- 68 500	- 43 800	- 77 200	- 121 800	- 201 100	- 187 800	- 86 100	...	Balance des services
Net primary income	- 15 580	- 26 500	- 7 300	- 34 100	- 34 100	- 30 200	- 38 800	- 43 000	...	Revenus primaires nets
Compensation of employees	87	5 249	3 443	2 426	3 156	2 081	...	...	...	Rémunération des salariés
Investment income	- 15 667	- 31 738	- 10 758	- 36 498	- 37 256	- 32 326	- 35 938	- 43 047	...	Revenus des investissements
Net secondary income	81 320	76 800	66 800	102 300	125 600	145 100	84 700	104 000	...	Revenus secondaires nets
Net official transfers	...	41 600	15 100	31 800	39 000	44 000	18 200	24 000	...	Transferts officiels nets
Workers' remittances	...	63 000	66 900	58 900	69 800	77 100	66 800	65 000	...	Envois de fonds des travailleurs
Other private transfers	...	...	...	...	...	...	...	...	...	Autres transferts privés
Current account balance	- 306 419	- 262 700	- 243 600	- 294 600	- 332 600	- 437 500	- 440 500	- 364 600	...	Solde du compte courant
Capital and financial account	260 252	341 900	222 800	354 700	423 600	605 300	521 800	285 600	...	Comptes de capital et financier
Capital account	76 081	75 600	125 200	85 000	91 900	125 200	74 100	95 100	...	Compte de capital
Financial account	184 171	266 300	97 600	269 700	331 700	480 100	447 700	190 500	...	Compte financier
Errors and omissions	- 2 724	3 900	8 800	9 400	8 100	7 200	2 300	...	...	Erreurs et omissions
Overall balance	- 48 891	83 100	- 11 900	69 500	99 100	175 100	83 600	- 79 000	...	Balance générale

BÉNIN

X DEBT AND FINANCIAL FLOWS - DETTE ET FLUX FINANCIERS

	2008	2009	2010	2011	2012	2013	2014	2015	2016	
X-1 DEBT *US $ (MILLIONS)*										**X-1 DETTE EXTÉRIEURE** *$ E.U (MILLIONS)*
Total external debt	1 070	1 187	1 233	1 278	1 580	1 788	1 731	1 836	2 336	Dette extérieure totale
Private	...	...	...	...	...	...	...	...	...	Privée
Public	1 070	1 187	1 233	1 278	1 580	1 788	1 731	1 836	...	Publique
Total external debt service	38	48	55	71	77	79	79	64	...	Service de la dette extérieure
Present value of external debt	...	...	...	...	...	...	...	1 585	...	Valeur actuelle de la dette extérieure
Total government domestic debt, National currency (millions)	...	...	...	...	...	...	...	...	...	Dette publique intérieure
X-2 FINANCIAL FLOWS *US $ (MILLIONS)*										**X-2 FLUX FINANCIERS** *$ E.U (MILLIONS)*
Net Foreign Direct Investment Inflows	134	177	161	230	360	405	150	161	...	Investissements étranger direct (flux nets entrants)
Main origin of FDI inflows	...									**Principales origines de l'IDE entrant:**
France	...	...	...	126	...	...	...	...	...	France
United States	- 10	...	...	...	...	...	...	...	...	États-Unis
...	...	...	...	...	...	...	...	...	...	...
...	...	...	...	...	...	...	...	...	...	...
Sweden	- 3	...	10	9	9	...	...	...	...	Suède
African countries	...	...	...	71	...	...	...	...	...	Pays africains
Net total official development assistance	678	689	673	508	660	599	430	493	...	Aide publique au développement (nette totale)
Main origin of net ODA										**Principales origines de l'APD nette**
France	50	49	42	41	38	37	28	28	...	France
International Development Association [IDA]	90	85	65	73	141	127	107	124	...	International Development Association
United States	59	100	189	42	24	39	36	58	...	États-Unis
Denmark	51	39	36	32	17	- 5	- 1	...	...	Danemark
...	...	...	...	...	...	...	...	...	...	...

BENIN

SOURCES AND NOTES - SOURCES ET NOTES

External trade - Total exports, fob: UNCTAD

External trade - Total import, cif: UNCTAD

ODA: OECD

Monetary statistics: IMF

National Accounts: The accounts are calculated using the new base year 2007

Poverty: World Bank

Commerce exterieur - Exportation, fab: CNUCED

Commerce exterieur - Imporations, caf: CNUCED

APD: OCDE

Statistiques monétaires: FMI

Comptes nationaux: Les comptes sont calculés selon la nouvelle année de base 2007

Pauvreté: Banque mondiale

	AREA (km2)	581 730	SUPERFICIE (KM2)	
	CAPITAL CITY	Gaborone	Gaborone	CAPITALE
	CURRENCY	Botswana Pula	Pula botswanais	MONNAIE

I SOCIAL AND DEMOGRAPHIC INDICATORS — INDICATEURS DEMOGRAPHIQUES ET SOCIAUX

	Year Année	Value Valeur	Charts / Graphiques	
Population				**Population**
Population ('000)	2017	2 200.0		Population ('000)
Female (%)	2017	50.9		Féminine (%)
Urban (%)	2017	70.7		Urbaine (%)
Average annual growth rate	2017	1.5		Taux de croissance annuel
Active population ('000)	2015	490.3		Population active ('000)
Population by age group ('000)				Population par groupe d'âge ('000)
0-14 years	2017	696.0		0-14 ans
15-64 years	2017	1 452.0		15-64 ans
65+ years	2017	106.0		65+ ans
Economically active population in agriculture (%)	2015	39.7		Participation de la population active agricole (%)
Crude birth rate	2017	20.3		Taux brut de natalité
Crude death rate	2017	7.4		Taux brut de mortalité
Total fertility rate	2017	2.3		Indice synthétique de fécondité
Life expectancy at birth - Total (years)	2015	64.5		Espérance de vie à la naissance - Totale (années)
Dependency ratio - Total (%)	2017	55.2		Taux de dépendance - Total (%)
Health				**Santé**
Percentage of children under-five and underweight	2015	3.5		% d'enfants de moins de cinq ans avec insuffisance pondérale
Prevalence of undernourishment	2017	26.0		Prévalence de la malnutrition
Under five mortality rate (per 1 000 live births)	2015	43.6		Taux de mortalité de moins de 5 ans (les deux sexes, pour 1000)
Infant mortality rate (per 1 000 live births)	2015	34.8		Taux de mortalité infantile (les deux sexes) par 1000
Neonatal mortality rate (per 1 000 live births)	2015	21.9		Le taux de mortalité néonatale (pour 1000 naissances vivantes)
Percentage of children provided the vaccines :				Pourcentage d'enfants vaccinés :
BCG	2016	83.0		BCG
DPT3	2016	89.0		DTC3
Polio	2016	80.0		polio
Measles	2016	95.0		rougeole
Percentage of mothers provided at least one antenatal care (%)	2007	94.4		Pourcentage de mères ayant au moins reçu un soin prénatal (%)
Percentage of deliveries attended by skilled health personnel	2007	94.6		% d'accouchements assistés par un personnel de santé qualifié
Number of doctors (per 10,000 population)	2006	3.4		Nombre de médecins (pour 10.000 habitants)
Number of nurses (per 10,000 population)	2006	28.4		Nombre d'infirmiers (pour 10.000 habitants)
Hospital beds - Total (per 10,000 population)	2011	26.0		Nombre de lits d'hôpitaux - Total (pour 10 000)
Births registered (per 1,000)	2015	24.6		Naissances enregistrées (pour 1000)
Deaths registered (per 1,000)	2015	7.5		Décès enregistrés (pour 1000)
Budget allocation to health (%)	2013	8.8		Dépenses publiques consacrées à la santé (% du budget)
Education				**Education**
Enrolment in primary education (000)	2015	345.0		Scolarisation dans le primaire (000)
Female	2015	168.0		Féminine
Enrolment in secondary education (000)	2014	182.0		Scolarisation dans le secondaire (000)
Female	2014	94.0		Féminine
Enrolment in tertiary education (000)	2014	60.6		Scolarisation dans le tertiaire (000)
Female	2014	38.8		Féminine
Literacy rate	2015	88.6		Taux d'alphabétisation (deux sexes)
Male	2015	87.5		Masculin
Female	2015	89.6		Féminin
Pupil teacher ratio - primary	2015	24.0		Ratio élève-enseignant
Budget allocation to education (%)	2009	16.2		Dépenses publiques consacrées à l'enseignement (% du budget)
Poverty				**Pauvreté**
GNI per capita, PPP (current int. $)	2016	16680.0		RNB par habitant, ($ PPA inter. courants)
Human Poverty Index (HPI-1) Value (%)	2007	22.9		Valeur de l'Indice de pauvreté (IPH-1) (%)
Population below Inter. poverty line ($2/ day) (%)	2009	18.2		Population sous le seuil inter. de pauvreté (2$/Jour) (%)
Share of income held by richest 10%	2009	49.6		% de revenu des 10% plus riches
Share of income held by poorest 10%	2009	1.1		% de revenu des 10% plus pauvres
GINI index	2009	60.5		Indice de GINI

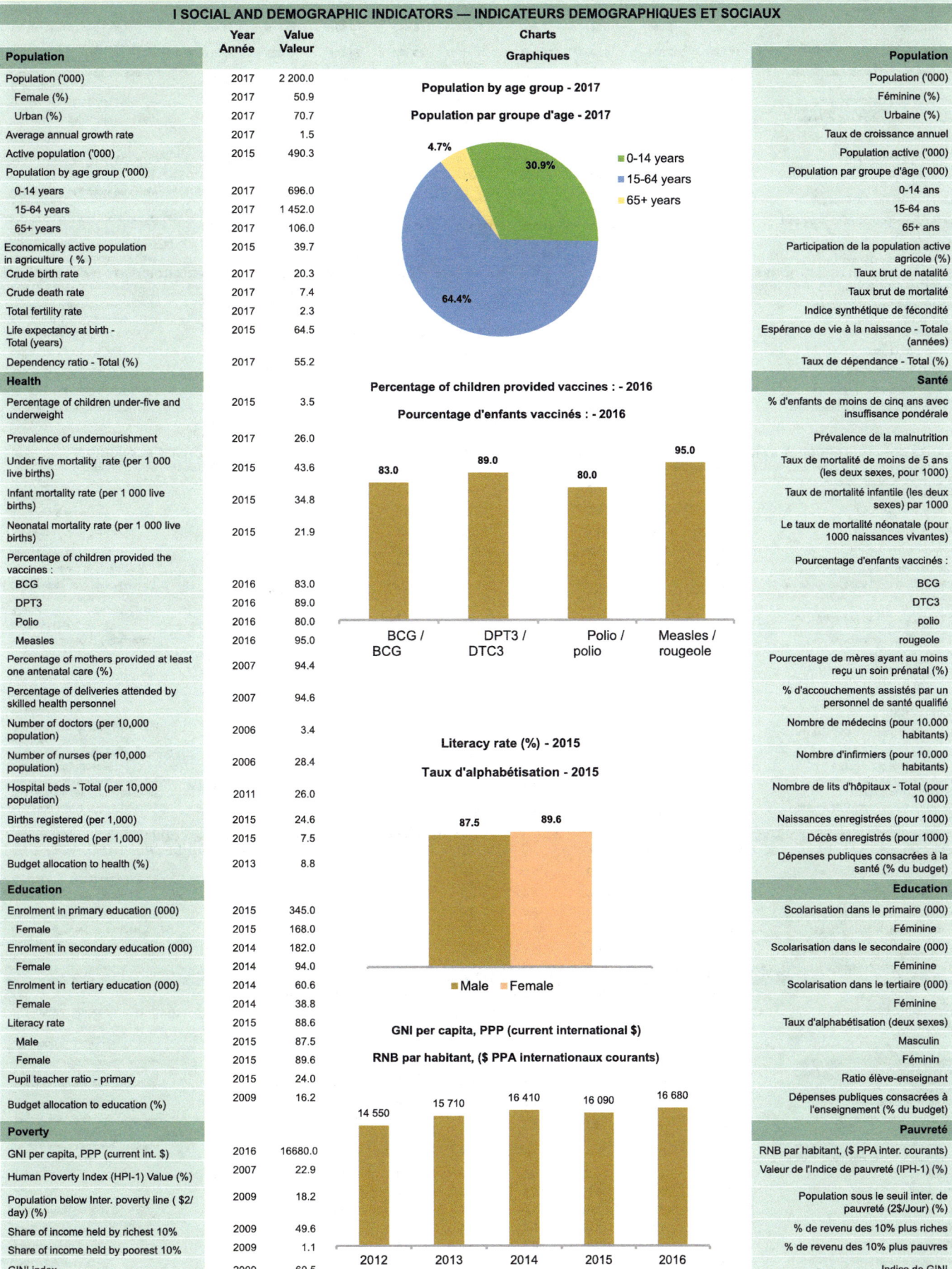

Population by age group - 2017
Population par groupe d'age - 2017

4.7% — 30.9% — 64.4%
- 0-14 years
- 15-64 years
- 65+ years

Percentage of children provided vaccines : - 2016
Pourcentage d'enfants vaccinés : - 2016

BCG / BCG 83.0 ; DPT3 / DTC3 89.0 ; Polio / polio 80.0 ; Measles / rougeole 95.0

Literacy rate (%) - 2015
Taux d'alphabétisation - 2015

Male 87.5 ; Female 89.6

GNI per capita, PPP (current international $)
RNB par habitant, ($ PPA internationaux courants)

2012 14 550 ; 2013 15 710 ; 2014 16 410 ; 2015 16 090 ; 2016 16 680

BOTSWANA

II NATIONAL ACCOUNTS — COMPTES NATIONAUX

	2009	2010	2011	2012	2013	2014	2015	2016	2017	
GROSS DOMESTIC PRODUCT BY KIND OF ECONOMIC ACTIVITY AT CURRENT PRICES BOTSWANA PULA (MILLIONS)										**PRODUIT INTÉRIEUR BRUT PAR BRANCHE D'ACTIVITÉ ÉCONOMIQUE AUX PRIX COURANTS** PULA BOTSWANAIS (MILLIONS)
Agriculture, hunting , forestry and Fishing	2 071	2 161	2 636	2 961	2 877	3 045	3 215	3 496	3 584	Agriculture, chasse sylviculture et Pêche
Mining and quarrying	11 210	16 661	24 529	19 287	24 243	32 403	25 962	34 913	32 538	Industries extractives
Manufacturing	4 662	5 548	6 074	6 523	7 285	7 740	8 442	8 860	9 238	Industries manufacturières
Electricity, gas & water	317	412	- 59	- 621	- 123	- 582	- 219	395	1 236	Electricité, gaz et eau
Construction	4 495	5 056	6 247	7 465	7 998	8 690	9 607	10 575	11 488	Bâtiments et travaux publics
Wholesale & retail trade, restaurants, hotels	11 163	13 084	15 595	16 897	21 211	26 182	23 711	31 021	35 308	Commerce de gros et de détail, restaurants et hôtels
Finance, insurance, real estate, etc.	9 695	11 610	13 979	16 468	17 717	19 284	21 518	23 349	25 048	Banques, assurances, affaires immobilières
Transport and communications	3 993	4 471	5 114	6 325	6 906	7 788	8 559	9 643	10 623	Transport(s) et communications
Public administration and defense	12 316	13 377	14 778	16 924	17 731	19 946	22 491	23 927	24 838	Administrations publiques et défense
Education	...	...	...	...	...	...	...	...	...	Education
Health And Social Work	...	...	...	...	...	...	...	...	...	Santé et Actions Sociales
Other services	4 593	5 243	5 881	6 750	7 344	8 138	8 653	9 259	9 899	Autres services
Less Imputed Service Charges	...	...	...	...	...	...	...	...	...	Moins Services d'intermédiation financière
Gross domestic product at factor cost / basic prices	64 515	77 623	94 774	98 978	113 190	132 636	131 938	155 438	163 798	Produit intérieur brut aux couts des facteurs / prix de base
Plus: Indirect Taxes / taxes on products, less subsidies	8 947	9 244	10 205	10 892	11 969	13 232	14 128	15 151	16 314	Plus taxes indirectes/impôts sur les produits, moins les subventions
EXPENDITURE ON GROSS DOMESTIC PRODUCT AT CURRENT PURCHASER'S VALUES BOTSWANA PULA (MILLIONS)										**EMPLOI DU PRODUIT INTÉRIEUR BRUT AUX PRIX COURANTS D'ACQUISITION** BOTSWANAIS (MILLIONS)
Government final consumption	15 493	17 162	19 407	21 196	23 215	29 078	30 057	31 033	33 158	Consommation finale des administrations publiques
Private final consumption	44 683	46 877	55 757	62 037	59 665	62 335	67 010	75 263	82 832	Consommation finale privée
Gross fixed capital formation	25 646	29 202	33 641	39 804	41 925	44 433	49 643	52 986	52 183	Formation brute de capital fixe
Change in inventories	192	254	1	188	- 262	165	1 486	69	1 313	Variation des stocks
Exports of goods and services	25 566	37 905	52 438	54 112	77 001	88 557	77 464	84 867	71 735	Exportations de biens et services
Less imports of goods and services	38 116	44 532	56 264	67 465	76 385	78 699	79 593	73 629	61 108	Moins importations de biens et services
GDP at purchasers' values	73 462	86 867	104 980	109 870	125 158	145 869	146 066	170 589	180 113	PIB aux prix d'acquisition
GROSS DOMESTIC PRODUCT BY KIND OF ECONOMIC ACTIVITY AT CONSTANT PRICES ANNUAL GROWTH RATES (%)										**PRODUIT INTÉRIEUR BRUT PAR BRANCHE D'ACTIVITÉ ÉCONOMIQUE AUX PRIX CONSTANTS** TAUX DE CROISSANCE ANNUEL (%)
Agriculture, hunting , forestry and Fishing	6.4	5.8	0.2	- 8.5	1.3	- 0.3	0.3	0.5	2.2	Agriculture, chasse sylviculture et Pêche
Mining and quarrying	- 42.4	20.4	- 6.5	- 5.8	24.2	0.5	- 19.6	- 3.5	- 11.2	Industries extractives
Manufacturing	5.0	3.9	11.4	3.7	6.5	0.5	3.2	1.6	1.9	Industries manufacturières
Electricity, gas & water	- 5.2	12.0	- 34.2	- 27.5	67.5	- 55.8	7.0	95.2	- 19.5	Electricité, gaz et eau
Construction	12.3	3.6	23.1	14.4	4.1	3.7	4.0	4.2	3.5	Bâtiments et travaux publics
Wholesale & retail trade, restaurants, hotels	3.9	9.3	13.8	6.8	16.0	10.7	- 3.9	13.5	7.3	Commerce de gros et de détail, restaurants et hôtels
Finance, insurance, real estate, etc.	1.5	11.5	7.7	9.1	8.7	2.7	4.5	3.3	5.0	Banques, assurances, affaires immobilières
Transport and communications	14.8	6.4	6.1	10.9	7.6	9.8	4.6	6.6	4.7	Transport(s) et communications
Public administration and defense	2.8	7.5	6.3	2.8	6.0	4.6	3.3	2.4	2.2	Administrations publiques et défense
Education	...	...	...	...	...	...	...	...	...	Education
Health And Social Work	...	...	...	...	...	...	...	...	...	Santé et Actions Sociales
Other services	11.3	6.2	8.3	10.7	8.0	4.2	3.6	3.5	2.8	Autres services
Less Imputed Service Charges	...	...	...	...	...	...	...	...	...	Moins Services d'intermédiation financière
Gross domestic product at factor cost / basic prices	- 9.1	10.2	6.1	4.5	11.8	4.1	- 2.0	4.9	2.2	Produit intérieur brut aux couts des facteurs / prix de base
Plus: Indirect Taxes / taxes on products, less subsidies	3.4	- 2.8	5.8	4.3	7.7	4.9	1.1	-	3.8	Plus taxes indirectes/impôts sur les produits, moins les subventions
Gross domestic product at market prices	- 7.7	8.6	6.0	4.5	11.3	4.1	- 1.7	4.3	2.4	Produit intérieur brut aux prix du marché
EXPENDITURE ON GROSS DOMESTIC PRODUCT AT CONSTANT PURCHASERS' VALUES ANNUAL GROWTH RATES (%)										**EMPLOIS DU PRODUIT INTÉRIEUR BRUT AUX PRIX CONSTANTS D'ACQUISITION** TAUX DE CROISSANCE ANNUEL (%)
Government final consumption	3.0	3.7	5.0	15.2	14.4	10.8	2.5	2.2	3.0	Consommation finale des administrations publiques
Private final consumption	5.1	4.4	- 0.6	8.9	- 6.3	- 6.0	12.6	- 0.3	- 3.4	Consommation finale privée
Gross fixed capital formation	9.5	9.2	12.2	13.6	2.0	1.5	8.8	3.6	- 9.4	Formation brute de capital fixe
Exports of goods and services	- 37.7	16.0	27.5	17.8	37.8	7.7	- 16.3	1.0	- 13.3	Exportations de biens et services
Less imports of goods and services	- 10.9	6.5	19.2	32.1	10.0	0.2	2.3	- 5.1	- 23.8	Moins importations de biens et services

III INFLATION

	2009	2010	2011	2012	2013	2014	2015	2016	2017	
Annual growth rates (%)										**Taux de croissance annuel (%)**
All item	8.1	6.9	8.5	7.5	5.9	4.4	3.1	2.8	3.3	Ensemble
of which:										dont:
Food and non-alcoholic beverages	14.7	3.6	6.9	8.0	5.4	3.0	1.3	2.7	3.4	Alimentation et boissons non alcoolisés
Alcoholic beverages, tobacco and narcotics	35.2	7.1	8.4	7.6	10.3	9.0	6.1	2.5	4.5	Boissons alcoolisées et tabacs
Clothing and footwear	8.4	8.0	8.9	7.5	6.3	6.0	7.6	6.5	3.2	Habillement et chaussures
Housing, water, electricity, gas and other fuels	4.8	6.4	8.4	7.7	4.3	3.9	7.1	6.3	5.4	Logement, eau, électricité, gaz et autres combustibles
Furnishings, household equipment and routine household maintenance	11.9	9.4	9.0	7.3	4.9	5.0	6.1	3.0	3.3	Meubles, articles de ménage et entretien courant
Health	5.5	2.7	4.5	5.9	5.5	8.3	6.3	3.0	2.4	Santé
Transport	- 8.4	12.1	13.2	10.8	7.3	1.2	- 5.1	- 2.7	1.6	Transport
Communication	- 0.3	1.2	- 3.0	- 1.4	0.3	0.3	0.3	0.2	0.5	Communication
Recreation and culture	5.0	6.0	8.3	5.8	4.5	4.2	5.7	3.0	2.2	Loisirs et culture
Education	3.9	5.8	10.6	6.4	4.7	7.4	6.4	3.7	4.1	Enseignement
Restaurants and hotels	18.8	9.0	9.3	8.4	7.9	7.6	5.5	4.0	3.7	Restaurants et hôtels
Miscellaneous goods and services	3.8	7.0	5.3	2.0	1.2	5.2	7.2	7.5	3.9	Biens et Services divers

IV AGRICULTURAL PRODUCTION - PRODUCTION AGRICOLE

TONNES (THOUSAND)	2009	2010	2011	2012	2013	2014	2015	2016	2017	Tonnes (milliers)
Sorghum	29	31	33	24	10	14	36	28	...	Sorgho
Maize	19	17	29	8	4	29	4	12	...	Maïs
Sunflower seed	2	4	16	6	2	...	2	4	...	Graines de tournesol
	...	...	...	...	...	...	...	...	...	
	...	...	...	...	...	...	...	...	...	

V MINING PRODUCTION - PRODUCTION MINIERE

	2009	2010	2011	2012	2013	2014	2015	2016	2017	
Hard Coal - Production, metric tons (thousands)	738	988	788	1 454	1 496	1 712	2 066	1 871	...	Houille - Production, tonnes métriques (milliers)
	...	...	...	...	...	...	...	...	...	
Diamonds and other precious stones, unworked - Production, carat (thousands)	17 733	22 019	22 903	20 619	23 134	24 658	20 824	20 891	...	Diamants et autres pierres gemmes (précieuses), bruts - Production, carat (milliers)

VI ENERGY - ENERGIE

	2009	2010	2011	2012	2013	2014	2015	2016	2017	
Total electricity generation (GWh)	444	430	699	2 257	2 626	2 362	...	...	...	Production électrique totale (GWh)
of which										dont
Production of electricity from fossil fuels (GWh)	444	430	694	2 250	2 617	99	...	...	...	Production d'électricité à partir de combustibles fossiles (GWh)
Production of hydro electricity (GWh)	...	...	...	...	...	...	...	...	...	Production d'électricité d'origine hydraulique (GWh)
Production of electricity from solar, wind, tide, wave and other sources (GWh)	...	...	5	8	9	11	12	...	...	Production d'électricité d'origine solaire, éolienne, marée motrice et autres (GWh)

VII TOURISM AND INFRASTRUCTURE - TOURISME ET INFRASTUCTURE

	2009	2010	2011	2012	2013	2014	2015	2016	2017	
VII-1 Tourism										**VII-1 Tourisme**
International tourist arrivals (thousands)	1 721	1 973	1 788	1 614	1 544	1 966	1 528	1 723	1 797	Arrivées de touristes internationaux (milliers)
Rooms in hotels and similar establishments (thousands)	6	7	7	7	8	8	9	11	...	Chambres d'hôtels et établissements assimilés (milliers)
Overnight stays (thousands)	- 1 363	10 188	9 055	7 995	10 102	12 700	9 528	12 901	13 435	Nuitées (milliers)
Tourism receipts (US$ thousand)	415 266	488 305	540 135	536 503	554 473	611 868	594 138	585 317	683 415	Recettes touristiques (milliers de $ EU)
Total contribution to GDP (%)	11.5	11.4	10.2	11.5	10.9	10.9	12.5	11.6	11.5	Contribution totale au PIB (%)
Total contribution to Employment (%)	7.3	7.3	7.1	8.1	7.6	7.8	8.6	7.6	7.6	Contribution totale à l'emploi (%)
VII-2 Infrastructure										**VII-2 Infrastructure**
Paved road (% of total)	75.8	75.8	50.2	37.1	37.4	33.0	33.0	...	...	Routes asphaltées (% du total)
Total network (Railways-km)	888	888	888	888	888	...	...	...	...	Réseau total voies ferrées-Km
Main telephone lines (per 100 inhabitants)	7.0	7.0	7.5	8.0	8.6	8.3	7.8	6.9	...	Lignes téléphoniques fixes (pour 100 habitants)
Mobile cellular subscribers (per 100 inhabitants)	96.0	120.0	146.0	153.8	160.6	167.3	169.0	158.5	...	Abonnés aux téléphones mobiles (pour 100 habitants)
Internet users per 100 inhabitants	6.2	6.0	9.0	16.0	30.0	36.7	37.3	39.4	...	Utilisateurs Internet par 100 Habitants
Fixed (wired)-broadband subscriptions per 100 inhabitants	0.5	0.6	1.0	1.1	1.1	1.6	1.8	2.8	...	Abonnements à l'Internet fixe (filaire) à large bande pour 100 habitants, par débit

VIII EXTERNAL TRADE - COMMERCE EXTERIEUR

	2009	2010	2011	2012	2013	2014	2015	2016	2017	
US$ (MILLIONS) EXPORTS, FOB										**$ E.U (MILLIONS) EXPORTATIONS, FÀB**
Exports - Total	3 456	4 693	5 882	5 971	7 573	7 915	6 319	7 321	...	Exportations - Total
Exports to Africa	994	1 051	899	965	1 100	1 375	1 482	1 478	...	Exportations vers l'Afrique
Main products										**Principaux produits**
Copper ores and concentrates; copper mattes, cemen	64	41	63	86	149	167	112	1	...	Minerais et concentrés de cuivre; mattes de cuivre, cemen
Equipment for distributing electricity, n.e.s.	14	55	43	45	42	50	111	116	...	Matériel de distribution d'électricité, n.d.a.
Meat of bovine animals, fresh, chilled or frozen	142	165	44	62	106	120	128	107	...	Viandes des animaux de l'espèce bovine, fraîches, réfrigérées ou congelées
Nickel ores & concentrates; nickel mattes, etc.	546	733	397	349	438	370	286	231	...	Minerais de nickel et concentrés; mattes de nickel, etc.
Pearls, precious & semi-precious stones	1 878	2 866	4 567	4 683	6 222	6 626	5 162	6 466	...	Perles, pierres précieuses et semi-précieuses
Main destinations										**Principales destinations**
Belgium	143	221	184	283	929	2 338	1 621	1 764	...	Belgique
India	6	43	56	70	217	1 207	774	1 061	...	Inde
South Africa	479	580	578	622	701	767	812	713	...	Afrique du Sud
United Arab Emirates	-	2	10	30	102	512	484	1 011	...	Emirates Arabes
United Kingdom	1 409	2 221	3 821	3 754	3 886	62	49	122	...	Royaume-Uni
IMPORTS, CIF										
Imports - Total	4 728	5 657	7 272	8 025	7 433	7 830	7 626	6 103	...	Importations - Total (millions)
Imports from Africa	3 793	4 494	5 245	6 052	5 456	6 118	6 048	4 794	...	Importations en provenance de l'Afrique
Main products										**Principaux produits**
Electric current	74	121	182	217	195	159	137	143	...	Courant électrique
Motor vehic. for transport of goods, special purpo.	163	153	236	207	179	215	148	141	...	Véhicule à moteur pour le transport de marchandises, spécial.
Motor vehicles for the transport of persons	145	172	200	211	158	171	177	141	...	Véhicules à moteur pour le transport de personnes
Pearls, precious & semi-precious stones	289	477	712	1 825	2 380	2 640	2 597	1 782	...	Perles, pierres précieuses et semi-précieuses
Petroleum oils or bituminous minerals > 70 % oil	518	960	1 011	1 051	971	1 031	786	601	...	Huiles de pétrole ou de minéraux bitumineux> 70% d'huile
Main origin										**Principales provenances**
Belgium	50	45	74	88	253	258	191	154	...	Belgique
Canada	6	4	6	4	259	718	582	324	...	Canada
Namibia	40	51	55	423	681	1 001	1 208	682	...	Namibie
South Africa	3 633	3 915	5 060	5 209	4 675	5 022	4 718	3 961	...	Afrique du Sud
United Kingdom	214	361	580	1 044	783	55	56	77	...	Royaume-Uni

BOTSWANA

IX FINANCIAL AND MONETARY STATISTICS - FINANCES ET STATISTIQUES MONETAIRES

	2009	2010	2011	2012	2013	2014	2015	2016	2017	
IX-1 MONETARY STATISTICS *BOTSWANA PULA (MILLIONS)*										**IX-1 STATISTIQUES MONÉTAIRES** *PULA BOTSWANAIS (MILLIONS)*
Money supply (M1)	38 717	43 534	39 372	39 667	40 167	39 891	40 687	46 490	49 112	Masse monétaire (M1)
Quasi-money	31 609	33 596	36 088	38 247	38 250	42 635	53 204	54 676	58 088	Quasi-monnaie
of which demand deposit	...	...	...	...	...	...	...	...	...	dont Monnaie scripturale
Net foreign assets	59 270	52 550	63 610	63 682	71 886	83 252	91 045	82 238	88 337	Avoirs extérieurs nets
Domestic credit	- 818	9 440	8 381	16 412	16 861	12 101	18 133	27 395	29 376	Crédit intérieur
of which claims on private sector	- 22 404	- 14 580	- 22 726	- 21 096	- 26 909	- 37 162	- 35 552	- 29 457	- 30 237	dont créances sur le secteur privé
of which claims on government sector, net	21 254	23 622	28 781	35 091	39 800	45 246	49 331	53 749	56 189	dont créances nettes sur le gouvernement
International reserves (millions US$)	8 679	7 893	8 010	7 627	7 768	8 313	7 553	8 142	9 045	Réserves internationales (millions $EU)
Average exchange rate (National currency per US$)	7	7	7	8	8	9	10	11	10	Taux de change (moyen) (monnaie nationale par $ EU)
IX-2 PUBLIC FINANCE *BOTSWANA PULA (MILLIONS)*										**IX-2 FINANCES PUBLIQUES** *PULA BOTSWANAIS (MILLIONS)*
Total Revenues and Grants	30 455	30 023	31 909	38 486	41 658	48 951	55 904	47 420	57 399	Recettes totales et dons
Direct taxes (on income, profits)	4 608	5 561	6 413	6 113	6 725	7 471	8 384	8 691	9 572	Taxes directes
Domestic indirect taxes revenues	4 644	3 944	4 638	4 851	5 283	4 885	5 710	5 548	6 643	Taxes Indirectes
Trade taxes	7 750	7 931	6 207	8 424	14 216	13 170	15 691	15 818	11 773	Taxes sur le commerce extérieur
Other taxes	10 182	9 209	11 076	13 107	11 359	16 573	17 903	12 398	21 679	Autres taxes
Other revenues	2 647	2 610	3 247	5 458	3 568	6 527	7 837	4 821	7 576	Autres recettes
Grants	623	769	329	533	507	326	380	146	156	Dons
Total Expenditures and Net Lending	35 151	39 489	38 417	38 667	40 736	41 730	50 564	54 411	56 275	Dépenses totales et prêts nets
Current expenditure	23 608	25 362	26 566	28 250	31 434	32 532	36 881	39 587	40 288	Dépenses courantes
Wages and Salaries	8 701	9 252	11 899	12 941	14 548	15 338	16 539	18 544	19 224	Rémunérations et salaires
Other purchases of goods and services	7 848	7 724	6 256	7 019	8 798	8 863	9 746	9 774	9 740	Achat de biens et services
Other current expenditure	...	...	...	...	...	...	...	...	...	Autres dépenses courantes
Current transfers	7 059	8 386	8 411	8 290	8 088	8 331	10 597	11 269	11 324	Transferts courants
Interest payments	282	370	524	587	672	687	702	827	878	Intérêts
Capital expenditure	11 458	13 006	11 372	9 956	8 280	8 909	13 072	12 773	15 161	Dépenses d'équipement
Net lending	- 197	752	- 44	- 124	351	- 399	- 91	1 225	826	Prêts nets
Fiscal balance	- 4 696	- 9 466	- 6 508	- 181	922	7 222	5 340	- 6 991	1 124	Solde global y compris les dons
IX-3 BALANCE OF PAYMENTS *BOTSWANA PULA (MILLIONS)*										**IX-3 BALANCE DES PAIEMENTS** *PULA BOTSWANAIS (MILLIONS)*
Trade balance	- 9 377	- 6 798	- 4 779	- 16 715	- 2 339	4 674	- 9 114	3 372	...	Balance commerciale
Services Balance	299	170	952	1 836	2 954	5 184	6 985	7 865	...	Balance des services
Net primary income	- 1 703	- 3 733	- 768	331	- 3 152	- 3 102	- 2 322	- 2 768	...	Revenus primaires nets
Compensation of employees	- 97	- 115	- 137	- 100	63	- 42	- 196	- 143	...	Rémunération des salariés
Investment income	- 1 606	- 3 619	- 631	431	- 3 214	- 3 060	- 2 126	- 2 625	...	Revenus des investissements
Net secondary income	6 101	7 942	7 846	13 272	14 156	15 463	16 504	11 409	...	Revenus secondaires nets
Net official transfers	6 207	8 283	7 492	12 784	13 314	15 275	15 717	11 771	...	Transferts officiels nets
Workers' remittances	...	...	...	...	...	...	...	...	...	Envois de fonds des travailleurs
Other private transfers	- 107	- 341	354	488	842	188	787	- 362	...	Autres transferts privés
Current account balance	- 4 680	- 2 420	3 250	- 1 275	11 619	22 219	12 052	19 878	...	Solde du compte courant
Capital and financial account	1 966	- 2 441	7 011	1 523	- 8 100	2 658	- 7 158	- 4 731	...	Comptes de capital et financier
Capital account	...	23	3	...	1	...	2	1	...	Compte de capital
Financial account	1 966	- 2 464	7 008	1 523	- 8 101	2 658	- 7 160	- 4 733	...	Compte financier
Errors and omissions	- 1 848	- 1 649	- 6 831	- 1 110	- 2 179	- 13 473	- 4 951	- 12 304	...	Erreurs et omissions
Overall balance	- 4 563	- 6 511	3 430	- 862	1 340	11 404	- 57	2 843	...	Balance générale

X-1 DEBT US $ (MILLIONS)	2008	2009	2010	2011	2012	2013	2014	2015	2016	X-1 DETTE EXTÉRIEURE $ E.U (MILLIONS)
Total external debt	3 262	3 803	3 644	4 251	4 165	3 709	4 012	4 841	4 833	Dette extérieure totale
Private	1 870	1 851	1 745	2 250	2 356	1 819	2 380	2 414	...	Privée
Public	1 392	1 952	1 899	2 001	1 809	1 890	1 633	2 427	...	Publique
Total external debt service	590	810	1 042	1 125	1 261	1 296	919	1 197	...	Service de la dette extérieure
Present value of external debt	...	...	...	...	...	...	...	1 380	...	Valeur actuelle de la dette extérieure
Total government domestic debt, National currency (millions)	3 600	4 650	18 790	6 484	6 358	7 018	...	...	...	Dette publique intérieure
X-2 FINANCIAL FLOWS US $ (MILLIONS)										**X-2 FLUX FINANCIERS** $ E.U (MILLIONS)
Net Foreign Direct Investment Inflows	209	218	1 371	487	398	515	679	10	...	Investissements étranger direct (flux nets entrants)
Main origin of FDI inflows										**Principales origines de l'IDE entrant:**
Luxembourg	565	384	1 774	1 976	2 204	595	...	...	...	Luxembourg
Netherlands	5	3	1	2	2	25	...	...	...	Pays-Bas
Other Europe, nes	7	29	50	23	97	121	...	...	...	Autres Europe
United Kingdom	125	53	179	157	268	187	...	...	...	Royaume-Uni
United States	...	20	30	-	36	14	...	...	...	États-Unis
African countries	551	355	423	630	873	1 064	...	...	...	Pays africains
Net total official development assistance	282	155	119	73	107	99	66	91	...	Aide publique au développement (nette totale)
Main origin of net ODA										**Principales origines de l'APD nette**
United States	214	74	77	49	74	57	50	67	...	États-Unis
Germany	2	2	2	-	1	-	-	-	...	Allemagne
France	1	6	1	1	1	0	-	-	...	France
Norway	2	1	1	0	-	-	-	-	...	Norvège
Sweden	3	5	2	7	6	-	-	-	...	Suède

BOTSWANA

SOURCES AND NOTES - SOURCES ET NOTES

External trade - Total exports, fob: UNCTAD

External trade - Total import, cif: UNCTAD

ODA: OECD

Monetary statistics: IMF

National Accounts: 2017:Estimates are provisional

National Accounts : The annual data   for 2016 are previsions based on the sum of four quarters of 2016.

Poverty: World Bank

Commerce exterieur - Exportation, fab: CNUCED

Commerce exterieur - Imporations, caf: CNUCED

APD: OCDE

Statistiques monétaires: FMI

Comptes nationaux: 2017:Données provisoires

Comptes Nationaux: Les données annuelles de L'année 2016 sont estimées à partir des comptes trimestriels.

Pauvreté: Banque mondiale

		AREA (km2)	274 220		SUPERFICIE (KM2)
	CAPITAL CITY	Ouagadougou		Ouagadougou	CAPITALE
	CURRENCY	CFA Franc		Franc CFA	MONNAIE

I SOCIAL AND DEMOGRAPHIC INDICATORS — INDICATEURS DEMOGRAPHIQUES ET SOCIAUX

Population	Year Année	Value Valeur	Charts Graphiques	Population
Population ('000)	2017	19 632.1		Population ('000)
Female (%)	2017	51.7		Féminine (%)
Urban (%)	2017	29.5		Urbaine (%)
Average annual growth rate	2015	3.0		Taux de croissance annuel
Active population ('000)	2016	836 652.8		Population active ('000)
Population by age group ('000)				Population par groupe d'âge ('000)
0-14 years	2017	9 245.9		0-14 ans
15-64 years	2017	9 818.5		15-64 ans
65+ years	2017	567.8		65+ ans
Economically active population in agriculture (%)	2015	102.6		Participation de la population active agricole (%)
Crude birth rate	2015	39.5		Taux brut de natalité
Crude death rate	2015	9.3		Taux brut de mortalité
Total fertility rate	2015	5.4		Indice synthétique de fécondité
Life expectancy at birth - Total (years)	2015	59.0		Espérance de vie à la naissance - Totale (années)
Dependency ratio - Total (%)	2017	100.0		Taux de dépendance - Total (%)
Health				**Santé**
Percentage of children under-five and underweight	2017	19.2		% d'enfants de moins de cinq ans avec insuffisance pondérale
Prevalence of undernourishment	2016	19.2		Prévalence de la malnutrition
Under five mortality rate (per 1 000 live births)	2015	88.6		Taux de mortalité de moins de 5 ans (les deux sexes, pour 1000)
Infant mortality rate (per 1 000 live births)	2015	60.9		Taux de mortalité infantile (les deux sexes) par 1000
Neonatal mortality rate (per 1 000 live births)	2015	26.7		Le taux de mortalité néonatale (pour 1000 naissances vivantes)
Percentage of children provided the vaccines :				Pourcentage d'enfants vaccinés :
BCG	2016	103.0		BCG
DPT3	2015	105.3		DTC3
Polio	2016	100.5		polio
Measles	2015	103.5		rougeole
Percentage of mothers provided at least one antenatal care (%)	2016	80.3		Pourcentage de mères ayant au moins reçu un soin prénatal (%)
Percentage of deliveries attended by skilled health personnel	2016	80.9		% d'accouchements assistés par un personnel de santé qualifié
Number of doctors (per 10,000 population)	2016	0.6		Nombre de médecins (pour 10.000 habitants)
Number of nurses (per 10,000 population)	2015	2.4		Nombre d'infirmiers (pour 10.000 habitants)
Hospital beds - Total (per 10,000 population)	2015	3.2		Nombre de lits d'hôpitaux - Total (pour 10 000)
Births registered (per 1,000)	2016	70.0		Naissances enregistrées (pour 1000)
Deaths registered (per 1,000)	2015	9.3		Décès enregistrés (pour 1000)
Budget allocation to health (%)	2016	12.4		Dépenses publiques consacrées à la santé (% du budget)
Education				**Education**
Enrolment in primary education (000)	2016	2 873.0		Scolarisation dans le primaire (000)
Female	2016	1 395.2		Féminine
Enrolment in secondary education (000)	2014	841.9		Scolarisation dans le secondaire (000)
Female	2014	385.1		Féminine
Enrolment in tertiary education (000)	2013	46.1		Scolarisation dans le tertiaire (000)
Female	2013	24.1		Féminine
Literacy rate	2014	34.5		Taux d'alphabétisation (deux sexes)
Male	2014	44.3		Masculin
Female	2014	26.1		Féminin
Pupil teacher ratio - primary	2015	49.6		Ratio élève-enseignant
Budget allocation to education (%)	2013	15.9		Dépenses publiques consacrées à l'enseignement (% du budget)
Poverty				**Pauvreté**
GNI per capita, PPP (current int. $)	2016	1730.0		RNB par habitant, ($ PPA inter. courants)
Human Poverty Index (HPI-1) Value (%)	2007	51.8		Valeur de l'Indice de pauvreté (IPH-1) (%)
Population below Inter. poverty line ($2/day) (%)	2009	55.3		Population sous le seuil inter. de pauvreté (2$/Jour) (%)
Share of income held by richest 10%	2009	32.1		% de revenu des 10% plus riches
Share of income held by poorest 10%	2009	2.7		% de revenu des 10% plus pauvres
GINI index	2009	39.8		Indice de GINI

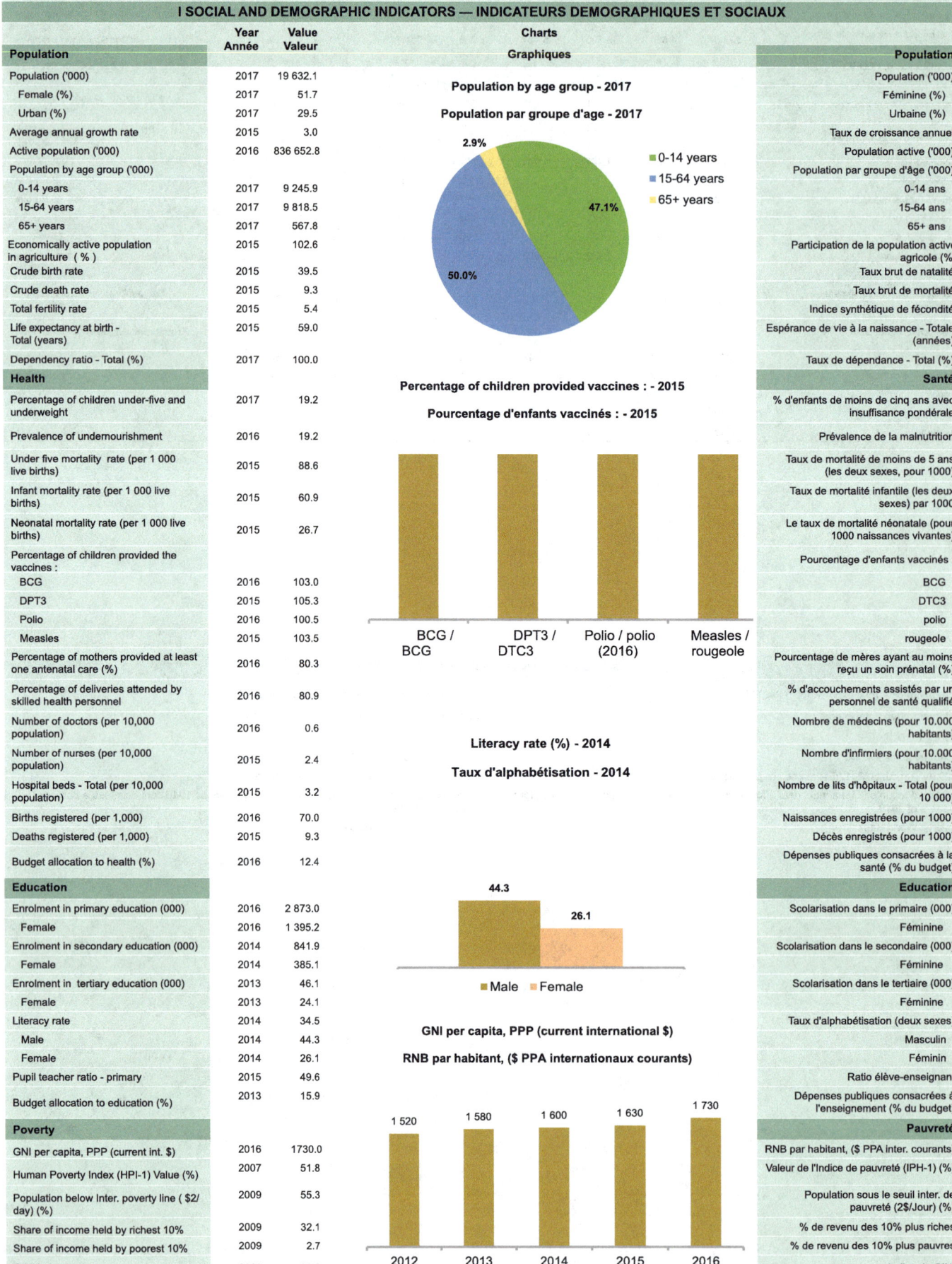

Population by age group - 2017
Population par groupe d'age - 2017

- 0-14 years 47.1%
- 15-64 years 50.0%
- 65+ years 2.9%

Percentage of children provided vaccines : - 2015
Pourcentage d'enfants vaccinés : - 2015

BCG / BCG — DPT3 / DTC3 — Polio / polio (2016) — Measles / rougeole

Literacy rate (%) - 2014
Taux d'alphabétisation - 2014

Male 44.3 — Female 26.1

GNI per capita, PPP (current international $)
RNB par habitant, ($ PPA internationaux courants)

2012: 1 520 — 2013: 1 580 — 2014: 1 600 — 2015: 1 630 — 2016: 1 730

	2009	2010	2011	2012	2013	2014	2015	2016	2017	
GROSS DOMESTIC PRODUCT BY KIND OF ECONOMIC ACTIVITY AT CURRENT PRICES *CFA FRANC (MILLIONS)*										**PRODUIT INTÉRIEUR BRUT PAR BRANCHE D'ACTIVITÉ ÉCONOMIQUE AUX PRIX COURANTS** *FRANC CFA (MILLIONS)*
Agriculture, hunting , forestry and Fishing	1 280 100	1 447 300	1 558 100	1 794 700	1 869 100	1 954 100	1 865 500	1 916 500	2 085 962	Agriculture, chasse sylviculture et Pêche
Mining and quarrying	117 400	313 400	535 100	583 600	463 300	456 000	455 800	574 200	847 554	Industries extractives
Manufacturing	332 100	321 000	355 100	384 900	310 300	327 900	408 100	543 501	409 146	Industries manufacturières
Electricity, gas & water	46 100	34 400	43 800	32 800	42 900	44 800	78 900	57 200	83 449	Electricité, gaz et eau
Construction	199 900	265 900	316 000	274 200	285 600	265 800	228 000	307 600	259 487	Bâtiments et travaux publics
Wholesale & retail trade, restaurants, hotels	461 600	470 800	487 600	547 000	688 300	724 300	690 600	824 400	788 479	Commerce de gros et de détail, restaurants et hôtels
Finance, insurance, real estate, etc.	232 700	259 300	270 100	329 200	337 600	391 900	436 000	435 900	511 200	Banques, assurances, affaires immobilières
Transport and communications	178 900	179 700	177 800	238 900	256 600	277 200	189 800	326 600	312 386	Transport(s) et communications
Public administration and defense	714 100	729 300	827 100	927 100	986 400	1 031 500	1 172 200	1 210 769	1 538 207	Administrations publiques et défense
Education	...	...	...	...	...	...	...	...	...	Education
Health And Social Work	...	...	...	...	...	...	...	...	...	Santé et Actions Sociales
Other services	86 500	88 500	90 500	92 600	94 700	96 800	98 900	101 930	125 300	Autres services
Less Imputed Service Charges	- 50 900	- 46 100	- 57 600	- 85 100	- 86 500	- 92 300	- 95 800	- 110 100	- 116 871	Moins Services d'intermédiation financière
Gross domestic product at factor cost / basic prices	3 598 500	4 063 500	4 603 600	5 119 900	5 248 300	5 478 000	5 528 000	6 188 499	6 844 300	Produit intérieur brut aux couts des facteurs / prix de base
Plus: Indirect Taxes / taxes on products, less subsidies	353 300	384 200	456 700	580 900	648 000	582 100	634 500	647 000	714 523	Plus taxes indirectes/impôts sur les produits, moins les subventions
EXPENDITURE ON GROSS DOMESTIC PRODUCT AT CURRENT PURCHASER'S VALUES *CFA FRANC (MILLIONS)*										**EMPLOI DU PRODUIT INTÉRIEUR BRUT AUX PRIX COURANTS D'ACQUISITION** *FRANC CFA (MILLIONS)*
Government final consumption	854 900	918 000	1 040 700	1 188 200	1 258 400	1 336 800	1 429 200	1 569 800	...	Consommation finale des administrations publiques
Private final consumption	2 707 700	2 795 000	3 016 700	3 226 200	3 607 300	3 690 000	3 820 700	3 773 300	...	Consommation finale privée
Gross fixed capital formation	905 600	1 089 700	1 336 600	1 672 000	1 876 800	1 840 700	1 521 500	2 125 900	...	Formation brute de capital fixe
Change in inventories	77 300	108 000	78 600	177 900	35 300	51 900	22 200	43 700	...	Variation des stocks
Exports of goods and services	501 900	855 100	1 265 300	1 554 700	1 544 400	1 571 700	1 605 100	1 951 300	...	Exportations de biens et services
Less imports of goods and services	1 095 500	1 318 300	1 677 500	2 118 400	2 426 000	2 431 200	2 236 200	2 628 600	...	Moins importations de biens et services
GDP at purchasers' values	3 951 800	4 447 600	5 060 300	5 700 600	5 896 200	6 059 900	6 162 500	6 835 500	7 558 823	PIB aux prix d'acquisition
GROSS DOMESTIC PRODUCT BY KIND OF ECONOMIC ACTIVITY AT CONSTANT PRICES *ANNUAL GROWTH RATES (%)*										**PRODUIT INTÉRIEUR BRUT PAR BRANCHE D'ACTIVITÉ ECONOMIQUE AUX PRIX CONSTANTS** *TAUX DE CROISSANCE ANNUEL (%)*
Agriculture, hunting , forestry and Fishing	- 9.2	11.3	- 3.4	7.9	2.9	2.7	- 2.8	5.2	0.8	Agriculture, chasse sylviculture et Pêche
Mining and quarrying	142.1	71.9	32.0	- 12.1	1.4	11.1	- 10.0	4.2	21.4	Industries extractives
Manufacturing	- 1.2	- 5.7	10.1	2.8	- 2.5	27.1	- 2.4	- 1.5	4.7	Industries manufacturières
Electricity, gas & water	3.2	- 22.8	54.6	- 17.9	21.7	26.0	20.2	5.2	11.0	Electricité, gaz et eau
Construction	5.9	21.8	21.1	- 11.7	- 7.7	- 1.0	23.3	9.6	8.3	Bâtiments et travaux publics
Wholesale & retail trade, restaurants, hotels	15.5	- 1.2	1.8	9.1	16.8	- 10.4	4.2	7.4	6.3	Commerce de gros et de détail, restaurants et hôtels
Finance, insurance, real estate, etc.	1.8	6.6	- 21.2	8.4	21.0	22.6	- 2.9	8.2	11.0	Banques, assurances, affaires immobilières
Transport and communications	- 4.9	27.6	18.7	26.2	7.2	1.2	2.7	6.6	4.9	Transport(s) et communications
Public administration and defense	3.6	- 1.3	14.4	5.2	1.4	4.4	14.3	8.6	9.1	Administrations publiques et défense
Education	...	...	...	...	...	...	...	...	...	Education
Health And Social Work	...	...	...	...	...	...	...	...	...	Santé et Actions Sociales
Other services	...	...	...	...	...	...	...	...	...	Autres services
Less Imputed Service Charges	- 5.2	- 9.2	25.0	46.7	- 0.2	5.9	7.1	7.7	10.9	Moins Services d'intermédiation financière
Gross domestic product at factor cost / basic prices	1.6	8.2	5.8	4.5	5.3	5.4	3.5	6.3	6.6	Produit intérieur brut aux couts des facteurs / prix de base
Plus: Indirect Taxes / taxes on products, less subsidies	19.4	10.9	14.7	24.3	9.6	- 3.6	7.2	3.1	7.6	Plus taxes indirectes/impôts sur les produits, moins les subventions
Gross domestic product at market prices	3.0	8.4	6.6	6.5	5.8	4.3	3.9	5.9	6.7	Produit intérieur brut aux prix du marché
EXPENDITURE ON GROSS DOMESTIC PRODUCT AT CONSTANT PURCHASERS' VALUES *ANNUAL GROWTH RATES (%)*										**EMPLOIS DU PRODUIT INTÉRIEUR BRUT AUX PRIX CONSTANTS D'ACQUISITION** *TAUX DE CROISSANCE ANNUEL (%)*
Government final consumption	2.5	5.7	7.6	8.1	4.6	5.4	13.7	3.6	1.5	Consommation finale des administrations publiques
Private final consumption	1.4	2.1	3.6	6.7	6.9	4.5	2.5	0.6	21.7	Consommation finale privée
Gross fixed capital formation	15.7	23.5	20.5	23.8	9.6	1.3	- 7.7	24.7	- 5.8	Formation brute de capital fixe
Exports of goods and services	17.5	52.1	26.0	4.2	18.0	- 4.4	14.8	- 2.7	10.0	Exportations de biens et services
Less imports of goods and services	13.2	22.3	22.9	24.3	13.6	- 1.1	0.4	8.8	13.4	Moins importations de biens et services

III INFLATION

Annual growth rates (%)	2009	2010	2011	2012	2013	2014	2015	2016	2017	Taux de croissance annuel (%)
All item	0.9	- 0.6	2.8	3.8	0.5	- 0.3	1.0	- 0.4	2.1	Ensemble
of which:										dont:
Food and non-alcoholic beverages	3.5	1.5	6.1	5.4	- 0.4	- 3.2	2.4	0.4	3.9	Alimentation et boissons non alcoolisés
Alcoholic beverages, tobacco and narcotics	- 1.4	- 0.9	1.9	5.3	- 1.4	- 2.9	- 1.8	0.4	- 0.3	Boissons alcoolisées et tabacs
Clothing and footwear	0.4	- 0.3	0.6	1.0	0.2	-	-	-	-	Habillement et chaussures
Housing, water, electricity, gas and other fuels	0.7	1.5	3.8	4.1	2.8	2.8	3.1	- 0.6	-	Logement, eau, électricité, gaz et autres combustibles
Furnishings, household equipment and routine household maintenance	- 0.5	- 1.3	0.4	- 0.1	0.1	0.2	- 0.6	- 0.2	0.3	Meubles, articles de ménage et entretien courant
Health	- 0.4	0.2	0.6	0.1	0.4	-	0.1	0.3	...	Santé
Transport	- 1.7	- 1.2	2.3	4.5	1.9	6.9	- 2.0	- 3.5	0.1	Transport
Communication	- 5.1	- 18.9	- 18.6	1.0	0.6	0.8	- 0.2	-	...	Communication
Recreation and culture	- 0.8	- 0.3	0.2	- 0.6	- 1.4	- 0.8	0.5	0.4	- 0.1	Loisirs et culture
Education	0.4	1.7	0.4	0.5	1.4	0.9	2.8	0.3	2.0	Enseignement
Restaurants and hotels	0.5	2.2	6.6	4.7	0.9	- 2.0	- 0.8	- 0.4	4.9	Restaurants et hôtels
Miscellaneous goods and services	2.3	- 0.7	0.7	0.9	0.6	0.8	0.1	0.1	...	Biens et Services divers

BURKINA FASO

IV AGRICULTURAL PRODUCTION - PRODUCTION AGRICOLE

TONNES (THOUSAND)	2009	2010	2011	2012	2013	2014	2015	2016	2017	Tonnes (milliers)
Sorghum	1 521	1 990	1 506	1 924	2 116	1 836	1 708	1 436	...	Sorgho
Millet	971	1 148	829	...	...	1 038	973	946	...	Millet
Maize	895	1 133	1 077	1 556	1 712	1 420	1 433	1 470	...	Maïs
Cotton lint	484	530	441	549	620	813	895	769	...	Fibre de coton
Cow peas, dry	454	626	730	641	705	797	563	571	...	Pois à vache secs

V MINING PRODUCTION - PRODUCTION MINIERE

	2009	2010	2011	2012	2013	2014	2015	2016	2017	
Gold ores and concentrates - Production (Kilograms)	11 581	22 939	31 774	...	...	36 283	36 451	38 530	43 473	Minerais d'or et leurs concentrés - Production (Kilogrammes)
Natural phosphates, P2O5 content - Production, metric tons (thousands)	2	2	2	...	...	145 022	137 301	155 680	167 715	Phosphates naturels, teneur en P2O5 - Production, tonnes métriques (milliers)
	...	...	...	...	...	...	...	...	...	

VI ENERGY - ENERGIE

	2009	2010	2011	2012	2013	2014	2015	2016	2017	
Total electricity generation (GWh)	700	565	612	479	731	791	799	...	...	Production électrique totale (GWh)
of which										dont
Production of electricity from fossil fuels (GWh)	567	448	530	382	625	722	722			Production d'électricité à partir de combustibles fossiles (GWh)
Production of hydro electricity (GWh)	132	118	82	97	106	64	70	...	...	Production d'électricité d'origine hydraulique (GWh)
Production of electricity from solar, wind, tide, wave and other sources (GWh)	...	...	...	...	...	5	7	...	...	Production d'électricité d'origine solaire, éolienne, marée motrice et autres (GWh)

VII TOURISM AND INFRASTRUCTURE - TOURISME ET INFRASTUCTURE

	2009	2010	2011	2012	2013	2014	2015	2016	2017	
VII-1 Tourism										**VII-1 Tourisme**
International tourist arrivals (thousands)	269	274	238	237	218	191	163	151	159	Arrivées de touristes internationaux (milliers)
Rooms in hotels and similar establishments (thousands)	...	7	...	7	8	8	11	11	...	Chambres d'hôtels et établissements assimilés (milliers)
Overnight stays (thousands)	793	815	708	710	697	544	481	451	481	Nuitées (milliers)
Tourism receipts (US$ thousand)	66 400	71 600	74 100	83 300	151 500	133 400	118 737	116 450	123 892	Recettes touristiques (milliers de $ EU)
Total contribution to GDP (%)	3.8	3.6	3.2	3.8	4.3	3.9	4.1	4.0	3.9	Contribution totale au PIB (%)
Total contribution to Employment (%)	3.4	3.0	3.0	3.4	3.8	3.3	3.6	3.4	3.3	Contribution totale à l'emploi (%)
VII-2 Infrastructure										**VII-2 Infrastructure**
Paved road (% of total)	15.3	16.0	20.6	...	...	...	...	...	...	Routes asphaltées (% du total)
Total network (Railways-km)	622	622	622	622	622	622	...	...	...	Réseau total voies ferrées-Km
Main telephone lines (per 100 inhabitants)	1.0	0.9	0.9	0.9	0.8	0.7	...	...	...	Lignes téléphoniques fixes (pour 100 habitants)
Mobile cellular subscribers (per 100 inhabitants)	25.3	36.7	48.0	60.6	66.4	71.7	80.6	83.6	...	Abonnés aux téléphones mobiles (pour 100 habitants)
Internet users per 100 inhabitants	1.1	2.4	3.0	3.7	9.1	9.4	11.4	14.0	...	Utilisateurs Internet par 100 Habitants
Fixed (wired)-broadband subscriptions per 100 inhabitants	...	...	...	...	...	...	...	...	...	Abonnements à l'Internet fixe (filaire) à large bande pour 100 habitants, par débit

VIII EXTERNAL TRADE - COMMERCE EXTERIEUR

	2009	2010	2011	2012	2013	2014	2015	2016	2017	
US$ (MILLIONS) EXPORTS, FOB										**$ E.U (MILLIONS) EXPORTATIONS, FÀB**
Exports - Total	900	1 591	2 312	2 411	2 356	2 453	2 177	2 401	...	Exportations - Total
Exports to Africa	119	273	511	324	416	531	246	350	...	Exportations vers l'Afrique
Main products										**Principaux produits**
Cotton	383	480	664	342	423	420	344	205	...	Coton
Fruits and nuts (excluding oil nuts), fresh or dried	10	23	113	36	48	46	93	62	...	Fruits et noix (à l'exclusion des oléagineux), frais ou secs
Gold, non-monetary (excluding gold ores and concentrates)	319	817	1 141	1 684	1 412	1 336	1 399	1 825	...	Or, non monétaire (à l'exclusion des minerais d'or et des concentrés)
Oil seeds and oleaginous fruits (excluding flour)	56	93	104	63	92	91	121	53	...	Graines oléagineuses et oléagineuses (à l'exclusion de la farine)
Petroleum oils or bituminous minerals > 70 % oil	...	...	1	96	192	230	1	36	...	Huiles de pétrole ou de minéraux bitumineux> 70% d'huile
Main destinations										**Principales destinations**
China	80	98	194	158	158	74	58	16	...	Chine
India	7	4	27	11	11	53	268	145	...	Inde
Mali	13	15	59	62	169	235	30	43	...	Mali
Singapore	128	99	189	59	67	91	117	105	...	Singapour
Switzerland	302	645	702	1 437	1 323	1 283	1 127	1 611	...	Suisse
IMPORTS, CIF										
Imports - Total	1 870	2 048	2 406	3 129	4 365	3 575	2 980	3 161	...	Importations - Total (millions)
Imports from Africa	750	753	974	1 115	1 650	1 890	1 052	720	...	Importations en provenance de l'Afrique
Main products										**Principaux produits**
Civil engineering & contractors' plant & equipment	33	38	62	139	174	73	78	142	...	Génie civil et installations et équipements des entrepreneurs
Fertilizers (other than those of group 272)	69	83	115	141	160	93	97	104	...	Engrais (autres que ceux du groupe 272)
Lime, cement, fabrica. constr. mat. (excludingglass, clay)	74	67	85	122	152	105	111	78	...	Chaux, ciment, tissu. constr. tapis. (sauf verre, argile)
Medicaments (incl. veterinary medicaments)	99	103	100	109	178	152	129	117	...	Médicaments (y compris les médicaments vétérinaires)
Petroleum oils or bituminous minerals > 70 % oil	326	325	328	542	827	752	595	429	...	Huiles de pétrole ou de minéraux bitumineux> 70% d'huile
Main origin										**Principales provenances**
China	119	138	147	194	303	252	248	385	...	Chine
Côte d'Ivoire	344	386	303	358	500	672	428	257	...	Côte d'Ivoire
France	288	288	300	319	470	432	304	223	...	France
Ghana	137	72	285	233	343	326	211	104	...	Ghana
Togo	88	66	105	158	215	291	113	88	...	Togo

BURKINA FASO

	2009	2010	2011	2012	2013	2014	2015	2016	2017	
IX-1 MONETARY STATISTICS *CFA FRANC (MILLIONS)*										**IX-1 STATISTIQUES MONÉTAIRES** *FRANC CFA (MILLIONS)*
Money supply (M1)	1 107 491	1 319 511	1 501 097	1 740 227	1 924 582	2 141 764	2 563 202	2 868 292	3 211 508	Masse monétaire (M1)
Quasi-money	432 994	591 273	630 901	744 716	849 263	924 934	1 066 103	1 172 887	1 347 761	Quasi-monnaie
of which demand deposit	...	...	...	...	...	...	...	...	...	dont Monnaie scripturale
Net foreign assets	574 706	657 749	681 958	680 015	547 674	94 747	162 531	400 058	384 468	Avoirs extérieurs nets
Domestic credit	583 578	718 269	864 380	1 055 593	1 454 362	1 826 942	1 981 432	1 994 011	2 372 610	Crédit intérieur
of which claims on private sector	- 88 489	- 52 346	- 87 219	- 125 579	- 37 952	50 015	24 056	- 80 495	63 907	dont créances sur le secteur privé
of which claims on government sector, net	671 077	769 405	950 539	1 180 112	1 491 476	1 572 875	1 705 167	1 909 007	2 202 360	dont créances nettes sur le gouvernement
International reserves (millions US$)	1 296	1 068	1 036	998	603	285	266	282	275	Réserves internationales (millions $EU)
Average exchange rate (National currency per US$)	472	495	472	511	494	494	591	593	582	Taux de change (moyen) (monnaie nationale par $ EU)
IX-2 PUBLIC FINANCE *CFA FRANC (MILLIONS)*										**IX-2 FINANCES PUBLIQUES** *FRANC CFA (MILLIONS)*
Total Revenues and Grants	771 524	880 286	1 047 249	1 276 671	1 441 993	1 321 439	1 288 519	1 412 575	1 583 575	Recettes totales et dons
Direct taxes (on income, profits)	116 421	143 221	210 912	267 797	288 713	307 919	280 102	348 396	343 005	Taxes directes
Domestic indirect taxes revenues	254 899	318 615	366 725	467 465	523 444	509 615	528 874	601 624	702 884	Taxes Indirectes
Trade taxes	117 773	96 760	111 977	148 870	180 873	157 047	153 426	159 139	181 189	Taxes sur le commerce extérieur
Other taxes	5 490	7 133	5 983	7 002	...	...	10 082	5 036	11 639	Autres taxes
Other revenues	44 513	115 614	97 982	108 036	124 661	90 410	86 034	116 343	151 030	Autres recettes
Grants	232 428	198 944	253 670	277 501	324 300	256 447	230 000	182 038	194 304	Dons
Total Expenditures and Net Lending	883 440	1 041 902	1 164 340	1 452 763	1 648 807	1 434 749	1 411 577	1 665 084	2 146 470	Dépenses totales et prêts nets
Current expenditure	445 835	474 820	600 425	786 860	784 223	842 692	879 454	1 053 401	1 318 661	Dépenses courantes
Wages and Salaries	228 436	245 820	281 445	332 340	355 523	437 292	468 530	554 474	617 951	Rémunérations et salaires
Other purchases of goods and services	92 901	90 856	97 556	120 571	118 600	102 400	109 443	127 983	174 079	Achat de biens et services
Other current expenditure	...	...	...	...	...	...	...	...	...	Autres dépenses courantes
Current transfers	124 497	138 145	221 424	333 950	310 100	303 000	301 481	370 944	527 116	Transferts courants
Interest payments	13 243	20 983	26 130	41 703	30 884	44 129	43 744	65 346	69 515	Intérêts
Capital expenditure	430 007	552 299	535 133	625 077	858 500	554 127	500 940	555 000	831 335	Dépenses d'équipement
Net lending	- 5 644	- 6 200	2 652	- 877	- 24 800	- 6 200	- 12 561	- 8 663	- 3 525	Prêts nets
Fiscal balance	- 111 917	- 161 616	- 117 092	- 176 092	- 206 815	- 113 310	- 123 058	- 252 509	- 562 895	Solde global y compris les dons
IX-3 BALANCE OF PAYMENTS *CFA FRANC (MILLIONS)*										**IX-3 BALANCE DES PAIEMENTS** *FRANC CFA (MILLIONS)*
Trade balance	- 227 599	- 65 584	14 173	108 482	- 328 836	- 128 639	- 142 726	- 88 152	- 162 400	Balance commerciale
Services Balance	- 192 078	- 265 075	- 343 076	- 407 564	- 459 401	- 423 169	- 458 740	- 476 159	- 499 200	Balance des services
Net primary income	- 2 592	- 3 206	- 3 718	- 39 056	- 93 250	- 177 518	- 199 478	- 176 684	- 189 100	Revenus primaires nets
Compensation of employees	- 2 169	- 1 375	- 1 499	- 15 365	- 13 639	- 7 002	- 7 861	- 8 453	- 617 951	Rémunération des salariés
Investment income	- 423	- 1 831	- 2 219	- 23 691	- 79 611	- 170 516	- 189 767	- 166 431	...	Revenus des investissements
Net secondary income	242 820	243 998	257 036	255 278	216 922	236 088	271 572	228 526	286 400	Revenus secondaires nets
Net official transfers	...	...	191 183	179 531	128 174	114 318	145 871	98 376	457 116	Transferts officiels nets
Workers' remittances	...	...	96 420	99 294	144 282	123 407	128 596	130 150	...	Envois de fonds des travailleurs
Other private transfers	...	...	...	...	...	...	...	...	...	Autres transferts privés
Current account balance	- 179 449	- 89 867	- 75 585	- 82 860	- 664 564	- 493 237	- 529 372	- 512 469	- 564 300	Solde du compte courant
Capital and financial account	405 559	174 348	123 981	76 081	521 347	363 681	808 641	811 954	567 300	Comptes de capital et financier
Capital account	132 904	98 895	91 070	137 779	238 412	200 189	153 774	150 143	257 700	Compte de capital
Financial account	272 655	75 453	32 911	- 61 698	282 935	163 492	654 867	661 811	309 600	Compte financier
Errors and omissions	- 1 422	1 512	- 4 274	3 408	- 3 800	- 3 360	4 301	- 3 970	...	Erreurs et omissions
Overall balance	224 688	85 993	44 122	- 3 371	- 147 018	- 132 916	283 570	295 515	3 000	Balance générale

BURKINA FASO

X DEBT AND FINANCIAL FLOWS - DETTE ET FLUX FINANCIERS

	2008	2009	2010	2011	2012	2013	2014	2015	2016	
X-1 DEBT *US $ (MILLIONS)*										**X-1 DETTE EXTÉRIEURE** *$ E.U (MILLIONS)*
Total external debt	2 146	2 393	2 333	2 562	2 637	2 708	2 704	2 920	3 120	Dette extérieure totale
Private	...	...	...	...	...	...	...	...		Privée
Public	2 146	2 393	2 333	2 562	2 637	2 708	2 704	2 920	...	Publique
Total external debt service	51	52	63	79	90	99	109	118	...	Service de la dette extérieure
Present value of external debt	1 394	1 704	1 787	1 960	...	...	...	1 846	...	Valeur actuelle de la dette extérieure
Total government domestic debt, National currency (millions)	259	315	438	555	434	523			...	Dette publique intérieure
X-2 FINANCIAL FLOWS *US $ (MILLIONS)*										**X-2 FLUX FINANCIERS** *$ E.U (MILLIONS)*
Net Foreign Direct Investment Inflows	101	35	144	329	490	356	232	309	...	Investissements étranger direct (flux nets entrants)
Main origin of FDI inflows										**Principales origines de l'IDE entrant:**
...	...	...	...	...	...	...	...	...	...	...
Norway	69	7	...	...	...	...	...	...	...	Norvège
...	...	...	...	...	...	...	...	...	...	...
...	...	...	...	...	...	...	...	...	...	...
...	...	...	...	...	...	...	...	...	...	...
African countries	...	...	...	...	...	...	...	...	...	Pays africains
Net total official development assistance	1 084	1 045	982	1 152	1 045	1 123	997	1 023	...	Aide publique au développement (nette totale)
Main origin of net ODA										**Principales origines de l'APD nette**
International Development Association [IDA]	224	191	219	216	177	238	262	330	...	International Development Association
France	77	64	79	65	62	59	67	66	...	France
...	...	...	...	...	...	...	...	...	...	...
Netherlands	66	54	54	41	43	...	...	...	...	Pays-Bas
Germany	48	53	44	51	44	50	47	44	...	Allemagne

SOURCES AND NOTES - SOURCES ET NOTES

External trade - Total exports, fob: UNCTAD

External trade - Total import, cif: UNCTAD

ODA: OECD

Monetary statistics: IMF

National Accounts:2013- 2014-2015 : Revised ; 2016-207: Provisional

Poverty: World Bank

Commerce exterieur - Exportation, fab: CNUCED

Commerce exterieur - Imporations, caf: CNUCED

APD: OCDE

Statistiques monétaires: FMI

Comptes nationaux:2013-2014- 2015 Révisées -2016-2017:Provisoires

Pauvreté: Banque mondiale

AREA (km2)		27 830	**SUPERFICIE (KM2)**
CAPITAL CITY	Bujumbura	Bujumbura	**CAPITALE**
CURRENCY	Burundi Franc	Franc du Burundi	**MONNAIE**

I SOCIAL AND DEMOGRAPHIC INDICATORS — INDICATEURS DEMOGRAPHIQUES ET SOCIAUX

	Year Année	Value Valeur	Charts Graphiques	
Population				**Population**
Population ('000)	2017	10 400.9		Population ('000)
Female (%)	2017	50.9		Féminine (%)
Urban (%)	2015	12.1		Urbaine (%)
Average annual growth rate	2015	3.2		Taux de croissance annuel
Active population ('000)	2017	5 610.8		Population active ('000)
Population by age group ('000)				Population par groupe d'âge ('000)
0-14 years	2017	4 563.2		0-14 ans
15-64 years	2017	5 610.8		15-64 ans
65+ years	2017	227.0		65+ ans
Economically active population in agriculture (%)	2015	78.0		Participation de la population active agricole (%)
Crude birth rate	2017	37.9		Taux brut de natalité
Crude death rate	2015	11.1		Taux brut de mortalité
Total fertility rate	2017	5.5		Indice synthétique de fécondité
Life expectancy at birth - Total (years)	2015	57.1		Espérance de vie à la naissance - Totale (années)
Dependency ratio - Total (%)	2017	85.4		Taux de dépendance - Total (%)
Health				**Santé**
Percentage of children under-five and underweight	2011	29.1		% d'enfants de moins de cinq ans avec insuffisance pondérale
Prevalence of undernourishment	...	...		Prévalence de la malnutrition
Under five mortality rate (per 1 000 live births)	2015	81.7		Taux de mortalité de moins de 5 ans (les deux sexes, pour 1000)
Infant mortality rate (per 1 000 live births)	2015	54.1		Taux de mortalité infantile (les deux sexes) par 1000
Neonatal mortality rate (per 1 000 live births)	2015	28.6		Le taux de mortalité néonatale (pour 1000 naissances vivantes)
Percentage of children provided the vaccines :				Pourcentage d'enfants vaccinés :
BCG	2016	82.8		BCG
DPT3	2014	95.0		DTC3
Polio	2016	100.0		polio
Measles	2014	94.0		rougeole
Percentage of mothers provided at least one antenatal care (%)	2010	98.9		Pourcentage de mères ayant au moins reçu un soin prénatal (%)
Percentage of deliveries attended by skilled health personnel	2010	60.3		% d'accouchements assistés par un personnel de santé qualifié
Number of doctors (per 10,000 population)	2016	0.5		Nombre de médecins (pour 10.000 habitants)
Number of nurses (per 10,000 population)	2016	6.8		Nombre d'infirmiers (pour 10.000 habitants)
Hospital beds - Total (per 10,000 population)	2014	1.3		Nombre de lits d'hôpitaux - Total (pour 10 000)
Births registered (per 1,000)	2015	43.5		Naissances enregistrées (pour 1000)
Deaths registered (per 1,000)	2015	11.1		Décès enregistrés (pour 1000)
Budget allocation to health (%)	2014	7.5		Dépenses publiques consacrées à la santé (% du budget)
Education				**Education**
Enrolment in primary education (000)	2015	2 202.8		Scolarisation dans le primaire (000)
Female	2015	1 114.9		Féminine
Enrolment in secondary education (000)	2015	533.8		Scolarisation dans le secondaire (000)
Female	2015	255.1		Féminine
Enrolment in tertiary education (000)	2013	44.9		Scolarisation dans le tertiaire (000)
Female	2013	13.9		Féminine
Literacy rate	2008	86.9		Taux d'alphabétisation (deux sexes)
Male	2008	88.8		Masculin
Female	2008	84.6		Féminin
Pupil teacher ratio - primary	...	...		Ratio élève-enseignant
Budget allocation to education (%)	2013	17.1		Dépenses publiques consacrées à l'enseignement (% du budget)
Poverty				**Pauvreté**
GNI per capita, PPP (current int. $)	2016	770.0		RNB par habitant, ($ PPA inter. courants)
Human Poverty Index (HPI-1) Value (%)	2014	44.2		Valeur de l'Indice de pauvreté (IPH-1) (%)
Population below Inter. poverty line ($2/day) (%)	2006	77.7		Population sous le seuil inter. de pauvreté (2$/Jour) (%)
Share of income held by richest 10%	2006	28.0		% de revenu des 10% plus riches
Share of income held by poorest 10%	2006	4.0		% de revenu des 10% plus pauvres
GINI index	2006	33.4		Indice de GINI

Population by age group - 2017

Population par groupe d'age - 2017

- 0-14 years: 43.9%
- 15-64 years: 53.9%
- 65+ years: 2.2%

Percentage of children provided vaccines : - 2014

Pourcentage d'enfants vaccinés : - 2014

BCG / BCG	DPT3 / DTC3	Polio / polio (2016)	Measles / rougeole
82.8	95.0	100.0	94.0

Literacy rate (%) - 2008

Taux d'alphabétisation - 2008

Male 88.8 — Female 84.6

GNI per capita, PPP (current international $)

RNB par habitant, ($ PPA internationaux courants)

2012	2013	2014	2015	2016
790	820	850	800	770

II NATIONAL ACCOUNTS — COMPTES NATIONAUX

	2009	2010	2011	2012	2013	2014	2015	2016	2017	
GROSS DOMESTIC PRODUCT BY KIND OF ECONOMIC ACTIVITY AT CURRENT PRICES BURUNDI FRANC (MILLIONS)										**PRODUIT INTÉRIEUR BRUT PAR BRANCHE D'ACTIVITÉ ÉCONOMIQUE AUX PRIX COURANTS** FRANC DU BURUNDI (MILLIONS)
Agriculture, hunting , forestry and Fishing	804 752	961 166	1 034 898	1 192 188	1 462 746	1 463 000	1 624 200	1 757 021	1 962 866	Agriculture, chasse sylviculture et Pêche
Mining and quarrying	12 334	12 153	10 419	13 281	15 471	14 300	13 900	14 644	17 348	Industries extractives
Manufacturing	248 042	256 177	282 775	353 777	409 740	458 500	476 300	507 608	519 702	Industries manufacturières
Electricity, gas & water	16 053	11 762	14 698	25 095	27 428	30 200	31 300	32 723	34 372	Electricité, gaz et eau
Construction	94 364	104 723	109 672	137 997	141 527	143 700	134 600	138 547	142 565	Bâtiments et travaux publics
Wholesale & retail trade, restaurants, hotels	415 991	454 534	512 982	615 324	613 736	703 100	719 100	757 475	793 149	Commerce de gros et de détail, restaurants et hôtels
Finance, insurance, real estate, etc.	65 280	93 005	108 267	119 026	120 532	144 800	194 300	232 966	275 994	Banques, assurances, affaires immobilières
Transport and communications	91 401	88 414	90 230	107 164	107 918	163 800	185 200	197 291	218 183	Transport(s) et communications
Public administration and defense	150 068	142 743	159 270	203 696	234 585	287 200	295 600	318 036	343 789	Administrations publiques et défense
Education	85 089	140 966	184 670	219 692	227 943	253 600	265 000	277 479	297 763	Education
Health And Social Work	25 475	38 386	66 971	98 387	106 437	121 500	126 500	149 510	175 706	Santé et Actions Sociales
Other services	53 601	57 228	54 865	49 659	67 578	99 200	117 400	138 136	156 571	Autres services
Less Imputed Service Charges	- 57 650	- 91 111	- 105 997	- 105 326	- 105 333	- 133 700	- 177 800	- 203 492	- 269 118	Moins Services d'intermédiation financière
Gross domestic product at factor cost / basic prices	2 004 800	2 270 146	2 523 720	3 029 960	3 430 308	3 749 200	4 005 600	4 317 943	4 668 891	Produit intérieur brut aux couts des facteurs / prix de base
Plus: Indirect Taxes / taxes on products, less subsidies	186 709	230 901	295 814	335 850	382 192	435 900	417 600	436 910	501 868	Plus taxes indirectes/impôts sur les produits, moins les subventions
EXPENDITURE ON GROSS DOMESTIC PRODUCT AT CURRENT PURCHASER'S VALUES BURUNDI FRANC (MILLIONS)										**EMPLOI DU PRODUIT INTÉRIEUR BRUT AUX PRIX COURANTS D'ACQUISITION** FRANC DU BURUNDI (MILLIONS)
Government final consumption	424 858	548 523	646 301	782 700	942 479	1 084 030	1 180 514	1 284 399	1 310 087	Consommation finale des administrations publiques
Private final consumption	1 907 004	2 038 000	2 430 149	2 840 200	3 396 350	3 578 055	3 753 408	3 941 078	4 138 132	Consommation finale privée
Gross fixed capital formation	331 246	398 277	435 105	498 700	512 343	604 897	543 123	551 429	648 952	Formation brute de capital fixe
Change in inventories	22 082	40 512	- 34 085	246 993	31 970	29 974	- 24 548	- 96 283	- 71 055	Variation des stocks
Exports of goods and services	145 587	222 431	297 190	328 117	344 070	318 470	280 004	301 573	310 620	Exportations de biens et services
Less imports of goods and services	639 268	746 695	955 126	1 330 900	1 414 712	1 430 326	1 309 301	1 227 345	1 165 977	Moins importations de biens et services
GDP at purchasers' values	2 191 509	2 501 047	2 819 534	3 365 810	3 812 500	4 185 100	4 423 200	4 754 853	5 170 759	PIB aux prix d'acquisition
GROSS DOMESTIC PRODUCT BY KIND OF ECONOMIC ACTIVITY AT CONSTANT PRICES ANNUAL GROWTH RATES (%)										**PRODUIT INTÉRIEUR BRUT PAR BRANCHE D'ACTIVITÉ ECONOMIQUE AUX PRIX CONSTANTS** TAUX DE CROISSANCE ANNUEL (%)
Agriculture, hunting , forestry and Fishing	- 1.2	1.6	- 1.4	2.1	8.4	- 3.6	0.3	- 2.0	- 0.3	Agriculture, chasse sylviculture et Pêche
Mining and quarrying	8.0	- 1.4	14.3	7.9	5.7	- 11.7	- 4.8	- 2.0	10.0	Industries extractives
Manufacturing	1.6	3.3	2.3	3.1	2.2	13.0	0.8	2.6	- 2.3	Industries manufacturières
Electricity, gas & water	- 12.8	- 27.0	- 21.7	15.4	5.5	2.5	- 10.1	1.5	1.0	Electricité, gaz et eau
Construction	34.4	1.5	2.1	8.9	2.3	- 5.4	- 10.1	- 1.5	- 2.0	Bâtiments et travaux publics
Wholesale & retail trade, restaurants, hotels	- 12.9	2.3	2.6	2.5	- 5.8	- 2.3	- 2.6	1.1	0.1	Commerce de gros et de détail, restaurants et hôtels
Finance, insurance, real estate, etc.	18.2	6.7	13.4	8.1	1.0	14.3	19.5	10.0	10.0	Banques, assurances, affaires immobilières
Transport and communications	32.6	- 7.0	1.5	9.1	- 5.6	31.6	0.1	5.4	5.3	Transport(s) et communications
Public administration and defense	19.8	- 5.0	12.6	11.3	13.6	19.6	5.6	6.0	6.5	Administrations publiques et défense
Education	13.7	73.3	22.0	15.0	0.5	4.0	4.7	4.5	5.0	Education
Health And Social Work	29.9	34.4	43.3	13.7	4.4	4.3	4.5	11.5	11.5	Santé et Actions Sociales
Other services	2.1	2.4	- 16.0	- 40.5	19.1	36.9	7.9	7.9	7.9	Autres services
Less Imputed Service Charges	4.7	40.1	18.9	- 4.7	- 0.1	29.2	20.5	9.0	15.0	Moins Services d'intermédiation financière
Gross domestic product at factor cost / basic prices	3.6	3.4	3.1	5.0	4.6	4.1	0.7	1.9	1.4	Produit intérieur brut aux couts des facteurs / prix de base
Plus: Indirect Taxes / taxes on products, less subsidies	5.7	23.5	12.8	- 0.2	8.0	5.2	- 9.1	- 0.4	12.6	Plus taxes indirectes/impôts sur les produits, moins les subventions
Gross domestic product at market prices	3.8	5.1	4.0	4.4	4.9	4.2	- 0.3	1.7	2.5	Produit intérieur brut aux prix du marché
EXPENDITURE ON GROSS DOMESTIC PRODUCT AT CONSTANT PURCHASERS' VALUES ANNUAL GROWTH RATES (%)										**EMPLOIS DU PRODUIT INTÉRIEUR BRUT AUX PRIX CONSTANTS D'ACQUISITION** TAUX DE CROISSANCE ANNUEL (%)
Government final consumption	10.6	35.4	15.2	10.8	17.7	7.1	5.7	3.1	- 1.0	Consommation finale des administrations publiques
Private final consumption	- 5.6	- 5.7	6.9	2.0	12.0	3.3	- 5.3	1.5	- 2.0	Consommation finale privée
Gross fixed capital formation	24.3	34.8	5.2	3.1	2.6	7.6	- 6.2	0.8	8.3	Formation brute de capital fixe
Exports of goods and services	- 26.4	26.0	9.8	39.5	- 3.6	0.3	- 24.3	27.3	2.8	Exportations de biens et services
Less imports of goods and services	- 14.4	20.7	5.9	12.3	21.6	- 0.5	- 15.1	18.4	- 10.9	Moins importations de biens et services

III INFLATION

	2009	2010	2011	2012	2013	2014	2015	2016	2017	
Annual growth rates (%)										**Taux de croissance annuel (%)**
All item	10.5	6.5	9.6	18.2	7.9	4.4	5.5	5.5	16.1	Ensemble
of which:										dont:
Food and non-alcoholic beverages	10.1	6.9	9.6	14.1	9.5	2.3	5.8	7.2	24.0	Alimentation et boissons non alcoolisés
Alcoholic beverages, tobacco and narcotics	...	...	...	...	7.3	- 0.9	- 0.4	12.7	9.3	Boissons alcoolisées et tabacs
Clothing and footwear	9.3	0.8	16.7	24.5	-	8.7	11.8	11.9	10.8	Habillement et chaussures
Housing, water, electricity, gas and other fuels	11.9	9.9	6.2	31.7	6.4	7.0	3.7	1.0	7.4	Logement, eau, électricité, gaz et autres combustibles
Furnishings, household equipment and routine household maintenance	24.2	8.7	6.3	7.1	14.4	17.3	6.7	8.9	9.5	Meubles, articles de ménage et entretien courant
Health	10.8	0.2	30.8	3.8	2.9	8.3	3.0	10.1	3.8	Santé
Transport	- 8.7	2.6	19.8	3.1	8.3	6.4	0.7	2.5	8.7	Transport
Communication	...	...	...	...	...	0.4	17.8	0.5	0.5	Communication
Recreation and culture	...	...	...	...	2.8	4.5	4.6	3.1	7.3	Loisirs et culture
Education	7.2	4.5	5.3	0.3	...	1.0	2.6	1.3	13.6	Enseignement
Restaurants and hotels	...	...	...	...	5.4	6.0	7.9	3.1	7.3	Restaurants et hôtels
Miscellaneous goods and services	15.0	2.0	11.6	17.7	18.0	10.4	6.4	6.3	7.2	Biens et Services divers

IV AGRICULTURAL PRODUCTION - PRODUCTION AGRICOLE

TONNES (THOUSAND)	2009	2010	2011	2012	2013	2014	2015	2016	2017	Tonnes (milliers)
Maize	120	126	128	110	162	128	59	160	...	Maïs
Sweet potatoes	484	303	300	1 167	840	664	414	581	...	Patates douces
Cassava	235	188	160	580	2 234	305	1 884	2 758	...	Manioc
Beans, dry	203	202	199	802	225	252	213	283	...	Haricots secs
Bananas	1 806	137	132	276	2 236	1 363	659	865	...	Bananes

V MINING PRODUCTION - PRODUCTION MINIERE

	2009	2010	2011	2012	2013	2014	2015	2016	2017	
Colombo-tantalite (kg) - Production (Kilograms)	44 207	67 365	158 782	258 578	73 518	81 672	44 480	32	...	Colombo-tantalite (kg) - Production (Kilogrammes)
Gold ores and concentrates - Production (metric tons)	980	310	1 052	2 147	2 823	650	549	396	...	Minerais d'or et leurs concentrés - Production (tonnes métriques)
Tin ores and concentrates, includes Cassiterite - Production (Kilograms)	28	29	52	117	31	35	65	67	...	Minerais d'étain et leurs concentrés - Production (Kilogrammes)

VI ENERGY - ENERGIE

	2009	2010	2011	2012	2013	2014	2015	2016	2017	
Total electricity generation (GWh)	122	241	153	184	184	174	180	...	...	Production électrique totale (GWh)
of which										dont
Production of electricity from fossil fuels (GWh)	2	11	2	4	4	34	43	...	...	Production d'électricité à partir de combustibles fossiles (GWh)
Production of hydro electricity (GWh)	120	230	150	179	179	140	138	...	...	Production d'électricité d'origine hydraulique (GWh)
Production of electricity from solar, wind, tide, wave and other sources (GWh)	...	...	1	1	1	2	2	...	...	Production d'électricité d'origine solaire, éolienne, marée motrice et autres (GWh)

VII TOURISM AND INFRASTRUCTURE - TOURISME ET INFRASTUCTURE

	2009	2010	2011	2012	2013	2014	2015	2016	2017	
VII-1 Tourism										**VII-1 Tourisme**
International tourist arrivals (thousands)	212	142	189	205	149	157	120	106	117	Arrivées de touristes internationaux (milliers)
Rooms in hotels and similar establishments (thousands)	...	...	...	...	...	2	4	...	...	Chambres d'hôtels et établissements assimilés (milliers)
Overnight stays (thousands)	1 274	874	1 162	912	1 452	1 459	813	717	732	Nuitées (milliers)
Tourism receipts (US$ thousand)	1 400	1 700	2 400	1 400	2 200	4 000	1 900	1 500	1 464	Recettes touristiques (milliers de $ EU)
Total contribution to GDP (%)	4.7	5.7	6.4	6.3	6.2	6.0	5.7	5.2	5.1	Contribution totale au PIB (%)
Total contribution to Employment (%)	4.2	5.0	5.7	5.5	5.1	5.2	4.9	4.5	4.4	Contribution totale à l'emploi (%)
VII-2 Infrastructure										**VII-2 Infrastructure**
Paved road (% of total)	15.1	15.5	16.3	16.7	14.8	14.8	15.0	...	...	Routes asphaltées (% du total)
Total network (Railways-km)	...	...	...	...	...	...	...	...	...	Réseau total voies ferrées-Km
Main telephone lines (per 100 inhabitants)	...	...	...	...	...	...	...	...	...	Lignes téléphoniques fixes (pour 100 habitants)
Mobile cellular subscribers (per 100 inhabitants)	10.3	18.2	20.1	22.8	25.0	30.5	46.2	48.0	...	Abonnés aux téléphones mobiles (pour 100 habitants)
Internet users per 100 inhabitants	0.9	1.0	1.1	1.2	1.3	1.4	4.9	5.2		Utilisateurs Internet par 100 Habitants
Fixed (wired)-broadband subscriptions per 100 inhabitants	...	...	...	...	...	...	...	...	...	Abonnements à l'Internet fixe (filaire) à large bande pour 100 habitants, par débit

VIII EXTERNAL TRADE - COMMERCE EXTERIEUR

US$ (MILLIONS) EXPORTS, FOB	2009	2010	2011	2012	2013	2014	2015	2016	2017	$ E.U (MILLIONS) EXPORTATIONS, FÀB
Exports - Total	67	101	123	134	94	142	114	103	...	Exportations - Total
Exports to Africa	12	16	19	19	12	31	26	25	...	Exportations vers l'Afrique
Main products										**Principaux produits**
Coffee and coffee substitutes	41	59	63	43	13	25	24	20	...	Café et succédanés du café
Gold, non-monetary (excluding gold ores and concentrates)	3	9	15	51	59	73	49	44	...	Or, non monétaire (à l'exclusion des minerais d'or et des concentrés)
Ores and concentrates of base metals, n.e.s.	1	4	11	6	4	2	2	2	...	Minerais et concentrés de métaux communs, n.d.a.
Soaps, cleansing and polishing preparations	1	1	2	7	2	4	4	4	...	Savons, préparations pour nettoyer et polir
Tea and mate	7	12	13	11	6	10	13	11	...	Thé et maté
Main destinations										**Principales destinations**
Democratic Republic of Congo	2	3	4	5	3	16	14	15	...	République Démocratique du Congo
Germany	13	15	15	11	3	5	3	5	...	Allemagne
Pakistan	5	8	8	8	3	7	9	7	...	Pakistan
Switzerland	6	12	11	8	2	5	4	1	...	Suisse
United Arab Emirates	3	9	14	51	60	73	49	44	...	Emirates Arabes
IMPORTS, CIF										
Imports - Total	402	509	752	751	811	769	722	616	...	Importations - Total (millions)
Imports from Africa	164	215	278	272	297	266	253	234	...	Importations en provenance de l'Afrique
Main products										**Principaux produits**
Lime, cement, fabrica. constr. mat. (excludingglass, clay)	15	38	33	28	26	22	14	17	...	Chaux, ciment, tissu. constr. tapis. (sauf verre, argile)
Medicaments (incl. veterinary medicaments)	24	31	37	37	47	45	45	39	...	Médicaments (y compris les médicaments vétérinaires)
Medicinal and pharmaceutical products, excluding 542	7	6	11	19	26	36	44	20	...	Produits médicinaux et pharmaceutiques, à l'exclusion de 542
Petroleum oils or bituminous minerals > 70 % oil	4	24	117	118	105	102	80	58	...	Huiles de pétrole ou de minéraux bitumineux> 70% d'huile
Telecommunication equipment, n.e.s.; & parts, n.e.s.	31	22	25	8	32	32	55	35	...	Matériel de télécommunication, n.es .; & parties, n.e.s.
Main origin										**Principales provenances**
Belgium	43	43	63	62	65	71	71	41	...	Belgique
China	36	44	58	63	76	77	74	67	...	Chine
India	16	22	34	50	68	62	62	55	...	Inde
Kenya	49	54	67	63	82	85	87	73	...	Kenya
Tanzania, United Republic of	23	47	70	60	70	61	57	57	...	Tanzanie, République Unie de

BURUNDI

IX FINANCIAL AND MONETARY STATISTICS - FINANCES ET STATISTIQUES MONETAIRES

	2009	2010	2011	2012	2013	2014	2015	2016	2017	
IX-1 MONETARY STATISTICS *BURUNDI FRANC (MILLIONS)*										**IX-1 STATISTIQUES MONÉTAIRES** *FRANC DU BURUNDI (MILLIONS)*
Money supply (M1)	530 770	633 490	725 532	856 091	939 528	1 045 337	1 061 261	1 129 690	1 218 412	Masse monétaire (M1)
Quasi-money	118 264	145 692	183 918	196 551	229 915	294 666	352 049	304 685	367 292	Quasi-monnaie
of which demand deposit	...	...	...	...	...	...	...	...	...	dont Monnaie scripturale
Net foreign assets	264 043	254 447	204 477	197 824	230 618	180 495	- 68 762	- 170 770	- 145 568	Avoirs extérieurs nets
Domestic credit	498 115	626 362	784 629	884 717	952 125	1 222 951	1 479 981	1 740 072	1 972 143	Crédit intérieur
of which claims on private sector	167 944	195 969	218 131	241 687	254 561	368 882	672 471	891 704	1 099 865	dont créances sur le secteur privé
of which claims on government sector, net	320 624	420 869	561 036	635 177	686 682	801 271	793 320	832 778	830 211	dont créances nettes sur le gouvernement
International reserves (millions US$)	323	332	296	309	321	317	136	112	195	Réserves internationales (millions $EU)
Average exchange rate (National currency per US$)	1 230	1 231	1 261	1 443	1 555	1 547	1 572	1 655	1 729	Taux de change (moyen) (monnaie nationale par $ EU)
IX-2 PUBLIC FINANCE *BURUNDI FRANC (MILLIONS)*										**IX-2 FINANCES PUBLIQUES** *FRANC DU BURUNDI (MILLIONS)(*
Total Revenues and Grants	411 800	634 700	778 200	937 068	1 014 563	828 607	737 087	756 830	...	Recettes totales et dons
Direct taxes (on income, profits)	84 700	108 600	131 000	155 900	146 014	133 359	132 037	147 680	...	Taxes directes
Domestic indirect taxes revenues	147 300	193 700	248 600	286 200	326 963	383 649	366 200	369 730	...	Taxes Indirectes
Trade taxes	44 500	39 600	44 500	49 650	50 525	51 500	51 450	67 180	...	Taxes sur le commerce extérieur
Other taxes	2 200	...	...	...	...	...	...	...	...	Autres taxes
Other revenues	25 900	21 500	32 900	34 918	37 761	83 700	41 000	53 240	...	Autres recettes
Grants	107 200	271 300	321 200	410 400	453 300	176 400	146 400	119 000	...	Dons
Total Expenditures and Net Lending	508 304	815 800	1 026 581	1 254 641	1 084 947	985 885	1 077 905	1 093 312	...	Dépenses totales et prêts nets
Current expenditure	389 700	522 200	648 900	751 679	613 244	658 444	846 486	768 823	...	Dépenses courantes
Wages and Salaries	185 000	214 900	258 200	282 200	295 917	314 387	322 820	359 090	...	Rémunérations et salaires
Other purchases of goods and services	104 100	100 300	98 000	96 128	117 882	114 652	140 230	152 742	...	Achat de biens et services
Other current expenditure	300	72 500	152 700	210 200	15 946	17 800	162 463	37 551	...	Autres dépenses courantes
Current transfers	100 300	134 500	140 000	163 151	183 500	211 604	220 972	219 440	...	Transferts courants
Interest payments	26 300	29 600	25 600	27 085	29 787	33 670	40 632	56 880	...	Intérêts
Capital expenditure	93 304	264 000	352 081	477 277	441 916	293 771	190 786	267 609	...	Dépenses d'équipement
Net lending	- 1 000	...	...	- 1 400	...	...	...	...	...	Prêts nets
Fiscal balance	- 96 504	- 181 100	- 248 381	- 317 573	- 70 384	- 157 278	- 340 817	- 336 482	...	Solde global y compris les dons
IX-3 BALANCE OF PAYMENTS *BURUNDI FRANC (MILLIONS)*										**IX-3 BALANCE DES PAIEMENTS** *FRANC DU BURUNDI (MILLIONS)*
Trade balance	- 338	- 415	- 540	- 831	- 513	- 634	- 521	- 464	- 512	Balance commerciale
Services Balance	- 156	- 109	- 128	- 171	- 21	- 152	- 146	- 124	- 121	Balance des services
Net primary income	- 21	- 13	- 22	- 9	3	- 16	- 3	- 3	...	Revenus primaires nets
Compensation of employees	...	...	...	...	15	9	13	11	...	Rémunération des salariés
Investment income	...	...	...	...	- 12	- 25	- 17	- 14	...	Revenus des investissements
Net secondary income	316	167	332	644	426	433	437	331	404	Revenus secondaires nets
Net official transfers	...	...	...	...	...	...	...	...	...	Transferts officiels nets
Workers' remittances	...	...	...	...	...	...	...	...	...	Envois de fonds des travailleurs
Other private transfers	...	...	...	...	...	...	...	...	...	Autres transferts privés
Current account balance	- 198	- 370	- 358	- 368	- 105	- 369	- 233	- 260	- 228	Solde du compte courant
Capital and financial account	214	374	335	360	187	205	86	125	115	Comptes de capital et financier
Capital account	1 261	96	122	222	167	127	87	117	134	Compte de capital
Financial account	- 1 048	278	213	139	20	78	- 1	9	- 19	Compte financier
Errors and omissions	- 15	- 4	23	8	...	...	...	...	...	Erreurs et omissions
Overall balance	...	...	...	...	82	- 164	- 147	- 134	- 114	Balance générale

BURUNDI

X DEBT AND FINANCIAL FLOWS - DETTE ET FLUX FINANCIERS

	2008	2009	2010	2011	2012	2013	2014	2015	2016	
X-1 DEBT *US $ (MILLIONS)*										**X-1 DETTE EXTÉRIEURE** *$ E.U (MILLIONS)*
Total external debt	376	455	536	528	540	555	545	525	929	Dette extérieure totale
Private	...	...	...	...	...	...	...	...	...	Privée
Public	376	455	536	528	540	555	545	525	...	Publique
Total external debt service	2	3	5	21	33	30	35	39	...	Service de la dette extérieure
Present value of external debt	...	...	...	...	...	...	...	360	...	Valeur actuelle de la dette extérieure
Total government domestic debt, National currency (millions)	335	387	450	522	596	...	759	...	...	Dette publique intérieure
X-2 FINANCIAL FLOWS *US $ (MILLIONS)*										**X-2 FLUX FINANCIERS** *$ E.U (MILLIONS)*
Net Foreign Direct Investment Inflows	...	1	3	1	7	47	7	...	...	Investissements étranger direct (flux nets entrants)
Main origin of FDI inflows										**Principales origines de l'IDE entrant:**
...	...	...	...	...	...	...	...	...	...	...
Belgium	...	3	1	...	...	...	...	...	...	Belgique
...	...	...	...	...	...	...	...	...	...	...
...	...	...	...	...	...	...	...	...	...	...
...	...	...	...	...	...	...	...	...	...	...
African countries	...	...	...	...	...	...	...	...	...	Pays africains
Net total official development assistance	561	628	572	524	559	515	367	742	...	Aide publique au développement (nette totale)
Main origin of net ODA										**Principales origines de l'APD nette**
International Development Association [IDA]	61	107	95	104	102	60	45	31	...	International Development Association
United States	48	43	47	42	36	40	42	389	...	États-Unis
Belgium	52	57	64	56	65	62	49	52	...	Belgique
Netherlands	18	19	20	17	33	28	27	34	...	Pays-Bas
Germany	28	29	33	24	25	26	17	46	...	Allemagne

BURUNDI

SOURCES AND NOTES - SOURCES ET NOTES

External trade - Total exports, fob: UNCTAD	Commerce exterieur - Exportation, fab: CNUCED
External trade - Total import, cif: UNCTAD	Commerce exterieur - Imporations, caf: CNUCED
ODA: OECD	APD: OCDE
Monetary statistics: IMF	Statistiques monétaires: FMI
National Accounts: 2017:Estimates are provisional	Comptes nationaux: 2017:Données provisoires
Poverty: World Bank	Pauvreté: Banque mondiale

AREA (km2)		4 030		SUPERFICIE (KM2)
CAPITAL CITY	Praia		Praia	CAPITALE
CURRENCY	Cape Verde Escudo		Escudo capverdien	MONNAIE

I SOCIAL AND DEMOGRAPHIC INDICATORS — INDICATEURS DEMOGRAPHIQUES ET SOCIAUX

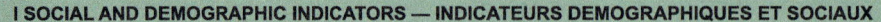

Population	Year Année	Value Valeur	Charts / Graphiques	Population
Population ('000)	2017	537 661.3		Population ('000)
Female (%)	2017	49.8		Féminine (%)
Urban (%)	2017	67.0		Urbaine (%)
Average annual growth rate	2017	1.3		Taux de croissance annuel
Active population ('000)	2017	232.2		Population active ('000)
Population by age group ('000)				Population par groupe d'âge ('000)
0-14 years	2017	153.8		0-14 ans
15-64 years	2017	354.3		15-64 ans
65+ years	2017	29.6		65+ ans
Economically active population in agriculture (%)	2017	13.6		Participation de la population active agricole (%)
Crude birth rate	2016	20.1		Taux brut de natalité
Crude death rate	2016	4.9		Taux brut de mortalité
Total fertility rate	2017	2.3		Indice synthétique de fécondité
Life expectancy at birth - Total (years)	2017	76.1		Espérance de vie à la naissance - Totale (années)
Dependency ratio - Total (%)	2017	51.8		Taux de dépendance - Total (%)
Health				**Santé**
Percentage of children under-five and underweight	...	...		% d'enfants de moins de cinq ans avec insuffisance pondérale
Prevalence of undernourishment	2015	9.4		Prévalence de la malnutrition
Under five mortality rate (per 1 000 live births)	2016	17.0		Taux de mortalité de moins de 5 ans (les deux sexes, pour 1000)
Infant mortality rate (per 1 000 live births)	2016	15.4		Taux de mortalité infantile (les deux sexes) par 1000
Neonatal mortality rate (per 1 000 live births)	2016	7.6		Le taux de mortalité néonatale (pour 1000 naissances vivantes)
Percentage of children provided the vaccines :				Pourcentage d'enfants vaccinés :
BCG	2016	92.0		BCG
DPT3	2016	95.3		DTC3
Polio	2016	95.3		polio
Measles	2016	92.0		rougeole
Percentage of mothers provided at least one antenatal care (%)	2016	87.3		Pourcentage de mères ayant au moins reçu un soin prénatal (%)
Percentage of deliveries attended by skilled health personnel	2016	92.0		% d'accouchements assistés par un personnel de santé qualifié
Number of doctors (per 10,000 population)	2017	7.5		Nombre de médecins (pour 10.000 habitants)
Number of nurses (per 10,000 population)	2017	12.8		Nombre d'infirmiers (pour 10.000 habitants)
Hospital beds - Total (per 10,000 population)	2017	20.2		Nombre de lits d'hôpitaux - Total (pour 10 000)
Births registered (per 1,000)	2017	19.0		Naissances enregistrées (pour 1000)
Deaths registered (per 1,000)	2017	5.0		Décès enregistrés (pour 1000)
Budget allocation to health (%)	2016	6.6		Dépenses publiques consacrées à la santé (% du budget)
Education				**Education**
Enrolment in primary education (000)	2017	63.6		Scolarisation dans le primaire (000)
Female	2017	30.4		Féminine
Enrolment in secondary education (000)	2017	56.5		Scolarisation dans le secondaire (000)
Female	2017	29.4		Féminine
Enrolment in tertiary education (000)	2017	12.8		Scolarisation dans le tertiaire (000)
Female	2017	7.6		Féminine
Literacy rate	2017	87.3		Taux d'alphabétisation (deux sexes)
Male	2017	90.5		Masculin
Female	2017	82.3		Féminin
Pupil teacher ratio - primary	2017	21.1		Ratio élève-enseignant
Budget allocation to education (%)	2017	18.4		Dépenses publiques consacrées à l'enseignement (% du budget)
Poverty				**Pauvreté**
GNI per capita, PPP (current int. $)	2016	6220.0		RNB par habitant, ($ PPA inter. courants)
Human Poverty Index (HPI-1) Value (%)	2007	14.5		Valeur de l'Indice de pauvreté (IPH-1) (%)
Population below Inter. poverty line ($2/ day) (%)	2007	17.6		Population sous le seuil inter. de pauvreté (2$/Jour) (%)
Share of income held by richest 10%	2007	37.1		% de revenu des 10% plus riches
Share of income held by poorest 10%	2007	2.0		% de revenu des 10% plus pauvres
GINI index	2007	47.2		Indice de GINI

Population by age group - 2017
Population par groupe d'age - 2017

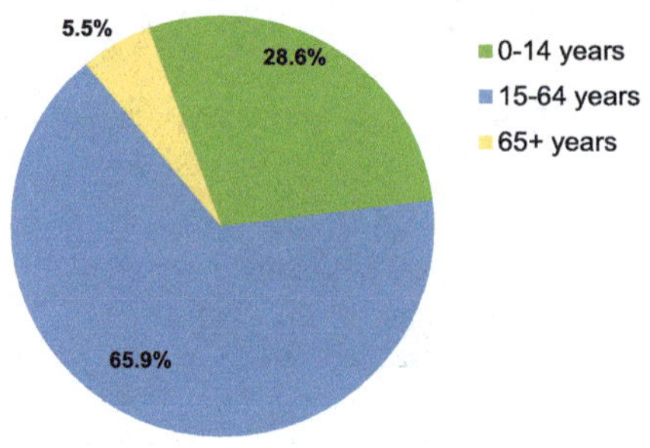

- 0-14 years: 28.6%
- 15-64 years: 65.9%
- 65+ years: 5.5%

Percentage of children provided vaccines : - 2016
Pourcentage d'enfants vaccinés : - 2016

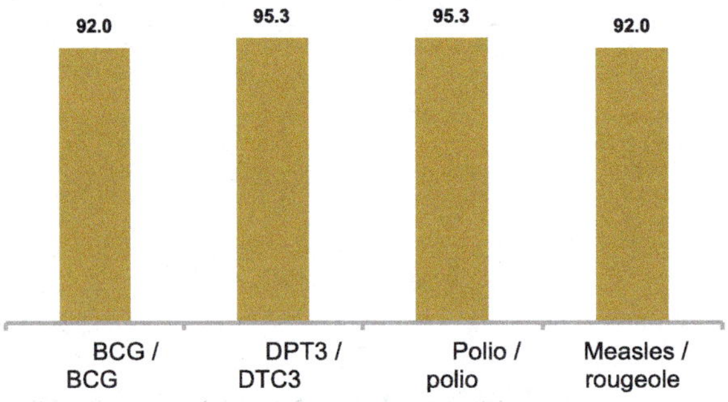

BCG / BCG	DPT3 / DTC3	Polio / polio	Measles / rougeole
92.0	95.3	95.3	92.0

Literacy rate (%) - 2017
Taux d'alphabétisation - 2017

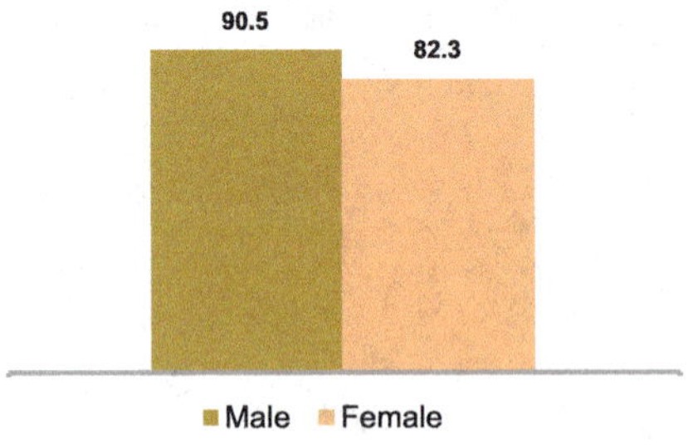

- Male: 90.5
- Female: 82.3

GNI per capita, PPP (current international $)
RNB par habitant, ($ PPA internationaux courants)

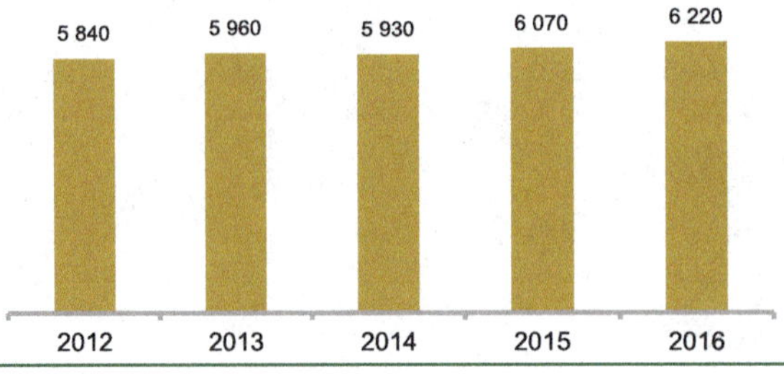

2012	2013	2014	2015	2016
5 840	5 960	5 930	6 070	6 220

	2009	2010	2011	2012	2013	2014	2015	2016	2017	
GROSS DOMESTIC PRODUCT BY KIND OF ECONOMIC ACTIVITY AT CURRENT PRICES *CAPE VERDE ESCUDO (MILLIONS)*										**PRODUIT INTÉRIEUR BRUT PAR BRANCHE D'ACTIVITÉ ÉCONOMIQUE AUX PRIX COURANTS** *ESCUDO CAPVERDIEN (MILLIONS)*
Agriculture, hunting , forestry and Fishing	11 304	11 071	11 602	12 699	12 727	12 379	13 866	13 825	...	Agriculture, chasse sylviculture et Pêche
Mining and quarrying	774	708	612	549	595	710	566	545	...	Industries extractives
Manufacturing	6 689	7 528	8 054	8 547	8 916	9 862	10 389	11 514	...	Industries manufacturières
Electricity, gas & water	2 125	1 940	2 157	3 268	3 999	4 071	5 234	4 648	...	Electricité, gaz et eau
Construction	16 584	14 973	15 455	13 203	13 415	14 278	12 569	11 765	...	Bâtiments et travaux publics
Wholesale & retail trade, restaurants, hotels	21 486	22 402	24 899	27 436	26 344	25 941	23 438	23 906	...	Commerce de gros et de détail, restaurants et hôtels
Finance, insurance, real estate, etc.	20 882	21 721	22 366	23 897	24 124	24 193	25 692	27 766	...	Banques, assurances, affaires immobilières
Transport and communications	20 917	21 035	20 283	19 630	20 794	19 227	21 012	20 683	...	Transport(s) et communications
Public administration and defense	18 497	19 592	22 097	22 501	23 783	25 203	25 901	27 375	...	Administrations publiques et défense
Education	...	...	...	...	...	...	...	...	...	Education
Health And Social Work	...	...	...	...	...	...	...	...	...	Santé et Actions Sociales
Other services	...	...	...	...	...	...	...	...	...	Autres services
Less Imputed Service Charges	...	...	...	...	...	...	...	...	...	Moins Services d'intermédiation financière
Gross domestic product at factor cost / basic prices	119 258	120 970	127 525	131 730	134 697	135 865	138 667	142 028	...	Produit intérieur brut aux couts des facteurs / prix de base
Plus: Indirect Taxes / taxes on products, less subsidies	16 621	17 598	20 399	18 621	19 026	18 571	20 032	21 354	...	Plus taxes indirectes/impôts sur les produits, moins les subventions
EXPENDITURE ON GROSS DOMESTIC PRODUCT AT CURRENT PURCHASER'S VALUES *CAPE VERDE ESCUDO (MILLIONS)*										**EMPLOI DU PRODUIT INTÉRIEUR BRUT AUX PRIX COURANTS D'ACQUISITION** *ESCUDO CAPVERDIEN (MILLIONS)*
Government final consumption	24 708	25 536	27 401	25 963	26 837	28 496	29 918	31 808	...	Consommation finale des administrations publiques
Private final consumption	86 839	87 328	92 864	97 656	100 330	100 180	103 491	106 964	...	Consommation finale privée
Gross fixed capital formation	52 337	62 625	69 128	52 844	46 337	53 317	45 681	44 837	...	Formation brute de capital fixe
Change in inventories	7 164	3 399	1 149	3 076	2 285	3 831	2 225	14 080	...	Variation des stocks
Exports of goods and services	42 228	45 271	52 541	60 790	62 246	62 332	71 268	62 871	...	Exportations de biens et services
Less imports of goods and services	77 396	85 591	95 159	89 978	84 312	93 720	93 884	97 179	...	Moins importations de biens et services
GDP at purchasers' values	135 879	138 569	147 924	150 351	153 723	154 436	158 699	163 381	...	PIB aux prix d'acquisition
GROSS DOMESTIC PRODUCT BY KIND OF ECONOMIC ACTIVITY AT CONSTANT PRICES *ANNUAL GROWTH RATES (%)*										**PRODUIT INTÉRIEUR BRUT PAR BRANCHE D'ACTIVITÉ ECONOMIQUE AUX PRIX CONSTANTS** *TAUX DE CROISSANCE ANNUEL (%)*
Agriculture, hunting , forestry and Fishing	10.5	- 3.6	4.4	9.4	- 1.3	- 1.7	8.2	2.7	...	Agriculture, chasse sylviculture et Pêche
Mining and quarrying	- 23.7	- 8.0	- 13.5	- 34.9	3.9	7.4	-27.6	-3.6	...	Industries extractives
Manufacturing	- 1.0	10.3	4.9	4.1	1.8	7.7	2.7	9.7	...	Industries manufacturières
Electricity, gas & water	11.8	- 21.6	- 16.1	18.8	- 11.8	0.6	36.5	4.9	...	Electricité, gaz et eau
Construction	- 7.7	- 11.0	0.6	- 13.0	0.5	7.4	-14.0	1.0	...	Bâtiments et travaux publics
Wholesale & retail trade, restaurants, hotels	3.5	0.9	6.1	6.5	- 4.3	2.4	2.7	-0.7	...	Commerce de gros et de détail, restaurants et hôtels
Finance, insurance, real estate, etc.	- 4.0	4.9	3.8	7.0	3.7	0.7	-8.2	7.6	...	Banques, assurances, affaires immobilières
Transport and communications	- 4.0	6.6	- 7.4	3.7	3.0	- 9.7	3.7	0.4	...	Transport(s) et communications
Public administration and defense	8.6	4.4	12.5	1.1	4.3	4.7	1.0	8.3	...	Administrations publiques et défense
Education	...	...	...	...	...	...	...	...	...	Education
Health And Social Work	...	...	...	...	...	...	...	...	...	Santé et Actions Sociales
Other services	...	...	...	...	...	...	...	...	...	Autres services
Less Imputed Service Charges	...	...	...	...	...	...	...	...	...	Moins Services d'intermédiation financière
Gross domestic product at factor cost / basic prices	0.1	1.2	3.0	3.0	0.7	1.1	0.0	4.0	...	Produit intérieur brut aux couts des facteurs / prix de base
Plus: Indirect Taxes / taxes on products, less subsidies	- 9.8	3.7	10.6	- 10.8	1.3	- 2.6	8.8	2.4	...	Plus taxes indirectes/impôts sur les produits, moins les subventions
Gross domestic product at market prices	- 1.3	1.5	4.0	1.1	0.8	0.6	1.0	3.8	...	Produit intérieur brut aux prix du marché
EXPENDITURE ON GROSS DOMESTIC PRODUCT AT CONSTANT PURCHASERS' VALUES *ANNUAL GROWTH RATES (%)*										**EMPLOIS DU PRODUIT INTÉRIEUR BRUT AUX PRIX CONSTANTS D'ACQUISITION** *TAUX DE CROISSANCE ANNUEL (%)*
Government final consumption	7.3	2.0	6.0	- 5.9	1.9	5.2	3.8	3.8	...	Consommation finale des administrations publiques
Private final consumption	6.1	- 1.2	2.2	3.3	1.8	1.2	3.2	3.5	...	Consommation finale privée
Gross fixed capital formation	- 8.5	19.0	5.6	- 23.5	- 12.0	14.9	-14.6	1.1	...	Formation brute de capital fixe
Exports of goods and services	- 16.8	6.9	10.9	13.5	0.6	- 1.2	14.8	-12.2	...	Exportations de biens et services
Less imports of goods and services	- 7.0	8.3	4.7	- 7.8	- 6.4	11.0	1.8	3.5	...	Moins importations de biens et services

III INFLATION

	2009	2010	2011	2012	2013	2014	2015	2016	2017	
Annual growth rates (%)										**Taux de croissance annuel (%)**
All item	1.0	2.1	4.5	2.5	1.5	- 0.2	0.1	- 1.4	0.8	Ensemble
of which:										dont:
Food and non-alcoholic beverages	2.0	2.2	5.2	2.6	0.7	- 1.2	1.5	- 0.6	- 0.2	Alimentation et boissons non alcoolisés
Alcoholic beverages, tobacco and narcotics	1.9	2.3	2.6	6.4	4.3	1.3	1.7	0.8	1.9	Boissons alcoolisées et tabacs
Clothing and footwear	- 1.8	3.0	2.3	0.3	1.3	1.5	1.0	- 0.4	1.4	Habillement et chaussures
Housing, water, electricity, gas and other fuels	-	2.7	6.4	5.5	4.9	- 0.2	- 6.0	- 8.3	1.7	Logement, eau, électricité, gaz et autres combustibles
Furnishings, household equipment and routine household maintenance	6.7	2.3	3.0	2.1	3.5	1.2	5.6	2.4	0.5	Meubles, articles de ménage et entretien courant
Health	6.2	2.4	0.4	0.4	0.7	1.3	1.0	2.0	2.9	Santé
Transport	- 6.0	2.7	7.4	4.3	- 3.7	- 1.7	- 2.6	- 3.2	1.7	Transport
Communication	- 2.8	- 8.6	...	- 14.2	3.7	0.7	...	...	...	Communication
Recreation and culture	- 2.2	- 1.7	0.2	- 2.0	- 5.6	- 1.2	0.9	2.0	1.7	Loisirs et culture
Education	-	0.1	-	- 0.3	-	- 0.7	- 0.9	...	1.8	Enseignement
Restaurants and hotels	1.2	5.7	3.4	8.1	6.5	- 0.1	1.2	2.2	0.7	Restaurants et hôtels
Miscellaneous goods and services	9.7	4.5	0.6	1.8	4.9	4.8	4.5	2.5	2.3	Biens et Services divers

CABO VERDE

IV AGRICULTURAL PRODUCTION - PRODUCTION AGRICOLE

	2009	2010	2011	2012	2013	2014	2015	2016	2017	
TONNES (THOUSAND)										**Tonnes (milliers)**
Tomatoes	14	15	17	14	17	16	15	15	...	Tomates
Bananas	7	7	9	10	10	11	10	10	...	Bananes
Dry onion	3	4	5	7	7	5	5	5	...	Oignons secs
Carrots and turnips	6	6	6	6	5	6	5	4	...	Carottes et navets
Mangoes, mangosteens, guavas	7	7	2	2	3	7	4	5	...	Mangues, mangoustans, goyaves

V MINING PRODUCTION - PRODUCTION MINIERE

	2009	2010	2011	2012	2013	2014	2015	2016	2017	
Salt and pure sodium chloride - Production (metric tons)	2 000	2 000	2 000	...	...	...	...	...	...	Sel et chlorure de sodium pur - Production (tonnes métriques)
	...	...	...	...	...	...	...	...	...	
	...	...	...	...	...	...	...	...	...	

VI ENERGY - ENERGIE

	2009	2010	2011	2012	2013	2014	2015	2016	2017	
Total electricity generation (GWh)	281	287	287	297	297	349	360	368	...	Production électrique totale (GWh)
of which										dont
Production of electricity from fossil fuels (GWh)	274	280	280	290	290	315	322	330	...	Production d'électricité à partir de combustibles fossiles (GWh)
Production of hydro electricity (GWh)	...	...	...	...	...	...	...	5 326	...	Production d'électricité d'origine hydraulique (GWh)
Production of electricity from solar, wind, tide, wave and other sources (GWh)	7	7	7	7	7	34	37	38	...	Production d'électricité d'origine solaire, éolienne, marée motrice et autres (GWh)

VII TOURISM AND INFRASTRUCTURE - TOURISME ET INFRASTUCTURE

	2009	2010	2011	2012	2013	2014	2015	2016	2017	
VII-1 Tourism										**VII-1 Tourisme**
International tourist arrivals (thousands)	287	336	428	482	503	494	520	598	717	Arrivées de touristes internationaux (milliers)
Rooms in hotels and similar establishments (thousands)	6	6	8	9	9	11	11	11	12	Chambres d'hôtels et établissements assimilés (milliers)
Overnight stays (thousands)	2 022	2 342	2 828	3 334	3 436	3 415	3 710	4 093	4 597	Nuitées (milliers)
Tourism receipts (US$ thousand)	286 000	278 200	367 887	413 854	462 172	418 303	377 877	419 451	440 811	Recettes touristiques (milliers de $ EU)
Total contribution to GDP (%)	6.1	5.7	6.1	6.4	6.9	6.9	6.8	6.8	6.8	Contribution totale au PIB (%)
Total contribution to Employment (%)	3.8	3.6	3.7	3.9	4.2	4.1	4.0	4.0	4.0	Contribution totale à l'emploi (%)
VII-2 Infrastructure										**VII-2 Infrastructure**
Paved road (% of total)	...	...	...	29.4	69.0	...	...	...	...	Routes asphaltées (% du total)
Total network (Railways-km)	...	...	...	...	...	...	...	...	...	Réseau total voies ferrées-Km
Main telephone lines (per 100 inhabitants)	14.8	14.8	15.2	14.2	13.3	11.6	11.5	11.6		Lignes téléphoniques fixes (pour 100 habitants)
Mobile cellular subscribers (per 100 inhabitants)	59.8	76.3	80.8	86.0	100.1	121.8	118.6	122.0	...	Abonnés aux téléphones mobiles (pour 100 habitants)
Internet users per 100 inhabitants	21.0	30.0	32.0	34.7	37.5	40.3	48.0	50.3	...	Utilisateurs Internet par 100 Habitants
Fixed (wired)-broadband subscriptions per 100 inhabitants	2.3	3.3	4.3	4.0	4.2	3.8	3.3	3.0	...	Abonnements à l'Internet fixe (filaire) à large bande pour 100 habitants, par débit

VIII EXTERNAL TRADE - COMMERCE EXTERIEUR

	2009	2010	2011	2012	2013	2014	2015	2016	2017	
US$ (MILLIONS) **EXPORTS, FOB**										**$ E.U (MILLIONS)** **EXPORTATIONS, FÀB**
Exports - Total	35	44	69	56	69	81	67	60	...	Exportations - Total
Exports to Africa	4	3	3	1	19	3	10	6	...	Exportations vers l'Afrique
Main products										**Principaux produits**
Fish, aqua. invertebrates, prepared, preserved, n.e.s.	4	6	14	8	9	13	10	9	...	Poisson, aqua. invertébrés, préparés, conservés, n.d.a.
Fish, fresh (live or dead), chilled or frozen	5	8	18	13	15	21	16	15	...	Poissons frais (vivants ou morts), réfrigérés ou congelés
Petroleum oils or bituminous minerals > 70 % oil	4	4	6	6	5	8	6	6	...	Huiles de pétrole ou de minéraux bitumineux> 70% d'huile
Ships, boats & floating structures	7	3	...	4	17	...	8	3	...	Navires, bateaux et structures flottantes
Trailers & semi-trailers	4	10	12	5	4	17	9	11	...	Remorques et semi-remorques
Main destinations										**Principales destinations**
Congo	3	2	...	...	17	-	8	3	...	Congo
Netherlands	3	4	6	6	4	8	5	5	...	Pays-Bas
Portugal	7	9	18	20	21	22	19	17	...	Portugal
Spain	12	18	26	18	16	25	18	18	...	Espagne
United States	-	0	0	1	1	7	4	5	...	États-Unis
IMPORTS, CIF										
Imports - Total	671	731	947	755	726	769	606	672	...	Importations - Total (millions)
Imports from Africa	17	13	15	14	11	19	12	15	...	Importations en provenance de l'Afrique
Main products										**Principaux produits**
Lime, cement, fabrica. constr. mat. (excludingglass, clay)	24	23	22	18	16	18	14	15	...	Chaux, ciment, tissu. constr. tapis. (sauf verre, argile)
Milk, cream and milk products (excluding butter, cheese)	21	21	28	21	23	26	20	22	...	Lait, crème et produits laitiers (à l'exclusion du beurre, du fromage)
Petroleum oils or bituminous minerals > 70 % oil	75	101	189	129	163	90	103	94	...	Huiles de pétrole ou de minéraux bitumineux> 70% d'huile
Rice	23	16	13	16	19	17	15	15	...	Riz
Rotating electric plant & parts thereof, n.e.s.	4	7	42	4	2	34	15	24	...	Installations électriques tournantes et leurs parties, n.d.a.
Main origin										**Principales provenances**
Brazil	59	58	73	61	52	23	30	26	...	Brazil
China	25	30	38	44	43	44	35	39	...	Chine
Netherlands	96	117	193	130	164	91	104	95	...	Pays-Bas
Portugal	285	313	341	284	254	295	223	253	...	Portugal
Spain	47	51	74	53	49	62	45	52	...	Espagne

	2009	2010	2011	2012	2013	2014	2015	2016	2017	
IX-1 MONETARY STATISTICS *CAPE VERDE ESCUDO (MILLIONS)*										**IX-1 STATISTIQUES MONÉTAIRES** *ESCUDO CAPVERDIEN (MILLIONS)*
Money supply (M1)	105 307	110 999	116 088	123 407	137 491	147 668	156 929	170 043	181 606	Masse monétaire (M1)
Quasi-money	60 768	62 877	70 756	75 662	82 523	86 668	92 635	97 336	95 461	Quasi-monnaie
of which demand deposit	...	...	...	...	...	...	...	...	...	dont Monnaie scripturale
Net foreign assets	27 376	28 482	19 986	25 375	33 541	42 617	48 463	58 018	60 227	Avoirs extérieurs nets
Domestic credit	99 192	105 489	121 514	125 018	129 209	131 578	134 141	138 782	148 766	Crédit intérieur
of which claims on private sector	18 550	17 196	20 456	24 928	26 856	29 475	29 068	29 947	32 479	dont créances sur le secteur privé
of which claims on government sector, net	78 761	85 815	97 248	96 712	98 668	97 747	98 105	101 613	108 207	dont créances nettes sur le gouvernement
International reserves (millions US$)	383	390	366	384	461	558	503	599	654	Réserves internationales (millions $EU)
Average exchange rate (National currency per US$)	79	83	79	86	83	83	99	100	98	Taux de change (moyen) (monnaie nationale par $ EU)
IX-2 PUBLIC FINANCE *CAPE VERDE ESCUDO (MILLIONS)*										**IX-2 FINANCES PUBLIQUES** *ESCUDO CAPVERDIEN (MILLIONS)*
Total Revenues and Grants	37 522	39 679	37 916	36 688	37 716	35 327	41 826	43 220	49 272	Recettes totales et dons
Direct taxes (on income, profits)	8 061	7 892	8 678	8 616	8 596	7 747	9 561	10 078	11 297	Taxes directes
Domestic indirect taxes revenues	11 081	12 015	13 840	11 903	12 187	11 676	12 762	13 536	16 836	Taxes Indirectes
Trade taxes	5 438	5 634	6 228	5 778	5 700	5 754	6 082	6 813	7 224	Taxes sur le commerce extérieur
Other taxes	951	701	835	1 276	1 616	1 883	1 848	1 877	552	Autres taxes
Other revenues	4 455	3 998	3 993	4 913	5 593	5 480	7 733	6 961	7 267	Autres recettes
Grants	7 536	9 440	4 342	4 203	4 024	2 787	3 841	3 955	6 097	Dons
Total Expenditures and Net Lending	45 455	54 250	49 235	55 289	52 039	47 393	48 168	49 018	54 917	Dépenses totales et prêts nets
Current expenditure	30 387	30 927	32 314	31 551	32 041	34 098	35 826	38 370	40 900	Dépenses courantes
Wages and Salaries	14 207	14 810	15 679	15 886	16 601	17 172	17 058	18 252	18 595	Rémunérations et salaires
Other purchases of goods and services	5 294	5 171	5 248	4 995	5 062	5 744	6 805	6 770	6 506	Achat de biens et services
Other current expenditure	3 252	2 362	2 107	2 421	2 053	2 339	2 321	3 136	4 099	Autres dépenses courantes
Current transfers	7 635	8 584	9 280	8 250	8 326	8 844	9 643	10 212	11 700	Transferts courants
Interest payments	1 818	2 159	2 276	2 858	3 383	3 444	4 134	4 223	4 522	Intérêts
Capital expenditure	13 249	21 164	14 644	20 880	16 615	9 850	8 207	6 425	9 496	Dépenses d'équipement
Net lending	...	...	...	...	...	...	...	...	...	Prêts nets
Fiscal balance	- 7 933	- 14 570	- 11 319	- 18 601	- 14 323	- 12 065	- 6 341	- 5 798	- 5 645	Solde global y compris les dons
IX-3 BALANCE OF PAYMENTS *CAPE VERDE ESCUDO (MILLIONS)*										**IX-3 BALANCE DES PAIEMENTS** *ESCUDO CAPVERDIEN (MILLIONS)*
Trade balance	- 53 735	- 56 822	- 67 206	- 56 398	- 51 533	- 50 277	- 47 029	- 53 236	- 63 186	Balance commerciale
Services Balance	12 782	16 529	20 449	19 475	25 207	21 888	22 608	26 164	27 780	Balance des services
Net primary income	- 3 442	- 6 710	- 5 655	- 6 438	- 5 367	- 7 692	- 5 870	- 6 259	- 6 525	Revenus primaires nets
Compensation of employees	...	...	...	58	9	- 67	- 39	715	402	Rémunération des salariés
Investment income	...	...	...	- 6 496	- 5 376	- 7 625	- 5 831	- 6 708	- 5 619	Revenus des investissements
Net secondary income	24 596	28 281	28 469	22 308	22 795	22 039	25 244	28 800	29 742	Revenus secondaires nets
Net official transfers	...	...	...	5 116	4 948	4 664	5 395	4 980	4 960	Transferts officiels nets
Workers' remittances	...	...	...	14 380	13 779	15 485	18 593	17 536	12 337	Envois de fonds des travailleurs
Other private transfers	...	...	...	2 812	4 068	1 890	1 256	6 244	4 635	Autres transferts privés
Current account balance	- 19 800	- 18 722	- 23 943	- 21 053	- 8 898	- 14 042	- 5 046	- 4 531	- 12 189	Solde du compte courant
Capital and financial account	25 570	32 473	30 564	27 393	14 619	23 421	13 559	13 382	11 487	Comptes de capital et financier
Capital account	3 670	3 311	985	1 122	533	659	1 884	1 255	1 163	Compte de capital
Financial account	21 900	29 162	29 579	26 271	14 085	22 762	11 675	12 127	10 324	Compte financier
Errors and omissions	- 2 502	- 6 937	- 65	- 2 283	- 117	- 1 534	- 4 989	300	- 3 780	Erreurs et omissions
Overall balance	3 269	6 814	6 556	4 058	5 604	7 845	3 524	9 150	- 4 481	Balance générale

CABO VERDE

X DEBT AND FINANCIAL FLOWS - DETTE ET FLUX FINANCIERS

	2008	2009	2010	2011	2012	2013	2014	2015	2016	
X-1 DEBT *US $ (MILLIONS)*										**X-1 DETTE EXTÉRIEURE** *$ E.U (MILLIONS)*
Total external debt	998	1 059	1 266	1 598	1 965	1 848	1 819	1 815	1 931	Dette extérieure totale
Private	196	173	254	269	264	216	199	194	...	Privée
Public	779	852	992	1 226	1 506	1 537	1 519	1 523	...	Publique
Total external debt service	53	53	65	73	81	91	77	72	...	Service de la dette extérieure
Present value of external debt	...	...	...	...	...	...	...	1 402	...	Valeur actuelle de la dette extérieure
Total government domestic debt, National currency (millions)	...	29 519	32 016	...	...	...	...	...	...	Dette publique intérieure
X-2 FINANCIAL FLOWS *US $ (MILLIONS)*										**X-2 FLUX FINANCIERS** *$ E.U (MILLIONS)*
Net Foreign Direct Investment Inflows	174	159	155	126	70	180	116	119	...	Investissements étranger direct (flux nets entrants)
Main origin of FDI inflows										**Principales origines de l'IDE entrant:**
Italy	- 36	8	...	- 5	...	...	...	...	...	Italie
...	...	...	...	...	...	...	...	...	...	...
Luxembourg	1	...	...	...	...	...	...	...	...	Luxembourg
...	...	...	...	...	...	...	...	...	...	...
...	...	...	...	...	...	...	...	...	...	...
African countries	...	...	...	...	...	...	...	...	...	Pays africains
Net total official development assistance	197	327	251	246	245	231	153	113	...	Aide publique au développement (nette totale)
Main origin of net ODA										**Principales origines de l'APD nette**
Portugal	53	142	147	168	159	137	50	31	...	Portugal
International Development Association [IDA]	...	22	- 2	12	4	21	12	- 4	...	International Development Association
United States	36	37	9	3	5	7	12	19	...	États-Unis
Luxembourg	14	17	15	18	19	15	15	11	...	Luxembourg
Spain	21	21	15	6	5	1	- 1	- 1	...	Espagne

CABO VERDE

SOURCES AND NOTES - SOURCES ET NOTES

External trade - Total exports, fob: UNCTAD

External trade - Total import, cif: UNCTAD

ODA: OECD

Monetary statistics: IMF

National Accounts: 2016: Provisional

National Accounts : The annual Growth Rates for 2016 are previsions based on the sum of four quarters of 2016.

Poverty: World Bank

Commerce exterieur - Exportation, fab: CNUCED

Commerce exterieur - Imporations, caf: CNUCED

APD: OCDE

Statistiques monétaires: FMI

Comptes nationaux: 2016: Provisioire

Comptes Nationaux: Les croissances annuelles de L'année 2016 sont estimées à partir des comptes trimestriels

Pauvreté: Banque mondiale

				AREA (km2)	475 440		SUPERFICIE (KM2)
			CAPITAL CITY	Yaoundé	Yaoundé	CAPITALE
			CURRENCY	CFA Franc	Franc CFA	MONNAIE

I SOCIAL AND DEMOGRAPHIC INDICATORS — INDICATEURS DEMOGRAPHIQUES ET SOCIAUX

Population	Year Année	Value Valeur	Charts Graphiques	Population
Population ('000)	2017	23 200.0		Population ('000)
Female (%)	2017	50.6		Féminine (%)
Urban (%)	2017	55.0		Urbaine (%)
Average annual growth rate	2017	2.4		Taux de croissance annuel
Active population ('000)	2015	9 732.8		Population active ('000)
Population by age group ('000)				Population par groupe d'âge ('000)
0-14 years	2017	9 880.0		0-14 ans
15-64 years	2017	12 531.0		15-64 ans
65+ years	2017	837.0		65+ ans
Economically active population in agriculture (%)	2015	36.6		Participation de la population active agricole (%)
Crude birth rate	2015	36.2		Taux brut de natalité
Crude death rate	2015	11.2		Taux brut de mortalité
Total fertility rate	2015	4.6		Indice synthétique de fécondité
Life expectancy at birth - Total (years)	2015	56.0		Espérance de vie à la naissance - Totale (années)
Dependency ratio - Total (%)	2017	85.5		Taux de dépendance - Total (%)
Health				**Santé**
Percentage of children under-five and underweight	2014	14.8		% d'enfants de moins de cinq ans avec insuffisance pondérale
Prevalence of undernourishment	2015	9.9		Prévalence de la malnutrition
Under five mortality rate (per 1 000 live births)	2015	87.9		Taux de mortalité de moins de 5 ans (les deux sexes, pour 1000)
Infant mortality rate (per 1 000 live births)	2015	57.1		Taux de mortalité infantile (les deux sexes) par 1000
Neonatal mortality rate (per 1 000 live births)	2015	25.7		Le taux de mortalité néonatale (pour 1000 naissances vivantes)
Percentage of children provided the vaccines :				Pourcentage d'enfants vaccinés :
BCG	2016	70.0		BCG
DPT3	2016	85.0		DTC3
Polio	2016	83.0		polio
Measles	2016	78.0		rougeole
Percentage of mothers provided at least one antenatal care (%)	2014	82.8		Pourcentage de mères ayant au moins reçu un soin prénatal (%)
Percentage of deliveries attended by skilled health personnel	2014	64.7		% d'accouchements assistés par un personnel de santé qualifié
Number of doctors (per 10,000 population)	2009	0.8		Nombre de médecins (pour 10.000 habitants)
Number of nurses (per 10,000 population)	2009	4.4		Nombre d'infirmiers (pour 10.000 habitants)
Hospital beds - Total (per 10,000 population)	2010	13.0		Nombre de lits d'hôpitaux - Total (pour 10 000)
Births registered (per 1,000)	2015	36.2		Naissances enregistrées (pour 1000)
Deaths registered (per 1,000)	2015	11.2		Décès enregistrés (pour 1000)
Budget allocation to health (%)	2017	4.8		Dépenses publiques consacrées à la santé (% du budget)
Education				**Education**
Enrolment in primary education (000)	2017	4 346.8		Scolarisation dans le primaire (000)
Female	2017	2 043.3		Féminine
Enrolment in secondary education (000)	2017	2 417.0		Scolarisation dans le secondaire (000)
Female	2016	1 031.8		Féminine
Enrolment in tertiary education (000)	2017	375.4		Scolarisation dans le tertiaire (000)
Female	2011	103.1		Féminine
Literacy rate	2014	73.4		Taux d'alphabétisation (deux sexes)
Male	2014	83.4		Masculin
Female	2014	71.0		Féminin
Pupil teacher ratio - primary	2017	44.7		Ratio élève-enseignant
Budget allocation to education (%)	2017	13.9		Dépenses publiques consacrées à l'enseignement (% du budget)
Poverty				**Pauvreté**
GNI per capita, PPP (current int. $)	2016	3540.0		RNB par habitant, ($ PPA inter. courants)
Human Poverty Index (HPI-1) Value (%)	2014	37.5		Valeur de l'Indice de pauvreté (IPH-1) (%)
Population below Inter. poverty line ($2/day) (%)	2007	29.3		Population sous le seuil inter. de pauvreté (2$/Jour) (%)
Share of income held by richest 10%	2007	33.0		% de revenu des 10% plus riches
Share of income held by poorest 10%	2007	2.5		% de revenu des 10% plus pauvres
GINI index	2007	42.8		Indice de GINI

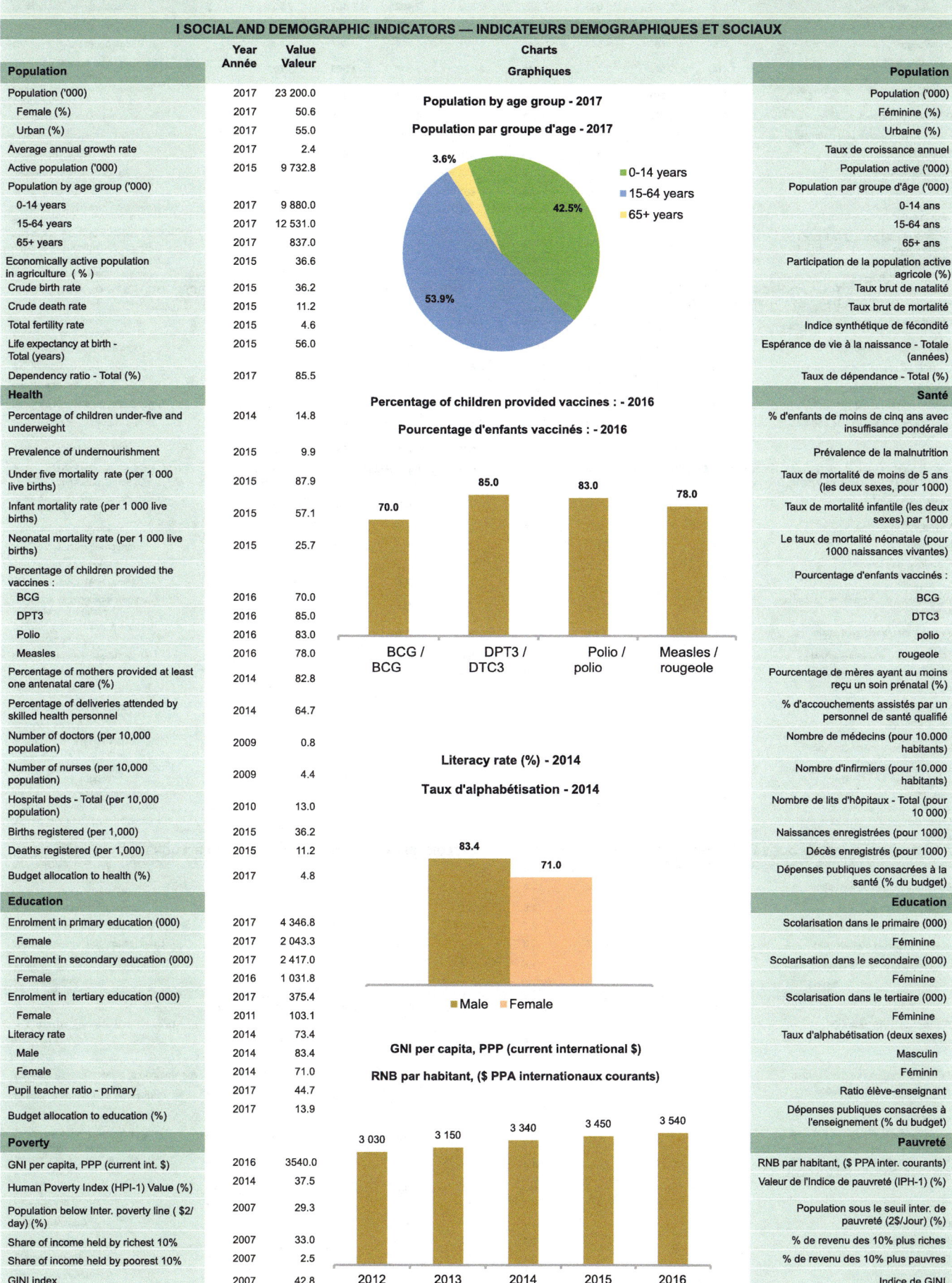

Population by age group - 2017
Population par groupe d'age - 2017

3.6% | 42.5% | 53.9%
■ 0-14 years
■ 15-64 years
□ 65+ years

Percentage of children provided vaccines : - 2016
Pourcentage d'enfants vaccinés : - 2016

BCG / BCG	DPT3 / DTC3	Polio / polio	Measles / rougeole
70.0	85.0	83.0	78.0

Literacy rate (%) - 2014
Taux d'alphabétisation - 2014

83.4 | 71.0
■ Male ■ Female

GNI per capita, PPP (current international $)
RNB par habitant, ($ PPA internationaux courants)

2012	2013	2014	2015	2016
3 030	3 150	3 340	3 450	3 540

II NATIONAL ACCOUNTS — COMPTES NATIONAUX

	2009	2010	2011	2012	2013	2014	2015	2016	2017	
GROSS DOMESTIC PRODUCT BY KIND OF ECONOMIC ACTIVITY AT CURRENT PRICES *CFA FRANC (BILLIONS)*										**PRODUIT INTÉRIEUR BRUT PAR BRANCHE D'ACTIVITÉ ÉCONOMIQUE AUX PRIX COURANTS** *FRANC CFA (MILLIARDS)*
Agriculture, hunting , forestry and Fishing	1 678	1 822	1 866	2 039	2 221	2 458	2 701	2 929	...	Agriculture, chasse sylviculture et Pêche
Mining and quarrying	776	925	983	1 102	1 092	1 164	803	679	...	Industries extractives
Manufacturing	1 872	1 873	2 033	2 240	2 396	2 492	2 681	2 803	...	Industries manufacturières
Electricity, gas & water	149	159	182	197	206	239	253	259	...	Electricité, gaz et eau
Construction	526	562	566	644	721	794	867	936	...	Bâtiments et travaux publics
Wholesale & retail trade, restaurants, hotels	2 414	2 569	2 726	2 919	3 120	3 346	3 569	3 707	...	Commerce de gros et de détail, restaurants et hôtels
Finance, insurance, real estate, etc.	267	291	466	381	431	467	499	532	...	Banques, assurances, affaires immobilières
Transport and communications	938	1 030	1 082	1 115	1 232	1 316	1 425	1 496	...	Transport(s) et communications
Public administration and defense	582	578	676	738	818	873	937	1 004	...	Administrations publiques et défense
Education	366	396	417	444	479	518	554	604	...	Education
Health And Social Work	275	286	307	324	344	367	365	384	...	Santé et Actions Sociales
Other services	1 618	1 599	1 672	1 798	1 961	2 069	2 173	2 243	...	Autres services
Less Imputed Service Charges	...	...	...	...	...	...	...	...	...	Moins Services d'intermédiation financière
Gross domestic product at factor cost / basic prices	11 459	12 091	12 977	13 941	15 022	16 102	16 828	17 576	...	Produit intérieur brut aux couts des facteurs / prix de base
Plus: Indirect Taxes / taxes on products, less subsidies	826	858	866	917	959	1 175	1 457	1 529	...	Plus taxes indirectes/impôts sur les produits, moins les subventions
EXPENDITURE ON GROSS DOMESTIC PRODUCT AT CURRENT PURCHASER'S VALUES *CFA FRANC (BILLIONS)*										**EMPLOI DU PRODUIT INTÉRIEUR BRUT AUX PRIX COURANTS D'ACQUISITION** *FRANC CFA (MILLIARDS)*
Government final consumption	1 425	1 475	1 677	1 815	1 970	2 100	2 245	2 353	...	Consommation finale des administrations publiques
Private final consumption	8 563	9 088	9 526	10 276	11 042	11 917	12 924	13 435	...	Consommation finale privée
Gross fixed capital formation	2 899	3 039	3 348	3 382	3 614	4 101	4 214	4 303	...	Formation brute de capital fixe
Change in inventories	8	- 34	- 6	1	69	55	- 119	- 63	...	Variation des stocks
Exports of goods and services	2 629	2 871	3 590	3 881	4 086	4 308	4 070	3 550	...	Exportations de biens et services
Less imports of goods and services	3 240	3 490	4 292	4 498	4 800	5 205	5 049	4 473	...	Moins importations de biens et services
GDP at purchasers' values	12 285	12 948	13 843	14 859	15 981	17 276	18 285	19 105	...	PIB aux prix d'acquisition
GROSS DOMESTIC PRODUCT BY KIND OF ECONOMIC ACTIVITY AT CONSTANT PRICES *ANNUAL GROWTH RATES (%)*										**PRODUIT INTÉRIEUR BRUT PAR BRANCHE D'ACTIVITÉ ECONOMIQUE AUX PRIX CONSTANTS** *TAUX DE CROISSANCE ANNUEL (%)*
Agriculture, hunting , forestry and Fishing	0.8	5.7	2.6	3.7	7.0	6.2	5.3	6.8	...	Agriculture, chasse sylviculture et Pêche
Mining and quarrying	- 7.7	- 9.0	- 6.7	3.5	8.4	14.3	24.8	- 3.5	...	Industries extractives
Manufacturing	3.9	2.2	7.9	5.7	5.9	1.1	3.1	4.0	...	Industries manufacturières
Electricity, gas & water	- 6.3	2.3	5.8	5.1	7.8	8.1	9.4	2.6	...	Electricité, gaz et eau
Construction	1.0	- 0.2	3.2	5.4	8.0	7.5	8.4	10.7	...	Bâtiments et travaux publics
Wholesale & retail trade, restaurants, hotels	3.1	5.1	2.4	5.6	1.6	5.5	3.3	4.8	...	Commerce de gros et de détail, restaurants et hôtels
Finance, insurance, real estate, etc.	- 1.2	8.8	12.7	17.4	14.6	5.6	6.9	5.2	...	Banques, assurances, affaires immobilières
Transport and communications	1.3	12.6	7.0	5.1	8.2	4.2	4.5	5.0	...	Transport(s) et communications
Public administration and defense	10.4	10.9	6.2	1.8	4.4	4.7	4.6	3.7	...	Administrations publiques et défense
Education	1.2	6.1	3.6	4.6	4.7	6.4	4.3	5.8	...	Education
Health And Social Work	1.9	2.7	4.9	3.7	4.1	4.5	- 2.9	3.2	...	Santé et Actions Sociales
Other services	3.9	- 1.4	3.2	2.9	4.3	3.5	2.2	3.8	...	Autres services
Less Imputed Service Charges	...	...	...	...	...	...	...	...	...	Moins Services d'intermédiation financière
Gross domestic product at factor cost / basic prices	2.0	3.5	3.8	4.7	5.5	5.2	5.4	4.4	...	Produit intérieur brut aux couts des facteurs / prix de base
Plus: Indirect Taxes / taxes on products, less subsidies	5.2	2.1	9.4	2.5	4.5	16.5	8.8	4.7	...	Plus taxes indirectes/impôts sur les produits, moins les subventions
Gross domestic product at market prices	2.2	3.4	4.1	4.5	5.4	5.9	5.7	4.5	...	Produit intérieur brut aux prix du marché
EXPENDITURE ON GROSS DOMESTIC PRODUCT AT CONSTANT PURCHASERS' VALUES *ANNUAL GROWTH RATES (%)*										**EMPLOIS DU PRODUIT INTÉRIEUR BRUT AUX PRIX CONSTANTS D'ACQUISITION** *TAUX DE CROISSANCE ANNUEL (%)*
Government final consumption	8.5	3.5	11.5	3.5	5.5	4.3	4.7	3.5	...	Consommation finale des administrations publiques
Private final consumption	3.2	3.3	6.4	4.6	6.2	5.3	5.3	3.7	...	Consommation finale privée
Gross fixed capital formation	1.1	4.8	- 1.3	2.7	5.5	13.0	2.5	6.5	...	Formation brute de capital fixe
Exports of goods and services	- 23.5	9.2	- 6.7	3.3	4.2	5.3	6.4	- 5.7	...	Exportations de biens et services
Less imports of goods and services	- 16.8	7.7	-	1.6	7.5	8.6	- 0.3	- 3.1	...	Moins importations de biens et services

III INFLATION

	2009	2010	2011	2012	2013	2014	2015	2016	2017	
Annual growth rates (%)										**Taux de croissance annuel (%)**
All item	3.0	1.3	2.9	2.4	2.1	1.9	2.7	0.9	0.6	Ensemble
of which:										dont:
Food and non-alcoholic beverages	5.8	1.2	4.8	3.4	3.3	0.8	2.0	1.1	-	Alimentation et boissons non alcoolisés
Alcoholic beverages, tobacco and narcotics	...	...	...	2.6	3.0	1.4	8.9	3.0	1.4	Boissons alcoolisées et tabacs
Clothing and footwear	...	...	...	2.2	1.3	1.6	0.2	0.1	1.0	Habillement et chaussures
Housing, water, electricity, gas and other fuels	- 4.2	- 0.1	3.1	3.3	2.8	2.0	2.9	1.4	1.2	Logement, eau, électricité, gaz et autres combustibles
Furnishings, household equipment and routine household maintenance	...	...	...	1.4	2.1	0.4	1.5	0.3	0.3	Meubles, articles de ménage et entretien courant
Health	0.1	- 0.5	- 0.7	0.3	0.6	0.7	0.5	- 0.3	0.3	Santé
Transport	- 0.7	0.9	0.3	2.3	1.9	7.7	7.5	- 0.7	0.8	Transport
Communication	...	...	...	- 0.7	- 2.9	- 2.5	- 2.7	- 2.2	0.7	Communication
Recreation and culture	...	...	...	0.1	0.2	0.7	0.4	1.0	0.6	Loisirs et culture
Education	...	...	...	3.3	3.0	1.1	2.2	2.6	1.0	Enseignement
Restaurants and hotels	...	...	...	2.6	1.9	3.6	5.9	3.4	0.9	Restaurants et hôtels
Miscellaneous goods and services	...	...	...	1.2	1.4	0.9	2.7	1.8	1.9	Biens et Services divers

IV AGRICULTURAL PRODUCTION - PRODUCTION AGRICOLE

TONNES (THOUSAND)	2009	2010	2011	2012	2013	2014	2015	2016	2017	Tonnes (milliers)
Cassava	2 941	3 808	4 083	4 287	4 502	4 601	4 991	5 285	...	Manioc
Plantains	2 550	3 182	3 426	3 569	3 719	3 834	3 916	5 285	...	Bananes plantains
	...	...	...	...	...	...	...	...	...	
Maize	1 625	1 670	1 572	1 750	1 948	2 063	2 149	5 285	...	Maïs
	...	...	...	...	...	...	...	...	...	

V MINING PRODUCTION - PRODUCTION MINIERE

	2009	2010	2011	2012	2013	2014	2015	2016	2017	
Crude petroleum - Production, metric tons (thousands)	27	23	22	23	24	28	35	34	29	Pétrole brut - Production, tonnes métriques (milliers)
Gold ores and concentrates - Production (Kilograms)	...	...	...	...	...	...	795	542	689	Minerais d'or et leurs concentrés - Production (Kilogrammes)
Marble, travertines, etc. - Production (metric tons)	5	2	...	-	...	...	...	...	...	Marbres, travertins, etc. - Production (tonnes métriques)

VI ENERGY - ENERGIE

	2009	2010	2011	2012	2013	2014	2015	2016	2017	
Total electricity generation (GWh)	5 874	5 958	5 874	6 167	5 442	6 080	6 531	...	...	Production électrique totale (GWh)
of which										dont
Production of electricity from fossil fuels (GWh)	1 716	1 580	1 537	1 574	1 613	1 652	1 693			Production d'électricité à partir de combustibles fossiles (GWh)
Production of hydro electricity (GWh)	4 016	4 260	4 217	4 470	4 783	5 118	5 476	...	...	Production d'électricité d'origine hydraulique (GWh)
Production of electricity from solar, wind, tide, wave and other sources (GWh)	71	59	59	60	64	68	72	...	...	Production d'électricité d'origine solaire, éolienne, marée motrice et autres (GWh)

VII TOURISM AND INFRASTRUCTURE - TOURISME ET INFRASTUCTURE

	2009	2010	2011	2012	2013	2014	2015	2016	2017	
VII-1 Tourism										**VII-1 Tourisme**
International tourist arrivals (thousands)	498	573	604	817	912	428	452	484	360	Arrivées de touristes internationaux (milliers)
Rooms in hotels and similar establishments (thousands)	27	...	...	38	30	31	33	36	36	Chambres d'hôtels et établissements assimilés (milliers)
Overnight stays (thousands)	1 126	1 268	1 167	1 353	1 717	3 274	3 355	3 504	1 888	Nuitées (milliers)
Tourism receipts (US$ thousand)	259 500	154 400	404 100	345 600	367 349	432 854	461 191	511 602	297 098	Recettes touristiques (milliers de $ EU)
Total contribution to GDP (%)	6.1	5.7	7.2	7.7	8.6	8.3	7.8	7.1	7.2	Contribution totale au PIB (%)
Total contribution to Employment (%)	5.6	5.3	6.3	6.9	7.7	7.3	6.8	6.2	6.0	Contribution totale à l'emploi (%)
VII-2 Infrastructure										**VII-2 Infrastructure**
Paved road (% of total)	...	10.1	8.0	...	...	...	...	...	...	Routes asphaltées (% du total)
Total network (Railways-km)	977	977	977	977	977	976	...	...	...	Réseau total voies ferrées-Km
Main telephone lines (per 100 inhabitants)	2.2	2.6	3.2	3.4	3.6	4.6	4.5	4.4	...	Lignes téléphoniques fixes (pour 100 habitants)
Mobile cellular subscribers (per 100 inhabitants)	39.8	41.9	49.6	60.4	70.4	75.7	71.8	68.1	...	Abonnés aux téléphones mobiles (pour 100 habitants)
Internet users per 100 inhabitants	3.8	4.3	5.0	7.5	10.0	16.2	20.7	25.0	...	Utilisateurs Internet par 100 Habitants
Fixed (wired)-broadband subscriptions per 100 inhabitants	...	...	...	...	...	...	...	...	...	Abonnements à l'Internet fixe (filaire) à large bande pour 100 habitants, par débit

VIII EXTERNAL TRADE - COMMERCE EXTERIEUR

US$ (MILLIONS) EXPORTS, FOB	2009	2010	2011	2012	2013	2014	2015	2016	2017	$ E.U (MILLIONS) EXPORTATIONS, FÂB
Exports - Total	3 552	3 878	4 517	4 275	4 521	5 160	4 053	4 275	...	Exportations - Total
Exports to Africa	491	585	880	731	646	651	502	535	...	Exportations vers l'Afrique
Main products										**Principaux produits**
Cocoa	771	595	543	452	454	602	609	562	...	Cacao
Petroleum oils or bituminous minerals > 70 % oil	208	423	319	510	430	395	244	297	...	Huiles de pétrole ou de minéraux bitumineux> 70 % d'huile
Petroleum oils, oils from bitumin. materials, crude	1 069	1 295	1 460	1 632	1 825	2 255	1 435	1 712	...	Huiles de pétrole, huiles de bitume. matériaux bruts
Wood in the rough or roughly squared	136	180	194	177	190	243	266	236	...	Bois bruts ou grossièrement équarris
Wood simply worked, and railway sleepers of wood	288	275	362	338	317	359	347	328	...	Le bois simplement travaillé, et les traverses de chemin de fer en bois
Main destinations										**Principales destinations**
China	332	340	472	644	271	624	562	550	...	Chine
India	42	145	216	249	234	481	580	492	...	Inde
Netherlands	610	472	429	401	390	440	431	404	...	Pays-Bas
Portugal	86	67	109	391	918	159	223	177	...	Portugal
Spain	385	605	600	417	491	723	222	438	...	Espagne
IMPORTS, CIF										
Imports - Total	4 442	5 133	6 800	6 515	6 657	7 561	6 037	6 213	...	Importations - Total (millions)
Imports from Africa	679	1 358	1 409	1 717	1 658	1 971	1 251	1 472	...	Importations en provenance de l'Afrique
Main products										**Principaux produits**
Fish, fresh (live or dead), chilled or frozen	177	135	269	204	221	227	243	215	...	Poissons frais (vivants ou morts), réfrigérés ou congelés
Petroleum oils or bituminous minerals > 70 % oil	103	123	80	410	350	390	244	290	...	Huiles de pétrole ou de minéraux bitumineux> 70 % d'huile
Petroleum oils, oils from bitumin. materials, crude	248	1 064	729	1 119	866	1 214	622	839	...	Huiles de pétrole, huiles de bitume. matériaux bruts
Rice	236	184	267	293	350	263	262	240	...	Riz
Telecommunication equipment, n.e.s.; & parts, n.e.s.	90	76	126	110	193	272	181	207	...	Matériel de télécommunication, n.es .; & parties, n.e.s.
Main origin										**Principales provenances**
Belgium	238	215	293	274	303	284	215	228	...	Belgique
China	499	564	935	888	1 144	1 620	1 492	1 422	...	Chine
France	851	801	1 034	839	818	821	666	679	...	France
Nigeria	255	753	782	1 009	905	1 142	579	786	...	Nigéria
United States	176	151	259	246	276	283	222	231	...	États-Unis

CAMEROUN

IX FINANCIAL AND MONETARY STATISTICS - FINANCES ET STATISTIQUES MONETAIRES

	2009	2010	2011	2012	2013	2014	2015	2016	2017	
IX-1 MONETARY STATISTICS CFA FRANC (MILLIONS)										**IX-1 STATISTIQUES MONÉTAIRES** FRANC CFA (MILLIONS)
Money supply (M1)	2 462 428	2 741 081	3 032 869	3 074 101	3 406 878	3 774 378	4 116 356	4 345 705	4 460 654	Masse monétaire (M1)
Quasi-money	883 223	1 038 490	1 104 879	1 147 735	1 257 690	1 339 830	1 465 490	1 537 245	1 591 725	Quasi-monnaie
of which demand deposit	976 757	1 091 818	1 272 143	...	...	...	...	...	...	dont Monnaie scripturale
Net foreign assets	1 780 800	1 849 441	1 629 648	1 541 390	1 552 978	1 669 823	2 112 961	1 451 133	2 003 994	Avoirs extérieurs nets
Domestic credit	866 188	1 202 407	1 670 682	1 939 998	2 261 673	2 576 475	2 549 602	3 555 527	3 366 496	Crédit intérieur
of which claims on private sector	- 558 227	- 496 171	- 373 849	- 162 092	- 155 097	- 79 424	- 468 911	245 730	261 086	dont créances sur le secteur privé
of which claims on government sector, net	1 266 887	1 466 950	1 779 274	1 910 943	2 159 135	2 466 360	2 753 902	2 984 734	2 947 799	dont créances nettes sur le gouvernement
International reserves (millions US$)	3 725	3 626	3 226	3 333	3 423	3 170	3 489	2 259	2 526	Réserves internationales (millions $EU)
Average exchange rate (National currency per US$)	472	495	472	511	494	494	591	593	582	Taux de change (moyen) (monnaie nationale par $ EU)
IX-2 PUBLIC FINANCE CFA FRANC (MILLIONS)										**IX-2 FINANCES PUBLIQUES** FRANC CFA (MILLIONS)
Total Revenues and Grants	1 926 400	1 920 200	2 222 700	2 424 600	2 591 300	2 903 800	3 013 200	2 866 200	3 161 000	Recettes totales et dons
Direct taxes (on income, profits)	334 900	342 800	404 800	471 000	513 000	613 400	683 900	635 600	699 600	Taxes directes
Domestic indirect taxes revenues	586 000	572 400	697 700	789 300	794 300	798 300	802 700	530 700	607 700	Taxes Indirectes
Trade taxes	235 900	252 700	273 600	294 100	289 700	356 600	338 100	348 400	335 200	Taxes sur le commerce extérieur
Other taxes	601 100	615 800	694 800	720 200	851 400	970 900	1 023 500	1 151 900	1 273 000	Autres taxes
Other revenues	81 600	77 200	86 000	94 000	96 600	119 300	153 900	145 500	160 000	Autres recettes
Grants	86 900	59 300	65 800	56 000	46 300	45 300	11 100	54 100	85 500	Dons
Total Expenditures and Net Lending	1 933 000	2 000 400	2 357 100	2 616 100	3 163 800	3 508 800	3 415 700	4 030 700	3 844 500	Dépenses totales et prêts nets
Current expenditure	1 459 800	1 558 000	1 703 500	1 753 700	2 053 300	2 215 300	2 257 700	2 204 000	2 059 300	Dépenses courantes
Wages and Salaries	629 400	634 500	681 600	706 100	790 000	851 600	910 700	942 200	998 500	Rémunérations et salaires
Other purchases of goods and services	541 000	592 200	526 300	567 300	655 100	765 600	786 600	767 900	693 600	Achat de biens et services
Other current expenditure	...	2 200	1 200	4 300	600	900	800	5 100	...	Autres dépenses courantes
Current transfers	289 400	329 100	494 400	476 000	607 600	597 200	559 600	488 800	367 200	Transferts courants
Interest payments	32 600	30 100	32 700	51 200	58 000	69 200	69 900	144 800	198 200	Intérêts
Capital expenditure	440 600	412 300	620 900	811 200	1 052 500	1 224 300	1 088 100	1 651 900	1 587 000	Dépenses d'équipement
Net lending	...	...	...	...	...	...	...	30 000	...	Prêts nets
Fiscal balance	- 6 600	- 80 200	- 134 400	- 191 500	- 572 500	- 605 000	- 402 500	-1 164 500	- 683 500	Solde global y compris les dons
IX-3 BALANCE OF PAYMENTS CFA FRANC (MILLIONS)										**IX-3 BALANCE DES PAIEMENTS** FRANC CFA (MILLIONS)
Trade balance	- 184	- 104	- 273	- 140	- 97	- 222	- 220	- 137	61	Balance commerciale
Services Balance	- 251	- 271	- 58	- 255	- 306	- 310	- 403	- 312	- 251	Balance des services
Net primary income	- 225	- 130	- 143	- 227	- 304	- 338	- 258	- 369	- 387	Revenus primaires nets
Compensation of employees	- 17	4	11	24	27	27	27	33	39	Rémunération des salariés
Investment income	- 209	- 135	- 154	- 251	- 331	- 365	- 285	- 394	- 418	Revenus des investissements
Net secondary income	132	110	122	134	150	177	187	205	218	Revenus secondaires nets
Net official transfers	62	52	62	44	45	54	43	49	48	Transferts officiels nets
Workers' remittances	42	35	54	47	62	72	72	78	85	Envois de fonds des travailleurs
Other private transfers	28	58	6	44	43	51	73	80	85	Autres transferts privés
Current account balance	- 528	- 396	- 353	- 488	- 557	- 692	- 694	- 613	- 358	Solde du compte courant
Capital and financial account	475	408	235	591	586	764	1 226	- 203	827	Comptes de capital et financier
Capital account	87	73	62	60	48	47	13	58	87	Compte de capital
Financial account	388	335	174	531	538	717	1 166	- 261	740	Compte financier
Errors and omissions	77	87	- 46	- 55	- 73	- 42	- 50	- 8	...	Erreurs et omissions
Overall balance	24	99	- 164	48	- 44	29	483	- 825	469	Balance générale

X DEBT AND FINANCIAL FLOWS - DETTE ET FLUX FINANCIERS										
	2009	2010	2011	2012	2013	2014	2015	2016	2017	
X-1 DEBT *US $ (MILLIONS)*										**X-1 DETTE EXTÉRIEURE** *$ E.U (MILLIONS)*
Total external debt	1 278	1 462	1 863	2 395	3 689	5 215	5 998	6 409	7 891	Dette extérieure totale
Private	...	...	...	...	...	...	...	...	...	Privée
Public	1 277 746	1 461 568	1 863 356	2 394 878	3 688 878	5 214 830	5 998 247	6 408 629	...	Publique
Total external debt service	215 114	176 013	161 692	183 254	237 571	301 192	408 305	369 627	...	Service de la dette extérieure
Present value of external debt	...	...	...	...	...	...	...	5 422 680	...	Valeur actuelle de la dette extérieure
Total government domestic debt, National currency (millions)	498 000	623 000	750 000	748 000	826 000	927 000	256 000	...	...	Dette publique intérieure
X-2 FINANCIAL FLOWS *US $ (MILLIONS)*										**X-2 FLUX FINANCIERS** *$ E.U (MILLIONS)*
Net Foreign Direct Investment Inflows	668	- 1	355	739	567	727	627	128	...	Investissements étranger direct (flux nets entrants)
Main origin of FDI inflows										**Principales origines de l'IDE entrant:**
France	57	103	- 330	85	204	...	...	...	...	France
United States	- 50	48	- 4	6	104	...	...	...	...	États-Unis
Netherlands	...	1	...	...	...	...	...	...	...	Pays-Bas
United Kingdom	- 3	19	- 6	11	...	...	...	...	...	Royaume-Uni
Italy	1	21	4	- 4	...	...	...	...	...	Italie
African countries	...	...	...	...	...	...	...	...	...	Pays africains
Net total official development assistance	644	540	612	597	752	856	663	756	...	Aide publique au développement (nette totale)
Main origin of net ODA										**Principales origines de l'APD nette**
Germany	91	91	97	89	84	87	72	88	...	Allemagne
France	91	82	149	89	172	167	162	238	...	France
Austria	...	...	...	-	-	-	-	2	...	Autriche
International Development Association [IDA]	48	83	73	88	158	126	91	127	...	International Development Association
Canada	7	7	12	5	3	3	4	8	...	Canada

CAMEROUN

SOURCES AND NOTES - SOURCES ET NOTES

External trade - Total exports, fob: UNCTAD	Commerce exterieur - Exportation, fab: CNUCED
External trade - Total import, cif: UNCTAD	Commerce exterieur - Imporations, caf: CNUCED
ODA: OECD	APD: OCDE
Monetary statistics: IMF	Statistiques monétaires: FMI
National Accounts: 2016:Provisional	Comptes nationaux: 2016: Provisoire.
Poverty: World Bank	Pauvreté: Banque mondiale

AREA (km2)		622 980			**SUPERFICIE (KM2)**
CAPITAL CITY	Bangui		Bangui		**CAPITALE**
CURRENCY	CFA Franc		Franc CFA		**MONNAIE**

I SOCIAL AND DEMOGRAPHIC INDICATORS — INDICATEURS DEMOGRAPHIQUES ET SOCIAUX

	Year Année	Value Valeur	Charts Graphiques	
Population				**Population**
Population ('000)	2015	4 900.3		Population ('000)
Female (%)	2015	50.7		Féminine (%)
Urban (%)	2015	39.2		Urbaine (%)
Average annual growth rate	2015	1.9		Taux de croissance annuel
Active population ('000)	2015	2 151.9		Population active ('000)
Population by age group ('000)				Population par groupe d'âge ('000)
0-14 years	2015	1 913.7		0-14 ans
15-64 years	2015	2 797.7		15-64 ans
65+ years	2015	188.9		65+ ans
Economically active population in agriculture (%)	2015	60.7		Participation de la population active agricole (%)
Crude birth rate	2015	33.4		Taux brut de natalité
Crude death rate	2015	14.1		Taux brut de mortalité
Total fertility rate	2015	4.2		Indice synthétique de fécondité
Life expectancy at birth - Total (years)	2015	51.5		Espérance de vie à la naissance - Totale (années)
Dependency ratio - Total (%)	2015	75.2		Taux de dépendance - Total (%)
Health				**Santé**
Percentage of children under-five and underweight	2011	23.5		% d'enfants de moins de cinq ans avec insuffisance pondérale
Prevalence of undernourishment	2015	47.7		Prévalence de la malnutrition
Under five mortality rate (per 1 000 live births)	2015	130.1		Taux de mortalité de moins de 5 ans (les deux sexes, pour 1000)
Infant mortality rate (per 1 000 live births)	2015	91.5		Taux de mortalité infantile (les deux sexes) par 1000
Neonatal mortality rate (per 1 000 live births)	2015	42.6		Le taux de mortalité néonatale (pour 1000 naissances vivantes)
Percentage of children provided the vaccines :				Pourcentage d'enfants vaccinés :
BCG	2014	74.0		BCG
DPT3	2014	47.0		DTC3
Polio	2012	47.0		polio
Measles	2014	49.0		rougeole
Percentage of mothers provided at least one antenatal care (%)	2006	57.3		Pourcentage de mères ayant au moins reçu un soin prénatal (%)
Percentage of deliveries attended by skilled health personnel	2010	53.8		% d'accouchements assistés par un personnel de santé qualifié
Number of doctors (per 10,000 population)	2004	0.9		Nombre de médecins (pour 10.000 habitants)
Number of nurses (per 10,000 population)	2009	2.6		Nombre d'infirmiers (pour 10.000 habitants)
Hospital beds - Total (per 10,000 population)	2011	10.0		Nombre de lits d'hôpitaux - Total (pour 10 000)
Births registered (per 1,000)	2015	33.4		Naissances enregistrées (pour 1000)
Deaths registered (per 1,000)	2015	14.1		Décès enregistrés (pour 1000)
Budget allocation to health (%)	2013	15.9		Dépenses publiques consacrées à la santé (% du budget)
Education				**Education**
Enrolment in primary education (000)	2012	662.3		Scolarisation dans le primaire (000)
Female	2012	284.5		Féminine
Enrolment in secondary education (000)	2012	125.9		Scolarisation dans le secondaire (000)
Female	2012	43.1		Féminine
Enrolment in tertiary education (000)	2012	12.5		Scolarisation dans le tertiaire (000)
Female	2012	3.4		Féminine
Literacy rate	2010	36.8		Taux d'alphabétisation (deux sexes)
Male	2010	50.7		Masculin
Female	2010	24.4		Féminin
Pupil teacher ratio - primary	...	...		Ratio élève-enseignant
Budget allocation to education (%)	2011	7.8		Dépenses publiques consacrées à l'enseignement (% du budget)
Poverty				**Pauvreté**
GNI per capita, PPP (current int. $)	2016	700.0		RNB par habitant, ($ PPA inter. courants)
Human Poverty Index (HPI-1) Value (%)	2007	42.4		Valeur de l'Indice de pauvreté (IPH-1) (%)
Population below Inter. poverty line ($2/day) (%)	2008	66.3		Population sous le seuil inter. de pauvreté (2$/Jour) (%)
Share of income held by richest 10%	2008	46.2		% de revenu des 10% plus riches
Share of income held by poorest 10%	2008	1.2		% de revenu des 10% plus pauvres
GINI index	2008	56.2		Indice de GINI

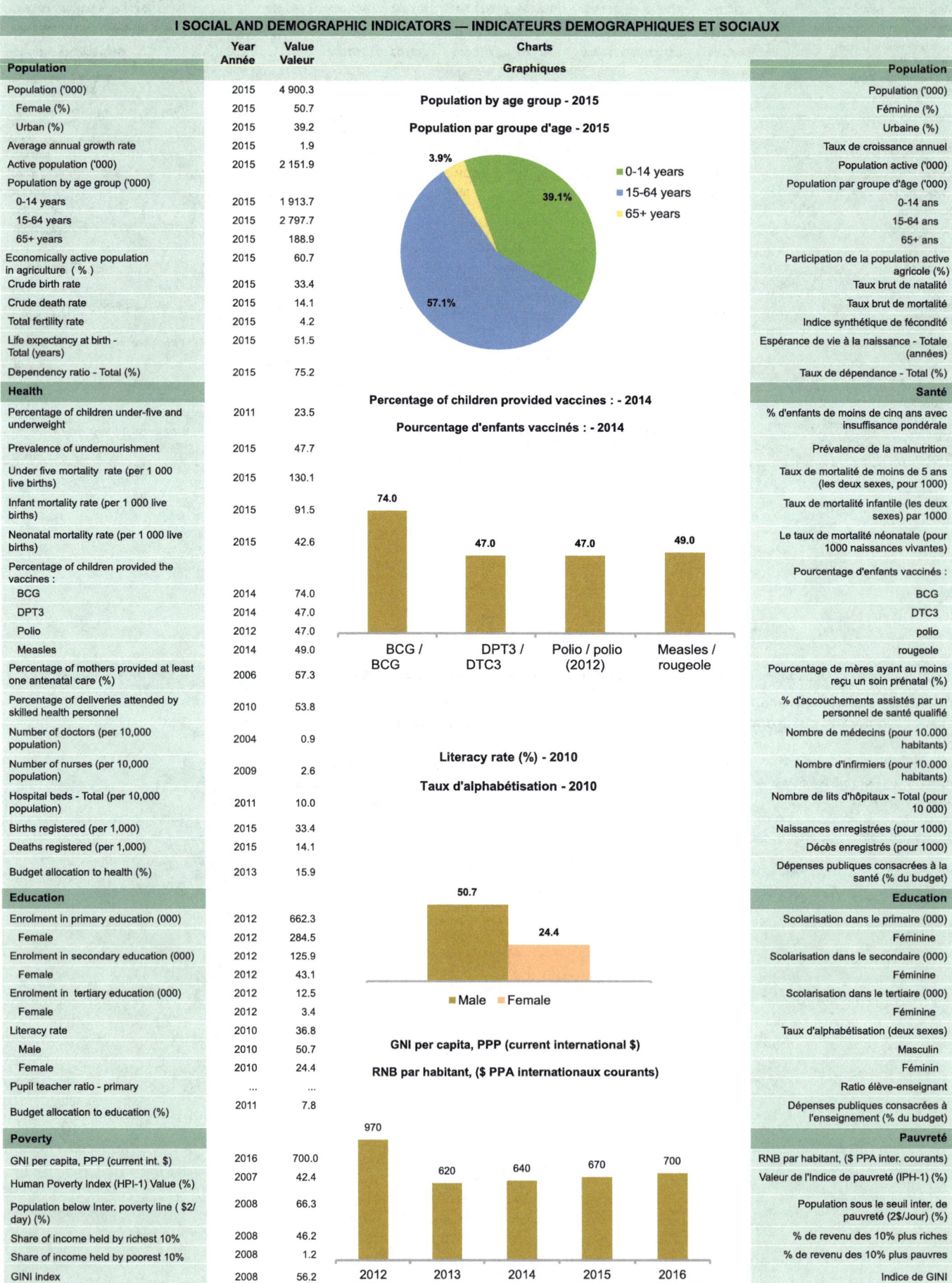

Population by age group - 2015

Population par groupe d'age - 2015

- 0-14 years 39.1%
- 15-64 years 57.1%
- 65+ years 3.9%

Percentage of children provided vaccines : - 2014

Pourcentage d'enfants vaccinés : - 2014

BCG / BCG 74.0 — DPT3 / DTC3 47.0 — Polio / polio (2012) 47.0 — Measles / rougeole 49.0

Literacy rate (%) - 2010

Taux d'alphabétisation - 2010

Male 50.7 — Female 24.4

GNI per capita, PPP (current international $)

RNB par habitant, ($ PPA internationaux courants)

2012: 970 — 2013: 620 — 2014: 640 — 2015: 670 — 2016: 700

	2009	2010	2011	2012	2013	2014	2015	2016	2017	
GROSS DOMESTIC PRODUCT BY KIND OF ECONOMIC ACTIVITY AT CURRENT PRICES *CFA FRANC (MILLIONS)*										**PRODUIT INTÉRIEUR BRUT PAR BRANCHE D'ACTIVITÉ ÉCONOMIQUE AUX PRIX COURANTS** *FRANC CFA (MILLIONS)*
Agriculture, hunting , forestry and Fishing	478 020	494 655	542 519	571 357	328 843	385 093	399 766	416 479	436 841	Agriculture, chasse sylviculture et Pêche
Mining and quarrying	16 231	18 009	20 484	22 473	7 465	3 626	2 960	2 559	4 103	Industries extractives
Manufacturing	59 446	61 549	64 735	68 122	60 901	65 446	63 716	67 073	72 350	Industries manufacturières
Electricity, gas & water	6 152	6 443	6 762	6 703	5 872	5 996	6 212	6 577	6 945	Electricité, gaz et eau
Construction	38 076	40 002	44 107	47 112	40 238	43 547	42 335	44 782	49 174	Bâtiments et travaux publics
Wholesale & retail trade, restaurants, hotels	114 321	120 694	135 503	141 649	111 548	118 254	122 270	127 137	132 814	Commerce de gros et de détail, restaurants et hôtels
Finance, insurance, real estate, etc.	57 315	61 396	68 929	71 707	55 716	55 810	60 363	63 728	64 358	Banques, assurances, affaires immobilières
Transport and communications	49 185	52 180	59 658	62 363	51 399	51 690	56 125	58 359	60 964	Transport(s) et communications
Public administration and defense	39 500	43 900	46 000	49 000	26 000	57 000	57 627	61 661	64 744	Administrations publiques et défense
Education	...	...	...	...	...	...	...	...	...	Education
Health And Social Work	...	...	...	...	...	...	...	...	...	Santé et Actions Sociales
Other services	16 700	13 800	...	11 400	8 700	19 635	29 952	37 440	35 568	Autres services
Less Imputed Service Charges	...	...	...	...	...	...	...	...	...	Moins Services d'intermédiation financière
Gross domestic product at factor cost / basic prices	874 945	912 627	988 698	1 051 885	696 682	806 096	841 326	885 793	927 861	Produit intérieur brut aux couts des facteurs / prix de base
Plus: Indirect Taxes / taxes on products, less subsidies	60 800	71 000	55 400	63 200	41 450	30 005	47 800	57 400	72 755	Plus taxes indirectes/impôts sur les produits, moins les subventions
EXPENDITURE ON GROSS DOMESTIC PRODUCT AT CURRENT PURCHASER'S VALUES *CFA FRANC (MILLIONS)*										**EMPLOI DU PRODUIT INTÉRIEUR BRUT AUX PRIX COURANTS D'ACQUISITION** *FRANC CFA (MILLIONS)*
Government final consumption	78 995	81 103	64 658	84 898	48 774	116 103	123 101	139 297	140 999	Consommation finale des administrations publiques
Private final consumption	862 362	883 440	933 195	978 933	742 123	798 732	870 373	894 801	935 234	Consommation finale privée
Gross fixed capital formation	105 575	138 771	155 160	163 495	71 757	106 506	101 452	122 383	146 164	Formation brute de capital fixe
Change in inventories	...	...	...	...	...	...	...	...	...	Variation des stocks
Exports of goods and services	89 289	102 333	119 297	129 037	66 261	37 960	118 100	137 711	170 217	Exportations de biens et services
Less imports of goods and services	200 476	222 020	228 212	241 279	190 783	223 200	323 900	351 000	392 000	Moins importations de biens et services
GDP at purchasers' values	935 745	983 627	1 044 098	1 115 085	738 132	836 101	889 126	943 193	1 000 616	PIB aux prix d'acquisition
GROSS DOMESTIC PRODUCT BY KIND OF ECONOMIC ACTIVITY AT CONSTANT PRICES *ANNUAL GROWTH RATES (%)*										**PRODUIT INTÉRIEUR BRUT PAR BRANCHE D'ACTIVITÉ ECONOMIQUE AUX PRIX CONSTANTS** *TAUX DE CROISSANCE ANNUEL (%)*
Agriculture, hunting , forestry and Fishing	- 0.9	2.3	6.8	2.9	- 45.1	- 6.5	3.0	3.1	1.3	Agriculture, chasse sylviculture et Pêche
Mining and quarrying	- 8.3	- 2.9	6.4	10.7	- 67.7	- 48.9	- 20.5	- 25.4	94.5	Industries extractives
Manufacturing	3.0	2.5	3.0	3.0	- 13.3	5.0	2.0	3.0	3.0	Industries manufacturières
Electricity, gas & water	1.1	2.5	4.0	- 1.4	- 13.3	2.1	1.9	3.0	3.2	Electricité, gaz et eau
Construction	3.5	3.0	8.1	3.5	- 17.2	4.5	1.9	3.5	4.9	Bâtiments et travaux publics
Wholesale & retail trade, restaurants, hotels	2.2	3.0	9.0	1.0	- 25.0	1.5	- 0.8	1.4	5.0	Commerce de gros et de détail, restaurants et hôtels
Finance, insurance, real estate, etc.	2.2	3.0	9.0	1.0	- 26.0	1.0	3.5	3.0	1.5	Banques, assurances, affaires immobilières
Transport and communications	2.2	3.0	11.0	1.0	- 20.0	1.4	3.9	1.4	5.0	Transport(s) et communications
Public administration and defense	2.9	7.4	1.7	2.4	- 48.6	95.6	- 0.9	6.9	4.0	Administrations publiques et défense
Education	...	...	...	...	...	...	...	...	...	Education
Health And Social Work	...	...	...	...	...	...	...	...	...	Santé et Actions Sociales
Other services	27.4	- 20.2	...	...	- 33.9	162.5	36.2	24.8	- 2.6	Autres services
Less Imputed Service Charges	...	...	...	...	...	...	...	...	...	Moins Services d'intermédiation financière
Gross domestic product at factor cost / basic prices	0.8	2.3	5.4	3.7	- 36.6	3.2	2.8	3.7	2.7	Produit intérieur brut aux couts des facteurs / prix de base
Plus: Indirect Taxes / taxes on products, less subsidies	16.6	14.5	- 24.1	9.7	- 37.2	- 35.5	56.9	18.3	24.3	Plus taxes indirectes/impôts sur les produits, moins les subventions
Gross domestic product at market prices	1.7	3.0	3.3	4.0	- 36.7	1.0	4.8	4.5	4.0	Produit intérieur brut aux prix du marché
EXPENDITURE ON GROSS DOMESTIC PRODUCT AT CONSTANT PURCHASERS' VALUES *ANNUAL GROWTH RATES (%)*										**EMPLOIS DU PRODUIT INTÉRIEUR BRUT AUX PRIX CONSTANTS D'ACQUISITION** *TAUX DE CROISSANCE ANNUEL (%)*
Government final consumption	51.1	10.0	- 2.4	- 16.6	- 3.0	78.1	- 12.1	- 2.5	1.2	Consommation finale des administrations publiques
Private final consumption	0.3	3.0	1.9	1.7	- 32.5	- 6.1	2.6	- 0.9	0.9	Consommation finale privée
Gross fixed capital formation	5.4	12.2	- 12.6	29.0	- 57.5	2.2	- 19.1	- 0.2	- 2.8	Formation brute de capital fixe
Exports of goods and services	- 17.0	9.8	5.2	10.1	- 24.4	55.4	218.7	20.4	21.3	Exportations de biens et services
Less imports of goods and services	5.5	13.4	- 13.3	9.1	- 15.6	12.7	13.2	- 8.4	- 0.6	Moins importations de biens et services

	III INFLATION									
	2009	2010	2011	2012	2013	2014	2015	2016	2017	
Annual growth rates (%)										**Taux de croissance annuel (%)**
All item	3.6	1.5	1.8	5.9	6.6	11.6	4.5	4.6	3.7	Ensemble
of which:										dont:
Food and non-alcoholic beverages	3.5	1.4	1.1	7.4	1.5	10.8	...	...	...	Alimentation et boissons non alcoolisés
Alcoholic beverages, tobacco and narcotics	6.8	- 0.1	1.6	- 0.2	1.9	6.1	...	...	...	Boissons alcoolisées et tabacs
Clothing and footwear	3.2	0.9	- 1.3	5.1	- 1.0	1.7	...	...	...	Habillement et chaussures
Housing, water, electricity, gas and other fuels	3.8	4.6	7.1	1.2	0.6	- 0.7	...	...	...	Logement, eau, électricité, gaz et autres combustibles
Furnishings, household equipment and routine household maintenance	5.2	- 1.4	3.8	6.0	- 4.9	- 5.5	...	...	...	Meubles, articles de ménage et entretien courant
Health	0.2	...	...	0.5	- 1.4	5.1	...	...	...	Santé
Transport	1.6	0.3	- 1.2	2.7	0.8	- 0.4	...	...	...	Transport
Communication	...	...	...	1.2	- 1.1	- 1.1	...	...	...	Communication
Recreation and culture	1.7	8.2	0.5	- 4.8	- 4.3	7.9	...	...	...	Loisirs et culture
Education	...	...	...	...	...	...	...	...	...	Enseignement
Restaurants and hotels	2.1	- 0.9	- 1.2	13.8	9.2	21.3	...	...	...	Restaurants et hôtels
Miscellaneous goods and services	5.3	7.6	6.3	6.0	20.4	23.6	...	...	...	Biens et Services divers

RÉPUBLIQUE CENTRAFRICAINE

IV AGRICULTURAL PRODUCTION - PRODUCTION AGRICOLE

TONNES (THOUSAND)	2009	2010	2011	2012	2013	2014	2015	2016	2017	Tonnes (milliers)
Cassava	643	679	706	684	675	695	706	714	...	Manioc
Yams	394	435	447	460	470	477	475	477	...	Ignames
Maize	163	140	160	149	162	122	116	135	...	Maïs
Groundnuts, with shell	151	150	160	162	121	80	80	92	...	Arachides (en coques)
Taro (cocoyam)	111	118	120	125	130	130	130	129	...	Taros (colocases)

V MINING PRODUCTION - PRODUCTION MINIERE

	2009	2010	2011	2012	2013	2014	2015	2016	2017	
Diamonds, industrial - Production (carat)	310 469	...	...	...	...	...	...	...	...	Diamants industriels - Production (carat)
	...	...	...	...	...	...	...	...	...	
Gold ores and concentrates - Production (Kilograms)	61	...	...	...	...	...	...	...	...	Minerais d'or et leurs concentrés - Production (Kilogrammes)

VI ENERGY - ENERGIE

	2009	2010	2011	2012	2013	2014	2015	2016	2017	
Total electricity generation (GWh)	159	160	165	176	144	146	148	150	...	Production électrique totale (GWh)
of which										dont
Production of electricity from fossil fuels (GWh)	24	25	25	27	1	-	-	-	...	Production d'électricité à partir de combustibles fossiles (GWh)
Production of hydro electricity (GWh)	135	135	139	149	138	139	141	142	...	Production d'électricité d'origine hydraulique (GWh)
Production of electricity from solar, wind, tide, wave and other sources (GWh)	...	...	1	1	5	7	7	7	...	Production d'électricité d'origine solaire, éolienne, marée motrice et autres (GWh)

VII TOURISM AND INFRASTRUCTURE - TOURISME ET INFRASTUCTURE

	2009	2010	2011	2012	2013	2014	2015	2016	2017	
VII-1 Tourism										**VII-1 Tourisme**
International tourist arrivals (thousands)	52	54	65	71	84	96	121	127	139	Arrivées de touristes internationaux (milliers)
Rooms in hotels and similar establishments (thousands)	...	...	...	1	1	1	1	...	...	Chambres d'hôtels et établissements assimilés (milliers)
Overnight stays (thousands)	52	49	52	55	37	74	106	125	150	Nuitées (milliers)
Tourism receipts (US$ thousand)	4 500	11 000	11 000	11 000	11 600	12 065	9 458	9 749	11 197	Recettes touristiques (milliers de $ EU)
Total contribution to GDP (%)	5.4	5.8	5.5	6.2	7.7	7.0	6.7	6.6	6.6	Contribution totale au PIB (%)
Total contribution to Employment (%)	4.9	5.4	5.2	5.8	5.8	5.4	5.1	5.0	5.0	Contribution totale à l'emploi (%)
VII-2 Infrastructure										**VII-2 Infrastructure**
Paved road (% of total)	6.8	6.8	...	...	...	...	...	...	...	Routes asphaltées (% du total)
Total network (Railways-km)	...	...	...	...	...	...	...	...	...	Réseau total voies ferrées-Km
Main telephone lines (per 100 inhabitants)	...	...	...	...	...	...	...	...	...	Lignes téléphoniques fixes (pour 100 habitants)
Mobile cellular subscribers (per 100 inhabitants)	20.2	22.5	22.4	25.3	29.5	24.5	25.9	25.5	...	Abonnés aux téléphones mobiles (pour 100 habitants)
Internet users per 100 inhabitants	1.8	2.0	2.2	3.0	3.4	3.6	3.8	4.0	...	Utilisateurs Internet par 100 Habitants
Fixed (wired)-broadband subscriptions per 100 inhabitants	...	...	...	...	...	...	...	...	...	Abonnements à l'Internet fixe (filaire) à large bande pour 100 habitants, par débit

VIII EXTERNAL TRADE - COMMERCE EXTERIEUR

US$ (MILLIONS) EXPORTS, FOB	2009	2010	2011	2012	2013	2014	2015	2016	2017	$ E.U (MILLIONS) EXPORTATIONS, FÀB
Exports - Total	120	140	190	203	116	96	85	93	...	Exportations - Total
Exports to Africa	14	14	29	15	13	11	10	11	...	Exportations vers l'Afrique
Main products										**Principaux produits**
Cotton	6	17	19	22	20	26	19	23	...	Coton
Natural abrasives, n.e.s. (incl. industri. diamonds)	11	19	39	28	5	...	2	1	...	Abrasifs naturels, n.e.s. (y compris les diamants industriels)
Pearls, precious & semi-precious stones	43	34	47	59	27	1	11	6	...	Perles, pierres précieuses et semi-précieuses
Wood in the rough or roughly squared	30	34	48	53	36	39	30	36	...	Bois bruts ou grossièrement équarris
Wood simply worked, and railway sleepers of wood	18	15	16	14	17	20	15	18	...	Le bois simplement travaillé, et les traverses de chemin de fer en bois
Main destinations										**Principales destinations**
Belgium	51	39	41	70	24	2	11	7	...	Belgique
China	13	20	27	47	30	30	25	28	...	Chine
France	9	12	24	12	5	6	5	5	...	France
Indonesia	5	7	8	6	14	23	15	19	...	Indonésie
Morocco	9	8	7	3	8	9	7	8	...	Maroc
IMPORTS, CIF										
Imports - Total	270	300	310	323	213	406	346	382	...	Importations - Total (millions)
Imports from Africa	50	52	35	57	28	81	61	72	...	Importations en provenance de l'Afrique
Main products										**Principaux produits**
Edible products and preparations, n.e.s.	8	5	5	9	5	14	11	13	...	Produits et préparations comestibles, n.d.a.
Medicaments (incl. veterinary medicaments)	19	13	8	17	14	33	27	30	...	Médicaments (y compris les médicaments vétérinaires)
Motor vehic. for transport of goods, special purpo.	7	7	4	8	2	26	16	21	...	Véhicule à moteur pour le transport de marchandises, spécial.
Petroleum oils or bituminous minerals > 70 % oil	19	106	168	88	87	3	50	27	...	Huiles de pétrole ou de minéraux bitumineux> 70% d'huile
Telecommunication equipment, n.e.s.; & parts, n.e.s.	11	9	4	10	11	21	18	20	...	Matériel de télécommunication, n.es .; & parties, n.e.s.
Main origin										**Principales provenances**
Cameroon	23	27	16	28	9	34	24	29	...	Cameroun
France	58	49	41	59	26	68	53	62	...	France
Republic of Korea	-	32	123	25	37	1	22	11	...	République de Corée
Netherlands	24	66	28	61	34	10	25	18	...	Pays-Bas
United States	39	9	5	9	7	41	27	35	...	États-Unis

IX FINANCIAL AND MONETARY STATISTICS - FINANCES ET STATISTIQUES MONETAIRES

	2009	2010	2011	2012	2013	2014	2015	2016	2017	
IX-1 MONETARY STATISTICS *CFA FRANC (MILLIONS)*										**IX-1 STATISTIQUES MONÉTAIRES** *FRANC CFA (MILLIONS)*
Money supply (M1)	150 733	175 045	199 191	202 289	213 650	244 800	257 805	272 629	296 444	Masse monétaire (M1)
Quasi-money	25 253	30 674	40 127	39 508	44 024	47 692	58 181	60 002	63 262	Quasi-monnaie
of which demand deposit	...	...	...	...	...	...	...	...	...	dont Monnaie scripturale
Net foreign assets	28 664	10 568	13 326	- 11 408	8 614	51 723	42 225	54 669	98 156	Avoirs extérieurs nets
Domestic credit	187 133	222 854	263 552	292 845	278 458	286 524	309 217	317 168	308 374	Crédit intérieur
of which claims on private sector	116 532	132 255	154 628	151 063	159 848	163 157	186 108	172 454	175 173	dont créances sur le secteur privé
of which claims on government sector, net	67 695	88 087	105 474	138 049	113 428	119 670	117 458	133 187	127 001	dont créances nettes sur le gouvernement
International reserves (millions US$)	203	184	184	172	199	279	199	220	319	Réserves internationales (millions $EU)
Average exchange rate (National currency per US$)	472	495	472	511	494	494	591	593	582	Taux de change (moyen) (monnaie nationale par $ EU)
IX-2 PUBLIC FINANCE *CFA FRANC (MILLIONS)*										**IX-2 FINANCES PUBLIQUES** *FRANC CFA (MILLIONS)*
Total Revenues and Grants	150	169	138	181	63	132	134	147	...	Recettes totales et dons
Direct taxes (on income, profits)	18	18	19	21	7	8	13	19	...	Taxes directes
Domestic indirect taxes revenues	44	47	36	58	23	20	33	39	...	Taxes Indirectes
Trade taxes	18	27	32	31	9	9	15	20	...	Taxes sur le commerce extérieur
Other taxes	...	...	...	...	...	...	...	...	...	Autres taxes
Other revenues	20	22	25	18	3	4	6	7	...	Autres recettes
Grants	49	54	26	54	21	91	68	62	...	Dons
Total Expenditures and Net Lending	156	183	163	181	112	107	140	131	...	Dépenses totales et prêts nets
Current expenditure	95	113	115	105	94	84	91	93	...	Dépenses courantes
Wages and Salaries	42	43	46	51	54	55	56	56	...	Rémunérations et salaires
Other purchases of goods and services	28	38	36	31	23	14	16	20	...	Achat de biens et services
Other current expenditure	25	32	33	23	18	15	19	18	...	Autres dépenses courantes
Current transfers	...	...	...	...	...	...	...	...	...	Transferts courants
Interest payments	15	10	7	8	5	6	5	6	...	Intérêts
Capital expenditure	46	59	41	68	13	18	44	32	...	Dépenses d'équipement
Net lending	...	...	...	...	...	...	...	...	...	Prêts nets
Fiscal balance	- 5	- 14	- 25	...	- 49	25	- 6	16	...	Solde global y compris les dons
IX-3 BALANCE OF PAYMENTS *CFA FRANC (MILLIONS)*										**IX-3 BALANCE DES PAIEMENTS** *FRANC CFA (MILLIONS)*
Trade balance	- 66 614	- 81 100	- 59 000	- 66 700	- 56 800	- 144 000	- 141 800	- 115 600	...	Balance commerciale
Services Balance	- 39 261	- 56 400	- 54 700	- 58 000	- 24 500	- 57 000	- 52 700	- 41 200	...	Balance des services
Net primary income	- 9 957	- 2 300	4 700	4 900	1 900	300	400	6 400	...	Revenus primaires nets
Compensation of employees	...	6 200	6 400	6 500	7 000	7 500	8 000	8 500	...	Rémunération des salariés
Investment income	...	- 8 500	- 1 700	- 1 600	- 5 100	- 7 200	- 7 600	- 2 100	...	Revenus des investissements
Net secondary income	48 600	39 600	30 600	69 700	53 500	149 100	130 100	135 500	...	Revenus secondaires nets
Net official transfers	...	36 100	23 600	35 900	35 100	55 800	62 900	70 700	...	Transferts officiels nets
Workers' remittances	...	...	...	...	...	...	...	...	...	Envois de fonds des travailleurs
Other private transfers	...	...	...	...	...	...	...	...	...	Autres transferts privés
Current account balance	- 67 232	- 100 200	- 78 400	- 50 100	- 25 900	- 51 600	- 64 000	- 14 900	...	Solde du compte courant
Capital and financial account	90 928	65 000	61 300	62 500	27 700	95 900	47 900	36 900	...	Comptes de capital et financier
Capital account	301 400	40 700	26 300	35 200	11 000	17 300	36 600	23 800	...	Compte de capital
Financial account	- 210 472	24 300	35 000	27 300	16 700	78 600	11 300	13 100	...	Compte financier
Errors and omissions	20 219	- 6 100	6 400	- 23 000	7 900	- 3 400	- 9 700	- 19 100	...	Erreurs et omissions
Overall balance	43 915	- 41 300	- 10 700	- 10 600	9 700	40 900	- 25 800	2 900	...	Balance générale

RÉPUBLIQUE CENTRAFRICAINE

X DEBT AND FINANCIAL FLOWS - DETTE ET FLUX FINANCIERS

	2009	2010	2011	2012	2013	2014	2015	2016	2017	
X-1 DEBT US $ (MILLIONS)										**X-1 DETTE EXTÉRIEURE** $ E.U (MILLIONS)
Total external debt	179	179	175	216	228	364	320	318	340	Dette extérieure totale
Private	...	...	...	...	...	...	...	...	...	Privée
Public	179	179	175	216	228	364	320	318	...	Publique
Total external debt service	23	11	11	25	20	17	18	21	...	Service de la dette extérieure
Present value of external debt	...	...	...	...	...	...	...	415	...	Valeur actuelle de la dette extérieure
Total government domestic debt, National currency (millions)	...	...	...	...	...	...	...	...	...	Dette publique intérieure
X-2 FINANCIAL FLOWS US $ (MILLIONS)										**X-2 FLUX FINANCIERS** $ E.U (MILLIONS)
Net Foreign Direct Investment Inflows	42	62	37	70	2	3	3	31	...	Investissements étranger direct (flux nets entrants)
Main origin of FDI inflows										**Principales origines de l'IDE entrant:**
...	...	...	...	...	...	...	...	...	...	...
...	...	...	...	...	...	...	...	...	...	...
...	...	...	...	...	...	...	...	...	...	...
...	...	...	...	...	...	...	...	...	...	...
...	...	...	...	...	...	...	...	...	...	...
African countries	...	...	5	...	...	...	...	...	...	Pays africains
Net total official development assistance	239	261	269	228	203	611	487	500	...	Aide publique au développement (nette totale)
Main origin of net ODA										**Principales origines de l'APD nette**
France	26	25	21	19	23	45	38	30	...	France
United States	31	20	12	15	32	62	68	78	...	États-Unis
International Development Association [IDA]	29	18	53	42	10	71	27	38	...	International Development Association
Japan	6	8	38	14	6	9	18	16	...	Japon
IMF (Concessional Trust Funds)	40	13	...	11	- 2	7	5	15	...	Financements concessionnels du FMI dans le cadre de la FASR

SOURCES AND NOTES - SOURCES ET NOTES

External trade - Total exports, fob: UNCTAD

External trade - Total import, cif: UNCTAD

ODA: OECD

Monetary statistics: IMF

National Accounts: 2013:Provisionnal;2014-2017: Projections

Poverty: World Bank

Commerce exterieur - Exportation, fab: CNUCED

Commerce exterieur - Imporations, caf: CNUCED

APD: OCDE

Statistiques monétaires: FMI

Comptes nationaux: 2013:Provisoire; 2014-2017: Projections

Pauvreté: Banque mondiale

		N'Djamena		
AREA (km2)		1 284 000		**SUPERFICIE (KM2)**
CAPITAL CITY	N'Djamena		N'Djamena	**CAPITALE**
CURRENCY	CFA Franc		Franc CFA	**MONNAIE**

I SOCIAL AND DEMOGRAPHIC INDICATORS — INDICATEURS DEMOGRAPHIQUES ET SOCIAUX

	Year Année	Value Valeur	Charts Graphiques	
Population				**Population**
Population ('000)	2017	14 600.0		Population ('000)
Female (%)	2017	51.0		Féminine (%)
Urban (%)	2017	24.2		Urbaine (%)
Average annual growth rate	2017	3.6		Taux de croissance annuel
Active population ('000)	2017	6.0		Population active ('000)
Population by age group ('000)				Population par groupe d'âge ('000)
0-14 years	2017	7.4		0-14 ans
15-64 years	2017	7.0		15-64 ans
65+ years	2017	0.3		65+ ans
Economically active population in agriculture (%)	2017	63.1		Participation de la population active agricole (%)
Crude birth rate	2017	49.6		Taux brut de natalité
Crude death rate	2017	14.8		Taux brut de mortalité
Total fertility rate	2017	6.8		Indice synthétique de fécondité
Life expectancy at birth - Total (years)	2017	53.0		Espérance de vie à la naissance - Totale (années)
Dependency ratio - Total (%)	2017	110.0		Taux de dépendance - Total (%)
Health				**Santé**
Percentage of children under-five and underweight	2016	22.1		% d'enfants de moins de cinq ans avec insuffisance pondérale
Prevalence of undernourishment	2017	37.0		Prévalence de la malnutrition
Under five mortality rate (per 1 000 live births)	2017	133.0		Taux de mortalité de moins de 5 ans (les deux sexes, pour 1000)
Infant mortality rate (per 1 000 live births)	2017	72.0		Taux de mortalité infantile (les deux sexes) par 1000
Neonatal mortality rate (per 1 000 live births)	2017	34.0		Le taux de mortalité néonatale (pour 1000 naissances vivantes)
Percentage of children provided the vaccines :				Pourcentage d'enfants vaccinés :
BCG	2016	84.6		BCG
DPT3	2016	92.7		DTC3
Polio	2016	81.6		polio
Measles	2016	85.9		rougeole
Percentage of mothers provided at least one antenatal care (%)	2015	85.2		Pourcentage de mères ayant au moins reçu un soin prénatal (%)
Percentage of deliveries attended by skilled health personnel	2015	40.1		% d'accouchements assistés par un personnel de santé qualifié
Number of doctors (per 10,000 population)	2015	19 641.0		Nombre de médecins (pour 10.000 habitants)
Number of nurses (per 10,000 population)	2015	2 837.0		Nombre d'infirmiers (pour 10.000 habitants)
Hospital beds - Total (per 10,000 population)	2015	1 992.0		Nombre de lits d'hôpitaux - Total (pour 10 000)
Births registered (per 1,000)	2017	45.0		Naissances enregistrées (pour 1000)
Deaths registered (per 1,000)	2017	14.0		Décès enregistrés (pour 1000)
Budget allocation to health (%)	2017	6.5		Dépenses publiques consacrées à la santé (% du budget)
Education				**Education**
Enrolment in primary education (000)	2017	3 856.0		Scolarisation dans le primaire (000)
Female	2017	1 850.0		Féminine
Enrolment in secondary education (000)	2017	890.0		Scolarisation dans le secondaire (000)
Female	2017	198.0		Féminine
Enrolment in tertiary education (000)	2014	42.5		Scolarisation dans le tertiaire (000)
Female	2017	139.0		Féminine
Literacy rate	2012	37.3		Taux d'alphabétisation (deux sexes)
Male	2012	46.9		Masculin
Female	2012	27.8		Féminin
Pupil teacher ratio - primary	2015	56.0		Ratio élève-enseignant
Budget allocation to education (%)	2013	12.5		Dépenses publiques consacrées à l'enseignement (% du budget)
Poverty				**Pauvreté**
GNI per capita, PPP (current int. $)	2016	1950.0		RNB par habitant, ($ PPA inter. courants)
Human Poverty Index (HPI-1) Value (%)	2007	53.1		Valeur de l'Indice de pauvreté (IPH-1) (%)
Population below Inter. poverty line ($2/day) (%)	2011	38.4		Population sous le seuil inter. de pauvreté (2$/Jour) (%)
Share of income held by richest 10%	2011	32.4		% de revenu des 10% plus riches
Share of income held by poorest 10%	2011	1.8		% de revenu des 10% plus pauvres
GINI index	2011	43.3		Indice de GINI

Population by age group - 2017

Population par groupe d'age - 2017

- 0-14 years — 50.3%
- 15-64 years — 47.6%
- 65+ years — 2.0%

Percentage of children provided vaccines : - 2016

Pourcentage d'enfants vaccinés : - 2016

- BCG / BCG — 84.6
- DPT3 / DTC3 — 92.7
- Polio / polio — 81.6
- Measles / rougeole — 85.9

Literacy rate (%) - 2012

Taux d'alphabétisation - 2012

- Male — 46.9
- Female — 27.8

GNI per capita, PPP (current international $)

RNB par habitant, ($ PPA internationaux courants)

2012	2013	2014	2015	2016
1 950	1 980	2 090	2 110	1 950

II NATIONAL ACCOUNTS — COMPTES NATIONAUX

	2009	2010	2011	2012	2013	2014	2015	2016	2017	
GROSS DOMESTIC PRODUCT BY KIND OF ECONOMIC ACTIVITY AT CURRENT PRICES *CFA FRANC (BILLIONS)*										**PRODUIT INTÉRIEUR BRUT PAR BRANCHE D'ACTIVITÉ ÉCONOMIQUE AUX PRIX COURANTS** *FRANC CFA (MILLIARDS)*
Agriculture, hunting , forestry and Fishing	1 284	1 696	1 452	1 743	2 014	2 025	2 025	2 111	...	Agriculture, chasse sylviculture et Pêche
Mining and quarrying	750	1 141	1 613	1 803	1 223	1 343	1 235	867	...	Industries extractives
Manufacturing	309	351	420	683	483	532	602	647	...	Industries manufacturières
Electricity, gas & water	1	9	9	14	8	9	12	11	...	Electricité, gaz et eau
Construction	250	250	286	415	413	419	279	113	...	Bâtiments et travaux publics
Wholesale & retail trade, restaurants, hotels	827	851	984	982	980	1 034	1 187	1 197	...	Commerce de gros et de détail, restaurants et hôtels
Finance, insurance, real estate, etc.	152	175	188	203	244	255	245	224	...	Banques, assurances, affaires immobilières
Transport and communications	296	306	352	411	398	470	462	441	...	Transport(s) et communications
Public administration and defense	219	235	349	394	411	469	373	360	...	Administrations publiques et défense
Education	89	98	100	113	144	145	132	134	...	Education
Health And Social Work	141	149	166	182	242	207	177	194	...	Santé et Actions Sociales
Other services	76	68	71	85	102	109	118	114	...	Autres services
Less Imputed Service Charges	- 33	- 24	- 24	- 30	- 35	- 37	- 29	- 40	...	Moins Services d'intermédiation financière
Gross domestic product at factor cost / basic prices	4 363	5 306	5 965	6 996	6 628	6 982	6 816	6 373	...	Produit intérieur brut aux couts des facteurs / prix de base
Plus: Indirect Taxes / taxes on products, less subsidies	87	127	159	153	194	187	125	123	...	Plus taxes indirectes/impôts sur les produits, moins les subventions
EXPENDITURE ON GROSS DOMESTIC PRODUCT AT CURRENT PURCHASER'S VALUES *CFA FRANC (BILLIONS)*										**EMPLOI DU PRODUIT INTÉRIEUR BRUT AUX PRIX COURANTS D'ACQUISITION** *FRANC CFA (MILLIARDS)*
Government final consumption	524	669	810	892	898	710	576	600	...	Consommation finale des administrations publiques
Private final consumption	3 292	3 352	3 526	3 864	4 069	4 358	4 556	4 643	...	Consommation finale privée
Gross fixed capital formation	982	1 097	1 623	1 458	1 466	1 466	1 316	903	...	Formation brute de capital fixe
Change in inventories	36	217	511	466	143	465	156	307	...	Variation des stocks
Exports of goods and services	1 429	2 078	2 043	2 656	2 218	1 643	1 996	1 655	...	Exportations de biens et services
Less imports of goods and services	1 813	1 979	2 390	2 188	1 973	1 473	1 657	1 612	...	Moins importations de biens et services
GDP at purchasers' values	4 450	5 433	6 123	7 149	6 821	7 169	6 942	6 496	...	PIB aux prix d'acquisition
GROSS DOMESTIC PRODUCT BY KIND OF ECONOMIC ACTIVITY AT CONSTANT PRICES *ANNUAL GROWTH RATES (%)*										**PRODUIT INTÉRIEUR BRUT PAR BRANCHE D'ACTIVITÉ ECONOMIQUE AUX PRIX CONSTANTS** *TAUX DE CROISSANCE ANNUEL (%)*
Agriculture, hunting , forestry and Fishing	- 5.2	42.5	- 11.6	8.1	9.5	1.6	4.5	9.7	...	Agriculture, chasse sylviculture et Pêche
Mining and quarrying	- 14.0	0.9	28.4	- 5.1	- 31.9	30.0	39.5	- 14.1	...	Industries extractives
Manufacturing	11.5	10.5	16.8	87.0	- 39.2	- 26.1	- 7.2	19.0	...	Industries manufacturières
Electricity, gas & water	21.4	1 189.4	- 5.1	6.1	- 31.3	15.2	19.2	5.3	...	Electricité, gaz et eau
Construction	- 2.4	- 2.9	19.9	32.8	- 9.4	- 1.3	- 29.8	- 67.9	...	Bâtiments et travaux publics
Wholesale & retail trade, restaurants, hotels	0.9	5.5	16.9	- 5.9	2.5	5.8	7.8	0.3	...	Commerce de gros et de détail, restaurants et hôtels
Finance, insurance, real estate, etc.	3.4	0.3	6.9	1.1	14.7	5.3	- 8.8	- 2.4	...	Banques, assurances, affaires immobilières
Transport and communications	27.8	5.4	5.9	20.8	3.1	11.8	- 2.2	- 2.1	...	Transport(s) et communications
Public administration and defense	- 12.9	0.5	15.4	- 11.0	8.3	13.2	- 27.0	- 13.1	...	Administrations publiques et défense
Education	- 0.8	9.7	- 6.1	- 1.7	15.5	- 6.7	- 20.0	- 10.7	...	Education
Health And Social Work	3.4	5.7	5.5	- 17.8	14.3	- 30.2	- 34.4	- 12.0	...	Santé et Actions Sociales
Other services	- 14.4	- 16.4	1.9	4.0	16.7	6.3	-	- 4.2	...	Autres services
Less Imputed Service Charges	4.2	- 26.8	0.4	- 4.4	12.2	3.6	- 26.5	37.8	...	Moins Services d'intermédiation financière
Gross domestic product at factor cost / basic prices	- 2.3	14.0	7.1	8.7	- 5.6	3.7	3.7	- 2.6	...	Produit intérieur brut aux couts des facteurs / prix de base
Plus: Indirect Taxes / taxes on products, less subsidies	11.6	55.7	25.3	- 0.3	23.8	- 2.7	6.7	- 4.7	...	Plus taxes indirectes/impôts sur les produits, moins les subventions
Gross domestic product at market prices	- 2.0	15.0	7.6	8.4	- 4.6	3.4	3.8	- 2.7	...	Produit intérieur brut aux prix du marché
EXPENDITURE ON GROSS DOMESTIC PRODUCT AT CONSTANT PURCHASERS' VALUES *ANNUAL GROWTH RATES (%)*										**EMPLOIS DU PRODUIT INTÉRIEUR BRUT AUX PRIX CONSTANTS D'ACQUISITION** *TAUX DE CROISSANCE ANNUEL (%)*
Government final consumption	- 2.2	- 1.6	26.6	24.6	17.2	- 12.4	- 0.4	1.6	...	Consommation finale des administrations publiques
Private final consumption	- 4.4	2.5	- 6.9	3.0	5.1	- 12.4	10.6	1.6	...	Consommation finale privée
Gross fixed capital formation	- 4.5	6.0	37.6	- 8.2	1.2	- 9.3	0.4	- 33.4	...	Formation brute de capital fixe
Exports of goods and services	- 12.3	12.0	- 17.5	26.9	- 10.8	- 27.2	74.1	- 8.7	...	Exportations de biens et services
Less imports of goods and services	- 1.4	3.6	9.3	- 4.0	- 7.4	- 31.5	21.2	- 1.2	...	Moins importations de biens et services

III INFLATION

	2009	2010	2011	2012	2013	2014	2015	2016	2017	
Annual growth rates (%)										**Taux de croissance annuel (%)**
All item	10.1	- 2.1	2.0	7.5	0.2	1.7	3.7	- 3.1	- 0.8	Ensemble
of which:										dont:
Food and non-alcoholic beverages	8.9	- 3.8	1.9	11.8	- 1.8	2.5	2.6	- 3.3	- 3.9	Alimentation et boissons non alcoolisés
Alcoholic beverages, tobacco and narcotics	9.1	- 4.7	5.9	- 2.6	- 0.3	12.7	1.7	17.9	- 1.8	Boissons alcoolisées et tabacs
Clothing and footwear	0.8	- 1.5	0.3	1.8	1.0	1.9	5.5	- 4.1	3.1	Habillement et chaussures
Housing, water, electricity, gas and other fuels	37.5	- 1.1	1.3	2.8	2.4	- 13.8	20.6	- 8.7	0.3	Logement, eau, électricité, gaz et autres combustibles
Furnishings, household equipment and routine household maintenance	3.8	- 1.9	3.5	5.6	4.6	5.8	1.7	4.2	- 2.7	Meubles, articles de ménage et entretien courant
Health	0.3	- 1.0	2.8	2.1	3.7	0.2	5.4	- 0.6	0.7	Santé
Transport	- 0.6	4.7	0.6	5.3	7.6	- 4.8	7.6	0.8	2.0	Transport
Communication	- 5.1	- 3.4	- 5.5	- 3.2	-	-	0.1	- 1.0	7.3	Communication
Recreation and culture	- 1.5	- 1.0	1.8	1.4	2.8	2.4	5.9	1.6	1.2	Loisirs et culture
Education	- 5.9	4.1	2.1	6.3	6.8	7.6	0.1	6.8	0.4	Enseignement
Restaurants and hotels	8.1	- 0.9	4.1	5.1	- 4.7	2.6	- 0.4	- 5.9	0.3	Restaurants et hôtels
Miscellaneous goods and services	- 1.6	12.1	18.4	24.2	4.9	1.4	7.4	3.8	- 4.1	Biens et Services divers

IV AGRICULTURAL PRODUCTION - PRODUCTION AGRICOLE

TONNES (THOUSAND)	2009	2010	2011	2012	2013	2014	2015	2016	2017	Tonnes (milliers)
Sorghum	685	570	870	512	1 171	1 241	1 316	...	...	Sorgho
Millet	523	298	300	577	341	361	383	...	...	Millet
Groundnuts, with shell	403	517	993	570	1 298	1 376	1 458	...	...	Arachides (en coques)
Cereals, nes	448	303	594	329	847	898	952	...	...	Céréales, nda
Yams	330	415	400	420	430	456	483	...	...	Ignames

V MINING PRODUCTION - PRODUCTION MINIERE

	2009	2010	2011	2012	2013	2014	2015	2016	2017	
Crude petroleum - Production, metric tons (thousands)	43 625	44 704	41 880	37 173	34 310	39 156	56 631	...	...	Pétrole brut - Production, tonnes métriques (milliers)
	...	...	...	...	...	...	...	...	...	
	...	...	...	...	...	...	...	...	...	

VI ENERGY - ENERGIE

	2009	2010	2011	2012	2013	2014	2015	2016	2017	
Total electricity generation (GWh) of which	97	100	203	235	269	286	290	294	...	Production électrique totale (GWh) dont
Production of electricity from fossil fuels (GWh)	97	100	203	235	269	286	290	294	...	Production d'électricité à partir de combustibles fossiles (GWh)
Production of hydro electricity (GWh)	...	...	...	...	...	...	...	...	...	Production d'électricité d'origine hydraulique (GWh)
Production of electricity from solar, wind, tide, wave and other sources (GWh)	...	...	...	...	...	...	...	...	...	Production d'électricité d'origine solaire, éolienne, marée motrice et autres (GWh)

VII TOURISM AND INFRASTRUCTURE - TOURISME ET INFRASTUCTURE

	2009	2010	2011	2012	2013	2014	2015	2016	2017	
VII-1 Tourism										**VII-1 Tourisme**
International tourist arrivals (thousands)	70	71	77	86	100	122	120	130	142	Arrivées de touristes internationaux (milliers)
Rooms in hotels and similar establishments (thousands)	...	...	2	1	1	2	2	...	...	Chambres d'hôtels et établissements assimilés (milliers)
Overnight stays (thousands)	63	37	59	70	86	84	89	90	99	Nuitées (milliers)
Tourism receipts (US$ thousand)	72 340	76 800	90 793	79 330	82 634	81 767	61 083	63 974	69 934	Recettes touristiques (milliers de $ EU)
Total contribution to GDP (%)	3.6	3.7	4.0	4.1	4.1	4.1	4.3	4.2	4.2	Contribution totale au PIB (%)
Total contribution to Employment (%)	3.1	3.4	3.6	3.4	3.4	3.5	3.6	3.5	3.5	Contribution totale à l'emploi (%)
VII-2 Infrastructure										**VII-2 Infrastructure**
Paved road (% of total)	...	...	1.0	...	...	...	...	...	...	Routes asphaltées (% du total)
Total network (Railways-km)	...	...	...	...	...	...	...	...	...	Réseau total voies ferrées-Km
Main telephone lines (per 100 inhabitants)	0.5	...	...	...	...	...	...	...	...	Lignes téléphoniques fixes (pour 100 habitants)
Mobile cellular subscribers (per 100 inhabitants)	20.1	24.5	30.3	35.4	35.6	39.8	40.2	44.5	...	Abonnés aux téléphones mobiles (pour 100 habitants)
Internet users per 100 inhabitants	1.5	1.7	1.9	2.1	2.5	2.9	3.5	5.0	...	Utilisateurs Internet par 100 Habitants
Fixed (wired)-broadband subscriptions per 100 inhabitants	...	...	...	...	...	...	...	...	...	Abonnements à l'Internet fixe (filaire) à large bande pour 100 habitants, par débit

VIII EXTERNAL TRADE - COMMERCE EXTERIEUR

	2009	2010	2011	2012	2013	2014	2015	2016	2017	
US$ (MILLIONS) EXPORTS, FOB										**$ E.U (MILLIONS) EXPORTATIONS, FÀB**
Exports - Total	2 800	3 600	4 800	4 800	3 800	3 800	2 600	1 600	...	Exportations - Total
Exports to Africa	13	51	24	15	28	9	6	4	...	Exportations vers l'Afrique
Main products										**Principaux produits**
Cotton	53	75	120	172	100	90	84	108	...	Coton
Crude vegetable materials, n.e.s.	32	26	32	50	39	35	33	21	...	Matières végétales brutes, n.e.s.
Gold, non-monetary (excluding gold ores and concentrates)	1	12	45	58	94	241	100	197	...	Or, non monétaire (à l'exclusion des minerais d'or et des concentrés)
Petroleum oils or bituminous minerals > 70 % oil	163	319	129	579	49	90	47	18	...	Huiles de pétrole ou de minéraux bitumineux> 70% d'huile
Petroleum oils, oils from bitumin. materials, crude	2 463	3 089	4 312	3 861	3 452	3 289	2 248	1 190	...	Huiles de pétrole, huiles de bitume. matériaux bruts
Main destinations										**Principales destinations**
China	89	597	328	325	134	138	104	100	...	Chine
India	9	2	2	59	162	18	382	123	...	Inde
Japan	1	-	-	51	206	338	256	58	...	Japon
United Arab Emirates	1	5	126	74	100	242	101	199	...	Emirates Arabes
United States	2 449	2 536	3 786	3 733	2 851	2 687	1 395	821	...	États-Unis
IMPORTS, CIF										
Imports - Total	2 000	2 400	3 300	2 800	3 000	3 100	2 600	2 200	...	Importations - Total (millions)
Imports from Africa	410	547	718	562	580	544	519	438	...	Importations en provenance de l'Afrique
Main products										**Principaux produits**
Aircraft & associated equipment; spacecraft, etc.	96	125	199	166	172	273	157	131	...	Aéronefs et équipement connexe; vaisseau spatial, etc.
Civil engineering & contractors' plant & equipment	181	202	274	247	307	316	227	180	...	Génie civil et installations et équipements des entrepreneurs
Iron & steel bars, rods, angles, shapes & sections	75	67	122	123	114	88	69	176	...	Barres, tiges, cornières et profilés en fer et en acier
Petroleum oils or bituminous minerals > 70 % oil	91	205	231	177	180	187	154	113	...	Huiles de pétrole ou de minéraux bitumineux> 70% d'huile
Tobacco, manufactured	71	84	118	94	96	89	88	74	...	Tabac fabriqué
Main origin										**Principales provenances**
Cameroon	173	300	401	276	284	295	285	246	...	Cameroun
China	138	265	124	187	344	283	138	105	...	Chine
France	447	517	784	687	657	654	615	509	...	France
Portugal	112	132	219	183	180	179	167	138	...	Portugal
United States	247	299	419	354	346	365	340	269	...	États-Unis

TCHAD

CHAD

	2009	2010	2011	2012	2013	2014	2015	2016	2017	
IX-1 MONETARY STATISTICS *CFA FRANC (MILLIONS)*										**IX-1 STATISTIQUES MONÉTAIRES** *FRANC CFA (MILLIONS)*
Money supply (M1)	482 881	605 276	691 330	784 283	852 112	1 077 709	1 027 048	948 039	1 002 683	Masse monétaire (M1)
Quasi-money	33 002	36 563	58 899	57 548	67 509	78 006	90 811	110 233	97 213	Quasi-monnaie
of which demand deposit	...	...	...	...	...	...	...	...	...	dont Monnaie scripturale
Net foreign assets	238 851	303 111	456 016	558 057	537 690	522 690	88 591	- 303 711	- 299 355	Avoirs extérieurs nets
Domestic credit	313 930	403 596	349 593	347 576	465 364	760 434	1 143 604	1 485 648	1 466 133	Crédit intérieur
of which claims on private sector	104 834	149 447	39 613	- 40 879	35 702	165 614	520 213	796 550	757 234	dont créances sur le secteur privé
of which claims on government sector, net	171 761	223 636	278 119	367 320	389 561	537 007	540 742	583 301	566 833	dont créances nettes sur le gouvernement
International reserves (millions US$)	617	632	951	1 156	1 183	1 076	369	8	- 46	Réserves internationales (millions $EU)
Average exchange rate (National currency per US$)	472	495	472	511	494	494	591	593	582	Taux de change (moyen) (monnaie nationale par $ EU)
IX-2 PUBLIC FINANCE *CFA FRANC (MILLIONS)*										**IX-2 FINANCES PUBLIQUES** *FRANC CFA (MILLIONS)*
Total Revenues and Grants	655 001	1 068 841	1 421 762	1 542 084	1 331 033	1 230 115	783 106	749 605	...	Recettes totales et dons
Direct taxes (on income, profits)	295 905	603 580	849 648	774 512	765 285	518 450	228 286	105 510	...	Taxes directes
Domestic indirect taxes revenues	40 321	58 495	54 783	69 648	76 887	86 867	58 495	76 914	...	Taxes Indirectes
Trade taxes	75 557	88 887	118 736	126 410	101 064	119 191	109 929	111 175	...	Taxes sur le commerce extérieur
Other taxes	21 229	30 523	31 528	40 493	44 967	51 249	52 985	50 942	...	Autres taxes
Other revenues	106 555	218 557	275 861	363 605	198 035	318 467	111 527	231 571	...	Autres recettes
Grants	115 434	68 799	91 206	167 416	144 795	135 891	221 884	173 493	...	Dons
Total Expenditures and Net Lending	1 057 776	1 288 501	1 284 476	1 512 111	1 463 564	1 519 220	1 101 711	869 684	...	Dépenses totales et prêts nets
Current expenditure	613 186	736 875	701 359	697 596	788 957	814 536	701 729	569 000	...	Dépenses courantes
Wages and Salaries	200 618	215 728	250 251	283 007	333 153	340 694	368 729	365 000	...	Rémunérations et salaires
Other purchases of goods and services	110 365	110 511	86 672	123 239	135 518	146 716	93 000	96 000	...	Achat de biens et services
Other current expenditure	...	...	...	...	...	...	...	...	...	Autres dépenses courantes
Current transfers	302 203	410 637	364 436	291 350	320 286	327 126	240 000	108 000	...	Transferts courants
Interest payments	20 789	29 285	35 000	27 930	33 987	40 481	23 190	120 684	...	Intérêts
Capital expenditure	423 801	522 340	548 117	786 585	640 620	664 203	376 792	180 000	...	Dépenses d'équipement
Net lending	...	...	...	...	...	...	...	...	...	Prêts nets
Fiscal balance	- 402 775	- 219 660	137 286	29 973	- 132 531	- 289 105	- 318 605	- 120 079	...	Solde global y compris les dons
IX-3 BALANCE OF PAYMENTS *CFA FRANC (MILLIONS)*										**IX-3 BALANCE DES PAIEMENTS** *FRANC CFA (MILLIONS)*
Trade balance	365 600	604 800	672 800	475 300	- 58 700	395 600	351 900	...	...	Balance commerciale
Services Balance	- 684 000	- 934 900	- 875 200	- 902 500	-1 026 700	-1 376 200	-1 441 500	...	...	Balance des services
Net primary income	- 182 100	- 176 100	- 176 800	- 167 300	- 153 400	- 171 100	- 190 100	...	...	Revenus primaires nets
Compensation of employees	10 400	9 900	- 1 100	- 1 200	- 1 400			...	...	Rémunération des salariés
Investment income	- 192 500	- 185 900	- 175 700	- 166 100	- 152 000	...	...	...	...	Revenus des investissements
Net secondary income	342 800	315 200	134 800	123 000	79 200	322 800	316 600	...	...	Revenus secondaires nets
Net official transfers	34 600	22 400	48 500	57 700	20 400	...	...	...	...	Transferts officiels nets
Workers' remittances	...	...	...	...	...	...	...	...	...	Envois de fonds des travailleurs
Other private transfers	...	...	...	...	...	...	...	...	...	Autres transferts privés
Current account balance	- 157 700	- 191 000	- 244 400	- 471 500	-1 159 600	- 828 900	- 963 100	...	...	Solde du compte courant
Capital and financial account	- 97 500	- 30 400	557 500	704 400	1 315 000	738 000	389 200	...	...	Comptes de capital et financier
Capital account	49 400	59 400	84 300	136 100	71 700	99 600	105 500	...	...	Compte de capital
Financial account	- 147 000	- 89 800	472 700	568 300	1 243 200	638 500	283 700	...	...	Compte financier
Errors and omissions	- 95 300	226 700	- 144 300	- 124 200	- 202 700	69 500	- 100	...	...	Erreurs et omissions
Overall balance	- 350 500	5 300	168 800	108 700	- 47 300	- 21 400	- 574 000	...	...	Balance générale

X DEBT AND FINANCIAL FLOWS - DETTE ET FLUX FINANCIERS

	2009	2010	2011	2012	2013	2014	2015	2016	2017	
X-1 DEBT *US $ (MILLIONS)*										**X-1 DETTE EXTÉRIEURE** *$ E.U (MILLIONS)*
Total external debt	2 549	2 626	2 513	2 538	2 833	3 785	2 680	2 609	2 781	Dette extérieure totale
Private	...	...	...	...	...	...	...	...	...	Privée
Public	2 549	2 626	2 513	2 538	2 833	3 785	2 680	2 609	...	Publique
Total external debt service	302	302	302	302	302	302	302	302	...	Service de la dette extérieure
Present value of external debt	...	...	...	...	...	...	...	2 783	...	Valeur actuelle de la dette extérieure
Total government domestic debt, National currency (millions)	...	...	...	...	...	...	...	...	...	Dette publique intérieure
X-2 FINANCIAL FLOWS *US $ (MILLIONS)*										**X-2 FLUX FINANCIERS** *$ E.U (MILLIONS)*
Net Foreign Direct Investment Inflows	375	313	282	580	520	- 676	560	560	...	Investissements étranger direct (flux nets entrants)
Main origin of FDI inflows										**Principales origines de l'IDE entrant:**
France	10	4	- 4	- 4	...	...	...	...	...	France
...	...	...	...	...	...	...	...	...	...	...
...	...	...	...	...	...	...	...	...	...	...
Italy	- 4	...	...	...	...	...	...	...	...	Italie
...	...	...	...	...	...	...	...	...	...	...
African countries	...	...	...	...	...	...	...	...	...	Pays africains
Net total official development assistance	558	490	457	475	459	392	607	624	...	Aide publique au développement (nette totale)
Main origin of net ODA										**Principales origines de l'APD nette**
United States	170	139	111	112	111	50	79	75	...	États-Unis
France	41	41	36	36	37	28	78	32	...	France
International Development Association [IDA]	4	- 4	4	- 2	- 5	1	72	87	...	International Development Association
Germany	28	20	15	15	11	14	15	19	...	Allemagne
...	...	...	...	...	...	...	...	...	...	...

TCHAD

SOURCES AND NOTES - SOURCES ET NOTES

External trade - Total exports, fob: UNCTAD	Commerce exterieur - Exportation, fab: CNUCED
External trade - Total import, cif: UNCTAD	Commerce exterieur - Imporations, caf: CNUCED
ODA: OECD	APD: OCDE
Monetary statistics: IMF	Statistiques monétaires: FMI
National Accounts: The serie is revised from 2008	Comptes nationaux:La série a été révisée à partir de 2008
Poverty: World Bank	Pauvreté: Banque mondiale

		AREA (km2)	1 861		SUPERFICIE (KM2)
		CAPITAL CITY	Moroni	Moroni	CAPITALE
		CURRENCY	Comoros Franc	Franc Comorien	MONNAIE

I SOCIAL AND DEMOGRAPHIC INDICATORS — INDICATEURS DEMOGRAPHIQUES ET SOCIAUX

Population	Year Année	Value Valeur	Charts Graphiques	Population
Population ('000)	2017	800.0		Population ('000)
Female (%)	2017	49.9		Féminine (%)
Urban (%)	2017	39.0		Urbaine (%)
Average annual growth rate	2017	2.7		Taux de croissance annuel
Active population ('000)	2017	267.0		Population active ('000)
Population by age group ('000)				Population par groupe d'âge ('000)
0-14 years	2017	323.0		0-14 ans
15-64 years	2017	471.0		15-64 ans
65+ years	2017	33.0		65+ ans
Economically active population in agriculture (%)	2012	94.6		Participation de la population active agricole (%)
Crude birth rate	2017	33.5		Taux brut de natalité
Crude death rate	2017	6.1		Taux brut de mortalité
Total fertility rate	2017	4.4		Indice synthétique de fécondité
Life expectancy at birth - Total (years)	2012	61.5		Espérance de vie à la naissance - Totale (années)
Dependency ratio - Total (%)	2017	75.6		Taux de dépendance - Total (%)
Health				**Santé**
Percentage of children under-five and underweight	...	...		% d'enfants de moins de cinq ans avec insuffisance pondérale
Prevalence of undernourishment	2012	23.0		Prévalence de la malnutrition
Under five mortality rate (per 1 000 live births)	2012	87.3		Taux de mortalité de moins de 5 ans (les deux sexes, pour 1000)
Infant mortality rate (per 1 000 live births)	2012	64.0		Taux de mortalité infantile (les deux sexes) par 1000
Neonatal mortality rate (per 1 000 live births)	2006	40.2		Le taux de mortalité néonatale (pour 1000 naissances vivantes)
Percentage of children provided the vaccines :				Pourcentage d'enfants vaccinés :
BCG	2011	76.0		BCG
DPT3	2011	83.0		DTC3
Polio	2011	85.0		polio
Measles	2011	72.0		rougeole
Percentage of mothers provided at least one antenatal care (%)	...	...		Pourcentage de mères ayant au moins reçu un soin prénatal (%)
Percentage of deliveries attended by skilled health personnel	...	...		% d'accouchements assistés par un personnel de santé qualifié
Number of doctors (per 10,000 population)	2006	2.0		Nombre de médecins (pour 10.000 habitants)
Number of nurses (per 10,000 population)	2006	7.0		Nombre d'infirmiers (pour 10.000 habitants)
Hospital beds - Total (per 10,000 population)	2006	22.0		Nombre de lits d'hôpitaux - Total (pour 10 000)
Births registered (per 1,000)	2012	36.1		Naissances enregistrées (pour 1000)
Deaths registered (per 1,000)	2012	8.4		Décès enregistrés (pour 1000)
Budget allocation to health (%)	2009	8.0		Dépenses publiques consacrées à la santé (% du budget)
Education				**Education**
Enrolment in primary education (000)	2012	119.4		Scolarisation dans le primaire (000)
Female	2008	52.3		Féminine
Enrolment in secondary education (000)	2011	34.1		Scolarisation dans le secondaire (000)
Female	2005	18.4		Féminine
Enrolment in tertiary education (000)	2011	23.9		Scolarisation dans le tertiaire (000)
Female	2010	2.1		Féminine
Literacy rate	2010	74.9		Taux d'alphabétisation (deux sexes)
Male	2010	80.2		Masculin
Female	2010	69.7		Féminin
Pupil teacher ratio - primary	2011	27.7		Ratio élève-enseignant
Budget allocation to education (%)	2002	24.1		Dépenses publiques consacrées à l'enseignement (% du budget)
Poverty				**Pauvreté**
GNI per capita, PPP (current int. $)	2016	1540.0		RNB par habitant, ($ PPA inter. courants)
Human Poverty Index (HPI-1) Value (%)	2007	20.4		Valeur de l'Indice de pauvreté (IPH-1) (%)
Population below Inter. poverty line ($2/ day) (%)	2004	13.5		Population sous le seuil inter. de pauvreté (2$/Jour) (%)
Share of income held by richest 10%	2004	48.1		% de revenu des 10% plus riches
Share of income held by poorest 10%	2004	1.5		% de revenu des 10% plus pauvres
GINI index	2004	55.9		Indice de GINI

Population by age group - 2017

Population par groupe d'age - 2017

- 0-14 years: 39.1%
- 15-64 years: 57.0%
- 65+ years: 4.0%

Percentage of children provided vaccines : - 2011

Pourcentage d'enfants vaccinés : - 2011

BCG / BCG	DPT3 / DTC3	Polio / polio	Measles / rougeole
76.0	83.0	85.0	72.0

Literacy rate (%) - 2010

Taux d'alphabétisation - 2010

Male 80.2, Female 69.7

GNI per capita, PPP (current international $)

RNB par habitant, ($ PPA internationaux courants)

2012	2013	2014	2015	2016
1 440	1 490	1 510	1 510	1 540

	2009	2010	2011	2012	2013	2014	2015	2016	2017	
GROSS DOMESTIC PRODUCT BY KIND OF ECONOMIC ACTIVITY AT CURRENT PRICES COMOROS FRANC (MILLIONS)									**PRODUIT INTÉRIEUR BRUT PAR BRANCHE D'ACTIVITÉ ÉCONOMIQUE AUX PRIX COURANTS** FRANC COMORIEN (MILLIONS)		
Agriculture, hunting , forestry and Fishing	139 260	160 452	164 040	186 093	206 313	213 639	205 879	211 105	219 814	Agriculture, chasse sylviculture et Pêche
Mining and quarrying	6 216	6 305	7 596	7 404	8 386	8 591	8 826	9 228	9 694	Industries extractives
Manufacturing	24 843	20 002	22 266	23 647	24 860	36 410	43 395	45 646	49 247	Industries manufacturières
Electricity, gas & water	2 986	1 936	1 794	2 561	2 938	2 277	2 577	2 653	2 977	Electricité, gaz et eau
Construction	7 829	3 970	1 783	3 760	3 828	1 182	1 721	1 694	1 769	Bâtiments et travaux publics
Wholesale & retail trade, restaurants, hotels	64 089	54 419	50 453	47 650	48 660	45 951	43 937	45 131	46 034	Commerce de gros et de détail, restaurants et hôtels
Finance, insurance, real estate, etc.	68 510	80 732	82 996	89 838	92 234	93 632	97 893	103 351	107 944	Banques, assurances, affaires immobilières
Transport and communications	16 469	24 078	30 687	35 666	39 286	43 525	44 411	44 563	45 726	Transport(s) et communications
Public administration and defense	36 048	35 523	35 485	35 902	35 796	35 145	36 682	38 919	33 692	Administrations publiques et défense
Education	...	...	...	...	...	...	...	...	...	Education
Health And Social Work	...	...	...	...	...	...	...	...	...	Santé et Actions Sociales
Other services	...	...	...	...	...	...	...	...	...	Autres services
Less Imputed Service Charges	- 2 481	- 2 748	- 2 857	- 3 937	- 4 068	- 2 257	- 2 299	- 2 408	- 2 483	Moins Services d'intermédiation financière
Gross domestic product at factor cost / basic prices	363 769	384 669	394 243	428 584	458 233	478 095	483 022	499 882	514 415	Produit intérieur brut aux couts des facteurs / prix de base
Plus: Indirect Taxes / taxes on products, less subsidies	14 718	12 072	12 684	11 873	8 599	8 622	6 901	11 500	22 080	Plus taxes indirectes/impôts sur les produits, moins les subventions
EXPENDITURE ON GROSS DOMESTIC PRODUCT AT CURRENT PURCHASER'S VALUES COMOROS FRANC (MILLIONS)								**EMPLOI DU PRODUIT INTÉRIEUR BRUT AUX PRIX COURANTS D'ACQUISITION** FRANC COMORIEN (MILLIONS)		
Government final consumption	36 649	37 532	38 546	39 068	38 564	42 243	44 528	54 088	42 010	Consommation finale des administrations publiques
Private final consumption	345 685	373 417	386 608	445 169	452 901	480 035	457 340	469 865	458 825	Consommation finale privée
Gross fixed capital formation	53 150	55 163	55 046	47 015	60 775	58 516	59 738	68 164	118 565	Formation brute de capital fixe
Change in inventories	6 766	- 1 144	- 2 552	- 2 118	5	3 392	2 329	1 907	1 965	Variation des stocks
Exports of goods and services	27 518	35 682	34 965	34 799	39 436	42 478	44 642	47 367	50 230	Exportations de biens et services
Less imports of goods and services	91 281	103 909	105 686	123 476	124 849	139 947	118 654	130 009	135 101	Moins importations de biens et services
GDP at purchasers' values	378 487	396 741	406 927	440 457	466 832	486 717	489 923	511 382	536 495	PIB aux prix d'acquisition
GROSS DOMESTIC PRODUCT BY KIND OF ECONOMIC ACTIVITY AT CONSTANT PRICES ANNUAL GROWTH RATES (%)								**PRODUIT INTÉRIEUR BRUT PAR BRANCHE D'ACTIVITÉ ECONOMIQUE AUX PRIX CONSTANTS** TAUX DE CROISSANCE ANNUEL (%)		
Agriculture, hunting , forestry and Fishing	3.1	7.8	1.3	1.4	5.7	2.8	- 1.9	- 0.1	1.2	Agriculture, chasse sylviculture et Pêche
Mining and quarrying	7.0	19.1	6.7	-4.5	-15.8	1.8	-1.5	2.0	3.0	Industries extractives
Manufacturing	4.9	-9.8	0.7	4.6	10.2	33.7	8.9	3.2	4.7	Industries manufacturières
Electricity, gas & water	-	-32.9	-13.5	65.0	8.1	-25.2	-40.4	4.0	10.0	Electricité, gaz et eau
Construction	-11.4	-48.9	-20.0	14.6	-2.5	23.5	19.8	1.5	6.0	Bâtiments et travaux publics
Wholesale & retail trade, restaurants, hotels	-5.5	-10.8	-9.0	-12.2	1.9	-9.6	-5.2	1.5	-	Commerce de gros et de détail, restaurants et hôtels
Finance, insurance, real estate, etc.	7.2	7.9	2.8	8.1	2.6	1.2	5.1	3.1	2.4	Banques, assurances, affaires immobilières
Transport and communications	3.4	27.8	28.6	12.7	10.1	11.3	-2.0	2.3	4.3	Transport(s) et communications
Public administration and defense	5.3	-2.5	-0.6	2.4	-1.6	-2.4	2.4	3.0	-17.6	Administrations publiques et défense
Education	...	...	...	...	...	...	...	...	...	Education
Health And Social Work	...	...	...	...	...	...	...	...	...	Santé et Actions Sociales
Other services	...	...	...	...	...	...	...	...	...	Autres services
Less Imputed Service Charges	2.2	8.9	4.7	35.9	1.1	-44.8	7.0	3.0	1.1	Moins Services d'intermédiation financière
Gross domestic product at factor cost / basic prices	2.3	1.8	1.4	2.2	4.2	3.6	0.1	1.5	0.6	Produit intérieur brut aux couts des facteurs / prix de base
Plus: Indirect Taxes / taxes on products, less subsidies	72.4	-6.9	8.0	-0.1	-25.4	-7.5	-16.2	52.0	84.6	Plus taxes indirectes/impôts sur les produits, moins les subventions
Gross domestic product at market prices	4.0	1.5	1.6	2.1	3.4	3.4	-0.2	2.2	2.5	Produit intérieur brut aux prix du marché
EXPENDITURE ON GROSS DOMESTIC PRODUCT AT CONSTANT PURCHASERS' VALUES ANNUAL GROWTH RATES (%)								**EMPLOIS DU PRODUIT INTÉRIEUR BRUT AUX PRIX CONSTANTS D'ACQUISITION** TAUX DE CROISSANCE ANNUEL (%)		
Government final consumption	0.1	0.6	-2.4	1.3	-1.6	9.5	4.8	19.1	-23.5	Consommation finale des administrations publiques
Private final consumption	3.0	6.3	1.3	3.1	-0.2	4.7	-3.6	-4.5	-9.0	Consommation finale privée
Gross fixed capital formation	-16.3	4.5	14.0	-13.2	30.6	-9.6	3.5	13.4	66.1	Formation brute de capital fixe
Exports of goods and services	13.9	24.9	-5.3	0.8	10.8	1.6	1.4	5.1	6.0	Exportations de biens et services
Less imports of goods and services	-9.5	18.9	2.7	-2.1	3.5	5.4	-9.2	-10.9	-15.0	Moins importations de biens et services

III INFLATION

Annual growth rates (%)	2009	2010	2011	2012	2013	2014	2015	2016	2017	Taux de croissance annuel (%)
All item	- 2.9	3.8	1.8	6.3	2.8	- 1.2	3.6	- 2.1	0.3	Ensemble
of which:										dont:
Food and non-alcoholic beverages	- 7.7	3.1	2.0	7.9	4.2	0.2	6.2	- 1.3	-	Alimentation et boissons non alcoolisés
Alcoholic beverages, tobacco and narcotics	...	...	...	...	0.6	- 4.5	1.4	7.4	- 3.3	Boissons alcoolisées et tabacs
Clothing and footwear	- 17.5	21.6	0.6	2.2	2.7	- 3.1	- 1.7	3.6	4.4	Habillement et chaussures
Housing, water, electricity, gas and other fuels	16.3	2.3	2.1	3.7	0.8	- 2.9	1.2	- 5.0	- 0.1	Logement, eau, électricité, gaz et autres combustibles
Furnishings, household equipment and routine household maintenance	- 5.1	10.4	1.6	2.5	3.2	- 2.1	3.0	4.5	- 1.2	Meubles, articles de ménage et entretien courant
Health	20.8	0.7	- 0.5	4.1	2.8	- 6.4	0.7	9.6	- 3.9	Santé
Transport	7.5	14.8	- 11.6	6.1	- 1.1	- 3.6	- 0.3	- 15.0	2.2	Transport
Communication	...	...	...	...	0.2	- 1.3	- 2.4	- 3.0	- 5.5	Communication
Recreation and culture	- 15.1	- 3.2	- 0.1	0.3	1.6	- 5.5	2.1	- 8.7	1.1	Loisirs et culture
Education	- 4.4	0.1	1.8	0.4	- 0.8	1.9	1.6	0.1	1.3	Enseignement
Restaurants and hotels	40.2	13.7	- 5.7	9.9	0.2	2.6	- 0.8	- 1.9	1.5	Restaurants et hôtels
Miscellaneous goods and services	- 18.1	20.5	17.2	7.2	- 0.1	- 4.4	- 2.2	4.5	5.7	Biens et Services divers

COMORES

COMOROS

IV AGRICULTURAL PRODUCTION - PRODUCTION AGRICOLE

TONNES (THOUSAND)	2009	2010	2011	2012	2013	2014	2015	2016	2017	Tonnes (milliers)
Coconuts	73	83	85	90	92	74	72	59	...	Noix de coco
Cassava	65	62	68	69	70	48	48	49	...	Manioc
Bananas	72	74	64	66	65	54	54	54	...	Bananes
Rice, paddy	22	24	27	27	29	31	51	50	...	Riz, Paddy
Taro (cocoyam)	10	13	12	12	13	22	22	23	...	Taros (colocases)

V MINING PRODUCTION - PRODUCTION MINIERE

	2009	2010	2011	2012	2013	2014	2015	2016	2017	
	...	...	...	...	...	...	...	...	...	
	...	...	...	...	...	...	...	...	...	
	...	...	...	...	...	...	...	...	...	

VI ENERGY - ENERGIE

	2009	2010	2011	2012	2013	2014	2015	2016	2017	
Total electricity generation (GWh) of which	37	37	60	62	66	65	68	70	...	Production électrique totale (GWh) dont
Production of electricity from fossil fuels (GWh)	32	32	55	57	60	60	66	65	...	Production d'électricité à partir de combustibles fossiles (GWh)
Production of hydro electricity (GWh)	5	5	5	5	6	5	2	5	...	Production d'électricité d'origine hydraulique (GWh)
Production of electricity from solar, wind, tide, wave and other sources (GWh)	...	...	...	...	...	...	...	...	...	Production d'électricité d'origine solaire, éolienne, marée motrice et autres (GWh)

VII TOURISM AND INFRASTRUCTURE - TOURISME ET INFRASTUCTURE

VII-1 Tourism	2009	2010	2011	2012	2013	2014	2015	2016	2017	VII-1 Tourisme
International tourist arrivals (thousands)	11	15	19	21	22	22	24	26	27	Arrivées de touristes internationaux (milliers)
Rooms in hotels and similar establishments (thousands)	...	5	5	5	5	5	5	5	5	Chambres d'hôtels et établissements assimilés (milliers)
Overnight stays (thousands)	79	107	131	146	150	159	168	187	201	Nuitées (milliers)
Tourism receipts (US$ thousand)	13 700	13 700	15 410	16 257	16 598	18 021	19 566	21 110	22 655	Recettes touristiques (milliers de $ EU)
Total contribution to GDP (%)	11.0	12.0	12.4	12.0	10.6	9.8	9.1	8.8	13.4	Contribution totale au PIB (%)
Total contribution to Employment (%)	9.2	9.9	10.2	9.7	8.4	8.5	7.9	7.7	12.3	Contribution totale à l'emploi (%)
VII-2 Infrastructure										**VII-2 Infrastructure**
Paved road (% of total)	77.0	...	...	...	...	...	...	...	...	Routes asphaltées (% du total)
Total network (Railways-km)	...	...	...	...	...	...	...	...	...	Réseau total voies ferrées-Km
Main telephone lines (per 100 inhabitants)	4.6	3.1	3.3	3.3	3.1	3.1	3.1	1.7	...	Lignes téléphoniques fixes (pour 100 habitants)
Mobile cellular subscribers (per 100 inhabitants)	18.4	24.2	30.9	39.5	47.3	50.9	55.2	57.7	...	Abonnés aux téléphones mobiles (pour 100 habitants)
Internet users per 100 inhabitants	3.5	5.1	5.5	6.0	6.5	7.0	7.5	7.9	...	Utilisateurs Internet par 100 Habitants
Fixed (wired)-broadband subscriptions per 100 inhabitants	...	...	...	...	...	...	...	...	...	Abonnements à l'Internet fixe (filaire) à large bande pour 100 habitants, par débit

VIII EXTERNAL TRADE - COMMERCE EXTERIEUR

US$ (MILLIONS) EXPORTS, FOB	2009	2010	2011	2012	2013	2014	2015	2016	2017	$ E.U (MILLIONS) EXPORTATIONS, FÀB
Exports - Total	15	21	26	20	21	23	17	31	...	Exportations - Total
Exports to Africa	...	2	2	1	2	2	1	2	...	Exportations vers l'Afrique
Main products										**Principaux produits**
Essential oils, perfume & flavour materials	2	3	2	1	2	4	2	5	...	Huiles essentielles, parfums et arômes
Ferrous waste, scrape; remelting ingots, iron, steel	1	...	...	...	...	...	...	...	...	Déchets ferreux, débris; lingots de refusion, fer, acier
...	...	...	...	...	...	...	...	...	...	...
Ships, boats & floating structures	5	5	4	3	2	...	1	1	...	Navires, bateaux et structures flottantes
Spices	6	10	17	12	13	16	11	21	...	Épices
Main destinations										**Principales destinations**
France	3	3	3	1	3	6	3	7	...	France
Germany	0	1	1	-	1	4	2	5	...	Allemagne
India	-	3	1	1	2	2	2	3	...	Inde
Netherlands	0	1	2	6	2	1	1	2	...	Pays-Bas
Singapore	2	3	9	2	3	2	2	3	...	Singapour
IMPORTS, CIF										
Imports - Total	210	233	277	273	284	278	214	219	...	Importations - Total (millions)
Imports from Africa	21	50	31	40	45	37	31	30	...	Importations en provenance de l'Afrique
Main products										**Principaux produits**
Lime, cement, fabrica. constr. mat. (excludingglass, clay)	15	14	17	18	15	15	12	12	...	Chaux, ciment, tissu. constr. tapis. (sauf verre, argile)
Motor vehicles for the transport of persons	8	11	12	9	14	11	9	9	...	Véhicules à moteur pour le transport de personnes
Other meat and edible meat offal	10	14	14	19	14	17	11	12	...	Autres viandes et abats comestibles
Petroleum oils or bituminous minerals > 70 % oil	9	7	11	6	6	8	5	6	...	Huiles de pétrole ou de minéraux bitumineux> 70% d'huile
Rice	23	20	37	36	24	26	19	20	...	Riz
Main origin										**Principales provenances**
China	11	14	10	18	35	36	27	28	...	Chine
France	33	35	45	41	53	46	37	37	...	France
India	12	7	9	20	19	17	14	14	...	Inde
Pakistan	25	22	29	37	30	31	23	24	...	Pakistan
United Arab Emirates	54	53	73	52	45	52	37	40	...	Emirates Arabes

	2009	2010	2011	2012	2013	2014	2015	2016	2017	
IX-1 MONETARY STATISTICS *COMOROS FRANC (MILLIONS)*										**IX-1 STATISTIQUES MONÉTAIRES** *FRANC COMORIEN (MILLIONS)*
Money supply (M1)	57 571	68 747	75 327	87 373	89 862	97 139	113 759	125 431	132 325	Masse monétaire (M1)
Quasi-money	21 817	26 097	26 506	30 871	32 985	34 886	37 380	41 180	41 776	Quasi-monnaie
of which demand deposit	...	...	...	...	...	...	...	...	...	dont Monnaie scripturale
Net foreign assets	44 114	45 974	53 860	62 709	56 567	57 566	79 363	69 000	76 198	Avoirs extérieurs nets
Domestic credit	37 172	43 704	45 845	49 366	59 694	67 525	64 417	85 809	85 522	Crédit intérieur
of which claims on private sector	7 266	5 743	6 016	1 604	5 511	8 457	- 4 264	10 241	5 946	dont créances sur le secteur privé
of which claims on government sector, net	28 048	35 304	38 431	47 062	52 946	58 020	67 773	72 669	77 229	dont créances nettes sur le gouvernement
International reserves (millions US$)	146	145	169	190	168	188	205	173	171	Réserves internationales (millions $EU)
Average exchange rate (National currency per US$)	354	371	354	383	371	371	444	445	437	Taux de change (moyen) (monnaie nationale par $ EU)
IX-2 PUBLIC FINANCE *COMOROS FRANC (MILLIONS)*										**IX-2 FINANCES PUBLIQUES** *FRANC COMORIEN (MILLIONS)*
Total Revenues and Grants	44 776	58 869	50 907	65 356	104 672	60 450	82 475	63 841	...	Recettes totales et dons
Direct taxes (on income, profits)	4 339	4 886	6 413	6 402	7 839	7 265	7 629	7 470	...	Taxes directes
Domestic indirect taxes revenues	6 514	6 569	5 526	10 733	16 039	16 902	17 409	22 966	...	Taxes Indirectes
Trade taxes	9 648	10 935	11 108	9 250	5 334	5 226	3 647	4 365	...	Taxes sur le commerce extérieur
Other taxes	13	58	472	465	324	548	257	564	...	Autres taxes
Other revenues	5 887	6 426	11 273	17 287	8 180	6 812	14 147	4 194	...	Autres recettes
Grants	18 374	29 994	16 114	21 219	66 956	23 698	39 386	24 283	...	Dons
Total Expenditures and Net Lending	43 627	44 703	47 793	57 803	61 305	61 789	71 087	83 651	...	Dépenses totales et prêts nets
Current expenditure	33 171	32 079	34 834	40 921	35 644	41 313	45 116	49 450	...	Dépenses courantes
Wages and Salaries	17 034	18 500	18 409	18 278	18 582	21 423	23 713	24 640	...	Rémunérations et salaires
Other purchases of goods and services	7 447	7 553	7 662	8 932	9 047	11 808	12 099	13 079	...	Achat de biens et services
Other current expenditure	3 365	2 191	4 874	9 317	2 787	2 995	2 408	3 651	...	Autres dépenses courantes
Current transfers	5 325	3 835	3 889	4 394	5 227	5 087	6 896	8 080	...	Transferts courants
Interest payments	1 069	1 036	952	977	457	201	104	138	...	Intérêts
Capital expenditure	8 939	11 588	11 708	15 444	23 904	20 275	21 965	27 948	...	Dépenses d'équipement
Net lending	448	...	300	461	1 300	...	3 902	6 115	...	Prêts nets
Fiscal balance	1 148	14 165	3 114	7 553	43 367	- 1 339	11 387	- 19 810	...	Solde global y compris les dons
IX-3 BALANCE OF PAYMENTS *COMOROS FRANC (MILLIONS)*										**IX-3 BALANCE DES PAIEMENTS** *FRANC COMORIEN (MILLIONS)*
Trade balance	- 53 361	- 57 488	- 60 438	- 75 941	- 76 743	- 79 536	- 74 647	- 68 167	...	Balance commerciale
Services Balance	1 210	- 9 731	- 11 049	- 12 383	- 10 066	1 716	- 860	- 2 576	...	Balance des services
Net primary income	- 439	- 316	- 277	- 597	81	1 669	2 222	2 453	...	Revenus primaires nets
Compensation of employees	62	- 395	- 152	- 484	143	868	901	1 688	...	Rémunération des salariés
Investment income	- 439	- 316	- 277	- 597	81	558	1 067	765	...	Revenus des investissements
Net secondary income	38 749	58 311	55 527	75 480	66 259	60 057	72 186	48 087	...	Revenus secondaires nets
Net official transfers	14 224	26 344	21 418	39 244	17 963	8 566	27 462	4 015	...	Transferts officiels nets
Workers' remittances	...	...	...	...	...	...	...	...	...	Envois de fonds des travailleurs
Other private transfers	34 662	31 967	34 109	36 236	48 296	51 491	44 724	44 072	...	Autres transferts privés
Current account balance	- 13 842	- 9 224	- 16 238	- 13 440	- 20 469	- 16 093	- 1 099	- 20 202	...	Solde du compte courant
Capital and financial account	12 448	13 328	15 267	15 570	22 381	14 456	- 119	24 164	...	Comptes de capital et financier
Capital account	16 532	26 445	20 972	19 258	63 578	17 855	13 772	8 370	...	Compte de capital
Financial account	- 4 084	- 13 117	- 5 705	- 3 689	- 41 197	- 3 399	- 13 890	15 795	...	Compte financier
Errors and omissions	1 395	- 4 104	971	- 2 129	- 1 912	1 638	1 217	- 3 962	...	Erreurs et omissions
Overall balance	...	...	...	...	...	...	...	...	...	Balance générale

COMORES

	2009	2010	2011	2012	2013	2014	2015	2016	2017	
X-1 DEBT US $ (MILLIONS)										**X-1 DETTE EXTÉRIEURE** $ E.U (MILLIONS)
Total external debt	278	266	274	247	123	133	141	174	178	Dette extérieure totale
Private	...	...	...	...	...	...	...	...	...	Privée
Public	278	266	274	247	123	133	141	174	...	Publique
Total external debt service	8	10	10	9	2	2	1	2	...	Service de la dette extérieure
Present value of external debt	197	200	209	80	...	...	...	66	...	Valeur actuelle de la dette extérieure
Total government domestic debt, National currency (millions)	...	...	...	...	...	...	...	...	...	Dette publique intérieure
X-2 FINANCIAL FLOWS US $ (MILLIONS)										**X-2 FLUX FINANCIERS** $ E.U (MILLIONS)
Net Foreign Direct Investment Inflows	14	8	23	10	4	5	5	8	...	Investissements étranger direct (flux nets entrants)
Main origin of FDI inflows										**Principales origines de l'IDE entrant:**
	...	...	...	...	...	...	...	...	...	
	...	...	...	...	...	...	...	...	...	
	...	...	...	...	...	...	...	...	...	
	...	...	...	...	...	...	...	...	...	
	...	...	...	...	...	...	...	...	...	
Net total official development assistance	51	68	52	102	81	75	66	55	...	Aide publique au développement (nette totale)
Main origin of net ODA										**Principales origines de l'APD nette**
France	22	21	22	24	36	26	20	19	...	France
International Development Association [IDA]	- 1	5	3	3	7	9	8	6	...	International Development Association
United Arab Emirates	...	16	1	8	...	...	...	...	...	Emirates Arabes
United Nation Development Programme	2	1	1	1	1	1	1	1	...	Programme des Nations Unies pour le développement
IMF (Concessional Trust Funds)	7	2	2	5	5	...	-	- 2	...	Financements concessionnels du FMI dans le cadre de la FASR

COMOROS

SOURCES AND NOTES - SOURCES ET NOTES

External trade - Total exports, fob: UNCTAD

External trade - Total import, cif: UNCTAD

ODA: OECD

Monetary statistics: IMF

National Accounts: 2017:Projection

National Accounts: The accounts are calculated using the new base year 2007

Poverty: World Bank

Commerce exterieur - Exportation, fab: CNUCED

Commerce exterieur - Imporations, caf: CNUCED

APD: OCDE

Statistiques monétaires: FMI

Comptes nationaux: 2017:Projection

Comptes Nationaux : Les comptes sont calculés selon la nouvelle année de base 2007

Pauvreté: Banque mondiale

	AREA (km2)	342 000		SUPERFICIE (KM2)	
	CAPITAL CITY	Brazzaville	Brazzaville	CAPITALE	
	CURRENCY	CFA Franc	Franc CFA	MONNAIE	

I SOCIAL AND DEMOGRAPHIC INDICATORS — INDICATEURS DEMOGRAPHIQUES ET SOCIAUX

Population	Year Année	Value Valeur	Charts Graphiques	Population
Population ('000)	2016	4 608.6		Population ('000)
Female (%)	2016	50.0		Féminine (%)
Urban (%)	2015	66.1		Urbaine (%)
Average annual growth rate	2015	2.8		Taux de croissance annuel
Active population ('000)	2015	1 717.0		Population active ('000)
Population by age group ('000)				Population par groupe d'âge ('000)
0-14 years	2015	1 969.7		0-14 ans
15-64 years	2015	2 481.5		15-64 ans
65+ years	2015	169.1		65+ ans
Economically active population in agriculture (%)	2015	30.9		Participation de la population active agricole (%)
Crude birth rate	2015	36.0		Taux brut de natalité
Crude death rate	2015	8.3		Taux brut de mortalité
Total fertility rate	2015	4.8		Indice synthétique de fécondité
Life expectancy at birth - Total (years)	2015	62.9		Espérance de vie à la naissance - Totale (années)
Dependency ratio - Total (%)	2015	86.2		Taux de dépendance - Total (%)
Health				**Santé**
Percentage of children under-five and underweight	2012	11.8		% d'enfants de moins de cinq ans avec insuffisance pondérale
Prevalence of undernourishment	2015	30.5		Prévalence de la malnutrition
Under five mortality rate (per 1 000 live births)	2015	45.0		Taux de mortalité de moins de 5 ans (les deux sexes, pour 1000)
Infant mortality rate (per 1 000 live births)	2015	33.2		Taux de mortalité infantile (les deux sexes) par 1000
Neonatal mortality rate (per 1 000 live births)	2015	18.0		Le taux de mortalité néonatale (pour 1000 naissances vivantes)
Percentage of children provided the vaccines :				Pourcentage d'enfants vaccinés :
BCG	2014	95.0		BCG
DPT3	2014	90.0		DTC3
Polio	2011	90.0		polio
Measles	2014	80.0		rougeole
Percentage of mothers provided at least one antenatal care	2005	85.8		Pourcentage de mères ayant au moins reçu un soin prénatal (%)
Percentage of deliveries attended by skilled health personnel	2012	93.6		% d'accouchements assistés par un personnel de santé qualifié
Number of doctors (per 10,000 population)	2007	1.0		Nombre de médecins (pour 10.000 habitants)
Number of nurses (per 10,000 population)	2007	8.2		Nombre d'infirmiers (pour 10.000 habitants)
Hospital beds - Total (per 10,000 population)	2005	16.0		Nombre de lits d'hôpitaux - Total (pour 10 000)
Births registered (per 1,000)	2015	36.0		Naissances enregistrées (pour 1000)
Deaths registered (per 1,000)	2015	8.3		Décès enregistrés (pour 1000)
Budget allocation to health (%)	2013	8.7		Dépenses publiques consacrées à la santé (% du budget)
Education				**Education**
Enrolment in primary education (000)	2015	842.2		Scolarisation dans le primaire (000)
Female	2012	378.3		Féminine
Enrolment in secondary education (000)	2015	525.0		Scolarisation dans le secondaire (000)
Female	2012	156.8		Féminine
Enrolment in tertiary education (000)	2014	44.7		Scolarisation dans le tertiaire (000)
Female	2014	18.8		Féminine
Literacy rate	2011	79.3		Taux d'alphabétisation (deux sexes)
Male	2011	86.4		Masculin
Female	2011	72.9		Féminin
Pupil teacher ratio - primary	2015	38.3		Ratio élève-enseignant
Budget allocation to education (%)	2010	29.0		Dépenses publiques consacrées à l'enseignement (% du budget)
Poverty				**Pauvreté**
GNI per capita, PPP (current int. $)	2016	5380.0		RNB par habitant, ($ PPA inter. courants)
Human Poverty Index (HPI-1) Value (%)	2007	38.0		Valeur de l'Indice de pauvreté (IPH-1) (%)
Population below Inter. poverty line ($2/day) (%)	2011	28.7		Population sous le seuil inter. de pauvreté (2$/Jour) (%)
Share of income held by richest 10%	2011	29.9		% de revenu des 10% plus riches
Share of income held by poorest 10%	2011	2.2		% de revenu des 10% plus pauvres
GINI index	2011	40.2		Indice de GINI

Population by age group - 2015
Population par groupe d'age - 2015

- 0-14 years: 42.6%
- 15-64 years: 53.7%
- 65+ years: 3.7%

Percentage of children provided vaccines : - 2014
Pourcentage d'enfants vaccinés : - 2014

BCG / BCG	DPT3 / DTC3	Polio / polio (2011)	Measles / rougeole
95.0	90.0	90.0	80.0

Literacy rate (%) - 2011
Taux d'alphabétisation - 2011

- Male: 86.4
- Female: 72.9

GNI per capita, PPP (current international $)
RNB par habitant, ($ PPA internationaux courants)

2012	2013	2014	2015	2016
4 140	4 320	4 830	5 840	5 380

CONGO

II NATIONAL ACCOUNTS — COMPTES NATIONAUX

	2009	2010	2011	2012	2013	2014	2015	2016	2017	
GROSS DOMESTIC PRODUCT BY KIND OF ECONOMIC ACTIVITY AT CURRENT PRICES CFA FRANC (BILLIONS)										**PRODUIT INTÉRIEUR BRUT PAR BRANCHE D'ACTIVITÉ ÉCONOMIQUE AUX PRIX COURANTS** FRANC CFA (MILLIARDS)
Agriculture, hunting , forestry and Fishing	201	220	248	274	304	345	374	...	...	Agriculture, chasse sylviculture et Pêche
Mining and quarrying	2 738	4 243	4 910	4 670	4 371	4 130	1 986	...	...	Industries extractives
Manufacturing	199	216	243	268	299	346	379	...	...	Industries manufacturières
Electricity, gas & water	33	35	40	44	48	53	56	...	...	Electricité, gaz et eau
Construction	158	178	205	231	262	293	320	...	...	Bâtiments et travaux publics
Wholesale & retail trade, restaurants, hotels	302	334	383	422	472	513	577	...	...	Commerce de gros et de détail, restaurants et hôtels
Finance, insurance, real estate, etc.	264	284	318	341	366	390	418	...	...	Banques, assurances, affaires immobilières
Transport and communications	223	247	282	310	346	375	421	...	...	Transport(s) et communications
Public administration and defense	206	222	235	283	316	356	353	...	...	Administrations publiques et défense
Education	...	...	...	...	...	...	...	...	...	Education
Health And Social Work	...	...	...	...	...	...	...	...	...	Santé et Actions Sociales
Other services	...	...	...	...	...	...	...	...	...	Autres services
Less Imputed Service Charges	...	...	...	...	...	...	...	...	...	Moins Services d'intermédiation financière
Gross domestic product at factor cost / basic prices	4 323	5 980	6 863	6 842	6 783	6 800	4 882	...	...	Produit intérieur brut aux couts des facteurs / prix de base
Plus: Indirect Taxes / taxes on products, less subsidies	86	103	119	130	144	160	175	...	...	Plus taxes indirectes/impôts sur les produits, moins les subventions
EXPENDITURE ON GROSS DOMESTIC PRODUCT AT CURRENT PURCHASER'S VALUES CFA FRANC (BILLIONS)										**EMPLOI DU PRODUIT INTÉRIEUR BRUT AUX PRIX COURANTS D'ACQUISITION** FRANC CFA (MILLIARDS)
Government final consumption	469	484	512	618	661	701	712	...	...	Consommation finale des administrations publiques
Private final consumption	1 348	1 468	1 553	1 729	1 922	2 260	2 650	...	...	Consommation finale privée
Gross fixed capital formation	1 853	1 805	2 406	3 012	3 079	4 078	2 336	...	...	Formation brute de capital fixe
Change in inventories	10	...	...	...	...	...	...	...	...	Variation des stocks
Exports of goods and services	3 438	5 609	5 930	5 732	5 689	5 560	2 974	...	...	Exportations de biens et services
Less imports of goods and services	2 708	3 283	3 419	4 118	4 424	5 639	3 616	...	...	Moins importations de biens et services
GDP at purchasers' values	4 410	6 083	6 982	6 972	6 927	6 960	5 056	...	...	PIB aux prix d'acquisition
GROSS DOMESTIC PRODUCT BY KIND OF ECONOMIC ACTIVITY AT CONSTANT PRICES ANNUAL GROWTH RATES (%)										**PRODUIT INTÉRIEUR BRUT PAR BRANCHE D'ACTIVITÉ ECONOMIQUE AUX PRIX CONSTANTS** TAUX DE CROISSANCE ANNUEL (%)
Agriculture, hunting , forestry and Fishing	- 3.0	6.2	7.1	7.3	7.9	7.6	6.4	...	...	Agriculture, chasse sylviculture et Pêche
Mining and quarrying	16.1	13.7	- 4.8	- 9.6	- 10.3	3.5	- 6.8	...	...	Industries extractives
Manufacturing	5.5	5.9	8.6	8.6	9.0	9.8	7.6	...	...	Industries manufacturières
Electricity, gas & water	1.3	5.5	7.4	7.5	7.0	7.8	2.3	...	...	Electricité, gaz et eau
Construction	8.7	8.8	10.5	10.5	10.2	11.8	3.9	...	...	Bâtiments et travaux publics
Wholesale & retail trade, restaurants, hotels	7.5	7.4	9.2	9.5	9.2	7.1	8.1	...	...	Commerce de gros et de détail, restaurants et hôtels
Finance, insurance, real estate, etc.	4.8	4.9	6.7	6.0	4.4	6.3	7.1	...	...	Banques, assurances, affaires immobilières
Transport and communications	6.1	6.9	9.2	9.1	9.1	7.8	7.3	...	...	Transport(s) et communications
Public administration and defense	2.9	3.2	3.2	17.7	7.9	9.4	- 2.9	...	...	Administrations publiques et défense
Education	...	...	...	...	...	...	...	...	...	Education
Health And Social Work	...	...	...	...	...	...	...	...	...	Santé et Actions Sociales
Other services	...	...	...	...	...	...	...	...	...	Autres services
Less Imputed Service Charges	...	...	...	...	...	...	...	...	...	Moins Services d'intermédiation financière
Gross domestic product at factor cost / basic prices	7.6	8.5	3.3	3.7	3.1	7.0	2.5	...	...	Produit intérieur brut aux couts des facteurs / prix de base
Plus: Indirect Taxes / taxes on products, less subsidies	4.5	16.0	6.6	8.1	8.1	1.9	5.1	...	...	Plus taxes indirectes/impôts sur les produits, moins les subventions
Gross domestic product at market prices	7.5	8.7	3.4	3.8	3.3	6.8	2.6	...	...	Produit intérieur brut aux prix du marché
EXPENDITURE ON GROSS DOMESTIC PRODUCT AT CONSTANT PURCHASERS' VALUES ANNUAL GROWTH RATES (%)										**EMPLOIS DU PRODUIT INTÉRIEUR BRUT AUX PRIX CONSTANTS D'ACQUISITION** TAUX DE CROISSANCE ANNUEL (%)
Government final consumption	4.6	3.2	3.2	17.7	6.5	1.6	- 0.4	...	...	Consommation finale des administrations publiques
Private final consumption	4.8	6.3	9.9	8.2	4.2	3.3	4.8	...	...	Consommation finale privée
Gross fixed capital formation	5.2	34.1	13.3	27.9	8.4	20.2	6.2	...	...	Formation brute de capital fixe
Exports of goods and services	0.2	7.1	- 5.9	- 5.2	- 4.6	4.1	- 4.1	...	...	Exportations de biens et services
Less imports of goods and services	- 0.3	17.0	10.3	26.3	5.7	12.9	4.0	...	...	Moins importations de biens et services

III INFLATION

	2009	2010	2011	2012	2013	2014	2015	2016	2017	
Annual growth rates (%)										**Taux de croissance annuel (%)**
All item	5.8	0.3	2.1	6.1	6.0	- 0.1	2.7	3.6	- 0.6	Ensemble
of which:										dont:
Food and non-alcoholic beverages	11.0	- 0.8	1.5	10.9	7.4	- 2.3	...	...	...	Alimentation et boissons non alcoolisés
Alcoholic beverages, tobacco and narcotics	...	...	...	5.8	5.9	- 6.5	...	...	...	Boissons alcoolisées et tabacs
Clothing and footwear	4.6	10.7	- 1.3	3.8	3.7	- 2.6	...	...	...	Habillement et chaussures
Housing, water, electricity, gas and other fuels	4.8	7.7	4.9	0.6	5.7	6.2	...	...	...	Logement, eau, électricité, gaz et autres combustibles
Furnishings, household equipment and routine household maintenance	...	...	...	4.7	2.4	2.0	...	...	...	Meubles, articles de ménage et entretien courant
Health	- 15.8	0.2	2.7	- 0.9	1.4	8.8	...	...	...	Santé
Transport	6.2	- 1.2	- 0.5	0.4	0.7	- 0.6	...	...	...	Transport
Communication	...	...	...	- 15.6	30.4	14.3	...	...	...	Communication
Recreation and culture	...	...	...	- 0.6	0.9	- 4.8	...	...	...	Loisirs et culture
Education	...	...	...	- 14.2	1.3	25.2	...	...	...	Enseignement
Restaurants and hotels	...	...	...	2.0	9.0	- 5.5	...	...	...	Restaurants et hôtels
Miscellaneous goods and services	...	...	...	3.6	1.3	- 2.9	...	...	...	Biens et Services divers

IV AGRICULTURAL PRODUCTION - PRODUCTION AGRICOLE

	2009	2010	2011	2012	2013	2014	2015	2016	2017	
TONNES (THOUSAND)										**Tonnes (milliers)**
Cassava	1 231	1 149	1 169	1 259	1 279	1 308	1 337	1 366	...	Manioc
Sugar cane	600	626	639	640	652	664	676	687	...	Canne à sucre
Bananas	140	141	142	144	144	144	147	148	...	Bananes
Plantains	80	81	82	85	85	85	85	86	...	Bananes plantains
Mangoes, mangosteens, guavas	81	83	82	81	81	81	81	81	...	Mangues, mangoustans, goyaves

V MINING PRODUCTION - PRODUCTION MINIERE

	2009	2010	2011	2012	2013	2014	2015	2016	2017	
Crude petroleum - Production, metric tons (thousands)	102 348	112 000	113 000	104 000	...	...	...	...	...	Pétrole brut - Production, tonnes métriques (milliers)
Natural gas - Production, terajoules (millions)	-	-	-	-	...	...	...	...	...	Gaz naturel - Production, térajoules (millions)
Gold ores and concentrates - Production (Kilograms)	100	150	150	150	...	...	...	...	...	Minerais d'or et leurs concentrés - Production (Kilogrammes)

VI ENERGY - ENERGIE

	2009	2010	2011	2012	2013	2014	2015	2016	2017	
Total electricity generation (GWh)	526	781	1 293	1 349	1 514	1 740	1 805	1 879	...	Production électrique totale (GWh)
of which										dont
Production of electricity from fossil fuels (GWh)	196	355	502	522	543	788	806	826	...	Production d'électricité à partir de combustibles fossiles (GWh)
Production of hydro electricity (GWh)	330	426	791	827	971	952	1 000	1 053	...	Production d'électricité d'origine hydraulique (GWh)
Production of electricity from solar, wind, tide, wave and other sources (GWh)	...	...	...	...	...	...	...	...	...	Production d'électricité d'origine solaire, éolienne, marée motrice et autres (GWh)

VII TOURISM AND INFRASTRUCTURE - TOURISME ET INFRASTUCTURE

	2009	2010	2011	2012	2013	2014	2015	2016	2017	
VII-1 Tourism										**VII-1 Tourisme**
International tourist arrivals (thousands)	94	194	218	256	343	227	264	163	166	Arrivées de touristes internationaux (milliers)
Rooms in hotels and similar establishments (thousands)	7	...	...	12	15	16	19	16	...	Chambres d'hôtels et établissements assimilés (milliers)
Overnight stays (thousands)	193	219	365	553	594	799	769	472	490	Nuitées (milliers)
Tourism receipts (US$ thousand)	76 900	27 200	37 899	62 302	51 105	53 805	39 392	41 529	44 814	Recettes touristiques (milliers de $ EU)
Total contribution to GDP (%)	4.1	2.7	2.5	3.0	3.5	3.9	3.9	3.9	4.0	Contribution totale au PIB (%)
Total contribution to Employment (%)	3.4	2.2	2.8	3.2	3.6	3.7	3.6	3.6	3.7	Contribution totale à l'emploi (%)
VII-2 Infrastructure										**VII-2 Infrastructure**
Paved road (% of total)	7.1	...	...	...	...	...	...	...	...	Routes asphaltées (% du total)
Total network (Railways-km)	...	...	...	...	...	...	...	...	...	Réseau total voies ferrées-Km
Main telephone lines (per 100 inhabitants)	...	...	...	...	...	...	...	...	...	Lignes téléphoniques fixes (pour 100 habitants)
Mobile cellular subscribers (per 100 inhabitants)	73.8	90.4	91.9	98.8	104.8	108.1	111.7	113.3	...	Abonnés aux téléphones mobiles (pour 100 habitants)
Internet users per 100 inhabitants	4.5	5.0	5.6	6.1	6.6	7.1	7.6	8.1	...	Utilisateurs Internet par 100 Habitants
Fixed (wired)-broadband subscriptions per 100 inhabitants	...	...	...	...	...	...	...	...	...	Abonnements à l'Internet fixe (filaire) à large bande pour 100 habitants, par débit

VIII EXTERNAL TRADE - COMMERCE EXTERIEUR

	2009	2010	2011	2012	2013	2014	2015	2016	2017	
US$ (MILLIONS) EXPORTS, FOB										**$ E.U (MILLIONS) EXPORTATIONS, FÀB**
Exports - Total	6 100	9 400	11 851	10 275	9 028	9 142	4 467	3 573	...	Exportations - Total
Exports to Africa	694	886	1 212	864	804	625	351	256	...	Exportations vers l'Afrique
Main products										**Principaux produits**
Copper	56	243	245	295	659	1 033	416	381	...	Cuivre
Petroleum oils or bituminous minerals > 70 % oil	158	181	303	150	326	275	148	111	...	Huiles de pétrole ou de minéraux bitumineux> 70% d'huile
Petroleum oils, oils from bitumin. materials, crude	4 465	7 018	9 158	8 271	6 416	6 071	3 070	2 400	...	Huiles de pétrole, huiles de bitume. matériaux bruts
Ships, boats & floating structures	828	1 087	1 245	680	1 025	1 058	512	412	...	Navires, bateaux et structures flottantes
Wood in the rough or roughly squared	105	182	246	223	160	196	88	74	...	Bois bruts ou grossièrement équarris
Main destinations										**Principales destinations**
Australia	-	116	604	757	711	686	344	270	...	Australie
China	1 282	2 324	3 917	3 455	4 108	4 035	2 002	1 585	...	Chine
France	586	733	757	1 050	442	241	168	107	...	France
Italy	42	132	396	252	170	618	194	213	...	Italie
United States	1 708	2 217	2 003	1 113	749	300	258	147	...	États-Unis
IMPORTS, CIF										
Imports - Total	2 900	4 369	5 007	5 485	6 249	6 564	5 481	4 951	...	Importations - Total (millions)
Imports from Africa	840	1 166	2 201	2 253	2 620	1 047	1 569	1 075	...	Importations en provenance de l'Afrique
Main products										**Principaux produits**
Civil engineering & contractors' plant & equipment	105	160	129	147	145	195	145	140	...	Génie civil et installations et équipements des entrepreneurs
Other meat and edible meat offal	51	87	83	117	126	206	142	143	...	Autres viandes et abats comestibles
Petroleum oils or bituminous minerals > 70 % oil	60	172	113	72	125	248	160	168	...	Huiles de pétrole ou de minéraux bitumineux> 70% d'huile
Ships, boats & floating structures	1 029	1 657	2 272	2 297	2 685	317	1 284	658	...	Navires, bateaux et structures flottantes
Tubes, pipes & hollow profiles, fittings, iron, steel	63	36	56	71	94	328	181	209	...	Tubes, tuyaux et profilés creux, raccords, fer, acier
Main origin										**Principales provenances**
Angola	310	255	553	1 285	936	109	447	229	...	Angola
Belgium	104	133	155	203	233	417	278	285	...	Belgique
China	195	284	307	373	561	1 104	712	747	...	Chine
France	402	584	501	586	666	1 017	720	714	...	France
Italy	152	202	205	180	202	456	282	303	...	Italie

	2009	2010	2011	2012	2013	2014	2015	2016	2017	
IX-1 MONETARY STATISTICS *CFA FRANC (MILLIONS)*										**IX-1 STATISTIQUES MONÉTAIRES** *FRANC CFA (MILLIONS)*
Money supply (M1)	1 018 661	1 414 519	1 902 698	2 304 376	2 320 041	2 624 912	2 330 127	1 971 832	1 906 330	Masse monétaire (M1)
Quasi-money	137 609	165 147	209 735	260 481	333 603	345 426	345 236	362 131	335 415	Quasi-monnaie
of which demand deposit	...	...	...	...	...	...	...	...	...	dont Monnaie scripturale
Net foreign assets	1 830 931	2 325 304	3 058 686	3 096 264	3 015 377	2 783 546	1 559 912	471 749	120 113	Avoirs extérieurs nets
Domestic credit	- 650 551	- 852 927	-1 098 254	- 623 791	- 503 550	57 093	1 088 914	1 805 328	1 853 086	Crédit intérieur
of which claims on private sector	- 893 102	-1 267 971	-1 641 869	-1 315 943	-1 312 975	- 971 576	- 133 672	518 680	578 600	dont créances sur le secteur privé
of which claims on government sector, net	222 798	389 027	528 927	669 611	787 521	987 401	1 115 777	1 162 119	1 109 747	dont créances nettes sur le gouvernement
International reserves (millions US$)	3 696	4 450	6 098	5 436	5 080	5 466	2 335	876	859	Réserves internationales (millions $EU)
Average exchange rate (National currency per US$)	472	495	472	511	494	494	591	593	582	Taux de change (moyen) (monnaie nationale par $ EU)
IX-2 PUBLIC FINANCE *CFA FRANC (MILLIONS)*										**IX-2 FINANCES PUBLIQUES** *FRANC CFA (MILLIONS)*
Total Revenues and Grants	1 334 761	2 231 200	2 894 000	2 975 800	3 123 400	2 832 327	1 537 977	1 507 582	1 506 618	Recettes totales et dons
Direct taxes (on income, profits)	139 824	176 400	215 232	241 056	321 048	293 227	356 596	316 874	313 727	Taxes directes
Domestic indirect taxes revenues	151 476	191 100	233 168	261 144	296 352	399 600	391 204	365 128	326 651	Taxes Indirectes
Trade taxes	66 624	77 900	101 100	117 500	147 600	154 900	148 400	125 900	143 455	Taxes sur le commerce extérieur
Other taxes	947 175	1 763 800	2 287 600	2 302 700	2 295 700	1 943 300	593 077	638 781	658 326	Autres taxes
Other revenues	15 162	17 900	21 500	43 400	35 800	9 700	5 800	20 500	21 372	Autres recettes
Grants	14 500	4 100	35 400	10 000	26 900	31 600	42 900	40 400	43 087	Dons
Total Expenditures and Net Lending	1 117 279	1 274 932	1 774 400	2 468 056	3 433 367	3 617 462	3 646 884	2 108 594	1 588 446	Dépenses totales et prêts nets
Current expenditure	554 100	620 900	679 800	1 010 200	924 900	1 090 500	1 056 300	1 044 900	997 201	Dépenses courantes
Wages and Salaries	175 000	179 500	206 700	248 400	274 700	322 500	356 400	380 400	410 000	Rémunérations et salaires
Other purchases of goods and services	354 900	398 800	429 500	723 400	650 200	743 000	690 200	652 100	575 971	Achat de biens et services
Other current expenditure	24 200	42 600	43 600	38 400	...	25 000	9 700	12 400	11 230	Autres dépenses courantes
Current transfers	...	...	...	...	...	...	...	...	...	Transferts courants
Interest payments	73 300	58 600	10 700	13 000	18 100	15 000	39 284	143 494	164 295	Intérêts
Capital expenditure	489 879	595 432	1 083 900	1 444 856	2 490 367	2 511 962	2 551 300	920 200	426 950	Dépenses d'équipement
Net lending	...	...	...	...	...	...	...	...	...	Prêts nets
Fiscal balance	217 482	956 268	1 119 600	507 744	- 309 967	- 785 135	-2 108 907	- 601 012	- 81 828	Solde global y compris les dons
IX-3 BALANCE OF PAYMENTS *CFA FRANC (MILLIONS)*										**IX-3 BALANCE DES PAIEMENTS** *FRANC CFA (MILLIONS)*
Trade balance	1 536	2 623	3 230	2 333	1 502	2 016	...	...	...	Balance commerciale
Services Balance	- 1 339	- 2 208	- 1 679	- 1 833	- 2 041	- 1 223	...	...	...	Balance des services
Net primary income	- 797	- 1 142	- 1 798	- 1 663	- 1 505	- 1 134	...	...	...	Revenus primaires nets
Compensation of employees	- 35	- 52	- 12	- 12	- 11		...	...	...	Rémunération des salariés
Investment income	- 762	- 1 091	- 1 787	- 1 652	- 1 494		...	...	...	Revenus des investissements
Net secondary income	- 21	- 21	- 101	- 106	- 118	- 190	...	...	...	Revenus secondaires nets
Net official transfers	7	7	13	13	8		...	...	...	Transferts officiels nets
Workers' remittances	...	...	...	...	...		...	...	...	Envois de fonds des travailleurs
Other private transfers	- 28	- 28	- 114	- 120	- 125		...	...	...	Autres transferts privés
Current account balance	- 621	- 749	- 348	- 1 269	- 2 162	- 531	...	...	...	Solde du compte courant
Capital and financial account	427	1 218	615	736	1 606		...	...	...	Comptes de capital et financier
Capital account	15	1 312	35	10	17		...	...	...	Compte de capital
Financial account	413	- 94	579	726	1 589		...	...	...	Compte financier
Errors and omissions	9	- 40	469	444	252		...	...	...	Erreurs et omissions
Overall balance	- 185	429	734	- 89	- 304		...	...	...	Balance générale

CONGO

X DEBT AND FINANCIAL FLOWS - DETTE ET FLUX FINANCIERS

	2009	2010	2011	2012	2013	2014	2015	2016	2017	
X-1 DEBT *US $ (MILLIONS)*										**X-1 DETTE EXTÉRIEURE** *$ E.U (MILLIONS)*
Total external debt	5 501	2 425	3 144	3 541	4 501	4 949	6 686	6 878	7 467	Dette extérieure totale
Private	...	...	...	...	...	...	...	...	...	Privée
Public	5 501	2 425	3 144	3 541	4 501	4 949	6 686	6 878	...	Publique
Total external debt service	539	145	139	122	288	398	365	753	...	Service de la dette extérieure
Present value of external debt	...	...	...	...	...	...	...	2 717	...	Valeur actuelle de la dette extérieure
Total government domestic debt, National currency (millions)	...	...	...	...	...	...	...	...	...	Dette publique intérieure
X-2 FINANCIAL FLOWS *US $ (MILLIONS)*										**X-2 FLUX FINANCIERS** *$ E.U (MILLIONS)*
Net Foreign Direct Investment Inflows	1 274	928	2 180	2 152	2 914	5 502	1 866	2 006	...	Investissements étranger direct (flux nets entrants)
Main origin of FDI inflows										**Principales origines de l'IDE entrant:**
France	315	- 9	318	335	...	...	...	...	...	France
Belgium	1 200	132	- 189	167	...	...	...	...	...	Belgique
...	...	...	...	...	...	...	...	...	...	...
Luxembourg	- 3	1	...	...	...	...	...	...	...	Luxembourg
...	...	...	...	...	...	...	...	...	...	...
African countries	...	68	...	...	...	...	...	...	...	Pays africains
Net total official development assistance	282	1 314	261	140	151	106	89	88	...	Aide publique au développement (nette totale)
Main origin of net ODA										**Principales origines de l'APD nette**
France	93	909	61	16	52	28	26	22	...	France
International Development Association [IDA]	12	21	25	30	21	12	10	12	...	International Development Association
Germany	26	9	100	9	1	1	0	-	...	Allemagne
Italy	29	97	...	-	-	1	1	1	...	Italie
Spain	44	...	1	2	1	-	-	-	...	Espagne

CONGO

SOURCES AND NOTES - SOURCES ET NOTES

External trade - Total exports, fob: UNCTAD

External trade - Total import, cif: UNCTAD

ODA: OECD

Monetary statistics: IMF

National Accounts: 2011-2013:Estimates;2014-2015:Provisoires

Poverty: World Bank

Commerce exterieur - Exportation, fab: CNUCED

Commerce exterieur - Imporations, caf: CNUCED

APD: OCDE

Statistiques monétaires: FMI

Comptes nationaux: 2011-2013:Estimées;2014-2015:Provisires

Pauvreté: Banque mondiale

AREA (km2)		322 460		SUPERFICIE (KM2)
CAPITAL CITY	Yamoussoukro		Yamoussoukro	CAPITALE
CURRENCY	CFA Franc		Franc CFA	MONNAIE

I SOCIAL AND DEMOGRAPHIC INDICATORS — INDICATEURS DEMOGRAPHIQUES ET SOCIAUX

	Year Année	Value Valeur	Charts Graphiques	
Population				**Population**
Population ('000)	2016	23 950.5		Population ('000)
Female (%)	2016	48.4		Féminine (%)
Urban (%)	2016	51.2		Urbaine (%)
Average annual growth rate	2016	2.6		Taux de croissance annuel
Active population ('000)	2015	7 914.7		Population active ('000)
Population by age group ('000)				Population par groupe d'âge ('000)
0-14 years	2016	10 001.9		0-14 ans
15-64 years	2016	13 345.6		15-64 ans
65+ years	2016	603.0		65+ ans
Economically active population in agriculture (%)	2015	35.5		Participation de la population active agricole (%)
Crude birth rate	2016	36.3		Taux brut de natalité
Crude death rate	2016	10.5		Taux brut de mortalité
Total fertility rate	2016	4.7		Indice synthétique de fécondité
Life expectancy at birth - Total (years)	2016	56.0		Espérance de vie à la naissance - Totale (années)
Dependency ratio - Total (%)	2016	79.5		Taux de dépendance - Total (%)
Health				**Santé**
Percentage of children under-five and underweight	2016	11.8		% d'enfants de moins de cinq ans avec insuffisance pondérale
Prevalence of undernourishment	2015	13.3		Prévalence de la malnutrition
Under five mortality rate (per 1 000 live births)	2016	96.0		Taux de mortalité de moins de 5 ans (les deux sexes, pour 1000)
Infant mortality rate (per 1 000 live births)	2016	68.0		Taux de mortalité infantile (les deux sexes) par 1000
Neonatal mortality rate (per 1 000 live births)	2016	38.0		Le taux de mortalité néonatale (pour 1000 naissances vivantes)
Percentage of children provided the vaccines :				Pourcentage d'enfants vaccinés :
BCG	2016	94.7		BCG
DPT3	2016	100.8		DTC3
Polio	2016	94.2		polio
Measles	2016	91.6		rougeole
Percentage of mothers provided at least one antenatal care (%)	2016	85.7		Pourcentage de mères ayant au moins reçu un soin prénatal (%)
Percentage of deliveries attended by skilled health personnel	2016	57.4		% d'accouchements assistés par un personnel de santé qualifié
Number of doctors (per 10,000 population)	2016	1.3		Nombre de médecins (pour 10.000 habitants)
Number of nurses (per 10,000 population)	2016	4.1		Nombre d'infirmiers (pour 10.000 habitants)
Hospital beds - Total (per 10,000 population)	2016	2.8		Nombre de lits d'hôpitaux - Total (pour 10 000)
Births registered (per 1,000)	2015	36.9		Naissances enregistrées (pour 1000)
Deaths registered (per 1,000)	2015	13.3		Décès enregistrés (pour 1000)
Budget allocation to health (%)	2016	6.0		Dépenses publiques consacrées à la santé (% du budget)
Education				**Education**
Enrolment in primary education (000)	2016	3 617.2		Scolarisation dans le primaire (000)
Female	2016	1 705.0		Féminine
Enrolment in secondary education (000)	2016	1 621.9		Scolarisation dans le secondaire (000)
Female	2016	672.1		Féminine
Enrolment in tertiary education (000)	2013	80.3		Scolarisation dans le tertiaire (000)
Female	2013	64.4		Féminine
Literacy rate	2016	45.0		Taux d'alphabétisation (deux sexes)
Male	...	...		Masculin
Female	...	...		Féminin
Pupil teacher ratio - primary	...	...		Ratio élève-enseignant
Budget allocation to education (%)	2014	20.7		Dépenses publiques consacrées à l'enseignement (% du budget)
Poverty				**Pauvreté**
GNI per capita, PPP (current int. $)	2016	3590.0		RNB par habitant, ($ PPA inter. courants)
Human Poverty Index (HPI-1) Value (%)	2007	37.4		Valeur de l'Indice de pauvreté (IPH-1) (%)
Population below Inter. poverty line ($2/day) (%)	2008	29.0		Population sous le seuil inter. de pauvreté (2$/Jour) (%)
Share of income held by richest 10%	2008	32.6		% de revenu des 10% plus riches
Share of income held by poorest 10%	2008	1.8		% de revenu des 10% plus pauvres
GINI index	2008	43.2		Indice de GINI

Population by age group - 2016

Population par groupe d'age - 2016

- 0-14 years 41.8%
- 15-64 years 55.7%
- 65+ years 2.5%

Percentage of children provided vaccines : - 2016

Pourcentage d'enfants vaccinés : - 2016

BCG / BCG	DPT3 / DTC3	Polio / polio	Measles / rougeole
94.7		94.2	91.6

Literacy rate (%) - 2008

Taux d'alphabétisation - 2008

- Male
- Female

GNI per capita, PPP (current international $)

RNB par habitant, ($ PPA internationaux courants)

2012	2013	2014	2015	2016
2 670	2 850	3 140	3 350	3 590

II NATIONAL ACCOUNTS — COMPTES NATIONAUX

	2009	2010	2011	2012	2013	2014	2015	2016	2017	
GROSS DOMESTIC PRODUCT BY KIND OF ECONOMIC ACTIVITY AT CURRENT PRICES CFA FRANC (MILLIONS)										**PRODUIT INTÉRIEUR BRUT PAR BRANCHE D'ACTIVITÉ ÉCONOMIQUE AUX PRIX COURANTS** FRANC CFA (MILLIONS)
Agriculture, hunting , forestry and Fishing	2 430 287	3 023 184	3 190 749	3 035 031	3 240 308	3 675 792	4 455 131	4 581 801	...	Agriculture, chasse sylviculture et Pêche
Mining and quarrying	703 046	807 956	1 097 017	928 093	926 802	801 279	961 815	1 164 141	...	Industries extractives
Manufacturing	1 888 817	1 674 356	1 555 503	1 912 423	2 502 672	2 942 393	2 887 234	3 160 956	...	Industries manufacturières
Electricity, gas & water	87 499	69 231	29 487	40 615	98 140	291 063	299 829	427 157	...	Electricité, gaz et eau
Construction	191 851	210 214	216 524	405 468	480 723	751 335	902 394	1 143 499	...	Bâtiments et travaux publics
Wholesale & retail trade, restaurants, hotels	1 213 676	1 374 719	1 399 454	1 385 326	1 480 946	1 650 676	1 849 467	2 053 245	...	Commerce de gros et de détail, restaurants et hôtels
Finance, insurance, real estate, etc.	1 112 857	1 122 116	1 049 288	1 093 788	1 182 257	1 301 709	1 448 861	1 671 407	...	Banques, assurances, affaires immobilières
Transport and communications	877 600	894 940	943 856	1 314 236	1 424 689	1 432 479	1 431 825	1 583 618	...	Transport(s) et communications
Public administration and defense	687 977	745 733	643 087	829 658	933 780	990 404	1 054 377	1 123 987	...	Administrations publiques et défense
Education	352 677	399 269	398 880	416 512	484 748	509 745	585 797	664 337	...	Education
Health And Social Work	80 831	86 781	93 999	131 295	110 659	126 646	149 662	169 728	...	Santé et Actions Sociales
Other services	1 062 557	1 206 919	947 849	1 191 372	1 411 565	1 568 684	1 881 599	2 078 518	...	Autres services
Less Imputed Service Charges	- 401 831	- 433 978	- 371 384	- 399 026	- 403 944	- 406 729	- 444 265	- 524 726	...	Moins Services d'intermédiation financière
Gross domestic product at factor cost / basic prices	10 287 844	11 181 440	11 194 309	12 284 791	13 873 345	15 635 476	17 463 726	19 297 668	...	Produit intérieur brut aux couts des facteurs / prix de base
Plus: Indirect Taxes / taxes on products, less subsidies	1 175 656	1 143 283	918 378	1 390 845	1 575 927	1 825 527	2 131 654	2 345 882	...	Plus taxes indirectes/impôts sur les produits, moins les subventions
EXPENDITURE ON GROSS DOMESTIC PRODUCT AT CURRENT PURCHASER'S VALUES CFA FRANC (MILLIONS)										**EMPLOI DU PRODUIT INTÉRIEUR BRUT AUX PRIX COURANTS D'ACQUISITION** FRANC CFA (MILLIONS)
Government final consumption	1 448 453	1 500 854	1 346 919	1 683 548	1 897 574	2 153 203	2 339 833	2 451 732	...	Consommation finale des administrations publiques
Private final consumption	7 765 162	8 267 366	8 298 424	9 219 282	9 899 393	11 004 773	12 635 956	14 020 775	...	Consommation finale privée
Gross fixed capital formation	1 246 199	1 517 979	1 072 050	1 751 362	2 625 056	3 296 497	3 826 937	4 488 732	...	Formation brute de capital fixe
Change in inventories	- 249 235	138 098	- 582 779	449 289	573 874	150 233	112 482	- 177 975	...	Variation des stocks
Exports of goods and services	5 829 699	6 240 333	6 449 568	6 692 155	6 414 786	6 857 748	7 390 982	6 351 071	...	Exportations de biens et services
Less imports of goods and services	4 576 778	5 339 907	4 471 495	6 120 000	5 961 411	6 001 451	6 710 810	5 490 785	...	Moins importations de biens et services
GDP at purchasers' values	11 463 500	12 324 723	12 112 687	13 675 636	15 449 272	17 461 003	19 595 380	21 643 550	...	PIB aux prix d'acquisition
GROSS DOMESTIC PRODUCT BY KIND OF ECONOMIC ACTIVITY AT CONSTANT PRICES ANNUAL GROWTH RATES (%)										**PRODUIT INTÉRIEUR BRUT PAR BRANCHE D'ACTIVITÉ ECONOMIQUE AUX PRIX CONSTANTS** TAUX DE CROISSANCE ANNUEL (%)
Agriculture, hunting , forestry and Fishing	- 2.9	- 4.1	3.8	1.1	3.9	15.9	3.0	- 3.1	...	Agriculture, chasse sylviculture et Pêche
Mining and quarrying	25.3	- 6.6	6.4	- 25.8	14.7	- 3.3	20.4	37.7	...	Industries extractives
Manufacturing	- 9.2	- 5.8	- 16.0	25.3	21.2	3.5	4.8	3.2	...	Industries manufacturières
Electricity, gas & water	26.0	19.6	- 11.9	155.2	129.3	1.5	5.2	37.7	...	Electricité, gaz et eau
Construction	17.2	12.2	- 21.4	40.5	17.9	32.2	18.3	2.9	...	Bâtiments et travaux publics
Wholesale & retail trade, restaurants, hotels	8.2	4.8	- 4.6	9.5	5.2	12.3	6.8	10.0	...	Commerce de gros et de détail, restaurants et hôtels
Finance, insurance, real estate, etc.	- 1.7	- 0.4	- 4.4	4.4	6.8	6.8	10.5	17.3	...	Banques, assurances, affaires immobilières
Transport and communications	15.6	20.8	1.8	22.0	9.4	5.4	10.8	7.6	...	Transport(s) et communications
Public administration and defense	4.0	8.8	- 14.0	- 1.6	3.3	1.8	7.9	5.4	...	Administrations publiques et défense
Education	1.7	14.9	- 1.6	2.2	1.5	5.9	7.3	19.5	...	Education
Health And Social Work	2.9	11.3	9.0	35.6	- 18.0	14.1	13.9	19.5	...	Santé et Actions Sociales
Other services	6.9	13.6	- 9.5	30.5	14.9	6.8	1.4	17.4	...	Autres services
Less Imputed Service Charges	- 3.4	6.0	- 9.4	6.4	1.2	0.7	9.2	14.1	...	Moins Services d'intermédiation financière
Gross domestic product at factor cost / basic prices	3.5	2.6	- 3.8	8.6	10.1	8.8	7.0	8.4	...	Produit intérieur brut aux couts des facteurs / prix de base
Plus: Indirect Taxes / taxes on products, less subsidies	1.0	- 2.9	- 7.9	28.4	2.4	8.3	25.0	6.4	...	Plus taxes indirectes/impôts sur les produits, moins les subventions
Gross domestic product at market prices	3.3	2.0	- 4.2	10.1	9.3	8.8	8.8	8.2	...	Produit intérieur brut aux prix du marché
EXPENDITURE ON GROSS DOMESTIC PRODUCT AT CONSTANT PURCHASERS' VALUES ANNUAL GROWTH RATES (%)										**EMPLOIS DU PRODUIT INTÉRIEUR BRUT AUX PRIX CONSTANTS D'ACQUISITION** TAUX DE CROISSANCE ANNUEL (%)
Government final consumption	4.7	4.1	- 10.6	8.3	3.8	10.0	5.4	5.4	...	Consommation finale des administrations publiques
Private final consumption	3.8	4.6	- 4.2	6.6	4.2	10.2	13.7	9.6	...	Consommation finale privée
Gross fixed capital formation	3.6	22.8	- 38.5	52.6	49.9	18.9	14.7	17.1	...	Formation brute de capital fixe
Exports of goods and services	18.1	- 4.3	- 1.5	6.0	- 7.9	4.7	7.2	- 2.8	...	Exportations de biens et services
Less imports of goods and services	14.7	12.4	- 21.8	34.8	- 5.5	0.2	16.6	1.2	...	Moins importations de biens et services

III INFLATION

	2009	2010	2011	2012	2013	2014	2015	2016	2017	
Annual growth rates (%)										**Taux de croissance annuel (%)**
All item	0.2	2.0	4.9	1.3	2.6	0.4	1.2	0.7	0.7	Ensemble
of which:										dont:
Food and non-alcoholic beverages	1.4	8.1	10.5	- 0.3	2.0	- 2.1	2.0	3.1	0.3	Alimentation et boissons non alcoolisés
Alcoholic beverages, tobacco and narcotics	0.1	- 0.7	3.6	- 0.3	0.2	0.4	1.4	0.4	1.6	Boissons alcoolisées et tabacs
Clothing and footwear	- 0.7	- 0.8	3.4	3.0	6.9	3.4	2.6	- 1.9	2.2	Habillement et chaussures
Housing, water, electricity, gas and other fuels	- 0.2	1.0	1.8	2.0	2.1	1.6	1.5	0.2	1.3	Logement, eau, électricité, gaz et autres combustibles
Furnishings, household equipment and routine household maintenance	- 0.2	- 1.0	5.9	4.5	3.3	2.6	1.8	0.3	2.7	Meubles, articles de ménage et entretien courant
Health	0.2	0.4	0.9	- 0.9	- 1.7	0.7	1.2	- 0.2	0.2	Santé
Transport	0.1	1.8	1.1	1.0	1.0	- 0.4	- 0.4	- 1.5	- 0.8	Transport
Communication	- 1.0	- 8.4	- 3.6	- 3.3	- 0.5	0.9	0.1	0.1	- 3.2	Communication
Recreation and culture	- 0.3	- 1.0	1.2	1.5	1.5	2.8	1.7	0.2	0.6	Loisirs et culture
Education	0.1	- 0.1	3.3	2.4	25.7	0.2	- 0.3	2.2	1.5	Enseignement
Restaurants and hotels	1.1	3.2	8.1	4.3	0.9	1.3	0.6	0.7	1.5	Restaurants et hôtels
Miscellaneous goods and services	- 0.4	0.6	3.3	2.3	1.3	1.5	0.9	1.3	1.5	Biens et Services divers

COTE D'IVOIRE

IV AGRICULTURAL PRODUCTION - PRODUCTION AGRICOLE

TONNES (THOUSAND)	2009	2010	2011	2012	2013	2014	2015	2016	2017	Tonnes (milliers)
Yams	5 313	5 392	5 532	5 675	6 414	7 039	6 650	6 895	...	Ignames
Cassava	2 129	2 307	2 359	2 412	2 436	4 239	5 087	4 548	...	Manioc
Rice, paddy	1 198	1 244	873	1 562	1 934	2 054	2 153	2 055	...	Riz, Paddy
Plantains	1 614	1 542	1 559	1 577	1 634	1 672	1 739	1 809	...	Bananes plantains
Cocoa, beans	1 304	1 302	1 559	1 499	1 670	1 679	1 826	1 634	...	Cacao en fèves

V MINING PRODUCTION - PRODUCTION MINIERE

	2009	2010	2011	2012	2013	2014	2015	2016	2017	
Crude petroleum - Production, metric tons (thousands)	2 948	2 315	1 970	1 716	1 456	1 099	1 707	...	...	Pétrole brut - Production, tonnes métriques (milliers)
Gold ores and concentrates - Production (Kilograms)	7 055	5 080	12 357	13 080	15 516	18 600	23 460	25 055	...	Minerais d'or et leurs concentrés - Production (Kilogrammes)
Natural gas - Production, terajoules (millions)	1 699	1 756	1 606	1 751	2 127	2 132	2 224	2 360	...	Gaz naturel - Production, térajoules (millions)

VI ENERGY - ENERGIE

	2009	2010	2011	2012	2013	2014	2015	2016	2017	
Total electricity generation (GWh)	...	...	...	8 977	8 799	8 395	8 714	9 057	...	Production électrique totale (GWh)
of which										dont
Production of electricity from fossil fuels (GWh)	3 656	4 278	4 261	7 016	7 016	6 303	6 575	6 869	...	Production d'électricité à partir de combustibles fossiles (GWh)
Production of hydro electricity (GWh)	2 117	1 602	1 774	1 789	1 606	1 913	1 947	1 981	...	Production d'électricité d'origine hydraulique (GWh)
Production of electricity from solar, wind, tide, wave and other sources (GWh)	107	109	109	109	109	109	109	...	...	Production d'électricité d'origine solaire, éolienne, marée motrice et autres (GWh)

VII TOURISM AND INFRASTRUCTURE - TOURISME ET INFRASTUCTURE

VII-1 Tourism	2009	2010	2011	2012	2013	2014	2015	2016	2017	VII-1 Tourisme
International tourist arrivals (thousands)	353	348	344	361	374	350	416	417	375	Arrivées de touristes internationaux (milliers)
Rooms in hotels and similar establishments (thousands)	...	...	...	23	27	28	34	38	...	Chambres d'hôtels et établissements assimilés (milliers)
Overnight stays (thousands)	4 412	4 200	4 390	4 769	4 958	4 591	5 369	5 380	4 888	Nuitées (milliers)
Tourism receipts (US$ thousand)	150 800	200 700	180 000	171 600	180 400	183 300	156 600	167 938	170 912	Recettes touristiques (milliers de $ EU)
Total contribution to GDP (%)	5.5	5.4	6.2	6.6	7.6	7.6	9.0	8.3	8.3	Contribution totale au PIB (%)
Total contribution to Employment (%)	4.7	4.8	5.5	6.0	6.9	6.8	7.9	7.3	7.3	Contribution totale à l'emploi (%)
VII-2 Infrastructure										**VII-2 Infrastructure**
Paved road (% of total)	7.9	...	...	...	...	...	...	...	...	Routes asphaltées (% du total)
Total network (Railways-km)	639	639	639	639	639	639	...	...	...	Réseau total voies ferrées-Km
Main telephone lines (per 100 inhabitants)	1.5	1.5	1.4	1.4	1.3	1.2	1.3	1.3	...	Lignes téléphoniques fixes (pour 100 habitants)
Mobile cellular subscribers (per 100 inhabitants)	70.9	82.2	89.4	91.2	95.4	106.2	119.3	126.0	...	Abonnés aux téléphones mobiles (pour 100 habitants)
Internet users per 100 inhabitants	2.0	2.7	2.9	5.0	12.0	19.3	21.9	26.5	...	Utilisateurs Internet par 100 Habitants
Fixed (wired)-broadband subscriptions per 100 inhabitants	...	...	...	...	...	0.6	0.5	0.6	...	Abonnements à l'Internet fixe (filaire) à large bande pour 100 habitants, par débit

VIII EXTERNAL TRADE - COMMERCE EXTERIEUR

US$ (MILLIONS) EXPORTS, FOB	2009	2010	2011	2012	2013	2014	2015	2016	2017	$ E.U (MILLIONS) EXPORTATIONS, FÀB
Exports - Total	10 280	10 284	12 635	10 861	12 084	12 985	11 845	11 913	...	Exportations - Total
Exports to Africa	3 069	3 263	3 319	3 782	5 276	4 214	3 301	3 340	...	Exportations vers l'Afrique
Main products										**Principaux produits**
Cocoa	3 606	3 699	4 054	3 287	3 114	4 559	5 023	4 552	...	Cacao
Fruits and nuts (excluding oil nuts), fresh or dried	322	488	449	528	530	1 001	923	1 092	...	Fruits et noix (à l'exclusion des oléagineux), frais ou secs
Gold, non-monetary (excluding gold ores and concentrates)	211	183	573	641	576	703	756	672	...	Or, non monétaire (à l'exclusion des minerais d'or et des concentrés)
Petroleum oils or bituminous minerals > 70 % oil	1 409	1 207	1 289	1 766	1 782	1 739	1 277	958	...	Huiles de pétrole ou de minéraux bitumineux> 70% d'huile
Petroleum oils, oils from bitumin. materials, crude	1 141	1 091	1 306	1 256	960	652	545	591	...	Huiles de pétrole, huiles de bitume. matériaux bruts
Main destinations										**Principales destinations**
France	1 123	716	630	502	788	800	762	810	...	France
Germany	738	522	819	815	750	547	721	615	...	Allemagne
Ghana	564	783	304	431	1 852	457	461	473	...	Ghana
Netherlands	1 428	1 462	1 296	950	966	1 297	1 428	1 338	...	Pays-Bas
United States	800	1 060	1 319	878	741	1 089	962	882	...	États-Unis
IMPORTS, CIF										
Imports - Total										Importations - Total (millions)
Imports from Africa										Importations en provenance de l'Afrique
Main products										**Principaux produits**
Fish, fresh (live or dead), chilled or frozen	354	278	327	330	359	387	445	412	...	Poissons frais (vivants ou morts), réfrigérés ou congelés
Medicaments (incl. veterinary medicaments)	214	213	236	259	250	339	256	259	...	Médicaments (y compris les médicaments vétérinaires)
Petroleum oils, oils from bitumin. materials, crude	1 623	1 690	1 749	2 753	2 928	2 613	1 517	1 398	...	Huiles de pétrole, huiles de bitume. matériaux bruts
Rice	597	460	568	685	472	437	488	445	...	Riz
Ships, boats & floating structures	5	845	2	401	2 702	637	28	256	...	Navires, bateaux et structures flottantes
Main origin										**Principales provenances**
Bahamas	-	-	...	-	1 460	613	...	...	...	Bahamas
China	501	546	461	716	1 424	981	1 114	1 187	...	Chine
France	991	931	791	1 210	1 306	1 364	1 312	1 355	...	France
India	128	144	179	389	321	556	366	356	...	Inde
Nigeria	1 435	2 064	1 570	2 511	2 887	2 434	1 444	1 339	...	Nigéria

IX FINANCIAL AND MONETARY STATISTICS - FINANCES ET STATISTIQUES MONETAIRES

	2009	2010	2011	2012	2013	2014	2015	2016	2017	
IX-1 MONETARY STATISTICS *CFA FRANC (MILLIONS)*										**IX-1 STATISTIQUES MONÉTAIRES** *FRANC CFA (MILLIONS)*
Money supply (M1)	1 620 200	1 933 543	2 265 700	2 093 378	2 297 249	2 615 034	3 060 500	3 274 900	3 654 816	Masse monétaire (M1)
Quasi-money	1 170 101	1 415 573	1 453 577	1 653 004	1 800 248	1 903 170	2 163 629	2 356 695	2 656 830	Quasi-monnaie
of which demand deposit	...	...	...	...	...	...	...	...	...	dont Monnaie scripturale
Net foreign assets	1 157 726	1 406 547	1 795 552	1 563 873	1 602 710	1 682 980	1 782 768	1 680 301	1 697 072	Avoirs extérieurs nets
Domestic credit	2 506 395	2 836 267	2 874 757	3 439 609	4 134 642	5 059 778	6 012 625	6 917 952	7 936 992	Crédit intérieur
of which claims on private sector	621 893	788 300	822 682	1 131 304	1 304 109	1 552 948	1 469 882	1 726 733	1 983 328	dont créances sur le secteur privé
of which claims on government sector, net	1 883 902	2 044 983	2 052 075	2 304 818	2 828 902	3 343 043	4 312 996	4 857 642	5 622 224	dont créances nettes sur le gouvernement
International reserves (millions US$)	3 267	3 624	4 316	3 928	4 225	3 158	3 029	2 618	3 181	Réserves internationales (millions $EU)
Average exchange rate (National currency per US$)	472	495	472	511	494	494	591	593	582	Taux de change (moyen) (monnaie nationale par $ EU)
IX-2 PUBLIC FINANCE *CFA FRANC (MILLIONS)*										**IX-2 FINANCES PUBLIQUES** *FRANC CFA (MILLIONS)*
Total Revenues and Grants	2 379 900	2 236 600	1 725 860	2 621 360	3 039 509	3 293 430	3 916 812	4 176 618	4 603 109	Recettes totales et dons
Direct taxes (on income, profits)	542 900	551 100	507 900	720 420	765 533	741 100	781 081	843 780	957 838	Taxes directes
Domestic indirect taxes revenues	503 300	476 900	265 600	382 040	401 578	463 221	696 569	937 481	997 701	Taxes Indirectes
Trade taxes	562 900	687 600	542 200	789 200	905 446	995 743	1 011 222	1 081 804	1 124 596	Taxes sur le commerce extérieur
Other taxes	186 500	212 900	177 500	321 300	336 040	373 258	465 983	528 429	547 250	Autres taxes
Other revenues	255 400	247 700	199 800	327 200	429 451	416 119	679 757	531 606	632 658	Autres recettes
Grants	328 900	60 400	32 860	81 200	201 460	303 989	282 200	253 518	343 066	Dons
Total Expenditures and Net Lending	2 147 253	2 464 357	2 208 735	3 054 046	3 385 584	3 669 539	4 469 802	5 014 557	5 655 090	Dépenses totales et prêts nets
Current expenditure	1 632 022	1 887 900	1 704 650	2 202 995	2 234 308	2 461 770	2 925 019	3 246 047	3 557 522	Dépenses courantes
Wages and Salaries	745 000	800 400	719 700	934 600	1 038 900	1 183 300	1 331 553	1 400 772	1 508 091	Rémunérations et salaires
Other purchases of goods and services	203 400	467 743	257 280	285 695	325 217	318 269	411 711	623 103	576 691	Achat de biens et services
Other current expenditure	467 551	491 600	413 060	572 100	545 211	656 108	767 072	836 405	1 106 892	Autres dépenses courantes
Current transfers	216 071	128 157	314 610	410 600	324 980	304 092	414 682	385 767	365 847	Transferts courants
Interest payments	168 500	194 457	219 285	232 951	214 779	213 600	297 505	360 135	433 640	Intérêts
Capital expenditure	334 331	348 600	285 700	615 800	934 198	994 169	1 247 278	1 408 375	1 663 928	Dépenses d'équipement
Net lending	12 400	33 400	- 900	2 300	2 300	...	...	...	...	Prêts nets
Fiscal balance	232 647	- 227 757	- 482 875	- 432 686	- 346 076	- 376 108	- 552 990	- 837 939	-1 051 981	Solde global y compris les dons
IX-3 BALANCE OF PAYMENTS *CFA FRANC (MILLIONS)*										**IX-3 BALANCE DES PAIEMENTS** *FRANC CFA (MILLIONS)*
Trade balance	2 010	1 794	2 816	1 566	1 479	1 915	1 874	1 818	...	Balance commerciale
Services Balance	- 757	- 893	- 842	- 994	- 1 026	- 1 068	- 1 194	- 1 179	...	Balance des services
Net primary income	- 442	- 453	- 466	- 470	- 445	- 449	- 596	- 638	...	Revenus primaires nets
Compensation of employees	...	80	81	82	83	83	84	73	...	Rémunération des salariés
Investment income	- 521	- 533	- 547	- 554	- 528	- 539	- 686	- 717	...	Revenus des investissements
Net secondary income	- 47	- 218	- 252	- 266	- 217	- 145	- 204	- 246	...	Revenus secondaires nets
Net official transfers	...	...	...	- 22	65	124	98	83	...	Transferts officiels nets
Workers' remittances	- 281	- 255	- 237	- 249	- 256	- 261	- 269	- 294	...	Envois de fonds des travailleurs
Other private transfers	...	2	- 1	5	- 25	- 9	- 33	...	...	Autres transferts privés
Current account balance	764	230	1 256	- 164	- 209	252	- 119	- 246	...	Solde du compte courant
Capital and financial account	- 746	- 218	- 807	- 61	175	49	406	198	...	Comptes de capital et financier
Capital account	106	584	73	4 141	95	139	156	111	...	Compte de capital
Financial account	- 853	- 801	- 880	- 4 202	80	- 90	250	87	...	Compte financier
Errors and omissions	- 17	- 12	- 21	- 39	37	- 27	- 39	- 6	...	Erreurs et omissions
Overall balance	128	235	429	- 264	3	274	249	- 53	...	Balance générale

COTE D'IVOIRE

X DEBT AND FINANCIAL FLOWS - DETTE ET FLUX FINANCIERS

	2009	2010	2011	2012	2013	2014	2015	2016	2017	
X-1 DEBT *US $ (MILLIONS)*										**X-1 DETTE EXTÉRIEURE** *$ E.U (MILLIONS)*
Total external debt	18 002	16 625	16 725	11 999	12 524	12 627	13 473	13 972	17 559	Dette extérieure totale
Private	...	...	...	...	...	...	...	...	...	Privée
Public	12 873	11 710	12 356	7 792	8 505	8 667	9 581	9 733	...	Publique
Total external debt service	1 883	1 560	3 119	1 227	1 635	1 145	1 290	1 531	...	Service de la dette extérieure
Present value of external debt	...	...	...	...	...	...	...	9 531	...	Valeur actuelle de la dette extérieure
Total government domestic debt, National currency (millions)	1 371	1 793	1 719	1 780	...	...	...	...	...	Dette publique intérieure
X-2 FINANCIAL FLOWS *US $ (MILLIONS)*										**X-2 FLUX FINANCIERS** *$ E.U (MILLIONS)*
Net Foreign Direct Investment Inflows	377	339	302	330	407	439	494	481	...	Investissements étranger direct (flux nets entrants)
Main origin of FDI inflows										**Principales origines de l'IDE entrant:**
France	122	91	- 11	117	...	...	...	...	...	France
Luxembourg	28	7	- 3	- 175	...	...	...	...	...	Luxembourg
Switzerland	105	114	19	43	...	...	...	...	...	Suisse
...	...	...	...	...	...	...	...	...	...	...
Belgium	3	7	11	3	...	...	...	...	...	Belgique
African countries	80	105	...	...	...	...	...	...	...	Pays africains
Net total official development assistance	2 402	844	1 436	2 908	1 273	925	653	658	...	Aide publique au développement (nette totale)
Main origin of net ODA										**Principales origines de l'APD nette**
United States	231	76	74	139	257	112	69	147	...	États-Unis
International Development Association [IDA]	185	186	165	108	126	192	246	179	...	International Development Association
...	...	...	...	...	...	...	...	...	...	...
France	1 199	139	553	1 279	81	68	22	16	...	France
...	...	...	...	...	...	...	...	...	...	...

SOURCES AND NOTES - SOURCES ET NOTES

External trade - Total exports, fob: UNCTAD	Commerce exterieur - Exportation, fab: CNUCED
External trade - Total import, cif: UNCTAD	Commerce exterieur - Imporations, caf: CNUCED
ODA: OECD	APD: OCDE
Monetary statistics: IMF	Statistiques monétaires: FMI
National Accounts: 2015:Revised;2016: Provisional	Comptes nationaux: 2015:Données Révisées; 2016: Données Provisoires
Poverty: World Bank	Pauvreté: Banque mondiale

AREA (km2)	2 344 860	SUPERFICIE (KM2)
CAPITAL CITY	Kinshasa	Kinshasa	CAPITALE
CURRENCY	Congolese Franc	Franc Congolais	MONNAIE

I SOCIAL AND DEMOGRAPHIC INDICATORS — INDICATEURS DEMOGRAPHIQUES ET SOCIAUX

Population	Year Année	Value Valeur	Charts Graphiques	Population
Population ('000)	2015	77 266.8		Population ('000)
Female (%)	2015	50.1		Féminine (%)
Urban (%)	2015	42.5		Urbaine (%)
Average annual growth rate	2015	3.1		Taux de croissance annuel
Active population ('000)	2015	28 542.3		Population active ('000)
Population by age group ('000)				Population par groupe d'âge ('000)
0-14 years	2015	35 537.3		0-14 ans
15-64 years	2015	39 439.4		15-64 ans
65+ years	2015	2 290.1		65+ ans
Economically active population in agriculture (%)	2015	54.2		Participation de la population active agricole (%)
Crude birth rate	2015	41.5		Taux brut de natalité
Crude death rate	2015	10.1		Taux brut de mortalité
Total fertility rate	2015	5.9		Indice synthétique de fécondité
Life expectancy at birth - Total (years)	2015	59.1		Espérance de vie à la naissance - Totale (années)
Dependency ratio - Total (%)	2015	95.9		Taux de dépendance - Total (%)
Health				**Santé**
Percentage of children under-five and underweight	2010	24.2		% d'enfants de moins de cinq ans avec insuffisance pondérale
Prevalence of undernourishment	...	...		Prévalence de la malnutrition
Under five mortality rate (per 1 000 live births)	2015	98.3		Taux de mortalité de moins de 5 ans (les deux sexes, pour 1000)
Infant mortality rate (per 1 000 live births)	2015	74.5		Taux de mortalité infantile (les deux sexes) par 1000
Neonatal mortality rate (per 1 000 live births)	2015	30.1		Le taux de mortalité néonatale (pour 1000 naissances vivantes)
Percentage of children provided the vaccines :				Pourcentage d'enfants vaccinés :
BCG	2014	90.0		BCG
DPT3	2014	80.0		DTC3
Polio	2011	78.0		polio
Measles	2014	77.0		rougeole
Percentage of mothers provided at least one antenatal care (%)	...	...		Pourcentage de mères ayant au moins reçu un soin prénatal (%)
Percentage of deliveries attended by skilled health personnel	2010	80.4		% d'accouchements assistés par un personnel de santé qualifié
Number of doctors (per 10,000 population)	2004	1.1		Nombre de médecins (pour 10.000 habitants)
Number of nurses (per 10,000 population)	2004	5.3		Nombre d'infirmiers (pour 10.000 habitants)
Hospital beds - Total (per 10,000 population)	2006	8.0		Nombre de lits d'hôpitaux - Total (pour 10 000)
Births registered (per 1,000)	2015	41.5		Naissances enregistrées (pour 1000)
Deaths registered (per 1,000)	2015	10.1		Décès enregistrés (pour 1000)
Budget allocation to health (%)	2014	4.3		Dépenses publiques consacrées à la santé (% du budget)
Education				**Education**
Enrolment in primary education (000)	2014	13 534.6		Scolarisation dans le primaire (000)
Female	2013	6 399.6		Féminine
Enrolment in secondary education (000)	2014	4 388.5		Scolarisation dans le secondaire (000)
Female	2014	1 674.2		Féminine
Enrolment in tertiary education (000)	2013	437.5		Scolarisation dans le tertiaire (000)
Female	2013	138.0		Féminine
Literacy rate	2007	61.2		Taux d'alphabétisation (deux sexes)
Male	2007	76.9		Masculin
Female	2007	46.1		Féminin
Pupil teacher ratio - primary	2011	37.4		Ratio élève-enseignant
Budget allocation to education (%)	2012	16.8		Dépenses publiques consacrées à l'enseignement (% du budget)
Poverty				**Pauvreté**
GNI per capita, PPP (current int. $)	2016	780.0		RNB par habitant, ($ PPA inter. courants)
Human Poverty Index (HPI-1) Value (%)	2007	24.3		Valeur de l'Indice de pauvreté (IPH-1) (%)
Population below Inter. poverty line ($2/day) (%)	2012	77.2		Population sous le seuil inter. de pauvreté (2$/Jour) (%)
Share of income held by richest 10%	2012	32.0		% de revenu des 10% plus riches
Share of income held by poorest 10%	2012	2.1		% de revenu des 10% plus pauvres
GINI index	2012	42.1		Indice de GINI

Population by age group - 2015

Population par groupe d'age - 2015

- 0-14 years
- 15-64 years
- 65+ years

3.0%
46.0%
51.0%

Percentage of children provided vaccines : - 2014

Pourcentage d'enfants vaccinés : - 2014

	90.0	80.0	78.0	77.0
	BCG / BCG	DPT3 / DTC3	Polio / polio (2011)	Measles / rougeole

Literacy rate (%) - 2007

Taux d'alphabétisation - 2007

76.9   46.1

■ Male ■ Female

GNI per capita, PPP (current international $)

RNB par habitant, ($ PPA internationaux courants)

630	650	700	740	780
2012	2013	2014	2015	2016

CONGO, DEM. REPUBLIC

GROSS DOMESTIC PRODUCT BY KIND OF ECONOMIC ACTIVITY AT CURRENT PRICES CONGOLEESE FRANC (MILLIONS) / PRODUIT INTÉRIEUR BRUT PAR BRANCHE D'ACTIVITÉ ÉCONOMIQUE AUX PRIX COURANTS FRANC CONGOLAIS (MILLIONS)

	2009	2010	2011	2012	2013	2014	2015	2016	2017	
Agriculture, hunting, forestry and Fishing	3 575 156	4 186 415	4 969 777	5 509 797	5 804 886	6 167 209	6 446 200	6 978 143	10 965 874	Agriculture, chasse sylviculture et Pêche
Mining and quarrying	1 356 595	3 388 941	4 790 423	5 186 984	6 057 094	7 332 235	6 214 400	6 419 161	9 567 747	Industries extractives
Manufacturing	2 850 452	3 169 171	3 649 184	4 140 583	4 623 444	5 167 797	5 753 400	6 852 324	10 840 274	Industries manufacturières
Electricity, gas & water	165 381	211 581	232 476	258 361	277 992	299 540	188 800	355 050	544 947	Electricité, gaz et eau
Construction	613 367	788 881	1 055 675	1 264 563	1 448 505	1 485 564	1 509 100	980 966	1 993 880	Bâtiments et travaux publics
Wholesale & retail trade, restaurants, hotels	1 708 910	2 080 030	2 391 108	2 842 133	3 110 795	3 299 680	3 763 200	4 129 906	6 690 797	Commerce de gros et de détail, restaurants et hôtels
Finance, insurance, real estate, etc.	1 183 700	1 487 205	1 697 813	1 889 869	2 027 803	2 268 802	2 762 400	2 716 312	4 287 753	Banques, assurances, affaires immobilières
Transport and communications	1 795 067	2 092 047	2 360 802	2 701 538	2 985 170	3 208 974	3 872 900	3 859 941	4 764 420	Transport(s) et communications
Public administration and defense	1 062 356	1 212 268	1 400 159	1 497 674	1 578 932	1 732 629	1 922 100	1 963 528	3 005 910	Administrations publiques et défense
Education	31 901	29 970	9 244	9 589	10 109	11 100	12 700	13 891	24 905	Education
Health And Social Work	9 866	10 053	8 620	3 275	3 453	5 900	6 600	7 594	12 961	Santé et Actions Sociales
Other services	...	...	...	...	...	...	...	...	...	Autres services
Less Imputed Service Charges	- 145 615	- 170 885	- 193 894	- 213 797	- 203 254	- 236 428	- 311 400	- 291 575	- 461 847	Moins Services d'intermédiation financière
Gross domestic product at factor cost / basic prices	14 207 135	18 485 677	22 371 387	25 090 569	27 724 927	30 743 003	32 140 400	33 985 241	52 237 620	Produit intérieur brut aux couts des facteurs / prix de base
Plus: Indirect Taxes / taxes on products, less subsidies	894 052	1 051 000	1 388 038	1 863 988	2 326 252	2 481 098	2 664 400	2 696 975	2 886 705	Plus taxes indirectes/impôts sur les produits, moins les subventions

EXPENDITURE ON GROSS DOMESTIC PRODUCT AT CURRENT PURCHASER'S VALUES CONGOLEESE FRANC (MILLIONS) / EMPLOI DU PRODUIT INTÉRIEUR BRUT AUX PRIX COURANTS D'ACQUISITION FRANC CONGOLAIS (MILLIONS)

	2009	2010	2011	2012	2013	2014	2015	2016	2017	
Government final consumption	1 692 459	2 312 825	2 559 922	3 491 076	3 770 362	3 882 500	4 204 500	4 931 024	3 038 146	Consommation finale des administrations publiques
Private final consumption	12 954 512	16 741 724	20 011 417	22 204 437	22 882 539	23 295 600	24 042 500	27 751 714	42 733 661	Consommation finale privée
Gross fixed capital formation	2 188 625	2 309 233	2 763 433	3 215 125	4 609 657	7 678 400	7 210 100	6 917 319	11 343 716	Formation brute de capital fixe
Change in inventories	10 627	11 612	18 236	21 635	31 019	37 400	54 200	88 174	119 114	Variation des stocks
Exports of goods and services	5 021 005	8 866 530	10 211 300	9 031 062	11 176 309	12 237 100	9 684 800	8 987 832	19 626 114	Exportations de biens et services
Less imports of goods and services	6 766 041	10 705 248	11 804 884	11 008 777	12 418 706	13 906 900	10 391 300	11 993 848	21 736 424	Moins importations de biens et services
GDP at purchasers' values	15 101 188	19 536 677	23 759 425	26 954 557	30 051 179	33 224 100	34 804 800	36 682 215	55 124 325	PIB aux prix d'acquisition

GROSS DOMESTIC PRODUCT BY KIND OF ECONOMIC ACTIVITY AT CONSTANT PRICES ANNUAL GROWTH RATES (%) / PRODUIT INTÉRIEUR BRUT PAR BRANCHE D'ACTIVITÉ ECONOMIQUE AUX PRIX CONSTANTS TAUX DE CROISSANCE ANNUEL (%)

	2009	2010	2011	2012	2013	2014	2015	2016	2017	
Agriculture, hunting, forestry and Fishing	2.8	3.6	3.6	3.5	4.2	4.7	5.0	2.9	1.6	Agriculture, chasse sylviculture et Pêche
Mining and quarrying	0.9	235.2	23.8	9.8	10.1	19.3	9.5	- 5.0	7.8	Industries extractives
Manufacturing	1.9	- 35.5	1.8	5.2	10.1	9.9	9.3	11.8	3.5	Industries manufacturières
Electricity, gas & water	- 16.0	6.4	- 3.2	6.8	7.2	6.3	- 1.2	5.6	5.3	Electricité, gaz et eau
Construction	5.8	1.3	17.9	15.1	14.1	1.2	1.1	- 25.5	31.4	Bâtiments et travaux publics
Wholesale & retail trade, restaurants, hotels	9.5	- 2.7	0.8	11.2	8.2	4.8	6.6	10.8	4.6	Commerce de gros et de détail, restaurants et hôtels
Finance, insurance, real estate, etc.	3.6	- 5.3	1.9	4.3	6.5	10.9	9.4	3.1	- 0.9	Banques, assurances, affaires immobilières
Transport and communications	- 2.5	- 5.3	0.6	5.9	9.5	6.0	10.1	3.3	2.5	Transport(s) et communications
Public administration and defense	7.2	- 6.7	1.9	- 0.8	4.3	7.8	5.6	5.3	- 1.0	Administrations publiques et défense
Education	45.4	- 11.2	- 13.5	- 9.5	4.3	4.6	6.8	5.9	0.4	Education
Health And Social Work	22.6	60.2	- 28.1	- 28.7	4.8	17.6	5.8	6.8	3.4	Santé et Actions Sociales
Other services	...	...	...	...	...	...	...	...	...	Autres services
Less Imputed Service Charges	16.6	- 3.4	1.3	2.3	- 6.0	14.7	15.3	21.2	- 14.7	Moins Services d'intermédiation financière
Gross domestic product at factor cost / basic prices	2.9	7.3	6.9	7.0	8.3	9.6	7.8	1.8	4.7	Produit intérieur brut aux couts des facteurs / prix de base
Plus: Indirect Taxes / taxes on products, less subsidies	1.7	1.9	6.3	11.5	14.1	5.2	6.7	- 1.8	- 32.2	Plus taxes indirectes/impôts sur les produits, moins les subventions
Gross domestic product at market prices	2.9	7.1	6.9	7.1	8.5	9.5	7.7	1.7	3.6	Produit intérieur brut aux prix du marché

EXPENDITURE ON GROSS DOMESTIC PRODUCT AT CONSTANT PURCHASERS' VALUES ANNUAL GROWTH RATES (%) / EMPLOIS DU PRODUIT INTÉRIEUR BRUT AUX PRIX CONSTANTS D'ACQUISITION TAUX DE CROISSANCE ANNUEL (%)

	2009	2010	2011	2012	2013	2014	2015	2016	2017	
Government final consumption	- 17.2	63.6	- 19.3	72.2	4.6	4.8	3.6	4.8	14.8	Consommation finale des administrations publiques
Private final consumption	2.3	15.9	2.5	- 2.0	12.7	7.8	7.1	1.8	- 9.3	Consommation finale privée
Gross fixed capital formation	66.2	20.8	21.9	33.7	- 0.8	5.4	0.9	- 11.0	19.7	Formation brute de capital fixe
Exports of goods and services	- 28.3	1.1	16.0	64.8	10.5	21.4	8.6	- 5.0	9.2	Exportations de biens et services
Less imports of goods and services	0.2	59.3	2.9	49.5	8.0	8.7	2.6	- 9.9	- 2.7	Moins importations de biens et services

III INFLATION

Annual growth rates (%)	2009	2010	2011	2012	2013	2014	2015	2016	2017	Taux de croissance annuel (%)
All item	29.0	17.2	12.6	3.7	1.3	1.3	1.3	1.1	1.7	Ensemble
of which:										dont:
Food and non-alcoholic beverages	30.3	20.1	5.3	4.2	1.2	1.6	1.7	1.3	1.6	Alimentation et boissons non alcoolisés
Alcoholic beverages, tobacco and narcotics	...	...	...	5.6	0.1	0.9	0.6	1.0	1.4	Boissons alcoolisées et tabacs
Clothing and footwear	53.7	14.5	7.5	2.2	2.2	1.4	1.2	1.3	1.9	Habillement et chaussures
Housing, water, electricity, gas and other fuels	20.2	21.4	12.4	0.4	0.3	1.2	1.2	2.5	3.7	Logement, eau, électricité, gaz et autres combustibles
Furnishings, household equipment and routine household maintenance	...	...	...	4.6	0.6	0.3	0.4	1.2	1.5	Meubles, articles de ménage et entretien courant
Health	15.7	11.8	22.1	1.6	1.6	0.9	0.7	1.1	1.9	Santé
Transport	53.6	12.5	2.8	13.3	1.8	1.1	1.1	1.3	1.4	Transport
Communication	29.6	1.8	12.8	0.8	...	0.2	0.2	1.1	1.5	Communication
Recreation and culture	...	...	...	5.0	0.9	0.3	0.3	1.2	1.6	Loisirs et culture
Education	...	...	...	3.7	3.7	0.4	0.1	1.1	1.9	Enseignement
Restaurants and hotels	...	...	...	4.5	0.2	0.9	- 0.7	1.0	1.2	Restaurants et hôtels
Miscellaneous goods and services	...	...	...	3.2	0.8	1.1	- 0.1	1.4	2.1	Biens et Services divers

IV AGRICULTURAL PRODUCTION - PRODUCTION AGRICOLE

TONNES (THOUSAND)	2009	2010	2011	2012	2013	2014	2015	2016	2017	Tonnes (milliers)
Cassava	15 054	15 014	15 634	16 069	16 517	16 963	17 434	36 804	...	Manioc
Maize	1 156	1 156	1 782	1 893	1 938	1 986	2 015	2 138	...	Maïs
Plantains	1 200	1 300	2 778	2 856	2 935	3 815	4 160	5 718	...	Bananes plantains
Groundnuts, with shell	371	388	389	405	405	413	422	439	...	Arachides (en coques)
Rice, paddy	317	318	755	709	645	811	1 020	1 295	...	Riz, Paddy

V MINING PRODUCTION - PRODUCTION MINIERE

	2009	2010	2011	2012	2013	2014	2015	2016	2017	
Copper ores and concentrates - Production, metric tons (thousands)	310	438	499	620	920	1 030	1 039	1 024	1 095	Minerais de cuivre et leurs concentrés - Production, tonnes métriques (milliers)
Diamonds and other precious stones, unworked - Production, carat (thousands)	21 298	20 166	19 249	21 524	16 653	16 455	15 753	15 523	18 903	Diamants et autres pierres gemmes (précieuses), bruts - Production, carat (milliers)
Cobalt - Production, Tonnes (thousands)	56	97	99	85	77	76	84	69	82	Cobalt - Production, tonnes (milliers)

VI ENERGY - ENERGIE

	2009	2010	2011	2012	2013	2014	2015	2016	2017	
Total electricity generation (GWh)	7 526	7 600	7 273	7 565	8 195	8 691	8 349	...	...	Production électrique totale (GWh)
of which										dont
Production of electricity from fossil fuels (GWh)	6	9	35	36	38	39	40	...	...	Production d'électricité à partir de combustibles fossiles (GWh)
Production of hydro electricity (GWh)	7 520	7 591	7 235	7 526	8 153	8 652	8 309	...	...	Production d'électricité d'origine hydraulique (GWh)
Production of electricity from solar, wind, tide, wave and other sources (GWh)	...	...	3	3	5	7	10	...	...	Production d'électricité d'origine solaire, éolienne, marée motrice et autres (GWh)

VII TOURISM AND INFRASTRUCTURE - TOURISME ET INFRASTUCTURE

	2009	2010	2011	2012	2013	2014	2015	2016	2017	
VII-1 Tourism										**VII-1 Tourisme**
International tourist arrivals (thousands)	53	81	186	167	191	195	215	232	240	Arrivées de touristes internationaux (milliers)
Rooms in hotels and similar establishments (thousands)	...	1	1	2	3	...	...	...	...	Chambres d'hôtels et établissements assimilés (milliers)
Overnight stays (thousands)	156	113	103	114	103	115	134	146	152	Nuitées (milliers)
Tourism receipts (US$ thousand)	18 169	8 100	8 630	5 223	6 359	34 369	76	3 255	2 808	Recettes touristiques (milliers de $ EU)
Total contribution to GDP (%)	2.3	1.6	1.3	2.2	2.0	1.8	1.6	1.8	1.8	Contribution totale au PIB (%)
Total contribution to Employment (%)	2.0	1.2	1.1	1.9	1.7	1.5	1.4	1.5	1.5	Contribution totale à l'emploi (%)
VII-2 Infrastructure										**VII-2 Infrastructure**
Paved road (% of total)	...	...	...	...	5.5	...	...	...	...	Routes asphaltées (% du total)
Total network (Railways-km)	3 641	3 641	3 641	3 641	3 641	3 641	...	...	...	Réseau total voies ferrées-Km
Main telephone lines (per 100 inhabitants)	...	...	...	...	...	...	...	...	...	Lignes téléphoniques fixes (pour 100 habitants)
Mobile cellular subscribers (per 100 inhabitants)	15.6	19.0	24.5	30.6	41.8	53.5	53.0	39.5	...	Abonnés aux téléphones mobiles (pour 100 habitants)
Internet users per 100 inhabitants	0.6	0.7	1.2	1.7	2.2	3.0	3.8	6.2	...	Utilisateurs Internet pour 100 Habitants
Fixed (wired)-broadband subscriptions per 100 inhabitants	...	...	...	...	...	...	...	...	...	Abonnements à l'Internet fixe (filaire) à large bande pour 100 habitants, par débit

VIII EXTERNAL TRADE - COMMERCE EXTERIEUR

US$ (MILLIONS) EXPORTS, FOB	2009	2010	2011	2012	2013	2014	2015	2016	2017	$ E.U (MILLIONS) EXPORTATIONS, FÀB
Exports - Total	3 500	5 300	6 600	6 300	6 300	6 600	5 800	5 526	...	Exportations - Total
Exports to Africa	753	1 368	1 544	1 346	1 814	1 551	1 268	230	...	Exportations vers l'Afrique
Main products										**Principaux produits**
Copper	744	1 763	2 264	2 985	2 527	2 886	2 806	2 751	...	Cuivre
Copper ores and concentrates; copper mattes, cemen	508	625	864	833	1 210	1 100	407	46	...	Minerais et concentrés de cuivre; mattes de cuivre, cemen
Miscellaneous no-ferrous base metals for metallur.	352	521	440	490	472	581	644	998	...	Métaux communs non ferreux divers pour métallur.
Ores and concentrates of base metals, n.e.s.	710	919	839	539	439	551	674	367	...	Minerais et concentrés de métaux communs, n.d.a.
Petroleum oils, oils from bitumin. materials, crude	563	498	1 029	631	756	768	290	346	...	Huiles de pétrole, huiles de bitume. matériaux bruts
Main destinations										**Principales destinations**
Belgium	287	267	332	318	247	245	253	398	...	Belgique
China	1 389	2 276	2 866	3 071	2 067	2 168	2 288	2 737	...	Chine
Republic of Korea	28	89	135	206	167	202	263	629	...	Corée, République de
Saudi Arabia	23	177	407	537	493	637	525	...	...	Arabie Saoudite
Zambia	633	1 180	1 269	1 193	1 581	1 246	979	...	...	Zambie
IMPORTS, CIF										**IMPORTS, CIF**
Imports - Total	3 900	4 500	5 500	6 100	6 300	6 500	6 200	5 648	...	Importations - Total (millions)
Imports from Africa	1 826	2 338	2 569	3 085	3 388	2 940	2 284	1 804	...	Importations en provenance de l'Afrique
Main products										**Principaux produits**
Civil engineering & contractors' plant & equipment	117	117	132	196	200	206	168	157	...	Génie civil et installations et équipements des entrepreneurs
Inorganic chemical elements, oxides & halogen salts	43	55	77	148	312	300	95	17	...	Eléments chimiques inorganiques, oxydes et sels halogénés
Medicaments (incl. veterinary medicaments)	151	135	139	157	176	164	239	312	...	Médicaments (y compris les médicaments vétérinaires)
Motor vehic. for transport of goods, special purpo.	77	110	150	207	216	151	146	117	...	Véhicule à moteur pour le transport de marchandises, spécial.
Petroleum oils or bituminous minerals > 70 % oil	262	348	426	350	295	334	202	167	...	Huiles de pétrole ou de minéraux bitumineux> 70% d'huile
Main origin										**Principales provenances**
Belgium	390	381	443	437	418	399	498	531	...	Belgique
China	384	505	833	813	812	1 286	1 474	1 372	...	Chine
France	275	242	246	267	256	197	283	364	...	France
South Africa	686	906	1 103	1 437	1 167	1 173	935	1 082	...	Afrique du Sud
Zambia	364	378	493	739	1 136	850	569	...	...	Zambie

RÉP. DÉMOCRATIQUE DU CONGO

IX FINANCIAL AND MONETARY STATISTICS - FINANCES ET STATISTIQUES MONETAIRES

	2009	2010	2011	2012	2013	2014	2015	2016	2017	
IX-1 MONETARY STATISTICS *CONGOLEESE FRANC (MILLIONS)*										**IX-1 STATISTIQUES MONÉTAIRES** *FRANC CONGOLAIS (MILLIONS)*
Money supply (M1)	1 501 869	1 964 597	2 403 325	2 927 433	3 470 705	3 907 420	4 317 891	5 257 623	7 356 800	Masse monétaire (M1)
Quasi-money	228 270	259 737	528 870	724 484	920 250	1 238 713	1 397 933	1 684 989	2 483 753	Quasi-monnaie
of which demand deposit	...	...	...	...	...	...	...	...	...	dont Monnaie scripturale
Net foreign assets	- 48 762	880 890	849 517	1 403 482	1 455 234	1 566 108	1 381 266	1 280 818	2 918 831	Avoirs extérieurs nets
Domestic credit	772 437	157 966	1 878 078	1 760 158	2 186 805	2 629 243	3 158 182	4 353 801	4 923 144	Crédit intérieur
of which claims on private sector	- 70 169	- 658 424	765 945	304 318	462 530	546 865	789 162	1 340 598	1 271 590	dont créances sur le secteur privé
of which claims on government sector, net	800 396	729 249	955 836	1 296 874	1 576 636	1 899 741	2 206 920	2 772 876	3 449 136	dont créances nettes sur le gouvernement
International reserves (millions US$)	999	1 085	1 232	1 578	1 871	1 722	1 225	626	631	Réserves internationales (millions $EU)
Average exchange rate (National currency per US$)	810	906	919	920	920	925	926	1 010	1 464	Taux de change (moyen) (monnaie nationale par $ EU)
IX-2 PUBLIC FINANCE *CONGOLEESE FRANC (MILLIONS)*										**IX-2 FINANCES PUBLIQUES** *FRANC CONGOLAIS (MILLIONS)*
Total Revenues and Grants	2 022 768	2 914 771	3 088 669	4 174 219	4 394 665	6 179 892	6 044 480	5 019 261	6 087 412	Recettes totales et dons
Direct taxes (on income, profits)	388 499	578 628	678 564	715 414	988 048	1 181 141	1 140 426	936 423	1 217 350	Taxes directes
Domestic indirect taxes revenues	573 906	772 446	1 008 515	1 377 888	1 294 695	1 742 634	1 890 052	1 420 161	1 507 791	Taxes Indirectes
Trade taxes	216 841	277 813	381 324	471 674	540 382	635 177	653 704	649 145	852 057	Taxes sur le commerce extérieur
Other taxes	410 184	629 463	598 300	1 073 048	1 049 467	1 176 560	1 252 236	962 799	1 422 177	Autres taxes
Other revenues	...	...	...	...	...	...	...	...	...	Autres recettes
Grants	433 338	656 421	421 965	536 194	522 072	1 444 380	1 108 062	1 050 733	1 088 037	Dons
Total Expenditures and Net Lending	1 883 583	3 110 983	3 323 353	3 702 547	3 477 003	5 770 601	6 153 412	5 366 823	6 699 023	Dépenses totales et prêts nets
Current expenditure	1 353 335	1 803 878	2 421 495	2 617 176	2 934 169	3 618 284	3 946 882	3 686 140	4 748 790	Dépenses courantes
Wages and Salaries	541 424	772 502	1 088 774	1 220 240	1 407 936	1 558 777	1 790 638	1 956 711	2 207 134	Rémunérations et salaires
Other purchases of goods and services	508 480	724 514	884 984	983 440	1 216 212	1 012 310	1 169 900	1 130 129	1 561 405	Achat de biens et services
Other current expenditure	...	...	...	...	...	...	...	...	...	Autres dépenses courantes
Current transfers	303 432	306 861	447 736	413 497	310 021	1 047 197	986 344	599 300	980 251	Transferts courants
Interest payments	48 978	56 754	169 844	158 118	155 206	117 904	114 147	103 077	248 283	Intérêts
Capital expenditure	481 269	1 250 351	732 015	927 253	387 628	2 034 413	2 092 383	1 577 606	1 701 951	Dépenses d'équipement
Net lending	...	...	...	...	...	...	...	...	...	Prêts nets
Fiscal balance	139 185	- 196 211	- 234 684	471 673	917 662	409 291	- 108 932	- 347 562	- 611 611	Solde global y compris les dons
IX-3 BALANCE OF PAYMENTS *CONGOLEESE FRANC (MILLIONS)*										**IX-3 BALANCE DES PAIEMENTS** *FRANC CONGOLAIS (MILLIONS)*
Trade balance	466 138	394 407	511 485	60 799	739 900	- 356 302	- 268 384	- 230 895	600 781	Balance commerciale
Services Balance	- 941 187	-2 059 968	-1 976 707	-1 879 070	-2 114 507	-2 560 476	-1 715 341	-1 702 331	-2 711 092	Balance des services
Net primary income	- 628 180	- 947 737	-1 009 454	- 963 066	-2 648 502	- 557 959	- 747 015	- 751 508	-1 805 561	Revenus primaires nets
Compensation of employees	- 9 207	- 37 593	68 958	- 39 631	- 94 543	- 67 240	- 11 765	- 12 649	350	Rémunération des salariés
Investment income	- 618 973	- 910 145	-1 078 412	- 923 436	-2 553 959	- 490 719	- 735 251	- 738 859	-1 805 911	Revenus des investissements
Net secondary income	1 129 883	763 388	1 297 239	1 622 518	1 164 035	1 880 928	1 299 516	1 336 840	2 137 656	Revenus secondaires nets
Net official transfers	...	...	...	...	...	...	...	...	...	Transferts officiels nets
Workers' remittances	...	...	...	...	...	...	...	...	...	Envois de fonds des travailleurs
Other private transfers	...	...	...	...	...	...	...	...	...	Autres transferts privés
Current account balance	26 655	-1 849 910	-1 177 438	-1 158 820	-2 859 075	-1 593 808	-1 431 223	-1 347 894	-1 778 216	Solde du compte courant
Capital and financial account	- 872 564	-1 990 435	565 257	- 237 012	-2 520 964	-1 012 642	-1 165 564	906 696	3 801 306	Comptes de capital et financier
Capital account	116 126	- 145 507	857 510	447 160	177 252	296 574	233 505	- 47 530	682 085	Compte de capital
Financial account	- 988 690	-1 844 928	- 292 253	- 684 172	-2 698 216	-1 309 216	-1 399 070	954 227	3 119 221	Compte financier
Errors and omissions	- 199 194	150 489	27 675	27 489	- 16 394	- 11 982	- 201 352	242 440	- 443 401	Erreurs et omissions
Overall balance	-1 045 103	-3 689 856	- 584 506	-1 368 343	-5 396 433	-2 618 432	-2 798 139	- 198 757	1 579 689	Balance générale

CONGO, DEM. REPUBLIC

X DEBT AND FINANCIAL FLOWS - DETTE ET FLUX FINANCIERS

	2009	2010	2011	2012	2013	2014	2015	2016	2017	
X-1 DEBT *US $ (MILLIONS)*										**X-1 DETTE EXTÉRIEURE** *$ E.U (MILLIONS)*
Total external debt	13 705	5 420	5 566	5 911	6 386	6 777	8 824	9 911	11 651	Dette extérieure totale
Private	1 422	480	795	803	884	1 591	3 698	5 037	...	Privée
Public	12 283	4 783	4 652	4 940	5 204	4 923	4 797	4 542	...	Publique
Total external debt service	188	177	160	182	195	213	267	349	...	Service de la dette extérieure
Present value of external debt	...	...	...	...	...	...	...	3 430	...	Valeur actuelle de la dette extérieure
Total government domestic debt, National currency (millions)	...	...	...	...	...	...	...	...	...	Dette publique intérieure
X-2 FINANCIAL FLOWS *US $ (MILLIONS)*										**X-2 FLUX FINANCIERS** *$ E.U (MILLIONS)*
Net Foreign Direct Investment Inflows	664	2 939	1 687	3 312	2 098	1 843	1 674	1 205	...	Investissements étranger direct (flux nets entrants)
Main origin of FDI inflows										**Principales origines de l'IDE entrant:**
Belgium	17	19	13	- 104	...	...	...	...	...	Belgique
...	...	...	...	...	...	...	...	...	...	...
...	...	...	...	...	...	...	...	...	...	...
Luxembourg	4	1	1	- 385	...	...	...	...	...	Luxembourg
...	...	...	...	...	...	...	...	...	...	...
African countries	...	...	...	...	...	...	...	...	...	Pays africains
Net total official development assistance	2 358	3 484	5 526	2 846	2 584	2 400	2 599	2 107	...	Aide publique au développement (nette totale)
Main origin of net ODA										**Principales origines de l'APD nette**
	...	...	...	...	...	...	...	...		
	...	...	...	...	...	...	...	...		
	...	...	...	...	...	...	...	...		
	...	...	...	...	...	...	...	...		
	...	...	...	...	...	...	...	...		

SOURCES AND NOTES - SOURCES ET NOTES

External trade - Total exports, fob: UNCTAD

External trade - Total import, cif: UNCTAD

ODA: OECD

Monetary statistics: IMF

National Accounts: 2012-2015:Estimates 2016-2017:Provisional

Poverty: World Bank

Commerce exterieur - Exportation, fab: CNUCED

Commerce exterieur - Imporations, caf: CNUCED

APD: OCDE

Statistiques monétaires: FMI

Comptes nationaux: 2012-2015:Estimées 2016-2017:Provisoire

Pauvreté: Banque mondiale

AREA (km2)		23 200		**SUPERFICIE (KM2)**	
CAPITAL CITY	Djibouti		Djibouti	**CAPITALE**	
CURRENCY	Djibouti Franc		Franc Djiboutien	**MONNAIE**	

I SOCIAL AND DEMOGRAPHIC INDICATORS — INDICATEURS DEMOGRAPHIQUES ET SOCIAUX

	Year Année	Value Valeur	Charts Graphiques	
Population				**Population**
Population ('000)	2016	992.6		Population ('000)
Female (%)	2016	0.5		Féminine (%)
Urban (%)	2015	78.4		Urbaine (%)
Average annual growth rate	2016	2.8		Taux de croissance annuel
Active population ('000)	2015	144.0		Population active ('000)
Population by age group ('000)				Population par groupe d'âge ('000)
0-14 years	2015	336.7		0-14 ans
15-64 years	2015	634.8		15-64 ans
65+ years	2015	30.6		65+ ans
Economically active population in agriculture (%)	2015	218.8		Participation de la population active agricole (%)
Crude birth rate	2016	13.1		Taux brut de natalité
Crude death rate	2016	1.2		Taux brut de mortalité
Total fertility rate	2015	3.1		Indice synthétique de fécondité
Life expectancy at birth - Total (years)	2016	52.9		Espérance de vie à la naissance - Totale (années)
Dependency ratio - Total (%)	2015	57.9		Taux de dépendance - Total (%)
Health				**Santé**
Percentage of children under-five and underweight	2012	29.8		% d'enfants de moins de cinq ans avec insuffisance pondérale
Prevalence of undernourishment	2015	15.9		Prévalence de la malnutrition
Under five mortality rate (per 1 000 live births)	2015	65.3		Taux de mortalité de moins de 5 ans (les deux sexes, pour 1000)
Infant mortality rate (per 1 000 live births)	2015	54.2		Taux de mortalité infantile (les deux sexes) par 1000
Neonatal mortality rate (per 1 000 live births)	2015	33.4		Le taux de mortalité néonatale (pour 1000 naissances vivantes)
Percentage of children provided the vaccines :				Pourcentage d'enfants vaccinés :
BCG	2015	89.9		BCG
DPT3	2014	78.0		DTC3
Polio	2013	94.4		polio
Measles	2014	71.0		rougeole
Percentage of mothers provided at least one antenatal care (%)	2012	87.7		Pourcentage de mères ayant au moins reçu un soin prénatal (%)
Percentage of deliveries attended by skilled health personnel	2006	92.9		% d'accouchements assistés par un personnel de santé qualifié
Number of doctors (per 10,000 population)	2015	0.8		Nombre de médecins (pour 10.000 habitants)
Number of nurses (per 10,000 population)	2015	3.1		Nombre d'infirmiers (pour 10.000 habitants)
Hospital beds - Total (per 10,000 population)	2015	13.7		Nombre de lits d'hôpitaux - Total (pour 10 000)
Births registered (per 1,000)	2016	13.0		Naissances enregistrées (pour 1000)
Deaths registered (per 1,000)	2016	1.2		Décès enregistrés (pour 1000)
Budget allocation to health (%)	2013	14.1		Dépenses publiques consacrées à la santé (% du budget)
Education				**Education**
Enrolment in primary education (000)	2016	61.8		Scolarisation dans le primaire (000)
Female	2016	28.8		Féminine
Enrolment in secondary education (000)	2016	39.1		Scolarisation dans le secondaire (000)
Female	2016	17.6		Féminine
Enrolment in tertiary education (000)	2016	21.7		Scolarisation dans le tertiaire (000)
Female	2016	9.7		Féminine
Literacy rate	...	...		Taux d'alphabétisation (deux sexes)
Male	...	...		Masculin
Female	...	...		Féminin
Pupil teacher ratio - primary	2016	26.2		Ratio élève-enseignant
Budget allocation to education (%)	2013	8.8		Dépenses publiques consacrées à l'enseignement (% du budget)
Poverty				**Pauvreté**
GNI per capita, PPP (current int. $)	2005	2200.0		RNB par habitant, ($ PPA inter. courants)
Human Poverty Index (HPI-1) Value (%)	2007	25.6		Valeur de l'Indice de pauvreté (IPH-1) (%)
Population below Inter. poverty line ($2/day) (%)	2012	18.3		Population sous le seuil inter. de pauvreté (2$/Jour) (%)
Share of income held by richest 10%	2012	34.4		% de revenu des 10% plus riches
Share of income held by poorest 10%	2012	1.3		% de revenu des 10% plus pauvres
GINI index	2012	45.1		Indice de GINI

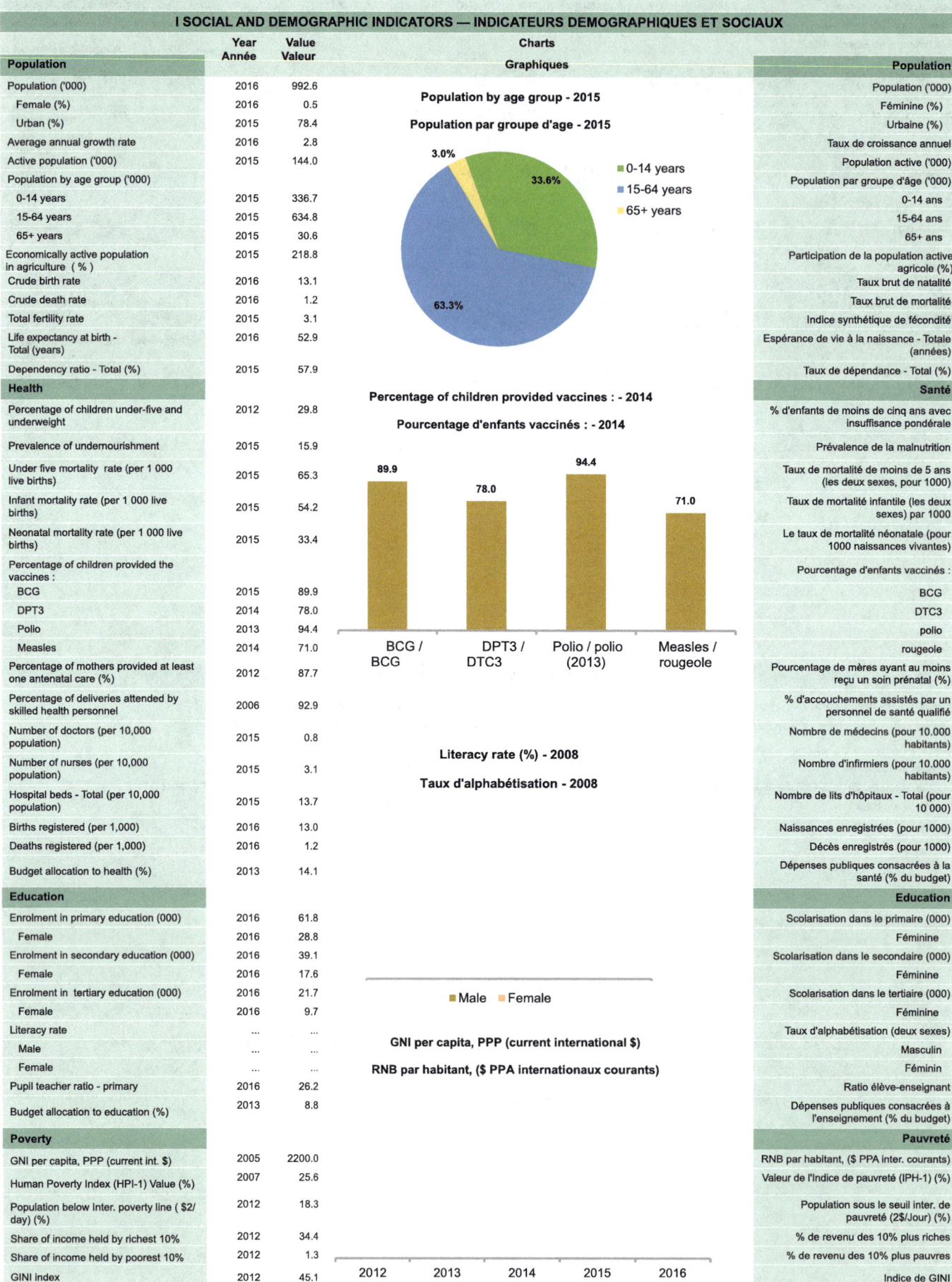

Population by age group - 2015
Population par groupe d'age - 2015

0-14 years — 33.6%
15-64 years — 63.3%
65+ years — 3.0%

Percentage of children provided vaccines : - 2014
Pourcentage d'enfants vaccinés : - 2014

BCG / BCG — 89.9
DPT3 / DTC3 — 78.0
Polio / polio (2013) — 94.4
Measles / rougeole — 71.0

Literacy rate (%) - 2008
Taux d'alphabétisation - 2008

Male   Female

GNI per capita, PPP (current international $)
RNB par habitant, ($ PPA internationaux courants)

2012   2013   2014   2015   2016

	2009	2010	2011	2012	2013	2014	2015	2016	2017	
GROSS DOMESTIC PRODUCT BY KIND OF ECONOMIC ACTIVITY AT CURRENT PRICES *DJIBOUTI FRANC (MILLIONS)*										**PRODUIT INTÉRIEUR BRUT PAR BRANCHE D'ACTIVITÉ ÉCONOMIQUE AUX PRIX COURANTS** *FRANC DJIBOUTIEN (MILLIONS)*
Agriculture, hunting , forestry and Fishing	6 613	6 819	7 006	7 777	8 664	8 332	9 251	9 899	...	Agriculture, chasse sylviculture et Pêche
Mining and quarrying	606	654	577	594	861	913	972	1 040	...	Industries extractives
Manufacturing	5 934	6 326	6 640	7 069	7 542	6 063	6 631	7 463	...	Industries manufacturières
Electricity, gas & water	4 884	5 446	6 328	10 295	13 527	14 339	15 271	16 340	...	Electricité, gaz et eau
Construction	21 532	23 198	21 908	22 529	26 324	38 952	38 465	42 397	...	Bâtiments et travaux publics
Wholesale & retail trade, restaurants, hotels	32 953	34 162	36 162	38 307	42 526	47 166	52 116	56 723	...	Commerce de gros et de détail, restaurants et hôtels
Finance, insurance, real estate, etc.	19 836	18 440	19 141	24 205	14 957	15 854	16 885	18 067	...	Banques, assurances, affaires immobilières
Transport and communications	45 764	48 427	54 773	59 258	65 785	71 957	78 884	86 337	...	Transport(s) et communications
Public administration and defense	28 551	32 323	34 738	37 794	45 866	48 618	51 778	55 403	...	Administrations publiques et défense
Education	...	...	...	...	...	...	...	...	...	Education
Health And Social Work	...	...	...	...	...	...	...	...	...	Santé et Actions Sociales
Other services	2 453	7 694	12 184	11 577	7 771	4 599	7 157	10 277	...	Autres services
Less Imputed Service Charges	...	...	...	...	...	...	...	...	...	Moins Services d'intermédiation financière
Gross domestic product at factor cost / basic prices	169 126	183 489	199 457	219 405	233 823	256 793	277 410	303 946	...	Produit intérieur brut aux couts des facteurs / prix de base
Plus: Indirect Taxes / taxes on products, less subsidies	17 323	17 089	20 765	21 164	24 835	25 610	31 278	32 215	...	Plus taxes indirectes/impôts sur les produits, moins les subventions
EXPENDITURE ON GROSS DOMESTIC PRODUCT AT CURRENT PURCHASER'S VALUES *DJIBOUTI FRANC (MILLIONS)*										**EMPLOI DU PRODUIT INTÉRIEUR BRUT AUX PRIX COURANTS D'ACQUISITION** *FRANC DJIBOUTIEN (MILLIONS)*
Government final consumption	40 635	47 786	51 383	57 143	61 191	63 674	68 938	76 977	...	Consommation finale des administrations publiques
Private final consumption	115 594	124 497	162 501	180 199	200 662	242 530	267 085	285 095	...	Consommation finale privée
Gross fixed capital formation	58 729	54 998	54 116	69 088	77 651	69 834	116 332	109 318	...	Formation brute de capital fixe
Change in inventories	3 284	- 13 879	- 2 509	- 3 203	- 3 600	- 1 517	- 8 189	- 6 022	...	Variation des stocks
Exports of goods and services	70 983	74 798	74 584	81 297	85 062	89 492	103 110	115 556	...	Exportations de biens et services
Less imports of goods and services	102 776	87 622	119 853	143 954	162 307	181 609	238 588	244 765	...	Moins importations de biens et services
GDP at purchasers' values	186 449	200 578	220 222	240 569	258 658	282 403	308 688	336 161	...	PIB aux prix d'acquisition
GROSS DOMESTIC PRODUCT BY KIND OF ECONOMIC ACTIVITY AT CONSTANT PRICES *ANNUAL GROWTH RATES (%)*										**PRODUIT INTÉRIEUR BRUT PAR BRANCHE D'ACTIVITÉ ECONOMIQUE AUX PRIX CONSTANTS** *TAUX DE CROISSANCE ANNUEL (%)*
Agriculture, hunting , forestry and Fishing	10.6	- 4.1	- 2.7	12.9	2.4	5.2	8.0	5.6	...	Agriculture, chasse sylviculture et Pêche
Mining and quarrying	6.8	5.9	9.3	1.0	6.1	6.6	5.7	6.6	...	Industries extractives
Manufacturing	1.1	0.7	-1.5	10.1	3.7	5.2	7.5	5.9	...	Industries manufacturières
Electricity, gas & water	...	...	...	...	...	...	...	...	...	Electricité, gaz et eau
Construction	12.0	3.8	-8.1	14.3	3.6	4.0	8.4	5.8	...	Bâtiments et travaux publics
Wholesale & retail trade, restaurants, hotels	30.6	9.3	5.2	2.5	6.3	5.9	6.1	6.6	...	Commerce de gros et de détail, restaurants et hôtels
Finance, insurance, real estate, etc.	...	...	...	...	...	...	...	...	...	Banques, assurances, affaires immobilières
Transport and communications	-10.2	1.7	11.6	0.9	5.4	7.1	5.6	6.5	...	Transport(s) et communications
Public administration and defense	10.3	1.3	1.6	7.5	4.2	5.6	7.0	6.1	...	Administrations publiques et défense
Education	...	...	...	...	...	...	...	...	...	Education
Health And Social Work	...	...	...	...	...	...	...	...	...	Santé et Actions Sociales
Other services	...	...	...	...	...	...	...	...	...	Autres services
Less Imputed Service Charges	...	...	...	...	...	...	...	...	...	Moins Services d'intermédiation financière
Gross domestic product at factor cost / basic prices	6.5	3.0	3.6	5.5	4.8	5.9	6.6	6.2	...	Produit intérieur brut aux couts des facteurs / prix de base
Plus: Indirect Taxes / taxes on products, less subsidies	-67.7	80.6	80.7	-33.3	21.8	13.7	-2.8	10.5	...	Plus taxes indirectes/impôts sur les produits, moins les subventions
Gross domestic product at market prices	5.0	3.5	4.5	4.8	5.0	6.0	6.5	6.3	...	Produit intérieur brut aux prix du marché
EXPENDITURE ON GROSS DOMESTIC PRODUCT AT CONSTANT PURCHASERS' VALUES *ANNUAL GROWTH RATES (%)*										**EMPLOIS DU PRODUIT INTÉRIEUR BRUT AUX PRIX CONSTANTS D'ACQUISITION** *TAUX DE CROISSANCE ANNUEL (%)*
Government final consumption	-5.6	6.3	3.5	3.4	4.6	1.1	6.0	8.4	...	Consommation finale des administrations publiques
Private final consumption	-7.3	12.9	27.7	13.7	-13.1	22.9	0.3	7.1	...	Consommation finale privée
Gross fixed capital formation	-18.3	-40.9	24.5	12.0	64.4	-10.4	55.0	-7.3	...	Formation brute de capital fixe
Exports of goods and services	6.6	1.4	-5.1	4.6	3.6	2.2	12.8	8.8	...	Exportations de biens et services
Less imports of goods and services	-19.1	-18.0	30.2	19.0	6.6	8.7	28.7	-0.4	...	Moins importations de biens et services

III INFLATION

	2009	2010	2011	2012	2013	2014	2015	2016	2017	
Annual growth rates (%)										**Taux de croissance annuel (%)**
All item	1.7	4.0	5.1	3.7	2.7	1.3	- 0.9	2.7	0.6	Ensemble
of which:										dont:
Food and non-alcoholic beverages	3.5	4.1	6.8	6.7	3.3	0.3	3.1	6.0	1.9	Alimentation et boissons non alcoolisés
Alcoholic beverages, tobacco and narcotics	...	...	...	...	...	- 6.0	- 7.5	3.3	- 3.7	Boissons alcoolisées et tabacs
Clothing and footwear	3.3	3.6	3.9	1.9	- 0.1	- 3.8	2.3	1.5	0.5	Habillement et chaussures
Housing, water, electricity, gas and other fuels	- 3.3	4.1	4.5	- 4.9	1.7	3.8	- 2.6	- 0.5	- 0.5	Logement, eau, électricité, gaz et autres combustibles
Furnishings, household equipment and routine household maintenance	0.4	2.0	1.0	2.6	0.1	8.2	- 8.6	1.0	- 0.5	Meubles, articles de ménage et entretien courant
Health	3.8	3.7	2.8	- 1.7	- 3.0	11.0	- 6.5	2.5	-	Santé
Transport	-	4.9	1.7	2.1	0.3	0.7	- 1.0	0.3	0.1	Transport
Communication	...	...	...	...	...	0.2	- 2.0	- 1.7	- 2.2	Communication
Recreation and culture	- 2.9	- 2.3	- 0.7	- 2.5	- 0.9	- 1.1	- 8.5	1.7	0.8	Loisirs et culture
Education	- 2.2	3.6	0.2	1.0	2.9	- 3.6	- 4.2	- 0.4	1.8	Enseignement
Restaurants and hotels	4.9	1.7	- 1.1	2.2	- 0.8	8.0	- 8.6	1.3	0.8	Restaurants et hôtels
Miscellaneous goods and services	2.5	4.6	4.8	12.8	6.3	1.4	1.7	- 2.2	0.6	Biens et Services divers

DJIBOUTI

IV AGRICULTURAL PRODUCTION - PRODUCTION AGRICOLE

TONNES (THOUSAND)	2009	2010	2011	2012	2013	2014	2015	2016	2017	Tonnes (milliers)
Beans, dry	2	2	2	3	3	2	2	2	...	Haricots secs
Lemons and limes	2	2	2	2	2	2	2	2	...	Citrons et limes
Tomatoes	1	1	1	1	1	1	1	1	...	Tomates
Mangoes, mangosteens, guavas	...	...	...	1	1	1	1	1	...	Mangues, mangoustans, goyaves
	...	...	...	...	...	...	...	...	...	

V MINING PRODUCTION - PRODUCTION MINIERE

	2009	2010	2011	2012	2013	2014	2015	2016	2017	
Salt and pure sodium chloride - Production (metric tons)	12 000	12 000	12 000	12 000	...	...	...	...	...	Sel et chlorure de sodium pur - Production (tonnes métriques)
	...	...	...	...	...	...	...	...	...	
	...	...	...	...	...	...	...	...	...	

VI ENERGY - ENERGIE

	2009	2010	2011	2012	2013	2014	2015	2016	2017	
Total electricity generation (GWh)	319	325	327	348	82	355	359	373	...	Production électrique totale (GWh)
of which										dont
Production of electricity from fossil fuels (GWh)	319	325	325	345	80	352	356	370	...	Production d'électricité à partir de combustibles fossiles (GWh)
Production of hydro electricity (GWh)	...	...	...	...	...	...	...	...	...	Production d'électricité d'origine hydraulique (GWh)
Production of electricity from solar, wind, tide, wave and other sources (GWh)	...	...	2	2	2	3	3	3	...	Production d'électricité d'origine solaire, éolienne, marée motrice et autres (GWh)

VII TOURISM AND INFRASTRUCTURE - TOURISME ET INFRASTUCTURE

VII-1 Tourism	2009	2010	2011	2012	2013	2014	2015	2016	2017	VII-1 Tourisme
International tourist arrivals (thousands)	58	51	32	61	67	100	118	126	...	Arrivées de touristes internationaux (milliers)
Rooms in hotels and similar establishments (thousands)	1	1	1	1	1	1	1	1	...	Chambres d'hôtels et établissements assimilés (milliers)
Overnight stays (thousands)	355	355	138	176	162	165	183	179	...	Nuitées (milliers)
Tourism receipts (US$ thousand)	...	...	...	...	...	...	...	...	...	Recettes touristiques (milliers de $ EU)
Total contribution to GDP (%)	...	...	...	...	...	...	...	...	...	Contribution totale au PIB (%)
Total contribution to Employment (%)	...	...	...	...	...	...	...	...	...	Contribution totale à l'emploi (%)
VII-2 Infrastructure										VII-2 Infrastructure
Paved road (% of total)	...	...	...	...	...	...	...	...	...	Routes asphaltées (% du total)
Total network (Railways-km)	781	...	...	...	...	...	...	...	...	Réseau total voies ferrées-Km
Main telephone lines (per 100 inhabitants)	2.0	2.2	2.2	2.3	2.4	2.5	2.6	2.7	...	Lignes téléphoniques fixes (pour 100 habitants)
Mobile cellular subscribers (per 100 inhabitants)	15.7	19.9	22.8	24.7	28.0	32.4	34.9	37.8	...	Abonnés aux téléphones mobiles (pour 100 habitants)
Internet users per 100 inhabitants	4.0	6.5	7.0	8.3	9.5	10.7	11.9	13.1	...	Utilisateurs Internet par 100 Habitants
Fixed (wired)-broadband subscriptions per 100 inhabitants	0.6	1.0	1.3	1.7	2.0	2.3	2.7	3.0	...	Abonnements à l'Internet fixe (filaire) à large bande pour 100 habitants, par débit

VIII EXTERNAL TRADE - COMMERCE EXTERIEUR

US$ (MILLIONS) EXPORTS, FOB	2009	2010	2011	2012	2013	2014	2015	2016	2017	$ E.U (MILLIONS) EXPORTATIONS, FÀB
Exports - Total	77	85	93	118	120	129	134	140	...	Exportations - Total
Exports to Africa	35	51	62	56	49	55	56	59	...	Exportations vers l'Afrique
Main products										**Principaux produits**
Ferrous waste, scrape; remelting ingots, iron, steel	...	...	9	7	9	10	11	11	...	Déchets ferreux, gratter; lingots de refusion, fer, acier
Fuel wood (excluding wood waste) and wood charcoal	2	...	...	1	11	12	12	13	...	Bois de chauffage (à l'exclusion des déchets de bois) et charbon de bois
Live animals other than animals of division 03	22	28	20	25	15	15	16	16	...	Animaux vivants autres que les animaux de la division 03
Petroleum oils or bituminous minerals > 70 % oil	7	1	16	4	3	6	5	6	...	Huiles de pétrole ou de minéraux bitumineux> 70% d'huile
Residual petroleum products, n.e.s., related mater.	...	2	3	10	22	26	25	27	...	Produits pétroliers résiduels, n.d.a.
Main destinations										**Principales destinations**
Eritrea	3	6	10	11	11	11	12	12	...	Erythrée
Ethiopia	17	25	23	33	29	34	34	37	...	Ethiopie
Saudi Arabia	17	7	6	12	14	15	16	16	...	Arabie Saoudite
United Arab Emirates	2	8	5	16	25	25	27	28	...	Emirates Arabes
Yemen	1	3	3	5	5	5	6	6	...	Yémen
IMPORTS, CIF										
Imports - Total	451	374	511	564	719	803	1 080	1 128	...	Importations - Total (millions)
Imports from Africa	24	18	25	35	39	47	61	65	...	Importations en provenance de l'Afrique
Main products										**Principaux produits**
Fixed vegetable fats & oils, crude, refined, fract.	25	22	32	30	39	43	58	61	...	Graisses et huiles végétales fixes, brutes, raffinées, fract.
Inorganic chemical elements, oxides & halogen salts	...	...	1	1	121	1	86	52	...	Eléments chimiques inorganiques, oxydes et sels halogénés
Motor vehic. for transport of goods, special purpo.	11	27	25	37	39	80	84	98	...	Véhicule à moteur pour le transport de marchandises, spécial.
Other plastics, in primary forms	5	7	11	24	12	28	28	34	...	Autres matières plastiques, sous formes primaires
Sugar, molasses and honey	7	17	33	23	24	19	31	30	...	Sucre, mélasse et miel
Main origin										**Principales provenances**
China	49	49	59	97	139	164	215	227	...	Chine
India	42	35	55	45	55	50	75	75	...	Inde
Indonesia	8	8	21	28	38	43	58	60	...	Indonésie
Saudi Arabia	81	96	148	156	190	188	268	273	...	Arabie Saoudite
United Arab Emirates	38	28	34	44	67	78	102	108	...	Emirates Arabes

	2009	2010	2011	2012	2013	2014	2015	2016	2017	
IX-1 MONETARY STATISTICS *DJIBOUTI FRANC (MILLIONS)*										**IX-1 STATISTIQUES MONÉTAIRES** *FRANC DJIBOUTIEN (MILLIONS)*
Money supply (M1)	167 191	187 589	179 209	206 184	220 397	234 774	279 444	303 886	328 337	Masse monétaire (M1)
Quasi-money	64 514	60 298	56 114	71 301	64 528	80 283	87 059	90 483	95 568	Quasi-monnaie
of which demand deposit	...	...	...	...	...	...	...	...	...	dont Monnaie scripturale
Net foreign assets	127 472	134 428	119 898	136 887	174 890	173 908	210 075	232 506	278 129	Avoirs extérieurs nets
Domestic credit	60 250	72 218	75 754	85 918	87 819	93 336	104 041	108 354	111 201	Crédit intérieur
of which claims on private sector	2 908	3 161	5 347	11 634	4 090	569	1 167	3 228	2 335	dont créances sur le secteur privé
of which claims on government sector, net	54 717	66 412	68 068	69 599	80 467	87 367	93 510	94 615	100 064	dont créances nettes sur le gouvernement
International reserves (millions US$)	218	231	228	234	411	381	355	398	424	Réserves internationales (millions $EU)
Average exchange rate (National currency per US$)	178	178	178	178	178	178	178	178	178	Taux de change (moyen) (monnaie nationale par $ EU)
IX-2 PUBLIC FINANCE *DJIBOUTI FRANC (MILLIONS)*										**IX-2 FINANCES PUBLIQUES** *FRANC DJIBOUTIEN (MILLIONS)*
Total Revenues and Grants	68 723	70 188	74 516	82 572	82 000	87 326	114 222	112 771	115 508	Recettes totales et dons
Direct taxes (on income, profits)	17 202	18 719	20 298	21 143	22 876	22 941	26 724	27 762	27 338	Taxes directes
Domestic indirect taxes revenues	14 022	15 092	17 090	16 303	19 941	21 077	25 493	25 945	27 111	Taxes Indirectes
Trade taxes	4 308	4 736	4 821	4 861	5 168	5 408	5 787	6 270	6 639	Taxes sur le commerce extérieur
Other taxes	1 890	2 029	2 242	2 144	3 232	3 175	3 775	4 814	4 350	Autres taxes
Other revenues	19 353	18 907	16 750	17 547	19 331	21 527	31 323	33 276	35 131	Autres recettes
Grants	11 948	10 705	13 315	20 574	11 452	13 199	21 120	14 704	14 939	Dons
Total Expenditures and Net Lending	78 562	73 054	78 180	89 473	97 425	114 392	180 805	173 711	117 201	Dépenses totales et prêts nets
Current expenditure	44 113	48 759	53 016	57 143	61 191	63 674	68 938	78 770	77 023	Dépenses courantes
Wages and Salaries	21 634	22 911	27 281	28 995	25 131	26 432	27 748	31 071	32 016	Rémunérations et salaires
Other purchases of goods and services	18 275	21 566	21 240	23 446	30 999	32 657	36 558	43 618	40 648	Achat de biens et services
Other current expenditure	1 780	1 729	1 798	1 851	2 039	1 456	1 357	623	801	Autres dépenses courantes
Current transfers	2 424	2 553	2 697	2 851	3 022	3 129	3 275	3 458	3 558	Transferts courants
Interest payments	803	803	745	1 027	847	892	1 747	3 807	4 049	Intérêts
Capital expenditure	33 646	23 491	24 419	31 303	35 387	49 827	110 120	91 134	36 129	Dépenses d'équipement
Net lending	...	...	...	...	...	...	...	...	...	Prêts nets
Fiscal balance	- 9 839	- 2 866	- 3 664	- 6 900	- 15 425	- 27 066	- 66 582	- 60 940	- 1 693	Solde global y compris les dons
IX-3 BALANCE OF PAYMENTS *DJIBOUTI FRANC (MILLIONS)*										**IX-3 BALANCE DES PAIEMENTS** *FRANC DJIBOUTIEN (MILLIONS)*
Trade balance	- 66 351	- 49 518	- 74 266	- 79 341	- 106 601	- 119 840	- 168 260	- 100 621	...	Balance commerciale
Services Balance	34 558	38 494	28 997	31 889	30 573	29 004	33 504	36 669	...	Balance des services
Net primary income	3 853	3 924	1 554	4 911	4 679	3 804	5 271	2 403	...	Revenus primaires nets
Compensation of employees	4 710	4 632	4 626	4 710	4 930	4 832	4 969	4 986	...	Rémunération des salariés
Investment income	- 857	- 708	- 3 072	201	- 251	- 1 028	302	- 2 583	...	Revenus des investissements
Net secondary income	15 304	16 912	13 175	16 244	16 516	16 914	32 134	31 331	...	Revenus secondaires nets
Net official transfers	...	...	...	...	...	...	...	...	...	Transferts officiels nets
Workers' remittances	...	...	...	...	...	...	...	...	...	Envois de fonds des travailleurs
Other private transfers	...	...	...	...	...	...	...	...	...	Autres transferts privés
Current account balance	- 12 635	9 812	- 30 540	- 26 297	- 54 833	- 70 118	- 97 351	- 30 218	...	Solde du compte courant
Capital and financial account	18 410	12 933	38 724	12 552	26 131	74 130	73 246	50 689	...	Comptes de capital et financier
Capital account	9 798	9 831	10 606	9 313	8 969	11 510	16 784	6 020	...	Compte de capital
Financial account	8 612	3 102	28 118	3 239	17 162	62 620	56 462	44 669	...	Compte financier
Errors and omissions	- 5 775	- 22 745	- 8 183	13 745	28 702	- 4 012	24 105	- 20 471	...	Erreurs et omissions
Overall balance	...	...	...	...	...	...	...	...	...	Balance générale

DJIBOUTI

X DEBT AND FINANCIAL FLOWS - DETTE ET FLUX FINANCIERS

	2009	2010	2011	2012	2013	2014	2015	2016	2017	
X-1 DEBT *US $ (MILLIONS)*										**X-1 DETTE EXTÉRIEURE** *$ E.U (MILLIONS)*
Total external debt	661	636	653	666	673	792	1 197	1 611	1 819	Dette extérieure totale
Private	...	...	...	...	5	10	...	...	...	Privée
Public	661	636	653	666	668	783	1 197	1 611	...	Publique
Total external debt service	27	28	33	39	40	64	42	68	...	Service de la dette extérieure
Present value of external debt	...	...	...	...	...	...	...	1 053	...	Valeur actuelle de la dette extérieure
Total government domestic debt, National currency (millions)	...	...	...	...	...	...	...	...	...	Dette publique intérieure
X-2 FINANCIAL FLOWS *US $ (MILLIONS)*										**X-2 FLUX FINANCIERS** *$ E.U (MILLIONS)*
Net Foreign Direct Investment Inflows	75	37	79	110	286	153	124	160	...	Investissements étranger direct (flux nets entrants)
Main origin of FDI inflows										**Principales origines de l'IDE entrant:**
...	...	...	...	...	...	...	...	...	...	...
Norway	17	- 2	...	...	...	...	...	...	...	Norvège
Luxembourg	...	...	...	-	...	...	...	...	...	Luxembourg
...	...	...	...	...	...	...	...	...	...	...
...	...	...	...	...	...	...	...	...	...	...
African countries	...	...	...	...	...	...	...	...	...	Pays africains
Net total official development assistance	166	132	141	148	149	166	170	185	...	Aide publique au développement (nette totale)
Main origin of net ODA										**Principales origines de l'APD nette**
France	42	46	44	40	42	41	56	49	...	France
Japan	29	38	17	25	6	26	18	9	...	Japon
International Development Association [IDA]	7	...	1	6	3	9	6	5	...	International Development Association
United States	6	12	15	9	9	8	6	7	...	États-Unis
...	...	...	...	...	...	...	...	...	...	...

DJIBOUTI

SOURCES AND NOTES - SOURCES ET NOTES

External trade - Total exports, fob: UNCTAD

External trade - Total import, cif: UNCTAD

ODA: OECD

Monetary statistics: IMF

National Accounts: 2014:Semi-Final;2015-2016:Provisional

Poverty: World Bank

Commerce exterieur - Exportation, fab: CNUCED

Commerce exterieur - Imporations, caf: CNUCED

APD: OCDE

Statistiques monétaires: FMI

Comptes nationaux: 2014:Semi-définitif;201-2016:Provisoire

Pauvreté: Banque mondiale

AREA (km2)	1 001 450	**SUPERFICIE (KM2)**
CAPITAL CITY	Cairo / Le Caire	**CAPITALE**
CURRENCY	Egyptian Pound / Livre egyptienne	**MONNAIE**

I SOCIAL AND DEMOGRAPHIC INDICATORS — INDICATEURS DEMOGRAPHIQUES ET SOCIAUX

Population	Year Année	Value Valeur	Charts / Graphiques	Population
Population ('000)	2017	95 200.0		Population ('000)
Female (%)	2017	48.4		Féminine (%)
Urban (%)	2017	42.3		Urbaine (%)
Average annual growth rate	2017	2.5		Taux de croissance annuel
Active population ('000)	2016	28 934.0		Population active ('000)
Population by age group ('000)				Population par groupe d'âge ('000)
0-14 years	2017	32 594.0		0-14 ans
15-64 years	2017	58 929.0		15-64 ans
65+ years	2017	3 678.0		65+ ans
Economically active population in agriculture (%)	2016	25.6		Participation de la population active agricole (%)
Crude birth rate	2017	26.8		Taux brut de natalité
Crude death rate	2017	5.7		Taux brut de mortalité
Total fertility rate	2014	3.5		Indice synthétique de fécondité
Life expectancy at birth - Total (years)	2017	72.2		Espérance de vie à la naissance - Totale (années)
Dependency ratio - Total (%)	2017	61.6		Taux de dépendance - Total (%)
Health				**Santé**
Percentage of children under-five and underweight	2014	7.0		% d'enfants de moins de cinq ans avec insuffisance pondérale
Prevalence of undernourishment	2015	5.0		Prévalence de la malnutrition
Under five mortality rate (per 1 000 live births)	2016	19.6		Taux de mortalité de moins de 5 ans (les deux sexes, pour 1000)
Infant mortality rate (per 1 000 live births)	2016	15.1		Taux de mortalité infantile (les deux sexes) par 1000
Neonatal mortality rate (per 1 000 live births)	2016	6.6		Le taux de mortalité néonatale (pour 1000 naissances vivantes)
Percentage of children provided the vaccines :				Pourcentage d'enfants vaccinés :
BCG	2014	96.0		BCG
DPT3	2014	94.0		DTC3
Polio	2014	94.0		polio
Measles	2014	93.0		rougeole
Percentage of mothers provided at least one antenatal care	2014	90.3		Pourcentage de mères ayant au moins reçu un soin prénatal (%)
Percentage of deliveries attended by skilled health personnel	2014	91.5		% d'accouchements assistés par un personnel de santé qualifié
Number of doctors (per 10,000 population)	2016	9.0		Nombre de médecins (pour 10.000 habitants)
Number of nurses (per 10,000 population)	2016	15.0		Nombre d'infirmiers (pour 10.000 habitants)
Hospital beds - Total (per 10,000 population)	2016	14.0		Nombre de lits d'hôpitaux - Total (pour 10 000)
Births registered (per 1,000)	2017	26.8		Naissances enregistrées (pour 1000)
Deaths registered (per 1,000)	2017	5.7		Décès enregistrés (pour 1000)
Budget allocation to health (%)	2017	4.5		Dépenses publiques consacrées à la santé (% du budget)
Education				**Education**
Enrolment in primary education (000)	2016	11 075.0		Scolarisation dans le primaire (000)
Female	2016	5 368.0		Féminine
Enrolment in secondary education (000)	2016	3 434.0		Scolarisation dans le secondaire (000)
Female	2016	1 646.0		Féminine
Enrolment in tertiary education (000)	2016	2 357.5		Scolarisation dans le tertiaire (000)
Female	2016	1 240.9		Féminine
Literacy rate	2017	74.0		Taux d'alphabétisation (deux sexes)
Male	2017	79.0		Masculin
Female	2017	69.0		Féminin
Pupil teacher ratio - primary	2016	26.3		Ratio élève-enseignant
Budget allocation to education (%)	2017	10.7		Dépenses publiques consacrées à l'enseignement (% du budget)
Poverty				**Pauvreté**
GNI per capita, PPP (current int. $)	2016	10980.0		RNB par habitant, ($ PPA inter. courants)
Human Poverty Index (HPI-1) Value (%)	2007	23.4		Valeur de l'Indice de pauvreté (IPH-1) (%)
Population below Inter. poverty line ($2/ day) (%)	...	...		Population sous le seuil inter. de pauvreté (2$/Jour) (%)
Share of income held by richest 10%	2008	26.6		% de revenu des 10% plus riches
Share of income held by poorest 10%	2008	4.0		% de revenu des 10% plus pauvres
GINI index	2008	30.8		Indice de GINI

Population by age group - 2017

Population par groupe d'age - 2017

- 0-14 years — 34.2%
- 15-64 years — 61.9%
- 65+ years — 3.9%

Percentage of children provided vaccines : - 2014

Pourcentage d'enfants vaccinés : - 2014

BCG / BCG	DPT3 / DTC3	Polio / polio	Measles / rougeole
96.0	94.0	94.0	93.0

Literacy rate (%) - 2017

Taux d'alphabétisation - 2017

- Male 79.0
- Female 69.0

GNI per capita, PPP (current international $)

RNB par habitant, ($ PPA internationaux courants)

2012	2013	2014	2015	2016
9 770	9 900	10 160	10 570	10 980

ÉGYPTE

EGYPT

	2009	2010	2011	2012	2013	2014	2015	2016	2017	
GROSS DOMESTIC PRODUCT BY KIND OF ECONOMIC ACTIVITY AT CURRENT PRICES *EGYPTIAN POUND (MILLIONS)*										**PRODUIT INTÉRIEUR BRUT PAR BRANCHE D'ACTIVITÉ ÉCONOMIQUE AUX PRIX COURANTS** *LIVRE ÉGYPTIENNE (MILLIONS)*
Agriculture, hunting , forestry and Fishing	135 465	160 970	190 159	188 785	209 748	241 493	278 459	318 878	398 539	Agriculture, chasse sylviculture et Pêche
Mining and quarrying	147 966	165 747	195 136	278 234	309 074	350 660	314 139	214 842	326 940	Industries extractives
Manufacturing	164 523	194 290	216 184	270 723	308 982	357 296	408 069	456 299	570 590	Industries manufacturières
Electricity, gas & water	16 020	18 287	21 544	37 438	41 526	46 576	53 463	62 772	78 524	Electricité, gaz et eau
Construction	44 026	52 609	60 070	70 947	82 475	95 133	119 535	145 450	195 098	Bâtiments et travaux publics
Wholesale & retail trade, restaurants, hotels	147 780	173 802	192 413	258 968	291 217	319 951	378 844	423 158	537 801	Commerce de gros et de détail, restaurants et hôtels
Finance, insurance, real estate, etc.	98 389	112 957	126 527	229 665	259 747	298 891	350 534	410 341	518 913	Banques, assurances, affaires immobilières
Transport and communications	101 103	110 448	122 681	148 435	159 390	181 215	203 060	229 522	308 569	Transport(s) et communications
Public administration and defense	98 575	114 944	133 688	150 521	174 234	213 144	249 288	276 488	301 772	Administrations publiques et défense
Education	11 133	12 828	14 558	29 373	32 486	37 424	43 518	50 519	63 907	Education
Health And Social Work	12 971	14 797	16 595	36 842	40 875	46 451	54 194	62 816	78 934	Santé et Actions Sociales
Other services	16 105	18 912	20 350	13 216	15 053	17 361	19 998	23 326	29 916	Autres services
Less Imputed Service Charges	...	...	...	...	...	...	...	...	...	Moins Services d'intermédiation financière
Gross domestic product at factor cost / basic prices	994 055	1 150 590	1 309 906	1 713 146	1 924 808	2 205 594	2 473 100	2 674 410	3 409 504	Produit intérieur brut aux couts des facteurs / prix de base
Plus: Indirect Taxes / taxes on products, less subsidies	48 245	56 010	61 094	- 38 446	- 64 408	- 75 594	- 29 200	34 991	60 496	Plus taxes indirectes/impôts sur les produits, moins les subventions
EXPENDITURE ON GROSS DOMESTIC PRODUCT AT CURRENT PURCHASER'S VALUES *EGYPTIAN POUND (MILLIONS)*										**EMPLOI DU PRODUIT INTÉRIEUR BRUT AUX PRIX COURANTS D'ACQUISITION** *LIVRE ÉGYPTIENNE (MILLIONS)*
Government final consumption	118 300	134 700	157 000	187 200	211 200	252 400	287 400	309 600	350 200	Consommation finale des administrations publiques
Private final consumption	793 200	899 800	1 036 000	1 351 700	1 502 700	1 766 600	2 014 500	2 251 400	3 012 700	Consommation finale privée
Gross fixed capital formation	197 100	231 800	229 100	246 100	241 600	265 100	333 700	392 000	514 300	Formation brute de capital fixe
Change in inventories	2 900	3 500	5 400	22 300	22 800	25 500	15 500	15 500	15 700	Variation des stocks
Exports of goods and services	260 100	257 600	282 000	274 600	316 600	303 400	322 200	280 300	565 600	Exportations de biens et services
Less imports of goods and services	329 300	320 800	338 500	407 200	434 500	483 000	529 400	539 400	988 500	Moins importations de biens et services
GDP at purchasers' values	1 042 300	1 206 600	1 371 000	1 674 700	1 860 400	2 130 000	2 443 900	2 709 400	3 470 000	PIB aux prix d'acquisition
GROSS DOMESTIC PRODUCT BY KIND OF ECONOMIC ACTIVITY AT CONSTANT PRICES *ANNUAL GROWTH RATES (%)*										**PRODUIT INTÉRIEUR BRUT PAR BRANCHE D'ACTIVITÉ ÉCONOMIQUE AUX PRIX CONSTANTS** *TAUX DE CROISSANCE ANNUEL (%)*
Agriculture, hunting , forestry and Fishing	3.2	3.5	2.7	2.9	3.0	3.0	3.1	3.1	3.2	Agriculture, chasse sylviculture et Pêche
Mining and quarrying	5.9	0.9	0.6	0.1	-2.3	- 3.8	- 4.1	- 5.3	- 1.8	Industries extractives
Manufacturing	3.7	5.1	- 0.9	0.7	2.3	4.8	3.1	0.8	2.1	Industries manufacturières
Electricity, gas & water	10.6	6.4	4.5	5.6	4.0	4.5	3.9	6.2	2.4	Electricité, gaz et eau
Construction	11.4	13.2	3.7	3.3	3.7	7.4	9.8	11.2	9.5	Bâtiments et travaux publics
Wholesale & retail trade, restaurants, hotels	2.4	7.7	- 0.5	2.1	3.6	0.2	5.9	0.2	5.1	Commerce de gros et de détail, restaurants et hôtels
Finance, insurance, real estate, etc.	4.6	5.3	3.0	3.9	3.1	5.9	3.4	4.4	4.8	Banques, assurances, affaires immobilières
Transport and communications	6.4	6.2	6.1	2.6	2.8	5.5	4.8	6.4	6.8	Transport(s) et communications
Public administration and defense	7.1	4.2	3.7	2.6	3.7	5.3	7.5	5.0	3.0	Administrations publiques et défense
Education	...	...	...	2.6	2.8	4.3	2.7	4.3	3.9	Education
Health And Social Work	...	...	...	2.6	3.1	5.3	3.2	4.1	3.8	Santé et Actions Sociales
Other services	- 2.4	5.0	2.8	2.6	2.6	5.2	3.1	4.3	4.6	Autres services
Less Imputed Service Charges	...	...	...	...	...	...	...	...	...	Moins Services d'intermédiation financière
Gross domestic product at factor cost / basic prices	4.7	5.1	4.5	2.2	2.2	2.9	3.4	2.3	3.6	Produit intérieur brut aux couts des facteurs / prix de base
Plus: Indirect Taxes / taxes on products, less subsidies	10.2	- 2.2	- 53.8	1.8	4.1	3.0	- 39.4	- 145.1	114.0	Plus taxes indirectes/impôts sur les produits, moins les subventions
Gross domestic product at market prices	4.9	4.8	1.8	2.2	2.2	2.9	4.4	4.3	4.2	Produit intérieur brut aux prix du marché
EXPENDITURE ON GROSS DOMESTIC PRODUCT AT CONSTANT PURCHASERS' VALUES *ANNUAL GROWTH RATES (%)*										**EMPLOIS DU PRODUIT INTÉRIEUR BRUT AUX PRIX CONSTANTS D'ACQUISITION** *TAUX DE CROISSANCE ANNUEL (%)*
Government final consumption	5.6	4.5	3.8	3.1	2.2	8.4	7.0	3.9	2.5	Consommation finale des administrations publiques
Private final consumption	5.7	4.1	5.5	5.9	3.3	4.4	3.1	4.6	4.2	Consommation finale privée
Gross fixed capital formation	- 9.1	5.8	- 5.6	0.7	-7.8	1.4	11.6	13.0	12.2	Formation brute de capital fixe
Exports of goods and services	- 14.5	- 3.0	1.2	- 2.3	4.5	- 10.9	-	- 15.0	86.0	Exportations de biens et services
Less imports of goods and services	- 17.9	- 3.2	8.4	10.8	0.6	0.1	1.0	- 2.2	52.5	Moins importations de biens et services

III INFLATION

	2009	2010	2011	2012	2013	2014	2015	2016	2017	
Annual growth rates (%)										**Taux de croissance annuel (%)**
All item	11.5	11.5	10.1	7.1	9.5	10.1	10.4	13.8	29.5	Ensemble
of which:										dont:
Food and non-alcoholic beverages	10.6	19.5	15.1	9.2	12.4	12.3	10.7	16.7	38.6	Alimentation et boissons non alcoolisés
Alcoholic beverages, tobacco and narcotics	-	14.9	34.7	17.7	7.9	17.3	22.3	9.3	32.1	Boissons alcoolisées et tabacs
Clothing and footwear	3.0	1.7	1.9	4.3	4.3	2.5	8.0	11.5	24.9	Habillement et chaussures
Housing, water, electricity, gas and other fuels	1.8	1.4	3.2	6.4	4.6	3.6	7.4	5.1	9.8	Logement, eau, électricité, gaz et autres combustibles
Furnishings, household equipment and routine household maintenance	3.4	1.8	3.4	6.6	9.2	9.1	4.7	14.3	28.9	Meubles, articles de ménage et entretien courant
Health	4.7	0.4	1.6	1.4	10.5	12.7	4.4	23.8	21.2	Santé
Transport	1.9	1.0	1.5	2.4	4.3	15.4	11.7	7.2	28.9	Transport
Communication	- 0.1	- 0.1	- 0.8	- 2.4	0.1	1.5	- 0.2	0.7	4.8	Communication
Recreation and culture	3.5	6.6	8.8	7.2	11.7	14.0	12.6	13.8	35.6	Loisirs et culture
Education	3.5	13.4	20.1	10.3	9.3	9.1	20.7	11.5	14.3	Enseignement
Restaurants and hotels	8.4	7.8	9.7	3.7	19.8	11.9	14.9	21.4	27.5	Restaurants et hôtels
Miscellaneous goods and services	12.2	12.6	2.6	1.6	0.6	2.5	3.7	12.8	28.5	Biens et Services divers

IV AGRICULTURAL PRODUCTION - PRODUCTION AGRICOLE

	2009	2010	2011	2012	2013	2014	2015	2016	2017	
TONNES (THOUSAND)										**Tonnes (milliers)**
Wheat	8 523	7 177	8 407	8 795	9 460	9 280	9 607	9 343	...	Blé
Maize	7 686	7 183	6 876	8 094	7 966	8 060	7 803	7 818	...	Maïs
Tomatoes	10 304	8 564	8 105	8 625	8 291	8 288	7 738	7 321	...	Tomates
Rice, paddy	5 520	4 329	5 675	5 911	5 724	5 467	4 818	5 309	...	Riz, Paddy
Sugar beet	5 334	7 840	7 486	9 126	10 044	11 046	11 983	11 209	...	betterave à sucre

V MINING PRODUCTION - PRODUCTION MINIERE

	2009	2010	2011	2012	2013	2014	2015	2016	2017	
Crude petroleum - Production, metric tons (thousands)	33 210	33 841	33 221	33 463	29 160	30 064	29 657	...	...	Pétrole brut - Production, tonnes métriques (milliers)
Natural gas - Production, terajoules (millions)	2	2	2	2	2	2	1	...	...	Gaz naturel - Production, térajoules (millions)
Iron ores and concentrates - Production, metric tons (thousands)	2	3	4	-	1	2	1	...	...	"Minerais de fer et leurs concentrés

VI ENERGY - ENERGIE

	2009	2010	2011	2012	2013	2014	2015	2016	2017	
Total electricity generation (GWh)	139 000	146 795	146 668	157 024	157 930	158 137	191 942	...	...	Production électrique totale (GWh)
of which										dont
Production of electricity from fossil fuels (GWh)	125 004	132 045	132 045	142 468	142 468	138 795	174 097	...	...	Production d'électricité à partir de combustibles fossiles (GWh)
Production of hydro electricity (GWh)	12 863	13 046	13 046	12 935	13 840	13 840	12 755	...	...	Production d'électricité d'origine hydraulique (GWh)
Production of electricity from solar, wind, tide, wave and other sources (GWh)	1 133	1 704	1 577	1 621	1 621	5 502	5 091	...	...	Production d'électricité d'origine solaire, éolienne, marée motrice et autres (GWh)

VII TOURISM AND INFRASTRUCTURE - TOURISME ET INFRASTUCTURE

	2009	2010	2011	2012	2013	2014	2015	2016	2017	
VII-1 Tourism										**VII-1 Tourisme**
International tourist arrivals (thousands)	12 536	14 731	9 845	11 532	9 464	9 878	9 071	5 399	8 292	Arrivées de touristes internationaux (milliers)
Rooms in hotels and similar establishments (thousands)	160	153	140	206	200	200	206	202	...	Chambres d'hôtels et établissements assimilés (milliers)
Overnight stays (thousands)	164 000	186 000	144 000	174 000	119 000	97 300	84 100	32 700	83 800	Nuitées (milliers)
Tourism receipts (US$ thousand)	10 510 300	12 282 600	8 462 040	9 695 140	5 827 030	6 968 420	5 826 030	2 540 640	7 250 400	Recettes touristiques (milliers de $ EU)
Total contribution to GDP (%)	17.5	17.1	13.6	13.7	11.3	11.6	11.0	11.3	...	Contribution totale au PIB (%)
Total contribution to Employment (%)	15.1	14.8	11.3	10.8	8.4	8.3	8.0	6.6	8.5	Contribution totale à l'emploi (%)
VII-2 Infrastructure										**VII-2 Infrastructure**
Paved road (% of total)	89.4	92.2	85.7	89.6	94.4	...	...	...	...	Routes asphaltées (% du total)
Total network (Railways-km)	5 195	5 195	5 195	5 195	5 195	5 195	...	...	...	Réseau total voies ferrées-Km
Main telephone lines (per 100 inhabitants)	13.4	12.3	11.0	10.6	8.3	7.6	7.4	7.1	...	Lignes téléphoniques fixes (pour 100 habitants)
Mobile cellular subscribers (per 100 inhabitants)	72.1	90.5	105.1	119.9	121.5	114.3	111.0	113.7	...	Abonnés aux téléphones mobiles (pour 100 habitants)
Internet users per 100 inhabitants	20.0	21.6	25.6	26.4	29.4	33.9	37.8	41.2	...	Utilisateurs Internet par 100 Habitants
Fixed (wired)-broadband subscriptions per 100 inhabitants	1.4	1.9	2.3	2.8	3.3	3.7	4.5	5.2	...	Abonnements à l'Internet fixe (filaire) à large bande pour 100 habitants, par débit

VIII EXTERNAL TRADE - COMMERCE EXTERIEUR

	2009	2010	2011	2012	2013	2014	2015	2016	2017	
US$ (MILLIONS) EXPORTS, FOB										**$ E.U (MILLIONS) EXPORTATIONS, FÀB**
Exports - Total	24 182	26 332	31 582	29 417	28 779	26 812	21 967	25 468	...	Exportations - Total
Exports to Africa	2 917	3 415	3 376	3 724	3 776	3 443	3 015	3 166	...	Exportations vers l'Afrique
Main products										**Principaux produits**
Fruits and nuts (excluding oil nuts), fresh or dried	924	869	956	931	1 021	997	1 065	1 320	...	Fruits et noix (à l'exclusion des oléagineux), frais ou secs
Gold, non-monetary (excluding gold ores and concentrates)	605	696	1 290	1 135	756	607	597	3 129	...	Or, non monétaire (à l'exclusion des minerais d'or et des concentrés)
Petroleum oils or bituminous minerals > 70 % oil	2 040	2 904	3 059	2 641	2 164	2 129	1 412	933	...	Huiles de pétrole ou de minéraux bitumineux> 70% d'huile
Petroleum oils, oils from bitumin. materials, crude	2 336	2 916	4 850	4 796	4 728	4 631	3 263	3 142	...	Huiles de pétrole, huiles de bitume. matériaux bruts
Vegetables	750	771	900	701	917	1 077	1 017	973	...	Légumes
Main destinations										**Principales destinations**
India	1 569	1 241	2 346	2 091	2 071	1 729	1 078	942	...	Inde
Italy	1 784	2 202	2 859	2 362	2 362	2 567	1 756	1 756	...	Italie
Saudi Arabia	1 376	1 493	1 750	1 701	1 856	1 907	1 946	1 726	...	Arabie Saoudite
Turkey	667	896	1 334	1 301	1 540	1 312	1 132	1 417	...	Turquie
United States	1 885	1 852	1 801	2 267	1 299	1 172	1 195	1 513	...	États-Unis
IMPORTS, CIF										
Imports - Total	44 912	53 003	62 282	69 866	66 666	71 338	63 574	58 053	...	Importations - Total (millions)
Imports from Africa	1 336	1 556	1 657	2 219	1 505	1 340	1 639	1 960	...	Importations en provenance de l'Afrique
Main products										**Principaux produits**
Motor vehicles for the transport of persons	1 062	1 415	1 148	1 469	1 451	2 269	2 375	1 896	...	Véhicules à moteur pour le transport de personnes
Petroleum oils or bituminous minerals > 70 % oil	1 896	2 984	4 532	7 092	5 210	5 708	4 744	3 331	...	Huiles de pétrole ou de minéraux bitumineux> 70% d'huile
Petroleum oils, oils from bitumin. materials, crude	736	1 050	1 225	2 454	1 778	2 403	1 327	1 207	...	Huiles de pétrole, huiles de bitume. matériaux bruts
Telecommunication equipment, n.e.s.; & parts, n.e.s.	886	1 197	1 361	1 512	1 583	2 253	2 025	1 836	...	Matériel de télécommunication, n.es .; & parties, n.e.s.
Wheat (including spelt) and meslin, unmilled	1 437	2 101	2 902	3 106	1 618	2 843	2 091	1 531	...	Blé (y compris l'épeautre) et méteil, non moulu
Main origin										**Principales provenances**
China	4 273	5 099	6 316	7 296	7 586	8 690	9 404	7 665	...	Chine
Germany	3 471	3 725	3 520	3 969	4 141	4 414	4 078	4 112	...	Allemagne
Italy	2 970	3 185	3 269	3 535	3 630	3 272	2 891	2 789	...	Italie
Russian Federation	1 575	1 677	2 364	3 468	2 156	3 520	2 938	2 781	...	Fédération Russe
United States	4 737	5 496	6 175	5 300	5 124	5 513	3 951	2 992	...	États-Unis

ÉGYPTE

EGYPT

	2009	2010	2011	2012	2013	2014	2015	2016	2017	
IX-1 MONETARY STATISTICS *EGYPTIAN POUND (MILLIONS)*										**IX-1 STATISTIQUES MONÉTAIRES** *LIVRE ÉGYPTIENNE (MILLIONS)*
Money supply (M1)	831 211	917 459	1 010 296	1 094 408	1 295 686	1 516 601	1 765 492	2 094 500	2 921 852	Masse monétaire (M1)
Quasi-money	640 257	716 434	742 440	828 237	956 770	1 099 997	1 315 922	1 896 381	2 329 399	Quasi-monnaie
of which demand deposit	...	...	...	...	...	...	...	...	...	dont Monnaie scripturale
Net foreign assets	255 846	305 209	190 209	132 822	117 592	84 397	- 17 215	- 204 238	213 713	Avoirs extérieurs nets
Domestic credit	782 844	837 646	1 022 981	1 223 477	1 511 332	1 854 288	2 328 230	3 240 446	3 436 963	Crédit intérieur
of which claims on private sector	311 935	333 250	501 884	663 851	912 637	1 172 147	1 482 054	1 878 654	1 916 931	dont créances sur le secteur privé
of which claims on government sector, net	376 158	399 050	427 165	458 674	487 842	545 422	643 146	924 850	989 646	dont créances nettes sur le gouvernement
International reserves (millions US$)	30 946	35 060	26 413	15 238	14 485	16 289	19 549	17 097	30 652	Réserves internationales (millions $EU)
Average exchange rate (National currency per US$)	6	6	6	6	7	7	8	10	18	Taux de change (moyen) (monnaie nationale par $ EU)
IX-2 PUBLIC FINANCE *EGYPTIAN POUND (MILLIONS)*										**IX-2 FINANCES PUBLIQUES** *LIVRE ÉGYPTIENNE (MILLIONS)*
Total Revenues and Grants	282 505	268 114	265 286	303 622	350 322	456 788	465 241	491 488	669 756	Recettes totales et dons
Direct taxes (on income, profits)	83 017	85 388	99 045	104 334	134 215	139 686	150 925	172 733	186 806	Taxes directes
Domestic indirect taxes revenues	62 650	67 095	76 068	84 594	92 924	91 867	122 930	140 525	201 178	Taxes Indirectes
Trade taxes	14 091	14 702	13 858	14 788	16 771	17 673	21 867	28 091	29 548	Taxes sur le commerce extérieur
Other taxes	3 464	3 309	3 102	3 694	7 208	11 062	10 235	10 966	15 768	Autres taxes
Other revenues	111 299	93 288	70 927	86 108	93 996	100 642	133 847	135 630	234 234	Autres recettes
Grants	7 984	4 333	2 287	10 104	5 208	95 856	25 437	3 543	2 213	Dons
Total Expenditures and Net Lending	354 330	366 153	399 746	470 327	590 041	712 227	744 671	830 983	989 216	Dépenses totales et prêts nets
Current expenditure	255 259	245 303	276 908	330 633	401 676	475 483	478 592	504 958	535 562	Dépenses courantes
Wages and Salaries	76 147	85 369	96 271	122 818	142 956	178 589	198 468	213 721	228 736	Rémunérations et salaires
Other purchases of goods and services	25 072	28 059	26 148	26 826	26 652	27 247	31 276	35 662	42 302	Achat de biens et services
Other current expenditure	27 007	28 901	31 364	30 796	34 975	41 068	50 279	54 551	58 100	Autres dépenses courantes
Current transfers	127 033	102 974	123 125	150 193	197 093	228 579	198 569	201 024	206 424	Transferts courants
Interest payments	52 810	72 333	85 077	104 441	146 995	173 150	193 008	243 635	292 520	Intérêts
Capital expenditure	43 430	48 350	39 881	35 918	39 516	52 882	61 750	69 250	146 711	Dépenses d'équipement
Net lending	2 831	166	- 2 120	- 665	1 854	10 713	11 321	13 139	14 422	Prêts nets
Fiscal balance	- 71 826	- 98 038	- 134 460	- 166 705	- 239 719	- 255 439	- 279 430	- 339 495	- 319 460	Solde global y compris les dons
IX-3 BALANCE OF PAYMENTS *US$ (MILLIONS)*										**IX-3 BALANCE DES PAIEMENTS** *$ E.U (MILLIONS)*
Trade balance	- 25 327	- 20 755	- 21 054	- 34 139	- 30 695	- 34 159	- 39 060	- 38 683	- 35 435	Balance commerciale
Services Balance	12 502	10 339	7 878	12 064	12 446	8 274	10 743	6 533	6 811	Balance des services
Net primary income	154	- 4 365	- 6 050	- 6 479	- 7 406	- 7 263	- 5 701	- 4 472	- 4 423	Revenus primaires nets
Compensation of employees	...	...	...	...	...	...	...	...	...	Rémunération des salariés
Investment income	154	- 4 365	- 6 050	- 6 479	- 7 406	- 7 263	- 5 701	- 4 472	- 4 423	Revenus des investissements
Net secondary income	8 247	10 463	13 137	18 408	19 265	30 368	21 876	16 791	17 472	Revenus secondaires nets
Net official transfers	614	954	753	632	836	11 920	2 670	102	149	Transferts officiels nets
Workers' remittances	7 806	9 753	12 593	17 971	18 668	18 519	19 330	17 077	17 453	Envois de fonds des travailleurs
Other private transfers	...	...	...	...	...	...	...	...	...	Autres transferts privés
Current account balance	- 4 424	- 4 318	- 6 088	- 10 146	- 6 390	- 2 780	- 12 143	- 19 831	- 15 575	Solde du compte courant
Capital and financial account	2 285	8 980	- 4 199	1 023	9 773	5 190	17 929	21 177	29 034	Comptes de capital et financier
Capital account	- 3	- 36	- 32	- 96	- 87	194	- 123	- 141	- 113	Compte de capital
Financial account	2 287	9 016	- 4 166	1 119	9 860	4 995	18 052	21 318	29 148	Compte financier
Errors and omissions	- 1 238	- 1 306	533	- 2 155	- 3 146	- 931	- 2 061	- 4 159	258	Erreurs et omissions
Overall balance	- 3 378	3 356	- 9 754	- 11 278	237	1 479	3 725	- 2 813	13 717	Balance générale

X DEBT AND FINANCIAL FLOWS - DETTE ET FLUX FINANCIERS

	2009	2010	2011	2012	2013	2014	2015	2016	2017	
X-1 DEBT *US $ (MILLIONS)*										**X-1 DETTE EXTÉRIEURE** *$ E.U (MILLIONS)*
Total external debt	31 531	33 694	34 906	34 419	43 239	46 056	48 063	55 765	76 275	Dette extérieure totale
Private	...	...	...	...	...	...	...	...	...	Privée
Public	29 888	31 447	32 863	32 236	41 947	42 894	43 960	47 219	...	Publique
Total external debt service	5 509	4 521	5 621	5 330	5 678	9 941	6 572	6 092	...	Service de la dette extérieure
Present value of external debt	554	554	545	- 521	8 849	2 834	...	42 002	...	Valeur actuelle de la dette extérieure
Total government domestic debt, National currency (millions)	562 327	663 818	808 113	990 529	1 261 141	1 538 459	1 871 332	...	...	Dette publique intérieure
X-2 FINANCIAL FLOWS *US $ (MILLIONS)*										**X-2 FLUX FINANCIERS** *$ E.U (MILLIONS)*
Net Foreign Direct Investment Inflows	6 712	6 386	- 483	6 031	4 256	4 612	6 925	8 107	...	Investissements étranger direct (flux nets entrants)
Main origin of FDI inflows										**Principales origines de l'IDE entrant:**
United States	2 258	1 791	578	2 183	2 230	2 116	...	...	...	États-Unis
United Kingdom	3 781	4 307	5 820	3 997	5 116	5 357	...	...	...	Royaume-Uni
France	244	227	316	266	347	230	...	...	...	France
Italy	82	247	193	75	17	37	...	...	...	Italie
Germany	85	275	203	186	194	190	...	...	...	Allemagne
African countries	14	...	...	...	...	...	...	...	...	Pays africains
Net total official development assistance	989	599	424	1 813	5 513	3 538	2 499	2 130	...	Aide publique au développement (nette totale)
Main origin of net ODA										**Principales origines de l'APD nette**
United States	185	49	- 98	- 15	58	- 173	- 155	- 130	...	États-Unis
France	112	140	116	140	55	56	83	207	...	France
Germany	139	104	164	103	188	144	141	13	...	Allemagne
United Arab Emirates	56	22	12	11	5	3	...	...	...	Emirates Arabes
...	...	...	...	...	...	...	...	...	...	...

ÉGYPTE

SOURCES AND NOTES - SOURCES ET NOTES

External trade - Total exports, fob: UNCTAD	Commerce exterieur - Exportation, fab: CNUCED
External trade - Total import, cif: UNCTAD	Commerce exterieur - Imporations, caf: CNUCED
ODA: OECD	APD: OCDE
Monetary statistics: IMF	Statistiques monétaires: FMI
National Accounts: 2017:Provisional	Comptes nationaux: 2017:Provisoire
National Accounts: Break in the serie from 2007 and 2012. data is in Fisical Year July (n-1) / June (n)	Comptes Nationaux: Repture de la serie à partir de 2007 et 2012 Les données sont exprimées en année fiscale juillet n-1/juin (n)
Poverty: World Bank	Pauvreté: Banque mondiale

AREA (km2)		28 050		SUPERFICIE (KM2)
CAPITAL CITY	Malabo		Malabo	CAPITALE
CURRENCY	CFA Franc		Franc CFA	MONNAIE

I SOCIAL AND DEMOGRAPHIC INDICATORS — INDICATEURS DEMOGRAPHIQUES ET SOCIAUX

Population	Year Année	Value Valeur	Charts Graphiques	Population
Population ('000)	2017	1 255.4		Population ('000)
Female (%)	2017	57.9		Féminine (%)
Urban (%)	2015	37.8		Urbaine (%)
Average annual growth rate	2017	3.4		Taux de croissance annuel
Active population ('000)	2017	68.6		Population active ('000)
Population by age group ('000)				Population par groupe d'âge ('000)
0-14 years	2017	48.0		0-14 ans
15-64 years	2017	68.2		15-64 ans
65+ years	...	...		65+ ans
Economically active population in agriculture (%)	2015	51.4		Participation de la population active agricole (%)
Crude birth rate	2017	36.0		Taux brut de natalité
Crude death rate	2017	10.4		Taux brut de mortalité
Total fertility rate	2017	5.1		Indice synthétique de fécondité
Life expectancy at birth - Total (years)	2017	59.3		Espérance de vie à la naissance - Totale (années)
Dependency ratio - Total (%)	2017	70.4		Taux de dépendance - Total (%)
Health				**Santé**
Percentage of children under-five and underweight	2017	6.0		% d'enfants de moins de cinq ans avec insuffisance pondérale
Prevalence of undernourishment	2016	5.6		Prévalence de la malnutrition
Under five mortality rate (per 1 000 live births)	2017	113.0		Taux de mortalité de moins de 5 ans (les deux sexes, pour 1000)
Infant mortality rate (per 1 000 live births)	2017	65.0		Taux de mortalité infantile (les deux sexes) par 1000
Neonatal mortality rate (per 1 000 live births)	2017	33.0		Le taux de mortalité néonatale (pour 1000 naissances vivantes)
Percentage of children provided the vaccines :				Pourcentage d'enfants vaccinés :
BCG	2017	70.8		BCG
DPT3	2017	41.0		DTC3
Polio	2017	33.0		polio
Measles	2017	40.3		rougeole
Percentage of mothers provided at least one antenatal care (%)	2017	91.0		Pourcentage de mères ayant au moins reçu un soin prénatal (%)
Percentage of deliveries attended by skilled health personnel	2017	68.0		% d'accouchements assistés par un personnel de santé qualifié
Number of doctors (per 10,000 population)	2017	4.0		Nombre de médecins (pour 10.000 habitants)
Number of nurses (per 10,000 population)	2017	5.0		Nombre d'infirmiers (pour 10.000 habitants)
Hospital beds - Total (per 10,000 population)	2017	9.3		Nombre de lits d'hôpitaux - Total (pour 10 000)
Births registered (per 1,000)	2017	36.0		Naissances enregistrées (pour 1000)
Deaths registered (per 1,000)	2017	10.4		Décès enregistrés (pour 1000)
Budget allocation to health (%)	2013	7.0		Dépenses publiques consacrées à la santé (% du budget)
Education				**Education**
Enrolment in primary education (000)	2017	93 396.0		Scolarisation dans le primaire (000)
Female	2017	45 855.0		Féminine
Enrolment in secondary education (000)	2017	34 968.0		Scolarisation dans le secondaire (000)
Female	2017	17 099.0		Féminine
Enrolment in tertiary education (000)	...	...		Scolarisation dans le tertiaire (000)
Female	...	...		Féminine
Literacy rate	2017	96.8		Taux d'alphabétisation (deux sexes)
Male	2017	97.9		Masculin
Female	2017	95.7		Féminin
Pupil teacher ratio - primary	2017	39.7		Ratio élève-enseignant
Budget allocation to education (%)	2003	4.0		Dépenses publiques consacrées à l'enseignement (% du budget)
Poverty				**Pauvreté**
GNI per capita, PPP (current int. $)	2016	18290.0		RNB par habitant, ($ PPA inter. courants)
Human Poverty Index (HPI-1) Value (%)	2007	31.9		Valeur de l'Indice de pauvreté (IPH-1) (%)
Population below Inter. poverty line ($2/day) (%)	2015	2.0		Population sous le seuil inter. de pauvreté (2$/Jour) (%)
Share of income held by richest 10%	...	...		% de revenu des 10% plus riches
Share of income held by poorest 10%	...	...		% de revenu des 10% plus pauvres
GINI index	...	...		Indice de GINI

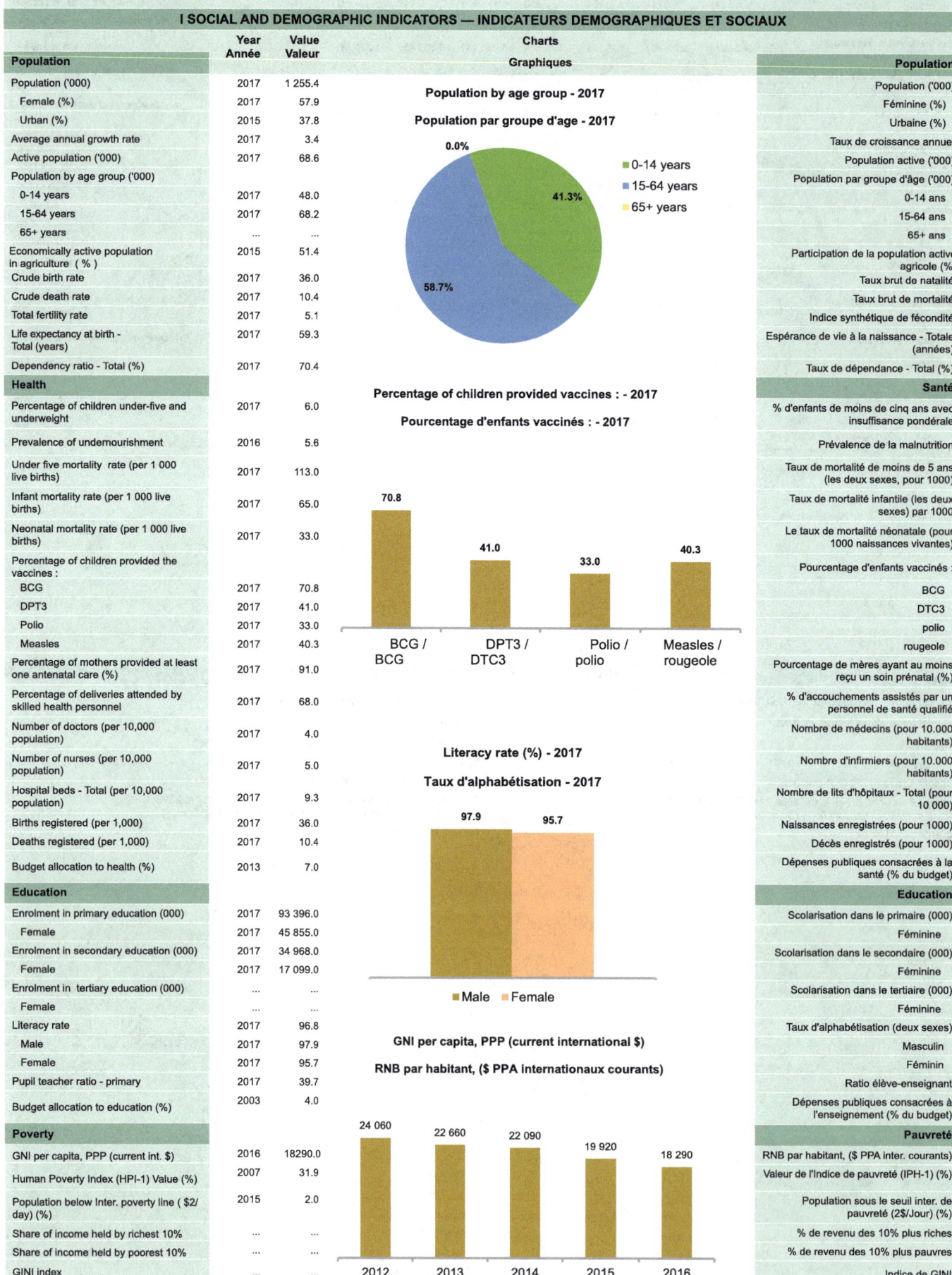

Population by age group - 2017
Population par groupe d'age - 2017

0.0%
41.3%
58.7%
- 0-14 years
- 15-64 years
- 65+ years

Percentage of children provided vaccines : - 2017
Pourcentage d'enfants vaccinés : - 2017

70.8   41.0   33.0   40.3
BCG / BCG   DPT3 / DTC3   Polio / polio   Measles / rougeole

Literacy rate (%) - 2017
Taux d'alphabétisation - 2017

97.9   95.7
- Male - Female

GNI per capita, PPP (current international $)
RNB par habitant, ($ PPA internationaux courants)

24 060   22 660   22 090   19 920   18 290
2012   2013   2014   2015   2016

II NATIONAL ACCOUNTS — COMPTES NATIONAUX

	2009	2010	2011	2012	2013	2014	2015	2016	2017	
GROSS DOMESTIC PRODUCT BY KIND OF ECONOMIC ACTIVITY AT CURRENT PRICES *CFA FRANC (MILLIONS)*										**PRODUIT INTÉRIEUR BRUT PAR BRANCHE D'ACTIVITÉ ÉCONOMIQUE AUX PRIX COURANTS** *FRANC CFA (MILLIONS)*
Agriculture, hunting , forestry and Fishing	75 089	85 677	106 031	120 667	129 218	139 091	147 208	158 402	166 263	Agriculture, chasse sylviculture et Pêche
Mining and quarrying	2 850 017	3 634 511	4 489 930	5 441 260	4 607 501	4 270 695	2 432 983	1 718 159	1 805 259	Industries extractives
Manufacturing	1 279 959	1 696 512	2 261 368	1 953 446	2 090 680	2 162 872	1 391 066	1 238 857	1 825 332	Industries manufacturières
Electricity, gas & water	23 926	24 045	42 658	50 747	56 292	66 161	56 939	63 075	64 692	Electricité, gaz et eau
Construction	1 191 080	678 532	1 062 976	1 391 647	1 099 404	1 043 589	726 151	450 152	383 106	Bâtiments et travaux publics
Wholesale & retail trade, restaurants, hotels	506 857	674 293	623 595	773 932	740 740	761 381	681 695	608 220	578 975	Commerce de gros et de détail, restaurants et hôtels
Finance, insurance, real estate, etc.	153 398	185 955	225 073	242 461	257 028	295 410	268 070	257 961	266 332	Banques, assurances, affaires immobilières
Transport and communications	281 234	290 511	406 291	452 293	486 478	501 309	480 858	529 617	539 441	Transport(s) et communications
Public administration and defense	667 298	769 737	892 001	1 063 591	1 360 554	1 451 033	1 504 796	1 529 343	1 585 992	Administrations publiques et défense
Education	47 495	51 661	54 945	60 374	66 218	70 977	73 638	78 433	80 934	Education
Health And Social Work	23 826	24 327	25 548	28 863	32 124	35 428	37 433	39 735	42 386	Santé et Actions Sociales
Other services	...	...	...	...	1 814	3 119	3 251	3 408	3 677	Autres services
Less Imputed Service Charges	- 58 162	- 71 082	- 100 392	- 115 287	- 100 065	- 123 662	- 106 391	- 101 635	- 98 159	Moins Services d'intermédiation financière
Gross domestic product at factor cost / basic prices	7 042 017	8 044 679	10 090 024	11 463 993	10 827 986	10 677 403	7 697 697	6 573 727	7 244 231	Produit intérieur brut aux couts des facteurs / prix de base
Plus: Indirect Taxes / taxes on products, less subsidies	53 902	27 614	- 25 405	- 33 482	12 535	69 449	97 723	100 385	79 502	Plus taxes indirectes/impôts sur les produits, moins les subventions
EXPENDITURE ON GROSS DOMESTIC PRODUCT AT CURRENT PURCHASER'S VALUES *CFA FRANC (MILLIONS)*										**EMPLOI DU PRODUIT INTÉRIEUR BRUT AUX PRIX COURANTS D'ACQUISITION** *FRANC CFA (MILLIONS)*
Government final consumption	790 085	943 347	1 185 718	1 323 864	1 675 732	1 715 884	1 708 874	1 707 211	1 708 372	Consommation finale des administrations publiques
Private final consumption	1 632 095	1 889 629	2 048 794	2 301 585	2 799 084	2 985 146	3 035 392	3 185 142	3 328 354	Consommation finale privée
Gross fixed capital formation	3 804 316	3 416 328	3 840 715	5 321 994	3 270 600	3 071 137	1 912 292	1 096 751	900 166	Formation brute de capital fixe
Change in inventories	-1 009 033	- 344 312	- 615 078	- 618 551	14 950	14 209	13 290	8 738	4 616	Variation des stocks
Exports of goods and services	5 275 263	6 922 672	7 558 057	8 219 108	7 333 972	7 088 977	4 416 766	3 424 797	4 109 744	Exportations de biens et services
Less imports of goods and services	3 396 807	4 755 371	3 953 587	5 117 489	4 253 817	4 128 501	3 291 194	2 748 527	2 727 519	Moins importations de biens et services
GDP at purchasers' values	7 095 919	8 072 293	10 064 619	11 430 511	10 840 521	10 746 852	7 795 420	6 674 112	7 323 733	PIB aux prix d'acquisition
GROSS DOMESTIC PRODUCT BY KIND OF ECONOMIC ACTIVITY AT CONSTANT PRICES *ANNUAL GROWTH RATES (%)*										**PRODUIT INTÉRIEUR BRUT PAR BRANCHE D'ACTIVITÉ ÉCONOMIQUE AUX PRIX CONSTANTS** *TAUX DE CROISSANCE ANNUEL (%)*
Agriculture, hunting , forestry and Fishing	- 8.7	18.5	11.6	8.1	7.8	7.2	11.8	8.5	5.4	Agriculture, chasse sylviculture et Pêche
Mining and quarrying	- 13.9	- 7.3	- 4.1	10.5	- 12.1	1.5	- 8.4	- 15.2	- 14.2	Industries extractives
Manufacturing	13.7	- 12.3	8.6	- 5.1	5.2	0.9	- 10.1	5.1	9.4	Industries manufacturières
Electricity, gas & water	15.8	12.2	98.0	41.4	4.0	14.8	- 15.7	9.7	1.3	Electricité, gaz et eau
Construction	72.5	- 44.3	60.7	20.9	- 22.9	- 8.4	- 32.1	- 39.2	- 12.5	Bâtiments et travaux publics
Wholesale & retail trade, restaurants, hotels	- 9.0	26.1	- 10.9	17.1	- 8.2	- 2.4	- 13.9	- 12.3	- 2.1	Commerce de gros et de détail, restaurants et hôtels
Finance, insurance, real estate, etc.	- 2.5	16.5	18.7	1.7	4.6	10.7	- 9.8	- 6.8	3.5	Banques, assurances, affaires immobilières
Transport and communications	1.0	1.7	38.0	3.4	5.8	- 2.1	- 4.1	3.4	3.4	Transport(s) et communications
Public administration and defense	14.1	11.8	14.8	11.4	25.8	1.3	3.4	- 2.9	4.6	Administrations publiques et défense
Education	2.5	4.1	4.1	3.6	8.3	1.7	0.8	2.8	3.4	Education
Health And Social Work	2.5	2.3	5.6	3.2	2.8	1.6	0.3	2.6	7.0	Santé et Actions Sociales
Other services	...	...	...	...	...	67.8	5.0	2.2	20.8	Autres services
Less Imputed Service Charges	- 1.9	16.5	37.8	8.8	- 13.6	23.6	- 14.0	- 4.4	- 3.4	Moins Services d'intermédiation financière
Gross domestic product at factor cost / basic prices	0.9	- 8.9	6.9	8.4	- 4.4	0.1	- 9.3	- 8.6	- 2.4	Produit intérieur brut aux couts des facteurs / prix de base
Plus: Indirect Taxes / taxes on products, less subsidies	- 677.0	- 28.9	- 141.7	90.8	- 134.1	436.5	46.4	3.2	- 6.2	Plus taxes indirectes/impôts sur les produits, moins les subventions
Gross domestic product at market prices	1.3	- 8.9	6.5	8.3	- 4.1	0.4	- 9.1	- 8.6	- 2.5	Produit intérieur brut aux prix du marché
EXPENDITURE ON GROSS DOMESTIC PRODUCT AT CONSTANT PURCHASERS' VALUES *ANNUAL GROWTH RATES (%)*										**EMPLOIS DU PRODUIT INTÉRIEUR BRUT AUX PRIX CONSTANTS D'ACQUISITION** *TAUX DE CROISSANCE ANNUEL (%)*
Government final consumption	14.8	12.7	22.7	6.0	25.8	- 1.0	- 0.7	- 4.5	1.7	Consommation finale des administrations publiques
Private final consumption	1.6	8.4	4.0	6.8	17.9	3.6	1.9	3.1	4.5	Consommation finale privée
Gross fixed capital formation	30.0	- 15.2	9.7	31.4	- 38.9	- 9.6	- 39.2	- 42.4	- 20.6	Formation brute de capital fixe
Exports of goods and services	- 6.1	- 0.2	- 10.7	4.6	- 7.6	0.5	- 6.4	- 9.3	- 4.3	Exportations de biens et services
Less imports of goods and services	- 10.2	29.5	- 19.4	23.8	- 17.7	- 5.6	- 15.5	- 16.3	- 3.9	Moins importations de biens et services

III INFLATION

	2009	2010	2011	2012	2013	2014	2015	2016	2017	
Annual growth rates (%)										**Taux de croissance annuel (%)**
All item	5.5	4.7	7.3	3.6	3.6	3.6	2.7	1.4	1.1	Ensemble
of which:										dont:
Food and non-alcoholic beverages	...	...	5.5	5.6	5.4	4.8	4.4	- 4.1	1.6	Alimentation et boissons non alcoolisés
Alcoholic beverages, tobacco and narcotics	...	...	2.2	2.1	2.3	2.1	4.3	4.0	- 0.3	Boissons alcoolisées et tabacs
Clothing and footwear	...	...	3.8	3.5	3.1	2.7	8.0	- 8.4	0.7	Habillement et chaussures
Housing, water, electricity, gas and other fuels	...	...	3.6	3.3	3.0	2.6	4.1	19.8	- 0.4	Logement, eau, électricité, gaz et autres combustibles
Furnishings, household equipment and routine household maintenance	...	...	3.4	3.8	3.6	3.2	6.0	8.2	0.1	Meubles, articles de ménage et entretien courant
Health	...	...	1.2	3.1	2.8	2.5	3.3	1.7	1.0	Santé
Transport	...	...	1.2	1.2	1.7	1.6	- 0.8	3.3	- 0.3	Transport
Communication	...	...	2.9	1.3	1.2	1.2	3.1	20.1	0.4	Communication
Recreation and culture	...	...	6.1	2.7	2.4	2.1	2.1	23.3	0.7	Loisirs et culture
Education	...	...	2.9	4.7	3.4	2.2	4.3	13.5	5.0	Enseignement
Restaurants and hotels	...	...	4.2	2.6	2.2	1.9	4.8	12.6	- 1.8	Restaurants et hôtels
Miscellaneous goods and services	...	...	...	...	...	...	...	5.7	- 1.0	Biens et Services divers

GUINÉE ÉQUATORIALE

IV AGRICULTURAL PRODUCTION - PRODUCTION AGRICOLE

TONNES (THOUSAND)	2009	2010	2011	2012	2013	2014	2015	2016	2017	Tonnes (milliers)
Sweet potatoes	92	90	91	95	92	...	...	...	...	Patates douces
Cassava	73	64	66	68	70	...	111	222	...	Manioc
Plantains	40	42	42	43	44	...	120	160	...	Bananes plantains
Bananas	27	27	28	29	30	...	18	33	...	Bananes
Coconuts	6	7	7	7	8	...	288	264	...	Noix de coco

V MINING PRODUCTION - PRODUCTION MINIERE

	2009	2010	2011	2012	2013	2014	2015	2016	2017	
Crude petroleum - Production, metric tons (thousands)	15 406	14 250	13 927	14 940	13 006	73 175	65 527	74 546 592	63 504 330	Pétrole brut - Production, tonnes métriques (milliers)
Natural gas - Production, terajoules (millions)	-	-	-	-	...	100	104	47	51	Gaz naturel - Production, térajoules (millions)
	...	...	...	...	...	...	...	...	...	

VI ENERGY - ENERGIE

	2009	2010	2011	2012	2013	2014	2015	2016	2017	
Total electricity generation (GWh)	94	410	410	410	413	888	916	...	...	Production électrique totale (GWh)
of which										dont
Production of electricity from fossil fuels (GWh)	87	396	396	396	396	505	523	...	...	Production d'électricité à partir de combustibles fossiles (GWh)
Production of hydro electricity (GWh)	7	14	14	14	18	383	393	...	...	Production d'électricité d'origine hydraulique (GWh)
Production of electricity from solar, wind, tide, wave and other sources (GWh)	...	...	...	...	...	...	9	...	...	Production d'électricité d'origine solaire, éolienne, marée motrice et autres (GWh)

VII TOURISM AND INFRASTRUCTURE - TOURISME ET INFRASTUCTURE

	2009	2010	2011	2012	2013	2014	2015	2016	2017	
VII-1 Tourism										**VII-1 Tourisme**
International tourist arrivals (thousands)	...	...	...	...	...	...	...	...	...	Arrivées de touristes internationaux (milliers)
Rooms in hotels and similar establishments (thousands)	...	...	...	...	...	...	...	...	...	Chambres d'hôtels et établissements assimilés (milliers)
Overnight stays (thousands)	...	...	...	...	...	...	...	...	...	Nuitées (milliers)
Tourism receipts (US$ thousand)	...	...	...	...	...	...	...	...	...	Recettes touristiques (milliers de $ EU)
Total contribution to GDP (%)	...	...	...	...	...	...	...	...	...	Contribution totale au PIB (%)
Total contribution to Employment (%)	...	...	...	...	...	...	...	...	...	Contribution totale à l'emploi (%)
VII-2 Infrastructure										**VII-2 Infrastructure**
Paved road (% of total)	...	...	...	...	...	...	...	...	...	Routes asphaltées (% du total)
Total network (Railways-km)	...	...	...	...	...	...	...	...	...	Réseau total voies ferrées-Km
Main telephone lines (per 100 inhabitants)	1.5	1.9	2.0	2.0	2.0	1.9	1.4	1.2	...	Lignes téléphoniques fixes (pour 100 habitants)
Mobile cellular subscribers (per 100 inhabitants)	29.5	57.4	66.9	68.1	67.5	66.4	66.7	65.9	...	Abonnés aux téléphones mobiles (pour 100 habitants)
Internet users per 100 inhabitants	2.1	6.0	11.5	13.9	16.4	18.9	21.3	23.8	...	Utilisateurs Internet par 100 Habitants
Fixed (wired)-broadband subscriptions per 100 inhabitants	...	...	...	...	...	...	...	...	...	Abonnements à l'Internet fixe (filaire) à large bande pour 100 habitants, par débit

VIII EXTERNAL TRADE - COMMERCE EXTERIEUR

	2009	2010	2011	2012	2013	2014	2015	2016	2017	
US$ (MILLIONS) **EXPORTS, FOB**										**$ E.U (MILLIONS)** **EXPORTATIONS, FÀB**
Exports - Total	9 100	10 000	13 500	15 500	14 700	12 600	6 500	4 800	...	Exportations - Total
Exports to Africa	315	562	494	285	726	544	295	100	...	Exportations vers l'Afrique
Main products										**Principaux produits**
Alcohols, phenols, halogenat., sulfonat., nitrat. der.	191	133	337	369	490	455	276	329	...	Alcools, phénols, halogénates, sulfonates, nitrates. der.
Liquefied propane and butane	220	323	364	284	418	299	137	118	...	Propane liquéfié et butane
Natural gas, whether or not liquefied	1 944	1 486	2 478	3 037	2 823	2 923	1 295	763	...	Gaz naturel, même liquéfié
Petroleum oils, oils from bitumin. materials, crude	6 394	7 418	9 641	11 341	9 846	8 593	4 341	3 255	...	Huiles de pétrole, huiles de bitume. matériaux bruts
Wood in the rough or roughly squared	9	91	132	132	151	174	172	281	...	Bois bruts ou grossièrement équarris
Main destinations										**Principales destinations**
China	1 052	623	1 706	1 805	2 482	3 095	1 086	670	...	Chine
France	337	387	613	2 475	1 524	957	370	53	...	France
Japan	779	374	1 349	2 872	2 023	822	194	135	...	Japon
Spain	637	996	1 931	1 104	1 085	670	587	601	...	Espagne
United Kingdom	66	17	518	491	1 857	1 867	369	193	...	Royaume-Uni
IMPORTS, CIF										
Imports - Total	5 200	5 200	6 500	6 900	5 600	5 500	3 400	2 800	...	Importations - Total (millions)
Imports from Africa	3 569	3 160	2 654	971	480	736	239	93	...	Importations en provenance de l'Afrique
Main products										**Principaux produits**
Alcoholic beverages	59	71	157	265	182	230	181	221	...	Boissons alcoolisées
Civil engineering & contractors' plant & equipment	200	193	267	366	1 091	234	79	45	...	Génie civil et installations et équipements des entrepreneurs
Petroleum oils or bituminous minerals > 70 % oil	119	137	325	515	280	323	150	20	...	Huiles de pétrole ou de minéraux bitumineux> 70% d'huile
Ships, boats & floating structures	38	173	199	169	516	190	531	460	...	Navires, bateaux et structures flottantes
Structures & parts, n.e.s., of iron, steel, aluminium	74	88	187	226	225	186	165	57	...	Structures et parties, n.d.a., de fer, d'acier, d'aluminium
Main origin										**Principales provenances**
China	349	460	491	1 068	626	729	510	372	...	Chine
France	160	236	502	493	273	284	166	120	...	France
Netherlands	59	56	150	175	135	196	689	132	...	Pays-Bas
Spain	264	302	692	1 130	787	879	569	657	...	Espagne
United States	298	275	526	689	1 323	1 189	316	699	...	États-Unis

IX FINANCIAL AND MONETARY STATISTICS - FINANCES ET STATISTIQUES MONETAIRES

	2009	2010	2011	2012	2013	2014	2015	2016	2017	
IX-1 MONETARY STATISTICS *CFA FRANC (MILLIONS)*										**IX-1 STATISTIQUES MONÉTAIRES** *FRANC CFA (MILLIONS)*
Money supply (M1)	744 181	993 563	1 069 869	1 688 615	1 811 990	1 557 006	1 386 845	1 159 964	1 389 921	Masse monétaire (M1)
Quasi-money	75 786	101 777	109 027	208 515	216 840	225 420	249 371	246 794	266 940	Quasi-monnaie
of which demand deposit	...	...	...	...	...	...	...	...	...	dont Monnaie scripturale
Net foreign assets	1 561 541	1 155 807	1 588 327	2 274 278	2 382 217	1 629 075	854 095	162 717	74 647	Avoirs extérieurs nets
Domestic credit	- 690 276	86 203	- 282 806	- 312 403	- 270 031	359 895	937 813	1 402 521	1 534 981	Crédit intérieur
of which claims on private sector	-1 131 055	- 496 718	-1 021 986	- 934 852	-1 103 645	- 618 563	- 175 650	224 263	338 730	dont créances sur le secteur privé
of which claims on government sector, net	412 944	539 111	704 847	608 999	817 723	968 304	1 104 787	1 151 487	1 166 964	dont créances nettes sur le gouvernement
International reserves (millions US$)	3 252	2 354	3 054	4 397	4 567	2 907	1 205	62	7	Réserves internationales (millions $EU)
Average exchange rate (National currency per US$)	472	495	472	511	494	494	591	593	582	Taux de change (moyen) (monnaie nationale par $ EU)
IX-2 PUBLIC FINANCE *CFA FRANC (MILLIONS)*										**IX-2 FINANCES PUBLIQUES** *FRANC CFA (MILLIONS)*
Total Revenues and Grants	2 608 087	2 150 932	2 849 081	3 195 000	2 696 000	2 585 000	2 071 000	1 565 000	1 485 200	Recettes totales et dons
Direct taxes (on income, profits)	94 000	99 000	113 000	131 000	130 000	137 000	171 000	120 000	309 745	Taxes directes
Domestic indirect taxes revenues	44 000	46 000	54 000	57 000	57 000	63 000	79 000	73 000	67 187	Taxes Indirectes
Trade taxes	10 000	12 000	14 000	15 000	17 000	18 000	18 000	17 000	23 724	Taxes sur le commerce extérieur
Other taxes	2 188 483	1 938 503	2 639 439	2 796 000	2 314 000	2 235 000	1 666 000	1 150 000	1 059 544	Autres taxes
Other revenues	271 604	55 429	28 642	196 000	178 000	132 000	137 000	205 000	25 000	Autres recettes
Grants	...	...	...	...	...	...	...	...	...	Dons
Total Expenditures and Net Lending	2 827 494	2 516 843	2 767 018	4 023 000	3 329 000	3 102 000	2 331 000	1 929 000	1 766 681	Dépenses totales et prêts nets
Current expenditure	341 834	434 365	472 819	783 000	834 000	714 000	654 000	784 000	732 331	Dépenses courantes
Wages and Salaries	70 654	77 800	79 822	100 000	110 000	112 000	121 000	147 000	146 769	Rémunérations et salaires
Other purchases of goods and services	154 187	186 552	210 588	433 000	488 000	417 000	345 000	404 000	382 979	Achat de biens et services
Other current expenditure	...	...	...	...	...	...	...	...	202 583	Autres dépenses courantes
Current transfers	116 992	170 013	182 409	250 000	236 000	185 000	188 000	233 000		Transferts courants
Interest payments	3 400	19 550	27 762	32 000	38 000	50 000	30 000	44 000	81 350	Intérêts
Capital expenditure	2 482 260	2 062 928	2 266 437	3 208 000	2 457 000	2 338 000	1 647 000	1 101 000	953 000	Dépenses d'équipement
Net lending	...	...	...	...	...	...	...	...	...	Prêts nets
Fiscal balance	- 219 407	- 365 911	82 063	- 828 000	- 633 000	- 517 000	- 260 000	- 364 000	- 281 481	Solde global y compris les dons
IX-3 BALANCE OF PAYMENTS *CFA FRANC (MILLIONS)*										**IX-3 BALANCE DES PAIEMENTS** *FRANC CFA (MILLIONS)*
Trade balance	2 981	3 048	4 850	5 430	4 093	3 538	1 279	1 616	1 696	Balance commerciale
Services Balance	- 1 134	- 1 251	- 1 536	- 1 661	- 1 603	- 1 674	- 1 202	- 545	- 558	Balance des services
Net primary income	- 2 403	- 3 351	- 3 674	- 3 611	- 2 662	- 2 058	- 1 075	- 851	- 890	Revenus primaires nets
Compensation of employees	...	- 58	- 146	- 106	- 115	- 63	- 50	- 47	- 49	Rémunération des salariés
Investment income	- 2 344	- 3 293	- 3 527	- 3 504	- 2 548	- 1 996	- 1 025	- 804	- 841	Revenus des investissements
Net secondary income	- 41	- 80	- 211	- 287	- 99	- 265	- 274	- 258	- 244	Revenus secondaires nets
Net official transfers	8	4	- 41	- 9	- 3	- 63	- 103	- 98	- 78	Transferts officiels nets
Workers' remittances	...	...	...	...	...	...	...	...	- 151	Envois de fonds des travailleurs
Other private transfers	- 49	- 85	- 170	- 278	- 95	- 201	- 171	- 160	- 167	Autres transferts privés
Current account balance	- 596	- 1 634	- 571	- 129	- 270	- 459	- 1 272	- 38	4	Solde du compte courant
Capital and financial account	527	1 148	1 518	1 377	648	426	253	1	195	Comptes de capital et financier
Capital account	...	...	...	...	...	...	...	...	...	Compte de capital
Financial account	527	1 148	1 513	1 377	648	426	253	1	195	Compte financier
Errors and omissions	- 559	160	- 551	- 620	- 397	- 553	172	- 674	...	Erreurs et omissions
Overall balance	- 627	- 327	395	628	- 20	- 587	- 846	- 712	199	Balance générale

GUINÉE ÉQUATORIALE

X DEBT AND FINANCIAL FLOWS - DETTE ET FLUX FINANCIERS

	2009	2010	2011	2012	2013	2014	2015	2016	2017	
X-1 DEBT *US $ (MILLIONS)*										**X-1 DETTE EXTÉRIEURE** *$ E.U (MILLIONS)*
Total external debt	673	1 294	1 164	1 677	1 400	1 022	1 030	1 024	1 555	Dette extérieure totale
Private	...	...	...	...	...	...	...	...	...	Privée
Public	673	1 294	1 164	1 677	1 400	1 022	1 030	1 024	...	Publique
Total external debt service	6	7	19	119	398	335	205	227	...	Service de la dette extérieure
Present value of external debt	...	...	...	...	...	...	...	...	...	Valeur actuelle de la dette extérieure
Total government domestic debt, National currency (millions)	...	...	...	...	...	...	...	...	...	Dette publique intérieure
X-2 FINANCIAL FLOWS *US $ (MILLIONS)*										**X-2 FLUX FINANCIERS** *$ E.U (MILLIONS)*
Net Foreign Direct Investment Inflows	1 636	2 734	1 975	985	583	168	233	54	...	Investissements étranger direct (flux nets entrants)
Main origin of FDI inflows										**Principales origines de l'IDE entrant:**
United States	342	- 90	37	...	...	...	...	...	...	États-Unis
Dem. People's Rep. of Korea	...	62	...	...	...	...	...	...	...	République de Corée
...	...	...	...	...	...	...	...	...	...	...
Sweden	...	...	7	6	...	...	...	...	...	Suède
Luxembourg	...	3	...	...	...	...	...	...	...	Luxembourg
African countries	...	...	...	...	...	...	...	...	...	Pays africains
Net total official development assistance	32	85	25	14	5	1	7	7	...	Aide publique au développement (nette totale)
Main origin of net ODA										**Principales origines de l'APD nette**
Spain	22	20	15	9	2	2	2	2	...	Espagne
Italy	...	55	...	...	-	...	-	...	...	Italie
France	3	3	4	3	3	3	2	2	...	France
Global Fund	3	7	3	-	...	-	...	...	...	Fonds Mondial
UNFPA	1	1	1	2	1	1	1	1	...	UNFPA

SOURCES AND NOTES - SOURCES ET NOTES

External trade - Total exports, fob: UNCTAD

External trade - Total import, cif: UNCTAD

ODA: OECD

Monetary statistics: IMF

National Accounts: 2014-2015:Estimated 2016-2017: Previsional

Poverty: World Bank

Commerce exterieur - Exportation, fab: CNUCED

Commerce exterieur - Imporations, caf: CNUCED

APD: OCDE

Statistiques monétaires: FMI

Comptes nationaux: 2014-2015: Données Estimées 2016-2017: Données Provisoires

Pauvreté: Banque mondiale

AREA (km2)		117 600		**SUPERFICIE (KM2)**
CAPITAL CITY	Asmara		Asmara	**CAPITALE**
CURRENCY	Eritrea Nakfa		Nafka érythréen	**MONNAIE**

I SOCIAL AND DEMOGRAPHIC INDICATORS — INDICATEURS DEMOGRAPHIQUES ET SOCIAUX

Population	**Year Année**	**Value Valeur**	**Charts / Graphiques**	**Population**
Population ('000)	2017	5 900.0		Population ('000)
Female (%)	...	...		Féminine (%)
Urban (%)	2017	23.6		Urbaine (%)
Average annual growth rate	2015	2.7		Taux de croissance annuel
Active population ('000)	2015	2 298.9		Population active ('000)
Population by age group ('000)				Population par groupe d'âge ('000)
0-14 years	2015	2 236.7		0-14 ans
15-64 years	2015	2 853.5		15-64 ans
65+ years	2015	137.6		65+ ans
Economically active population in agriculture (%)	2015	77.1		Participation de la population active agricole (%)
Crude birth rate	2015	33.4		Taux brut de natalité
Crude death rate	2015	6.4		Taux brut de mortalité
Total fertility rate	2016	4.2		Indice synthétique de fécondité
Life expectancy at birth - Total (years)	2015	64.2		Espérance de vie à la naissance - Totale (années)
Dependency ratio - Total (%)	2015	83.2		Taux de dépendance - Total (%)
Health				**Santé**
Percentage of children under-five and underweight	2002	34.5		% d'enfants de moins de cinq ans avec insuffisance pondérale
Prevalence of undernourishment	...	...		Prévalence de la malnutrition
Under five mortality rate (per 1 000 live births)	2016	44.5		Taux de mortalité de moins de 5 ans (les deux sexes, pour 1000)
Infant mortality rate (per 1 000 live births)	2016	32.9		Taux de mortalité infantile (les deux sexes) par 1000
Neonatal mortality rate (per 1 000 live births)	2016	17.7		Le taux de mortalité néonatale (pour 1000 naissances vivantes)
Percentage of children provided the vaccines :				Pourcentage d'enfants vaccinés :
BCG	2014	97.0		BCG
DPT3	2014	94.0		DTC3
Polio	2012	99.0		polio
Measles	2014	96.0		rougeole
Percentage of mothers provided at least one antenatal care (%)	2002	70.0		Pourcentage de mères ayant au moins reçu un soin prénatal (%)
Percentage of deliveries attended by skilled health personnel	2002	28.3		% d'accouchements assistés par un personnel de santé qualifié
Number of doctors (per 10,000 population)	2004	0.5		Nombre de médecins (pour 10.000 habitants)
Number of nurses (per 10,000 population)	2004	5.8		Nombre d'infirmiers (pour 10.000 habitants)
Hospital beds - Total (per 10,000 population)	2011	7.0		Nombre de lits d'hôpitaux - Total (pour 10 000)
Births registered (per 1,000)	2015	33.4		Naissances enregistrées (pour 1000)
Deaths registered (per 1,000)	2015	6.4		Décès enregistrés (pour 1000)
Budget allocation to health (%)	2014	3.3		Dépenses publiques consacrées à la santé (% du budget)
Education				**Education**
Enrolment in primary education (000)	2012	334.2		Scolarisation dans le primaire (000)
Female	2013	157.5		Féminine
Enrolment in secondary education (000)	2013	268.6		Scolarisation dans le secondaire (000)
Female	2013	117.5		Féminine
Enrolment in tertiary education (000)	2014	12.6		Scolarisation dans le tertiaire (000)
Female	2014	4.1		Féminine
Literacy rate	2012	70.5		Taux d'alphabétisation (deux sexes)
Male	2012	80.1		Masculin
Female	2012	61.3		Féminin
Pupil teacher ratio - primary	...	...		Ratio élève-enseignant
Budget allocation to education (%)	2005	5.2		Dépenses publiques consacrées à l'enseignement (% du budget)
Poverty				**Pauvreté**
GNI per capita, PPP (current int. $)	2011	1500.0		RNB par habitant, ($ PPA inter. courants)
Human Poverty Index (HPI-1) Value (%)	2007	33.7		Valeur de l'Indice de pauvreté (IPH-1) (%)
Population below Inter. poverty line ($2/day) (%)	...	...		Population sous le seuil inter. de pauvreté (2$/Jour) (%)
Share of income held by richest 10%	...	...		% de revenu des 10% plus riches
Share of income held by poorest 10%	...	...		% de revenu des 10% plus pauvres
GINI index	...	...		Indice de GINI

Population by age group - 2015
Population par groupe d'age - 2015

0-14 years 42.8%
15-64 years 54.6%
65+ years 2.6%

Percentage of children provided vaccines : - 2014
Pourcentage d'enfants vaccinés : - 2014

BCG / BCG	DPT3 / DTC3	Polio / polio (2012)	Measles / rougeole
97.0	94.0	99.0	96.0

Literacy rate (%) - 2012
Taux d'alphabétisation - 2012

Male 80.1 Female 61.3

GNI per capita, PPP (current international $)
RNB par habitant, ($ PPA internationaux courants)

2012 2013 2014 2015 2016

ERYTHRÉE

II NATIONAL ACCOUNTS — COMPTES NATIONAUX

	2009	2010	2011	2012	2013	2014	2015	2016	2017	
GROSS DOMESTIC PRODUCT BY KIND OF ECONOMIC ACTIVITY AT CURRENT PRICES *ERITREA NAKFA (MILLIONS)*										**PRODUIT INTÉRIEUR BRUT PAR BRANCHE D'ACTIVITÉ ÉCONOMIQUE AUX PRIX COURANTS)** *NAFKA ÉRYTHRÉEN (MILLIONS)*
Agriculture, hunting , forestry and Fishing	4 032	5 985	6 588	7 756	9 179	10 339	11 947	13 794	...	Agriculture, chasse sylviculture et Pêche
Mining and quarrying	471	541	704	803	917	1 069	1 222	1 405	...	Industries extractives
Manufacturing	1 568	1 897	2 385	2 736	3 146	3 643	4 172	4 801	...	Industries manufacturières
Electricity, gas & water	...	...	...	...	...	...	...	...	...	Electricité, gaz et eau
Construction	4 190	4 824	6 273	7 154	8 169	9 524	10 882	12 514	...	Bâtiments et travaux publics
Wholesale & retail trade, restaurants, hotels	5 667	5 880	7 399	8 933	9 927	11 563	13 341	15 247	...	Commerce de gros et de détail, restaurants et hôtels
Finance, insurance, real estate, etc.	...	...	...	...	...	...	...	...	...	Banques, assurances, affaires immobilières
Transport and communications	3 629	3 766	4 739	5 721	6 359	7 406	8 545	9 766	...	Transport(s) et communications
Public administration and defense	8 195	8 498	10 694	12 913	14 350	16 712	19 284	22 039	...	Administrations publiques et défense
Education	...	...	...	...	...	...	...	...	...	Education
Health And Social Work	...	...	...	...	...	...	...	...	...	Santé et Actions Sociales
Other services	...	...	...	...	...	...	...	...	...	Autres services
Less Imputed Service Charges	...	...	...	...	...	...	...	...	...	Moins Services d'intermédiation financière
Gross domestic product at factor cost / basic prices	27 752	31 391	38 782	46 016	52 047	60 256	69 393	79 567	...	Produit intérieur brut aux couts des facteurs / prix de base
Plus: Indirect Taxes / taxes on products, less subsidies	795	1 158	1 313	1 523	1 802	2 040	2 349	2 714	...	Plus taxes indirectes/impôts sur les produits, moins les subventions
EXPENDITURE ON GROSS DOMESTIC PRODUCT AT CURRENT PURCHASER'S VALUES *ERITREA NAKFA (MILLIONS)*										**EMPLOI DU PRODUIT INTÉRIEUR BRUT AUX PRIX COURANTS D'ACQUISITION** *NAFKA ÉRYTHRÉEN (MILLIONS)*
Government final consumption	5 741	7 764	8 439	9 148	10 326	11 958	13 754	15 767	...	Consommation finale des administrations publiques
Private final consumption	25 561	27 799	31 167	35 601	41 596	47 838	57 035	63 243	...	Consommation finale privée
Gross fixed capital formation	2 645	3 027	4 008	4 536	4 697	4 918	5 463	6 069	...	Formation brute de capital fixe
Change in inventories	...	...	...	...	...	...	...	...	...	Variation des stocks
Exports of goods and services	1 293	1 559	5 764	9 080	9 145	11 189	9 489	12 989	...	Exportations de biens et services
Less imports of goods and services	6 692	7 599	9 283	10 826	11 914	13 606	13 999	15 786	...	Moins importations de biens et services
GDP at purchasers' values	28 547	32 549	40 095	47 539	53 849	62 296	71 742	82 281	...	PIB aux prix d'acquisition
GROSS DOMESTIC PRODUCT BY KIND OF ECONOMIC ACTIVITY AT CONSTANT PRICES *ANNUAL GROWTH RATES (%)*										**PRODUIT INTÉRIEUR BRUT PAR BRANCHE D'ACTIVITÉ ECONOMIQUE AUX PRIX CONSTANTS** *TAUX DE CROISSANCE ANNUEL (%)*
Agriculture, hunting , forestry and Fishing	- 12.5	33.0	- 2.9	6.3	7.7	2.2	5.1	4.4	...	Agriculture, chasse sylviculture et Pêche
Mining and quarrying	- 12.4	2.9	14.8	3.0	3.9	5.8	4.0	3.9	...	Industries extractives
Manufacturing	- 12.5	8.4	10.9	3.5	4.6	5.1	4.2	4.0	...	Industries manufacturières
Electricity, gas & water	...	...	...	...	...	...	...	...	...	Electricité, gaz et eau
Construction	- 12.6	3.2	14.7	2.9	3.9	5.8	4.0	3.9	...	Bâtiments et travaux publics
Wholesale & retail trade, restaurants, hotels	18.2	- 7.0	11.0	9.0	1.1	5.7	5.0	3.3	...	Commerce de gros et de détail, restaurants et hôtels
Finance, insurance, real estate, etc.	...	...	...	...	...	...	...	...	...	Banques, assurances, affaires immobilières
Transport and communications	18.2	- 7.0	11.0	9.0	1.1	5.7	5.0	3.3	...	Transport(s) et communications
Public administration and defense	18.3	- 7.1	11.0	9.0	1.1	5.7	5.0	3.3	...	Administrations publiques et défense
Education	...	...	...	...	...	...	...	...	...	Education
Health And Social Work	...	...	...	...	...	...	...	...	...	Santé et Actions Sociales
Other services	...	...	...	...	...	...	...	...	...	Autres services
Less Imputed Service Charges	...	...	...	...	...	...	...	...	...	Moins Services d'intermédiation financière
Gross domestic product at factor cost / basic prices	4.6	1.4	9.0	7.1	2.9	5.1	4.8	3.6	...	Produit intérieur brut aux couts des facteurs / prix de base
Plus: Indirect Taxes / taxes on products, less subsidies	- 17.1	30.7	-	4.7	7.6	2.8	4.7	4.4	...	Plus taxes indirectes/impôts sur les produits, moins les subventions
Gross domestic product at market prices	3.9	2.2	8.7	7.0	3.1	5.0	4.8	3.7	...	Produit intérieur brut aux prix du marché
EXPENDITURE ON GROSS DOMESTIC PRODUCT AT CONSTANT PURCHASERS' VALUES *ANNUAL GROWTH RATES (%)*										**EMPLOIS DU PRODUIT INTÉRIEUR BRUT AUX PRIX CONSTANTS D'ACQUISITION** *TAUX DE CROISSANCE ANNUEL (%)*
Government final consumption	- 5.8	30.6	- 1.6	- 1.1	2.9	5.5	4.8	4.4	...	Consommation finale des administrations publiques
Private final consumption	6.8	- 2.7	- 1.2	2.1	7.1	4.0	10.3	- 1.7	...	Consommation finale privée
Gross fixed capital formation	- 14.0	8.0	24.6	6.9	- 2.2	- 1.4	4.7	4.7	...	Formation brute de capital fixe
Exports of goods and services	34.8	18.1	262.2	54.3	- 1.3	19.9	- 16.9	34.1	...	Exportations de biens et services
Less imports of goods and services	19.3	11.9	20.2	14.7	8.3	11.9	0.8	10.5	...	Moins importations de biens et services

III INFLATION

	2009	2010	2011	2012	2013	2014	2015	2016	2017	
Annual growth rates (%)										**Taux de croissance annuel (%)**
All item	33.0	11.2	3.9	6.0	6.5	10.0	9.0	8.9	9.0	Ensemble
of which:										dont:
Food and non-alcoholic beverages	...	...	...	...	...	...	...	...	...	Alimentation et boissons non alcoolisés
Alcoholic beverages, tobacco and narcotics	...	...	...	...	...	...	...	...	...	Boissons alcoolisées et tabacs
Clothing and footwear	...	...	...	...	...	...	...	...	...	Habillement et chaussures
Housing, water, electricity, gas and other fuels	...	...	...	...	...	...	...	...	...	Logement, eau, électricité, gaz et autres combustibles
Furnishings, household equipment and routine household maintenance	...	...	...	...	...	...	...	...	...	Meubles, articles de ménage et entretien courant
Health	...	...	...	...	...	...	...	...	...	Santé
Transport	...	...	...	...	...	...	...	...	...	Transport
Communication	...	...	...	...	...	...	...	...	...	Communication
Recreation and culture	...	...	...	...	...	...	...	...	...	Loisirs et culture
Education	...	...	...	...	...	...	...	...	...	Enseignement
Restaurants and hotels	...	...	...	...	...	...	...	...	...	Restaurants et hôtels
Miscellaneous goods and services	...	...	...	...	...	...	...	...	...	Biens et Services divers

IV AGRICULTURAL PRODUCTION - PRODUCTION AGRICOLE

TONNES (THOUSAND)	2009	2010	2011	2012	2013	2014	2015	2016	2017	Tonnes (milliers)
Sorghum	65	67	65	70	65	65	65	67	...	Sorgho
Barley	59	33	29	33	30	30	30	50	...	Orge
Wheat	26	33	29	33	30	30	30	31	...	Blé
Millet	17	20	20	20	20	20	20	22	...	Millet
Sesame seed	17	18	20	22	20	18	20	19	...	Sésame

V MINING PRODUCTION - PRODUCTION MINIERE

	2009	2010	2011	2012	2013	2014	2015	2016	2017	
Gold ores and concentrates - Production (Kilograms)	30	50	12	...	...	...	...	...	...	Minerais d'or et leurs concentrés - Production (Kilogrammes)
Salt and pure sodium chloride - Production (metric tons)	7 500	7 800	7 800	...	...	...	...	...	...	Sel et chlorure de sodium pur - Production (tonnes métriques)
	...	...	...	...	...	...	...	...	...	

VI ENERGY - ENERGIE

	2009	2010	2011	2012	2013	2014	2015	2016	2017	
Total electricity generation (GWh)	295	311	339	387	404	421	438	...	...	Production électrique totale (GWh)
of which										dont
Production of electricity from fossil fuels (GWh)	293	309	335	383	398	414	430	...	...	Production d'électricité à partir de combustibles fossiles (GWh)
Production of hydro electricity (GWh)	...	...	...	...	...	...	...	...	...	Production d'électricité d'origine hydraulique (GWh)
Production of electricity from solar, wind, tide, wave and other sources (GWh)	2	2	4	4	6	7	8	...	...	Production d'électricité d'origine solaire, éolienne, marée motrice et autres (GWh)

VII TOURISM AND INFRASTRUCTURE - TOURISME ET INFRASTUCTURE

	2009	2010	2011	2012	2013	2014	2015	2016	2017	
VII-1 Tourism										**VII-1 Tourisme**
International tourist arrivals (thousands)	79	...	...	...	...	...	...	...	...	Arrivées de touristes internationaux (milliers)
Rooms in hotels and similar establishments (thousands)	...	...	...	6	5	6	5	6	...	Chambres d'hôtels et établissements assimilés (milliers)
Overnight stays (thousands)	...	...	...	...	...	...	...	...	...	Nuitées (milliers)
Tourism receipts (US$ thousand)	...	...	...	...	...	...	...	...	...	Recettes touristiques (milliers de $ EU)
Total contribution to GDP (%)	...	...	...	...	...	...	...	...	...	Contribution totale au PIB (%)
Total contribution to Employment (%)	...	...	...	...	...	...	...	...	...	Contribution totale à l'emploi (%)
VII-2 Infrastructure										**VII-2 Infrastructure**
Paved road (% of total)	...	...	...	...	...	...	...	...	...	Routes asphaltées (% du total)
Total network (Railways-km)	...	...	...	...	...	...	...	...	...	Réseau total voies ferrées-Km
Main telephone lines (per 100 inhabitants)	0.9	0.9	1.0	1.0	1.0	1.0	1.0	1.0	...	Lignes téléphoniques fixes (pour 100 habitants)
Mobile cellular subscribers (per 100 inhabitants)	2.5	3.2	4.1	5.0	5.6	6.4	7.0	7.3	...	Abonnés aux téléphones mobiles (pour 100 habitants)
Internet users per 100 inhabitants	0.5	0.6	0.7	0.8	0.9	1.0	1.1	1.2	...	Utilisateurs Internet par 100 Habitants
Fixed (wired)-broadband subscriptions per 100 inhabitants	...	...	...	...	...	...	...	...	...	Abonnements à l'Internet fixe (filaire) à large bande pour 100 habitants, par débit

VIII EXTERNAL TRADE - COMMERCE EXTERIEUR

US$ (MILLIONS) EXPORTS, FOB	2009	2010	2011	2012	2013	2014	2015	2016	2017	$ E.U (MILLIONS) EXPORTATIONS, FÀB
Exports - Total	11	13	418	467	307	626	485	335	...	Exportations - Total
Exports to Africa	2	3	30	10	14	13	14	8	...	Exportations vers l'Afrique
Main products										**Principaux produits**
Copper ores and concentrates; copper mattes, cemen	...	...	...	...	39	291	172	140	...	Minerais et concentrés de cuivre; mattes de cuivre, cemen
Cotton	...	1	23	16	11	46	30	23	...	Coton
Gold, non-monetary (excluding gold ores and concentrates)	1	1	253	329	132	7	72	24	...	Or, non monétaire (à l'exclusion des minerais d'or et des concentrés)
Hides and skins (except furskins), raw	...	...	10	12	10	48	30	24	...	Cuirs et peaux (sauf les pelleteries), bruts
Vegetables	...	1	11	9	15	34	25	18	...	Légumes
Main destinations										**Principales destinations**
Canada	-	-	248	220	108	-	56	17	...	Canada
China	-	1	14	12	47	270	165	132	...	Chine
India	1	1	44	43	30	211	125	102	...	Inde
Republic of Korea	-	-	-	-	18	20	20	12	...	Corée, République de
Switzerland	-	-	-	119	7	-	4	1	...	Suisse
IMPORTS, CIF										
Imports - Total	580	649	934	954	1 023	1 111	1 003	1 037	...	Importations - Total (millions)
Imports from Africa	95	161	121	184	164	162	153	155	...	Importations en provenance de l'Afrique
Main products										**Principaux produits**
Meal and flour of wheat and flour of meslin	13	20	21	21	24	36	28	31	...	Repas et farine de blé et farine de méteil
Motor vehicles for the transport of persons	14	15	14	77	39	50	42	45	...	Véhicules à moteur pour le transport de personnes
Rubber tyres, tyre treads or flaps & inner tubes	17	15	29	29	28	32	28	29	...	Pneus en caoutchouc, bandes de roulement ou flaps et chambres à air
Sugar, molasses and honey	57	56	73	49	51	52	48	49	...	Sucre, mélasse et miel
Wheat (including spelt) and meslin, unmilled	36	39	64	62	69	65	63	63	...	Blé (y compris l'épeautre) et méteil, non moulu
Main origin										**Principales provenances**
China	56	54	172	89	173	163	158	158	...	Chine
Italy	71	55	86	116	96	102	93	96	...	Italie
Saudi Arabia	48	49	86	86	93	107	94	99	...	Arabie Saoudite
Sudan	...	...	...	70	59	38	46	41	...	Soudan
United Arab Emirates	88	85	162	158	172	195	172	180	...	Emirates Arabes

ERYTHRÉE

IX FINANCIAL AND MONETARY STATISTICS - FINANCES ET STATISTIQUES MONETAIRES										
	2009	2010	2011	2012	2013	2014	2015	2016	2017	
IX-1 MONETARY STATISTICS *ERITREA NAKFA (MILLIONS)*										**IX-1 STATISTIQUES MONÉTAIRES** *NAFKA ÉRYTHRÉEN (MILLIONS)*
Money supply (M1)	34 699	40 117	45 993	54 233	63 716	74 677	85 091	98 472	113 768	Masse monétaire (M1)
Quasi-money	17 397	20 388	23 635	26 444	30 279	28 489	33 302	...	...	Quasi-monnaie
of which demand deposit	...	...	...	...	...	...	...	...	...	dont Monnaie scripturale
Net foreign assets	4 031	5 744	7 017	8 253	8 158	8 719	11 051	...	...	Avoirs extérieurs nets
Domestic credit	32 293	37 224	41 679	46 641	56 074	58 547	65 138	...	...	Crédit intérieur
of which claims on private sector	26 949	31 328	35 400	39 283	40 040	39 152	41 089	...	...	dont créances sur le secteur privé
of which claims on government sector, net	4 787	5 201	5 577	6 665	15 307	20 822	23 235	...	...	dont créances nettes sur le gouvernement
International reserves (millions US$)	91	123	163	264	294	354	297	360	475	Réserves internationales (millions $EU)
Average exchange rate (National currency per US$)	15	15	15	15	15	15	15	15	15	Taux de change (moyen) (monnaie nationale par $ EU)
IX-2 PUBLIC FINANCE *ERITREA NAKFA (MILLIONS)*										**IX-2 FINANCES PUBLIQUES** *NAFKA ÉRYTHRÉEN (MILLIONS)*
Total Revenues and Grants	4 542	6 048	6 987	7 291	7 847	9 021	10 243	11 687	...	Recettes totales et dons
Direct taxes (on income, profits)	1 580	1 801	2 230	2 642	2 994	3 464	3 989	4 575	...	Taxes directes
Domestic indirect taxes revenues	464	537	642	739	827	950	1 087	1 241	...	Taxes Indirectes
Trade taxes	360	405	490	564	613	698	704	790	...	Taxes sur le commerce extérieur
Other taxes	...	...	...	...	...	...	...	...	...	Autres taxes
Other revenues	1 401	1 597	2 351	2 787	3 157	3 652	4 206	4 824	...	Autres recettes
Grants	737	1 707	1 275	560	256	256	256	256	...	Dons
Total Expenditures and Net Lending	8 826	11 811	12 677	13 616	15 135	17 469	20 444	23 204	...	Dépenses totales et prêts nets
Current expenditure	4 829	6 165	6 963	7 723	8 996	10 237	11 878	13 571	...	Dépenses courantes
Wages and Salaries	2 430	2 667	3 189	3 720	4 330	5 048	5 896	6 740	...	Rémunérations et salaires
Other purchases of goods and services	2 398	2 703	3 108	3 606	4 359	4 883	5 668	6 500	...	Achat de biens et services
Other current expenditure	1	795	666	397	307	306	314	331	...	Autres dépenses courantes
Current transfers	931	1 060	1 221	1 404	1 604	1 835	1 904	1 987	...	Transferts courants
Interest payments	932	1 054	1 181	1 323	1 447	1 602	2 138	2 476	...	Intérêts
Capital expenditure	2 134	3 532	3 312	3 166	3 088	3 795	4 523	5 170	...	Dépenses d'équipement
Net lending	...	...	...	...	...	...	...	...	...	Prêts nets
Fiscal balance	- 4 284	- 5 763	- 5 690	- 6 325	- 7 288	- 8 448	- 10 201	- 11 518	...	Solde global y compris les dons
IX-3 BALANCE OF PAYMENTS *ERITREA NAKFA (MILLIONS)*										**IX-3 BALANCE DES PAIEMENTS** *NAFKA ÉRYTHRÉEN (MILLIONS)*
Trade balance	- 5 691	- 6 377	- 4 140	- 2 185	- 3 085	- 2 624	- 4 589	- 2 729	- 2 230	Balance commerciale
Services Balance	292	337	621	439	316	207	80	- 69	- 208	Balance des services
Net primary income	- 248	- 302	- 455	- 605	- 472	- 436	- 274	- 463	- 245	Revenus primaires nets
Compensation of employees	...	...	...	...	...	...	...	...	...	Rémunération des salariés
Investment income	...	...	...	...	...	...	...	...	...	Revenus des investissements
Net secondary income	3 474	4 512	4 196	3 455	3 192	3 200	3 210	3 210	3 300	Revenus secondaires nets
Net official transfers	...	...	...	...	...	...	...	...	...	Transferts officiels nets
Workers' remittances	...	...	...	...	...	...	...	...	...	Envois de fonds des travailleurs
Other private transfers	...	...	...	...	...	...	...	...	...	Autres transferts privés
Current account balance	- 2 174	- 1 830	222	1 104	- 50	347	- 1 574	- 50	617	Solde du compte courant
Capital and financial account	...	...	...	...	...	...	...	...	...	Comptes de capital et financier
Capital account	...	...	...	...	...	...	...	...	...	Compte de capital
Financial account	...	...	...	...	...	...	...	...	...	Compte financier
Errors and omissions	...	...	...	...	...	...	...	...	...	Erreurs et omissions
Overall balance	...	...	...	...	...	...	...	...	...	Balance générale

X DEBT AND FINANCIAL FLOWS - DETTE ET FLUX FINANCIERS

X-1 DEBT US $ (MILLIONS)	2009	2010	2011	2012	2013	2014	2015	2016	2017	X-1 DETTE EXTÉRIEURE $ E.U (MILLIONS)
Total external debt	912	969	935	900	883	894	1 003	1 025	1 170	Dette extérieure totale
Private	...	...	...	...	...	...	...	...	...	Privée
Public	912	969	935	900	883	894	1 003	1 025	...	Publique
Total external debt service	30	34	49	49	49	50	49	34	...	Service de la dette extérieure
Present value of external debt	...	...	...	...	...	...	...	627	...	Valeur actuelle de la dette extérieure
Total government domestic debt, National currency (millions)	...	...	...	...	...	...	...	...	...	Dette publique intérieure
X-2 FINANCIAL FLOWS US $ (MILLIONS)										**X-2 FLUX FINANCIERS** $ E.U (MILLIONS)
Net Foreign Direct Investment Inflows	91	91	39	41	44	47	49	52	...	Investissements étranger direct (flux nets entrants)
Main origin of FDI inflows										**Principales origines de l'IDE entrant:**
Italy	- 15	- 1	1	- 2	...	...	...	...	...	Italie
...	...	...	...	...	...	...	...	...	...	...
...	...	...	...	...	...	...	...	...	...	...
...	...	...	...	...	...	...	...	...	...	...
...	...	...	...	...	...	...	...	...	...	...
African countries	...	...	...	...	...	...	...	...	...	Pays africains
Net total official development assistance	143	162	133	136	81	84	94	67	...	Aide publique au développement (nette totale)
Main origin of net ODA										**Principales origines de l'APD nette**
United States	4	1	...	-	-	-	-	-	...	États-Unis
International Development Association [IDA]	5	1	12	1	...	...	...	...	...	International Development Association
Norway	10	10	8	3	-	-	1	2	...	Norvège
Italy	1	...	2	1	2	1	1	-	...	Italie
Global Fund	13	41	14	28	28	31	...	...	...	Fonds Mondial

ERYTHRÉE

SOURCES AND NOTES - SOURCES ET NOTES

External trade - Total exports, fob: UNCTAD

External trade - Total import, cif: UNCTAD

ODA: OECD

Monetary statistics: IMF

Nationl Accounts:The data are estimated by the statistics division of the United Nations.

Poverty: World Bank

Commerce exterieur - Exportation, fab: CNUCED

Commerce exterieur - Imporations, caf: CNUCED

APD: OCDE

Statistiques monétaires: FMI

Comptes Nationaux:Les données sont estimées par la division des statistiques des Nations Unies.

Pauvreté: Banque mondiale

AREA (km2)	1 104 300	**SUPERFICIE (KM2)**
CAPITAL CITY	Addis Ababa / Addis-Abeba	**CAPITALE**
CURRENCY	Ethiopian Birr / Birr Éthiopien	**MONNAIE**

I SOCIAL AND DEMOGRAPHIC INDICATORS — INDICATEURS DEMOGRAPHIQUES ET SOCIAUX

Population	Year Année	Value Valeur	Charts Graphiques	Population
Population ('000)	2017	94 352.0		Population ('000)
Female (%)	2017	49.8		Féminine (%)
Urban (%)	2017	20.3		Urbaine (%)
Average annual growth rate	2017	1.9		Taux de croissance annuel
Active population ('000)	2015	45 654.1		Population active ('000)
Population by age group ('000)				Population par groupe d'âge ('000)
0-14 years	2017	39 684.5		0-14 ans
15-64 years	2017	51 846.4		15-64 ans
65+ years	2017	2 821.1		65+ ans
Economically active population in agriculture (%)	2015	77.3		Participation de la population active agricole (%)
Crude birth rate	2017	30.3		Taux brut de natalité
Crude death rate	2017	7.2		Taux brut de mortalité
Total fertility rate	2017	3.9		Indice synthétique de fécondité
Life expectancy at birth - Total (years)	2017	65.0		Espérance de vie à la naissance - Totale (années)
Dependency ratio - Total (%)	2017	82.0		Taux de dépendance - Total (%)
Health				**Santé**
Percentage of children under-five and underweight	2016	24.0		% d'enfants de moins de cinq ans avec insuffisance pondérale
Prevalence of undernourishment	2015	32.0		Prévalence de la malnutrition
Under five mortality rate (per 1 000 live births)	2016	67.0		Taux de mortalité de moins de 5 ans (les deux sexes, pour 1000)
Infant mortality rate (per 1 000 live births)	2016	48.0		Taux de mortalité infantile (les deux sexes) par 1000
Neonatal mortality rate (per 1 000 live births)	2017	32.0		Le taux de mortalité néonatale (pour 1000 naissances vivantes)
Percentage of children provided the vaccines :				Pourcentage d'enfants vaccinés :
BCG	2017	100.0		BCG
DPT3	2017	97.4		DTC3
Polio	2016	81.0		polio
Measles	2017	93.6		rougeole
Percentage of mothers provided at least one antenatal care (%)	2016	62.0		Pourcentage de mères ayant au moins reçu un soin prénatal (%)
Percentage of deliveries attended by skilled health personnel	2016	28.0		% d'accouchements assistés par un personnel de santé qualifié
Number of doctors (per 10,000 population)	2017	1.0		Nombre de médecins (pour 10.000 habitants)
Number of nurses (per 10,000 population)	2017	8.4		Nombre d'infirmiers (pour 10.000 habitants)
Hospital beds - Total (per 10,000 population)	2011	63.0		Nombre de lits d'hôpitaux - Total (pour 10 000)
Births registered (per 1,000)	2015	31.9		Naissances enregistrées (pour 1000)
Deaths registered (per 1,000)	2015	7.2		Décès enregistrés (pour 1000)
Budget allocation to health (%)	2017	11.7		Dépenses publiques consacrées à la santé (% du budget)
Education				**Education**
Enrolment in primary education (000)	2017	20 783.1		Scolarisation dans le primaire (000)
Female	2017	9 753.6		Féminine
Enrolment in secondary education (000)	2017	2 559.1		Scolarisation dans le secondaire (000)
Female	2017	1 201.0		Féminine
Enrolment in tertiary education (000)	2017	860.4		Scolarisation dans le tertiaire (000)
Female	2017	294.3		Féminine
Literacy rate	2016	53.3		Taux d'alphabétisation (deux sexes)
Male	2016	62.8		Masculin
Female	2016	44.4		Féminin
Pupil teacher ratio - primary	2017	43.0		Ratio élève-enseignant
Budget allocation to education (%)	2014	25.0		Dépenses publiques consacrées à l'enseignement (% du budget)
Poverty				**Pauvreté**
GNI per capita, PPP (current int. $)	2016	1730.0		RNB par habitant, ($ PPA inter. courants)
Human Poverty Index (HPI-1) Value (%)	2007	50.9		Valeur de l'Indice de pauvreté (IPH-1) (%)
Population below Inter. poverty line ($2/ day) (%)	2010	33.5		Population sous le seuil inter. de pauvreté (2$/Jour) (%)
Share of income held by richest 10%	2010	27.4		% de revenu des 10% plus riches
Share of income held by poorest 10%	2010	3.2		% de revenu des 10% plus pauvres
GINI index	2010	33.2		Indice de GINI

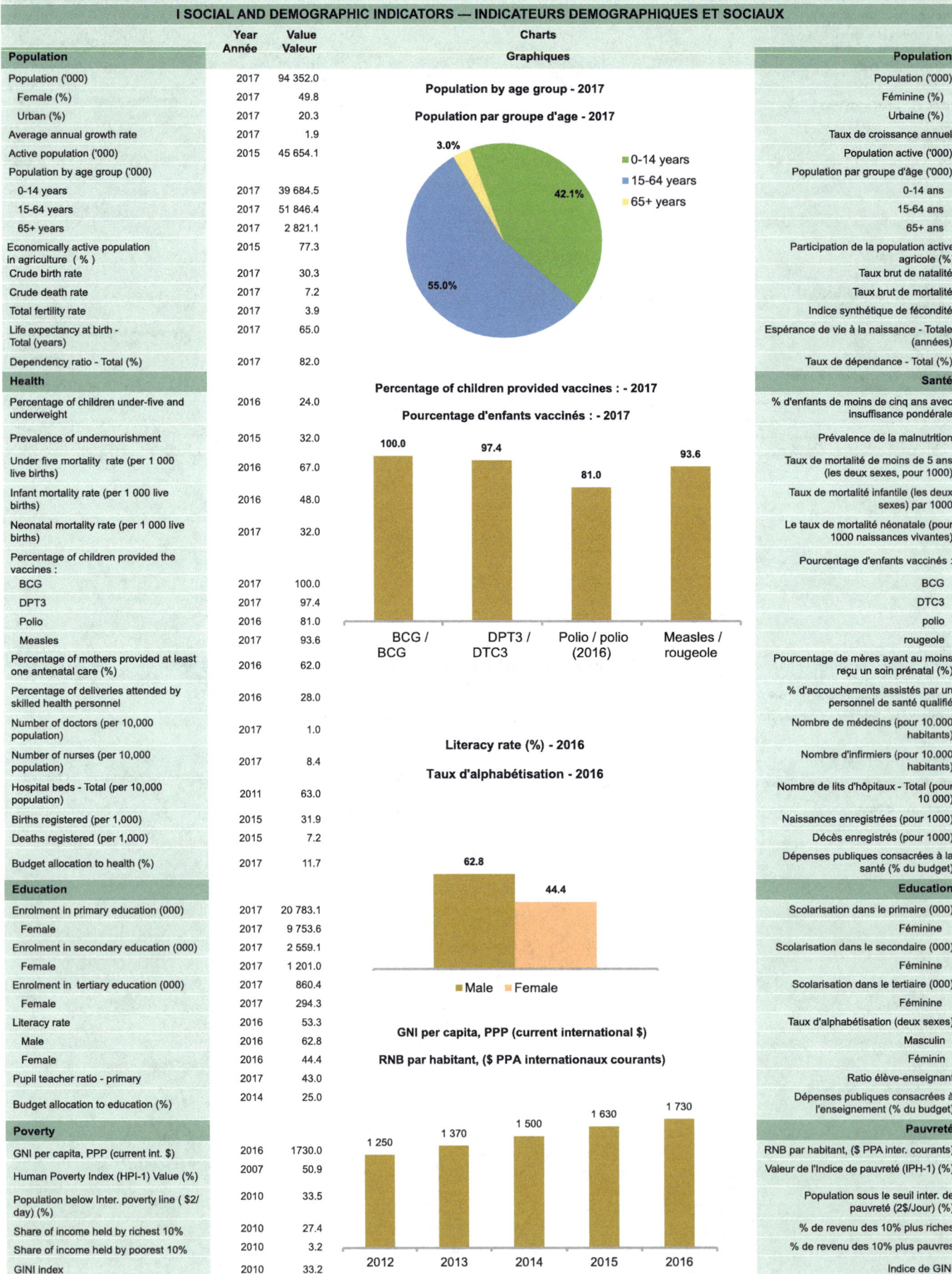

Population by age group - 2017

Population par groupe d'age - 2017

- 0-14 years: 42.1%
- 15-64 years: 55.0%
- 65+ years: 3.0%

Percentage of children provided vaccines : - 2017

Pourcentage d'enfants vaccinés : - 2017

BCG / BCG	DPT3 / DTC3	Polio / polio (2016)	Measles / rougeole
100.0	97.4	81.0	93.6

Literacy rate (%) - 2016

Taux d'alphabétisation - 2016

- Male: 62.8
- Female: 44.4

GNI per capita, PPP (current international $)

RNB par habitant, ($ PPA internationaux courants)

2012	2013	2014	2015	2016
1 250	1 370	1 500	1 630	1 730

II NATIONAL ACCOUNTS — COMPTES NATIONAUX

	2009	2010	2011	2012	2013	2014	2015	2016	2017	
GROSS DOMESTIC PRODUCT BY KIND OF ECONOMIC ACTIVITY AT CURRENT PRICES *ETHIOPIAN BIRR (MILLIONS)*										**PRODUIT INTÉRIEUR BRUT PAR BRANCHE D'ACTIVITÉ ÉCONOMIQUE AUX PRIX COURANTS** *BIRR ÉTHIOPIEN (MILLIONS)*
Agriculture, hunting, forestry and Fishing	160 627	165 668	212 470	331 297	357 514	408 630	468 006	535 675	614 210	Agriculture, chasse sylviculture et Pêche
Mining and quarrying	1 270	2 475	6 810	9 301	9 687	8 665	6 036	6 117	4 840	Industries extractives
Manufacturing	11 813	14 467	18 968	25 559	32 095	42 341	57 170	85 971	102 920	Industries manufacturières
Electricity, gas & water	3 717	4 457	4 902	6 187	7 355	8 234	8 087	11 012	13 105	Electricité, gaz et eau
Construction	16 074	15 882	19 100	29 771	45 744	83 665	140 246	237 545	292 902	Bâtiments et travaux publics
Wholesale & retail trade, restaurants, hotels	56 629	66 432	87 937	126 427	145 478	191 218	241 521	229 352	260 307	Commerce de gros et de détail, restaurants et hôtels
Finance, insurance, real estate, etc.	26 748	38 718	55 992	70 576	85 728	97 397	112 514	115 763	127 417	Banques, assurances, affaires immobilières
Transport and communications	12 766	15 967	19 891	29 721	38 340	45 776	53 555	69 351	78 927	Transport(s) et communications
Public administration and defense	10 320	11 577	25 736	29 274	34 582	40 353	50 328	63 354	90 125	Administrations publiques et défense
Education	7 390	8 841	10 772	13 283	16 814	22 334	27 501	39 380	57 138	Education
Health And Social Work	2 085	2 422	4 132	4 999	6 363	8 279	10 824	13 899	18 375	Santé et Actions Sociales
Other services	6 026	6 659	12 157	17 915	24 521	27 579	31 580	32 564	37 025	Autres services
Less Imputed Service Charges	- 2 544	- 2 843	- 3 219	- 3 864	- 7 918	- 9 745	- 14 535	- 17 380	- 20 444	Moins Services d'intermédiation financière
Gross domestic product at factor cost / basic prices	312 921	350 723	475 648	690 444	796 303	974 727	1 192 833	1 422 601	1 676 848	Produit intérieur brut aux couts des facteurs / prix de base
Plus: Indirect Taxes / taxes on products, less subsidies	19 139	28 412	39 431	56 882	70 618	86 098	105 129	118 676	129 808	Plus taxes indirectes/impôts sur les produits, moins les subventions
EXPENDITURE ON GROSS DOMESTIC PRODUCT AT CURRENT PURCHASER'S VALUES *ETHIOPIAN BIRR (MILLIONS)*										**EMPLOI DU PRODUIT INTÉRIEUR BRUT AUX PRIX COURANTS D'ACQUISITION** *BIRR ÉTHIOPIEN (MILLIONS)*
Government final consumption	29 810	32 888	53 147	62 044	77 637	98 121	116 995	174 120	222 865	Consommation finale des administrations publiques
Private final consumption	287 116	325 901	373 089	541 536	636 902	744 977	941 006	1 083 741	1 167 790	Consommation finale privée
Gross fixed capital formation	76 185	94 497	165 380	277 243	295 456	402 922	511 618	585 665	704 596	Formation brute de capital fixe
Change in inventories	...	...	...	...	...	...	...	...	...	Variation des stocks
Exports of goods and services	35 233	52 168	85 950	102 887	108 227	123 496	121 532	122 501	139 805	Exportations de biens et services
Less imports of goods and services	96 285	126 319	162 487	236 384	251 301	308 691	393 189	424 750	428 400	Moins importations de biens et services
GDP at purchasers' values	332 060	379 135	515 079	747 326	866 921	1 060 825	1 297 961	1 541 277	1 806 656	PIB aux prix d'acquisition
GROSS DOMESTIC PRODUCT BY KIND OF ECONOMIC ACTIVITY AT CONSTANT PRICES *ANNUAL GROWTH RATES (%)*										**PRODUIT INTÉRIEUR BRUT PAR BRANCHE D'ACTIVITÉ ECONOMIQUE AUX PRIX CONSTANTS** *TAUX DE CROISSANCE ANNUEL (%)*
Agriculture, hunting, forestry and Fishing	6.4	7.6	9.0	4.9	7.1	5.4	6.4	2.3	6.7	Agriculture, chasse sylviculture et Pêche
Mining and quarrying	12.8	44.2	57.7	12.7	6.3	- 3.2	- 25.6	-3.3	- 29.8	Industries extractives
Manufacturing	9.1	10.0	12.1	11.8	16.9	16.6	18.2	18.4	17.4	Industries manufacturières
Electricity, gas & water	5.0	5.1	19.1	13.5	10.0	6.8	4.5	15.0	11.4	Electricité, gaz et eau
Construction	11.7	10.9	12.8	31.5	38.7	23.9	31.6	25.0	20.7	Bâtiments et travaux publics
Wholesale & retail trade, restaurants, hotels	14.0	11.7	5.9	12.0	11.8	19.5	16.0	8.2	8.1	Commerce de gros et de détail, restaurants et hôtels
Finance, insurance, real estate, etc.	16.0	18.5	9.7	8.0	-	6.1	4.9	14.8	8.4	Banques, assurances, affaires immobilières
Transport and communications	8.9	13.8	23.7	12.6	16.5	12.7	13.3	13.7	12.1	Transport(s) et communications
Public administration and defense	18.4	3.4	5.2	3.1	7.6	11.0	6.0	7.4	22.1	Administrations publiques et défense
Education	13.0	17.0	5.2	4.5	10.1	2.6	9.2	8.8	11.0	Education
Health And Social Work	19.3	8.3	5.2	9.4	12.3	19.3	13.0	10.8	15.0	Santé et Actions Sociales
Other services	6.1	7.5	5.2	12.7	17.4	3.9	3.8	3.0	3.1	Autres services
Less Imputed Service Charges	12.5	8.7	11.1	-10.6	6.4	19.4	17.9	16.9	18.0	Moins Services d'intermédiation financière
Gross domestic product at factor cost / basic prices	10.0	10.4	11.4	8.7	9.9	10.3	10.4	8.0	10.9	Produit intérieur brut aux couts des facteurs / prix de base
Plus: Indirect Taxes / taxes on products, less subsidies	- 8.3	45.4	11.4	8.0	18.3	9.9	10.2	2.9	2.9	Plus taxes indirectes/impôts sur les produits, moins les subventions
Gross domestic product at market prices	8.8	12.4	11.2	8.6	10.6	10.3	10.4	7.6	10.3	Produit intérieur brut aux prix du marché
EXPENDITURE ON GROSS DOMESTIC PRODUCT AT CONSTANT PURCHASERS' VALUES *ANNUAL GROWTH RATES (%)*										**EMPLOIS DU PRODUIT INTÉRIEUR BRUT AUX PRIX CONSTANTS D'ACQUISITION** *TAUX DE CROISSANCE ANNUEL (%)*
Government final consumption	...	...	...	...	...	...	...	...	...	Consommation finale des administrations publiques
Private final consumption	...	...	...	...	...	...	...	...	...	Consommation finale privée
Gross fixed capital formation	...	...	...	...	...	...	...	...	...	Formation brute de capital fixe
Exports of goods and services	...	...	...	...	...	...	...	...	...	Exportations de biens et services
Less imports of goods and services	...	...	...	...	...	...	...	...	...	Moins importations de biens et services

III INFLATION

	2009	2010	2011	2012	2013	2014	2015	2016	2017	
Annual growth rates (%)										**Taux de croissance annuel (%)**
All item	36.4	2.8	33.2	23.0	7.7	8.1	7.7	9.7	7.2	Ensemble
of which:										dont:
Food and non-alcoholic beverages	9.1	13.5	23.8	25.9	5.1	5.9	7.5	11.2	7.4	Alimentation et boissons non alcoolisés
Alcoholic beverages, tobacco and narcotics	...	...	30.5	6.3	13.1	10.6	8.0	8.1	1.1	Boissons alcoolisées et tabacs
Clothing and footwear	...	...	33.4	28.9	12.0	13.9	15.2	6.7	3.0	Habillement et chaussures
Housing, water, electricity, gas and other fuels	18.6	23.3	20.7	15.4	12.0	11.4	9.7	6.2	10.6	Logement, eau, électricité, gaz et autres combustibles
Furnishings, household equipment and routine household maintenance	...	...	25.5	26.6	12.8	11.8	8.5	9.9	6.9	Meubles, articles de ménage et entretien courant
Health	20.4	11.5	11.4	15.1	20.5	9.9	7.4	8.2	7.4	Santé
Transport	27.1	20.8	35.6	2.6	- 2.7	14.1	8.4	9.3	5.6	Transport
Communication	...	...	...	...	...	0.8	0.1	- 0.2	1.4	Communication
Recreation and culture	...	...	36.8	22.0	10.8	...	0.7	1.2	10.5	Loisirs et culture
Education	...	...	25.4	15.2	4.1	7.0	0.1	15.0	2.3	Enseignement
Restaurants and hotels	...	...	...	...	10.2	1.9	0.7	12.0	8.6	Restaurants et hôtels
Miscellaneous goods and services	...	...	12.2	17.1	10.1	12.5	5.9	10.4	4.9	Biens et Services divers

ÉTHIOPIE

IV AGRICULTURAL PRODUCTION - PRODUCTION AGRICOLE

TONNES (THOUSAND)	2009	2010	2011	2012	2013	2014	2015	2016	2017	Tonnes (milliers)
Maize	30 722	32 758	35 394	35 331	38 326	44 274	48 127	45 871	...	Maïs
Sorghum	16 635	19 065	18 201	16 734	19 069	19 103	20 708	20 616	...	Sorgho
Wheat	27 035	33 458	30 769	31 400	36 412	41 830	45 577	45 496	...	Blé
Barley	44 625	49 165	57 964	66 202	69 729	68 367	80 955	85 791	...	Orge
Coffee, green	29 934	31 934	41 492	41 069	38 300	40 849	46 152	46 147	...	Café, vert

V MINING PRODUCTION - PRODUCTION MINIERE

	2009	2010	2011	2012	2013	2014	2015	2016	2017	
Gold ores and concentrates - Production (Kilograms)	3 585	6 002	10 322	4 139	4 314	16 985	9 071	8 297	9 089	Minerais d'or et leurs concentrés - Production (Kilogrammes)
Silver ores and concentrates - Production, Kilograms (thousands)	1	1	1	2	2	...	...	...	...	Minerais d'argent et leurs concentrés - Production, Kilogrammes (milliers)
Tantalum (Tantalite) - Production (metric tons)	166	198	207	...	...	...	105	90	223	Tantalum (Tantalite) - Production (tonnes métriques)

VI ENERGY - ENERGIE

	2009	2010	2011	2012	2013	2014	2015	2016	2017	
Total electricity generation (GWh)	3 982	4 931	7 308	6 584	8 077	9 201	9 796	10 328	...	Production électrique totale (GWh)
of which										dont
Production of electricity from fossil fuels (GWh)	434	31	11	12	8	9	9	9	...	Production d'électricité à partir de combustibles fossiles (GWh)
Production of hydro electricity (GWh)	3 524	4 882	4 931	6 241	7 388	8 338	8 807	9 302	...	Production d'électricité d'origine hydraulique (GWh)
Production of electricity from solar, wind, tide, wave and other sources (GWh)	...	...	126	294	489	498	545	551	...	Production d'électricité d'origine solaire, éolienne, marée motrice et autres (GWh)

VII TOURISM AND INFRASTRUCTURE - TOURISME ET INFRASTUCTURE

	2009	2010	2011	2012	2013	2014	2015	2016	2017	
VII-1 Tourism										**VII-1 Tourisme**
International tourist arrivals (thousands)	427	468	523	597	681	770	864	902	1 013	Arrivées de touristes internationaux (milliers)
Rooms in hotels and similar establishments (thousands)	...	...	...	20	20	22	24	25	...	Chambres d'hôtels et établissements assimilés (milliers)
Overnight stays (thousands)	1 386	1 568	1 765	1 959	2 247	2 562	2 872	2 988	3 398	Nuitées (milliers)
Tourism receipts (US$ thousand)	316 500	519 200	750 700	604 300	585 500	352 400	403 700	344 300	348 135	Recettes touristiques (milliers de $ EU)
Total contribution to GDP (%)	9.2	11.9	12.6	9.8	9.9	8.6	8.0	7.2	6.8	Contribution totale au PIB (%)
Total contribution to Employment (%)	8.1	10.3	10.9	9.1	9.1	7.8	7.3	6.4	6.1	Contribution totale à l'emploi (%)
VII-2 Infrastructure										**VII-2 Infrastructure**
Paved road (% of total)	14.8	15.3	15.4	15.7	13.1	12.7	13.0	...	...	Routes asphaltées (% du total)
Total network (Railways-km)	...	...	...	...	...	...	...	...	...	Réseau total voies ferrées-Km
Main telephone lines (per 100 inhabitants)	1.1	1.0	0.9	0.9	0.8	0.8	0.9	1.1	...	Lignes téléphoniques fixes (pour 100 habitants)
Mobile cellular subscribers (per 100 inhabitants)	4.8	7.9	15.8	22.4	27.3	31.6	42.8	50.5	...	Abonnés aux téléphones mobiles (pour 100 habitants)
Internet users per 100 inhabitants	0.5	0.8	1.1	2.9	4.6	7.7	13.9	15.4	...	Utilisateurs Internet par 100 Habitants
Fixed (wired)-broadband subscriptions per 100 inhabitants	...	...	...	...	...	...	...	0.6	...	Abonnements à l'Internet fixe (filaire) à large bande pour 100 habitants, par débit

VIII EXTERNAL TRADE - COMMERCE EXTERIEUR

US$ (MILLIONS) EXPORTS, FOB	2009	2010	2011	2012	2013	2014	2015	2016	2017	$ E.U (MILLIONS) EXPORTATIONS, FÀB
Exports - Total	1 618	2 330	2 615	2 891	3 112	3 427	3 050	2 919	...	Exportations - Total
Exports to Africa	255	470	455	542	857	787	732	684	...	Exportations vers l'Afrique
Main products										**Principaux produits**
Coffee and coffee substitutes	378	736	896	880	594	616	614	554	...	Café et succédanés du café
Crude vegetable materials, n.e.s.	169	208	231	231	373	360	349	320	...	Matières végétales brutes, n.e.s.
Oil seeds and oleaginous fruits (excluding flour)	335	361	352	453	404	512	316	373	...	Graines oléagineuses et oléagineuses (à l'exclusion de la farine)
Petroleum oils or bituminous minerals > 70 % oil	...	...	...	...	152	441	257	314	...	Huiles de pétrole ou de minéraux bitumineux> 70% d'huile
Vegetables	236	384	381	452	695	646	581	553	...	Légumes
Main destinations										**Principales destinations**
China	229	283	297	325	277	372	262	285	...	Chine
Germany	147	262	341	298	201	201	175	170	...	Allemagne
Netherlands	125	125	131	130	243	220	280	225	...	Pays-Bas
Saudi Arabia	112	161	168	201	237	282	192	213	...	Arabie Saoudite
Somalia	138	251	256	273	570	524	473	449	...	Somalie
IMPORTS, CIF										
Imports - Total	7 974	8 602	8 896	11 913	12 224	15 551	16 914	16 588	...	Importations - Total (millions)
Imports from Africa	512	594	678	614	499	648	802	741	...	Importations en provenance de l'Afrique
Main products										**Principaux produits**
Civil engineering & contractors' plant & equipment	253	163	304	511	522	321	335	335	...	Génie civil et installations et équipements des entrepreneurs
Medicaments (incl. veterinary medicaments)	268	258	223	230	487	291	448	377	...	Médicaments (y compris les médicaments vétérinaires)
Motor vehic. for transport of goods, special purpo.	228	409	369	546	680	616	817	733	...	Véhicule à moteur pour le transport de marchandises, spécial.
Petroleum oils or bituminous minerals > 70 % oil	919	1 060	1 015	2 020	1 384	2 582	1 695	2 185	...	Huiles de pétrole ou de minéraux bitumineux> 70% d'huile
Telecommunication equipment, n.e.s.; & parts, n.e.s.	555	562	150	190	116	552	904	744	...	Matériel de télécommunication, n.es .; & parties, n.e.s.
Main origin										**Principales provenances**
China	2 030	2 024	1 550	2 423	3 109	4 732	5 771	5 367	...	Chine
India	588	545	696	966	1 355	1 063	1 154	1 133	...	Inde
Kuwait	3	3	195	852	572	1 436	1 182	1 338	...	Koweit
Saudi Arabia	628	678	596	1 059	803	946	363	669	...	Arabie Saoudite
United States	481	775	700	1 001	777	1 321	1 423	1 402	...	États-Unis

	2009	2010	2011	2012	2013	2014	2015	2016	2017	
IX-1 MONETARY STATISTICS *ETHIOPIAN BIRR (MILLIONS)*										**IX-1 STATISTIQUES MONÉTAIRES** *BIRR ÉTHIOPIEN (MILLIONS)*
Money supply (M1)	83 744	104 143	142 111	188 838	234 572	297 599	369 747	445 049	527 562	Masse monétaire (M1)
Quasi-money	...	...	...	...	...	...	...	...	...	Quasi-monnaie
of which demand deposit	...	...	...	...	...	...	...	...	...	dont Monnaie scripturale
Net foreign assets	...	...	...	...	...	...	...	...	...	Avoirs extérieurs nets
Domestic credit	...	...	...	...	...	...	...	...	...	Crédit intérieur
of which claims on private sector	...	...	...	...	...	...	...	...	...	dont créances sur le secteur privé
of which claims on government sector, net	...	...	...	...	...	...	...	...	...	dont créances nettes sur le gouvernement
International reserves (millions US$)	1 581	1 979	3 046	2 262	2 368	2 496	3 248	3 402	3 061	Réserves internationales (millions $EU)
Average exchange rate (National currency per US$)	12	14	17	18	19	20	21	22	23	Taux de change (moyen) (monnaie nationale par $ EU)
IX-2 PUBLIC FINANCE *ETHIOPIAN BIRR (MILLIONS)*										**IX-2 FINANCES PUBLIQUES** *BIRR ÉTHIOPIEN (MILLIONS)*
Total Revenues and Grants	54 637	66 240	85 611	115 659	137 192	158 077	199 609	244 819	270 214	Recettes totales et dons
Direct taxes (on income, profits)	9 868	14 906	19 550	28 858	36 393	47 021	60 149	71 844	81 417	Taxes directes
Domestic indirect taxes revenues	7 325	10 727	15 705	23 326	32 440	40 499	52 339	55 953	62 553	Taxes Indirectes
Trade taxes	11 814	17 685	23 726	33 556	38 177	45 599	52 790	62 723	66 202	Taxes sur le commerce extérieur
Other taxes	...	...	...	...	...	...	...	...	...	Autres taxes
Other revenues	11 176	10 546	10 139	17 124	17 067	13 055	21 312	41 285	47 565	Autres recettes
Grants	14 454	12 376	16 491	12 795	13 115	11 904	13 020	13 014	12 477	Dons
Total Expenditures and Net Lending	57 774	72 598	93 943	124 451	154 009	185 472	224 881	280 893	337 906	Dépenses totales et prêts nets
Current expenditure	25 890	30 950	38 748	49 215	59 814	74 293	101 861	129 477	176 635	Dépenses courantes
Wages and Salaries	16 282	14 700	19 067	24 662	31 209	37 981	53 763	69 650	...	Rémunérations et salaires
Other purchases of goods and services	7 440	3 950	4 750	6 604	6 548	7 649	14 787	13 992	...	Achat de biens et services
Other current expenditure	1 827	11 669	14 593	17 949	22 058	28 663	33 311	45 835	66 529	Autres dépenses courantes
Current transfers	340	631	338							Transferts courants
Interest payments	1 286	1 587	1 913	2 230	2 931	3 794	5 338	7 232	8 248	Intérêts
Capital expenditure	30 599	40 061	53 283	72 971	91 263	107 385	117 683	144 184	153 023	Dépenses d'équipement
Net lending	...	...	● ...	35	...	...	...	...	...	Prêts nets
Fiscal balance	- 3 137	- 6 358	- 8 332	- 8 793	- 16 816	- 27 395	- 25 272	- 36 073	- 67 692	Solde global y compris les dons
IX-3 BALANCE OF PAYMENTS *US $ (MILLIONS)*										**IX-3 BALANCE DES PAIEMENTS** *$ E.U (MILLIONS)*
Trade balance	- 6 066	- 5 810	- 6 330	- 8 510	- 9 046	- 11 992	- 13 789	- 13 616	- 12 744	Balance commerciale
Services Balance	415	483	292	311	920	- 29	- 448	- 803	- 157	Balance des services
Net primary income	- 38	- 64	- 93	- 97	- 129	- 196	- 322	- 436	- 499	Revenus primaires nets
Compensation of employees	...	- 2	...	...	...	...	...	...	...	Rémunération des salariés
Investment income	- 38	- 62	- 93	- 97	- 129	- 196	- 322	- 436	- 499	Revenus des investissements
Net secondary income	4 214	4 763	5 054	5 252	5 226	6 444	7 423	7 530	7 741	Revenus secondaires nets
Net official transfers	1 595	2 023	2 042	1 591	1 457	1 547	1 302	1 562	1 292	Transferts officiels nets
Workers' remittances	1 792	1 756	1 809	2 336	2 749	3 580	4 254	4 037	4 830	Envois de fonds des travailleurs
Other private transfers	788	920	1 109	1 228	999	1 121	1 546	1 496	1 121	Autres transferts privés
Current account balance	- 1 475	- 628	- 1 077	- 3 044	- 3 029	- 5 773	- 7 135	- 7 324	- 5 657	Solde du compte courant
Capital and financial account	2 196	2 672	2 455	3 153	3 105	6 994	5 998	7 353	6 100	Comptes de capital et financier
Capital account	2 196	2 672	2 455	3 153	3 105	6 994	5 998	7 353	6 100	Compte de capital
Financial account	...	...	...	...	...	...	...	...	...	Compte financier
Errors and omissions	- 94	- 1 246	- 935	- 780	- 497	- 1 019	668	- 777	- 363	Erreurs et omissions
Overall balance	626	798	443	- 670	- 421	202	- 469	- 748	79	Balance générale

ÉTHIOPIE

X DEBT AND FINANCIAL FLOWS - DETTE ET FLUX FINANCIERS

	2009	2010	2011	2012	2013	2014	2015	2016	2017	
X-1 DEBT *US $ (MILLIONS)*										**X-1 DETTE EXTÉRIEURE** *$ E.U (MILLIONS)*
Total external debt	4 759	5 632	7 798	8 889	11 223	14 005	22 542	25 491	27 291	Dette extérieure totale
Private	...	...	...	...	...	...	...	...	...	Privée
Public	4 759	5 632	7 798	8 889	11 223	14 005	22 542	24 691	...	Publique
Total external debt service	95	128	199	366	483	675	1 228	1 647	...	Service de la dette extérieure
Present value of external debt	...	...	...	...	...	...	...	17 291	...	Valeur actuelle de la dette extérieure
Total government domestic debt, National currency (millions)	56 695	80 138	116 571	156 013	202 542	228 978	294 608	...	...	Dette publique intérieure
X-2 FINANCIAL FLOWS *US $ (MILLIONS)*										**X-2 FLUX FINANCIERS** *$ E.U (MILLIONS)*
Net Foreign Direct Investment Inflows	221	288	627	279	1 344	1 855	2 193	3 196	...	Investissements étranger direct (flux nets entrants)
Main origin of FDI inflows										**Principales origines de l'IDE entrant:**
Italy	32	10	8	- 39	...	...	...	...	...	Italie
United Kingdom	...	...	...	11	...	...	...	...	...	Royaume-Uni
...	...	...	...	...	...	...	...	...	...	...
United States	...	4	2	...	...	...	...	...	...	États-Unis
Turkey	...	...	...	1	...	...	...	...	...	Turquie
African countries	...	...	...	...	...	...	...	...	...	Pays africains
Net total official development assistance	3 824	3 455	3 493	3 243	3 886	3 584	3 234	4 074	...	Aide publique au développement (nette totale)
Main origin of net ODA										**Principales origines de l'APD nette**
United States	726	803	659	693	679	665	746	877	...	États-Unis
International Development Association [IDA]	1 038	665	712	760	955	877	692	1 177	...	International Development Association
United Kingdom	343	407	552	421	515	530	518	451	...	Royaume-Uni
...	...	...	...	...	...	...	...	...	...	...
Global Fund	130	257	195	94	272	101	...	...	...	Fonds Mondial

SOURCES AND NOTES - SOURCES ET NOTES

External trade - Total exports, fob: UNCTAD

External trade - Total import, cif: UNCTAD

ODA: OECD

Monetary statistics: IMF

National Accounts: Break in the serie from 2011 and 2016

Nationl Accounts:The data is in Ethiopian Fisical Year July (n-1) / June (n)

Poverty: World Bank

Commerce extérieur - Exportation, fab: CNUCED

Commerce extérieur - Imporations, caf: CNUCED

APD: OCDE

Statistiques monétaires: FMI

Comptes nationaux: Rupture dans la série à partir de 2011 et 2016

Comptes Nationaux:Les données sont exprimées en année fiscale juillet n-1/juin (n)

Pauvreté: Banque mondiale

		267 670		
AREA (km2)				**SUPERFICIE (KM2)**
CAPITAL CITY	Libreville		Libreville	**CAPITALE**
CURRENCY	CFA Franc		Franc CFA	**MONNAIE**

I SOCIAL AND DEMOGRAPHIC INDICATORS — INDICATEURS DEMOGRAPHIQUES ET SOCIAUX

	Year Année	Value Valeur	Charts Graphiques	
Population				**Population**
Population ('000)	2017	2 042.0		Population ('000)
Female (%)	2017	49.8		Féminine (%)
Urban (%)	2017	87.7		Urbaine (%)
Average annual growth rate	2017	2.5		Taux de croissance annuel
Active population ('000)	2015	420.8		Population active ('000)
Population by age group ('000)				Population par groupe d'âge ('000)
0-14 years	2017	724.9		0-14 ans
15-64 years	2017	1 233.6		15-64 ans
65+ years	2017	89.2		65+ ans
Economically active population in agriculture (%)	2015	44.9		Participation de la population active agricole (%)
Crude birth rate	2017	29.5		Taux brut de natalité
Crude death rate	2017	7.3		Taux brut de mortalité
Total fertility rate	2015	3.8		Indice synthétique de fécondité
Life expectancy at birth - Total (years)	2017	66.9		Espérance de vie à la naissance - Totale (années)
Dependency ratio - Total (%)	2017	66.0		Taux de dépendance - Total (%)
Health				**Santé**
Percentage of children under-five and underweight	2012	6.5		% d'enfants de moins de cinq ans avec insuffisance pondérale
Prevalence of undernourishment	2017	5.0		Prévalence de la malnutrition
Under five mortality rate (per 1 000 live births)	2015	50.8		Taux de mortalité de moins de 5 ans (les deux sexes, pour 1000)
Infant mortality rate (per 1 000 live births)	2015	36.1		Taux de mortalité infantile (les deux sexes) par 1000
Neonatal mortality rate (per 1 000 live births)	2015	23.2		Le taux de mortalité néonatale (pour 1000 naissances vivantes)
Percentage of children provided the vaccines :				Pourcentage d'enfants vaccinés :
BCG	2017	75.0		BCG
DPT3	2017	75.0		DTC3
Polio	2017	74.0		polio
Measles	2017	63.0		rougeole
Percentage of mothers provided at least one antenatal care (%)	2012	94.7		Pourcentage de mères ayant au moins reçu un soin prénatal (%)
Percentage of deliveries attended by skilled health personnel	2012	89.3		% d'accouchements assistés par un personnel de santé qualifié
Number of doctors (per 10,000 population)	2004	2.9		Nombre de médecins (pour 10.000 habitants)
Number of nurses (per 10,000 population)	2004	50.2		Nombre d'infirmiers (pour 10.000 habitants)
Hospital beds - Total (per 10,000 population)	2010	63.0		Nombre de lits d'hôpitaux - Total (pour 10 000)
Births registered (per 1,000)	2015	29.7		Naissances enregistrées (pour 1000)
Deaths registered (per 1,000)	2015	8.4		Décès enregistrés (pour 1000)
Budget allocation to health (%)	2013	4.0		Dépenses publiques consacrées à la santé (% du budget)
Education				**Education**
Enrolment in primary education (000)	2011	317.9		Scolarisation dans le primaire (000)
Female	2011	155.2		Féminine
Enrolment in secondary education (000)	2002	105.2		Scolarisation dans le secondaire (000)
Female	...	...		Féminine
Enrolment in tertiary education (000)	...	...		Scolarisation dans le tertiaire (000)
Female	2003	3.7		Féminine
Literacy rate	2012	82.3		Taux d'alphabétisation (deux sexes)
Male	2012	84.9		Masculin
Female	2012	79.9		Féminin
Pupil teacher ratio - primary	2011	24.5		Ratio élève-enseignant
Budget allocation to education (%)	...	...		Dépenses publiques consacrées à l'enseignement (% du budget)
Poverty				**Pauvreté**
GNI per capita, PPP (current int. $)	2016	16720.0		RNB par habitant, ($ PPA inter. courants)
Human Poverty Index (HPI-1) Value (%)	2007	17.5		Valeur de l'Indice de pauvreté (IPH-1) (%)
Population below Inter. poverty line ($2/ day) (%)	2005	8.0		Population sous le seuil inter. de pauvreté (2$/Jour) (%)
Share of income held by richest 10%	2005	33.2		% de revenu des 10% plus riches
Share of income held by poorest 10%	2005	2.3		% de revenu des 10% plus pauvres
GINI index	2005	42.2		Indice de GINI

Population by age group - 2017

Population par groupe d'age - 2017

- 0-14 years
- 15-64 years
- 65+ years

Percentage of children provided vaccines : - 2017

Pourcentage d'enfants vaccinés : - 2017

BCG / BCG	DPT3 / DTC3	Polio / polio	Measles / rougeole
75.0	75.0	74.0	63.0

Literacy rate (%) - 2012

Taux d'alphabétisation - 2012

- Male 84.9
- Female 79.9

GNI per capita, PPP (current international $)

RNB par habitant, ($ PPA internationaux courants)

2012	2013	2014	2015	2016
14 810	15 420	16 660	16 430	16 720

II NATIONAL ACCOUNTS — COMPTES NATIONAUX

	2009	2010	2011	2012	2013	2014	2015	2016	2017	
GROSS DOMESTIC PRODUCT BY KIND OF ECONOMIC ACTIVITY AT CURRENT PRICES *CFA FRANC (BILLIONS)*										**PRODUIT INTÉRIEUR BRUT PAR BRANCHE D'ACTIVITÉ ÉCONOMIQUE AUX PRIX COURANTS** *FRANC CFA (MILLIARDS)*
Agriculture, hunting , forestry and Fishing	287	278	295	294	289	326	367	413	473	Agriculture, chasse sylviculture et Pêche
Mining and quarrying	2 373	3 279	4 325	4 154	3 828	3 622	2 977	2 262	1 715	Industries extractives
Manufacturing	263	318	392	457	461	526	536	586	624	Industries manufacturières
Electricity, gas & water	53	58	61	65	71	85	91	96	104	Electricité, gaz et eau
Construction	185	270	446	480	561	506	496	505	510	Bâtiments et travaux publics
Wholesale & retail trade, restaurants, hotels	307	330	363	410	433	450	441	446	455	Commerce de gros et de détail, restaurants et hôtels
Finance, insurance, real estate, etc.	898	953	970	991	1 067	1 112	1 167	1 187	1 097	Banques, assurances, affaires immobilières
Transport and communications	306	314	335	365	388	434	452	516	560	Transport(s) et communications
Public administration and defense	559	631	669	766	802	1 033	1 070	1 230	1 111	Administrations publiques et défense
Education	86	97	103	118	123	159	165	189	197	Education
Health And Social Work	55	62	66	75	79	101	105	121	86	Santé et Actions Sociales
Other services	...	...	...	...	...	...	...	...	1 002	Autres services
Less Imputed Service Charges	- 113	- 81	- 144	- 132	- 123	- 112	- 104	- 90	- 112	Moins Services d'intermédiation financière
Gross domestic product at factor cost / basic prices	5 259	6 510	7 881	8 043	7 978	8 241	7 761	7 462	7 821	Produit intérieur brut aux couts des facteurs / prix de base
Plus: Indirect Taxes / taxes on products, less subsidies	438	602	701	723	713	747	721	676	691	Plus taxes indirectes/impôts sur les produits, moins les subventions
EXPENDITURE ON GROSS DOMESTIC PRODUCT AT CURRENT PURCHASER'S VALUES *CFA FRANC (BILLIONS)*										**EMPLOI DU PRODUIT INTÉRIEUR BRUT AUX PRIX COURANTS D'ACQUISITION** *FRANC CFA (MILLIARDS)*
Government final consumption	919	959	1 098	1 230	1 256	1 335	1 268	1 238	1 156	Consommation finale des administrations publiques
Private final consumption	1 997	2 179	2 366	2 581	2 806	3 100	3 218	3 503	3 131	Consommation finale privée
Gross fixed capital formation	1 682	2 234	2 461	2 432	2 602	3 208	2 488	2 317	2 449	Formation brute de capital fixe
Change in inventories	- 88	- 121	- 175	- 68	- 67	- 50	...	...	...	Variation des stocks
Exports of goods and services	2 972	4 101	5 299	5 343	4 985	4 002	3 891	3 470	3 723	Exportations de biens et services
Less imports of goods and services	1 785	2 240	2 468	2 752	2 892	2 607	2 384	2 390	1 947	Moins importations de biens et services
GDP at purchasers' values	5 697	7 112	8 582	8 767	8 691	8 988	8 481	8 137	8 512	PIB aux prix d'acquisition
GROSS DOMESTIC PRODUCT BY KIND OF ECONOMIC ACTIVITY AT CONSTANT PRICES *ANNUAL GROWTH RATES (%)*										**PRODUIT INTÉRIEUR BRUT PAR BRANCHE D'ACTIVITÉ ÉCONOMIQUE AUX PRIX CONSTANTS** *TAUX DE CROISSANCE ANNUEL (%)*
Agriculture, hunting , forestry and Fishing	- 7.0	- 5.2	2.3	4.7	4.6	9.7	8.2	16.6	- 12.6	Agriculture, chasse sylviculture et Pêche
Mining and quarrying	- 5.0	10.6	- 0.1	- 1.8	0.2	1.2	4.1	- 4.1	- 33.0	Industries extractives
Manufacturing	- 2.0	19.4	2.2	8.1	- 0.3	9.8	2.8	12.3	4.2	Industries manufacturières
Electricity, gas & water	- 15.2	9.1	5.1	6.4	5.8	12.8	4.4	6.0	1.3	Electricité, gaz et eau
Construction	7.5	23.3	68.0	- 2.4	12.7	- 10.8	- 3.7	- 1.1	- 1.3	Bâtiments et travaux publics
Wholesale & retail trade, restaurants, hotels	2.1	2.7	3.4	6.2	5.0	3.4	- 0.7	- 0.3	0.1	Commerce de gros et de détail, restaurants et hôtels
Finance, insurance, real estate, etc.	- 6.5	7.6	2.4	7.1	8.1	5.6	1.3	4.7	- 35.0	Banques, assurances, affaires immobilières
Transport and communications	- 2.5	5.1	7.5	9.7	10.2	8.3	12.7	6.6	3.7	Transport(s) et communications
Public administration and defense	7.5	5.7	17.0	12.4	7.6	5.8	4.4	2.5	- 31.3	Administrations publiques et défense
Education	7.5	5.7	17.0	12.4	7.6	5.8	4.4	2.5	132.6	Education
Health And Social Work	7.5	5.7	17.0	12.4	7.6	5.8	4.4	2.5	75.9	Santé et Actions Sociales
Other services	...	...	...	...	...	...	...	...	...	Autres services
Less Imputed Service Charges	5.9	- 1.8	29.3	0.9	- 0.2	1.4	- 13.9	- 7.9	7.1	Moins Services d'intermédiation financière
Gross domestic product at factor cost / basic prices	- 2.4	8.5	7.2	5.3	5.7	4.1	4.3	3.3	0.1	Produit intérieur brut aux couts des facteurs / prix de base
Plus: Indirect Taxes / taxes on products, less subsidies	24.2	- 2.8	6.2	5.0	4.9	5.7	- 0.1	- 0.5	2.2	Plus taxes indirectes/impôts sur les produits, moins les subventions
Gross domestic product at market prices	0.1	7.1	7.1	5.2	5.6	4.3	3.9	2.9	0.3	Produit intérieur brut aux prix du marché
EXPENDITURE ON GROSS DOMESTIC PRODUCT AT CONSTANT PURCHASERS' VALUES *ANNUAL GROWTH RATES (%)*										**EMPLOIS DU PRODUIT INTÉRIEUR BRUT AUX PRIX CONSTANTS D'ACQUISITION** *TAUX DE CROISSANCE ANNUEL (%)*
Government final consumption	6.3	8.2	10.2	5.8	11.8	1.6	- 7.3	- 0.5	- 11.0	Consommation finale des administrations publiques
Private final consumption	5.0	7.5	7.2	6.2	8.2	5.5	4.1	3.1	- 13.5	Consommation finale privée
Gross fixed capital formation	- 1.3	32.7	20.9	12.4	7.0	7.8	- 14.3	3.8	- 0.8	Formation brute de capital fixe
Exports of goods and services	- 1.6	14.8	5.0	- 3.6	- 0.3	0.4	8.7	0.4	- 0.3	Exportations de biens et services
Less imports of goods and services	0.1	31.6	12.5	9.1	2.5	7.9	- 9.3	0.2	- 19.8	Moins importations de biens et services

III INFLATION

	2009	2010	2011	2012	2013	2014	2015	2016	2017	
Annual growth rates (%)										**Taux de croissance annuel (%)**
All item	1.9	1.4	1.3	2.7	0.5	4.5	- 0.3	2.1	2.7	Ensemble
of which:										dont:
Food and non-alcoholic beverages	3.7	4.4	4.0	5.3	- 0.4	3.2	2.8	- 0.1	- 0.7	Alimentation et boissons non alcoolisés
Alcoholic beverages, tobacco and narcotics	1.7	11.1	1.7	0.3	2.9	- 1.6	1.6	2.5	2.4	Boissons alcoolisées et tabacs
Clothing and footwear	- 2.1	- 1.9	1.4	2.1	1.5	4.8	16.9	0.1	1.3	Habillement et chaussures
Housing, water, electricity, gas and other fuels	4.1	0.5	0.5	0.8	2.2	8.0	- 10.2	1.4	9.9	Logement, eau, électricité, gaz et autres combustibles
Furnishings, household equipment and routine household maintenance	- 0.7	- 3.3	- 5.5	0.5	4.6	12.3	- 0.7	4.2	0.7	Meubles, articles de ménage et entretien courant
Health	2.9	0.9	3.8	- 0.1	1.2	1.2	- 11.8	- 5.4	1.7	Santé
Transport	- 6.3	1.1	3.5	4.8	- 1.1	4.5	1.7	10.5	4.2	Transport
Communication	4.4	- 8.7	- 13.4	- 3.8	- 10.0	0.1	- 21.8	- 23.2	- 0.2	Communication
Recreation and culture	1.7	1.7	- 0.8	2.0	0.9	2.5	10.2	2.6	- 0.1	Loisirs et culture
Education	2.7	6.4	- 4.2	- 6.2	9.8	1.5	- 0.5	3.9	12.6	Enseignement
Restaurants and hotels	2.3	4.6	2.9	3.0	0.7	3.2	0.8	4.1	- 0.4	Restaurants et hôtels
Miscellaneous goods and services	3.9	- 2.9	- 0.5	- 4.7	0.1	1.3	7.1	35.1	2.3	Biens et Services divers

IV AGRICULTURAL PRODUCTION - PRODUCTION AGRICOLE

TONNES (THOUSAND)	2009	2010	2011	2012	2013	2014	2015	2016	2017	Tonnes (milliers)
Cassava	245	250	255	300	315	...	...	...	...	Manioc
Sugar cane	240	245	265	260	280	266	282	289	...	Canne à sucre
Plantains	317	325	295	285	272	184	...	...	...	Bananes plantains
Yams	188	190	195	200	210	...	...	...	...	Ignames
Taro (cocoyam)	58	58	60	63	65	...	...	...	...	Taros (colocases)

V MINING PRODUCTION - PRODUCTION MINIERE

	2009	2010	2011	2012	2013	2014	2015	2016	2017	
Crude petroleum - Production, metric tons (thousands)	11 829	12 431	12 512	12 655	11 270	10 980	11 922	11 484	11 060	Pétrole brut - Production, tonnes métriques (milliers)
Natural gas - Production, terajoules (millions)	258	338	336	...	...	438	466	530	565	Gaz naturel - Production, térajoules (millions)
	...	...	...	...	...	...	...	...		

VI ENERGY - ENERGIE

	2009	2010	2011	2012	2013	2014	2015	2016	2017	
Total electricity generation (GWh)	1 674	1 776	1 845	2 017	2 113	2 213	2 318	...	...	Production électrique totale (GWh)
of which										dont
Production of electricity from fossil fuels (GWh)	718	855	851	974	1 017	1 063	1 111	...	...	Production d'électricité à partir de combustibles fossiles (GWh)
Production of hydro electricity (GWh)	948	912	981	1 030	1 082	1 136	1 193	...	...	Production d'électricité d'origine hydraulique (GWh)
Production of electricity from solar, wind, tide, wave and other sources (GWh)	...	...	4	4	4	4	4	...	...	Production d'électricité d'origine solaire, éolienne, marée motrice et autres (GWh)

VII TOURISM AND INFRASTRUCTURE - TOURISME ET INFRASTUCTURE

	2009	2010	2011	2012	2013	2014	2015	2016	2017	
VII-1 Tourism										**VII-1 Tourisme**
International tourist arrivals (thousands)	368	398	463	544	548	586	624	664	586	Arrivées de touristes internationaux (milliers)
Rooms in hotels and similar establishments (thousands)	...	...	...	...	...	...	...	...	...	Chambres d'hôtels et établissements assimilés (milliers)
Overnight stays (thousands)	1 769	1 914	2 152	2 487	2 606	2 680	2 852	3 036	2 678	Nuitées (milliers)
Tourism receipts (US$ thousand)	7 099	7 129	10 367	11 755	12 098	12 386	10 445	10 981	10 731	Recettes touristiques (milliers de $ EU)
Total contribution to GDP (%)	3.9	3.3	2.5	2.6	2.8	3.2	2.9	2.9	2.9	Contribution totale au PIB (%)
Total contribution to Employment (%)	4.3	3.6	2.6	2.2	2.3	2.7	2.6	2.6	2.6	Contribution totale à l'emploi (%)
VII-2 Infrastructure										**VII-2 Infrastructure**
Paved road (% of total)	...	...	...	...	...	...	...	...	...	Routes asphaltées (% du total)
Total network (Railways-km)	810	810	810	810	810	810	...	...	...	Réseau total voies ferrées-Km
Main telephone lines (per 100 inhabitants)	2.4	2.0	1.4	1.4	1.2	1.1	1.1	1.1	...	Lignes téléphoniques fixes (pour 100 habitants)
Mobile cellular subscribers (per 100 inhabitants)	95.4	103.5	148.7	156.7	164.2	171.4	161.1	144.2	...	Abonnés aux téléphones mobiles (pour 100 habitants)
Internet users per 100 inhabitants	9.5	13.0	18.0	24.0	30.5	38.1	45.8	48.1	...	Utilisateurs Internet par 100 Habitants
Fixed (wired)-broadband subscriptions per 100 inhabitants	...	...	...	...	0.5	0.6	0.6	0.7	...	Abonnements à l'Internet fixe (filaire) à large bande pour 100 habitants, par débit

VIII EXTERNAL TRADE - COMMERCE EXTERIEUR

	2009	2010	2011	2012	2013	2014	2015	2016	2017	
US$ (MILLIONS) **EXPORTS, FOB**										**$ E.U (MILLIONS)** **EXPORTATIONS, FÁB**
Exports - Total	5 356	8 686	9 766	9 493	9 715	9 346	6 473	5 871	...	Exportations - Total
Exports to Africa	369	318	476	446	451	438	302	274	...	Exportations vers l'Afrique
Main products										**Principaux produits**
Ores and concentrates of base metals, n.e.s.	299	327	374	321	332	316	264	309	...	Minerais et concentrés de métaux communs, n.d.a.
Petroleum oils or bituminous minerals > 70 % oil	92	173	206	203	210	203	140	121	...	Huiles de pétrole ou de minéraux bitumineux> 70% d'huile
Petroleum oils, oils from bitumin. materials, crude	4 027	7 169	7 971	7 787	8 001	7 629	5 098	4 531	...	Huiles de pétrole, huiles de bitume. matériaux bruts
Veneers, plywood, and other wood, worked, n.e.s.	116	154	145	150	144	132	122	133	...	Placages, contreplaqués et autres bois, travaillés, n.d.a.
Wood in the rough or roughly squared	448	284	409	432	418	479	368	322	...	Bois bruts ou grossièrement équarris
Main destinations										**Principales destinations**
China	571	585	898	821	836	812	561	509	...	Chine
Malaysia	262	553	540	547	559	536	372	337	...	Malaisie
Netherlands	98	517	473	473	490	468	325	294	...	Pays-Bas
Spain	296	313	403	389	394	381	264	239	...	Espagne
United States	2 222	5 122	5 283	5 217	5 356	5 136	3 561	3 230	...	États-Unis
IMPORTS, CIF										**IMPORTATIONS, CAF**
Imports - Total	2 501	2 983	3 665	3 629	3 909	4 046	3 061	2 977	...	Importations - Total (millions)
Imports from Africa	400	276	337	358	778	432	329	304	...	Importations en provenance de l'Afrique
Main products										**Principaux produits**
Civil engineering & contractors' plant & equipment	133	150	196	208	208	261	182	149	...	Génie civil et installations et équipements des entrepreneurs
Other meat and edible meat offal	75	79	90	94	101	139	92	202	...	Autres viandes et abats comestibles
Petroleum oils or bituminous minerals > 70 % oil	91	129	181	203	280	202	106	97	...	Huiles de pétrole ou de minéraux bitumineux> 70% d'huile
Ships, boats & floating structures	158	155	118	140	144	148	113	87	...	Navires, bateaux et structures flottantes
Tubes, pipes & hollow profiles, fittings, iron, steel	125	119	144	173	166	169	133	114	...	Tubes, tuyaux et profilés creux, raccords, fer, acier
Main origin										**Principales provenances**
Belgium	252	463	575	564	590	605	331	436	...	Belgique
China	140	185	205	317	287	347	550	378	...	Chine
France	765	912	1 195	1 058	914	1 046	719	731	...	France
Italy	100	155	174	164	132	150	88	72	...	Italie
United States	176	263	206	313	269	444	222	109	...	États-Unis

GABON

IX FINANCIAL AND MONETARY STATISTICS - FINANCES ET STATISTIQUES MONETAIRES

	2009	2010	2011	2012	2013	2014	2015	2016	2017	
IX-1 MONETARY STATISTICS *CFA FRANC (MILLIONS)*										**IX-1 STATISTIQUES MONÉTAIRES** *FRANC CFA (MILLIONS)*
Money supply (M1)	1 165 151	1 389 187	1 757 157	2 033 579	2 157 071	2 191 764	2 180 025	2 026 426	2 201 834	Masse monétaire (M1)
Quasi-money	393 408	465 067	540 012	731 987	734 554	779 387	742 229	718 150	565 186	Quasi-monnaie
of which demand deposit	...	...	...	...	...	...	...	...	...	dont Monnaie scripturale
Net foreign assets	973 962	896 436	1 046 542	1 097 428	1 420 204	1 307 523	1 119 099	459 618	521 199	Avoirs extérieurs nets
Domestic credit	449 821	745 382	982 873	1 236 393	1 117 640	1 242 611	1 435 389	1 926 971	1 591 526	Crédit intérieur
of which claims on private sector	- 151 789	121 475	131 845	169 459	- 311 125	- 141 894	88 313	635 002	643 501	dont créances sur le secteur privé
of which claims on government sector, net	574 890	583 852	817 625	990 797	1 304 694	1 307 060	1 234 375	1 149 277	892 062	dont créances nettes sur le gouvernement
International reserves (millions US$)	1 922	1 731	2 341	2 312	2 908	2 742	2 273	844	1 153	Réserves internationales (millions $EU)
Average exchange rate (National currency per US$)	472	495	472	511	494	494	591	593	582	Taux de change (moyen) (monnaie nationale par $ EU)
IX-2 PUBLIC FINANCE *CFA FRANC (MILLIONS)*										**IX-2 FINANCES PUBLIQUES** *FRANC CFA (MILLIONS)*
Total Revenues and Grants	1 685 163	1 834 003	2 015 249	2 643 426	2 746 678	2 672 688	1 797 300	1 424 246	1 584 770	Recettes totales et dons
Direct taxes (on income, profits)	651 625	443 362	601 887	719 725	743 997	738 832	680 985	385 498	419 052	Taxes directes
Domestic indirect taxes revenues	141 773	163 200	148 152	161 947	270 106	373 686	167 000	222 762	235 985	Taxes Indirectes
Trade taxes	277 322	361 300	358 430	411 130	425 009	425 603	354 800	277 249	309 907	Taxes sur le commerce extérieur
Other taxes	613 943	866 141	906 780	1 350 624	1 307 566	1 134 567	594 515	523 736	606 826	Autres taxes
Other revenues	...	...	...	...	...	...	...	...	...	Autres recettes
Grants	500	...	...	...	...	...	...	15 000	13 001	Dons
Total Expenditures and Net Lending	1 296 716	1 642 091	1 865 706	2 099 537	3 013 399	2 135 220	1 892 300	1 815 682	1 891 184	Dépenses totales et prêts nets
Current expenditure	832 097	886 643	874 377	1 005 924	1 471 133	1 308 463	1 277 000	1 219 547	1 089 188	Dépenses courantes
Wages and Salaries	379 700	412 400	414 942	452 587	561 425	712 959	714 700	730 924	710 000	Rémunérations et salaires
Other purchases of goods and services	215 700	238 964	229 837	264 143	419 884	244 115	241 200	251 736	188 000	Achat de biens et services
Other current expenditure	236 697	235 279	229 598	289 194	489 824	351 389	321 100	236 887	191 188	Autres dépenses courantes
Current transfers	...	...	...	...	...	...	...	...	...	Transferts courants
Interest payments	82 192	96 800	94 559	93 720	135 169	145 231	172 300	193 174	267 643	Intérêts
Capital expenditure	382 427	658 648	896 770	999 893	1 407 098	681 526	443 000	402 961	534 354	Dépenses d'équipement
Net lending	...	...	...	...	...	...	...	...	...	Prêts nets
Fiscal balance	388 447	191 912	149 543	543 889	- 266 722	537 468	- 95 000	- 391 436	- 306 414	Solde global y compris les dons
IX-3 BALANCE OF PAYMENTS *CFA FRANC (MILLIONS)*										**IX-3 BALANCE DES PAIEMENTS** *FRANC CFA (MILLIONS)*
Trade balance	1 794	2 618	3 065	3 046	2 491	2 192	1 439	1 700	1 496	Balance commerciale
Services Balance	- 665	- 667	- 1 055	- 985	- 1 048	- 1 033	- 1 005	- 1 172	- 824	Balance des services
Net primary income	- 579	- 844	- 598	- 794	- 790	- 721	- 492	- 578	- 613	Revenus primaires nets
Compensation of employees	...	...	...	...	...	...	...	...	...	Rémunération des salariés
Investment income	...	...	...	...	...	...	...	...	...	Revenus des investissements
Net secondary income	- 170	- 113	- 184	- 186	- 194	- 190	- 192	- 194	...	Revenus secondaires nets
Net official transfers	...	...	...	...	...	...	...	...	...	Transferts officiels nets
Workers' remittances	...	...	...	...	...	...	...	...	...	Envois de fonds des travailleurs
Other private transfers	...	...	...	...	...	...	...	...	...	Autres transferts privés
Current account balance	380	994	1 229	1 080	459	249	- 251	- 245	...	Solde du compte courant
Capital and financial account	- 377	- 683	- 540	- 587	81	- 52	67	- 101	...	Comptes de capital et financier
Capital account	- 1	- 14	...	...	...	...	...	...	...	Compte de capital
Financial account	- 376	- 669	- 540	- 587	81	- 52	67	- 101	...	Compte financier
Errors and omissions	- 98	- 366	- 448	- 413	- 289	- 311	...	...	...	Erreurs et omissions
Overall balance	- 95	- 55	241	80	252	- 114	- 184	- 346	...	Balance générale

X DEBT AND FINANCIAL FLOWS - DETTE ET FLUX FINANCIERS

	2009	2010	2011	2012	2013	2014	2015	2016	2017	
X-1 DEBT *US $ (MILLIONS)*										**X-1 DETTE EXTÉRIEURE** *$ E.U (MILLIONS)*
Total external debt	2 443	2 448	2 801	2 854	4 260	4 613	4 783	4 991	6 530	Dette extérieure totale
Private	...	...	...	...	...	...	...	...	...	Privée
Public	2 443	2 448	2 801	2 854	4 260	4 613	4 783	4 991	...	Publique
Total external debt service	834	931	619	592	1 246	526	593	1 326	...	Service de la dette extérieure
Present value of external debt	...	...	...	...	...	...	...	4 973	...	Valeur actuelle de la dette extérieure
Total government domestic debt, National currency (millions)	256	89	57	57	244	206	281	...	...	Dette publique intérieure
X-2 FINANCIAL FLOWS *US $ (MILLIONS)*										**X-2 FLUX FINANCIERS** *$ E.U (MILLIONS)*
Net Foreign Direct Investment Inflows	573	499	696	832	771	1 011	624	703	...	Investissements étranger direct (flux nets entrants)
Main origin of FDI inflows										**Principales origines de l'IDE entrant:**
France	54	- 8	26	207	...	...	...	...	...	France
Belgium	13	29	58	76	...	...	...	...	...	Belgique
...	...	...	...	...	...	...	...	...	...	...
Italy	41	- 10	6	11	...	...	...	...	...	Italie
Germany	1	...	...	...	...	...	...	...	...	Allemagne
African countries	23	151	2	...	...	...	...	...	...	Pays africains
Net total official development assistance	78	106	69	69	87	111	99	42	...	Aide publique au développement (nette totale)
Main origin of net ODA										**Principales origines de l'APD nette**
France	54	58	51	57	64	88	72	17	...	France
Japan	...	25	11	3	4	4	2	3	...	Japon
Global Fund	7	2	1	- 1	1	-	...	...	...	Fonds Mondial
United States	1	...	...	-	-	-	-	-	...	États-Unis
United Nations High Commissioner for Refugees	1	1	...	-	...	...	-	...	...	L'agence des Nations Unies pour les réfugiés

GABON

SOURCES AND NOTES - SOURCES ET NOTES

External trade - Total exports, fob: UNCTAD	Commerce exterieur - Exportation, fab: CNUCED
External trade - Total import, cif: UNCTAD	Commerce exterieur - Imporations, caf: CNUCED
ODA: OECD	APD: OCDE
Monetary statistics: IMF	Statistiques monétaires: FMI
National Accounts: 2017:Projection	Comptes nationaux: 2017: Projection
Poverty: World Bank	Pauvreté: Banque mondiale

	AREA (km2)		11 300		SUPERFICIE (KM2)
	CAPITAL CITY	Banjul		Banjul	CAPITALE
	CURRENCY	Gambian Dalasi		Dalasi Gambien	MONNAIE

I SOCIAL AND DEMOGRAPHIC INDICATORS — INDICATEURS DEMOGRAPHIQUES ET SOCIAUX

	Year Année	Value Valeur	Charts Graphiques	
Population				**Population**
Population ('000)	2016	2 052.6		Population ('000)
Female (%)	2016	52.1		Féminine (%)
Urban (%)	2016	60.8		Urbaine (%)
Average annual growth rate	2016	3.4		Taux de croissance annuel
Active population ('000)	2016	596.7		Population active ('000)
Population by age group ('000)				Population par groupe d'âge ('000)
0-14 years	2016	948.0		0-14 ans
15-64 years	2016	1 057.1		15-64 ans
65+ years	2016	47.5		65+ ans
Economically active population in agriculture (%)	2016	124.0		Participation de la population active agricole (%)
Crude birth rate	2016	43.0		Taux brut de natalité
Crude death rate	2016	8.8		Taux brut de mortalité
Total fertility rate	2016	5.8		Indice synthétique de fécondité
Life expectancy at birth - Total (years)	2015	60.5		Espérance de vie à la naissance - Totale (années)
Dependency ratio – Total (%)	2016	94.2		Taux de dépendance – Total (%)
Health				**Santé**
Percentage of children under-five and underweight	2013	11.7		% d'enfants de moins de cinq ans avec insuffisance pondérale
Prevalence of undernourishment	2016	5.5		Prévalence de la malnutrition
Under five mortality rate (per 1 000 live births)	2015	68.9		Taux de mortalité de moins de 5 ans (les deux sexes, pour 1000)
Infant mortality rate (per 1 000 live births)	2015	47.9		Taux de mortalité infantile (les deux sexes) par 1000
Neonatal mortality rate (per 1 000 live births)	2015	29.9		Le taux de mortalité néonatale (pour 1000 naissances vivantes)
Percentage of children provided the vaccines :				Pourcentage d'enfants vaccinés :
BCG	2014	96.0		BCG
DPT3	2014	96.0		DTC3
Polio	2013	96.0		polio
Measles	2014	96.0		rougeole
Percentage of mothers provided at least one antenatal care (%)	2013	98.9		Pourcentage de mères ayant au moins reçu un soin prénatal (%)
Percentage of deliveries attended by skilled health personnel	2013	57.1		% d'accouchements assistés par un personnel de santé qualifié
Number of doctors (per 10,000 population)	2013	1.0		Nombre de médecins (pour 10.000 habitants)
Number of nurses (per 10,000 population)	2013	13.7		Nombre d'infirmiers (pour 10.000 habitants)
Hospital beds - Total (per 10,000 population)	2013	264.3		Nombre de lits d'hôpitaux – Total (pour 10 000)
Births registered (per 1,000)	2015	41.7		Naissances enregistrées (pour 1000)
Deaths registered (per 1,000)	2015	8.6		Décès enregistrés (pour 1000)
Budget allocation to health (%)	2013	13.0		Dépenses publiques consacrées à la santé (% du budget)
Education				**Education**
Enrolment in primary education (000)	2016	358.0		Scolarisation dans le primaire (000)
Female	2014	139.3		Féminine
Enrolment in secondary education (000)	2016	155.0		Scolarisation dans le secondaire (000)
Female	2014	67.6		Féminine
Enrolment in tertiary education (000)	2008	6.5		Scolarisation dans le tertiaire (000)
Female	2014	21.7		Féminine
Literacy rate	2013	62.5		Taux d'alphabétisation (deux sexes)
Male	2013	71.0		Masculin
Female	2013	46.0		Féminin
Pupil teacher ratio - primary	2011	37.6		Ratio élève-enseignant
Budget allocation to education (%)	2014	46.4		Dépenses publiques consacrées à l'enseignement (% du budget)
Poverty				**Pauvreté**
GNI per capita, PPP (current int. $)	2016	1630.0		RNB par habitant, ($ PPA inter. courants)
Human Poverty Index (HPI-1) Value (%)	2007	40.9		Valeur de l'Indice de pauvreté (IPH-1) (%)
Population below Inter. poverty line ($2/day) (%)	2003	45.3		Population sous le seuil inter. de pauvreté (2$/Jour) (%)
Share of income held by richest 10%	2003	36.9		% de revenu des 10% plus riches
Share of income held by poorest 10%	2003	1.8		% de revenu des 10% plus pauvres
GINI index	2003	47.3		Indice de GINI

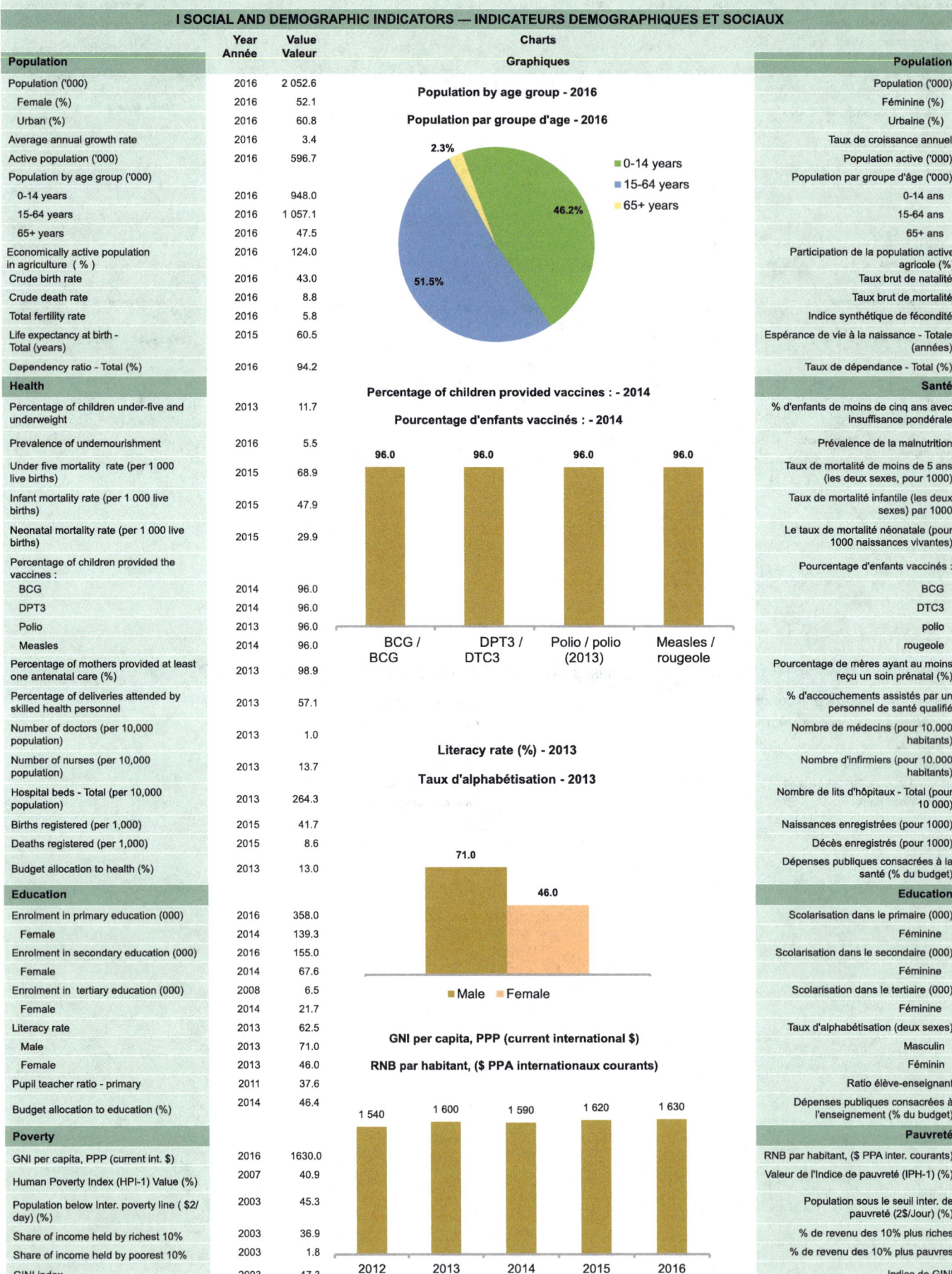

Population by age group - 2016
Population par groupe d'age - 2016

- 0-14 years 46.2%
- 15-64 years 51.5%
- 65+ years 2.3%

Percentage of children provided vaccines : - 2014
Pourcentage d'enfants vaccinés : - 2014

BCG / BCG	DPT3 / DTC3	Polio / polio (2013)	Measles / rougeole
96.0	96.0	96.0	96.0

Literacy rate (%) - 2013
Taux d'alphabétisation - 2013

Male 71.0 — Female 46.0

GNI per capita, PPP (current international $)
RNB par habitant, ($ PPA internationaux courants)

2012	2013	2014	2015	2016
1 540	1 600	1 590	1 620	1 630

GAMBIA

	2009	2010	2011	2012	2013	2014	2015	2016	2017	
GROSS DOMESTIC PRODUCT BY KIND OF ECONOMIC ACTIVITY AT CURRENT PRICES *GAMBIA DALASI (MILLIONS)*										**PRODUIT INTÉRIEUR BRUT PAR BRANCHE D'ACTIVITÉ ÉCONOMIQUE AUX PRIX COURANTS** *DALASI GAMBIEN (MILLIONS)*
Agriculture, hunting , forestry and Fishing	6 292	7 719	5 942	6 533	6 939	6 850	7 647	8 429	...	Agriculture, chasse sylviculture et Pêche
Mining and quarrying	603	705	792	897	1 014	871	851	851	...	Industries extractives
Manufacturing	1 195	1 260	1 460	1 671	1 777	1 848	1 916	1 971	...	Industries manufacturières
Electricity, gas & water	299	331	331	335	366	432	492	546	...	Electricité, gaz et eau
Construction	910	992	1 131	1 329	1 468	1 726	2 288	2 309	...	Bâtiments et travaux publics
Wholesale & retail trade, restaurants, hotels	6 460	6 675	7 154	7 778	8 397	9 820	10 556	11 788	...	Commerce de gros et de détail, restaurants et hôtels
Finance, insurance, real estate, etc.	3 034	3 193	3 668	3 936	4 386	5 095	5 631	6 276	...	Banques, assurances, affaires immobilières
Transport and communications	2 653	3 114	3 464	3 939	4 896	5 254	6 061	6 700	...	Transport(s) et communications
Public administration and defense	440	526	565	608	687	802	879	968	...	Administrations publiques et défense
Education	249	276	297	321	366	419	440	497	...	Education
Health And Social Work	253	283	293	295	323	423	467	537	...	Santé et Actions Sociales
Other services	100	104	108	114	126	133	139	149	...	Autres services
Less Imputed Service Charges	- 1 017	- 848	- 1 058	- 1 126	- 1 389	- 2 086	- 2 341	- 2 892	...	Moins Services d'intermédiation financière
Gross domestic product at factor cost / basic prices	21 470	24 331	24 147	26 628	29 355	31 587	35 025	38 130	...	Produit intérieur brut aux couts des facteurs / prix de base
Plus: Indirect Taxes / taxes on products, less subsidies	2 527	2 349	2 494	2 645	3 143	3 849	4 902	5 147	...	Plus taxes indirectes/impôts sur les produits, moins les subventions
EXPENDITURE ON GROSS DOMESTIC PRODUCT AT CURRENT PURCHASER'S VALUES *GAMBIA DALASI (MILLIONS)*										**EMPLOI DU PRODUIT INTÉRIEUR BRUT AUX PRIX COURANTS D'ACQUISITION** *DALASI GAMBIEN (MILLIONS)*
Government final consumption	2 511	2 676	2 836	2 802	3 110	3 803	4 023	4 687	...	Consommation finale des administrations publiques
Private final consumption	20 147	24 806	22 895	26 282	28 293	32 748	37 339	40 084	...	Consommation finale privée
Gross fixed capital formation	6 421	4 903	6 755	6 845	7 118	7 518	8 355	8 131	...	Formation brute de capital fixe
Change in inventories	...	...	...	...	...	...	...	...	...	Variation des stocks
Exports of goods and services	1 847	1 185	2 790	3 794	4 732	5 141	4 551	4 884	...	Exportations de biens et services
Less imports of goods and services	6 929	6 890	8 636	10 451	10 755	13 774	14 341	14 508	...	Moins importations de biens et services
GDP at purchasers' values	23 997	26 679	26 641	29 273	32 498	35 436	39 927	43 277	...	PIB aux prix d'acquisition
GROSS DOMESTIC PRODUCT BY KIND OF ECONOMIC ACTIVITY AT CONSTANT PRICES *ANNUAL GROWTH RATES (%)*										**PRODUIT INTÉRIEUR BRUT PAR BRANCHE D'ACTIVITÉ ECONOMIQUE AUX PRIX CONSTANTS** *TAUX DE CROISSANCE ANNUEL (%)*
Agriculture, hunting , forestry and Fishing	11.7	11.2	- 24.2	6.2	- 1.8	- 7.1	3.8	0.5	...	Agriculture, chasse sylviculture et Pêche
Mining and quarrying	12.1	14.2	7.6	9.0	7.4	- 10.2	- 6.5	- 10.3	...	Industries extractives
Manufacturing	- 4.3	0.4	3.9	2.5	3.2	2.8	1.5	1.5	...	Industries manufacturières
Electricity, gas & water	2.2	7.7	- 3.9	- 4.1	2.2	7.4	9.2	7.3	...	Electricité, gaz et eau
Construction	3.0	3.8	9.2	12.7	4.5	10.6	24.1	- 5.9	...	Bâtiments et travaux publics
Wholesale & retail trade, restaurants, hotels	- 0.6	- 2.1	2.4	4.5	2.9	6.8	1.4	3.0	...	Commerce de gros et de détail, restaurants et hôtels
Finance, insurance, real estate, etc.	19.9	1.2	10.6	3.9	6.3	9.9	4.4	4.5	...	Banques, assurances, affaires immobilières
Transport and communications	8.0	11.4	5.5	9.2	18.6	0.2	6.9	8.0	...	Transport(s) et communications
Public administration and defense	30.5	13.8	2.4	3.2	7.0	10.1	2.7	2.7	...	Administrations publiques et défense
Education	5.4	10.5	4.7	7.0	13.7	13.8	4.2	12.3	...	Education
Health And Social Work	21.2	11.6	3.7	0.1	9.1	7.1	5.3	12.4	...	Santé et Actions Sociales
Other services	2.7	2.7	2.7	2.7	7.0	3.1	3.1	3.1	...	Autres services
Less Imputed Service Charges	29.9	- 20.6	19.0	2.1	16.8	41.7	5.1	15.2	...	Moins Services d'intermédiation financière
Gross domestic product at factor cost / basic prices	6.4	6.5	- 4.3	5.9	4.8	0.9	4.3	2.2	...	Produit intérieur brut aux couts des facteurs / prix de base
Plus: Indirect Taxes / taxes on products, less subsidies	27.6	- 7.0	6.2	6.1	18.8	22.5	27.4	5.0	...	Plus taxes indirectes/impôts sur les produits, moins les subventions
Gross domestic product at market prices	6.4	6.5	- 4.3	5.9	4.8	0.9	4.3	2.2	...	Produit intérieur brut aux prix du marché
EXPENDITURE ON GROSS DOMESTIC PRODUCT AT CONSTANT PURCHASERS' VALUES *ANNUAL GROWTH RATES (%)*										**EMPLOIS DU PRODUIT INTÉRIEUR BRUT AUX PRIX CONSTANTS D'ACQUISITION** *TAUX DE CROISSANCE ANNUEL (%)*
Government final consumption	15.1	1.5	1.1	- 5.3	5.0	15.4	- 1.0	8.7	...	Consommation finale des administrations publiques
Private final consumption	- 1.5	17.7	- 11.3	10.5	1.6	6.8	5.5	1.2	...	Consommation finale privée
Gross fixed capital formation	8.0	- 29.8	33.5	- 3.4	- 2.5	0.1	4.2	- 9.6	...	Formation brute de capital fixe
Exports of goods and services	492.6	- 41.5	128.8	29.4	16.5	3.3	- 16.8	- 0.7	...	Exportations de biens et services
Less imports of goods and services	9.6	- 9.3	21.8	15.1	- 3.9	21.8	- 2.2	- 6.3	...	Moins importations de biens et services

	2009	2010	2011	2012	2013	2014	2015	2016	2017	
Annual growth rates (%)										**Taux de croissance annuel (%)**
All item	4.6	5.0	4.8	4.3	5.7	6.0	6.8	7.2	8.0	Ensemble
of which:										dont:
Food and non-alcoholic beverages	5.3	6.6	6.4	5.0	6.7	6.5	9.0	8.2	...	Alimentation et boissons non alcoolisés
Alcoholic beverages, tobacco and narcotics	1.6	0.9	1.0	1.5	2.3	1.7	1.9	2.8	...	Boissons alcoolisées et tabacs
Clothing and footwear	3.6	1.8	0.9	2.1	2.9	3.3	5.1	7.6	...	Habillement et chaussures
Housing, water, electricity, gas and other fuels	4.0	2.1	3.9	8.9	11.6	5.6	4.6	3.6	...	Logement, eau, électricité, gaz et autres combustibles
Furnishings, household equipment and routine household maintenance	2.8	1.3	1.7	1.8	2.5	2.3	2.7	5.4	...	Meubles, articles de ménage et entretien courant
Health	0.7	0.1	0.1	0.3	0.4	17.9	1.5	2.3	...	Santé
Transport	2.0	13.3	13.4	7.7	16.6	12.2	5.5	- 0.9	...	Transport
Communication	0.5	0.4	0.1	0.3	0.4	0.3	0.7	0.4	...	Communication
Recreation and culture	0.9	1.2	1.9	2.2	2.8	2.8	1.8	4.0	...	Loisirs et culture
Education	0.6	1.3	1.9	0.8	0.5	0.5	0.6	0.6	...	Enseignement
Restaurants and hotels	4.8	6.6	7.7	5.3	6.5	4.4	8.2	7.8	...	Restaurants et hôtels
Miscellaneous goods and services	9.6	6.7	4.1	4.9	5.5	5.8	7.6	11.2	...	Biens et Services divers

GAMBIE

IV AGRICULTURAL PRODUCTION - PRODUCTION AGRICOLE

TONNES (THOUSAND)	2009	2010	2011	2012	2013	2014	2015	2016	2017	Tonnes (milliers)
Groundnuts, with shell	122	138	84	120	81	91	92	110	...	Arachides (en coques)
Millet	145	158	87	116	77	86	78	102	...	Millet
Rice, paddy	79	100	51	54	47	57	53	60	...	Riz, Paddy
Maize	55	66	24	30	30	31	31	39	...	Maïs
Sorghum	32	39	21	23	20	23	22	...	...	Sorgho

V MINING PRODUCTION - PRODUCTION MINIERE

	2009	2010	2011	2012	2013	2014	2015	2016	2017	
	...	...	...	...	...	...	...	...	...	
	...	...	...	...	...	...	...	...	...	
	...	...	...	...	...	...	...	...	...	

VI ENERGY - ENERGIE

	2009	2010	2011	2012	2013	2014	2015	2016	2017	
Total electricity generation (GWh) of which	155	205	205	238	238	310	323	...	...	Production électrique totale (GWh) dont
Production of electricity from fossil fuels (GWh)	155	203	203	236	236	304	313			Production d'électricité à partir de combustibles fossiles (GWh)
Production of hydro electricity (GWh)	...	...	...	...	...	...	...	...	...	Production d'électricité d'origine hydraulique (GWh)
Production of electricity from solar, wind, tide, wave and other sources (GWh)	...	2	2	2	2	6	10	...	...	Production d'électricité d'origine solaire, éolienne, marée motrice et autres (GWh)

VII TOURISM AND INFRASTRUCTURE - TOURISME ET INFRASTUCTURE

VII-1 Tourism	2009	2010	2011	2012	2013	2014	2015	2016	2017	VII-1 Tourisme
International tourist arrivals (thousands)	142	91	106	157	171	156	135	145	159	Arrivées de touristes internationaux (milliers)
Rooms in hotels and similar establishments (thousands)	9	9	9	9	9	9	9	...	...	Chambres d'hôtels et établissements assimilés (milliers)
Overnight stays (thousands)	1 488	934	1 117	1 430	1 430	1 352	1 086	1 213	1 395	Nuitées (milliers)
Tourism receipts (US$ thousand)	57 904	64 986	64 164	80 464	57 064	91 464	99 064	101 606	110 479	Recettes touristiques (milliers de $ EU)
Total contribution to GDP (%)	17.5	17.2	20.5	23.0	17.9	22.6	21.6	19.6	20.1	Contribution totale au PIB (%)
Total contribution to Employment (%)	16.0	15.8	17.7	19.9	15.3	19.9	18.5	16.9	17.2	Contribution totale à l'emploi (%)
VII-2 Infrastructure										**VII-2 Infrastructure**
Paved road (% of total)	0.8	0.8	19.0	20.6	20.6	20.6	20.6	...	...	Routes asphaltées (% du total)
Total network (Railways-km)	...	...	...	...	...	...	...	...	...	Réseau total voies ferrées-Km
Main telephone lines (per 100 inhabitants)	3.0	2.9	2.9	3.6	3.5	2.9	2.3	1.9	...	Lignes téléphoniques fixes (pour 100 habitants)
Mobile cellular subscribers (per 100 inhabitants)	80.6	88.0	80.8	85.2	100.0	119.6	137.8	139.6	...	Abonnés aux téléphones mobiles (pour 100 habitants)
Internet users per 100 inhabitants	7.6	9.2	10.9	12.4	14.0	15.6	16.5	18.5	...	Utilisateurs Internet par 100 Habitants
Fixed (wired)-broadband subscriptions per 100 inhabitants	...	...	...	...	...	...	...	...	...	Abonnements à l'Internet fixe (filaire) à large bande pour 100 habitants, par débit

VIII EXTERNAL TRADE - COMMERCE EXTERIEUR

US$ (MILLIONS) EXPORTS, FOB	2009	2010	2011	2012	2013	2014	2015	2016	2017	$ E.U (MILLIONS) EXPORTATIONS, FÀB
Exports - Total	66	68	95	119	106	104	109	107	...	Exportations - Total
Exports to Africa	27	21	33	48	43	46	46	46	...	Exportations vers l'Afrique
Main products										**Principaux produits**
Fabrics, woven, of man-made fabrics	8	8	13	25	26	31	30	31	...	Tissus tissés en tissus synthétiques ou artificiels
Fruits and nuts (excluding oil nuts), fresh or dried	17	8	15	12	15	21	19	20	...	Fruits et noix (à l'exclusion des oléagineux), frais ou secs
Ores and concentrates of base metals, n.e.s.	3	4	8	3	6	2	4	3	...	Minerais et concentrés de métaux communs, n.d.a.
Petroleum oils or bituminous minerals > 70 % oil	1	2	1	7	4	1	2	2	...	Huiles de pétrole ou de minéraux bitumineux> 70% d'huile
Wood in the rough or roughly squared	...	4	15	36	29	16	23	20	...	Bois bruts ou grossièrement équarris
Main destinations										**Principales destinations**
China	4	9	24	40	35	20	29	25	...	Chine
Guinea	9	7	9	18	11	9	10	10	...	Guinée
India	15	8	14	11	13	16	15	16	...	Inde
Mali	-	1	6	17	22	24	24	24	...	Mali
Senegal	9	8	11	6	7	7	7	7	...	Sénégal
IMPORTS, CIF										
Imports - Total	304	284	341	380	350	387	417	368	...	Importations - Total (millions)
Imports from Africa	64	57	70	84	70	68	78	67	...	Importations en provenance de l'Afrique
Main products										**Principaux produits**
Cotton fabrics, woven	26	29	36	39	43	46	50	44	...	Tissus de coton, tissés
Edible products and preparations, n.e.s.	10	11	14	15	20	20	22	19	...	Produits et préparations comestibles, n.d.a.
Petroleum oils or bituminous minerals > 70 % oil	31	23	36	43	31	31	35	30	...	Huiles de pétrole ou de minéraux bitumineux> 70% d'huile
Rice	18	16	21	26	21	28	28	26	...	Riz
Sugar, molasses and honey	17	18	15	18	18	20	22	19	...	Sucre, mélasse et miel
Main origin										**Principales provenances**
Brazil	23	30	34	29	30	35	37	33	...	Brazil
China	56	57	77	82	83	97	102	91	...	Chine
Côte d'Ivoire	22	22	24	34	24	24	27	23	...	Côte d'Ivoire
India	12	14	18	20	22	29	28	26	...	Inde
Senegal	22	21	23	31	29	27	32	27	...	Sénégal

GAMBIA

	2009	2010	2011	2012	2013	2014	2015	2016	2017	
IX-1 MONETARY STATISTICS *GAMBIA DALASI (MILLIONS)*										**IX-1 STATISTIQUES MONÉTAIRES** *DALASI GAMBIEN (MILLIONS)*
Money supply (M1)	11 695	13 292	14 753	15 902	18 309	20 365	20 179	23 259	25 911	Masse monétaire (M1)
Quasi-money	5 941	7 096	7 914	8 255	8 493	9 243	...	...	11 507	Quasi-monnaie
of which demand deposit	...	...	...	...	...	...	...	...	...	dont Monnaie scripturale
Net foreign assets	3 023	3 571	4 307	4 552	4 049	3 535	2 750	...	525	Avoirs extérieurs nets
Domestic credit	7 480	10 389	11 601	12 912	16 057	19 063	19 024	...	...	Crédit intérieur
of which claims on private sector	3 247	5 394	6 455	7 559	10 299	13 796	13 927	...	...	dont créances sur le secteur privé
of which claims on government sector, net	3 542	4 103	4 322	4 575	4 937	4 531	4 481	...	3 585	dont créances nettes sur le gouvernement
International reserves (millions US$)	178	158	170	184	161	112	76	60	85	Réserves internationales (millions $EU)
Average exchange rate (National currency per US$)	27	28	29	32	36	42	43	44	46	Taux de change (moyen) (monnaie nationale par $ EU)
IX-2 PUBLIC FINANCE *GAMBIA DALASI (MILLIONS)*										**IX-2 FINANCES PUBLIQUES** *DALASI GAMBIEN (MILLIONS)*
Total Revenues and Grants	4 909	5 026	5 619	7 397	5 992	7 720	8 346	8 477	...	Recettes totales et dons
Direct taxes (on income, profits)	974	1 109	1 225	1 520	1 384	1 595	1 717	1 831	...	Taxes directes
Domestic indirect taxes revenues	1 395	1 500	1 683	1 833	1 899	2 349	2 925	3 055	...	Taxes Indirectes
Trade taxes	1 148	867	830	856	1 286	1 544	2 109	2 110	...	Taxes sur le commerce extérieur
Other taxes	...	53	42	12	10	41	57	56	...	Autres taxes
Other revenues	371	433	484	565	688	906	805	706	...	Autres recettes
Grants	1 021	1 065	1 355	2 611	725	1 285	733	718	...	Dons
Total Expenditures and Net Lending	5 684	6 292	6 871	8 686	8 742	9 740	11 469	12 585	...	Dépenses totales et prêts nets
Current expenditure	2 880	3 182	3 612	4 000	5 133	5 356	6 297	6 615	...	Dépenses courantes
Wages and Salaries	1 192	1 516	1 693	1 815	1 878	1 910	1 826	2 117	...	Rémunérations et salaires
Other purchases of goods and services	1 198	1 106	1 273	1 540	2 009	2 117	2 066	2 747	...	Achat de biens et services
Other current expenditure	490	561	646	645	1 246	1 328	2 405	1 752	...	Autres dépenses courantes
Current transfers	...	...	...	...	...	...	...	...	...	Transferts courants
Interest payments	741	766	967	1 079	1 307	1 895	2 798	3 261	...	Intérêts
Capital expenditure	1 924	2 344	2 292	3 607	2 302	2 490	2 374	2 709	...	Dépenses d'équipement
Net lending	138	...	...	...	...	...	...	...	...	Prêts nets
Fiscal balance	- 775	- 1 266	- 1 252	- 1 289	- 2 750	- 2 020	- 3 123	- 4 108	...	Solde global y compris les dons
IX-3 BALANCE OF PAYMENTS *GAMBIA DALASI (MILLIONS)*										**IX-3 BALANCE DES PAIEMENTS** *DALASI GAMBIEN (MILLIONS)*
Trade balance	- 635	- 2 964	- 5 600	- 6 392	- 6 023	- 8 633	- 9 789	- 8 416	...	Balance commerciale
Services Balance	226	1 585	1 917	2 589	2 313	1 207	1 628	344	...	Balance des services
Net primary income	- 47	- 231	- 1 226	- 1 212	- 1 064	- 1 207	- 1 186	- 1 586	...	Revenus primaires nets
Compensation of employees	38	116	- 800	- 690	- 264	- 433	- 405	- 416	...	Rémunération des salariés
Investment income	- 84	- 347	- 426	- 521	- 800	- 775	- 781	- 1 147	...	Revenus des investissements
Net secondary income	777	2 152	1 547	2 547	1 248	5 142	5 312	5 639	...	Revenus secondaires nets
Net official transfers	- 3	- 10	- 10	286	- 32	- 87	- 234	...	...	Transferts officiels nets
Workers' remittances	243	1 478	799	2 004	1 727	5 118	5 371	...	...	Envois de fonds des travailleurs
Other private transfers	...	...	...	...	...	...	...	...	...	Autres transferts privés
Current account balance	321	542	- 3 363	- 2 467	- 3 526	- 3 491	- 4 036	- 4 020	...	Solde du compte courant
Capital and financial account	- 143	365	5 860	4 466	2 956	- 280	3 799	859	...	Comptes de capital et financier
Capital account	251	1 065	1 355	1 973	566	1 631	821	456	...	Compte de capital
Financial account	- 393	- 701	4 505	2 492	2 391	- 1 912	2 978	404	...	Compte financier
Errors and omissions	99	- 1 229	- 1 594	- 876	383	1 373	258	1 818	...	Erreurs et omissions
Overall balance	278	- 321	903	1 123	- 187	- 2 398	21	- 1 343	...	Balance générale

GAMBIE

X DEBT AND FINANCIAL FLOWS - DETTE ET FLUX FINANCIERS

	2009	2010	2011	2012	2013	2014	2015	2016	2017	
X-1 DEBT *US $ (MILLIONS)*										**X-1 DETTE EXTÉRIEURE** *$ E.U (MILLIONS)*
Total external debt	389	406	403	415	430	474	535	541	550	Dette extérieure totale
Private	...	...	...	...	...	...	...	...	...	Privée
Public	369	378	386	376	394	449	499	504	...	Publique
Total external debt service	72	76	80	86	88	100	101	96	...	Service de la dette extérieure
Present value of external debt	...	...	...	...	...	...	...	354	...	Valeur actuelle de la dette extérieure
Total government domestic debt, National currency (millions)	7 239	8 707	9 652	10 737	13 520	15 320	...	...	...	Dette publique intérieure
X-2 FINANCIAL FLOWS *US $ (MILLIONS)*										**X-2 FLUX FINANCIERS** *$ E.U (MILLIONS)*
Net Foreign Direct Investment Inflows	1	20	66	41	25	35	11	- 2	...	Investissements étranger direct (flux nets entrants)
Main origin of FDI inflows										**Principales origines de l'IDE entrant:**
Germany	1	...	...	...	...	...	...	...	...	Allemagne
...	...	...	...	...	...	...	...	...	...	...
...	...	...	...	...	...	...	...	...	...	...
...	...	...	...	...	...	...	...	...	...	...
Hungary	...	...	...	-	...	...	...	...	...	Hongrie
African countries	...	...	...	...	...	...	...	...	...	Pays africains
Net total official development assistance	125	121	136	139	112	100	108	92	...	Aide publique au développement (nette totale)
Main origin of net ODA										**Principales origines de l'APD nette**
International Development Association [IDA]	16	11	11	29	7	13	9	18	...	International Development Association
...	...	...	...	...	...	...	...	...	...	...
Japan	11	17	11	7	7	-	3	2	...	Japon
Global Fund	13	19	16	11	21	9	...	...	...	Fonds Mondial
Islamic Development Bank [IsDB]	9	10	12	11	...	...	...	...	...	Banque islamique de développement (BID)

SOURCES AND NOTES - SOURCES ET NOTES

External trade - Total exports, fob: UNCTAD

External trade - Total import, cif: UNCTAD

ODA: OECD

Monetary statistics: IMF

National Accounts: 2014-2015: Revised 2016:Provisional

Poverty: World Bank

Commerce exterieur - Exportation, fab: CNUCED

Commerce exterieur - Imporations, caf: CNUCED

APD: OCDE

Statistiques monétaires: FMI

Comptes nationaux: 2014-2015: Révisée   2016: Provisoire

Pauvreté: Banque mondiale

GAMBIA

GHANA

GHANA

AREA (km2)	238 540	SUPERFICIE (KM2)
CAPITAL CITY	Accra	Accra	CAPITALE
CURRENCY	Ghanian Cedi	Cedi ghanéen	MONNAIE

I SOCIAL AND DEMOGRAPHIC INDICATORS — INDICATEURS DEMOGRAPHIQUES ET SOCIAUX

Population	Year Année	Value Valeur	Charts Graphiques	Population
Population ('000)	2017	28 939.7		Population ('000)
Female (%)	2017	50.9		Féminine (%)
Urban (%)	2017	54.2		Urbaine (%)
Average annual growth rate	2017	2.3		Taux de croissance annuel
Active population ('000)	2017	12 855.4		Population active ('000)
Population by age group ('000)				Population par groupe d'âge ('000)
0-14 years	2017	10 790.8		0-14 ans
15-64 years	2017	16 972.6		15-64 ans
65+ years	2017	1 176.2		65+ ans
Economically active population in agriculture (%)	2017	56.0		Participation de la population active agricole (%)
Crude birth rate	2017	31.9		Taux brut de natalité
Crude death rate	2017	8.6		Taux brut de mortalité
Total fertility rate	2017	4.1		Indice synthétique de fécondité
Life expectancy at birth - Total (years)	2017	61.9		Espérance de vie à la naissance - Totale (années)
Dependency ratio - Total (%)	2017	70.5		Taux de dépendance - Total (%)
Health				**Santé**
Percentage of children under-five and underweight	2017	13.3		% d'enfants de moins de cinq ans avec insuffisance pondérale
Prevalence of undernourishment	2017	4.2		Prévalence de la malnutrition
Under five mortality rate (per 1 000 live births)	2017	56.0		Taux de mortalité de moins de 5 ans (les deux sexes, pour 1000)
Infant mortality rate (per 1 000 live births)	2017	39.6		Taux de mortalité infantile (les deux sexes) par 1000
Neonatal mortality rate (per 1 000 live births)	2017	27.6		Le taux de mortalité néonatale (pour 1000 naissances vivantes)
Percentage of children provided the vaccines :				Pourcentage d'enfants vaccinés :
BCG	2017	98.5		BCG
DPT3	2017	88.6		DTC3
Polio	2017	83.6		polio
Measles	2017	92.0		rougeole
Percentage of mothers provided at least one antenatal care (%)	2017	95.8		Pourcentage de mères ayant au moins reçu un soin prénatal (%)
Percentage of deliveries attended by skilled health personnel	2017	65.1		% d'accouchements assistés par un personnel de santé qualifié
Number of doctors (per 10,000 population)	2017	1.8		Nombre de médecins (pour 10.000 habitants)
Number of nurses (per 10,000 population)	2017	12.0		Nombre d'infirmiers (pour 10.000 habitants)
Hospital beds - Total (per 10,000 population)	2017	14.0		Nombre de lits d'hôpitaux - Total (pour 10 000)
Births registered (per 1,000)	2017	32.1		Naissances enregistrées (pour 1000)
Deaths registered (per 1,000)	2017	8.6		Décès enregistrés (pour 1000)
Budget allocation to health (%)	2017	10.6		Dépenses publiques consacrées à la santé (% du budget)
Education				**Education**
Enrolment in primary education (000)	2017	4 274.2		Scolarisation dans le primaire (000)
Female	2017	2 101.8		Féminine
Enrolment in secondary education (000)	2017	2 231.9		Scolarisation dans le secondaire (000)
Female	2017	1 091.8		Féminine
Enrolment in tertiary education (000)	2017	317.7		Scolarisation dans le tertiaire (000)
Female	2017	108.0		Féminine
Literacy rate	2017	72.3		Taux d'alphabétisation (deux sexes)
Male	2017	81.1		Masculin
Female	2017	65.3		Féminin
Pupil teacher ratio - primary	2017	29.5		Ratio élève-enseignant
Budget allocation to education (%)	2017	12.8		Dépenses publiques consacrées à l'enseignement (% du budget)
Poverty				**Pauvreté**
GNI per capita, PPP (current int. $)	2016	4150.0		RNB par habitant, ($ PPA inter. courants)
Human Poverty Index (HPI-1) Value (%)	2007	28.1		Valeur de l'Indice de pauvreté (IPH-1) (%)
Population below Inter. poverty line ($2/day) (%)	2005	25.2		Population sous le seuil inter. de pauvreté (2$/Jour) (%)
Share of income held by richest 10%	2005	32.7		% de revenu des 10% plus riches
Share of income held by poorest 10%	2005	1.9		% de revenu des 10% plus pauvres
GINI index	2005	42.8		Indice de GINI

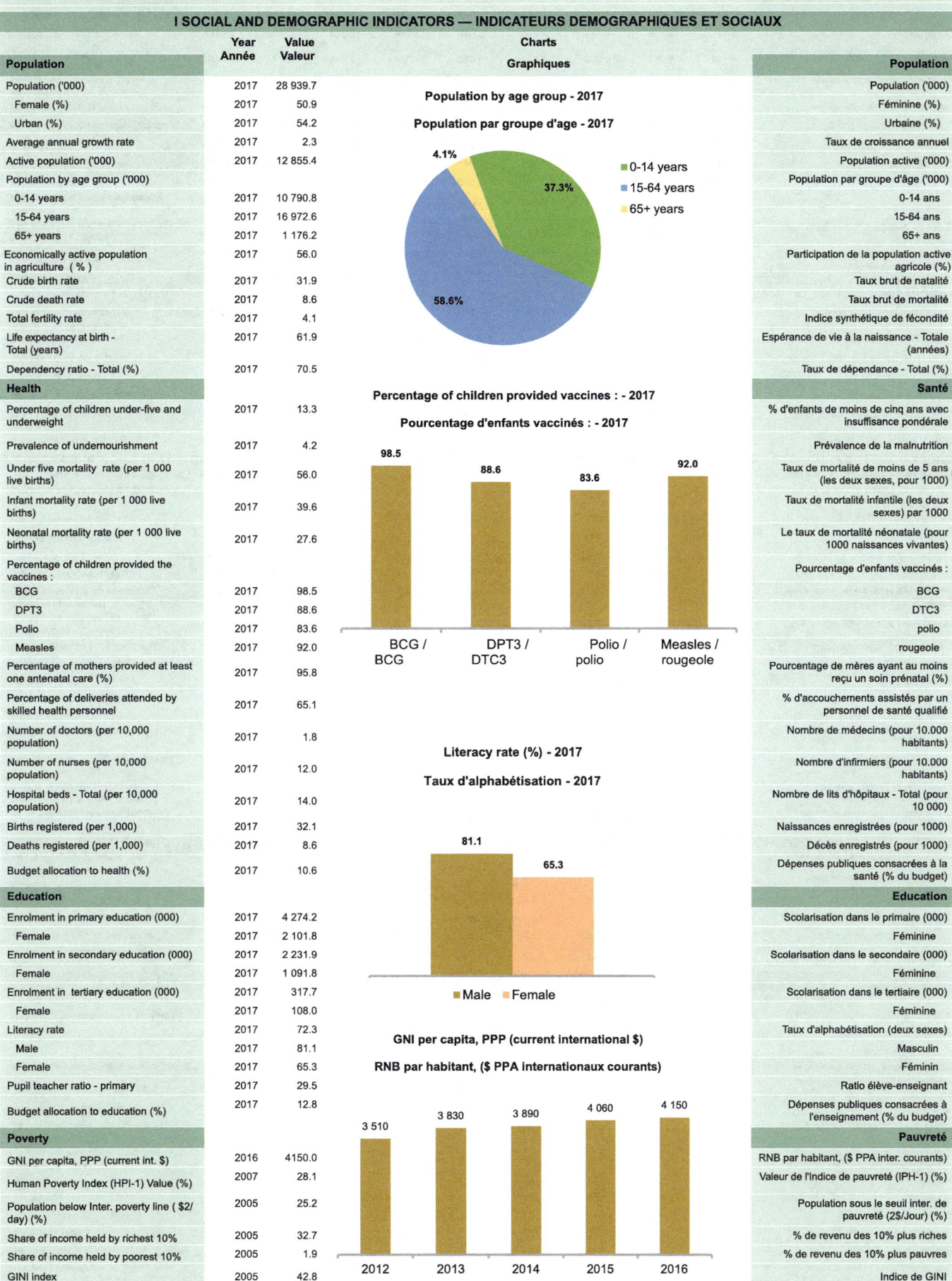

Population by age group - 2017 / Population par groupe d'age - 2017
- 0-14 years 37.3%
- 15-64 years 58.6%
- 65+ years 4.1%

Percentage of children provided vaccines : - 2017 / Pourcentage d'enfants vaccinés : - 2017
BCG/BCG 98.5, DPT3/DTC3 88.6, Polio/polio 83.6, Measles/rougeole 92.0

Literacy rate (%) - 2017 / Taux d'alphabétisation - 2017
Male 81.1, Female 65.3

GNI per capita, PPP (current international $) / RNB par habitant, ($ PPA internationaux courants)
2012 3 510, 2013 3 830, 2014 3 890, 2015 4 060, 2016 4 150

II NATIONAL ACCOUNTS — COMPTES NATIONAUX

	2009	2010	2011	2012	2013	2014	2015	2016	2017	
GROSS DOMESTIC PRODUCT BY KIND OF ECONOMIC ACTIVITY AT CURRENT PRICES *GHANIAN CEDI (MILLIONS)*										**PRODUIT INTÉRIEUR BRUT PAR BRANCHE D'ACTIVITÉ ÉCONOMIQUE AUX PRIX COURANTS** *CEDI GHANÉEN (MILLIONS)*
Agriculture, hunting , forestry and Fishing	11 343	12 910	14 155	16 668	20 232	23 278	26 134	29 565	35 047	Agriculture, chasse sylviculture et Pêche
Mining and quarrying	740	1 013	4 690	6 961	8 503	8 640	6 851	6 616	11 187	Industries extractives
Manufacturing	2 478	2 941	3 842	4 263	4 800	5 342	6 219	7 273	8 571	Industries manufacturières
Electricity, gas & water	413	634	747	844	962	1 019	1 914	2 585	2 836	Electricité, gaz et eau
Construction	3 144	3 706	4 995	8 370	10 848	13 766	17 310	21 491	26 168	Bâtiments et travaux publics
Wholesale & retail trade, restaurants, hotels	4 304	5 294	6 290	7 577	10 478	12 184	15 378	19 274	23 261	Commerce de gros et de détail, restaurants et hôtels
Finance, insurance, real estate, etc.	3 009	4 185	5 057	6 954	9 370	13 009	16 539	21 035	24 767	Banques, assurances, affaires immobilières
Transport and communications	4 414	5 410	6 986	9 631	11 721	15 792	20 189	25 905	31 390	Transport(s) et communications
Public administration and defense	2 479	3 024	3 897	4 952	5 305	5 843	6 835	8 514	10 299	Administrations publiques et défense
Education	1 506	1 877	2 307	3 101	3 248	3 883	4 758	6 270	8 143	Education
Health And Social Work	513	674	728	921	956	1 091	1 529	2 206	2 922	Santé et Actions Sociales
Other services	1 318	1 722	2 159	2 701	3 886	4 445	4 931	5 742	6 621	Autres services
Less Imputed Service Charges	- 1 192	- 1 512	- 1 458	- 2 317	- 2 919	- 4 354	- 5 469	- 6 716	- 8 137	Moins Services d'intermédiation financière
Gross domestic product at factor cost / basic prices	34 470	41 876	54 394	70 627	87 390	103 939	123 118	149 761	183 076	Produit intérieur brut aux couts des facteurs / prix de base
Plus: Indirect Taxes / taxes on products, less subsidies	2 128	4 166	5 422	4 689	6 026	9 404	13 839	17 593	22 838	Plus taxes indirectes/impôts sur les produits, moins les subventions
EXPENDITURE ON GROSS DOMESTIC PRODUCT AT CURRENT PURCHASER'S VALUES *GHANIAN CEDI (MILLIONS)*										**EMPLOI DU PRODUIT INTÉRIEUR BRUT AUX PRIX COURANTS D'ACQUISITION** *CEDI GHANÉEN (MILLIONS)*
Government final consumption	2 772	3 255	8 248	8 860	8 694	10 606	13 353	15 175	17 614	Consommation finale des administrations publiques
Private final consumption	32 574	43 102	51 337	63 052	84 717	92 136	113 800	139 970	175 821	Consommation finale privée
Gross fixed capital formation	5 665	5 416	7 164	12 133	11 811	20 341	21 762	23 010	24 374	Formation brute de capital fixe
Change in inventories	349	615	498	646	595	1 020	1 127	1 235	1 342	Variation des stocks
Exports of goods and services	10 720	13 572	22 094	30 397	31 938	44 797	62 344	68 567	82 339	Exportations de biens et services
Less imports of goods and services	15 482	19 918	29 525	39 773	44 338	55 556	75 428	80 604	95 577	Moins importations de biens et services
GDP at purchasers' values	36 598	46 042	59 816	75 315	93 416	113 343	136 957	167 353	205 914	PIB aux prix d'acquisition
GROSS DOMESTIC PRODUCT BY KIND OF ECONOMIC ACTIVITY AT CONSTANT PRICES *ANNUAL GROWTH RATES (%)*										**PRODUIT INTÉRIEUR BRUT PAR BRANCHE D'ACTIVITÉ ECONOMIQUE AUX PRIX CONSTANTS** *TAUX DE CROISSANCE ANNUEL (%)*
Agriculture, hunting , forestry and Fishing	7.2	5.3	0.8	2.3	5.7	4.6	2.8	3.0	8.4	Agriculture, chasse sylviculture et Pêche
Mining and quarrying	6.8	18.8	206.5	16.4	11.6	3.2	- 6.1	- 7.6	46.7	Industries extractives
Manufacturing	- 1.3	7.6	17.0	2.0	- 0.5	- 0.8	2.2	2.7	3.7	Industries manufacturières
Electricity, gas & water	7.6	7.9	1.5	5.7	5.7	- 0.5	6.3	2.5	6.6	Electricité, gaz et eau
Construction	9.3	2.5	17.2	16.4	8.6		2.2	2.9	4.6	Bâtiments et travaux publics
Wholesale & retail trade, restaurants, hotels	1.4	9.0	8.1	9.3	18.1	0.6	6.7	2.3	2.2	Commerce de gros et de détail, restaurants et hôtels
Finance, insurance, real estate, etc.	3.8	15.1	8.5	19.7	- 1.1	10.7	5.3	3.7	2.6	Banques, assurances, affaires immobilières
Transport and communications	4.3	11.0	12.2	16.1	6.0	11.9	10.0	10.4	6.3	Transport(s) et communications
Public administration and defense	11.7	3.4	7.4	4.2	8.4	- 4.7	1.4	2.2	1.5	Administrations publiques et défense
Education	12.4	5.3	3.8	6.7	6.9	7.1	7.9	8.3	9.9	Education
Health And Social Work	15.2	11.2	5.0	10.9	7.8	- 1.7	15.7	16.8	14.4	Santé et Actions Sociales
Other services	7.5	10.8	12.9	4.2	36.5	- 1.6	- 6.4	- 5.2	- 3.8	Autres services
Less Imputed Service Charges	41.4	7.9	13.4	12.4	29.5	6.0	2.5	- 0.6	0.9	Moins Services d'intermédiation financière
Gross domestic product at factor cost / basic prices	4.8	7.9	14.0	9.3	7.3	4.0	3.8	3.7	8.5	Produit intérieur brut aux couts des facteurs / prix de base
Plus: Indirect Taxes / taxes on products, less subsidies	4.8	7.9	14.0	9.3	7.3	4.0	3.8	3.7	8.5	Plus taxes indirectes/impôts sur les produits, moins les subventions
Gross domestic product at market prices	4.8	7.9	14.0	9.3	7.3	4.0	3.8	3.7	8.5	Produit intérieur brut aux prix du marché
EXPENDITURE ON GROSS DOMESTIC PRODUCT AT CONSTANT PURCHASERS' VALUES *ANNUAL GROWTH RATES (%)*										**EMPLOIS DU PRODUIT INTÉRIEUR BRUT AUX PRIX CONSTANTS D'ACQUISITION** *TAUX DE CROISSANCE ANNUEL (%)*
Government final consumption	- 10.7	17.4	80.0	- 10.6	- 16.1	6.5	16.5	11.1	11.8	Consommation finale des administrations publiques
Private final consumption	2.1	17.3	5.9	6.4	19.8	- 6.9	3.1	1.7	8.8	Consommation finale privée
Gross fixed capital formation	- 25.2	- 25.3	25.6	42.4	- 26.1	19.7	6.6	- 12.0	0.2	Formation brute de capital fixe
Exports of goods and services	7.6	24.7	53.8	15.2	- 3.6	- 5.8	8.1	5.9	6.6	Exportations de biens et services
Less imports of goods and services	- 12.6	26.7	40.1	12.8	2.3	- 15.9	9.8	- 1.1	5.6	Moins importations de biens et services

III INFLATION

	2009	2010	2011	2012	2013	2014	2015	2016	2017	
Annual growth rates (%)										**Taux de croissance annuel (%)**
All item	19.2	10.7	8.7	9.2	11.8	15.5	17.1	17.5	12.4	Ensemble
of which:										dont:
Food and non-alcoholic beverages	15.7	6.1	4.0	4.6	7.3	6.8	7.5	8.7	7.3	Alimentation et boissons non alcoolisés
Alcoholic beverages, tobacco and narcotics	29.2	18.5	14.0	12.8	15.6	14.8	19.7	15.2	11.9	Boissons alcoolisées et tabacs
Clothing and footwear	20.9	16.0	12.9	13.8	17.0	16.4	23.8	21.0	17.2	Habillement et chaussures
Housing, water, electricity, gas and other fuels	4.6	10.3	10.6	7.9	22.6	46.8	25.5	30.7	7.1	Logement, eau, électricité, gaz et autres combustibles
Furnishings, household equipment and routine household maintenance	31.6	15.3	11.9	13.8	14.6	12.3	23.2	22.0	21.8	Meubles, articles de ménage et entretien courant
Health	48.3	10.3	7.8	8.9	10.5	15.1	16.3	15.8	12.5	Santé
Transport	2.8	9.7	22.2	19.7	12.9	29.2	25.9	31.9	21.3	Transport
Communication	6.0	- 0.1	0.2	0.5	0.5	8.4	13.4	12.2	10.5	Communication
Recreation and culture	74.2	20.8	8.5	13.4	13.5	15.4	24.9	25.6	16.1	Loisirs et culture
Education	11.9	1.1	2.5	15.1	11.4	7.0	25.2	29.0	12.7	Enseignement
Restaurants and hotels	29.4	18.3	8.6	7.5	9.9	9.0	18.7	14.9	12.3	Restaurants et hôtels
Miscellaneous goods and services	14.3	8.6	16.5	15.7	14.7	15.9	19.2	15.8	15.4	Biens et Services divers

IV AGRICULTURAL PRODUCTION - PRODUCTION AGRICOLE

TONNES (THOUSAND)	2009	2010	2011	2012	2013	2014	2015	2016	2017	Tonnes (milliers)
Cassava	12 231	13 504	14 241	14 547	16 116	16 524	17 213	17 798	...	Manioc
Yams	5 778	5 960	6 295	6 639	7 260	7 119	7 296	7 440	...	Ignames
Plantains	3 563	3 538	3 620	3 557	3 565	3 828	3 952	4 000	...	Bananes plantains
Maize	1 620	1 872	1 684	1 950	1 817	1 769	1 692	1 722	...	Maïs
Taro (cocoyam)	1 504	1 355	1 300	1 270	1 268	1 299	1 301	1 344	...	Taros (colocases)

V MINING PRODUCTION - PRODUCTION MINIERE

	2009	2010	2011	2012	2013	2014	2015	2016	2017	
Crude petroleum - Production, metric tons (thousands)	...	...	3 396	3 702	4 994	5 217	5 242	3 949	5 832	Pétrole brut - Production, tonnes métriques (milliers)
Gold ores and concentrates - Production (Kilograms)	88 446	94 483	105 953	119 910	124 650	126 790	102 731	107 073	76 052	Minerais d'or et leurs concentrés - Production (Kilogrammes)
	...	...	...	...	...	...	...	...	...	

VI ENERGY - ENERGIE

	2009	2010	2011	2012	2013	2014	2015	2016	2017	
Total electricity generation (GWh)	9	10	10	11	13	13	11	...	...	Production électrique totale (GWh)
of which										dont
Production of electricity from fossil fuels (GWh)	2	3	4	4	5	7	6	...	...	Production d'électricité à partir de combustibles fossiles (GWh)
Production of hydro electricity (GWh)	7	7	8	8	8	6	6	...	...	Production d'électricité d'origine hydraulique (GWh)
Production of electricity from solar, wind, tide, wave and other sources (GWh)	...	...	...	...	3	4	44	...	...	Production d'électricité d'origine solaire, éolienne, marée motrice et autres (GWh)

VII TOURISM AND INFRASTRUCTURE - TOURISME ET INFRASTUCTURE

	2009	2010	2011	2012	2013	2014	2015	2016	2017	
VII-1 Tourism										**VII-1 Tourisme**
International tourist arrivals (thousands)	668	747	828	903	994	1 093	1 134	1 206	1 278	Arrivées de touristes internationaux (milliers)
Rooms in hotels and similar establishments (thousands)	26	28	34	34	37	41	42	45	47	Chambres d'hôtels et établissements assimilés (milliers)
Overnight stays (thousands)	12 839	14 000	16 340	17 047	19 709	21 705	23 033	24 778	26 523	Nuitées (milliers)
Tourism receipts (US$ thousand)	1 211 200	1 400 000	1 634 000	1 704 700	1 877 000	2 067 100	2 218 547	2 382 050	2 545 553	Recettes touristiques (milliers de $ EU)
Total contribution to GDP (%)	8.4	6.8	7.4	8.6	7.9	7.5	6.9	6.4	6.3	Contribution totale au PIB (%)
Total contribution to Employment (%)	7.9	6.5	6.1	5.9	5.5	6.0	6.0	5.1	4.8	Contribution totale à l'emploi (%)
VII-2 Infrastructure										**VII-2 Infrastructure**
Paved road (% of total)	12.6	5.5	...	...	...	...	...	...	...	Routes asphaltées (% du total)
Total network (Railways-km)	...	...	...	...	...	...	...	...	...	Réseau total voies ferrées-Km
Main telephone lines (per 100 inhabitants)	1.1	1.1	1.1	1.1	1.0	1.0	1.0	0.9	...	Lignes téléphoniques fixes (pour 100 habitants)
Mobile cellular subscribers (per 100 inhabitants)	63.8	71.9	85.3	101.0	108.2	114.8	129.7	139.1	...	Abonnés aux téléphones mobiles (pour 100 habitants)
Internet users per 100 inhabitants	5.4	7.8	9.0	10.6	15.0	25.5	31.4	34.7	...	Utilisateurs Internet par 100 Habitants
Fixed (wired)-broadband subscriptions per 100 inhabitants	...	...	...	...	...	...	...	...	...	Abonnements à l'Internet fixe (filaire) à large bande pour 100 habitants, par débit

VIII EXTERNAL TRADE - COMMERCE EXTERIEUR

US$ (MILLIONS) EXPORTS, FOB	2009	2010	2011	2012	2013	2014	2015	2016	2017	$ E.U (MILLIONS) EXPORTATIONS, FÁB
Exports - Total	5 840	7 960	12 785	13 552	12 644	12 317	9 683	10 656	...	Exportations - Total
Exports to Africa	1 988	2 528	3 989	3 146	2 736	2 646	2 088	2 293	...	Exportations vers l'Afrique
Main products										**Principaux produits**
Cocoa	2 315	3 118	2 853	2 737	1 991	2 327	1 675	1 939	...	Cacao
Fruits and nuts (excluding oil nuts), fresh or dried	158	201	511	252	466	308	300	295	...	Fruits et noix (à l'exclusion des oléagineux), frais ou secs
Gold, non-monetary (excluding gold ores and concentrates)	1 772	2 646	2 532	4 908	4 020	4 102	3 151	3 513	...	Or, non monétaire (à l'exclusion des minerais d'or et des concentrés)
Ores and concentrates of base metals, n.e.s.	260	272	272	213	202	176	147	156	...	Minerais et concentrés de métaux communs, n.d.a.
Petroleum oils, oils from bitumin. materials, crude	9	...	2 565	3 219	3 494	3 248	2 615	2 840	...	Huiles de pétrole, huiles de bitume. matériaux bruts
Main destinations										**Principales destinations**
France	245	336	1 687	1 315	1 015	889	738	788	...	France
Italy	89	110	811	1 165	917	739	642	669	...	Italie
South Africa	1 307	1 758	1 111	1 897	1 408	1 634	1 180	1 363	...	Afrique du Sud
Switzerland	350	240	369	1 499	1 470	1 316	1 081	1 161	...	Suisse
United Arab Emirates	126	705	1 107	1 830	1 724	1 318	1 180	1 210	...	Emirates Arabes
IMPORTS, CIF										
Imports - Total	8 046	10 922	15 838	17 763	17 600	14 600	13 465	13 352	...	Importations - Total (millions)
Imports from Africa	1 373	1 744	2 461	2 458	3 185	2 416	2 342	2 264	...	Importations en provenance de l'Afrique
Main products										**Principaux produits**
Civil engineering & contractors' plant & equipment	200	340	556	778	582	570	482	500	...	Génie civil et installations et équipements des entrepreneurs
Motor vehicles for the transport of persons	385	471	756	864	923	731	692	677	...	Véhicules à moteur pour le transport de personnes
Petroleum oils or bituminous minerals > 70 % oil	214	470	686	994	1 003	754	735	708	...	Huiles de pétrole ou de minéraux bitumineux> 70% d'huile
Petroleum oils, oils from bitumin. materials, crude	317	408	1 056	729	630	650	535	564	...	Huiles de pétrole, huiles de bitume. matériaux bruts
Ships, boats & floating structures	34	474	50	465	934	510	604	530	...	Navires, bateaux et structures flottantes
Main origin										**Principales provenances**
Belgium	317	425	677	708	920	694	675	652	...	Belgique
China	1 256	1 720	2 947	3 934	3 547	3 006	2 740	2 734	...	Chine
Netherlands	275	419	766	1 046	944	798	728	726	...	Pays-Bas
Nigeria	345	454	1 147	970	921	805	722	727	...	Nigéria
United States	613	1 199	1 428	1 579	1 277	1 159	1 018	1 036	...	États-Unis

GHANA

	2009	2010	2011	2012	2013	2014	2015	2016	2017	
IX-1 MONETARY STATISTICS *GHANIAN CEDI (MILLIONS)*										**IX-1 STATISTIQUES MONÉTAIRES** *CEDI GHANÉEN (MILLIONS)*
Money supply (M1)	10 241	13 766	18 195	22 620	26 937	36 843	45 432	56 692	69 561	Masse monétaire (M1)
Quasi-money	3 955	4 998	6 216	7 051	8 665	11 950	15 990	19 651	24 746	Quasi-monnaie
of which demand deposit	977	1 092	1 272	...	...	...	...	...	...	dont Monnaie scripturale
Net foreign assets	3 600	5 436	7 336	6 976	5 464	8 880	11 389	15 496	20 860	Avoirs extérieurs nets
Domestic credit	10 504	13 062	16 438	23 601	32 622	43 305	49 053	57 378	62 910	Crédit intérieur
of which claims on private sector	3 577	4 787	6 289	9 740	13 409	16 778	16 102	20 463	18 944	dont créances sur le secteur privé
of which claims on government sector, net	5 730	7 040	9 002	11 783	15 947	22 563	28 367	33 052	35 571	dont créances nettes sur le gouvernement
International reserves (millions US$)	3 168	4 644	5 382	5 348	4 587	4 349	4 403	4 862	5 783	Réserves internationales (millions $EU)
Average exchange rate (National currency per US$)	1	1	2	2	2	3	4	4	4	Taux de change (moyen) (monnaie nationale par $ EU)
IX-2 PUBLIC FINANCE *GHANIAN CEDI (MILLIONS)*										**IX-2 FINANCES PUBLIQUES** *CEDI GHANÉEN (MILLIONS)*
Total Revenues and Grants	6 457	8 424	12 273	15 889	18 630	23 528	29 982	33 678	43 097	Recettes totales et dons
Direct taxes (on income, profits)	1 717	2 454	4 037	5 536	6 302	8 487	8 707	9 107	12 951	Taxes directes
Domestic indirect taxes revenues	1 948	2 446	3 589	4 212	4 833	6 434	9 927	12 231	15 445	Taxes Indirectes
Trade taxes	763	1 146	1 516	1 990	2 331	3 091	3 449	4 390	6 703	Taxes sur le commerce extérieur
Other taxes	58	72	79	138	159	218	289	1 926	296	Autres taxes
Other revenues	870	1 226	1 822	2 853	4 265	4 483	4 921	4 882	6 170	Autres recettes
Grants	1 101	1 080	1 231	1 160	739	814	2 689	1 141	1 532	Dons
Total Expenditures and Net Lending	8 417	11 532	13 430	20 945	27 463	31 962	39 951	47 231	54 984	Dépenses totales et prêts nets
Current expenditure	5 303	7 705	9 498	14 924	18 275	18 786	22 442	27 707	31 900	Dépenses courantes
Wages and Salaries	2 479	3 183	4 535	6 666	8 243	9 449	10 556	11 723	12 850	Rémunérations et salaires
Other purchases of goods and services	650	962	724	1 322	1 449	1 777	1 388	2 127	2 114	Achat de biens et services
Other current expenditure	775	1 175	965	1 851	1 640	1 218	2 059	1 234	1 520	Autres dépenses courantes
Current transfers	1 400	2 386	3 274	5 086	6 943	6 343	8 439	12 623	15 416	Transferts courants
Interest payments	1 032	1 439	1 611	2 436	4 397	7 081	9 075	10 490	12 292	Intérêts
Capital expenditure	2 082	2 388	2 320	3 584	4 791	6 096	7 134	7 234	7 959	Dépenses d'équipement
Net lending	...	...	...	...	...	...	1 300	1 800	2 833	Prêts nets
Fiscal balance	- 1 960	- 3 108	- 1 156	- 5 055	- 8 833	- 8 434	- 9 969	- 13 553	- 11 887	Solde global y compris les dons
IX-3 BALANCE OF PAYMENTS *US $ (MILLIONS)*										**IX-3 BALANCE DES PAIEMENTS** *$ E.U (MILLIONS)*
Trade balance	- 2 207	- 2 962	- 3 057	- 4 211	- 3 848	- 1 383	- 3 144	- 5 951	- 8 061	Balance commerciale
Services Balance	- 1 173	- 1 526	- 1 795	- 979	- 2 444	- 2 602	- 1 167	- 1 883	- 1 165	Balance des services
Net primary income	- 595	- 582	- 1 249	- 2 131	- 1 351	- 1 717	- 1 132	- 1 212	- 849	Revenus primaires nets
Compensation of employees	- 595	- 582	- 1 249	- 2 131	- 1 351	- 1 717	- 1 132	- 1 212	- 849	Rémunération des salariés
Investment income	...	...	...	...	...	...	...	...	...	Revenus des investissements
Net secondary income	2 078	2 322	2 597	2 689	1 939	2 008	2 598	3 098	3 658	Revenus secondaires nets
Net official transfers	...	...	...	...	...	...	...	...	...	Transferts officiels nets
Workers' remittances	...	...	...	...	...	...	...	...	...	Envois de fonds des travailleurs
Other private transfers	...	...	...	...	...	...	...	...	...	Autres transferts privés
Current account balance	- 1 897	- 2 748	- 3 504	- 4 632	- 5 704	- 3 694	- 2 845	- 5 948	- 6 417	Solde du compte courant
Capital and financial account	4 372	4 604	5 291	4 656	5 367	3 753	3 123	5 686	6 121	Comptes de capital et financier
Capital account	564	338	445	283	349	...	474	499	823	Compte de capital
Financial account	3 808	4 266	4 846	4 373	5 018	3 753	2 649	5 187	5 297	Compte financier
Errors and omissions	- 1 342	- 721	- 691	- 190	- 829	- 144	- 407	- 25	- 73	Erreurs et omissions
Overall balance	1 133	1 135	1 096	- 166	- 1 166	- 85	- 129	- 287	- 370	Balance générale

GHANA

X DEBT AND FINANCIAL FLOWS - DETTE ET FLUX FINANCIERS

	2009	2010	2011	2012	2013	2014	2015	2016	2017	
X-1 DEBT *US $ (MILLIONS)*										**X-1 DETTE EXTÉRIEURE** *$ E.U (MILLIONS)*
Total external debt	6 811	8 377	9 938	10 556	14 029	15 551	17 258	18 172	18 170	Dette extérieure totale
Private	...	...	...	...	...	...	...	...	...	Privée
Public	5 008	6 255	7 653	9 154	11 902	13 872	15 782	16 461	...	Publique
Total external debt service	316	370	463	633	733	1 025	1 483	2 234	...	Service de la dette extérieure
Present value of external debt	...	...	...	...	...	...	...	16 888	...	Valeur actuelle de la dette extérieure
Total government domestic debt, National currency (millions)	6 083	8 280	11 841	18 535	26 666	34 651	40 264	...	...	Dette publique intérieure
X-2 FINANCIAL FLOWS *US $ (MILLIONS)*										**X-2 FLUX FINANCIERS** *$ E.U (MILLIONS)*
Net Foreign Direct Investment Inflows	2 897	2 527	3 237	3 293	3 226	3 357	3 192	3 485	...	Investissements étranger direct (flux nets entrants)
Main origin of FDI inflows										**Principales origines de l'IDE entrant:**
United States	205	- 313	328	461	594	727	860	...	...	États-Unis
United Kingdom	97	127	159	162	165	168	171	...	...	Royaume-Uni
Sweden	64	66	55	65	76	87	98	...	...	Suède
Belgium	- 25	73	- 91	428	947	1 465	1 984	...	...	Belgique
...	...	...	...	...	...	...	...	...	...	...
African countries	...	...	...	...	...	...	...	...	...	Pays africains
Net total official development assistance	1 585	1 697	1 804	1 799	1 328	1 123	1 769	1 316	...	Aide publique au développement (nette totale)
Main origin of net ODA										**Principales origines de l'APD nette**
International Development Association [IDA]	247	319	422	365	317	312	519	283	...	International Development Association
United Kingdom	154	167	130	84	162	109	93	78	...	Royaume-Uni
United States	151	206	304	211	114	139	185	227	...	États-Unis
Netherlands	98	73	63	41	22	31	32	31	...	Pays-Bas
...	...	...	...	...	...	...	...	...	...	...

GHANA

SOURCES AND NOTES - SOURCES ET NOTES

External trade - Total exports, fob: UNCTAD

External trade - Total import, cif: UNCTAD

ODA: OECD

Monetary statistics: IMF

National Accounts: 2014:Final; 2015:Revised ; 2016:Provisional

National Accounts : Private final consumption includes statistical discripancy

Poverty: World Bank

Commerce exterieur - Exportation, fab: CNUCED

Commerce exterieur - Imporations, caf: CNUCED

APD: OCDE

Statistiques monétaires: FMI

Comptes nationaux: 2014:Définitives;2015:Revisées;2016:Provisoires

Comptes Nationaux: La consommation finale privée inclut les écarts dûs aux changement de l'année de base

Pauvreté: Banque mondiale

AREA (km2)		245 850	**SUPERFICIE (KM2)**
CAPITAL CITY	Conakry	Conakry	**CAPITALE**
CURRENCY	Guinea Franc	Franc Guinéen	**MONNAIE**

I SOCIAL AND DEMOGRAPHIC INDICATORS — INDICATEURS DEMOGRAPHIQUES ET SOCIAUX

	Year Année	Value Valeur	Charts Graphiques	
Population				**Population**
Population ('000)	2017	11 600.0		Population ('000)
Female (%)	2017	51.6		Féminine (%)
Urban (%)	2017	35.6		Urbaine (%)
Average annual growth rate	2017	2.8		Taux de croissance annuel
Active population ('000)	2014	2 009.0		Population active ('000)
Population by age group ('000)				Population par groupe d'âge ('000)
0-14 years	2017	5 209.0		0-14 ans
15-64 years	2017	5 918.0		15-64 ans
65+ years	2017	428.0		65+ ans
Economically active population in agriculture (%)	2014	94.5		Participation de la population active agricole (%)
Crude birth rate	2017	38.2		Taux brut de natalité
Crude death rate	2017	10.3		Taux brut de mortalité
Total fertility rate	2017	4.7		Indice synthétique de fécondité
Life expectancy at birth - Total (years)	2017	61.4		Espérance de vie à la naissance - Totale (années)
Dependency ratio - Total (%)	2017	95.3		Taux de dépendance - Total (%)
Health				**Santé**
Percentage of children under-five and underweight	2016	18.3		% d'enfants de moins de cinq ans avec insuffisance pondérale
Prevalence of undernourishment	2016	18.3		Prévalence de la malnutrition
Under five mortality rate (per 1 000 live births)	2016	88.0		Taux de mortalité de moins de 5 ans (les deux sexes, pour 1000)
Infant mortality rate (per 1 000 live births)	2017	66.1		Taux de mortalité infantile (les deux sexes) par 1000
Neonatal mortality rate (per 1 000 live births)	2016	20.0		Le taux de mortalité néonatale (pour 1000 naissances vivantes)
Percentage of children provided the vaccines :				Pourcentage d'enfants vaccinés :
BCG	2013	66.0		BCG
DPT3	2013	63.0		DTC3
Polio	2011	97.4		polio
Measles	2013	62.0		rougeole
Percentage of mothers provided at least one antenatal care (%)	2016	84.3		Pourcentage de mères ayant au moins reçu un soin prénatal (%)
Percentage of deliveries attended by skilled health personnel	2016	67.2		% d'accouchements assistés par un personnel de santé qualifié
Number of doctors (per 10,000 population)	2014	0.9		Nombre de médecins (pour 10.000 habitants)
Number of nurses (per 10,000 population)	2014	1.0		Nombre d'infirmiers (pour 10.000 habitants)
Hospital beds - Total (per 10,000 population)	2014	2.2		Nombre de lits d'hôpitaux - Total (pour 10 000)
Births registered (per 1,000)	2014	36.5		Naissances enregistrées (pour 1000)
Deaths registered (per 1,000)	2014	11.3		Décès enregistrés (pour 1000)
Budget allocation to health (%)	2016	4.4		Dépenses publiques consacrées à la santé (% du budget)
Education				**Education**
Enrolment in primary education (000)	2017	1 930.0		Scolarisation dans le primaire (000)
Female	2017	872.5		Féminine
Enrolment in secondary education (000)	2017	678.0		Scolarisation dans le secondaire (000)
Female	2017	263.1		Féminine
Enrolment in tertiary education (000)	2014	105.4		Scolarisation dans le tertiaire (000)
Female	2014	30.0		Féminine
Literacy rate	2014	32.0		Taux d'alphabétisation (deux sexes)
Male	2014	43.6		Masculin
Female	2014	22.0		Féminin
Pupil teacher ratio - primary	2016	47.1		Ratio élève-enseignant
Budget allocation to education (%)	2016	14.9		Dépenses publiques consacrées à l'enseignement (% du budget)
Poverty				**Pauvreté**
GNI per capita, PPP (current int. $)	2016	1840.0		RNB par habitant, ($ PPA inter. courants)
Human Poverty Index (HPI-1) Value (%)	2007	50.5		Valeur de l'Indice de pauvreté (IPH-1) (%)
Population below Inter. poverty line ($2/day) (%)	...	...		Population sous le seuil inter. de pauvreté (2$/Jour) (%)
Share of income held by richest 10%	2012	26.5		% de revenu des 10% plus riches
Share of income held by poorest 10%	2012	3.1		% de revenu des 10% plus pauvres
GINI index	2012	33.7		Indice de GINI

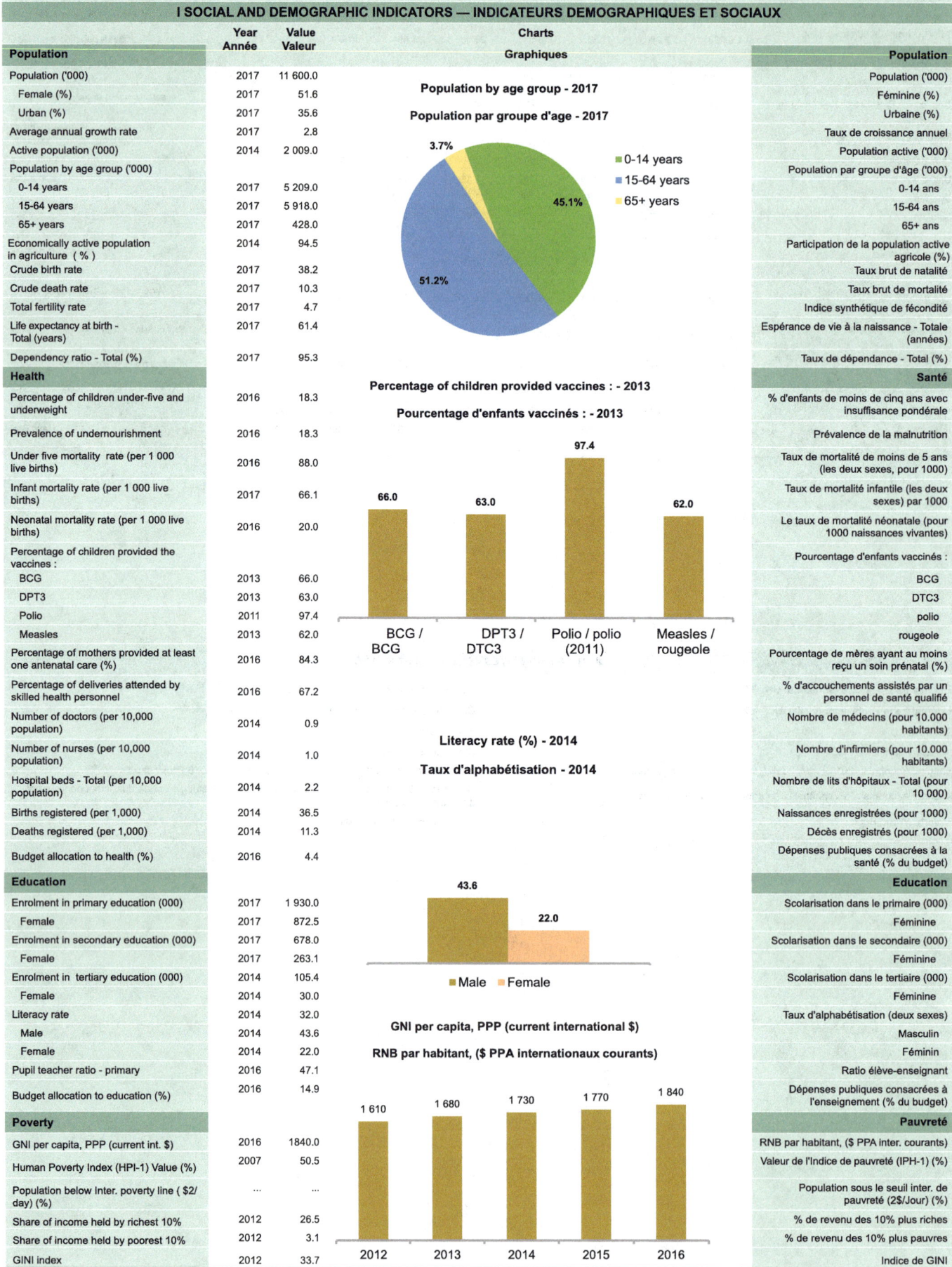

Population by age group - 2017
Population par groupe d'age - 2017
0-14 years 45.1% — 15-64 years 51.2% — 65+ years 3.7%

Percentage of children provided vaccines : - 2013
Pourcentage d'enfants vaccinés : - 2013
BCG / BCG 66.0 — DPT3 / DTC3 63.0 — Polio / polio (2011) 97.4 — Measles / rougeole 62.0

Literacy rate (%) - 2014
Taux d'alphabétisation - 2014
Male 43.6 — Female 22.0

GNI per capita, PPP (current international $)
RNB par habitant, ($ PPA internationaux courants)
2012 1 610 — 2013 1 680 — 2014 1 730 — 2015 1 770 — 2016 1 840

GUINEA

GROSS DOMESTIC PRODUCT BY KIND OF ECONOMIC ACTIVITY AT CURRENT PRICES *GUINEA FRANC (BILLIONS)* — PRODUIT INTÉRIEUR BRUT PAR BRANCHE D'ACTIVITÉ ÉCONOMIQUE AUX PRIX COURANTS *FRANC GUINÉEN (MILLIARDS)*

	2009	2010	2011	2012	2013	2014	2015	2016	2017	
Agriculture, hunting , forestry and Fishing	5 276	6 862	7 260	8 981	10 153	10 790	12 164	13 887	...	Agriculture, chasse sylviculture et Pêche
Mining and quarrying	3 346	5 492	7 064	7 762	7 314	7 657	5 354	10 584	...	Industries extractives
Manufacturing	4 051	4 172	4 730	5 618	6 249	6 823	7 977	8 941	...	Industries manufacturières
Electricity, gas & water	401	409	301	350	406	402	421	514	...	Electricité, gaz et eau
Construction	2 614	2 607	2 639	3 118	3 182	3 401	3 577	4 147	...	Bâtiments et travaux publics
Wholesale & retail trade, restaurants, hotels	6 215	7 833	9 018	11 212	12 350	12 560	14 063	15 207	...	Commerce de gros et de détail, restaurants et hôtels
Finance, insurance, real estate, etc.	2 596	3 181	3 865	4 421	4 829	4 557	5 204	5 980	...	Banques, assurances, affaires immobilières
Transport and communications	1 787	1 918	2 208	2 488	2 743	2 765	3 277	3 585	...	Transport(s) et communications
Public administration and defense	1 538	2 772	2 619	2 694	3 877	4 556	4 780	5 236	...	Administrations publiques et défense
Education	1 655	887	1 727	1 355	867	1 381	1 922	2 001	...	Education
Health And Social Work	413	350	505	479	612	935	862	924	...	Santé et Actions Sociales
Other services	461	481	591	680	795	832	992	984	...	Autres services
Less Imputed Service Charges	- 385	- 388	- 712	- 799	- 887	- 891	- 1 143	- 1 593	...	Moins Services d'intermédiation financière
Gross domestic product at factor cost / basic prices	29 968	36 576	41 815	48 359	52 490	55 768	59 450	70 397	...	Produit intérieur brut aux couts des facteurs / prix de base
Plus: Indirect Taxes / taxes on products, less subsidies	2 280	2 667	3 361	4 999	5 375	5 806	6 379	7 502	...	Plus taxes indirectes/impôts sur les produits, moins les subventions

EXPENDITURE ON GROSS DOMESTIC PRODUCT AT CURRENT PURCHASER'S VALUES *GUINEA FRANC (BILLIONS)* — EMPLOI DU PRODUIT INTÉRIEUR BRUT AUX PRIX COURANTS D'ACQUISITION *FRANC GUINÉEN (MILLIARDS)*

	2009	2010	2011	2012	2013	2014	2015	2016	2017	
Government final consumption	3 213	4 932	6 768	7 724	10 921	10 956	12 838	12 745	...	Consommation finale des administrations publiques
Private final consumption	30 156	31 383	36 915	42 634	49 253	50 974	56 505	65 392	...	Consommation finale privée
Gross fixed capital formation	6 751	7 510	10 662	13 402	13 557	13 984	15 779	40 086	...	Formation brute de capital fixe
Change in inventories	120	466	204	482	37	65	93	281	...	Variation des stocks
Exports of goods and services	7 261	11 907	14 728	17 681	15 317	16 433	14 151	22 920	...	Exportations de biens et services
Less imports of goods and services	15 253	16 955	24 102	28 566	31 221	30 838	33 537	63 525	...	Moins importations de biens et services
GDP at purchasers' values	32 248	39 243	45 176	53 358	57 865	61 573	65 829	77 899	...	PIB aux prix d'acquisition

GROSS DOMESTIC PRODUCT BY KIND OF ECONOMIC ACTIVITY AT CONSTANT PRICES *ANNUAL GROWTH RATES (%)* — PRODUIT INTÉRIEUR BRUT PAR BRANCHE D'ACTIVITÉ ECONOMIQUE AUX PRIX CONSTANTS *TAUX DE CROISSANCE ANNUEL (%)*

	2009	2010	2011	2012	2013	2014	2015	2016	2017	
Agriculture, hunting , forestry and Fishing	- 5.9	19.7	6.4	4.9	5.4	4.5	6.1	4.4	...	Agriculture, chasse sylviculture et Pêche
Mining and quarrying	- 1.0	- 2.8	3.2	- 6.0	- 8.1	11.0	- 18.0	46.1	...	Industries extractives
Manufacturing	- 8.3	2.5	- 1.2	15.1	- 1.1	7.1	10.0	5.6	...	Industries manufacturières
Electricity, gas & water	4.7	1.2	- 1.5	1.7	- 0.5	1.2	3.6	22.0	...	Electricité, gaz et eau
Construction	- 1.8	9.7	- 1.0	11.1	- 6.5	3.0	- 3.1	9.5	...	Bâtiments et travaux publics
Wholesale & retail trade, restaurants, hotels	- 4.0	4.0	9.0	10.9	3.2	0.7	5.0	5.1	...	Commerce de gros et de détail, restaurants et hôtels
Finance, insurance, real estate, etc.	- 2.3	4.5	8.2	12.3	20.7	- 16.7	19.7	3.0	...	Banques, assurances, affaires immobilières
Transport and communications	- 7.1	- 5.8	1.3	7.8	6.5	1.8	13.5	11.1	...	Transport(s) et communications
Public administration and defense	33.2	82.1	- 4.4	- 2.0	42.0	20.5	2.2	9.3	...	Administrations publiques et défense
Education	77.4	- 47.8	83.5	- 16.1	- 39.9	5.1	54.7	3.9	...	Education
Health And Social Work	16.5	- 20.1	12.6	11.4	21.4	12.8	- 14.3	6.8	...	Santé et Actions Sociales
Other services	- 0.8	1.5	- 4.8	- 9.6	- 4.3	10.6	5.5	6.1	...	Autres services
Less Imputed Service Charges	- 3.1	- 12.4	15.2	- 2.0	0.5	- 6.8	35.9	23.5	...	Moins Services d'intermédiation financière
Gross domestic product at factor cost / basic prices	- 0.5	5.9	5.7	5.5	3.9	3.7	4.3	9.7	...	Produit intérieur brut aux couts des facteurs / prix de base
Plus: Indirect Taxes / taxes on products, less subsidies	- 8.2	- 7.9	3.7	11.6	4.1	3.3	- 2.6	20.7	...	Plus taxes indirectes/impôts sur les produits, moins les subventions
Gross domestic product at market prices	- 1.1	4.8	5.6	5.9	3.9	3.7	3.8	10.5	...	Produit intérieur brut aux prix du marché

EXPENDITURE ON GROSS DOMESTIC PRODUCT AT CONSTANT PURCHASERS' VALUES *ANNUAL GROWTH RATES (%)* — EMPLOIS DU PRODUIT INTÉRIEUR BRUT AUX PRIX CONSTANTS D'ACQUISITION *TAUX DE CROISSANCE ANNUEL (%)*

	2009	2010	2011	2012	2013	2014	2015	2016	2017	
Government final consumption	68.0	53.5	40.1	14.4	41.4	0.4	15.8	- 1.5	...	Consommation finale des administrations publiques
Private final consumption	-	- 1.8	4.0	7.9	8.5	- 2.2	4.5	7.0	...	Consommation finale privée
Gross fixed capital formation	- 8.1	5.2	30.3	10.8	0.7	5.0	8.8	139.0	...	Formation brute de capital fixe
Exports of goods and services	5.7	3.8	- 0.9	6.2	- 9.7	6.6	5.5	24.1	...	Exportations de biens et services
Less imports of goods and services	1.6	3.8	19.2	12.8	8.5	- 5.0	13.2	65.2	...	Moins importations de biens et services

III INFLATION

Annual growth rates (%)	2009	2010	2011	2012	2013	2014	2015	2016	2017	Taux de croissance annuel (%)
All item	4.7	15.5	21.4	15.2	11.9	9.7	8.2	8.2	8.9	Ensemble
of which:										dont:
Food and non-alcoholic beverages	6.9	20.4	27.4	15.6	12.7	10.6	11.5	11.5	13.6	Alimentation et boissons non alcoolisés
Alcoholic beverages, tobacco and narcotics	15.1	19.2	13.9	23.6	15.6	4.6	2.5	- 2.5	1.1	Boissons alcoolisées et tabacs
Clothing and footwear	8.1	13.2	12.5	19.3	14.6	13.3	7.5	5.1	2.0	Habillement et chaussures
Housing, water, electricity, gas and other fuels	8.8	9.5	10.0	12.7	15.1	7.2	8.4	6.0	3.8	Logement, eau, électricité, gaz et autres combustibles
Furnishings, household equipment and routine household maintenance	11.7	5.0	21.2	17.0	9.0	10.7	6.7	5.9	2.5	Meubles, articles de ménage et entretien courant
Health	9.1	7.9	13.1	24.2	17.3	15.5	8.6	5.8	4.3	Santé
Transport	- 16.0	19.2	16.5	7.5	1.6	1.7	0.3	- 0.1	0.1	Transport
Communication	...	1.5	4.4	...	- 0.2	- 1.7	- 0.4	...	...	Communication
Recreation and culture	6.0	3.2	13.2	16.8	10.4	4.1	13.0	3.2	1.3	Loisirs et culture
Education	1.0	1.8	12.4	19.9	4.1	6.1	- 50.2	5.9	5.7	Enseignement
Restaurants and hotels	9.5	8.2	22.9	16.1	15.8	2.8	3.1	0.7	0.4	Restaurants et hôtels
Miscellaneous goods and services	4.2	7.4	10.3	6.0	8.4	6.9	13.6	1.0	0.2	Biens et Services divers

GUINÉE

IV AGRICULTURAL PRODUCTION - PRODUCTION AGRICOLE

	2009	2010	2011	2012	2013	2014	2015	2016	2017	
TONNES (THOUSAND)										**Tonnes (milliers)**
Rice, paddy	1 456	1 633	1 793	1 852	1 913	1 971	2 047	2 136	...	Riz, Paddy
Maize	290	584	611	641	672	698	727	749	...	Maïs
Fonio	345	384	409	429	451	473	497	483	...	Fonio
Groundnuts, with shell	300	309	313	348	363	422	490	535	...	Arachides (en coques)
Cassava	1 051	1 062	1 113	1 217	1 332	1 427	1 528	1 599	...	Manioc

V MINING PRODUCTION - PRODUCTION MINIERE

	2009	2010	2011	2012	2013	2014	2015	2016	2017	
Aluminium ores and concentrates (Bauxite) - Production, metric tons (thousands)	15 285	15 549	15 940	17 906	18 363	18 494	19 470	30 800	...	Minerais d'aluminium et leurs concentrés (Bauxite) - Production, tonnes métriques (milliers)
Gold ores and concentrates - Production (Kilograms)	20 946	22 637	14 382	14 723	16 695	21 381	19 558	27 593	...	Minerais d'or et leurs concentrés - Production (Kilogrammes)
Diamonds and other precious stones, unworked - Production, carat (thousands)	417	311	235	279	197	162	162	117	...	Diamants et autres pierres gemmes (précieuses), bruts - Production, carat (milliers)

VI ENERGY - ENERGIE

	2009	2010	2011	2012	2013	2014	2015	2016	2017	
Total electricity generation (GWh)	962	969	973	1 145	1 183	1 182	1 263	1 301	...	Production électrique totale (GWh)
of which										dont
Production of electricity from fossil fuels (GWh)	445	450	450	598	598	521	547	569	...	Production d'électricité à partir de combustibles fossiles (GWh)
Production of hydro electricity (GWh)	517	519	519	542	580	654	706	725	...	Production d'électricité d'origine hydraulique (GWh)
Production of electricity from solar, wind, tide, wave and other sources (GWh)	...	...	4	4	4	7	10	8	...	Production d'électricité d'origine solaire, éolienne, marée motrice et autres (GWh)

VII TOURISM AND INFRASTRUCTURE - TOURISME ET INFRASTUCTURE

	2009	2010	2011	2012	2013	2014	2015	2016	2017	
VII-1 Tourism										**VII-1 Tourisme**
International tourist arrivals (thousands)	18	12	131	96	56	33	35	60	63	Arrivées de touristes internationaux (milliers)
Rooms in hotels and similar establishments (thousands)	...	5	5	5	5	5	5	5	6	Chambres d'hôtels et établissements assimilés (milliers)
Overnight stays (thousands)	584	469	5 581	3 306	8 523	4 318	2 681	1 337	1 482	Nuitées (milliers)
Tourism receipts (US$ thousand)	600	600	700	400	1 246	4 771	6 571	4 457	4 562	Recettes touristiques (milliers de $ EU)
Total contribution to GDP (%)	5.0	5.2	5.5	5.6	5.4	5.6	5.2	5.2	5.3	Contribution totale au PIB (%)
Total contribution to Employment (%)	4.2	4.4	4.2	4.4	4.2	4.5	4.2	4.2	4.3	Contribution totale à l'emploi (%)
VII-2 Infrastructure										**VII-2 Infrastructure**
Paved road (% of total)	...	...	...	...	...	...	...	...	...	Routes asphaltées (% du total)
Total network (Railways-km)	...	...	...	...	...	...	...	...	...	Réseau total voies ferrées-Km
Main telephone lines (per 100 inhabitants)	...	...	...	...	...	...	...	...	...	Lignes téléphoniques fixes (pour 100 habitants)
Mobile cellular subscribers (per 100 inhabitants)	32.9	36.8	43.5	48.8	63.3	72.1	87.2	85.3	...	Abonnés aux téléphones mobiles (pour 100 habitants)
Internet users per 100 inhabitants	0.9	1.0	2.0	3.1	4.5	6.4	8.2	9.8	...	Utilisateurs Internet par 100 Habitants
Fixed (wired)-broadband subscriptions per 100 inhabitants	...	...	...	...	...	...	...	...	...	Abonnements à l'Internet fixe (filaire) à large bande pour 100 habitants, par débit

VIII EXTERNAL TRADE - COMMERCE EXTERIEUR

	2009	2010	2011	2012	2013	2014	2015	2016	2017	
US$ (MILLIONS) EXPORTS, FOB										**$ E.U (MILLIONS) EXPORTATIONS, FÀB**
Exports - Total	1 055	1 434	1 374	1 834	1 780	1 947	1 781	2 414	...	Exportations - Total
Exports to Africa	77	105	50	89	124	194	152	224	...	Exportations vers l'Afrique
Main products										**Principaux produits**
Aluminium ores and concentrates (incl. alumina)	613	526	517	674	565	569	542	719	...	Minerais d'aluminium et leurs concentrés (y compris l'alumine)
Gold, non-monetary (excluding gold ores and concentrates)	173	149	156	567	569	550	535	702	...	Or, non monétaire (à l'exclusion des minerais d'or et des concentrés)
Natural gas, whether or not liquefied	3	311	409	178	26	...	13	8	...	Gaz naturel, même liquéfié
Petroleum oils, oils from bitumin. materials, crude	33	191	71	116	308	504	388	578	...	Huiles de pétrole, huiles de bitume. matériaux bruts
Printed matter	2	1	1	4	41	111	73	119	...	Imprimé
Main destinations										**Principales destinations**
France	214	165	186	290	199	80	134	139	...	France
India	35	152	60	118	272	331	288	401	...	Inde
Republic of Korea	17	19	4	5	92	370	221	383	...	Corée, République de
Switzerland	3	-	4	257	251	53	145	128	...	Suisse
United Arab Emirates	6	38	40	112	182	302	231	345	...	Emirates Arabes
IMPORTS, CIF										
Imports - Total	1 060	1 405	2 106	2 254	1 869	2 509	2 139	2 092	...	Importations - Total (millions)
Imports from Africa	124	160	241	181	190	233	207	198	...	Importations en provenance de l'Afrique
Main products										**Principaux produits**
Civil engineering & contractors' plant & equipment	53	67	102	101	31	42	36	35	...	Génie civil et installations et équipements des entrepreneurs
Meal and flour of wheat and flour of meslin	15	19	32	54	47	61	52	51	...	Repas et farine de blé et farine de méteil
Medicaments (incl. veterinary medicaments)	23	28	42	53	53	65	58	55	...	Médicaments (y compris les médicaments vétérinaires)
Petroleum oils or bituminous minerals > 70 % oil	211	303	484	546	487	579	520	495	...	Huiles de pétrole ou de minéraux bitumineux> 70% d'huile
Rice	59	69	93	125	124	190	153	154	...	Riz
Main origin										**Principales provenances**
Belgium	67	87	127	110	66	85	74	71	...	Belgique
China	116	154	231	256	344	573	448	459	...	Chine
France	112	149	224	199	96	120	105	101	...	France
India	46	59	87	182	111	201	152	159	...	Inde
Netherlands	141	193	291	502	437	560	487	471	...	Pays-Bas

GUINEA

	2009	2010	2011	2012	2013	2014	2015	2016	2017	
IX-1 MONETARY STATISTICS *GUINEA FRANC (MILLIONS)*										**IX-1 STATISTIQUES MONÉTAIRES** *FRANC GUINÉEN (MILLIONS)*
Money supply (M1)	5 945 121	10 366 376	11 337 946	11 450 219	13 067 542	14 671 809	17 644 344	19 394 614	21 638 742	Masse monétaire (M1)
Quasi-money	1 203 057	1 561 738	2 485 029	2 960 170	3 810 910	3 515 588	4 191 258	4 710 200	5 277 225	Quasi-monnaie
of which demand deposit	...	...	...	7 744 320	9 015 540	10 346 910	12 466 310	...	...	dont Monnaie scripturale
Net foreign assets	1 169 908	- 200 745	4 871 762	4 521 990	4 489 520	2 187 223	143 933	1 124 670	2 410 541	Avoirs extérieurs nets
Domestic credit	4 682 363	10 116 304	10 869 001	8 164 100	10 553 160	13 210 820	17 204 891	17 816 153	17 573 297	Crédit intérieur
of which claims on private sector	3 781 953	8 490 836	7 691 250	3 068 590	4 143 840	7 465 963	9 949 994	10 309 834	10 354 382	dont créances sur le secteur privé
of which claims on government sector, net	857 766	1 547 252	3 080 028	5 025 490	6 304 620	5 674 693	7 213 399	7 496 291	7 209 640	dont créances nettes sur le gouvernement
International reserves (millions US$)	344	254	855	634	697	752	461	594	741	Réserves internationales (millions $EU)
Average exchange rate (National currency per US$)	4 801	5 726	6 658	6 986	6 908	7 014	7 486	8 960	9 118	Taux de change (moyen) (monnaie nationale par $ EU)
IX-2 PUBLIC FINANCE *GUINEA FRANC (MILLIONS)*										**IX-2 FINANCES PUBLIQUES** *FRANC GUINÉEN (MILLIONS)*
Total Revenues and Grants	3 492 790	4 257 698	11 912 705	9 000 916	9 115 230	9 702 407	9 325 985	12 225 180	14 310 181	Recettes totales et dons
Direct taxes (on income, profits)	473 887	505 465	582 939	836 466	925 992	925 091	1 249 892	1 328 406	1 662 382	Taxes directes
Domestic indirect taxes revenues	416 385	564 544	693 090	950 077	1 068 666	1 289 979	1 457 948	2 096 108	2 589 813	Taxes Indirectes
Trade taxes	2 428 069	2 927 131	3 974 688	5 801 608	5 651 350	5 911 673	5 923 880	7 510 109	8 198 141	Taxes sur le commerce extérieur
Other taxes	...	...	...	...	...	...	...	...	...	Autres taxes
Other revenues	93 870	157 738	5 499 648	387 408	830 222	410 394	356 696	456 949	451 603	Autres recettes
Grants	80 580	102 820	1 162 339	1 025 356	639 000	1 165 270	337 569	833 607	1 408 242	Dons
Total Expenditures and Net Lending	5 220 675	7 961 184	6 608 626	7 894 263	11 386 190	12 407 574	14 285 164	12 058 908	16 372 406	Dépenses totales et prêts nets
Current expenditure	3 194 650	5 023 110	4 748 684	5 634 540	6 776 960	7 819 180	8 739 852	7 615 475	10 148 957	Dépenses courantes
Wages and Salaries	1 109 230	1 551 190	1 764 234	1 756 890	2 190 170	2 370 180	2 720 000	2 936 900	3 409 194	Rémunérations et salaires
Other purchases of goods and services	1 360 700	2 545 980	1 745 430	2 372 950	2 943 540	3 368 000	3 313 000	2 576 203	3 436 196	Achat de biens et services
Other current expenditure	...	...	...	...	...	...	...	...	...	Autres dépenses courantes
Current transfers	724 720	925 940	1 239 020	1 504 700	1 643 250	2 081 000	2 706 852	2 102 372	3 303 566	Transferts courants
Interest payments	460 500	538 840	565 580	477 470	648 230	595 920	542 072	746 682	756 304	Intérêts
Capital expenditure	1 557 785	2 399 114	1 293 848	1 531 673	3 911 000	3 940 000	4 990 000	3 694 751	5 394 999	Dépenses d'équipement
Net lending	7 740	120	514	250 580	50 000	52 474	13 240	2 000	72 146	Prêts nets
Fiscal balance	-1 727 885	-3 703 486	5 304 079	1 106 653	-2 270 960	-2 705 167	-4 959 179	166 272	-2 062 225	Solde global y compris les dons
IX-3 BALANCE OF PAYMENTS *GUINEA FRANC (MILLIONS)*										**IX-3 BALANCE DES PAIEMENTS** *FRANC GUINÉEN (MILLIONS)*
Trade balance	- 49 501	396 692	-4 532 385	-2 274 418	-1 745 880	-2 596 333	-3 090 561	-18 370 216	10 119 212	Balance commerciale
Services Balance	-1 234 291	-1 994 656	-3 331 675	-5 036 514	-4 080 672	-4 081 709	-3 199 097	-5 979 033	-6 413 608	Balance des services
Net primary income	- 803 098	- 461 719	- 898 528	- 850 058	-2 798 215	-1 800 163	-1 078 132	-1 411 298	- 461 560	Revenus primaires nets
Compensation of employees	...	...	...	...	...	- 167 972	- 41 539	- 142 439	...	Rémunération des salariés
Investment income	...	...	...	...	...	-1 371 167	- 970 293	-1 331 286	...	Revenus des investissements
Net secondary income	160 963	102 092	939 484	923 022	606 731	151 244	- 311 006	736 964	1 481 859	Revenus secondaires nets
Net official transfers	...	...	...	...	...	- 173 826	- 169 119	- 309 509	...	Transferts officiels nets
Workers' remittances	...	...	...	...	...	...	...	...	...	Envois de fonds des travailleurs
Other private transfers	...	...	...	...	...	786 446	880 972	311 169	...	Autres transferts privés
Current account balance	-1 925 928	-1 957 591	-7 823 104	-7 237 969	-8 018 035	-8 326 962	-7 678 796	-25 023 584	4 725 903	Solde du compte courant
Capital and financial account	2 213 342	1 520 542	11 771 200	5 871 938	6 136 443	5 879 158	3 919 482	25 014 832	-5 126 474	Comptes de capital et financier
Capital account	188 698	283 223	5 656 101	1 730 779	1 683 446	2 187 475	1 738 003	1 497 083	1 328 249	Compte de capital
Financial account	2 024 644	1 237 319	6 115 099	4 141 159	4 452 998	3 691 683	2 181 479	23 517 749	-6 454 723	Compte financier
Errors and omissions	- 191	- 120	38 733	8 990	6 078	288 491	- 3 613	1 276	- 1 003	Erreurs et omissions
Overall balance	287 223	- 437 169	3 986 828	-1 357 041	-1 875 514	-2 159 313	-3 762 926	- 7 567	- 401 574	Balance générale

GUINÉE

X DEBT AND FINANCIAL FLOWS - DETTE ET FLUX FINANCIERS

	2009	2010	2011	2012	2013	2014	2015	2016	2017	
X-1 DEBT *US $ (MILLIONS)*										**X-1 DETTE EXTÉRIEURE** *$ E.U (MILLIONS)*
Total external debt	3 224	3 155	3 214	1 306	1 577	1 829	1 878	1 934	2 226	Dette extérieure totale
Private	...	...	...	...	...	...	...	...	...	Privée
Public	3 224	3 155	3 214	1 306	1 577	1 829	1 878	1 934	...	Publique
Total external debt service	80	55	128	2 058	55	65	103	78	...	Service de la dette extérieure
Present value of external debt	...	...	...	...	...	...	...	843	...	Valeur actuelle de la dette extérieure
Total government domestic debt, National currency (millions)	...	...	...	...	...	...	...	...	...	Dette publique intérieure
X-2 FINANCIAL FLOWS *US $ (MILLIONS)*										**X-2 FLUX FINANCIERS** *$ E.U (MILLIONS)*
Net Foreign Direct Investment Inflows	141	101	956	606	134	77	48	104	...	Investissements étranger direct (flux nets entrants)
Main origin of FDI inflows										**Principales origines de l'IDE entrant:**
Belgium	4	37	45	89	...	...	...	...	...	Belgique
...	...	...	...	...	...	...	...	...	...	...
...	...	...	...	...	...	...	...	...	...	...
...	...	...	...	...	...	...	...	...	...	...
...	...	...	...	...	...	...	...	...	...	...
African countries	...	...	...	...	...	...	...	...	...	Pays africains
Net total official development assistance	218	221	202	633	468	563	538	561	...	Aide publique au développement (nette totale)
Main origin of net ODA										**Principales origines de l'APD nette**
France	82	36	36	80	114	77	30	28	...	France
United States	35	22	16	20	27	42	77	125	...	États-Unis
International Development Association [IDA]	- 25	...	20	53	35	100	73	71	...	International Development Association
Germany	19	13	14	8	5	12	13	23	...	Allemagne
Japan	18	11	2	23	70	23	26	18	...	Japon

SOURCES AND NOTES - SOURCES ET NOTES

External trade - Total exports, fob: UNCTAD	Commerce exterieur - Exportation, fab: CNUCED
External trade - Total import, cif: UNCTAD	Commerce exterieur - Imporations, caf: CNUCED
ODA: OECD	APD: OCDE
Monetary statistics: IMF	Statistiques monétaires: FMI
National Accounts: 2009-2015 Estimates;2016:Provisional	Comptes nationaux: 2009-2015Estimées ;2016:Provisoire
Poverty: World Bank	Pauvreté: Banque mondiale

GUINEA

	AREA (km2)	36 130		SUPERFICIE (KM2)
	CAPITAL CITY	Bissau	Bissau	CAPITALE
	CURRENCY	Guinea-Bissau Peso	Guinea-Bissau Peso	MONNAIE

I SOCIAL AND DEMOGRAPHIC INDICATORS — INDICATEURS DEMOGRAPHIQUES ET SOCIAUX

Population	Year Année	Value Valeur	Charts / Graphiques	Population
Population ('000)	2015	1 844.3		Population ('000)
Female (%)	2015	50.4		Féminine (%)
Urban (%)	2015	47.8		Urbaine (%)
Average annual growth rate	2015	2.5		Taux de croissance annuel
Active population ('000)	2015	733.7		Population active ('000)
Population by age group ('000)				Population par groupe d'âge ('000)
0-14 years	2015	752.4		0-14 ans
15-64 years	2015	1 033.5		15-64 ans
65+ years	2015	58.4		65+ ans
Economically active population in agriculture (%)	2015	66.5		Participation de la population active agricole (%)
Crude birth rate	2015	36.6		Taux brut de natalité
Crude death rate	2015	11.9		Taux brut de mortalité
Total fertility rate	2015	4.8		Indice synthétique de fécondité
Life expectancy at birth - Total (years)	2015	55.5		Espérance de vie à la naissance - Totale (années)
Dependency ratio - Total (%)	2015	78.4		Taux de dépendance - Total (%)

Population by age group - 2015
Population par groupe d'age - 2015

Health				Santé
Percentage of children under-five and underweight	2015	16.5		% d'enfants de moins de cinq ans avec insuffisance pondérale
Prevalence of undernourishment	2015	20.7		Prévalence de la malnutrition
Under five mortality rate (per 1 000 live births)	2015	92.5		Taux de mortalité de moins de 5 ans (les deux sexes, pour 1000)
Infant mortality rate (per 1 000 live births)	2015	60.3		Taux de mortalité infantile (les deux sexes) par 1000
Neonatal mortality rate (per 1 000 live births)	2015	39.7		Le taux de mortalité néonatale (pour 1000 naissances vivantes)
Percentage of children provided the vaccines :				Pourcentage d'enfants vaccinés :
BCG	2015	95.3		BCG
DPT3	2015	81.6		DTC3
Polio	2015	85.2		polio
Measles	2014	69.0		rougeole
Percentage of mothers provided at least one antenatal care (%)	2015	93.7		Pourcentage de mères ayant au moins reçu un soin prénatal (%)
Percentage of deliveries attended by skilled health personnel	2015	45.3		% d'accouchements assistés par un personnel de santé qualifié
Number of doctors (per 10,000 population)	2015	2.0		Nombre de médecins (pour 10.000 habitants)
Number of nurses (per 10,000 population)	2015	14.0		Nombre d'infirmiers (pour 10.000 habitants)
Hospital beds - Total (per 10,000 population)	2015	96.0		Nombre de lits d'hôpitaux - Total (pour 10 000)
Births registered (per 1,000)	2015	36.6		Naissances enregistrées (pour 1000)
Deaths registered (per 1,000)	2015	11.9		Décès enregistrés (pour 1000)
Budget allocation to health (%)	2015	11.2		Dépenses publiques consacrées à la santé (% du budget)

Percentage of children provided vaccines : - 2014
Pourcentage d'enfants vaccinés : - 2014

Education				Education
Enrolment in primary education (000)	2015	347.3		Scolarisation dans le primaire (000)
Female	2015	198.7		Féminine
Enrolment in secondary education (000)	2015	82.3		Scolarisation dans le secondaire (000)
Female	2015	33.2		Féminine
Enrolment in tertiary education (000)	2006	3.7		Scolarisation dans le tertiaire (000)
Female	...	...		Féminine
Literacy rate	2015	53.2		Taux d'alphabétisation (deux sexes)
Male	2015	58.0		Masculin
Female	2015	41.3		Féminin
Pupil teacher ratio - primary	2015	46.1		Ratio élève-enseignant
Budget allocation to education (%)	2015	11.0		Dépenses publiques consacrées à l'enseignement (% du budget)

Literacy rate (%) - 2015
Taux d'alphabétisation - 2015

Poverty				Pauvreté
GNI per capita, PPP (current int. $)	2016	1550.0		RNB par habitant, ($ PPA inter. courants)
Human Poverty Index (HPI-1) Value (%)	2007	34.9		Valeur de l'Indice de pauvreté (IPH-1) (%)
Population below Inter. poverty line ($2/ day) (%)	2010	67.1		Population sous le seuil inter. de pauvreté (2$/Jour) (%)
Share of income held by richest 10%	2010	42.0		% de revenu des 10% plus riches
Share of income held by poorest 10%	2010	1.6		% de revenu des 10% plus pauvres
GINI index	2010	50.7		Indice de GINI

GNI per capita, PPP (current international $)
RNB par habitant, ($ PPA internationaux courants)

	2009	2010	2011	2012	2013	2014	2015	2016	2017	
GROSS DOMESTIC PRODUCT BY KIND OF ECONOMIC ACTIVITY AT CURRENT PRICES *GUINEA-BISSAU PESO (MILLIONS)*										**PRODUIT INTÉRIEUR BRUT PAR BRANCHE D'ACTIVITÉ ÉCONOMIQUE AUX PRIX COURANTS** *GUINEA-BISSAU PESO (MILLIONS)*
Agriculture, hunting , forestry and Fishing	171 777	189 602	233 346	236 844	228 032	214 247	284 045	317 884	...	Agriculture, chasse sylviculture et Pêche
Mining and quarrying	111	166	85	93	157	172	137	114	...	Industries extractives
Manufacturing	46 894	47 695	57 512	61 679	65 515	64 493	66 327	79 023	...	Industries manufacturières
Electricity, gas & water	1 699	2 326	3 571	2 795	2 377	3 322	3 754	3 652	...	Electricité, gaz et eau
Construction	3 458	5 076	3 109	3 833	6 478	7 097	5 723	4 794	...	Bâtiments et travaux publics
Wholesale & retail trade, restaurants, hotels	81 718	77 428	105 575	94 997	111 282	111 767	108 108	131 622	...	Commerce de gros et de détail, restaurants et hôtels
Finance, insurance, real estate, etc.	8 670	11 551	15 242	15 678	15 081	15 443	16 991	17 390	...	Banques, assurances, affaires immobilières
Transport and communications	16 389	18 460	26 012	26 144	26 331	27 025	29 750	30 490	...	Transport(s) et communications
Public administration and defense	40 545	46 012	51 338	42 578	43 446	53 056	54 346	56 025	...	Administrations publiques et défense
Education	7 347	7 869	8 414	8 643	7 146	7 054	11 038	11 620	...	Education
Health And Social Work	3 032	3 248	2 675	3 225	2 895	2 989	3 132	3 309	...	Santé et Actions Sociales
Other services	904	968	969	998	1 051	1 064	1 088	1 122	...	Autres services
Less Imputed Service Charges	- 5 521	- 6 579	- 9 773	- 10 893	- 10 216	- 10 611	- 9 773	- 9 773	...	Moins Services d'intermédiation financière
Gross domestic product at factor cost / basic prices	377 023	403 822	498 075	486 614	499 575	497 118	574 666	647 272	...	Produit intérieur brut aux couts des facteurs / prix de base
Plus: Indirect Taxes / taxes on products, less subsidies	12 920	16 693	20 213	18 465	17 087	23 754	37 844	43 200	...	Plus taxes indirectes/impôts sur les produits, moins les subsidions
EXPENDITURE ON GROSS DOMESTIC PRODUCT AT CURRENT PURCHASER'S VALUES *GUINEA-BISSAU PESO (MILLIONS)*										**EMPLOI DU PRODUIT INTÉRIEUR BRUT AUX PRIX COURANTS D'ACQUISITION** *GUINEA-BISSAU PESO (MILLIONS)*
Government final consumption	60 365	63 956	69 815	65 836	65 454	86 885	96 208	93 079	...	Consommation finale des administrations publiques
Private final consumption	368 499	393 324	441 559	453 207	454 568	444 510	521 445	569 224	...	Consommation finale privée
Gross fixed capital formation	23 600	27 169	27 379	33 145	29 438	31 360	34 162	34 074	...	Formation brute de capital fixe
Change in inventories	1 400	497	551	4 111	5 344	9 449	- 8 425	522	...	Variation des stocks
Exports of goods and services	73 588	83 742	139 392	78 595	95 275	116 016	170 643	180 312	...	Exportations de biens et services
Less imports of goods and services	137 510	148 173	160 409	129 817	133 417	167 347	201 522	186 739	...	Moins importations de biens et services
GDP at purchasers' values	389 943	420 515	518 288	505 079	516 662	520 872	612 511	690 472	...	PIB aux prix d'acquisition
GROSS DOMESTIC PRODUCT BY KIND OF ECONOMIC ACTIVITY AT CONSTANT PRICES *ANNUAL GROWTH RATES (%)*										**PRODUIT INTÉRIEUR BRUT PAR BRANCHE D'ACTIVITÉ ECONOMIQUE AUX PRIX CONSTANTS** *TAUX DE CROISSANCE ANNUEL (%)*
Agriculture, hunting , forestry and Fishing	3.6	0.7	9.6	- 0.1	3.7	- 6.5	2.9	5.3	...	Agriculture, chasse sylviculture et Pêche
Mining and quarrying	6.9	43.5	- 48.4	10.0	63.6	8.3	- 23.7	- 17.6	...	Industries extractives
Manufacturing	3.0	1.9	3.5	5.1	1.5	5.3	9.6	9.8	...	Industries manufacturières
Electricity, gas & water	10.6	41.1	32.1	- 9.4	- 18.1	37.8	6.5	- 3.1	...	Electricité, gaz et eau
Construction	22.6	41.1	- 46.4	17.8	62.8	8.0	- 23.7	- 17.8	...	Bâtiments et travaux publics
Wholesale & retail trade, restaurants, hotels	- 4.4	0.7	10.9	2.3	1.4	0.1	5.7	7.0	...	Commerce de gros et de détail, restaurants et hôtels
Finance, insurance, real estate, etc.	- 8.7	30.1	31.9	- 5.7	0.1	9.5	- 4.6	2.5	...	Banques, assurances, affaires immobilières
Transport and communications	7.3	20.6	14.2	- 3.6	- 0.9	8.4	13.5	4.1	...	Transport(s) et communications
Public administration and defense	23.0	13.5	7.9	- 19.3	13.7	17.3	7.1	3.1	...	Administrations publiques et défense
Education	3.3	4.8	6.2	2.1	- 16.3	- 3.0	5.2	3.9	...	Education
Health And Social Work	3.3	4.8	- 18.5	19.5	- 8.9	3.0	4.5	6.1	...	Santé et Actions Sociales
Other services	3.3	4.8	...	2.2	1.9	2.7	2.1	2.0	...	Autres services
Less Imputed Service Charges	18.1	2.9	45.5	- 3.0	4.9	19.0	- 27.8	1.3	...	Moins Services d'intermédiation financière
Gross domestic product at factor cost / basic prices	3.3	4.8	8.1	- 1.4	3.4	0.4	5.8	5.5	...	Produit intérieur brut aux couts des facteurs / prix de base
Plus: Indirect Taxes / taxes on products, less subsidies	2.1	0.8	6.2	- 15.9	- 1.8	26.8	20.4	14.3	...	Plus taxes indirectes/impôts sur les produits, moins les subsidions
Gross domestic product at market prices	3.3	4.7	8.1	- 1.7	3.3	1.0	6.1	5.8	...	Produit intérieur brut aux prix du marché
EXPENDITURE ON GROSS DOMESTIC PRODUCT AT CONSTANT PURCHASERS' VALUES *ANNUAL GROWTH RATES (%)*										**EMPLOIS DU PRODUIT INTÉRIEUR BRUT AUX PRIX CONSTANTS D'ACQUISITION** *TAUX DE CROISSANCE ANNUEL (%)*
Government final consumption	36.6	18.6	5.4	- 9.2	7.3	28.0	12.2	- 2.8	...	Consommation finale des administrations publiques
Private final consumption	3.1	0.3	4.1	- 4.2	- 0.2	2.5	10.0	8.9	...	Consommation finale privée
Gross fixed capital formation	2.4	32.6	- 2.5	19.5	- 11.8	2.1	6.6	- 2.1	...	Formation brute de capital fixe
Exports of goods and services	- 1.9	31.1	14.6	- 29.6	17.3	11.8	12.4	- 15.5	...	Exportations de biens et services
Less imports of goods and services	11.0	16.1	- 0.6	- 24.5	- 1.4	33.5	14.0	- 2.9	...	Moins importations de biens et services

	2009	2010	2011	2012	2013	2014	2015	2016	2017	
Annual growth rates (%)										**Taux de croissance annuel (%)**
All item	- 2.8	2.2	4.8	2.3	1.2	- 1.5	1.4	1.7	1.4	Ensemble
of which:										dont:
Food and non-alcoholic beverages	- 2.4	1.9	6.8	3.5	2.1	- 2.5	3.2	2.4	1.8	Alimentation et boissons non alcoolisés
Alcoholic beverages, tobacco and narcotics	- 4.8	1.2	0.7	1.6	0.7	- 0.3	- 1.2	0.7	- 0.4	Boissons alcoolisées et tabacs
Clothing and footwear	- 4.3	5.0	4.1	-	0.3	- 3.9	- 3.2	0.1	0.1	Habillement et chaussures
Housing, water, electricity, gas and other fuels	2.2	0.6	- 1.5	-	2.5	1.7	7.4	1.1	6.0	Logement, eau, électricité, gaz et autres combustibles
Furnishings, household equipment and routine household maintenance	0.3	2.0	2.1	0.3	0.2	0.3	- 0.2	1.0	- 0.3	Meubles, articles de ménage et entretien courant
Health	- 1.6	3.5	8.5	- 0.1	0.7	1.9	- 4.4	- 1.4	- 1.1	Santé
Transport	- 1.9	2.3	3.5	4.3	0.1	1.5	3.8	2.6	0.2	Transport
Communication	- 8.1	0.9	5.3	0.2	1.0	- 9.2	- 8.2	- 1.8	- 0.3	Communication
Recreation and culture	- 1.8	1.9	0.3	- 0.2	0.6	- 2.7	- 3.6	- 1.6	1.0	Loisirs et culture
Education	- 4.6	0.5	5.7	0.0	1.8	4.6	3.0	6.1	- 3.8	Enseignement
Restaurants and hotels	14.3	1.2	0.3	1.5	1.5	4.9	0.3	- 0.7	- 0.2	Restaurants et hôtels
Miscellaneous goods and services	- 0.3	- 3.0	4.5	3.9	0.6	- 0.4	1.1	1.8	0.2	Biens et Services divers

GUINEA-BISSAU

IV AGRICULTURAL PRODUCTION - PRODUCTION AGRICOLE

TONNES (THOUSAND)	2009	2010	2011	2012	2013	2014	2015	2016	2017	Tonnes (milliers)
Rice, paddy	184	209	175	199	210	133	142	186	...	Riz, Paddy
Cashew nuts, with shell	154	137	200	181	176	188	195	154	...	Noix d'Acajou
Palm nuts	80	80	80	80	80	80	80	...	...	Noix de palme
Coconuts	46	46	47	47	47	48	45	...	...	Noix de coco
Millet	12	15	14	17	18	11	13	...	...	Millet

V MINING PRODUCTION - PRODUCTION MINIERE

	2009	2010	2011	2012	2013	2014	2015	2016	2017	
	...	...	...	...	...	...	...	...	...	
	...	...	...	...	...	...	...	...	...	
	...	...	...	...	...	...	...	...	...	

VI ENERGY - ENERGIE

	2009	2010	2011	2012	2013	2014	2015	2016	2017	
Total electricity generation (GWh) of which	67	67	101	75	75	139	147	148	...	Production électrique totale (GWh) dont
Production of electricity from fossil fuels (GWh)	67	67	101	75	75	136	144	145	...	Production d'électricité à partir de combustibles fossiles (GWh)
Production of hydro electricity (GWh)	...	...	...	...	...	...	...	...	...	Production d'électricité d'origine hydraulique (GWh)
Production of electricity from solar, wind, tide, wave and other sources (GWh)	...	...	...	...	...	3	3	3	...	Production d'électricité d'origine solaire, éolienne, marée motrice et autres (GWh)

VII TOURISM AND INFRASTRUCTURE - TOURISME ET INFRASTUCTURE

	2009	2010	2011	2012	2013	2014	2015	2016	2017	
VII-1 Tourism										**VII-1 Tourisme**
International tourist arrivals (thousands)	67	67	101	75	75	139	147	148	...	Arrivées de touristes internationaux (milliers)
Rooms in hotels and similar establishments (thousands)										Chambres d'hôtels et établissements assimilés (milliers)
Overnight stays (thousands)	67	67	101	75	75	136	144	145	...	Nuitées (milliers)
Tourism receipts (US$ thousand)	...	...	...	...	...	...	...	...	...	Recettes touristiques (milliers de $ EU)
Total contribution to GDP (%)	...	...	...	...	...	3	3	3	...	Contribution totale au PIB (%)
Total contribution to Employment (%)										Contribution totale à l'emploi (%)
VII-2 Infrastructure										**VII-2 Infrastructure**
Paved road (% of total)	32.8	33.0	33.0	33.0	33.0	33.0	33.0	...	...	Routes asphaltées (% du total)
Total network (Railways-km)	...	...	...	...	...	...	...	...	...	Réseau total voies ferrées-Km
Main telephone lines (per 100 inhabitants)	...	...	...	...	...	...	...	...	...	Lignes téléphoniques fixes (pour 100 habitants)
Mobile cellular subscribers (per 100 inhabitants)	36.1	42.7	45.1	63.1	55.2	63.5	69.3	70.3	...	Abonnés aux téléphones mobiles (pour 100 habitants)
Internet users per 100 inhabitants	2.3	2.5	2.7	2.9	3.1	3.3	3.5	3.8	...	Utilisateurs Internet par 100 Habitants
Fixed (wired)-broadband subscriptions per 100 inhabitants	...	...	...	...	...	...	...	...	...	Abonnements à l'Internet fixe (filaire) à large bande pour 100 habitants, par débit

VIII EXTERNAL TRADE - COMMERCE EXTERIEUR

US$ (MILLIONS) EXPORTS, FOB	2009	2010	2011	2012	2013	2014	2015	2016	2017	$ E.U (MILLIONS) EXPORTATIONS, FÀB
Exports - Total	122	127	242	131	153	166	252	263	...	Exportations - Total
Exports to Africa	6	6	11	6	7	8	12	12	...	Exportations vers l'Afrique
Main products										**Principaux produits**
Fish, fresh (live or dead), chilled or frozen	4	4	8	4	5	5	8	8	...	Poissons frais (vivants ou morts), réfrigérés ou congelés
Fruits and nuts (excluding oil nuts), fresh or dried	107	112	213	116	135	147	223	233	...	Fruits et noix (à l'exclusion des oléagineux), frais ou secs
Ingots, primary forms, of iron or steel; semi-finis.	...	...	1	1	1	1	1	1	...	Lingots, formes primaires, en fer ou en acier; semi-finis.
Petroleum oils, oils from bitumin. materials, crude	5	5	10	6	6	7	10	11	...	Huiles de pétrole, huiles de bitume. matériaux bruts
Wood in the rough or roughly squared	1	1	1	1	1	1	1	1	...	Bois bruts ou grossièrement équarris
Main destinations										**Principales destinations**
Ghana	4	4	7	4	5	5	8	8	...	Ghana
India	99	103	197	107	124	135	205	214	...	Inde
Mali	1	2	3	2	2	2	3	3	...	Mali
Singapore	9	9	17	9	11	12	18	19	...	Singapour
United States	5	5	10	6	7	7	11	11	...	États-Unis
IMPORTS, CIF										
Imports - Total	183	178	218	165	166	194	206	226	...	Importations - Total (millions)
Imports from Africa	41	40	45	36	45	44	40	47	...	Importations en provenance de l'Afrique
Main products										**Principaux produits**
Alcoholic beverages	6	8	10	7	8	9	10	11	...	Boissons alcoolisées
Edible products and preparations, n.e.s.	4	7	5	5	10	9	11	11	...	Produits et préparations comestibles, n.d.a.
Non-alcoholic beverages, n.e.s.	7	10	15	10	10	12	15	17	...	Boissons non alcoolisées, n.d.a.
Petroleum oils or bituminous minerals > 70 % oil	31	12	21	23	24	42	20	19	...	Huiles de pétrole ou de minéraux bitumineux> 70% d'huile
Rice	26	28	28	16	13	16	22	26	...	Riz
Main origin										**Principales provenances**
China	15	7	10	8	7	9	13	15	...	Chine
Netherlands	18	7	9	5	6	5	8	9	...	Pays-Bas
Pakistan	1	12	7	6	4	6	10	12	...	Pakistan
Portugal	39	54	77	60	60	57	76	80	...	Portugal
Senegal	30	32	34	28	40	36	31	37	...	Sénégal

GUINÉE-BISSAU

GUINEA-BISSAU

	2009	2010	2011	2012	2013	2014	2015	2016	2017	
IX-1 MONETARY STATISTICS *GUINEA-BISSAU PESO (MILLIONS)*										**IX-1 STATISTIQUES MONÉTAIRES** *GUINEA-BISSAU PESO (MILLIONS)*
Money supply (M1)	96 111	124 578	173 296	162 832	199 453	241 467	302 919	326 323	373 143	Masse monétaire (M1)
Quasi-money	7 807	13 637	28 253	31 020	29 988	29 943	31 953	30 617	26 495	Quasi-monnaie
of which demand deposit	...	...	...	...	...	...	...	...	...	dont Monnaie scripturale
Net foreign assets	82 270	93 048	132 522	87 594	95 173	150 934	167 232	201 006	150 130	Avoirs extérieurs nets
Domestic credit	19 378	31 980	62 060	85 369	88 280	102 328	148 221	163 547	110 882	Crédit intérieur
of which claims on private sector	- 2 692	6 224	7 950	21 145	21 719	37 339	94 079	111 338	64 010	dont créances sur le secteur privé
of which claims on government sector, net	22 070	25 756	54 110	64 224	66 561	59 407	50 294	47 680	46 144	dont créances nettes sur le gouvernement
International reserves (millions US$)	177	158	222	164	186	288	332	322	397	Réserves internationales (millions $EU)
Average exchange rate (National currency per US$)	472	495	472	511	494	494	591	593	582	Taux de change (moyen) (monnaie nationale par $ EU)
IX-2 PUBLIC FINANCE *GUINEA-BISSAU PESO (MILLIONS)*										**IX-2 FINANCES PUBLIQUES** *GUINEA-BISSAU PESO (MILLIONS)*
Total Revenues and Grants	98 502	91 279	90 905	74 131	61 150	105 888	124 858	114 801	131 448	Recettes totales et dons
Direct taxes (on income, profits)	7 422	9 468	11 679	12 019	10 570	11 176	16 609	17 880	19 141	Taxes directes
Domestic indirect taxes revenues	8 483	12 091	14 573	13 142	12 529	14 538	21 332	24 909	29 883	Taxes Indirectes
Trade taxes	9 417	9 635	12 050	11 312	11 585	17 029	21 050	21 097	24 844	Taxes sur le commerce extérieur
Other taxes	1 281	1 955	2 129	2 538	697	1 432	2 959	2 224	2 204	Autres taxes
Other revenues	8 791	11 518	12 350	7 111	5 765	21 374	22 863	21 070	21 070	Autres recettes
Grants	63 107	46 612	38 123	28 011	20 004	40 339	40 046	27 621	34 306	Dons
Total Expenditures and Net Lending	82 316	90 869	81 200	84 429	76 620	118 083	141 072	142 380	153 152	Dépenses totales et prêts nets
Current expenditure	45 299	49 145	54 732	62 424	50 303	74 878	86 292	95 068	95 663	Dépenses courantes
Wages and Salaries	20 083	26 224	28 717	24 341	24 380	31 390	30 992	31 511	33 798	Rémunérations et salaires
Other purchases of goods and services	6 770	8 619	7 500	12 316	8 864	11 015	16 500	11 970	20 616	Achat de biens et services
Other current expenditure	6 869	7 525	11 318	9 239	4 159	12 826	19 900	20 017	16 777	Autres dépenses courantes
Current transfers	11 577	6 778	7 197	16 527	12 900	19 647	18 900	31 570	24 473	Transferts courants
Interest payments	1 000	1 125	400	400	200	3 212	6 380	4 808	5 123	Intérêts
Capital expenditure	36 017	40 599	26 069	21 605	26 117	39 993	48 401	42 503	52 365	Dépenses d'équipement
Net lending	...	...	...	...	...	...	...	...	...	Prêts nets
Fiscal balance	16 186	410	9 704	- 10 298	- 15 470	- 12 195	- 16 214	- 27 578	- 21 704	Solde global y compris les dons
IX-3 BALANCE OF PAYMENTS *GUINEA-BISSAU PESO (MILLIONS)*										**IX-3 BALANCE DES PAIEMENTS** *GUINEA-BISSAU PESO (MILLIONS)*
Trade balance	- 38 097	- 34 644	- 1 046	- 25 732	- 14 843	- 24 583	26 801	27 491	...	Balance commerciale
Services Balance	- 25 378	- 13 685	- 19 042	- 17 063	- 14 903	- 19 019	- 24 569	- 29 040	...	Balance des services
Net primary income	- 5 197	862	- 244	- 1 810	- 309	8 458	8 173	9 622	...	Revenus primaires nets
Compensation of employees	- 55	- 2 005	- 8 490	- 15 022	- 3 654	- 2 530	- 6 036	- 2 625	...	Rémunération des salariés
Investment income	- 5 142	...	...	- 32	...	12 531	12 988	10 625	...	Revenus des investissements
Net secondary income	46 251	12 428	13 702	2 108	4 113	38 263	1 981	1 983	...	Revenus secondaires nets
Net official transfers	31 156	11 200	15 782	11 900	2 400	2 400	5 600	1 425	...	Transferts officiels nets
Workers' remittances	11 024	12 131	10 697	12 363	12 363	19 178	...	...	...	Envois de fonds des travailleurs
Other private transfers	4 071	3 406	1 118	1 771	2 888	76	...	...	...	Autres transferts privés
Current account balance	- 22 421	- 35 040	- 6 630	- 42 497	- 25 942	3 120	12 386	10 056	...	Solde du compte courant
Capital and financial account	40 532	49 334	35 661	14 174	31 694	66 987	31 254	36 246	...	Comptes de capital et financier
Capital account	33 268	485 428	26 958	15 863	15 822	27 396	35 382	29 564	...	Compte de capital
Financial account	7 264	- 436 094	8 703	- 1 689	15 872	39 592	- 4 129	6 682	...	Compte financier
Errors and omissions	- 4 368	- 2 114	- 2 262	- 4 765	5 130	6 140	- 7 839	- 12 456	...	Erreurs et omissions
Overall balance	13 743	12 180	26 770	- 33 088	10 882	76 247	35 801	33 846	...	Balance générale

GUINEA-BISSAU

X DEBT AND FINANCIAL FLOWS - DETTE ET FLUX FINANCIERS

	2009	2010	2011	2012	2013	2014	2015	2016	2017	
X-1 DEBT *US $ (MILLIONS)*										**X-1 DETTE EXTÉRIEURE** *$ E.U (MILLIONS)*
Total external debt	1 067	310	269	270	268	240	242	248	265	Dette extérieure totale
Private	...	...	...	...	...	...	...	...	...	Privée
Public	1 067	310	269	270	268	240	242	248	...	Publique
Total external debt service	11	896	3	2	...	2	4	3	...	Service de la dette extérieure
Present value of external debt	...	...	...	...	...	...	...	215	...	Valeur actuelle de la dette extérieure
Total government domestic debt, National currency (millions)	...	...	...	...	...	...	...	...	...	Dette publique intérieure
X-2 FINANCIAL FLOWS *US $ (MILLIONS)*										**X-2 FLUX FINANCIERS** *$ E.U (MILLIONS)*
Net Foreign Direct Investment Inflows	17	33	25	7	20	29	19	20	...	Investissements étranger direct (flux nets entrants)
Main origin of FDI inflows										**Principales origines de l'IDE entrant:**
...	...	...	...	...	...	...	...	...	...	...
...	...	...	...	...	...	...	...	...	...	...
...	...	...	...	...	...	...	...	...	...	...
Slovenia	...	...	...	-	...	...	...	...	...	Slovénie
...	...	...	...	...	...	...	...	...	...	...
African countries	...	...	...	...	...	...	...	...	...	Pays africains
Net total official development assistance	148	128	121	80	106	110	95	199	...	Aide publique au développement (nette totale)
Main origin of net ODA										**Principales origines de l'APD nette**
Portugal	14	16	14	10	8	11	14	13	...	Portugal
International Development Association [IDA]	14	8	11	10	6	17	7	9	...	International Development Association
Italy	2	...	1	-	-	1	1	102	...	Italie
Spain	13	8	6	4	5	0	2	4	...	Espagne
France	6	2	14	1	1	1	1	1	...	France

GUINÉE-BISSAU

SOURCES AND NOTES - SOURCES ET NOTES

External trade - Total exports, fob: UNCTAD

External trade - Total import, cif: UNCTAD

ODA: OECD

Monetary statistics: IMF

National Accounts: 2013:Estimates;2014-2015-2016:Projections

Poverty: World Bank

Commerce exterieur - Exportation, fab: CNUCED

Commerce exterieur - Imporations, caf: CNUCED

APD: OCDE

Statistiques monétaires: FMI

Comptes nationaux: 2013:Estimées;2014-2015-2016:Projections

Pauvreté: Banque mondiale

	AREA (km2)	580 370		SUPERFICIE (KM2)
	CAPITAL CITY	Nairobi	Nairobi	CAPITALE
	CURRENCY	Kenyan Shilling	Shilling Kenyan	MONNAIE

I SOCIAL AND DEMOGRAPHIC INDICATORS — INDICATEURS DEMOGRAPHIQUES ET SOCIAUX

Population	Year Année	Value Valeur	Charts Graphiques	Population
Population ('000)	2017	46 500.0		Population ('000)
Female (%)	2017	50.0		Féminine (%)
Urban (%)	2015	26.0		Urbaine (%)
Average annual growth rate	2017	2.6		Taux de croissance annuel
Active population ('000)	2015	16 294.2		Population active ('000)
Population by age group ('000)				Population par groupe d'âge ('000)
0-14 years	2017	19 209.0		0-14 ans
15-64 years	2017	25 866.0		15-64 ans
65+ years	2017	1 521.0		65+ ans
Economically active population in agriculture (%)	2015	90.2		Participation de la population active agricole (%)
Crude birth rate	2017	30.5		Taux brut de natalité
Crude death rate	2017	10.0		Taux brut de mortalité
Total fertility rate	2017	3.9		Indice synthétique de fécondité
Life expectancy at birth - Total (years)	2017	60.0		Espérance de vie à la naissance - Totale (années)
Dependency ratio - Total (%)	2017	80.1		Taux de dépendance - Total (%)
Health				**Santé**
Percentage of children under-five and underweight	2017	11.0		% d'enfants de moins de cinq ans avec insuffisance pondérale
Prevalence of undernourishment	2015	21.2		Prévalence de la malnutrition
Under five mortality rate (per 1 000 live births)	2017	52.0		Taux de mortalité de moins de 5 ans (les deux sexes, pour 1000)
Infant mortality rate (per 1 000 live births)	2017	39.0		Taux de mortalité infantile (les deux sexes) par 1000
Neonatal mortality rate (per 1 000 live births)	2017	22.0		Le taux de mortalité néonatale (pour 1000 naissances vivantes)
Percentage of children provided the vaccines :				Pourcentage d'enfants vaccinés :
BCG	2017	95.9		BCG
DPT3	2017	88.3		DTC3
Polio	2017	88.1		polio
Measles	2017	78.9		rougeole
Percentage of mothers provided at least one antenatal care (%)	2017	96.0		Pourcentage de mères ayant au moins reçu un soin prénatal (%)
Percentage of deliveries attended by skilled health personnel	2017	62.0		% d'accouchements assistés par un personnel de santé qualifié
Number of doctors (per 10,000 population)	2017	2.4		Nombre de médecins (pour 10.000 habitants)
Number of nurses (per 10,000 population)	2017	17.0		Nombre d'infirmiers (pour 10.000 habitants)
Hospital beds - Total (per 10,000 population)	2014	14.8		Nombre de lits d'hôpitaux - Total (pour 10 000)
Births registered (per 1,000)	2015	34.1		Naissances enregistrées (pour 1000)
Deaths registered (per 1,000)	2015	8.0		Décès enregistrés (pour 1000)
Budget allocation to health (%)	2017	7.0		Dépenses publiques consacrées à la santé (% du budget)
Education				**Education**
Enrolment in primary education (000)	2017	10 462.0		Scolarisation dans le primaire (000)
Female	2017	5 143.0		Féminine
Enrolment in secondary education (000)	2017	2 831.0		Scolarisation dans le secondaire (000)
Female	2017	1 380.0		Féminine
Enrolment in tertiary education (000)	2017	838.2		Scolarisation dans le tertiaire (000)
Female	2017	339.0		Féminine
Literacy rate	2017	89.1		Taux d'alphabétisation (deux sexes)
Male	2017	92.4		Masculin
Female	2017	87.8		Féminin
Pupil teacher ratio - primary	2016	40.1		Ratio élève-enseignant
Budget allocation to education (%)	2014	15.2		Dépenses publiques consacrées à l'enseignement (% du budget)
Poverty				**Pauvreté**
GNI per capita, PPP (current int. $)	2016	3120.0		RNB par habitant, ($ PPA inter. courants)
Human Poverty Index (HPI-1) Value (%)	2007	29.5		Valeur de l'Indice de pauvreté (IPH-1) (%)
Population below Inter. poverty line ($2/ day) (%)	2005	33.6		Population sous le seuil inter. de pauvreté (2$/Jour) (%)
Share of income held by richest 10%	2005	38.8		% de revenu des 10% plus riches
Share of income held by poorest 10%	2005	1.7		% de revenu des 10% plus pauvres
GINI index	2005	48.5		Indice de GINI

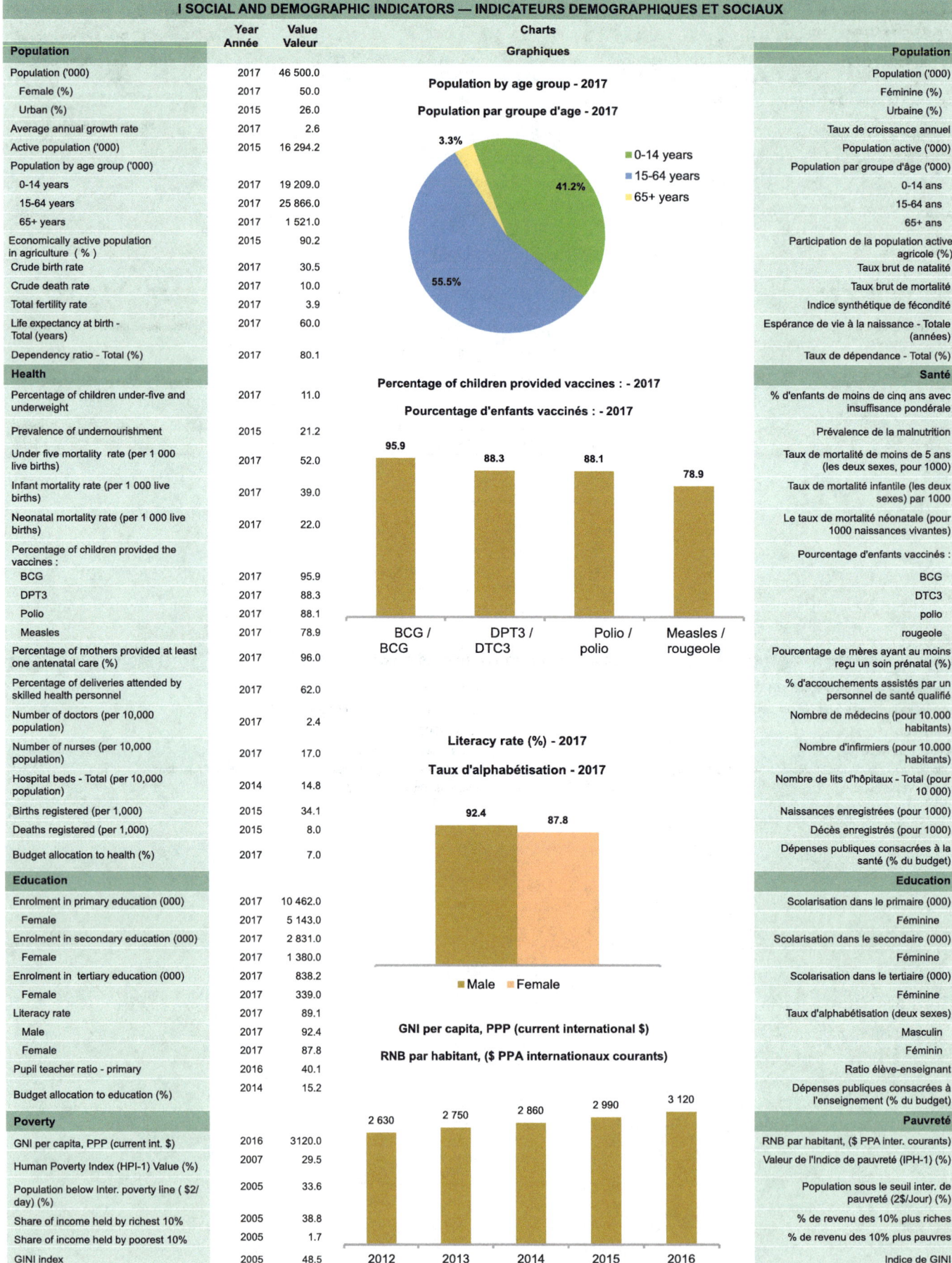

Population by age group - 2017
Population par groupe d'age - 2017

- 0-14 years 41.2%
- 15-64 years 55.5%
- 65+ years 3.3%

Percentage of children provided vaccines : - 2017
Pourcentage d'enfants vaccinés : - 2017

BCG / BCG 95.9 — DPT3 / DTC3 88.3 — Polio / polio 88.1 — Measles / rougeole 78.9

Literacy rate (%) - 2017
Taux d'alphabétisation - 2017

Male 92.4 — Female 87.8

GNI per capita, PPP (current international $)
RNB par habitant, ($ PPA internationaux courants)

2012: 2 630 — 2013: 2 750 — 2014: 2 860 — 2015: 2 990 — 2016: 3 120

KENYA

	2009	2010	2011	2012	2013	2014	2015	2016	2017	
GROSS DOMESTIC PRODUCT BY KIND OF ECONOMIC ACTIVITY AT CURRENT PRICES *KENYAN SHILLING (MILLIONS)*										**PRODUIT INTÉRIEUR BRUT PAR BRANCHE D'ACTIVITÉ ÉCONOMIQUE AUX PRIX COURANTS** *SHILLING KENYAN (MILLIONS)*
Agriculture, hunting , forestry and Fishing	669 069	788 649	982 191	1 115 198	1 254 813	1 482 840	1 900 965	2 334 147	...	Agriculture, chasse sylviculture et Pêche
Mining and quarrying	18 134	26 029	32 514	46 628	40 742	44 936	54 806	59 402	...	Industries extractives
Manufacturing	342 531	356 731	437 883	469 104	506 612	537 999	589 597	657 950	...	Industries manufacturières
Electricity, gas & water	64 032	62 486	69 502	86 001	94 343	97 292	136 170	171 822	...	Electricité, gaz et eau
Construction	112 221	142 666	164 635	190 851	213 565	262 090	309 046	359 656	...	Bâtiments et travaux publics
Wholesale & retail trade, restaurants, hotels	251 542	292 984	350 973	391 505	438 683	481 136	522 507	571 984	...	Commerce de gros et de détail, restaurants et hôtels
Finance, insurance, real estate, etc.	474 193	521 158	600 548	692 631	794 370	897 652	1 017 630	1 165 109	...	Banques, assurances, affaires immobilières
Transport and communications	279 465	285 416	327 372	407 972	447 003	528 049	578 529	632 537	...	Transport(s) et communications
Public administration and defense	127 814	138 748	158 673	185 689	208 647	243 526	267 675	290 280	...	Administrations publiques et défense
Education	177 993	174 481	199 165	229 193	251 958	279 543	308 424	312 971	...	Education
Health And Social Work	58 686	66 041	67 839	70 459	75 157	91 969	107 936	119 537	...	Santé et Actions Sociales
Other services	42 593	45 798	49 586	56 381	62 206	70 086	78 197	84 390	...	Autres services
Less Imputed Service Charges	- 59 373	- 71 891	- 90 687	- 111 574	- 124 136	- 134 588	- 163 233	- 202 720	...	Moins Services d'intermédiation financière
Gross domestic product at factor cost / basic prices	2 558 899	2 829 296	3 350 194	3 830 038	4 263 964	4 882 532	5 708 251	6 557 066	...	Produit intérieur brut aux couts des facteurs / prix de base
Plus: Indirect Taxes / taxes on products, less subsidies	304 896	341 391	377 223	431 332	481 179	519 878	552 396	601 629	...	Plus taxes indirectes/impôts sur les produits, moins les subventions
EXPENDITURE ON GROSS DOMESTIC PRODUCT AT CURRENT PURCHASER'S VALUES *KENYAN SHILLING (MILLIONS)*										**EMPLOI DU PRODUIT INTÉRIEUR BRUT AUX PRIX COURANTS D'ACQUISITION** *SHILLING KENYAN (MILLIONS)*
Government final consumption	435 705	448 876	520 941	590 538	670 936	750 450	894 853	976 510	...	Consommation finale des administrations publiques
Private final consumption	2 183 685	2 437 237	2 997 858	3 322 882	3 750 433	4 234 481	4 707 392	5 579 393	...	Consommation finale privée
Gross fixed capital formation	529 936	647 363	754 175	901 305	976 086	1 236 107	1 360 448	1 236 835	...	Formation brute de capital fixe
Change in inventories	23 702	14 855	48 959	13 850	- 22 059	- 24 203	- 9 125	- 4 808	...	Variation des stocks
Exports of goods and services	573 672	686 298	851 985	947 190	945 478	988 521	1 042 700	1 043 002	...	Exportations de biens et services
Less imports of goods and services	882 904	1 063 942	1 446 502	1 514 394	1 575 731	1 782 945	1 735 621	1 672 236	...	Moins importations de biens et services
GDP at purchasers' values	2 863 796	3 170 687	3 727 416	4 261 370	4 745 143	5 402 410	6 260 647	7 158 695	...	PIB aux prix d'acquisition
GROSS DOMESTIC PRODUCT BY KIND OF ECONOMIC ACTIVITY AT CONSTANT PRICES *ANNUAL GROWTH RATES (%)*										**PRODUIT INTÉRIEUR BRUT PAR BRANCHE D'ACTIVITÉ ECONOMIQUE AUX PRIX CONSTANTS** *TAUX DE CROISSANCE ANNUEL (%)*
Agriculture, hunting , forestry and Fishing	- 2.3	10.3	2.4	2.8	5.4	4.3	5.5	4.0	...	Agriculture, chasse sylviculture et Pêche
Mining and quarrying	11.3	31.7	19.0	19.0	- 4.2	14.9	12.4	9.5	...	Industries extractives
Manufacturing	- 1.1	4.5	7.2	- 0.6	5.6	2.5	3.6	3.5	...	Industries manufacturières
Electricity, gas & water	7.0	6.3	9.4	9.6	6.6	6.1	8.5	7.1	...	Electricité, gaz et eau
Construction	17.6	19.1	4.0	11.3	6.1	13.1	13.9	9.2	...	Bâtiments et travaux publics
Wholesale & retail trade, restaurants, hotels	9.9	7.5	7.5	6.3	6.1	3.1	5.0	5.0	...	Commerce de gros et de détail, restaurants et hôtels
Finance, insurance, real estate, etc.	4.7	8.7	4.4	4.7	5.5	6.2	7.3	7.4	...	Banques, assurances, affaires immobilières
Transport and communications	7.9	8.3	11.5	2.6	4.8	8.5	7.8	8.9	...	Transport(s) et communications
Public administration and defense	7.1	1.4	2.4	4.0	2.8	5.6	5.5	5.3	...	Administrations publiques et défense
Education	5.4	10.2	7.5	11.1	6.3	7.8	4.5	6.3	...	Education
Health And Social Work	4.7	6.2	- 2.6	- 2.8	7.7	8.1	6.1	5.8	...	Santé et Actions Sociales
Other services	1.2	3.6	1.5	2.3	4.6	4.2	3.9	4.2	...	Autres services
Less Imputed Service Charges	10.6	15.9	9.1	10.1	5.2	11.3	13.5	3.0	...	Moins Services d'intermédiation financière
Gross domestic product at factor cost / basic prices	3.3	8.4	5.3	4.1	5.4	5.6	6.1	6.0	...	Produit intérieur brut aux couts des facteurs / prix de base
Plus: Indirect Taxes / taxes on products, less subsidies	3.0	9.0	12.5	7.7	9.5	3.4	2.8	4.5	...	Plus taxes indirectes/impôts sur les produits, moins les subventions
Gross domestic product at market prices	3.3	8.4	6.1	4.5	5.9	5.4	5.7	5.8	...	Produit intérieur brut aux prix du marché
EXPENDITURE ON GROSS DOMESTIC PRODUCT AT CONSTANT PURCHASERS' VALUES *ANNUAL GROWTH RATES (%)*										**EMPLOIS DU PRODUIT INTÉRIEUR BRUT AUX PRIX CONSTANTS D'ACQUISITION** *TAUX DE CROISSANCE ANNUEL (%)*
Government final consumption	8.1	3.5	4.0	7.1	6.1	1.7	13.0	7.0	...	Consommation finale des administrations publiques
Private final consumption	5.5	7.0	8.4	4.0	7.0	6.5	2.5	7.2	...	Consommation finale privée
Gross fixed capital formation	10.0	14.4	3.4	13.3	2.1	14.2	6.7	- 9.3	...	Formation brute de capital fixe
Exports of goods and services	- 6.0	14.2	10.6	0.4	- 2.2	5.8	6.2	0.6	...	Exportations de biens et services
Less imports of goods and services	9.0	8.1	13.4	5.1	- 0.4	10.4	1.2	- 4.7	...	Moins importations de biens et services

III INFLATION

	2009	2010	2011	2012	2013	2014	2015	2016	2017	
Annual growth rates (%)										**Taux de croissance annuel (%)**
All item	9.5	4.1	14.0	9.4	5.7	6.9	6.6	6.3	8.0	Ensemble
of which:										dont:
Food and non-alcoholic beverages	15.4	5.9	20.5	10.0	7.3	8.9	11.4	10.1	13.4	Alimentation et boissons non alcoolisés
Alcoholic beverages, tobacco and narcotics	9.4	7.5	9.4	9.0	6.0	5.5	3.1	13.2	3.2	Boissons alcoolisées et tabacs
Clothing and footwear	4.3	3.4	7.1	9.6	5.2	4.8	4.6	4.2	3.7	Habillement et chaussures
Housing, water, electricity, gas and other fuels	4.4	3.2	11.4	9.3	4.6	5.6	3.3	1.6	3.1	Logement, eau, électricité, gaz et autres combustibles
Furnishings, household equipment and routine household maintenance	6.4	3.2	8.6	10.0	4.3	5.1	4.4	4.0	3.2	Meubles, articles de ménage et entretien courant
Health	9.5	4.4	7.2	5.9	4.3	6.1	4.8	4.1	3.3	Santé
Transport	4.6	5.3	21.4	7.4	4.8	9.2	-	0.2	3.9	Transport
Communication	- 0.3	- 10.3	- 15.7	5.7	- 1.5	- 0.9	0.2	2.0	0.4	Communication
Recreation and culture	2.7	1.2	7.9	9.6	6.1	10.6	2.7	4.2	1.6	Loisirs et culture
Education	0.1	1.4	4.4	6.7	5.2	5.4	4.1	4.2	3.0	Enseignement
Restaurants and hotels	8.6	4.0	14.6	14.4	7.1	6.7	5.1	5.5	5.5	Restaurants et hôtels
Miscellaneous goods and services	7.3	2.2	7.2	9.5	4.6	4.4	4.8	4.1	3.6	Biens et Services divers

KENYA

IV AGRICULTURAL PRODUCTION - PRODUCTION AGRICOLE

	2009	2010	2011	2012	2013	2014	2015	2016	2017	
TONNES (THOUSAND)										**Tonnes (milliers)**
Maize	2 250	3 060	3 096	3 771	3 663	3 510	3 825	3 339	...	Maïs
Tea	314	399	378	369	432	445	399	473	...	Thé
Sugar cane	5 611	5 695	5 307	5 824	6 674	6 478	6 995	7 152	...	Canne à sucre
Coffee, green	57	42	36	50	40	50	42	46	...	Café, vert
Wheat	129	200	106	163	195	229	239	222	...	Blé

V MINING PRODUCTION - PRODUCTION MINIERE

	2009	2010	2011	2012	2013	2014	2015	2016	2017	
Soda Ash - Production (metric tons)	464 900	473 700	499 100	449 300	468 200	409 800	295 400	301 700	303 600	Bicarbonate de soude - Production (tonnes métriques)
Fluorspar - Production, metric tons (thousands)	6	41	95	91	72	97	70	43	7	Spath fluor - Production, tonnes métriques (milliers)
Gold ores and concentrates - Production (Kilograms)	1 135	2 035	1 642	3 643	2 100	237	337	197	503	Minerais d'or et leurs concentrés - Production (Kilogrammes)

VI ENERGY - ENERGIE

	2009	2010	2011	2012	2013	2014	2015	2016	2017	
Total electricity generation (GWh)	6 507	6 976	7 560	7 851	8 448	9 139	10 109	...	...	Production électrique totale (GWh)
of which										dont
Production of electricity from fossil fuels (GWh)	3 029	2 201	2 801	2 200	2 162	2 585	3 683	...	...	Production d'électricité à partir de combustibles fossiles (GWh)
Production of hydro electricity (GWh)	2 160	3 224	3 217	4 016	4 435	3 569	...	...	...	Production d'électricité d'origine hydraulique (GWh)
Production of electricity from solar, wind, tide, wave and other sources (GWh)	1 318	1 551	1 542	1 635	1 851	2 985	...	...	...	Production d'électricité d'origine solaire, éolienne, marée motrice et autres (GWh)

VII TOURISM AND INFRASTRUCTURE - TOURISME ET INFRASTUCTURE

	2009	2010	2011	2012	2013	2014	2015	2016	2017	
VII-1 Tourism										**VII-1 Tourisme**
International tourist arrivals (thousands)	1 392	1 470	1 750	1 619	1 434	1 261	1 114	1 301	1 428	Arrivées de touristes internationaux (milliers)
Rooms in hotels and similar establishments (thousands)	10	10	11	12	11	12	12	14	...	Chambres d'hôtels et établissements assimilés (milliers)
Overnight stays (thousands)	4 062	4 260	4 353	4 027	3 840	3 234	2 622	3 355	3 774	Nuitées (milliers)
Tourism receipts (US$ thousand)	689 900	800 100	925 900	934 800	880 700	810 700	724 000	823 800	969 184	Recettes touristiques (milliers de $ EU)
Total contribution to GDP (%)	10.4	11.1	11.4	11.4	10.5	10.2	9.7	9.3	9.7	Contribution totale au PIB (%)
Total contribution to Employment (%)	9.7	10.4	10.8	10.6	9.8	9.5	9.1	8.7	9.0	Contribution totale à l'emploi (%)
VII-2 Infrastructure										**VII-2 Infrastructure**
Paved road (% of total)	13.6	14.0	14.0	15.7	12.0	17.1	...	...	...	Routes asphaltées (% du total)
Total network (Railways-km)	2 064	2 064	2 064	2 064	...	...	...	...	...	Réseau total voies ferrées-Km
Main telephone lines (per 100 inhabitants)	1.7	0.9	0.7	0.6	...	...	...	...	...	Lignes téléphoniques fixes (pour 100 habitants)
Mobile cellular subscribers (per 100 inhabitants)	48.6	61.0	66.8	71.2	71.8	73.8	80.7	81.3	...	Abonnés aux téléphones mobiles (pour 100 habitants)
Internet users per 100 inhabitants	6.1	7.2	8.8	10.5	13.0	16.5	21.0	26.0	...	Utilisateurs Internet par 100 Habitants
Fixed (wired)-broadband subscriptions per 100 inhabitants	...	...	...	...	...	...	...	...	...	Abonnements à l'Internet fixe (filaire) à large bande pour 100 habitants, par débit

VIII EXTERNAL TRADE - COMMERCE EXTERIEUR

	2009	2010	2011	2012	2013	2014	2015	2016	2017	
US$ (MILLIONS) **EXPORTS, FOB**										**$ E.U (MILLIONS)** **EXPORTATIONS, FÂB**
Exports - Total	4 463	5 169	5 599	5 877	5 537	5 782	5 585	5 385	...	Exportations - Total
Exports to Africa	1 961	2 197	2 734	2 754	2 374	2 507	2 359	2 201	...	Exportations vers l'Afrique
Main products										**Principaux produits**
Coffee and coffee substitutes	211	226	242	246	183	268	227	245	...	Café et succédanés du café
Crude vegetable materials, n.e.s.	584	624	579	600	640	694	581	568	...	Matières végétales brutes, n.e.s.
Petroleum oils or bituminous minerals > 70 % oil	196	224	256	303	450	292	195	130	...	Huiles de pétrole ou de minéraux bitumineux> 70% d'huile
Tea and mate	846	1 092	1 135	1 202	1 150	971	1 113	1 063	...	Thé et maté
Vegetables	235	293	262	263	233	265	244	251	...	Légumes
Main destinations										**Principales destinations**
Netherlands	407	417	364	371	405	463	402	401	...	Pays-Bas
Uganda	548	603	842	803	578	677	644	560	...	Ouganda
United Kingdom	518	527	517	486	402	409	398	397	...	Royaume-Uni
Tanzania, United Republic of	345	359	460	550	357	487	486	472	...	Tanzanie, République Unie de
United States	259	314	283	316	366	436	422	416	...	États-Unis
IMPORTS, CIF										
Imports - Total	10 202	12 093	14 799	16 317	16 394	18 437	16 129	14 137	...	Importations - Total (millions)
Imports from Africa	1 481	1 557	1 710	1 672	1 695	1 644	1 637	1 642	...	Importations en provenance de l'Afrique
Main products										**Principaux produits**
Fixed vegetable fats & oils, crude, refined, fract.	182	269	496	453	346	452	385	358	...	Graisses et huiles végétales fixes, brutes, raffinées, fract.
Motor vehicles for the transport of persons	289	358	334	375	481	492	492	423	...	Véhicules à moteur pour le transport de personnes
Petroleum oils or bituminous minerals > 70 % oil	1 390	1 692	2 456	2 912	3 039	2 960	1 841	1 417	...	Huiles de pétrole ou de minéraux bitumineux> 70% d'huile
Petroleum oils, oils from bitumin. materials, crude	414	790	1 385	1 186	325	788	511	411	...	Huiles de pétrole, huiles de bitume. matériaux bruts
Telecommunication equipment, n.e.s.; & parts, n.e.s.	362	503	404	461	422	501	528	483	...	Matériel de télécommunication, n.es ; & parties, n.e.s.
Main origin										**Principales provenances**
China	1 092	1 603	1 620	1 987	2 451	2 819	3 332	3 390	...	Chine
India	1 184	1 601	1 691	2 319	3 103	3 007	1 898	1 581	...	Inde
Japan	567	656	662	750	864	984	930	762	...	Japon
United Arab Emirates	939	1 138	2 254	1 784	1 165	1 175	1 084	1 059	...	Emirates Arabes
United States	633	419	503	786	598	1 913	1 071	451	...	États-Unis

	2009	2010	2011	2012	2013	2014	2015	2016	2017	
IX-1 MONETARY STATISTICS *KENYAN SHILLING (MILLIONS)*										**IX-1 STATISTIQUES MONÉTAIRES** *SHILLING KENYAN (MILLIONS)*
Money supply (M1)	1 045 657	1 271 638	1 514 152	1 727 324	1 996 241	2 329 979	2 658 166	2 753 528	3 119 599	Masse monétaire (M1)
Quasi-money	515 682	597 485	764 029	886 752	996 984	1 245 995	1 447 512	1 258 438	1 345 095	Quasi-monnaie
of which demand deposit	...	...	...	...	...	...	...	...	...	dont Monnaie scripturale
Net foreign assets	243 450	269 412	294 295	328 307	390 135	483 262	492 963	496 241	518 557	Avoirs extérieurs nets
Domestic credit	1 018 813	1 301 978	1 552 896	1 799 875	2 037 491	2 417 379	2 841 228	3 062 443	3 303 237	Crédit intérieur
of which claims on private sector	228 125	361 825	314 659	419 853	409 199	423 630	503 346	580 623	746 807	dont créances sur le secteur privé
of which claims on government sector, net	716 541	862 950	1 139 112	1 258 645	1 504 813	1 844 124	2 152 112	2 351 930	2 399 613	dont créances nettes sur le gouvernement
International reserves (millions US$)	3 847	4 002	4 248	5 702	6 560	7 895	7 534	7 546	9 012	Réserves internationales (millions $EU)
Average exchange rate (National currency per US$)	77	79	89	85	86	88	98	102	103	Taux de change (moyen) (monnaie nationale par $ EU)
IX-2 PUBLIC FINANCE *KENYAN SHILLING (MILLIONS)*										**IX-2 FINANCES PUBLIQUES** *SHILLING KENYAN (MILLIONS)*
Total Revenues and Grants	505 958	617 567	678 857	763 772	896 497	1 001 375	1 140 407	1 254 876	1 524 210	Recettes totales et dons
Direct taxes (on income, profits)	184 447	216 760	272 439	312 463	373 086	449 590	509 160	569 811	662 854	Taxes directes
Domestic indirect taxes revenues	196 726	221 436	252 448	255 270	308 930	367 981	411 396	451 896	543 696	Taxes Indirectes
Trade taxes	36 181	41 372	46 072	51 712	81 813	94 233	101 041	104 433	119 643	Taxes sur le commerce extérieur
Other taxes	...	...	...	...	...	...	...	...	...	Autres taxes
Other revenues	70 539	106 809	88 645	128 682	111 679	62 614	90 693	99 139	176 705	Autres recettes
Grants	18 065	31 190	19 253	15 645	20 990	26 957	28 117	29 597	21 312	Dons
Total Expenditures and Net Lending	595 598	792 943	819 767	945 313	1 132 126	1 300 589	1 639 199	1 746 452	2 152 083	Dépenses totales et prêts nets
Current expenditure	383 363	471 566	505 245	568 495	695 120	617 682	688 686	798 721	910 604	Dépenses courantes
Wages and Salaries	155 220	173 499	197 959	218 833	274 407	281 197	297 978	307 421	340 000	Rémunérations et salaires
Other purchases of goods and services	200 952	269 626	280 616	323 580	393 102	306 330	353 200	437 899	507 671	Achat de biens et services
Other current expenditure	...	...	...	...	...	...	...	...	...	Autres dépenses courantes
Current transfers	27 191	28 441	26 670	26 082	27 611	30 155	37 508	53 401	62 933	Transferts courants
Interest payments	52 058	64 779	78 876	81 913	121 235	134 821	171 876	193 328	240 000	Intérêts
Capital expenditure	160 177	255 398	233 146	292 305	313 371	545 786	775 737	749 403	1 001 479	Dépenses d'équipement
Net lending	...	1 200	2 500	2 600	2 400	2 300	2 900	5 000	...	Prêts nets
Fiscal balance	- 89 640	- 175 376	- 140 910	- 181 541	- 235 629	- 299 214	- 498 792	- 491 576	- 627 873	Solde global y compris les dons
IX-3 BALANCE OF PAYMENTS *KENYAN SHILLING (MILLIONS)*										**IX-3 BALANCE DES PAIEMENTS** *SHILLING KENYAN (MILLIONS)*
Trade balance	- 383 078	- 492 544	- 742 044	- 787 364	- 882 179	- 941 665	- 822 276	- 800 888	...	Balance commerciale
Services Balance	83 861	138 282	177 194	220 159	251 926	147 242	129 355	171 654	...	Balance des services
Net primary income	- 11 318	- 17 709	- 11 572	- 26 684	- 51 671	- 76 338	- 67 161	- 69 415	...	Revenus primaires nets
Compensation of employees	...	...	...	...	...	...	...	...	...	Rémunération des salariés
Investment income	...	...	...	...	...	...	...	...	...	Revenus des investissements
Net secondary income	177 853	184 393	237 227	237 499	264 905	310 000	339 001	327 847	...	Revenus secondaires nets
Net official transfers	...	...	...	...	...	...	...	...	...	Transferts officiels nets
Workers' remittances	...	...	...	...	...	...	...	...	...	Envois de fonds des travailleurs
Other private transfers	...	...	...	...	...	...	...	...	...	Autres transferts privés
Current account balance	- 132 683	- 187 577	- 339 195	- 356 389	- 417 020	- 560 761	- 421 082	- 370 802	...	Solde du compte courant
Capital and financial account	312 206	276 864	324 990	489 865	459 882	674 570	409 439	440 876	...	Comptes de capital et financier
Capital account	20 178	19 030	20 861	19 890	13 644	24 204	25 718	20 878	...	Compte de capital
Financial account	292 028	257 834	304 130	469 975	446 238	650 366	383 721	419 998	...	Compte financier
Errors and omissions	- 93 788	- 75 408	- 65 409	- 30 119	- 11 096	14 034	- 13 262	- 56 978	...	Erreurs et omissions
Overall balance	85 735	13 879	- 79 613	103 357	31 766	127 842	- 24 905	13 096	...	Balance générale

KENYA

	2009	2010	2011	2012	2013	2014	2015	2016	2017	
X-1 DEBT US $ (MILLIONS)										**X-1 DETTE EXTÉRIEURE** $ E.U (MILLIONS)
Total external debt	10 648	11 976	12 972	15 244	16 162	22 097	25 632	29 122	34 275	Dette extérieure totale
Private	...	...	...	...	...	...	...	...	...	Privée
Public	7 748	8 607	9 316	10 642	10 642	14 047	15 787	17 880	...	Publique
Total external debt service	1 851	2 390	3 717	4 688	5 969	7 754	5 397	5 810	...	Service de la dette extérieure
Present value of external debt	...	...	...	...	...	...	...	14 772	...	Valeur actuelle de la dette extérieure
Total government domestic debt, National currency (millions)	585 536	711 123	807 831	768 569	889 121	1 078 807	...	...	...	Dette publique intérieure
X-2 FINANCIAL FLOWS US $ (MILLIONS)										**X-2 FLUX FINANCIERS** $ E.U (MILLIONS)
Net Foreign Direct Investment Inflows	115	178	335	1 380	1 119	821	620	394	...	Investissements étranger direct (flux nets entrants)
Main origin of FDI inflows										**Principales origines de l'IDE entrant:**
United Kingdom	179	301	101	- 9	...	...	...	...	...	Royaume-Uni
France	13	- 1	17	45	...	...	...	...	...	France
Belgium	215	123	21	- 331	...	...	...	...	...	Belgique
Germany	- 18	...	...	...	...	...	...	...	...	Allemagne
...	...	...	...	...	...	...	...	...	...	...
African countries	...	...	1	...	...	...	...	...	...	Pays africains
Net total official development assistance	1 782	1 631	2 479	2 654	3 307	2 661	2 464	2 189	...	Aide publique au développement (nette totale)
Main origin of net ODA										**Principales origines de l'APD nette**
United States	590	562	712	818	894	807	712	806	...	États-Unis
United Kingdom	131	105	142	161	249	222	238	181	...	Royaume-Uni
International Development Association [IDA]	83	133	165	193	383	478	422	343	...	International Development Association
Germany	86	80	157	157	99	106	47	29	...	Allemagne
Japan	34	37	81	132	270	46	163	83	...	Japon

KENYA

SOURCES AND NOTES - SOURCES ET NOTES

External trade - Total exports, fob: UNCTAD	Commerce exterieur - Exportation, fab: CNUCED
External trade - Total import, cif: UNCTAD	Commerce exterieur - Imporations, caf: CNUCED
ODA: OECD	APD: OCDE
Monetary statistics: IMF	Statistiques monétaires: FMI
National Accounts: The accounts are calculated using the new base year 2009	Comptes nationaux:Les comptes sont calculés selon la nouvelle année de base 2009
Poverty: World Bank	Pauvreté: Banque mondiale

		Maseru	
AREA (km2)		30 360	**SUPERFICIE (KM2)**
CAPITAL CITY	Maseru	Maseru	**CAPITALE**
CURRENCY	Lesotho Loti	Loti lesothan	**MONNAIE**

I SOCIAL AND DEMOGRAPHIC INDICATORS — INDICATEURS DEMOGRAPHIQUES ET SOCIAUX

	Year Année	Value Valeur	Charts / Graphiques	
Population				**Population**
Population ('000)	2016	2 200.0		Population ('000)
Female (%)	2016	50.8		Féminine (%)
Urban (%)	2015	27.1		Urbaine (%)
Average annual growth rate	2015	1.4		Taux de croissance annuel
Active population ('000)	2015	657.1		Population active ('000)
Population by age group ('000)				Population par groupe d'âge ('000)
0-14 years	2016	783.0		0-14 ans
15-64 years	...	...		15-64 ans
65+ years	...	...		65+ ans
Economically active population in agriculture (%)	2015	57.4		Participation de la population active agricole (%)
Crude birth rate	2015	28.5		Taux brut de natalité
Crude death rate	2015	14.7		Taux brut de mortalité
Total fertility rate	2015	3.1		Indice synthétique de fécondité
Life expectancy at birth - Total (years)	2015	50.1		Espérance de vie à la naissance - Totale (années)
Dependency ratio - Total (%)	2015	67.3		Taux de dépendance - Total (%)
Health				**Santé**
Percentage of children under-five and underweight	2010	13.5		% d'enfants de moins de cinq ans avec insuffisance pondérale
Prevalence of undernourishment	2015	11.2		Prévalence de la malnutrition
Under five mortality rate (per 1 000 live births)	2015	90.2		Taux de mortalité de moins de 5 ans (les deux sexes, pour 1000)
Infant mortality rate (per 1 000 live births)	2015	69.2		Taux de mortalité infantile (les deux sexes) par 1000
Neonatal mortality rate (per 1 000 live births)	2015	32.7		Le taux de mortalité néonatale (pour 1000 naissances vivantes)
Percentage of children provided the vaccines :				Pourcentage d'enfants vaccinés :
BCG	2014	87.0		BCG
DPT3	2014	96.0		DTC3
Polio	2013	95.0		polio
Measles	2014	92.0		rougeole
Percentage of mothers provided at least one antenatal care (%)	2009	91.8		Pourcentage de mères ayant au moins reçu un soin prénatal (%)
Percentage of deliveries attended by skilled health personnel	2009	61.5		% d'accouchements assistés par un personnel de santé qualifié
Number of doctors (per 10,000 population)	2003	0.5		Nombre de médecins (pour 10.000 habitants)
Number of nurses (per 10,000 population)	2003	6.2		Nombre d'infirmiers (pour 10.000 habitants)
Hospital beds - Total (per 10,000 population)	2006	13.3		Nombre de lits d'hôpitaux - Total (pour 10 000)
Births registered (per 1,000)	2015	28.5		Naissances enregistrées (pour 1000)
Deaths registered (per 1,000)	2015	14.7		Décès enregistrés (pour 1000)
Budget allocation to health (%)	2013	14.5		Dépenses publiques consacrées à la santé (% du budget)
Education				**Education**
Enrolment in primary education (000)	2014	366.0		Scolarisation dans le primaire (000)
Female	2014	179.4		Féminine
Enrolment in secondary education (000)	2013	127.1		Scolarisation dans le secondaire (000)
Female	2013	72.5		Féminine
Enrolment in tertiary education (000)	2014	23.5		Scolarisation dans le tertiaire (000)
Female	2014	13.8		Féminine
Literacy rate	2011	87.4		Taux d'alphabétisation (deux sexes)
Male	...	...		Masculin
Female	...	...		Féminin
Pupil teacher ratio - primary	2013	33.0		Ratio élève-enseignant
Budget allocation to education (%)	2011	21.5		Dépenses publiques consacrées à l'enseignement (% du budget)
Poverty				**Pauvreté**
GNI per capita, PPP (current int. $)	2016	3340.0		RNB par habitant, ($ PPA inter. courants)
Human Poverty Index (HPI-1) Value (%)	2007	34.3		Valeur de l'Indice de pauvreté (IPH-1) (%)
Population below Inter. poverty line ($2/ day) (%)	2010	59.7		Population sous le seuil inter. de pauvreté (2$/Jour) (%)
Share of income held by richest 10%	2010	40.9		% de revenu des 10% plus riches
Share of income held by poorest 10%	2010	0.9		% de revenu des 10% plus pauvres
GINI index	2010	54.2		Indice de GINI

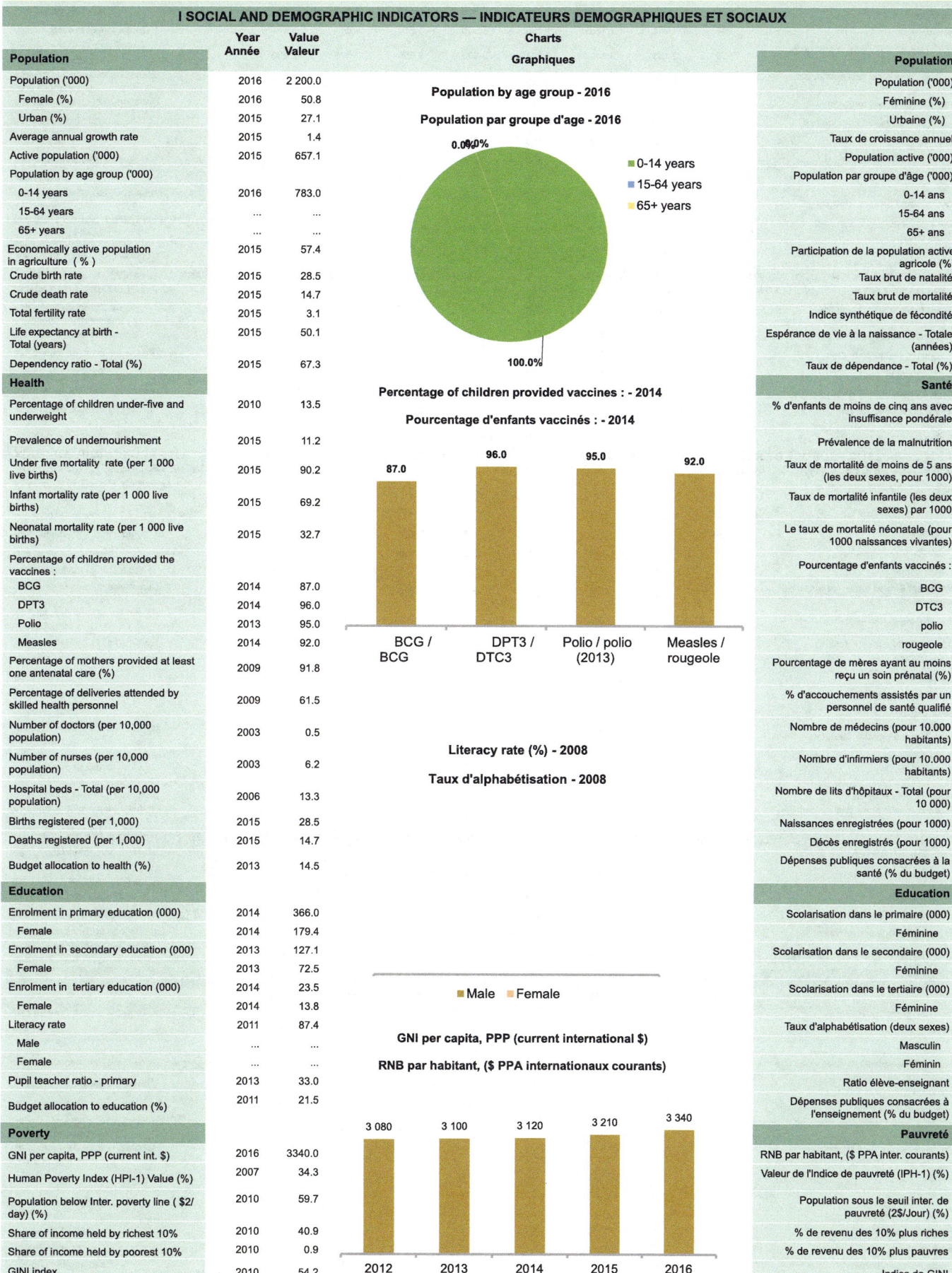

Population by age group - 2016
Population par groupe d'age - 2016

0.0% 0.0%
- 0-14 years
- 15-64 years
- 65+ years

100.0%

Percentage of children provided vaccines : - 2014
Pourcentage d'enfants vaccinés : - 2014

BCG / BCG	DPT3 / DTC3	Polio / polio (2013)	Measles / rougeole
87.0	96.0	95.0	92.0

Literacy rate (%) - 2008
Taux d'alphabétisation - 2008

■ Male ■ Female

GNI per capita, PPP (current international $)
RNB par habitant, ($ PPA internationaux courants)

2012	2013	2014	2015	2016
3 080	3 100	3 120	3 210	3 340

	2009	2010	2011	2012	2013	2014	2015	2016	2017	
GROSS DOMESTIC PRODUCT BY KIND OF ECONOMIC ACTIVITY AT CURRENT PRICES *LESOTHO LOTI (MILLIONS)*										**PRODUIT INTÉRIEUR BRUT PAR BRANCHE D'ACTIVITÉ ÉCONOMIQUE AUX PRIX COURANTS** *LOTI LESOTHAN (MILLIONS)*
Agriculture, hunting , forestry and Fishing	907	895	1 043	1 099	1 445	1 595	1 589	1 752	...	Agriculture, chasse sylviculture et Pêche
Mining and quarrying	716	893	1 657	1 211	1 430	2 390	2 590	2 775	...	Industries extractives
Manufacturing	2 612	2 189	2 437	2 385	2 590	3 402	4 675	5 247	...	Industries manufacturières
Electricity, gas & water	774	979	1 092	1 209	1 316	1 451	1 591	1 657	...	Electricité, gaz et eau
Construction	944	1 211	1 166	1 608	1 505	1 519	1 641	1 457	...	Bâtiments et travaux publics
Wholesale & retail trade, restaurants, hotels	1 959	2 165	2 445	2 911	3 383	3 555	3 525	3 835	...	Commerce de gros et de détail, restaurants et hôtels
Finance, insurance, real estate, etc.	2 268	2 442	2 664	2 865	3 396	4 076	4 871	4 742	...	Banques, assurances, affaires immobilières
Transport and communications	885	1 012	1 117	1 215	1 377	1 617	1 716	1 848	...	Transport(s) et communications
Public administration and defense	1 969	2 155	2 400	2 709	2 711	2 971	3 379	3 594	...	Administrations publiques et défense
Education	1 405	1 578	1 798	1 808	2 024	2 125	2 247	2 401	...	Education
Health And Social Work	272	289	433	590	672	834	917	1 021	...	Santé et Actions Sociales
Other services	200	218	217	239	249	268	265	287	...	Autres services
Less Imputed Service Charges	- 179	- 168	- 166	- 185	- 230	- 299	- 355	- 377	...	Moins Services d'intermédiation financière
Gross domestic product at factor cost / basic prices	14 734	15 860	18 303	19 664	21 867	25 504	28 649	30 240	...	Produit intérieur brut aux couts des facteurs / prix de base
Plus: Indirect Taxes / taxes on products, less subsidies	1 078	1 608	1 941	2 327	2 522	2 871	3 324	3 465	...	Plus taxes indirectes/impôts sur les produits, moins les subventions
EXPENDITURE ON GROSS DOMESTIC PRODUCT AT CURRENT PURCHASER'S VALUES *LESOTHO LOTI (MILLIONS)*										**EMPLOI DU PRODUIT INTÉRIEUR BRUT AUX PRIX COURANTS D'ACQUISITION** *LOTI LESOTHAN (MILLIONS)*
Government final consumption	6 077	6 550	7 064	8 206	8 455	10 386	11 193	11 760	...	Consommation finale des administrations publiques
Private final consumption	15 586	16 728	18 770	20 293	21 688	22 316	24 807	26 186	...	Consommation finale privée
Gross fixed capital formation	4 063	4 643	5 094	7 092	6 838	7 754	8 330	8 073	...	Formation brute de capital fixe
Change in inventories	319	319	- 506	- 46	396	1 163	871	1 466	...	Variation des stocks
Exports of goods and services	6 603	6 891	8 937	8 504	8 737	10 107	12 913	14 239	...	Exportations de biens et services
Less imports of goods and services	16 836	17 663	19 115	22 059	21 725	23 351	26 142	28 020	...	Moins importations de biens et services
GDP at purchasers' values	15 812	17 468	20 244	21 990	24 389	28 375	31 972	33 704	...	PIB aux prix d'acquisition
GROSS DOMESTIC PRODUCT BY KIND OF ECONOMIC ACTIVITY AT CONSTANT PRICES *ANNUAL GROWTH RATES (%)*										**PRODUIT INTÉRIEUR BRUT PAR BRANCHE D'ACTIVITÉ ECONOMIQUE AUX PRIX CONSTANTS** *TAUX DE CROISSANCE ANNUEL (%)*
Agriculture, hunting , forestry and Fishing	5.4	- 5.2	5.3	- 3.4	24.5	3.5	- 6.9	7.2	...	Agriculture, chasse sylviculture et Pêche
Mining and quarrying	- 32.4	5.3	44.3	- 0.3	- 27.5	11.8	0.8	- 2.4	...	Industries extractives
Manufacturing	- 3.5	4.0	- 3.0	- 3.6	- 2.5	- 8.4	12.3	21.7	...	Industries manufacturières
Electricity, gas & water	- 1.7	0.6	- 2.3	- 1.1	- 3.2	1.6	- 2.4	- 2.6	...	Electricité, gaz et eau
Construction	13.7	22.5	- 5.9	35.1	- 9.0	- 2.6	4.8	- 13.5	...	Bâtiments et travaux publics
Wholesale & retail trade, restaurants, hotels	- 0.5	6.8	7.6	12.3	11.3	0.3	- 5.4	0.6	...	Commerce de gros et de détail, restaurants et hôtels
Finance, insurance, real estate, etc.	3.8	7.1	8.1	7.7	9.8	11.9	10.3	- 3.3	...	Banques, assurances, affaires immobilières
Transport and communications	7.6	12.0	9.1	5.7	11.6	13.6	7.7	8.7	...	Transport(s) et communications
Public administration and defense	13.4	2.1	9.7	4.9	- 7.9	1.8	6.9	1.7	...	Administrations publiques et défense
Education	14.7	10.5	3.2	- 1.7	0.4	...	- 0.4	1.5	...	Education
Health And Social Work	12.8	...	46.7	26.9	7.3	18.8	4.1	6.1	...	Santé et Actions Sociales
Other services	- 0.5	5.1	- 1.3	6.7	1.7	5.3	- 4.7	7.4	...	Autres services
Less Imputed Service Charges	- 6.3	21.8	11.7	2.2	14.1	5.7	9.4	0.8	...	Moins Services d'intermédiation financière
Gross domestic product at factor cost / basic prices	2.2	5.8	6.5	5.9	1.3	3.4	3.3	2.5	...	Produit intérieur brut aux couts des facteurs / prix de base
Plus: Indirect Taxes / taxes on products, less subsidies	2.1	8.9	10.1	6.9	6.3	1.1	- 4.2	1.4	...	Plus taxes indirectes/impôts sur les produits, moins les subventions
Gross domestic product at market prices	2.2	6.1	6.9	6.0	1.8	3.1	2.5	2.4	...	Produit intérieur brut aux prix du marché
EXPENDITURE ON GROSS DOMESTIC PRODUCT AT CONSTANT PURCHASERS' VALUES *ANNUAL GROWTH RATES (%)*										**EMPLOIS DU PRODUIT INTÉRIEUR BRUT AUX PRIX CONSTANTS D'ACQUISITION** *TAUX DE CROISSANCE ANNUEL (%)*
Government final consumption	8.0	3.3	3.0	10.8	- 3.6	14.8	0.2	2.9	...	Consommation finale des administrations publiques
Private final consumption	3.5	5.8	6.3	0.5	0.6	- 4.2	5.7	- 0.9	...	Consommation finale privée
Gross fixed capital formation	4.8	12.7	6.1	32.3	- 9.9	5.6	3.5	- 6.2	...	Formation brute de capital fixe
Exports of goods and services	- 7.4	0.5	11.9	- 0.3	- 8.3	- 9.0	13.0	7.8	...	Exportations de biens et services
Less imports of goods and services	2.5	3.9	2.8	8.5	- 7.6	- 1.0	7.8	0.8	...	Moins importations de biens et services

III INFLATION

	2009	2010	2011	2012	2013	2014	2015	2016	2017	
Annual growth rates (%)										**Taux de croissance annuel (%)**
All item	7.4	3.6	5.0	6.1	5.0	5.3	3.2	6.6	5.3	Ensemble
of which:										dont:
Food and non-alcoholic beverages	8.5	3.5	7.0	9.9	5.4	5.3	6.1	11.9	6.9	Alimentation et boissons non alcoolisés
Alcoholic beverages, tobacco and narcotics	6.9	9.3	6.4	6.9	5.6	6.5	6.0	4.2	4.9	Boissons alcoolisées et tabacs
Clothing and footwear	6.4	3.3	1.5	1.0	1.6	3.7	4.3	4.6	3.6	Habillement et chaussures
Housing, water, electricity, gas and other fuels	- 0.3	3.3	11.6	8.4	10.6	7.7	- 6.9	0.4	6.8	Logement, eau, électricité, gaz et autres combustibles
Furnishings, household equipment and routine household maintenance	7.2	3.0	3.3	2.9	3.8	2.8	3.8	4.0	3.5	Meubles, articles de ménage et entretien courant
Health	2.4	2.3	1.4	0.5	0.6	1.0	1.1	1.8	0.4	Santé
Transport	5.8	4.1	2.9	7.0	4.1	10.2	0.3	1.1	1.1	Transport
Communication	- 0.8	1.4	1.1	- 0.5	- 0.1	...	...	...	...	Communication
Recreation and culture	7.1	2.0	1.4	2.3	0.9	1.2	3.3	1.4	4.5	Loisirs et culture
Education	2.0	6.2	1.0	0.7	13.5	7.1	3.9	4.9	5.9	Enseignement
Restaurants and hotels	9.0	5.0	3.7	0.2	0.8	2.2	3.1	2.4	1.4	Restaurants et hôtels
Miscellaneous goods and services	6.7	3.7	2.6	2.1	2.8	4.4	4.1	4.2	4.5	Biens et Services divers

LESOTHO

IV AGRICULTURAL PRODUCTION - PRODUCTION AGRICOLE

	2009	2010	2011	2012	2013	2014	2015	2016	2017	
TONNES (THOUSAND)										**Tonnes (milliers)**
Maize	91	99	112	115	125	131	121	122	...	Maïs
Sorghum	57	128	73	78	86	90	71	25	...	Sorgho
Wheat	7	20	20	11	13	13	10	4	...	Blé
Beans, dry	10	24	10	2	7	5	5	5	...	Haricots secs
Peas	3	9	7	5	3	2	3	4	...	Pois

V MINING PRODUCTION - PRODUCTION MINIERE

	2009	2010	2011	2012	2013	2014	2015	2016	2017	
Diamonds and other precious stones, unworked - Production, carat (thousands)	-	-	-	0	-	...	...	...	...	Diamants et autres pierres gemmes (précieuses), bruts - Production, carat (milliers)
	...	...	...	...	...	...	...	...	...	
	...	...	...	...	...	...	...	...	...	

VI ENERGY - ENERGIE

	2009	2010	2011	2012	2013	2014	2015	2016	2017	
Total electricity generation (GWh)	648	694	566	280	385	385	385	...	...	Production électrique totale (GWh)
of which										dont
Production of electricity from fossil fuels (GWh)	...	...	...	...	...	...	...	...	...	Production d'électricité à partir de combustibles fossiles (GWh)
Production of hydro electricity (GWh)	648	694	566	280	385	385	385	...	...	Production d'électricité d'origine hydraulique (GWh)
Production of electricity from solar, wind, tide, wave and other sources (GWh)	...	...	...	...	...	...	...	...	...	Production d'électricité d'origine solaire, éolienne, marée motrice et autres (GWh)

VII TOURISM AND INFRASTRUCTURE - TOURISME ET INFRASTUCTURE

	2009	2010	2011	2012	2013	2014	2015	2016	2017	
VII-1 Tourism										**VII-1 Tourisme**
International tourist arrivals (thousands)	320	414	397	317	320	797	800	884	1 001	Arrivées de touristes internationaux (milliers)
Rooms in hotels and similar establishments (thousands)	2	3	3	3	3	3	3	3		Chambres d'hôtels et établissements assimilés (milliers)
Overnight stays (thousands)	903	1 179	1 133	904	911	2 219	2 257	2 179	2 493	Nuitées (milliers)
Tourism receipts (US$ thousand)	29 501	22 600	23 502	21 207	16 995	15 994	34 198	47 898	57 843	Recettes touristiques (milliers de $ EU)
Total contribution to GDP (%)	16.5	11.5	12.7	12.5	12.8	12.1	14.0	14.7	13.8	Contribution totale au PIB (%)
Total contribution to Employment (%)	16.6	11.9	11.3	10.6	11.0	10.5	12.5	13.6	13.5	Contribution totale à l'emploi (%)
VII-2 Infrastructure										**VII-2 Infrastructure**
Paved road (% of total)	19.8	...	18.0	...	...	...	...	...	...	Routes asphaltées (% du total)
Total network (Railways-km)	...	...	...	...	...	...	...	...	...	Réseau total voies ferrées-Km
Main telephone lines (per 100 inhabitants)	2.0	1.9	1.9	2.5	2.4	2.4	2.1	1.9	...	Lignes téléphoniques fixes (pour 100 habitants)
Mobile cellular subscribers (per 100 inhabitants)	33.2	49.2	60.7	75.3	86.3	102.0	100.9	106.6	...	Abonnés aux téléphones mobiles (pour 100 habitants)
Internet users per 100 inhabitants	3.7	3.9	7.0	10.0	15.0	22.0	25.0	27.4	...	Utilisateurs Internet par 100 Habitants
Fixed (wired)-broadband subscriptions per 100 inhabitants	...	...	...	...	...	...	...	...	...	Abonnements à l'Internet fixe (filaire) à large bande pour 100 habitants, par débit

VIII EXTERNAL TRADE - COMMERCE EXTERIEUR

	2009	2010	2011	2012	2013	2014	2015	2016	2017	
US$ (MILLIONS) EXPORTS, FOB										**$ E.U (MILLIONS) EXPORTATIONS, FÂB**
Exports - Total	734	878	1 172	972	847	826	844	894	...	Exportations - Total
Exports to Africa	259	403	439	392	338	328	336	356	...	Exportations vers l'Afrique
Main products										**Principaux produits**
Apparatus for electrical circuits; board, panels	19	53	71	60	56	57	57	61	...	Appareils pour circuits électriques; panneau, panneaux
Articles of apparel, of textile fabrics, n.e.s.	117	80	118	99	82	79	83	87	...	Vêtements, en tissus, n.d.a.
Men's clothing of textile fabrics, not knitted	92	90	173	134	119	122	125	132	...	Vêtements pour hommes en matières textiles, non tricotés
Pearls, precious & semi-precious stones	107	224	274	195	189	184	183	196	...	Perles, pierres précieuses et semi-précieuses
Women's clothing, of textile, knitted or crocheted	43	53	94	103	76	77	84	86	...	Vêtements pour femmes, en textile, en bonneterie
Main destinations										**Principales destinations**
Belgium	89	206	223	178	162	156	160	169	...	Belgique
Canada	62	14	35	9	14	14	13	14	...	Canada
South Africa	247	369	390	347	302	293	300	317	...	Afrique du Sud
Swaziland	2	29	33	30	26	25	26	27	...	Swaziland
United States	311	238	438	362	308	305	310	329	...	États-Unis
IMPORTS, CIF										
Imports - Total	1 850	2 300	2 500	2 602	2 175	2 144	2 018	1 851	...	Importations - Total (millions)
Imports from Africa	1 620	1 862	2 277	2 274	1 909	1 889	1 774	1 629	...	Importations en provenance de l'Afrique
Main products										**Principaux produits**
Apparatus for electrical circuits; board, panels	29	99	58	51	59	54	56	49	...	Principaux produits
Knitted or crocheted fabrics, n.e.s.	75	87	83	109	85	87	80	74	...	Appareils pour circuits électriques; panneau, panneaux
Motor vehicles for the transport of persons	14	57	57	67	54	55	60	51	...	Tissus tricotés ou crochetés, n.d.a.
Other meat and edible meat offal	46	53	52	50	51	55	51	47	...	Véhicules à moteur pour le transport de personnes
Petroleum oils or bituminous minerals > 70 % oil	97	161	342	353	272	284	187	210	...	Autres viandes et abats comestibles
Main origin										**Principales provenances**
China	32	74	59	104	75	75	72	65	...	Chine
China, Hong Kong SAR	33	28	16	21	18	17	16	15	...	China, Hong Kong
TAIWAN, PROVINCE OF CHINA	60	97	64	115	84	83	80	72	...	TAÏWAN, PROVINCE DE CHINE
India	8	31	23	19	19	18	17	15	...	Inde
South Africa	1 580	1 837	2 248	2 259	1 893	1 873	1 759	1 616	...	Afrique du Sud

LÉSOTHO

IX FINANCIAL AND MONETARY STATISTICS - FINANCES ET STATISTIQUES MONETAIRES

	2009	2010	2011	2012	2013	2014	2015	2016	2017	
IX-1 MONETARY STATISTICS *LESOTHO LOTI (MILLIONS)*										**IX-1 STATISTIQUES MONÉTAIRES** *LOTI LESOTHAN (MILLIONS)*
Money supply (M1)	5 747	6 578	6 504	6 922	9 105	9 240	9 829	10 561	11 974	Masse monétaire (M1)
Quasi-money	1 568	1 589	3 859	3 672	4 673	4 907	4 839	4 769	5 945	Quasi-monnaie
of which demand deposit	...	...	...	...	...	...	...	...	...	dont Monnaie scripturale
Net foreign assets	10 840	10 104	9 906	10 141	12 835	13 964	16 133	13 017	12 619	Avoirs extérieurs nets
Domestic credit	- 2 136	- 1 001	127	640	390	171	743	3 160	5 456	Crédit intérieur
of which claims on private sector	- 3 996	- 3 198	- 2 572	- 3 149	- 4 178	- 4 963	- 4 790	- 2 584	- 770	dont créances sur le secteur privé
of which claims on government sector, net	1 860	2 194	2 687	3 778	4 556	5 121	5 502	5 665	6 148	dont créances nettes sur le gouvernement
International reserves (millions US$)	1 180	1 076	950	1 016	1 045	1 071	916	841	816	Réserves internationales (millions $EU)
Average exchange rate (National currency per US$)	8	7	7	8	10	11	13	15	13	Taux de change (moyen) (monnaie nationale par $ EU)
IX-2 PUBLIC FINANCE *LESOTHO LOTI (MILLIONS)*										**IX-2 FINANCES PUBLIQUES** *LOTI LESOTHAN (MILLIONS)*
Total Revenues and Grants	9 094	9 438	9 114	9 627	13 145	13 274	14 594	15 321	14 051	Recettes totales et dons
Direct taxes (on income, profits)	1 613	1 868	2 078	2 520	2 498	2 808	3 198	3 644	3 727	Taxes directes
Domestic indirect taxes revenues	1 098	1 170	1 402	1 590	1 819	1 887	2 355	2 683	2 669	Taxes Indirectes
Trade taxes	4 901	4 918	2 628	2 753	5 966	6 055	7 034	6 399	4 519	Taxes sur le commerce extérieur
Other taxes	147	50	401	173	279	453	244	251	613	Autres taxes
Other revenues	841	797	1 404	1 155	879	1 025	1 267	1 378	1 657	Autres recettes
Grants	495	635	1 200	1 437	1 703	1 047	496	966	867	Dons
Total Expenditures and Net Lending	6 528	8 226	7 330	8 522	8 766	10 415	10 734	14 775	15 588	Dépenses totales et prêts nets
Current expenditure	5 372	6 814	6 024	7 059	6 860	8 365	8 587	10 907	12 008	Dépenses courantes
Wages and Salaries	2 144	2 684	2 871	3 129	3 226	3 938	4 219	5 400	5 787	Rémunérations et salaires
Other purchases of goods and services	2 297	2 464	1 815	2 045	2 356	2 972	2 819	2 829	3 412	Achat de biens et services
Other current expenditure	...	...	...	...	...	...	...	...	...	Autres dépenses courantes
Current transfers	932	1 666	1 338	1 886	1 277	1 455	1 549	2 677	2 809	Transferts courants
Interest payments	129	137	96	137	166	189	177	274	255	Intérêts
Capital expenditure	1 027	1 275	1 210	1 325	1 740	1 862	1 970	3 594	3 325	Dépenses d'équipement
Net lending	...	...	...	...	...	...	...	...	...	Prêts nets
Fiscal balance	2 566	1 212	1 783	1 105	4 379	2 860	3 859	546	- 1 536	Solde global y compris les dons
IX-3 BALANCE OF PAYMENTS *LESOTHO LOTI (MILLIONS)*										**IX-3 BALANCE DES PAIEMENTS** *LOTI LESOTHAN (MILLIONS)*
Trade balance	- 7 114	- 8 004	- 7 124	- 10 457	- 9 940	- 11 201	- 11 297	...	...	Balance commerciale
Services Balance	- 3 245	- 2 918	- 3 049	- 3 001	- 2 914	- 3 271	- 3 688	...	...	Balance des services
Net primary income	4 805	4 827	4 624	4 379	4 478	3 308	3 944	...	...	Revenus primaires nets
Compensation of employees	4 536	4 417	4 648	4 496	4 410	...	...	...	...	Rémunération des salariés
Investment income	269	410	- 24	- 117	- 172	...	...	...	...	Revenus des investissements
Net secondary income	6 079	4 894	4 452	7 133	7 986	8 678	8 535	...	...	Revenus secondaires nets
Net official transfers	4 967	3 713	3 159	5 785	6 571	...	...	...	...	Transferts officiels nets
Workers' remittances	...	...	...	...	...	...	...	...	...	Envois de fonds des travailleurs
Other private transfers	...	...	...	...	...	...	...	...	...	Autres transferts privés
Current account balance	525	- 1 200	- 1 097	- 1 946	- 391	- 2 487	- 2 505	...	...	Solde du compte courant
Capital and financial account	735	- 353	1 614	3 088	1 642	...	...	...	...	Comptes de capital et financier
Capital account	592	991	1 379	1 611	1 085	...	...	...	...	Compte de capital
Financial account	142	- 1 344	235	1 477	557	...	...	...	...	Compte financier
Errors and omissions	- 743	605	- 646	- 342	524	...	...	...	...	Erreurs et omissions
Overall balance	- 644	- 1 211	589	1 221	2 401	...	...	...	...	Balance générale

X-1 DEBT US $ (MILLIONS)	2009	2010	2011	2012	2013	2014	2015	2016	2017	X-1 DETTE EXTÉRIEURE $ E.U (MILLIONS)
Total external debt	684	739	766	791	835	914	904	931	949	Dette extérieure totale
Private	...	...	...	...	...	...	...	...	...	Privée
Public	684	739	766	791	835	914	904	931	...	Publique
Total external debt service	44	37	38	32	39	38	63	42	...	Service de la dette extérieure
Present value of external debt	744	1 201	1 034	1 065	884	825	...	679	...	Valeur actuelle de la dette extérieure
Total government domestic debt, National currency (millions)	2 238	1 067	615	369	1 239	639		...	...	Dette publique intérieure
X-2 FINANCIAL FLOWS US $ (MILLIONS)										**X-2 FLUX FINANCIERS** $ E.U (MILLIONS)
Net Foreign Direct Investment Inflows	92	51	149	139	123	162	169	132	...	Investissements étranger direct (flux nets entrants)
Main origin of FDI inflows										**Principales origines de l'IDE entrant:**
	...	...	...	...	...	...	...	...	...	
	...	...	...	...	...	...	...	...	...	
	...	...	...	...	...	...	...	...	...	
	...	...	...	...	...	...	...	...	...	
	...	...	...	...	...	...	...	...	...	
African countries	57	14	...	...	...	...	...	...	...	Pays africains
Net total official development assistance	122	256	257	276	321	107	83	113	...	Aide publique au développement (nette totale)
Main origin of net ODA										**Principales origines de l'APD nette**
United States	25	...	...	-	-	-	-	-	...	États-Unis
Ireland	17	16	16	11	3	2	0	-	...	Irlande
International Development Association [IDA]	11	34	17	- 4	34	5	8	11	...	International Development Association
Global Fund	16	1	1	2	1	4	3	4	...	Fonds Mondial
Japan	3	9	20	3	3	2	2	-	...	Japon

LÉSOTHO

SOURCES AND NOTES - SOURCES ET NOTES

External trade - Total exports, fob: UNCTAD

External trade - Total import, cif: UNCTAD

ODA: OECD

Monetary statistics: IMF

National Accounts: 2013-2014:Estimates   2015:Projection

Poverty: World Bank

Commerce exterieur - Exportation, fab: CNUCED

Commerce exterieur - Imporations, caf: CNUCED

APD: OCDE

Statistiques monétaires: FMI

Comptes nationaux: 2013-2014:Estimées   2015:Projection

Pauvreté: Banque mondiale

AREA (km2)		111 370		**SUPERFICIE (KM2)**
CAPITAL CITY	Monrovia		Monrovia	**CAPITALE**
CURRENCY	Liberian Dollar		Dollar Liberien	**MONNAIE**

I SOCIAL AND DEMOGRAPHIC INDICATORS — INDICATEURS DEMOGRAPHIQUES ET SOCIAUX

	Year Année	Value Valeur	Charts Graphiques	
Population				**Population**
Population ('000)	2016	4 615.0		Population ('000)
Female (%)	2016	49.6		Féminine (%)
Urban (%)	2015	49.7		Urbaine (%)
Average annual growth rate	2016	2.5		Taux de croissance annuel
Active population ('000)	2015	1 517.4		Population active ('000)
Population by age group ('000)				Population par groupe d'âge ('000)
0-14 years	2016	1 940.0		0-14 ans
15-64 years	2016	3 725.0		15-64 ans
65+ years	2016	140.0		65+ ans
Economically active population in agriculture (%)	2015	65.7		Participation de la population active agricole (%)
Crude birth rate	2016	33.7		Taux brut de natalité
Crude death rate	2016	8.1		Taux brut de mortalité
Total fertility rate	2016	4.5		Indice synthétique de fécondité
Life expectancy at birth - Total (years)	2015	61.2		Espérance de vie à la naissance - Totale (années)
Dependency ratio - Total (%)	2016	55.8		Taux de dépendance - Total (%)
Health				**Santé**
Percentage of children under-five and underweight	2013	15.3		% d'enfants de moins de cinq ans avec insuffisance pondérale
Prevalence of undernourishment	2015	31.9		Prévalence de la malnutrition
Under five mortality rate (per 1 000 live births)	2015	69.9		Taux de mortalité de moins de 5 ans (les deux sexes, pour 1000)
Infant mortality rate (per 1 000 live births)	2015	52.8		Taux de mortalité infantile (les deux sexes) par 1000
Neonatal mortality rate (per 1 000 live births)	2015	24.1		Le taux de mortalité néonatale (pour 1000 naissances vivantes)
Percentage of children provided the vaccines :				Pourcentage d'enfants vaccinés :
BCG	2015	93.9		BCG
DPT3	2015	71.4		DTC3
Polio	2015	69.0		polio
Measles	2015	60.0		rougeole
Percentage of mothers provided at least one antenatal care (%)	2013	75.8		Pourcentage de mères ayant au moins reçu un soin prénatal (%)
Percentage of deliveries attended by skilled health personnel	2013	61.1		% d'accouchements assistés par un personnel de santé qualifié
Number of doctors (per 10,000 population)	2008	0.1		Nombre de médecins (pour 10.000 habitants)
Number of nurses (per 10,000 population)	2008	2.7		Nombre d'infirmiers (pour 10.000 habitants)
Hospital beds - Total (per 10,000 population)	2010	8.0		Nombre de lits d'hôpitaux - Total (pour 10 000)
Births registered (per 1,000)	2015	34.6		Naissances enregistrées (pour 1000)
Deaths registered (per 1,000)	2015	8.5		Décès enregistrés (pour 1000)
Budget allocation to health (%)	2013	13.2		Dépenses publiques consacrées à la santé (% du budget)
Education				**Education**
Enrolment in primary education (000)	2015	684.0		Scolarisation dans le primaire (000)
Female	2015	318.0		Féminine
Enrolment in secondary education (000)	2015	227.0		Scolarisation dans le secondaire (000)
Female	2015	97.0		Féminine
Enrolment in tertiary education (000)	2012	44.0		Scolarisation dans le tertiaire (000)
Female	2012	16.7		Féminine
Literacy rate	2015	47.6		Taux d'alphabétisation (deux sexes)
Male	2015	62.4		Masculin
Female	2015	32.8		Féminin
Pupil teacher ratio - primary	2015	53.3		Ratio élève-enseignant
Budget allocation to education (%)	...	...		Dépenses publiques consacrées à l'enseignement (% du budget)
Poverty				**Pauvreté**
GNI per capita, PPP (current int. $)	2016	700.0		RNB par habitant, ($ PPA inter. courants)
Human Poverty Index (HPI-1) Value (%)	2007	35.2		Valeur de l'Indice de pauvreté (IPH-1) (%)
Population below Inter. poverty line ($2/day) (%)	2015	56.3		Population sous le seuil inter. de pauvreté (2$/Jour) (%)
Share of income held by richest 10%	2007	28.3		% de revenu des 10% plus riches
Share of income held by poorest 10%	2007	2.4		% de revenu des 10% plus pauvres
GINI index	2007	36.5		Indice de GINI

Population by age group - 2016

Population par groupe d'age - 2016

- 0-14 years 33.4%
- 15-64 years 64.2%
- 65+ years 2.4%

Percentage of children provided vaccines : - 2015

Pourcentage d'enfants vaccinés : - 2015

BCG / BCG	DPT3 / DTC3	Polio / polio	Measles / rougeole
93.9	71.4	69.0	60.0

Literacy rate (%) - 2015

Taux d'alphabétisation - 2015

Male 62.4 — Female 32.8

GNI per capita, PPP (current international $)

RNB par habitant, ($ PPA internationaux courants)

2012	2013	2014	2015	2016
670	720	710	720	700

II NATIONAL ACCOUNTS — COMPTES NATIONAUX

	2009	2010	2011	2012	2013	2014	2015	2016	2017	
GROSS DOMESTIC PRODUCT BY KIND OF ECONOMIC ACTIVITY AT CURRENT PRICES *LIBERIAN DOLLAR (MILLIONS)*										**PRODUIT INTÉRIEUR BRUT PAR BRANCHE D'ACTIVITÉ ÉCONOMIQUE AUX PRIX COURANTS** *DOLLAR LIBÉRIEN (MILLIONS)*
Agriculture, hunting , forestry and Fishing	663	696	745	968	1 258	1 636	2 126	2 185	...	Agriculture, chasse sylviculture et Pêche
Mining and quarrying	28	29	32	41	53	69	89	53	...	Industries extractives
Manufacturing	54	57	61	79	103	133	173	163	...	Industries manufacturières
Electricity, gas & water	6	6	7	9	11	15	19	16	...	Electricité, gaz et eau
Construction	25	26	28	36	47	61	79	47	...	Bâtiments et travaux publics
Wholesale & retail trade, restaurants, hotels	48	50	53	68	89	116	150	154	...	Commerce de gros et de détail, restaurants et hôtels
Finance, insurance, real estate, etc.	17	18	19	25	33	43	55	45	...	Banques, assurances, affaires immobilières
Transport and communications	53	54	58	75	98	127	165	169	...	Transport(s) et communications
Public administration and defense	69	73	77	101	132	171	222	228	...	Administrations publiques et défense
Education	...	...	...	...	...	...	...	...	...	Education
Health And Social Work	...	...	...	...	...	...	...	...	...	Santé et Actions Sociales
Other services	19	20	21	27	36	46	60	60	...	Autres services
Less Imputed Service Charges	- 8	- 9	- 9	- 12	- 16	- 21	- 21	- 14	...	Moins Services d'intermédiation financière
Gross domestic product at factor cost / basic prices	974	1 020	1 092	1 417	1 844	2 396	3 118	3 106	...	Produit intérieur brut aux couts des facteurs / prix de base
Plus: Indirect Taxes / taxes on products, less subsidies	...	...	...	...	...	...	...	...	...	Plus taxes indirectes/impôts sur les produits, moins les subventions
EXPENDITURE ON GROSS DOMESTIC PRODUCT AT CURRENT PURCHASER'S VALUES *LIBERIAN DOLLAR (MILLIONS)*										**EMPLOI DU PRODUIT INTÉRIEUR BRUT AUX PRIX COURANTS D'ACQUISITION** *DOLLAR LIBÉRIEN (MILLIONS)*
Government final consumption	222	280	374	461	456	481	654	657	...	Consommation finale des administrations publiques
Private final consumption	1 147	1 229	1 218	1 123	961	1 498	1 667	1 701	...	Consommation finale privée
Gross fixed capital formation	208	242	569	738	1 107	466	1 089	1 109	...	Formation brute de capital fixe
Change in inventories	...	...	...	...	...	...	...	...	...	Variation des stocks
Exports of goods and services	153	215	374	479	558	613	768	804	...	Exportations de biens et services
Less imports of goods and services	574	674	996	1 067	1 146	1 006	1 510	1 514	...	Moins importations de biens et services
GDP at purchasers' values	1 155	1 292	1 538	1 734	1 936	2 053	2 669	2 757	...	PIB aux prix d'acquisition
GROSS DOMESTIC PRODUCT BY KIND OF ECONOMIC ACTIVITY AT CONSTANT PRICES *ANNUAL GROWTH RATES (%)*										**PRODUIT INTÉRIEUR BRUT PAR BRANCHE D'ACTIVITÉ ECONOMIQUE AUX PRIX CONSTANTS** *TAUX DE CROISSANCE ANNUEL (%)*
Agriculture, hunting , forestry and Fishing	6.7	6.7	7.3	11.1	4.4	5.1	9.2	...	...	Agriculture, chasse sylviculture et Pêche
Mining and quarrying	6.7	6.7	7.3	11.1	4.4	5.1	9.2	...	...	Industries extractives
Manufacturing	6.7	6.7	7.3	11.1	4.4	5.1	9.2	...	...	Industries manufacturières
Electricity, gas & water	6.7	6.7	7.3	11.1	4.4	5.1	9.2	...	...	Electricité, gaz et eau
Construction	6.7	6.7	7.3	11.1	4.4	5.1	9.2	...	...	Bâtiments et travaux publics
Wholesale & retail trade, restaurants, hotels	6.7	6.7	7.3	11.1	4.4	5.1	9.2	...	...	Commerce de gros et de détail, restaurants et hôtels
Finance, insurance, real estate, etc.	6.7	6.7	7.3	11.1	4.4	5.1	9.2	...	...	Banques, assurances, affaires immobilières
Transport and communications	6.7	6.7	7.3	11.1	4.4	5.1	9.2	...	...	Transport(s) et communications
Public administration and defense	6.7	6.7	7.3	11.1	4.4	5.1	9.2	...	...	Administrations publiques et défense
Education	...	...	...	...	...	...	...	...	...	Education
Health And Social Work	...	...	...	...	...	...	...	...	...	Santé et Actions Sociales
Other services	6.7	6.7	7.3	11.1	4.4	5.1	9.2	...	...	Autres services
Less Imputed Service Charges	...	...	...	...	...	...	...	...	...	Moins Services d'intermédiation financière
Gross domestic product at factor cost / basic prices	6.7	6.7	7.3	11.1	4.4	5.1	9.2	...	...	Produit intérieur brut aux couts des facteurs / prix de base
Plus: Indirect Taxes / taxes on products, less subsidies	18.1	12.2	16.2	13.1	6.8	6.4	10.3	...	...	Plus taxes indirectes/impôts sur les produits, moins les subventions
Gross domestic product at market prices	7.8	7.3	8.2	11.3	4.6	5.2	9.3	...	...	Produit intérieur brut aux prix du marché
EXPENDITURE ON GROSS DOMESTIC PRODUCT AT CONSTANT PURCHASERS' VALUES *ANNUAL GROWTH RATES (%)*										**EMPLOIS DU PRODUIT INTÉRIEUR BRUT AUX PRIX CONSTANTS D'ACQUISITION** *TAUX DE CROISSANCE ANNUEL (%)*
Government final consumption	...	...	...	...	...	...	...	...	...	Consommation finale des administrations publiques
Private final consumption	...	...	...	...	...	...	...	...	...	Consommation finale privée
Gross fixed capital formation	...	...	...	...	...	...	...	...	...	Formation brute de capital fixe
Exports of goods and services	...	...	...	...	...	...	...	...	...	Exportations de biens et services
Less imports of goods and services	...	...	...	...	...	...	...	...	...	Moins importations de biens et services

III INFLATION

	2009	2010	2011	2012	2013	2014	2015	2016	2017	
Annual growth rates (%)										**Taux de croissance annuel (%)**
All item	7.4	7.3	8.5	6.8	7.6	9.9	7.8	8.8	12.4	Ensemble
of which:										dont:
Food and non-alcoholic beverages	2.6	7.2	11.4	10.3	10.3	9.1	10.1	7.9	6.4	Alimentation et boissons non alcoolisés
Alcoholic beverages, tobacco and narcotics	12.8	10.5	10.3	3.7	6.2	10.3	4.9	12.0	25.1	Boissons alcoolisées et tabacs
Clothing and footwear	16.1	8.6	5.9	3.3	5.0	16.8	13.7	15.7	27.5	Habillement et chaussures
Housing, water, electricity, gas and other fuels	- 2.2	3.3	5.7	4.0	0.8	1.9	- 0.4	- 5.4	11.6	Logement, eau, électricité, gaz et autres combustibles
Furnishings, household equipment and routine household maintenance	25.6	6.9	1.8	4.2	5.7	10.5	9.0	14.1	16.1	Meubles, articles de ménage et entretien courant
Health	3.1	0.8	- 0.1	- 0.6	0.1	16.1	- 4.3	- 0.6	0.4	Santé
Transport	3.9	4.7	18.2	5.4	5.6	16.7	3.9	20.4	21.2	Transport
Communication	- 0.2	3.3	2.9	0.2	0.6	1.1	- 8.6	- 0.7	7.3	Communication
Recreation and culture	4.4	2.4	4.4	2.8	8.6	7.1	20.7	11.6	21.3	Loisirs et culture
Education	...	...	...	...	...	...	...	...	...	Enseignement
Restaurants and hotels	67.4	23.5	2.8	2.0	7.0	10.8	- 1.6	9.4	17.4	Restaurants et hôtels
Miscellaneous goods and services	8.6	4.5	- 0.3	4.1	6.8	16.6	5.5	8.9	19.0	Biens et Services divers

LIBÉRIA

IV AGRICULTURAL PRODUCTION - PRODUCTION AGRICOLE

TONNES (THOUSAND)	2009	2010	2011	2012	2013	2014	2015	2016	2017	Tonnes (milliers)
Cassava	495	493	496	522	517	521	525	529	...	Manioc
Rice, paddy	293	296	290	291	270	237	286	309	...	Riz, Paddy
Bananas	265	265	265	265	265	267	272	273	...	Bananes
Plantains	174	174	173	172	171	175	178	177	...	Bananes plantains
Taro (cocoyam)	123	125	125	127	129	135	136	138	...	Taros (colocases)

V MINING PRODUCTION - PRODUCTION MINIERE

	2009	2010	2011	2012	2013	2014	2015	2016	2017	
Gold ores and concentrates - Production (Kilograms)	524	666	448	641	600	598	...	...	...	Minerais d'or et leurs concentrés - Production (Kilogrammes)
Diamonds and other precious stones, unworked - Production, carat (thousands)	28	27	42	34	54	79	...	...	...	Diamants et autres pierres gemmes (précieuses), bruts - Production, carat (milliers)
	...	...	...	...	...	...	...	...	...	

VI ENERGY - ENERGIE

	2009	2010	2011	2012	2013	2014	2015	2016	2017	
Total electricity generation (GWh)	20	30	39	40	40	105	109	113	...	Production électrique totale (GWh)
of which										dont
Production of electricity from fossil fuels (GWh)	20	30	39	40	40	104	108	112	...	Production d'électricité à partir de combustibles fossiles (GWh)
Production of hydro electricity (GWh)	...	...	...	...	...	...	...	...	...	Production d'électricité d'origine hydraulique (GWh)
Production of electricity from solar, wind, tide, wave and other sources (GWh)	...	...	...	...	...	1	1	1	...	Production d'électricité d'origine solaire, éolienne, marée motrice et autres (GWh)

VII TOURISM AND INFRASTRUCTURE - TOURISME ET INFRASTUCTURE

VII-1 Tourism	2009	2010	2011	2012	2013	2014	2015	2016	2017	VII-1 Tourisme
International tourist arrivals (thousands)	...	...	...	...	...	...	...	...	...	Arrivées de touristes internationaux (milliers)
Rooms in hotels and similar establishments (thousands)	...	...	...	...	...	...	...	...	...	Chambres d'hôtels et établissements assimilés (milliers)
Overnight stays (thousands)	...	...	...	...	...	...	...	...	...	Nuitées (milliers)
Tourism receipts (US$ thousand)	...	...	...	...	...	...	...	...	...	Recettes touristiques (milliers de $ EU)
Total contribution to GDP (%)	...	...	...	...	...	...	...	...	...	Contribution totale au PIB (%)
Total contribution to Employment (%)	...	...	...	...	...	...	...	...	...	Contribution totale à l'emploi (%)
VII-2 Infrastructure										**VII-2 Infrastructure**
Paved road (% of total)	...	...	...	...	...	...	...	...	...	Routes asphaltées (% du total)
Total network (Railways-km)	...	...	...	...	...	...	...	...	...	Réseau total voies ferrées-Km
Main telephone lines (per 100 inhabitants)	...	...	...	...	...	...	...	...	...	Lignes téléphoniques fixes (pour 100 habitants)
Mobile cellular subscribers (per 100 inhabitants)	28.4	39.7	49.5	56.8	59.4	73.4	81.1	83.1	...	Abonnés aux téléphones mobiles (pour 100 habitants)
Internet users per 100 inhabitants	2.0	2.3	2.5	2.6	3.2	5.4	5.9	7.3	...	Utilisateurs Internet par 100 Habitants
Fixed (wired)-broadband subscriptions per 100 inhabitants	...	...	...	...	...	...	...	...	...	Abonnements à l'Internet fixe (filaire) à large bande pour 100 habitants, par débit

VIII EXTERNAL TRADE - COMMERCE EXTERIEUR

US$ (MILLIONS) EXPORTS, FOB	2009	2010	2011	2012	2013	2014	2015	2016	2017	$ E.U (MILLIONS) EXPORTATIONS, FÀB
Exports - Total	149	222	367	460	559	444	265	170	...	Exportations - Total
Exports to Africa	23	12	43	53	45	4	3	19	...	Exportations vers l'Afrique
Main products										**Principaux produits**
Gold, non-monetary (excluding gold ores and concentrates)	2	13	36	52	47	40	34	38	...	Or, non monétaire (à l'exclusion des minerais d'or et des concentrés)
Iron ore and concentrates	...	3	3	84	178	161	58	13	...	Minerai de fer et ses concentrés
Natural rubber & similar gums, in primary forms	17	54	117	99	83	65	27	17	...	Caoutchouc naturel et gommes similaires, sous formes primaires
Ships, boats & floating structures	101	76	95	99	158	124	107	41	...	Navires, bateaux et structures flottantes
Wood in the rough or roughly squared	...	1	7	20	24	14	11	5	...	Bois bruts ou grossièrement équarris
Main destinations										**Principales destinations**
China	-	5	13	82	67	113	43	8	...	Chine
Poland	36	47	29	55	162	53	75	33	...	Pologne
Spain	-	17	25	38	37	17	6	1	...	Espagne
United Arab Emirates	2	12	35	51	47	41	29	21	...	Emirates Arabes
United States	9	39	52	52	40	34	12	11	...	États-Unis
IMPORTS, CIF										
Imports - Total	551	710	1 044	1 005	1 150	1 997	1 687	1 311	...	Importations - Total (millions)
Imports from Africa	5	4	43	44	16	40	23	9	...	Importations en provenance de l'Afrique
Main products										**Principaux produits**
Non-electric parts & accessor. of machinery, n.e.s.	2	1	4	3	4	10	18	11	...	Pièces non électriques et accessor. de machines, n.e.s.
Petroleum oils or bituminous minerals > 70 % oil	22	29	77	89	76	125	103	48	...	Huiles de pétrole ou de minéraux bitumineux> 70% d'huile
Rice	2	3	7	6	11	18	20	11	...	Riz
Ships, boats & floating structures	409	512	863	552	633	933	804	844	...	Navires, bateaux et structures flottantes
Structures & parts, n.e.s., of iron, steel, aluminium	10	5	15	16	4	17	13	7	...	Structures et parties, n.d.a., de fer, d'acier, d'aluminium
Main origin										**Principales provenances**
China	88	188	280	214	195	288	272	219	...	Chine
Germany	5	6	25	6	10	74	68	30	...	Allemagne
Japan	69	84	186	143	146	176	173	151	...	Japon
Republic of Korea	228	231	416	236	294	501	260	500	...	Corée, République de
Singapore	77	123	...	258	323	664	489	248	...	Singapour

LIBERIA

	2009	2010	2011	2012	2013	2014	2015	2016	2017	
IX-1 MONETARY STATISTICS *LIBERIAN DOLLAR (MILLIONS)*										**IX-1 STATISTIQUES MONÉTAIRES** *DOLLAR LIBÉRIEN (MILLIONS)*
Money supply (M1)	358	458	647	634	682	697	709	677	664	Masse monétaire (M1)
Quasi-money	5 884	7 573	11 356	13 273	16 252	17 011	19 496	20 764	22 302	Quasi-monnaie
of which demand deposit	...	...	...	...	...	...	...	...	...	dont Monnaie scripturale
Net foreign assets	- 44 804	25 574	28 005	25 162	26 185	28 307	26 314	24 992	23 926	Avoirs extérieurs nets
Domestic credit	89 441	29 458	38 655	43 233	57 001	60 760	64 133	80 915	83 707	Crédit intérieur
of which claims on private sector	78 551	15 187	19 479	21 046	25 476	27 557	24 843	32 466	33 208	dont créances sur le secteur privé
of which claims on government sector, net	9 626	13 676	18 356	20 415	29 548	31 202	36 183	42 885	45 727	dont créances nettes sur le gouvernement
International reserves (millions US$)	313	386	401	381	393	411	446	462	460	Réserves internationales (millions $EU)
Average exchange rate (National currency per US$)	68	71	72	74	78	84	86	94	113	Taux de change (moyen) (monnaie nationale par $ EU)
IX-2 PUBLIC FINANCE *LIBERIAN DOLLAR (MILLIONS)*										**IX-2 FINANCES PUBLIQUES** *DOLLAR LIBÉRIEN (MILLIONS)*
Total Revenues and Grants	235	288	375	459	554	544	658	646	651	Recettes totales et dons
Direct taxes (on income, profits)	66	70	111	145	156	160	160	147	163	Taxes directes
Domestic indirect taxes revenues	34	39	48	54	67	63	44	50	47	Taxes Indirectes
Trade taxes	88	92	105	149	140	154	144	168	185	Taxes sur le commerce extérieur
Other taxes	3	7	4	9	5	15	17	4	6	Autres taxes
Other revenues	21	67	65	74	140	74	91	78	51	Autres recettes
Grants	24	13	40	28	46	77	202	199	199	Dons
Total Expenditures and Net Lending	249	282	383	514	582	582	827	842	738	Dépenses totales et prêts nets
Current expenditure	208	246	305	433	486	477	639	637	567	Dépenses courantes
Wages and Salaries	91	114	139	181	211	199	259	255	277	Rémunérations et salaires
Other purchases of goods and services	75	77	86	114	161	161	263	267	214	Achat de biens et services
Other current expenditure	...	...	...	...	...	...	...	...	...	Autres dépenses courantes
Current transfers	41	56	81	138	113	117	117	115	76	Transferts courants
Interest payments	8	4	4	5	6	6	10	10	9	Intérêts
Capital expenditure	34	32	74	76	91	99	178	195	162	Dépenses d'équipement
Net lending	- 14	6	- 8	- 55	2	...	...	...	...	Prêts nets
Fiscal balance	- 14	6	- 8	- 55	- 28	- 38	- 170	- 196	- 87	Solde global y compris les dons
IX-3 BALANCE OF PAYMENTS *US $ (MILLIONS)*										**IX-3 BALANCE DES PAIEMENTS** *$ E.U (MILLIONS)*
Trade balance	- 421	- 459	- 677	- 632	- 667	- 1 513	- 1 978	...	...	Balance commerciale
Services Balance	- 741	- 830	- 865	- 658	- 668	- 1 082	- 1 039	...	...	Balance des services
Net primary income	- 145	- 182	- 688	- 944	- 634	- 497	- 500	...	...	Revenus primaires nets
Compensation of employees	...	...	...	...	...	20	19	...	...	Rémunération des salariés
Investment income	...	...	- 688	- 944	- 634	- 516	- 519	...	...	Revenus des investissements
Net secondary income	970	1 041	1 233	1 097	681	1 217	1 668	...	...	Revenus secondaires nets
Net official transfers	...	...	977	957	650	1 020	1 124	...	...	Transferts officiels nets
Workers' remittances	...	...	257	140	31	159	368	...	...	Envois de fonds des travailleurs
Other private transfers	...	...	...	...	...	38	175	...	...	Autres transferts privés
Current account balance	- 337	- 430	- 996	- 1 137	- 1 288	- 1 875	- 1 975	...	...	Solde du compte courant
Capital and financial account	...	...	1 231	1 871	1 529	662	878	...	...	Comptes de capital et financier
Capital account	...	...	...	312	133	117	362	...	...	Compte de capital
Financial account	...	...	1 231	1 559	1 396	546	516	...	...	Compte financier
Errors and omissions	...	...	- 1 508	- 519	- 316	1 175	919	...	...	Erreurs et omissions
Overall balance	...	...	- 20	44	- 177	- 38	- 52	...	...	Balance générale

LIBÉRIA

X DEBT AND FINANCIAL FLOWS - DETTE ET FLUX FINANCIERS

	2009	2010	2011	2012	2013	2014	2015	2016	2017	
X-1 DEBT *US $ (MILLIONS)*										**X-1 DETTE EXTÉRIEURE** *$ E.U (MILLIONS)*
Total external debt	1 689	138	165	180	230	360	529	678	820	Dette extérieure totale
Private	...	...	...	...	...	...	...	...	...	Privée
Public	1 689	138	165	180	230	360	529	678	...	Publique
Total external debt service	21	33	27	40	20	34	38	35	...	Service de la dette extérieure
Present value of external debt	...	...	...	...	...	...	...	340	...	Valeur actuelle de la dette extérieure
Total government domestic debt, National currency (millions)	...	...	...	...	...	...	...	...	...	Dette publique intérieure
X-2 FINANCIAL FLOWS *US $ (MILLIONS)*										**X-2 FLUX FINANCIERS** *$ E.U (MILLIONS)*
Net Foreign Direct Investment Inflows	218	450	785	985	1 061	277	627	453	...	Investissements étranger direct (flux nets entrants)
Main origin of FDI inflows										**Principales origines de l'IDE entrant:**
United States	52	80	113	...	...	...	...	...	...	États-Unis
...	...	...	...	...	...	...	...	...	...	...
Japan	40	137	413	149	...	...	...	...	...	Japon
Germany	1	...	...	...	...	...	...	...	...	Allemagne
United States	52	80	113	...	...	...	...	...	...	États-Unis
African countries	...	...	...	...	...	...	...	...	...	Pays africains
Net total official development assistance	511	1 414	762	567	536	750	1 094	815	...	Aide publique au développement (nette totale)
Main origin of net ODA										**Principales origines de l'APD nette**
United States	97	127	149	175	158	209	514	399	...	États-Unis
IMF (Concessional Trust Funds)	28	540	14	18	22	57	56	38	...	Financements concessionnels du FMI dans le cadre de la FASR
International Development Association [IDA]	42	42	63	42	44	100	185	119	...	International Development Association
Germany	28	50	110	16	24	41	15	45	...	Allemagne
France	...	232	1	1	1	1	-	-	...	France

LIBERIA

SOURCES AND NOTES - SOURCES ET NOTES

External trade - Total exports, fob: UNCTAD

External trade - Total import, cif: UNCTAD

ODA: OECD

Monetary statistics: IMF

National Accounts:The data is in US$

Poverty: World Bank

Commerce exterieur - Exportation, fab: CNUCED

Commerce exterieur - Imporations, caf: CNUCED

APD: OCDE

Statistiques monétaires: FMI

Comptes nationaux: sont exprimées en $ EU

Pauvreté: Banque mondiale

	AREA (km2)	1 759 540	SUPERFICIE (KM2)
	CAPITAL CITY	Tripoli	Tripoli	CAPITALE
	CURRENCY	Libyan Dinar	Dinar lybien	MONNAIE

I SOCIAL AND DEMOGRAPHIC INDICATORS — INDICATEURS DEMOGRAPHIQUES ET SOCIAUX

	Year Année	Value Valeur	Charts / Graphiques	
Population				**Population**
Population ('000)	2016	6 400.0		Population ('000)
Female (%)	2016	49.0		Féminine (%)
Urban (%)	2016	79.0		Urbaine (%)
Average annual growth rate	2016	1.6		Taux de croissance annuel
Active population ('000)	2013	1 688.0		Population active ('000)
Population by age group ('000)				Population par groupe d'âge ('000)
0-14 years	2013	2 087.9		0-14 ans
15-64 years	2013	3 665.8		15-64 ans
65+ years	2013	248.0		65+ ans
Economically active population in agriculture (%)	2015	2.9		Participation de la population active agricole (%)
Crude birth rate	2015	24.9		Taux brut de natalité
Crude death rate	2015	4.1		Taux brut de mortalité
Total fertility rate	2016	2.6		Indice synthétique de fécondité
Life expectancy at birth - Total (years)	2015	72.0		Espérance de vie à la naissance - Totale (années)
Dependency ratio - Total (%)	2016	53.0		Taux de dépendance - Total (%)
Health				**Santé**
Percentage of children under-five and underweight	2015	5.0		% d'enfants de moins de cinq ans avec insuffisance pondérale
Prevalence of undernourishment	...	...		Prévalence de la malnutrition
Under five mortality rate (per 1 000 live births)	2015	13.0		Taux de mortalité de moins de 5 ans (les deux sexes, pour 1000)
Infant mortality rate (per 1 000 live births)	2015	11.0		Taux de mortalité infantile (les deux sexes) par 1000
Neonatal mortality rate (per 1 000 live births)	2011	5.2		Le taux de mortalité néonatale (pour 1000 naissances vivantes)
Percentage of children provided the vaccines :				Pourcentage d'enfants vaccinés :
BCG	2015	100.0		BCG
DPT3	2015	93.7		DTC3
Polio	2015	98.0		polio
Measles	2015	96.5		rougeole
Percentage of mothers provided at least one antenatal care (%)	2015	93.0		Pourcentage de mères ayant au moins reçu un soin prénatal (%)
Percentage of deliveries attended by skilled health personnel	2015	99.0		% d'accouchements assistés par un personnel de santé qualifié
Number of doctors (per 10,000 population)	2015	20.0		Nombre de médecins (pour 10.000 habitants)
Number of nurses (per 10,000 population)	2015	66.0		Nombre d'infirmiers (pour 10.000 habitants)
Hospital beds - Total (per 10,000 population)	2015	37.0		Nombre de lits d'hôpitaux - Total (pour 10 000)
Births registered (per 1,000)	2015	24.9		Naissances enregistrées (pour 1000)
Deaths registered (per 1,000)	2015	4.1		Décès enregistrés (pour 1000)
Budget allocation to health (%)	2015	8.3		Dépenses publiques consacrées à la santé (% du budget)
Education				**Education**
Enrolment in primary education (000)	2016	1 390.5		Scolarisation dans le primaire (000)
Female	2016	689.7		Féminine
Enrolment in secondary education (000)	2011	220.2		Scolarisation dans le secondaire (000)
Female	2011	130.0		Féminine
Enrolment in tertiary education (000)	2015	374.7		Scolarisation dans le tertiaire (000)
Female	2015	216.1		Féminine
Literacy rate	2012	89.9		Taux d'alphabétisation (deux sexes)
Male	2012	96.1		Masculin
Female	2012	83.7		Féminin
Pupil teacher ratio - primary	2012	9.0		Ratio élève-enseignant
Budget allocation to education (%)	...	...		Dépenses publiques consacrées à l'enseignement (% du budget)
Poverty				**Pauvreté**
GNI per capita, PPP (current int. $)	2011	11210.0		RNB par habitant, ($ PPA inter. courants)
Human Poverty Index (HPI-1) Value (%)	2007	13.4		Valeur de l'Indice de pauvreté (IPH-1) (%)
Population below Inter. poverty line ($2/day) (%)	2007	68.6		Population sous le seuil inter. de pauvreté (2$/Jour) (%)
Share of income held by richest 10%	...	...		% de revenu des 10% plus riches
Share of income held by poorest 10%	...	...		% de revenu des 10% plus pauvres
GINI index	...	...		Indice de GINI

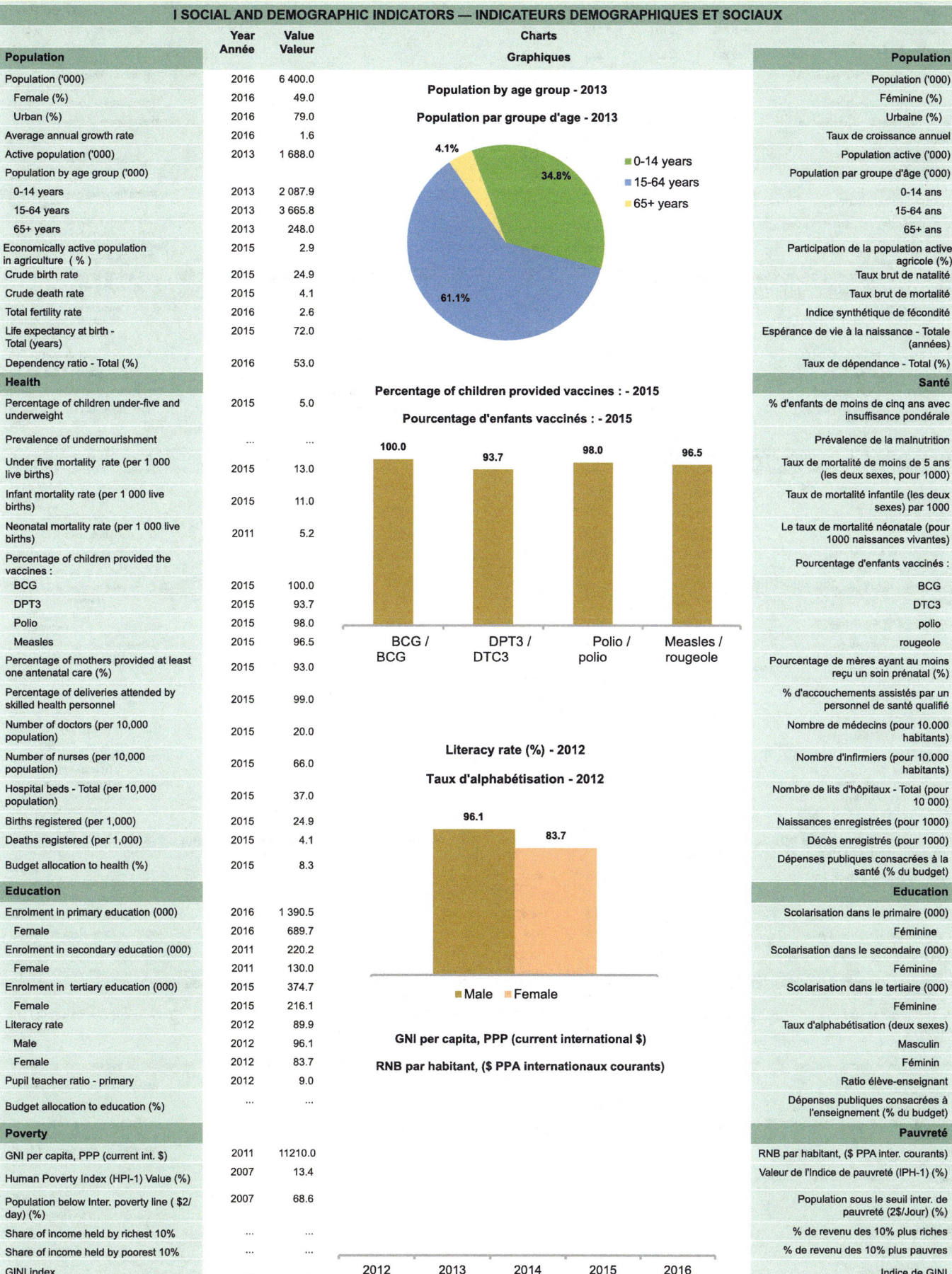

Population by age group - 2013 / Population par groupe d'age - 2013
- 0-14 years: 34.8%
- 15-64 years: 61.1%
- 65+ years: 4.1%

Percentage of children provided vaccines : - 2015 / Pourcentage d'enfants vaccinés : - 2015
- BCG / BCG: 100.0
- DPT3 / DTC3: 93.7
- Polio / polio: 98.0
- Measles / rougeole: 96.5

Literacy rate (%) - 2012 / Taux d'alphabétisation - 2012
- Male: 96.1
- Female: 83.7

GNI per capita, PPP (current international $) / RNB par habitant, ($ PPA internationaux courants)
2012   2013   2014   2015   2016

II NATIONAL ACCOUNTS — COMPTES NATIONAUX

	2009	2010	2011	2012	2013	2014	2015	2016	2017	
GROSS DOMESTIC PRODUCT BY KIND OF ECONOMIC ACTIVITY AT CURRENT PRICES *LIBYAN DINAR (MILLIONS)*										**PRODUIT INTÉRIEUR BRUT PAR BRANCHE D'ACTIVITÉ ÉCONOMIQUE AUX PRIX COURANTS** *FRANC CFA (MILLIONS)*
Agriculture, hunting , forestry and Fishing	679	725	572	745	...	...	...	...	...	Agriculture, chasse sylviculture et Pêche
Mining and quarrying	45 740	66 801	29 475	84 572	...	...	...	...	...	Industries extractives
Manufacturing	4 299	4 463	1 163	3 796	...	...	...	...	...	Industries manufacturières
Electricity, gas & water	1 105	1 157	394	1 168	...	...	...	...	...	Electricité, gaz et eau
Construction	5 332	5 677	1 110	1 222	...	...	...	...	...	Bâtiments et travaux publics
Wholesale & retail trade, restaurants, hotels	2 883	3 123	1 830	3 597	...	...	...	...	...	Commerce de gros et de détail, restaurants et hôtels
Finance, insurance, real estate, etc.	4 213	4 503	2 667	3 820	...	...	...	...	...	Banques, assurances, affaires immobilières
Transport and communications	915	983	750	978	...	...	...	...	...	Transport(s) et communications
Public administration and defense	5 305	5 505	9 523	11 860	...	...	...	...	...	Administrations publiques et défense
Education	695	735	269	587	...	...	...	...	...	Education
Health And Social Work	457	486	339	447	...	...	...	...	...	Santé et Actions Sociales
Other services	2 590	2 795	1 806	3 158	...	...	...	...	...	Autres services
Less Imputed Service Charges	- 3 720	- 3 973	- 2 348	- 3 358	...	...	...	...	...	Moins Services d'intermédiation financière
Gross domestic product at factor cost / basic prices	70 493	92 979	47 549	112 591	79 953	43 030	...	...	...	Produit intérieur brut aux couts des facteurs / prix de base
Plus: Indirect Taxes / taxes on products, less subsidies	- 6 804	- 5 603	- 8 378	- 11 964	- 13 958	- 12 159	...	...	...	Plus taxes indirectes/impôts sur les produits, moins les subventions
EXPENDITURE ON GROSS DOMESTIC PRODUCT AT CURRENT PURCHASER'S VALUES *LIBYAN DINAR (MILLIONS)*										**EMPLOI DU PRODUIT INTÉRIEUR BRUT AUX PRIX COURANTS D'ACQUISITION** *FRANC CFA (MILLIONS)*
Government final consumption	21 913	23 807	21 692	31 410	30 945	31 424	24 035	...	...	Consommation finale des administrations publiques
Private final consumption	14 653	16 249	10 264	17 169	16 926	16 095	15 223	...	...	Consommation finale privée
Gross fixed capital formation	21 807	23 947	6 333	13 743	13 453	6 841	15 300	...	...	Formation brute de capital fixe
Change in inventories	- 330	- 220	726	- 392	...	...	...	...	...	Variation des stocks
Exports of goods and services	51 415	76 306	27 451	87 576	58 671	24 612	15 112	...	...	Exportations de biens et services
Less imports of goods and services	31 116	36 465	17 031	31 709	54 002	48 101	28 980	...	...	Moins importations de biens et services
GDP at purchasers' values	63 689	87 375	39 171	100 627	65 995	30 871	40 690	...	...	PIB aux prix d'acquisition
GROSS DOMESTIC PRODUCT BY KIND OF ECONOMIC ACTIVITY AT CONSTANT PRICES *ANNUAL GROWTH RATES (%)*										**PRODUIT INTÉRIEUR BRUT PAR BRANCHE D'ACTIVITÉ ECONOMIQUE AUX PRIX CONSTANTS** *TAUX DE CROISSANCE ANNUEL (%)*
Agriculture, hunting , forestry and Fishing	1.9	- 1.0	- 71.8	37.1	...	...	...	...	...	Agriculture, chasse sylviculture et Pêche
Mining and quarrying	- 7.0	2.4	- 70.8	148.2	...	...	...	...	...	Industries extractives
Manufacturing	8.8	- 4.1	- 78.9	234.1	...	...	...	...	...	Industries manufacturières
Electricity, gas & water	3.1	- 2.1	- 48.5	125.7	...	...	...	...	...	Electricité, gaz et eau
Construction	12.3	5.6	- 79.0	11.9	...	...	...	...	...	Bâtiments et travaux publics
Wholesale & retail trade, restaurants, hotels	5.3	6.5	- 63.3	84.6	...	...	...	...	...	Commerce de gros et de détail, restaurants et hôtels
Finance, insurance, real estate, etc.	6.9	6.2	- 46.1	33.7	...	...	...	...	...	Banques, assurances, affaires immobilières
Transport and communications	6.3	6.6	- 57.4	19.1	...	...	...	...	...	Transport(s) et communications
Public administration and defense	3.0	2.7	2.2	23.8	...	...	...	...	...	Administrations publiques et défense
Education	52.5	1.0	- 72.0	94.7	...	...	...	...	...	Education
Health And Social Work	22.0	2.3	1.3	30.2	...	...	...	...	...	Santé et Actions Sociales
Other services	0.3	4.6	- 53.7	60.1	...	...	...	...	...	Autres services
Less Imputed Service Charges	6.1	6.3	- 46.0	32.4	...	...	...	...	...	Moins Services d'intermédiation financière
Gross domestic product at factor cost / basic prices	- 3.1	2.5	- 64.2	106.5	- 30.8	- 47.7	...	...	...	Produit intérieur brut aux couts des facteurs / prix de base
Plus: Indirect Taxes / taxes on products, less subsidies	- 4.6	- 4.5	- 36.9	0.4	248.0	- 12.9	...	...	...	Plus taxes indirectes/impôts sur les produits, moins les subventions
Gross domestic product at market prices	- 3.0	3.2	- 66.7	124.7	- 52.1	- 67.2	...	...	...	Produit intérieur brut aux prix du marché
EXPENDITURE ON GROSS DOMESTIC PRODUCT AT CONSTANT PURCHASERS' VALUES *ANNUAL GROWTH RATES (%)*										**EMPLOIS DU PRODUIT INTÉRIEUR BRUT AUX PRIX CONSTANTS D'ACQUISITION** *TAUX DE CROISSANCE ANNUEL (%)*
Government final consumption	10.2	7.4	- 32.5	40.0	...	...	...	...	...	Consommation finale des administrations publiques
Private final consumption	...	...	...	...	...	...	...	...	...	Consommation finale privée
Gross fixed capital formation	1.9	6.5	- 74.5	144.9	...	...	...	...	...	Formation brute de capital fixe
Exports of goods and services	- 1.8	2.7	- 76.6	180.4	...	...	...	...	...	Exportations de biens et services
Less imports of goods and services	14.4	7.1	- 64.1	70.1	...	...	...	...	...	Moins importations de biens et services

III INFLATION

	2009	2010	2011	2012	2013	2014	2015	2016	2017	
Annual growth rates (%)										**Taux de croissance annuel (%)**
All item	2.4	2.4	15.9	6.1	2.6	2.4	9.8	25.9	28.5	Ensemble
of which:										dont:
Food and non-alcoholic beverages	3.1	2.8	16.3	- 3.8	3.7	4.5	15.3	29.8	35.1	Alimentation et boissons non alcoolisés
Alcoholic beverages, tobacco and narcotics	...	...	...	...	...	...	...	...	...	Boissons alcoolisées et tabacs
Clothing and footwear	3.6	8.9	13.1	16.7	7.4	- 1.8	20.5	42.4	27.5	Habillement et chaussures
Housing, water, electricity, gas and other fuels	0.3	0.1	11.8	22.0	4.8	2.0	1.4	3.1	2.9	Logement, eau, électricité, gaz et autres combustibles
Furnishings, household equipment and routine household maintenance	4.6	3.1	23.4	16.3	0.6	...	3.4	65.3	32.7	Meubles, articles de ménage et entretien courant
Health	- 0.1	...	50.8	7.5	- 3.6	1.2	7.6	34.9	19.2	Santé
Transport	2.2	- 0.4	9.2	7.6	0.5	1.5	0.3	10.4	15.3	Transport
Communication	...	...	...	...	...	...	...	...	...	Communication
Recreation and culture	...	...	...	...	...	...	...	...	...	Loisirs et culture
Education	6.2	5.4	4.8	10.4	0.9	1.4	7.8	34.5	49.7	Enseignement
Restaurants and hotels	...	...	...	...	...	...	...	...	...	Restaurants et hôtels
Miscellaneous goods and services	2.2	7.1	22.7	0.4	- 6.2	0.4	21.4	38.3	58.1	Biens et Services divers

IV AGRICULTURAL PRODUCTION - PRODUCTION AGRICOLE

TONNES (THOUSAND)	2009	2010	2011	2012	2013	2014	2015	2016	2017	Tonnes (milliers)
Potatoes	291	290	352	291	295	283	336	337	...	Pommes de terre
Tomatoes	220	230	223	225	221	213	215	216	...	Tomates
Dates	155	161	166	170	174	...	...	...	...	Dattes
Olives	171	180	139	135	138	187	188	189	...	Olives
Dry onion	186	195	206	208	211	184	184	185	...	Oignons secs

V MINING PRODUCTION - PRODUCTION MINIERE

	2009	2010	2011	2012	2013	2014	2015	2016	2017	
Crude petroleum - Production, metric tons (thousands)	1	1	-	1	-	-	-	-	-	Pétrole brut - Production, tonnes métriques (milliers)
	...	...	...	...	...	...	...	...	...	
Salt and pure sodium chloride - Production (metric tons)	40 000	40 000	20 000	30 000	...	...	...	...	...	Sel et chlorure de sodium pur - Production (tonnes métriques)

VI ENERGY - ENERGIE

	2009	2010	2011	2012	2013	2014	2015	2016	2017	
Total electricity generation (GWh)	30 426	32 753	28 657	31 183	31 183	34 378	36 106	39 732	...	Production électrique totale (GWh)
of which										dont
Production of electricity from fossil fuels (GWh)	30 426	32 753	28 649	31 174	31 174	34 369	36 088	39 723	...	Production d'électricité à partir de combustibles fossiles (GWh)
Production of hydro electricity (GWh)	...	...	...	...	...	...	...	...	...	Production d'électricité d'origine hydraulique (GWh)
Production of electricity from solar, wind, tide, wave and other sources (GWh)	...	...	9	9	9	9	18	9	...	Production d'électricité d'origine solaire, éolienne, marée motrice et autres (GWh)

VII TOURISM AND INFRASTRUCTURE - TOURISME ET INFRASTUCTURE

VII-1 Tourism	2009	2010	2011	2012	2013	2014	2015	2016	2017	VII-1 Tourisme
International tourist arrivals (thousands)	36	32	...	...	...	...	...	...	...	Arrivées de touristes internationaux (milliers)
Rooms in hotels and similar establishments (thousands)	15	16	16	16	17	17	17	17	...	Chambres d'hôtels et établissements assimilés (milliers)
Overnight stays (thousands)	201	150	...	...	...	...	...	...	...	Nuitées (milliers)
Tourism receipts (US$ thousand)	50 000	60 000	...	...	...	...	...	...	...	Recettes touristiques (milliers de $ EU)
Total contribution to GDP (%)	5.5	4.5	6.9	4.1	3.8	9.2	7.3	6.9	5.3	Contribution totale au PIB (%)
Total contribution to Employment (%)	5.3	4.3	4.7	4.2	4.2	5.9	5.5	5.2	5.1	Contribution totale à l'emploi (%)
VII-2 Infrastructure										VII-2 Infrastructure
Paved road (% of total)	...	...	...	...	...	...	...	...	...	Routes asphaltées (% du total)
Total network (Railways-km)	...	...	...	...	...	...	...	...	...	Réseau total voies ferrées-Km
Main telephone lines (per 100 inhabitants)	17.8	20.3	16.4	13.2	12.7	11.3	10.0	21.5	...	Lignes téléphoniques fixes (pour 100 habitants)
Mobile cellular subscribers (per 100 inhabitants)	159.9	180.4	163.8	155.8	165.0	161.1	154.3	119.8	...	Abonnés aux téléphones mobiles (pour 100 habitants)
Internet users per 100 inhabitants	10.8	14.0	14.0	...	16.5	17.8	19.0	20.3	...	Utilisateurs Internet par 100 Habitants
Fixed (wired)-broadband subscriptions per 100 inhabitants	1.1	1.2	1.1	1.1	1.0	1.0	1.0	2.6	...	Abonnements à l'Internet fixe (filaire) à large bande pour 100 habitants, par débit

VIII EXTERNAL TRADE - COMMERCE EXTERIEUR

US$ (MILLIONS) EXPORTS, FOB	2009	2010	2011	2012	2013	2014	2015	2016	2017	$ E.U (MILLIONS) EXPORTATIONS, FÀB
Exports - Total	36 951	48 673	18 996	60 946	43 500	21 000	10 200	6 000	...	Exportations - Total
Exports to Africa	918	702	214	741	790	319	352	651	...	Exportations vers l'Afrique
Main products										Principaux produits
Gold, non-monetary (excluding gold ores and concentrates)	419	621	376	565	302	401	613	942	...	Or, non monétaire (à l'exclusion des minerais d'or et des concentrés)
Natural gas, whether or not liquefied	2 777	3 149	824	3 030	2 132	1 732	1 205	395	...	Gaz naturel, même liquéfié
Petroleum gases, other gaseous hydrocarbons, n.e.s.	133	1 325	390	1 856	1 959	941	227	132	...	Gaz de pétrole, autres hydrocarbures gazeux, n.d.a.
Petroleum oils or bituminous minerals > 70 % oil	3 390	2 769	1 155	3 531	3 579	1 247	565	364	...	Huiles de pétrole ou de minéraux bitumineux> 70% d'huile
Petroleum oils, oils from bitumin. materials, crude	28 656	38 925	15 439	50 614	34 065	15 560	6 340	3 233	...	Huiles de pétrole, huiles de bitume. matériaux bruts
Main destinations										Principales destinations
China	3 280	4 394	2 046	6 829	2 206	786	887	234	...	Chine
France	3 361	6 507	2 995	6 369	4 975	2 793	938	398	...	France
Germany	3 329	3 119	1 881	5 512	4 917	1 776	942	322	...	Allemagne
Italy	13 036	17 114	6 217	18 673	11 895	6 392	3 532	1 344	...	Italie
Spain	2 793	4 329	1 013	4 340	2 567	1 096	564	585	...	Espagne
IMPORTS, CIF										
Imports - Total	12 859	17 674	8 000	22 000	27 000	19 000	13 000	10 600	...	Importations - Total (millions)
Imports from Africa	1 148	1 507	1 037	2 037	2 202	1 628	1 122	859	...	Importations en provenance de l'Afrique
Main products										Principaux produits
Aircraft & associated equipment; spacecraft, etc.	501	611	129	421	662	270	604	175	...	Aéronefs et équipement connexe; vaisseau spatial, etc.
Motor vehic. for transport of goods, special purpo.	481	514	154	554	765	468	285	246	...	Véhicule à moteur pour le transport de marchandises, spécial.
Motor vehicles for the transport of persons	801	895	274	1 272	1 339	882	463	410	...	Véhicules à moteur pour le transport de personnes
Petroleum oils or bituminous minerals > 70 % oil	937	1 563	618	2 368	2 583	1 785	831	912	...	Huiles de pétrole ou de minéraux bitumineux> 70% d'huile
Wheat (including spelt) and meslin, unmilled	236	407	260	552	713	555	332	284	...	Blé (y compris l'épeautre) et méteil, non moulu
Main origin										Principales provenances
China	1 439	1 802	881	2 681	3 207	2 381	2 000	1 374	...	Chine
Germany	1 005	1 170	552	1 175	1 535	950	581	487	...	Allemagne
Italy	1 944	2 666	780	2 881	3 522	2 641	1 584	1 193	...	Italie
Republic of Korea	949	1 389	262	1 420	1 507	1 188	767	896	...	Corée
Turkey	1 225	1 778	977	2 547	3 219	2 345	1 635	1 136	...	Turquie

LIBYE

IX FINANCIAL AND MONETARY STATISTICS - FINANCES ET STATISTIQUES MONETAIRES

	2009	2010	2011	2012	2013	2014	2015	2016	2017	
IX-1 MONETARY STATISTICS *LIBYAN DINAR (MILLIONS)*										**IX-1 STATISTIQUES MONÉTAIRES** *DINAR LIBYEN (MILLIONS)*
Money supply (M1)	44 721	46 351	57 941	65 609	70 148	78 248	80 987	83 822	...	Masse monétaire (M1)
Quasi-money	7 992	5 030	4 504	5 655	4 707	2 681	1 823	1 712	2 233	Quasi-monnaie
of which demand deposit	...	...	...	...	...	...	...	...	...	dont Monnaie scripturale
Net foreign assets	128 810	134 192	140 155	158 549	154 232	130 049	114 439	106 479	109 996	Avoirs extérieurs nets
Domestic credit	- 51 560	- 57 220	- 48 721	- 59 346	- 48 262	- 21 986	1 097	20 328	28 137	Crédit intérieur
of which claims on private sector	- 69 953	- 78 831	- 69 067	- 82 995	- 74 034	- 49 768	- 27 115	- 6 595	2 267	dont créances sur le secteur privé
of which claims on government sector, net	8 521	8 843	8 363	10 903	13 163	14 103	14 481	13 104	12 265	dont créances nettes sur le gouvernement
International reserves (millions US$)	98 979	99 894	104 999	118 609	115 399	89 283	73 856	69 335	...	Réserves internationales (millions $EU)
Average exchange rate (National currency per US$)	1	1	1	1	1	1	1	1	1	Taux de change (moyen) (monnaie nationale par $ EU)
IX-2 PUBLIC FINANCE *LIBYAN DINAR (MILLIONS)*										**IX-2 FINANCES PUBLIQUES** *DINAR LIBYEN (MILLIONS)*
Total Revenues and Grants	41 785	61 503	16 813	70 131	54 763	21 543	16 843	8 595	13 766	Recettes totales et dons
Direct taxes (on income, profits)	...	...	...	...	...	...	...	717	493	Taxes directes
Domestic indirect taxes revenues	2 504	2 248	461	618	851	660	671	...	...	Taxes Indirectes
Trade taxes	876	1 393	238	249	142	60	46	64	83	Taxes sur le commerce extérieur
Other taxes	...	...	...	...	...	...	...	...	...	Autres taxes
Other revenues	3 057	2 149	285	2 333	1 995	846	5 528	7 813	13 190	Autres recettes
Grants	-	-	72	-	-	-	...	...	...	Dons
Total Expenditures and Net Lending	35 677	54 499	23 367	53 942	65 284	43 814	43 179	28 788	20 640	Dépenses totales et prêts nets
Current expenditure	17 568	28 486	18 964	40 278	51 283	40 408	...	...	...	Dépenses courantes
Wages and Salaries	10 253	15 121	17 580	36 733	42 598	26 892	29 196	21 316	15 912	Rémunérations et salaires
Other purchases of goods and services	...	...	...	...	...	...	...	1 398	398	Achat de biens et services
Other current expenditure	...	...	...	...	...	...	...	5 724	4 330	Autres dépenses courantes
Current transfers	...	...	...	...	...	...	...	...	...	Transferts courants
Interest payments	...	...	...	...	...	...	...	...	...	Intérêts
Capital expenditure	18 984	24 176	3 403	4 800	8 700	6 461	...	...	...	Dépenses d'équipement
Net lending	800	1 280	1 000	900	600	2 000	...	...	...	Prêts nets
Fiscal balance	4 434	7 561	- 6 752	28 736	- 5 821	- 25 476	- 26 336	- 20 193	- 6 874	Solde global y compris les dons
IX-3 BALANCE OF PAYMENTS *LIBYAN DINAR (MILLIONS)*										**IX-3 BALANCE DES PAIEMENTS** *LIBYAN DINAR (MILLIONS)*
Trade balance	18 816	31 020	9 590	44 650	15 199	- 14 120	- 7 687	- 2 645	6 712	Balance commerciale
Services Balance	- 5 848	- 7 510	- 5 326	- 8 623	- 10 530	- 9 368	- 5 507	- 3 888	- 4 987	Balance des services
Net primary income	721	- 37	68	- 2 434	- 527	741	1 641	1 044	882	Revenus primaires nets
Compensation of employees	...	...	...	...	...	...	...	...	...	Rémunération des salariés
Investment income	721	- 37	68	- 2 434	- 527	741	1 708	1 044	882	Revenus des investissements
Net secondary income	- 1 965	- 2 303	- 460	- 3 559	- 4 130	- 1 424	- 1 159	- 1 050	- 1 270	Revenus secondaires nets
Net official transfers	- 264	- 276	333	- 1 075	- 67	- 2	...	...	...	Transferts officiels nets
Workers' remittances	- 1 076	1 271	- 610	- 1 665	- 3 613	- 1 229	- 1 063	- 998	- 1 164	Envois de fonds des travailleurs
Other private transfers	- 2 326	- 2 783	- 976	- 3 303	- 4 513	- 1 422	- 1 257	- 1 103	...	Autres transferts privés
Current account balance	11 724	21 170	3 872	30 034	12	- 24 172	- 12 713	- 6 540	1 337	Solde du compte courant
Capital and financial account	- 4 445	- 12 356	- 3 002	- 9 937	- 5 643	- 535	- 3 939	- 1 300	- 530	Comptes de capital et financier
Capital account	...	...	...	...	...	...	...	...	...	Compte de capital
Financial account	...	...	...	...	...	...	...	...	...	Compte financier
Errors and omissions	- 826	- 3 143	3 345	- 3 199	- 3 042	- 2 698	287	- 1 894	2 887	Erreurs et omissions
Overall balance	6 453	5 671	4 215	16 898	- 8 672	- 27 406	- 16 365	- 9 735	3 694	Balance générale

LIBYA

X DEBT AND FINANCIAL FLOWS - DETTE ET FLUX FINANCIERS

	2009	2010	2011	2012	2013	2014	2015	2016	2017	
X-1 DEBT *US $ (MILLIONS)*										**X-1 DETTE EXTÉRIEURE** *$ E.U (MILLIONS)*
Total external debt	...	...	...	...	...	...	...	...	...	Dette extérieure totale
Private	...	...	...	...	...	...	...	...	...	Privée
Public	...	...	...	...	...	...	...	...	...	Publique
Total external debt service	...	...	...	...	...	...	...	...	...	Service de la dette extérieure
Present value of external debt	...	...	...	...	...	...	...	...	...	Valeur actuelle de la dette extérieure
Total government domestic debt, National currency (millions)	...	...	...	...	...	...	...	...	...	Dette publique intérieure
X-2 FINANCIAL FLOWS *US $ (MILLIONS)*										**X-2 FLUX FINANCIERS** *$ E.U (MILLIONS)*
Net Foreign Direct Investment Inflows	3 310	1 909	...	1 425	702	50	726	493	...	Investissements étranger direct (flux nets entrants)
Main origin of FDI inflows										**Principales origines de l'IDE entrant:**
Germany	261	...	...	...	...	...	...	...	...	Allemagne
France	- 25	69	- 628	- 477	...	...	...	...	...	France
...	...	...	...	...	...	...	...	...	...	...
Spain	...	...	...	- 725	...	...	...	...	...	Espagne
...	...	...	...	...	...	...	...	...	...	...
African countries	10	11	...	3	...	...	...	...	...	Pays africains
Net total official development assistance	40	8	641	87	129	210	157	179	...	Aide publique au développement (nette totale)
Main origin of net ODA										**Principales origines de l'APD nette**
United States	6	7	289	39	12	21	21	20	...	États-Unis
France	19	4	14	4	6	4	3	5	...	France
Turkey	1	1	53	3	...	...	...	...	...	Turquie
United Arab Emirates	...	...	58	-	...	...	...	...	...	Emirates Arabes
Australia	...	...	41	1	-	...	...	...	...	Australie

LIBYE

SOURCES AND NOTES - SOURCES ET NOTES

External trade - Total exports, fob: UNCTAD

External trade - Total import, cif: UNCTAD

ODA: OECD

Monetary statistics: IMF

National Accounts: 2014-2015 Preliminary data

Nationl Accounts:The data for 2014-2015 are estimated by the Africain Developement bank Group

Poverty: World Bank

Commerce exterieur - Exportation, fab: CNUCED

Commerce exterieur - Imporations, caf: CNUCED

APD: OCDE

Statistiques monétaires: FMI

Comptes nationaux:2014-2015 Données préliminaires

Comptes Nationaux:Les données pour les années 2014-2015 sont estimées par la Banque africaine de développement

Pauvreté: Banque mondiale

AREA (km2)	587 295		SUPERFICIE (KM2)
CAPITAL CITY	Antananarivo	Tananarive	CAPITALE
CURRENCY	Malagascy Ariary	Ariary malgache	MONNAIE

I SOCIAL AND DEMOGRAPHIC INDICATORS — INDICATEURS DEMOGRAPHIQUES ET SOCIAUX

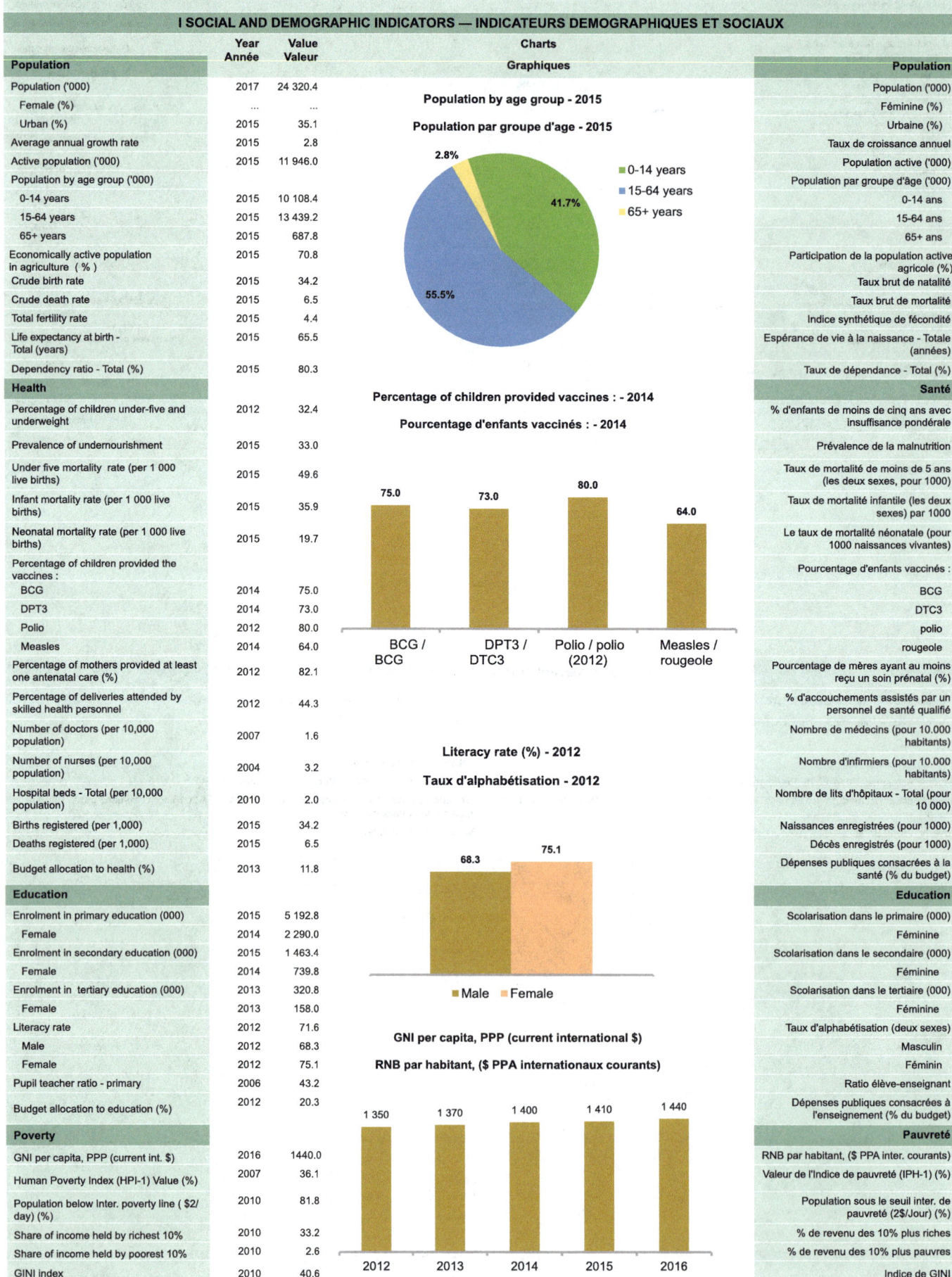

Population	Year Année	Value Valeur		Population
Population ('000)	2017	24 320.4		Population ('000)
Female (%)	...	...		Féminine (%)
Urban (%)	2015	35.1		Urbaine (%)
Average annual growth rate	2015	2.8		Taux de croissance annuel
Active population ('000)	2015	11 946.0		Population active ('000)
Population by age group ('000)				Population par groupe d'âge ('000)
0-14 years	2015	10 108.4		0-14 ans
15-64 years	2015	13 439.2		15-64 ans
65+ years	2015	687.8		65+ ans
Economically active population in agriculture (%)	2015	70.8		Participation de la population active agricole (%)
Crude birth rate	2015	34.2		Taux brut de natalité
Crude death rate	2015	6.5		Taux brut de mortalité
Total fertility rate	2015	4.4		Indice synthétique de fécondité
Life expectancy at birth - Total (years)	2015	65.5		Espérance de vie à la naissance - Totale (années)
Dependency ratio - Total (%)	2015	80.3		Taux de dépendance - Total (%)
Health				**Santé**
Percentage of children under-five and underweight	2012	32.4		% d'enfants de moins de cinq ans avec insuffisance pondérale
Prevalence of undernourishment	2015	33.0		Prévalence de la malnutrition
Under five mortality rate (per 1 000 live births)	2015	49.6		Taux de mortalité de moins de 5 ans (les deux sexes, pour 1000)
Infant mortality rate (per 1 000 live births)	2015	35.9		Taux de mortalité infantile (les deux sexes) par 1000
Neonatal mortality rate (per 1 000 live births)	2015	19.7		Le taux de mortalité néonatale (pour 1000 naissances vivantes)
Percentage of children provided the vaccines :				Pourcentage d'enfants vaccinés :
BCG	2014	75.0		BCG
DPT3	2014	73.0		DTC3
Polio	2012	80.0		polio
Measles	2014	64.0		rougeole
Percentage of mothers provided at least one antenatal care (%)	2012	82.1		Pourcentage de mères ayant au moins reçu un soin prénatal (%)
Percentage of deliveries attended by skilled health personnel	2012	44.3		% d'accouchements assistés par un personnel de santé qualifié
Number of doctors (per 10,000 population)	2007	1.6		Nombre de médecins (pour 10.000 habitants)
Number of nurses (per 10,000 population)	2004	3.2		Nombre d'infirmiers (pour 10.000 habitants)
Hospital beds - Total (per 10,000 population)	2010	2.0		Nombre de lits d'hôpitaux - Total (pour 10 000)
Births registered (per 1,000)	2015	34.2		Naissances enregistrées (pour 1000)
Deaths registered (per 1,000)	2015	6.5		Décès enregistrés (pour 1000)
Budget allocation to health (%)	2013	11.8		Dépenses publiques consacrées à la santé (% du budget)
Education				**Education**
Enrolment in primary education (000)	2015	5 192.8		Scolarisation dans le primaire (000)
Female	2014	2 290.0		Féminine
Enrolment in secondary education (000)	2015	1 463.4		Scolarisation dans le secondaire (000)
Female	2014	739.8		Féminine
Enrolment in tertiary education (000)	2013	320.8		Scolarisation dans le tertiaire (000)
Female	2013	158.0		Féminine
Literacy rate	2012	71.6		Taux d'alphabétisation (deux sexes)
Male	2012	68.3		Masculin
Female	2012	75.1		Féminin
Pupil teacher ratio - primary	2006	43.2		Ratio élève-enseignant
Budget allocation to education (%)	2012	20.3		Dépenses publiques consacrées à l'enseignement (% du budget)
Poverty				**Pauvreté**
GNI per capita, PPP (current int. $)	2016	1440.0		RNB par habitant, ($ PPA inter. courants)
Human Poverty Index (HPI-1) Value (%)	2007	36.1		Valeur de l'Indice de pauvreté (IPH-1) (%)
Population below Inter. poverty line ($2/ day) (%)	2010	81.8		Population sous le seuil inter. de pauvreté (2$/Jour) (%)
Share of income held by richest 10%	2010	33.2		% de revenu des 10% plus riches
Share of income held by poorest 10%	2010	2.6		% de revenu des 10% plus pauvres
GINI index	2010	40.6		Indice de GINI

	2009	2010	2011	2012	2013	2014	2015	2016	2017	
GROSS DOMESTIC PRODUCT BY KIND OF ECONOMIC ACTIVITY AT CURRENT PRICES *MALAGASCY ARIARY (BILLIONS)*										**PRODUIT INTÉRIEUR BRUT PAR BRANCHE D'ACTIVITÉ ÉCONOMIQUE AUX PRIX COURANTS** *FRANC CFA (MILLIARDS)*
Agriculture, hunting , forestry and Fishing	4 490	4 701	5 201	5 612	5 684	6 276	6 714	7 666	8 482	Agriculture, chasse sylviculture et Pêche
Mining and quarrying	16	24	29	40	62	80	90	72	91	Industries extractives
Manufacturing	2 250	2 431	2 682	2 908	3 116	3 419	3 601	3 954	4 437	Industries manufacturières
Electricity, gas & water	191	215	222	245	271	284	331	355	429	Electricité, gaz et eau
Construction	647	654	703	718	724	760	849	933	1 110	Bâtiments et travaux publics
Wholesale & retail trade, restaurants, hotels	2 085	2 250	2 492	2 675	2 844	3 113	3 404	3 769	4 198	Commerce de gros et de détail, restaurants et hôtels
Finance, insurance, real estate, etc.	208	288	374	437	604	632	703	799	908	Banques, assurances, affaires immobilières
Transport and communications	3 071	3 534	3 863	4 366	5 192	5 617	6 771	7 711	9 264	Transport(s) et communications
Public administration and defense	664	769	876	952	1 097	1 345	1 300	1 467	1 618	Administrations publiques et défense
Education	280	317	349	376	421	501	506	571	635	Education
Health And Social Work	390	434	463	493	537	619	655	738	829	Santé et Actions Sociales
Other services	1 297	1 406	1 441	1 511	1 584	1 735	1 972	2 220	2 524	Autres services
Less Imputed Service Charges	- 182	- 267	- 360	- 432	- 623	- 656	- 739	- 844	- 964	Moins Services d'intermédiation financière
Gross domestic product at factor cost / basic prices	15 407	16 755	18 333	19 900	21 514	23 725	26 157	29 410	33 559	Produit intérieur brut aux couts des facteurs / prix de base
Plus: Indirect Taxes / taxes on products, less subsidies	1 319	1 491	1 701	1 873	1 883	2 049	2 305	2 756	3 022	Plus taxes indirectes/impôts sur les produits, moins les subvention
EXPENDITURE ON GROSS DOMESTIC PRODUCT AT CURRENT PURCHASER'S VALUES *MALAGASCY ARIARY (BILLIONS)*										**EMPLOI DU PRODUIT INTÉRIEUR BRUT AUX PRIX COURANTS D'ACQUISITION** *FRANC CFA (MILLIARDS)*
Government final consumption	1 581	1 941	2 041	2 100	2 269	2 806	2 643	2 825	3 114	Consommation finale des administrations publiques
Private final consumption	14 224	15 812	17 588	19 156	20 776	21 984	23 759	24 431	26 777	Consommation finale privée
Gross fixed capital formation	5 815	3 790	3 528	3 774	3 650	3 782	4 723	6 164	8 010	Formation brute de capital fixe
Change in inventories	...	...	...	...	...	...	...	...	...	Variation des stocks
Exports of goods and services	3 742	4 557	5 358	6 317	6 842	8 224	9 078	11 312	13 297	Exportations de biens et services
Less imports of goods and services	8 635	7 854	8 481	9 573	10 140	11 022	11 740	12 565	14 617	Moins importations de biens et services
GDP at purchasers' values	16 726	18 245	20 034	21 774	23 397	25 775	28 463	32 166	36 581	PIB aux prix d'acquisition
GROSS DOMESTIC PRODUCT BY KIND OF ECONOMIC ACTIVITY AT CONSTANT PRICES *ANNUAL GROWTH RATES (%)*										**PRODUIT INTÉRIEUR BRUT PAR BRANCHE D'ACTIVITÉ ECONOMIQUE AUX PRIX CONSTANTS** *TAUX DE CROISSANCE ANNUEL (%)*
Agriculture, hunting , forestry and Fishing	8.5	- 3.4	0.7	1.5	- 6.1	3.3	- 0.9	1.8	2.2	Agriculture, chasse sylviculture et Pêche
Mining and quarrying	- 8.9	55.3	31.1	183.2	219.2	25.9	19.5	- 10.8	1.2	Industries extractives
Manufacturing	- 8.8	- 2.1	3.9	2.7	1.7	2.8	2.3	6.7	7.2	Industries manufacturières
Electricity, gas & water	- 0.4	7.5	- 0.9	3.9	5.6	4.2	3.7	6.5	3.1	Electricité, gaz et eau
Construction	- 17.7	2.6	3.7	3.4	- 2.2	3.1	9.4	5.9	10.3	Bâtiments et travaux publics
Wholesale & retail trade, restaurants, hotels	3.9	- 1.4	2.1	1.9	- 3.4	2.9	1.1	24.2	3.6	Commerce de gros et de détail, restaurants et hôtels
Finance, insurance, real estate, etc.	16.5	9.9	1.5	5.2	8.1	5.1	5.1	2.5	5.8	Banques, assurances, affaires immobilières
Transport and communications	- 9.0	2.9	- 2.3	5.1	4.5	2.2	2.4	3.1	6.0	Transport(s) et communications
Public administration and defense	- 5.0	1.0	1.0	1.1	1.0	1.4	1.0	1.0	3.0	Administrations publiques et défense
Education	- 8.9	0.9	-	1.0	0.9	1.3	6.5	- 1.1	3.9	Education
Health And Social Work	- 11.7	0.8	- 0.7	0.9	0.9	1.3	3.7	4.1	4.5	Santé et Actions Sociales
Other services	- 14.4	0.7	- 1.5	0.8	0.8	1.2	4.4	- 17.3	5.2	Autres services
Less Imputed Service Charges	16.7	9.7	1.3	5.3	8.1	5.3	5.3	2.4	5.8	Moins Services d'intermédiation financière
Gross domestic product at factor cost / basic prices	- 3.0	- 0.6	0.6	3.2	1.4	3.5	2.6	2.7	4.4	Produit intérieur brut aux couts des facteurs / prix de base
Plus: Indirect Taxes / taxes on products, less subsidies	- 11.4	7.2	7.8	2.0	8.4	2.1	6.5	11.8	1.2	Plus taxes indirectes/impôts sur les produits, moins les subventions
Gross domestic product at market prices	- 4.0	0.3	1.5	3.0	2.3	3.3	3.1	4.0	3.9	Produit intérieur brut aux prix du marché
EXPENDITURE ON GROSS DOMESTIC PRODUCT AT CONSTANT PURCHASERS' VALUES *ANNUAL GROWTH RATES (%)*										**EMPLOIS DU PRODUIT INTÉRIEUR BRUT AUX PRIX CONSTANTS D'ACQUISITION** *TAUX DE CROISSANCE ANNUEL (%)*
Government final consumption	- 0.3	7.6	- 5.6	- 3.4	- 4.1	6.0	- 4.5	- 8.0	- 0.3	Consommation finale des administrations publiques
Private final consumption	0.1	0.8	1.6	3.3	1.2	- 0.2	0.3	- 4.7	1.5	Consommation finale privée
Gross fixed capital formation	- 18.9	- 12.3	1.3	5.8	- 2.7	1.2	3.0	29.2	13.5	Formation brute de capital fixe
Exports of goods and services	- 11.3	3.1	7.8	1.8	30.0	8.6	12.2	7.0	4.9	Exportations de biens et services
Less imports of goods and services	- 12.1	- 6.1	3.4	3.6	10.7	- 2.5	1.5	1.8	7.8	Moins importations de biens et services

III INFLATION

	2009	2010	2011	2012	2013	2014	2015	2016	2017	
Annual growth rates (%)										**Taux de croissance annuel (%)**
All item	9.0	9.2	9.5	5.7	5.8	6.1	7.4	6.7	8.3	Ensemble
of which:										dont:
Food and non-alcoholic beverages	8.3	6.5	13.3	5.2	5.0	5.4	6.5	6.4	8.3	Alimentation et boissons non alcoolisés
Alcoholic beverages, tobacco and narcotics	...	...	...	...	...	...	...	...	...	Boissons alcoolisées et tabacs
Clothing and footwear	15.6	15.2	3.6	6.6	8.4	8.7	6.5	3.6	6.0	Habillement et chaussures
Housing, water, electricity, gas and other fuels	11.6	12.4	6.7	7.6	6.1	6.6	11.6	9.2	7.9	Logement, eau, électricité, gaz et autres combustibles
Furnishings, household equipment and routine household maintenance	14.7	20.4	- 0.8	4.5	4.2	3.3	3.7	4.3	8.9	Meubles, articles de ménage et entretien courant
Health	9.8	19.1	8.1	7.6	5.6	6.1	11.6	12.5	13.4	Santé
Transport	2.5	3.0	3.1	2.6	4.5	4.6	2.9	1.3	9.3	Transport
Communication	...	...	...	...	...	...	...	...	...	Communication
Recreation and culture	4.6	13.3	- 5.7	2.6	6.8	7.2	8.0	7.0	5.7	Loisirs et culture
Education	6.9	14.5	14.7	11.1	13.6	9.9	6.2	4.7	5.6	Enseignement
Restaurants and hotels	9.5	17.1	8.2	3.8	8.5	8.0	7.1	8.9	11.8	Restaurants et hôtels
Miscellaneous goods and services	8.4	8.6	10.1	9.4	9.8	11.7	9.0	12.3	11.6	Biens et Services divers

MADAGASCAR

IV AGRICULTURAL PRODUCTION - PRODUCTION AGRICOLE

	2009	2010	2011	2012	2013	2014	2015	2016	2017	
TONNES (THOUSAND)										**Tonnes (milliers)**
Rice, paddy	4 540	4 738	4 300	4 551	3 611	3 978	3 722	3 650	...	Riz, Paddy
Cassava	3 020	3 009	3 490	3 621	3 115	2 930	2 677	2 629	...	Manioc
Bananas	352	361	350	356	355	...	...	...	...	Bananes
Maize	425	412	428	448	379	366	329	316	...	Maïs
Sugar cane	3 000	3 000	3 050	3 270	3 250	...	...	...	...	Canne à sucre

V MINING PRODUCTION - PRODUCTION MINIERE

	2009	2010	2011	2012	2013	2014	2015	2016	2017	
	...	...	...	...	...	...	...	...	...	
Chromium ores and concentrates - Production (metric tons)	...	...	...	...	...	...	197 750	79 345	...	Minerais de chrome et leurs concentrés - Production (tonnes métriques)
	...	...	...	...	...	...	...	...	...	

VI ENERGY - ENERGIE

	2009	2010	2011	2012	2013	2014	2015	2016	2017	
Total electricity generation (GWh)	1 242	1 196	3 469	2 349	2 422	2 498	2 599	2 876	...	Production électrique totale (GWh)
of which										dont
Production of electricity from fossil fuels (GWh)	501	478	1 482	1 512	1 542	1 573	1 604	1 802	...	Production d'électricité à partir de combustibles fossiles (GWh)
Production of hydro electricity (GWh)	734	711	1 967	817	858	901	946	1 047	...	Production d'électricité d'origine hydraulique (GWh)
Production of electricity from solar, wind, tide, wave and other sources (GWh)	7	7	19	20	21	23	48	27	...	Production d'électricité d'origine solaire, éolienne, marée motrice et autres (GWh)

VII TOURISM AND INFRASTRUCTURE - TOURISME ET INFRASTUCTURE

	2009	2010	2011	2012	2013	2014	2015	2016	2017	
VII-1 Tourism										**VII-1 Tourisme**
International tourist arrivals (thousands)	163	196	225	256	196	222	244	293	254	Arrivées de touristes internationaux (milliers)
Rooms in hotels and similar establishments (thousands)	16	18	19	21	22	23	24	25	...	Chambres d'hôtels et établissements assimilés (milliers)
Overnight stays (thousands)	2 413	3 298	3 764	5 052	3 690	4 545	3 551	4 480	5 015	Nuitées (milliers)
Tourism receipts (US$ thousand)	255 700	308 000	477 200	559 300	572 000	666 200	620 400	749 100	786 110	Recettes touristiques (milliers de $ EU)
Total contribution to GDP (%)	10.3	11.4	11.5	12.9	12.5	13.9	14.8	16.9	16.6	Contribution totale au PIB (%)
Total contribution to Employment (%)	8.8	9.5	9.6	11.0	10.6	11.7	12.4	14.2	13.9	Contribution totale à l'emploi (%)
VII-2 Infrastructure										**VII-2 Infrastructure**
Paved road (% of total)	15.9	16.3	16.3	...	...	...	...	...	...	Routes asphaltées (% du total)
Total network (Railways-km)	...	...	...	...	...	...	...	...	...	Réseau total voies ferrées-Km
Main telephone lines (per 100 inhabitants)	0.9	0.7	1.1	1.1	1.1	1.1	1.0	0.6	...	Lignes téléphoniques fixes (pour 100 habitants)
Mobile cellular subscribers (per 100 inhabitants)	30.7	36.6	40.0	39.4	36.9	41.2	44.1	41.8	...	Abonnés aux téléphones mobiles (pour 100 habitants)
Internet users per 100 inhabitants	1.6	1.7	1.9	2.3	3.0	3.7	4.2	4.7	...	Utilisateurs Internet par 100 Habitants
Fixed (wired)-broadband subscriptions per 100 inhabitants	...	...	...	...	...	...	...	...	...	Abonnements à l'Internet fixe (filaire) à large bande pour 100 habitants, par débit

VIII EXTERNAL TRADE - COMMERCE EXTERIEUR

	2009	2010	2011	2012	2013	2014	2015	2016	2017	
US$ (MILLIONS) EXPORTS, FOB										**$ E.U (MILLIONS) EXPORTATIONS, FÀB**
Exports - Total	1 096	1 082	1 590	1 516	1 923	2 243	2 164	2 256	...	Exportations - Total
Exports to Africa	57	107	94	108	177	209	188	182	...	Exportations vers l'Afrique
Main products										**Principaux produits**
Articles of apparel, of textile fabrics, n.e.s.	197	160	191	195	223	227	225	224	...	Vêtements, en tissus, n.d.a.
Men's clothing of textile fabrics, not knitted	69	55	65	75	103	112	107	127	...	Vêtements pour hommes en matières textiles, non tricotés
Nickel	...	...	...	32	357	555	538	355	...	Nickel
Ores and concentrates of base metals, n.e.s.	34	69	115	146	126	105	78	58	...	Minerais et concentrés de métaux communs, n.d.a.
Spices	114	76	345	269	190	277	397	612	...	Épices
Main destinations										**Principales destinations**
China	51	76	96	110	147	105	149	138	...	Chine
France	349	326	445	393	456	477	399	475	...	France
Germany	72	75	92	94	112	114	131	184	...	Allemagne
Netherlands	20	31	26	29	102	135	123	82	...	Pays-Bas
United States	214	74	63	84	157	194	261	336	...	États-Unis
IMPORTS, CIF										
Imports - Total	3 159	2 546	2 730	3 094	3 260	3 355	2 961	2 965	...	Importations - Total (millions)
Imports from Africa	328	392	374	408	371	377	342	365	...	Importations en provenance de l'Afrique
Main products										**Principaux produits**
Cotton fabrics, woven	51	39	56	53	71	72	68	90	...	Tissus de coton, tissés
Petroleum oils or bituminous minerals > 70 % oil	303	351	553	530	537	528	381	383	...	Huiles de pétrole ou de minéraux bitumineux> 70% d'huile
Rice	43	52	87	88	182	131	86	81	...	Riz
Sulphur and unroasted iron pyrites	...	...	9	25	56	66	137	47	...	Soufre et pyrites de fer non grillées
Textile yarn	98	102	111	105	101	97	93	89	...	Fils de textile
Main origin										**Principales provenances**
China	446	378	411	513	581	644	709	800	...	Chine
France	292	362	366	303	309	301	275	281	...	France
India	120	67	108	159	209	207	182	171	...	Inde
South Africa	147	201	174	180	176	157	134	152	...	Afrique du Sud
United Arab Emirates	43	63	344	335	471	460	150	134	...	Emirates Arabes

	2009	2010	2011	2012	2013	2014	2015	2016	2017	
IX-1 MONETARY STATISTICS *MALAGASCY ARIARY (MILLIONS)*										**IX-1 STATISTIQUES MONÉTAIRES** *ARIARY MALGACHE (MILLIONS)*
Money supply (M1)	4 105 519	4 498 493	5 235 491	5 599 333	5 893 928	6 549 306	7 502 259	8 993 062	10 339 800	Masse monétaire (M1)
Quasi-money	1 497 797	1 661 577	1 749 856	1 963 858	2 026 697	1 829 165	2 259 078	2 535 936	2 920 099	Quasi-monnaie
of which demand deposit	...	...	...	...	...	...	...	...	...	dont Monnaie scripturale
Net foreign assets	1 924 641	2 307 952	2 625 962	2 530 094	1 779 374	2 087 203	2 611 552	3 583 180	3 582 405	Avoirs extérieurs nets
Domestic credit	1 951 522	1 911 702	2 368 453	2 827 916	3 662 433	4 454 889	5 363 904	5 965 605	6 802 768	Crédit intérieur
of which claims on private sector	19 764	- 228 821	154 566	420 739	860 753	977 751	1 447 308	1 672 392	1 813 944	dont créances sur le secteur privé
of which claims on government sector, net	1 926 169	2 133 735	2 206 138	2 398 532	2 792 644	3 319 051	3 809 541	4 160 861	4 215 479	dont créances nettes sur le gouvernement
International reserves (millions US$)	990	826	1 147	1 049	772	780	831	1 136	1 219	Réserves internationales (millions $EU)
Average exchange rate (National currency per US$)	1 956	2 090	2 025	2 195	2 207	2 415	2 934	3 177	3 116	Taux de change (moyen) (monnaie nationale par $ EU)
IX-2 PUBLIC FINANCE *MALAGASCY ARIARY (MILLIONS)*										**IX-2 FINANCES PUBLIQUES** *ARIARY MALGACHE (MILLIONS)*
Total Revenues and Grants	1 927 400	2 403 500	2 338 900	2 358 100	2 550 000	3 204 000	3 382 850	4 451 500	4 395 429	Recettes totales et dons
Direct taxes (on income, profits)	367 400	428 000	411 800	418 100	455 000	694 000	706 719	871 200	1 024 114	Taxes directes
Domestic indirect taxes revenues	432 368	519 400	499 700	507 900	556 000	601 000	712 899	693 200	784 457	Taxes Indirectes
Trade taxes	753 432	829 700	997 100	1 048 600	1 172 000	1 252 000	1 458 246	1 680 900	1 896 171	Taxes sur le commerce extérieur
Other taxes	16 500	3 600	3 700	3 100	...	...	...	13 700	12 171	Autres taxes
Other revenues	80 200	268 300	36 300	117 500	71 000	64 000	80 786	103 300	169 371	Autres recettes
Grants	277 500	354 500	390 300	262 900	296 000	593 000	424 200	1 089 200	509 143	Dons
Total Expenditures and Net Lending	2 353 200	2 562 100	2 816 900	2 926 804	3 484 050	3 797 000	4 332 160	5 256 300	5 271 429	Dépenses totales et prêts nets
Current expenditure	1 411 700	1 499 700	1 804 800	2 176 504	2 594 050	2 639 000	3 100 760	3 340 700	3 850 286	Dépenses courantes
Wages and Salaries	803 200	944 900	1 060 400	1 167 300	1 342 000	1 445 000	1 566 106	1 788 500	1 940 400	Rémunérations et salaires
Other purchases of goods and services	514 800	477 700	626 500	836 000	1 117 000	1 046 000	1 122 250	1 201 200	1 617 429	Achat de biens et services
Other current expenditure	93 425	77 100	117 800	173 146	135 000	148 000	412 404	351 000	292 457	Autres dépenses courantes
Current transfers	275	...	100	58	50	...	...	...	...	Transferts courants
Interest payments	128 500	147 900	170 300	155 100	159 000	142 000	230 900	64 700	68 571	Intérêts
Capital expenditure	813 000	914 500	841 800	595 200	731 000	1 016 000	1 000 500	1 621 600	1 226 743	Dépenses d'équipement
Net lending	...	...	...	...	...	...	...	229 300	125 829	Prêts nets
Fiscal balance	- 425 800	- 158 600	- 478 000	- 568 704	- 934 050	- 593 000	- 949 310	- 804 800	- 876 000	Solde global y compris les dons
IX-3 BALANCE OF PAYMENTS *MALAGASCY ARIARY (MILLIONS)*										**IX-3 BALANCE DES PAIEMENTS** *ARIARY MALGACHE (MILLIONS)*
Trade balance	- 3 259	- 2 188	- 2 018	- 2 445	- 1 872	- 1 320	- 964	- 839	- 1 392	Balance commerciale
Services Balance	- 697	- 408	- 259	158	- 157	191	- 161	121	- 33	Balance des services
Net primary income	- 179	- 273	- 314	- 691	- 741	- 722	- 1 103	- 1 294	- 1 096	Revenus primaires nets
Compensation of employees	40	74	62	33	36	35	- 33	9	10	Rémunération des salariés
Investment income	27	57	111	41	3	...	- 1 072	- 1 330	- 1 136	Revenus des investissements
Net secondary income	599	1 016	1 192	1 312	1 400	1 771	1 554	2 194	2 316	Revenus secondaires nets
Net official transfers	12	127	131	149	149	310	226	443	484	Transferts officiels nets
Workers' remittances	...	...	...	...	...	...	...	...	...	Envois de fonds des travailleurs
Other private transfers	588	890	1 061	1 164	1 250	1 460	1 328	1 751	1 832	Autres transferts privés
Current account balance	- 3 535	- 1 853	- 1 400	- 1 665	- 1 371	- 81	- 675	181	- 205	Solde du compte courant
Capital and financial account	3 306	1 974	1 755	1 541	811	177	1 378	- 56	865	Comptes de capital et financier
Capital account	148	157	372	262	296	382	382	882	891	Compte de capital
Financial account	3 158	1 818	1 383	1 279	516	- 205	996	- 938	- 26	Compte financier
Errors and omissions	183	2	- 97	- 62	- 24	- 42	- 736	- 116	- 651	Erreurs et omissions
Overall balance	- 47	124	258	- 186	- 584	54	- 33	9	10	Balance générale

MADAGASCAR

X DEBT AND FINANCIAL FLOWS - DETTE ET FLUX FINANCIERS

	2009	2010	2011	2012	2013	2014	2015	2016	2017	
X-1 DEBT *US $ (MILLIONS)*										**X-1 DETTE EXTÉRIEURE** *$ E.U (MILLIONS)*
Total external debt	3 107	3 368	3 873	4 324	4 639	4 528	4 490	4 367	4 713	Dette extérieure totale
Private	...	...	...	...	...	...	...	...	...	Privée
Public	2 221	2 051	2 136	2 258	2 381	2 419	2 534	2 562	...	Publique
Total external debt service	338	462	607	711	769	745	684	666	...	Service de la dette extérieure
Present value of external debt	...	...	...	...	...	...	...	1 940	...	Valeur actuelle de la dette extérieure
Total government domestic debt, National currency (millions)	...	...	...	...	...	...	...	...	...	Dette publique intérieure
X-2 FINANCIAL FLOWS *US $ (MILLIONS)*										**X-2 FLUX FINANCIERS** *$ E.U (MILLIONS)*
Net Foreign Direct Investment Inflows	1 066	808	810	812	567	351	441	541	...	Investissements étranger direct (flux nets entrants)
Main origin of FDI inflows										**Principales origines de l'IDE entrant:**
France	8	33	- 36	1	...	...	...	...	...	France
...	...	...	...	...	...	...	...	...	...	...
...	...	...	...	...	...	...	...	...	...	...
Germany	3	- 2	- 2	...	...	...	...	...	...	Allemagne
...	...	...	...	...	...	...	...	...	...	...
African countries	...	...	...	...	...	...	...	...	...	Pays africains
Net total official development assistance	434	477	447	368	499	588	677	622	...	Aide publique au développement (nette totale)
Main origin of net ODA										**Principales origines de l'APD nette**
International Development Association [IDA]	36	79	44	47	80	118	106	128	...	International Development Association
France	97	84	89	73	74	65	99	51	...	France
United States	77	79	64	49	56	64	152	116	...	États-Unis
...	...	...	...	...	...	...	...	...	...	...
Japan	19	10	11	14	51	10	17	8	...	Japon

SOURCES AND NOTES - SOURCES ET NOTES

External trade - Total exports, fob: UNCTAD	Commerce exterieur - Exportation, fab: CNUCED
External trade - Total import, cif: UNCTAD	Commerce exterieur - Imporations, caf: CNUCED
ODA: OECD	APD: OCDE
Monetary statistics: IMF	Statistiques monétaires: FMI
National Accounts:2014-2015: Revised;2016:Prevision; 2017 Projection	Comptes nationaux: 2014-2015: Révisées;2016:Prévison;2017 Projection
Poverty: World Bank	Pauvreté: Banque mondiale

	AREA (km2)	118 480		SUPERFICIE (KM2)
	CAPITAL CITY	Lilongwe	Lilongwe	CAPITALE
	CURRENCY	Malawi Kwacha	Kwacha malawite	MONNAIE

I SOCIAL AND DEMOGRAPHIC INDICATORS — INDICATEURS DEMOGRAPHIQUES ET SOCIAUX

	Year Année	Value Valeur	Charts Graphiques	
Population				**Population**
Population ('000)	2017	17 373.2		Population ('000)
Female (%)	2017	50.8		Féminine (%)
Urban (%)	2017	16.6		Urbaine (%)
Average annual growth rate	2017	3.2		Taux de croissance annuel
Active population ('000)	2016	6 873.4		Population active ('000)
Population by age group ('000)				Population par groupe d'âge ('000)
0-14 years	2017	8 026.4		0-14 ans
15-64 years	2017	8 828.0		15-64 ans
65+ years	2017	519.0		65+ ans
Economically active population in agriculture (%)	2015	80.7		Participation de la population active agricole (%)
Crude birth rate	2017	42.0		Taux brut de natalité
Crude death rate	2017	10.4		Taux brut de mortalité
Total fertility rate	2017	5.4		Indice synthétique de fécondité
Life expectancy at birth - Total (years)	2017	58.4		Espérance de vie à la naissance - Totale (années)
Dependency ratio - Total (%)	2017	96.8		Taux de dépendance - Total (%)
Health				**Santé**
Percentage of children under-five and underweight	2015	12.0		% d'enfants de moins de cinq ans avec insuffisance pondérale
Prevalence of undernourishment	2015	20.7		Prévalence de la malnutrition
Under five mortality rate (per 1 000 live births)	2015	64.0		Taux de mortalité de moins de 5 ans (les deux sexes, pour 1000)
Infant mortality rate (per 1 000 live births)	2017	63.3		Taux de mortalité infantile (les deux sexes) par 1000
Neonatal mortality rate (per 1 000 live births)	2015	21.8		Le taux de mortalité néonatale (pour 1000 naissances vivantes)
Percentage of children provided the vaccines :				Pourcentage d'enfants vaccinés :
BCG	2015	97.6		BCG
DPT3	2015	93.0		DTC3
Polio	2015	81.2		polio
Measles	2015	91.2		rougeole
Percentage of mothers provided at least one antenatal care (%)	2015	94.8		Pourcentage de mères ayant au moins reçu un soin prénatal (%)
Percentage of deliveries attended by skilled health personnel	2015	89.8		% d'accouchements assistés par un personnel de santé qualifié
Number of doctors (per 10,000 population)	2009	0.2		Nombre de médecins (pour 10.000 habitants)
Number of nurses (per 10,000 population)	2009	3.4		Nombre d'infirmiers (pour 10.000 habitants)
Hospital beds - Total (per 10,000 population)	2011	13.0		Nombre de lits d'hôpitaux - Total (pour 10 000)
Births registered (per 1,000)	2015	38.5		Naissances enregistrées (pour 1000)
Deaths registered (per 1,000)	2015	7.5		Décès enregistrés (pour 1000)
Budget allocation to health (%)	2014	10.0		Dépenses publiques consacrées à la santé (% du budget)
Education				**Education**
Enrolment in primary education (000)	2017	5 074.0		Scolarisation dans le primaire (000)
Female	2017	2 560.0		Féminine
Enrolment in secondary education (000)	2017	373.0		Scolarisation dans le secondaire (000)
Female	2017	178.0		Féminine
Enrolment in tertiary education (000)	2015	13.4		Scolarisation dans le tertiaire (000)
Female	2015	7.3		Féminine
Literacy rate	2017	72.8		Taux d'alphabétisation (deux sexes)
Male	2017	80.9		Masculin
Female	2017	65.8		Féminin
Pupil teacher ratio - primary	2017	72.0		Ratio élève-enseignant
Budget allocation to education (%)	2016	27.0		Dépenses publiques consacrées à l'enseignement (% du budget)
Poverty				**Pauvreté**
GNI per capita, PPP (current int. $)	2016	1140.0		RNB par habitant, ($ PPA inter. courants)
Human Poverty Index (HPI-1) Value (%)	2007	28.2		Valeur de l'Indice de pauvreté (IPH-1) (%)
Population below Inter. poverty line ($2/day) (%)	2010	70.9		Population sous le seuil inter. de pauvreté (2$/Jour) (%)
Share of income held by richest 10%	2010	37.5		% de revenu des 10% plus riches
Share of income held by poorest 10%	2010	2.2		% de revenu des 10% plus pauvres
GINI index	2010	46.1		Indice de GINI

Population by age group - 2017
Population par groupe d'age - 2017

- 0-14 years: 46.2%
- 15-64 years: 50.8%
- 65+ years: 3.0%

Percentage of children provided vaccines : - 2015
Pourcentage d'enfants vaccinés : - 2015

BCG / BCG	DPT3 / DTC3	Polio / polio	Measles / rougeole
97.6	93.0	81.2	91.2

Literacy rate (%) - 2017
Taux d'alphabétisation - 2017

- Male: 80.9
- Female: 65.8

GNI per capita, PPP (current international $)
RNB par habitant, ($ PPA internationaux courants)

2012	2013	2014	2015	2016
1 040	1 070	1 120	1 120	1 140

MALAWI

II NATIONAL ACCOUNTS — COMPTES NATIONAUX

	2009	2010	2011	2012	2013	2014	2015	2016	2017	
GROSS DOMESTIC PRODUCT BY KIND OF ECONOMIC ACTIVITY AT CURRENT PRICES *MALAWI KWACHA (MILLIONS)*										**PRODUIT INTÉRIEUR BRUT PAR BRANCHE D'ACTIVITÉ ÉCONOMIQUE AUX PRIX COURANTS** *KWACHA MALAWITE (MILLIONS)*
Agriculture, hunting , forestry and Fishing	265 944	310 167	360 446	426 653	577 064	758 977	922 098	1 064 942	1 318 052	Agriculture, chasse sylviculture et Pêche
Mining and quarrying	7 156	10 528	12 393	14 676	19 980	23 593	29 289	33 992	39 919	Industries extractives
Manufacturing	90 708	103 789	126 146	136 188	182 996	240 726	306 839	359 247	439 971	Industries manufacturières
Electricity, gas & water	11 738	13 640	17 374	18 712	25 128	32 044	40 294	46 630	55 715	Electricité, gaz et eau
Construction	24 385	31 393	37 183	42 231	54 817	71 107	90 368	107 988	129 230	Bâtiments et travaux publics
Wholesale & retail trade, restaurants, hotels	156 761	181 450	229 580	248 811	340 659	447 952	576 961	684 667	842 071	Commerce de gros et de détail, restaurants et hôtels
Finance, insurance, real estate, etc.	103 875	134 876	156 253	195 908	256 895	332 162	421 562	507 366	615 530	Banques, assurances, affaires immobilières
Transport and communications	49 608	65 576	75 000	93 673	127 087	171 566	225 254	273 172	332 603	Transport(s) et communications
Public administration and defense	13 960	20 058	39 303	29 058	37 986	49 411	64 478	79 156	97 635	Administrations publiques et défense
Education	22 668	25 135	28 551	36 726	49 285	63 413	82 630	103 044	132 431	Education
Health And Social Work	22 713	27 229	32 009	38 419	51 378	66 266	84 300	104 413	128 551	Santé et Actions Sociales
Other services	40 964	47 768	39 261	69 578	93 455	121 963	158 527	193 228	232 821	Autres services
Less Imputed Service Charges	...	...	...	...	...	...	...	...	...	Moins Services d'intermédiation financière
Gross domestic product at factor cost / basic prices	810 479	971 608	1 153 499	1 350 632	1 816 731	2 379 181	3 002 601	3 557 846	4 364 528	Produit intérieur brut aux couts des facteurs / prix de base
Plus: Indirect Taxes / taxes on products, less subsidies	63 504	75 728	99 251	74 597	111 109	155 291	210 083	254 155	312 355	Plus taxes indirectes/impôts sur les produits, moins les subventions
EXPENDITURE ON GROSS DOMESTIC PRODUCT AT CURRENT PURCHASER'S VALUES *MALAWI KWACHA (MILLIONS)*										**EMPLOI DU PRODUIT INTÉRIEUR BRUT AUX PRIX COURANTS D'ACQUISITION** *KWACHA MALAWITE (MILLIONS)*
Government final consumption	107 993	95 281	116 055	137 992	201 072	250 738	296 623	371 749	476 419	Consommation finale des administrations publiques
Private final consumption	813 241	1 021 561	1 053 597	1 252 750	1 825 424	2 276 310	2 692 872	3 374 898	4 325 139	Consommation finale privée
Gross fixed capital formation	142 538	159 734	158 489	188 447	274 592	342 418	405 080	507 675	650 616	Formation brute de capital fixe
Change in inventories	- 25 796	10 129	124 637	148 196	215 941	269 279	318 557	399 238	511 648	Variation des stocks
Exports of goods and services	187 363	183 055	251 093	344 240	508 488	697 721	773 209	863 049	760 305	Exportations de biens et services
Less imports of goods and services	351 357	422 425	451 120	646 394	1 097 678	1 301 994	1 273 657	1 704 609	2 047 245	Moins importations de biens et services
GDP at purchasers' values	873 982	1 047 336	1 252 750	1 425 230	1 927 840	2 534 472	3 212 684	3 812 000	4 676 882	PIB aux prix d'acquisition
GROSS DOMESTIC PRODUCT BY KIND OF ECONOMIC ACTIVITY AT CONSTANT PRICES *ANNUAL GROWTH RATES (%)*										**PRODUIT INTÉRIEUR BRUT PAR BRANCHE D'ACTIVITÉ ECONOMIQUE AUX PRIX CONSTANTS** *TAUX DE CROISSANCE ANNUEL (%)*
Agriculture, hunting , forestry and Fishing	4.0	6.8	4.3	1.0	6.2	6.3	- 1.0	- 0.1	7.1	Agriculture, chasse sylviculture et Pêche
Mining and quarrying	17.6	23.9	1.4	5.3	6.9	- 4.6	1.1	0.4	1.6	Industries extractives
Manufacturing	29.1	11.4	1.4	- 0.9	5.6	6.3	3.8	1.3	6.0	Industries manufacturières
Electricity, gas & water	2.3	2.9	6.0	- 0.9	5.5	3.0	2.4	0.1	3.4	Electricité, gaz et eau
Construction	1.8	- 2.4	2.3	0.7	2.0	4.8	3.5	3.4	3.6	Bâtiments et travaux publics
Wholesale & retail trade, restaurants, hotels	8.7	3.1	3.8	1.2	7.6	6.2	4.9	2.7	6.4	Commerce de gros et de détail, restaurants et hôtels
Finance, insurance, real estate, etc.	7.6	10.0	7.2	3.8	3.0	4.5	3.4	4.2	5.0	Banques, assurances, affaires immobilières
Transport and communications	3.9	9.3	3.7	5.5	6.6	9.1	7.0	4.9	5.4	Transport(s) et communications
Public administration and defense	7.3	8.9	80.2	- 38.4	2.7	5.1	6.3	6.2	6.7	Administrations publiques et défense
Education	11.1	7.6	4.3	7.3	5.4	4.0	6.1	7.9	11.2	Education
Health And Social Work	14.1	11.7	6.0	1.9	5.1	4.2	3.6	7.2	6.5	Santé et Actions Sociales
Other services	9.0	5.1	- 25.2	49.2	5.5	5.4	5.9	5.5	4.3	Autres services
Less Imputed Service Charges	...	...	...	...	...	...	...	...	...	Moins Services d'intermédiation financière
Gross domestic product at factor cost / basic prices	8.3	7.0	4.3	2.0	5.7	5.8	2.8	2.5	6.2	Produit intérieur brut aux couts des facteurs / prix de base
Plus: Indirect Taxes / taxes on products, less subsidies	8.7	5.2	11.4	- 32.3	17.0	12.9	10.2	4.7	6.4	Plus taxes indirectes/impôts sur les produits, moins les subventions
Gross domestic product at market prices	8.3	6.9	4.9	- 0.6	6.3	6.2	3.3	2.7	6.2	Produit intérieur brut aux prix du marché
EXPENDITURE ON GROSS DOMESTIC PRODUCT AT CONSTANT PURCHASERS' VALUES *ANNUAL GROWTH RATES (%)*										**EMPLOIS DU PRODUIT INTÉRIEUR BRUT AUX PRIX CONSTANTS D'ACQUISITION** *TAUX DE CROISSANCE ANNUEL (%)*
Government final consumption	3.3	- 26.9	13.0	- 0.6	6.3	6.2	3.3	2.7	6.4	Consommation finale des administrations publiques
Private final consumption	9.8	3.5	1.5	- 0.6	6.3	6.2	3.3	2.7	6.2	Consommation finale privée
Gross fixed capital formation	- 32.5	- 7.0	- 7.6	- 0.6	6.3	6.2	3.3	2.7	6.4	Formation brute de capital fixe
Exports of goods and services	13.6	- 2.3	24.2	- 0.6	6.3	6.2	3.3	2.7	6.4	Exportations de biens et services
Less imports of goods and services	- 19.6	- 9.4	1.0	- 0.6	6.3	6.2	3.3	2.7	6.4	Moins importations de biens et services

III INFLATION

	2009	2010	2011	2012	2013	2014	2015	2016	2017	
Annual growth rates (%)										**Taux de croissance annuel (%)**
All item	8.4	7.4	7.6	21.3	27.3	23.8	21.9	21.7	12.2	Ensemble
of which:										dont:
Food and non-alcoholic beverages	7.4	5.1	3.2	18.8	23.3	21.2	23.9	24.8	13.6	Alimentation et boissons non alcoolisés
Alcoholic beverages, tobacco and narcotics	11.5	13.1	10.4	18.1	27.0	11.9	10.3	17.9	12.8	Boissons alcoolisées et tabacs
Clothing and footwear	9.0	7.9	10.2	12.9	24.2	20.0	17.1	14.2	12.2	Habillement et chaussures
Housing, water, electricity, gas and other fuels	2.9	6.7	12.1	33.9	41.5	32.3	29.4	19.3	19.3	Logement, eau, électricité, gaz et autres combustibles
Furnishings, household equipment and routine household maintenance	18.1	13.1	10.2	20.7	25.0	34.3	14.4	15.9	10.4	Meubles, articles de ménage et entretien courant
Health	...	...	...	...	18.7	17.4	14.5	16.2	20.4	Santé
Transport	12.1	12.7	17.0	21.0	23.5	22.5	16.5	14.0	5.4	Transport
Communication	...	...	...	...	30.6	30.8	7.7	10.9	0.2	Communication
Recreation and culture	...	...	...	...	39.5	38.7	15.5	20.3	19.1	Loisirs et culture
Education	...	...	...	...	26.9	4.0	28.1	21.5	9.1	Enseignement
Restaurants and hotels	...	...	...	...	94.4	19.2	13.1	13.6	10.4	Restaurants et hôtels
Miscellaneous goods and services	13.3	9.4	14.6	18.1	18.1	12.0	19.6	11.2	8.6	Biens et Services divers

IV AGRICULTURAL PRODUCTION - PRODUCTION AGRICOLE

TONNES (THOUSAND)	2009	2010	2011	2012	2013	2014	2015	2016	2017	Tonnes (milliers)
Maize	3 767	3 419	3 895	3 624	3 640	3 978	2 776	2 369	...	Maïs
Tobacco, unmanufactured	232	220	237	73	133	139	127	120	...	Tabac brut
Tea	53	52	47	42	46	...	42	...	...	Thé
Sugar cane	2 600	2 500	2 500	2 800	2 900	...	...	...	...	Canne à sucre
Rice, paddy	301	110	118	110	125	115	111	84	...	Riz, Paddy

V MINING PRODUCTION - PRODUCTION MINIERE

	2009	2010	2011	2012	2013	2014	2015	2016	2017	
Hard Coal - Production, metric tons (thousands)	59	79	77	71	67	64	59	43	60	Houille - Production, tonnes métriques (milliers)
Cement, except in the form of clinkers - Production (metric tons)	47 150	57 296	60 161	64 100	60 895	57 850	65 560	188 946	200 000	Ciments, autres que sous forme de "clinkers" - Production (tonnes métriques)
	...	...	...	...	...	...	...	...		

VI ENERGY - ENERGIE

	2009	2010	2011	2012	2013	2014	2015	2016	2017	
Total electricity generation (GWh)	1 899	1 943	1 745	2 180	2 442	2 640	2 927	...	...	Production électrique totale (GWh)
of which										dont
Production of electricity from fossil fuels (GWh)	240	210	6	7	43	8	9	...	...	Production d'électricité à partir de combustibles fossiles (GWh)
Production of hydro electricity (GWh)	1 659	1 733	1 733	2 164	2 380	2 618	2 880	...	...	Production d'électricité d'origine hydraulique (GWh)
Production of electricity from solar, wind, tide, wave and other sources (GWh)	...	...	3	3	12	13	34	...	...	Production d'électricité d'origine solaire, éolienne, marée motrice et autres (GWh)

VII TOURISM AND INFRASTRUCTURE - TOURISME ET INFRASTUCTURE

VII-1 Tourism	2009	2010	2011	2012	2013	2014	2015	2016	2017	VII-1 Tourisme
International tourist arrivals (thousands)	755	746	767	770	795	819	805	823	840	Arrivées de touristes internationaux (milliers)
Rooms in hotels and similar establishments (thousands)	...	...	...	...	...	...	...	...	...	Chambres d'hôtels et établissements assimilés (milliers)
Overnight stays (thousands)	5 167	6 057	5 821	6 702	7 476	8 274	7 244	7 980	8 218	Nuitées (milliers)
Tourism receipts (US$ thousand)	31 000	29 100	28 900	29 100	26 800	30 300	32 600	29 433	31 315	Recettes touristiques (milliers de $ EU)
Total contribution to GDP (%)	8.0	7.5	7.1	7.0	6.8	7.0	7.3	7.4	7.0	Contribution totale au PIB (%)
Total contribution to Employment (%)	6.5	6.1	6.2	6.2	6.1	6.1	6.2	6.2	6.2	Contribution totale à l'emploi (%)
VII-2 Infrastructure										VII-2 Infrastructure
Paved road (% of total)	26.0	...	45.0	...	...	...	...	...	...	Routes asphaltées (% du total)
Total network (Railways-km)	...	...	...	...	...	...	...	...	...	Réseau total voies ferrées-Km
Main telephone lines (per 100 inhabitants)	0.8	1.0	1.1	1.4	...	...	...	...	...	Lignes téléphoniques fixes (pour 100 habitants)
Mobile cellular subscribers (per 100 inhabitants)	17.1	20.8	25.6	29.2	32.3	33.5	37.9	40.3	...	Abonnés aux téléphones mobiles (pour 100 habitants)
Internet users per 100 inhabitants	1.1	2.3	3.3	4.4	5.1	5.8	9.3	9.6	...	Utilisateurs Internet par 100 Habitants
Fixed (wired)-broadband subscriptions per 100 inhabitants	...	...	...	...	...	...	...	...	...	Abonnements à l'Internet fixe (filaire) à large bande pour 100 habitants, par débit

VIII EXTERNAL TRADE - COMMERCE EXTERIEUR

US$ (MILLIONS) EXPORTS, FOB	2009	2010	2011	2012	2013	2014	2015	2016	2017	$ E.U (MILLIONS) EXPORTATIONS, FAB
Exports - Total	1 188	1 066	1 425	1 183	1 208	1 342	1 080	1 087	...	Exportations - Total
Exports to Africa	311	304	531	314	302	422	324	474	...	Exportations vers l'Afrique
Main products										Principaux produits
Oil seeds and oleaginous fruits (excluding flour)	16	13	30	63	54	58	19	39	...	Graines oléagineuses et oléagineuses (à l'exclusion de la farine)
Sugar, molasses and honey	73	71	163	73	98	58	91	93	...	Sucre, mélasse et miel
Tea and mate	72	74	90	71	84	86	66	70	...	Thé et maté
Tobacco, unmanufactured; tobacco refuse	760	584	611	607	579	672	543	468	...	Tabac, non manufacturé; déchets de tabac
Vegetables	65	34	26	45	37	60	70	48	...	Des légumes
Main destinations										Principales destinations
Belgium	208	132	93	85	100	172	114	...	...	Belgique
Zimbabwe	36	58	122	47	48	89	100	...	...	Zimbabwe
Mozambique	64	36	45	33	31	131	100	...	...	Mozambique
South Africa	122	62	117	90	92	105	80	...	...	Afrique du Sud
United Kingdom	50	49	109	40	71	64	64	...	...	Royaume-Uni
IMPORTS, CIF										
Imports - Total	2 022	2 173	2 428	2 330	2 845	2 774	2 312	2 084	...	Importations - Total (millions)
Imports from Africa	1 172	1 060	1 090	1 022	1 287	1 176	808	791	...	Importations en provenance de l'Afrique
Main products										Principaux produits
Petroleum oils and oils obtained from bituminous minerals, other than crude	198	199	199	314	389	359	235	...	...	Huiles de pétrole ou de minéraux bitumineux autres que bruts;
Medicaments	86	101	130	156	162	185	148	...	...	Médicaments
Mineral or chemical fertilisers, nitrogenous.	91	130	137	186	212	134	123	...	...	Engrais minéraux ou chimiques azotés.
Mineral or chemical fertilisers	80	66	46	78	120	69	97	...	...	Engrais minéraux ou chimiques
Motor cars and other motor vehicles	66	58	48	53	59	55	58	...	...	Véhicules automobiles et autres véhicules automobiles
Main origin										Principales provenances
South Africa	691	654	606	570	618	527	417	...	...	Afrique du Sud
China	120	198	225	252	265	276	304	...	...	Chine
United Arab Emirates	80	108	113	116	178	151	254	...	...	Emirates Arabes
India	96	165	280	191	223	326	238	...	...	Inde
Zambia	73	121	110	80	130	111	118	...	...	Zambie

MALAWI

	2009	2010	2011	2012	2013	2014	2015	2016	2017	
IX-1 MONETARY STATISTICS *MALAWI KWACHA (MILLIONS)*										**IX-1 STATISTIQUES MONÉTAIRES** *KWACHA MALAWITE (MILLIONS)*
Money supply (M1)	173 050	231 711	314 331	386 461	521 963	629 763	778 808	897 266	1 052 062	Masse monétaire (M1)
Quasi-money	92 132	124 841	172 396	233 082	324 190	348 782	466 536	508 219	498 968	Quasi-monnaie
of which demand deposit	...	...	...	...	...	...	...	...	...	dont Monnaie scripturale
Net foreign assets	- 2 045	21 234	3 968	32 819	116 207	240 925	333 032	354 992	328 394	Avoirs extérieurs nets
Domestic credit	213 801	243 602	334 320	377 907	421 544	389 159	539 753	764 342	813 641	Crédit intérieur
of which claims on private sector	112 517	94 096	139 757	139 673	153 257	92 186	144 352	346 823	398 911	dont créances sur le secteur privé
of which claims on government sector, net	95 044	144 843	174 538	218 866	250 446	293 038	390 325	408 305	405 445	dont créances nettes sur le gouvernement
International reserves (millions US$)	130	272	194	221	397	588	670	605	670	Réserves internationales (millions $EU)
Average exchange rate (National currency per US$)	141	150	157	249	364	425	496	718	730	Taux de change (moyen) (monnaie nationale par $ EU)
IX-2 PUBLIC FINANCE *MALAWI KWACHA (MILLIONS)*										**IX-2 FINANCES PUBLIQUES** *KWACHA MALAWITE (MILLIONS)*
Total Revenues and Grants	210 270	257 499	271 901	257 474	483 017	522 212	617 490	765 000	946 000	Recettes totales et dons
Direct taxes (on income, profits)	50 549	66 411	81 117	89 924	139 017	192 212	242 490	289 000	384 000	Taxes directes
Domestic indirect taxes revenues	57 845	64 451	79 425	84 000	111 000	168 000	189 000	225 000	309 000	Taxes Indirectes
Trade taxes	13 571	14 993	17 488	17 550	33 000	41 000	46 000	53 000	68 000	Taxes sur le commerce extérieur
Other taxes	- 2 943	- 4 100	- 2 335	- 3 000	- 4 000	- 2 000	- 6 000	- 3 000	- 6 000	Autres taxes
Other revenues	15 269	37 296	31 877	26 000	28 000	53 000	67 000	70 000	97 000	Autres recettes
Grants	75 979	78 448	64 329	43 000	176 000	70 000	79 000	131 000	94 000	Dons
Total Expenditures and Net Lending	247 520	255 948	295 197	324 621	500 582	661 927	805 046	1 005 000	1 176 000	Dépenses totales et prêts nets
Current expenditure	182 917	174 364	207 407	222 621	363 582	463 927	538 046	704 000	771 500	Dépenses courantes
Wages and Salaries	37 595	44 792	58 092	70 000	97 000	140 000	197 000	226 000	271 000	Rémunérations et salaires
Other purchases of goods and services	86 137	84 120	95 054	95 000	168 582	198 927	202 046	202 000	276 000	Achat de biens et services
Other current expenditure	407			...	...	...	...	104 000	59 500	Autres dépenses courantes
Current transfers	58 778	45 452	54 261	57 621	98 000	125 000	139 000	172 000	165 000	Transferts courants
Interest payments	17 863	21 498	22 819	24 000	33 000	98 000	115 000	133 000	184 000	Intérêts
Capital expenditure	46 740	60 086	64 971	78 000	104 000	100 000	152 000	168 000	220 500	Dépenses d'équipement
Net lending	...	...	...	...	...	...	...	...	...	Prêts nets
Fiscal balance	- 37 250	1 551	- 23 296	- 67 147	- 17 564	- 139 715	- 187 556	- 240 000	- 230 000	Solde global y compris les dons
IX-3 BALANCE OF PAYMENTS *MALAWI KWACHA (MILLIONS)*										**IX-3 BALANCE DES PAIEMENTS** *KWACHA MALAWITE (MILLIONS)*
Trade balance	- 104 461	- 189 623	- 174 438	- 261 680	- 520 448	- 515 265	- 394 070	- 577 909	- 567 410	Balance commerciale
Services Balance	- 21 186	- 24 050	- 25 590	- 40 474	- 68 742	- 89 010	- 106 380	- 123 588	- 154 038	Balance des services
Net primary income	- 17 247	- 28 666	- 59 093	- 10 429	- 97 039	- 127 222	- 163 083	- 145 791	- 138 673	Revenus primaires nets
Compensation of employees	- 937	- 924	- 880	- 1 456	- 1 970	- 2 590	- 3 282	- 3 895	- 4 742	Rémunération des salariés
Investment income	- 16 310	- 27 742	- 58 213	- 8 972	- 95 069	- 124 633	- 159 801	- 141 896	- 133 930	Revenus des investissements
Net secondary income	66 150	96 474	81 208	117 042	215 864	230 691	198 778	317 974	307 258	Revenus secondaires nets
Net official transfers	30 530	56 960	37 893	47 042	118 278	102 388	36 154	52 181	70 190	Transferts officiels nets
Workers' remittances	1 408	1 956	2 112	4 074	8 412	11 060	14 018	16 634	20 254	Envois de fonds des travailleurs
Other private transfers	34 211	37 558	41 203	65 925	89 174	117 243	148 606	249 160	216 814	Autres transferts privés
Current account balance	- 76 744	- 145 864	- 177 913	- 195 541	- 470 364	- 500 806	- 464 755	- 529 314	- 552 863	Solde du compte courant
Capital and financial account	89 184	107 801	191 000	123 972	495 762	508 238	527 616	659 873	677 850	Comptes de capital et financier
Capital account	57 692	106 853	71 732	89 587	222 667	194 104	114 025	170 641	218 606	Compte de capital
Financial account	31 492	948	119 268	34 385	273 095	314 135	413 591	489 232	459 244	Compte financier
Errors and omissions	- 12 440	38 063	- 13 087	71 569	- 25 397	- 7 432	- 62 861	- 130 559	- 124 987	Erreurs et omissions
Overall balance	- 12 964	20 380	- 17 018	6 305	68 594	76 309	45 114	- 47 685	68 375	Balance générale

MALAWI

X DEBT AND FINANCIAL FLOWS - DETTE ET FLUX FINANCIERS

	2009	2010	2011	2012	2013	2014	2015	2016	2017	
X-1 DEBT *US $ (MILLIONS)*										**X-1 DETTE EXTÉRIEURE** *$ E.U (MILLIONS)*
Total external debt	952	1 112	1 118	1 430	1 664	2 037	2 002	2 014	2 149	Dette extérieure totale
Private	...	...	...	...	...	...	...	...	...	Privée
Public	799	866	908	1 200	1 447	1 818	1 783	1 789	...	Publique
Total external debt service	13	18	20	28	74	81	121	197	...	Service de la dette extérieure
Present value of external debt	...	...	...	...	...	...	...	1 088		Valeur actuelle de la dette extérieure
Total government domestic debt, National currency (millions)	172	154	206	254	...	...	...	...	...	Dette publique intérieure
X-2 FINANCIAL FLOWS *US $ (MILLIONS)*										**X-2 FLUX FINANCIERS** *$ E.U (MILLIONS)*
Net Foreign Direct Investment Inflows	49	97	129	130	446	599	288	326	...	Investissements étranger direct (flux nets entrants)
Main origin of FDI inflows										**Principales origines de l'IDE entrant:**
Netherlands	...	2	4	20	...	...	...	...	...	Pays-Bas
France	...	7	21	3	...	...	...	...	...	France
Denmark	4	7	12	- 11	...	...	...	...	...	Danemark
Germany	...	...	...	16	...	...	...	...	...	Allemagne
France	...	7	21	3	...	...	...	...	...	France
African countries	...	47	313	- 142	...	...	...	...	...	Pays africains
Net total official development assistance	774	1 017	797	1 171	1 133	931	1 049	1 243	...	Aide publique au développement (nette totale)
Main origin of net ODA										**Principales origines de l'APD nette**
United Kingdom	112	148	104	197	177	100	131	139	...	Royaume-Uni
International Development Association [IDA]	82	132	71	158	195	169	154	150	...	International Development Association
United States	111	118	152	180	200	182	249	372	...	États-Unis
Norway	64	65	67	69	107	84	73	63	...	Norvège
Global Fund	67	2	2	3	6	5	5	6	...	Fonds Mondial

MALAWI

SOURCES AND NOTES - SOURCES ET NOTES

External trade - Total exports, fob: UNCTAD	Commerce exterieur - Exportation, fab: CNUCED
External trade - Total import, cif: UNCTAD	Commerce exterieur - Imporations, caf: CNUCED
ODA: OECD	APD: OCDE
Monetary statistics: IMF	Statistiques monétaires: FMI
National Accounts: 2017:Projection	Comptes nationaux: 2017:Projection
Poverty: World Bank	Pauvreté: Banque mondiale

AREA (km2)		1 240 190			**SUPERFICIE (KM2)**
CAPITAL CITY	Bamako			Bamako	**CAPITALE**
CURRENCY	CFA Franc			Franc CFA	**MONNAIE**

I SOCIAL AND DEMOGRAPHIC INDICATORS — INDICATEURS DEMOGRAPHIQUES ET SOCIAUX

	Year Année	Value Valeur	Charts Graphiques	
Population				**Population**
Population ('000)	2017	18 900.0		Population ('000)
Female (%)	...	...		Féminine (%)
Urban (%)	2017	41.4		Urbaine (%)
Average annual growth rate	2016	3.6		Taux de croissance annuel
Active population ('000)	2016	5 953.0		Population active ('000)
Population by age group ('000)				Population par groupe d'âge ('000)
0-14 years	2016	8 697.0		0-14 ans
15-64 years	2016	9 141.0		15-64 ans
65+ years	2016	461.0		65+ ans
Economically active population in agriculture (%)	2015	61.5		Participation de la population active agricole (%)
Crude birth rate	2016	42.0		Taux brut de natalité
Crude death rate	2015	10.1		Taux brut de mortalité
Total fertility rate	2016	6.1		Indice synthétique de fécondité
Life expectancy at birth - Total (years)	2015	58.5		Espérance de vie à la naissance - Totale (années)
Dependency ratio - Total (%)	2016	100.2		Taux de dépendance - Total (%)
Health				**Santé**
Percentage of children under-five and underweight	2006	27.9		% d'enfants de moins de cinq ans avec insuffisance pondérale
Prevalence of undernourishment	2016	5.0		Prévalence de la malnutrition
Under five mortality rate (per 1 000 live births)	2016	122.9		Taux de mortalité de moins de 5 ans (les deux sexes, pour 1000)
Infant mortality rate (per 1 000 live births)	2016	77.6		Taux de mortalité infantile (les deux sexes) par 1000
Neonatal mortality rate (per 1 000 live births)	2016	39.4		Le taux de mortalité néonatale (pour 1000 naissances vivantes)
Percentage of children provided the vaccines :				Pourcentage d'enfants vaccinés :
BCG	2014	79.0		BCG
DPT3	2014	77.0		DTC3
Polio	2013	79.0		polio
Measles	2014	80.0		rougeole
Percentage of mothers provided at least one antenatal care (%)	2006	70.4		Pourcentage de mères ayant au moins reçu un soin prénatal (%)
Percentage of deliveries attended by skilled health personnel	2014	59.0		% d'accouchements assistés par un personnel de santé qualifié
Number of doctors (per 10,000 population)	2014	0.8		Nombre de médecins (pour 10.000 habitants)
Number of nurses (per 10,000 population)	2014	2.3		Nombre d'infirmiers (pour 10.000 habitants)
Hospital beds - Total (per 10,000 population)	2015	2.0		Nombre de lits d'hôpitaux - Total (pour 10 000)
Births registered (per 1,000)	2017	43.9		Naissances enregistrées (pour 1000)
Deaths registered (per 1,000)	2017	9.8		Décès enregistrés (pour 1000)
Budget allocation to health (%)	2014	6.9		Dépenses publiques consacrées à la santé (% du budget)
Education				**Education**
Enrolment in primary education (000)	2016	1 972.0		Scolarisation dans le primaire (000)
Female	2016	850.5		Féminine
Enrolment in secondary education (000)	2016	513.8		Scolarisation dans le secondaire (000)
Female	2016	229.1		Féminine
Enrolment in tertiary education (000)	2016	147.7		Scolarisation dans le tertiaire (000)
Female	2012	28.1		Féminine
Literacy rate	2016	31.0		Taux d'alphabétisation (deux sexes)
Male	2016	41.4		Masculin
Female	2016	21.6		Féminin
Pupil teacher ratio - primary	2013	45.7		Ratio élève-enseignant
Budget allocation to education (%)	2014	3.6		Dépenses publiques consacrées à l'enseignement (% du budget)
Poverty				**Pauvreté**
GNI per capita, PPP (current int. $)	2016	2050.0		RNB par habitant, ($ PPA inter. courants)
Human Poverty Index (HPI-1) Value (%)	2007	54.5		Valeur de l'Indice de pauvreté (IPH-1) (%)
Population below Inter. poverty line ($2/day) (%)	2009	49.3		Population sous le seuil inter. de pauvreté (2$/Jour) (%)
Share of income held by richest 10%	2009	25.7		% de revenu des 10% plus riches
Share of income held by poorest 10%	2009	3.3		% de revenu des 10% plus pauvres
GINI index	2009	33.0		Indice de GINI

Population by age group - 2016

Population par groupe d'age - 2016

2.5%
47.5%
50.0%

- 0-14 years
- 15-64 years
- 65+ years

Percentage of children provided vaccines : - 2014

Pourcentage d'enfants vaccinés : - 2014

BCG / BCG	DPT3 / DTC3	Polio / polio (2013)	Measles / rougeole
79.0	77.0	79.0	80.0

Literacy rate (%) - 2016

Taux d'alphabétisation - 2016

Male	Female
41.4	21.6

GNI per capita, PPP (current international $)

RNB par habitant, ($ PPA internationaux courants)

2012	2013	2014	2015	2016
1 760	1 800	1 910	1 980	2 050

	2009	2010	2011	2012	2013	2014	2015	2016	2017	
GROSS DOMESTIC PRODUCT BY KIND OF ECONOMIC ACTIVITY AT CURRENT PRICES *CFA FRANC (BILLIONS)*										**PRODUIT INTÉRIEUR BRUT PAR BRANCHE D'ACTIVITÉ ÉCONOMIQUE AUX PRIX COURANTS** *FRANC CFA (MILLIARDS)*
Agriculture, hunting , forestry and Fishing	1 503	1 710	2 086	2 384	2 368	2 617	2 843	3 058	...	Agriculture, chasse sylviculture et Pêche
Mining and quarrying	24	37	31	37	35	37	39	43	...	Industries extractives
Manufacturing	785	787	863	1 007	904	1 000	984	1 014	...	Industries manufacturières
Electricity, gas & water	23	26	27	14	23	26	29	32	...	Electricité, gaz et eau
Construction	364	389	375	240	292	321	343	383	...	Bâtiments et travaux publics
Wholesale & retail trade, restaurants, hotels	539	629	732	729	781	816	867	960	...	Commerce de gros et de détail, restaurants et hôtels
Finance, insurance, real estate, etc.	286	305	326	331	358	380	402	433	...	Banques, assurances, affaires immobilières
Transport and communications	256	276	283	285	349	386	423	469	...	Transport(s) et communications
Public administration and defense	400	479	706	645	693	746	835	898	...	Administrations publiques et défense
Education	...	...	...	...	...	...	...	...	...	Education
Health And Social Work	...	...	...	...	...	...	...	...	...	Santé et Actions Sociales
Other services	236	255	271	270	308	334	357	383	...	Autres services
Less Imputed Service Charges	- 70	- 69	- 69	- 86	- 77	- 81	- 87	- 91	...	Moins Services d'intermédiation financière
Gross domestic product at factor cost / basic prices	4 346	4 824	5 630	5 857	6 034	6 582	7 034	7 584	...	Produit intérieur brut aux couts des facteurs / prix de base
Plus: Indirect Taxes / taxes on products, less subsidies	461	465	494	495	509	532	678	719	...	Plus taxes indirectes/impôts sur les produits, moins les subventions
EXPENDITURE ON GROSS DOMESTIC PRODUCT AT CURRENT PURCHASER'S VALUES *CFA FRANC (BILLIONS)*										**EMPLOI DU PRODUIT INTÉRIEUR BRUT AUX PRIX COURANTS D'ACQUISITION** *FRANC CFA (MILLIARDS)*
Government final consumption	700	830	1 151	984	1 091	1 157	1 255	1 371	...	Consommation finale des administrations publiques
Private final consumption	3 390	3 840	4 283	4 494	4 764	5 319	5 694	6 046	...	Consommation finale privée
Gross fixed capital formation	973	1 099	1 143	941	1 106	1 199	1 293	1 428	...	Formation brute de capital fixe
Change in inventories	86	172	65	150	59	55	19	20	...	Variation des stocks
Exports of goods and services	1 045	1 208	1 392	1 770	1 659	1 600	1 690	1 690	...	Exportations de biens et services
Less imports of goods and services	1 386	1 859	1 910	1 986	2 135	2 217	2 239	2 253	...	Moins importations de biens et services
GDP at purchasers' values	4 807	5 289	6 124	6 352	6 544	7 114	7 711	8 303	...	PIB aux prix d'acquisition
GROSS DOMESTIC PRODUCT BY KIND OF ECONOMIC ACTIVITY AT CONSTANT PRICES *ANNUAL GROWTH RATES (%)*										**PRODUIT INTÉRIEUR BRUT PAR BRANCHE D'ACTIVITÉ ECONOMIQUE AUX PRIX CONSTANTS** *TAUX DE CROISSANCE ANNUEL (%)*
Agriculture, hunting , forestry and Fishing	4.8	9.8	- 2.1	8.9	- 2.8	9.3	7.6	5.8	...	Agriculture, chasse sylviculture et Pêche
Mining and quarrying	- 49.1	60.7	- 2.8	16.4	- 8.7	3.9	3.4	7.1	...	Industries extractives
Manufacturing	0.7	- 10.2	- 0.3	3.7	1.7	9.8	- 2.7	1.7	...	Industries manufacturières
Electricity, gas & water	8.7	21.3	18.4	4.1	9.2	11.3	7.2	8.3	...	Electricité, gaz et eau
Construction	4.1	4.5	1.1	- 35.4	4.6	7.0	5.7	7.9	...	Bâtiments et travaux publics
Wholesale & retail trade, restaurants, hotels	- 3.9	12.6	14.7	- 8.1	7.4	3.4	4.8	7.8	...	Commerce de gros et de détail, restaurants et hôtels
Finance, insurance, real estate, etc.	5.7	8.4	- 3.2	1.3	8.7	3.5	4.0	4.6	...	Banques, assurances, affaires immobilières
Transport and communications	13.2	19.6	18.7	7.2	12.2	7.4	9.9	8.8	...	Transport(s) et communications
Public administration and defense	- 8.5	4.5	1.7	- 8.2	2.3	6.2	9.7	4.7	...	Administrations publiques et défense
Education	...	...	...	...	...	...	...	...	...	Education
Health And Social Work	...	...	...	...	...	...	...	...	...	Santé et Actions Sociales
Other services	2.8	7.0	3.2	- 0.4	6.5	5.5	6.1	4.6	...	Autres services
Less Imputed Service Charges	- 1.0	- 4.4	- 4.4	25.3	- 9.1	4.2	5.8	2.9	...	Moins Services d'intermédiation financière
Gross domestic product at factor cost / basic prices	1.4	6.5	2.6	- 0.4	2.0	7.5	5.6	5.5	...	Produit intérieur brut aux couts des facteurs / prix de base
Plus: Indirect Taxes / taxes on products, less subsidies	41.8	- 5.0	10.1	- 6.3	6.0	1.0	10.0	4.6	...	Plus taxes indirectes/impôts sur les produits, moins les subventions
Gross domestic product at market prices	4.7	5.4	3.2	- 0.8	2.3	7.0	6.0	5.4	...	Produit intérieur brut aux prix du marché
EXPENDITURE ON GROSS DOMESTIC PRODUCT AT CONSTANT PURCHASERS' VALUES *ANNUAL GROWTH RATES (%)*										**EMPLOIS DU PRODUIT INTÉRIEUR BRUT AUX PRIX CONSTANTS D'ACQUISITION** *TAUX DE CROISSANCE ANNUEL (%)*
Government final consumption	2.8	7.4	12.2	- 14.5	6.2	2.0	8.1	7.0	...	Consommation finale des administrations publiques
Private final consumption	5.7	10.6	2.2	1.2	2.6	7.5	5.8	3.9	...	Consommation finale privée
Gross fixed capital formation	- 1.0	10.7	15.1	- 24.1	15.9	5.2	7.5	6.9	...	Formation brute de capital fixe
Exports of goods and services	- 11.1	- 0.2	6.2	8.8	2.5	1.1	4.7	4.0	...	Exportations de biens et services
Less imports of goods and services	- 4.7	26.7	5.5	- 5.3	5.9	5.5	5.7	3.5	...	Moins importations de biens et services

III INFLATION

	2009	2010	2011	2012	2013	2014	2015	2016	2017	
Annual growth rates (%)										**Taux de croissance annuel (%)**
All item	2.4	1.2	3.0	5.3	- 0.6	0.9	1.5	- 1.8	1.8	Ensemble
of which:										dont:
Food and non-alcoholic beverages	3.8	3.4	5.1	8.0	- 3.3	- 0.2	3.1	- 3.3	2.6	Alimentation et boissons non alcoolisés
Alcoholic beverages, tobacco and narcotics	0.5	7.0	- 0.4	- 0.4	5.9	13.1	6.6	0.3	- 1.2	Boissons alcoolisées et tabacs
Clothing and footwear	0.5	1.9	0.1	3.6	- 0.5	2.1	0.3	0.5	- 1.7	Habillement et chaussures
Housing, water, electricity, gas and other fuels	1.5	- 2.8	3.0	2.0	3.8	3.1	1.7	1.8	- 0.6	Logement, eau, électricité, gaz et autres combustibles
Furnishings, household equipment and routine household maintenance	4.4	- 0.5	2.7	4.1	- 2.3	- 0.4	0.5	2.0	19.1	Meubles, articles de ménage et entretien courant
Health	0.7	- 0.9	1.6	- 1.2	- 0.2	0.9	1.8	- 2.5	- 0.2	Santé
Transport	0.2	2.1	2.1	2.2	4.0	3.4	- 1.9	- 4.8	0.7	Transport
Communication	- 2.0	- 4.3	- 3.7	3.8	3.4	- 0.9	- 1.7	0.3	- 6.5	Communication
Recreation and culture	0.2	- 2.2	1.0	0.6	- 0.8	- 1.6	- 0.6	- 0.5	- 1.7	Loisirs et culture
Education	2.4	2.8	0.8	- 0.9	0.5	1.2	0.2	0.2	4.5	Enseignement
Restaurants and hotels	3.5	- 2.8	- 0.4	7.8	1.9	- 1.4	0.2	- 0.1	6.3	Restaurants et hôtels
Miscellaneous goods and services	5.4	- 6.3	-	6.0	2.0	0.4	- 0.1	1.9	2.6	Biens et Services divers

MALI

IV AGRICULTURAL PRODUCTION - PRODUCTION AGRICOLE

TONNES (THOUSAND)	2009	2010	2011	2012	2013	2014	2015	2016	2017	Tonnes (milliers)
Cottonseed	1 614	1 296	1 741	2 076	1 978	2 167	2 331	2 781	...	Graines de coton
Rice, paddy	1 477	1 356	1 298	1 419	1 636	1 744	2 276	2 811	...	Riz, Paddy
Millet	1 450	1 373	1 462	1 680	1 854	1 715	1 864	1 807	...	Millet
Sorghum	1 466	1 251	1 191	1 322	1 468	1 272	1 527	1 394	...	Sorgho
Maize	301	314	524	479	515	509	521	374	...	Maïs

V MINING PRODUCTION - PRODUCTION MINIERE

	2009	2010	2011	2012	2013	2014	2015	2016	2017	
Gold ores and concentrates - Production (Kilograms)	53 726	46 033	46 038	50 272	50 994	51 147	47 400	...	...	Minerais d'or et leurs concentrés - Production (Kilogrammes)
Silver ores and concentrates - Production, Kilograms (thousands)	...	...	188	268	149	604	...	...	...	Minerais d'argent et leurs concentrés - Production, Kilogrammes (milliers)
	...	...	...	...	...	...	...	...	...	

VI ENERGY - ENERGIE

	2009	2010	2011	2012	2013	2014	2015	2016	2017	
Total electricity generation (GWh)	1 575	1 691	1 729	1 682	1 736	2 081	2 619	...	...	Production électrique totale (GWh)
of which										dont
Production of electricity from fossil fuels (GWh)	844	944	953	864	864	1 320	1 520	...	...	Production d'électricité à partir de combustibles fossiles (GWh)
Production of hydro electricity (GWh)	679	695	724	766	820	701	1 016	...	...	Production d'électricité d'origine hydraulique (GWh)
Production of electricity from solar, wind, tide, wave and other sources (GWh)	...	...	...	...	...	7	8	...	...	Production d'électricité d'origine solaire, éolienne, marée motrice et autres (GWh)

VII TOURISM AND INFRASTRUCTURE - TOURISME ET INFRASTUCTURE

VII-1 Tourism	2009	2010	2011	2012	2013	2014	2015	2016	2017	VII-1 Tourisme
International tourist arrivals (thousands)	160	169	160	134	142	168	168	180	...	Arrivées de touristes internationaux (milliers)
Rooms in hotels and similar establishments (thousands)	8	9	10	10	10	...	...	...	...	Chambres d'hôtels et établissements assimilés (milliers)
Overnight stays (thousands)	699	563	564	122	214	150	131	174	...	Nuitées (milliers)
Tourism receipts (US$ thousand)	170 000	186 100	210 100	140 100	158 800	169 269	157 228	164 048	...	Recettes touristiques (milliers de $ EU)
Total contribution to GDP (%)	9.0	10.6	9.6	8.7	9.6	9.6	9.4	9.4	...	Contribution totale au PIB (%)
Total contribution to Employment (%)	7.3	7.9	7.0	6.8	6.2	7.0	6.7	6.8	...	Contribution totale à l'emploi (%)
VII-2 Infrastructure										**VII-2 Infrastructure**
Paved road (% of total)	24.6	...	...	...	...	...	...	...	...	Routes asphaltées (% du total)
Total network (Railways-km)	...	...	...	...	...	...	...	...	...	Réseau total voies ferrées-Km
Main telephone lines (per 100 inhabitants)	0.6	0.8	0.7	0.8	0.8	1.0	1.0	1.2	...	Lignes téléphoniques fixes (pour 100 habitants)
Mobile cellular subscribers (per 100 inhabitants)	32.9	53.2	75.1	98.4	129.1	149.1	139.6	120.3	...	Abonnés aux téléphones mobiles (pour 100 habitants)
Internet users per 100 inhabitants	1.8	2.0	2.2	2.8	3.5	7.0	10.3	11.1	...	Utilisateurs Internet par 100 Habitants
Fixed (wired)-broadband subscriptions per 100 inhabitants	...	...	...	...	...	...	...	...	...	Abonnements à l'Internet fixe (filaire) à large bande pour 100 habitants, par débit

VIII EXTERNAL TRADE - COMMERCE EXTERIEUR

US$ (MILLIONS) EXPORTS, FOB	2009	2010	2011	2012	2013	2014	2015	2016	2017	$ E.U (MILLIONS) EXPORTATIONS, FÀB
Exports - Total	1 698	1 996	2 374	2 610	2 339	2 779	2 717	2 538	...	Exportations - Total
Exports to Africa	1 127	953	1 153	767	193	193	174	695	...	Exportations vers l'Afrique
Main products										**Principaux produits**
Cotton	257	284	389	438	241	291	247	255	...	Coton
Fertilizers (other than those of group 272)	47	40	155	123	135	119	102	59	...	Engrais (autres que ceux du groupe 272)
Gold, non-monetary (excluding gold ores and concentrates)	1 110	1 300	1 397	1 776	1 743	2 076	2 126	1 892	...	Or, non monétaire (à l'exclusion des minerais d'or et des concentrés)
Live animals other than animals of division 03	30	51	48	47	29	36	31	87	...	Animaux vivants autres que les animaux de la division 03
Oil seeds and oleaginous fruits (excluding flour)	18	32	44	42	25	31	29	57	...	Graines oléagineuses et oléagineuses (à l'exclusion de la farine)
Main destinations										**Principales destinations**
China	66	99	194	303	116	84	79	70	...	Chine
India	6	3	8	25	68	77	101	119	...	Inde
South Africa	978	744	812	543	31	40	45	474	...	Afrique du Sud
Switzerland	18	158	168	441	198	255	304	485	...	Suisse
United Arab Emirates	82	285	396	772	1 454	1 712	1 696	848	...	Emirates Arabes
IMPORTS, CIF										
Imports - Total	2 486	3 428	3 352	3 463	3 956	4 178	4 111	3 845	...	Importations - Total (millions)
Imports from Africa	982	1 499	1 454	1 623	1 801	1 775	1 497	1 619	...	Importations en provenance de l'Afrique
Main products										**Principaux produits**
Civil engineering & contractors' plant & equipment	65	97	127	116	133	138	178	87	...	Génie civil et installations et équipements des entrepreneurs
Fertilizers (other than those of group 272)	145	78	124	116	128	196	194	144	...	Engrais (autres que ceux du groupe 272)
Lime, cement, fabrica. constr. mat. (excludingglass, clay)	151	179	219	193	229	317	286	187	...	Chaux, ciment, tissu. constr. tapis. (sauf verre, argile)
Medicaments (incl. veterinary medicaments)	105	216	130	150	177	196	202	160	...	Médicaments (y compris les médicaments vétérinaires)
Petroleum oils or bituminous minerals > 70 % oil	288	725	619	733	855	669	411	711	...	Huiles de pétrole ou de minéraux bitumineux> 70% d'huile
Main origin										**Principales provenances**
China	251	336	362	367	418	501	517	490	...	Chine
Côte d'Ivoire	318	287	282	325	356	502	401	408	...	Côte d'Ivoire
France	384	484	429	426	501	609	547	374	...	France
Germany	90	95	127	101	125	138	161	161	...	Allemagne
Senegal	342	557	625	688	756	1 003	758	611	...	Sénégal

	2009	2010	2011	2012	2013	2014	2015	2016	2017	
IX-1 MONETARY STATISTICS *CFA FRANC (MILLIONS)*										**IX-1 STATISTIQUES MONÉTAIRES** *FRANC CFA (MILLIONS)*
Money supply (M1)	1 187 904	1 294 463	1 491 953	1 718 048	1 845 371	1 976 807	2 237 133	2 401 333	2 666 692	Masse monétaire (M1)
Quasi-money	344 368	333 886	337 488	373 590	456 177	483 969	592 199	717 820	646 597	Quasi-monnaie
of which demand deposit	...	...	...	...	...	...	...	...	...	dont Monnaie scripturale
Net foreign assets	769 405	760 875	710 798	713 300	808 215	623 602	573 781	243 465	86 592	Avoirs extérieurs nets
Domestic credit	453 007	572 083	846 128	1 045 033	1 127 274	1 525 054	1 892 238	2 390 340	2 428 051	Crédit intérieur
of which claims on private sector	- 287 704	- 269 583	- 203 192	- 54 162	- 104 892	- 66 649	- 27 946	207 618	35 954	dont créances sur le secteur privé
of which claims on government sector, net	740 711	841 666	1 049 320	1 099 195	1 232 166	1 461 937	1 824 675	2 079 077	2 280 821	dont créances nettes sur le gouvernement
International reserves (millions US$)	1 605	1 351	1 379	1 341	1 300	976	794	276	51	Réserves internationales (millions $EU)
Average exchange rate (National currency per US$)	472	495	472	511	494	494	591	593	582	Taux de change (moyen) (monnaie nationale par $ EU)
IX-2 PUBLIC FINANCE *CFA FRANC (MILLIONS)*										**IX-2 FINANCES PUBLIQUES** *FRANC CFA (MILLIONS)*
Total Revenues and Grants	919	940	1 095	983	1 137	1 215	1 481	1 594	...	Recettes totales et dons
Direct taxes (on income, profits)	177	205	221	263	258	324	331	368	...	Taxes directes
Domestic indirect taxes revenues	87	93	310	287	265	273	327	467	...	Taxes Indirectes
Trade taxes	267	285	117	126	134	143	235	258	...	Taxes sur le commerce extérieur
Other taxes	94	98	120	141	147	150	190	218	...	Autres taxes
Other revenues	101	126	132	154	147	167	191	150	...	Autres recettes
Grants	194	134	194	13	186	158	208	133	...	Dons
Total Expenditures and Net Lending	1 098	1 050	1 265	995	1 292	1 420	1 622	1 850	...	Dépenses totales et prêts nets
Current expenditure	605	644	785	795	877	923	1 015	1 062	...	Dépenses courantes
Wages and Salaries	214	232	265	291	291	313	358	401	...	Rémunérations et salaires
Other purchases of goods and services	190	213	236	208	240	241	261	268	...	Achat de biens et services
Other current expenditure	72	62	103	108	109	117	139	105	...	Autres dépenses courantes
Current transfers	130	137	181	187	238	252	257	288	...	Transferts courants
Interest payments	16	21	35	33	32	42	46	56	...	Intérêts
Capital expenditure	455	370	448	171	390	460	566	740	...	Dépenses d'équipement
Net lending	22	15	- 3	- 3	- 6	- 5	- 5	- 8	...	Prêts nets
Fiscal balance	- 179	- 110	- 170	- 12	- 155	- 205	- 141	- 256	...	Solde global y compris les dons
IX-3 BALANCE OF PAYMENTS *CFA FRANC (MILLIONS)*										**IX-3 BALANCE DES PAIEMENTS** *FRANC CFA (MILLIONS)*
Trade balance	- 100 409	- 329 170	- 157 100	57 000	- 122 800	- 251 300	- 281 300	...	...	Balance commerciale
Services Balance	- 222 505	- 318 900	- 338 600	- 367 200	- 854 100	- 850 100	- 923 600	...	...	Balance des services
Net primary income	- 215 955	- 207 520	- 217 900	- 234 800	- 213 700	- 190 000	- 174 800	...	...	Revenus primaires nets
Compensation of employees	1 065	1 680	- 4 300	- 1 500	1 100	2 600	1 300	...	...	Rémunération des salariés
Investment income	- 217 020	- 209 200	- 208 300	- 235 100	- 213 400	- 197 400	- 173 500	...	...	Revenus des investissements
Net secondary income	229 650	266 230	403 800	405 800	1 005 500	957 200	967 300	...	...	Revenus secondaires nets
Net official transfers	82 344	98 110	81 000	29 000	625 400	569 800	542 900	...	...	Transferts officiels nets
Workers' remittances	147 306	168 120	313 400	367 400	374 700	379 600	403 100	...	...	Envois de fonds des travailleurs
Other private transfers	...	...	9 400	9 400	5 400	7 800	21 300	...	...	Autres transferts privés
Current account balance	- 309 219	- 589 360	- 309 700	- 139 200	- 185 100	- 334 100	- 412 500	...	...	Solde du compte courant
Capital and financial account	344 252	- 300 400	78 300	- 44 000	- 8 600	7 800	40 600	...	...	Comptes de capital et financier
Capital account	194 371	124 730	184 300	53 400	129 300	114 100	202 500	...	...	Compte de capital
Financial account	149 881	- 425 130	- 106 000	- 97 400	- 137 900	- 106 300	- 161 900	...	...	Compte financier
Errors and omissions	- 35 033	19 000	186 900	184 300	257 800	193 400	285 200	...	...	Erreurs et omissions
Overall balance	...	- 870 760	- 44 600	1 100	64 100	- 133 000	- 86 600	...	...	Balance générale

MALI

X DEBT AND FINANCIAL FLOWS - DETTE ET FLUX FINANCIERS

	2009	2010	2011	2012	2013	2014	2015	2016	2017	
X-1 DEBT US $ (MILLIONS)										**X-1 DETTE EXTÉRIEURE** $ E.U (MILLIONS)
Total external debt	2 132	2 285	2 470	2 764	2 940	2 810	2 909	3 332	3 646	Dette extérieure totale
Private	...	...	...	...	...	...	...	...	...	Privée
Public	2 132	2 285	2 470	2 764	2 940	2 810	2 909	3 332	...	Publique
Total external debt service	104	108	173	142	152	190	243	193	...	Service de la dette extérieure
Present value of external debt	...	...	...	...	...	...	...	2 614	...	Valeur actuelle de la dette extérieure
Total government domestic debt, National currency (millions)	128	169	186	172	494			...	...	Dette publique intérieure
X-2 FINANCIAL FLOWS US $ (MILLIONS)										**X-2 FLUX FINANCIERS** $ E.U (MILLIONS)
Net Foreign Direct Investment Inflows	748	406	556	398	308	144	275	126	...	Investissements étranger direct (flux nets entrants)
Main origin of FDI inflows										**Principales origines de l'IDE entrant:**
...	...	...	...	...	...	...	...	...	...	...
Belgium	...	...	3	- 1	...	...	...	...	...	Belgique
Italy	...	1	...	1	...	...	...	...	...	Italie
Luxembourg	...	- 1	1	...	...	...	...	...	...	Luxembourg
...	...	...	...	...	...	...	...	...	...	...
African countries	204	187	23	...	...	...	...	...	...	Pays africains
Net total official development assistance	985	1 091	1 268	996	1 398	1 236	1 204	1 209	...	Aide publique au développement (nette totale)
Main origin of net ODA										**Principales origines de l'APD nette**
International Development Association [IDA]	167	153	151	69	150	120	233	95	...	International Development Association
France	75	78	73	41	82	96	148	60	...	France
United States	111	198	261	342	158	155	162	209	...	États-Unis
Netherlands	77	57	59	46	60	44	37	34	...	Pays-Bas
Canada	83	96	116	94	65	100	88	87	...	Canada

MALI

SOURCES AND NOTES - SOURCES ET NOTES

External trade - Total exports, fob: UNCTAD

External trade - Total import, cif: UNCTAD

ODA: OECD

Monetary statistics: IMF

National Accounts: 2015:Semi-final;2016:Provisional

* The accounts at constant prices are based on chained prices with 1999 as reference year

Poverty: World Bank

Commerce exterieur - Exportation, fab: CNUCED

Commerce exterieur - Imporations, caf: CNUCED

APD: OCDE

Statistiques monétaires: FMI

Comptes nationaux:2015:Semi-définitives;-2016:Provisoires

* les comptes en prix constant sont publiés aux prix de l'année précédente chaînés (1999 année de référence)

Pauvreté: Banque mondiale

AREA (km2)		1 030 700			**SUPERFICIE (KM2)**
CAPITAL CITY	Nouakchott		Nouakchott		**CAPITALE**
CURRENCY	Mauritanian Ouguiya		Ouguiya mauritanien		**MONNAIE**

I SOCIAL AND DEMOGRAPHIC INDICATORS — INDICATEURS DEMOGRAPHIQUES ET SOCIAUX

	Year Année	Value Valeur	Charts Graphiques	
Population				**Population**
Population ('000)	2017	3 893.8		Population ('000)
Female (%)	2017	50.6		Féminine (%)
Urban (%)	2017	50.5		Urbaine (%)
Average annual growth rate	2017	2.8		Taux de croissance annuel
Active population ('000)	2013	1 909.9		Population active ('000)
Population by age group ('000)				Population par groupe d'âge ('000)
0-14 years	2017	1 660.0		0-14 ans
15-64 years	2017	2 089.6		15-64 ans
65+ years	2017	144.2		65+ ans
Economically active population in agriculture (%)	2006	111.6		Participation de la population active agricole (%)
Crude birth rate	2013	32.0		Taux brut de natalité
Crude death rate	2013	10.9		Taux brut de mortalité
Total fertility rate	2013	4.3		Indice synthétique de fécondité
Life expectancy at birth - Total (years)	2017	60.3		Espérance de vie à la naissance - Totale (années)
Dependency ratio - Total (%)	2017	86.3		Taux de dépendance - Total (%)
Health				**Santé**
Percentage of children under-five and underweight	...	...		% d'enfants de moins de cinq ans avec insuffisance pondérale
Prevalence of undernourishment	2006	11.1		Prévalence de la malnutrition
Under five mortality rate (per 1 000 live births)	2006	107.9		Taux de mortalité de moins de 5 ans (les deux sexes, pour 1000)
Infant mortality rate (per 1 000 live births)	2007	77.0		Taux de mortalité infantile (les deux sexes) par 1000
Neonatal mortality rate (per 1 000 live births)	2006	41.8		Le taux de mortalité néonatale (pour 1000 naissances vivantes)
Percentage of children provided the vaccines :				Pourcentage d'enfants vaccinés :
BCG	2017	103.4		BCG
DPT3	2017	89.8		DTC3
Polio	2017	87.3		polio
Measles	2006	62.0		rougeole
Percentage of mothers provided at least one antenatal care (%)	...	...		Pourcentage de mères ayant au moins reçu un soin prénatal (%)
Percentage of deliveries attended by skilled health personnel	...	...		% d'accouchements assistés par un personnel de santé qualifié
Number of doctors (per 10,000 population)	2015	615.0		Nombre de médecins (pour 10.000 habitants)
Number of nurses (per 10,000 population)	2004	6.4		Nombre d'infirmiers (pour 10.000 habitants)
Hospital beds - Total (per 10,000 population)	2006	4.0		Nombre de lits d'hôpitaux - Total (pour 10 000)
Births registered (per 1,000)	2006	36.5		Naissances enregistrées (pour 1000)
Deaths registered (per 1,000)	2006	9.1		Décès enregistrés (pour 1000)
Budget allocation to health (%)	2013	4.6		Dépenses publiques consacrées à la santé (% du budget)
Education				**Education**
Enrolment in primary education (000)	2017	627.7		Scolarisation dans le primaire (000)
Female	2017	317 763.0		Féminine
Enrolment in secondary education (000)	2017	209.1		Scolarisation dans le secondaire (000)
Female	2017	100.8		Féminine
Enrolment in tertiary education (000)	2006	10.2		Scolarisation dans le tertiaire (000)
Female	2006	2.6		Féminine
Literacy rate	...	...		Taux d'alphabétisation (deux sexes)
Male	...	...		Masculin
Female	...	...		Féminin
Pupil teacher ratio - primary	2017	32.7		Ratio élève-enseignant
Budget allocation to education (%)	...	...		Dépenses publiques consacrées à l'enseignement (% du budget)
Poverty				**Pauvreté**
GNI per capita, PPP (current int. $)	2016	3760.0		RNB par habitant, ($ PPA inter. courants)
Human Poverty Index (HPI-1) Value (%)	2007	36.2		Valeur de l'Indice de pauvreté (IPH-1) (%)
Population below Inter. poverty line ($2/day) (%)	2008	10.9		Population sous le seuil inter. de pauvreté (2$/Jour) (%)
Share of income held by richest 10%	2008	27.9		% de revenu des 10% plus riches
Share of income held by poorest 10%	2008	2.5		% de revenu des 10% plus pauvres
GINI index	2008	37.5		Indice de GINI

Population by age group - 2017

Population par groupe d'age - 2017

- 0-14 years: 42.6%
- 15-64 years: 53.7%
- 65+ years: 3.7%

Percentage of children provided vaccines : - 2006

Pourcentage d'enfants vaccinés : - 2006

| BCG / BCG | DPT3 / DTC3 89.8 | Polio / polio (2017) 87.3 | Measles / rougeole 62.0 |

Literacy rate (%) - 2008

Taux d'alphabétisation - 2008

■ Male ■ Female

GNI per capita, PPP (current international $)

RNB par habitant, ($ PPA internationaux courants)

2012	2013	2014	2015	2016
3 400	3 580	3 750	3 690	3 760

MAURITANIE

II NATIONAL ACCOUNTS — COMPTES NATIONAUX

	2009	2010	2011	2012	2013	2014	2015	2016	2017	
GROSS DOMESTIC PRODUCT BY KIND OF ECONOMIC ACTIVITY AT CURRENT PRICES *MAURITANIAN OUGUIYA (MILLIONS)*										**PRODUIT INTÉRIEUR BRUT PAR BRANCHE D'ACTIVITÉ ÉCONOMIQUE AUX PRIX COURANTS** *OUGUIYA MAURITANIEN (MILLIONS)*
Agriculture, hunting , forestry and Fishing	231 680	242 864	248 240	278 240	305 176	356 306	387 615	398 711	...	Agriculture, chasse sylviculture et Pêche
Mining and quarrying	181 251	304 345	477 733	406 702	455 371	245 474	152 068	203 978	...	Industries extractives
Manufacturing	77 064	85 219	98 634	116 444	115 924	130 451	140 736	129 812	...	Industries manufacturières
Electricity, gas & water	5 554	5 562	80	- 2 200	997	3 685	4 020	4 442	...	Electricité, gaz et eau
Construction	53 775	71 772	81 387	99 134	127 592	156 479	124 374	129 437	...	Bâtiments et travaux publics
Wholesale & retail trade, restaurants, hotels	82 136	86 825	98 734	112 243	117 499	132 099	136 535	143 123	...	Commerce de gros et de détail, restaurants et hôtels
Finance, insurance, real estate, etc.	145 863	171 293	184 308	200 464	220 197	227 158	243 059	272 000	...	Banques, assurances, affaires immobilières
Transport and communications	38 994	53 403	61 103	81 407	79 805	90 223	90 920	91 702	...	Transport(s) et communications
Public administration and defense	96 233	120 179	132 375	142 856	149 434	157 664	170 377	175 694	...	Administrations publiques et défense
Education	...	...	...	...	...	...	...	...		Education
Health And Social Work	...	...	...	...	...	...	...	...		Santé et Actions Sociales
Other services	...	...	...	...	...	...	...	...		Autres services
Less Imputed Service Charges	- 13 832	- 19 813	- 23 227	- 26 221	- 23 925	- 31 016	- 32 094	- 32 895	...	Moins Services d'intermédiation financière
Gross domestic product at factor cost / basic prices	898 718	1 121 649	1 359 367	1 409 069	1 548 070	1 468 523	1 417 612	1 516 004	...	Produit intérieur brut aux couts des facteurs / prix de base
Plus: Indirect Taxes / taxes on products, less subsidies	62 140	75 122	92 986	142 626	147 722	157 953	151 382	156 642	...	Plus taxes indirectes/impôts sur les produits, moins les subventions
EXPENDITURE ON GROSS DOMESTIC PRODUCT AT CURRENT PURCHASER'S VALUES *MAURITANIAN OUGUIYA (MILLIONS)*										**EMPLOI DU PRODUIT INTÉRIEUR BRUT AUX PRIX COURANTS D'ACQUISITION** *OUGUIYA MAURITANIEN (MILLIONS)*
Government final consumption	207 245	237 921	263 112	307 353	327 154	348 800	361 811	362 019	...	Consommation finale des administrations publiques
Private final consumption	570 686	614 636	650 786	741 901	795 355	861 847	909 726	931 568	...	Consommation finale privée
Gross fixed capital formation	287 164	437 401	548 251	780 894	931 588	882 731	688 005	673 129	...	Formation brute de capital fixe
Change in inventories	47 745	31 646	82 488	131 908	18 405	- 33 770	- 81 555	...	...	Variation des stocks
Exports of goods and services	393 397	607 298	815 248	822 770	844 952	636 730	529 474	586 661	...	Exportations de biens et services
Less imports of goods and services	545 379	732 131	907 532	1 233 131	1 221 662	1 069 862	838 468	880 731	...	Moins importations de biens et services
GDP at purchasers' values	960 858	1 196 771	1 452 353	1 551 695	1 695 792	1 626 476	1 568 993	1 672 646	...	PIB aux prix d'acquisition
GROSS DOMESTIC PRODUCT BY KIND OF ECONOMIC ACTIVITY AT CONSTANT PRICES *ANNUAL GROWTH RATES (%)*										**PRODUIT INTÉRIEUR BRUT PAR BRANCHE D'ACTIVITÉ ECONOMIQUE AUX PRIX CONSTANTS** *TAUX DE CROISSANCE ANNUEL (%)*
Agriculture, hunting , forestry and Fishing	1.3	5.2	- 2.2	7.5	- 1.0	2.2	4.3	2.7	...	Agriculture, chasse sylviculture et Pêche
Mining and quarrying	- 3.4	1.9	- 4.7	- 4.7	15.1	4.2	- 6.7	- 1.4	...	Industries extractives
Manufacturing	0.1	- 1.1	12.5	10.1	2.4	- 8.5	7.4	- 9.1	...	Industries manufacturières
Electricity, gas & water	- 5.2	- 2.3	1.5	- 31.9	- 230.8	- 160.0	9.1	10.4	...	Electricité, gaz et eau
Construction	- 8.9	3.9	14.3	12.3	18.0	18.5	- 20.9	2.6	...	Bâtiments et travaux publics
Wholesale & retail trade, restaurants, hotels	6.5	7.4	5.4	7.5	- 1.0	10.4	2.9	3.3	...	Commerce de gros et de détail, restaurants et hôtels
Finance, insurance, real estate, etc.	11.0	6.6	6.1	- 1.1	7.3	1.9	6.5	4.4	...	Banques, assurances, affaires immobilières
Transport and communications	- 16.2	15.1	14.3	29.5	4.0	28.4	3.6	4.7	...	Transport(s) et communications
Public administration and defense	- 8.5	5.3	0.4	2.1	0.5	1.9	1.6	- 2.2	...	Administrations publiques et défense
Education	...	...	...	...	...	...	...	...		Education
Health And Social Work	...	...	...	...	...	...	...	...		Santé et Actions Sociales
Other services	...	...	...	...	...	...	...	...		Autres services
Less Imputed Service Charges	- 9.8	34.7	10.9	7.6	- 12.3	25.2	1.5	1.9	...	Moins Services d'intermédiation financière
Gross domestic product at factor cost / basic prices	- 0.7	4.4	2.4	6.1	4.7	5.9	0.3	1.5	...	Produit intérieur brut aux couts des facteurs / prix de base
Plus: Indirect Taxes / taxes on products, less subsidies	- 5.4	9.1	30.7	3.0	18.7	2.9	6.0	3.9	...	Plus taxes indirectes/impôts sur les produits, moins les subventions
Gross domestic product at market prices	- 1.0	4.8	4.7	5.8	6.1	5.6	0.9	1.7	...	Produit intérieur brut aux prix du marché
EXPENDITURE ON GROSS DOMESTIC PRODUCT AT CONSTANT PURCHASERS' VALUES *ANNUAL GROWTH RATES (%)*										**EMPLOIS DU PRODUIT INTÉRIEUR BRUT AUX PRIX CONSTANTS D'ACQUISITION** *TAUX DE CROISSANCE ANNUEL (%)*
Government final consumption	- 4.5	10.0	3.9	11.4	2.3	4.0	- 0.2	- 2.5	...	Consommation finale des administrations publiques
Private final consumption	2.6	8.9	- 2.4	8.6	2.4	3.1	6.4	0.9	...	Consommation finale privée
Gross fixed capital formation	- 13.5	48.0	35.7	24.1	14.8	- 8.8	- 4.7	- 9.1	...	Formation brute de capital fixe
Exports of goods and services	2.2	2.4	0.7	6.0	1.2	2.7	- 19.3	4.8	...	Exportations de biens et services
Less imports of goods and services	- 6.1	32.1	2.7	30.8	- 4.6	- 15.0	- 11.2	5.2	...	Moins importations de biens et services

III INFLATION

	2009	2010	2011	2012	2013	2014	2015	2016	2017	
Annual growth rates (%)										**Taux de croissance annuel (%)**
All item	2.2	6.3	5.7	4.9	4.1	3.5	0.5	1.5	1.7	Ensemble
of which:										dont:
Food and non-alcoholic beverages	2.6	7.7	6.4	4.3	4.4	5.1	- 1.2	5.1	3.1	Alimentation et boissons non alcoolisés
Alcoholic beverages, tobacco and narcotics	15.9	12.6	13.0	16.5	- 2.9	1.8	- 0.4	22.5	7.0	Boissons alcoolisées et tabacs
Clothing and footwear	6.9	6.8	6.3	7.8	5.1	1.3	-	1.4	0.9	Habillement et chaussures
Housing, water, electricity, gas and other fuels	- 2.9	4.6	4.1	3.4	3.9	1.6	3.0	- 0.2	0.7	Logement, eau, électricité, gaz et autres combustibles
Furnishings, household equipment and routine household maintenance	7.0	4.3	3.9	3.0	1.5	2.3	1.8	2.9	2.6	Meubles, articles de ménage et entretien courant
Health	3.3	1.2	...	3.8	2.0	- 0.1	0.5	3.2	3.3	Santé
Transport	- 0.9	3.0	6.5	10.9	5.9	1.0	4.3	- 0.1	0.1	Transport
Communication	...	...	...	...	...	...	...	- 21.2	- 3.4	Communication
Recreation and culture	0.2	0.5	3.6	1.1	1.1	1.2	0.9	- 1.5	2.8	Loisirs et culture
Education	0.1	0.5	0.9	0.3	0.2	...	...	16.4	0.6	Enseignement
Restaurants and hotels	2.3	4.4	3.3	4.8	3.4	...	21.3	- 17.0	1.7	Restaurants et hôtels
Miscellaneous goods and services	2.3	3.0	1.2	2.7	6.8	3.0	1.0	- 1.7	1.9	Biens et Services divers

IV AGRICULTURAL PRODUCTION - PRODUCTION AGRICOLE

TONNES (THOUSAND)	2009	2010	2011	2012	2013	2014	2015	2016	2017	Tonnes (milliers)
Sorghum	85	102	118	25	130	95	59	96	...	Sorgho
Rice, paddy	67	53	134	159	184	203	293	223	...	Riz, Paddy
Maize	23	15	22	14	29	13	20	22	...	Maïs
	...	...	...	...	...	...	...	...	...	
	...	...	...	...	...	...	...	...	...	

V MINING PRODUCTION - PRODUCTION MINIERE

	2009	2010	2011	2012	2013	2014	2015	2016	2017	
Iron ores and concentrates - Production, metric tons (thousands) - Production, tonnes métriques (milliers)	10 524	11 534	11 176	11 169	11 975	13 306	11 607	13 268	8 938	"Minerais de fer et leurs concentrés
Gold ores and concentrates - Production (Kilograms)	252 300	267 700	263 600	243 000	304 300	309 500	283 000	229 100	219	Minerais d'or et leurs concentrés - Production (Kilogrammes)

Copper ores and concentrates - Production, metric tons (thousands)

	2009	2010	2011	2012	2013	2014	2015	2016	2017	
Total electricity generation (GWh)	712	701	378	383	391	605	709	732	...	Production électrique totale (GWh)
of which										dont
Production of electricity from fossil fuels (GWh)	602	585	268	268	268	394	498	519	...	Production d'électricité à partir de combustibles fossiles (GWh)
Production of hydro electricity (GWh)	110	116	110	115	123	87	184	186	...	Production d'électricité d'origine hydraulique (GWh)
Production of electricity from solar, wind, tide, wave and other sources (GWh)	...	...	...	...	...	24	26	27	...	Production d'électricité d'origine solaire, éolienne, marée motrice et autres (GWh)

VII TOURISM AND INFRASTRUCTURE - TOURISME ET INFRASTUCTURE

VII-1 Tourism	2009	2010	2011	2012	2013	2014	2015	2016	2017	VII-1 Tourisme
International tourist arrivals (thousands)	...	...	...	...	...	...	...	...	...	Arrivées de touristes internationaux (milliers)
Rooms in hotels and similar establishments (thousands)	...	...	...	...	...	...	...	...	...	Chambres d'hôtels et établissements assimilés (milliers)
Overnight stays (thousands)	...	...	...	...	...	...	...	...	...	Nuitées (milliers)
Tourism receipts (US$ thousand)	...	...	...	...	...	...	...	...	...	Recettes touristiques (milliers de $ EU)
Total contribution to GDP (%)	...	...	...	...	...	...	...	...	...	Contribution totale au PIB (%)
Total contribution to Employment (%)	...	...	...	...	...	...	...	...	...	Contribution totale à l'emploi (%)
VII-2 Infrastructure										**VII-2 Infrastructure**
Paved road (% of total)	27.8	29.7	34.6	36.1	...	...	...	...	...	Routes asphaltées (% du total)
Total network (Railways-km)	728	728	728	728	728	728	...	...	...	Réseau total voies ferrées-Km
Main telephone lines (per 100 inhabitants)	2.1	2.0	2.0	1.7	1.4	1.3	1.3	1.3	...	Lignes téléphoniques fixes (pour 100 habitants)
Mobile cellular subscribers (per 100 inhabitants)	62.1	76.9	89.5	106.0	102.5	94.2	89.3	86.5	...	Abonnés aux téléphones mobiles (pour 100 habitants)
Internet users per 100 inhabitants	2.3	4.0	4.5	5.0	6.2	10.7	15.2	18.0	...	Utilisateurs Internet par 100 Habitants
Fixed (wired)-broadband subscriptions per 100 inhabitants	...	...	...	...	...	...	...	...	...	Abonnements à l'Internet fixe (filaire) à large bande pour 100 habitants, par débit

VIII EXTERNAL TRADE - COMMERCE EXTERIEUR

US$ (MILLIONS) EXPORTS, FOB	2009	2010	2011	2012	2013	2014	2015	2016	2017	$ E.U (MILLIONS) EXPORTATIONS, FÂB
Exports - Total	1 387	2 074	2 458	2 624	2 463	2 140	1 462	1 399	...	Exportations - Total
Exports to Africa	194	360	305	265	189	323	327	240	...	Exportations vers l'Afrique
Main products										**Principaux produits**
Copper ores and concentrates; copper mattes, cemen	109	210	217	350	303	147	157	157	...	Minerais et concentrés de cuivre; mattes de cuivre, cemen
Crustaceans, mollusks and aquatic invertebrates	182	174	207	301	189	191	219	194	...	Crustacés, mollusques et invertébrés aquatiques
Fish, fresh (live or dead), chilled or frozen	182	335	326	308	236	379	374	281	...	Poissons frais (vivants ou morts), réfrigérés ou congelés
Gold, non-monetary (excluding gold ores and concentrates)	54	197	136	300	273	245	177	165	...	Or, non monétaire (à l'exclusion des minerais d'or et des concentrés)
Iron ore and concentrates	464	921	923	1 076	1 126	872	338	381	...	Minerai de fer et ses concentrés
Main destinations										**Principales destinations**
China	531	724	1 014	1 158	1 239	768	423	478	...	Chine
Italy	139	115	214	181	175	125	82	68	...	Italie
Japan	111	146	111	189	105	75	90	88	...	Japon
Spain	95	139	124	109	76	118	134	128	...	Espagne
Switzerland	54	57	96	259	263	268	185	156	...	Suisse
IMPORTS, CIF										
Imports - Total	1 337	1 727	2 453	2 971	3 044	2 646	1 948	1 951	...	Importations - Total (millions)
Imports from Africa	119	161	201	251	212	273	199	206	...	Importations en provenance de l'Afrique
Main products										**Principaux produits**
Civil engineering & contractors' plant & equipment	58	77	175	154	180	110	80	46	...	Génie civil et installations et équipements des entrepreneurs
Petroleum oils or bituminous minerals > 70 % oil	174	344	623	763	649	477	163	221	...	Huiles de pétrole ou de minéraux bitumineux> 70% d'huile
Ships, boats & floating structures	9	62	24	14	300	186	99	77	...	Navires, bateaux et structures flottantes
Sugar, molasses and honey	48	76	77	71	83	48	75	94	...	Sucre, mélasse et miel
Wheat (including spelt) and meslin, unmilled	69	69	72	94	90	79	75	53	...	Blé (y compris l'épeautre) et méteil, non moulu
Main origin										**Principales provenances**
China	160	183	228	285	320	375	406	464	...	Chine
France	214	211	224	255	241	207	151	115	...	France
Netherlands	112	200	153	187	214	147	115	95	...	Pays-Bas
United Arab Emirates	24	161	473	528	520	436	141	186	...	Emirates Arabes
United States	46	63	143	195	175	274	158	133	...	États-Unis

MAURITANIE

IX FINANCIAL AND MONETARY STATISTICS - FINANCES ET STATISTIQUES MONETAIRES

	2009	2010	2011	2012	2013	2014	2015	2016	2017	
IX-1 MONETARY STATISTICS *MAURITANIAN OUGUIYA (MILLIONS)*										**IX-1 STATISTIQUES MONÉTAIRES** *OUGUIYA MAURITANIEN (MILLIONS)*
Money supply (M1)	276 521	312 063	374 154	413 438	469 673	510 162	512 051	548 424	588 692	Masse monétaire (M1)
Quasi-money	45 924	48 810	50 329	51 620	64 936	70 058	83 917	...	...	Quasi-monnaie
of which demand deposit	148 967	172 001	222 926	246 525	272 009	309 182	298 463	...	...	dont Monnaie scripturale
Net foreign assets	- 3 474	9 083	70 810	192 201	196 652	108 055	77 009	...	...	Avoirs extérieurs nets
Domestic credit	420 031	463 095	502 240	458 854	516 635	609 343	654 942	...	...	Crédit intérieur
of which claims on private sector	247 114	284 065	312 852	358 537	398 404	442 977	485 743	...	...	dont créances sur le secteur privé
of which claims on government sector, net	172 917	179 030	189 388	100 317	118 232	166 356	169 199	...	...	dont créances nettes sur le gouvernement
International reserves (millions US$)	238	288	505	962	996	639	823	825	779	Réserves internationales (millions $EU)
Average exchange rate (National currency per US$)	262	276	281	297	301	303	325	352	358	Taux de change (moyen) (monnaie nationale par $ EU)
IX-2 PUBLIC FINANCE *MAURITANIAN OUGUIYA (MILLIONS)*										**IX-2 FINANCES PUBLIQUES** *OUGUIYA MAURITANIEN (MILLIONS)*
Total Revenues and Grants	198 736	262 560	324 100	462 900	422 800	424 000	460 210	495 140	489 340	Recettes totales et dons
Direct taxes (on income, profits)	34 600	43 440	54 950	80 490	85 770	94 370	95 230	97 780	97 630	Taxes directes
Domestic indirect taxes revenues	53 750	79 260	100 490	133 530	136 400	137 990	130 850	145 510	157 100	Taxes Indirectes
Trade taxes	14 182	17 600	22 340	29 090	31 980	37 330	38 840	46 930	50 000	Taxes sur le commerce extérieur
Other taxes	4 073	15 300	5 920	7 390	15 050	10 710	4 690	22 070	14 000	Autres taxes
Other revenues	89 781	97 100	132 690	144 600	142 300	141 450	162 300	142 670	158 950	Autres recettes
Grants	2 350	9 860	7 710	67 800	11 300	2 150	28 300	40 180	11 660	Dons
Total Expenditures and Net Lending	227 400	269 000	341 400	430 000	436 700	479 100	513 688	494 400	491 860	Dépenses totales et prêts nets
Current expenditure	170 276	185 871	218 100	270 430	240 740	260 570	272 990	254 520	290 600	Dépenses courantes
Wages and Salaries	76 970	83 683	90 100	94 671	103 710	110 450	119 350	123 100	131 000	Rémunérations et salaires
Other purchases of goods and services	51 639	47 147	51 277	54 573	60 120	64 720	62 350	61 930	66 260	Achat de biens et services
Other current expenditure	21 347	37 103	11 322	15 487	6 690	12 900	23 500	7 760	37 230	Autres dépenses courantes
Current transfers	20 320	17 938	65 401	105 699	70 220	72 500	67 790	61 730	56 110	Transferts courants
Interest payments	16 224	15 040	18 400	12 616	15 680	15 810	17 798	17 200	18 000	Intérêts
Capital expenditure	36 900	54 880	91 800	136 166	169 580	191 460	210 980	210 250	198 260	Dépenses d'équipement
Net lending	4 000	13 209	13 100	10 788	10 700	11 260	11 920	12 430	3 000	Prêts nets
Fiscal balance	- 28 664	- 6 440	- 17 300	32 901	- 13 900	- 55 100	- 53 478	740	- 2 530	Solde global y compris les dons
IX-3 BALANCE OF PAYMENTS *MAURITANIAN OUGUIYA (MILLIONS)*										**IX-3 BALANCE DES PAIEMENTS** *OUGUIYA MAURITANIEN (MILLIONS)*
Trade balance	- 17 054	38 132	86 751	- 157 509	- 117 839	- 215 196	- 180 753	- 175 481	- 101 600	Balance commerciale
Services Balance	- 126 736	- 151 996	- 155 110	- 250 705	- 246 545	- 187 550	- 127 759	- 118 235	- 125 636	Balance des services
Net primary income	- 17 786	- 18 911	- 43 734	- 56 001	- 59 134	- 76 380	- 58 103	- 40 860	- 32 649	Revenus primaires nets
Compensation of employees	...	...	...	...	...	...	...	...	...	Rémunération des salariés
Investment income	...	...	...	...	...	...	...	...	...	Revenus des investissements
Net secondary income	34 281	44 728	42 538	92 915	42 218	34 379	58 034	86 625	38 509	Revenus secondaires nets
Net official transfers	16 875	18 919	22 313	80 291	25 102	19 311	32 793	60 165	17 138	Transferts officiels nets
Workers' remittances	...	...	...	...	...	...	...	...	...	Envois de fonds des travailleurs
Other private transfers	17 406	15 574	10 663	12 624	17 116	15 068	25 241	26 460	21 371	Autres transferts privés
Current account balance	- 127 295	- 88 047	- 69 555	- 371 300	- 381 300	- 444 747	- 308 581	- 247 950	- 221 376	Solde du compte courant
Capital and financial account	102 839	151 924	140 267	537 542	472 143	369 882	404 943	172 329	181 192	Comptes de capital et financier
Capital account	...	57 663	...	11 944	1 446	4 829	10 049	2 961	2 718	Compte de capital
Financial account	- 102 839	- 94 261	- 140 267	- 525 598	- 470 698	- 365 053	- 394 895	- 169 368	- 178 474	Compte financier
Errors and omissions	21 898	1 205	423	- 20 397	- 86 299	- 18 682	- 44 900	47 716	50 526	Erreurs et omissions
Overall balance	- 2 558	65 083	71 135	145 844	4 544	- 93 547	51 462	- 27 905	10 341	Balance générale

X DEBT AND FINANCIAL FLOWS - DETTE ET FLUX FINANCIERS									
	2009	2010	2011	2012	2013	2014	2015	2016	2017
X-1 DEBT *US $ (MILLIONS)*									**X-1 DETTE EXTÉRIEURE** *$ E.U (MILLIONS)*
Total external debt	3 283	3 441	3 800	4 242	4 658	4 655	5 040	5 164	4 257	Dette extérieure totale
Private	139	215	329	573	694	618	547	480	...	Privée
Public	2 998	3 102	3 351	3 494	3 770	3 856	4 292	4 408	...	Publique
Total external debt service	58	77	96	131	133	143	174	212	...	Service de la dette extérieure
Present value of external debt	...	...	...	...	...	...	...	2 922	...	Valeur actuelle de la dette extérieure
Total government domestic debt, National currency (millions)	...	...	...	...	...	...	...	...	...	Dette publique intérieure
X-2 FINANCIAL FLOWS *US $ (MILLIONS)*									**X-2 FLUX FINANCIERS** *$ E.U (MILLIONS)*
Net Foreign Direct Investment Inflows	- 3	131	589	1 389	1 126	501	502	272	...	Investissements étranger direct (flux nets entrants)
Main origin of FDI inflows									**Principales origines de l'IDE entrant:**
...	...	...	...	...	...	...	...	...	...	...
Luxembourg	49	56	...	20	...	...	...	...	...	Luxembourg
France	23	31	...	...	...	...	...	...	...	France
...	...	...	...	...	...	...	...	...	...	...
...	...	...	...	...	...	...	...	...	...	...
African countries	11	13	...	...	...	...	...	...	...	Pays africains
Net total official development assistance	376	374	382	410	295	261	318	291	...	Aide publique au développement (nette totale)
Main origin of net ODA									**Principales origines de l'APD nette**
International Development Association [IDA]	38	38	33	38	10	9	13	60	...	International Development Association
France	35	32	57	84	34	24	18	18	...	France
Spain	45	35	35	9	15	8	15	3	...	Espagne
Japan	10	15	10	13	24	22	20	16	...	Japon
United States	10	7	10	20	25	15	24	12	...	États-Unis

MAURITANIE

SOURCES AND NOTES - SOURCES ET NOTES

External trade - Total exports, fob: UNCTAD

External trade - Total import, cif: UNCTAD

ODA: OECD

Monetary statistics: IMF

National Accounts: 2016:Provisional

National Account: The accounts are calculated using the new base year 2004

Poverty: World Bank

Commerce exterieur - Exportation, fab: CNUCED

Commerce exterieur - Imporations, caf: CNUCED

APD: OCDE

Statistiques monétaires: FMI

Comptes nationaux: 2016:Provisioires

Comptes Nationaux: Les comptes sont calculées selon la nouvelle année de base 2004

Pauvreté: Banque mondiale

AREA (km2)		2 040	**SUPERFICIE (KM2)**
CAPITAL CITY	Port Louis	Port Louis	**CAPITALE**
CURRENCY	Mauritian Rupee	Roupie Mauricienne	**MONNAIE**

I SOCIAL AND DEMOGRAPHIC INDICATORS — INDICATEURS DEMOGRAPHIQUES ET SOCIAUX

	Year Année	Value Valeur	Charts Graphiques	
Population				**Population**
Population ('000)	2017	1 300.0		Population ('000)
Female (%)	2017	50.5		Féminine (%)
Urban (%)	2017	40.7		Urbaine (%)
Average annual growth rate	2017	0.1		Taux de croissance annuel
Active population ('000)	2015	612.9		Population active ('000)
Population by age group ('000)				Population par groupe d'âge ('000)
0-14 years	2017	234.0		0-14 ans
15-64 years	2017	898.0		15-64 ans
65+ years	2017	133.0		65+ ans
Economically active population in agriculture (%)	2015	7.2		Participation de la population active agricole (%)
Crude birth rate	2017	10.7		Taux brut de natalité
Crude death rate	2017	8.0		Taux brut de mortalité
Total fertility rate	2016	1.4		Indice synthétique de fécondité
Life expectancy at birth - Total (years)	2016	74.5		Espérance de vie à la naissance - Totale (années)
Dependency ratio - Total (%)	2017	40.9		Taux de dépendance - Total (%)
Health				**Santé**
Percentage of children under-five and underweight	...	...		% d'enfants de moins de cinq ans avec insuffisance pondérale
Prevalence of undernourishment	2015	5.0		Prévalence de la malnutrition
Under five mortality rate (per 1 000 live births)	2016	13.0		Taux de mortalité de moins de 5 ans (les deux sexes, pour 1000)
Infant mortality rate (per 1 000 live births)	2017	12.0		Taux de mortalité infantile (les deux sexes) par 1000
Neonatal mortality rate (per 1 000 live births)	2016	8.0		Le taux de mortalité néonatale (pour 1000 naissances vivantes)
Percentage of children provided the vaccines :				Pourcentage d'enfants vaccinés :
BCG	2016	98.0		BCG
DPT3	2016	96.0		DTC3
Polio	2016	96.0		polio
Measles	2016	92.0		rougeole
Percentage of mothers provided at least one antenatal care (%)	2014	100.0		Pourcentage de mères ayant au moins reçu un soin prénatal (%)
Percentage of deliveries attended by skilled health personnel	2016	99.7		% d'accouchements assistés par un personnel de santé qualifié
Number of doctors (per 10,000 population)	2016	22.0		Nombre de médecins (pour 10.000 habitants)
Number of nurses (per 10,000 population)	2016	33.0		Nombre d'infirmiers (pour 10.000 habitants)
Hospital beds - Total (per 10,000 population)	2016	36.0		Nombre de lits d'hôpitaux - Total (pour 10 000)
Births registered (per 1,000)	2017	13.0		Naissances enregistrées (pour 1000)
Deaths registered (per 1,000)	2017	10.0		Décès enregistrés (pour 1000)
Budget allocation to health (%)	2016	8.0		Dépenses publiques consacrées à la santé (% du budget)
Education				**Education**
Enrolment in primary education (000)	2017	93.0		Scolarisation dans le primaire (000)
Female	2017	46.0		Féminine
Enrolment in secondary education (000)	2017	120.0		Scolarisation dans le secondaire (000)
Female	2017	61.0		Féminine
Enrolment in tertiary education (000)	2016	21.0		Scolarisation dans le tertiaire (000)
Female	2015	12.6		Féminine
Literacy rate	2011	90.0		Taux d'alphabétisation (deux sexes)
Male	2011	92.0		Masculin
Female	2011	86.7		Féminin
Pupil teacher ratio - primary	2017	24.0		Ratio élève-enseignant
Budget allocation to education (%)	2017	11.3		Dépenses publiques consacrées à l'enseignement (% du budget)
Poverty				**Pauvreté**
GNI per capita, PPP (current int. $)	2016	20990.0		RNB par habitant, ($ PPA inter. courants)
Human Poverty Index (HPI-1) Value (%)	2009	9.5		Valeur de l'Indice de pauvreté (IPH-1) (%)
Population below Inter. poverty line ($2/day) (%)	2012	0.5		Population sous le seuil inter. de pauvreté (2$/Jour) (%)
Share of income held by richest 10%	2012	29.0		% de revenu des 10% plus riches
Share of income held by poorest 10%	2012	3.0		% de revenu des 10% plus pauvres
GINI index	2012	35.8		Indice de GINI

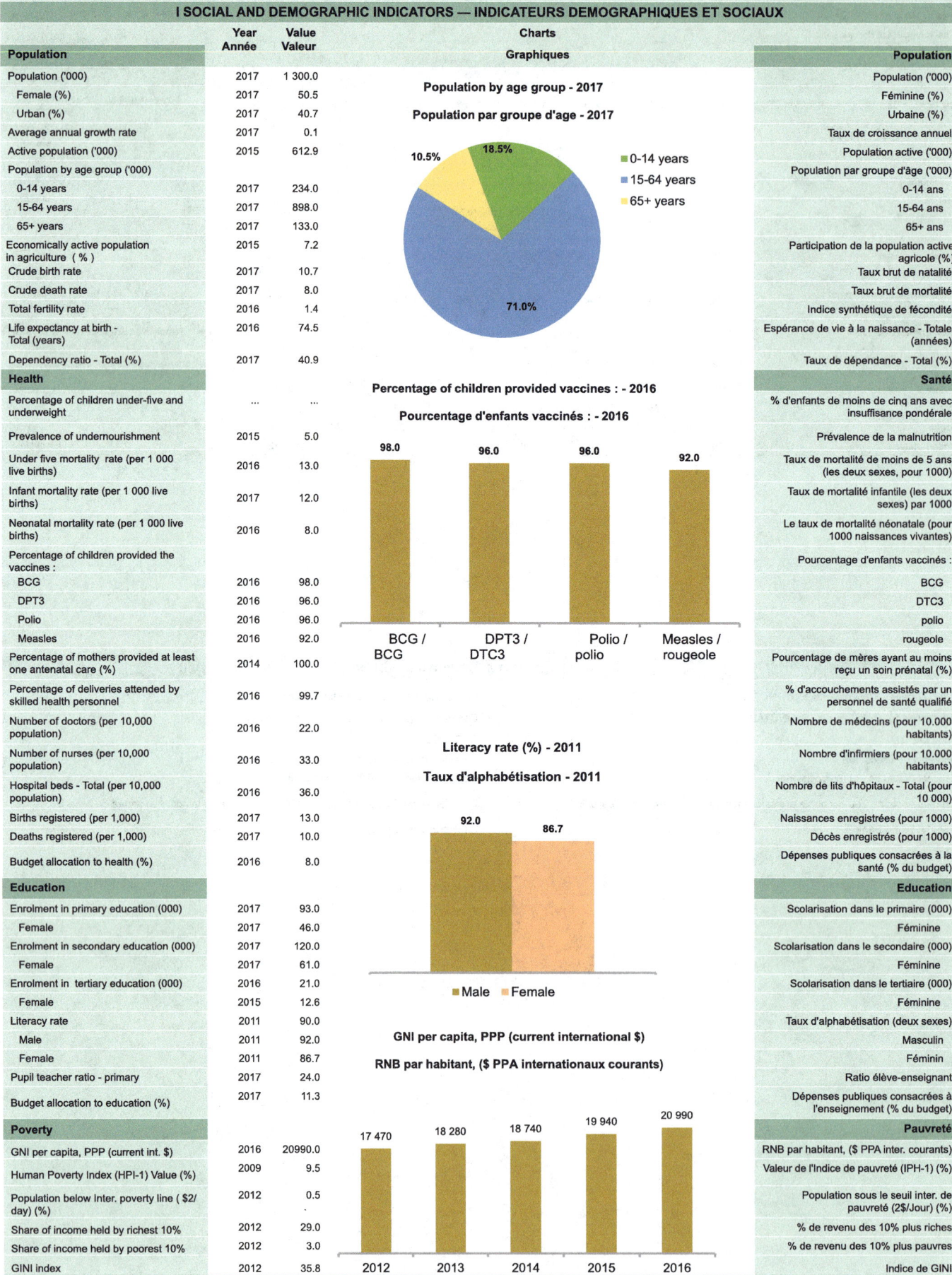

Population by age group - 2017
Population par groupe d'age - 2017

- 0-14 years: 18.5%
- 15-64 years: 71.0%
- 65+ years: 10.5%

Percentage of children provided vaccines : - 2016
Pourcentage d'enfants vaccinés : - 2016

BCG / BCG	DPT3 / DTC3	Polio / polio	Measles / rougeole
98.0	96.0	96.0	92.0

Literacy rate (%) - 2011
Taux d'alphabétisation - 2011

Male	Female
92.0	86.7

GNI per capita, PPP (current international $)
RNB par habitant, ($ PPA internationaux courants)

2012	2013	2014	2015	2016
17 470	18 280	18 740	19 940	20 990

	2009	2010	2011	2012	2013	2014	2015	2016	2017	
GROSS DOMESTIC PRODUCT BY KIND OF ECONOMIC ACTIVITY AT CURRENT PRICES *RUPEE (MILLIONS)*										**PRODUIT INTÉRIEUR BRUT PAR BRANCHE D'ACTIVITÉ ÉCONOMIQUE AUX PRIX COURANTS** *RUPEE (MILLIONS)*
Agriculture, hunting , forestry and Fishing	11 322	11 215	12 246	12 824	12 570	12 778	12 928	13 706	14 274	Agriculture, chasse sylviculture et Pêche
Mining and quarrying	1 041	1 173	1 041	1 000	990	1 000	893	908	944	Industries extractives
Manufacturing	43 498	43 620	45 848	47 855	51 787	53 274	53 436	53 631	54 236	Industries manufacturières
Electricity, gas & water	5 821	5 860	5 603	5 526	6 016	6 851	8 525	9 917	10 823	Electricité, gaz et eau
Construction	17 764	18 551	18 927	19 043	17 923	16 631	16 018	16 027	17 358	Bâtiments et travaux publics
Wholesale & retail trade, restaurants, hotels	45 136	49 222	53 394	57 416	58 792	63 281	67 258	72 641	77 741	Commerce de gros et de détail, restaurants et hôtels
Finance, insurance, real estate, etc.	63 047	65 957	71 246	76 564	81 756	88 162	92 689	98 462	104 671	Banques, assurances, affaires immobilières
Transport and communications	27 954	30 081	31 755	32 431	34 177	36 108	38 454	40 719	42 638	Transport(s) et communications
Public administration and defense	14 705	15 498	16 483	17 327	20 196	21 543	22 419	24 878	25 884	Administrations publiques et défense
Education	11 338	11 934	12 837	13 804	15 725	16 562	17 636	18 944	19 614	Education
Health And Social Work	8 903	9 446	10 269	11 179	13 123	14 431	15 199	16 501	17 907	Santé et Actions Sociales
Other services	10 488	11 444	12 967	14 351	15 955	17 391	18 094	19 140	20 693	Autres services
Less Imputed Service Charges	...	...	...	...	...	...	...	...	...	Moins Services d'intermédiation financière
Gross domestic product at factor cost / basic prices	261 017	274 000	292 617	309 319	329 009	348 011	363 547	385 472	406 781	Produit intérieur brut aux couts des facteurs / prix de base
Plus: Indirect Taxes / taxes on products, less subsidies	30 739	33 957	38 030	41 325	43 388	44 051	46 346	48 879	54 100	Plus taxes indirectes/impôts sur les produits, moins les subventions
EXPENDITURE ON GROSS DOMESTIC PRODUCT AT CURRENT PURCHASER'S VALUES *RUPEE (MILLIONS)*										**EMPLOI DU PRODUIT INTÉRIEUR BRUT AUX PRIX COURANTS D'ACQUISITION** *RUPEE (MILLIONS)*
Government final consumption	40 619	42 555	44 517	46 838	54 388	58 114	61 211	66 870	70 366	Consommation finale des administrations publiques
Private final consumption	208 277	215 749	248 781	260 099	284 876	300 589	315 710	330 511	363 100	Consommation finale privée
Gross fixed capital formation	74 430	74 395	77 567	79 185	77 618	73 989	71 155	74 990	79 961	Formation brute de capital fixe
Change in inventories	- 5 092	9 077	1 611	6 304	4 429	3 152	2 999	2 837	- 1 746	Variation des stocks
Exports of goods and services	139 101	157 790	173 405	188 619	180 305	200 198	200 007	193 230	196 641	Exportations de biens et services
Less imports of goods and services	165 579	191 609	215 234	230 401	229 219	243 980	241 189	234 087	247 441	Moins importations de biens et services
GDP at purchasers' values	291 756	307 957	330 647	350 644	372 397	392 062	409 893	434 351	460 881	PIB aux prix d'acquisition
GROSS DOMESTIC PRODUCT BY KIND OF ECONOMIC ACTIVITY AT CONSTANT PRICES *ANNUAL GROWTH RATES (%)*										**PRODUIT INTÉRIEUR BRUT PAR BRANCHE D'ACTIVITÉ ECONOMIQUE AUX PRIX CONSTANTS** *TAUX DE CROISSANCE ANNUEL (%)*
Agriculture, hunting , forestry and Fishing	10.2	- 0.4	3.5	1.1	0.5	3.7	0.3	3.7	- 0.2	Agriculture, chasse sylviculture et Pêche
Mining and quarrying	- 5.4	4.4	- 19.0	- 8.2	- 4.6	- 2.5	- 3.4	1.0	1.6	Industries extractives
Manufacturing	2.4	1.9	0.7	2.1	4.7	1.8	0.1	0.3	1.2	Industries manufacturières
Electricity, gas & water	- 0.1	3.4	3.9	4.0	3.9	3.8	3.7	3.7	3.1	Electricité, gaz et eau
Construction	5.9	4.3	- 2.0	- 3.0	- 8.2	- 8.5	- 4.9	0.0	7.5	Bâtiments et travaux publics
Wholesale & retail trade, restaurants, hotels	- 1.4	5.7	3.3	2.2	2.8	4.2	5.2	5.6	4.1	Commerce de gros et de détail, restaurants et hôtels
Finance, insurance, real estate, etc.	4.6	5.3	6.3	6.1	5.5	5.1	4.4	4.6	4.8	Banques, assurances, affaires immobilières
Transport and communications	6.8	7.3	6.3	5.6	4.7	4.6	5.2	5.0	4.7	Transport(s) et communications
Public administration and defense	1.2	3.2	4.9	2.6	0.9	5.4	1.3	2.7	2.4	Administrations publiques et défense
Education	1.1	3.7	3.7	4.2	1.6	2.6	3.1	0.8	1.9	Education
Health And Social Work	4.4	4.9	5.4	6.3	5.3	6.8	3.6	2.2	5.1	Santé et Actions Sociales
Other services	7.4	5.7	6.3	6.6	6.6	5.7	4.2	4.2	4.2	Autres services
Less Imputed Service Charges	...	...	...	...	...	...	...	...	...	Moins Services d'intermédiation financière
Gross domestic product at factor cost / basic prices	3.4	4.5	3.9	3.6	3.4	3.6	3.1	3.6	3.7	Produit intérieur brut aux couts des facteurs / prix de base
Plus: Indirect Taxes / taxes on products, less subsidies	2.6	3.4	5.6	2.4	2.9	4.9	7.0	5.7	5.0	Plus taxes indirectes/impôts sur les produits, moins les subventions
Gross domestic product at market prices	3.3	4.4	4.1	3.5	3.4	3.7	3.6	3.8	3.9	Produit intérieur brut aux prix du marché
EXPENDITURE ON GROSS DOMESTIC PRODUCT AT CONSTANT PURCHASERS' VALUES *ANNUAL GROWTH RATES (%)*										**EMPLOIS DU PRODUIT INTÉRIEUR BRUT AUX PRIX CONSTANTS D'ACQUISITION** *TAUX DE CROISSANCE ANNUEL (%)*
Government final consumption	5.3	2.6	2.6	2.8	1.8	4.6	3.1	2.4	3.6	Consommation finale des administrations publiques
Private final consumption	- 7.3	2.9	6.1	3.1	10.4	4.7	11.2	7.1	4.2	Consommation finale privée
Gross fixed capital formation	8.9	- 0.7	1.4	- 0.8	- 3.3	- 6.0	- 5.4	3.7	5.0	Formation brute de capital fixe
Exports of goods and services	- 1.7	14.1	5.2	3.6	- 5.9	10.9	- 0.7	- 4.9	0.1	Exportations de biens et services
Less imports of goods and services	- 10.9	9.2	6.2	1.4	- 0.5	8.5	6.2	- 0.2	1.4	Moins importations de biens et services

III INFLATION										
	2009	2010	2011	2012	2013	2014	2015	2016	2017	
Annual growth rates (%)										**Taux de croissance annuel (%)**
All item	2.5	2.9	6.5	3.9	2.9	3.0	1.3	1.0	3.7	Ensemble
of which:										dont:
Food and non-alcoholic beverages	4.1	3.7	5.8	2.2	2.1	4.2	3.2	1.1	3.7	Alimentation et boissons non alcoolisés
Alcoholic beverages, tobacco and narcotics	4.6	2.8	18.4	14.8	10.1	4.7	1.8	6.2	13.2	Boissons alcoolisées et tabacs
Clothing and footwear	5.8	7.4	5.6	4.7	2.6	5.1	3.6	5.3	3.0	Habillement et chaussures
Housing, water, electricity, gas and other fuels	- 3.2	- 0.3	2.3	4.8	0.9	0.9	- 0.1	- 3.1	- 2.2	Logement, eau, électricité, gaz et autres combustibles
Furnishings, household equipment and routine household maintenance	4.6	3.6	2.7	3.4	2.5	- 0.1	2.8	2.7	0.6	Meubles, articles de ménage et entretien courant
Health	5.4	4.6	5.5	3.6	3.2	5.1	4.2	2.9	5.3	Santé
Transport	0.2	2.4	9.7	- 0.1	1.8	2.4	- 2.9	- 4.2	4.2	Transport
Communication	- 2.1	- 0.3	- 2.2	- 1.9	-	- 0.4	- 3.8	- 1.4	...	Communication
Recreation and culture	0.9	2.3	1.4	2.9	0.1	3.6	2.3	2.0	0.7	Loisirs et culture
Education	3.5	1.2	5.2	2.1	2.6	1.6	1.9	6.1	3.4	Enseignement
Restaurants and hotels	4.1	3.7	9.8	7.4	4.7	4.6	1.5	2.5	3.6	Restaurants et hôtels
Miscellaneous goods and services	5.7	4.2	2.6	2.5	2.5	2.1	0.7	1.1	1.3	Biens et Services divers

MAURICE

MAURITIUS

IV AGRICULTURAL PRODUCTION - PRODUCTION AGRICOLE

	2009	2010	2011	2012	2013	2014	2015	2016	2017	
TONNES (THOUSAND)										**Tonnes (milliers)**
Potatoes	20	22	22	20	16	19	16	16	...	Pommes de terre
Tomatoes	13	12	11	13	11	11	9	10	...	Tomates
Pumpkins, squash and gourds	17	19	19	19	20	18	16	18	...	Citrouilles, courges et potirons
Sugar cane	4 667	4 366	4 230	3 947	3 816	4 044	4 009	3 798	...	Canne à sucre
Bananas	11	12	11	10	10	9	8	8	...	Bananes

V MINING PRODUCTION - PRODUCTION MINIERE

	2009	2010	2011	2012	2013	2014	2015	2016	2017	
Salt and pure sodium chloride - Production (metric tons)	2 000	3 000	3 000	3 800	4 000	3 800	2 000	100	...	Sel et chlorure de sodium pur - Production (tonnes métriques)
	...	...	...	...	...	...	...	...	...	
	...	...	...	...	...	...	...	...	...	

VI ENERGY - ENERGIE

	2009	2010	2011	2012	2013	2014	2015	2016	2017	
Total electricity generation (GWh)	2 577	2 689	2 739	2 797	2 885	2 937	2 651	...	...	Production électrique totale (GWh)
of which										dont
Production of electricity from fossil fuels (GWh)	1 968	2 111	2 190	2 230	2 291	2 341	1 823	...	...	Production d'électricité à partir de combustibles fossiles (GWh)
Production of hydro electricity (GWh)	122	101	56	74	95	91	100	...	...	Production d'électricité d'origine hydraulique (GWh)
Production of electricity from solar, wind, tide, wave and other sources (GWh)	2	3	3	4	6	28	27	...	...	Production d'électricité d'origine solaire, éolienne, marée motrice et autres (GWh)

VII TOURISM AND INFRASTRUCTURE - TOURISME ET INFRASTUCTURE

	2009	2010	2011	2012	2013	2014	2015	2016	2017	
VII-1 Tourism										**VII-1 Tourisme**
International tourist arrivals (thousands)	871	935	965	965	993	1 038	1 151	1 275	1 342	Arrivées de touristes internationaux (milliers)
Rooms in hotels and similar establishments (thousands)	11	12	12	13	12	13	14	14	14	Chambres d'hôtels et établissements assimilés (milliers)
Overnight stays (thousands)	8 639	9 336	9 494	10 044	10 676	11 267	12 050	13 118	13 641	Nuitées (milliers)
Tourism receipts (US$ thousand)	1 117 467	1 277 307	1 485 809	1 482 726	1 322 842	1 447 039	1 429 047	1 558 563	1 732 696	Recettes touristiques (milliers de $ EU)
Total contribution to GDP (%)	7.5	8.0	8.1	8.0	6.8	7.0	7.4	7.8	8.0	Contribution totale au PIB (%)
Total contribution to Employment (%)	9.2	9.1	9.3	9.3	9.3	9.4	9.4	9.8	9.8	Contribution totale à l'emploi (%)
VII-2 Infrastructure										**VII-2 Infrastructure**
Paved road (% of total)	98.1	98.0	98.0	98.0	98.0	98.0	98.0	...	...	Routes asphaltées (% du total)
Total network (Railways-km)	...	...	...	...	...	...	...	...	...	Réseau total voies ferrées-Km
Main telephone lines (per 100 inhabitants)	30.6	31.5	30.3	28.2	29.2	29.8	30.3	30.7	...	Lignes téléphoniques fixes (pour 100 habitants)
Mobile cellular subscribers (per 100 inhabitants)	88.6	96.8	104.8	119.9	123.2	132.2	140.6	144.2	...	Abonnés aux téléphones mobiles (pour 100 habitants)
Internet users per 100 inhabitants	22.5	28.3	35.0	35.4	40.1	44.8	50.1	52.2	...	Utilisateurs Internet par 100 Habitants
Fixed (wired)-broadband subscriptions per 100 inhabitants	5.9	7.6	9.6	11.4	13.1	14.6	15.7	16.9	...	Abonnements à l'Internet fixe (filaire) à large bande pour 100 habitants, par débit

VIII EXTERNAL TRADE - COMMERCE EXTERIEUR

	2009	2010	2011	2012	2013	2014	2015	2016	2017	
US$ (MILLIONS) EXPORTS, FOB										**$ E.U (MILLIONS) EXPORTATIONS, FÀB**
Exports - Total	1 766	2 261	2 565	2 649	2 869	3 094	2 481	2 194	...	Exportations - Total
Exports to Africa	250	248	382	451	419	427	463	430	...	Exportations vers l'Afrique
Main products										**Principaux produits**
Articles of apparel, of textile fabrics, n.e.s.	376	295	442	359	296	328	299	250	...	Vêtements, en tissus, n.d.a.
Fish, aqua. invertebrates, prepared, preserved, n.e.s.	221	250	278	345	376	320	256	263	...	Poisson, aqua. invertébrés, préparés, conservés, n.d.a.
Men's clothing of textile fabrics, not knitted	190	198	243	266	275	285	293	265	...	Vêtements pour hommes en matières textiles, non tricotés
Sugar, molasses and honey	224	267	305	272	314	260	222	237	...	Sucre, mélasse et miel
Telecommunication equipment, n.e.s.; & parts, n.e.s.	5	14	6	12	56	301	290	97	...	Matériel de télécommunication, n.es .; & parties, n.e.s
Main destinations										**Principales destinations**
France	366	300	392	362	342	387	295	325	...	France
Italy	97	138	182	149	217	174	135	149	...	Italie
South Africa	80	84	174	221	197	188	214	179	...	Afrique du Sud
United Kingdom	480	439	481	423	389	362	325	264	...	Royaume-Uni
United States	145	202	237	227	236	279	264	250	...	États-Unis
IMPORTS, CIF										
Imports - Total	3 725	4 402	5 159	5 772	5 395	5 607	4 458	4 655	...	Importations - Total (millions)
Imports from Africa	459	543	584	609	572	597	524	625	...	Importations en provenance de l'Afrique
Main products										**Principaux produits**
Fish, fresh (live or dead), chilled or frozen	195	223	285	342	348	296	225	274	...	Poissons frais (vivants ou morts), réfrigérés ou congelés
Medicaments (incl. veterinary medicaments)	87	119	94	103	94	106	104	110	...	Médicaments (y compris les médicaments vétérinaires)
Motor vehicles for the transport of persons	96	123	138	183	166	183	168	188	...	Véhicules à moteur pour le transport de personnes
Petroleum oils or bituminous minerals > 70 % oil	482	704	940	1 019	1 019	890	554	507	...	Huiles de pétrole ou de minéraux bitumineux> 70% d'huile
Telecommunication equipment, n.e.s.; & parts, n.e.s.	72	92	81	122	146	388	358	219	...	Matériel de télécommunication, n.es .; & parties, n.e.s.
Main origin										**Principales provenances**
China	469	586	724	931	792	906	813	825	...	Chine
France	439	389	465	479	441	431	319	365	...	France
India	703	984	1 208	1 302	1 300	1 212	808	768	...	Inde
South Africa	322	371	365	378	333	370	288	349	...	Afrique du Sud
Spain	88	119	153	190	214	194	133	139	...	Espagne

IX FINANCIAL AND MONETARY STATISTICS - FINANCES ET STATISTIQUES MONETAIRES										
	2009	2010	2011	2012	2013	2014	2015	2016	2017	
IX-1 MONETARY STATISTICS *RUPEE (MILLIONS)*										**IX-1 STATISTIQUES MONÉTAIRES** *RUPEE (MILLIONS)*
Money supply (M1)	280 827	300 231	319 537	345 617	365 609	397 557	437 999	477 789	501 387	Masse monétaire (M1)
Quasi-money	194 053	213 064	227 842	246 842	258 832	276 088	297 846	319 948	346 956	Quasi-monnaie
of which demand deposit	...	...	...	...	...	...	...	...	...	dont Monnaie scripturale
Net foreign assets	336 656	396 026	370 755	401 321	396 300	457 823	529 026	549 151	566 913	Avoirs extérieurs nets
Domestic credit	281 514	308 855	341 302	391 022	448 175	446 806	476 653	493 258	574 578	Crédit intérieur
of which claims on private sector	30 192	29 843	30 173	26 748	34 759	44 771	41 980	54 205	69 678	dont créances sur le secteur privé
of which claims on government sector, net	233 629	262 857	295 286	346 603	395 882	387 243	421 023	418 546	468 055	dont créances nettes sur le gouvernement
International reserves (millions US$)	2 303	2 601	2 779	3 046	3 491	3 919	4 228	4 939	5 341	Réserves internationales (millions $EU)
Average exchange rate (National currency per US$)	32	31	29	30	31	31	35	36	34	Taux de change (moyen) (monnaie nationale par $ EU)
IX-2 PUBLIC FINANCE *RUPEE (MILLIONS)*										**IX-2 FINANCES PUBLIQUES** *RUPEE (MILLIONS)*
Total Revenues and Grants	62 216	65 480	69 223	73 791	78 211	79 675	84 159	90 228	103 249	Recettes totales et dons
Direct taxes (on income, profits)	15 296	13 976	13 620	14 634	15 920	17 089	18 607	20 320	22 813	Taxes directes
Domestic indirect taxes revenues	31 002	34 633	38 818	43 008	44 964	45 971	48 412	50 999	56 510	Taxes Indirectes
Trade taxes	5 441	1 525	1 560	1 506	1 389	1 239	1 297	1 245	1 288	Taxes sur le commerce extérieur
Other taxes	594	5 074	5 183	5 771	5 718	7 429	7 182	7 181	7 957	Autres taxes
Other revenues	7 102	8 279	7 698	6 477	8 826	7 540	6 833	7 866	6 553	Autres recettes
Grants	2 781	1 991	2 344	2 395	1 394	407	1 829	2 615	8 129	Dons
Total Expenditures and Net Lending	70 648	75 059	79 570	80 045	91 058	92 213	95 574	107 640	111 928	Dépenses totales et prêts nets
Current expenditure	54 415	56 721	61 308	60 126	70 257	72 581	79 839	90 909	93 645	Dépenses courantes
Wages and Salaries	16 247	17 541	18 001	18 684	22 717	24 025	24 963	27 779	28 619	Rémunérations et salaires
Other purchases of goods and services	5 124	6 150	6 195	6 516	7 070	7 547	7 571	8 431	8 847	Achat de biens et services
Other current expenditure	30 265	29 948	34 791	32 554	37 434	38 907	44 577	48 926	51 856	Autres dépenses courantes
Current transfers	2 778	3 083	2 322	2 373	3 037	2 102	2 728	5 773	4 324	Transferts courants
Interest payments	10 687	10 262	9 629	10 303	9 638	10 105	9 845	10 541	11 106	Intérêts
Capital expenditure	5 546	8 076	8 633	9 616	11 162	9 528	5 890	6 190	7 177	Dépenses d'équipement
Net lending	...	...	...	...	...	...	...	...	...	Prêts nets
Fiscal balance	- 8 432	- 9 580	- 10 346	- 6 254	- 12 847	- 12 539	- 11 415	- 17 413	- 8 679	Solde global y compris les dons
IX-3 BALANCE OF PAYMENTS *RUPEE (MILLIONS)*										**IX-3 BALANCE DES PAIEMENTS** *RUPEE (MILLIONS)*
Trade balance	- 49 473	- 58 289	- 67 585	- 73 813	- 69 625	- 69 394	- 65 398	- 72 782	...	Balance commerciale
Services Balance	20 050	21 949	22 869	28 837	17 364	21 154	21 095	28 496	...	Balance des services
Net primary income	1 678	- 274	- 3 389	15 658	31 969	32 867	31 748	33 648	...	Revenus primaires nets
Compensation of employees	- 307	- 235	- 256	- 221	- 238	- 245	- 204	- 195	...	Rémunération des salariés
Investment income	1 985	- 39	- 3 133	15 879	32 207	33 112	31 952	33 843	...	Revenus des investissements
Net secondary income	6 909	5 629	3 475	4 259	- 2 832	- 6 451	- 7 917	- 8 243	...	Revenus secondaires nets
Net official transfers	3 049	1 699	2 463	3 018	1 539	486	1 531	2 453	...	Transferts officiels nets
Workers' remittances	...	...	...	...	...	...	...	...	...	Envois de fonds des travailleurs
Other private transfers	3 860	3 930	1 012	1 242	- 4 371	- 6 937	- 9 448	- 10 696	...	Autres transferts privés
Current account balance	- 20 836	- 30 985	- 44 630	- 25 059	- 23 124	- 21 824	- 20 472	- 18 881	...	Solde du compte courant
Capital and financial account	11 626	26 139	39 188	35 464	16 091	18 586	17 871	24 014	...	Comptes de capital et financier
Capital account	- 59	- 148	- 53	- 241	- 123	- 146	- 136	- 36	...	Compte de capital
Financial account	11 685	26 287	39 241	35 705	16 214	18 732	18 007	24 050	...	Compte financier
Errors and omissions	9 210	4 846	5 442	- 10 405	7 033	3 238	2 601	- 5 132	...	Erreurs et omissions
Overall balance	12 103	6 177	5 247	6 041	16 580	23 019	19 960	26 227	...	Balance générale

MAURICE

X DEBT AND FINANCIAL FLOWS - DETTE ET FLUX FINANCIERS

	2009	2010	2011	2012	2013	2014	2015	2016	2017	
X-1 DEBT US $ (MILLIONS)										**X-1 DETTE EXTÉRIEURE** $ E.U (MILLIONS)
Total external debt	7 124	7 791	9 374	10 061	12 414	13 253	10 601	10 701	12 142	Dette extérieure totale
Private	...	...	...	...	...	...	...	...	...	Privée
Public	974	1 158	1 432	1 515	1 925	1 981	1 880	1 781	...	Publique
Total external debt service	129	217	215	230	231	309	223	256	...	Service de la dette extérieure
Present value of external debt	...	...	...	...	...	...	...	1 572	...	Valeur actuelle de la dette extérieure
Total government domestic debt, National currency (millions)	125 644	128 557	137 219	140 806	149 960	165 285	181 649	...	...	Dette publique intérieure
X-2 FINANCIAL FLOWS US $ (MILLIONS)										**X-2 FLUX FINANCIERS** $ E.U (MILLIONS)
Net Foreign Direct Investment Inflows	248	430	433	589	293	418	208	349	...	Investissements étranger direct (flux nets entrants)
Main origin of FDI inflows										**Principales origines de l'IDE entrant:**
Luxembourg	2	8	6	12	10	25	...	...	...	Luxembourg
Japan	...	...	2	1	1	...	...	...	...	Japon
France	73	52	142	143	112	114	...	...	...	France
Netherlands	4	15	7	1	6	2	...	...	...	Pays-Bas
France	73	52	142	143	112	114	...	...	...	France
African countries	33	66	123	195	80	47	...	...	...	Pays africains
Net total official development assistance	156	125	186	177	146	45	78	42	...	Aide publique au développement (nette totale)
Main origin of net ODA										**Principales origines de l'APD nette**
France	43	54	101	84	62	71	36	5	...	France
United Kingdom	21	6	14	-	1	1	1	-	...	Royaume-Uni
Japan	- 2	- 3	- 2	1	- 1	1	0	1	...	Japon
...	...	...	...	...	...	...	...	...	...	...
United Nation Development Programme	1	1	1	1	-	1	1	1	...	Programme des Nations Unies pour le développement

SOURCES AND NOTES - SOURCES ET NOTES

External trade - Total exports, fob: UNCTAD	Commerce exterieur - Exportation, fab: CNUCED
External trade - Total import, cif: UNCTAD	Commerce exterieur - Imporations, caf: CNUCED
ODA: OECD	APD: OCDE
Monetary statistics: IMF	Statistiques monétaires: FMI
National Accounts: 2016Semi-final ;2017:Provisional	Comptes nationaux: 2016:Semi-définitives;2017:Provisoires
Poverty: World Bank	Pauvreté: Banque mondiale

	AREA (km2)		446550		SUPERFICIE (KM2)
	CAPITAL CITY	Rabat		Rabat	CAPITALE
	CURRENCY	Moroccan Dirham		Dirham marocain	MONNAIE

I SOCIAL AND DEMOGRAPHIC INDICATORS — INDICATEURS DEMOGRAPHIQUES ET SOCIAUX

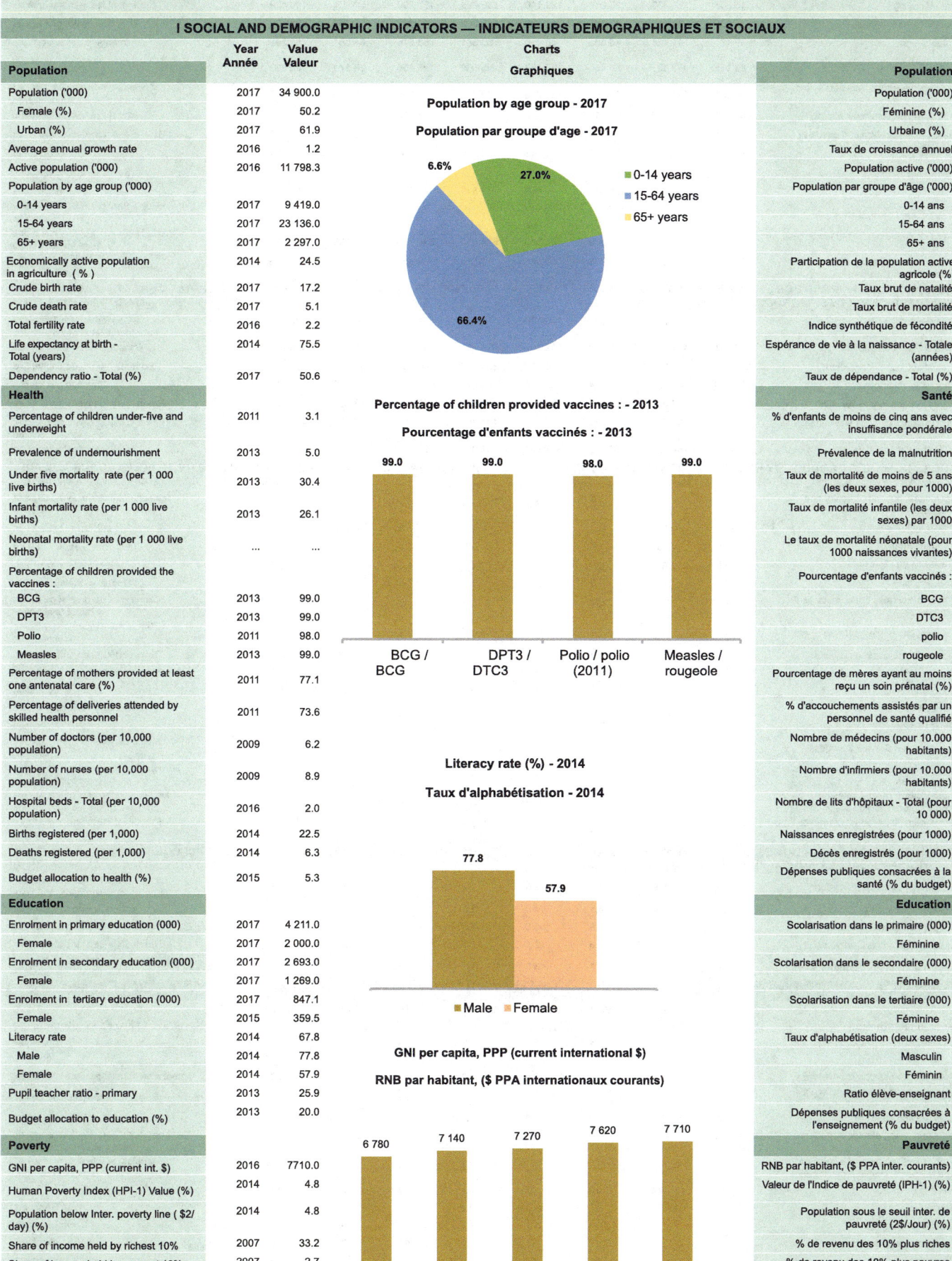

Population	Year Année	Value Valeur	Charts Graphiques	Population
Population ('000)	2017	34 900.0		Population ('000)
Female (%)	2017	50.2		Féminine (%)
Urban (%)	2017	61.9		Urbaine (%)
Average annual growth rate	2016	1.2		Taux de croissance annuel
Active population ('000)	2016	11 798.3		Population active ('000)
Population by age group ('000)				Population par groupe d'âge ('000)
0-14 years	2017	9 419.0		0-14 ans
15-64 years	2017	23 136.0		15-64 ans
65+ years	2017	2 297.0		65+ ans
Economically active population in agriculture (%)	2014	24.5		Participation de la population active agricole (%)
Crude birth rate	2017	17.2		Taux brut de natalité
Crude death rate	2017	5.1		Taux brut de mortalité
Total fertility rate	2016	2.2		Indice synthétique de fécondité
Life expectancy at birth - Total (years)	2014	75.5		Espérance de vie à la naissance - Totale (années)
Dependency ratio - Total (%)	2017	50.6		Taux de dépendance - Total (%)
Health				**Santé**
Percentage of children under-five and underweight	2011	3.1		% d'enfants de moins de cinq ans avec insuffisance pondérale
Prevalence of undernourishment	2013	5.0		Prévalence de la malnutrition
Under five mortality rate (per 1 000 live births)	2013	30.4		Taux de mortalité de moins de 5 ans (les deux sexes, pour 1000)
Infant mortality rate (per 1 000 live births)	2013	26.1		Taux de mortalité infantile (les deux sexes) par 1000
Neonatal mortality rate (per 1 000 live births)	...	...		Le taux de mortalité néonatale (pour 1000 naissances vivantes)
Percentage of children provided the vaccines :				Pourcentage d'enfants vaccinés :
BCG	2013	99.0		BCG
DPT3	2013	99.0		DTC3
Polio	2011	98.0		polio
Measles	2013	99.0		rougeole
Percentage of mothers provided at least one antenatal care (%)	2011	77.1		Pourcentage de mères ayant au moins reçu un soin prénatal (%)
Percentage of deliveries attended by skilled health personnel	2011	73.6		% d'accouchements assistés par un personnel de santé qualifié
Number of doctors (per 10,000 population)	2009	6.2		Nombre de médecins (pour 10.000 habitants)
Number of nurses (per 10,000 population)	2009	8.9		Nombre d'infirmiers (pour 10.000 habitants)
Hospital beds - Total (per 10,000 population)	2016	2.0		Nombre de lits d'hôpitaux - Total (pour 10 000)
Births registered (per 1,000)	2014	22.5		Naissances enregistrées (pour 1000)
Deaths registered (per 1,000)	2014	6.3		Décès enregistrés (pour 1000)
Budget allocation to health (%)	2015	5.3		Dépenses publiques consacrées à la santé (% du budget)
Education				**Education**
Enrolment in primary education (000)	2017	4 211.0		Scolarisation dans le primaire (000)
Female	2017	2 000.0		Féminine
Enrolment in secondary education (000)	2017	2 693.0		Scolarisation dans le secondaire (000)
Female	2017	1 269.0		Féminine
Enrolment in tertiary education (000)	2017	847.1		Scolarisation dans le tertiaire (000)
Female	2015	359.5		Féminine
Literacy rate	2014	67.8		Taux d'alphabétisation (deux sexes)
Male	2014	77.8		Masculin
Female	2014	57.9		Féminin
Pupil teacher ratio - primary	2013	25.9		Ratio élève-enseignant
Budget allocation to education (%)	2013	20.0		Dépenses publiques consacrées à l'enseignement (% du budget)
Poverty				**Pauvreté**
GNI per capita, PPP (current int. $)	2016	7710.0		RNB par habitant, ($ PPA inter. courants)
Human Poverty Index (HPI-1) Value (%)	2014	4.8		Valeur de l'Indice de pauvreté (IPH-1) (%)
Population below Inter. poverty line ($2/day) (%)	2014	4.8		Population sous le seuil inter. de pauvreté (2$/Jour) (%)
Share of income held by richest 10%	2007	33.2		% de revenu des 10% plus riches
Share of income held by poorest 10%	2007	2.7		% de revenu des 10% plus pauvres
GINI index	2014	39.5		Indice de GINI

MAROC

II NATIONAL ACCOUNTS — COMPTES NATIONAUX

	2009	2010	2011	2012	2013	2014	2015	2016	2017	
GROSS DOMESTIC PRODUCT BY KIND OF ECONOMIC ACTIVITY AT CURRENT PRICES MOROCCAN DIRHAM (MILLIONS)										**PRODUIT INTÉRIEUR BRUT PAR BRANCHE D'ACTIVITÉ ÉCONOMIQUE AUX PRIX COURANTS** DIRHAM MAROCAIN (MILLIONS)
Agriculture, hunting , forestry and Fishing	97 517	101 558	107 594	104 540	120 228	107 905	124 799	122 187	...	Agriculture, chasse sylviculture et Pêche
Mining and quarrying	13 063	22 632	31 650	33 420	30 027	22 691	22 692	21 145	...	Industries extractives
Manufacturing	116 007	122 330	127 057	129 146	139 296	152 599	159 424	160 428	...	Industries manufacturières
Electricity, gas & water	12 875	14 931	13 930	12 657	15 269	16 272	21 095	24 908	...	Electricité, gaz et eau
Construction	39 474	41 421	45 603	48 680	50 381	53 576	54 584	58 248	...	Bâtiments et travaux publics
Wholesale & retail trade, restaurants, hotels	82 136	83 323	89 460	95 459	95 560	98 155	98 171	103 032	...	Commerce de gros et de détail, restaurants et hôtels
Finance, insurance, real estate, etc.	116 124	121 605	129 188	136 240	138 052	142 516	149 700	156 843	...	Banques, assurances, affaires immobilières
Transport and communications	54 631	55 906	56 010	55 826	53 541	54 882	57 592	58 347	...	Transport(s) et communications
Public administration and defense	61 763	63 731	74 383	79 431	84 200	88 038	90 630	92 911	...	Administrations publiques et défense
Education	60 502	64 627	68 797	74 345	79 318	81 053	81 816	83 824	...	Education
Health And Social Work	...	...	...	...	...	...	...	...		Santé et Actions Sociales
Other services	10 360	11 248	11 637	12 069	12 541	13 021	13 547	14 121	...	Autres services
Less Imputed Service Charges	...	...	...	...	...	...	...	...		Moins Services d'intermédiation financière
Gross domestic product at factor cost / basic prices	664 452	703 312	755 309	781 813	818 413	830 708	874 050	895 994	...	Produit intérieur brut aux couts des facteurs / prix de base
Plus: Indirect Taxes / taxes on products, less subsidies	84 031	81 312	64 768	66 068	79 510	94 668	113 971	120 125	...	Plus taxes indirectes/impôts sur les produits, moins les subventions
EXPENDITURE ON GROSS DOMESTIC PRODUCT AT CURRENT PURCHASER'S VALUES MOROCCAN DIRHAM (MILLIONS)										**EMPLOI DU PRODUIT INTÉRIEUR BRUT AUX PRIX COURANTS D'ACQUISION** DIRHAM MAROCAIN (MILLIONS)
Government final consumption	136 522	140 823	153 360	168 190	178 309	184 303	190 450	195 598	...	Consommation finale des administrations publiques
Private final consumption	438 781	461 040	488 348	512 207	538 145	555 716	568 292	588 651	...	Consommation finale privée
Gross fixed capital formation	236 985	240 536	258 285	276 390	276 496	276 237	280 271	306 910	...	Formation brute de capital fixe
Change in inventories	25 330	26 820	35 114	20 530	34 860	24 861	24 072	29 014	...	Variation des stocks
Exports of goods and services	209 599	252 908	284 567	296 161	294 318	320 480	343 807	356 559	...	Exportations de biens et services
Less imports of goods and services	298 734	337 503	399 597	425 597	424 205	436 221	418 871	460 613	...	Moins importations de biens et services
GDP at purchasers' values	748 483	784 624	820 077	847 881	897 923	925 376	988 021	1 016 119	...	PIB aux prix d'acquisition
GROSS DOMESTIC PRODUCT BY KIND OF ECONOMIC ACTIVITY AT CONSTANT PRICES ANNUAL GROWTH RATES (%)										**PRODUIT INTÉRIEUR BRUT PAR BRANCHE D'ACTIVITÉ ÉCONOMIQUE AUX PRIX CONSTANTS** TAUX DE CROISSANCE ANNUEL (%)
Agriculture, hunting , forestry and Fishing	23.9	1.1	6.7	- 7.9	17.9	- 2.4	11.6	- 11.5	...	Agriculture, chasse sylviculture et Pêche
Mining and quarrying	- 28.9	42.1	5.0	- 2.1	- 1.2	3.0	- 2.1	2.2	...	Industries extractives
Manufacturing	- 3.6	8.6	7.5	1.6	- 0.7	4.1	2.3	0.8	...	Industries manufacturières
Electricity, gas & water	- 13.5	18.2	8.3	- 6.7	14.9	1.3	6.2	2.5	...	Electricité, gaz et eau
Construction	4.5	2.4	4.9	2.2	1.6	2.6	0.7	1.7	...	Bâtiments et travaux publics
Wholesale & retail trade, restaurants, hotels	- 1.0	- 1.3	5.7	3.8	- 0.8	1.7	0.2	4.1	...	Commerce de gros et de détail, restaurants et hôtels
Finance, insurance, real estate, etc.	- 4.2	9.5	4.1	28.9	- 0.6	8.5	3.6	3.2	...	Banques, assurances, affaires immobilières
Transport and communications	4.7	5.0	8.3	16.2	2.1	4.5	2.9	3.7	...	Transport(s) et communications
Public administration and defense	11.4	0.8	9.9	- 27.0	3.7	2.6	0.5	0.9	...	Administrations publiques et défense
Education	1.6	4.4	1.6	19.1	5.0	1.4	0.1	1.8	...	Education
Health And Social Work	...	...	...	...	...	...	...	...	...	Santé et Actions Sociales
Other services	2.3	2.4	2.1	3.0	2.9	0.2	3.4	3.0	...	Autres services
Less Imputed Service Charges	...	...	...	...	...	...	...	...	...	Moins Services d'intermédiation financière
Gross domestic product at factor cost / basic prices	3.3	4.7	6.3	2.7	3.7	2.9	3.3	0.1	...	Produit intérieur brut aux couts des facteurs / prix de base
Plus: Indirect Taxes / taxes on products, less subsidies	12.2	- 2.9	- 3.7	6.0	12.3	0.4	15.0	10.1	...	Plus taxes indirectes/impôts sur les produits, moins les subventions
Gross domestic product at market prices	4.2	3.8	5.2	3.0	4.5	2.7	4.5	1.2	...	Produit intérieur brut aux prix du marché
EXPENDITURE ON GROSS DOMESTIC PRODUCT AT CONSTANT PURCHASERS' VALUES ANNUAL GROWTH RATES (%)										**EMPLOIS DU PRODUIT INTÉRIEUR BRUT AUX PRIX CONSTANTS D'ACQUISION** TAUX DE CROISSANCE ANNUEL (%)
Government final consumption	12.2	0.9	3.4	8.5	4.2	2.0	2.4	2.1	...	Consommation finale des administrations publiques
Private final consumption	3.7	4.4	5.4	4.5	2.6	3.6	2.5	1.8	...	Consommation finale privée
Gross fixed capital formation	- 2.6	- 1.4	7.8	3.6	- 0.5	- 1.3	0.2	9.3	...	Formation brute de capital fixe
Exports of goods and services	- 9.2	17.9	5.6	2.7	-	9.0	5.5	5.1	...	Exportations de biens et services
Less imports of goods and services	- 8.4	7.8	9.1	3.3	- 0.1	3.8	- 1.1	15.4	...	Moins importations de biens et services

III INFLATION

	2009	2010	2011	2012	2013	2014	2015	2016	2017	
Annual growth rates (%)										**Taux de croissance annuel (%)**
All item	1.0	0.9	0.9	1.3	1.9	0.4	1.6	1.6	0.8	Ensemble
of which:										dont:
Food and non-alcoholic beverages	0.5	0.6	1.4	2.4	2.2	- 1.2	2.6	2.8	-	Alimentation et boissons non alcoolisés
Alcoholic beverages, tobacco and narcotics	...	...	...	0.1	5.4	1.7	3.9	1.5	1.1	Boissons alcoolisées et tabacs
Clothing and footwear	1.4	0.7	1.7	2.0	1.5	2.1	0.7	1.0	1.4	Habillement et chaussures
Housing, water, electricity, gas and other fuels	0.7	0.5	0.4	0.5	1.1	2.5	3.4	1.0	1.2	Logement, eau, électricité, gaz et autres combustibles
Furnishings, household equipment and routine household maintenance	1.4	0.8	0.9	0.1	0.2	0.8	0.3	0.5	0.6	Meubles, articles de ménage et entretien courant
Health	1.0	0.4	0.2	0.7	0.9	- 0.2	- 0.3	0.3	0.7	Santé
Transport	0.7	- 0.3	- 0.1	3.2	3.2	2.6	- 3.2	- 0.1	1.7	Transport
Communication	...	...	- 5.4	- 19.7	- 9.2	- 4.6	0.1	- 0.1	- 0.1	Communication
Recreation and culture	1.8	...	- 0.7	0.5	0.5	- 0.9	0.3	1.6	0.6	Loisirs et culture
Education	...	...	4.1	3.9	5.5	3.4	2.8	2.4	2.6	Enseignement
Restaurants and hotels	...	...	1.7	2.0	3.2	2.5	2.3	2.5	3.2	Restaurants et hôtels
Miscellaneous goods and services	2.2	1.8	2.0	1.3	1.3	1.2	0.6	0.2	0.8	Biens et Services divers

IV AGRICULTURAL PRODUCTION - PRODUCTION AGRICOLE

	2009	2010	2011	2012	2013	2014	2015	2016	2017	
TONNES (THOUSAND)										**Tonnes (milliers)**
Wheat	6 371	4 876	6 018	3 878	6 934	5 116	8 075	2 731	...	Blé
Potatoes	2 753	2 436	3 035	1 627	2 142	3 209	3 876	4 219	...	Pommes de terre
Tomatoes	3 770	2 566	2 318	1 201	2 723	1 638	3 397	620	...	Tomates
Olives	1 234	1 605	1 721	1 657	1 929	1 951	1 924	1 744	...	Olives
Dry onion	1 230	1 434	1 218	1 219	1 293	1 231	1 231		...	Oignons secs

V MINING PRODUCTION - PRODUCTION MINIERE

	2009	2010	2011	2012	2013	2014	2015	2016	2017	
Zinc ores and concentrates - Production, metric tons (thousands)	88	83	72	92	82	90	106	106	...	Minerais de zinc et leurs concentrés - Production, tonnes métriques (milliers)
Copper ores and concentrates - Production, metric tons (thousands)	42	38	40	59	46	66	73	119	...	Minerais de cuivre et leurs concentrés - Production, tonnes métriques (milliers)
Natural phosphates, P2O5 content - Production, metric tons (thousands)	18 307	26 628	28 052	27 060	26 431	27 389	26 264	26 928	...	Phosphates naturels, teneur en P2O5 - Production, tonnes métriques (milliers)

VI ENERGY - ENERGIE

	2009	2010	2011	2012	2013	2014	2015	2016	2017	
Total electricity generation (GWh)	21 345	23 637	25 005	26 356	26 868	29 142	29 762	30 426	...	Production électrique totale (GWh)
of which										dont
Production of electricity from fossil fuels (GWh)	18 412	19 545	22 308	23 812	22 663	25 185	25 675	26 184	...	Production d'électricité à partir de combustibles fossiles (GWh)
Production of hydro electricity (GWh)	2 542	3 433	2 005	1 816	2 990	2 033	2 067	2 102	...	Production d'électricité d'origine hydraulique (GWh)
Production of electricity from solar, wind, tide, wave and other sources (GWh)	391	659	692	728	1 215	1 924	2 020	2 139	...	Production d'électricité d'origine solaire, éolienne, marée motrice et autres (GWh)

VII TOURISM AND INFRASTRUCTURE - TOURISME ET INFRASTUCTURE

	2009	2010	2011	2012	2013	2014	2015	2016	2017	
VII-1 Tourism										**VII-1 Tourisme**
International tourist arrivals (thousands)	8 341	9 288	9 342	9 375	10 046	10 283	10 177	10 332	11 310	Arrivées de touristes internationaux (milliers)
Rooms in hotels and similar establishments (thousands)	78	82	86	94	99	103	107	112		Chambres d'hôtels et établissements assimilés (milliers)
Overnight stays (thousands)	16 212	17 585	15 649	15 812	17 472	18 882	17 886	18 614	20 869	Nuitées (milliers)
Tourism receipts (US$ thousand)	6 586 490	6 658 580	7 277 780	6 654 280	6 808 280	7 313 100	6 188 400	6 481 930	6 942 090	Recettes touristiques (milliers de $ EU)
Total contribution to GDP (%)	19.0	19.1	19.3	19.2	18.2	18.8	18.1	18.5	18.6	Contribution totale au PIB (%)
Total contribution to Employment (%)	17.3	17.5	17.6	17.2	16.4	16.8	16.2	16.5	16.4	Contribution totale à l'emploi (%)
VII-2 Infrastructure										**VII-2 Infrastructure**
Paved road (% of total)	70.3	70.4	70.6	...	...	...	...	...	...	Routes asphaltées (% du total)
Total network (Railways-km)	2 110	2 109	2 109	2 109	2 109	2 109	...	...	...	Réseau total voies ferrées-Km
Main telephone lines (per 100 inhabitants)	11.2	11.8	11.1	10.1	8.9	7.4	6.5	6.0	...	Lignes téléphoniques fixes (pour 100 habitants)
Mobile cellular subscribers (per 100 inhabitants)	80.9	101.1	114.0	120.0	128.5	131.7	126.9	120.7	...	Abonnés aux téléphones mobiles (pour 100 habitants)
Internet users per 100 inhabitants	41.3	52.0	46.1	55.4	56.0	56.8	57.1	58.3	...	Utilisateurs Internet par 100 Habitants
Fixed (wired)-broadband subscriptions per 100 inhabitants	1.5	1.6	1.9	2.1	2.6	3.0	3.4	3.7	...	Abonnements à l'Internet fixe (filaire) à large bande pour 100 habitants, par débit

VIII EXTERNAL TRADE - COMMERCE EXTERIEUR

	2009	2010	2011	2012	2013	2014	2015	2016	2017	
US$ (MILLIONS) EXPORTS, FOB										**$ E.U (MILLIONS) EXPORTATIONS, FÀB**
Exports - Total	14 069	17 765	21 650	21 417	21 965	23 816	22 037	22 858	...	Exportations - Total
Exports to Africa	906	1 205	1 295	1 755	1 641	1 763	2 002	2 086	...	Exportations vers l'Afrique
Main products										**Principaux produits**
Equipment for distributing electricity, n.e.s.	1 138	1 614	2 023	1 778	2 071	2 391	2 281	2 494	...	Matériel de distribution d'électricité, n.d.a.
Fertilizers (other than those of group 272)	718	1 434	2 291	2 329	1 942	1 994	1 794	2 090	...	Engrais (autres que ceux du groupe 272)
Inorganic chemical elements, oxides & halogen salts	978	1 472	1 935	1 652	1 376	1 449	1 676	1 147	...	Eléments chimiques inorganiques, oxydes et sels halogénés
Motor vehicles for the transport of persons	53	72	249	766	1 230	1 929	2 016	2 455	...	Véhicules à moteur pour le transport de personnes
Women's clothing, of textile fabrics	1 359	1 397	1 485	1 458	1 532	1 768	1 456	1 654	...	Vêtements pour femmes en tissus
Main destinations										**Principales destinations**
Brazil	302	645	1 122	1 213	1 326	1 143	714	595	...	Brazil
France	3 223	3 629	4 071	4 076	4 203	4 539	4 024	4 375	...	France
India	724	943	1 404	1 236	837	830	969	756	...	Inde
Spain	2 974	3 253	3 936	3 595	4 157	5 076	4 827	5 467	...	Espagne
United States	466	693	968	921	919	903	886	868	...	États-Unis
IMPORTS, CIF										
Imports - Total	32 882	35 379	44 263	44 790	45 186	46 192	37 546	41 696	...	Importations - Total (millions)
Imports from Africa	1 709	2 089	2 356	2 280	2 353	2 414	1 901	1 602	...	Importations en provenance de l'Afrique
Main products										**Principaux produits**
Liquefied propane and butane	996	1 376	1 782	1 957	1 811	1 856	1 049	925	...	Propane liquéfié et butane
Motor vehicles for the transport of persons	1 182	1 279	1 375	1 609	1 503	1 647	1 593	1 983	...	Véhicules à moteur pour le transport de personnes
Petroleum oils or bituminous minerals > 70 % oil	2 214	2 633	4 197	4 608	4 533	4 271	3 326	3 546	...	Huiles de pétrole ou de minéraux bitumineux> 70% d'huile
Petroleum oils, oils from bitumin. materials, crude	2 139	2 980	3 888	4 352	4 321	3 374	1 121	...	...	Huiles de pétrole, huiles de bitume. matériaux bruts
Wheat (including spelt) and meslin, unmilled	683	878	1 440	1 400	978	1 514	876	1 304	...	Blé (y compris l'épeautre) et méteil, non moulu
Main origin										**Principales provenances**
China	2 568	2 968	2 885	2 968	3 137	3 508	3 153	3 804	...	Chine
France	5 118	5 508	6 309	5 548	5 849	6 225	4 755	5 514	...	France
Germany	1 792	1 626	1 981	2 139	2 167	2 398	2 180	2 452	...	Allemagne
Spain	4 004	3 753	4 859	5 901	6 120	6 161	5 225	6 554	...	Espagne
United States	2 282	2 495	3 591	2 859	3 397	3 220	2 441	2 659	...	États-Unis

MAROC

IX FINANCIAL AND MONETARY STATISTICS - FINANCES ET STATISTIQUES MONETAIRES

	2009	2010	2011	2012	2013	2014	2015	2016	2017	
IX-1 MONETARY STATISTICS *MOROCCAN DIRHAM (MILLIONS)*										**IX-1 STATISTIQUES MONÉTAIRES** *FRANC CFA (MILLIONS)*
Money supply (M1)	855 955	891 866	949 287	992 176	1 022 816	1 086 227	1 148 039	1 205 770	1 278 117	Masse monétaire (M1)
Quasi-money	298 490	319 022	329 717	339 099	353 000	380 502	397 175	399 554	404 498	Quasi-monnaie
of which demand deposit	388 716	404 818	428 489	...	...	...	...	...	...	dont Monnaie scripturale
Net foreign assets	192 714	192 491	168 456	140 403	141 661	173 809	223 778	241 386	262 251	Avoirs extérieurs nets
Domestic credit	731 954	796 465	891 970	955 366	1 008 380	1 033 964	1 052 148	1 100 026	1 163 698	Crédit intérieur
of which claims on private sector	87 797	81 218	102 143	125 402	149 281	143 720	147 974	142 379	170 712	dont créances sur le secteur privé
of which claims on government sector, net	473 778	524 623	577 761	607 405	612 429	632 097	630 472	648 581	671 112	dont créances nettes sur le gouvernement
International reserves (millions US$)	23 579	23 959	20 449	17 390	19 049	20 522	23 008	25 366	24 986	Réserves internationales (millions $EU)
Average exchange rate (National currency per US$)	8	8	8	9	8	8	10	10	10	Taux de change (moyen) (monnaie nationale par $ EU)
IX-2 PUBLIC FINANCE *MOROCCAN DIRHAM (MILLIONS)*										**IX-2 FINANCES PUBLIQUES** *FRANC CFA (MILLIONS)*
Total Revenues and Grants	189 119	193 667	208 046	228 564	234 567	236 954	240 347	244 459	...	Recettes totales et dons
Direct taxes (on income, profits)	71 734	65 004	70 850	78 911	77 390	77 593	80 835	84 795	...	Taxes directes
Domestic indirect taxes revenues	74 708	86 324	93 178	97 530	98 005	97 276	100 003	101 914	...	Taxes Indirectes
Trade taxes	11 830	12 242	10 286	9 003	7 681	7 738	7 715	9 074	...	Taxes sur le commerce extérieur
Other taxes	9 104	9 992	10 667	13 060	13 454	15 579	16 092	16 590	...	Autres taxes
Other revenues	18 943	18 236	21 755	25 560	31 896	36 268	28 521	28 713	...	Autres recettes
Grants	2 800	1 869	1 310	4 500	6 141	2 500	7 181	3 373	...	Dons
Total Expenditures and Net Lending	215 475	228 609	265 633	289 645	280 475	282 294	281 902	286 557	...	Dépenses totales et prêts nets
Current expenditure	151 930	164 004	197 370	218 962	209 778	206 935	195 920	196 215	...	Dépenses courantes
Wages and Salaries	75 527	78 768	88 973	96 673	99 044	101 505	102 959	104 320	...	Rémunérations et salaires
Other purchases of goods and services	46 604	38 483	38 171	44 983	46 556	50 754	56 593	55 064	...	Achat de biens et services
Other current expenditure	13 276	27 195	48 830	54 870	41 600	32 648	13 977	14 097	...	Autres dépenses courantes
Current transfers	16 523	19 558	21 396	22 436	22 578	22 028	22 391	22 734	...	Transferts courants
Interest payments	17 326	17 574	18 240	19 225	22 502	21 052	27 291	27 100	...	Intérêts
Capital expenditure	46 219	47 031	50 023	51 458	48 195	54 307	58 691	63 242	...	Dépenses d'équipement
Net lending	...	...	...	...	...	...	...	...	...	Prêts nets
Fiscal balance	- 26 356	- 34 942	- 57 587	- 61 081	- 45 908	- 45 340	- 41 555	- 42 098	...	Solde global y compris les dons
IX-3 BALANCE OF PAYMENTS *MOROCCAN DIRHAM (MILLIONS)*										**IX-3 BALANCE DES PAIEMENTS** *FRANC CFA (MILLIONS)*
Trade balance	- 133 332	- 126 033	- 157 161	- 173 043	- 171 300	- 172 120	- 141 548	- 173 650	...	Balance commerciale
Services Balance	45 427	42 837	43 498	45 280	46 712	59 513	62 089	66 366	...	Balance des services
Net primary income	- 7 352	- 12 555	- 16 561	- 19 234	- 14 896	- 21 158	- 18 412	- 17 651	...	Revenus primaires nets
Compensation of employees	...	...	...	...	...	...	...	...	...	Rémunération des salariés
Investment income	...	...	...	...	...	...	...	...	...	Revenus des investissements
Net secondary income	58 449	61 429	65 615	66 350	73 317	81 543	76 728	80 440	...	Revenus secondaires nets
Net official transfers	...	...	...	...	...	...	...	...	...	Transferts officiels nets
Workers' remittances	...	...	...	...	...	...	...	...	...	Envois de fonds des travailleurs
Other private transfers	...	...	...	...	...	...	...	...	...	Autres transferts privés
Current account balance	- 36 808	- 34 322	- 64 608	- 80 648	- 66 166	- 52 222	- 21 144	- 44 496	...	Solde du compte courant
Capital and financial account	44 038	37 194	66 636	83 117	63 373	72 161	12 710	16 503	...	Comptes de capital et financier
Capital account	- 4	- 1	- 2	1	- 1	16	6	...	...	Compte de capital
Financial account	44 042	37 194	67 398	83 116	63 374	72 145	12 704	16 503	...	Compte financier
Errors and omissions	- 4 164	- 2 871	- 2 793	- 2 469	2 792	- 8 687	6 733	8 150	...	Erreurs et omissions
Overall balance	...	- 10 148	21 226	29 944	- 11 760	26 692	42 379	27 113	...	Balance générale

X DEBT AND FINANCIAL FLOWS - DETTE ET FLUX FINANCIERS

	2009	2010	2011	2012	2013	2014	2015	2016	2017	
X-1 DEBT *US $ (MILLIONS)*										**X-1 DETTE EXTÉRIEURE** *$ E.U (MILLIONS)*
Total external debt	22 213	23 457	24 928	28 612	32 308	34 093	33 780	34 799	37 715	Dette extérieure totale
Private	1 421	1 330	1 440	1 695	1 754	1 671	1 697	1 929	...	Privée
Public	19 372	20 798	22 048	25 222	28 801	30 752	30 385	30 940	...	Publique
Total external debt service	1 979	2 004	2 348	2 515	2 825	2 892	2 703	3 184	...	Service de la dette extérieure
Present value of external debt	...	...	...	...	...	...	...	31 540	...	Valeur actuelle de la dette extérieure
Total government domestic debt, National currency (millions)	...	...	...	...	...	...	...	...	...	Dette publique intérieure
X-2 FINANCIAL FLOWS *US $ (MILLIONS)*										**X-2 FLUX FINANCIERS** *$ E.U (MILLIONS)*
Net Foreign Direct Investment Inflows	1 952	1 574	2 568	2 728	3 298	3 561	3 255	2 322	...	Investissements étranger direct (flux nets entrants)
Main origin of FDI inflows										**Principales origines de l'IDE entrant:**
Spain	...	- 750	162	116	...	...	...	...	...	Espagne
Belgium	44	922	52	- 45	...	...	...	...	...	Belgique
Switzerland	100	55	40	- 2	...	...	...	...	...	Suisse
United Kingdom	6	- 2	- 42	- 17	...	...	...	...	...	Royaume-Uni
...	...	...	...	...	...	...	...	...	...	...
African countries	...	...	...	...	...	...	...	...	...	Pays africains
Net total official development assistance	1 046	986	1 440	1 471	2 009	2 240	1 481	1 992	...	Aide publique au développement (nette totale)
Main origin of net ODA										**Principales origines de l'APD nette**
France	238	254	524	507	682	539	214	303	...	France
United Arab Emirates	- 125	- 5	9	3	...	...	...	...	...	Emirates Arabes
Japan	98	121	31	76	77	27	34	83	...	Japon
Spain	191	91	37	34	30	16	18	8	...	Espagne
Germany	82	39	56	12	54	415	352	463	...	Allemagne

MAROC

SOURCES AND NOTES - SOURCES ET NOTES

External trade - Total exports, fob: UNCTAD	Commerce exterieur - Exportation, fab: CNUCED
External trade - Total import, cif: UNCTAD	Commerce exterieur - Imporations, caf: CNUCED
ODA: OECD	APD: OCDE
Monetary statistics: IMF	Statistiques monétaires: FMI
National Accounts: 2014: Semi-final; 2015-2106:Provisional	Comptes nationaux: 2014 semi-définitives;2015-2016:Provisoires
National Accounts : The annual Growth Rates for 2016 are previsions based on the sum of four quarters of 2016	Comptes Nationaux: Les croissances annuelles de L'année 2016 sont estimées à partir des comptes trimestriels
Poverty: World Bank	Pauvreté: Banque mondiale

AREA (km2)		799 380			**SUPERFICIE (KM2)**
CAPITAL CITY	Maputo		Maputo		**CAPITALE**
CURRENCY	Mozambique Metical		Metical mozambicain		**MONNAIE**

I SOCIAL AND DEMOGRAPHIC INDICATORS — INDICATEURS DEMOGRAPHIQUES ET SOCIAUX

	Year Année	Value Valeur	Charts Graphiques	
Population				**Population**
Population ('000)	2017	27 000.0		Population ('000)
Female (%)	2017	51.7		Féminine (%)
Urban (%)	2017	32.3		Urbaine (%)
Average annual growth rate	2017	2.6		Taux de croissance annuel
Active population ('000)	2017	15 053.9		Population active ('000)
Population by age group ('000)				Population par groupe d'âge ('000)
0-14 years	2017	12 075.0		0-14 ans
15-64 years	2017	14 226.0		15-64 ans
65+ years	2017	828.0		65+ ans
Economically active population in agriculture (%)	2015	81.0		Participation de la population active agricole (%)
Crude birth rate	2017	38.2		Taux brut de natalité
Crude death rate	2017	12.0		Taux brut de mortalité
Total fertility rate	2017	5.1		Indice synthétique de fécondité
Life expectancy at birth - Total (years)	2016	54.1		Espérance de vie à la naissance - Totale (années)
Dependency ratio - Total (%)	2017	90.7		Taux de dépendance - Total (%)
Health				**Santé**
Percentage of children under-five and underweight	2011	15.6		% d'enfants de moins de cinq ans avec insuffisance pondérale
Prevalence of undernourishment	2013	27.2		Prévalence de la malnutrition
Under five mortality rate (per 1 000 live births)	2013	85.6		Taux de mortalité de moins de 5 ans (les deux sexes, pour 1000)
Infant mortality rate (per 1 000 live births)	2013	60.9		Taux de mortalité infantile (les deux sexes) par 1000
Neonatal mortality rate (per 1 000 live births)	2013	28.4		Le taux de mortalité néonatale (pour 1000 naissances vivantes)
Percentage of children provided the vaccines :				Pourcentage d'enfants vaccinés :
BCG	2017	103.9		BCG
DPT3	2017	100.6		DTC3
Polio	2017	87.0		polio
Measles	2017	98.8		rougeole
Percentage of mothers provided at least one antenatal care (%)	2017	112.9		Pourcentage de mères ayant au moins reçu un soin prénatal (%)
Percentage of deliveries attended by skilled health personnel	2016	76.6		% d'accouchements assistés par un personnel de santé qualifié
Number of doctors (per 10,000 population)	2017	1.0		Nombre de médecins (pour 10.000 habitants)
Number of nurses (per 10,000 population)	2017	2.9		Nombre d'infirmiers (pour 10.000 habitants)
Hospital beds - Total (per 10,000 population)	2017	8.0		Nombre de lits d'hôpitaux - Total (pour 10 000)
Births registered (per 1,000)	2014	38.4		Naissances enregistrées (pour 1000)
Deaths registered (per 1,000)	2014	13.9		Décès enregistrés (pour 1000)
Budget allocation to health (%)	2014	8.3		Dépenses publiques consacrées à la santé (% du budget)
Education				**Education**
Enrolment in primary education (000)	2017	6 140.1		Scolarisation dans le primaire (000)
Female	2017	2 950.5		Féminine
Enrolment in secondary education (000)	2017	1 103.9		Scolarisation dans le secondaire (000)
Female	2017	541.3		Féminine
Enrolment in tertiary education (000)	2015	174.8		Scolarisation dans le tertiaire (000)
Female	2015	74.2		Féminine
Literacy rate	2015	55.1		Taux d'alphabétisation (deux sexes)
Male	2015	69.9		Masculin
Female	2015	42.2		Féminin
Pupil teacher ratio - primary	2015	56.0		Ratio élève-enseignant
Budget allocation to education (%)	2017	17.7		Dépenses publiques consacrées à l'enseignement (% du budget)
Poverty				**Pauvreté**
GNI per capita, PPP (current int. $)	2016	1190.0		RNB par habitant, ($ PPA inter. courants)
Human Poverty Index (HPI-1) Value (%)	2007	46.8		Valeur de l'Indice de pauvreté (IPH-1) (%)
Population below Inter. poverty line ($2/day) (%)	2008	68.7		Population sous le seuil inter. de pauvreté (2$/Jour) (%)
Share of income held by richest 10%	2008	36.8		% de revenu des 10% plus riches
Share of income held by poorest 10%	2008	1.9		% de revenu des 10% plus pauvres
GINI index	2008	45.6		Indice de GINI

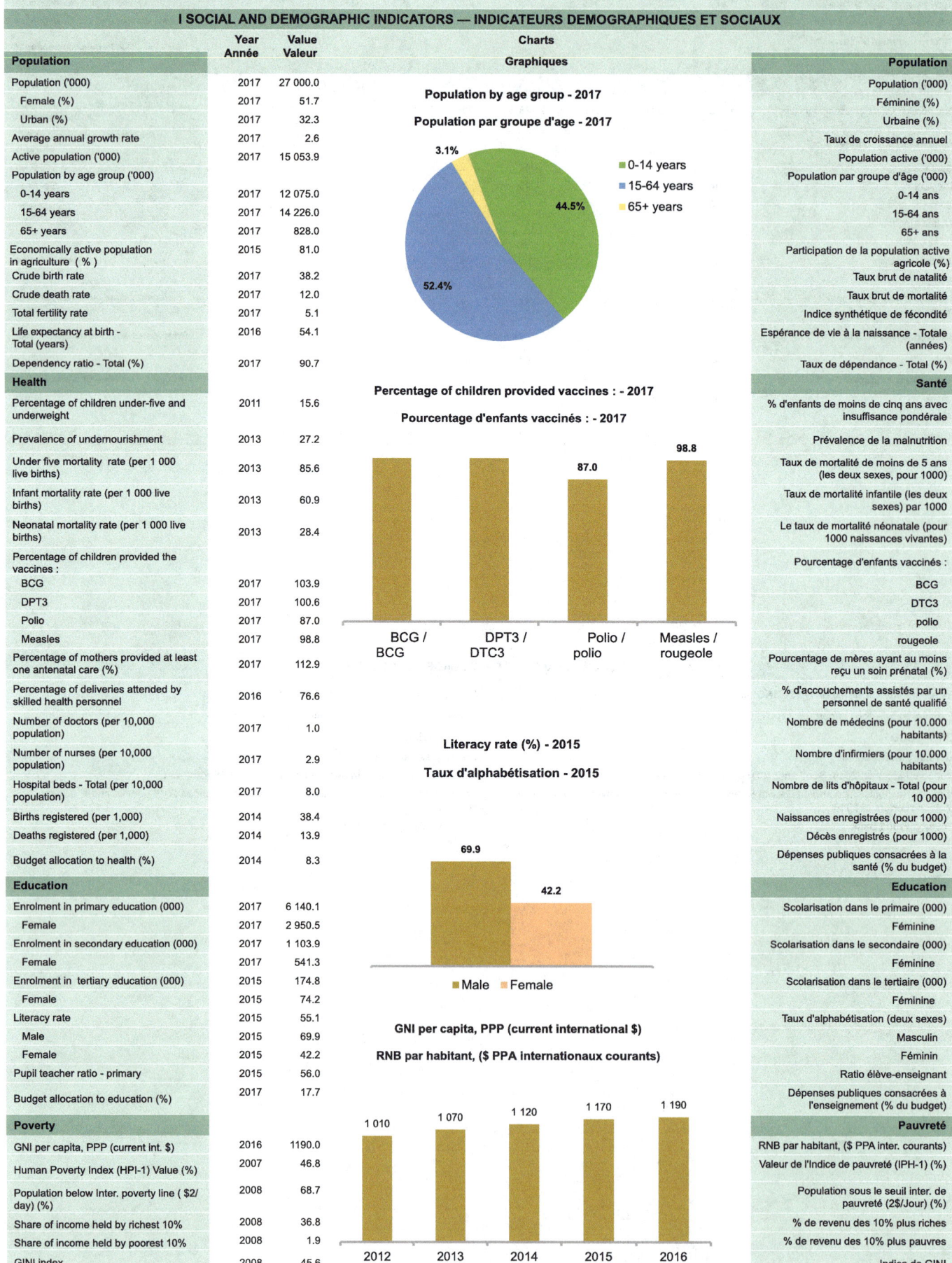

Population by age group - 2017
Population par groupe d'age - 2017
0-14 years 44.5%; 15-64 years 52.4%; 65+ years 3.1%

Percentage of children provided vaccines : - 2017
Pourcentage d'enfants vaccinés : - 2017
BCG / BCG; DPT3 / DTC3; Polio / polio 87.0; Measles / rougeole 98.8

Literacy rate (%) - 2015
Taux d'alphabétisation - 2015
Male 69.9; Female 42.2

GNI per capita, PPP (current international $)
RNB par habitant, ($ PPA internationaux courants)
2012 1 010; 2013 1 070; 2014 1 120; 2015 1 170; 2016 1 190

MOZAMBIQUE

II NATIONAL ACCOUNTS — COMPTES NATIONAUX

	2009	2010	2011	2012	2013	2014	2015	2016	2017	
GROSS DOMESTIC PRODUCT BY KIND OF ECONOMIC ACTIVITY AT CURRENT PRICES *MOZAMBIQUE METICAL (NEW) (MILLIONS)*										**PRODUIT INTÉRIEUR BRUT PAR BRANCHE D'ACTIVITÉ ÉCONOMIQUE AUX PRIX COURANTS** *METICAL MOZAMBICAIN (NOUVEAU) (MILLIONS)*
Agriculture, hunting , forestry and Fishing	83 779	94 292	100 369	109 287	116 129	120 982	135 754	155 412	...	Agriculture, chasse sylviculture et Pêche
Mining and quarrying	4 346	5 557	8 428	13 081	15 230	23 894	30 309	42 957	...	Industries extractives
Manufacturing	33 231	36 104	39 299	39 413	41 591	47 821	53 917	59 806	...	Industries manufacturières
Electricity, gas & water	9 889	11 997	12 085	13 841	16 301	17 116	18 296	18 614	...	Electricité, gaz et eau
Construction	5 553	6 862	7 948	9 158	8 737	10 960	13 714	14 399	...	Bâtiments et travaux publics
Wholesale & retail trade, restaurants, hotels	35 295	43 575	49 902	56 943	66 438	72 496	79 499	93 757	...	Commerce de gros et de détail, restaurants et hôtels
Finance, insurance, real estate, etc.	30 819	35 825	44 167	48 410	53 940	55 583	61 534	70 530	...	Banques, assurances, affaires immobilières
Transport and communications	39 162	44 657	44 126	50 998	59 569	57 639	60 325	67 075	...	Transport(s) et communications
Public administration and defense	13 579	16 749	19 324	21 662	25 271	31 291	37 462	44 381	...	Administrations publiques et défense
Education	20 041	22 202	25 806	31 314	33 972	42 271	46 821	56 163	...	Education
Health And Social Work	4 790	5 248	6 137	7 624	7 922	10 497	11 296	13 593	...	Santé et Actions Sociales
Other services	2 673	2 940	3 225	3 337	3 482	3 603	3 920	4 089	...	Autres services
Less Imputed Service Charges	- 4 561	- 6 626	- 9 386	- 9 798	- 11 520	- 11 226	- 14 065	- 16 694	...	Moins Services d'intermédiation financière
Gross domestic product at factor cost / basic prices	278 597	319 384	351 430	395 269	437 064	482 926	538 782	624 083	...	Produit intérieur brut aux couts des facteurs / prix de base
Plus: Indirect Taxes / taxes on products, less subsidies	21 675	25 455	30 262	37 853	45 169	48 851	52 895	63 033	...	Plus taxes indirectes/impôts sur les produits, moins les subventions
EXPENDITURE ON GROSS DOMESTIC PRODUCT AT CURRENT PURCHASER'S VALUES *MOZAMBIQUE METICAL (NEW) (MILLIONS)*										**EMPLOI DU PRODUIT INTÉRIEUR BRUT AUX PRIX COURANTS D'ACQUISITION** *METICAL MOZAMBICAIN (NOUVEAU) (MILLIONS)*
Government final consumption	54 299	64 131	76 137	90 282	115 101	138 592	157 807	194 588	...	Consommation finale des administrations publiques
Private final consumption	235 826	268 348	289 576	337 190	363 123	372 134	401 021	488 801	...	Consommation finale privée
Gross fixed capital formation	42 340	61 599	82 232	152 145	189 791	228 937	189 089	154 470	...	Formation brute de capital fixe
Change in inventories	1 760	1 491	15 738	53 076	72 875	65 469	79 092	107 447	...	Variation des stocks
Exports of goods and services	89 990	108 659	127 587	140 228	146 451	177 397	190 616	252 787	...	Exportations de biens et services
Less imports of goods and services	123 944	159 389	209 578	339 800	405 108	450 752	425 947	510 977	...	Moins importations de biens et services
GDP at purchasers' values	300 271	344 839	381 692	433 121	482 233	531 777	591 679	687 116	...	PIB aux prix d'acquisition
GROSS DOMESTIC PRODUCT BY KIND OF ECONOMIC ACTIVITY AT CONSTANT PRICES *ANNUAL GROWTH RATES (%)*										**PRODUIT INTÉRIEUR BRUT PAR BRANCHE D'ACTIVITÉ ECONOMIQUE AUX PRIX CONSTANTS** *TAUX DE CROISSANCE ANNUEL (%)*
Agriculture, hunting , forestry and Fishing	5.1	5.2	4.2	2.0	1.9	3.7	3.1	2.6	4.6	Agriculture, chasse sylviculture et Pêche
Mining and quarrying	8.6	3.0	26.5	67.9	15.7	24.6	22.5	15.6	32.4	Industries extractives
Manufacturing	-	3.1	2.1	0.1	4.1	2.6	9.0	3.9	- 0.8	Industries manufacturières
Electricity, gas & water	14.0	3.5	4.6	- 1.1	5.5	5.1	11.6	0.3	- 11.0	Electricité, gaz et eau
Construction	25.0	12.5	9.5	1.3	7.2	12.1	12.0	1.1	- 4.6	Bâtiments et travaux publics
Wholesale & retail trade, restaurants, hotels	1.8	12.8	6.6	12.2	13.5	8.5	7.3	3.1	- 15.6	Commerce de gros et de détail, restaurants et hôtels
Finance, insurance, real estate, etc.	3.1	13.6	17.7	8.7	9.5	12.6	5.0	2.1	0.7	Banques, assurances, affaires immobilières
Transport and communications	13.3	6.4	4.1	7.0	8.5	3.3	6.5	1.2	5.2	Transport(s) et communications
Public administration and defense	10.1	15.5	15.3	13.4	3.7	10.6	14.9	1.2	4.1	Administrations publiques et défense
Education	15.5	5.9	10.3	13.8	3.0	7.6	7.4	7.4	6.4	Education
Health And Social Work	6.9	6.7	0.6	3.3	- 3.3	16.7	10.2	4.0	5.6	Santé et Actions Sociales
Other services	5.6	6.0	4.8	5.0	4.8	5.0	5.4	4.9	0.1	Autres services
Less Imputed Service Charges	4.0	39.8	35.8	6.1	18.2	- 1.3	22.6	3.0	- 208.8	Moins Services d'intermédiation financière
Gross domestic product at factor cost / basic prices	6.6	7.1	6.6	7.2	6.0	7.4	6.8	3.3	8.0	Produit intérieur brut aux couts des facteurs / prix de base
Plus: Indirect Taxes / taxes on products, less subsidies	3.8	1.7	14.3	7.1	22.1	8.2	4.2	9.2	4.7	Plus taxes indirectes/impôts sur les produits, moins les subventions
Gross domestic product at market prices	6.4	6.7	7.1	7.2	7.1	7.4	6.6	3.8	3.7	Produit intérieur brut aux prix du marché
EXPENDITURE ON GROSS DOMESTIC PRODUCT AT CONSTANT PURCHASERS' VALUES *ANNUAL GROWTH RATES (%)*										**EMPLOIS DU PRODUIT INTÉRIEUR BRUT AUX PRIX CONSTANTS D'ACQUISITION** *TAUX DE CROISSANCE ANNUEL (%)*
Government final consumption	7.1	11.9	14.3	15.3	14.4	4.2	11.8	4.8	...	Consommation finale des administrations publiques
Private final consumption	6.2	3.6	4.9	8.2	5.9	4.7	4.9	2.8	...	Consommation finale privée
Gross fixed capital formation	7.2	17.6	17.1	73.8	53.2	24.0	- 22.8	- 23.1	...	Formation brute de capital fixe
Exports of goods and services	15.5	1.5	17.2	13.3	2.2	15.7	- 1.2	9.4	...	Exportations de biens et services
Less imports of goods and services	13.2	1.6	25.6	62.4	28.8	14.6	- 6.7	3.7	...	Moins importations de biens et services

III INFLATION

	2009	2010	2011	2012	2013	2014	2015	2016	2017	
Annual growth rates (%)										**Taux de croissance annuel (%)**
All item	3.8	12.4	11.2	2.6	4.3	2.6	3.6	17.4	15.1	Ensemble
of which:										dont:
Food and non-alcoholic beverages	7.0	15.3	13.2	3.1	5.4	3.8	5.2	27.2	16.4	Alimentation et boissons non alcoolisés
Alcoholic beverages, tobacco and narcotics	6.3	13.3	6.8	3.8	7.7	2.2	2.4	21.6	14.1	Boissons alcoolisées et tabacs
Clothing and footwear	2.6	2.8	5.7	3.5	2.7	2.2	4.1	17.7	21.5	Habillement et chaussures
Housing, water, electricity, gas and other fuels	- 7.4	10.8	9.0	4.3	4.8	3.4	0.9	4.7	15.7	Logement, eau, électricité, gaz et autres combustibles
Furnishings, household equipment and routine household maintenance	3.1	6.1	8.3	2.0	1.9	-	2.7	17.0	17.1	Meubles, articles de ménage et entretien courant
Health	6.1	6.1	1.0	1.1	4.6	3.0	0.4	7.4	11.4	Santé
Transport	- 3.5	7.2	6.4	0.7	3.5	0.2	1.2	8.0	13.0	Transport
Communication	- 0.1	- 0.3	- 0.1	- 1.2	1.6	- 1.1	0.8	2.9	2.6	Communication
Recreation and culture	1.5	3.9	5.7	- 2.9	- 0.4	- 0.7	2.5	7.7	7.6	Loisirs et culture
Education	9.0	5.3	22.1	6.2	9.7	5.8	13.3	10.3	14.1	Enseignement
Restaurants and hotels	10.4	11.3	14.9	3.3	4.8	3.9	3.1	19.1	17.4	Restaurants et hôtels
Miscellaneous goods and services	5.6	10.0	13.5	1.8	2.4	0.6	1.1	11.0	18.8	Biens et Services divers

MOZAMBIQUE

IV AGRICULTURAL PRODUCTION - PRODUCTION AGRICOLE

	2009	2010	2011	2012	2013	2014	2015	2016	2017	
TONNES (THOUSAND)										**Tonnes (milliers)**
Cassava	...	...	...	4 099	...	4 136	3 579	...	...	Manioc
Sugar cane	2 207	2 729	3 396	3 394	3 166	3 620	3 084	2 763	...	Canne à sucre
Maize	...	...	...	1 177	1 174	1 357	1 001	...	...	Maïs
Sweet potatoes	...	...	...	587	...	503	390	...	...	Patates douces
Bananas	34	321	341	470	570	575	670	517	...	Bananes

V MINING PRODUCTION - PRODUCTION MINIERE

	2009	2010	2011	2012	2013	2014	2015	2016	2017	
Hard Coal - Production, metric tons (thousands)	26	38	648	4 954	6 343	6 331	6 600	6 186	11 778	Houille - Production, tonnes métriques (milliers)
Natural gas - Production, terajoules (millions)	108	125	132	147	150	177	190	194	193	Gaz naturel - Production, térajoules (millions)
	...	...	...	...	...	...	...			

VI ENERGY - ENERGIE

	2009	2010	2011	2012	2013	2014	2015	2016	2017	
Total electricity generation (GWh)	16 967	16 658	16 734	16 744	15 026	17 555	19 617	...	...	Production électrique totale (GWh)
of which										dont
Production of electricity from fossil fuels (GWh)	17	18	20	21	318	1 417	2 533	...	...	Production d'électricité à partir de combustibles fossiles (GWh)
Production of hydro electricity (GWh)	16 950	16 640	16 567	16 567	14 542	16 136	17 082			Production d'électricité d'origine hydraulique (GWh)
Production of electricity from solar, wind, tide, wave and other sources (GWh)	...	...	2	5	7	1	14	...	...	Production d'électricité d'origine solaire, éolienne, marée motrice et autres (GWh)

VII TOURISM AND INFRASTRUCTURE - TOURISME ET INFRASTUCTURE

	2009	2010	2011	2012	2013	2014	2015	2016	2017	
VII-1 Tourism										**VII-1 Tourisme**
International tourist arrivals (thousands)	1 461	1 718	1 902	2 113	1 886	1 661	1 552	1 639	2 016	Arrivées de touristes internationaux (milliers)
Rooms in hotels and similar establishments (thousands)	16	21	21	22	22	22	30	34	32	Chambres d'hôtels et établissements assimilés (milliers)
Overnight stays (thousands)	924	1 036	1 195	867	867	912	789	702	639	Nuitées (milliers)
Tourism receipts (US$ thousand)	64 289	70 067	106 787	91 324	91 038	108 286	94 926	59 671	77 386	Recettes touristiques (milliers de $ EU)
Total contribution to GDP (%)	7.5	7.7	7.2	8.2	9.2	9.5	9.2	9.0	8.8	Contribution totale au PIB (%)
Total contribution to Employment (%)	6.9	6.3	5.6	6.9	7.9	8.3	8.1	8.0	7.9	Contribution totale à l'emploi (%)
VII-2 Infrastructure										**VII-2 Infrastructure**
Paved road (% of total)	24.3	17.9	17.9	18.0	21.0	23.0	25.4	...	...	Routes asphaltées (% du total)
Total network (Railways-km)	3 116	3 116	3 116	3 116	3 116	3 116	...	...	...	Réseau total voies ferrées-Km
Main telephone lines (per 100 inhabitants)	...	...	...	...	...	...	...	...	...	Lignes téléphoniques fixes (pour 100 habitants)
Mobile cellular subscribers (per 100 inhabitants)	25.6	30.1	32.0	34.9	48.0	69.8	74.2	66.3	...	Abonnés aux téléphones mobiles (pour 100 habitants)
Internet users per 100 inhabitants	2.7	4.2	4.3	6.0	7.3	9.2	16.9	17.5	...	Utilisateurs Internet par 100 Habitants
Fixed (wired)-broadband subscriptions per 100 inhabitants	...	...	...	...	...	...	...	...	...	Abonnements à l'Internet fixe (filaire) à large bande pour 100 habitants, par débit

VIII EXTERNAL TRADE - COMMERCE EXTERIEUR

	2009	2010	2011	2012	2013	2014	2015	2016	2017	
US$ (MILLIONS) EXPORTS, FOB										**$ E.U (MILLIONS) EXPORTATIONS, FÀB**
Exports - Total	2 147	3 000	3 604	3 470	4 024	4 725	3 196	3 142	...	Exportations - Total
Exports to Africa	689	723	1 054	1 121	1 324	1 207	869	778	...	Exportations vers l'Afrique
Main products										**Principaux produits**
Aluminium	565	1 571	1 548	1 057	1 118	1 191	987	819	...	Aluminium
Coal, whether or not pulverized, not agglomerated	11	11	44	217	287	298	246	328	...	Charbon, même pulvérisé, non aggloméré
Electric current	204	239	225	163	153	213	254	174	...	Courant électrique
Natural gas, whether or not liquefied	113	157	163	179	242	338	212	135	...	Gaz naturel, même liquéfié
Petroleum oils or bituminous minerals > 70 % oil	157	61	339	488	426	334	145	121	...	Huiles de pétrole ou de minéraux bitumineux> 70 % d'huile
Main destinations										**Principales destinations**
China	125	148	193	375	256	887	240	226	...	Chine
India	46	57	93	161	373	289	273	368	...	Inde
Italy	132	262	266	201	244	243	218	201	...	Italie
Netherlands	420	592	629	380	497	489	421	567	...	Pays-Bas
South Africa	398	490	768	822	912	817	591	470	...	Afrique du Sud
IMPORTS, CIF										
Imports - Total	3 764	4 600	6 306	8 688	10 099	8 743	7 908	5 024	...	Importations - Total (millions)
Imports from Africa	1 487	1 752	2 201	2 850	3 100	2 724	2 362	1 887	...	Importations en provenance de l'Afrique
Main products										**Principaux produits**
Aluminium	4	7	289	337	212	223	225	122	...	Aluminium
Electric current	98	122	190	272	261	229	230	149	...	Courant électrique
Motor vehic. for transport of goods, special purpo.	117	140	219	248	277	230	226	116	...	Véhicule à moteur pour le transport de marchandises, spécial.
Petroleum oils or bituminous minerals > 70 % oil	421	570	908	1 280	2 708	1 717	1 100	598	...	Huiles de pétrole ou de minéraux bitumineux> 70 % d'huile
Rice	138	111	139	194	213	176	164	119	...	Riz
Main origin										**Principales provenances**
China	239	333	487	802	886	1 144	1 346	725	...	Chine
India	269	357	397	700	935	1 014	868	386	...	Inde
Portugal	136	168	230	386	405	331	354	176	...	Portugal
South Africa	1 298	1 519	1 944	2 459	2 679	2 256	1 944	1 617	...	Afrique du Sud
United Arab Emirates	71	48	323	482	732	369	285	187	...	Emirates Arabes

	2009	2010	2011	2012	2013	2014	2015	2016	2017	
IX-1 MONETARY STATISTICS *MOZAMBIQUE METICAL (NEW) (MILLIONS)*										**IX-1 STATISTIQUES MONÉTAIRES** *METICAL MOZAMBICAIN (NOUVEAU) (MILLIONS)*
Money supply (M1)	72 537	85 275	105 697	132 716	160 840	204 815	249 291	255 207	279 452	Masse monétaire (M1)
Quasi-money	33 174	42 274	46 223	56 817	70 404	82 868	115 071	123 654	138 755	Quasi-monnaie
of which demand deposit	977	1 092	1 272	...	...	...	...	...	...	dont Monnaie scripturale
Net foreign assets	63 737	79 875	72 999	94 333	99 960	104 761	115 298	154 238	191 645	Avoirs extérieurs nets
Domestic credit	60 111	80 170	92 601	117 768	137 637	185 775	255 417	302 847	255 910	Crédit intérieur
of which claims on private sector	- 11 330	- 12 202	- 5 650	- 62	- 14 026	- 8 895	23 290	41 473	29 939	dont créances sur le secteur privé
of which claims on government sector, net	65 981	83 901	88 898	106 211	135 963	170 164	207 728	237 790	206 424	dont créances nettes sur le gouvernement
International reserves (millions US$)	1 951	2 180	2 423	2 799	3 192	3 072	2 472	1 973	2 652	Réserves internationales (millions $EU)
Average exchange rate (National currency per US$)	28	34	29	28	30	31	40	63	64	Taux de change (moyen) (monnaie nationale par $ EU)
IX-2 PUBLIC FINANCE *MOZAMBIQUE METICAL (NEW) (MILLIONS)*										**IX-2 FINANCES PUBLIQUES** *METICAL MOZAMBICAIN (NOUVEAU) (MILLIONS)*
Total Revenues and Grants	72 865	89 754	109 691	120 376	151 219	179 036	178 839	180 438	225 965	Recettes totales et dons
Direct taxes (on income, profits)	13 727	18 480	24 896	36 797	49 386	63 097	57 930	64 273	97 579	Taxes directes
Domestic indirect taxes revenues	19 743	27 624	33 765	36 914	44 595	67 846	63 897	56 370	55 996	Taxes Indirectes
Trade taxes	4 138	5 264	6 726	7 538	10 018	11 961	11 260	12 339	12 471	Taxes sur le commerce extérieur
Other taxes	1 787	2 340	2 877	3 207	3 544	4 142	6 570	5 512	7 354	Autres taxes
Other revenues	8 170	9 858	12 795	14 020	18 776	9 290	14 982	27 102	40 351	Autres recettes
Grants	25 300	26 188	28 632	21 900	24 900	22 700	24 200	14 843	12 215	Dons
Total Expenditures and Net Lending	83 700	105 423	135 726	151 279	194 709	189 863	191 918	216 533	227 061	Dépenses totales et prêts nets
Current expenditure	42 422	56 683	67 488	79 680	91 685	121 247	112 069	126 111	129 949	Dépenses courantes
Wages and Salaries	22 544	29 106	35 807	41 592	49 521	59 831	64 092	78 175	85 082	Rémunérations et salaires
Other purchases of goods and services	9 081	10 126	10 989	14 322	18 859	26 038	22 453	23 970	21 515	Achat de biens et services
Other current expenditure	2 884	8 019	9 406	10 240	7 907	17 045	5 666	2 458	3 175	Autres dépenses courantes
Current transfers	7 913	9 432	11 286	13 526	15 398	18 333	19 858	21 509	20 177	Transferts courants
Interest payments	1 371	2 673	3 501	4 125	3 970	5 193	7 577	16 309	18 020	Intérêts
Capital expenditure	35 624	43 904	51 012	53 457	72 301	58 394	58 651	60 645	53 104	Dépenses d'équipement
Net lending	4 283	2 163	13 725	14 017	26 753	5 029	13 621	13 467	25 988	Prêts nets
Fiscal balance	- 10 835	- 15 669	- 26 035	- 30 903	- 43 490	- 10 827	- 13 079	- 36 095	- 1 096	Solde global y compris les dons
IX-3 BALANCE OF PAYMENTS *US $ (MILLIONS)*										**IX-3 BALANCE DES PAIEMENTS** *$ E.U (MILLIONS)*
Trade balance	- 1 275	- 1 179	- 2 249	- 4 048	- 4 357	- 4 035	- 4 163	- 1 405	- 465	Balance commerciale
Services Balance	- 433	- 969	- 1 885	- 3 706	- 3 259	- 2 932	- 2 306	- 2 701	- 2 235	Balance des services
Net primary income	- 282	- 360	- 255	- 75	- 59	- 202	- 300	- 261	- 420	Revenus primaires nets
Compensation of employees	55	62	88	45	55	- 17	1	22	8	Rémunération des salariés
Investment income	- 337	- 422	- 343	- 121	- 114	- 185	- 301	- 282	- 428	Revenus des investissements
Net secondary income	763	828	1 004	1 039	1 421	1 372	802	520	679	Revenus secondaires nets
Net official transfers	682	604	781	714	1 088	1 087	540	440	511	Transferts officiels nets
Workers' remittances	- 9	...	1	33	- 3	- 22	- 48	- 27	38	Envois de fonds des travailleurs
Other private transfers	90	224	223	292	336	307	310	107	130	Autres transferts privés
Current account balance	- 1 226	- 1 680	- 3 385	- 6 790	- 6 253	- 5 797	- 5 968	- 3 846	- 2 440	Solde du compte courant
Capital and financial account	1 275	1 627	3 337	6 758	6 231	5 820	5 942	3 875	2 503	Comptes de capital et financier
Capital account	424	357	446	490	423	375	288	206	194	Compte de capital
Financial account	851	1 270	2 891	6 268	5 808	5 445	5 654	3 668	2 310	Compte financier
Errors and omissions	- 49	53	48	32	22	- 23	26	- 29	- 63	Erreurs et omissions
Overall balance	208	198	245	377	396	- 106	- 678	462	- 1 091	Balance générale

MOZAMBIQUE

X DEBT AND FINANCIAL FLOWS - DETTE ET FLUX FINANCIERS

	2009	2010	2011	2012	2013	2014	2015	2016	2017	
X-1 DEBT *US $ (MILLIONS)*										**X-1 DETTE EXTÉRIEURE** *$ E.U (MILLIONS)*
Total external debt	8 989	9 531	9 562	10 579	13 289	15 214	17 030	16 915	17 372	Dette extérieure totale
Private	...	...	...	...	...	...	...	...	...	Privée
Public	4 139	4 010	4 422	5 040	7 529	8 835	9 850	9 816	...	Publique
Total external debt service	176	155	720	590	628	683	737	897	...	Service de la dette extérieure
Present value of external debt	...	...	...	...	...	...	...	7 935	...	Valeur actuelle de la dette extérieure
Total government domestic debt, National currency (millions)	11 914	18 747	22 330	23 738	...	...	...	...	...	Dette publique intérieure
X-2 FINANCIAL FLOWS *US $ (MILLIONS)*										**X-2 FLUX FINANCIERS** *$ E.U (MILLIONS)*
Net Foreign Direct Investment Inflows	898	1 018	3 559	5 629	6 175	4 902	3 867	3 093	...	Investissements étranger direct (flux nets entrants)
Main origin of FDI inflows										**Principales origines de l'IDE entrant:**
United States	4	1	35	915	1 207	1 750	741	...	...	États-Unis
United Arab Emirates	6	7	44	217	1 652	1 505	1 474	...	...	Emirates Arabes
Mauritius	197	234	461	473	145	500	440	...	...	Maurice, île
India	2	- 2	10	409	899	4	149	...	...	Inde
...	...	...	...	...	...	...	...	...	...	...
African countries	240	378	591	429	...	...	...	...	...	Pays africains
Net total official development assistance	2 014	1 943	2 065	2 072	2 313	2 106	1 815	1 531	...	Aide publique au développement (nette totale)
Main origin of net ODA										**Principales origines de l'APD nette**
World Bank	213	164	96	223	369	317	...	...	...	World Bank
United States	256	267	378	413	541	395	302	392	...	États-Unis
EU	55	192	153	169	115	83	71	- 66	...	UE
African Development Bank	...	...	...	50	30	...	...	-	...	African Development Bank
Department for International Development	105	85	113	79	89	...	...	...	...	Department for International Development

SOURCES AND NOTES - SOURCES ET NOTES

External trade - Total exports, fob: UNCTAD

External trade - Total import, cif: UNCTAD

ODA: OECD

Monetary statistics: IMF

National Accounts: The Accounts are calculated using the new base year 2009 from 2007

National Accounts : The annual Growth Rates for 2016 are previsions based on the sum of four quarters of 2016

Poverty: World Bank

Commerce exterieur - Exportation, fab: CNUCED

Commerce exterieur - Imporations, caf: CNUCED

APD: OCDE

Statistiques monétaires: FMI

Comptes nationaux: Les comptes sont calculés selon la nouvelle année de base 2009 à partir de 2007

Comptes Nationaux: Les croissances annuelles de L'année 2016 sont estimées à partir des comptes trimestriels

Pauvreté: Banque mondiale

AREA (km2)	824 290	**SUPERFICIE (KM2)**
CAPITAL CITY	Windhoek	Windhoek **CAPITALE**
CURRENCY	Namibian Dollar	Dollar de namibie **MONNAIE**

I SOCIAL AND DEMOGRAPHIC INDICATORS — INDICATEURS DEMOGRAPHIQUES ET SOCIAUX

Population	Year Année	Value Valeur	Charts Graphiques	Population
Population ('000)	2017	2 368.7		Population ('000)
Female (%)	2017	51.4		Féminine (%)
Urban (%)	2017	48.9		Urbaine (%)
Average annual growth rate	2017	1.9		Taux de croissance annuel
Active population ('000)	2017	1 505.2		Population active ('000)
Population by age group ('000)				Population par groupe d'âge ('000)
0-14 years	2017	863.5		0-14 ans
15-64 years	2017	1 402.0		15-64 ans
65+ years	2017	103.2		65+ ans
Economically active population in agriculture (%)	2015	40.0		Participation de la population active agricole (%)
Crude birth rate	2017	29.4		Taux brut de natalité
Crude death rate	2017	10.6		Taux brut de mortalité
Total fertility rate	2011	3.9		Indice synthétique de fécondité
Life expectancy at birth - Total (years)	2015	65.1		Espérance de vie à la naissance - Totale (années)
Dependency ratio - Total (%)	2017	69.0		Taux de dépendance - Total (%)
Health				**Santé**
Percentage of children under-five and underweight	2007	17.5		% d'enfants de moins de cinq ans avec insuffisance pondérale
Prevalence of undernourishment	2015	42.3		Prévalence de la malnutrition
Under five mortality rate (per 1 000 live births)	2015	45.4		Taux de mortalité de moins de 5 ans (les deux sexes, pour 1000)
Infant mortality rate (per 1 000 live births)	2015	32.8		Taux de mortalité infantile (les deux sexes) par 1000
Neonatal mortality rate (per 1 000 live births)	2015	15.9		Le taux de mortalité néonatale (pour 1000 naissances vivantes)
Percentage of children provided the vaccines :				Pourcentage d'enfants vaccinés :
BCG	2014	97.0		BCG
DPT3	2014	88.0		DTC3
Polio	2011	85.0		polio
Measles	2014	83.0		rougeole
Percentage of mothers provided at least one antenatal care (%)	2007	94.6		Pourcentage de mères ayant au moins reçu un soin prénatal (%)
Percentage of deliveries attended by skilled health personnel	2007	81.4		% d'accouchements assistés par un personnel de santé qualifié
Number of doctors (per 10,000 population)	2007	3.7		Nombre de médecins (pour 10.000 habitants)
Number of nurses (per 10,000 population)	2007	27.8		Nombre d'infirmiers (pour 10.000 habitants)
Hospital beds - Total (per 10,000 population)	2009	26.7		Nombre de lits d'hôpitaux - Total (pour 10 000)
Births registered (per 1,000)	2015	29.4		Naissances enregistrées (pour 1000)
Deaths registered (per 1,000)	2015	7.0		Décès enregistrés (pour 1000)
Budget allocation to health (%)	2013	13.9		Dépenses publiques consacrées à la santé (% du budget)
Education				**Education**
Enrolment in primary education (000)	2015	442.7		Scolarisation dans le primaire (000)
Female	2015	238.8		Féminine
Enrolment in secondary education (000)	2015	195.7		Scolarisation dans le secondaire (000)
Female	2015	53.0		Féminine
Enrolment in tertiary education (000)	2014	47.0		Scolarisation dans le tertiaire (000)
Female	2014	29.6		Féminine
Literacy rate	2007	76.5		Taux d'alphabétisation (deux sexes)
Male	2007	74.3		Masculin
Female	2007	78.4		Féminin
Pupil teacher ratio - primary	2015	25.1		Ratio élève-enseignant
Budget allocation to education (%)	2015	23.9		Dépenses publiques consacrées à l'enseignement (% du budget)
Poverty				**Pauvreté**
GNI per capita, PPP (current int. $)	2016	10380.0		RNB par habitant, ($ PPA inter. courants)
Human Poverty Index (HPI-1) Value (%)	2007	17.1		Valeur de l'Indice de pauvreté (IPH-1) (%)
Population below Inter. poverty line ($2/day) (%)	2009	22.6		Population sous le seuil inter. de pauvreté (2$/Jour) (%)
Share of income held by richest 10%	2009	51.8		% de revenu des 10% plus riches
Share of income held by poorest 10%	2009	1.3		% de revenu des 10% plus pauvres
GINI index	2009	61.0		Indice de GINI

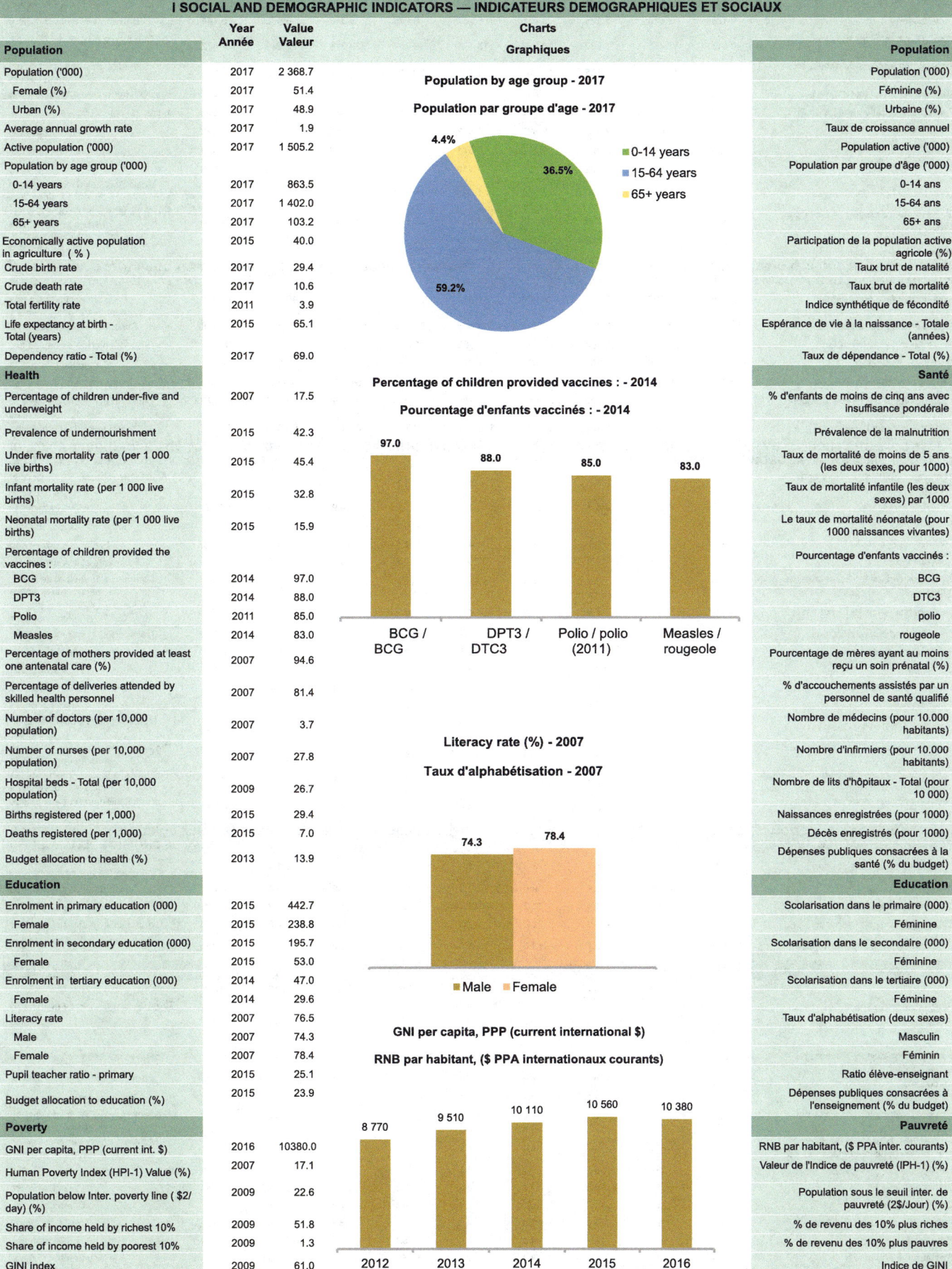

Population by age group - 2017
Population par groupe d'age - 2017

- 0-14 years: 36.5%
- 15-64 years: 59.2%
- 65+ years: 4.4%

Percentage of children provided vaccines : - 2014
Pourcentage d'enfants vaccinés : - 2014

- BCG / BCG: 97.0
- DPT3 / DTC3: 88.0
- Polio / polio (2011): 85.0
- Measles / rougeole: 83.0

Literacy rate (%) - 2007
Taux d'alphabétisation - 2007

- Male: 74.3
- Female: 78.4

GNI per capita, PPP (current international $)
RNB par habitant, ($ PPA internationaux courants)

- 2012: 8 770
- 2013: 9 510
- 2014: 10 110
- 2015: 10 560
- 2016: 10 380

II NATIONAL ACCOUNTS — COMPTES NATIONAUX

	2009	2010	2011	2012	2013	2014	2015	2016	2017	
GROSS DOMESTIC PRODUCT BY KIND OF ECONOMIC ACTIVITY AT CURRENT PRICES *NAMIBIAN DOLLAR (MILLIONS)*										**PRODUIT INTÉRIEUR BRUT PAR BRANCHE D'ACTIVITÉ ÉCONOMIQUE AUX PRIX COURANTS** *DOLLAR DE NAMIBIE (MILLIONS)*
Agriculture, hunting, forestry and Fishing	6 208	7 085	7 418	8 607	7 790	9 282	8 834	10 146	12 208	Agriculture, chasse sylviculture et Pêche
Mining and quarrying	8 177	8 598	7 833	13 562	16 218	16 939	17 627	19 894	21 460	Industries extractives
Manufacturing	9 801	10 306	12 303	13 027	13 509	13 911	14 603	18 483	19 042	Industries manufacturières
Electricity, gas & water	1 497	1 538	1 795	1 997	2 332	2 691	2 305	3 871	4 512	Electricité, gaz et eau
Construction	2 429	2 618	3 126	3 515	4 747	6 999	8 318	6 495	5 141	Bâtiments et travaux publics
Wholesale & retail trade, restaurants, hotels	9 613	10 705	11 895	13 226	16 141	19 767	20 315	22 539	24 472	Commerce de gros et de détail, restaurants et hôtels
Finance, insurance, real estate, etc.	12 328	13 966	15 358	16 566	19 233	20 482	24 008	25 668	26 913	Banques, assurances, affaires immobilières
Transport and communications	3 891	4 238	4 606	5 012	5 765	6 717	7 039	8 110	8 597	Transport(s) et communications
Public administration and defense	7 624	9 100	8 769	11 770	13 974	15 440	17 381	18 278	18 962	Administrations publiques et défense
Education	5 546	5 872	7 403	8 827	10 523	12 757	14 212	15 771	17 228	Education
Health And Social Work	2 225	2 531	2 923	3 200	3 571	3 957	4 507	4 848	5 328	Santé et Actions Sociales
Other services	749	853	972	1 126	1 110	1 234	1 298	1 405	1 506	Autres services
Less Imputed Service Charges	- 795	- 1 011	- 1 100	- 1 315	- 1 525	- 1 774	- 1 931	- 1 937	- 2 001	Moins Services d'intermédiation financière
Gross domestic product at factor cost / basic prices	69 294	76 398	83 303	99 119	113 389	128 402	138 516	153 571	163 368	Produit intérieur brut aux couts des facteurs / prix de base
Plus: Indirect Taxes / taxes on products, less subsidies	5 920	6 202	6 805	7 745	9 403	10 361	11 644	12 775	12 956	Plus taxes indirectes/impôts sur les produits, moins les subventions
EXPENDITURE ON GROSS DOMESTIC PRODUCT AT CURRENT PURCHASER'S VALUES *Namibian Dollar (Millions)*										**EMPLOI DU PRODUIT INTÉRIEUR BRUT AUX PRIX COURANTS D'ACQUISITION** *DOLLAR DE NAMIBIE (MILLIONS)*
Government final consumption	17 945	21 107	20 895	26 684	31 912	36 415	38 460	40 312	43 221	Consommation finale des administrations publiques
Private final consumption	53 005	52 220	59 817	69 514	80 808	90 015	106 386	124 544	121 068	Consommation finale privée
Gross fixed capital formation	21 025	20 884	20 453	27 514	32 565	46 370	50 032	37 192	28 299	Formation brute de capital fixe
Change in inventories	- 1 129	- 958	- 291	1 044	- 1 785	259	779	2 271	2 817	Variation des stocks
Exports of goods and services	39 372	39 447	41 023	46 391	50 572	53 721	57 650	68 431	64 668	Exportations de biens et services
Less imports of goods and services	55 005	50 102	51 789	64 284	71 280	88 016	103 146	106 405	83 749	Moins importations de biens et services
GDP at purchasers' values	75 214	82 599	90 108	106 864	122 792	138 763	150 160	166 345	176 324	PIB aux prix d'acquisition
GROSS DOMESTIC PRODUCT BY KIND OF ECONOMIC ACTIVITY AT CONSTANT PRICES *ANNUAL GROWTH RATES (%)*										**PRODUIT INTÉRIEUR BRUT PAR BRANCHE D'ACTIVITÉ ECONOMIQUE AUX PRIX CONSTANTS** *TAUX DE CROISSANCE ANNUEL (%)*
Agriculture, hunting, forestry and Fishing	17.7	4.9	- 1.3	2.0	- 11.4	5.5	- 5.6	4.8	7.8	Agriculture, chasse sylviculture et Pêche
Mining and quarrying	- 31.7	22.2	- 5.4	25.1	1.7	- 6.0	- 4.9	- 5.8	12.8	Industries extractives
Manufacturing	2.0	7.5	5.7	- 6.8	4.4	- 0.1	- 4.3	5.2	1.4	Industries manufacturières
Electricity, gas & water	- 16.4	2.4	1.7	15.4	- 4.4	1.5	13.6	6.8	1.8	Electricité, gaz et eau
Construction	- 17.5	6.8	15.9	7.5	28.7	42.6	24.3	- 26.3	- 25.6	Bâtiments et travaux publics
Wholesale & retail trade, restaurants, hotels	9.4	7.4	6.3	4.8	14.0	13.4	7.2	2.8	- 6.5	Commerce de gros et de détail, restaurants et hôtels
Finance, insurance, real estate, etc.	2.9	4.1	6.6	1.8	7.2	5.9	5.6	2.4	2.2	Banques, assurances, affaires immobilières
Transport and communications	16.0	6.7	4.9	8.0	6.4	5.7	6.9	7.0	0.8	Transport(s) et communications
Public administration and defense	5.3	2.8	5.3	2.7	3.8	1.4	14.0	3.3	0.3	Administrations publiques et défense
Education	3.0	- 0.2	17.4	4.4	3.3	10.3	4.1	2.8	- 1.2	Education
Health And Social Work	5.5	9.5	5.7	5.7	8.9	10.2	17.5	7.2	- 1.3	Santé et Actions Sociales
Other services	8.6	8.6	8.6	8.6	- 6.7	5.5	1.7	1.4	1.0	Autres services
Less Imputed Service Charges	- 7.3	23.4	10.6	4.5	18.8	5.3	0.1	2.1	- 0.2	Moins Services d'intermédiation financière
Gross domestic product at factor cost / basic prices	- 0.3	6.6	5.1	4.8	5.1	6.6	5.6	0.7	- 0.3	Produit intérieur brut aux couts des facteurs / prix de base
Plus: Indirect Taxes / taxes on products, less subsidies	8.0	0.0	5.3	8.9	11.5	4.1	12.5	0.9	- 5.5	Plus taxes indirectes/impôts sur les produits, moins les subventions
Gross domestic product at market prices	0.3	6.0	5.1	5.1	5.6	6.4	6.1	0.7	- 0.8	Produit intérieur brut aux prix du marché
EXPENDITURE ON GROSS DOMESTIC PRODUCT AT CONSTANT PURCHASERS' VALUES *ANNUAL GROWTH RATES (%)*										**EMPLOIS DU PRODUIT INTÉRIEUR BRUT AUX PRIX CONSTANTS D'ACQUISITION** *TAUX DE CROISSANCE ANNUEL (%)*
Government final consumption	3.8	1.0	6.7	3.3	4.8	4.6	12.2	- 1.4	1.9	Consommation finale des administrations publiques
Private final consumption	13.9	- 5.5	8.9	9.6	9.5	6.9	12.9	10.4	- 7.6	Consommation finale privée
Gross fixed capital formation	14.5	- 1.2	- 4.4	31.2	13.5	33.7	7.9	- 28.7	- 24.4	Formation brute de capital fixe
Exports of goods and services	1.8	2.8	- 3.3	1.0	2.8	- 0.5	- 0.4	7.9	- 12.2	Exportations de biens et services
Less imports of goods and services	15.1	- 10.2	- 0.7	19.6	6.9	17.6	12.3	- 1.8	- 20.8	Moins importations de biens et services

III INFLATION

Annual growth rates (%)	2009	2010	2011	2012	2013	2014	2015	2016	2017	Taux de croissance annuel (%)
All item	9.5	4.9	5.0	6.7	5.6	5.4	3.4	6.7	6.1	Ensemble
of which:										dont:
Food and non-alcoholic beverages	10.7	3.2	4.9	9.1	6.5	8.3	5.6	10.8	5.6	Alimentation et boissons non alcoolisés
Alcoholic beverages, tobacco and narcotics	12.3	10.2	6.4	8.7	8.7	6.6	7.3	6.7	4.6	Boissons alcoolisées et tabacs
Clothing and footwear	10.0	3.2	1.2	0.5	3.5	3.4	1.3	0.1	- 0.4	Habillement et chaussures
Housing, water, electricity, gas and other fuels	7.6	4.5	7.8	5.8	5.2	3.2	2.6	7.7	9.2	Logement, eau, électricité, gaz et autres combustibles
Furnishings, household equipment and routine household maintenance	11.7	2.0	1.7	6.0	6.1	4.7	3.6	5.7	4.6	Meubles, articles de ménage et entretien courant
Health	5.8	5.0	4.9	3.3	3.1	2.1	5.0	7.1	5.7	Santé
Transport	5.9	5.5	5.2	7.1	5.3	7.2	- 2.1	3.2	5.0	Transport
Communication	6.1	1.1	1.3	0.7	2.3	- 0.5	0.8	2.6	3.6	Communication
Recreation and culture	8.0	2.3	3.4	7.5	4.4	5.7	3.8	5.8	4.1	Loisirs et culture
Education	3.8	5.0	4.3	4.5	4.0	8.1	4.3	7.6	7.8	Enseignement
Restaurants and hotels	10.8	7.9	4.5	4.9	8.9	5.9	6.0	7.9	7.3	Restaurants et hôtels
Miscellaneous goods and services	10.6	3.3	2.5	2.5	1.8	4.4	6.2	4.7	5.5	Biens et Services divers

NAMIBIA

IV AGRICULTURAL PRODUCTION - PRODUCTION AGRICOLE

	2009	2010	2011	2012	2013	2014	2015	2016	2017	
TONNES (THOUSAND)										**Tonnes (milliers)**
Millet	37	73	41	56	25	44	15	...	...	Millet
Maize	57	54	69	88	40	73	38	...	...	Maïs
Wheat	15	12	12	17	15	10	13	...	...	Blé
Grapes	20	21	25	26	25	30	30	...	...	Raisins
Sorghum	5	8	6	8	2	4	2	...	...	Sorgho

V MINING PRODUCTION - PRODUCTION MINIERE

	2009	2010	2011	2012	2013	2014	2015	2016	2017	
Silver ores and concentrates - Production, Kilograms (thousands)	3	...	...	1	2	1	1	5	6	Minerais d'argent et leurs concentrés - Production, Kilogrammes (milliers)
Lead ores and concentrates - Production, metric tons (thousands)	7 250	20 018	18 249	13 322	10 771	21 571	10 308	14 862	18 675	Minerais de plomb et leurs concentrés - Production, tonnes métriques (milliers)
Uranium ores and concentrates - Production (metric tons)	8 000 000	5 807 520	4 359 160	5 540 850	5 157 500	4 649 000	3 810 000	4 329 000	5 340 260	Minerais et concentrés d'uranium - Production (tonnes métriques)

VI ENERGY - ENERGIE

	2009	2010	2011	2012	2013	2014	2015	2016	2017	
Total electricity generation (GWh)	1 510	1 293	1 424	1 454	1 331	1 498	...	...	...	Production électrique totale (GWh)
of which										dont
Production of electricity from fossil fuels (GWh)	81	58	39	41	59	13	49	...	...	Production d'électricité à partir de combustibles fossiles (GWh)
Production of hydro electricity (GWh)	1 429	1 235	1 386	1 413	1 272	1 485	1 470	...	...	Production d'électricité d'origine hydraulique (GWh)
Production of electricity from solar, wind, tide, wave and other sources (GWh)	...	...	...	...	5	7	10	...	...	Production d'électricité d'origine solaire, éolienne, marée motrice et autres (GWh)

VII TOURISM AND INFRASTRUCTURE - TOURISME ET INFRASTUCTURE

	2009	2010	2011	2012	2013	2014	2015	2016	2017	
VII-1 Tourism										**VII-1 Tourisme**
International tourist arrivals (thousands)	980	984	1 030	1 080	1 180	1 320	1 330	1 469	1 528	Arrivées de touristes internationaux (milliers)
Rooms in hotels and similar establishments (thousands)	13	12	10	16	16	17	17	18	19	Chambres d'hôtels et établissements assimilés (milliers)
Overnight stays (thousands)	12 100	12 200	12 400	12 900	13 900	15 600	15 600	15 400	16 170	Nuitées (milliers)
Tourism receipts (US$ thousand)	405 299	439 097	517 896	485 192	411 294	408 393	444 046	556 210	589 583	Recettes touristiques (milliers de $ EU)
Total contribution to GDP (%)	11.0	10.0	11.0	11.0	9.0	11.0	10.0	11.0	11.0	Contribution totale au PIB (%)
Total contribution to Employment (%)	14.0	14.0	14.0	15.0	14.0	13.0	15.0	15.0	16.0	Contribution totale à l'emploi (%)
VII-2 Infrastructure										**VII-2 Infrastructure**
Paved road (% of total)	14.1	14.5	15.4	15.4	15.4	15.4	...	...	...	Routes asphaltées (% du total)
Total network (Railways-km)	...	...	...	...	...	...	...	...	...	Réseau total voies ferrées-Km
Main telephone lines (per 100 inhabitants)	6.9	7.2	7.2	7.6	8.0	7.8	7.6	7.7	...	Lignes téléphoniques fixes (pour 100 habitants)
Mobile cellular subscribers (per 100 inhabitants)	76.1	89.5	99.0	95.0	118.4	113.8	106.6	109.2	...	Abonnés aux téléphones mobiles (pour 100 habitants)
Internet users per 100 inhabitants	6.5	11.6	12.0	12.9	13.9	14.8	25.7	31.0	...	Utilisateurs Internet par 100 Habitants
Fixed (wired)-broadband subscriptions per 100 inhabitants	...	...	0.8	1.1	1.6	1.8	1.9	2.2	...	Abonnements à l'Internet fixe (filaire) à large bande pour 100 habitants, par débit

VIII EXTERNAL TRADE - COMMERCE EXTERIEUR

	2009	2010	2011	2012	2013	2014	2015	2016	2017	
US$ (MILLIONS) EXPORTS, FOB										**$ E.U (MILLIONS) EXPORTATIONS, FÀB**
Exports - Total	3 146	4 026	4 407	4 389	4 629	4 612	4 067	3 979	...	Exportations - Total
Exports to Africa	1 587	1 555	1 616	1 857	2 462	2 151	2 248	1 773	...	Exportations vers l'Afrique
Main products										**Principaux produits**
Pearls, precious & semi-precious stones	295	542	778	996	833	937	769	...	...	Perles, pierres précieuses et semi-précieuses
Fish, fresh, chilled or frozen	387	479	522	578	634	621	545	...	...	Poissons frais, réfrigérés ou congelés
Ores and concentrates of uranium or thorium	379	381	349	351	384	376	330	...	...	Minerais et concentrés d'uranium ou de thorium
Ships, boats & floating structures	24	27	87	108	406	263	291	...	...	Navires, bateaux et structures flottantes
Coppe	165	186	348	267	226	253	208	...	...	Cuivre
Main destinations										**Principales destinations**
South Africa	762	881	1 024	699	973	857	795	...	...	Afrique du Sud
Botswana	30	46	42	374	643	521	505	...	...	Botswana
Angola	498	473	411	457	433	456	386	...	...	Angola
Belgium	33	88	304	404	290	356	280	...	...	Belgique
United Kingdom	243	449	656	539	120	338	199	...	...	Royaume-Uni
IMPORTS, CIF										
Imports - Total	4 980	5 980	6 457	7 132	7 575	8 531	7 697	6 721	...	Importations - Total (millions)
Imports from Africa	3 657	4 417	4 830	5 266	5 139	5 563	5 637	4 895	...	Importations en provenance de l'Afrique
Main products										**Principaux produits**
Petroleum oils or bituminous minerals > 70 % oil	322	351	360	517	639	671	670	...	...	Huiles de pétrole ou minéraux bitumineux> 70 % Huile
Ships, boats & floating structures	28	18	36	314	462	450	466	...	...	Navires, bateaux et structures flottantes
Copper ores and concentrates; copper mattes, cemen	105	295	372	367	362	423	401	...	...	Minerais et concentrés de cuivre; Mattes de cuivre, cemen
Motor vehicles for the transport of persons	348	373	369	385	336	418	386	...	...	Véhicules automobiles pour le transport de personnes
Motor vehic. for transport of goods, special purpo.	159	221	264	259	307	328	325	...	...	Véhicule motorisé. Pour le transport de marchandises,.
Main origin										**Principales provenances**
South Africa	3 591	4 272	4 562	4 669	4 494	5 315	5 013	...	...	Afrique du Sud
China	237	234	275	414	410	478	454	...	...	Chine
Marshall Islands	-	...	-	-	316	183	255	...	...	Iles Marshall
United States	136	104	108	147	209	207	213	...	...	États-Unis
Germany	127	133	190	172	190	210	204	...	...	Allemagne

NAMIBIE

	2009	2010	2011	2012	2013	2014	2015	2016	2017	
IX-1 MONETARY STATISTICS *NAMIBIAN DOLLAR (MILLIONS)*										**IX-1 STATISTIQUES MONÉTAIRES** *DOLLAR DE NAMIBIE (MILLIONS)*
Money supply (M1)	49 472	53 194	57 713	61 169	69 567	74 366	81 934	85 949	92 996	Masse monétaire (M1)
Quasi-money	27 180	28 506	31 391	36 381	35 078	37 650	41 792	46 297	49 615	Quasi-monnaie
of which demand deposit	...	...	...	...	...	...	...	...	...	dont Monnaie scripturale
Net foreign assets	24 600	19 635	23 172	20 902	23 332	19 512	29 792	26 502	29 168	Avoirs extérieurs nets
Domestic credit	34 504	42 738	46 365	53 160	62 866	77 066	83 316	95 879	106 208	Crédit intérieur
of which claims on private sector	- 5 227	- 1 721	- 554	- 1 306	269	4 002	- 1 608	3 905	9 671	dont créances sur le secteur privé
of which claims on government sector, net	36 591	40 589	44 441	51 970	59 486	69 282	78 863	85 606	89 902	dont créances nettes sur le gouvernement
International reserves (millions US$)	1 891	1 550	1 780	1 750	1 505	1 198	1 524	1 313	1 482	Réserves internationales (millions $EU)
Average exchange rate (National currency per US$)	8	7	7	8	10	11	13	15	13	Taux de change (moyen) (monnaie nationale par $ EU)
IX-2 PUBLIC FINANCE *NAMIBIAN DOLLAR (MILLIONS)*										**IX-2 FINANCES PUBLIQUES** *DOLLAR DE NAMIBIE (MILLIONS)*
Total Revenues and Grants	23 998	23 396	29 892	36 586	40 922	49 954	52 200	50 848	58 804	Recettes totales et dons
Direct taxes (on income, profits)	8 137	9 912	11 597	13 099	12 390	17 216	18 516	19 910	20 979	Taxes directes
Domestic indirect taxes revenues	5 227	5 366	8 086	7 090	10 098	10 269	11 902	12 188	12 982	Taxes Indirectes
Trade taxes	8 585	5 976	7 137	13 796	14 727	18 117	17 355	14 071	19 597	Taxes sur le commerce extérieur
Other taxes	187	152	210	245	258	1 234	1 129	1 472	1 552	Autres taxes
Other revenues	1 662	1 966	2 684	2 172	3 171	3 008	3 146	3 207	3 644	Autres recettes
Grants	201	24	179	184	278	110	152	...	50	Dons
Total Expenditures and Net Lending	25 246	28 074	36 740	37 682	47 351	59 334	65 262	66 066	67 671	Dépenses totales et prêts nets
Current expenditure	18 950	22 510	28 902	29 586	37 522	48 132	52 572	53 348	55 580	Dépenses courantes
Wages and Salaries	9 053	9 390	12 317	13 557	17 932	21 655	23 961	26 738	29 411	Rémunérations et salaires
Other purchases of goods and services	4 298	4 096	5 470	5 289	7 331	11 310	10 794	10 281	9 191	Achat de biens et services
Other current expenditure	932	1 385	3 333	1 213	1 984	2 415	2 461	2 721	1 721	Autres dépenses courantes
Current transfers	4 668	7 639	7 781	9 527	10 275	12 752	15 356	13 608	15 257	Transferts courants
Interest payments	1 195	967	1 131	1 719	1 796	2 066	2 633	4 312	5 075	Intérêts
Capital expenditure	4 426	4 597	5 465	5 673	8 039	9 132	10 050	8 396	7 006	Dépenses d'équipement
Net lending	675	...	1 243	705	- 6	4	7	10	10	Prêts nets
Fiscal balance	- 1 248	- 4 678	- 6 848	- 1 096	- 6 428	- 9 380	- 13 062	- 15 218	- 8 867	Solde global y compris les dons
IX-3 BALANCE OF PAYMENTS *US $ (MILLIONS)*										**IX-3 BALANCE DES PAIEMENTS** *$ E.U (MILLIONS)*
Trade balance	- 12 082	- 10 312	- 12 314	- 18 898	- 22 823	- 32 328	- 39 668	- 31 697	- 18 463	Balance commerciale
Services Balance	698	- 41	1 076	2 798	- 1 519	1 278	1 969	- 1 291	- 494	Balance des services
Net primary income	- 825	- 2 051	- 811	- 4 534	- 357	- 835	- 1 346	- 5 257	- 3 527	Revenus primaires nets
Compensation of employees	66	- 39	- 116	- 87	- 109	- 296	- 142	- 22	- 136	Rémunération des salariés
Investment income	- 857	- 1 883	- 565	- 4 299	- 111	- 379	- 955	- 5 125	...	Revenus des investissements
Net secondary income	9 786	8 514	6 087	13 369	15 072	18 695	17 979	15 239	18 540	Revenus secondaires nets
Net official transfers	9 305	8 094	7 118	13 191	14 717	18 306	17 775	14 929	18 014	Transferts officiels nets
Workers' remittances	12	- 54	- 130	- 104	- 75	- 250	- 167	247	...	Envois de fonds des travailleurs
Other private transfers	...	...	...	...	...	...	...	...	Autres transferts privés
Current account balance	- 2 424	- 3 890	- 5 962	- 7 265	- 9 628	- 13 191	- 21 066	- 23 006	- 3 944	Solde du compte courant
Capital and financial account	3 589	- 3 831	- 503	- 7 791	- 6 767	- 7 969	- 20 109	- 16 996	- 2 390	Comptes de capital et financier
Capital account	1 730	1 371	2 085	1 948	2 896	1 701	1 378	1 689	2 053	Compte de capital
Financial account	1 859	- 5 202	- 2 588	- 9 739	- 9 663	- 9 670	- 21 487	- 18 685	- 4 443	Compte financier
Errors and omissions	2 553	- 2 684	1 289	- 4 422	- 2 931	1 821	- 1 800	2 631	- 2 552	Erreurs et omissions
Overall balance	1 022	- 3 794	4 114	231	598	- 1 768	10 048	906	5 355	Balance générale

NAMIBIA

X DEBT AND FINANCIAL FLOWS - DETTE ET FLUX FINANCIERS

	2009	2010	2011	2012	2013	2014	2015	2016	2017	
X-1 DEBT *US $ (MILLIONS)*										**X-1 DETTE EXTÉRIEURE** *$ E.U (MILLIONS)*
Total external debt	2 506	3 481	5 146	4 626	4 972	5 501	5 842	6 488	7 005	Dette extérieure totale
Private	2 073	2 998	4 357	3 607	3 968	4 523	4 338	4 578	...	Privée
Public	433	483	790	1 018	1 004	978	1 503	1 911	...	Publique
Total external debt service	923	1 185	1 708	2 217	1 709	2 183	2 118	2 269	...	Service de la dette extérieure
Present value of external debt	170	246	338	283	320	370	...	...	...	Valeur actuelle de la dette extérieure
Total government domestic debt, National currency (millions)	10 177	9 983	16 029	17 278	19 023	...	...	...	...	Dette publique intérieure
X-2 FINANCIAL FLOWS *US $ (MILLIONS)*										**X-2 FLUX FINANCIERS** *$ E.U (MILLIONS)*
Net Foreign Direct Investment Inflows	506	793	1 120	1 133	801	432	1 095	275	...	Investissements étranger direct (flux nets entrants)
Main origin of FDI inflows										**Principales origines de l'IDE entrant:**
Germany	164	...	...	...	...	...	...	...	...	Allemagne
...	...	...	...	...	...	...	...	...	...	...
...	...	...	...	...	...	...	...	...	...	...
Italy	4	...	1	...	...	...	...	...	...	Italie
...	...	...	...	...	...	...	...	...	...	...
African countries	...	...	...	...	...	...	...	...	...	Pays africains
Net total official development assistance	331	261	278	252	261	226	142	170	...	Aide publique au développement (nette totale)
Main origin of net ODA										**Principales origines de l'APD nette**
United States	90	117	114	139	161	149	62	58	...	États-Unis
Germany	37	24	69	43	27	24	50	74	...	Allemagne
Global Fund	38	7	2	1	4	3	3	3	...	Fonds Mondial
Japan	40	41	25	- 7	- 4	- 4	- 4	- 6	...	Japon
Spain	12	9	4	1	0	-	- 2	- 1	...	Espagne

NAMIBIE

SOURCES AND NOTES - SOURCES ET NOTES

External trade - Total exports, fob: UNCTAD

External trade - Total import, cif: UNCTAD

ODA: OECD

Monetary statistics: IMF

National Accounts: The Accounts are calculated using the new base year 2010 from 2007

National Accounts : The annual Growth Rates   for 2017 are previsions based on the sum of four quarters of 2017

Poverty: World Bank

Commerce exterieur - Exportation, fab: CNUCED

Commerce exterieur - Imporations, caf: CNUCED

APD: OCDE

Statistiques monétaires: FMI

Comptes nationaux: Les comptes sont calculés selon la nouvelle année de base 2010 à partir de 2007

Comptes Nationaux: Les croissances annuelles de L'année 2017 sont estimées à partir des comptes trimestriels

Pauvreté: Banque mondiale

	AREA (km2)		1 267 000		SUPERFICIE (KM2)
	CAPITAL CITY	Niamey	Niamey		CAPITALE
	CURRENCY	CFA Franc	Franc CFA		MONNAIE

I SOCIAL AND DEMOGRAPHIC INDICATORS — INDICATEURS DEMOGRAPHIQUES ET SOCIAUX

	Year Année	Value Valeur	Charts Graphiques	
Population				**Population**
Population ('000)	2017	20 651.1		Population ('000)
Female (%)	2017	50.1		Féminine (%)
Urban (%)	2017	16.3		Urbaine (%)
Average annual growth rate	2017	3.8		Taux de croissance annuel
Active population ('000)	2017	6 258.1		Population active ('000)
Population by age group ('000)				Population par groupe d'âge ('000)
0-14 years	2017	10 666.2		0-14 ans
15-64 years	2017	9 440.1		15-64 ans
65+ years	2017	544.8		65+ ans
Economically active population in agriculture (%)	2015	80.7		Participation de la population active agricole (%)
Crude birth rate	2017	45.5		Taux brut de natalité
Crude death rate	2017	7.2		Taux brut de mortalité
Total fertility rate	2017	7.2		Indice synthétique de fécondité
Life expectancy at birth - Total (years)	2017	64.5		Espérance de vie à la naissance - Totale (années)
Dependency ratio - Total (%)	2017	118.8		Taux de dépendance - Total (%)
Health				**Santé**
Percentage of children under-five and underweight	2016	31.7		% d'enfants de moins de cinq ans avec insuffisance pondérale
Prevalence of undernourishment	2015	9.5		Prévalence de la malnutrition
Under five mortality rate (per 1 000 live births)	2016	127.0		Taux de mortalité de moins de 5 ans (les deux sexes, pour 1000)
Infant mortality rate (per 1 000 live births)	2016	51.0		Taux de mortalité infantile (les deux sexes) par 1000
Neonatal mortality rate (per 1 000 live births)	2016	1.3		Le taux de mortalité néonatale (pour 1000 naissances vivantes)
Percentage of children provided the vaccines :				Pourcentage d'enfants vaccinés :
BCG	2015	99.0		BCG
DPT3	2015	96.0		DTC3
Polio	2012	74.7		polio
Measles	2014	72.0		rougeole
Percentage of mothers provided at least one antenatal care (%)	2016	110.4		Pourcentage de mères ayant au moins reçu un soin prénatal (%)
Percentage of deliveries attended by skilled health personnel	2016	29.3		% d'accouchements assistés par un personnel de santé qualifié
Number of doctors (per 10,000 population)	2016	0.4		Nombre de médecins (pour 10.000 habitants)
Number of nurses (per 10,000 population)	2016	2.8		Nombre d'infirmiers (pour 10.000 habitants)
Hospital beds - Total (per 10,000 population)	2016	5 609.0		Nombre de lits d'hôpitaux - Total (pour 10 000)
Births registered (per 1,000)	2015	57.7		Naissances enregistrées (pour 1000)
Deaths registered (per 1,000)	2015	8.8		Décès enregistrés (pour 1000)
Budget allocation to health (%)	2015	6.6		Dépenses publiques consacrées à la santé (% du budget)
Education				**Education**
Enrolment in primary education (000)	2017	2 768.3		Scolarisation dans le primaire (000)
Female	2017	1 261.4		Féminine
Enrolment in secondary education (000)	2017	730.1		Scolarisation dans le secondaire (000)
Female	2017	302.0		Féminine
Enrolment in tertiary education (000)	2017	64.7		Scolarisation dans le tertiaire (000)
Female	2017	23.3		Féminine
Literacy rate	2017	28.4		Taux d'alphabétisation (deux sexes)
Male	2017	40.9		Masculin
Female	2017	17.8		Féminin
Pupil teacher ratio - primary	2017	36.0		Ratio élève-enseignant
Budget allocation to education (%)	2017	7.4		Dépenses publiques consacrées à l'enseignement (% du budget)
Poverty				**Pauvreté**
GNI per capita, PPP (current int. $)	2016	970.0		RNB par habitant, ($ PPA inter. courants)
Human Poverty Index (HPI-1) Value (%)	2007	55.8		Valeur de l'Indice de pauvreté (IPH-1) (%)
Population below Inter. poverty line ($2/ day) (%)	2011	50.3		Population sous le seuil inter. de pauvreté (2$/Jour) (%)
Share of income held by richest 10%	2011	26.4		% de revenu des 10% plus riches
Share of income held by poorest 10%	2011	3.8		% de revenu des 10% plus pauvres
GINI index	2011	31.5		Indice de GINI

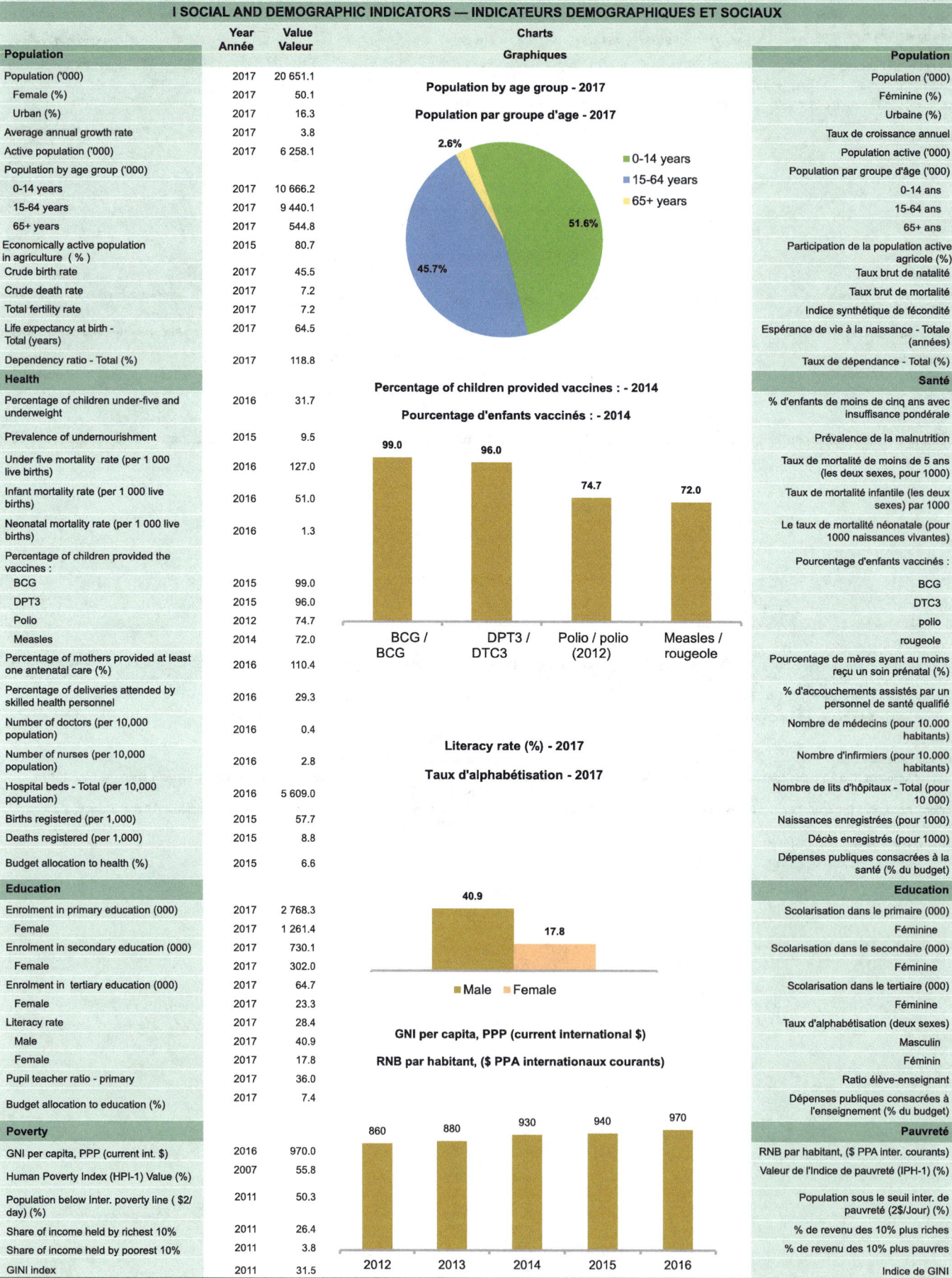

Population by age group - 2017
Population par groupe d'age - 2017
- 0-14 years: 51.6%
- 15-64 years: 45.7%
- 65+ years: 2.6%

Percentage of children provided vaccines : - 2014
Pourcentage d'enfants vaccinés : - 2014
- BCG / BCG: 99.0
- DPT3 / DTC3: 96.0
- Polio / polio (2012): 74.7
- Measles / rougeole: 72.0

Literacy rate (%) - 2017
Taux d'alphabétisation - 2017
- Male: 40.9
- Female: 17.8

GNI per capita, PPP (current international $)
RNB par habitant, ($ PPA internationaux courants)
- 2012: 860
- 2013: 880
- 2014: 930
- 2015: 940
- 2016: 970

NIGER

	2009	2010	2011	2012	2013	2014	2015	2016	2017	
GROSS DOMESTIC PRODUCT BY KIND OF ECONOMIC ACTIVITY AT CURRENT PRICES *CFA FRANC (MILLIONS)*										**PRODUIT INTÉRIEUR BRUT PAR BRANCHE D'ACTIVITÉ ÉCONOMIQUE AUX PRIX COURANTS** *FRANC CFA (MILLIONS)*
Agriculture, hunting , forestry and Fishing	999 357	1 158 359	1 158 647	1 349 697	1 356 240	1 493 523	1 542 643	1 760 233	...	Agriculture, chasse sylviculture et Pêche
Mining and quarrying	162 627	203 462	221 494	388 975	410 499	364 517	347 790	318 422	...	Industries extractives
Manufacturing	128 256	134 918	143 942	214 407	252 214	256 216	242 617	253 297	...	Industries manufacturières
Electricity, gas & water	28 600	32 293	40 498	42 919	46 729	49 830	53 767	56 401	...	Electricité, gaz et eau
Construction	64 096	71 643	76 173	100 412	109 887	117 834	128 304	123 416	...	Bâtiments et travaux publics
Wholesale & retail trade, restaurants, hotels	384 236	403 338	435 528	454 091	495 262	518 573	563 409	591 136	...	Commerce de gros et de détail, restaurants et hôtels
Finance, insurance, real estate, etc.	128 504	138 232	124 844	173 848	182 966	195 499	220 268	237 882	...	Banques, assurances, affaires immobilières
Transport and communications	156 493	171 911	193 196	209 426	237 193	258 719	269 292	274 324	...	Transport(s) et communications
Public administration and defense	225 082	215 784	251 651	201 177	223 401	276 072	303 666	326 019	...	Administrations publiques et défense
Education	37 082	40 197	43 413	143 180	154 523	188 753	204 204	210 584	...	Education
Health And Social Work	39 390	42 620	46 243	48 256	48 908	52 745	60 880	63 636	...	Santé et Actions Sociales
Other services	30 884	30 117	32 053	35 890	36 995	40 837	47 571	43 424	...	Autres services
Less Imputed Service Charges	- 21 690	- 22 668	- 24 341	- 27 005	- 26 945	- 28 609	- 32 008	- 35 800	...	Moins Services d'intermédiation financière
Gross domestic product at factor cost / basic prices	2 362 917	2 620 206	2 743 341	3 335 273	3 527 872	3 784 509	3 952 403	4 222 974	...	Produit intérieur brut aux couts des facteurs / prix de base
Plus: Indirect Taxes / taxes on products, less subsidies	185 530	212 080	280 930	208 913	260 403	284 394	336 389	287 890	...	Plus taxes indirectes/impôts sur les produits, moins les subventions
EXPENDITURE ON GROSS DOMESTIC PRODUCT AT CURRENT PURCHASER'S VALUES *CFA FRANC (MILLIONS)*										**EMPLOI DU PRODUIT INTÉRIEUR BRUT AUX PRIX COURANTS D'ACQUISITION** *FRANC CFA (MILLIONS)*
Government final consumption	412 978	386 440	436 487	468 482	497 935	627 969	662 795	700 934	...	Consommation finale des administrations publiques
Private final consumption	1 926 410	2 076 008	2 237 605	2 389 277	2 537 905	2 643 309	2 870 742	3 036 850	...	Consommation finale privée
Gross fixed capital formation	883 824	1 101 631	1 161 156	1 282 221	1 369 486	1 522 982	1 717 561	1 527 542	...	Formation brute de capital fixe
Change in inventories	1 464	29 912	2 082	24 503	5 939	17 476	1 459	14 005	...	Variation des stocks
Exports of goods and services	517 883	628 718	632 144	774 877	857 495	855 274	780 082	729 296	...	Exportations de biens et services
Less imports of goods and services	1 194 112	1 390 424	1 445 203	1 395 174	1 480 486	1 598 107	1 743 847	1 497 763	...	Moins importations de biens et services
GDP at purchasers' values	2 548 447	2 832 285	3 024 271	3 544 186	3 788 274	4 068 903	4 288 792	4 510 864	...	PIB aux prix d'acquisition
GROSS DOMESTIC PRODUCT BY KIND OF ECONOMIC ACTIVITY AT CONSTANT PRICES *ANNUAL GROWTH RATES (%)*										**PRODUIT INTÉRIEUR BRUT PAR BRANCHE D'ACTIVITÉ ECONOMIQUE AUX PRIX CONSTANTS** *TAUX DE CROISSANCE ANNUEL (%)*
Agriculture, hunting , forestry and Fishing	- 9.5	15.8	- 3.0	14.9	- 0.3	8.3	1.9	11.0	...	Agriculture, chasse sylviculture et Pêche
Mining and quarrying	39.5	17.2	16.4	115.2	12.3	- 2.4	- 7.9	2.5	...	Industries extractives
Manufacturing	4.4	3.3	4.1	45.8	16.5	1.3	1.8	5.9	...	Industries manufacturières
Electricity, gas & water	8.4	9.7	- 12.1	5.0	8.8	5.7	6.4	4.3	...	Electricité, gaz et eau
Construction	7.9	9.5	4.3	1.0	6.2	5.3	5.2	0.1	...	Bâtiments et travaux publics
Wholesale & retail trade, restaurants, hotels	5.8	1.6	4.7	0.9	4.6	3.5	5.4	1.8	...	Commerce de gros et de détail, restaurants et hôtels
Finance, insurance, real estate, etc.	6.6	4.6	- 18.9	15.2	6.0	5.2	10.3	5.6	...	Banques, assurances, affaires immobilières
Transport and communications	5.0	4.3	6.8	4.3	9.4	5.8	6.2	- 0.1	...	Transport(s) et communications
Public administration and defense	8.2	- 3.3	5.9	- 25.6	10.3	26.8	7.1	4.3	...	Administrations publiques et défense
Education	- 1.4	4.6	16.1	143.8	6.1	15.2	7.0	2.0	...	Education
Health And Social Work	1.5	1.7	15.8	4.5	1.4	5.9	13.6	3.2	...	Santé et Actions Sociales
Other services	1.7	1.7	74.3	4.2	1.5	8.6	13.3	10.3	...	Autres services
Less Imputed Service Charges	13.2	9.2	- 1.5	10.9	- 0.2	6.2	11.9	11.8	...	Moins Services d'intermédiation financière
Gross domestic product at factor cost / basic prices	- 1.3	8.8	1.4	14.8	4.4	7.4	3.5	6.6	...	Produit intérieur brut aux couts des facteurs / prix de base
Plus: Indirect Taxes / taxes on products, less subsidies	7.1	3.8	13.2	- 20.6	19.6	9.2	16.0	- 14.8	...	Plus taxes indirectes/impôts sur les produits, moins les subventions
Gross domestic product at market prices	- 0.7	8.4	2.3	11.8	5.3	7.5	4.3	4.9	...	Produit intérieur brut aux prix du marché
EXPENDITURE ON GROSS DOMESTIC PRODUCT AT CONSTANT PURCHASERS' VALUES *ANNUAL GROWTH RATES (%)*										**EMPLOIS DU PRODUIT INTÉRIEUR BRUT AUX PRIX CONSTANTS D'ACQUISITION** *TAUX DE CROISSANCE ANNUEL (%)*
Government final consumption	10.6	- 7.5	6.0	3.7	4.6	25.9	4.9	5.2	...	Consommation finale des administrations publiques
Private final consumption	5.8	5.2	5.3	4.2	4.1	3.6	7.1	5.5	...	Consommation finale privée
Gross fixed capital formation	9.6	17.1	0.9	2.1	6.7	9.9	13.4	- 12.9	...	Formation brute de capital fixe
Exports of goods and services	18.0	19.7	- 0.9	18.9	8.9	- 0.5	- 9.0	- 7.2	...	Exportations de biens et services
Less imports of goods and services	32.2	11.5	3.1	- 4.3	5.7	5.0	7.4	- 14.5	...	Moins importations de biens et services

				III INFLATION						
	2009	2010	2011	2012	2013	2014	2015	2016	2017	
Annual growth rates (%)										**Taux de croissance annuel (%)**
All item	0.5	0.9	2.9	0.5	2.3	- 0.9	1.0	0.2	2.4	Ensemble
of which:										dont:
Food and non-alcoholic beverages	8.4	2.1	3.4	3.2	4.4	- 1.3	0.5	- 1.2	0.7	Alimentation et boissons non alcoolisés
Alcoholic beverages, tobacco and narcotics	6.4	- 11.8	8.7	6.4	- 9.6	- 0.8	0.8	2.3	6.6	Boissons alcoolisées et tabacs
Clothing and footwear	0.9	1.0	0.2	1.1	- 0.6	-	1.4	0.8	2.3	Habillement et chaussures
Housing, water, electricity, gas and other fuels	- 0.4	- 0.8	5.7	- 2.7	1.2	0.7	2.4	2.4	6.2	Logement, eau, électricité, gaz et autres combustibles
Furnishings, household equipment and routine household maintenance	4.4	- 5.1	- 2.6	5.2	0.6	- 0.1	1.8	0.6	- 0.6	Meubles, articles de ménage et entretien courant
Health	- 2.5	0.9	2.7	0.7	1.7	1.1	2.6	0.7	3.5	Santé
Transport	- 13.4	0.4	11.3	- 3.1	- 0.5	1.5	-	2.0	- 0.3	Transport
Communication	- 14.1	- 9.5	- 8.1	- 6.8	- 2.7	- 16.1	- 3.9	1.6	10.7	Communication
Recreation and culture	5.7	- 1.0	1.0	- 0.7	- 0.6	1.0	1.3	5.4	1.7	Loisirs et culture
Education	-	0.6	0.5	0.1	-	2.5	3.2	1.8	1.2	Enseignement
Restaurants and hotels	- 12.8	16.8	1.9	- 7.3	7.1	- 0.8	4.5	0.3	10.0	Restaurants et hôtels
Miscellaneous goods and services	10.2	- 8.1	- 4.3	4.6	- 2.2	- 0.1	0.4	- 2.1	0.2	Biens et Services divers

NIGER

IV AGRICULTURAL PRODUCTION - PRODUCTION AGRICOLE

TONNES (THOUSAND)	2009	2010	2011	2012	2013	2014	2015	2016	2017	Tonnes (milliers)
Millet	2 678	3 838	2 761	3 862	2 816	2 922	3 405	3 886	...	Millet
Sorghum	739	1 305	770	1 376	1 222	1 320	1 917	1 808	...	Sorgho
Rice, paddy	20	30	12	5	5	13	11	11	...	Riz, Paddy
Cow peas, dry	787	1 773	1 569	1 330	1 790	1 586	1 668	1 982	...	Pois à vache secs
Groundnuts, with shell	254	406	396	292	343	403	403	453	...	Arachides (en coques)

V MINING PRODUCTION - PRODUCTION MINIERE

	2009	2010	2011	2012	2013	2014	2015	2016	2017	
Uranium ores and concentrates - Production (metric tons)	3 245	4 199	4 264	4 773	4 277	4 156	4 116	3 478	3 485	Minerais et concentrés d'uranium - Production (tonnes métriques)
Gold ores and concentrates - Production (Kilograms)	1 770	1 596	1 453	1 549	962	668	877	713	800	Minerais d'or et leurs concentrés - Production (Kilogrammes)
Hard Coal - Production, metric tons (thousands)	225	247	246	235	242	256	221	247	233	Houille - Production, tonnes métriques (milliers)

VI ENERGY - ENERGIE

	2009	2010	2011	2012	2013	2014	2015	2016	2017	
Total electricity generation (GWh)	234	269	273	399	693	383	678	...	...	Production électrique totale (GWh)
of which										dont
Production of electricity from fossil fuels (GWh)	234	269	273	399	693	383	671	...	...	Production d'électricité à partir de combustibles fossiles (GWh)
Production of hydro electricity (GWh)	...	...	...	...	...	...	...	...	...	Production d'électricité d'origine hydraulique (GWh)
Production of electricity from solar, wind, tide, wave and other sources (GWh)	...	...	...	...	4	6	7	...	...	Production d'électricité d'origine solaire, éolienne, marée motrice et autres (GWh)

VII TOURISM AND INFRASTRUCTURE - TOURISME ET INFRASTUCTURE

	2009	2010	2011	2012	2013	2014	2015	2016	2017	
VII-1 Tourism										**VII-1 Tourisme**
International tourist arrivals (thousands)	...	...	...	...	...	31	32	47	37	Arrivées de touristes internationaux (milliers)
Rooms in hotels and similar establishments (thousands)	2	2	2	2	3	2	3	3	3	Chambres d'hôtels et établissements assimilés (milliers)
Overnight stays (thousands)	142	148	131	216	203	160	171	177	120	Nuitées (milliers)
Tourism receipts (US$ thousand)	65 600	104 900	50 800	49 500	57 300	89 100	72 900	74 935	80 276	Recettes touristiques (milliers de $ EU)
Total contribution to GDP (%)	4.6	5.2	5.1	4.2	4.5	4.4	4.7	5.0	4.9	Contribution totale au PIB (%)
Total contribution to Employment (%)	3.8	4.3	4.3	3.6	3.9	3.9	4.0	4.2	4.2	Contribution totale à l'emploi (%)
VII-2 Infrastructure										**VII-2 Infrastructure**
Paved road (% of total)	20.9	20.6	21.0	21.5	21.4	...	...	...	...	Routes asphaltées (% du total)
Total network (Railways-km)	...	...	...	...	...	...	...	...	...	Réseau total voies ferrées-Km
Main telephone lines (per 100 inhabitants)	...	0.5	0.5	0.6	0.6	0.6	0.6	0.6		Lignes téléphoniques fixes (pour 100 habitants)
Mobile cellular subscribers (per 100 inhabitants)	17.0	23.1	28.7	31.4	39.3	44.4	46.5	48.9		Abonnés aux téléphones mobiles (pour 100 habitants)
Internet users per 100 inhabitants	0.8	0.8	1.3	1.4	1.7	2.0	2.5	4.3		Utilisateurs Internet par 100 Habitants
Fixed (wired)-broadband subscriptions per 100 inhabitants	...	...	...	...	...	...	...	...		Abonnements à l'Internet fixe (filaire) à large bande pour 100 habitants, par débit

VIII EXTERNAL TRADE - COMMERCE EXTERIEUR

US$ (MILLIONS) EXPORTS, FOB	2009	2010	2011	2012	2013	2014	2015	2016	2017	$ E.U (MILLIONS) EXPORTATIONS, FÀB
Exports - Total	1 000	1 150	1 250	1 380	1 585	1 445	1 087	1 053	...	Exportations - Total
Exports to Africa	285	224	135	310	268	378	173	171	...	Exportations vers l'Afrique
Main products										**Principaux produits**
Gold, non-monetary (excluding gold ores and concentrates)	37	98	...	34	21	88	145	134	...	Or, non monétaire (à l'exclusion des minerais d'or et des concentrés)
Oil seeds and oleaginous fruits (excluding flour)	...	...	2	3	3	30	68	70	...	Graines oléagineuses et oléagineuses (à l'exclusion de la farine)
Ores and concentrates of uranium or thorium	272	296	423	...	255	365	231	180	...	Minerais et concentrés d'uranium ou de thorium
Petroleum oils or bituminous minerals > 70 % oil	106	64	205	245	271	318	134	130	...	Huiles de pétrole ou de minéraux bitumineux> 70% d'huile
Radio-actives and associated materials	248	333	300	327	377	415	351	200	...	Radio-actifs et matériaux associés
Main destinations										**Principales destinations**
Burkina Faso	4	6	5	31	22	224	37	34	...	Burkina Faso
China	3	49	30	58	53	103	87	107	...	Chine
France	497	395	539	591	681	684	495	325	...	France
Nigeria	229	139	69	88	95	106	78	73	...	Nigéria
United States	129	140	264	90	214	63	85	26	...	États-Unis
IMPORTS, CIF										
Imports - Total	2 200	2 273	2 190	1 900	2 533	2 757	2 458	1 861	...	Importations - Total (millions)
Imports from Africa	463	379	445	423	537	886	514	413	...	Importations en provenance de l'Afrique
Main products										**Principaux produits**
Aircraft & associated equipment; spacecraft, etc.	2	5	1	7	5	105	409	259	...	Aéronefs et équipement connexe; vaisseau spatial, etc.
Civil engineering & contractors' plant & equipment	188	109	98	121	136	126	67	50	...	Génie civil et installations et équipements des entrepreneurs
Lime, cement, fabrica. constr. mat. (excludingglass, clay)	71	63	76	72	91	124	89	70	...	Chaux, ciment, tissu. constr. tapis. (sauf verre, argile)
Petroleum oils or bituminous minerals > 70 % oil	210	200	261	107	228	368	66	41	...	Huiles de pétrole ou de minéraux bitumineux> 70% d'huile
Rice	69	70	47	127	108	130	134	147	...	Riz
Main origin										**Principales provenances**
China	576	789	440	332	478	466	475	256	...	Chine
France	329	330	314	260	355	361	628	428	...	France
Nigeria	121	109	119	67	115	379	79	93	...	Nigéria
Togo	66	53	111	117	141	120	71	54	...	Togo
United States	101	117	107	96	126	110	131	135	...	États-Unis

	2009	2010	2011	2012	2013	2014	2015	2016	2017	
IX-1 MONETARY STATISTICS *CFA FRANC (MILLIONS)*										**IX-1 STATISTIQUES MONÉTAIRES** *FRANC CFA (MILLIONS)*
Money supply (M1)	472 297	576 020	611 560	802 500	883 510	1 110 730	1 151 260	1 249 650	1 383 297	Masse monétaire (M1)
Quasi-money	116 182	102 466	116 731	141 389	152 881	179 447	223 987	229 191	235 678	Quasi-monnaie
of which demand deposit	...	...	...	...	...	...	...	...	...	dont Monnaie scripturale
Net foreign assets	238 383	342 947	316 336	487 341	615 092	704 028	591 317	569 815	575 016	Avoirs extérieurs nets
Domestic credit	311 277	351 213	418 432	454 863	433 319	510 571	701 710	819 940	902 049	Crédit intérieur
of which claims on private sector	386	4 065	15 825	- 45 123	- 86 449	- 85 239	11 650	82 216	121 755	dont créances sur le secteur privé
of which claims on government sector, net	310 891	347 148	402 607	499 986	519 768	527 014	594 470	669 973	684 368	dont créances nettes sur le gouvernement
International reserves (millions US$)	656	760	508	772	891	1 120	760	825	810	Réserves internationales (millions $EU)
Average exchange rate (National currency per US$)	472	495	472	511	494	494	591	593	582	Taux de change (moyen) (monnaie nationale par $ EU)
IX-2 PUBLIC FINANCE *CFA FRANC (MILLIONS)*										**IX-2 FINANCES PUBLIQUES** *FRANC CFA (MILLIONS)*
Total Revenues and Grants	474 500	515 800	627 600	759 500	933 300	931 611	992 958	905 109	...	Recettes totales et dons
Direct taxes (on income, profits)	102 300	86 900	96 500	152 200	175 800	190 844	167 417	156 222	...	Taxes directes
Domestic indirect taxes revenues	99 000	109 900	162 100	178 800	202 200	228 000	252 027	239 015	...	Taxes Indirectes
Trade taxes	116 600	135 000	192 400	123 900	146 600	153 373	188 568	164 712	...	Taxes sur le commerce extérieur
Other taxes	25 100	29 900	34 900	40 800	57 700	60 938	76 846	46 972	...	Autres taxes
Other revenues	20 600	23 900	28 200	47 300	46 200	76 332	75 500	27 934	...	Autres recettes
Grants	110 900	130 200	113 500	216 500	304 800	222 124	232 600	270 255	...	Dons
Total Expenditures and Net Lending	609 884	584 050	561 919	799 269	1 030 301	1 263 729	1 384 580	1 187 914	...	Dépenses totales et prêts nets
Current expenditure	295 014	360 300	345 701	394 288	500 097	579 126	631 152	589 357	...	Dépenses courantes
Wages and Salaries	93 574	103 185	134 584	155 239	189 827	214 497	250 233	265 145	...	Rémunérations et salaires
Other purchases of goods and services	83 900	94 300	87 600	80 400	105 800	127 386	157 937	107 134	...	Achat de biens et services
Other current expenditure	20 300	27 300	26 700	9 000	16 500	16 200	18 500	19 429	...	Autres dépenses courantes
Current transfers	97 241	135 515	96 818	149 649	187 969	221 043	204 483	197 649	...	Transferts courants
Interest payments	5 800	6 000	10 200	10 800	11 500	16 073	26 600	41 930	...	Intérêts
Capital expenditure	309 069	217 750	206 017	394 181	518 704	668 530	726 827	556 627	...	Dépenses d'équipement
Net lending	...	...	...	...	...	...	...	...	...	Prêts nets
Fiscal balance	- 135 384	- 68 250	65 681	- 39 769	- 97 001	- 332 118	- 391 622	- 282 805	...	Solde global y compris les dons
IX-3 BALANCE OF PAYMENTS *CFA FRANC (MILLIONS)*										**IX-3 BALANCE DES PAIEMENTS** *FRANC CFA (MILLIONS)*
Trade balance	- 376 487	- 402 812	- 435 062	- 235 223	- 212 277	- 367 896	- 525 406	- 405 478	...	Balance commerciale
Services Balance	- 299 742	- 358 894	- 378 000	- 403 668	- 433 833	- 374 937	- 438 359	- 362 989	...	Balance des services
Net primary income	- 16 324	- 21 837	- 24 100	- 69 100	- 91 267	- 75 011	- 90 479	- 96 693	...	Revenus primaires nets
Compensation of employees	15 085	15 572	12 059	13 264	10 316	8 890	9 592	7 473	...	Rémunération des salariés
Investment income	- 31 409	- 37 409	- 36 159	- 82 366	- 101 583	- 84 443	- 89 739	- 97 093	...	Revenus des investissements
Net secondary income	71 231	222 076	161 900	186 391	169 096	172 537	175 575	164 903	...	Revenus secondaires nets
Net official transfers	17 298	156 726	79 033	117 853	78 724	91 768	94 525	82 828	...	Transferts officiels nets
Workers' remittances	21 046	15 191	13 636	17 955	16 544	26 566	31 980	32 367	...	Envois de fonds des travailleurs
Other private transfers	32 887	50 159	69 231	31 992	50 709	53 454	...	...	...	Autres transferts privés
Current account balance	- 621 322	- 561 467	- 675 262	- 521 600	- 568 281	- 645 307	- 878 669	- 700 258	...	Solde du compte courant
Capital and financial account	538 631	664 551	652 150	689 285	674 761	832 348	751 202	680 015	...	Comptes de capital et financier
Capital account	120 358	96 985	68 523	139 109	282 070	184 072	173 913	229 635	...	Compte de capital
Financial account	418 273	567 566	583 627	550 176	392 691	648 276	577 289	450 380	...	Compte financier
Errors and omissions	- 7 063	- 6 496	- 4 962	- 5 000	- 7 428	- 5 678	- 5 180	...	...	Erreurs et omissions
Overall balance	- 89 754	96 588	- 28 074	162 685	99 053	181 363	- 132 646	- 20 243	...	Balance générale

NIGER

X DEBT AND FINANCIAL FLOWS - DETTE ET FLUX FINANCIERS

	2009	2010	2011	2012	2013	2014	2015	2016	2017	
X-1 DEBT *US $ (MILLIONS)*										**X-1 DETTE EXTÉRIEURE** *$ E.U (MILLIONS)*
Total external debt	2 156	2 855	3 124	3 483	3 642	3 891	4 112	4 470	4 835	Dette extérieure totale
Private	1 097	1 888	2 130	2 298	2 247	2 197	2 147	2 192	...	Privée
Public	1 059	967	994	1 185	1 395	1 694	1 966	2 277	...	Publique
Total external debt service	24	30	58	78	104	71	76	93	...	Service de la dette extérieure
Present value of external debt	...	...	...	...	...	...	...	2 145	...	Valeur actuelle de la dette extérieure
Total government domestic debt, National currency (millions)	...	...	...	...	...	...	...	...	...	Dette publique intérieure
X-2 FINANCIAL FLOWS *US $ (MILLIONS)*										**X-2 FLUX FINANCIERS** *$ E.U (MILLIONS)*
Net Foreign Direct Investment Inflows	791	940	1 066	841	719	822	529	293	...	Investissements étranger direct (flux nets entrants)
Main origin of FDI inflows										**Principales origines de l'IDE entrant:**
...	...	...	...	...	...	...	...	...	...	...
Italy	1	...	...	- 5	...	...	...	...	...	Italie
Japan	3	1	- 1	...	...	...	...	...	...	Japon
...	...	...	...	...	...	...	...	...	...	...
...	...	...	...	...	...	...	...	...	...	...
African countries	...	...	...	...	...	...	...	...	...	Pays africains
Net total official development assistance	471	741	645	891	797	918	868	951	...	Aide publique au développement (nette totale)
Main origin of net ODA										**Principales origines de l'APD nette**
France	57	50	47	102	67	53	51	73	...	France
International Development Association [IDA]	39	72	103	113	114	143	93	202	...	International Development Association
United States	37	97	88	100	78	79	112	106	...	États-Unis
...	...	...	...	...	...	...	...	...	...	...
Germany	22	23	30	39	23	27	24	42	...	Allemagne

NIGER

SOURCES AND NOTES - SOURCES ET NOTES

External trade - Total exports, fob: UNCTAD

External trade - Total import, cif: UNCTAD

ODA: OECD

Monetary statistics: IMF

National Accounts: 2015 : Provisional;2016:Estimates

Poverty: World Bank

Commerce exterieur - Exportation, fab: CNUCED

Commerce exterieur - Imporations, caf: CNUCED

APD: OCDE

Statistiques monétaires: FMI

Comptes nationaux: 2015:Provisoires;2016:Estimations

Pauvreté: Banque mondiale

		NIGÉRIA
AREA (km2)	923 770	SUPERFICIE (KM2)
CAPITAL CITY	Abuja Abuja	CAPITALE
CURRENCY	Nigerian Naira Naira nigerian	MONNAIE

I SOCIAL AND DEMOGRAPHIC INDICATORS — INDICATEURS DEMOGRAPHIQUES ET SOCIAUX

Population	Year Année	Value Valeur	Charts Graphiques	Population
Population ('000)	2017	188 100.0		Population ('000)
Female (%)	2017	49.1		Féminine (%)
Urban (%)	2017	48.2		Urbaine (%)
Average annual growth rate	2017	2.7		Taux de croissance annuel
Active population ('000)	2017	55 264.1		Population active ('000)
Population by age group ('000)				Population par groupe d'âge ('000)
0-14 years	2017	80 153.0		0-14 ans
15-64 years	2017	97 069.0		15-64 ans
65+ years	2017	48 987.0		65+ ans
Economically active population in agriculture (%)	2016	22.0		Participation de la population active agricole (%)
Crude birth rate	2017	37.7		Taux brut de natalité
Crude death rate	2017	12.7		Taux brut de mortalité
Total fertility rate	2017	5.6		Indice synthétique de fécondité
Life expectancy at birth - Total (years)	2015	53.1		Espérance de vie à la naissance - Totale (années)
Dependency ratio - Total (%)	2017	133.0		Taux de dépendance - Total (%)
Health				**Santé**
Percentage of children under-five and underweight	2016	31.5		% d'enfants de moins de cinq ans avec insuffisance pondérale
Prevalence of undernourishment	2017	7.0		Prévalence de la malnutrition
Under five mortality rate (per 1 000 live births)	2016	120.0		Taux de mortalité de moins de 5 ans (les deux sexes, pour 1000)
Infant mortality rate (per 1 000 live births)	2016	70.0		Taux de mortalité infantile (les deux sexes) par 1000
Neonatal mortality rate (per 1 000 live births)	2016	39.0		Le taux de mortalité néonatale (pour 1000 naissances vivantes)
Percentage of children provided the vaccines :				Pourcentage d'enfants vaccinés :
BCG	2016	53.1		BCG
DPT3	2016	34.4		DTC3
Polio	2016	46.9		polio
Measles	2016	41.8		rougeole
Percentage of mothers provided at least one antenatal care (%)	2015	63.2		Pourcentage de mères ayant au moins reçu un soin prénatal (%)
Percentage of deliveries attended by skilled health personnel	2016	43.0		% d'accouchements assistés par un personnel de santé qualifié
Number of doctors (per 10,000 population)	2009	4.1		Nombre de médecins (pour 10.000 habitants)
Number of nurses (per 10,000 population)	2008	16.1		Nombre d'infirmiers (pour 10.000 habitants)
Hospital beds - Total (per 10,000 population)	2004	5.3		Nombre de lits d'hôpitaux - Total (pour 10 000)
Births registered (per 1,000)	2016	47.0		Naissances enregistrées (pour 1000)
Deaths registered (per 1,000)	2015	12.7		Décès enregistrés (pour 1000)
Budget allocation to health (%)	2013	18.0		Dépenses publiques consacrées à la santé (% du budget)
Education				**Education**
Enrolment in primary education (000)	2016	25 591.2		Scolarisation dans le primaire (000)
Female	2016	12 155.2		Féminine
Enrolment in secondary education (000)	2016	10 314.3		Scolarisation dans le secondaire (000)
Female	2016	4 782.7		Féminine
Enrolment in tertiary education (000)	2005	1 391.5		Scolarisation dans le tertiaire (000)
Female	2005	566.5		Féminine
Literacy rate	2008	51.1		Taux d'alphabétisation (deux sexes)
Male	2008	61.3		Masculin
Female	2008	41.4		Féminin
Pupil teacher ratio - primary	2014	40.0		Ratio élève-enseignant
Budget allocation to education (%)	2016	7.9		Dépenses publiques consacrées à l'enseignement (% du budget)
Poverty				**Pauvreté**
GNI per capita, PPP (current int. $)	2016	5740.0		RNB par habitant, ($ PPA inter. courants)
Human Poverty Index (HPI-1) Value (%)	2007	36.2		Valeur de l'Indice de pauvreté (IPH-1) (%)
Population below Inter. poverty line ($2/ day) (%)	2009	53.5		Population sous le seuil inter. de pauvreté (2$/Jour) (%)
Share of income held by richest 10%	2009	32.7		% de revenu des 10% plus riches
Share of income held by poorest 10%	2009	2.0		% de revenu des 10% plus pauvres
GINI index	2009	43.0		Indice de GINI

Population by age group - 2017
Population par groupe d'age - 2017

- 0-14 years: 35.4%
- 15-64 years: 42.9%
- 65+ years: 21.7%

Percentage of children provided vaccines : - 2016
Pourcentage d'enfants vaccinés : - 2016

BCG / BCG: 53.1 DPT3 / DTC3: 34.4 Polio / polio: 46.9 Measles / rougeole: 41.8

Literacy rate (%) - 2008
Taux d'alphabétisation - 2008

Male: 61.3 Female: 41.4

GNI per capita, PPP (current international $)
RNB par habitant, ($ PPA internationaux courants)

2012	2013	2014	2015	2016
5 180	5 390	5 780	5 880	5 740

II NATIONAL ACCOUNTS — COMPTES NATIONAUX

	2009	2010	2011	2012	2013	2014	2015	2016	2017	
GROSS DOMESTIC PRODUCT BY KIND OF ECONOMIC ACTIVITY AT CURRENT PRICES *NIGERIAN NAIRA (MILLIONS)*										**PRODUIT INTÉRIEUR BRUT PAR BRANCHE D'ACTIVITÉ ÉCONOMIQUE AUX PRIX COURANTS** *NAIRA NIGERIAN (MILLIONS)*
Agriculture, hunting, forestry and Fishing	9 186 306	13 048 893	14 037 826	15 815 998	16 816 553	18 018 613	19 636 969	21 523 510	23 952 554	Agriculture, chasse sylviculture et Pêche
Mining and quarrying	7 458 762	8 454 554	11 098 978	11 386 523	10 380 972	9 716 761	6 100 009	5 578 533	10 489 386	Industries extractives
Manufacturing	612 309	3 578 642	4 527 445	5 588 822	7 233 322	8 685 430	8 973 773	8 903 229	10 044 485	Industries manufacturières
Electricity, gas & water	62 148	222 265	321 116	423 658	563 267	621 992	642 540	661 823	831 669	Electricité, gaz et eau
Construction	347 691	1 570 973	1 905 575	2 188 719	2 676 284	3 188 823	3 472 255	3 606 560	4 281 776	Bâtiments et travaux publics
Wholesale & retail trade, restaurants, hotels	4 181 313	9 238 411	10 608 942	12 196 752	14 351 227	16 523 912	18 922 565	21 600 924	22 557 932	Commerce de gros et de détail, restaurants et hôtels
Finance, insurance, real estate, etc.	1 657 246	7 761 631	8 269 246	10 222 163	12 039 975	13 688 206	15 397 594	16 466 038	18 968 645	Banques, assurances, affaires immobilières
Transport and communications	762 725	6 649 831	7 158 914	8 184 038	9 410 628	10 786 011	12 142 142	13 052 989	11 978 642	Transport(s) et communications
Public administration and defense	197 262	1 998 471	2 471 239	2 210 046	2 384 904	2 644 232	2 552 450	2 783 828	2 921 585	Administrations publiques et défense
Education	47 096	826 672	1 110 721	1 252 722	1 549 934	1 804 405	2 116 348	2 445 952	2 590 856	Education
Health And Social Work	11 086	330 964	387 195	442 939	518 736	615 026	682 697	745 582	784 803	Santé et Actions Sociales
Other services	270 295	930 958	1 083 201	1 801 556	2 166 761	2 750 204	3 505 619	4 229 514	4 316 714	Autres services
Less Imputed Service Charges	...	...	...	...	...	...	...	...	...	Moins Services d'intermédiation financière
Gross domestic product at factor cost / basic prices	24 794 239	54 612 264	62 980 397	71 713 935	80 092 563	89 043 615	94 144 960	101 598 482	113 719 048	Produit intérieur brut aux couts des facteurs / prix de base
Plus: Indirect Taxes / taxes on products, less subsidies	441 818	857 086	732 962	885 695	917 401	1 093 369	1 032 775	1 085 925	1 187 615	Plus taxes indirectes/impôts sur les produits, moins les subventions
EXPENDITURE ON GROSS DOMESTIC PRODUCT AT CURRENT PURCHASER'S VALUES *NIGERIAN NAIRA (MILLIONS)*										**EMPLOI DU PRODUIT INTÉRIEUR BRUT AUX PRIX COURANTS D'ACQUISITION** *NAIRA NIGERIAN (MILLIONS)*
Government final consumption	3 269 928	4 832 148	5 412 006	5 953 206	5 796 440	5 826 893	5 648 950	5 522 950	...	Consommation finale des administrations publiques
Private final consumption	18 980 959	36 676 905	41 686 511	42 394 482	59 043 367	64 671 261	74 652 864	83 771 534	...	Consommation finale privée
Gross fixed capital formation	3 050 576	9 183 059	9 897 197	10 281 952	11 478 080	13 595 842	14 112 170	15 076 795	...	Formation brute de capital fixe
Change in inventories	1 626	408 003	432 000	540 976	595 569	648 238	630 960	658 309	...	Variation des stocks
Exports of goods and services	7 764 785	14 013 841	19 961 271	22 824 414	14 615 287	16 616 867	10 119 235	9 455 515	...	Exportations de biens et services
Less imports of goods and services	7 831 818	9 644 605	13 675 626	9 395 401	10 518 778	11 222 116	9 986 444	11 800 696	...	Moins importations de biens et services
GDP at purchasers' values	25 236 056	55 469 350	63 713 359	72 599 630	81 009 965	90 136 985	95 177 736	102 684 407	114 906 664	PIB aux prix d'acquisition
GROSS DOMESTIC PRODUCT BY KIND OF ECONOMIC ACTIVITY AT CONSTANT PRICES *ANNUAL GROWTH RATES (%)*										**PRODUIT INTÉRIEUR BRUT PAR BRANCHE D'ACTIVITÉ ÉCONOMIQUE AUX PRIX CONSTANTS** *TAUX DE CROISSANCE ANNUEL (%)*
Agriculture, hunting, forestry and Fishing	5.9	5.8	2.9	6.7	2.9	4.3	3.7	4.1	3.4	Agriculture, chasse sylviculture et Pêche
Mining and quarrying	0.7	5.4	2.4	- 4.8	- 12.8	- 1.1	- 5.3	- 13.7	3.8	Industries extractives
Manufacturing	7.9	7.6	17.8	13.5	21.8	14.7	- 1.5	- 4.3	- 0.2	Industries manufacturières
Electricity, gas & water	3.2	3.3	32.5	13.0	18.8	- 3.3	- 4.0	- 8.7	12.6	Electricité, gaz et eau
Construction	12.0	11.9	15.7	9.4	14.2	13.0	4.4	- 5.9	1.0	Bâtiments et travaux publics
Wholesale & retail trade, restaurants, hotels	11.5	11.2	7.3	2.6	8.7	6.5	5.0	- 0.5	- 1.1	Commerce de gros et de détail, restaurants et hôtels
Finance, insurance, real estate, etc.	6.1	22.6	-2.3	9.0	9.0	5.8	3.9	- 7.1	10.0	Banques, assurances, affaires immobilières
Transport and communications	21.0	6.1	2.5	2.4	7.8	6.7	6.1	1.8	- 8.5	Transport(s) et communications
Public administration and defense	4.4	4.2	15.5	- 20.3	- 0.5	2.5	- 12.3	- 4.6	- 0.4	Administrations publiques et défense
Education	10.0	9.8	31.6	1.7	15.6	8.9	7.7	1.3	- 0.7	Education
Health And Social Work	10.0	10.0	13.0	4.3	9.6	10.5	2.5	- 1.8	- 0.3	Santé et Actions Sociales
Other services	9.8	9.6	8.6	48.2	11.0	17.5	17.3	16.6	- 13.6	Autres services
Less Imputed Service Charges	...	25.0	...	...	...	...	...	...	...	Moins Services d'intermédiation financière
Gross domestic product at factor cost / basic prices	7.0	8.0	5.3	4.2	5.5	6.2	2.8	- 1.5	0.8	Produit intérieur brut aux couts des facteurs / prix de base
Plus: Indirect Taxes / taxes on products, less subsidies	5.9	2.0	-21.9	10.6	- 2.2	13.9	- 8.2	- 4.7	- 0.9	Plus taxes indirectes/impôts sur les produits, moins les subventions
Gross domestic product at market prices	6.9	7.8	4.9	4.3	5.4	6.3	2.7	- 1.5	0.7	Produit intérieur brut aux prix du marché
EXPENDITURE ON GROSS DOMESTIC PRODUCT AT CONSTANT PURCHASERS' VALUES *ANNUAL GROWTH RATES (%)*										**EMPLOIS DU PRODUIT INTÉRIEUR BRUT AUX PRIX CONSTANTS D'ACQUISITION** *TAUX DE CROISSANCE ANNUEL (%)*
Government final consumption	0.7	11.9	4.6	- 2.0	1.4	- 6.5	- 22.4	- 15.1	...	Consommation finale des administrations publiques
Private final consumption	31.7	- 9.0	2.6	0.3	29.1	- 10.0	0.1	- 5.5	...	Consommation finale privée
Gross fixed capital formation	34.8	18.3	-29.8	1.9	10.5	41.8	- 1.3	- 5.0	...	Formation brute de capital fixe
Exports of goods and services	- 30.7	53.5	25.8	- 3.6	- 45.8	66.8	7.0	11.9	...	Exportations de biens et services
Less imports of goods and services	11.7	12.7	-7.8	- 32.9	12.1	6.1	- 26.9	- 8.9	...	Moins importations de biens et services

III INFLATION

	2009	2010	2011	2012	2013	2014	2015	2016	2017	
Annual growth rates (%)										**Taux de croissance annuel (%)**
All item	12.5	13.7	10.8	12.2	8.5	8.1	9.0	15.7	16.5	Ensemble
of which:										dont:
Food and non-alcoholic beverages	14.7	14.9	10.2	11.2	9.5	9.5	9.9	14.7	19.6	Alimentation et boissons non alcoolisés
Alcoholic beverages, tobacco and narcotics	1.3	8.2	6.8	7.1	6.3	6.7	8.6	13.2	10.6	Boissons alcoolisées et tabacs
Clothing and footwear	6.7	10.6	8.9	12.7	8.5	7.4	9.1	14.9	16.2	Habillement et chaussures
Housing, water, electricity, gas and other fuels	8.3	10.0	15.5	17.7	9.6	5.8	7.2	21.9	12.9	Logement, eau, électricité, gaz et autres combustibles
Furnishings, household equipment and routine household maintenance	11.4	15.2	8.3	10.8	7.3	7.2	8.6	11.3	12.9	Meubles, articles de ménage et entretien courant
Health	10.8	8.3	9.3	9.7	6.9	6.8	8.2	10.2	10.7	Santé
Transport	7.1	13.9	10.6	13.5	7.3	6.8	8.6	15.8	13.4	Transport
Communication	5.8	2.6	4.4	7.8	3.9	4.3	3.1	4.9	3.6	Communication
Recreation and culture	6.3	8.8	5.2	7.8	6.3	7.5	6.9	9.3	10.1	Loisirs et culture
Education	18.3	13.2	5.2	10.9	7.0	6.4	8.8	16.7	15.2	Enseignement
Restaurants and hotels	10.7	7.2	6.5	7.6	5.6	7.1	8.8	9.3	9.1	Restaurants et hôtels
Miscellaneous goods and services	12.7	11.5	8.9	11.8	6.6	6.9	8.7	11.8	11.3	Biens et Services divers

IV AGRICULTURAL PRODUCTION - PRODUCTION AGRICOLE

	2009	2010	2011	2012	2013	2014	2015	2016	2017	
TONNES (THOUSAND)										**Tonnes (milliers)**
Cassava	36 822	42 533	46 190	50 950	54 023	56 328	57 172	60 530	...	Manioc
Yams	29 092	37 328	33 134	32 319	42 849	45 152	45 678	48 983	...	Ignames
Sorghum	5 279	7 141	5 690	5 837	6 725	6 883	7 005	5 723	...	Sorgho
Maize	7 358	7 677	8 878	8 695	10 280	10 059	10 562	10 532	...	Maïs
Millet	4 930	5 170	1 271	1 281	1 314	1 399	1 485	1 539	...	Millet

V MINING PRODUCTION - PRODUCTION MINIERE

	2009	2010	2011	2012	2013	2014	2015	2016	2017	
Crude petroleum - Production, metric tons (thousands)	1 062 400	896 040	866 250	852 780	800 490	798 500	773 500	669 900	...	Pétrole brut - Production, tonnes métriques (milliers)
Gypsum; anhydrite; limestone and other calcareous stone - Production, metric tons (thousands)	3	5	...	...	...	...	...	28	...	Gypse; anhydrite; pierres à chaux ou à ciment - Production, tonnes métriques (milliers)
Natural gas - Production, terajoules (millions)	1 837	2 393	2 400	2 580	2 325	2 486	2 930	2 778	...	Gaz naturel - Production, térajoules (millions)

VI ENERGY - ENERGIE

	2009	2010	2011	2012	2013	2014	2015	2016	2017	
Total electricity generation (GWh)	19 777	26 057	27 034	25 391	25 200	36 042	78 367	...	...	Production électrique totale (GWh)
of which										dont
Production of electricity from fossil fuels (GWh)	15 248	19 747	21 384	20 084	19 934	29 748	71 741			Production d'électricité à partir de combustibles fossiles (GWh)
Production of hydro electricity (GWh)	4 529	6 310	5 650	5 307	5 267	6 220	6 531	...	...	Production d'électricité d'origine hydraulique (GWh)
Production of electricity from solar, wind, tide, wave and other sources (GWh)	...	...	...	...	...	74	95	...	...	Production d'électricité d'origine solaire, éolienne, marée motrice et autres (GWh)

VII TOURISM AND INFRASTRUCTURE - TOURISME ET INFRASTUCTURE

	2009	2010	2011	2012	2013	2014	2015	2016	2017	
VII-1 Tourism										**VII-1 Tourisme**
International tourist arrivals (thousands)	1 414	1 555	715	486	600	858	1 255	1 401	1 530	Arrivées de touristes internationaux (milliers)
Rooms in hotels and similar establishments (thousands)	...	...	...	...	...	...	...	...	...	Chambres d'hôtels et établissements assimilés (milliers)
Overnight stays (thousands)	8 498	9 569	3 322	2 346	2 422	2 790	4 492	5 316	6 017	Nuitées (milliers)
Tourism receipts (US$ thousand)	601 800	569 100	623 200	554 500	538 000	538 700	412 400	1 066 900	891 579	Recettes touristiques (milliers de $ EU)
Total contribution to GDP (%)	5.1	4.0	3.6	3.9	4.6	4.6	4.5	5.2	5.1	Contribution totale au PIB (%)
Total contribution to Employment (%)	4.7	4.0	3.6	3.7	4.3	4.3	4.2	4.9	4.8	Contribution totale à l'emploi (%)
VII-2 Infrastructure										**VII-2 Infrastructure**
Paved road (% of total)	...	...	...	...	...	...	...	...	...	Routes asphaltées (% du total)
Total network (Railways-km)	...	...	...	...	...	...	...	...	...	Réseau total voies ferrées-Km
Main telephone lines (per 100 inhabitants)	1.0	0.7	...	...	...	...	...	...	...	Lignes téléphoniques fixes (pour 100 habitants)
Mobile cellular subscribers (per 100 inhabitants)	48.0	54.7	58.0	66.8	73.3	77.8	82.2	81.8	...	Abonnés aux téléphones mobiles (pour 100 habitants)
Internet users per 100 inhabitants	9.3	11.5	13.8	16.1	19.1	21.0	24.5	25.7	...	Utilisateurs Internet par 100 Habitants
Fixed (wired)-broadband subscriptions per 100 inhabitants	...	...	...	...	...	...	...	...	...	Abonnements à l'Internet fixe (filaire) à large bande pour 100 habitants, par débit

VIII EXTERNAL TRADE - COMMERCE EXTERIEUR

	2009	2010	2011	2012	2013	2014	2015	2016	2017	
US$ (MILLIONS) EXPORTS, FOB										**$ E.U (MILLIONS) EXPORTATIONS, FÂB**
Exports - Total	56 742	86 568	125 641	114 700	102 400	102 878	56 135	35 822	...	Exportations - Total
Exports to Africa	7 806	9 386	10 768	10 048	9 479	10 884	6 728	4 484	...	Exportations vers l'Afrique
Main products										**Principaux produits**
Cocoa	727	837	887	999	1 155	850	910	768	...	Cacao
Liquefied propane and butane	617	1 059	1 179	1 121	890	1 331	774	468	...	Propane liquéfié et butane
Natural gas, whether or not liquefied	3 441	5 184	9 233	10 678	9 417	10 839	6 704	3 357	...	Gaz naturel, même liquéfié
Petroleum oils or bituminous minerals > 70 % oil	828	4 418	8 302	5 706	3 217	4 110	2 194	1 302	...	Huiles de pétrole ou de minéraux bitumineux> 70% d'huile
Petroleum oils, oils from bitumin. materials, crude	48 774	70 076	99 985	89 229	83 096	80 777	41 324	26 636	...	Huiles de pétrole, huiles de bitume. matériaux bruts
Main destinations										**Principales destinations**
Brazil	4 791	6 215	9 343	8 520	10 203	10 203	4 898	1 800	...	Brazil
India	7 112	13 350	18 832	17 910	17 171	21 191	12 752	8 530	...	Inde
Netherlands	1 606	2 858	4 280	8 244	6 677	7 719	4 349	1 857	...	Pays-Bas
Spain	3 278	4 903	7 810	7 982	6 756	8 023	4 418	2 820	...	Espagne
United States	17 833	29 765	33 556	18 430	11 159	3 815	2 377	3 347	...	États-Unis
IMPORTS, CIF										
Imports - Total	33 906	44 235	56 000	51 000	56 000	60 000	48 000	39 000	...	Importations - Total (millions)
Imports from Africa	2 253	2 475	2 585	2 927	3 610	2 862	2 574	2 415	...	Importations en provenance de l'Afrique
Main products										**Principaux produits**
Fish, fresh (live or dead), chilled or frozen	462	660	1 183	1 252	1 024	1 107	1 348	1 301	...	Poissons frais (vivants ou morts), réfrigérés ou congelés
Motor vehicles for the transport of persons	1 916	2 776	2 238	3 573	2 138	2 308	2 776	1 765	...	Véhicules à moteur pour le transport de personnes
Petroleum oils or bituminous minerals > 70 % oil	3 391	4 801	7 296	5 980	9 493	8 842	5 239	4 557	...	Huiles de pétrole ou de minéraux bitumineux> 70% d'huile
Telecommunication equipment, n.e.s.; & parts, n.e.s.	1 030	1 127	1 608	1 772	1 533	1 592	1 597	1 421	...	Matériel de télécommunication, n.es .; & parties, n.e.s.
Wheat (including spelt) and meslin, unmilled	1 230	916	2 129	1 870	1 887	2 015	1 678	1 044	...	Blé (y compris l'épeautre) et méteil, non moulu
Main origin										**Principales provenances**
Belgium	1 367	1 299	2 072	2 306	3 179	3 100	3 352	3 687	...	Belgique
China	5 125	6 809	8 361	10 064	12 394	15 307	12 494	9 821	...	Chine
Netherlands	2 157	3 160	3 700	2 881	3 398	3 504	2 416	1 980	...	Pays-Bas
United Kingdom	1 875	2 075	2 292	2 932	2 778	2 593	2 540	2 137	...	Royaume-Uni
United States	3 658	5 943	7 023	6 891	7 694	7 589	7 019	4 010	...	États-Unis

NIGÉRIA

	2009	2010	2011	2012	2013	2014	2015	2016	2017	
IX-1 MONETARY STATISTICS *NIGERIAN NAIRA (MILLIONS)*										**IX-1 STATISTIQUES MONÉTAIRES** *NAIRA NIGERIAN (MILLIONS)*
Money supply (M1)	10 780 627	11 525 530	11 987 104	15 480 439	15 632 181	18 813 898	19 924 740	23 193 376	26 587 484	Masse monétaire (M1)
Quasi-money	5 707 989	5 941 368	6 526 685	8 021 190	9 603 453	11 312 731	10 967 750	11 750 107	12 566 619	Quasi-monnaie
of which demand deposit	4 089 879	4 488 975	5 526 446	6 119 786	5 586 178	4 885 264	7 115 604	...	9 253 687	dont Monnaie scripturale
Net foreign assets	7 287 925	6 195 141	6 643 739	8 715 632	8 262 158	6 730 504	5 297 042	7 647 759	11 999 549	Avoirs extérieurs nets
Domestic credit	9 363 895	10 426 949	14 112 185	15 102 802	17 702 702	19 727 840	22 027 652	27 239 036	26 753 591	Crédit intérieur
of which claims on private sector	-1 844 274	446 896	749 633	760 129	1 838 341	706 056	2 415 080	4 397 068	3 413 205	dont créances sur le secteur privé
of which claims on government sector, net	9 687 254	8 554 239	7 949 079	8 569 594	10 202 487	13 077 826	13 524 119	16 083 411	16 325 859	dont créances nettes sur le gouvernement
International reserves (millions US$)	42 382	32 339	32 640	43 830	42 847	34 250	28 285	26 991	28 740	Réserves internationales (millions \$EU)
Average exchange rate (National currency per US$)	149	150	155	157	157	159	192	253	305	Taux de change (moyen) (monnaie nationale par \$ EU)
IX-2 PUBLIC FINANCE *NIGERIAN NAIRA (MILLIONS)*										**IX-2 FINANCES PUBLIQUES** *NAIRA NIGERIAN (MILLIONS)*
Total Revenues and Grants	4 844 600	7 303 800	11 116 900	10 654 900	9 759 900	10 068 800	7 224 000	5 694 000	...	Recettes totales et dons
Direct taxes (on income, profits)	1 036 500	1 220 200	1 350 000	1 558 800	1 781 100	2 001 500	1 802 000	1 799 000	...	Taxes directes
Domestic indirect taxes revenues	212 700	268 100	284 200	421 400	555 400	488 400	1 211 000	729 000	...	Taxes Indirectes
Trade taxes	297 500	309 200	438 300	474 900	433 600	566 200	546 000	567 000	...	Taxes sur le commerce extérieur
Other taxes	3 191 900	5 396 100	8 879 000	8 026 000	6 809 200	6 793 800	3 299 000	2 200 000	...	Autres taxes
Other revenues	106 000	110 200	165 400	173 800	180 600	218 900	366 000	399 000	...	Autres recettes
Grants	...	...	...	...	...	...	...	...	...	Dons
Total Expenditures and Net Lending	7 681 485	8 409 101	12 295 796	11 839 324	12 331 187	11 406 985	10 555 202	9 727 054	...	Dépenses totales et prêts nets
Current expenditure	4 430 085	4 784 801	8 709 896	7 872 013	8 708 909	8 172 948	7 888 915	7 259 000	...	Dépenses courantes
Wages and Salaries	1 148 300	1 564 000	1 854 000	1 811 000	1 860 000	1 810 326	1 862 013	1 875 000	...	Rémunérations et salaires
Other purchases of goods and services	564 200	982 300	673 300	589 600	648 560	713 416	784 758	538 000	...	Achat de biens et services
Other current expenditure	2 252 085	1 710 201	5 226 419	4 325 813	4 758 394	4 234 234	3 757 657	3 470 000	...	Autres dépenses courantes
Current transfers	465 500	528 300	956 177	1 145 600	1 441 955	1 414 973	1 484 487	1 376 000	...	Transferts courants
Interest payments	384 700	586 000	759 400	711 800	770 062	733 093	551 283	575 054	...	Intérêts
Capital expenditure	2 866 700	3 038 300	2 826 500	3 255 511	2 852 216	2 500 943	2 115 004	1 893 000	...	Dépenses d'équipement
Net lending	...	...	...	...	...	...	...	...	...	Prêts nets
Fiscal balance	-2 836 885	-1 105 301	-1 178 896	-1 184 424	-2 571 287	-1 338 185	-3 331 202	-4 033 054	...	Solde global y compris les dons
IX-3 BALANCE OF PAYMENTS *NIGERIAN NAIRA (MILLIONS)*										**IX-3 BALANCE DES PAIEMENTS** *NAIRA NIGERIAN (MILLIONS)*
Trade balance	3 780 287	4 523 691	5 051 021	6 172 471	6 634 108	3 302 989	-1 266 752	- 135 456	...	Balance commerciale
Services Balance	-2 453 708	-2 743 227	-3 259 469	-3 392 667	-3 052 899	-3 595 575	-3 232 725	-2 025 222	...	Balance des services
Net primary income	-2 144 671	-2 921 789	-3 505 308	-3 478 448	-4 014 681	-3 013 614	-2 496 902	-2 177 291	...	Revenus primaires nets
Compensation of employees	17 789	22 213	21 108	26 116	26 206	28 765	40 230	45 415	...	Rémunération des salariés
Investment income	-2 162 460	-2 944 002	-3 526 416	-3 504 563	-4 040 888	-3 042 379	-2 537 131	-2 222 707	...	Revenus des investissements
Net secondary income	2 882 981	3 111 917	3 355 220	3 435 092	3 430 100	3 448 772	3 962 894	5 025 788	...	Revenus secondaires nets
Net official transfers	219 407	215 078	264 024	276 879	270 080	286 819	299 024	353 600	...	Transferts officiels nets
Workers' remittances	2 710 253	2 938 239	3 139 423	3 203 293	3 237 475	3 265 166	3 809 058	4 743 855	...	Envois de fonds des travailleurs
Other private transfers	- 46 679	- 41 400	- 48 228	- 45 080	- 77 455	- 103 214	- 145 188	- 71 666	...	Autres transferts privés
Current account balance	2 064 890	1 970 592	1 641 463	2 736 448	2 996 627	142 571	-3 033 485	687 818	...	Solde du compte courant
Capital and financial account	1 862 598	305 561	- 831 406	-1 949 197	1 209 070	1 932 253	- 201 971	417 187	...	Comptes de capital et financier
Capital account	...	...	...	...	...	...	...	...	...	Compte de capital
Financial account	1 862 598	305 561	- 831 406	-1 949 197	1 209 070	1 932 253	- 201 971	417 187	...	Compte financier
Errors and omissions	-3 927 488	-2 276 153	- 810 057	- 787 251	-4 205 697	-2 074 824	3 235 456	-1 105 005	...	Erreurs et omissions
Overall balance	-1 563 694	-1 491 478	47 064	1 747 900	- 154 179	-1 329 318	-1 150 133	- 247 841	...	Balance générale

NIGERIA

X DEBT AND FINANCIAL FLOWS - DETTE ET FLUX FINANCIERS

	2009	2010	2011	2012	2013	2014	2015	2016	2017	
X-1 DEBT *US $ (MILLIONS)*										**X-1 DETTE EXTÉRIEURE** *$ E.U (MILLIONS)*
Total external debt	24 268	24 486	29 899	32 356	32 363	42 115	47 194	44 507	51 593	Dette extérieure totale
Private	13 978	12 790	15 351	14 929	18 741	27 604	31 975	28 173	...	Privée
Public	10 289	11 696	14 549	17 427	13 622	14 511	15 218	16 334	...	Publique
Total external debt service	9 749	9 269	9 168	11 173	11 724	12 249	16 043	17 590	...	Service de la dette extérieure
Present value of external debt	...	...	...	...	...	...	...	9 073	...	Valeur actuelle de la dette extérieure
Total government domestic debt, National currency (millions)	3 228	4 552	5 623	...	...	...	...	...	...	Dette publique intérieure
X-2 FINANCIAL FLOWS *US $ (MILLIONS)*										**X-2 FLUX FINANCIERS** *$ E.U (MILLIONS)*
Net Foreign Direct Investment Inflows	8 650	6 099	8 915	7 127	5 608	4 694	3 064	4 449	...	Investissements étranger direct (flux nets entrants)
Main origin of FDI inflows										**Principales origines de l'IDE entrant:**
United States	57	40	119	4 532	...	...	...	...	...	États-Unis
France	...	...	2 529	214	...	...	...	...	...	France
United Kingdom	1 367	964	10	3 464	...	...	...	...	...	Royaume-Uni
Italy	...	...	- 1 753	28	...	...	...	...	...	Italie
...	...	...	...	...	...	...	...	...	...	...
African countries	2 232	1 574	774	18 610	...	...	...	...	...	Pays africains
Net total official development assistance	1 639	2 052	1 768	1 916	2 516	2 479	2 432	2 501	...	Aide publique au développement (nette totale)
Main origin of net ODA										**Principales origines de l'APD nette**
United Kingdom	189	265	299	313	389	390	401	431	...	Royaume-Uni
France	9	9	11	7	46	82	33	59	...	France
International Development Association [IDA]	476	975	646	481	630	859	709	650	...	International Development Association
Germany	27	39	22	38	73	22	34	72	...	Allemagne
United States	354	442	405	415	544	486	491	532	...	États-Unis

NIGÉRIA

SOURCES AND NOTES - SOURCES ET NOTES

External trade - Total exports, fob: UNCTAD

External trade - Total import, cif: UNCTAD

ODA: OECD

Monetary statistics: IMF

National Account: The accounts are calculated using the new base year 2010

National Accounts : The annual Growth Rates for 2016 are previsions based on the sum of four quarters of 2016.

Poverty: World Bank

Commerce exterieur - Exportation, fab: CNUCED

Commerce exterieur - Imporations, caf: CNUCED

APD: OCDE

Statistiques monétaires: FMI

Comptes Nationaux : Les comptes sont calculés selon la nouvelle année de base 2010

Comptes Nationaux: Les croissances annuelles de L'année 2016 sont estimées à partir des comptes trimestriels

Pauvreté: Banque mondiale

AREA (km2)		26 340		**SUPERFICIE (KM2)**
CAPITAL CITY	Kigali		Kigali	**CAPITALE**
CURRENCY	Rwandan Franc		Franc Rwandais	**MONNAIE**

I SOCIAL AND DEMOGRAPHIC INDICATORS — INDICATEURS DEMOGRAPHIQUES ET SOCIAUX

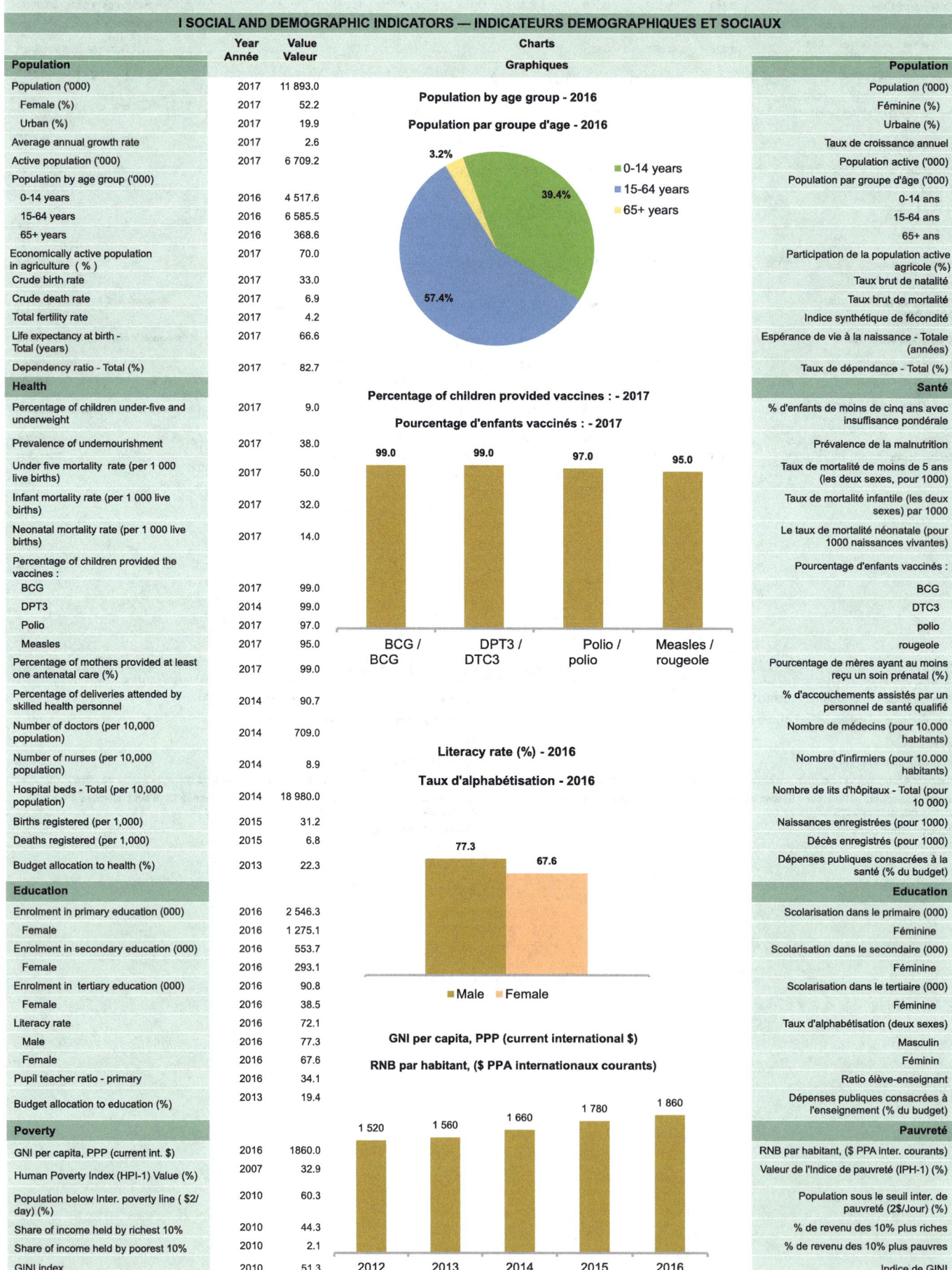

Population	Year / Année	Value / Valeur	Charts / Graphiques	Population
Population ('000)	2017	11 893.0		Population ('000)
Female (%)	2017	52.2		Féminine (%)
Urban (%)	2017	19.9		Urbaine (%)
Average annual growth rate	2017	2.6		Taux de croissance annuel
Active population ('000)	2017	6 709.2		Population active ('000)
Population by age group ('000)				Population par groupe d'âge ('000)
0-14 years	2016	4 517.6		0-14 ans
15-64 years	2016	6 585.5		15-64 ans
65+ years	2016	368.6		65+ ans
Economically active population in agriculture (%)	2017	70.0		Participation de la population active agricole (%)
Crude birth rate	2017	33.0		Taux brut de natalité
Crude death rate	2017	6.9		Taux brut de mortalité
Total fertility rate	2017	4.2		Indice synthétique de fécondité
Life expectancy at birth - Total (years)	2017	66.6		Espérance de vie à la naissance - Totale (années)
Dependency ratio - Total (%)	2017	82.7		Taux de dépendance - Total (%)
Health				**Santé**
Percentage of children under-five and underweight	2017	9.0		% d'enfants de moins de cinq ans avec insuffisance pondérale
Prevalence of undernourishment	2017	38.0		Prévalence de la malnutrition
Under five mortality rate (per 1 000 live births)	2017	50.0		Taux de mortalité de moins de 5 ans (les deux sexes, pour 1000)
Infant mortality rate (per 1 000 live births)	2017	32.0		Taux de mortalité infantile (les deux sexes) par 1000
Neonatal mortality rate (per 1 000 live births)	2017	14.0		Le taux de mortalité néonatale (pour 1000 naissances vivantes)
Percentage of children provided the vaccines :				Pourcentage d'enfants vaccinés :
BCG	2017	99.0		BCG
DPT3	2014	99.0		DTC3
Polio	2017	97.0		polio
Measles	2017	95.0		rougeole
Percentage of mothers provided at least one antenatal care (%)	2017	99.0		Pourcentage de mères ayant au moins reçu un soin prénatal (%)
Percentage of deliveries attended by skilled health personnel	2014	90.7		% d'accouchements assistés par un personnel de santé qualifié
Number of doctors (per 10,000 population)	2014	709.0		Nombre de médecins (pour 10.000 habitants)
Number of nurses (per 10,000 population)	2014	8.9		Nombre d'infirmiers (pour 10.000 habitants)
Hospital beds - Total (per 10,000 population)	2014	18 980.0		Nombre de lits d'hôpitaux - Total (pour 10 000)
Births registered (per 1,000)	2015	31.2		Naissances enregistrées (pour 1000)
Deaths registered (per 1,000)	2015	6.8		Décès enregistrés (pour 1000)
Budget allocation to health (%)	2013	22.3		Dépenses publiques consacrées à la santé (% du budget)
Education				**Education**
Enrolment in primary education (000)	2016	2 546.3		Scolarisation dans le primaire (000)
Female	2016	1 275.1		Féminine
Enrolment in secondary education (000)	2016	553.7		Scolarisation dans le secondaire (000)
Female	2016	293.1		Féminine
Enrolment in tertiary education (000)	2016	90.8		Scolarisation dans le tertiaire (000)
Female	2016	38.5		Féminine
Literacy rate	2016	72.1		Taux d'alphabétisation (deux sexes)
Male	2016	77.3		Masculin
Female	2016	67.6		Féminin
Pupil teacher ratio - primary	2016	34.1		Ratio élève-enseignant
Budget allocation to education (%)	2013	19.4		Dépenses publiques consacrées à l'enseignement (% du budget)
Poverty				**Pauvreté**
GNI per capita, PPP (current int. $)	2016	1860.0		RNB par habitant, ($ PPA inter. courants)
Human Poverty Index (HPI-1) Value (%)	2007	32.9		Valeur de l'Indice de pauvreté (IPH-1) (%)
Population below Inter. poverty line ($2/day) (%)	2010	60.3		Population sous le seuil inter. de pauvreté (2$/Jour) (%)
Share of income held by richest 10%	2010	44.3		% de revenu des 10% plus riches
Share of income held by poorest 10%	2010	2.1		% de revenu des 10% plus pauvres
GINI index	2010	51.3		Indice de GINI

	2009	2010	2011	2012	2013	2014	2015	2016	2017	
GROSS DOMESTIC PRODUCT BY KIND OF ECONOMIC ACTIVITY AT CURRENT PRICES *RWANDAN FRANC (BILLIONS)*										**PRODUIT INTÉRIEUR BRUT PAR BRANCHE D'ACTIVITÉ ÉCONOMIQUE AUX PRIX COURANTS** *FRANC RWANDAIS (MILLIARDS)*
Agriculture, hunting , forestry and Fishing	896	949	1 091	1 300	1 424	1 572	1 670	1 956	2 352	Agriculture, chasse sylviculture et Pêche
Mining and quarrying	33	45	102	97	124	147	132	137	179	Industries extractives
Manufacturing	184	208	235	270	291	322	352	389	451	Industries manufacturières
Electricity, gas & water	40	47	55	65	73	78	90	118	128	Electricité, gaz et eau
Construction	176	198	259	313	359	392	440	450	442	Bâtiments et travaux publics
Wholesale & retail trade, restaurants, hotels	301	341	384	445	472	529	581	628	655	Commerce de gros et de détail, restaurants et hôtels
Finance, insurance, real estate, etc.	692	736	793	851	898	957	1 069	1 201	1 426	Banques, assurances, affaires immobilières
Transport and communications	158	182	205	255	273	287	318	350	382	Transport(s) et communications
Public administration and defense	116	137	165	210	238	260	283	329	356	Administrations publiques et défense
Education	56	68	85	104	140	154	156	166	171	Education
Health And Social Work	66	78	80	102	117	133	136	140	153	Santé et Actions Sociales
Other services	141	153	161	185	214	257	313	342	382	Autres services
Less Imputed Service Charges	...	...	...	...	...	...	...	...	...	Moins Services d'intermédiation financière
Gross domestic product at factor cost / basic prices	2 859	3 142	3 615	4 197	4 623	5 088	5 540	6 206	7 077	Produit intérieur brut aux couts des facteurs / prix de base
Plus: Indirect Taxes / taxes on products, less subsidies	198	225	282	297	306	377	416	466	520	Plus taxes indirectes/impôts sur les produits, moins les subventions
EXPENDITURE ON GROSS DOMESTIC PRODUCT AT CURRENT PURCHASER'S VALUES *RWANDAN FRANC (BILLIONS)*										**EMPLOI DU PRODUIT INTÉRIEUR BRUT AUX PRIX COURANTS D'ACQUISITION** *FRANC RWANDAIS (MILLIARDS)*
Government final consumption	422	479	510	625	667	824	874	1 006	1 156	Consommation finale des administrations publiques
Private final consumption	2 469	2 718	3 127	3 567	3 833	4 254	4 743	5 154	5 768	Consommation finale privée
Gross fixed capital formation	692	749	887	1 118	1 254	1 333	1 541	1 689	1 741	Formation brute de capital fixe
Change in inventories	22	24	27	41	53	50	38	38	37	Variation des stocks
Exports of goods and services	359	405	538	576	695	804	850	994	1 385	Exportations de biens et services
Less imports of goods and services	907	1 010	1 192	1 432	1 574	1 799	2 089	2 208	2 490	Moins importations de biens et services
GDP at purchasers' values	3 057	3 367	3 897	4 494	4 929	5 466	5 956	6 672	7 597	PIB aux prix d'acquisition
GROSS DOMESTIC PRODUCT BY KIND OF ECONOMIC ACTIVITY AT CONSTANT PRICES *ANNUAL GROWTH RATES (%)*										**PRODUIT INTÉRIEUR BRUT PAR BRANCHE D'ACTIVITÉ ECONOMIQUE AUX PRIX CONSTANTS** *TAUX DE CROISSANCE ANNUEL (%)*
Agriculture, hunting , forestry and Fishing	7.7	5.0	4.7	6.5	3.3	6.6	5.0	3.9	6.5	Agriculture, chasse sylviculture et Pêche
Mining and quarrying	- 17.7	- 10.1	49.3	- 7.5	20.4	24.6	- 4.8	10.0	21.4	Industries extractives
Manufacturing	3.2	9.2	8.4	5.6	4.9	7.7	8.4	6.9	6.2	Industries manufacturières
Electricity, gas & water	15.0	15.2	13.2	13.3	7.4	6.8	6.4	7.2	5.6	Electricité, gaz et eau
Construction	1.5	9.1	23.2	14.6	10.9	9.8	15.6	4.9	- 2.9	Bâtiments et travaux publics
Wholesale & retail trade, restaurants, hotels	2.0	8.8	7.0	12.2	5.2	9.1	11.9	6.9	2.2	Commerce de gros et de détail, restaurants et hôtels
Finance, insurance, real estate, etc.	6.8	3.5	2.3	4.0	3.3	4.7	9.8	6.6	11.9	Banques, assurances, affaires immobilières
Transport and communications	9.3	9.0	4.4	22.0	5.0	4.7	11.8	8.1	11.8	Transport(s) et communications
Public administration and defense	7.7	14.3	14.4	21.9	9.4	6.6	5.8	11.3	4.2	Administrations publiques et défense
Education	15.6	8.7	18.6	6.7	4.2	3.4	1.3	5.1	2.4	Education
Health And Social Work	15.9	15.0	2.2	23.4	6.0	8.1	9.8	5.5	7.1	Santé et Actions Sociales
Other services	- 5.6	7.2	- 0.6	10.7	12.2	16.3	19.1	6.9	8.6	Autres services
Less Imputed Service Charges	...	...	...	...	...	...	...	...	...	Moins Services d'intermédiation financière
Gross domestic product at factor cost / basic prices	5.4	6.3	7.2	8.8	5.5	7.5	8.5	6.0	6.9	Produit intérieur brut aux couts des facteurs / prix de base
Plus: Indirect Taxes / taxes on products, less subsidies	9.5	4.8	1.4	2.0	- 3.3	8.0	14.1	4.7	- 4.2	Plus taxes indirectes/impôts sur les produits, moins les subventions
Gross domestic product at market prices	6.3	7.3	7.8	8.8	4.7	7.6	8.9	6.0	6.1	Produit intérieur brut aux prix du marché
EXPENDITURE ON GROSS DOMESTIC PRODUCT AT CONSTANT PURCHASERS' VALUES *ANNUAL GROWTH RATES (%)*										**EMPLOIS DU PRODUIT INTÉRIEUR BRUT AUX PRIX CONSTANTS D'ACQUISITION** *TAUX DE CROISSANCE ANNUEL (%)*
Government final consumption	11.7	10.3	3.9	15.9	- 0.3	20.8	5.1	9.1	10.9	Consommation finale des administrations publiques
Private final consumption	5.0	6.9	9.9	4.0	6.9	5.9	6.1	5.3	10.8	Consommation finale privée
Gross fixed capital formation	2.5	7.2	10.8	21.0	7.8	4.9	18.8	10.5	6.6	Formation brute de capital fixe
Exports of goods and services	- 2.4	8.0	22.6	8.8	18.7	7.2	6.3	13.1	33.5	Exportations de biens et services
Less imports of goods and services	17.4	1.4	17.4	18.1	9.6	14.6	23.0	8.4	10.1	Moins importations de biens et services

III INFLATION

	2009	2010	2011	2012	2013	2014	2015	2016	2017	
Annual growth rates (%)										**Taux de croissance annuel (%)**
All item	10.4	2.3	5.7	6.3	4.2	1.8	2.5	5.7	4.8	Ensemble
of which:										dont:
Food and non-alcoholic beverages	16.3	1.7	6.5	12.4	5.1	1.2	3.9	10.8	9.5	Alimentation et boissons non alcoolisés
Alcoholic beverages, tobacco and narcotics	18.1	7.3	2.1	4.1	5.1	7.3	5.9	5.1	7.9	Boissons alcoolisées et tabacs
Clothing and footwear	3.0	1.4	6.8	3.7	1.2	5.5	2.3	1.7	5.9	Habillement et chaussures
Housing, water, electricity, gas and other fuels	6.7	1.0	3.7	4.8	0.9	0.9	4.0	2.4	2.0	Logement, eau, électricité, gaz et autres combustibles
Furnishings, household equipment and routine household maintenance	7.4	- 1.9	2.1	4.5	2.7	1.0	1.7	3.2	2.9	Meubles, articles de ménage et entretien courant
Health	3.2	1.1	0.6	1.4	0.5	10.4	- 0.1	0.3	6.6	Santé
Transport	3.2	8.0	9.0	1.8	1.4	- 0.8	- 0.8	7.1	4.5	Transport
Communication	- 3.7	-	- 1.6	- 5.3	- 1.0	- 1.1	0.2	4.7	2.1	Communication
Recreation and culture	4.3	1.0	4.2	- 1.0	1.6	0.9	4.9	3.2	2.8	Loisirs et culture
Education	16.6	6.6	20.3	1.9	35.2	7.1	0.4	1.8	- 0.7	Enseignement
Restaurants and hotels	8.8	2.4	0.8	1.8	4.2	7.5	2.6	2.8	- 0.9	Restaurants et hôtels
Miscellaneous goods and services	2.0	- 0.9	6.1	3.4	3.4	3.5	1.8	2.2	3.1	Biens et Services divers

RWANDA

IV AGRICULTURAL PRODUCTION - PRODUCTION AGRICOLE

	2009	2010	2011	2012	2013	2014	2015	2016	2017	
TONNES (THOUSAND)										**Tonnes (milliers)**
Bananas	1 857	2 749	3 036	3 219	3 292	1 804 649	1 862 841	1 898 726	...	Bananes
Cassava	1 137	2 377	2 579	2 716	2 948	900 227	924 651	930 220	...	Manioc
Potatoes	893	1 789	2 172	2 172	2 241	719 006	742 626	751 284	...	Pommes de terre
Sweet potatoes	540	840	845	1 005	1 081	940 787	931 027	919 123	...	Patates douces
Maize	262	432	526	573	668	357 083	370 140	374 267	...	Maïs

V MINING PRODUCTION - PRODUCTION MINIERE

	2009	2010	2011	2012	2013	2014	2015	2016	2017	
Tin ores and concentrates, includes Cassiterite - Production (metric tons)	4 269	3 874	6 952	4 637	4 895	5 954	3 846	3 550	...	Minerais d'étain et leurs concentrés - Production (tonnes métriques)
	...	...	...	...	...	...	...	...	...	
	...	...	...	...	...	...	...	...	...	

VI ENERGY - ENERGIE

	2009	2010	2011	2012	2013	2014	2015	2016	2017	
Total electricity generation (GWh)	238	280	340	348	769	821	839	863	...	Production électrique totale (GWh)
of which										dont
Production of electricity from fossil fuels (GWh)	140	170	190	196	256	308	311	315	...	Production d'électricité à partir de combustibles fossiles (GWh)
Production of hydro electricity (GWh)	98	110	149	150	214	214	217	219	...	Production d'électricité d'origine hydraulique (GWh)
Production of electricity from solar, wind, tide, wave and other sources (GWh)	...	...	1	3	298	298	310	328	...	Production d'électricité d'origine solaire, éolienne, marée motrice et autres (GWh)

VII TOURISM AND INFRASTRUCTURE - TOURISME ET INFRASTUCTURE

	2009	2010	2011	2012	2013	2014	2015	2016	2017	
VII-1 Tourism										**VII-1 Tourisme**
International tourist arrivals (thousands)	502	504	688	815	864	926	987	1 104	1 073	Arrivées de touristes internationaux (milliers)
Rooms in hotels and similar establishments (thousands)	4	5	7	6	7	8	8	8	...	Chambres d'hôtels et établissements assimilés (milliers)
Overnight stays (thousands)	3 017	3 102	4 102	5 237	6 020	6 607	7 586	...	...	Nuitées (milliers)
Tourism receipts (US$ thousand)	174 200	200 400	251 500	281 000	292 300	301 900	365 400	387 400	396 918	Recettes touristiques (milliers de $ EU)
Total contribution to GDP (%)	9.7	8.9	9.6	11.1	11.8	12.0	12.9	12.8	12.7	Contribution totale au PIB (%)
Total contribution to Employment (%)	8.6	7.7	8.4	9.8	10.4	10.4	11.2	11.1	11.1	Contribution totale à l'emploi (%)
VII-2 Infrastructure										**VII-2 Infrastructure**
Paved road (% of total)	...	25.0	25.0	25.7	...	1.3	...	...	...	Routes asphaltées (% du total)
Total network (Railways-km)	...	...	...	...	...	...	...	...	...	Réseau total voies ferrées-Km
Main telephone lines (per 100 inhabitants)	...	...	...	...	...	...	...	...	...	Lignes téléphoniques fixes (pour 100 habitants)
Mobile cellular subscribers (per 100 inhabitants)	23.1	32.7	39.9	49.7	56.8	64.0	70.5	69.9	...	Abonnés aux téléphones mobiles (pour 100 habitants)
Internet users per 100 inhabitants	7.7	8.0	7.0	8.0	9.0	10.6	18.0	20.0	...	Utilisateurs Internet par 100 Habitants
Fixed (wired)-broadband subscriptions per 100 inhabitants	...	...	...	...	...	...	...	...	...	Abonnements à l'Internet fixe (filaire) à large bande pour 100 habitants, par débit

VIII EXTERNAL TRADE - COMMERCE EXTERIEUR

	2009	2010	2011	2012	2013	2014	2015	2016	2017	
US$ (MILLIONS) **EXPORTS, FOB**										**$ E.U (MILLIONS)** **EXPORTATIONS, FÀB**
Exports - Total	261	297	464	591	703	653	684	744	...	Exportations - Total
Exports to Africa	115	82	114	352	433	363	244	250	...	Exportations vers l'Afrique
Main products										**Principaux produits**
Coffee and coffee substitutes	59	70	81	90	64	64	89	83	...	Café et succédanés du café
Gold, non-monetary (excluding gold ores and concentrates)	1	...	...	...	...	7	65	189	...	Or, non monétaire (à l'exclusion des minerais d'or et des concentrés)
Ores and concentrates of base metals, n.e.s.	82	110	222	201	305	228	173	139	...	Minerais et concentrés de métaux communs, n.d.a.
Petroleum oils or bituminous minerals > 70 % oil	1	-2	19	39	68	93	58	71	...	Huiles de pétrole ou de minéraux bitumineux> 70 % d'huile
Tea and mate	52	47	50	82	50	46	101	88	...	Thé et maté
Main destinations										**Principales destinations**
China	20	35	63	51	79	63	44	32	...	Chine
Democratic Republic of Congo	15	22	54	129	141	162	131	136	...	République Démocratique du Congo
Kenya	45	26	34	52	55	37	56	65	...	Kenya
United Arab Emirates	2	-	2	3	12	13	77	198	...	Emirates Arabes
Tanzania, United Republic of	2	3	2	95	152	93	2	3	...	Tanzanie, République Unie de
IMPORTS, CIF										
Imports - Total	1 308	1 405	2 039	2 300	2 302	2 468	2 378	2 293	...	Importations - Total (millions)
Imports from Africa	494	600	873	926	803	897	854	748	...	Importations en provenance de l'Afrique
Main products										**Principaux produits**
Aircraft & associated equipment; spacecraft, etc.	18	39	9	51	7	34	35	218	...	Aéronefs et équipement connexe; vaisseau spatial, etc.
Lime, cement, fabrica. constr. mat. (excludingglass, clay)	53	62	93	118	117	118	109	84	...	Chaux, ciment, tissu. constr. tapis. (sauf verre, argile)
Medicaments (incl. veterinary medicaments)	39	48	56	68	66	84	84	85	...	Médicaments (y compris les médicaments vétérinaires)
Petroleum oils or bituminous minerals > 70 % oil	85	50	149	142	113	89	28	19	...	Huiles de pétrole ou de minéraux bitumineux> 70% d'huile
Telecommunication equipment, n.e.s.; & parts, n.e.s.	128	52	66	90	81	135	150	147	...	Matériel de télécommunication, n.es.; & parties, n.e.s.
Main origin										**Principales provenances**
China	95	134	163	222	289	328	327	301	...	Chine
India	50	61	94	152	160	232	224	147	...	Inde
Kenya	164	165	215	259	209	263	253	222	...	Kenya
Uganda	192	201	315	370	340	399	362	285	...	Ouganda
United Arab Emirates	106	104	147	191	184	187	139	138	...	Emirates Arabes

	2009	2010	2011	2012	2013	2014	2015	2016	2017	
IX-1 MONETARY STATISTICS *RWANDAN FRANC (MILLIONS)*										**IX-1 STATISTIQUES MONÉTAIRES** *FRANC RWANDAIS (MILLIONS)*
Money supply (M1)	527 100	615 936	780 354	890 157	1 030 377	1 223 871	1 482 101	1 594 683	1 801 360	Masse monétaire (M1)
Quasi-money	133 524	153 491	214 109	232 605	228 051	258 782	281 289	356 460	390 442	Quasi-monnaie
of which demand deposit	...	...	...	...	...	...	...	...	...	dont Monnaie scripturale
Net foreign assets	429 573	506 461	649 419	522 382	704 723	641 206	627 194	725 876	785 577	Avoirs extérieurs nets
Domestic credit	219 635	283 146	360 861	604 502	614 598	946 248	1 143 787	1 263 120	1 439 773	Crédit intérieur
of which claims on private sector	- 154 305	- 136 124	- 276 300	- 238 195	- 351 861	- 218 439	- 136 550	- 188 473	- 209 088	dont créances sur le secteur privé
of which claims on government sector, net	359 886	410 416	623 645	831 475	944 970	1 135 709	1 261 115	1 401 172	1 584 397	dont créances nettes sur le gouvernement
International reserves (millions US$)	893	961	1 346	1 133	1 070	951	922	1 001	1 037	Réserves internationales (millions $EU)
Average exchange rate (National currency per US$)	568	583	600	614	647	682	721	787	832	Taux de change (moyen) (monnaie nationale par $ EU)
IX-2 PUBLIC FINANCE *RWANDAN FRANC (MILLIONS)*										**IX-2 FINANCES PUBLIQUES** *FRANC RWANDAIS (MILLIONS)*
Total Revenues and Grants	670 800	800 700	863 357	1 049 100	1 101 322	1 338 763	1 426 794	1 541 628	1 615 800	Recettes totales et dons
Direct taxes (on income, profits)	130 100	148 800	180 871	228 500	282 038	311 632	375 700	406 159	468 400	Taxes directes
Domestic indirect taxes revenues	179 300	195 000	245 078	282 600	315 061	393 937	432 400	510 270	544 600	Taxes Indirectes
Trade taxes	52 000	32 600	37 760	45 900	54 822	57 856	63 500	83 885	91 200	Taxes sur le commerce extérieur
Other taxes	...	...	...	...	...	...	...	...	...	Autres taxes
Other revenues	51 700	15 000	20 623	34 700	84 500	101 049	131 200	167 600	181 400	Autres recettes
Grants	257 700	409 300	379 026	457 400	364 900	474 289	423 994	373 714	330 200	Dons
Total Expenditures and Net Lending	731 300	804 000	984 289	1 098 100	1 335 600	1 542 605	1 725 687	1 757 642	1 942 900	Dépenses totales et prêts nets
Current expenditure	390 300	444 400	511 396	595 700	603 200	736 273	817 087	890 821	997 400	Dépenses courantes
Wages and Salaries	90 800	106 900	122 017	144 800	168 900	187 872	203 900	242 300	263 700	Rémunérations et salaires
Other purchases of goods and services	103 200	106 300	124 083	149 500	123 100	142 516	159 500	180 621	207 400	Achat de biens et services
Other current expenditure	54 700	51 600	68 134	75 800	80 400	119 108	121 100	138 462	54 200	Autres dépenses courantes
Current transfers	141 600	179 600	197 161	225 600	230 800	286 776	332 587	329 438	472 100	Transferts courants
Interest payments	11 400	14 700	15 600	18 400	30 700	43 661	45 600	56 699	72 200	Intérêts
Capital expenditure	306 700	316 700	438 592	482 900	564 500	712 452	769 800	721 700	759 500	Dépenses d'équipement
Net lending	22 900	28 200	18 701	1 100	137 200	50 220	93 200	88 422	113 800	Prêts nets
Fiscal balance	- 60 500	- 3 300	- 120 932	- 49 000	- 234 278	- 203 842	- 298 894	- 216 014	- 327 100	Solde global y compris les dons
IX-3 BALANCE OF PAYMENTS *RWANDAN FRANC (MILLIONS)*										**IX-3 BALANCE DES PAIEMENTS** *FRANC RWANDAIS (MILLIONS)*
Trade balance	- 764	- 787	- 1 105	- 1 274	- 1 151	- 1 269	- 1 237	- 1 310	- 872	Balance commerciale
Services Balance	- 182	- 170	- 104	- 3	- 15	- 77	- 273	- 254	- 30	Balance des services
Net primary income	- 37	- 51	- 57	- 103	- 132	- 176	- 228	- 296	- 317	Revenus primaires nets
Compensation of employees	- 32	- 35	- 39	- 43	- 58	- 62	- 67	- 69	- 69	Rémunération des salariés
Investment income	10	- 15	- 12	- 31	- 18	- 41	- 74	- 122	- 132	Revenus des investissements
Net secondary income	604	581	798	632	741	578	536	524	596	Revenus secondaires nets
Net official transfers	458	490	665	449	560	398	370	344	376	Transferts officiels nets
Workers' remittances	53	65	110	118	115	119	102	107	150	Envois de fonds des travailleurs
Other private transfers	27	26	23	65	67	60	64	73	71	Autres transferts privés
Current account balance	- 379	- 427	- 469	- 747	- 556	- 943	- 1 201	- 1 336	- 622	Solde du compte courant
Capital and financial account	427	565	730	569	896	986	990	1 157	745	Comptes de capital et financier
Capital account	200	286	197	171	235	337	300	190	190	Compte de capital
Financial account	227	279	533	397	661	649	690	967	556	Compte financier
Errors and omissions	5	- 66	- 27	- 34	- 111	- 133	183	169	- 31	Erreurs et omissions
Overall balance	54	72	234	- 212	229	- 90	- 29	- 10	93	Balance générale

RWANDA

X DEBT AND FINANCIAL FLOWS - DETTE ET FLUX FINANCIERS

	2009	2010	2011	2012	2013	2014	2015	2016	2017	
X-1 DEBT US $ (MILLIONS)										**X-1 DETTE EXTÉRIEURE** $ E.U (MILLIONS)
Total external debt	837	1 015	1 313	1 481	1 922	2 141	2 488	3 163	3 576	Dette extérieure totale
Private	100	238	328	418	367	312	261	270	...	Privée
Public	737	777	985	1 062	1 556	1 829	2 227	2 893	...	Publique
Total external debt service	10	14	34	36	43	71	75	90	...	Service de la dette extérieure
Present value of external debt	...	...	...	...	...	...	...	1 754	...	Valeur actuelle de la dette extérieure
Total government domestic debt, National currency (millions)	254	288	298	399	...	...	...	...	...	Dette publique intérieure
X-2 FINANCIAL FLOWS US $ (MILLIONS)										**X-2 FLUX FINANCIERS** $ E.U (MILLIONS)
Net Foreign Direct Investment Inflows	119	251	119	255	258	459	380	410	...	Investissements étranger direct (flux nets entrants)
Main origin of FDI inflows										**Principales origines de l'IDE entrant:**
United States	...	...	16	...	...	...	...	...	...	États-Unis
...	...	...	...	...	...	...	...	...	...	...
Luxembourg	3	...	...	-	...	...	...	...	...	Luxembourg
Belgium	...	...	...	1	...	...	...	...	...	Belgique
United States	...	...	16	...	...	...	...	...	...	États-Unis
African countries	...	...	159	...	...	...	...	...	...	Pays africains
Net total official development assistance	934	1 033	1 263	879	1 086	1 035	1 085	1 148	...	Aide publique au développement (nette totale)
Main origin of net ODA										**Principales origines de l'APD nette**
International Development Association [IDA]	114	146	289	95	153	200	292	225	...	International Development Association
United States	146	140	178	159	156	157	198	178	...	États-Unis
United Kingdom	90	106	136	45	162	79	155	93	...	Royaume-Uni
Global Fund	81	3	2	1	3	4	3	5	...	Fonds Mondial
Belgium	82	70	77	54	48	42	36	26	...	Belgique

RWANDA

SOURCES AND NOTES - SOURCES ET NOTES

External trade - Total exports, fob: UNCTAD	Commerce exterieur - Exportation, fab: CNUCED
External trade - Total import, cif: UNCTAD	Commerce exterieur - Imporations, caf: CNUCED
ODA: OECD	APD: OCDE
Monetary statistics: IMF	Statistiques monétaires: FMI
National Accounts: The Accounts are calculated using the new base year 2014	Comptes nationaux: Les comptes sont calculés selon la nouvelle année de base 2014
National Accounts : The annual data for 2016 are previsions based on the sum of four quarters of 2016.	Comptes Nationaux: Les données de l'année 2016 sont estimées à partir des comptes trimestriels
Poverty: World Bank	Pauvreté: Banque mondiale

AREA (km2)		960	**SUPERFICIE (KM2)**
CAPITAL CITY	São Tomé	São Tomé	**CAPITALE**
CURRENCY	Sao Tome Dobra	Dobra santoméen	**MONNAIE**

I SOCIAL AND DEMOGRAPHIC INDICATORS — INDICATEURS DEMOGRAPHIQUES ET SOCIAUX

Population	Year Année	Value Valeur	Charts / Graphiques	Population
Population ('000)	2016	193.7		Population ('000)
Female (%)	2016	50.4		Féminine (%)
Urban (%)	2016	67.5		Urbaine (%)
Average annual growth rate	2016	2.0		Taux de croissance annuel
Active population ('000)	2015	56.9		Population active ('000)
Population by age group ('000)				Population par groupe d'âge ('000)
0-14 years	2016	76.5		0-14 ans
15-64 years	2016	110.6		15-64 ans
65+ years	2016	6.6		65+ ans
Economically active population in agriculture (%)	2015	63.3		Participation de la population active agricole (%)
Crude birth rate	2016	26.4		Taux brut de natalité
Crude death rate	2016	6.3		Taux brut de mortalité
Total fertility rate	2016	3.4		Indice synthétique de fécondité
Life expectancy at birth - Total (years)	2015	66.6		Espérance de vie à la naissance - Totale (années)
Dependency ratio - Total (%)	2016	75.1		Taux de dépendance - Total (%)

Population by age group - 2016
Population par groupe d'age - 2016

- 0-14 years: 39.5%
- 15-64 years: 57.1%
- 65+ years: 3.4%

Health				Santé
Percentage of children under-five and underweight	2009	14.4		% d'enfants de moins de cinq ans avec insuffisance pondérale
Prevalence of undernourishment	2015	6.6		Prévalence de la malnutrition
Under five mortality rate (per 1 000 live births)	2016	42.4		Taux de mortalité de moins de 5 ans (les deux sexes, pour 1000)
Infant mortality rate (per 1 000 live births)	2016	34.7		Taux de mortalité infantile (les deux sexes) par 1000
Neonatal mortality rate (per 1 000 live births)	2015	17.1		Le taux de mortalité néonatale (pour 1000 naissances vivantes)
Percentage of children provided the vaccines :				Pourcentage d'enfants vaccinés :
BCG	2014	95.0		BCG
DPT3	2014	95.0		DTC3
Polio	2011	96.0		polio
Measles	2014	92.0		rougeole
Percentage of mothers provided at least one antenatal care (%)	2009	97.5		Pourcentage de mères ayant au moins reçu un soin prénatal (%)
Percentage of deliveries attended by skilled health personnel	2009	81.7		% d'accouchements assistés par un personnel de santé qualifié
Number of doctors (per 10,000 population)	2004	4.9		Nombre de médecins (pour 10.000 habitants)
Number of nurses (per 10,000 population)	2004	18.7		Nombre d'infirmiers (pour 10.000 habitants)
Hospital beds - Total (per 10,000 population)	2011	29.0		Nombre de lits d'hôpitaux - Total (pour 10 000)
Births registered (per 1,000)	2015	33.5		Naissances enregistrées (pour 1000)
Deaths registered (per 1,000)	2015	6.8		Décès enregistrés (pour 1000)
Budget allocation to health (%)	2013	5.6		Dépenses publiques consacrées à la santé (% du budget)

Percentage of children provided vaccines : - 2014
Pourcentage d'enfants vaccinés : - 2014

- BCG / BCG: 95.0
- DPT3 / DTC3: 95.0
- Polio / polio (2011): 96.0
- Measles / rougeole: 92.0

Education				Education
Enrolment in primary education (000)	2015	35.6		Scolarisation dans le primaire (000)
Female	2015	17.3		Féminine
Enrolment in secondary education (000)	2015	22.1		Scolarisation dans le secondaire (000)
Female	2013	8.4		Féminine
Enrolment in tertiary education (000)	2015	2.3		Scolarisation dans le tertiaire (000)
Female	2014	1.2		Féminine
Literacy rate	2008	69.5		Taux d'alphabétisation (deux sexes)
Male	2008	80.3		Masculin
Female	2008	60.1		Féminin
Pupil teacher ratio - primary	...	...		Ratio élève-enseignant
Budget allocation to education (%)	2010	19.3		Dépenses publiques consacrées à l'enseignement (% du budget)

Literacy rate (%) - 2008
Taux d'alphabétisation - 2008

- Male: 80.3
- Female: 60.1

Poverty				Pauvreté
GNI per capita, PPP (current int. $)	2016	3250.0		RNB par habitant, ($ PPA inter. courants)
Human Poverty Index (HPI-1) Value (%)	2007	12.6		Valeur de l'Indice de pauvreté (IPH-1) (%)
Population below Inter. poverty line ($2/ day) (%)	2010	33.9		Population sous le seuil inter. de pauvreté (2$/Jour) (%)
Share of income held by richest 10%	2010	24.2		% de revenu des 10% plus riches
Share of income held by poorest 10%	2010	3.5		% de revenu des 10% plus pauvres
GINI index	2010	30.8		Indice de GINI

GNI per capita, PPP (current international $)
RNB par habitant, ($ PPA internationaux courants)

- 2012: 2 720
- 2013: 2 910
- 2014: 3 110
- 2015: 3 130
- 2016: 3 250

SAO TOMÉ-ET-PRINCIPE

II NATIONAL ACCOUNTS — COMPTES NATIONAUX

	2009	2010	2011	2012	2013	2014	2015	2016	2017	
GROSS DOMESTIC PRODUCT BY KIND OF ECONOMIC ACTIVITY AT CURRENT PRICES SAO TOME DOBRA (MILLIONS)										**PRODUIT INTÉRIEUR BRUT PAR BRANCHE D'ACTIVITÉ ÉCONOMIQUE AUX PRIX COURANTS** DOBRA SANTOMÉEN (MILLIONS)
Agriculture, hunting , forestry and Fishing	329 223	411 359	464 425	553 952	672 573	732 984	833 605	847 799	...	Agriculture, chasse sylviculture et Pêche
Mining and quarrying	12 056	13 222	14 212	15 659	16 737	18 322	18 914	21 353	...	Industries extractives
Manufacturing	277 990	309 857	342 458	355 491	406 445	416 654	435 013	533 187	...	Industries manufacturières
Electricity, gas & water	106 964	111 336	118 994	119 560	131 960	128 476	135 107	142 280	...	Electricité, gaz et eau
Construction	171 956	200 807	209 379	273 236	324 422	525 132	402 414	536 579	...	Bâtiments et travaux publics
Wholesale & retail trade, restaurants, hotels	1 190 721	1 378 357	1 680 002	1 620 520	1 693 712	1 912 196	2 179 204	2 287 210	...	Commerce de gros et de détail, restaurants et hôtels
Finance, insurance, real estate, etc.	268 525	309 179	352 008	389 617	438 429	517 965	564 895	631 809	...	Banques, assurances, affaires immobilières
Transport and communications	386 177	457 597	582 052	612 227	635 487	719 201	852 471	847 468	...	Transport(s) et communications
Public administration and defense	135 133	190 286	191 920	407 383	505 364	569 453	630 812	676 084	...	Administrations publiques et défense
Education	85 750	120 632	138 106	204 645	294 888	377 992	391 330	427 297	...	Education
Health And Social Work	39 995	46 887	49 921	50 793	69 084	80 269	82 465	92 455	...	Santé et Actions Sociales
Other services	130 200	156 507	190 032	223 305	256 399	291 353	325 712	356 567	...	Autres services
Less Imputed Service Charges	- 92 918	- 109 623	- 123 527	- 144 771	- 168 306	- 196 578	- 207 595	- 229 722	...	Moins Services d'intermédiation financière
Gross domestic product at factor cost / basic prices	3 041 772	3 596 403	4 209 981	4 681 616	5 277 194	6 093 421	6 644 346	7 170 365	...	Produit intérieur brut aux couts des facteurs / prix de base
Plus: Indirect Taxes / taxes on products, less subsidies	198 985	263 890	259 433	270 635	303 973	342 174	373 604	423 438	...	Plus taxes indirectes/impôts sur les produits, moins les subventions
EXPENDITURE ON GROSS DOMESTIC PRODUCT AT CURRENT PURCHASER'S VALUES Sao Tome Dobra (Millions)										**EMPLOI DU PRODUIT INTÉRIEUR BRUT AUX PRIX COURANTS D'ACQUISITION** DOBRA SANTOMÉEN (MILLIONS)
Government final consumption	423 925	1 060 181	2 615 213	1 215 225	1 517 744	1 618 412	1 757 096	1 019 171	...	Consommation finale des administrations publiques
Private final consumption	3 764 408	3 195 179	3 742 077	4 010 852	4 832 255	5 154 145	5 603 000	6 242 648	...	Consommation finale privée
Gross fixed capital formation	711 317	1 371 234	164 076	1 773 869	1 363 380	2 173 409	2 470 206	2 105 505	...	Formation brute de capital fixe
Change in inventories	- 152 247	28 005	47 022	132 915	143 409	160 553	224 787	147 776	...	Variation des stocks
Exports of goods and services	273 656	487 083	554 257	591 623	677 208	724 470	822 744	2 180 545	...	Exportations de biens et services
Less imports of goods and services	1 780 303	2 281 389	2 653 231	2 772 233	2 952 828	3 395 395	3 859 882	4 101 842	...	Moins importations de biens et services
GDP at purchasers' values	3 240 757	3 860 293	4 469 415	4 952 251	5 581 167	6 435 595	7 017 950	7 593 803	...	PIB aux prix d'acquisition
GROSS DOMESTIC PRODUCT BY KIND OF ECONOMIC ACTIVITY AT CONSTANT PRICES ANNUAL GROWTH RATES (%)										**PRODUIT INTÉRIEUR BRUT PAR BRANCHE D'ACTIVITÉ ECONOMIQUE AUX PRIX CONSTANTS** TAUX DE CROISSANCE ANNUEL (%)
Agriculture, hunting , forestry and Fishing	3.8	0.7	3.0	1.6	- 0.4	4.2	2.3	2.0	...	Agriculture, chasse sylviculture et Pêche
Mining and quarrying	6.5	3.8	1.4	7.8	6.2	8.9	- 0.8	8.2	...	Industries extractives
Manufacturing	13.1	4.8	6.9	- 1.5	6.0	- 3.6	0.4	8.2	...	Industries manufacturières
Electricity, gas & water	- 0.2	4.3	4.7	- 0.4	10.7	- 3.0	7.4	- 2.6	...	Electricité, gaz et eau
Construction	11.9	5.9	1.0	8.5	10.6	15.6	- 3.2	13.7	...	Bâtiments et travaux publics
Wholesale & retail trade, restaurants, hotels	5.9	3.6	3.5	3.5	3.1	5.4	1.4	5.3	...	Commerce de gros et de détail, restaurants et hôtels
Finance, insurance, real estate, etc.	11.0	10.1	8.0	- 1.9	- 0.6	8.3	12.5	- 5.7	...	Banques, assurances, affaires immobilières
Transport and communications	7.3	5.7	4.3	2.0	4.9	5.0	3.6	4.4	...	Transport(s) et communications
Public administration and defense	1.1	1.1	2.0	2.0	2.0	2.0	2.0	2.0	...	Administrations publiques et défense
Education	-	22.4	10.5	31.9	28.8	17.7	1.0	0.3	...	Education
Health And Social Work	- 1.9	- 8.1	2.0	2.0	2.1	2.2	2.0	2.0	...	Santé et Actions Sociales
Other services	6.4	6.1	6.2	6.2	6.2	6.2	6.2	6.2	...	Autres services
Less Imputed Service Charges	4.2	4.8	4.4	2.8	5.0	5.2	2.8	3.9	...	Moins Services d'intermédiation financière
Gross domestic product at factor cost / basic prices	6.2	4.7	4.4	3.0	4.3	5.5	3.3	3.1	...	Produit intérieur brut aux couts des facteurs / prix de base
Plus: Indirect Taxes / taxes on products, less subsidies	- 34.0	37.0	4.2	5.2	10.2	17.3	9.4	13.3	...	Plus taxes indirectes/impôts sur les produits, moins les subventions
Gross domestic product at market prices	2.4	6.7	4.4	3.1	4.8	6.5	3.8	4.1	...	Produit intérieur brut aux prix du marché
EXPENDITURE ON GROSS DOMESTIC PRODUCT AT CONSTANT PURCHASERS' VALUES ANNUAL GROWTH RATES (%)										**EMPLOIS DU PRODUIT INTÉRIEUR BRUT AUX PRIX CONSTANTS D'ACQUISITION** TAUX DE CROISSANCE ANNUEL (%)
Government final consumption	2.7	6.7	4.4	3.1	149.3	6.9	3.9	- 3.0	...	Consommation finale des administrations publiques
Private final consumption	- 7.8	6.7	4.4	3.1	- 14.7	6.5	3.8	4.8	...	Consommation finale privée
Gross fixed capital formation	- 0.7	6.7	4.4	3.1	5.0	6.9	3.9	- 10.1	...	Formation brute de capital fixe
Exports of goods and services	8.5	6.7	4.4	3.1	5.0	6.9	3.9	5.7	...	Exportations de biens et services
Less imports of goods and services	- 0.9	6.7	4.4	3.1	5.0	6.9	3.9	- 4.5	...	Moins importations de biens et services

III INFLATION

	2009	2010	2011	2012	2013	2014	2015	2016	2017	
Annual growth rates (%)										**Taux de croissance annuel (%)**
All item	16.1	12.9	11.9	10.4	7.1	6.4	4.0	5.1	5.7	Ensemble
of which:										dont:
Food and non-alcoholic beverages	20.6	14.9	11.8	12.3	...	...	13.2	6.5	6.6	Alimentation et boissons non alcoolisés
Alcoholic beverages, tobacco and narcotics	...	...	...	...	...	...	...	1.6	11.7	Boissons alcoolisées et tabacs
Clothing and footwear	...	...	...	...	...	...	...	8.4	- 0.6	Habillement et chaussures
Housing, water, electricity, gas and other fuels	- 6.2	5.5	8.6	1.4	...	...	6.1	- 1.2	1.5	Logement, eau, électricité, gaz et autres combustibles
Furnishings, household equipment and routine household maintenance	...	...	...	...	...	...	8.1	1.1	2.9	Meubles, articles de ménage et entretien courant
Health	9.5	6.1	- 8.8	1.6	...	...	0.7	0.9	- 0.6	Santé
Transport	2.1	1.1	25.1	0.8	...	...	5.4	- 0.5	2.6	Transport
Communication	...	...	...	...	...	...	...	0.1	- 3.3	Communication
Recreation and culture	...	...	...	...	...	...	1.1	1.5	- 3.1	Loisirs et culture
Education	...	...	...	...	...	...	2.5	- 0.2	5.1	Enseignement
Restaurants and hotels	...	...	...	...	...	...	43.0	0.1	7.7	Restaurants et hôtels
Miscellaneous goods and services	...	...	...	...	...	...	21.9	5.4	7.1	Biens et Services divers

IV AGRICULTURAL PRODUCTION - PRODUCTION AGRICOLE

	2009	2010	2011	2012	2013	2014	2015	2016	2017	
TONNES (THOUSAND)										**Tonnes (milliers)**
Maize	3	1	2	1	1	1	...	...	...	Maïs
Cassava	2	1	2	2	2	3	...	...	...	Manioc
Coconuts	31	1	...	...	...	...	1	1	...	Noix de coco
Bananas	34	41	54	56	57	61	...	...	...	Bananes
Taro (cocoyam)	16	11	11	12	11	12	...	...	...	Taros (colocases)

V MINING PRODUCTION - PRODUCTION MINIERE

	2009	2010	2011	2012	2013	2014	2015	2016	2017
	...	...	...	...	...	...	...	...	...
	...	...	...	...	...	...	...	...	...
	...	...	...	...	...	...	...	...	...

VI ENERGY - ENERGIE

	2009	2010	2011	2012	2013	2014	2015	2016	2017	
Total electricity generation (GWh) of which	27	25	28	28	28	29	29	30	...	Production électrique totale (GWh) dont
Production of electricity from fossil fuels (GWh)	20	20	18	18	18	18	18	19	...	Production d'électricité à partir de combustibles fossiles (GWh)
Production of hydro electricity (GWh)	7	5	10	11	11	11	11	11	...	Production d'électricité d'origine hydraulique (GWh)
Production of electricity from solar, wind, tide, wave and other sources (GWh)	...	...	...	...	...	...	...	...	...	Production d'électricité d'origine solaire, éolienne, marée motrice et autres (GWh)

VII TOURISM AND INFRASTRUCTURE - TOURISME ET INFRASTUCTURE

	2009	2010	2011	2012	2013	2014	2015	2016	2017	
VII-1 Tourism										**VII-1 Tourisme**
International tourist arrivals (thousands)	15	8	12	12	24	44	46	47	42	Arrivées de touristes internationaux (milliers)
Rooms in hotels and similar establishments (thousands)	...	...	...	...	...	...	...	...	...	Chambres d'hôtels et établissements assimilés (milliers)
Overnight stays (thousands)	91	49	76	71	146	270	281	281	252	Nuitées (milliers)
Tourism receipts (US$ thousand)	8 300	11 100	15 900	15 000	30 600	56 000	62 200	68 800	65 240	Recettes touristiques (milliers de $ EU)
Total contribution to GDP (%)	12.1	13.2	15.6	13.7	17.8	22.2	27.5	27.8	24.3	Contribution totale au PIB (%)
Total contribution to Employment (%)	11.3	11.5	13.1	11.8	16.4	20.7	25.9	26.4	23.6	Contribution totale à l'emploi (%)
VII-2 Infrastructure										**VII-2 Infrastructure**
Paved road (% of total)	...	...	...	...	...	...	...	...	...	Routes asphaltées (% du total)
Total network (Railways-km)	...	...	...	...	...	...	...	...	...	Réseau total voies ferrées-Km
Main telephone lines (per 100 inhabitants)	4.4	4.4	4.3	4.3	3.6	3.4	3.5	2.8	...	Lignes téléphoniques fixes (pour 100 habitants)
Mobile cellular subscribers (per 100 inhabitants)	46.7	57.6	62.8	65.0	64.9	64.9	91.2	85.3	...	Abonnés aux téléphones mobiles (pour 100 habitants)
Internet users per 100 inhabitants	16.4	18.8	20.2	21.6	23.0	24.4	25.8	28.0	...	Utilisateurs Internet par 100 Habitants
Fixed (wired)-broadband subscriptions per 100 inhabitants	...	...	...	...	0.5	0.6	0.6	0.7	...	Abonnements à l'Internet fixe (filaire) à large bande pour 100 habitants, par débit

VIII EXTERNAL TRADE - COMMERCE EXTERIEUR

	2009	2010	2011	2012	2013	2014	2015	2016	2017	
US$ (MILLIONS) EXPORTS, FOB										**$ E.U (MILLIONS) EXPORTATIONS, FÀB**
Exports - Total	8	11	11	12	7	10	9	10	...	Exportations - Total
Exports to Africa	1	2	1	1	1	1	1	1	...	Exportations vers l'Afrique
Main products										**Principaux produits**
Cocoa	4	4	4	6	4	6	6	6	...	Cacao
Jewellery & articles of precious materia., n.e.s.	1	2	2	1	...	...	...	...	...	Bijoux et articles en matières précieuses, n.d.a.
...	...	...	...	...	...	...	...	...	...	...
Ships, boats & floating structures	...	...	...	...	...	1	1	1	...	Navires, bateaux et structures flottantes
Watches & clocks	1	2	3	2	...	...	...	...	...	Montres et horloges
Main destinations										**Principales destinations**
Aruba	3	4	5	4	...	...	...	...	...	Aruba
Belgium	1	1	1	1	1	2	2	2	...	Belgique
Netherlands	1	2	2	2	2	1	2	2	...	Pays-Bas
Spain	-	-	-	1	1	1	1	1	...	Espagne
Turkey	-	-	-	-	-	2	1	2	...	Turquie
IMPORTS, CIF										
Imports - Total	103	112	134	141	152	170	142	139	...	Importations - Total (millions)
Imports from Africa	20	26	20	36	43	42	37	35	...	Importations en provenance de l'Afrique
Main products										**Principaux produits**
Alcoholic beverages	4	7	8	7	8	9	8	8	...	Boissons alcoolisées
Lime, cement, fabrica. constr. mat. (excludingglass, clay)	3	4	4	4	4	6	4	5	...	Chaux, ciment, tissu. constr. tapis. (sauf verre, argile)
Motor vehicles for the transport of persons	6	7	5	7	5	7	5	5	...	Véhicules à moteur pour le transport de personnes
Petroleum oils or bituminous minerals > 70 % oil	15	18	20	35	39	38	34	32	...	Huiles de pétrole ou de minéraux bitumineux> 70% d'huile
Rice	5	4	6	5	5	6	5	5	...	Riz
Main origin										**Principales provenances**
Angola	15	18	15	32	38	36	33	31	...	Angola
Belgium	2	3	2	5	3	3	3	2	...	Belgique
China	1	2	2	3	2	4	3	3	...	Chine
Portugal	58	70	80	73	90	104	86	85	...	Portugal
United States	-	-	6	3	3	4	3	3	...	États-Unis

IX FINANCIAL AND MONETARY STATISTICS - FINANCES ET STATISTIQUES MONETAIRES

	2009	2010	2011	2012	2013	2014	2015	2016	2017	
IX-1 MONETARY STATISTICS *SAO TOME DOBRA (MILLIONS)*										**IX-1 STATISTIQUES MONÉTAIRES** *DOBRA SANTOMÉEN (MILLIONS)*
Money supply (M1)	1 130 355	1 414 604	1 561 892	1 879 479	2 140 380	2 499 681	2 828 229	2 691 193	2 664 041	Masse monétaire (M1)
Quasi-money	266 164	331 373	433 626	640 270	556 082	685 402	658 323	566 463	555 647	Quasi-monnaie
of which demand deposit	...	...	...	...	...	...	...	...	...	dont Monnaie scripturale
Net foreign assets	1 278 631	1 364 142	1 262 714	1 487 478	1 647 562	2 198 522	2 526 748	2 105 609	1 582 105	Avoirs extérieurs nets
Domestic credit	809 573	1 465 504	1 727 691	1 765 270	1 651 328	1 650 892	1 660 557	1 719 213	1 971 589	Crédit intérieur
of which claims on private sector	- 280 124	- 60 444	- 22 072	- 123 437	- 250 177	- 252 119	- 323 265	- 395 501	- 196 337	dont créances sur le secteur privé
of which claims on government sector, net	1 063 451	1 444 314	1 667 451	1 820 799	1 789 752	1 784 634	1 923 373	2 051 190	2 077 292	dont créances nettes sur le gouvernement
International reserves (millions US$)	67	47	52	52	64	64	73	63	71	Réserves internationales (millions $EU)
Average exchange rate (National currency per US$)	16 208	18 499	17 623	19 068	18 450	18 466	22 091	22 150	21 740	Taux de change (moyen) (monnaie nationale par $ EU)
IX-2 PUBLIC FINANCE *SAO TOME DOBRA (MILLIONS)*										**IX-2 FINANCES PUBLIQUES** *DOBRA SANTOMÉEN (MILLIONS)*
Total Revenues and Grants	994 860	1 396 610	1 621 718	1 681 771	1 720 919	1 690 292	2 070 924	2 177 578	...	Recettes totales et dons
Direct taxes (on income, profits)	144 308	153 295	225 588	206 588	322 244	299 807	344 072	377 287	...	Taxes directes
Domestic indirect taxes revenues	147 380	244 022	196 265	53 847	61 107	82 389	94 721	91 882	...	Taxes Indirectes
Trade taxes	96 750	115 484	158 846	334 043	398 388	407 478	515 308	371 286	...	Taxes sur le commerce extérieur
Other taxes	73 131	104 551	145 310	109 256	125 512	101 463	131 973	157 973	...	Autres taxes
Other revenues	67 296	59 989	96 466	101 680	93 951	154 081	180 850	28 598	...	Autres recettes
Grants	465 994	719 269	799 243	876 357	719 717	645 075	804 000	1 150 552	...	Dons
Total Expenditures and Net Lending	1 546 099	1 824 361	2 145 376	2 225 316	1 650 893	1 873 708	2 486 809	2 438 531	...	Dépenses totales et prêts nets
Current expenditure	623 266	720 457	826 714	845 635	914 889	1 043 056	1 304 284	1 244 859	...	Dépenses courantes
Wages and Salaries	252 090	308 783	369 185	419 418	521 351	569 453	623 355	684 309	...	Rémunérations et salaires
Other purchases of goods and services	194 846	190 862	233 682	197 632	171 854	157 645	238 988	172 293	...	Achat de biens et services
Other current expenditure	32 196	28 312	42 870	38 823	33 856	86 446	194 154	106 110	...	Autres dépenses courantes
Current transfers	144 133	192 500	180 997	189 761	187 829	229 512	247 787	282 147	...	Transferts courants
Interest payments	23 010	16 225	23 824	29 500	28 399	27 702	51 525	33 728	...	Intérêts
Capital expenditure	934 823	1 087 679	1 294 838	1 350 181	707 605	802 950	1 131 000	1 159 944	...	Dépenses d'équipement
Net lending	- 35 000	...	...	...	...	...	...	...	...	Prêts nets
Fiscal balance	- 551 239	- 427 751	- 523 658	- 543 545	70 026	- 183 416	- 415 885	- 260 953	...	Solde global y compris les dons
IX-3 BALANCE OF PAYMENTS *US $ (MILLIONS)*										**IX-3 BALANCE DES PAIEMENTS** *$ E.U (MILLIONS)*
Trade balance	-1 225 424	-1 626 248	-1 751 011	-1 881 942	-2 135 744	-2 352 787	-2 377 868	-2 336 159	-2 436 711	Balance commerciale
Services Balance	- 139 060	- 202 413	- 229 149	- 128 410	- 221 370	- 271 277	255 952	380 911	240 254	Balance des services
Net primary income	- 4 607	- 6 827	- 7 488	- 42 383	36 781	123 503	62 895	63 054	- 30 892	Revenus primaires nets
Compensation of employees	...	...	...	...	...	...	...	...	...	Rémunération des salariés
Investment income	...	...	...	...	...	...	...	...	...	Revenus des investissements
Net secondary income	75 220	166 438	218 571	268 635	821 079	581 228	541 532	530 103	637 177	Revenus secondaires nets
Net official transfers	5 570	6 000	9 570	9 170	26 280	8 140	6 370	11 110	...	Transferts officiels nets
Workers' remittances	32 417	117 711	121 269	121 254	480 885	464 534	433 532	386 796	395 496	Envois de fonds des travailleurs
Other private transfers	...	...	...	...	...	...	...	...	...	Autres transferts privés
Current account balance	-1 293 871	-1 669 050	-1 769 077	-1 784 100	-1 499 255	-1 919 332	-1 517 488	-1 362 091	-1 590 172	Solde du compte courant
Capital and financial account	1 432 169	1 803 921	1 983 424	1 992 256	- 103 175	1 662 401	1 215 737	2 131 425	1 695 070	Comptes de capital et financier
Capital account	646 478	770 126	819 140	738 253	542 742	546 370	709 122	658 438	645 836	Compte de capital
Financial account	785 692	1 033 796	1 164 284	1 254 003	- 645 917	1 116 031	506 615	1 472 987	1 049 234	Compte financier
Errors and omissions	- 138 298	- 134 872	- 214 347	- 208 156	1 602 430	256 931	301 752	- 769 334	- 104 898	Erreurs et omissions
Overall balance	- 647 394	- 898 924	- 949 937	-1 045 847	- 956 514	-1 372 963	- 808 367	- 703 653	- 944 336	Balance générale

X DEBT AND FINANCIAL FLOWS - DETTE ET FLUX FINANCIERS

	2009	2010	2011	2012	2013	2014	2015	2016	2017	
X-1 DEBT *US $ (MILLIONS)*										**X-1 DETTE EXTÉRIEURE** *$ E.U (MILLIONS)*
Total external debt	136	157	182	205	216	242	273	279	276	Dette extérieure totale
Private	...	...	...	...	...	...	...	...	...	Privée
Public	136	157	182	205	216	242	273	279	...	Publique
Total external debt service	2	2	2	2	5	3	3	3	...	Service de la dette extérieure
Present value of external debt	...	...	...	...	...	...	...	208	...	Valeur actuelle de la dette extérieure
Total government domestic debt, National currency (millions)	...	...	...	...	...	...	...	...	...	Dette publique intérieure
X-2 FINANCIAL FLOWS *US $ (MILLIONS)*										**X-2 FLUX FINANCIERS** *$ E.U (MILLIONS)*
Net Foreign Direct Investment Inflows	16	51	32	23	12	27	29	22	...	Investissements étranger direct (flux nets entrants)
Main origin of FDI inflows										**Principales origines de l'IDE entrant:**
...	...	...	...	...	...	...	...	...	...	...
...	...	...	...	...	...	...	...	...	...	...
...	...	...	...	...	...	...	...	...	...	...
...	...	...	...	...	...	...	...	...	...	...
...	...	...	...	...	...	...	...	...	...	...
African countries	...	...	...	...	...	...	...	...	...	Pays africains
Net total official development assistance	31	50	73	51	54	41	49	47	...	Aide publique au développement (nette totale)
Main origin of net ODA										**Principales origines de l'APD nette**
Portugal	15	26	29	21	17	13	25	15	...	Portugal
International Development Association [IDA]	1	2	19	6	6	1	1	6	...	International Development Association
France	2	2	2	2	2	2	1	0	...	France
Japan	...	4	4	4	3	2	2	2	...	Japon
...	...	...	...	...	...	...	...	...	...	...

SAO TOMÉ-ET-PRINCIPE

SOURCES AND NOTES - SOURCES ET NOTES

External trade - Total exports, fob: UNCTAD

External trade - Total import, cif: UNCTAD

ODA: OECD

Monetary statistics: IMF

National Accounts: 2013-2014:Provisional; 2015- 2016:Estimates

Poverty: World Bank

Commerce exterieur - Exportation, fab: CNUCED

Commerce exterieur - Imporations, caf: CNUCED

APD: OCDE

Statistiques monétaires: FMI

Comptes nationaux: 2013-2014:Provisoires;2015-2016:Estimations

Pauvreté: Banque mondiale

AREA (km2)		196 710		**SUPERFICIE (KM2)**
CAPITAL CITY	Dakar		Dakar	**CAPITALE**
CURRENCY	CFA Franc		Franc CFA	**MONNAIE**

I SOCIAL AND DEMOGRAPHIC INDICATORS — INDICATEURS DEMOGRAPHIQUES ET SOCIAUX

Population	Year Année	Value Valeur	Charts Graphiques	Population
Population ('000)	2017	14 942.7		Population ('000)
Female (%)	2017	0.5		Féminine (%)
Urban (%)	2017	0.5		Urbaine (%)
Average annual growth rate	2017	-		Taux de croissance annuel
Active population ('000)	2015	4 402.8		Population active ('000)
Population by age group ('000)				Population par groupe d'âge ('000)
0-14 years	2017	6 371.4		0-14 ans
15-64 years	2017	7 952.2		15-64 ans
65+ years	2017	619.1		65+ ans
Economically active population in agriculture (%)	2017	100.2		Participation de la population active agricole (%)
Crude birth rate	2017	37.1		Taux brut de natalité
Crude death rate	2017	7.3		Taux brut de mortalité
Total fertility rate	2017	5.0		Indice synthétique de fécondité
Life expectancy at birth - Total (years)	2017	66.5		Espérance de vie à la naissance - Totale (années)
Dependency ratio - Total (%)	2017	87.9		Taux de dépendance - Total (%)
Health				**Santé**
Percentage of children under-five and underweight	2017	14.4		% d'enfants de moins de cinq ans avec insuffisance pondérale
Prevalence of undernourishment	2015	24.6		Prévalence de la malnutrition
Under five mortality rate (per 1 000 live births)	2017	56.0		Taux de mortalité de moins de 5 ans (les deux sexes, pour 1000)
Infant mortality rate (per 1 000 live births)	2017	42.0		Taux de mortalité infantile (les deux sexes) par 1000
Neonatal mortality rate (per 1 000 live births)	2017	28.0		Le taux de mortalité néonatale (pour 1000 naissances vivantes)
Percentage of children provided the vaccines :				Pourcentage d'enfants vaccinés :
BCG	2016	94.1		BCG
DPT3	2015	88.3		DTC3
Polio	2016	94.6		polio
Measles	2016	80.6		rougeole
Percentage of mothers provided at least one antenatal care (%)	2016	95.9		Pourcentage de mères ayant au moins reçu un soin prénatal (%)
Percentage of deliveries attended by skilled health personnel	2016	59.0		% d'accouchements assistés par un personnel de santé qualifié
Number of doctors (per 10,000 population)	2015	1 382.0		Nombre de médecins (pour 10.000 habitants)
Number of nurses (per 10,000 population)	2015	2 571.0		Nombre d'infirmiers (pour 10.000 habitants)
Hospital beds - Total (per 10,000 population)	2008	3.4		Nombre de lits d'hôpitaux - Total (pour 10 000)
Births registered (per 1,000)	2016	34.6		Naissances enregistrées (pour 1000)
Deaths registered (per 1,000)	2015	6.0		Décès enregistrés (pour 1000)
Budget allocation to health (%)	2013	7.6		Dépenses publiques consacrées à la santé (% du budget)
Education				**Education**
Enrolment in primary education (000)	2016	2 014.0		Scolarisation dans le primaire (000)
Female	2016	1 046.0		Féminine
Enrolment in secondary education (000)	2016	1 435.0		Scolarisation dans le secondaire (000)
Female	2016	726.0		Féminine
Enrolment in tertiary education (000)	2010	92.1		Scolarisation dans le tertiaire (000)
Female	2010	34.3		Féminine
Literacy rate	2011	52.1		Taux d'alphabétisation (deux sexes)
Male	2011	66.3		Masculin
Female	2011	40.4		Féminin
Pupil teacher ratio - primary	...	...		Ratio élève-enseignant
Budget allocation to education (%)	2010	20.7		Dépenses publiques consacrées à l'enseignement (% du budget)
Poverty				**Pauvreté**
GNI per capita, PPP (current int. $)	2016	2480.0		RNB par habitant, ($ PPA inter. courants)
Human Poverty Index (HPI-1) Value (%)	2007	41.6		Valeur de l'Indice de pauvreté (IPH-1) (%)
Population below Inter. poverty line ($2/day) (%)	2011	38.0		Population sous le seuil inter. de pauvreté (2$/Jour) (%)
Share of income held by richest 10%	2011	31.1		% de revenu des 10% plus riches
Share of income held by poorest 10%	2011	2.3		% de revenu des 10% plus pauvres
GINI index	2011	40.3		Indice de GINI

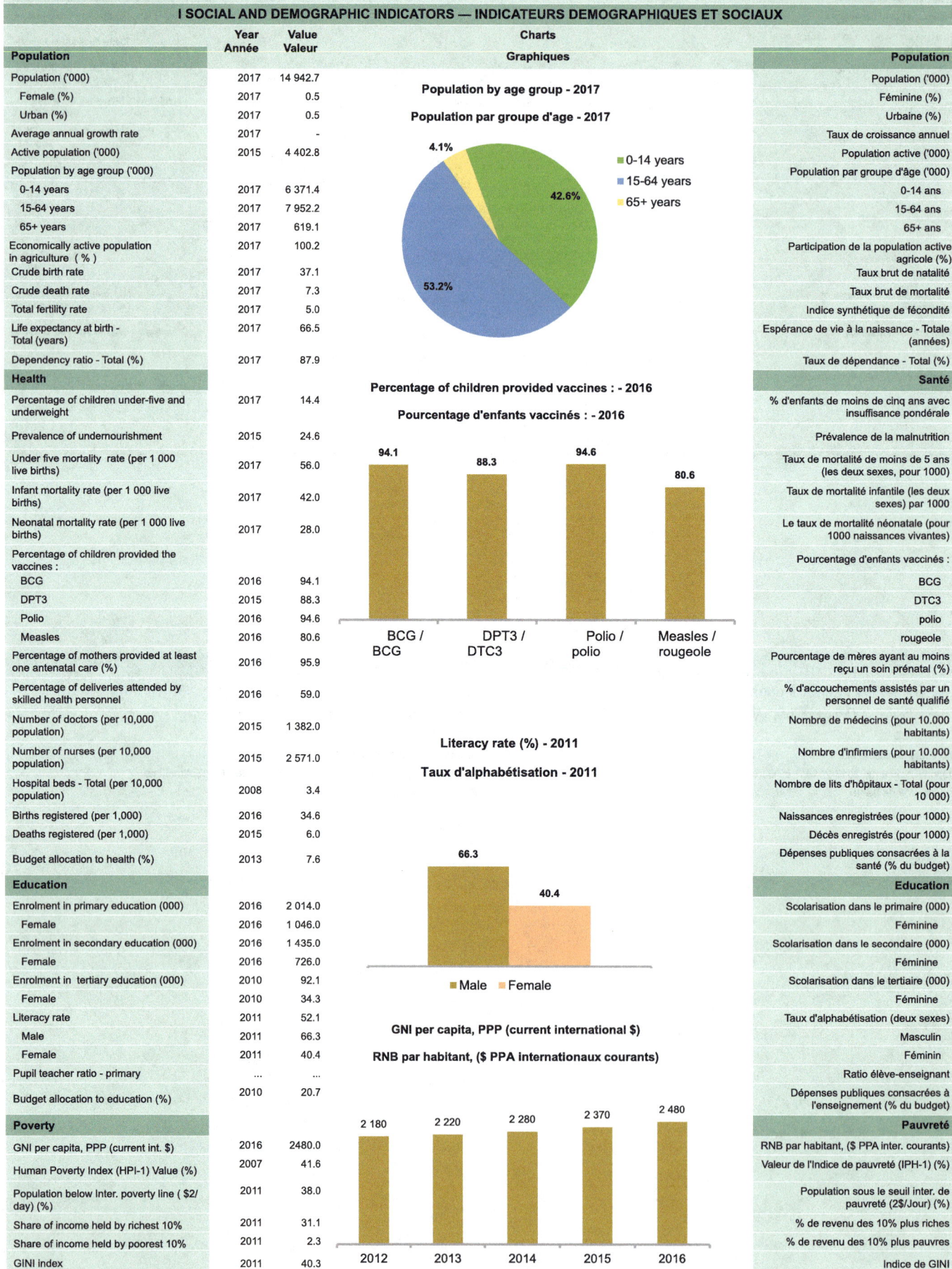

Population by age group - 2017
Population par groupe d'age - 2017
- 0-14 years — 42.6%
- 15-64 years — 53.2%
- 65+ years — 4.1%

Percentage of children provided vaccines : - 2016
Pourcentage d'enfants vaccinés : - 2016
- BCG / BCG: 94.1
- DPT3 / DTC3: 88.3
- Polio / polio: 94.6
- Measles / rougeole: 80.6

Literacy rate (%) - 2011
Taux d'alphabétisation - 2011
- Male: 66.3
- Female: 40.4

GNI per capita, PPP (current international $)
RNB par habitant, ($ PPA internationaux courants)
- 2012: 2 180
- 2013: 2 220
- 2014: 2 280
- 2015: 2 370
- 2016: 2 480

II NATIONAL ACCOUNTS — COMPTES NATIONAUX

	2009	2010	2011	2012	2013	2014	2015	2016	2017	
GROSS DOMESTIC PRODUCT BY KIND OF ECONOMIC ACTIVITY AT CURRENT PRICES *CFA FRANC (MILLIONS))*										**PRODUIT INTÉRIEUR BRUT PAR BRANCHE D'ACTIVITÉ ÉCONOMIQUE AUX PRIX COURANTS** *FRANC CFA (MILLIONS))*
Agriculture, hunting, forestry and Fishing	919 213	978 872	864 580	994 752	1 004 972	1 017 875	1 228 070	1 378 928	1 303 499	Agriculture, chasse sylviculture et Pêche
Mining and quarrying	101 667	117 822	141 523	193 062	147 019	151 103	143 745	170 467	157 106	Industries extractives
Manufacturing	737 062	767 722	854 308	876 657	867 733	877 841	927 449	1 035 132	981 290	Industries manufacturières
Electricity, gas & water	153 232	171 795	170 969	188 456	199 728	224 205	202 802	211 548	207 175	Electricité, gaz et eau
Construction	244 185	246 447	284 111	282 983	298 374	336 347	365 719	416 097	390 908	Bâtiments et travaux publics
Wholesale & retail trade, restaurants, hotels	1 054 130	1 105 001	1 196 428	1 276 176	1 295 577	1 319 478	1 369 218	1 479 935	1 559 654	Commerce de gros et de détail, restaurants et hôtels
Finance, insurance, real estate, etc.	805 098	850 248	921 798	980 045	1 006 814	1 031 144	1 077 518	1 161 815	987 557	Banques, assurances, affaires immobilières
Transport and communications	641 809	666 206	703 335	761 265	789 739	785 095	830 477	884 839	857 658	Transport(s) et communications
Public administration and defense	368 919	391 840	439 886	481 486	486 153	518 222	548 217	575 916	562 067	Administrations publiques et défense
Education	222 892	242 858	266 223	275 482	276 974	290 672	300 964	314 613	307 788	Education
Health And Social Work	78 811	81 566	87 787	90 311	91 991	88 972	91 582	98 193	94 887	Santé et Actions Sociales
Other services	110 266	111 896	116 835	123 871	127 651	128 857	130 838	135 988	130 445	Autres services
Less Imputed Service Charges	- 133 088	- 132 725	- 151 651	- 164 178	- 173 529	- 174 008	- 196 388	- 220 170	- 208 279	Moins Services d'intermédiation financière
Gross domestic product at factor cost / basic prices	5 304 195	5 599 548	5 896 132	6 360 368	6 419 194	6 595 803	7 020 212	7 643 301	7 331 756	Produit intérieur brut aux couts des facteurs / prix de base
Plus: Indirect Taxes / taxes on products, less subsidies	726 432	796 524	876 102	886 117	895 800	961 162	1 029 410	1 112 766	1 071 088	Plus taxes indirectes/impôts sur les produits, moins les subventions
EXPENDITURE ON GROSS DOMESTIC PRODUCT AT CURRENT PURCHASER'S VALUES *CFA FRANC (MILLIONS))*										**EMPLOI DU PRODUIT INTÉRIEUR BRUT AUX PRIX COURANTS D'ACQUISITION** *FRANC CFA (MILLIONS))*
Government final consumption	861 020	947 438	1 052 533	1 110 511	1 140 693	1 253 099	1 323 858	1 390 746	1 357 302	Consommation finale des administrations publiques
Private final consumption	4 857 682	5 024 020	5 234 696	5 551 164	5 686 508	5 878 299	6 178 386	6 547 719	6 363 053	Consommation finale privée
Gross fixed capital formation	1 386 191	1 421 476	1 660 016	1 709 649	1 860 776	1 935 863	2 078 350	2 264 292	2 171 321	Formation brute de capital fixe
Change in inventories	- 55 791	- 11 731	67 223	399 004	153 952	- 61 474	- 172 692	- 7 311	- 88 022	Variation des stocks
Exports of goods and services	1 471 790	1 592 644	1 787 320	2 025 435	2 079 096	2 124 433	2 353 341	2 516 685	2 433 033	Exportations de biens et services
Less imports of goods and services	2 490 265	2 577 776	3 029 554	3 549 278	3 606 030	3 573 257	3 711 621	3 956 065	3 833 843	Moins importations de biens et services
GDP at purchasers' values	6 030 626	6 396 072	6 772 234	7 246 485	7 314 994	7 556 965	8 049 622	8 756 067	8 402 844	PIB aux prix d'acquisition
GROSS DOMESTIC PRODUCT BY KIND OF ECONOMIC ACTIVITY AT CONSTANT PRICES *ANNUAL GROWTH RATES (%)*										**PRODUIT INTÉRIEUR BRUT PAR BRANCHE D'ACTIVITÉ ECONOMIQUE AUX PRIX CONSTANTS** *TAUX DE CROISSANCE ANNUEL (%)*
Agriculture, hunting, forestry and Fishing	13.0	5.8	- 14.8	8.9	1.8	2.4	18.2	9.0	1.8	Agriculture, chasse sylviculture et Pêche
Mining and quarrying	51.2	6.5	8.7	8.0	- 13.3	6.3	-	14.0	4.3	Industries extractives
Manufacturing	5.4	2.6	7.4	3.2	2.9	2.0	8.0	8.4	5.1	Industries manufacturières
Electricity, gas & water	- 4.6	7.5	- 1.7	12.1	5.1	9.7	6.2	6.9	6.7	Electricité, gaz et eau
Construction	- 4.5	4.7	7.3	- 1.0	11.7	11.3	7.0	11.0	3.8	Bâtiments et travaux publics
Wholesale & retail trade, restaurants, hotels	2.2	2.0	2.8	3.8	5.5	5.1	3.7	5.0	9.4	Commerce de gros et de détail, restaurants et hôtels
Finance, insurance, real estate, etc.	- 0.7	5.3	6.2	7.0	3.2	4.4	5.2	7.2	6.8	Banques, assurances, affaires immobilières
Transport and communications	1.4	7.1	2.8	6.3	7.3	2.0	4.9	5.9	7.9	Transport(s) et communications
Public administration and defense	1.0	2.4	5.6	3.4	2.2	4.1	4.6	3.5	9.6	Administrations publiques et défense
Education	1.6	1.8	5.1	2.6	1.1	4.5	3.0	3.5	10.2	Education
Health And Social Work	1.3	3.3	4.3	1.2	1.5	3.4	2.7	4.1	9.9	Santé et Actions Sociales
Other services	0.6	1.2	1.6	5.0	2.6	1.6	1.4	2.4	6.7	Autres services
Less Imputed Service Charges	- 0.3	1.5	15.4	11.6	4.2	0.2	12.7	11.0	2.1	Moins Services d'intermédiation financière
Gross domestic product at factor cost / basic prices	3.4	4.3	1.2	5.0	4.1	4.1	6.6	6.7	6.7	Produit intérieur brut aux couts des facteurs / prix de base
Plus: Indirect Taxes / taxes on products, less subsidies	- 4.9	3.1	6.3	- 0.2	- 1.1	6.0	5.4	6.5	7.3	Plus taxes indirectes/impôts sur les produits, moins les subventions
Gross domestic product at market prices	2.4	4.2	1.8	4.4	3.5	4.3	6.5	6.6	6.8	Produit intérieur brut aux prix du marché
EXPENDITURE ON GROSS DOMESTIC PRODUCT AT CONSTANT PURCHASERS' VALUES *ANNUAL GROWTH RATES (%)*										**EMPLOIS DU PRODUIT INTÉRIEUR BRUT AUX PRIX CONSTANTS D'ACQUISITION** *TAUX DE CROISSANCE ANNUEL (%)*
Government final consumption	1.7	2.6	5.5	2.8	1.6	3.9	4.6	3.5	9.6	Consommation finale des administrations publiques
Private final consumption	3.9	2.1	1.3	3.1	2.3	5.2	5.0	4.7	8.6	Consommation finale privée
Gross fixed capital formation	- 4.3	1.5	9.0	2.9	17.8	7.5	6.3	7.7	6.1	Formation brute de capital fixe
Exports of goods and services	6.2	5.7	7.7	9.1	7.8	6.8	12.7	8.4	3.7	Exportations de biens et services
Less imports of goods and services	- 3.9	- 5.0	8.7	11.0	11.0	4.4	12.0	7.9	4.2	Moins importations de biens et services

III INFLATION

	2009	2010	2011	2012	2013	2014	2015	2016	2017	
Annual growth rates (%)										**Taux de croissance annuel (%)**
All item	- 2.2	1.2	3.4	1.4	0.7	- 1.1	0.1	0.8	1.3	Ensemble
of which:										dont:
Food and non-alcoholic beverages	- 3.2	4.0	6.7	2.5	1.3	- 1.9	1.8	3.3	3.7	Alimentation et boissons non alcoolisés
Alcoholic beverages, tobacco and narcotics	- 0.7	4.3	- 1.0	- 2.2	11.7	-	- 0.5	- 0.1	- 0.2	Boissons alcoolisées et tabacs
Clothing and footwear	- 1.8	0.3	- 1.1	- 0.2	- 0.7	- 0.4	0.1	- 0.3	0.6	Habillement et chaussures
Housing, water, electricity, gas and other fuels	- 0.1	2.1	3.1	0.2	- 0.3	- 1.1	- 6.3	- 1.8	- 1.4	Logement, eau, électricité, gaz et autres combustibles
Furnishings, household equipment and routine household maintenance	1.2	- 1.2	0.4	1.1	- 0.3	0.5	- 0.1	0.1	0.1	Meubles, articles de ménage et entretien courant
Health	1.5	1.0	0.8	1.0	3.0	1.0	0.3	0.5	0.2	Santé
Transport	- 4.8	2.9	5.5	1.8	0.4	1.7	- 3.6	- 1.5	-	Transport
Communication	- 15.0	- 7.9	0.2	0.4	- 5.3	3.8	- 0.1	0.8	- 2.2	Communication
Recreation and culture	1.6	- 3.8	0.3	0.5	- 1.4	1.0	1.9	1.2	1.2	Loisirs et culture
Education	0.8	1.1	2.6	2.7	2.6	0.8	0.5	0.7	1.1	Enseignement
Restaurants and hotels	0.9	0.3	1.2	2.3	6.6	0.6	- 0.1	- 0.2	1.2	Restaurants et hôtels
Miscellaneous goods and services	- 1.9	- 2.8	2.8	0.9	0.1	- 0.2	- 1.1	- 1.4	0.1	Biens et Services divers

SÉNÉGAL

IV AGRICULTURAL PRODUCTION - PRODUCTION AGRICOLE

TONNES (THOUSAND)	2009	2010	2011	2012	2013	2014	2015	2016	2017	Tonnes (milliers)
Sugar cane	836	850	880	900	841	1 228	...	...	...	Canne à sucre
Groundnuts, with shell	1 033	1 287	528	673	677	669	1 050	945	...	Arachides (en coques)
Millet	810	813	481	662	515	409	750	699	...	Millet
Rice, paddy	502	604	406	631	436	559	906	951	...	Riz, Paddy
Maize	160	160	190	210	226	179	304	400	...	Maïs

V MINING PRODUCTION - PRODUCTION MINIERE

	2009	2010	2011	2012	2013	2014	2015	2016	2017	
Natural phosphates, P2O5 content - Production, metric tons (thousands)	949	1 131	1 437	1 416	882	821	1 063	1 609	1 385	Phosphates naturels, teneur en P2O5 - Production, tonnes métriques (milliers)
Salt and pure sodium chloride - Production (metric tons)	222 298	231 595	258 250	237 400	241 311	245 192	265 700	263 200	265 000	Sel et chlorure de sodium pur - Production (tonnes métriques)
	...	...	...	...	...	...	...	...	...	

VI ENERGY - ENERGIE

	2009	2010	2011	2012	2013	2014	2015	2016	2017	
Total electricity generation (GWh)	2 811	3 032	2 965	2 932	3 497	3 684	3 760	3 842	...	Production électrique totale (GWh)
of which										dont
Production of electricity from fossil fuels (GWh)	2 519	2 724	2 651	2 586	3 126	3 273	3 345	3 420	...	Production d'électricité à partir de combustibles fossiles (GWh)
Production of hydro electricity (GWh)	239	253	257	290	308	323	324	324	...	Production d'électricité d'origine hydraulique (GWh)
Production of electricity from solar, wind, tide, wave and other sources (GWh)	3	3	3	4	4	26	27	28	...	Production d'électricité d'origine solaire, éolienne, marée motrice et autres (GWh)

VII TOURISM AND INFRASTRUCTURE - TOURISME ET INFRASTUCTURE

	2009	2010	2011	2012	2013	2014	2015	2016	2017	
VII-1 Tourism										**VII-1 Tourisme**
International tourist arrivals (thousands)	810	900	968	962	1 063	963	1 007	1 071	1 074	Arrivées de touristes internationaux (milliers)
Rooms in hotels and similar establishments (thousands)	...	...	...	17	17	17	18	...	...	Chambres d'hôtels et établissements assimilés (milliers)
Overnight stays (thousands)	1 318	1 511	1 674	1 713	1 947	1 813	1 532	1 722	1 790	Nuitées (milliers)
Tourism receipts (US$ thousand)	430 500	432 300	439 200	378 200	410 200	452 373	408 221	416 682	482 000	Recettes touristiques (milliers de $ EU)
Total contribution to GDP (%)	11.4	11.0	11.3	10.9	10.8	10.8	10.4	10.5	10.4	Contribution totale au PIB (%)
Total contribution to Employment (%)	9.7	9.4	9.6	9.2	9.4	9.5	9.1	9.2	9.1	Contribution totale à l'emploi (%)
VII-2 Infrastructure										**VII-2 Infrastructure**
Paved road (% of total)	32.0	35.5	...	...	...	...	35.3	...	...	Routes asphaltées (% du total)
Total network (Railways-km)	...	...	...	...	...	...	...	...	...	Réseau total voies ferrées-Km
Main telephone lines (per 100 inhabitants)	2.2	2.6	2.6	2.5	2.4	2.1	2.0	1.9	...	Lignes téléphoniques fixes (pour 100 habitants)
Mobile cellular subscribers (per 100 inhabitants)	54.8	64.4	70.2	83.6	92.9	98.8	99.9	98.7	...	Abonnés aux téléphones mobiles (pour 100 habitants)
Internet users per 100 inhabitants	7.5	8.0	9.8	10.8	13.1	17.7	21.7	25.7	...	Utilisateurs Internet par 100 Habitants
Fixed (wired)-broadband subscriptions per 100 inhabitants	...	0.6	0.7	0.7	0.8	0.7	0.7	0.6	...	Abonnements à l'Internet fixe (filaire) à large bande pour 100 habitants, par débit

VIII EXTERNAL TRADE - COMMERCE EXTERIEUR

US$ (MILLIONS) EXPORTS, FOB	2009	2010	2011	2012	2013	2014	2015	2016	2017	$ E.U (MILLIONS) EXPORTATIONS, FÀB
Exports - Total	2 017	2 088	2 542	2 532	2 661	2 750	2 612	2 640	...	Exportations - Total
Exports to Africa	884	1 059	1 121	1 146	1 255	1 285	1 237	1 162	...	Exportations vers l'Afrique
Main products										**Principaux produits**
Fish, fresh (live or dead), chilled or frozen	193	182	228	226	265	286	259	276		Poissons frais (vivants ou morts), réfrigérés ou congelés
Gold, non-monetary (excluding gold ores and concentrates)	125	156	171	408	364	341	277	349		Or, non monétaire (à l'exclusion des minerais d'or et des concentrés)
Inorganic chemical elements, oxides & halogen salts	197	179	306	190	129	125	143	207		Eléments chimiques inorganiques, oxydes et sels halogénés
Lime, cement, fabrica. constr. mat. (excludingglass, clay)	123	182	210	180	193	223	178	192		Chaux, ciment, tissu. constr. tapis. (sauf verre, argile)
Petroleum oils or bituminous minerals > 70 % oil	472	521	513	493	543	549	538	392		Huiles de pétrole ou de minéraux bitumineux> 70% d'huile
Main destinations										**Principales destinations**
Côte d'Ivoire	61	52	59	67	91	89	112	116	...	Côte d'Ivoire
India	212	204	348	218	151	134	170	249	...	Inde
Mali	420	586	551	576	603	667	476	551	...	Mali
Switzerland	69	73	83	308	265	257	209	252	...	Suisse
United Arab Emirates	52	82	97	114	119	138	104	106	...	Emirates Arabes
IMPORTS, CIF										
Imports - Total	4 713	4 782	5 909	6 434	6 552	6 503	5 595	5 478	...	Importations - Total (millions)
Imports from Africa	861	818	1 011	1 301	1 191	992	864	869	...	Importations en provenance de l'Afrique
Main products										**Principaux produits**
Edible products and preparations, n.e.s.	72	81	121	138	172	191	131	146		Produits et préparations comestibles, n.d.a.
Petroleum oils or bituminous minerals > 70 % oil	606	885	1 159	1 396	1 293	1 191	588	527		Huiles de pétrole ou de minéraux bitumineux> 70% d'huile
Petroleum oils, oils from bitumin. materials, crude	400	398	503	685	659	530	442	360		Huiles de pétrole, huiles de bitume. matériaux bruts
Rice	316	259	342	390	369	348	314	258		Riz
Telecommunication equipment, n.e.s.; & parts, n.e.s.	119	87	106	98	142	150	150	157		Matériel de télécommunication, n.e.s.; & parties, n.e.s
Main origin										**Principales provenances**
China	389	409	455	493	648	897	1 108	1 092	...	Chine
France	874	848	955	850	868	871	722	668	...	France
India	130	150	171	379	376	358	344	394	...	Inde
Netherlands	201	239	384	227	585	554	249	247	...	Pays-Bas
Nigeria	427	427	507	745	665	532	445	366	...	Nigéria

	2009	2010	2011	2012	2013	2014	2015	2016	2017	
IX-1 MONETARY STATISTICS *CFA FRANC (MILLIONS)*										**IX-1 STATISTIQUES MONÉTAIRES** *FRANC CFA (MILLIONS)*
Money supply (M1)	2 225 998	2 540 249	2 711 427	2 894 664	3 127 078	3 484 519	3 953 097	4 427 584	4 868 708	Masse monétaire (M1)
Quasi-money	867 492	991 161	1 062 657	1 118 402	1 139 869	1 065 430	1 211 457	1 299 276	1 479 516	Quasi-monnaie
of which demand deposit	...	...	...	...	...	...	...	...	...	dont Monnaie scripturale
Net foreign assets	896 442	1 028 641	903 926	928 052	910 169	837 130	1 118 860	1 165 087	1 427 742	Avoirs extérieurs nets
Domestic credit	1 606 811	1 847 310	2 122 292	2 241 881	2 565 366	2 805 492	3 163 152	3 677 975	4 182 692	Crédit intérieur
of which claims on private sector	114 819	200 322	169 291	101 109	151 104	41 069	202 513	434 072	402 103	dont créances sur le secteur privé
of which claims on government sector, net	1 491 992	1 646 988	1 953 001	2 140 772	2 414 262	2 512 019	2 661 625	2 897 321	3 397 622	dont créances nettes sur le gouvernement
International reserves (millions US$)	2 123	2 048	1 946	2 082	2 253	2 039	2 139	2 228	2 366	Réserves internationales (millions $EU)
Average exchange rate (National currency per US$)	472	495	472	511	494	494	591	593	582	Taux de change (moyen) (monnaie nationale par $ EU)
IX-2 PUBLIC FINANCE *CFA FRANC (MILLIONS)*										**IX-2 FINANCES PUBLIQUES** *FRANC CFA (MILLIONS)*
Total Revenues and Grants	1 304 700	1 398 330	1 525 400	1 670 300	1 659 580	1 877 500	2 026 030	2 335 000	2 384 000	Recettes totales et dons
Direct taxes (on income, profits)	285 076	338 983	355 600	367 348	368 828	406 000	435 500	513 000	556 000	Taxes directes
Domestic indirect taxes revenues	558 717	610 569	658 600	693 106	697 298	780 000	855 500	960 000	978 000	Taxes Indirectes
Trade taxes	163 808	181 591	203 800	217 932	221 761	219 000	228 000	235 000	260 000	Taxes sur le commerce extérieur
Other taxes	76 999	63 597	88 900	94 614	88 953	78 000	78 000	81 000	192 000	Autres taxes
Other revenues	37 300	41 740	68 500	91 000	95 200	141 000	197 000	302 000	148 000	Autres recettes
Grants	182 800	161 850	150 000	206 300	187 540	253 500	232 030	244 000	250 000	Dons
Total Expenditures and Net Lending	1 607 970	1 728 110	1 980 310	2 090 110	2 059 251	2 256 700	2 413 506	2 704 225	2 559 400	Dépenses totales et prêts nets
Current expenditure	952 530	947 440	1 129 400	1 191 000	1 160 580	1 230 600	1 344 565	1 424 825	1 310 000	Dépenses courantes
Wages and Salaries	364 350	392 340	427 500	461 500	464 700	490 000	526 100	572 000	584 000	Rémunérations et salaires
Other purchases of goods and services	339 540	314 900	366 900	374 500	359 640	360 700	384 285	322 000	343 000	Achat de biens et services
Other current expenditure	...	...	...	...	...	...	...	...	...	Autres dépenses courantes
Current transfers	248 640	240 200	335 000	355 000	336 240	379 900	434 180	530 825	383 000	Transferts courants
Interest payments	45 340	60 100	66 110	66 110	102 471	127 000	159 740	188 000	204 000	Intérêts
Capital expenditure	606 900	722 670	756 400	813 700	801 300	899 100	909 200	1 091 400	1 045 400	Dépenses d'équipement
Net lending	3 200	- 2 100	28 400	19 300	- 5 100	...	...	...	...	Prêts nets
Fiscal balance	- 303 270	- 329 780	- 454 910	- 419 810	- 399 671	- 379 200	- 387 476	- 369 225	- 175 400	Solde global y compris les dons
IX-3 BALANCE OF PAYMENTS *CFA FRANC (MILLIONS)*										**IX-3 BALANCE DES PAIEMENTS** *FRANC CFA (MILLIONS)*
Trade balance	- 957 702	- 949 997	-1 183 579	-1 468 911	-1 471 022	-1 383 184	-1 288 110	-1 259 177	-1 435 500	Balance commerciale
Services Balance	- 60 773	- 34 990	- 58 600	- 55 000	- 55 913	- 65 600	- 70 100	- 70 500	- 80 900	Balance des services
Net primary income	- 80 149	- 74 290	- 132 794	- 153 840	- 159 476	- 186 428	- 242 878	- 292 010	- 30 900	Revenus primaires nets
Compensation of employees	38 421	38 075	39 338	46 976	51 034	51 225	52 271	53 337	...	Rémunération des salariés
Investment income	- 118 570	- 112 365	- 172 132	- 200 816	- 210 510	- 237 653	- 295 148	- 345 347	...	Revenus des investissements
Net secondary income	695 636	767 540	833 973	897 551	920 931	969 312	1 042 388	1 088 487	839 300	Revenus secondaires nets
Net official transfers	23 147	33 441	62 273	75 788	42 528	52 625	49 426	53 380	...	Transferts officiels nets
Workers' remittances	516 857	586 582	713 553	750 447	815 060	889 282	968 646	1 017 078	1 059 900	Envois de fonds des travailleurs
Other private transfers	155 632	147 513	58 147	71 316	63 343	27 405	24 316	18 029	...	Autres transferts privés
Current account balance	- 402 988	- 291 737	- 541 000	- 780 200	- 765 480	- 665 900	- 558 700	- 533 200	- 708 000	Solde du compte courant
Capital and financial account	400 219	409 840	482 204	722 613	733 359	880 686	713 570	473 278	974 000	Comptes de capital et financier
Capital account	144 050	149 510	119 404	202 813	181 512	217 486	208 070	210 078	221 200	Compte de capital
Financial account	256 169	260 330	362 800	519 800	551 847	663 200	505 500	263 200	752 800	Compte financier
Errors and omissions	2 769	- 2 100	3 746	4 053	5 666	4 914	30	22	...	Erreurs et omissions
Overall balance	...	116 003	- 55 050	- 53 534	- 26 455	219 700	154 900	- 59 900	266 000	Balance générale

SÉNÉGAL

X DEBT AND FINANCIAL FLOWS - DETTE ET FLUX FINANCIERS

	2009	2010	2011	2012	2013	2014	2015	2016	2017	
X-1 DEBT US $ (MILLIONS)										**X-1 DETTE EXTÉRIEURE** $ E.U (MILLIONS)
Total external debt	6 869	6 550	7 615	8 792	10 409	10 490	9 929	10 078	11 938	Dette extérieure totale
Private	...	...	...	...	...	...	...	...	...	Privée
Public	3 615	3 525	4 003	4 442	4 996	5 730	5 502	5 920	...	Publique
Total external debt service	193	207	548	315	387	496	538	677	...	Service de la dette extérieure
Present value of external debt	...	...	...	...	...	...	...	4 988	...	Valeur actuelle de la dette extérieure
Total government domestic debt, National currency (millions)	...	...	...	...	...	...	...	...	...	Dette publique intérieure
X-2 FINANCIAL FLOWS US $ (MILLIONS)										**X-2 FLUX FINANCIERS** $ E.U (MILLIONS)
Net Foreign Direct Investment Inflows	320	266	338	276	311	403	409	393	...	Investissements étranger direct (flux nets entrants)
Main origin of FDI inflows										**Principales origines de l'IDE entrant:**
Luxembourg	1	...	29	14	...	...	...	...	...	Luxembourg
Italy	...	...	...	-	...	...	...	...	...	Italie
Turkey	...	6	...	6	...	...	...	...	...	Turquie
Germany	- 4	4	1	3	...	...	...	...	...	Allemagne
...	...	...	...	...	...	...	...	...	...	...
African countries	...	...	309	...	...	...	...	...	...	Pays africains
Net total official development assistance	1 018	936	1 055	1 076	994	1 109	879	736	...	Aide publique au développement (nette totale)
Main origin of net ODA										**Principales origines de l'APD nette**
France	141	157	177	304	190	294	110	87	...	France
International Development Association [IDA]	134	110	172	137	131	137	161	124	...	International Development Association
United States	68	102	114	123	203	271	268	125	...	États-Unis
...	...	...	...	...	...	...	...	...	...	...
Japan	47	55	83	81	42	45	38	28	...	Japon

SENEGAL

SOURCES AND NOTES - SOURCES ET NOTES

External trade - Total exports, fob: UNCTAD

External trade - Total import, cif: UNCTAD

ODA: OECD

Monetary statistics: IMF

National Accounts: 2014: Semi-Final 2015:Provional 2016-2017:Projection

Poverty: World Bank

Commerce exterieur - Exportation, fab: CNUCED

Commerce exterieur - Imporations, caf: CNUCED

APD: OCDE

Statistiques monétaires: FMI

Comptes nationaux: 2014: Semi-Définitive 2015:Provisoire 2016-2017:Projection

Pauvreté: Banque mondiale

AREA (km2)		460	**SUPERFICIE (KM2)**
CAPITAL CITY	Victoria	Victoria	**CAPITALE**
CURRENCY	Seychelles Rupee	Roupie seychelloise	**MONNAIE**

I SOCIAL AND DEMOGRAPHIC INDICATORS — INDICATEURS DEMOGRAPHIQUES ET SOCIAUX

Population	Year Année	Value Valeur	Charts Graphiques	Population
Population ('000)	2017	100.0		Population ('000)
Female (%)	2017	50.0		Féminine (%)
Urban (%)	2015	52.4		Urbaine (%)
Average annual growth rate	2007	1.2		Taux de croissance annuel
Active population ('000)	2017	48.8		Population active ('000)
Population by age group ('000)				Population par groupe d'âge ('000)
0-14 years	2017	19.0		0-14 ans
15-64 years	2017	67.0		15-64 ans
65+ years	2017	9.0		65+ ans
Economically active population in agriculture (%)	...	...		Participation de la population active agricole (%)
Crude birth rate	2017	17.2		Taux brut de natalité
Crude death rate	2017	7.8		Taux brut de mortalité
Total fertility rate	2017	3.6		Indice synthétique de fécondité
Life expectancy at birth - Total (years)	2017	74.3		Espérance de vie à la naissance - Totale (années)
Dependency ratio - Total (%)	2017	41.8		Taux de dépendance - Total (%)
Health				**Santé**
Percentage of children under-five and underweight	...	...		% d'enfants de moins de cinq ans avec insuffisance pondérale
Prevalence of undernourishment	...	...		Prévalence de la malnutrition
Under five mortality rate (per 1 000 live births)	2016	14.6		Taux de mortalité de moins de 5 ans (les deux sexes, pour 1000)
Infant mortality rate (per 1 000 live births)	2017	10.9		Taux de mortalité infantile (les deux sexes) par 1000
Neonatal mortality rate (per 1 000 live births)	2016	9.1		Le taux de mortalité néonatale (pour 1000 naissances vivantes)
Percentage of children provided the vaccines :				Pourcentage d'enfants vaccinés :
BCG	2017	99.0		BCG
DPT3	2017	99.0		DTC3
Polio	2011	99.0		polio
Measles	2017	99.0		rougeole
Percentage of mothers provided at least one antenatal care (%)	2009	99.8		Pourcentage de mères ayant au moins reçu un soin prénatal (%)
Percentage of deliveries attended by skilled health personnel	...	...		% d'accouchements assistés par un personnel de santé qualifié
Number of doctors (per 10,000 population)	2016	178.0		Nombre de médecins (pour 10.000 habitants)
Number of nurses (per 10,000 population)	2016	2 879.0		Nombre d'infirmiers (pour 10.000 habitants)
Hospital beds - Total (per 10,000 population)	2016	32.0		Nombre de lits d'hôpitaux - Total (pour 10 000)
Births registered (per 1,000)	2017	16.5		Naissances enregistrées (pour 1000)
Deaths registered (per 1,000)	2017	7.8		Décès enregistrés (pour 1000)
Budget allocation to health (%)	2014	3.4		Dépenses publiques consacrées à la santé (% du budget)
Education				**Education**
Enrolment in primary education (000)	2016	9.0		Scolarisation dans le primaire (000)
Female	2016	4.0		Féminine
Enrolment in secondary education (000)	2016	7.0		Scolarisation dans le secondaire (000)
Female	2016	4.0		Féminine
Enrolment in tertiary education (000)	2016	3.0		Scolarisation dans le tertiaire (000)
Female	...	...		Féminine
Literacy rate	2012	91.8		Taux d'alphabétisation (deux sexes)
Male	2012	91.4		Masculin
Female	2012	92.3		Féminin
Pupil teacher ratio - primary	...	...		Ratio élève-enseignant
Budget allocation to education (%)	2011	10.4		Dépenses publiques consacrées à l'enseignement (% du budget)
Poverty				**Pauvreté**
GNI per capita, PPP (current int. $)	2016	28380.0		RNB par habitant, ($ PPA inter. courants)
Human Poverty Index (HPI-1) Value (%)	...	...		Valeur de l'Indice de pauvreté (IPH-1) (%)
Population below Inter. poverty line ($2/day) (%)	2006	0.4		Population sous le seuil inter. de pauvreté (2$/Jour) (%)
Share of income held by richest 10%	2006	33.8		% de revenu des 10% plus riches
Share of income held by poorest 10%	2006	2.4		% de revenu des 10% plus pauvres
GINI index	2006	42.8		Indice de GINI

Population by age group - 2017
Population par groupe d'age - 2017

Pie chart: 0-14 years 20.0%; 15-64 years 70.5%; 65+ years 9.5%

Percentage of children provided vaccines : - 2017
Pourcentage d'enfants vaccinés : - 2017

Bar chart: BCG / BCG 99.0; DPT3 / DTC3 99.0; Polio / polio (2011) 99.0; Measles / rougeole 99.0

Literacy rate (%) - 2012
Taux d'alphabétisation - 2012

Bar chart: Male 91.4; Female 92.3

GNI per capita, PPP (current international $)
RNB par habitant, ($ PPA internationaux courants)

Bar chart: 2012 22 930; 2013 24 350; 2014 24 950; 2015 25 670; 2016 28 380

II NATIONAL ACCOUNTS — COMPTES NATIONAUX

	2009	2010	2011	2012	2013	2014	2015	2016	2017	
GROSS DOMESTIC PRODUCT BY KIND OF ECONOMIC ACTIVITY AT CURRENT PRICES *SEYCHELLES RUPEE (MILLIONS)*										**PRODUIT INTÉRIEUR BRUT PAR BRANCHE D'ACTIVITÉ ÉCONOMIQUE AUX PRIX COURANTS** *ROUPIE SEYCHELLOISE (MILLIONS)*
Agriculture, hunting , forestry and Fishing	260	265	286	297	427	406	375	382	398	Agriculture, chasse sylviculture et Pêche
Mining and quarrying	...	...	...	...	...	...	...	...	...	Industries extractives
Manufacturing	902	940	970	1 224	1 156	1 113	1 097	1 093	1 229	Industries manufacturières
Electricity, gas & water	147	167	57	210	409	424	495	514	579	Electricité, gaz et eau
Construction	568	534	788	634	457	544	575	551	508	Bâtiments et travaux publics
Wholesale & retail trade, restaurants, hotels	2 955	2 788	2 422	2 798	3 322	3 380	3 560	3 713	3 752	Commerce de gros et de détail, restaurants et hôtels
Finance, insurance, real estate, etc.	2 619	2 798	3 001	3 614	3 889	3 994	4 286	4 505	4 698	Banques, assurances, affaires immobilières
Transport and communications	1 453	1 269	1 619	1 787	2 131	2 492	2 968	3 076	3 429	Transport(s) et communications
Public administration and defense	559	604	731	852	1 013	1 100	1 234	1 279	1 325	Administrations publiques et défense
Education	243	261	305	342	361	369	392	405	409	Education
Health And Social Work	161	170	208	237	272	296	310	318	321	Santé et Actions Sociales
Other services	121	126	144	176	179	203	190	197	196	Autres services
Less Imputed Service Charges	- 225	- 182	- 205	- 275	- 224	- 208	- 283	- 334	- 340	Moins Services d'intermédiation financière
Gross domestic product at factor cost / basic prices	9 765	9 740	10 327	11 896	13 392	14 111	15 200	15 700	16 503	Produit intérieur brut aux couts des facteurs / prix de base
Plus: Indirect Taxes / taxes on products, less subsidies	1 768	1 965	2 283	2 623	2 623	3 008	3 140	3 314	3 787	Plus taxes indirectes/impôts sur les produits, moins les subventions
EXPENDITURE ON GROSS DOMESTIC PRODUCT AT CURRENT PURCHASER'S VALUES *SEYCHELLES RUPEE (MILLIONS)*										**EMPLOI DU PRODUIT INTÉRIEUR BRUT AUX PRIX COURANTS D'ACQUISITION** *ROUPIE SEYCHELLOISE (MILLIONS)*
Government final consumption	3 308	3 183	3 496	4 045	2 918	3 382	3 728	3 833	4 257	Consommation finale des administrations publiques
Private final consumption	7 221	6 908	7 328	7 981	8 837	9 845	9 538	10 608	11 820	Consommation finale privée
Gross fixed capital formation	2 934	4 142	4 569	5 812	5 495	6 739	6 759	6 922	6 725	Formation brute de capital fixe
Change in inventories	...	...	...	...	...	...	...	...	...	Variation des stocks
Exports of goods and services	11 566	10 146	11 730	12 776	14 539	15 033	14 755	15 313	18 442	Exportations de biens et services
Less imports of goods and services	13 495	12 673	14 514	16 095	15 776	17 879	16 441	17 663	20 955	Moins importations de biens et services
GDP at purchasers' values	11 533	11 705	12 609	14 519	16 015	17 119	18 340	19 014	20 290	PIB aux prix d'acquisition
GROSS DOMESTIC PRODUCT BY KIND OF ECONOMIC ACTIVITY AT CONSTANT PRICES *ANNUAL GROWTH RATES (%)*										**PRODUIT INTÉRIEUR BRUT PAR BRANCHE D'ACTIVITÉ ECONOMIQUE AUX PRIX CONSTANTS** *TAUX DE CROISSANCE ANNUEL (%)*
Agriculture, hunting , forestry and Fishing	- 16.5	- 6.2	5.0	0.4	22.5	- 7.1	- 4.0	0.9	- 8.2	Agriculture, chasse sylviculture et Pêche
Mining and quarrying	...	...	...	...	...	...	...	...	...	Industries extractives
Manufacturing	- 11.3	8.4	13.0	17.7	- 13.1	- 6.3	7.4	1.7	7.9	Industries manufacturières
Electricity, gas & water	- 2.3	12.9	0.3	- 10.3	- 14.0	2.0	16.1	- 14.2	- 6.0	Electricité, gaz et eau
Construction	- 4.9	- 5.3	22.1	- 28.0	- 28.8	14.1	3.5	- 2.2	0.7	Bâtiments et travaux publics
Wholesale & retail trade, restaurants, hotels	3.3	12.8	8.2	4.2	14.1	0.4	4.2	3.6	4.9	Commerce de gros et de détail, restaurants et hôtels
Finance, insurance, real estate, etc.	9.2	8.2	5.9	7.9	6.5	1.3	5.6	6.0	5.3	Banques, assurances, affaires immobilières
Transport and communications	- 1.9	3.5	- 7.2	4.7	21.9	16.9	6.5	8.9	12.3	Transport(s) et communications
Public administration and defense	- 12.6	- 15.2	- 3.4	8.9	13.9	7.0	4.7	2.2	0.2	Administrations publiques et défense
Education	2.4	5.1	8.0	- 2.9	- 2.1	2.3	- 1.6	2.9	5.6	Education
Health And Social Work	- 9.1	5.0	- 4.2	7.8	10.2	6.2	3.0	1.6	1.3	Santé et Actions Sociales
Other services	9.7	5.5	14.1	14.4	- 2.1	7.5	- 9.5	5.6	- 1.3	Autres services
Less Imputed Service Charges	- 0.2	- 13.0	- 12.3	24.9	0.6	- 9.7	10.7	8.1	4.4	Moins Services d'intermédiation financière
Gross domestic product at factor cost / basic prices	- 0.7	5.2	5.2	3.7	7.2	4.4	4.7	4.4	5.8	Produit intérieur brut aux couts des facteurs / prix de base
Plus: Indirect Taxes / taxes on products, less subsidies	- 3.6	10.3	6.6	3.7	- 0.6	5.0	6.4	5.0	9.2	Plus taxes indirectes/impôts sur les produits, moins les subventions
Gross domestic product at market prices	- 1.1	5.9	5.4	3.7	6.0	4.5	4.9	4.5	6.3	Produit intérieur brut aux prix du marché
EXPENDITURE ON GROSS DOMESTIC PRODUCT AT CONSTANT PURCHASERS' VALUES *ANNUAL GROWTH RATES (%)*										**EMPLOIS DU PRODUIT INTÉRIEUR BRUT AUX PRIX CONSTANTS D'ACQUISITION** *TAUX DE CROISSANCE ANNUEL (%)*
Government final consumption	0.8	- 1.6	10.5	6.1	6.0	4.5	5.0	1.5	...	Consommation finale des administrations publiques
Private final consumption	- 20.1	26.5	17.6	2.8	6.0	4.5	5.0	5.5	...	Consommation finale privée
Gross fixed capital formation	- 5.1	47.8	0.6	11.4	6.0	4.5	5.0	1.5	...	Formation brute de capital fixe
Exports of goods and services	14.3	- 15.5	- 5.2	0.6	6.0	4.5	5.0	1.5	...	Exportations de biens et services
Less imports of goods and services	- 2.8	4.3	6.2	3.6	6.0	4.5	5.0	1.5	...	Moins importations de biens et services

III INFLATION

	2009	2010	2011	2012	2013	2014	2015	2016	2017	
Annual growth rates (%)										**Taux de croissance annuel (%)**
All item	31.8	- 2.4	2.6	7.1	4.3	1.4	4.0	- 1.0	2.9	Ensemble
of which:										dont:
Food and non-alcoholic beverages	40.8	- 3.8	4.2	6.0	6.8	0.5	0.5	-	0.3	Alimentation et boissons non alcoolisés
Alcoholic beverages, tobacco and narcotics	44.5	- 3.2	0.2	4.1	3.9	0.2	12.8	1.9	5.4	Boissons alcoolisées et tabacs
Clothing and footwear	...	29.9	3.7	6.2	6.4	9.6	1.0	2.2	- 1.7	Habillement et chaussures
Housing, water, electricity, gas and other fuels	12.0	3.4	1.0	14.4	2.4	1.1	- 1.9	- 8.3	12.1	Logement, eau, électricité, gaz et autres combustibles
Furnishings, household equipment and routine household maintenance	25.1	- 0.2	1.1	3.7	6.1	1.5	4.3	2.3	-	Meubles, articles de ménage et entretien courant
Health	13.6	0.4	1.9	5.8	3.9	2.4	14.5	3.5	5.3	Santé
Transport	32.8	- 7.3	5.0	9.9	0.7	1.0	5.7	- 3.4	5.1	Transport
Communication	25.1	- 0.3	-	0.4	0.1	0.3	0.9	- 1.1	- 4.5	Communication
Recreation and culture	30.8	- 7.1	5.6	8.7	5.4	8.4	3.4	1.4	0.2	Loisirs et culture
Education	19.8	...	4.4	15.2	7.9	...	33.5	4.2	2.9	Enseignement
Restaurants and hotels	17.5	3.3	4.5	13.9	9.4	1.7	3.4	0.9	6.5	Restaurants et hôtels
Miscellaneous goods and services	24.1	- 6.0	1.5	4.8	2.6	3.3	4.7	- 3.0	- 0.5	Biens et Services divers

IV AGRICULTURAL PRODUCTION - PRODUCTION AGRICOLE

	2009	2010	2011	2012	2013	2014	2015	2016	2017	
TONNES (THOUSAND)										**Tonnes (milliers)**
Coconuts	2	2	2	3	3	4	12	6	...	Noix de coco
Bananas	2	2	2	2	2	2	...	...	...	Bananes
	...	...	...	...	...	...	...	...	...	
	...	...	...	...	...	...	...	...	...	
	...	...	...	...	...	...	...	...	...	

V MINING PRODUCTION - PRODUCTION MINIERE

	2009	2010	2011	2012	2013	2014	2015	2016	2017
	...	...	...	...	...	...	...	...	...
	...	...	...	...	...	...	...	...	...
	...	...	...	...	...	...	...	...	...

VI ENERGY - ENERGIE

	2009	2010	2011	2012	2013	2014	2015	2016	2017	
Total electricity generation (GWh)	825	283	401	405	409	430	438	...	...	Production électrique totale (GWh)
of which										dont
Production of electricity from fossil fuels (GWh)	259	283	400	404	408	412	416			Production d'électricité à partir de combustibles fossiles (GWh)
Production of hydro electricity (GWh)	...	...	...	...	...	...	...			Production d'électricité d'origine hydraulique (GWh)
Production of electricity from solar, wind, tide, wave and other sources (GWh)	...	...	1	1	1	4	7	...	...	Production d'électricité d'origine solaire, éolienne, marée motrice et autres (GWh)

VII TOURISM AND INFRASTRUCTURE - TOURISME ET INFRASTUCTURE

	2009	2010	2011	2012	2013	2014	2015	2016	2017	
VII-1 Tourism										**VII-1 Tourisme**
International tourist arrivals (thousands)	158	175	194	208	230	233	276	303	350	Arrivées de touristes internationaux (milliers)
Rooms in hotels and similar establishments (thousands)	3	2	3	3	3	5	5	5	5	Chambres d'hôtels et établissements assimilés (milliers)
Overnight stays (thousands)	1 607	1 815	1 945	2 060	2 349	2 373	2 735	3 001	3 324	Nuitées (milliers)
Tourism receipts (US$ thousand)	256 500	274 400	291 000	388 500	430 200	397 555	392 718	413 710	483 327	Recettes touristiques (milliers de $ EU)
Total contribution to GDP (%)	...	...	...	27.0	26.0	25.0	25.0	25.0	25.0	Contribution totale au PIB (%)
Total contribution to Employment (%)	...	...	...	25.0	25.0	24.0	24.0	25.0	25.0	Contribution totale à l'emploi (%)
VII-2 Infrastructure										**VII-2 Infrastructure**
Paved road (% of total)	96.5	96.5	96.5	...	...	...	97.7	...	...	Routes asphaltées (% du total)
Total network (Railways-km)	...	...	...	...	...	...	...	...	...	Réseau total voies ferrées-Km
Main telephone lines (per 100 inhabitants)	28.8	24.2	30.4	22.7	23.4	22.7	22.8	22.1	...	Lignes téléphoniques fixes (pour 100 habitants)
Mobile cellular subscribers (per 100 inhabitants)	122.2	128.9	137.9	147.8	147.3	162.2	158.1	161.2	...	Abonnés aux téléphones mobiles (pour 100 habitants)
Internet users per 100 inhabitants	...	41.0	43.2	47.1	50.4	51.3	54.3	56.5	...	Utilisateurs Internet par 100 Habitants
Fixed (wired)-broadband subscriptions per 100 inhabitants	5.0	7.4	10.3	11.5	13.4	12.7	14.3	14.9	...	Abonnements à l'Internet fixe (filaire) à large bande pour 100 habitants, par débit

VIII EXTERNAL TRADE - COMMERCE EXTERIEUR

	2009	2010	2011	2012	2013	2014	2015	2016	2017	
US$ (MILLIONS) **EXPORTS, FOB**										**$ E.U (MILLIONS)** **EXPORTATIONS, FÀB**
Exports - Total	404	418	483	497	574	551	474	484	...	Exportations - Total
Exports to Africa	40	34	103	21	38	33	44	59	...	Exportations vers l'Afrique
Main products										**Principaux produits**
Feeding stuff for animals (no unmilled cereals)	3	5	4	7	6	8	7	8	...	Nourriture pour animaux (pas de céréales non moulues)
Fish, aqua. invertebrates, prepared, preserved, n.e.s.	158	192	174	283	361	313	230	236	...	Poisson, aqua. invertébrés, préparés, conservés, n.d.a.
Fish, fresh (live or dead), chilled or frozen	55	58	38	54	82	71	75	102	...	Poissons frais (vivants ou morts), réfrigérés ou congelés
Petroleum oils or bituminous minerals > 70 % oil	92	87	73	80	68	93	72	62	...	Huiles de pétrole ou de minéraux bitumineux> 70% d'huile
Ships, boats & floating structures	1	6	87	2	1	3	3	18	...	Navires, bateaux et structures flottantes
Main destinations										**Principales destinations**
France	76	73	150	141	167	132	93	102	...	France
Italy	28	40	28	53	66	63	38	47	...	Italie
Japan	19	21	15	31	28	27	26	24	...	Japon
United Arab Emirates	8	80	69	81	69	94	72	58	...	Emirates Arabes
United Kingdom	83	74	63	87	113	105	88	73	...	Royaume-Uni
IMPORTS, CIF										
Imports - Total	757	984	1 049	1 071	1 098	1 075	975	1 043	...	Importations - Total (millions)
Imports from Africa	145	105	87	101	114	115	141	91	...	Importations en provenance de l'Afrique
Main products										**Principaux produits**
Fish, fresh (live or dead), chilled or frozen	119	78	81	143	162	120	76	71	...	Poissons frais (vivants ou morts), réfrigérés ou congelés
Motor vehicles for the transport of persons	15	14	18	18	21	23	16	27	...	Véhicules à moteur pour le transport de personnes
Petroleum oils or bituminous minerals > 70 % oil	17	286	274	208	155	196	167	87	...	Huiles de pétrole ou de minéraux bitumineux> 70% d'huile
Ships, boats & floating structures	85	35	187	29	55	48	78	384	...	Navires, bateaux et structures flottantes
Telecommunication equipment, n.e.s.; & parts, n.e.s.	10	11	16	14	31	21	22	15	...	Matériel de télécommunication, n.es.; & parties, n.e.s.
Main origin										**Principales provenances**
Cayman Islands	...	-	-	1	-	-	4	343	...	Îles Caïmans
France	85	57	52	74	94	85	64	73	...	France
South Africa	84	59	47	52	52	60	64	55	...	Afrique du Sud
Spain	85	66	86	225	163	145	112	69	...	Espagne
United Arab Emirates	...	407	484	279	235	289	196	136	...	Emirates Arabes

SEYCHELLES

IX FINANCIAL AND MONETARY STATISTICS - FINANCES ET STATISTIQUES MONETAIRES

	2009	2010	2011	2012	2013	2014	2015	2016	2017	
IX-1 MONETARY STATISTICS *SEYCHELLES RUPEE (MILLIONS)*										**IX-1 STATISTIQUES MONÉTAIRES** *ROUPIE SEYCHELLOISE (MILLIONS)*
Money supply (M1)	6 401	7 266	7 596	7 554	9 340	11 825	12 173	13 648	15 010	Masse monétaire (M1)
Quasi-money	1 617	1 921	1 264	1 204	1 398	1 574	1 143	1 359	1 576	Quasi-monnaie
of which demand deposit	1 517	1 674	1 040	1 061	...	...	...	...	...	dont Monnaie scripturale
Net foreign assets	2 751	3 489	4 262	5 072	7 081	9 477	9 188	9 603	10 521	Avoirs extérieurs nets
Domestic credit	4 966	5 807	5 796	5 306	6 047	6 018	6 533	7 643	9 018	Crédit intérieur
of which claims on private sector	2 235	2 559	2 380	1 760	2 335	1 414	1 309	1 791	2 209	dont créances sur le secteur privé
of which claims on government sector, net	2 315	2 861	2 936	3 114	3 412	4 307	4 644	5 122	6 032	dont créances nettes sur le gouvernement
International reserves (millions US$)	196	254	277	307	425	463	537	523	508	Réserves internationales (millions $EU)
Average exchange rate (National currency per US$)	14	12	12	14	12	13	13	13	14	Taux de change (moyen) (monnaie nationale par $ EU)
IX-2 PUBLIC FINANCE *SEYCHELLES RUPEE (MILLIONS)*										**IX-2 FINANCES PUBLIQUES** *ROUPIE SEYCHELLOISE (MILLIONS)*
Total Revenues and Grants	3 944	3 584	4 135	6 076	5 869	6 784	6 810	7 296	7 448	Recettes totales et dons
Direct taxes (on income, profits)	1 028	1 025	1 109	1 517	1 685	2 144	2 150	2 468	2 419	Taxes directes
Domestic indirect taxes revenues	1 316	1 282	1 413	2 192	2 280	2 608	2 754	2 781	3 462	Taxes Indirectes
Trade taxes	437	356	421	401	411	376	326	359	285	Taxes sur le commerce extérieur
Other taxes	350	346	304	491	354	473	585	581	434	Autres taxes
Other revenues	497	474	569	772	796	652	715	868	675	Autres recettes
Grants	317	101	319	702	343	532	279	240	173	Dons
Total Expenditures and Net Lending	4 176	4 704	5 824	6 962	5 595	5 992	6 175	7 330	7 293	Dépenses totales et prêts nets
Current expenditure	2 893	3 372	4 371	4 816	3 798	4 470	4 601	5 672	6 058	Dépenses courantes
Wages and Salaries	736	677	866	965	1 068	1 229	1 138	1 258	2 075	Rémunérations et salaires
Other purchases of goods and services	677	763	854	963	1 026	1 288	1 038	1 156	2 562	Achat de biens et services
Other current expenditure	19	12	15	23	31	21	29	27	41	Autres dépenses courantes
Current transfers	1 461	1 920	2 636	2 866	1 672	1 931	2 396	3 231	1 380	Transferts courants
Interest payments	1 046	712	384	540	631	404	438	714	631	Intérêts
Capital expenditure	608	1 009	1 061	1 613	1 160	998	1 021	909	605	Dépenses d'équipement
Net lending	- 372	- 389	9	- 6	6	120	115	35	...	Prêts nets
Fiscal balance	- 232	- 1 121	- 1 689	- 887	275	791	635	- 34	155	Solde global y compris les dons
IX-3 BALANCE OF PAYMENTS *US $ (MILLIONS)*										**IX-3 BALANCE DES PAIEMENTS** *$ E.U (MILLIONS)*
Trade balance	- 319	- 381	- 438	- 469	- 445	- 542	- 473	- 532	- 590	Balance commerciale
Services Balance	242	242	272	287	356	331	350	386	446	Balance des services
Net primary income	- 56	- 52	- 70	- 4	- 82	- 102	- 105	- 132	- 136	Revenus primaires nets
Compensation of employees	- 8	- 2	- 2	- 9	- 11	- 7	- 15	- 7	- 9	Rémunération des salariés
Investment income	- 48	- 50	- 68	4	- 72	- 95	- 90	- 125	- 127	Revenus des investissements
Net secondary income	7	5	7	25	15	3	- 27	- 10	- 16	Revenus secondaires nets
Net official transfers	45	26	29	55	52	38	19	31	22	Transferts officiels nets
Workers' remittances	- 38	- 22	- 23	- 30	- 38	- 35	- 42	- 34	- 37	Envois de fonds des travailleurs
Other private transfers	...	...	...	...	...	...	- 4	- 6	- 1	Autres transferts privés
Current account balance	- 125	- 186	- 230	- 161	- 157	- 310	- 256	- 287	- 296	Solde du compte courant
Capital and financial account	38	401	- 159	- 135	8	- 175	- 179	- 171	- 195	Comptes de capital et financier
Capital account	52	275	61	64	71	39	37	54	52	Compte de capital
Financial account	15	125	220	199	62	214	216	225	247	Compte financier
Errors and omissions	58	36	- 50	- 102	25	57	3	8	- 3	Erreurs et omissions
Overall balance	- 121	- 81	- 37	- 28	- 97	- 43	- 73	...	- 18	Balance générale

X DEBT AND FINANCIAL FLOWS - DETTE ET FLUX FINANCIERS

	2009	2010	2011	2012	2013	2014	2015	2016	2017	
X-1 DEBT *US $ (MILLIONS)*										**X-1 DETTE EXTÉRIEURE** *$ E.U (MILLIONS)*
Total external debt	1 567	1 658	1 863	1 778	1 663	1 588	1 372	1 404	1 498	Dette extérieure totale
Private	...	...	...	...	...	...	...	...	...	Privée
Public	743	478	490	512	521	501	486	454	...	Publique
Total external debt service	113	78	32	33	86	27	79	106	...	Service de la dette extérieure
Present value of external debt	...	...	...	...	...	...	...	...	...	Valeur actuelle de la dette extérieure
Total government domestic debt, National currency (millions)	...	...	...	...	...	...	...	...	...	Dette publique intérieure
X-2 FINANCIAL FLOWS *US $ (MILLIONS)*										**X-2 FLUX FINANCIERS** *$ E.U (MILLIONS)*
Net Foreign Direct Investment Inflows	171	211	207	261	170	230	195	155	...	Investissements étranger direct (flux nets entrants)
Main origin of FDI inflows										**Principales origines de l'IDE entrant:**
...	...	...	...	...	...	...	...	...	...	...
...	...	...	...	...	...	...	...	...	...	...
United Kingdom	- 8	...	8	...	...	...	...	...	...	Royaume-Uni
Hungary	3	2	- 1	- 3	...	...	...	...	...	Hongrie
...	...	...	...	...	...	...	...	...	...	...
African countries	...	...	...	...	...	...	...	...	...	Pays africains
Net total official development assistance	23	54	23	35	27	12	7	6	...	Aide publique au développement (nette totale)
Main origin of net ODA										**Principales origines de l'APD nette**
United Arab Emirates	...	17	6	12	...	...	...	...	...	Emirates Arabes
France	2	10	2	2	4	1	1	- 9	...	France
Japan	9	10	1	2	1	1	1	1	...	Japon
Global Environment Facility [GEF]	1	1	2	1	2	2	2	1	...	Fonds pour l'environnement mondial (FEM)
Arab Bank for Economic Development in Africa (B	- 1	2	2	2	...	...	...	...	...	Arab Bank for Economic Development in Africa (B

SEYCHELLES

SOURCES AND NOTES - SOURCES ET NOTES

External trade - Total exports, fob: UNCTAD

External trade - Total import, cif: UNCTAD

ODA: OECD

Monetary statistics: IMF

National Accounts: 2016-2017 Provisional

National Accounts: The data for 2017 are previsions based on the sum of four quarters of 2017.

Poverty: World Bank

Commerce exterieur - Exportation, fab: CNUCED

Commerce exterieur - Imporations, caf: CNUCED

APD: OCDE

Statistiques monétaires: FMI

Comptes nationaux: 2016-2017 Provisoire

Comptes Nationaux : Les données de L'année 2017 sont estimées à partir des comptes trimestriels

Pauvreté: Banque mondiale

	AREA (km2)		72 300		SUPERFICIE (KM2)
	CAPITAL CITY	Freetown		Freetown	CAPITALE
	CURRENCY	Leone		Leone	MONNAIE

I SOCIAL AND DEMOGRAPHIC INDICATORS — INDICATEURS DEMOGRAPHIQUES ET SOCIAUX

	Year Année	Value Valeur	Charts Graphiques	

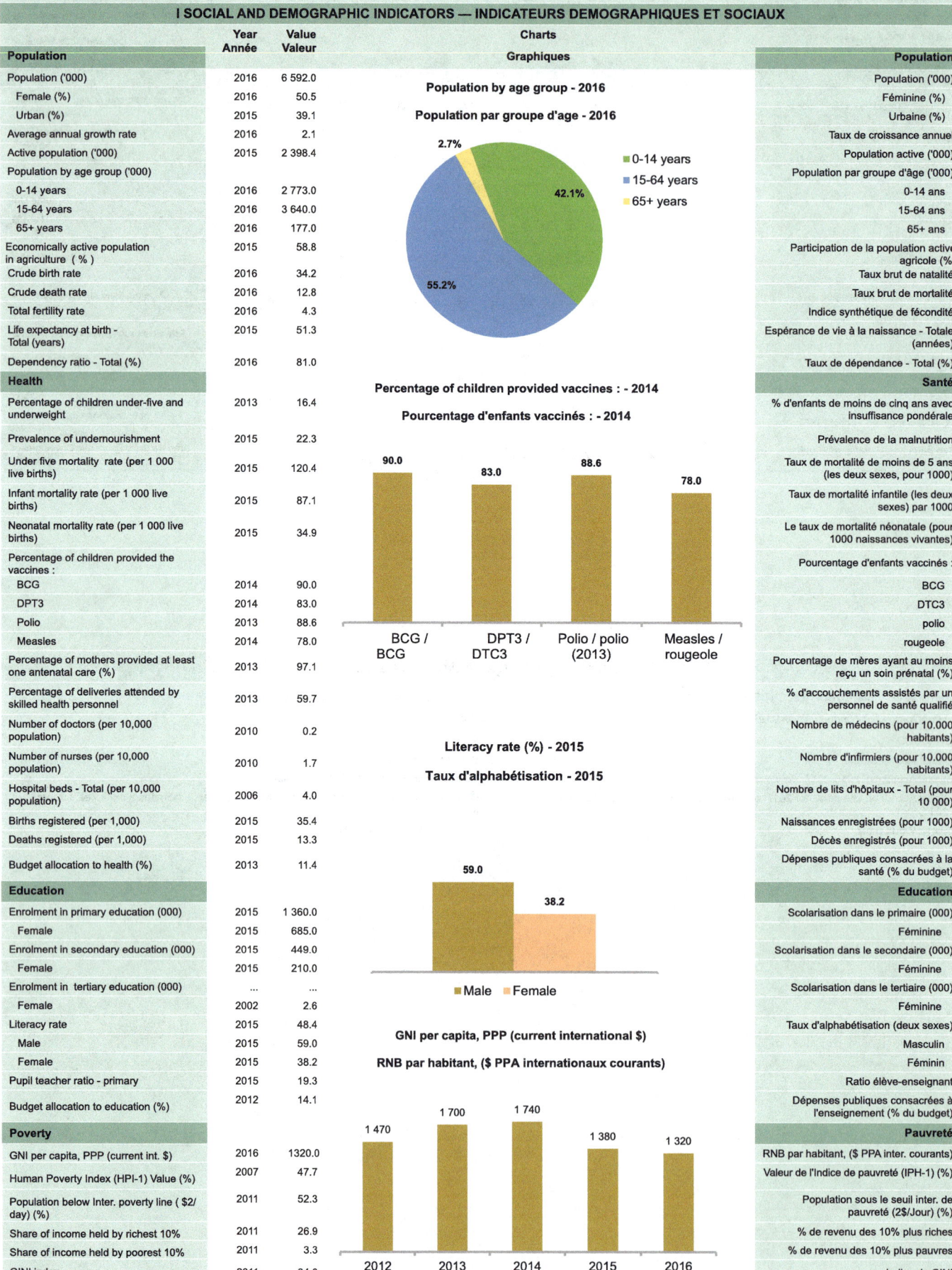

Population				**Population**
Population ('000)	2016	6 592.0		Population ('000)
Female (%)	2016	50.5		Féminine (%)
Urban (%)	2015	39.1		Urbaine (%)
Average annual growth rate	2016	2.1		Taux de croissance annuel
Active population ('000)	2015	2 398.4		Population active ('000)
Population by age group ('000)				Population par groupe d'âge ('000)
0-14 years	2016	2 773.0		0-14 ans
15-64 years	2016	3 640.0		15-64 ans
65+ years	2016	177.0		65+ ans
Economically active population in agriculture (%)	2015	58.8		Participation de la population active agricole (%)
Crude birth rate	2016	34.2		Taux brut de natalité
Crude death rate	2016	12.8		Taux brut de mortalité
Total fertility rate	2016	4.3		Indice synthétique de fécondité
Life expectancy at birth - Total (years)	2015	51.3		Espérance de vie à la naissance - Totale (années)
Dependency ratio - Total (%)	2016	81.0		Taux de dépendance - Total (%)
Health				**Santé**
Percentage of children under-five and underweight	2013	16.4		% d'enfants de moins de cinq ans avec insuffisance pondérale
Prevalence of undernourishment	2015	22.3		Prévalence de la malnutrition
Under five mortality rate (per 1 000 live births)	2015	120.4		Taux de mortalité de moins de 5 ans (les deux sexes, pour 1000)
Infant mortality rate (per 1 000 live births)	2015	87.1		Taux de mortalité infantile (les deux sexes) par 1000
Neonatal mortality rate (per 1 000 live births)	2015	34.9		Le taux de mortalité néonatale (pour 1000 naissances vivantes)
Percentage of children provided the vaccines :				Pourcentage d'enfants vaccinés :
BCG	2014	90.0		BCG
DPT3	2014	83.0		DTC3
Polio	2013	88.6		polio
Measles	2014	78.0		rougeole
Percentage of mothers provided at least one antenatal care (%)	2013	97.1		Pourcentage de mères ayant au moins reçu un soin prénatal (%)
Percentage of deliveries attended by skilled health personnel	2013	59.7		% d'accouchements assistés par un personnel de santé qualifié
Number of doctors (per 10,000 population)	2010	0.2		Nombre de médecins (pour 10.000 habitants)
Number of nurses (per 10,000 population)	2010	1.7		Nombre d'infirmiers (pour 10.000 habitants)
Hospital beds - Total (per 10,000 population)	2006	4.0		Nombre de lits d'hôpitaux - Total (pour 10 000)
Births registered (per 1,000)	2015	35.4		Naissances enregistrées (pour 1000)
Deaths registered (per 1,000)	2015	13.3		Décès enregistrés (pour 1000)
Budget allocation to health (%)	2013	11.4		Dépenses publiques consacrées à la santé (% du budget)
Education				**Education**
Enrolment in primary education (000)	2015	1 360.0		Scolarisation dans le primaire (000)
Female	2015	685.0		Féminine
Enrolment in secondary education (000)	2015	449.0		Scolarisation dans le secondaire (000)
Female	2015	210.0		Féminine
Enrolment in tertiary education (000)	...	...		Scolarisation dans le tertiaire (000)
Female	2002	2.6		Féminine
Literacy rate	2015	48.4		Taux d'alphabétisation (deux sexes)
Male	2015	59.0		Masculin
Female	2015	38.2		Féminin
Pupil teacher ratio - primary	2015	19.3		Ratio élève-enseignant
Budget allocation to education (%)	2012	14.1		Dépenses publiques consacrées à l'enseignement (% du budget)
Poverty				**Pauvreté**
GNI per capita, PPP (current int. $)	2016	1320.0		RNB par habitant, ($ PPA inter. courants)
Human Poverty Index (HPI-1) Value (%)	2007	47.7		Valeur de l'Indice de pauvreté (IPH-1) (%)
Population below Inter. poverty line ($2/day) (%)	2011	52.3		Population sous le seuil inter. de pauvreté (2$/Jour) (%)
Share of income held by richest 10%	2011	26.9		% de revenu des 10% plus riches
Share of income held by poorest 10%	2011	3.3		% de revenu des 10% plus pauvres
GINI index	2011	34.0		Indice de GINI

	2009	2010	2011	2012	2013	2014	2015	2016	2017	
GROSS DOMESTIC PRODUCT BY KIND OF ECONOMIC ACTIVITY AT CURRENT PRICES SIERRA LEONE LEONE (MILLIONS)										**PRODUIT INTÉRIEUR BRUT PAR BRANCHE D'ACTIVITÉ ÉCONOMIQUE AUX PRIX COURANTS** LEONE (MILLIONS)
Agriculture, hunting , forestry and Fishing	4 591 100	5 429 597	6 986 660	8 355 508	10 228 785	11 751 396	12 559 859	13 454 507	...	Agriculture, chasse sylviculture et Pêche
Mining and quarrying	240 340	410 642	528 777	1 831 856	3 922 351	2 957 664	332 618	601 388	...	Industries extractives
Manufacturing	176 800	223 299	288 488	333 221	349 867	347 739	378 738	420 843	...	Industries manufacturières
Electricity, gas & water	17 512	24 443	30 237	37 805	43 890	42 001	46 138	52 796	...	Electricité, gaz et eau
Construction	109 294	139 643	159 623	197 533	209 255	195 329	218 123	221 897	...	Bâtiments et travaux publics
Wholesale & retail trade, restaurants, hotels	738 286	941 678	1 251 769	1 508 625	1 805 401	1 888 985	1 995 965	2 195 312	...	Commerce de gros et de détail, restaurants et hôtels
Finance, insurance, real estate, etc.	384 955	479 134	583 534	684 079	769 540	915 121	893 765	988 010	...	Banques, assurances, affaires immobilières
Transport and communications	528 442	586 426	688 455	733 836	804 167	855 262	885 296	919 204	...	Transport(s) et communications
Public administration and defense	291 966	420 731	582 523	768 692	900 937	1 136 633	1 318 578	1 515 026	...	Administrations publiques et défense
Education	203 609	237 666	290 722	350 979	379 766	422 719	443 291	468 758	...	Education
Health And Social Work	273 170	437 171	479 580	538 252	564 594	617 082	667 831	724 036	...	Santé et Actions Sociales
Other services	453 997	513 435	635 032	792 139	846 690	931 719	1 048 565	883 481	...	Autres services
Less Imputed Service Charges	- 121 928	- 152 963	- 186 728	- 224 582	- 252 006	- 281 933	- 311 201	- 348 305	...	Moins Services d'intermédiation financière
Gross domestic product at factor cost / basic prices	7 887 543	9 690 903	12 318 673	15 907 945	20 573 237	21 779 717	20 477 565	22 096 953	...	Produit intérieur brut aux couts des facteurs / prix de base
Plus: Indirect Taxes / taxes on products, less subsidies	420 503	564 711	478 940	607 489	744 146	909 649	936 677	1 017 285	...	Plus taxes indirectes/impôts sur les produits, moins les subventions
EXPENDITURE ON GROSS DOMESTIC PRODUCT AT CURRENT PURCHASER'S VALUES SIERRA LEONE LEONE (MILLIONS)										**EMPLOI DU PRODUIT INTÉRIEUR BRUT AUX PRIX COURANTS D'ACQUISION** LEONE (MILLIONS)
Government final consumption	873 436	1 074 174	1 289 136	1 684 737	1 855 847	1 621 292	2 194 055	2 409 591	...	Consommation finale des administrations publiques
Private final consumption	7 795 507	7 796 737	12 295 070	14 828 523	22 965 681	22 877 912	21 924 945	23 627 203	...	Consommation finale privée
Gross fixed capital formation	799 404	3 150 100	5 315 874	4 227 645	3 080 211	2 974 524	3 315 839	3 877 103	...	Formation brute de capital fixe
Change in inventories	39 131	48 577	63 879	310 239	- 146 659	131 451	- 8 007	220 099	...	Variation des stocks
Exports of goods and services	1 121 567	1 722 427	2 081 748	5 434 458	6 102 475	6 979 258	4 146 342	5 442 019	...	Exportations de biens et services
Less imports of goods and services	2 320 999	3 536 401	8 248 094	9 970 168	12 540 173	11 895 072	10 158 931	12 461 777	...	Moins importations de biens et services
GDP at purchasers' values	8 308 046	10 255 614	12 797 613	16 515 434	21 317 382	22 689 366	21 414 242	23 114 237	...	PIB aux prix d'acquisition
GROSS DOMESTIC PRODUCT BY KIND OF ECONOMIC ACTIVITY AT CONSTANT PRICES ANNUAL GROWTH RATES (%)										**PRODUIT INTÉRIEUR BRUT PAR BRANCHE D'ACTIVITÉ ECONOMIQUE AUX PRIX CONSTANTS** TAUX DE CROISSANCE ANNUEL (%)
Agriculture, hunting , forestry and Fishing	4.0	3.5	4.9	3.8	4.6	0.8	3.1	3.4	...	Agriculture, chasse sylviculture et Pêche
Mining and quarrying	- 1.2	15.7	1.8	296.7	134.1	16.8	- 85.3	51.4	...	Industries extractives
Manufacturing	- 6.8	9.1	15.0	4.0	2.4	- 7.1	0.3	4.6	...	Industries manufacturières
Electricity, gas & water	- 8.8	2.7	3.9	5.6	- 18.2	5.6	5.9	4.4	...	Electricité, gaz et eau
Construction	- 8.3	13.2	24.1	12.0	6.2	- 7.6	3.1	4.1	...	Bâtiments et travaux publics
Wholesale & retail trade, restaurants, hotels	3.4	8.5	12.1	5.5	9.3	- 4.6	- 3.0	2.1	...	Commerce de gros et de détail, restaurants et hôtels
Finance, insurance, real estate, etc.	5.4	4.1	3.0	4.2	3.2	1.4	2.6	3.8	...	Banques, assurances, affaires immobilières
Transport and communications	8.8	4.0	5.3	5.8	4.8	- 2.8	- 0.6	3.8	...	Transport(s) et communications
Public administration and defense	3.3	22.4	16.9	16.0	6.7	16.5	6.5	7.4	...	Administrations publiques et défense
Education	- 6.1	5.1	6.7	4.2	7.1	3.3	3.6	4.7	...	Education
Health And Social Work	3.3	4.8	3.2	4.1	2.8	6.5	5.7	5.3	...	Santé et Actions Sociales
Other services	4.7	2.5	3.0	3.4	6.0	4.4	3.1	3.6	...	Autres services
Less Imputed Service Charges	9.2	6.5	3.0	5.7	2.1	3.3	1.3	2.7	...	Moins Services d'intermédiation financière
Gross domestic product at factor cost / basic prices	3.2	5.3	6.3	15.7	21.4	4.7	- 21.5	6.2	...	Produit intérieur brut aux couts des facteurs / prix de base
Plus: Indirect Taxes / taxes on products, less subsidies	3.2	5.3	6.1	5.4	5.6	0.9	1.9	3.7	...	Plus taxes indirectes/impôts sur les produits, moins les subventions
Gross domestic product at market prices	3.2	5.3	6.3	15.2	20.7	4.6	- 20.6	6.1	...	Produit intérieur brut aux prix du marché
EXPENDITURE ON GROSS DOMESTIC PRODUCT AT CONSTANT PURCHASERS' VALUES ANNUAL GROWTH RATES (%)										**EMPLOIS DU PRODUIT INTÉRIEUR BRUT AUX PRIX CONSTANTS D'ACQUISITION** TAUX DE CROISSANCE ANNUEL (%)
Government final consumption	10.9	4.4	1.3	14.9	0.3	- 19.3	24.2	2.6	...	Consommation finale des administrations publiques
Private final consumption	7.9	- 14.6	35.4	7.2	29.6	- 15.1	- 2.6	10.5	...	Consommation finale privée
Gross fixed capital formation	9.0	239.8	42.2	- 26.0	- 15.8	- 5.3	- 15.4	- 0.4	...	Formation brute de capital fixe
Exports of goods and services	7.4	18.9	- 1.3	157.3	37.3	60.5	- 51.2	31.6	...	Exportations de biens et services
Less imports of goods and services	28.9	22.6	101.1	9.9	19.9	- 1.3	- 17.9	25.1	...	Moins importations de biens et services

III INFLATION

	2009	2010	2011	2012	2013	2014	2015	2016	2017	
Annual growth rates (%)										**Taux de croissance annuel (%)**
All item	7.5	7.2	6.8	6.6	5.5	4.7	6.7	10.9	18.2	Ensemble
of which:										dont:
Food and non-alcoholic beverages	8.3	8.6	7.8	6.7	5.7	4.7	8.4	12.6	19.4	Alimentation et boissons non alcoolisés
Alcoholic beverages, tobacco and narcotics	5.2	5.1	6.7	6.4	6.0	5.2	5.8	8.6	23.0	Boissons alcoolisées et tabacs
Clothing and footwear	4.5	7.0	8.8	9.8	10.0	6.7	5.3	10.7	26.9	Habillement et chaussures
Housing, water, electricity, gas and other fuels	6.6	5.9	5.6	5.2	4.4	3.7	3.4	7.6	12.2	Logement, eau, électricité, gaz et autres combustibles
Furnishings, household equipment and routine household maintenance	8.9	8.0	8.0	7.4	7.4	5.6	8.6	12.3	22.6	Meubles, articles de ménage et entretien courant
Health	7.5	7.7	6.5	8.5	4.9	5.0	5.8	10.6	11.7	Santé
Transport	10.2	4.8	4.4	4.8	4.3	3.1	2.8	7.9	21.2	Transport
Communication	6.7	3.0	2.6	2.4	2.7	2.4	4.7	5.5	16.9	Communication
Recreation and culture	6.5	5.6	5.8	4.9	4.9	5.6	6.8	12.9	11.6	Loisirs et culture
Education	6.6	3.1	2.2	1.8	1.5	1.7	4.5	5.8	6.2	Enseignement
Restaurants and hotels	7.3	3.7	1.9	2.8	4.7	4.5	13.2	12.4	19.6	Restaurants et hôtels
Miscellaneous goods and services	5.3	5.2	6.0	5.8	3.8	5.2	8.0	10.3	23.7	Biens et Services divers

SIERRA LEONE

IV AGRICULTURAL PRODUCTION - PRODUCTION AGRICOLE

TONNES (THOUSAND)	2009	2010	2011	2012	2013	2014	2015	2016	2017	Tonnes (milliers)
Groundnuts, with shell	2 815	3 250	3 460	3 585	3 810	4 109	4 783	4 778	...	Arachides (en coques)
Coffee, green	888	1 027	1 129	1 141	1 256	1 204	872	1 560	...	Café, vert
Oil, palm	177	206	210	221	225	244	274	311	...	Palmistes
Rice, paddy	209	212	212	210	210	210	208	211	...	Riz, Paddy
Cassava	70	81	83	85	86	86	79	66	...	Manioc

V MINING PRODUCTION - PRODUCTION MINIERE

	2009	2010	2011	2012	2013	2014	2015	2016	2017	
Diamonds and other precious stones, unworked - Production, carat (thousands)	400	525	357	541	609	...	...	...	...	Diamants et autres pierres gemmes (précieuses), bruts - Production, carat (milliers)
Aluminium ores and concentrates (Bauxite) - Production, metric tons (thousands)	743	905	1 300	776	616	...	...	...	...	Minerais d'aluminium et leurs concentrés (Bauxite) - Production, tonnes métriques (milliers)
	...	...	...	...	...	...	...	...	...	

VI ENERGY - ENERGIE

	2009	2010	2011	2012	2013	2014	2015	2016	2017	
Total electricity generation (GWh)	281	298	302	313	332	314	326	...	...	Production électrique totale (GWh)
of which										dont
Production of electricity from fossil fuels (GWh)	42	45	45	45	45	142	151	...	...	Production d'électricité à partir de combustibles fossiles (GWh)
Production of hydro electricity (GWh)	239	253	257	268	287	145	145	...	...	Production d'électricité d'origine hydraulique (GWh)
Production of electricity from solar, wind, tide, wave and other sources (GWh)	...	...	...	...	...	16	19	...	...	Production d'électricité d'origine solaire, éolienne, marée motrice et autres (GWh)

VII TOURISM AND INFRASTRUCTURE - TOURISME ET INFRASTUCTURE

	2009	2010	2011	2012	2013	2014	2015	2016	2017	
VII-1 Tourism										**VII-1 Tourisme**
International tourist arrivals (thousands)	37	39	52	60	81	44	24	55	51	Arrivées de touristes internationaux (milliers)
Rooms in hotels and similar establishments (thousands)	3	3	4	4	...	...	2	2	...	Chambres d'hôtels et établissements assimilés (milliers)
Overnight stays (thousands)	257	270	367	418	569	306	167	376	151	Nuitées (milliers)
Tourism receipts (US$ thousand)	25 400	25 800	44 300	46 800	65 800	34 600	37 500	40 897	40 979	Recettes touristiques (milliers de $ EU)
Total contribution to GDP (%)	6.6	7.1	7.3	4.7	3.9	2.9	3.8	3.8	3.5	Contribution totale au PIB (%)
Total contribution to Employment (%)	6.3	7.0	7.2	4.8	4.1	3.2	3.6	3.3	3.2	Contribution totale à l'emploi (%)
VII-2 Infrastructure										**VII-2 Infrastructure**
Paved road (% of total)	...	...	...	...	...	...	...	...	...	Routes asphaltées (% du total)
Total network (Railways-km)	...	...	...	...	...	...	...	...	...	Réseau total voies ferrées-Km
Main telephone lines (per 100 inhabitants)	0.6	...	...	...	...	...	...	...	...	Lignes téléphoniques fixes (pour 100 habitants)
Mobile cellular subscribers (per 100 inhabitants)	20.6	34.8	36.4	37.0	65.7	76.7	89.5	97.6		Abonnés aux téléphones mobiles (pour 100 habitants)
Internet users per 100 inhabitants	...	0.6	0.9	2.5	4.0	6.1	6.3	11.8		Utilisateurs Internet par 100 Habitants
Fixed (wired)-broadband subscriptions per 100 inhabitants	...	...	...	...	...	...	...	...		Abonnements à l'Internet fixe (filaire) à large bande pour 100 habitants, par débit

VIII EXTERNAL TRADE - COMMERCE EXTERIEUR

US$ (MILLIONS) EXPORTS, FOB	2009	2010	2011	2012	2013	2014	2015	2016	2017	$ E.U (MILLIONS) EXPORTATIONS, FÀB
Exports - Total	231	341	350	1 122	1 917	1 552	512	635	...	Exportations - Total
Exports to Africa	51	42	51	159	265	33	44	24	...	Exportations vers l'Afrique
Main products										**Principaux produits**
Aluminium ores and concentrates (incl. alumina)	18	55	55	40	31	55	13	21	...	Minerais d'aluminium et leurs concentrés (y compris l'alumine)
Iron ore and concentrates	...	...	3	295	830	1 095	284	424	...	Minerai de fer et ses concentrés
Live animals other than animals of division 03	4	8	9	34	108	2	16	6	...	Animaux vivants autres que les animaux de la division 03
Ores and concentrates of base metals, n.e.s.	17	19	19	115	99	133	34	51	...	Minerais et concentrés de métaux communs, n.d.a.
Pearls, precious & semi-precious stones	39	68	68	146	205	132	50	56	...	Perles, pierres précieuses et semi-précieuses
Main destinations										**Principales destinations**
Belgium	35	65	62	162	183	119	44	50	...	Belgique
China	8	12	19	368	997	1 142	315	448	...	Chine
Côte d'Ivoire	34	32	29	135	219	2	33	11	...	Côte d'Ivoire
United Kingdom	18	23	25	69	109	9	17	8	...	Royaume-Uni
United States	18	34	27	76	133	18	22	12	...	États-Unis
IMPORTS, CIF										
Imports - Total	520	770	1 717	1 604	1 780	1 568	1 530	1 560	...	Importations - Total (millions)
Imports from Africa	214	317	707	661	733	479	554	520	...	Importations en provenance de l'Afrique
Main products										**Principaux produits**
Motor vehic. for transport of goods, special purpo.	8	11	24	23	28	39	31	35	...	Véhicule à moteur pour le transport de marchandises, spécial.
Motor vehicles for the transport of persons	13	18	38	36	41	67	49	59	...	Véhicules à moteur pour le transport de personnes
Petroleum oils or bituminous minerals > 70 % oil	200	298	673	630	701	395	501	451	...	Huiles de pétrole ou de minéraux bitumineux> 70 % d'huile
Rice	38	52	113	109	119	63	83	74	...	Riz
Worn clothing and other worn textile articles	36	53	118	110	122	14	62	38	...	Vêtements usés et autres articles textiles usés
Main origin										**Principales provenances**
Belgium	8	12	26	25	27	170	90	131	...	Belgique
Benin	...	...	...	...	...	337	154	247	...	Bénin
China	18	26	58	55	61	152	97	126	...	Chine
Côte d'Ivoire	186	275	613	572	635	34	306	171	...	Côte d'Ivoire
United Kingdom	22	32	72	67	75	100	80	91	...	Royaume-Uni

	2009	2010	2011	2012	2013	2014	2015	2016	2017	
IX-1 MONETARY STATISTICS *SIERRA LEONE LEONE (MILLIONS)*										**IX-1 STATISTIQUES MONÉTAIRES** *LEONE (MILLIONS)*
Money supply (M1)	1 878 987	2 413 927	2 958 294	3 623 234	4 228 684	4 929 146	5 172 265	6 096 130	6 786 223	Masse monétaire (M1)
Quasi-money	559 702	644 379	901 074	1 170 936	1 347 432	1 358 100	1 417 141	1 613 572	1 852 286	Quasi-monnaie
of which demand deposit	387 437	490 794	645 024	...	...	...	...	...	...	dont Monnaie scripturale
Net foreign assets	832 407	839 494	1 270 385	1 628 700	1 882 963	2 395 784	2 354 853	2 439 514	2 178 026	Avoirs extérieurs nets
Domestic credit	1 195 143	1 777 761	2 092 063	2 313 066	2 601 936	3 291 775	3 974 144	5 039 571	6 057 503	Crédit intérieur
of which claims on private sector	448 855	891 347	1 012 095	1 141 863	1 289 160	1 869 026	2 536 133	3 429 667	4 374 198	dont créances sur le secteur privé
of which claims on government sector, net	683 295	802 381	981 148	1 027 103	1 016 691	1 109 320	1 153 425	1 346 365	1 412 985	dont créances nettes sur le gouvernement
International reserves (millions US$)	324	341	374	417	474	548	580	503	506	Réserves internationales (millions $EU)
Average exchange rate (National currency per US$)	3 386	3 978	4 349	4 344	4 332	4 524	5 081	6 290	7 353	Taux de change (moyen) (monnaie nationale par $ EU)
IX-2 PUBLIC FINANCE *SIERRA LEONE LEONE (MILLIONS)*										**IX-2 FINANCES PUBLIQUES** *LEONE (MILLIONS)*
Total Revenues and Grants	1 250 546	1 550 248	2 170 476	2 337 118	2 828 600	3 186 000	3 361 000	3 719 600	...	Recettes totales et dons
Direct taxes (on income, profits)	211 901	291 747	472 073	774 000	924 000	888 000	895 000	1 587 600	...	Taxes directes
Domestic indirect taxes revenues	103 299	246 362	351 449	417 643	440 000	459 000	593 000	666 000	...	Taxes Indirectes
Trade taxes	317 204	322 817	282 308	237 000	269 000	285 000	329 000	382 000	...	Taxes sur le commerce extérieur
Other taxes	1 619	18 400	61 322	99 000	221 000	222 000	216 000	184 000	...	Autres taxes
Other revenues	116 186	128 307	295 003	346 000	427 000	373 000	163 000	173 000	...	Autres recettes
Grants	500 337	542 615	708 321	463 475	547 600	959 000	1 165 000	727 000	...	Dons
Total Expenditures and Net Lending	1 414 150	2 038 895	2 525 756	2 928 791	3 004 032	4 069 000	4 477 000	5 521 000	...	Dépenses totales et prêts nets
Current expenditure	858 624	1 092 429	1 153 655	1 489 065	1 724 341	2 630 000	2 686 000	3 431 000	...	Dépenses courantes
Wages and Salaries	401 536	535 669	681 346	935 912	999 093	1 446 000	1 587 000	1 818 000	...	Rémunérations et salaires
Other purchases of goods and services	349 754	426 350	396 251	464 445	421 247	681 000	700 000	1 139 000	...	Achat de biens et services
Other current expenditure	...	...	...	...	...	138 000	57 000	79 000	...	Autres dépenses courantes
Current transfers	107 334	130 410	76 058	88 708	304 000	365 000	342 000	395 000	...	Transferts courants
Interest payments	103 248	159 179	250 382	282 511	301 158	222 000	175 000	202 000	...	Intérêts
Capital expenditure	452 278	787 287	1 121 719	1 157 215	1 146 533	1 205 000	1 616 000	2 039 000	...	Dépenses d'équipement
Net lending	...	...	...	...	- 168 000	12 000	...	- 151 000	...	Prêts nets
Fiscal balance	- 163 604	- 488 647	- 355 280	- 591 673	- 175 432	- 883 000	-1 116 000	-1 801 400	...	Solde global y compris les dons
IX-3 BALANCE OF PAYMENTS *SIERRA LEONE LEONE (MILLIONS)*										**IX-3 BALANCE DES PAIEMENTS** *LEONE (MILLIONS)*
Trade balance	-1 210 134	-2 090 721	-7 313 137	-3 851 918	- 118 277	-1 538 214	- 759 695	...	...	Balance commerciale
Services Balance	- 115 670	- 786 258	-1 196 697	-1 516 944	-2 247 991	-5 274 061	-2 268 926	...	...	Balance des services
Net primary income	- 120 799	- 195 358	- 948 391	- 579 158	-2 414 483	- 582 271	- 555 905	...	...	Revenus primaires nets
Compensation of employees	4 888	3 632	4 931	6 098				...	...	Rémunération des salariés
Investment income	- 125 686	- 198 990	- 953 323	- 585 256				...	...	Revenus des investissements
Net secondary income	304 679	713 378	1 087 408	1 026 572	875 402	3 716 495	1 252 309	...	...	Revenus secondaires nets
Net official transfers	130 873	503 746	490 599	407 562	...	...	...	...	...	Transferts officiels nets
Workers' remittances	104 824	130 222	161 210	171 590	...	...	...	...	...	Envois de fonds des travailleurs
Other private transfers	68 982	79 409	435 599	447 421	...	...	...	...	...	Autres transferts privés
Current account balance	-1 141 924	-2 358 960	-8 370 818	-4 921 448	-3 905 349	-3 678 050	-2 332 218	...	...	Solde du compte courant
Capital and financial account	1 129 591	2 335 627	8 325 618	4 791 701	...	...	...	...	...	Comptes de capital et financier
Capital account	507 628	521 140	683 236	535 984	...	...	...	...	...	Compte de capital
Financial account	621 963	1 814 487	7 642 382	4 255 717	...	...	...	...	...	Compte financier
Errors and omissions	- 22 535	- 7 263	- 3 349	- 4 161	...	...	...	...	...	Erreurs et omissions
Overall balance	- 12 333	- 23 332	- 45 200	- 129 747	...	...	...	...	...	Balance générale

SIERRA LEONE

X DEBT AND FINANCIAL FLOWS - DETTE ET FLUX FINANCIERS

	2009	2010	2011	2012	2013	2014	2015	2016	2017	
X-1 DEBT US $ (MILLIONS)										**X-1 DETTE EXTÉRIEURE** $ E.U (MILLIONS)
Total external debt	693	783	955	981	1 045	1 128	1 250	1 368	1 691	Dette extérieure totale
Private	...	...	...	...	...	...	...	...	...	Privée
Public	693	783	955	981	1 045	1 128	1 250	1 368	...	Publique
Total external debt service	15	16	23	25	34	46	60	41	...	Service de la dette extérieure
Present value of external debt	...	...	...	...	...	...	...	793	...	Valeur actuelle de la dette extérieure
Total government domestic debt, National currency (millions)	...	...	...	...	...	...	...	...	...	Dette publique intérieure
X-2 FINANCIAL FLOWS US $ (MILLIONS)										**X-2 FLUX FINANCIERS** $ E.U (MILLIONS)
Net Foreign Direct Investment Inflows	111	238	950	722	430	404	263	516	...	Investissements étranger direct (flux nets entrants)
Main origin of FDI inflows										**Principales origines de l'IDE entrant:**
...	...	...	...	...	...	...	...	...	...	...
...	...	...	...	...	...	...	...	...	...	...
...	...	...	...	...	...	...	...	...	...	...
...	...	...	...	...	...	...	...	...	...	...
Luxembourg	3	...	6	5	...	...	...	...	...	Luxembourg
African countries	...	...	...	...	...	...	...	...	...	Pays africains
Net total official development assistance	447	458	424	440	449	914	946	693	...	Aide publique au développement (nette totale)
Main origin of net ODA										**Principales origines de l'APD nette**
United Kingdom	80	85	74	100	109	391	333	207	...	Royaume-Uni
International Development Association [IDA]	36	57	61	65	44	119	78	25	...	International Development Association
United States	17	21	20	20	15	15	113	128	...	États-Unis
...	...	...	...	...	...	...	...	...	...	...
IMF (Concessional Trust Funds)	19	41	9	-	6	41	131	67	...	Financements concessionnels du FMI dans le cadre de la FASR

SIERRA LEONE

SOURCES AND NOTES - SOURCES ET NOTES

External trade - Total exports, fob: UNCTAD	Commerce exterieur - Exportation, fab: CNUCED
External trade - Total import, cif: UNCTAD	Commerce exterieur - Imporations, caf: CNUCED
ODA: OECD	APD: OCDE
Monetary statistics: IMF	Statistiques monétaires: FMI
National Accounts: 2014-2016:provisional	Comptes nationaux: 2014-2016:provisoire
National Accounts: annual accounts are based on new prices of 2006	Comptes Nationaux : publication des comptes annuels selon la nouvelle base des prix 2006
Poverty: World Bank	Pauvreté: Banque mondiale

AREA (km2)		637 660		**SUPERFICIE (KM2)**
CAPITAL CITY	Mogadishu		Mogadiscio	**CAPITALE**
CURRENCY	Somali Shilling		Shilling de Somalie	**MONNAIE**

I SOCIAL AND DEMOGRAPHIC INDICATORS — INDICATEURS DEMOGRAPHIQUES ET SOCIAUX

Population	Year Année	Value Valeur	Charts Graphiques	Population
Population				**Population**
Population ('000)	2017	14 700.0		Population ('000)
Female (%)	...	...		Féminine (%)
Urban (%)	2015	40.8		Urbaine (%)
Average annual growth rate	2015	3.2		Taux de croissance annuel
Active population ('000)	2015	2 884.3		Population active ('000)
Population by age group ('000)				Population par groupe d'âge ('000)
0-14 years	2015	5 038.1		0-14 ans
15-64 years	2015	5 444.3		15-64 ans
65+ years	2015	304.6		65+ ans
Economically active population in agriculture (%)	2015	94.9		Participation de la population active agricole (%)
Crude birth rate	2015	43.4		Taux brut de natalité
Crude death rate	2015	11.8		Taux brut de mortalité
Total fertility rate	2015	6.4		Indice synthétique de fécondité
Life expectancy at birth - Total (years)	2017	52.8		Espérance de vie à la naissance - Totale (années)
Dependency ratio - Total (%)	2015	98.1		Taux de dépendance - Total (%)
Health				**Santé**
Percentage of children under-five and underweight	2006	32.8		% d'enfants de moins de cinq ans avec insuffisance pondérale
Prevalence of undernourishment	...	...		Prévalence de la malnutrition
Under five mortality rate (per 1 000 live births)	2015	136.8		Taux de mortalité de moins de 5 ans (les deux sexes, pour 1000)
Infant mortality rate (per 1 000 live births)	2017	94.8		Taux de mortalité infantile (les deux sexes) par 1000
Neonatal mortality rate (per 1 000 live births)	2015	39.7		Le taux de mortalité néonatale (pour 1000 naissances vivantes)
Percentage of children provided the vaccines :				Pourcentage d'enfants vaccinés :
BCG	2014	37.0		BCG
DPT3	2014	42.0		DTC3
Polio	2012	47.0		polio
Measles	2014	46.0		rougeole
Percentage of mothers provided at least one antenatal care (%)	2006	22.0		Pourcentage de mères ayant au moins reçu un soin prénatal (%)
Percentage of deliveries attended by skilled health personnel	2006	33.0		% d'accouchements assistés par un personnel de santé qualifié
Number of doctors (per 10,000 population)	2006	0.4		Nombre de médecins (pour 10.000 habitants)
Number of nurses (per 10,000 population)	2006	1.1		Nombre d'infirmiers (pour 10.000 habitants)
Hospital beds - Total (per 10,000 population)	...	...		Nombre de lits d'hôpitaux - Total (pour 10 000)
Births registered (per 1,000)	2017	39.6		Naissances enregistrées (pour 1000)
Deaths registered (per 1,000)	2017	13.1		Décès enregistrés (pour 1000)
Budget allocation to health (%)	...	...		Dépenses publiques consacrées à la santé (% du budget)
Education				**Education**
Enrolment in primary education (000)	2007	457.1		Scolarisation dans le primaire (000)
Female	2007	162.1		Féminine
Enrolment in secondary education (000)	2007	86.9		Scolarisation dans le secondaire (000)
Female	2007	27.4		Féminine
Enrolment in tertiary education (000)	...	...		Scolarisation dans le tertiaire (000)
Female	...	...		Féminine
Literacy rate	...	...		Taux d'alphabétisation (deux sexes)
Male	...	...		Masculin
Female	...	...		Féminin
Pupil teacher ratio - primary	...	...		Ratio élève-enseignant
Budget allocation to education (%)	...	...		Dépenses publiques consacrées à l'enseignement (% du budget)
Poverty				**Pauvreté**
GNI per capita, PPP (current int. $)	...	...		RNB par habitant, ($ PPA inter. courants)
Human Poverty Index (HPI-1) Value (%)	...	...		Valeur de l'Indice de pauvreté (IPH-1) (%)
Population below Inter. poverty line ($2/day) (%)	...	...		Population sous le seuil inter. de pauvreté (2$/Jour) (%)
Share of income held by richest 10%	...	...		% de revenu des 10% plus riches
Share of income held by poorest 10%	...	...		% de revenu des 10% plus pauvres
GINI index	...	...		Indice de GINI

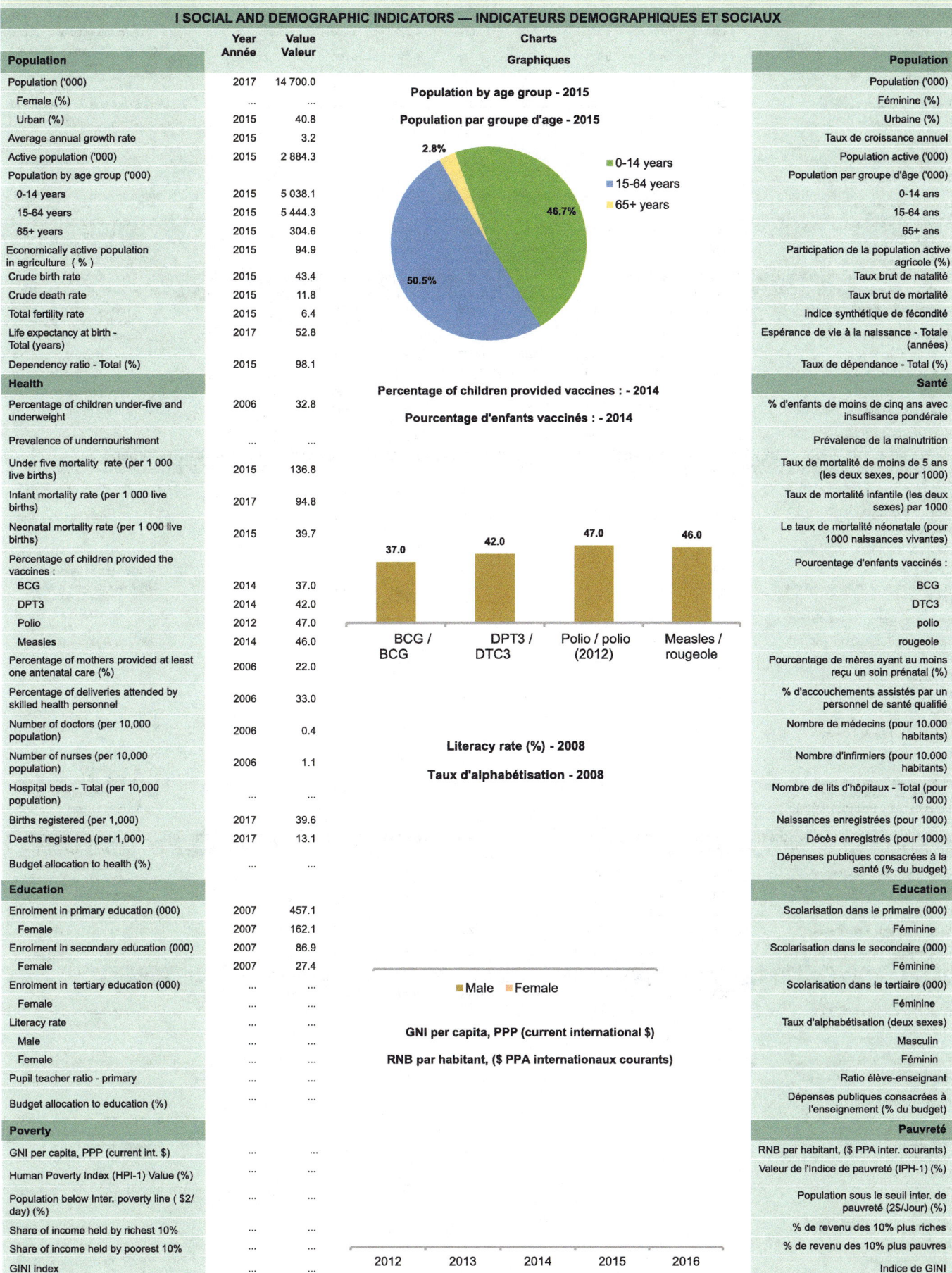

Population by age group - 2015

Population par groupe d'age - 2015

2.8% — 0-14 years
50.5% — 15-64 years
46.7% — 65+ years

Percentage of children provided vaccines : - 2014

Pourcentage d'enfants vaccinés : - 2014

BCG / BCG 37.0 — DPT3 / DTC3 42.0 — Polio / polio (2012) 47.0 — Measles / rougeole 46.0

Literacy rate (%) - 2008

Taux d'alphabétisation - 2008

■ Male ■ Female

GNI per capita, PPP (current international $)

RNB par habitant, ($ PPA internationaux courants)

2012 — 2013 — 2014 — 2015 — 2016

SOMALIE

	2009	2010	2011	2012	2013	2014	2015	2016	2017	
GROSS DOMESTIC PRODUCT BY KIND OF ECONOMIC ACTIVITY AT CURRENT PRICES *SOMALI SHILLING (BILLIONS)*										**PRODUIT INTÉRIEUR BRUT PAR BRANCHE D'ACTIVITÉ ÉCONOMIQUE AUX PRIX COURANTS** *SHILLING DE SOMALIE (MILLIARDS)*
Agriculture, hunting , forestry and Fishing	20 802	18 075	18 001	18 092	17 975	17 663	17 120	...	...	Agriculture, chasse sylviculture et Pêche
Mining and quarrying	233	203	202	203	202	198	192	...	...	Industries extractives
Manufacturing	859	746	743	747	742	729	707	...	...	Industries manufacturières
Electricity, gas & water	...	...	...	...	...	...	...	...	...	Electricité, gaz et eau
Construction	1 451	1 261	1 256	1 262	1 254	1 232	1 194	...	...	Bâtiments et travaux publics
Wholesale & retail trade, restaurants, hotels	3 671	3 190	3 177	3 193	3 172	3 117	3 021	...	...	Commerce de gros et de détail, restaurants et hôtels
Finance, insurance, real estate, etc.	...	...	...	...	...	...	...	...	...	Banques, assurances, affaires immobilières
Transport and communications	3 234	2 821	2 810	2 820	2 804	2 755	2 670	...	...	Transport(s) et communications
Public administration and defense	4 311	3 740	3 724	3 745	3 720	3 655	3 543	...	...	Administrations publiques et défense
Education	...	...	...	...	...	...	...	...	...	Education
Health And Social Work	...	...	...	...	...	...	...	...	...	Santé et Actions Sociales
Other services	...	...	...	...	...	...	...	...	...	Autres services
Less Imputed Service Charges	...	...	...	...	...	...	...	...	...	Moins Services d'intermédiation financière
Gross domestic product at factor cost / basic prices	34 561	30 036	29 913	30 063	29 869	29 350	28 447	...	...	Produit intérieur brut aux couts des facteurs / prix de base
Plus: Indirect Taxes / taxes on products, less subsidies	4 782	4 135	4 134	4 151	4 121	4 053	3 927	...	...	Plus taxes indirectes/impôts sur les produits, moins les subventions
EXPENDITURE ON GROSS DOMESTIC PRODUCT AT CURRENT PURCHASER'S VALUES *SOMALI SHILLING (BLLIONS)*										**EMPLOI DU PRODUIT INTÉRIEUR BRUT AUX PRIX COURANTS D'ACQUISITION** *SHILLING DE SOMALIE (MILLIARDS)*
Government final consumption	3 430	2 985	2 969	2 985	2 966	2 914	2 825	...	...	Consommation finale des administrations publiques
Private final consumption	28 569	24 839	24 725	24 854	24 694	24 263	23 518	...	...	Consommation finale privée
Gross fixed capital formation	7 863	6 797	6 802	6 826	6 778	6 666	6 459	...	...	Formation brute de capital fixe
Change in inventories	22	18	19	19	18	18	18	...	...	Variation des stocks
Exports of goods and services	120	104	104	104	104	102	99	...	...	Exportations de biens et services
Less imports of goods and services	661	573	572	574	571	561	544	...	...	Moins importations de biens et services
GDP at purchasers' values	39 343	34 171	34 047	34 214	33 990	33 403	32 375	...	...	PIB aux prix d'acquisition
GROSS DOMESTIC PRODUCT BY KIND OF ECONOMIC ACTIVITY AT CONSTANT PRICES *ANNUAL GROWTH RATES (%)*										**PRODUIT INTÉRIEUR BRUT PAR BRANCHE D'ACTIVITÉ ECONOMIQUE AUX PRIX CONSTANTS** *TAUX DE CROISSANCE ANNUEL (%)*
Agriculture, hunting , forestry and Fishing	2.9	2.4	2.6	...	2.6	4.6	2.1	...	...	Agriculture, chasse sylviculture et Pêche
Mining and quarrying	1.9	2.9	2.6	...	2.5	4.7	2.1	...	...	Industries extractives
Manufacturing	2.1	2.8	2.6	...	2.5	4.7	2.1	...	...	Industries manufacturières
Electricity, gas & water	...	...	...	...	...	...	...	...	...	Electricité, gaz et eau
Construction	2.4	2.7	2.6	...	2.6	4.6	2.1	...	...	Bâtiments et travaux publics
Wholesale & retail trade, restaurants, hotels	2.5	2.6	2.6	...	2.6	4.6	2.1	...	...	Commerce de gros et de détail, restaurants et hôtels
Finance, insurance, real estate, etc.	...	...	...	...	...	...	...	...	...	Banques, assurances, affaires immobilières
Transport and communications	2.5	2.6	2.6	...	2.6	4.6	2.1	...	...	Transport(s) et communications
Public administration and defense	2.5	2.7	2.6	-	2.6	4.6	2.1	...	...	Administrations publiques et défense
Education	...	...	...	...	...	...	...	...	...	Education
Health And Social Work	...	...	...	...	...	...	...	...	...	Santé et Actions Sociales
Other services	...	...	...	...	...	...	...	...	...	Autres services
Less Imputed Service Charges	...	...	...	...	...	...	...	...	...	Moins Services d'intermédiation financière
Gross domestic product at factor cost / basic prices	2.7	2.5	2.6	-	2.6	4.6	2.1	...	...	Produit intérieur brut aux couts des facteurs / prix de base
Plus: Indirect Taxes / taxes on products, less subsidies	1.7	3.3	2.6	21.9	2.6	- 1.8	6.5	...	...	Plus taxes indirectes/impôts sur les produits, moins les subventions
Gross domestic product at market prices	2.6	2.6	2.6	2.6	2.6	3.7	2.7	...	...	Produit intérieur brut aux prix du marché
EXPENDITURE ON GROSS DOMESTIC PRODUCT AT CONSTANT PURCHASERS' VALUES *ANNUAL GROWTH RATES (%)*										**EMPLOIS DU PRODUIT INTÉRIEUR BRUT AUX PRIX CONSTANTS D'ACQUISITION** *TAUX DE CROISSANCE ANNUEL (%)*
Government final consumption	3.0	2.4	2.6	2.7	2.6	2.7	2.6	...	...	Consommation finale des administrations publiques
Private final consumption	2.4	2.7	2.6	2.5	2.6	4.1	2.7	...	...	Consommation finale privée
Gross fixed capital formation	3.3	2.3	2.5	2.8	2.5	2.7	2.6	...	...	Formation brute de capital fixe
Exports of goods and services	6.6	- 0.6	3.4	3.2	2.0	2.9	2.2	...	...	Exportations de biens et services
Less imports of goods and services	5.3	0.7	2.9	3.0	2.2	2.8	2.3	...	...	Moins importations de biens et services

III INFLATION

	2009	2010	2011	2012	2013	2014	2015	2016	2017	
Annual growth rates (%)										**Taux de croissance annuel (%)**
All item	...	...	...	...	...	...	...	...	...	Ensemble
of which:										dont:
Food and non-alcoholic beverages	...	...	...	...	...	...	...	...	...	Alimentation et boissons non alcoolisés
Alcoholic beverages, tobacco and narcotics	...	...	...	...	...	...	...	...	...	Boissons alcoolisées et tabacs
Clothing and footwear	...	...	...	...	...	...	...	...	...	Habillement et chaussures
Housing, water, electricity, gas and other fuels	...	...	...	...	...	...	...	...	...	Logement, eau, électricité, gaz et autres combustibles
Furnishings, household equipment and routine household maintenance	...	...	...	...	...	...	...	...	...	Meubles, articles de ménage et entretien courant
Health	...	...	...	...	...	...	...	...	...	Santé
Transport	...	...	...	...	...	...	...	...	...	Transport
Communication	...	...	...	...	...	...	...	...	...	Communication
Recreation and culture	...	...	...	...	...	...	...	...	...	Loisirs et culture
Education	...	...	...	...	...	...	...	...	...	Enseignement
Restaurants and hotels	...	...	...	...	...	...	...	...	...	Restaurants et hôtels
Miscellaneous goods and services	...	...	...	...	...	...	...	...	...	Biens et Services divers

SOMALIA

IV AGRICULTURAL PRODUCTION - PRODUCTION AGRICOLE

TONNES (THOUSAND)	2009	2010	2011	2012	2013	2014	2015	2016	2017	Tonnes (milliers)
Maize	230	230	230	220	220	214	210	211	...	Maïs
Sorghum	95	214	48	234	231	132	130	77	...	Sorgho
Cassava	129	133	65	145	149	111	107	63	...	Manioc
Bananas	86	87	88	90	90	91	93	93	...	Bananes
Sesame seed	29	28	26	25	24	23	22	22	...	Sésame

V MINING PRODUCTION - PRODUCTION MINIERE

	2009	2010	2011	2012	2013	2014	2015	2016	2017	
	...	...	...	...	...	...	...	...	...	
	...	...	...	...	...	...	...	...	...	
	...	...	...	...	...	...	...	...	...	

VI ENERGY - ENERGIE

	2009	2010	2011	2012	2013	2014	2015	2016	2017	
Total electricity generation (GWh) of which	305	310	323	342	362	383	406	...	...	Production électrique totale (GWh) dont
Production of electricity from fossil fuels (GWh)	305	310	312	331	351	372	394	...	...	Production d'électricité à partir de combustibles fossiles (GWh)
Production of hydro electricity (GWh)	...	...	11	11	11	11	12	...	...	Production d'électricité d'origine hydraulique (GWh)
Production of electricity from solar, wind, tide, wave and other sources (GWh)	...	...	...	...	...	...	...	...	...	Production d'électricité d'origine solaire, éolienne, marée motrice et autres (GWh)

VII TOURISM AND INFRASTRUCTURE - TOURISME ET INFRASTUCTURE

VII-1 Tourism	2009	2010	2011	2012	2013	2014	2015	2016	2017	VII-1 Tourisme
International tourist arrivals (thousands)	...	...	...	...	...	...	...	...	...	Arrivées de touristes internationaux (milliers)
Rooms in hotels and similar establishments (thousands)	...	...	...	...	...	...	...	...	...	Chambres d'hôtels et établissements assimilés (milliers)
Overnight stays (thousands)	...	...	...	...	...	...	...	...	...	Nuitées (milliers)
Tourism receipts (US$ thousand)	...	...	...	...	...	...	...	...	...	Recettes touristiques (milliers de $ EU)
Total contribution to GDP (%)	...	...	...	...	...	...	...	...	...	Contribution totale au PIB (%)
Total contribution to Employment (%)	...	...	...	...	...	...	...	...	...	Contribution totale à l'emploi (%)
VII-2 Infrastructure										**VII-2 Infrastructure**
Paved road (% of total)	...	...	...	...	...	...	...	...	...	Routes asphaltées (% du total)
Total network (Railways-km)	...	...	...	...	...	...	...	...	...	Réseau total voies ferrées-Km
Main telephone lines (per 100 inhabitants)	1.1	1.0	0.9	0.7	0.6	0.5	...	...	...	Lignes téléphoniques fixes (pour 100 habitants)
Mobile cellular subscribers (per 100 inhabitants)	6.8	6.7	18.2	22.6	49.4	50.9	52.5	58.1	...	Abonnés aux téléphones mobiles (pour 100 habitants)
Internet users per 100 inhabitants	1.2	...	1.3	1.4	1.5	1.6	1.8	1.9	...	Utilisateurs Internet par 100 Habitants
Fixed (wired)-broadband subscriptions per 100 inhabitants	...	...	...	0.6	0.6	0.7	0.8	...		Abonnements à l'Internet fixe (filaire) à large bande pour 100 habitants, par débit

VIII EXTERNAL TRADE - COMMERCE EXTERIEUR

US$ (MILLIONS) EXPORTS, FOB	2009	2010	2011	2012	2013	2014	2015	2016	2017	$ E.U (MILLIONS) EXPORTATIONS, FÀB
Exports - Total	435	450	520	540	520	510	440	440	...	Exportations - Total
Exports to Africa	31	2	32	1	22	1	5	5	...	Exportations vers l'Afrique
Main products										**Principaux produits**
Crude vegetable materials, n.e.s.	5	4	4	5	4	4	8	23	...	Matières végétales brutes, n.e.s.
Fuel wood (excluding wood waste) and wood charcoal	56	57	61	45	1	...	...	1	...	Bois de chauffage (à l'exclusion des déchets de bois) et charbon de bois
Gold, non-monetary (excluding gold ores and concentrates)	66	50	28	24	16	18	25	83	...	Or, non monétaire (à l'exclusion des minerais d'or et des concentrés)
Live animals other than animals of division 03	215	281	330	418	386	390	338	193	...	Animaux vivants autres que les animaux de la division 03
Oil seeds and oleaginous fruits (excluding flour)	6	12	5	9	52	67	22	36	...	Graines oléagineuses et oléagineuses (à l'exclusion de la farine)
Main destinations										**Principales destinations**
India	6	11	3	9	33	42	11	24	...	Inde
Oman	102	84	78	99	91	105	88	190	...	Oman
Saudi Arabia	65	155	231	250	238	229	201	...	...	Arabie Saoudite
United Arab Emirates	147	109	82	81	57	65	82	104	...	Emirates Arabes
Yemen	65	47	37	53	36	19	13	...	...	Yémen
IMPORTS, CIF										
Imports - Total	750	840	1 200	1 200	1 300	1 250	1 100	1 080	...	Importations - Total (millions)
Imports from Africa	198	292	253	158	315	261	212	31	...	Importations en provenance de l'Afrique
Main products										**Principaux produits**
Meal and flour of wheat and flour of meslin	40	23	57	42	103	55	42	42	...	Repas et farine de blé et farine de méteil
Milk, cream and milk products (excluding butter, cheese)	34	28	56	70	52	81	48	39	...	Lait, crème et produits laitiers (à l'exclusion du beurre, du fromage)
Motor vehicles for the transport of persons	11	11	24	58	46	48	31	35	...	Véhicules à moteur pour le transport de personnes
Sugar, molasses and honey	96	114	132	113	65	95	83	143	...	Sucre, mélasse et miel
Vegetables	79	142	154	116	176	179	144	7	...	Légumes
Main origin										**Principales provenances**
China	41	44	67	52	54	93	117	173	...	Chine
Ethiopia	84	153	187	139	230	237	186	4	...	Ethiopie
India	11	43	89	101	76	152	165	221	...	Inde
Oman	74	49	98	123	158	88	74	78	...	Oman
United Arab Emirates	233	207	363	545	487	379	318	346	...	Emirates Arabes

SOMALIE

IX FINANCIAL AND MONETARY STATISTICS - FINANCES ET STATISTIQUES MONETAIRES

	2009	2010	2011	2012	2013	2014	2015	2016	2017	
IX-1 MONETARY STATISTICS *SOMALI SHILLING (MILLIONS)*										**IX-1 STATISTIQUES MONÉTAIRES** *SHILLING DE SOMALIE (MILLIONS)*
Money supply (M1)	...	...	...	...	...	...	...	...	...	Masse monétaire (M1)
Quasi-money	...	...	...	...	...	...	...	...	...	Quasi-monnaie
of which demand deposit	...	...	...	...	...	...	...	...	...	dont Monnaie scripturale
Net foreign assets	...	...	...	...	...	...	...	...	...	Avoirs extérieurs nets
Domestic credit	...	...	...	...	...	...	...	...	...	Crédit intérieur
of which claims on private sector	...	...	...	...	...	...	...	...	...	dont créances sur le secteur privé
of which claims on government sector, net	...	...	...	...	...	...	...	...	...	dont créances nettes sur le gouvernement
International reserves (millions US$)	...	...	...	...	...	...	...	...	...	Réserves internationales (millions $EU)
Average exchange rate (National currency per US$)	...	...	...	...	...	...	...	...	...	Taux de change (moyen) (monnaie nationale par $ EU)
IX-2 PUBLIC FINANCE *SOMALI SHILLING (MILLIONS)*										**IX-2 FINANCES PUBLIQUES** *SHILLING DE SOMALIE (MILLIONS)*
Total Revenues and Grants	...	...	...	...	...	...	...	...	...	Recettes totales et dons
Direct taxes (on income, profits)	...	...	...	...	...	...	...	...	...	Taxes directes
Domestic indirect taxes revenues	...	...	...	...	...	...	...	...	...	Taxes Indirectes
Trade taxes	...	...	...	...	...	...	...	...	...	Taxes sur le commerce extérieur
Other taxes	...	...	...	...	...	...	...	...	...	Autres taxes
Other revenues	...	...	...	...	...	...	...	...	...	Autres recettes
Grants	...	...	...	...	...	...	...	...	...	Dons
Total Expenditures and Net Lending	...	...	...	...	...	...	...	...	...	Dépenses totales et prêts nets
Current expenditure	...	...	...	...	...	...	...	...	...	Dépenses courantes
Wages and Salaries	...	...	...	...	...	...	...	...	...	Rémunérations et salaires
Other purchases of goods and services	...	...	...	...	...	...	...	...	...	Achat de biens et services
Other current expenditure	...	...	...	...	...	...	...	...	...	Autres dépenses courantes
Current transfers	...	...	...	...	...	...	...	...	...	Transferts courants
Interest payments	...	...	...	...	...	...	...	...	...	Intérêts
Capital expenditure	...	...	...	...	...	...	...	...	...	Dépenses d'équipement
Net lending	...	...	...	...	...	...	...	...	...	Prêts nets
Fiscal balance	...	...	...	...	...	...	...	...	...	Solde global y compris les dons
IX-3 BALANCE OF PAYMENTS *SOMALI SHILLING (MILLIONS)*										**IX-3 BALANCE DES PAIEMENTS** *SHILLING DE SOMALIE (MILLIONS)*
Trade balance	...	...	...	...	...	...	...	...	...	Balance commerciale
Services Balance	...	...	...	...	...	...	...	...	...	Balance des services
Net primary income	...	...	...	...	...	...	...	...	...	Revenus primaires nets
Compensation of employees	...	...	...	...	...	...	...	...	...	Rémunération des salariés
Investment income	...	...	...	...	...	...	...	...	...	Revenus des investissements
Net secondary income	...	...	...	...	...	...	...	...	...	Revenus secondaires nets
Net official transfers	...	...	...	...	...	...	...	...	...	Transferts officiels nets
Workers' remittances	...	...	...	...	...	...	...	...	...	Envois de fonds des travailleurs
Other private transfers	...	...	...	...	...	...	...	...	...	Autres transferts privés
Current account balance	...	...	...	...	...	...	...	...	...	Solde du compte courant
Capital and financial account	...	...	...	...	...	...	...	...	...	Comptes de capital et financier
Capital account	...	...	...	...	...	...	...	...	...	Compte de capital
Financial account	...	...	...	...	...	...	...	...	...	Compte financier
Errors and omissions	...	...	...	...	...	...	...	...	...	Erreurs et omissions
Overall balance	...	...	...	...	...	...	...	...	...	Balance générale

X DEBT AND FINANCIAL FLOWS - DETTE ET FLUX FINANCIERS										
	2009	2010	2011	2012	2013	2014	2015	2016	2017	
X-1 DEBT *US $ (MILLIONS)*										**X-1 DETTE EXTÉRIEURE** *$ E.U (MILLIONS)*
Total external debt	...	...	...	...	...	...	...	...	...	Dette extérieure totale
Private	...	...	...	...	...	...	...	...	...	Privée
Public	...	...	...	...	...	...	...	...	...	Publique
Total external debt service	...	...	...	...	...	...	...	...	...	Service de la dette extérieure
Present value of external debt	...	...	...	...	...	...	...	2 792	...	Valeur actuelle de la dette extérieure
Total government domestic debt, National currency (millions)	...	...	...	...	...	...	...	...	...	Dette publique intérieure
X-2 FINANCIAL FLOWS *US $ (MILLIONS)*										**X-2 FLUX FINANCIERS** *$ E.U (MILLIONS)*
Net Foreign Direct Investment Inflows	108	112	102	107	258	283	306	339	...	Investissements étranger direct (flux nets entrants)
Main origin of FDI inflows										**Principales origines de l'IDE entrant:**
...	...	...	...	...	...	...	...	...	...	...
...	...	...	...	...	...	...	...	...	...	...
...	...	...	...	...	...	...	...	...	...	...
...	...	...	...	...	...	...	...	...	...	...
...	...	...	...	...	...	...	...	...	...	...
African countries	...	...	...	...	...	...	...	...	...	Pays africains
Net total official development assistance	662	506	1 099	990	1 055	1 109	1 253	1 169	...	Aide publique au développement (nette totale)
Main origin of net ODA										**Principales origines de l'APD nette**
United States	195	68	125	211	245	203	204	214	...	États-Unis
United Kingdom	44	62	152	142	168	204	186	205	...	Royaume-Uni
Norway	33	32	84	35	63	63	42	40	...	Norvège
Sweden	29	26	64	42	58	83	61	64	...	Suède
Netherlands	15	9	28	18	6	6	2	8	...	Pays-Bas

SOMALIE

SOURCES AND NOTES - SOURCES ET NOTES

External trade - Total exports, fob: UNCTAD

External trade - Total import, cif: UNCTAD

ODA: OECD

Monetary statistics: IMF

National Accounts: 2015:Provisional

National Accounts: The data are estimated by the statistics division of the United Nations.

Poverty: World Bank

Commerce exterieur - Exportation, fab: CNUCED

Commerce exterieur - Imporations, caf: CNUCED

APD: OCDE

Statistiques monétaires: FMI

Comptes nationaux: 2015:Provisoire

Comptes Nationaux : Les données sont estimées par la division des statistiques des Nations Unies.

Pauvreté: Banque mondiale

AREA (km2)		1 219 090			**SUPERFICIE (KM2)**
CAPITAL CITY	Pretoria		Pretoria		**CAPITALE**
CURRENCY	South African Rand		Rand Sud-africain		**MONNAIE**

I SOCIAL AND DEMOGRAPHIC INDICATORS — INDICATEURS DEMOGRAPHIQUES ET SOCIAUX

	Year Année	Value Valeur	Charts / Graphiques	
Population				**Population**
Population ('000)	2016	55 653.7		Population ('000)
Female (%)	2016	51.0		Féminine (%)
Urban (%)	2016	65.3		Urbaine (%)
Average annual growth rate	2015	0.8		Taux de croissance annuel
Active population ('000)	2016	21 849.0		Population active ('000)
Population by age group ('000)				Population par groupe d'âge ('000)
0-14 years	2016	16 786.0		0-14 ans
15-64 years	2016	35 915.0		15-64 ans
65+ years	2016	2 952.0		65+ ans
Economically active population in agriculture (%)	2016	4.2		Participation de la population active agricole (%)
Crude birth rate	2016	19.6		Taux brut de natalité
Crude death rate	2015	12.4		Taux brut de mortalité
Total fertility rate	2016	2.3		Indice synthétique de fécondité
Life expectancy at birth - Total (years)	2015	57.7		Espérance de vie à la naissance - Totale (années)
Dependency ratio - Total (%)	2016	55.0		Taux de dépendance - Total (%)
Health				**Santé**
Percentage of children under-five and underweight	2008	8.7		% d'enfants de moins de cinq ans avec insuffisance pondérale
Prevalence of undernourishment	2016	5.0		Prévalence de la malnutrition
Under five mortality rate (per 1 000 live births)	2015	40.5		Taux de mortalité de moins de 5 ans (les deux sexes, pour 1000)
Infant mortality rate (per 1 000 live births)	2015	33.6		Taux de mortalité infantile (les deux sexes) par 1000
Neonatal mortality rate (per 1 000 live births)	2015	11.0		Le taux de mortalité néonatale (pour 1000 naissances vivantes)
Percentage of children provided the vaccines :				Pourcentage d'enfants vaccinés :
BCG	2015	69.0		BCG
DPT3	2015	69.0		DTC3
Polio	2015	95.0		polio
Measles	2015	76.0		rougeole
Percentage of mothers provided at least one antenatal care (%)	2003	91.7		Pourcentage de mères ayant au moins reçu un soin prénatal (%)
Percentage of deliveries attended by skilled health personnel	2003	91.2		% d'accouchements assistés par un personnel de santé qualifié
Number of doctors (per 10,000 population)	2013	7.8		Nombre de médecins (pour 10.000 habitants)
Number of nurses (per 10,000 population)	2012	49.0		Nombre d'infirmiers (pour 10.000 habitants)
Hospital beds - Total (per 10,000 population)	2005	28.4		Nombre de lits d'hôpitaux - Total (pour 10 000)
Births registered (per 1,000)	2015	20.4		Naissances enregistrées (pour 1000)
Deaths registered (per 1,000)	2015	12.4		Décès enregistrés (pour 1000)
Budget allocation to health (%)	2014	14.2		Dépenses publiques consacrées à la santé (% du budget)
Education				**Education**
Enrolment in primary education (000)	2014	7 195.2		Scolarisation dans le primaire (000)
Female	2014	3 494.0		Féminine
Enrolment in secondary education (000)	2013	5 201.2		Scolarisation dans le secondaire (000)
Female	2013	2 698.1		Féminine
Enrolment in tertiary education (000)	2014	1 018.5		Scolarisation dans le tertiaire (000)
Female	2014	591.8		Féminine
Literacy rate	2015	95.3		Taux d'alphabétisation (deux sexes)
Male	2015	95.9		Masculin
Female	2015	94.7		Féminin
Pupil teacher ratio - primary	2014	33.6		Ratio élève-enseignant
Budget allocation to education (%)	2013	19.1		Dépenses publiques consacrées à l'enseignement (% du budget)
Poverty				**Pauvreté**
GNI per capita, PPP (current int. $)	2016	12830.0		RNB par habitant, ($ PPA inter. courants)
Human Poverty Index (HPI-1) Value (%)	2007	25.4		Valeur de l'Indice de pauvreté (IPH-1) (%)
Population below Inter. poverty line ($2/day) (%)	2011	16.6		Population sous le seuil inter. de pauvreté (2$/Jour) (%)
Share of income held by richest 10%	2011	51.3		% de revenu des 10% plus riches
Share of income held by poorest 10%	2011	0.9		% de revenu des 10% plus pauvres
GINI index	2011	63.4		Indice de GINI

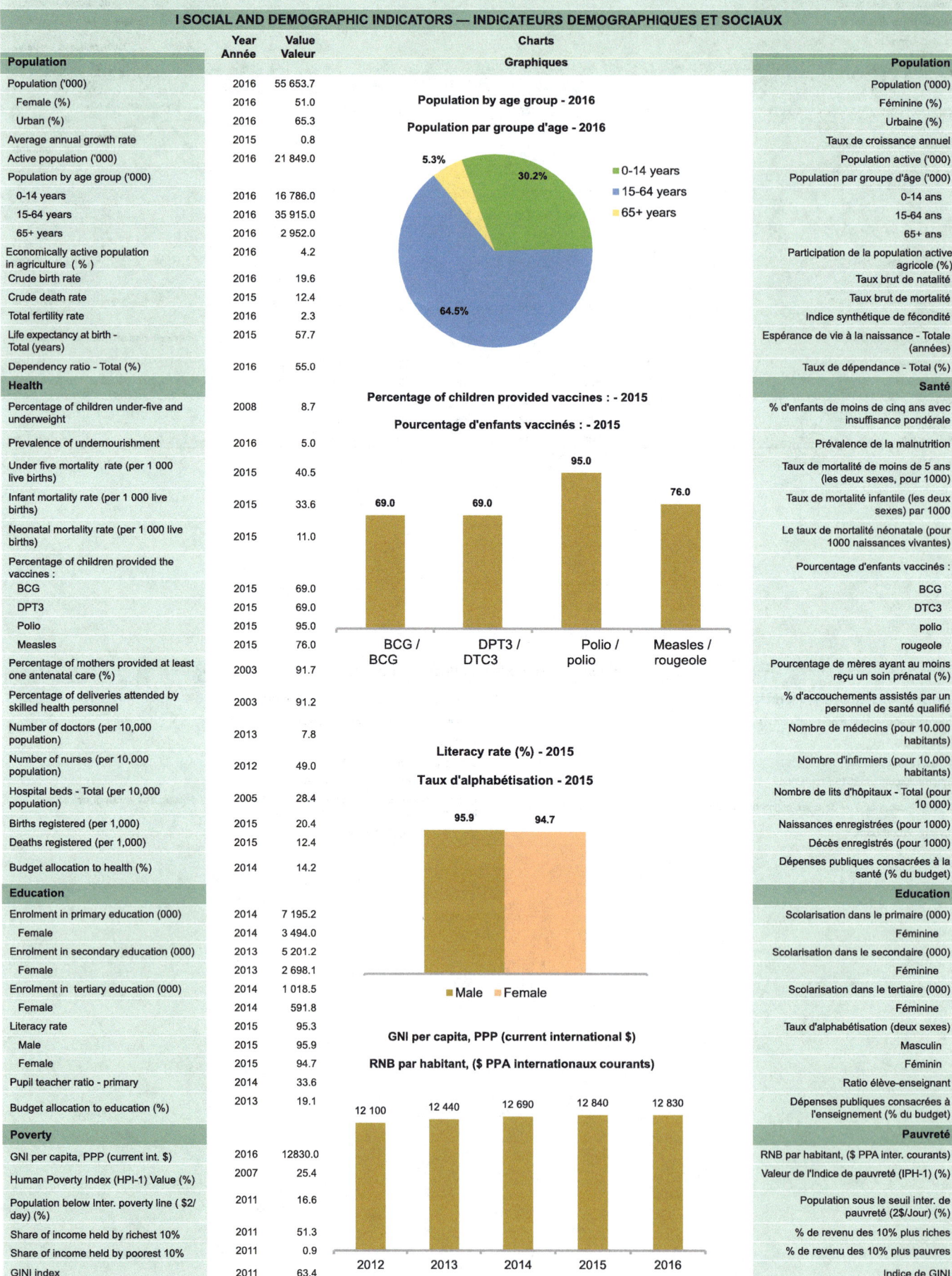

Population by age group - 2016
Population par groupe d'age - 2016

5.3% — 30.2% — 64.5%
- 0-14 years
- 15-64 years
- 65+ years

Percentage of children provided vaccines : - 2015
Pourcentage d'enfants vaccinés : - 2015

BCG / BCG: 69.0 DPT3 / DTC3: 69.0 Polio / polio: 95.0 Measles / rougeole: 76.0

Literacy rate (%) - 2015
Taux d'alphabétisation - 2015

Male: 95.9 Female: 94.7

GNI per capita, PPP (current international $)
RNB par habitant, ($ PPA internationaux courants)

2012: 12 100 2013: 12 440 2014: 12 690 2015: 12 840 2016: 12 830

SOUTH AFRICA

	2009	2010	2011	2012	2013	2014	2015	2016	2017	
GROSS DOMESTIC PRODUCT BY KIND OF ECONOMIC ACTIVITY AT CURRENT PRICES *SOUTH AFRICAN RAND (MILLIONS)*										**PRODUIT INTÉRIEUR BRUT PAR BRANCHE D'ACTIVITÉ ÉCONOMIQUE AUX PRIX COURANTS** *RAND SUD-AFRICAIN (MILLIONS)*
Agriculture, hunting , forestry and Fishing	68 044	65 605	69 105	70 592	74 260	82 755	84 303	94 757	106 421	Agriculture, chasse sylviculture et Pêche
Mining and quarrying	200 824	230 350	261 575	267 344	288 300	287 488	282 888	307 302	334 667	Industries extractives
Manufacturing	341 658	358 699	362 693	381 267	410 670	458 404	486 292	523 785	551 621	Industries manufacturières
Electricity, gas & water	53 473	67 940	86 547	105 731	116 468	124 341	136 969	146 024	155 155	Electricité, gaz et eau
Construction	95 753	95 453	103 835	113 820	128 606	139 903	148 951	154 368	163 307	Bâtiments et travaux publics
Wholesale & retail trade, restaurants, hotels	317 655	370 580	404 469	437 982	473 488	503 804	542 200	578 213	626 802	Commerce de gros et de détail, restaurants et hôtels
Finance, insurance, real estate, etc.	482 872	523 526	566 117	605 674	644 910	685 292	734 068	784 066	840 700	Banques, assurances, affaires immobilières
Transport and communications	223 427	229 499	257 335	289 003	326 646	351 475	370 985	384 503	411 483	Transport(s) et communications
Public administration and defense	356 819	404 647	448 778	485 222	534 550	585 108	626 892	684 959	739 459	Administrations publiques et défense
Education	...	...	...	...	...	...	...	...	...	Education
Health And Social Work	...	...	...	...	...	...	...	...	...	Santé et Actions Sociales
Other services	136 621	148 561	163 946	176 244	185 719	196 372	212 164	222 846	242 113	Autres services
Less Imputed Service Charges	...	...	...	...	...	...	...	...	...	Moins Services d'intermédiation financière
Gross domestic product at factor cost / basic prices	2 277 146	2 494 860	2 724 400	2 932 879	3 183 618	3 414 943	3 625 714	3 880 824	4 171 729	Produit intérieur brut aux couts des facteurs / prix de base
Plus: Indirect Taxes / taxes on products, less subsidies	230 531	253 148	299 259	320 972	356 359	390 407	425 707	469 490	480 056	Plus taxes indirectes/impôts sur les produits, moins les subventions
EXPENDITURE ON GROSS DOMESTIC PRODUCT AT CURRENT PURCHASER'S VALUES *SOUTH AFRICAN RAND (MILLIONS)*										**EMPLOI DU PRODUIT INTÉRIEUR BRUT AUX PRIX COURANTS D'ACQUISITION** *RAND SUD-AFRICAIN (MILLIONS)*
Government final consumption	486 027	555 912	600 566	659 228	728 350	791 348	828 934	905 164	973 820	Consommation finale des administrations publiques
Private final consumption	1 492 269	1 621 762	1 802 329	1 992 204	2 143 829	2 290 898	2 424 696	2 576 491	2 749 095	Consommation finale privée
Gross fixed capital formation	539 440	529 431	578 014	625 644	721 234	775 950	828 245	848 912	871 476	Formation brute de capital fixe
Change in inventories	- 20 228	6 787	18 280	24 020	27 951	4 128	21 730	- 6 992	- 6 157	Variation des stocks
Exports of goods and services	699 940	786 349	921 035	967 171	1 096 378	1 197 492	1 221 748	1 335 659	1 384 971	Exportations de biens et services
Less imports of goods and services	689 771	752 233	896 566	1 014 415	1 177 766	1 254 466	1 273 933	1 308 919	1 321 420	Moins importations de biens et services
GDP at purchasers' values	2 507 677	2 748 008	3 023 659	3 253 852	3 539 977	3 805 350	4 051 421	4 350 314	4 651 785	PIB aux prix d'acquisition
GROSS DOMESTIC PRODUCT BY KIND OF ECONOMIC ACTIVITY AT CONSTANT PRICES *ANNUAL GROWTH RATES (%)*										**PRODUIT INTÉRIEUR BRUT PAR BRANCHE D'ACTIVITÉ ECONOMIQUE AUX PRIX CONSTANTS** *TAUX DE CROISSANCE ANNUEL (%)*
Agriculture, hunting , forestry and Fishing	- 1.9	- 0.3	2.0	1.8	4.5	6.8	- 6.4	- 10.2	17.7	Agriculture, chasse sylviculture et Pêche
Mining and quarrying	- 5.1	5.3	- 0.7	- 2.9	4.0	- 1.7	3.1	- 4.2	4.6	Industries extractives
Manufacturing	- 10.6	5.9	3.0	2.1	1.0	0.3	- 0.4	0.9	- 0.2	Industries manufacturières
Electricity, gas & water	- 1.8	2.4	1.5	- 0.4	- 0.6	- 1.0	- 1.7	- 2.3	0.2	Electricité, gaz et eau
Construction	8.5	0.7	0.4	2.6	4.6	3.5	1.8	1.1	- 0.3	Bâtiments et travaux publics
Wholesale & retail trade, restaurants, hotels	- 1.1	4.4	4.1	4.0	2.0	1.4	1.9	1.7	- 0.6	Commerce de gros et de détail, restaurants et hôtels
Finance, insurance, real estate, etc.	1.1	1.2	4.3	3.0	2.6	2.7	2.6	2.3	1.9	Banques, assurances, affaires immobilières
Transport and communications	- 0.2	1.7	3.5	2.4	2.9	3.5	1.4	0.8	1.5	Transport(s) et communications
Public administration and defense	3.2	2.7	4.7	3.0	3.2	3.2	1.0	1.4	0.3	Administrations publiques et défense
Education	...	...	...	...	...	...	...	...	...	Education
Health And Social Work	...	...	...	...	...	...	...	...	...	Santé et Actions Sociales
Other services	- 0.8	0.4	2.5	2.1	2.6	1.8	1.0	1.5	1.2	Autres services
Less Imputed Service Charges	...	...	...	...	...	...	...	...	...	Moins Services d'intermédiation financière
Gross domestic product at factor cost / basic prices	- 1.4	2.9	3.2	2.2	2.6	1.9	1.2	0.7	1.3	Produit intérieur brut aux couts des facteurs / prix de base
Plus: Indirect Taxes / taxes on products, less subsidies	- 2.6	4.2	4.0	2.0	1.8	0.9	1.6	- 0.4	1.3	Plus taxes indirectes/impôts sur les produits, moins les subventions
Gross domestic product at market prices	- 1.5	3.0	3.3	2.2	2.5	1.8	1.3	0.6	1.3	Produit intérieur brut aux prix du marché
EXPENDITURE ON GROSS DOMESTIC PRODUCT AT CONSTANT PURCHASERS' VALUES *ANNUAL GROWTH RATES (%)*										**EMPLOIS DU PRODUIT INTÉRIEUR BRUT AUX PRIX CONSTANTS D'ACQUISITION** *TAUX DE CROISSANCE ANNUEL (%)*
Government final consumption	4.6	3.0	2.8	3.5	3.1	1.7	- 0.3	1.9	0.6	Consommation finale des administrations publiques
Private final consumption	- 2.6	3.9	5.7	3.2	1.5	1.1	1.7	0.7	2.4	Consommation finale privée
Gross fixed capital formation	- 6.7	- 3.9	5.5	2.6	7.2	0.7	3.4	- 4.1	0.4	Formation brute de capital fixe
Exports of goods and services	- 17.0	7.7	3.5	0.8	4.0	3.6	2.8	1.0	- 0.1	Exportations de biens et services
Less imports of goods and services	- 17.7	10.8	11.9	4.2	5.0	- 0.6	5.4	- 3.8	1.9	Moins importations de biens et services

III INFLATION

	2009	2010	2011	2012	2013	2014	2015	2016	2017	
Annual growth rates (%)										**Taux de croissance annuel (%)**
All item	7.3	4.1	5.0	5.7	5.8	6.1	4.5	6.6	5.2	Ensemble
of which:										dont:
Food and non-alcoholic beverages	9.3	1.2	7.1	7.2	5.7	8.0	5.0	11.7	6.8	Alimentation et boissons non alcoolisés
Alcoholic beverages, tobacco and narcotics	11.2	9.1	6.1	7.2	7.0	6.4	8.3	5.8	3.9	Boissons alcoolisées et tabacs
Clothing and footwear	4.9	2.0	2.3	3.8	3.2	5.4	5.4	5.0	3.3	Habillement et chaussures
Housing, water, electricity, gas and other fuels	8.1	6.7	6.8	6.4	5.7	5.6	5.9	5.9	5.1	Logement, eau, électricité, gaz et autres combustibles
Furnishings, household equipment and routine household maintenance	6.0	0.2	1.3	2.5	3.2	3.0	2.3	3.7	2.4	Meubles, articles de ménage et entretien courant
Health	10.8	7.7	5.9	5.3	4.6	5.3	6.1	5.5	6.6	Santé
Transport	- 0.5	2.5	5.0	6.4	6.2	6.4	- 1.0	4.2	4.9	Transport
Communication	0.5	- 2.0	- 1.9	- 0.9	1.1	- 0.7	- 0.9	- 0.1	- 1.2	Communication
Recreation and culture	11.4	0.1	- 0.6	0.9	3.3	2.7	2.3	6.9	2.5	Loisirs et culture
Education	9.6	9.5	8.9	9.0	9.0	8.9	9.3	5.3	6.6	Enseignement
Restaurants and hotels	11.0	7.1	4.9	6.2	6.7	8.4	5.9	6.1	4.7	Restaurants et hôtels
Miscellaneous goods and services	11.7	6.5	4.1	5.3	7.1	6.7	7.0	7.0	7.2	Biens et Services divers

AFRIQUE DU SUD

IV AGRICULTURAL PRODUCTION - PRODUCTION AGRICOLE

TONNES (THOUSAND)	2009	2010	2011	2012	2013	2014	2015	2016	2017	Tonnes (milliers)
Sugar cane	18 655	16 016	16 800	17 278	20 033	17 756	14 861	15 075	...	Canne à sucre
Maize	12 050	12 815	10 360	12 121	11 811	14 250	9 955	7 779	...	Maïs
Potatoes	1 867	2 090	2 197	2 229	2 174	2 247	2 487	2 151	...	Pommes de terre
Wheat	1 749	1 743	1 680	1 841	1 980	1 949	2 007	2 009	...	Blé
Grapes	1 958	1 430	2 005	1 915	1 870	1 750	1 457	1 910	...	Raisins

V MINING PRODUCTION - PRODUCTION MINIERE

	2009	2010	2011	2012	2013	2014	2015	2016	2017	
Hard Coal - Production, metric tons (thousands)	250 538	254 522	252 757	...	...	...	...	...	...	Houille - Production, tonnes métriques (milliers)
Iron ores and concentrates - Production, metric tons (thousands)	55 313	58 709	58 056	67 100	...	...	...	...	...	Minerais de fer et leurs concentrés - Production, tonnes métriques (milliers)
Copper ores and concentrates - Production, metric tons (thousands)	107 600	102 600	96 600	81 000	...	...	...	...	...	Minerais de cuivre et leurs concentrés - Production, tonnes métriques (milliers)

VI ENERGY - ENERGIE

	2009	2010	2011	2012	2013	2014	2015	2016	2017	
Total electricity generation (GWh)	240 444	245 840	279 585	258 237	283 728	286 710	295 389	...	...	Production électrique totale (GWh)
of which										dont
Production of electricity from fossil fuels (GWh)	222 603	227 552	257 857	235 766	260 017	262 952	265 886	...	...	Production d'électricité à partir de combustibles fossiles (GWh)
Production of hydro electricity (GWh)	4 194	5 091	7 858	7 858	7 858	7 858	12 960	...	...	Production d'électricité d'origine hydraulique (GWh)
Production of electricity from solar, wind, tide, wave and other sources (GWh)	564	110	123	131	142	152	756	...	...	Production d'électricité d'origine solaire, éolienne, marée motrice et autres (GWh)

VII TOURISM AND INFRASTRUCTURE - TOURISME ET INFRASTUCTURE

	2009	2010	2011	2012	2013	2014	2015	2016	2017	
VII-1 Tourism										**VII-1 Tourisme**
International tourist arrivals (thousands)	7 000	7 883	8 135	8 603	8 962	9 549	8 904	10 044	10 273	Arrivées de touristes internationaux (milliers)
Rooms in hotels and similar establishments (thousands)	...	...	...	77	78	78	79	80		Chambres d'hôtels et établissements assimilés (milliers)
Overnight stays (thousands)	42 140	49 686	52 467	55 377	57 272	60 288	56 293	65 084	66 796	Nuitées (milliers)
Tourism receipts (US$ thousand)	7 466 010	8 912 830	9 331 820	9 886 190	9 134 450	9 227 410	8 147 910	7 812 870	8 580 610	Recettes touristiques (milliers de $ EU)
Total contribution to GDP (%)	9.3	9.0	8.6	9.1	9.2	9.3	9.1	9.2	8.9	Contribution totale au PIB (%)
Total contribution to Employment (%)	10.0	9.8	9.5	9.9	9.7	9.9	9.8	9.8	9.5	Contribution totale à l'emploi (%)
VII-2 Infrastructure										**VII-2 Infrastructure**
Paved road (% of total)	...	...	...	...	...	21.3	...	...	...	Routes asphaltées (% du total)
Total network (Railways-km)	22 051	22 051	20 500	20 500	20 500	20 500	...	...	...	Réseau total voies ferrées-Km
Main telephone lines (per 100 inhabitants)	9.6	9.4	9.3	9.3	7.3	6.9	7.7	6.6	...	Lignes téléphoniques fixes (pour 100 habitants)
Mobile cellular subscribers (per 100 inhabitants)	91.2	97.9	123.2	130.6	145.6	149.2	164.5	142.4	...	Abonnés aux téléphones mobiles (pour 100 habitants)
Internet users per 100 inhabitants	10.0	24.0	34.0	41.0	46.5	49.0	51.9	54.0	...	Utilisateurs Internet par 100 Habitants
Fixed (wired)-broadband subscriptions per 100 inhabitants	0.9	1.4	1.7	2.1	3.1	3.2	2.6	2.8	...	Abonnements à l'Internet fixe (filaire) à large bande pour 100 habitants, par débit

VIII EXTERNAL TRADE - COMMERCE EXTERIEUR

US$ (MILLIONS) EXPORTS, FOB	2009	2010	2011	2012	2013	2014	2015	2016	2017	$ E.U (MILLIONS) EXPORTATIONS, FÀB
Exports - Total	53 864	82 626	107 946	98 872	95 112	90 612	69 631	74 111	...	Exportations - Total
Exports to Africa	10 523	23 328	26 652	27 645	27 371	27 628	21 741	21 363	...	Exportations vers l'Afrique
Main products										**Principaux produits**
Coal, whether or not pulverized, not agglomerated	4 204	5 504	7 421	6 718	5 773	5 145	4 231	3 829	...	Charbon, même pulvérisé, non aggloméré
Gold, non-monetary (excluding gold ores and concentrates)	200	230	10 634	8 874	6 813	4 866	2 103	3 700	...	Or, non monétaire (à l'exclusion des minerais d'or et des concentrés)
Iron ore and concentrates	3 135	5 462	9 006	7 751	8 458	6 739	2 652	3 582	...	Minerai de fer et ses concentrés
Motor vehicles for the transport of persons	3 062	4 596	4 721	4 028	3 667	4 372	4 727	5 274	...	Véhicules à moteur pour le transport de personnes
Silver, platinum, other metals of the platinum group	6 770	9 349	11 052	7 930	8 443	6 510	6 506	6 036	...	Argent, platine, autres métaux du groupe du platine
Main destinations										**Principales destinations**
Botswana	...	4 174	4 570	5 046	4 602	4 775	3 792	3 712	...	Botswana
China	5 670	8 095	12 495	10 337	12 046	8 680	5 803	6 812	...	Chine
Germany	3 513	5 494	5 468	4 047	3 828	4 236	4 237	5 260	...	Allemagne
Japan	4 096	6 428	7 624	5 696	5 572	4 869	3 644	3 450	...	Japon
United States	4 860	7 183	8 172	7 822	6 886	6 420	5 248	5 474	...	États-Unis
IMPORTS, CIF										
Imports - Total										Importations - Total (millions)
Imports from Africa										Importations en provenance de l'Afrique
Main products										**Principaux produits**
Automatic data processing machines, n.e.s.	1 286	1 731	2 050	2 054	2 109	2 020	1 751	1 496	...	Machines automatiques de traitement de l'information, n.d.a.
Motor vehicles for the transport of persons	2 336	4 068	5 072	5 168	5 494	4 706	4 038	3 342	...	Véhicules à moteur pour le transport de personnes
Petroleum oils or bituminous minerals > 70 % oil	2 463	3 367	5 742	5 856	6 433	5 806	4 263	2 557	...	Huiles de pétrole ou de minéraux bitumineux> 70% d'huile
Petroleum oils, oils from bitumin. materials, crude	10 294	11 199	14 086	15 788	14 722	16 212	8 475	6 535	...	Huiles de pétrole, huiles de bitume. matériaux bruts
Telecommunication equipment, n.e.s.; & parts, n.e.s.	2 627	3 734	4 108	3 793	4 139	3 886	3 663	3 522	...	Matériel de télécommunication, n.e.s .; & parties, n.e.s.
Main origin										**Principales provenances**
China	8 325	11 480	14 195	14 611	16 006	15 449	14 603	13 537	...	Chine
Germany	7 438	9 072	10 662	10 228	10 698	10 003	9 424	8 817	...	Allemagne
India	1 812	2 841	4 015	4 592	5 377	4 551	3 940	3 104	...	Inde
Saudi Arabia	3 204	3 240	4 444	7 936	8 026	7 129	2 218	2 836	...	Arabie Saoudite
United States	4 949	5 982	7 982	7 477	6 564	6 596	5 293	4 978	...	États-Unis

	2009	2010	2011	2012	2013	2014	2015	2016	2017	
IX-1 MONETARY STATISTICS *SOUTH AFRICAN RAND (MILLIONS)*										**IX-1 STATISTIQUES MONÉTAIRES** *RAND SUD-AFRICAIN (MILLIONS)*
Money supply (M1)	1 948 222	2 083 114	2 255 299	2 373 439	2 513 865	2 696 862	2 975 276	3 156 157	3 355 591	Masse monétaire (M1)
Quasi-money	1 154 303	1 217 424	1 420 874	1 475 003	1 552 370	1 690 421	1 853 685	1 893 556	2 014 519	Quasi-monnaie
of which demand deposit	...	...	...	...	...	...	...	...	...	dont Monnaie scripturale
Net foreign assets	333 510	337 781	504 824	504 105	641 393	600 238	785 383	703 621	698 526	Avoirs extérieurs nets
Domestic credit	2 108 473	2 238 120	2 292 052	2 524 945	2 586 829	2 833 667	3 061 742	3 353 894	3 662 174	Crédit intérieur
of which claims on private sector	55 124	51 900	- 16 724	- 24 842	- 115 106	- 108 153	- 199 429	- 56 912	50 154	dont créances sur le secteur privé
of which claims on government sector, net	1 870 685	1 933 351	2 043 637	2 233 178	2 381 470	2 551 944	2 763 817	2 903 518	3 051 522	dont créances nettes sur le gouvernement
International reserves (millions US$)	39 674	43 827	48 866	50 697	49 583	49 091	45 780	47 356	47 356	Réserves internationales (millions $EU)
Average exchange rate (National currency per US$)	8	7	7	8	10	11	13	15	13	Taux de change (moyen) (monnaie nationale par $ EU)
IX-2 PUBLIC FINANCE *SOUTH AFRICAN RAND (MILLIONS)*										**IX-2 FINANCES PUBLIQUES** *RAND SUD-AFRICAIN (MILLIONS)*
Total Revenues and Grants	682 995	664 842	762 873	842 165	907 566	1 008 051	1 095 322	1 215 270	1 285 690	Recettes totales et dons
Direct taxes (on income, profits)	383 483	359 045	379 941	426 584	457 314	507 759	561 790	606 821	664 526	Taxes directes
Domestic indirect taxes revenues	218 220	220 298	267 245	281 865	316 789	347 384	382 882	416 021	433 165	Taxes Indirectes
Trade taxes	- 6 069	- 8 596	9 071	12 361	- 2 602	1 358	- 10 275	- 4 080	6 654	Taxes sur le commerce extérieur
Other taxes	544	44	20	6	18	13	- 16	...	12	Autres taxes
Other revenues	86 817	94 051	106 596	121 349	136 047	151 537	160 941	196 508	181 333	Autres recettes
Grants	...	...	...	...	...	...	...	...	...	Dons
Total Expenditures and Net Lending	674 643	782 227	879 947	952 309	1 043 433	1 143 422	1 234 987	1 366 250	1 441 777	Dépenses totales et prêts nets
Current expenditure	579 104	660 436	726 255	805 223	878 764	953 988	1 021 949	1 104 514	1 196 534	Dépenses courantes
Wages and Salaries	211 164	248 612	309 862	347 424	376 325	407 961	437 364	472 800	510 803	Rémunérations et salaires
Other purchases of goods and services	96 075	106 219	137 693	150 789	162 924	174 172	186 009	195 265	214 596	Achat de biens et services
Other current expenditure	...	...	...	...	...	...	...	...	...	Autres dépenses courantes
Current transfers	271 865	305 605	278 699	307 010	339 515	371 856	398 577	436 449	471 136	Transferts courants
Interest payments	54 645	57 472	75 298	81 712	93 286	109 577	121 358	138 463	156 802	Intérêts
Capital expenditure	29 861	32 608	55 957	62 330	66 297	75 662	85 514	92 236	80 263	Dépenses d'équipement
Net lending	11 033	31 711	22 438	3 044	5 087	4 194	6 165	31 037	8 177	Prêts nets
Fiscal balance	8 352	- 117 385	- 117 074	- 110 145	- 135 868	- 135 371	- 139 665	- 150 980	- 156 088	Solde global y compris les dons
IX-3 BALANCE OF PAYMENTS *SOUTH AFRICAN RAND (MILLIONS)*										**IX-3 BALANCE DES PAIEMENTS** *RAND SUD-AFRICAIN (MILLIONS)*
Trade balance	28 104	59 744	49 213	- 36 790	- 69 408	- 54 871	- 46 147	34 705	68 856	Balance commerciale
Services Balance	- 17 935	- 25 628	- 24 744	- 10 454	- 11 979	- 2 103	- 6 038	- 7 965	- 5 306	Balance des services
Net primary income	- 56 159	- 58 599	- 77 331	- 88 336	- 92 788	- 101 544	- 100 366	- 120 470	- 139 564	Revenus primaires nets
Compensation of employees	...	34 099	38 118	48 501	64 441	82 235	98 016	87 773	81 637	Rémunération des salariés
Investment income	...	...	...	...	...	...	...	...	...	Revenus des investissements
Net secondary income	- 22 428	- 16 762	- 14 199	- 31 369	- 30 666	- 34 448	- 33 533	- 27 458	- 38 303	Revenus secondaires nets
Net official transfers	...	...	...	...	...	...	...	...	...	Transferts officiels nets
Workers' remittances	...	...	...	...	...	...	...	...	...	Envois de fonds des travailleurs
Other private transfers	...	...	...	...	...	...	...	...	...	Autres transferts privés
Current account balance	- 68 418	- 41 245	- 67 061	- 166 949	- 204 841	- 192 966	- 186 084	- 121 188	- 114 317	Solde du compte courant
Capital and financial account	114 503	56 353	90 512	201 741	179 859	248 499	209 587	131 673	101 371	Comptes de capital et financier
Capital account	216	225	241	239	243	236	243	241	246	Compte de capital
Financial account	114 287	56 128	90 271	201 502	179 616	248 263	209 344	131 432	101 125	Compte financier
Errors and omissions	...	...	...	...	...	...	...	...	...	Erreurs et omissions
Overall balance	46 085	15 108	23 451	34 792	- 24 982	55 533	23 503	10 485	- 12 946	Balance générale

AFRIQUE DU SUD

X DEBT AND FINANCIAL FLOWS - DETTE ET FLUX FINANCIERS

X-1 DEBT US $ (MILLIONS)	2009	2010	2011	2012	2013	2014	2015	2016	2017	X-1 DETTE EXTÉRIEURE $ E.U (MILLIONS)
Total external debt	82 893	111 256	118 180	141 791	136 516	145 082	124 132	142 833	158 395	Dette extérieure totale
Private	38 244	51 596	55 227	59 968	60 370	59 491	55 103	59 390	...	Privée
Public	22 602	35 819	41 541	55 918	52 809	53 829	40 933	56 001	...	Publique
Total external debt service	36 626	35 532	38 365	39 052	49 234	44 034	54 241	47 428	...	Service de la dette extérieure
Present value of external debt	...	...	...	...	...	...	...	62 427	...	Valeur actuelle de la dette extérieure
Total government domestic debt, National currency (millions)	658	840	1 030	1 209	...	...	...	...	...	Dette publique intérieure
X-2 FINANCIAL FLOWS US $ (MILLIONS)										**X-2 FLUX FINANCIERS** $ E.U (MILLIONS)
Net Foreign Direct Investment Inflows	7 502	3 636	4 243	4 559	8 300	5 771	1 729	2 270	...	Investissements étranger direct (flux nets entrants)
Main origin of FDI inflows										**Principales origines de l'IDE entrant:**
Switzerland	- 225	122	245	129	...	...	...	...	...	Suisse
United States	410	779	722	250	...	...	...	...	...	États-Unis
Germany	307	740	605	316	...	...	...	...	...	Allemagne
France	393	277	366	217	...	...	...	...	...	France
...	...	...	...	...	...	...	...	...	...	...
African countries	...	...	...	...	...	...	...	...	...	Pays africains
Net total official development assistance	1 074	1 036	1 397	1 066	1 295	1 077	1 420	1 181	...	Aide publique au développement (nette totale)
Main origin of net ODA										**Principales origines de l'APD nette**
United States	524	526	556	504	477	515	336	491	...	États-Unis
Germany	87	40	105	54	52	103	387	356	...	Allemagne
United Kingdom	67	39	47	- 22	56	- 30	29	17	...	Royaume-Uni
France	- 16	48	144	58	301	54	123	36	...	France
Netherlands	49	36	33	22	10	3	3	3	...	Pays-Bas

SOURCES AND NOTES - SOURCES ET NOTES

External trade - Total exports, fob: UNCTAD	Commerce exterieur - Exportation, fab: CNUCED
External trade - Total import, cif: UNCTAD	Commerce exterieur - Imporations, caf: CNUCED
ODA: OECD	APD: OCDE
Monetary statistics: IMF	Statistiques monétaires: FMI
National Accounts: The Accounts are calculated using the new base year 2010	Comptes nationaux: Les comptes Annuels sont élaborés selon la nouvelle année de base 2010
Poverty: World Bank	Pauvreté: Banque mondiale

		644 330		
AREA (km2)				**SUPERFICIE (KM2)**
CAPITAL CITY	Juba		Djouba	**CAPITALE**
CURRENCY	South Sudanese Pound		Livre Sud-Sudanais	**MONNAIE**

I SOCIAL AND DEMOGRAPHIC INDICATORS — INDICATEURS DEMOGRAPHIQUES ET SOCIAUX

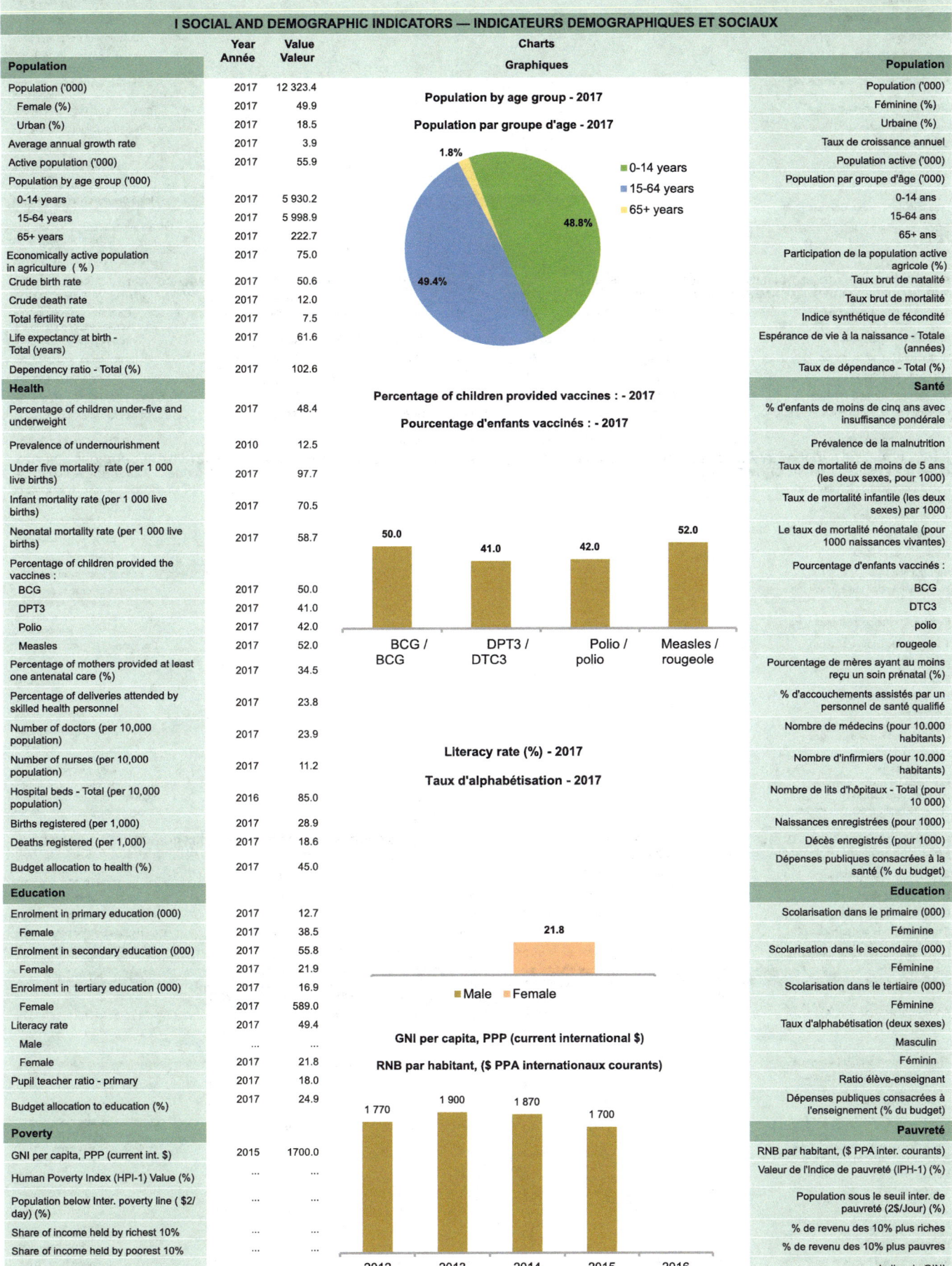

Population	Year Année	Value Valeur	Charts / Graphiques	Population
Population ('000)	2017	12 323.4		Population ('000)
Female (%)	2017	49.9		Féminine (%)
Urban (%)	2017	18.5		Urbaine (%)
Average annual growth rate	2017	3.9		Taux de croissance annuel
Active population ('000)	2017	55.9		Population active ('000)
Population by age group ('000)				Population par groupe d'âge ('000)
0-14 years	2017	5 930.2		0-14 ans
15-64 years	2017	5 998.9		15-64 ans
65+ years	2017	222.7		65+ ans
Economically active population in agriculture (%)	2017	75.0		Participation de la population active agricole (%)
Crude birth rate	2017	50.6		Taux brut de natalité
Crude death rate	2017	12.0		Taux brut de mortalité
Total fertility rate	2017	7.5		Indice synthétique de fécondité
Life expectancy at birth - Total (years)	2017	61.6		Espérance de vie à la naissance - Totale (années)
Dependency ratio - Total (%)	2017	102.6		Taux de dépendance - Total (%)
Health				**Santé**
Percentage of children under-five and underweight	2017	48.4		% d'enfants de moins de cinq ans avec insuffisance pondérale
Prevalence of undernourishment	2010	12.5		Prévalence de la malnutrition
Under five mortality rate (per 1 000 live births)	2017	97.7		Taux de mortalité de moins de 5 ans (les deux sexes, pour 1000)
Infant mortality rate (per 1 000 live births)	2017	70.5		Taux de mortalité infantile (les deux sexes) par 1000
Neonatal mortality rate (per 1 000 live births)	2017	58.7		Le taux de mortalité néonatale (pour 1000 naissances vivantes)
Percentage of children provided the vaccines :				Pourcentage d'enfants vaccinés :
BCG	2017	50.0		BCG
DPT3	2017	41.0		DTC3
Polio	2017	42.0		polio
Measles	2017	52.0		rougeole
Percentage of mothers provided at least one antenatal care (%)	2017	34.5		Pourcentage de mères ayant au moins reçu un soin prénatal (%)
Percentage of deliveries attended by skilled health personnel	2017	23.8		% d'accouchements assistés par un personnel de santé qualifié
Number of doctors (per 10,000 population)	2017	23.9		Nombre de médecins (pour 10.000 habitants)
Number of nurses (per 10,000 population)	2017	11.2		Nombre d'infirmiers (pour 10.000 habitants)
Hospital beds - Total (per 10,000 population)	2016	85.0		Nombre de lits d'hôpitaux - Total (pour 10 000)
Births registered (per 1,000)	2017	28.9		Naissances enregistrées (pour 1000)
Deaths registered (per 1,000)	2017	18.6		Décès enregistrés (pour 1000)
Budget allocation to health (%)	2017	45.0		Dépenses publiques consacrées à la santé (% du budget)
Education				**Education**
Enrolment in primary education (000)	2017	12.7		Scolarisation dans le primaire (000)
Female	2017	38.5		Féminine
Enrolment in secondary education (000)	2017	55.8		Scolarisation dans le secondaire (000)
Female	2017	21.9		Féminine
Enrolment in tertiary education (000)	2017	16.9		Scolarisation dans le tertiaire (000)
Female	2017	589.0		Féminine
Literacy rate	2017	49.4		Taux d'alphabétisation (deux sexes)
Male	...	...		Masculin
Female	2017	21.8		Féminin
Pupil teacher ratio - primary	2017	18.0		Ratio élève-enseignant
Budget allocation to education (%)	2017	24.9		Dépenses publiques consacrées à l'enseignement (% du budget)
Poverty				**Pauvreté**
GNI per capita, PPP (current int. $)	2015	1700.0		RNB par habitant, ($ PPA inter. courants)
Human Poverty Index (HPI-1) Value (%)	...	...		Valeur de l'Indice de pauvreté (IPH-1) (%)
Population below Inter. poverty line ($2/day) (%)	...	...		Population sous le seuil inter. de pauvreté (2$/Jour) (%)
Share of income held by richest 10%	...	...		% de revenu des 10% plus riches
Share of income held by poorest 10%	...	...		% de revenu des 10% plus pauvres
GINI index	...	...		Indice de GINI

SOUTH SUDAN

	2009	2010	2011	2012	2013	2014	2015	2016	2017	
GROSS DOMESTIC PRODUCT BY KIND OF ECONOMIC ACTIVITY AT CURRENT PRICES *SUDANESE POUND (MILLIONS)*										**PRODUIT INTÉRIEUR BRUT PAR BRANCHE D'ACTIVITÉ ÉCONOMIQUE AUX PRIX COURANTS** *POUND SOUDANAIS (MILLIONS)*
Agriculture, hunting , forestry and Fishing	...	...	...	...	...	...	...	...	...	Agriculture, chasse sylviculture et Pêche
Mining and quarrying	...	...	...	...	...	...	...	...	...	Industries extractives
Manufacturing	...	...	...	...	...	...	...	...	...	Industries manufacturières
Electricity, gas & water	...	...	...	...	...	...	...	...	...	Electricité, gaz et eau
Construction	...	...	...	...	...	...	...	...	...	Bâtiments et travaux publics
Wholesale & retail trade, restaurants, hotels	...	...	...	...	...	...	...	...	...	Commerce de gros et de détail, restaurants et hôtels
Finance, insurance, real estate, etc.	...	...	...	...	...	...	...	...	...	Banques, assurances, affaires immobilières
Transport and communications	...	...	...	...	...	...	...	...	...	Transport(s) et communications
Public administration and defense	...	...	...	...	...	...	...	...	...	Administrations publiques et défense
Education	...	...	...	...	...	...	...	...	...	Education
Health And Social Work	...	...	...	...	...	...	...	...	...	Santé et Actions Sociales
Other services	...	...	...	...	...	...	...	...	...	Autres services
Less Imputed Service Charges	...	...	...	...	...	...	...	...	...	Moins Services d'intermédiation financière
Gross domestic product at factor cost / basic prices	...	...	...	...	...	...	...	...	...	Produit intérieur brut aux couts des facteurs / prix de base
Plus: Indirect Taxes / taxes on products, less subsidies	...	...	...	...	...	...	...	...	...	Plus taxes indirectes/impôts sur les produits, moins les subventions
EXPENDITURE ON GROSS DOMESTIC PRODUCT AT CURRENT PURCHASER'S VALUES *SUDANESE POUND (MILLIONS)*										**EMPLOI DU PRODUIT INTÉRIEUR BRUT AUX PRIX COURANTS D'ACQUISITION** *POUND SOUDANAIS (MILLIONS)*
Government final consumption	4 362	5 854	6 782	7 001	8 228	9 880	14 964	30 890	...	Consommation finale des administrations publiques
Private final consumption	12 972	14 414	21 108	28 846	30 976	32 002	48 988	243 781	...	Consommation finale privée
Gross fixed capital formation	3 857	3 730	5 056	3 463	4 488	4 553	5 319	19 363	...	Formation brute de capital fixe
Change in inventories	8	10	7	17	17	113	22	113	...	Variation des stocks
Exports of goods and services	17 041	22 272	35 204	3 084	11 449	16 493	9 874	91 722	...	Exportations de biens et services
Less imports of goods and services	10 060	11 216	14 986	14 180	15 545	16 290	24 337	63 022	...	Moins importations de biens et services
GDP at purchasers' values	28 180	35 065	53 171	28 231	39 612	46 751	54 830	322 846	...	PIB aux prix d'acquisition
GROSS DOMESTIC PRODUCT BY KIND OF ECONOMIC ACTIVITY AT CONSTANT PRICES *ANNUAL GROWTH RATES (%)*										**PRODUIT INTÉRIEUR BRUT PAR BRANCHE D'ACTIVITÉ ECONOMIQUE AUX PRIX CONSTANTS** *TAUX DE CROISSANCE ANNUEL (%)*
Agriculture, hunting , forestry and Fishing	...	...	...	...	...	...	...	...	...	Agriculture, chasse sylviculture et Pêche
Mining and quarrying	...	...	...	...	...	...	...	...	...	Industries extractives
Manufacturing	...	...	...	...	...	...	...	...	...	Industries manufacturières
Electricity, gas & water	...	...	...	...	...	...	...	...	...	Electricité, gaz et eau
Construction	...	...	...	...	...	...	...	...	...	Bâtiments et travaux publics
Wholesale & retail trade, restaurants, hotels	...	...	...	...	...	...	...	...	...	Commerce de gros et de détail, restaurants et hôtels
Finance, insurance, real estate, etc.	...	...	...	...	...	...	...	...	...	Banques, assurances, affaires immobilières
Transport and communications	...	...	...	...	...	...	...	...	...	Transport(s) et communications
Public administration and defense	...	...	...	...	...	...	...	...	...	Administrations publiques et défense
Education	...	...	...	...	...	...	...	...	...	Education
Health And Social Work	...	...	...	...	...	...	...	...	...	Santé et Actions Sociales
Other services	...	...	...	...	...	...	...	...	...	Autres services
Less Imputed Service Charges	...	...	...	...	...	...	...	...	...	Moins Services d'intermédiation financière
Gross domestic product at factor cost / basic prices	...	...	...	...	...	...	...	...	...	Produit intérieur brut aux couts des facteurs / prix de base
Plus: Indirect Taxes / taxes on products, less subsidies	...	...	...	...	...	...	...	...	...	Plus taxes indirectes/impôts sur les produits, moins les subventions
Gross domestic product at market prices	7.4	- 1.8	1.9	- 51.5	30.2	22.2	5.1	0.3	...	Produit intérieur brut aux prix du marché
EXPENDITURE ON GROSS DOMESTIC PRODUCT AT CONSTANT PURCHASERS' VALUES *ANNUAL GROWTH RATES (%)*										**EMPLOIS DU PRODUIT INTÉRIEUR BRUT AUX PRIX CONSTANTS D'ACQUISITION** *TAUX DE CROISSANCE ANNUEL (%)*
Government final consumption	- 11.3	6.5	3.1	- 9.6	12.5	22.7	29.4	8.3	...	Consommation finale des administrations publiques
Private final consumption	6.4	9.1	1.3	- 7.2	7.6	1.3	-	4.8	...	Consommation finale privée
Gross fixed capital formation	- 19.8	- 7.8	3.9	- 49.7	25.6	- 1.6	- 17.9	- 26.9	...	Formation brute de capital fixe
Exports of goods and services	10.8	- 1.6	- 2.1	- 91.9	255.5	59.1	- 1.0	- 15.9	...	Exportations de biens et services
Less imports of goods and services	- 9.1	14.0	- 3.5	- 35.2	18.3	1.8	1.4	- 4.9	...	Moins importations de biens et services

	2009	2010	2011	2012	2013	2014	2015	2016	2017	
					III INFLATION					
Annual growth rates (%)										**Taux de croissance annuel (%)**
All item	5.0	1.2	47.3	45.1	-	1.7	52.8	379.9	187.9	Ensemble
of which:										dont:
Food and non-alcoholic beverages	5.1	0.6	53.6	44.0	- 4.0	2.6	60.3	375.3	175.4	Alimentation et boissons non alcoolisés
Alcoholic beverages, tobacco and narcotics	1.3	4.7	75.8	134.2	33.1	- 13.2	6.9	350.3	159.2	Boissons alcoolisées et tabacs
Clothing and footwear	...	...	...	30.0	10.5	- 1.5	89.1	415.2	222.3	Habillement et chaussures
Housing, water, electricity, gas and other fuels	5.4	- 3.3	25.7	40.2	- 7.9	12.3	28.0	388.9	216.0	Logement, eau, électricité, gaz et autres combustibles
Furnishings, household equipment and routine household maintenance	9.2	7.0	58.5	46.0	- 0.3	2.6	68.3	361.7	185.4	Meubles, articles de ménage et entretien courant
Health	...	...	...	7.0	- 8.6	11.6	39.1	718.3	200.4	Santé
Transport	- 2.8	4.8	35.0	26.8	- 2.5	- 8.1	12.8	300.3	215.7	Transport
Communication	...	...	...	0.9	- 1.0	- 5.8	19.9	351.7	282.9	Communication
Recreation and culture	29.2	9.7	14.7	33.4	11.8	14.5	33.7	221.9	193.0	Loisirs et culture
Education	...	...	...	43.4	12.3	3.8	0.1	...	295.2	Enseignement
Restaurants and hotels	11.6	6.3	25.2	34.9	17.5	3.3	40.9	272.8	305.4	Restaurants et hôtels
Miscellaneous goods and services	4.8	6.3	10.8	29.7	12.4	3.2	60.3	319.1	281.5	Biens et Services divers

IV AGRICULTURAL PRODUCTION - PRODUCTION AGRICOLE

	2009	2010	2011	2012	2013	2014	2015	2016	2017	
TONNES (THOUSAND)										**Tonnes (milliers)**
Cereals, nes	825	874	703	952	112	127	115	788	...	Céréales, nda
Olives	...	...	75 100	601 349	601 349	35 550	35 550	40 317	...	Olives
Dates	...	...	64 588	52 718	52 718	59 550	559 550	561 010	...	Dattes
	...	...	...	...	...	...	...	...	...	
	...	...	...	...	...	...	...	...	...	

V MINING PRODUCTION - PRODUCTION MINIERE

	2009	2010	2011	2012	2013	2014	2015	2016	2017	
Crude petroleum - Production, metric tons (thousands)	1 255	3 196	122	338	1 591	5 572	21 951	30 855	3 171	Pétrole brut - Production, tonnes métriques (milliers)
	...	...	...	...	...	...	...	...	...	
	...	...	...	...	...	...	...	...	...	

VI ENERGY - ENERGIE

	2009	2010	2011	2012	2013	2014	2015	2016	2017	
Total electricity generation (GWh)	...	...	172	193	271	297	325	...	...	Production électrique totale (GWh)
of which										dont
Production of electricity from fossil fuels (GWh)	...	...	158	175	250	275	302	...	...	Production d'électricité à partir de combustibles fossiles (GWh)
Production of hydro electricity (GWh)	...	...	14	18	21	21	21	...	...	Production d'électricité d'origine hydraulique (GWh)
Production of electricity from solar, wind, tide, wave and other sources (GWh)	...	...	...	...	...	1	2	...	...	Production d'électricité d'origine solaire, éolienne, marée motrice et autres (GWh)

VII TOURISM AND INFRASTRUCTURE - TOURISME ET INFRASTUCTURE

	2009	2010	2011	2012	2013	2014	2015	2016	2017	
VII-1 Tourism										**VII-1 Tourisme**
International tourist arrivals (thousands)	...	...	...	...	...	...	...	...	...	Arrivées de touristes internationaux (milliers)
Rooms in hotels and similar establishments (thousands)	...	...	...	...	...	...	...	...	...	Chambres d'hôtels et établissements assimilés (milliers)
Overnight stays (thousands)	...	...	...	...	...	...	...	...	...	Nuitées (milliers)
Tourism receipts (US$ thousand)	...	...	694	897	313	342	763	987	104	Recettes touristiques (milliers de $ EU)
Total contribution to GDP (%)	...	...	...	...	...	...	...	...	...	Contribution totale au PIB (%)
Total contribution to Employment (%)	...	...	...	...	...	...	...	...	...	Contribution totale à l'emploi (%)
VII-2 Infrastructure										**VII-2 Infrastructure**
Paved road (% of total)	...	...	...	2.7	...	...	...	...	...	Routes asphaltées (% du total)
Total network (Railways-km)	...	...	...	...	...	...	...	...	...	Réseau total voies ferrées-Km
Main telephone lines (per 100 inhabitants)	...	...	...	...	...	...	...	...	...	Lignes téléphoniques fixes (pour 100 habitants)
Mobile cellular subscribers (per 100 inhabitants)	...	14.4	17.3	21.2	25.3	24.5	23.9	21.5	...	Abonnés aux téléphones mobiles (pour 100 habitants)
Internet users per 100 inhabitants	...	...	...	...	...	...	...	...	...	Utilisateurs Internet par 100 Habitants
Fixed (wired)-broadband subscriptions per 100 inhabitants	...	...	...	...	...	...	...	...	...	Abonnements à l'Internet fixe (filaire) à large bande pour 100 habitants, par débit

VIII EXTERNAL TRADE - COMMERCE EXTERIEUR

	2009	2010	2011	2012	2013	2014	2015	2016	2017	
US$ (MILLIONS) **EXPORTS, FOB**										**$ E.U (MILLIONS)** **EXPORTATIONS, FÀB**
Exports - Total	...	...	...	...	...	...	...	...	...	Exportations - Total
Exports to Africa	...	...	...	...	...	...	...	...	...	Exportations vers l'Afrique
Main products										**Principaux produits**
...	...	...	...	...	...	...	...	...	...	...
...	...	...	...	...	...	...	...	...	...	...
...	...	...	...	...	...	...	...	...	...	...
...	...	...	...	...	...	...	...	...	...	...
...	...	...	...	...	...	...	...	...	...	...
Main destinations										**Principales destinations**
...	...	...	...	...	...	...	...	...	...	...
...	...	...	...	...	...	...	...	...	...	...
...	...	...	...	...	...	...	...	...	...	...
...	...	...	...	...	...	...	...	...	...	...
...	...	...	...	...	...	...	...	...	...	...
IMPORTS, CIF										
Imports - Total	...	...	...	...	...	...	...	...	...	Importations - Total (millions)
Imports from Africa	...	...	...	...	...	...	...	...	...	Importations en provenance de l'Afrique
Main products										**Principaux produits**
...	...	...	...	...	...	...	...	...	...	...
...	...	...	...	...	...	...	...	...	...	...
...	...	...	...	...	...	...	...	...	...	...
...	...	...	...	...	...	...	...	...	...	...
...	...	...	...	...	...	...	...	...	...	...
Main origin										**Principales provenances**
...	...	...	...	...	...	...	...	...	...	...
...	...	...	...	...	...	...	...	...	...	...
...	...	...	...	...	...	...	...	...	...	...
...	...	...	...	...	...	...	...	...	...	...

SOUDAN DU SUD

IX FINANCIAL AND MONETARY STATISTICS - FINANCES ET STATISTIQUES MONETAIRES

	2009	2010	2011	2012	2013	2014	2015	2016	2017	
IX-1 MONETARY STATISTICS *SUDANESE POUND (MILLIONS)*										**IX-1 STATISTIQUES MONÉTAIRES** *POUND SOUDANAIS (MILLIONS)*
Money supply (M1)	...	...	4 913	6 576	6 473	7 844	17 052	41 349	42 009	Masse monétaire (M1)
Quasi-money	...	...	454	586	949	1 017	2 763	7 182	7 497	Quasi-monnaie
of which demand deposit	...	...								dont Monnaie scripturale
Net foreign assets	...	...	7 521	3 876	2 973	1 560	- 7 298	- 40 124	- 54 907	Avoirs extérieurs nets
Domestic credit	...	...	- 3 273	1 964	3 755	8 852	14 572	19 181	29 883	Crédit intérieur
of which claims on private sector	...	...	- 3 530	1 533	3 099	8 106	13 576	16 376	21 517	dont créances sur le secteur privé
of which claims on government sector, net	...	...	229	402	616	746	997	2 800	8 360	dont créances nettes sur le gouvernement
International reserves (millions US$)	...	...	2 017	1 314	990	426	50	34	42	Réserves internationales (millions $EU)
Average exchange rate (National currency per US$)	...	...	...	3	3	3	4	49	115	Taux de change (moyen) (monnaie nationale par $ EU)
IX-2 PUBLIC FINANCE *SUDANESE POUND (MILLIONS)*										**IX-2 FINANCES PUBLIQUES** *POUND SOUDANAIS (MILLIONS)*
Total Revenues and Grants	4 240	5 757	10 183	6 970	16 637	6 158	10 642	11 743	14 169	Recettes totales et dons
Direct taxes (on income, profits)	4 121	5 630	9 883	374	10 039	4 666	7 342	6 118	6 900	Taxes directes
Domestic indirect taxes revenues	118	127	300	915	951	1 402	2 568	2 113	364	Taxes Indirectes
Trade taxes	29	3	4	40	7	5	7	2 876	184	Taxes sur le commerce extérieur
Other taxes	118	127	111	300	915	1 968	725	637	115	Autres taxes
Other revenues	4 121	5 630	5 656	9 883	374	10 411	457	789	287	Autres recettes
Grants	...	...	...	...	50	89 459	127 586	987 099	414	Dons
Total Expenditures and Net Lending	5 325	6 966	11 271	6 813	17 367	14 366	10 642	12 246	1 477	Dépenses totales et prêts nets
Current expenditure	4 323	5 876	9 411	208	15 865	13 713	10 304	11 212	2 230	Dépenses courantes
Wages and Salaries	1 977	2 206	3 801	3 202	3 636	5 740	5 463	7 877	2 241	Rémunérations et salaires
Other purchases of goods and services	1 255	2 280	2 076	2 197	1 303	1 927	1 672	1 551	890	Achat de biens et services
Other current expenditure	...	167	720	45	8 666	2 622	8	8	590	Autres dépenses courantes
Current transfers	1 090	1 224	2 694	1 658	1 658	2 589	2 795	4 863	1 118	Transferts courants
Interest payments	...	...	...	...	...	...	...	...	702	Intérêts
Capital expenditure	1 002	1 091	1 258	1 859	605	1 501	266	345	3 470	Dépenses d'équipement
Net lending	...	...	...	...	...	...	...	...	...	Prêts nets
Fiscal balance	- 1 085	- 1 210	- 1 088	- 157	- 730	- 8 208	- 985	- 876	- 605	Solde global y compris les dons
IX-3 BALANCE OF PAYMENTS *SUDANESE POUND (MILLIONS)*										**IX-3 BALANCE DES PAIEMENTS** *POUND SOUDANAIS (MILLIONS)*
Trade balance	...	...	8 448	- 2 212	277	1 438	245	109	- 212	Balance commerciale
Services Balance	...	...	- 1 213	- 585	- 557	- 1 079	- 713	- 503	- 563	Balance des services
Net primary income	...	...	- 4 859	...	- 1 294	- 1 274	- 595	- 394	- 290	Revenus primaires nets
Compensation of employees	...	...	...	- 20	- 91	- 304	- 221	- 113	- 144	Rémunération des salariés
Investment income	...	...	...	- 398	- 1 288	- 866	- 374	- 281	- 146	Revenus des investissements
Net secondary income	...	...	783	1 003	994	693	665	875	604	Revenus secondaires nets
Net official transfers	...	...	...	288	721	627	762	794	583	Transferts officiels nets
Workers' remittances	...	...	...	213	189	87	- 38	45	42	Envois de fonds des travailleurs
Other private transfers	...	...	...	...	...	...	...	...	...	Autres transferts privés
Current account balance	...	...	3 158	- 1 793	- 581	- 222	- 398	87	- 461	Solde du compte courant
Capital and financial account	...	...	- 1 379	289	- 212	- 385	892	- 187	276	Comptes de capital et financier
Capital account	...	...	70	237	118	...	...	...	63	Compte de capital
Financial account	...	...	- 1 450	52	- 330	- 385	892	- 187	213	Compte financier
Errors and omissions	...	...	- 1 779	641	469	33	- 944	- 105	81	Erreurs et omissions
Overall balance	...	...	...	- 1 504	- 793	- 607	495	- 99	- 186	Balance générale

X DEBT AND FINANCIAL FLOWS - DETTE ET FLUX FINANCIERS

	2009	2010	2011	2012	2013	2014	2015	2016	2017	
X-1 DEBT *US $ (MILLIONS)*										**X-1 DETTE EXTÉRIEURE** *$ E.U (MILLIONS)*
Total external debt	...	...	...	...	...	...	...	...	...	Dette extérieure totale
Private	...	...	...	...	...	...	...	...	...	Privée
Public	...	...	...	...	...	...	...	...	...	Publique
Total external debt service	...	...	...	...	...	...	...	...	...	Service de la dette extérieure
Present value of external debt	...	...	...	...	...	...	...	...	...	Valeur actuelle de la dette extérieure
Total government domestic debt, National currency (millions)	...	...	...	...	...	...	...	...	...	Dette publique intérieure
X-2 FINANCIAL FLOWS *US $ (MILLIONS)*										**X-2 FLUX FINANCIERS** *$ E.U (MILLIONS)*
Net Foreign Direct Investment Inflows	...	...	...	161	- 793	44	- 71	- 17	...	Investissements étranger direct (flux nets entrants)
Main origin of FDI inflows										**Principales origines de l'IDE entrant:**
...	...	...	...	...	...	...	...	...	...	...
...	...	...	...	...	...	...	...	...	...	...
...	...	...	...	...	...	...	...	...	...	...
...	...	...	...	...	...	...	...	...	...	...
...	...	...	...	...	...	...	...	...	...	...
African countries	...	...	...	...	...	...	...	...	...	Pays africains
Net total official development assistance	...	...	436	1 186	1 399	1 964	1 675	1 590	...	Aide publique au développement (nette totale)
Main origin of net ODA										**Principales origines de l'APD nette**
United States	...	...	56	382	410	796	595	547	...	États-Unis
United Kingdom	...	...	83	172	213	275	318	217	...	Royaume-Uni
Norway	...	...	60	74	91	95	59	67	...	Norvège
Canada	...	...	49	66	66	87	88	67	...	Canada
Denmark	...	...	36	37	34	36	10	20	...	Danemark

SOURCES AND NOTES - SOURCES ET NOTES

External trade - Total exports, fob: UNCTAD	Commerce exterieur - Exportation, fab: CNUCED
External trade - Total import, cif: UNCTAD	Commerce exterieur - Imporations, caf: CNUCED
ODA: OECD	APD: OCDE
Monetary statistics: IMF	Statistiques monétaires: FMI
Poverty: World Bank	Pauvreté: Banque mondiale

AREA (km2)		1 879 358			**SUPERFICIE (KM2)**
CAPITAL CITY	Khartoum		Khartoum		**CAPITALE**
CURRENCY	Sudanese Pound		Pound soudanais		**MONNAIE**

I SOCIAL AND DEMOGRAPHIC INDICATORS — INDICATEURS DEMOGRAPHIQUES ET SOCIAUX

	Year Année	Value Valeur	Charts Graphiques	
Population				**Population**
Population ('000)	2017	40 800.0		Population ('000)
Female (%)	2017	49.3		Féminine (%)
Urban (%)	2017	37.8		Urbaine (%)
Average annual growth rate	2017	2.8		Taux de croissance annuel
Active population ('000)	2015	9 953.8		Population active ('000)
Population by age group ('000)				Population par groupe d'âge ('000)
0-14 years	2017	16 901.8		0-14 ans
15-64 years	2017	22 693.0		15-64 ans
65+ years	2017	1 189.0		65+ ans
Economically active population in agriculture (%)	2017	0.8		Participation de la population active agricole (%)
Crude birth rate	2017	37.9		Taux brut de natalité
Crude death rate	2017	8.8		Taux brut de mortalité
Total fertility rate	2017	5.1		Indice synthétique de fécondité
Life expectancy at birth - Total (years)	2015	63.7		Espérance de vie à la naissance - Totale (années)
Dependency ratio - Total (%)	2017	79.7		Taux de dépendance - Total (%)
Health				**Santé**
Percentage of children under-five and underweight	2014	33.0		% d'enfants de moins de cinq ans avec insuffisance pondérale
Prevalence of undernourishment	2010	24.3		Prévalence de la malnutrition
Under five mortality rate (per 1 000 live births)	2015	70.1		Taux de mortalité de moins de 5 ans (les deux sexes, pour 1000)
Infant mortality rate (per 1 000 live births)	2015	47.6		Taux de mortalité infantile (les deux sexes) par 1000
Neonatal mortality rate (per 1 000 live births)	2015	29.8		Le taux de mortalité néonatale (pour 1000 naissances vivantes)
Percentage of children provided the vaccines :				Pourcentage d'enfants vaccinés :
BCG	2014	95.0		BCG
DPT3	2014	94.0		DTC3
Polio	2011	93.0		polio
Measles	2014	86.0		rougeole
Percentage of mothers provided at least one antenatal care (%)	2014	62.8		Pourcentage de mères ayant au moins reçu un soin prénatal (%)
Percentage of deliveries attended by skilled health personnel	2014	77.5		% d'accouchements assistés par un personnel de santé qualifié
Number of doctors (per 10,000 population)	2008	2.8		Nombre de médecins (pour 10.000 habitants)
Number of nurses (per 10,000 population)	2008	8.4		Nombre d'infirmiers (pour 10.000 habitants)
Hospital beds - Total (per 10,000 population)	2013	12.0		Nombre de lits d'hôpitaux - Total (pour 10 000)
Births registered (per 1,000)	2015	32.6		Naissances enregistrées (pour 1000)
Deaths registered (per 1,000)	2015	7.7		Décès enregistrés (pour 1000)
Budget allocation to health (%)	2013	11.4		Dépenses publiques consacrées à la santé (% du budget)
Education				**Education**
Enrolment in primary education (000)	2013	5 158.0		Scolarisation dans le primaire (000)
Female	2013	2 480.0		Féminine
Enrolment in secondary education (000)	2012	1 723.7		Scolarisation dans le secondaire (000)
Female	2012	811.9		Féminine
Enrolment in tertiary education (000)	2013	537.6		Scolarisation dans le tertiaire (000)
Female	2013	334.1		Féminine
Literacy rate	2012	73.4		Taux d'alphabétisation (deux sexes)
Male	2012	81.7		Masculin
Female	2012	65.3		Féminin
Pupil teacher ratio - primary	2009	38.4		Ratio élève-enseignant
Budget allocation to education (%)	2010	12.9		Dépenses publiques consacrées à l'enseignement (% du budget)
Poverty				**Pauvreté**
GNI per capita, PPP (current int. $)	2016	4290.0		RNB par habitant, ($ PPA inter. courants)
Human Poverty Index (HPI-1) Value (%)	2007	34.0		Valeur de l'Indice de pauvreté (IPH-1) (%)
Population below Inter. poverty line ($2/day) (%)	2009	14.9		Population sous le seuil inter. de pauvreté (2$/Jour) (%)
Share of income held by richest 10%	2009	26.7		% de revenu des 10% plus riches
Share of income held by poorest 10%	2009	2.6		% de revenu des 10% plus pauvres
GINI index	2009	35.4		Indice de GINI

Population by age group - 2017

Population par groupe d'age - 2017

- 0.6% 65+ years
- 11.8% 15-64 years
- 87.6% 0-14 years

Percentage of children provided vaccines : - 2014

Pourcentage d'enfants vaccinés : - 2014

BCG / BCG	DPT3 / DTC3	Polio / polio (2011)	Measles / rougeole
95.0	94.0	93.0	86.0

Literacy rate (%) - 2012

Taux d'alphabétisation - 2012

Male 81.7   Female 65.3

GNI per capita, PPP (current international $)

RNB par habitant, ($ PPA internationaux courants)

2012	2013	2014	2015	2016
3 820	2 700	3 980	4 150	4 290

	2009	2010	2011	2012	2013	2014	2015	2016	2017	
GROSS DOMESTIC PRODUCT BY KIND OF ECONOMIC ACTIVITY AT CURRENT PRICES *SUDANESE POUND (MILLIONS)*										**PRODUIT INTÉRIEUR BRUT PAR BRANCHE D'ACTIVITÉ ÉCONOMIQUE AUX PRIX COURANTS** *POUND SOUDANAIS (MILLIONS)*
Agriculture, hunting, forestry and Fishing	44 971	54 465	63 609	80 675	115 739	150 113	183 150	224 044	262 215	Agriculture, chasse sylviculture et Pêche
Mining and quarrying	15 777	14 943	11 428	12 847	17 239	23 626	24 188	27 433	54 062	Industries extractives
Manufacturing	11 769	12 975	16 285	21 677	31 786	47 758	60 091	72 181	83 655	Industries manufacturières
Electricity, gas & water	794	893	1 606	2 181	3 055	4 097	5 503	6 465	2 778	Electricité, gaz et eau
Construction	6 087	7 340	8 718	11 525	16 022	22 428	28 080	34 057	29 958	Bâtiments et travaux publics
Wholesale & retail trade, restaurants, hotels	20 613	23 381	30 709	40 720	56 232	77 760	99 166	124 451	138 028	Commerce de gros et de détail, restaurants et hôtels
Finance, insurance, real estate, etc.	14 264	18 924	16 499	21 475	29 785	40 362	50 483	52 492	106 003	Banques, assurances, affaires immobilières
Transport and communications	14 252	15 633	24 426	32 511	45 271	66 741	84 454	101 312	113 003	Transport(s) et communications
Public administration and defense	9 370	10 157	9 998	15 248	21 337	29 721	36 857	44 067	42 972	Administrations publiques et défense
Education	...	...	...	...	...	...	...	...	...	Education
Health And Social Work	...	...	...	...	...	...	...	...	...	Santé et Actions Sociales
Other services	1 583	1 831	1 502	1 954	2 717	3 771	4 647	5 023	19 238	Autres services
Less Imputed Service Charges	- 1 707	- 1 719	- 1 625	- 2 123	- 2 946	- 4 105	- 5 104	- 5 766	- 7 050	Moins Services d'intermédiation financière
Gross domestic product at factor cost / basic prices	137 773	158 823	183 155	238 690	336 238	462 272	571 515	685 759	844 862	Produit intérieur brut aux couts des facteurs / prix de base
Plus: Indirect Taxes / taxes on products, less subsidies	1 614	1 824	3 535	4 723	6 565	9 024	11 422	13 210	16 275	Plus taxes indirectes/impôts sur les produits, moins les subventions
EXPENDITURE ON GROSS DOMESTIC PRODUCT AT CURRENT PURCHASER'S VALUES *SUDANESE POUND (MILLIONS)*										**EMPLOI DU PRODUIT INTÉRIEUR BRUT AUX PRIX COURANTS D'ACQUISITION** *POUND SOUDANAIS (MILLIONS)*
Government final consumption	11 758	12 001	12 742	16 903	25 212	45 844	56 626	63 383	70 989	Consommation finale des administrations publiques
Private final consumption	105 783	112 731	129 986	184 880	261 478	357 822	443 706	521 457	624 765	Consommation finale privée
Gross fixed capital formation	25 376	31 705	41 616	51 493	67 553	90 681	117 324	140 340	189 661	Formation brute de capital fixe
Change in inventories	3 208	3 099	4 868	...	...	...	...	...	...	Variation des stocks
Exports of goods and services	19 119	27 522	27 198	17 960	39 563	20 630	19 370	18 857	23 232	Exportations de biens et services
Less imports of goods and services	25 859	26 411	29 719	27 824	51 003	43 682	54 088	45 068	47 510	Moins importations de biens et services
GDP at purchasers' values	139 387	160 647	186 690	243 413	342 803	471 295	582 937	698 969	861 137	PIB aux prix d'acquisition
GROSS DOMESTIC PRODUCT BY KIND OF ECONOMIC ACTIVITY AT CONSTANT PRICES *ANNUAL GROWTH RATES (%)*										**PRODUIT INTÉRIEUR BRUT PAR BRANCHE D'ACTIVITÉ ECONOMIQUE AUX PRIX CONSTANTS** *TAUX DE CROISSANCE ANNUEL (%)*
Agriculture, hunting, forestry and Fishing	- 3.3	11.7	3.4	11.8	- 2.6	9.6	5.5	5.5	6.7	Agriculture, chasse sylviculture et Pêche
Mining and quarrying	1.8	- 2.2	- 35.9	- 67.9	59.1	- 5.9	- 10.8	- 13.6	10.1	Industries extractives
Manufacturing	19.3	10.0	8.1	13.2	1.1	- 0.6	4.1	5.1	5.5	Industries manufacturières
Electricity, gas & water	7.4	7.0	6.3	6.3	6.7	6.7	10.9	5.8	5.4	Electricité, gaz et eau
Construction	5.2	2.8	10.2	- 47.0	38.3	- 12.6	5.0	5.5	5.5	Bâtiments et travaux publics
Wholesale & retail trade, restaurants, hotels	3.9	5.5	5.3	5.6	5.4	4.2	4.3	4.4	4.5	Commerce de gros et de détail, restaurants et hôtels
Finance, insurance, real estate, etc.	7.0	5.1	- 5.5	10.4	5.3	2.8	4.9	5.4	5.5	Banques, assurances, affaires immobilières
Transport and communications	8.8	5.7	5.1	1.2	15.3	21.0	4.2	4.6	5.5	Transport(s) et communications
Public administration and defense	4.6	2.1	4.0	12.5	21.0	6.8	3.1	6.0	5.0	Administrations publiques et défense
Education	...	...	...	...	...	...	...	...	...	Education
Health And Social Work	...	...	...	...	...	...	...	...	...	Santé et Actions Sociales
Other services	2.4	2.4	169.1	23.5	6.3	26.3	3.2	5.9	5.0	Autres services
Less Imputed Service Charges	- 10.8	0.7	6.0	2.2	1.1	4.8	5.9	4.9	5.8	Moins Services d'intermédiation financière
Gross domestic product at factor cost / basic prices	4.7	6.6	0.9	3.6	6.9	7.1	4.3	4.9	5.8	Produit intérieur brut aux couts des facteurs / prix de base
Plus: Indirect Taxes / taxes on products, less subsidies	- 5.6	1.6	2.1	3.0	0.8	4.9	6.6	4.9	5.8	Plus taxes indirectes/impôts sur les produits, moins les subventions
Gross domestic product at market prices	4.5	6.5	0.9	3.5	6.8	7.0	4.3	4.9	5.8	Produit intérieur brut aux prix du marché
EXPENDITURE ON GROSS DOMESTIC PRODUCT AT CONSTANT PURCHASERS' VALUES *ANNUAL GROWTH RATES (%)*										**EMPLOIS DU PRODUIT INTÉRIEUR BRUT AUX PRIX CONSTANTS D'ACQUISITION** *TAUX DE CROISSANCE ANNUEL (%)*
Government final consumption	- 14.8	1.1	0.9	0.5	3.6	...	...	...	...	Consommation finale des administrations publiques
Private final consumption	7.9	3.9	0.9	6.7	9.9	...	...	...	...	Consommation finale privée
Gross fixed capital formation	4.1	10.8	0.9	0.5	3.6	...	...	...	...	Formation brute de capital fixe
Exports of goods and services	- 90.8	30.5	0.9	0.5	3.6	...	...	...	...	Exportations de biens et services
Less imports of goods and services	- 90.3	8.4	0.9	0.5	3.6	...	...	...	...	Moins importations de biens et services

	2009	2010	2011	2012	2013	2014	2015	2016	2017	
Annual growth rates (%)										**Taux de croissance annuel (%)**
All item	11.3	13.0	18.0	35.6	36.4	36.9	16.9	11.8	33.1	Ensemble
of which:										dont:
Food and non-alcoholic beverages	12.2	15.6	20.4	38.8	30.7	31.0	13.8	7.9	35.0	Alimentation et boissons non alcoolisés
Alcoholic beverages, tobacco and narcotics	4.3	8.3	11.3	41.9	24.4	34.1	22.0	20.8	22.0	Boissons alcoolisées et tabacs
Clothing and footwear	10.0	9.9	17.4	49.5	54.7	49.6	26.9	16.4	17.7	Habillement et chaussures
Housing, water, electricity, gas and other fuels	8.6	9.9	11.0	13.4	19.5	19.9	20.8	13.2	15.5	Logement, eau, électricité, gaz et autres combustibles
Furnishings, household equipment and routine household maintenance	9.1	8.3	20.5	39.6	91.9	45.5	15.1	13.0	21.8	Meubles, articles de ménage et entretien courant
Health	9.6	5.1	20.1	37.4	47.8	30.3	11.9	10.6	53.1	Santé
Transport	4.4	2.4	14.8	53.6	66.3	73.8	17.2	16.1	53.0	Transport
Communication	7.0	3.4	5.9	31.7	139.6	41.8	34.3	32.5	14.7	Communication
Recreation and culture	5.5	6.6	8.6	63.7	32.1	46.4	33.8	18.8	28.5	Loisirs et culture
Education	18.7	31.3	25.6	13.4	54.0	38.1	32.8	23.1	17.2	Enseignement
Restaurants and hotels	34.8	19.4	14.5	12.9	32.2	37.1	16.8	18.3	41.0	Restaurants et hôtels
Miscellaneous goods and services	11.6	10.3	17.1	36.5	53.8	45.9	13.0	16.7	29.4	Biens et Services divers

SOUDAN

IV AGRICULTURAL PRODUCTION - PRODUCTION AGRICOLE

	2009	2010	2011	2012	2013	2014	2015	2016	2017	
TONNES (THOUSAND)										**Tonnes (milliers)**
Sugar cane	7 527	6 728	6 055	6 173	6 798	702	652	792	...	Canne à sucre
Sorghum	4 192	2 630	4 605	1 883	4 524	2 249	6 208	2 744	...	Sorgho
Groundnuts, with shell	942	763	1 185	1 032	1 767	963	856	1 042	...	Arachides (en coques)
Onions, dry	1 024	1 116	1 116	1 036	1 037	...	...	...	...	Oignons secs
Bananas	624	684	687	750	758	...	...	...	...	Bananes

V MINING PRODUCTION - PRODUCTION MINIERE

	2009	2010	2011	2012	2013	2014	2015	2016	2017	
Crude petroleum - Production, metric tons (thousands)	24.2	23.5	23.0	5.2	45.1	42.4	28.7	31.0	...	Pétrole brut - Production, tonnes métriques (milliers)
Gold ores and concentrates - Production (Kilograms)	26.3	23.7	46.1	...	70.0	73.3	82.4	93.4	...	Minerais d'or et leurs concentrés - Production (Kilogrammes)
Gypsum; anhydrite; limestone and other calcareous stone - Production, metric tons (thousands)	30.0	31.0	31.0	11.7	132.0	111.3	241.0	349.2	...	"Gypse; anhydrite; pierres à chaux ou à ciment

VI ENERGY - ENERGIE

	2009	2010	2011	2012	2013	2014	2015	2016	2017	
Total electricity generation (GWh)	6 883	8 009	11 508	11 554	11 599	118 480	...	...	...	Production électrique totale (GWh)
of which										dont
Production of electricity from fossil fuels (GWh)	3 137	1 297	3 416	3 460	3 504	2 021	5 011			Production d'électricité à partir de combustibles fossiles (GWh)
Production of hydro electricity (GWh)	3 236	6 202	7 884	7 884	7 884	1 205	9 671			Production d'électricité d'origine hydraulique (GWh)
Production of electricity from solar, wind, tide, wave and other sources (GWh)	...	...	5	7	9	9	9	...	...	Production d'électricité d'origine solaire, éolienne, marée motrice et autres (GWh)

VII TOURISM AND INFRASTRUCTURE - TOURISME ET INFRASTUCTURE

	2009	2010	2011	2012	2013	2014	2015	2016	2017	
VII-1 Tourism										**VII-1 Tourisme**
International tourist arrivals (thousands)	420	495	536	575	591	684	741	682	698	Arrivées de touristes internationaux (milliers)
Rooms in hotels and similar establishments (thousands)	5	...	...	...	...	...	...	...	...	Chambres d'hôtels et établissements assimilés (milliers)
Overnight stays (thousands)	2 524	3 046	3 171	2 508	3 203	3 958	4 327	3 762	3 967	Nuitées (milliers)
Tourism receipts (US$ thousand)	230 700	82 300	179 300	771 800	773 000	967 100	948 900	1 008 600	1 144 100	Recettes touristiques (milliers de $ EU)
Total contribution to GDP (%)	4.4	4.0	3.3	4.4	5.1	5.9	5.9	5.4	5.4	Contribution totale au PIB (%)
Total contribution to Employment (%)	3.8	3.4	3.2	3.9	5.4	6.0	4.8	4.4	4.3	Contribution totale à l'emploi (%)
VII-2 Infrastructure										**VII-2 Infrastructure**
Paved road (% of total)	32.0	51.6	90.6	90.6	90.6	90.6	...	...	...	Routes asphaltées (% du total)
Total network (Railways-km)	4 508	4 508	4 708	4 313	4 313	4 313	...	...	...	Réseau total voies ferrées-Km
Main telephone lines (per 100 inhabitants)	0.9	1.3	1.3	1.1	1.1	1.1	...	...	...	Lignes téléphoniques fixes (pour 100 habitants)
Mobile cellular subscribers (per 100 inhabitants)	36.1	41.5	68.8	74.4	72.9	72.2	70.5	68.6	...	Abonnés aux téléphones mobiles (pour 100 habitants)
Internet users per 100 inhabitants	...	16.7	17.5	21.0	22.7	24.6	26.6	28.0	...	Utilisateurs Internet par 100 Habitants
Fixed (wired)-broadband subscriptions per 100 inhabitants	...	...	...	...	...	...	...	...	...	Abonnements à l'Internet fixe (filaire) à large bande pour 100 habitants, par débit

VIII EXTERNAL TRADE - COMMERCE EXTERIEUR

	2009	2010	2011	2012	2013	2014	2015	2016	2017	
US$ (MILLIONS) EXPORTS, FOB										**$ E.U (MILLIONS) EXPORTATIONS, FÅB**
Exports - Total	9 080	11 529	10 193	4 066	7 086	5 463	2 985	1 735	...	Exportations - Total
Exports to Africa	189	299	261	167	216	171	92	54	...	Exportations vers l'Afrique
Main products										**Principaux produits**
Gold, non-monetary (excluding gold ores and concentrates)	844	1 356	1 166	2 068	1 733	1 462	760	456	...	Or, non monétaire (à l'exclusion des minerais d'or et des concentrés)
Live animals other than animals of division 03	210	160	195	198	204	170	89	53	...	Animaux vivants autres que les animaux de la division 03
Oil seeds and oleaginous fruits (excluding flour)	166	187	145	161	152	122	65	39	...	Graines oléagineuses et oléagineuses (à l'exclusion de la farine)
Petroleum oils or bituminous minerals > 70 % oil	197	80	120	59	73	64	32	20	...	Huiles de pétrole ou de minéraux bitumineux> 70% d'huile
Petroleum oils, oils from bitumin. materials, crude	7 386	9 404	8 231	1 157	4 575	3 323	1 879	1 068	...	Huiles de pétrole, huiles de bitume. matériaux bruts
Main destinations										**Principales destinations**
China	5 641	7 619	6 722	1 006	3 647	2 693	1 508	863	...	Chine
India	309	415	200	82	164	120	68	39	...	Inde
Japan	715	907	972	176	522	394	218	126	...	Japon
Saudi Arabia	227	181	220	232	234	193	102	61	...	Arabie Saoudite
United Arab Emirates	683	1 443	1 184	2 057	1 819	1 511	792	473	...	Emirates Arabes
IMPORTS, CIF										
Imports - Total	9 691	10 045	9 546	9 230	9 819	9 084	8 413	5 549	...	Importations - Total (millions)
Imports from Africa	1 084	1 151	1 082	1 103	1 145	1 061	982	648	...	Importations en provenance de l'Afrique
Main products										**Principaux produits**
Civil engineering & contractors' plant & equipment	215	324	272	283	307	288	265	176	...	Génie civil et installations et équipements des entrepreneurs
Medicaments (incl. veterinary medicaments)	279	286	276	330	295	275	253	167	...	Médicaments (y compris les médicaments vétérinaires)
Petroleum oils or bituminous minerals > 70 % oil	230	432	537	436	495	453	422	278	...	Huiles de pétrole ou de minéraux bitumineux> 70% d'huile
Sugar, molasses and honey	190	432	454	500	412	388	356	236	...	Sucre, mélasse et miel
Wheat (including spelt) and meslin, unmilled	448	716	556	391	664	573	551	356	...	Blé (y compris l'épeautre) et méteil, non moulu
Main origin										**Principales provenances**
China	1 860	2 005	2 036	2 008	2 104	1 955	1 807	1 193	...	Chine
Egypt	573	636	530	546	576	531	493	325	...	Egypte
India	601	504	675	803	762	722	660	438	...	Inde
Saudi Arabia	674	604	657	735	727	682	627	415	...	Arabie Saoudite
United Arab Emirates	609	924	768	528	673	606	569	373	...	Emirates Arabes

	2009	2010	2011	2012	2013	2014	2015	2016	2017	
IX-1 MONETARY STATISTICS *SUDANESE POUND (MILLIONS)*										**IX-1 STATISTIQUES MONÉTAIRES** *POUND SOUDANAIS (MILLIONS)*
Money supply (M1)	28 519	35 612	41 914	58 792	66 446	77 739	93 103	121 064	157 488	Masse monétaire (M1)
Quasi-money	10 621	13 800	15 247	23 504	26 217	29 736	36 004	43 327	70 457	Quasi-monnaie
of which demand deposit	8 040	9 840	12 000	...	...	...	...	...	...	dont Monnaie scripturale
Net foreign assets	- 1 107	- 202	- 1 605	- 212	- 3 658	- 3 644	- 17 937	- 27 739	- 28 280	Avoirs extérieurs nets
Domestic credit	26 600	33 344	42 622	60 919	75 739	88 674	105 638	133 320	176 006	Crédit intérieur
of which claims on private sector	8 085	11 748	19 300	29 650	37 104	43 460	51 011	64 232	80 705	dont créances sur le secteur privé
of which claims on government sector, net	15 513	17 959	19 427	26 966	33 034	35 920	41 606	52 561	73 649	dont créances nettes sur le gouvernement
International reserves (millions US$)	1 370	1 566	1 317	1 689	1 612	1 461	900	1 016	1 155	Réserves internationales (millions $EU)
Average exchange rate (National currency per US$)	2	2	3	4	5	6	6	6	7	Taux de change (moyen) (monnaie nationale par $ EU)
IX-2 PUBLIC FINANCE *SUDANESE POUND (MILLIONS)*										**IX-2 FINANCES PUBLIQUES** *POUND SOUDANAIS (MILLIONS)*
Total Revenues and Grants	18 986	29 245	32 385	22 266	34 349	49 022	54 500	57 365	...	Recettes totales et dons
Direct taxes (on income, profits)	928	1 136	1 061	1 433	1 764	3 094	3 188	3 478	...	Taxes directes
Domestic indirect taxes revenues	5 163	5 966	6 877	6 014	11 241	23 896	29 608	34 098	...	Taxes Indirectes
Trade taxes	2 505	2 882	3 443	4 685	6 825	7 901	9 063	9 058	...	Taxes sur le commerce extérieur
Other taxes	22	24	46	58	77	90	104	125	...	Autres taxes
Other revenues	10 320	18 261	20 340	9 062	12 410	11 475	10 856	8 849	...	Autres recettes
Grants	47	976	618	1 013	2 033	2 566	1 680	1 758	...	Dons
Total Expenditures and Net Lending	25 198	28 815	32 229	29 749	41 456	54 817	63 376	67 538	...	Dépenses totales et prêts nets
Current expenditure	21 144	25 104	27 507	25 215	36 613	46 664	52 938	57 636	...	Dépenses courantes
Wages and Salaries	6 836	7 516	9 763	10 730	14 870	15 794	18 509	21 109	...	Rémunérations et salaires
Other purchases of goods and services	2 375	2 417	2 603	2 032	2 828	5 738	6 872	8 729	...	Achat de biens et services
Other current expenditure	10 920	13 040	14 028	10 900	18 345	22 432	23 971	24 830	...	Autres dépenses courantes
Current transfers	1 012	2 131	1 112	1 553	570	2 700	3 587	2 968	...	Transferts courants
Interest payments	1 254	1 669	2 210	2 525	1 511	3 521	3 587	2 968	...	Intérêts
Capital expenditure	7 876	2 591	4 525	4 893	3 331	4 631	6 851	6 934	...	Dépenses d'équipement
Net lending	- 5 077	- 548	- 2 013	- 2 884	...	...	...	...	...	Prêts nets
Fiscal balance	- 6 211	430	156	- 7 483	- 7 106	- 5 795	- 8 876	- 10 173	...	Solde global y compris les dons
IX-3 BALANCE OF PAYMENTS *SUDANESE POUND (MILLIONS)*										**IX-3 BALANCE DES PAIEMENTS** *POUND SOUDANAIS (MILLIONS)*
Trade balance	- 623	5 915	4 075	- 16 989	- 18 733	- 30 006	- 42 715	- 4 231	- 4 186	Balance commerciale
Services Balance	- 4 112	- 5 324	- 4 017	- 3 123	- 1 077	1 485	123	848	- 237	Balance des services
Net primary income	- 9 476	- 9 729	- 6 657	- 8 654	- 15 089	- 19 575	- 1 785	1 617	- 1 653	Revenus primaires nets
Compensation of employees	...	...	...	...	...	...	...	...	...	Rémunération des salariés
Investment income	...	...	...	...	...	...	...	...	...	Revenus des investissements
Net secondary income	2 815	5 060	3 015	3 083	7 229	5 446	1 148	15 322	974	Revenus secondaires nets
Net official transfers	...	...	...	...	...	...	...	...	...	Transferts officiels nets
Workers' remittances	...	...	...	...	...	...	...	...	...	Envois de fonds des travailleurs
Other private transfers	...	...	...	...	...	...	...	...	...	Autres transferts privés
Current account balance	- 11 397	- 4 078	- 3 584	- 25 682	- 27 670	- 42 651	- 5 712	- 5 461	- 5 102	Solde du compte courant
Capital and financial account	4 747	2 672	750	3 768	4 029	2 106	...	...	3 583	Comptes de capital et financier
Capital account	...	...	...	320	408	213	...	...	227	Compte de capital
Financial account	4 747	2 672	750	3 448	3 621	1 894	...	...	3 357	Compte financier
Errors and omissions	- 376	- 983	- 89	2 449	434	1 436	...	...	1 506	Erreurs et omissions
Overall balance	- 556	- 27	- 680	- 24	- 18	- 3	...	...	13	Balance générale

SOUDAN

X DEBT AND FINANCIAL FLOWS - DETTE ET FLUX FINANCIERS

	2009	2010	2011	2012	2013	2014	2015	2016	2017	
X-1 DEBT *US $ (MILLIONS)*										**X-1 DETTE EXTÉRIEURE** *$ E.U (MILLIONS)*
Total external debt	34 866	39 486	41 450	43 191	45 022	46 781	49 772	52 400	55 306	Dette extérieure totale
Private	...	...	...	...	...	...	...	...	...	Privée
Public	34 866	39 486	41 450	43 191	45 022	46 781	49 772	52 400	...	Publique
Total external debt service	262	382	283	261	177	128	418	153	...	Service de la dette extérieure
Present value of external debt	...	...	...	...	...	...	...	20 182	...	Valeur actuelle de la dette extérieure
Total government domestic debt, National currency (millions)	14	16	20	27	...	...	...	...	...	Dette publique intérieure
X-2 FINANCIAL FLOWS *US $ (MILLIONS)*										**X-2 FLUX FINANCIERS** *$ E.U (MILLIONS)*
Net Foreign Direct Investment Inflows	1 726	2 064	1 734	2 311	1 688	1 251	1 728	1 064	...	Investissements étranger direct (flux nets entrants)
Main origin of FDI inflows										**Principales origines de l'IDE entrant:**
...	...	...	...	...	...	...	...	...	...	...
Turkey	2	...	...	...	...	...	...	...	...	Turquie
...	...	...	...	...	...	...	...	...	...	...
...	...	...	...	...	...	...	...	...	...	...
...	...	...	...	...	...	...	...	...	...	...
African countries	...	...	...	...	...	...	...	...	...	Pays africains
Net total official development assistance	2 352	2 026	1 742	1 369	1 507	875	900	810	...	Aide publique au développement (nette totale)
Main origin of net ODA										**Principales origines de l'APD nette**
United States	955	696	658	454	714	256	272	228	...	États-Unis
United Kingdom	292	119	157	82	108	82	83	88	...	Royaume-Uni
Netherlands	97	87	45	15	11	6	4	11	...	Pays-Bas
Norway	92	117	47	33	34	27	12	14	...	Norvège
Canada	105	108	52	29	21	14	13	14	...	Canada

SOURCES AND NOTES - SOURCES ET NOTES

External trade - Total exports, fob: UNCTAD

External trade - Total import, cif: UNCTAD

ODA: OECD

Monetary statistics: IMF

National Accounts: 2014 -2015: Estimated; 2016-2017:Projection

Poverty: World Bank

Commerce exterieur - Exportation, fab: CNUCED

Commerce exterieur - Imporations, caf: CNUCED

APD: OCDE

Statistiques monétaires: FMI

Comptes nationaux: 2014-2015: Estimées;2016-2017:Projections

Pauvreté: Banque mondiale

AREA (km2)		17 360		SUPERFICIE (KM2)
CAPITAL CITY	Mbabane		Mbabane	CAPITALE
CURRENCY	Swadziland Lilangani		Lilangani swadzilandais	MONNAIE

I SOCIAL AND DEMOGRAPHIC INDICATORS — INDICATEURS DEMOGRAPHIQUES ET SOCIAUX

	Year Année	Value Valeur	Charts Graphiques	
Population				**Population**
Population ('000)	2017	1 146.0		Population ('000)
Female (%)	2017	52.5		Féminine (%)
Urban (%)	2017	23.7		Urbaine (%)
Average annual growth rate	2017	1.2		Taux de croissance annuel
Active population ('000)	2017	347.6		Population active ('000)
Population by age group ('000)				Population par groupe d'âge ('000)
0-14 years	2017	417.2		0-14 ans
15-64 years	2017	689.7		15-64 ans
65+ years	2017	39.0		65+ ans
Economically active population in agriculture (%)	2017	48.0		Participation de la population active agricole (%)
Crude birth rate	2017	30.4		Taux brut de natalité
Crude death rate	2017	17.1		Taux brut de mortalité
Total fertility rate	2017	3.4		Indice synthétique de fécondité
Life expectancy at birth - Total (years)	2017	45.9		Espérance de vie à la naissance - Totale (années)
Dependency ratio - Total (%)	2017	66.2		Taux de dépendance - Total (%)
Health				**Santé**
Percentage of children under-five and underweight	2017	5.8		% d'enfants de moins de cinq ans avec insuffisance pondérale
Prevalence of undernourishment	2017	25.0		Prévalence de la malnutrition
Under five mortality rate (per 1 000 live births)	2017	61.0		Taux de mortalité de moins de 5 ans (les deux sexes, pour 1000)
Infant mortality rate (per 1 000 live births)	2017	45.0		Taux de mortalité infantile (les deux sexes) par 1000
Neonatal mortality rate (per 1 000 live births)	2017	14.0		Le taux de mortalité néonatale (pour 1000 naissances vivantes)
Percentage of children provided the vaccines :				Pourcentage d'enfants vaccinés :
BCG	2017	98.0		BCG
DPT3	2017	90.0		DTC3
Polio	2017	90.0		polio
Measles	2017	94.0		rougeole
Percentage of mothers provided at least one antenatal care	2017	99.0		Pourcentage de mères ayant au moins reçu un soin prénatal (%)
Percentage of deliveries attended by skilled health personnel	2017	88.3		% d'accouchements assistés par un personnel de santé qualifié
Number of doctors (per 10,000 population)	2009	1.7		Nombre de médecins (pour 10.000 habitants)
Number of nurses (per 10,000 population)	2015	20.0		Nombre d'infirmiers (pour 10.000 habitants)
Hospital beds - Total (per 10,000 population)	2015	20.0		Nombre de lits d'hôpitaux - Total (pour 10 000)
Births registered (per 1,000)	2017	29.0		Naissances enregistrées (pour 1000)
Deaths registered (per 1,000)	2017	14.0		Décès enregistrés (pour 1000)
Budget allocation to health (%)	2017	9.1		Dépenses publiques consacrées à la santé (% du budget)
Education				**Education**
Enrolment in primary education (000)	2016	238.0		Scolarisation dans le primaire (000)
Female	2016	113.0		Féminine
Enrolment in secondary education (000)	2016	104.0		Scolarisation dans le secondaire (000)
Female	2016	41.0		Féminine
Enrolment in tertiary education (000)	2016	12.6		Scolarisation dans le tertiaire (000)
Female	2016	6.8		Féminine
Literacy rate	2016	92.0		Taux d'alphabétisation (deux sexes)
Male	2016	91.0		Masculin
Female	2016	93.0		Féminin
Pupil teacher ratio - primary	2016	27.0		Ratio élève-enseignant
Budget allocation to education (%)	2016	15.7		Dépenses publiques consacrées à l'enseignement (% du budget)
Poverty				**Pauvreté**
GNI per capita, PPP (current int. $)	2016	8310.0		RNB par habitant, ($ PPA inter. courants)
Human Poverty Index (HPI-1) Value (%)	2015	35.1		Valeur de l'Indice de pauvreté (IPH-1) (%)
Population below Inter. poverty line ($2/day) (%)	2009	42.0		Population sous le seuil inter. de pauvreté (2$/Jour) (%)
Share of income held by richest 10%	2015	57.0		% de revenu des 10% plus riches
Share of income held by poorest 10%	2009	1.5		% de revenu des 10% plus pauvres
GINI index	2009	51.5		Indice de GINI

Population by age group - 2017

Population par groupe d'âge - 2017

3.4%　36.4%　60.2%

- 0-14 years
- 15-64 years
- 65+ years

Percentage of children provided vaccines : - 2017

Pourcentage d'enfants vaccinés : - 2017

BCG / BCG	DPT3 / DTC3	Polio / polio	Measles / rougeole
98.0	90.0	90.0	94.0

Literacy rate (%) - 2016

Taux d'alphabétisation - 2016

Male 91.0　Female 93.0

GNI per capita, PPP (current international $)

RNB par habitant, ($ PPA internationaux courants)

2012	2013	2014	2015	2016
7 630	8 220	8 310	8 340	8 310

II NATIONAL ACCOUNTS — COMPTES NATIONAUX

GROSS DOMESTIC PRODUCT BY KIND OF ECONOMIC ACTIVITY AT CURRENT PRICES SWADZILAND LILANGANI (MILLIONS) — PRODUIT INTÉRIEUR BRUT PAR BRANCHE D'ACTIVITÉ ÉCONOMIQUE AUX PRIX COURANTS LILANGANI SWADZILANDAIS (MILLIONS)

	2009	2010	2011	2012	2013	2014	2015	2016	2017	
Agriculture, hunting , forestry and Fishing	2 807	3 301	3 403	3 733	4 008	4 009	3 895	5 176	...	Agriculture, chasse sylviculture et Pêche
Mining and quarrying	29	40	82	463	146	132	75	38	...	Industries extractives
Manufacturing	10 522	10 533	11 070	12 390	13 146	14 545	16 167	17 196	...	Industries manufacturières
Electricity, gas & water	391	528	593	529	478	530	623	438	...	Electricité, gaz et eau
Construction	1 133	1 114	1 106	1 143	1 225	1 303	1 366	1 757	...	Bâtiments et travaux publics
Wholesale & retail trade, restaurants, hotels	4 603	4 963	5 356	5 491	6 349	7 253	7 245	8 170	...	Commerce de gros et de détail, restaurants et hôtels
Finance, insurance, real estate, etc.	4 369	4 772	5 414	6 075	6 697	7 119	7 862	8 099	...	Banques, assurances, affaires immobilières
Transport and communications	1 505	1 623	1 680	1 931	2 237	2 469	2 483	2 716	...	Transport(s) et communications
Public administration and defense	1 926	2 062	2 371	2 344	2 685	2 958	3 393	4 120	...	Administrations publiques et défense
Education	1 914	2 199	2 194	2 247	2 501	2 691	2 843	3 456	...	Education
Health And Social Work	551	610	597	716	846	892	957	1 046	...	Santé et Actions Sociales
Other services	335	349	342	342	363	407	436	278	...	Autres services
Less Imputed Service Charges	- 609	- 605	- 485	- 527	- 580	- 640	- 703	- 746	...	Moins Services d'intermédiation financière
Gross domestic product at factor cost / basic prices	29 475	31 490	33 723	36 876	40 102	43 669	46 643	51 745	...	Produit intérieur brut aux couts des facteurs / prix de base
Plus: Indirect Taxes / taxes on products, less subsidies	1 300	1 446	1 656	2 159	2 558	2 978	3 467	2 986	...	Plus taxes indirectes/impôts sur les produits, moins les subventions

EXPENDITURE ON GROSS DOMESTIC PRODUCT AT CURRENT PURCHASER'S VALUES SWADZILAND LILANGANI (MILLIONS) — EMPLOI DU PRODUIT INTÉRIEUR BRUT AUX PRIX COURANTS D'ACQUISITION LILANGANI SWADZILANDAIS (MILLIONS)

	2009	2010	2011	2012	2013	2014	2015	2016	2017	
Government final consumption	6 452	6 747	6 763	7 175	8 070	9 021	10 433	12 198	...	Consommation finale des administrations publiques
Private final consumption	24 094	25 741	28 549	31 097	31 901	33 946	33 942	40 775	...	Consommation finale privée
Gross fixed capital formation	4 668	4 707	4 515	4 715	5 404	6 005	5 958	3 489	...	Formation brute de capital fixe
Change in inventories	...	...	...	...	...	...	...	...	...	Variation des stocks
Exports of goods and services	15 762	15 102	16 014	17 802	20 545	23 870	25 479	27 101	...	Exportations de biens et services
Less imports of goods and services	20 200	19 361	20 461	21 753	23 261	26 195	25 703	28 832	...	Moins importations de biens et services
GDP at purchasers' values	30 775	32 935	35 379	39 035	42 659	46 646	50 109	54 731	...	PIB aux prix d'acquisition

GROSS DOMESTIC PRODUCT BY KIND OF ECONOMIC ACTIVITY AT CONSTANT PRICES ANNUAL GROWTH RATES (%) — PRODUIT INTÉRIEUR BRUT PAR BRANCHE D'ACTIVITÉ ECONOMIQUE AUX PRIX CONSTANTS TAUX DE CROISSANCE ANNUEL (%)

	2009	2010	2011	2012	2013	2014	2015	2016	2017	
Agriculture, hunting , forestry and Fishing	8.2	- 12.3	5.8	0.8	4.6	0.3	- 4.2	6.2	...	Agriculture, chasse sylviculture et Pêche
Mining and quarrying	- 23.8	21.4	65.4	476.2	- 11.3	- 44.3	- 77.4	10.2	...	Industries extractives
Manufacturing	6.3	10.9	1.8	5.0	1.5	4.8	4.8	- 5.0	...	Industries manufacturières
Electricity, gas & water	7.8	2.3	3.4	- 6.3	- 7.7	- 3.2	1.1	- 42.2	...	Electricité, gaz et eau
Construction	1.2	- 2.7	- 4.7	- 0.9	0.3	- 0.1	4.4	26.8	...	Bâtiments et travaux publics
Wholesale & retail trade, restaurants, hotels	0.9	0.2	0.7	- 4.5	11.0	8.3	- 5.9	6.7	...	Commerce de gros et de détail, restaurants et hôtels
Finance, insurance, real estate, etc.	- 0.5	3.5	2.5	6.5	6.2	3.4	3.4	- 5.1	...	Banques, assurances, affaires immobilières
Transport and communications	- 7.6	- 5.8	5.8	9.6	15.8	7.6	- 3.1	3.5	...	Transport(s) et communications
Public administration and defense	6.2	2.7	8.8	- 5.9	9.6	5.4	7.0	14.3	...	Administrations publiques et défense
Education	12.1	8.7	- 6.8		0.3	2.4	2.1	4.6	...	Education
Health And Social Work	12.9	8.1	- 5.4	10.9	8.3	- 0.4	1.5	5.5	...	Santé et Actions Sociales
Other services	9.2	- 0.1	- 7.2	- 2.9	4.0	8.8	1.2	- 42.0	...	Autres services
Less Imputed Service Charges	- 8.6	- 4.9	- 24.6	- 0.6	4.7	4.7	4.3	- 2.2	...	Moins Services d'intermédiation financière
Gross domestic product at factor cost / basic prices	4.3	3.2	2.4	3.3	4.9	3.9	0.8	0.5	...	Produit intérieur brut aux couts des facteurs / prix de base
Plus: Indirect Taxes / taxes on products, less subsidies	10.4	9.8	- 5.4	7.1	2.2	- 0.9	6.4	3.8	...	Plus taxes indirectes/impôts sur les produits, moins les subventions
Gross domestic product at market prices	4.5	3.5	2.0	3.5	4.8	3.6	1.1	0.7	...	Produit intérieur brut aux prix du marché

EXPENDITURE ON GROSS DOMESTIC PRODUCT AT CONSTANT PURCHASERS' VALUES ANNUAL GROWTH RATES (%) — EMPLOIS DU PRODUIT INTÉRIEUR BRUT AUX PRIX CONSTANTS D'ACQUISITION TAUX DE CROISSANCE ANNUEL (%)

	2009	2010	2011	2012	2013	2014	2015	2016	2017	
Government final consumption	13.7	0.6	- 5.6	1.8	6.1	6.6	9.4	6.7	...	Consommation finale des administrations publiques
Private final consumption	2.9	3.6	5.1	- 0.3	- 3.9	- 3.0	- 4.8	6.1	...	Consommation finale privée
Gross fixed capital formation	5.3		- 6.7	- 0.1	6.0	2.9	- 0.5	8.8	...	Formation brute de capital fixe
Exports of goods and services	1.7	- 4.6	5.9	4.2	10.4	13.1	0.7	- 6.6	...	Exportations de biens et services
Less imports of goods and services	3.3	- 4.5	4.5	- 2.6	- 2.2	4.3	- 4.3	4.6	...	Moins importations de biens et services

III INFLATION

Annual growth rates (%)	2009	2010	2011	2012	2013	2014	2015	2016	2017	Taux de croissance annuel (%)
All item	7.4	4.5	6.1	8.9	5.6	5.7	5.0	7.9	6.2	Ensemble
of which:										dont:
Food and non-alcoholic beverages	10.0	0.4	6.0	13.1	5.7	6.4	4.2	15.1	7.1	Alimentation et boissons non alcoolisés
Alcoholic beverages, tobacco and narcotics	9.6	6.8	4.5	5.6	4.5	6.7	3.7	3.5	5.9	Boissons alcoolisées et tabacs
Clothing and footwear	6.1	6.8	1.1	4.6	3.6	7.4	7.8	6.8	4.2	Habillement et chaussures
Housing, water, electricity, gas and other fuels	10.0	8.7	6.7	8.5	5.5	3.4	4.6	4.6	6.7	Logement, eau, électricité, gaz et autres combustibles
Furnishings, household equipment and routine household maintenance	9.5	5.0	3.3	5.2	5.0	4.6	3.9	6.3	6.2	Meubles, articles de ménage et entretien courant
Health	5.3	2.1	3.0	10.3	12.8	7.1	2.8	0.3	0.5	Santé
Transport	1.0	5.0	13.3	8.1	2.4	8.8	3.8	9.6	3.7	Transport
Communication	7.2	7.2	0.4	-	-	- 0.2	4.0	4.6	0.1	Communication
Recreation and culture	2.9	16.3	3.0	2.8	6.7	6.7	7.1	4.5	...	Loisirs et culture
Education	- 1.7	11.7	12.3	7.4	9.4	9.6	6.5	3.1	6.4	Enseignement
Restaurants and hotels	13.1	1.4	2.6	5.9	- 0.4	4.3	9.3	2.0	3.1	Restaurants et hôtels
Miscellaneous goods and services	3.8	5.0	6.0	2.4	0.3	4.1	9.8	5.6	3.6	Biens et Services divers

IV AGRICULTURAL PRODUCTION - PRODUCTION AGRICOLE

TONNES (THOUSAND)	2009	2010	2011	2012	2013	2014	2015	2016	2017	Tonnes (milliers)
Sugar cane	500	500	500	540	545	653	687	695	...	Canne à sucre
Maize	57	68	85	76	82	101	82	34	...	Maïs
Oranges	36	43	43	45	46	46	...	...	...	Oranges
Pineapples	25	27	31	32	34	34	...	...	...	Ananas
Grapes	36	37	37	53	58	39	39	...	...	Raisins

V MINING PRODUCTION - PRODUCTION MINIERE

	2009	2010	2011	2012	2013	2014	2015	2016	2017	
Hard Coal - Production, metric tons (thousands)	130	146	121	152	257	178	142	158	202	Houille - Production, tonnes métriques (milliers)
Iron ores and concentrates - Production, metric tons (thousands)	...	...	79	1 032	1 258	603	...	...	...	"Minerais de fer et leurs concentrés - Production, tonnes métriques (milliers)"
Gravel and crushed stone - Production, cubic meters (thousands)	-	-	-	308	292	310	396	420	291	Graviers et pierres concassées - Production, mètres cubes (milliers)

VI ENERGY - ENERGIE

	2009	2010	2011	2012	2013	2014	2015	2016	2017	
Total electricity generation (GWh)	544	653	700	700	700	572	577	...	...	Production électrique totale (GWh)
of which										dont
Production of electricity from fossil fuels (GWh)	256	260	315	315	315	315	315	...	...	Production d'électricité à partir de combustibles fossiles (GWh)
Production of hydro electricity (GWh)	288	288	333	272	240	302	231	...	...	Production d'électricité d'origine hydraulique (GWh)
Production of electricity from solar, wind, tide, wave and other sources (GWh)	...	...	1	1	1	4	7	...	...	Production d'électricité d'origine solaire, éolienne, marée motrice et autres (GWh)

VII TOURISM AND INFRASTRUCTURE - TOURISME ET INFRASTUCTURE

VII-1 Tourism	2009	2010	2011	2012	2013	2014	2015	2016	2017	VII-1 Tourisme
International tourist arrivals (thousands)	908	868	879	888	968	939	873	947	995	Arrivées de touristes internationaux (milliers)
Rooms in hotels and similar establishments (thousands)	656	573	569	569	570	598	574	574	601	Chambres d'hôtels et établissements assimilés (milliers)
Overnight stays (thousands)	951	1 157	1 172	1 189	1 009	1 008	1 014	1 064	1 133	Nuitées (milliers)
Tourism receipts (US$ thousand)	28 300	31 700	5 200	18 800	1 800	10 000	8 100	6 900	8 008	Recettes touristiques (milliers de $ EU)
Total contribution to GDP (%)	4.5	4.0	3.3	5.4	6.5	7.0	6.7	6.9	6.9	Contribution totale au PIB (%)
Total contribution to Employment (%)	3.9	3.4	2.8	4.4	5.4	5.7	5.5	5.7	5.7	Contribution totale à l'emploi (%)
VII-2 Infrastructure										**VII-2 Infrastructure**
Paved road (% of total)	37.6	37.6	42.0	43.9	45.0	45.0	45.6	...	...	Routes asphaltées (% du total)
Total network (Railways-km)	300	300	300	300	300	300	...	...	...	Réseau total voies ferrées-Km
Main telephone lines (per 100 inhabitants)	3.8	4.4	6.3	3.7	3.7	3.5	3.3	3.2	...	Lignes téléphoniques fixes (pour 100 habitants)
Mobile cellular subscribers (per 100 inhabitants)	56.6	60.8	63.2	65.4	71.5	72.3	73.2	76.4	...	Abonnés aux téléphones mobiles (pour 100 habitants)
Internet users per 100 inhabitants	8.9	11.0	18.1	20.8	24.7	26.2	25.6	28.6	...	Utilisateurs Internet par 100 Habitants
Fixed (wired)-broadband subscriptions per 100 inhabitants	...	...	0.7	...	...	...	...	0.5	...	Abonnements à l'Internet fixe (filaire) à large bande pour 100 habitants, par débit

VIII EXTERNAL TRADE - COMMERCE EXTERIEUR

US$ (MILLIONS) EXPORTS, FOB	2009	2010	2011	2012	2013	2014	2015	2016	2017	$ E.U (MILLIONS) EXPORTATIONS, FÀB
Exports - Total	1 660	1 800	1 910	1 926	1 895	1 802	1 648	1 578	...	Exportations - Total
Exports to Africa	976	1 054	1 284	1 335	1 275	1 243	996	949	...	Exportations vers l'Afrique
Main products										**Principaux produits**
Carboxylic acids, anhydrides, halides, per.; derivati.	32	37	45	57	46	45	41	39	...	Acides carboxyliques, anhydrides, halogénures, par. dérivés
Essential oils, perfume & flavour materials	319	363	330	322	328	290	276	259	...	Huiles essentielles, parfums et arômes
Miscellaneous chemical products, n.e.s.	148	169	184	202	189	184	166	160	...	Produits chimiques divers, n.e.s.
Pulp and waste paper	99	117	110	187	186	132	142	125	...	Pâte et papier de rebut
Sugar, molasses and honey	298	330	231	186	235	153	173	149	...	Sucre, mélasse et miel
Main destinations										**Principales destinations**
China	18	19	-	89	92	36	57	43	...	Chine
India	26	28	59	59	24	96	54	68	...	Inde
Nigeria	...	...	50	58	91	118	...	...	...	Nigéria
South Africa	634	701	994	1 027	934	903	819	788	...	Afrique du Sud
United States	115	124	99	62	50	67	52	55	...	États-Unis
IMPORTS, CIF										
Imports - Total	1 780	1 960	1 950	1 848	1 693	1 676	1 385	1 406	...	Importations - Total (millions)
Imports from Africa	1 513	1 666	1 663	1 649	1 506	1 476	1 225	1 240	...	Importations en provenance de l'Afrique
Main products										**Principaux produits**
Essential oils, perfume & flavour materials	68	68	76	56	62	58	49	49	...	Huiles essentielles, parfums et arômes
Fruits and nuts (excluding oil nuts), fresh or dried	13	16	13	75	23	140	67	95	...	Fruits et noix (à l'exclusion des oléagineux), frais ou secs
Maize (not including sweet corn), unmilled	46	62	70	66	58	48	44	42	...	Maïs (à l'exclusion du maïs sucré), non moulu
Motor vehic. for transport of goods, special purpo.	39	40	33	33	33	30	26	26	...	Véhicule à moteur pour le transport de marchandises, spécial.
Petroleum oils or bituminous minerals > 70 % oil	164	207	242	236	237	200	180	174	...	Huiles de pétrole ou de minéraux bitumineux> 70% d'huile
Main origin										**Principales provenances**
China	38	43	31	29	24	23	19	19	...	Chine
India	14	16	87	46	27	22	20	20	...	Inde
Nigeria	1	1	-	67	6	138	59	91	...	Nigéria
South Africa	1 458	1 605	1 599	1 499	1 473	1 285	1 134	1 111	...	Afrique du Sud
United States	26	30	20	40	22	22	18	18	...	États-Unis

	2009	2010	2011	2012	2013	2014	2015	2016	2017	
IX-1 MONETARY STATISTICS *SWADZILAND LILANGANI (MILLIONS)*										**IX-1 STATISTIQUES MONÉTAIRES** *LILANGANI SWADZILANDAIS (MILLIONS)*
Money supply (M1)	7 713	8 323	8 778	9 658	11 197	11 639	13 219	16 708	17 919	Masse monétaire (M1)
Quasi-money	5 376	5 784	5 896	6 219	6 783	7 375	8 462	10 682	11 655	Quasi-monnaie
of which demand deposit	...	...	...	...	...	...	...	...	...	dont Monnaie scripturale
Net foreign assets	7 811	5 744	4 024	6 269	7 867	7 714	8 898	8 949	7 955	Avoirs extérieurs nets
Domestic credit	2 273	4 668	7 660	6 473	6 751	7 907	8 688	12 211	14 162	Crédit intérieur
of which claims on private sector	- 4 238	- 2 232	- 619	- 1 589	- 3 008	- 2 965	- 2 738	- 833	- 63	dont créances sur le secteur privé
of which claims on government sector, net	6 250	6 215	7 833	7 698	9 254	10 159	10 590	11 816	12 275	dont créances nettes sur le gouvernement
International reserves (millions US$)	878	678	520	664	767	690	547	564	474	Réserves internationales (millions $EU)
Average exchange rate (National currency per US$)	8	7	7	8	10	11	13	15	13	Taux de change (moyen) (monnaie nationale par $ EU)
IX-2 PUBLIC FINANCE *SWADZILAND LILANGANI (MILLIONS)*										**IX-2 FINANCES PUBLIQUES** *LILANGANI SWADZILANDAIS (MILLIONS)*
Total Revenues and Grants	9 595	9 176	6 831	7 184	12 035	12 910	14 881	14 667	13 944	Recettes totales et dons
Direct taxes (on income, profits)	1 780	2 050	2 577	2 713	2 359	2 826	3 562	3 859	4 590	Taxes directes
Domestic indirect taxes revenues	1 279	1 337	1 326	1 340	2 195	2 432	2 738	3 135	3 341	Taxes Indirectes
Trade taxes	6 009	5 190	2 631	2 884	7 066	7 154	7 500	6 931	5 252	Taxes sur le commerce extérieur
Other taxes	14	14	51	109	94	20	12	46	99	Autres taxes
Other revenues	471	420	187	104	278	282	291	367	237	Autres recettes
Grants	41	165	59	34	43	196	778	329	426	Dons
Total Expenditures and Net Lending	9 242	10 213	10 338	9 132	10 567	12 582	15 303	16 999	19 830	Dépenses totales et prêts nets
Current expenditure	6 858	7 534	8 262	7 849	8 790	9 874	11 241	12 639	15 120	Dépenses courantes
Wages and Salaries	3 519	3 773	4 138	3 822	4 062	5 231	5 487	6 090	7 777	Rémunérations et salaires
Other purchases of goods and services	1 821	2 074	2 401	2 343	3 026	2 357	2 770	3 470	3 070	Achat de biens et services
Other current expenditure	192	36	30	18	28	...	...	...	...	Autres dépenses courantes
Current transfers	1 326	1 651	1 693	1 667	1 675	2 286	2 984	3 080	4 273	Transferts courants
Interest payments	252	208	204	265	350	344	452	634	866	Intérêts
Capital expenditure	2 132	2 470	1 873	1 019	1 427	2 364	3 610	3 725	3 843	Dépenses d'équipement
Net lending	...	...	...	...	...	...	...	...	...	Prêts nets
Fiscal balance	353	- 1 037	- 3 508	- 1 948	1 467	328	- 422	- 2 332	- 5 885	Solde global y compris les dons
IX-3 BALANCE OF PAYMENTS *SWADZILAND LILANGANI (MILLIONS)*										**IX-3 BALANCE DES PAIEMENTS** *LILANGANI SWADZILANDAIS (MILLIONS)*
Trade balance	- 1 028	- 1 097	- 319	639	1 951	5 499	7 352	5 874	...	Balance commerciale
Services Balance	- 3 411	- 3 162	- 4 128	- 4 799	- 4 858	- 3 541	- 2 482	- 3 061	...	Balance des services
Net primary income	- 640	- 1 656	- 1 857	- 2 576	- 3 544	114	507	- 151	...	Revenus primaires nets
Compensation of employees	...	...	...	...	...	...	...	...	...	Rémunération des salariés
Investment income	...	...	...	...	...	...	...	...	...	Revenus des investissements
Net secondary income	1 601	2 968	3 845	8 006	8 699	8 030	8 003	6 781	...	Revenus secondaires nets
Net official transfers	...	...	...	...	...	...	...	...	...	Transferts officiels nets
Workers' remittances	...	...	...	...	...	...	...	...	...	Envois de fonds des travailleurs
Other private transfers	...	...	...	...	...	...	...	...	...	Autres transferts privés
Current account balance	- 3 478	- 2 947	- 2 459	1 270	2 248	10 101	13 380	9 443	...	Solde du compte courant
Capital and financial account	2 390	891	982	277	- 1 386	7 381	9 566	9 305	...	Comptes de capital et financier
Capital account	91	106	147	930	249	- 3	- 24	6	...	Compte de capital
Financial account	2 299	785	836	- 654	- 1 635	7 384	9 590	9 299	...	Compte financier
Errors and omissions	1 096	363	786	- 243	947	- 2 715	- 3 766	- 151	...	Erreurs et omissions
Overall balance	8	- 1 693	- 690	1 303	1 809	14 768	19 180	18 598	...	Balance générale

SWAZILAND

X DEBT AND FINANCIAL FLOWS - DETTE ET FLUX FINANCIERS

	2009	2010	2011	2012	2013	2014	2015	2016	2017	
X-1 DEBT *US $ (MILLIONS)*										**X-1 DETTE EXTÉRIEURE** *$ E.U (MILLIONS)*
Total external debt	592	708	643	575	611	515	563	523	636	Dette extérieure totale
Private	...	...	...	...	...	...	...	...	...	Privée
Public	357	358	353	338	343	329	371	353	...	Publique
Total external debt service	58	1 079	430	158	198	264	214	178	...	Service de la dette extérieure
Present value of external debt	...	...	...	...	...	...	...	302	...	Valeur actuelle de la dette extérieure
Total government domestic debt, National currency (millions)	...	2	2	2	3	3	3	...	...	Dette publique intérieure
X-2 FINANCIAL FLOWS *US $ (MILLIONS)*										**X-2 FLUX FINANCIERS** *$ E.U (MILLIONS)*
Net Foreign Direct Investment Inflows	66	136	93	90	29	27	32	- 11	...	Investissements étranger direct (flux nets entrants)
Main origin of FDI inflows										**Principales origines de l'IDE entrant:**
Poland	...	- 24	29	...	...	...	...	...	...	Pologne
Italy	- 67	19	- 1	- 23	...	...	...	...	...	Italie
...	...	...	...	...	...	...	...	...	...	...
...	...	...	...	...	...	...	...	...	...	...
...	...	...	...	...	...	...	...	...	...	...
African countries	...	...	...	...	...	...	...	...	...	Pays africains
Net total official development assistance	56	91	124	90	118	86	93	147	...	Aide publique au développement (nette totale)
Main origin of net ODA										**Principales origines de l'APD nette**
Global Fund	17	1	1	1	2	2	1	1	...	Fonds Mondial
United States	16	23	45	44	38	44	36	56	...	États-Unis
Japan	1	4	13	- 2	-	- 1	- 1	- 1	...	Japon
...	...	...	...	...	...	...	...	...	...	...
Italy	...	...	...	...	...	-	-	-	...	Italie

SWAZILAND

SOURCES AND NOTES - SOURCES ET NOTES

External trade - Total exports, fob: UNCTAD

External trade - Total import, cif: UNCTAD

ODA: OECD

Monetary statistics: IMF

National Account: The Accounts are calculated using the new base year 2011 from 2008.

Poverty: World Bank

Commerce exterieur - Exportation, fab: CNUCED

Commerce exterieur - Imporations, caf: CNUCED

APD: OCDE

Statistiques monétaires: FMI

Comptes Nationaux : Les comptes sont calculés selon la nouvelle année de base 2011 à partir de 2008.

Pauvreté: Banque mondiale

AREA (km2)		947 303		**SUPERFICIE (KM2)**
CAPITAL CITY	Dar es Salaam		Dar es Salaam	**CAPITALE**
CURRENCY	Tanzanian Shilling		Shilling Tanzanien	**MONNAIE**

I SOCIAL AND DEMOGRAPHIC INDICATORS — INDICATEURS DEMOGRAPHIQUES ET SOCIAUX

	Year Année	Value Valeur	Charts Graphiques	
Population				**Population**
Population ('000)	2015	53 470.4		Population ('000)
Female (%)	2015	50.3		Féminine (%)
Urban (%)	2015	30.9		Urbaine (%)
Average annual growth rate	2017	3.1		Taux de croissance annuel
Active population ('000)	2015	22 284.4		Population active ('000)
Population by age group ('000)				Population par groupe d'âge ('000)
0-14 years	2015	24 167.9		0-14 ans
15-64 years	2015	27 590.4		15-64 ans
65+ years	2015	1 712.1		65+ ans
Economically active population in agriculture (%)	2015	87.1		Participation de la population active agricole (%)
Crude birth rate	2015	38.5		Taux brut de natalité
Crude death rate	2015	6.7		Taux brut de mortalité
Total fertility rate	2017	5.1		Indice synthétique de fécondité
Life expectancy at birth - Total (years)	2015	65.5		Espérance de vie à la naissance - Totale (années)
Dependency ratio - Total (%)	2015	93.8		Taux de dépendance - Total (%)
Health				**Santé**
Percentage of children under-five and underweight	2011	13.6		% d'enfants de moins de cinq ans avec insuffisance pondérale
Prevalence of undernourishment	2015	32.1		Prévalence de la malnutrition
Under five mortality rate (per 1 000 live births)	2015	48.7		Taux de mortalité de moins de 5 ans (les deux sexes, pour 1000)
Infant mortality rate (per 1 000 live births)	2015	35.2		Taux de mortalité infantile (les deux sexes) par 1000
Neonatal mortality rate (per 1 000 live births)	2015	18.8		Le taux de mortalité néonatale (pour 1000 naissances vivantes)
Percentage of children provided the vaccines :				Pourcentage d'enfants vaccinés :
BCG	2014	99.0		BCG
DPT3	2014	97.0		DTC3
Polio	2011	88.0		polio
Measles	2014	99.0		rougeole
Percentage of mothers provided at least one antenatal care (%)	2010	87.8		Pourcentage de mères ayant au moins reçu un soin prénatal (%)
Percentage of deliveries attended by skilled health personnel	2010	48.9		% d'accouchements assistés par un personnel de santé qualifié
Number of doctors (per 10,000 population)	2006	0.1		Nombre de médecins (pour 10.000 habitants)
Number of nurses (per 10,000 population)	2013	2.1		Nombre d'infirmiers (pour 10.000 habitants)
Hospital beds - Total (per 10,000 population)	2013	5.0		Nombre de lits d'hôpitaux - Total (pour 10 000)
Births registered (per 1,000)	2015	38.5		Naissances enregistrées (pour 1000)
Deaths registered (per 1,000)	2015	6.7		Décès enregistrés (pour 1000)
Budget allocation to health (%)	2013	11.2		Dépenses publiques consacrées à la santé (% du budget)
Education				**Education**
Enrolment in primary education (000)	2017	9 317.8		Scolarisation dans le primaire (000)
Female	2017	4 688.6		Féminine
Enrolment in secondary education (000)	2017	1 909.0		Scolarisation dans le secondaire (000)
Female	2017	961.0		Féminine
Enrolment in tertiary education (000)	2016	306.9		Scolarisation dans le tertiaire (000)
Female	2016	126.4		Féminine
Literacy rate	2014	72.2		Taux d'alphabétisation (deux sexes)
Male	2014	77.4		Masculin
Female	2014	67.6		Féminin
Pupil teacher ratio - primary	2017	50.0		Ratio élève-enseignant
Budget allocation to education (%)	2016	17.2		Dépenses publiques consacrées à l'enseignement (% du budget)
Poverty				**Pauvreté**
GNI per capita, PPP (current int. $)	2016	2740.0		RNB par habitant, ($ PPA inter. courants)
Human Poverty Index (HPI-1) Value (%)	2007	30.0		Valeur de l'Indice de pauvreté (IPH-1) (%)
Population below Inter. poverty line ($2/day) (%)	2011	46.6		Population sous le seuil inter. de pauvreté (2$/Jour) (%)
Share of income held by richest 10%	2011	31.0		% de revenu des 10% plus riches
Share of income held by poorest 10%	2011	3.1		% de revenu des 10% plus pauvres
GINI index	2011	37.8		Indice de GINI

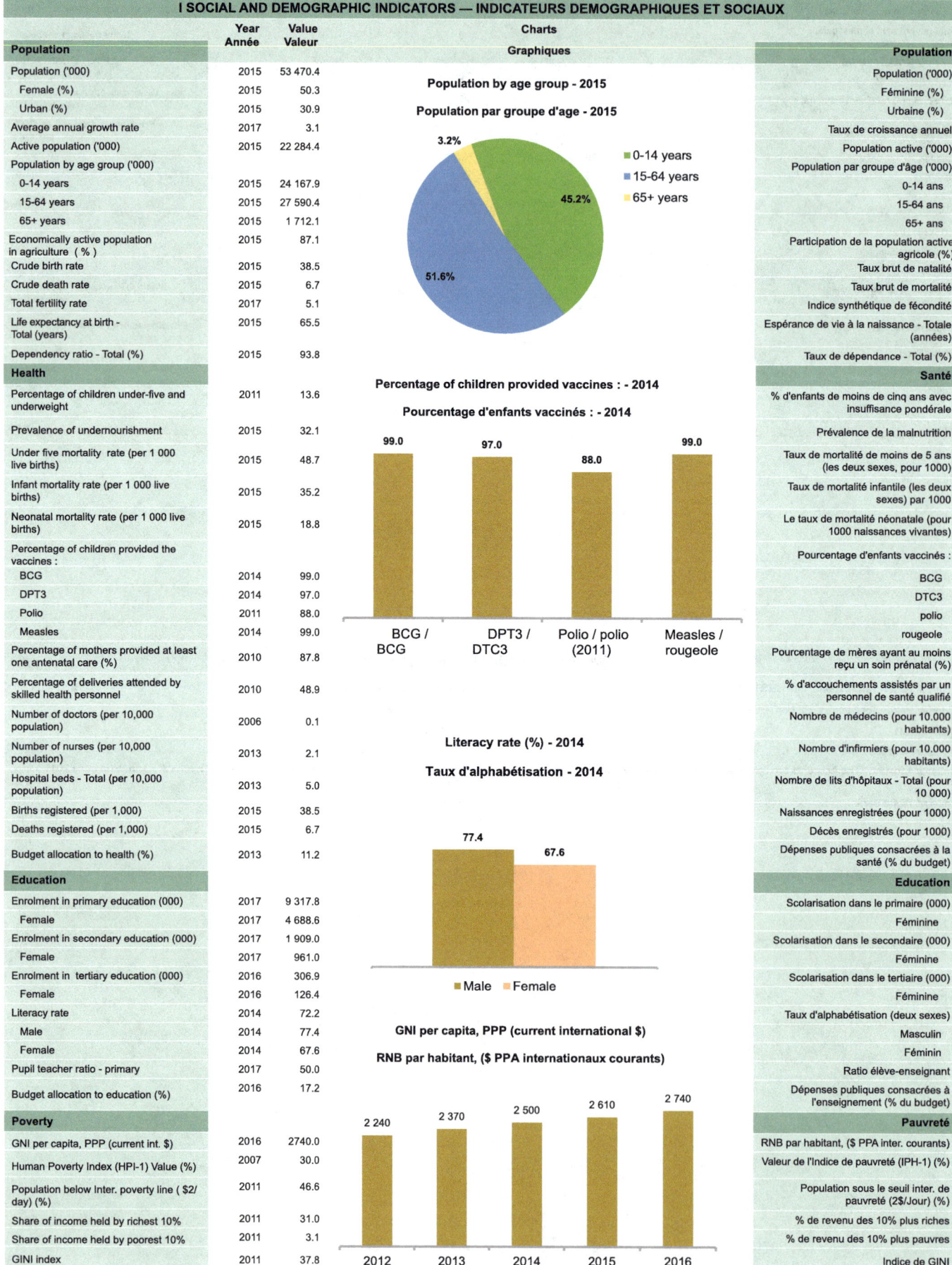

Population by age group - 2015
Population par groupe d'age - 2015

- 0-14 years — 45.2%
- 15-64 years — 51.6%
- 65+ years — 3.2%

Percentage of children provided vaccines : - 2014
Pourcentage d'enfants vaccinés : - 2014

- BCG / BCG: 99.0
- DPT3 / DTC3: 97.0
- Polio / polio (2011): 88.0
- Measles / rougeole: 99.0

Literacy rate (%) - 2014
Taux d'alphabétisation - 2014

- Male: 77.4
- Female: 67.6

GNI per capita, PPP (current international $)
RNB par habitant, ($ PPA internationaux courants)

- 2012: 2 240
- 2013: 2 370
- 2014: 2 500
- 2015: 2 610
- 2016: 2 740

TANZANIA

GROSS DOMESTIC PRODUCT BY KIND OF ECONOMIC ACTIVITY AT CURRENT PRICES *TANZANIAN SHILLING (MILLIONS)* — PRODUIT INTÉRIEUR BRUT PAR BRANCHE D'ACTIVITÉ ÉCONOMIQUE AUX PRIX COURANTS *SHILLING TANZANIEN (MILLIONS)*

	2009	2010	2011	2012	2013	2014	2015	2016	2017	
Agriculture, hunting , forestry and Fishing	11 408 000	13 110 000	15 488 000	19 096 000	22 129 000	22 969 225	26 346 665	30 160 064	...	Agriculture, chasse sylviculture et Pêche
Mining and quarrying	1 073 000	1 780 000	2 689 000	3 001 000	2 986 000	2 923 420	3 659 599	4 975 991	...	Industries extractives
Manufacturing	2 597 000	3 022 000	4 032 000	4 416 000	4 812 000	4 445 568	4 768 917	5 305 097	...	Industries manufacturières
Electricity, gas & water	620 000	667 000	551 000	808 000	873 000	1 247 855	1 291 238	1 337 639	...	Electricité, gaz et eau
Construction	2 740 000	3 146 000	4 340 000	5 009 000	6 480 000	9 899 350	12 374 188	14 477 799	...	Bâtiments et travaux publics
Wholesale & retail trade, restaurants, hotels	4 440 000	5 163 000	6 330 000	7 312 000	8 282 000	9 250 790	10 671 932	12 139 938	...	Commerce de gros et de détail, restaurants et hôtels
Finance, insurance, real estate, etc.	4 480 000	3 877 000	4 615 000	5 748 000	9 215 000	5 649 861	6 186 930	6 793 671	...	Banques, assurances, affaires immobilières
Transport and communications	3 234 000	3 689 000	3 974 000	4 189 000	4 425 000	5 138 488	5 674 378	6 499 777	...	Transport(s) et communications
Public administration and defense	2 512 000	2 669 000	3 338 000	4 017 000	4 936 000	8 233 830	9 115 935	10 017 139	...	Administrations publiques et défense
Education	1 193 000	1 380 000	1 464 000	1 607 000	1 893 000	2 172 080	2 309 345	2 425 025	...	Education
Health And Social Work	664 000	736 000	821 000	919 000	1 020 000	1 151 978	1 275 702	1 429 936	...	Santé et Actions Sociales
Other services	572 000	613 000	679 000	782 000	872 000	1 008 782	1 110 013	1 222 602	...	Autres services
Less Imputed Service Charges	- 327 000	- 376 000	- 558 000	- 638 000	- 867 000	- 826 396	-1 037 814	-1 082 044	...	Moins Services d'intermédiation financière
Gross domestic product at factor cost / basic prices	35 206 000	39 476 000	47 763 000	56 266 000	67 056 000	73 264 831	83 747 037	95 702 634	...	Produit intérieur brut aux couts des facteurs / prix de base
Plus: Indirect Taxes / taxes on products, less subsidies	2 520 824	4 360 018	4 999 581	5 168 214	3 897 227	6 453 585	7 116 789	8 041 972	...	Plus taxes indirectes sur les produits, moins les subventions

EXPENDITURE ON GROSS DOMESTIC PRODUCT AT CURRENT PURCHASER'S VALUES *Tanzanian Shilling (Millions)* — EMPLOI DU PRODUIT INTÉRIEUR BRUT AUX PRIX COURANTS D'ACQUISITION *SHILLING TANZANIEN (MILLIONS)*

	2009	2010	2011	2012	2013	2014	2015	2016	2017	
Government final consumption	6 599 152	6 451 836	7 293 792	9 055 182	11 580 484	10 996 641	12 454 217	14 407 309	...	Consommation finale des administrations publiques
Private final consumption	25 008 001	29 970 434	35 993 661	42 134 008	47 377 326	52 972 167	56 557 244	67 025 286	...	Consommation finale privée
Gross fixed capital formation	10 883 740	12 572 205	17 324 767	18 786 138	21 625 331	25 968 851	31 122 533	34 768 001	...	Formation brute de capital fixe
Change in inventories	-1 404 814	- 606 714	213 708	-1 275 622	- 109 266	-1 949 131	-6 405 326	-9 209 861	...	Variation des stocks
Exports of goods and services	6 554 600	8 217 681	10 951 622	13 076 463	12 524 115	15 476 677	19 645 876	20 213 109	...	Exportations de biens et services
Less imports of goods and services	9 913 855	12 769 425	19 014 968	20 341 955	22 044 763	23 746 791	22 510 717	23 459 238	...	Moins importations de biens et services
GDP at purchasers' values	37 726 824	43 836 018	52 762 581	61 434 214	70 953 227	79 718 416	90 863 827	103 744 606	...	PIB aux prix d'acquisition

GROSS DOMESTIC PRODUCT BY KIND OF ECONOMIC ACTIVITY AT CONSTANT PRICES *ANNUAL GROWTH RATES (%)* — PRODUIT INTÉRIEUR BRUT PAR BRANCHE D'ACTIVITÉ ECONOMIQUE AUX PRIX CONSTANTS *TAUX DE CROISSANCE ANNUEL (%)*

	2009	2010	2011	2012	2013	2014	2015	2016	2017	
Agriculture, hunting , forestry and Fishing	5.1	2.7	3.5	3.2	3.2	3.4	2.3	2.1	...	Agriculture, chasse sylviculture et Pêche
Mining and quarrying	18.7	7.3	6.3	6.7	3.9	9.4	9.1	11.5	...	Industries extractives
Manufacturing	4.7	8.9	6.9	4.1	6.5	6.8	6.5	7.8	...	Industries manufacturières
Electricity, gas & water	4.4	7.8	- 2.9	3.1	8.1	6.8	3.3	6.7	...	Electricité, gaz et eau
Construction	- 3.8	10.3	22.9	3.2	14.6	14.1	16.8	13.0	...	Bâtiments et travaux publics
Wholesale & retail trade, restaurants, hotels	2.5	9.0	10.3	4.2	4.2	9.0	7.1	6.3	...	Commerce de gros et de détail, restaurants et hôtels
Finance, insurance, real estate, etc.	12.9	15.4	5.9	10.9	12.7	- 10.6	6.8	6.6	...	Banques, assurances, affaires immobilières
Transport and communications	7.0	9.5	6.5	6.0	6.0	21.4	8.3	9.6	...	Transport(s) et communications
Public administration and defense	- 0.7	- 5.0	15.9	9.1	7.8	3.9	4.6	6.7	...	Administrations publiques et défense
Education	9.2	6.4	5.6	7.4	4.3	4.8	6.3	8.1	...	Education
Health And Social Work	7.4	3.3	5.3	11.4	8.8	8.1	4.7	5.2	...	Santé et Actions Sociales
Other services	4.6	5.6	5.8	6.6	5.6	5.8	6.0	6.8	...	Autres services
Less Imputed Service Charges	20.0	7.9	22.6	1.2	0.1	9.7	11.7	16.3	...	Moins Services d'intermédiation financière
Gross domestic product at factor cost / basic prices	4.8	6.6	7.6	5.5	6.7	6.9	6.7	6.9	...	Produit intérieur brut aux couts des facteurs / prix de base
Plus: Indirect Taxes / taxes on products, less subsidies	12.8	3.8	12.1	0.4	14.2	7.7	9.6	7.8	...	Plus taxes indirectes/impôts sur les produits, moins les subventions
Gross domestic product at market prices	5.4	6.4	7.9	5.1	7.3	7.0	7.0	7.0	...	Produit intérieur brut aux prix du marché

EXPENDITURE ON GROSS DOMESTIC PRODUCT AT CONSTANT PURCHASERS' VALUES *ANNUAL GROWTH RATES (%)* — EMPLOIS DU PRODUIT INTÉRIEUR BRUT AUX PRIX CONSTANTS D'ACQUISITION *TAUX DE CROISSANCE ANNUEL (%)*

	2009	2010	2011	2012	2013	2014	2015	2016	2017	
Government final consumption	12.8	- 9.7	5.3	13.3	18.1	- 0.5	- 4.0	12.3	...	Consommation finale des administrations publiques
Private final consumption	8.0	7.4	5.6	3.3	7.6	4.3	2.4	17.0	...	Consommation finale privée
Gross fixed capital formation	- 0.8	11.5	21.7	1.0	4.4	12.8	10.6	12.4	...	Formation brute de capital fixe
Exports of goods and services	3.5	6.8	10.1	16.0	0.6	17.7	23.3	- 11.7	...	Exportations de biens et services
Less imports of goods and services	- 2.4	14.7	25.9	- 0.8	11.0	2.9	- 6.0	1.6	...	Moins importations de biens et services

III INFLATION

	2009	2010	2011	2012	2013	2014	2015	2016	2017	
Annual growth rates (%)										**Taux de croissance annuel (%)**
All item	12.1	8.2	12.7	16.0	7.9	6.1	5.6	5.2	5.3	Ensemble
of which:										dont:
Food and non-alcoholic beverages	17.5	9.7	16.0	20.6	8.5	7.4	8.7	7.2	9.1	Alimentation et boissons non alcoolisés
Alcoholic beverages, tobacco and narcotics	8.8	13.8	4.8	14.8	14.0	5.9	3.6	4.0	3.3	Boissons alcoolisées et tabacs
Clothing and footwear	6.3	- 0.3	9.5	13.8	5.7	3.0	4.1	3.9	3.5	Habillement et chaussures
Housing, water, electricity, gas and other fuels	12.5	- 0.9	18.7	16.3	14.2	10.7	1.6	6.3	7.6	Logement, eau, électricité, gaz et autres combustibles
Furnishings, household equipment and routine household maintenance	- 1.6	18.6	13.8	9.0	4.1	1.9	1.6	3.6	2.9	Meubles, articles de ménage et entretien courant
Health	6.1	2.1	2.1	3.1	2.8	3.6	3.0	5.6	2.6	Santé
Transport	5.2	4.9	7.4	6.1	6.3	3.8	- 0.6	0.6	0.5	Transport
Communication	6.8	2.1	- 1.5	- 1.2	- 0.3	0.7	0.3	- 0.7	- 0.9	Communication
Recreation and culture	9.2	2.7	3.0	9.9	2.1	0.7	1.6	2.7	1.3	Loisirs et culture
Education	-	5.9	4.1	4.6	2.4	5.3	2.9	2.7	0.9	Enseignement
Restaurants and hotels	10.1	4.9	8.1	16.6	5.5	2.7	4.6	4.1	1.2	Restaurants et hôtels
Miscellaneous goods and services	3.2	- 0.7	4.7	10.7	5.7	6.1	2.9	3.4	3.2	Biens et Services divers

IV AGRICULTURAL PRODUCTION - PRODUCTION AGRICOLE

	2009	2010	2011	2012	2013	2014	2015	2016	2017	
TONNES (THOUSAND)										**Tonnes (milliers)**
Maize	3 326	4 733	4 341	5 104	5 356	6 734	5 903	6 149	...	Maïs
Cassava	5 916	4 548	4 647	5 462	4 755	1 664	1 962	2 205	...	Manioc
Sweet potatoes	1 417	2 424	3 573	3 018	3 470	1 167	1 090	1 044	...	Patates douces
Bananas	3 006	3 156	3 144	2 525	2 679	1 064	1 195	1 061	...	Bananes
Rice, paddy	1 335	2 650	2 248	1 801	2 195	1 681	1 937	2 229	...	Riz, Paddy

V MINING PRODUCTION - PRODUCTION MINIERE

	2009	2010	2011	2012	2013	2014	2015	2016	2017	
Hard Coal - Production, metric tons (thousands)	-	-	81	79	85	246	257	276	551	Houille - Production, tonnes métriques (milliers)
Gold ores and concentrates - Production (Kilograms)	8 231	12 470	10 399	11 227	12 159	40 400	43 293	45 155	43 171	Minerais d'or et leurs concentrés - Production (Kilogrammes)
Silver ores and concentrates - Production, Kilograms (thousands)	39	39	37	39	43	15	16	18	11	Minerais d'argent et leurs concentrés - Production, Kilogrammes (milliers)

VI ENERGY - ENERGIE

	2009	2010	2011	2012	2013	2014	2015	2016	2017	
Total electricity generation (GWh)	3 341	3 680	3 078	3 134	5 938	4 074	3 936	...	...	Production électrique totale (GWh)
of which										dont
Production of electricity from fossil fuels (GWh)	650	915	957	1 204	4 042	1 292	1 555	...	...	Production d'électricité à partir de combustibles fossiles (GWh)
Production of hydro electricity (GWh)	2 640	2 701	1 993	1 767	1 717	2 591	2 108	...	...	Production d'électricité d'origine hydraulique (GWh)
Production of electricity from solar, wind, tide, wave and other sources (GWh)	51	65	128	164	179	192	273	...	...	Production d'électricité d'origine solaire, éolienne, marée motrice et autres (GWh)

VII TOURISM AND INFRASTRUCTURE - TOURISME ET INFRASTUCTURE

	2009	2010	2011	2012	2013	2014	2015	2016	2017	
VII-1 Tourism										**VII-1 Tourisme**
International tourist arrivals (thousands)	695	754	843	1 043	1 063	1 113	1 104	1 247	1 236	Arrivées de touristes internationaux (milliers)
Rooms in hotels and similar establishments (thousands)	32	...	...	...	...	...	...	...	...	Chambres d'hôtels et établissements assimilés (milliers)
Overnight stays (thousands)	8 599	9 263	10 161	12 880	13 244	13 906	13 740	15 736	15 548	Nuitées (milliers)
Tourism receipts (US$ thousand)	1 159 800	1 254 500	1 353 200	1 712 700	1 880 400	2 010 100	1 902 000	2 131 600	2 153 670	Recettes touristiques (milliers de $ EU)
Total contribution to GDP (%)	10.8	9.7	10.6	10.9	11.4	11.4	11.4	10.0	9.1	Contribution totale au PIB (%)
Total contribution to Employment (%)	9.0	8.2	8.9	9.2	9.9	9.9	9.9	8.8	8.2	Contribution totale à l'emploi (%)
VII-2 Infrastructure										**VII-2 Infrastructure**
Paved road (% of total)	14.9	8.2	21.3	21.3	21.6	24.2	23.0	...	...	Routes asphaltées (% du total)
Total network (Railways-km)	2 707	2 707	2 707	2 707	2 707	2 707	...	...	...	Réseau total voies ferrées-Km
Main telephone lines (per 100 inhabitants)	...	...	...	...	...	...	...	...	...	Lignes téléphoniques fixes (pour 100 habitants)
Mobile cellular subscribers (per 100 inhabitants)	40.0	46.7	55.4	57.0	55.7	62.8	75.9	74.4	...	Abonnés aux téléphones mobiles (pour 100 habitants)
Internet users per 100 inhabitants	2.4	2.9	3.2	4.0	4.4	7.0	10.0	13.0	...	Utilisateurs Internet par 100 Habitants
Fixed (wired)-broadband subscriptions per 100 inhabitants	...	...	...	...	...	...	...	...	...	Abonnements à l'Internet fixe (filaire) à large bande pour 100 habitants, par débit

VIII EXTERNAL TRADE - COMMERCE EXTERIEUR

	2009	2010	2011	2012	2013	2014	2015	2016	2017	
US$ (MILLIONS) **EXPORTS, FOB**										**$ E.U (MILLIONS)** **EXPORTATIONS, FÀB**
Exports - Total	2 982	4 051	4 735	5 547	4 413	4 628	4 931	4 742	...	Exportations - Total
Exports to Africa	709	1 218	1 384	1 582	1 252	1 387	1 487	1 241	...	Exportations vers l'Afrique
Main products										**Principaux produits**
Fruits and nuts (excluding oil nuts), fresh or dried	99	156	140	198	165	233	256	333	...	ruits et noix (à l'exclusion des oléagineux), frais ou secs
Gold, non-monetary (excluding gold ores and concentrates)	757	927	1 452	2 077	1 563	1 241	1 351	1 571	...	Or, non monétaire (à l'exclusion des minerais d'or et des concentrés)
Ores & concentrates of precious metals; waste, scrap	340	418	541	356	229	290	286	267	...	Minerais et concentrés de métaux précieux; déchets, débris
Tobacco, unmanufactured; tobacco refuse	149	200	222	269	217	253	287	360	...	Tabac, non manufacturé; déchets de tabac
Vegetables	84	126	86	136	113	181	235	235	...	Légumes
Main destinations										**Principales destinations**
China	325	603	620	464	388	465	411	311	...	Chine
India	242	290	249	506	711	906	942	710	...	Inde
South Africa	121	283	502	535	391	307	309	304	...	Afrique du Sud
Switzerland	338	416	511	828	358	130	136	659	...	Suisse
United Arab Emirates	293	350	558	709	541	461	476	426	...	Emirates Arabes
IMPORTS, CIF										
Imports - Total	6 531	8 013	11 184	11 716	12 525	12 691	10 789	9 488	...	Importations - Total (millions)
Imports from Africa	1 099	1 245	1 510	1 806	1 380	1 361	872	1 085	...	Importations en provenance de l'Afrique
Main products										**Principaux produits**
Fixed vegetable fats & oils, crude, refined, fract.	131	204	320	287	234	352	229	323	...	Graisses et huiles végétales fixes, brutes, raffinées, fract.
Medicaments (incl. veterinary medicaments)	112	148	224	218	230	298	271	322	...	Médicaments (y compris les médicaments vétérinaires)
Motor vehicles for the transport of persons	209	253	237	269	315	257	179	179	...	Véhicules à moteur pour le transport de personnes
Petroleum oils or bituminous minerals > 70 % oil	1 198	1 733	2 775	2 731	4 050	3 179	3 629	1 299	...	Huiles de pétrole ou de minéraux bitumineux> 70% d'huile
Telecommunication equipment, n.e.s.; & parts, n.e.s.	180	137	277	231	192	219	328	300	...	Matériel de télécommunication, n.e.s .; & parties, n.e.s.
Main origin										**Principales provenances**
China	839	1 108	1 424	1 670	2 199	2 690	2 523	2 738	...	Chine
India	867	1 051	1 756	1 274	2 663	2 748	1 205	1 658	...	Inde
Saudi Arabia	241	307	383	456	397	368	2 606	317	...	Arabie Saoudite
South Africa	592	692	820	789	576	500	415	475	...	Afrique du Sud
United Arab Emirates	598	654	1 116	1 013	1 074	1 012	614	562	...	Emirates Arabes

TANZANIA

	2009	2010	2011	2012	2013	2014	2015	2016	2017	
IX-1 MONETARY STATISTICS *TANZANIAN SHILLING (MILLIONS)*										**IX-1 STATISTIQUES MONÉTAIRES** *SHILLING TANZANIEN (MILLIONS)*
Money supply (M1)	8 780 143	11 012 664	13 021 322	14 647 105	16 106 768	18 614 151	22 115 315	23 642 279	26 621 150	Masse monétaire (M1)
Quasi-money	3 924 470	4 715 501	5 219 938	5 795 699	6 458 737	7 711 642	8 935 753	9 203 317	9 249 992	Quasi-monnaie
of which demand deposit	...	...	...	...	...	...	...	...	...	dont Monnaie scripturale
Net foreign assets	4 930 809	6 086 780	6 296 384	6 371 084	6 572 437	6 562 045	8 206 591	8 252 158	8 011 983	Avoirs extérieurs nets
Domestic credit	5 120 245	6 798 432	9 093 572	11 045 512	12 947 217	16 063 918	20 374 364	20 890 861	21 991 105	Crédit intérieur
of which claims on private sector	128 358	806 665	1 471 255	2 035 131	2 554 554	3 651 622	4 881 635	4 281 968	5 190 117	dont créances sur le secteur privé
of which claims on government sector, net	4 326 349	5 235 706	6 668 738	7 988 285	9 149 395	10 989 336	13 787 773	14 813 462	15 243 141	dont créances nettes sur le gouvernement
International reserves (millions US$)	3 553	3 948	3 745	4 077	4 497	4 461	4 078	4 170	4 754	Réserves internationales (millions $EU)
Average exchange rate (National currency per US$)	1 320	1 409	1 572	1 583	1 598	1 653	1 991	2 177	2 228	Taux de change (moyen) (monnaie nationale par $ EU)
IX-2 PUBLIC FINANCE *TANZANIAN SHILLING (MILLIONS)*										**IX-2 FINANCES PUBLIQUES** *SHILLING TANZANIEN (MILLIONS)*
Total Revenues and Grants	5 550 383	6 066 788	7 204 900	9 076 096	10 260 027	11 770 103	11 681 980	14 912 915	17 732 600	Recettes totales et dons
Direct taxes (on income, profits)	1 257 861	1 388 700	1 719 800	2 247 000	3 065 737	3 778 546	3 720 000	4 600 000	4 829 600	Taxes directes
Domestic indirect taxes revenues	1 333 789	1 488 400	1 632 900	1 677 464	2 883 854	1 707 136	1 194 740	2 423 600	3 915 000	Taxes Indirectes
Trade taxes	1 130 860	1 214 600	1 512 100	2 555 536	1 861 268	3 535 759	3 928 467	4 898 988	3 100 000	Taxes sur le commerce extérieur
Other taxes	321 189	336 100	428 400	545 000	456 765	372 977	498 556	917 327	2 211 000	Autres taxes
Other revenues	249 401	233 700	284 700	196 000	205 173	888 038	946 085	1 588 000	2 585 000	Autres recettes
Grants	1 257 283	1 405 288	1 627 000	1 855 096	1 787 230	1 487 649	1 394 133	485 000	1 092 000	Dons
Total Expenditures and Net Lending	6 811 859	8 311 300	9 439 000	10 765 000	13 437 325	14 411 133	14 339 359	18 460 045	18 889 000	Dépenses totales et prêts nets
Current expenditure	4 438 790	5 451 000	6 337 000	6 553 961	8 636 203	9 508 009	9 581 659	12 633 769	9 901 000	Dépenses courantes
Wages and Salaries	1 608 591	1 723 000	2 346 000	2 722 000	3 333 865	4 137 816	4 355 359	5 653 257	5 599 000	Rémunérations et salaires
Other purchases of goods and services	2 830 199	3 728 000	3 991 000	3 831 961	5 302 338	5 370 193	5 226 300	6 980 512	4 302 000	Achat de biens et services
Other current expenditure	...	...	...	...	...	...	...	...	...	Autres dépenses courantes
Current transfers	...	...	...	...	...	...	...	...	...	Transferts courants
Interest payments	242 669	249 000	353 000	436 317	763 306	977 082	1 197 900	1 486 276	1 715 000	Intérêts
Capital expenditure	2 130 400	2 611 300	2 749 000	3 774 722	4 037 817	3 926 042	3 559 800	4 340 000	7 273 000	Dépenses d'équipement
Net lending	...	...	...	...	...	...	...	...	...	Prêts nets
Fiscal balance	-1 261 476	-2 244 512	-2 234 100	-1 688 904	-3 177 299	-2 641 030	-2 657 379	-3 547 130	-1 156 400	Solde global y compris les dons
IX-3 BALANCE OF PAYMENTS *US$ (MILLIONS)*										**IX-3 BALANCE DES PAIEMENTS** *$ E.U (MILLIONS)*
Trade balance	- 2 536	- 2 841	- 4 730	- 4 430	- 5 771	- 5 724	- 4 526	- 2 803	...	Balance commerciale
Services Balance	146	157	92	428	713	727	743	1 376	...	Balance des services
Net primary income	- 298	- 578	- 646	- 574	- 706	- 325	- 348	- 1 110	...	Revenus primaires nets
Compensation of employees	- 28	- 32	- 16	- 36	- 38	- 17	- 5	- 10	...	Rémunération des salariés
Investment income	- 269	- 545	- 626	- 535	- 665	- 606	- 690	- 663	...	Revenus des investissements
Net secondary income	891	1 051	902	807	775	477	480	382	...	Revenus secondaires nets
Net official transfers	...	...	...	...	...	...	...	...	...	Transferts officiels nets
Workers' remittances	...	...	...	...	...	...	...	...	...	Envois de fonds des travailleurs
Other private transfers	...	...	...	...	...	...	...	...	...	Autres transferts privés
Current account balance	- 1 797	- 2 211	- 4 381	- 3 770	- 4 989	- 4 844	- 3 651	- 2 155	...	Solde du compte courant
Capital and financial account	2 336	3 598	3 534	4 657	5 680	3 767	3 187	2 333	...	Comptes de capital et financier
Capital account	447	538	691	777	659	522	313	11	...	Compte de capital
Financial account	1 890	3 061	2 843	3 880	5 021	3 245	2 874	2 322	...	Compte financier
Errors and omissions	- 173	- 1 018	645	- 561	- 183	826	224	- 282	...	Erreurs et omissions
Overall balance	366	370	- 202	326	508	- 252	- 241	- 104	...	Balance générale

TANZANIE

X DEBT AND FINANCIAL FLOWS - DETTE ET FLUX FINANCIERS

	2009	2010	2011	2012	2013	2014	2015	2016	2017	
X-1 DEBT US $ (MILLIONS)										**X-1 DETTE EXTÉRIEURE** $ E.U (MILLIONS)
Total external debt	5 996	7 177	8 358	9 893	11 591	13 172	14 564	15 676	17 077	Dette extérieure totale
Private	...	...	...	...	...	...	...	...	...	Privée
Public	4 960	6 012	7 081	8 497	10 124	11 370	12 388	13 321	...	Publique
Total external debt service	196	220	243	230	270	353	585	760	...	Service de la dette extérieure
Present value of external debt	...	...	...	...	...	...	...	9 545	...	Valeur actuelle de la dette extérieure
Total government domestic debt, National currency (millions)	2 495	3 232	3 892	4 318	...	...	...	...	...	Dette publique intérieure
X-2 FINANCIAL FLOWS US $ (MILLIONS)										**X-2 FLUX FINANCIERS** $ E.U (MILLIONS)
Net Foreign Direct Investment Inflows	953	1 813	1 229	1 800	2 087	1 673	1 605	1 365	...	Investissements étranger direct (flux nets entrants)
Main origin of FDI inflows										**Principales origines de l'IDE entrant:**
Sweden	5	16	1	33	...	...	...	...	...	Suède
Netherlands	22	110	15	...	...	...	...	...	...	Pays-Bas
Norway	- 1	21	66	...	...	...	...	...	...	Norvège
Italy	13	...	...	1	...	...	...	...	...	Italie
...	...	...	...	...	...	...	...	...	...	...
African countries	434	517	873	...	...	...	...	...	...	Pays africains
Net total official development assistance	2 928	2 960	2 442	2 822	3 433	2 651	2 582	2 318	...	Aide publique au développement (nette totale)
Main origin of net ODA										**Principales origines de l'APD nette**
International Development Association [IDA]	627	693	258	535	697	606	581	398	...	International Development Association
United States	284	456	532	562	735	509	453	500	...	États-Unis
United Kingdom	217	241	159	250	237	245	313	251	...	Royaume-Uni
...	...	...	...	...	...	...	...	...	...	...
...	...	...	...	...	...	...	...	...	...	...

TANZANIA

SOURCES AND NOTES - SOURCES ET NOTES

External trade - Total exports, fob: UNCTAD

External trade - Total import, cif: UNCTAD

ODA: OECD

Monetary statistics: IMF

National Accounts: NA data : 2014-2015:Revised;2016: Provisional

National Account: The accounts are calculated using the new base year 2007

Poverty: World Bank

Commerce exterieur - Exportation, fab: CNUCED

Commerce exterieur - Imporations, caf: CNUCED

APD: OCDE

Statistiques monétaires: FMI

Comptes nationaux: Données des CN: 2014-2015:Données Révisées; 2016: Données Provisoires

Comptes Nationaux : Les Comptes Natioanux :Les comptes annuels sont élaborés selon la nouvelle base des prix 2007

Pauvreté: Banque mondiale

AREA (km2)	56 790	**SUPERFICIE (KM2)**
CAPITAL CITY	Lomé · Lomé	**CAPITALE**
CURRENCY	CFA Franc · Franc CFA	**MONNAIE**

I SOCIAL AND DEMOGRAPHIC INDICATORS — INDICATEURS DEMOGRAPHIQUES ET SOCIAUX

	Year / Année	Value / Valeur	Charts / Graphiques	
Population				**Population**
Population ('000)	2017	7 300.0		Population ('000)
Female (%)	2017	51.3		Féminine (%)
Urban (%)	2017	40.0		Urbaine (%)
Average annual growth rate	2017	2.4		Taux de croissance annuel
Active population ('000)	2017	3 306.5		Population active ('000)
Population by age group ('000)				Population par groupe d'âge ('000)
0-14 years	2017	2 913.4		0-14 ans
15-64 years	2017	4 084.2		15-64 ans
65+ years	2017	267.7		65+ ans
Economically active population in agriculture (%)	2016	44.0		Participation de la population active agricole (%)
Crude birth rate	2017	34.0		Taux brut de natalité
Crude death rate	2017	8.3		Taux brut de mortalité
Total fertility rate	2017	4.6		Indice synthétique de fécondité
Life expectancy at birth - Total (years)	2017	60.0		Espérance de vie à la naissance - Totale (années)
Dependency ratio - Total (%)	2017	77.9		Taux de dépendance - Total (%)
Health				**Santé**
Percentage of children under-five and underweight	2017	5.0		% d'enfants de moins de cinq ans avec insuffisance pondérale
Prevalence of undernourishment	2017	27.5		Prévalence de la malnutrition
Under five mortality rate (per 1 000 live births)	2017	83.0		Taux de mortalité de moins de 5 ans (les deux sexes, pour 1000)
Infant mortality rate (per 1 000 live births)	2017	51.0		Taux de mortalité infantile (les deux sexes) par 1000
Neonatal mortality rate (per 1 000 live births)	2017	27.0		Le taux de mortalité néonatale (pour 1000 naissances vivantes)
Percentage of children provided the vaccines :				Pourcentage d'enfants vaccinés :
BCG	2017	87.0		BCG
DPT3	2017	87.0		DTC3
Polio	2017	85.0		polio
Measles	2017	84.0		rougeole
Percentage of mothers provided at least one antenatal care	2010	84.3		Pourcentage de mères ayant au moins reçu un soin prénatal (%)
Percentage of deliveries attended by skilled health personnel	2013	43.8		% d'accouchements assistés par un personnel de santé qualifié
Number of doctors (per 10,000 population)	2017	1.0		Nombre de médecins (pour 10.000 habitants)
Number of nurses (per 10,000 population)	2017	2.0		Nombre d'infirmiers (pour 10.000 habitants)
Hospital beds - Total (per 10,000 population)	2017	7.0		Nombre de lits d'hôpitaux - Total (pour 10 000)
Births registered (per 1,000)	2017	37.0		Naissances enregistrées (pour 1000)
Deaths registered (per 1,000)	2017	9.0		Décès enregistrés (pour 1000)
Budget allocation to health (%)	2017	6.4		Dépenses publiques consacrées à la santé (% du budget)
Education				**Education**
Enrolment in primary education (000)	2017	1 668.1		Scolarisation dans le primaire (000)
Female	2017	815.3		Féminine
Enrolment in secondary education (000)	2017	540.9		Scolarisation dans le secondaire (000)
Female	2017	239.7		Féminine
Enrolment in tertiary education (000)	2017	144.8		Scolarisation dans le tertiaire (000)
Female	2017	48.6		Féminine
Literacy rate	2017	67.7		Taux d'alphabétisation (deux sexes)
Male	2017	77.1		Masculin
Female	2017	53.0		Féminin
Pupil teacher ratio - primary	2017	40.0		Ratio élève-enseignant
Budget allocation to education (%)	2017	9.8		Dépenses publiques consacrées à l'enseignement (% du budget)
Poverty				**Pauvreté**
GNI per capita, PPP (current int. $)	2016	1370.0		RNB par habitant, ($ PPA inter. courants)
Human Poverty Index (HPI-1) Value (%)	2007	36.6		Valeur de l'Indice de pauvreté (IPH-1) (%)
Population below Inter. poverty line ($2/ day) (%)	2011	54.2		Population sous le seuil inter. de pauvreté (2$/Jour) (%)
Share of income held by richest 10%	2011	34.5		% de revenu des 10% plus riches
Share of income held by poorest 10%	2011	1.9		% de revenu des 10% plus pauvres
GINI index	2011	46.0		Indice de GINI

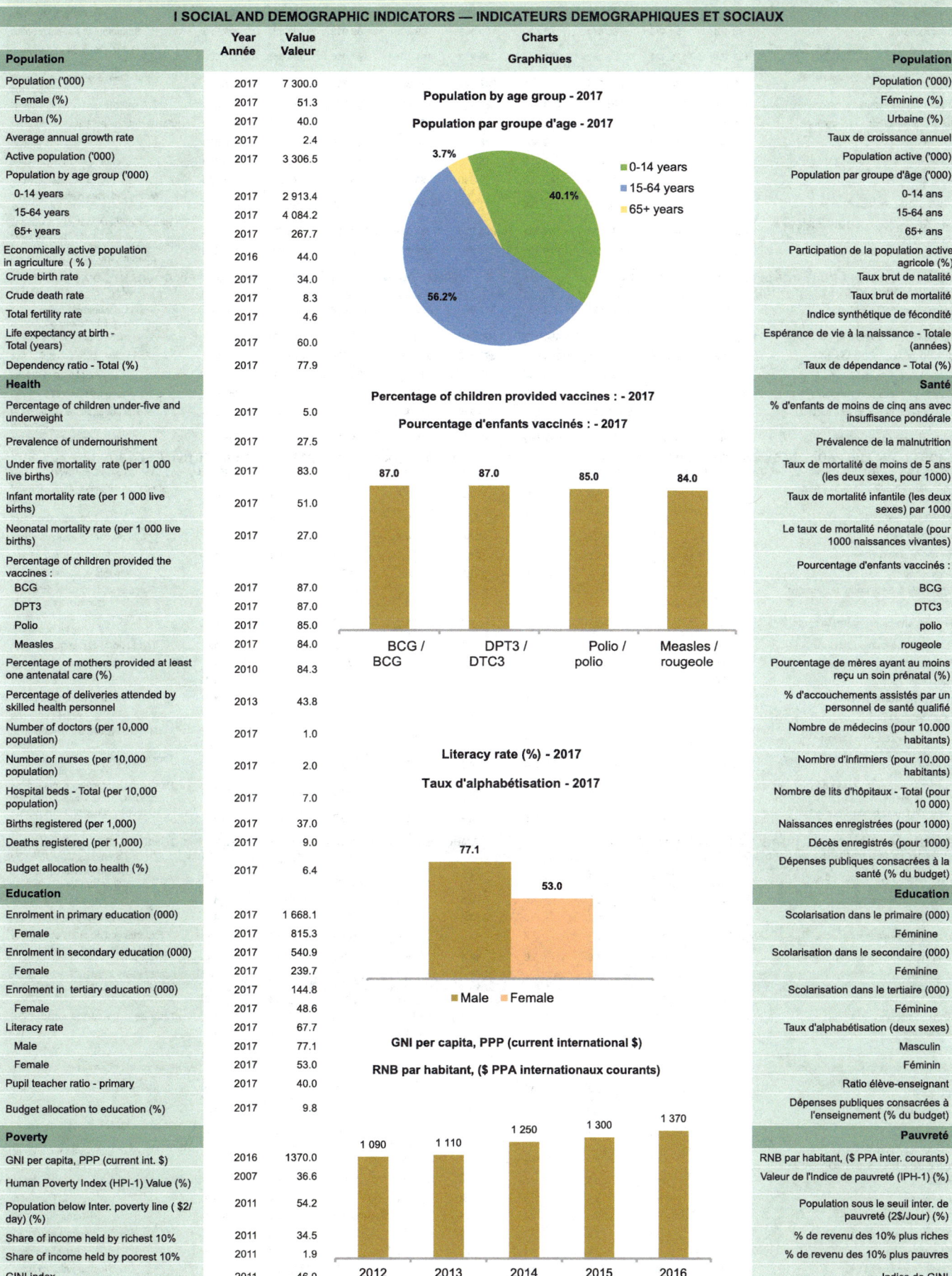

Population by age group - 2017
Population par groupe d'âge - 2017

- 0-14 years — 40.1%
- 15-64 years — 56.2%
- 65+ years — 3.7%

Percentage of children provided vaccines : - 2017
Pourcentage d'enfants vaccinés : - 2017

BCG / BCG	DPT3 / DTC3	Polio / polio	Measles / rougeole
87.0	87.0	85.0	84.0

Literacy rate (%) - 2017
Taux d'alphabétisation - 2017

Male 77.1 · Female 53.0

GNI per capita, PPP (current international $)
RNB par habitant, ($ PPA internationaux courants)

2012	2013	2014	2015	2016
1 090	1 110	1 250	1 300	1 370

II NATIONAL ACCOUNTS — COMPTES NATIONAUX

	2009	2010	2011	2012	2013	2014	2015	2016	2017	
GROSS DOMESTIC PRODUCT BY KIND OF ECONOMIC ACTIVITY AT CURRENT PRICES *CFA Franc (Millions)*										**PRODUIT INTÉRIEUR BRUT PAR BRANCHE D'ACTIVITÉ ÉCONOMIQUE AUX PRIX COURANTS** *FRANC CFA (MILLIONS)*
Agriculture, hunting , forestry and Fishing	514 309	521 168	518 689	563 974	567 190	580 204	602 471	658 919	680 281	Agriculture, chasse sylviculture et Pêche
Mining and quarrying	39 897	38 073	40 939	64 198	61 244	55 303	66 209	72 412	74 760	Industries extractives
Manufacturing	131 391	129 815	131 490	126 939	167 881	167 666	168 254	184 018	189 984	Industries manufacturières
Electricity, gas & water	19 978	24 932	38 785	41 487	49 859	52 678	61 042	66 761	68 926	Electricité, gaz et eau
Construction	48 661	54 472	85 874	86 630	80 669	89 706	89 913	98 337	101 525	Bâtiments et travaux publics
Wholesale & retail trade, restaurants, hotels	166 186	178 428	185 083	188 211	209 213	199 701	187 016	204 538	211 169	Commerce de gros et de détail, restaurants et hôtels
Finance, insurance, real estate, etc.	169 727	170 033	201 681	239 531	237 949	246 874	289 764	316 913	327 187	Banques, assurances, affaires immobilières
Transport and communications	168 208	197 977	199 823	213 027	228 138	248 625	263 210	287 871	297 204	Transport(s) et communications
Public administration and defense	85 713	100 502	136 179	149 509	164 037	173 858	225 940	247 109	255 120	Administrations publiques et défense
Education	62 540	85 078	84 874	79 305	88 189	106 326	99 710	109 052	112 588	Education
Health And Social Work	16 719	16 697	15 348	14 779	15 716	17 871	17 333	18 957	19 572	Santé et Actions Sociales
Other services	27 505	28 028	40 519	47 256	54 240	53 970	65 379	71 505	73 823	Autres services
Less Imputed Service Charges	- 29 889	- 35 422	- 46 832	- 56 495	- 61 100	- 61 463	- 62 318	- 68 157	- 70 366	Moins Services d'intermédiation financière
Gross domestic product at factor cost / basic prices	1 420 945	1 509 781	1 632 452	1 758 351	1 863 225	1 931 319	2 073 923	2 268 238	2 341 773	Produit intérieur brut aux couts des facteurs / prix de base
Plus: Indirect Taxes / taxes on products, less subsidies	168 298	187 097	192 439	219 191	271 239	327 728	397 854	369 902	393 343	Plus taxes indirectes/impôts sur les produits, moins les subventions
EXPENDITURE ON GROSS DOMESTIC PRODUCT AT CURRENT PURCHASER'S VALUES *CFA FRANC (MILLIONS)*										**EMPLOI DU PRODUIT INTÉRIEUR BRUT AUX PRIX COURANTS D'ACQUISITION** *FRANC CFA (MILLIONS)*
Government final consumption	181 994	226 751	308 421	302 606	321 867	373 694	444 658	373 280	452 504	Consommation finale des administrations publiques
Private final consumption	1 304 751	1 367 306	1 427 394	1 490 777	1 603 962	1 662 048	1 773 608	2 131 707	2 381 789	Consommation finale privée
Gross fixed capital formation	321 071	359 596	507 735	504 447	582 737	677 572	773 105	693 100	693 689	Formation brute de capital fixe
Change in inventories	14 360	6 698	- 38 435	- 43 430	48 713	- 46 939	23 383	- 3 812	- 3 858	Variation des stocks
Exports of goods and services	565 007	642 071	796 303	893 955	992 014	897 164	886 042	1 097 435	983 078	Exportations de biens et services
Less imports of goods and services	797 940	905 544	1 176 527	1 170 813	1 414 829	1 304 492	1 429 019	1 653 571	1 772 085	Moins importations de biens et services
GDP at purchasers' values	1 589 243	1 696 878	1 824 891	1 977 542	2 134 464	2 259 047	2 471 777	2 638 140	2 735 117	PIB aux prix d'acquisition
GROSS DOMESTIC PRODUCT BY KIND OF ECONOMIC ACTIVITY AT CONSTANT PRICES *ANNUAL GROWTH RATES (%)*										**PRODUIT INTÉRIEUR BRUT PAR BRANCHE D'ACTIVITÉ ECONOMIQUE AUX PRIX CONSTANTS** *TAUX DE CROISSANCE ANNUEL (%)*
Agriculture, hunting , forestry and Fishing	2.9	-	0.3	2.0	- 3.2	7.4	-	5.1	4.4	Agriculture, chasse sylviculture et Pêche
Mining and quarrying	128.6	33.1	- 72.9	254.4	13.2	8.9	- 41.2	5.1	4.4	Industries extractives
Manufacturing	22.2	4.5	10.5	8.3	27.6	4.8	3.4	5.1	4.4	Industries manufacturières
Electricity, gas & water	- 0.5	13.0	33.2	- 3.7	21.0	3.7	14.0	5.1	4.4	Electricité, gaz et eau
Construction	- 24.2	- 5.3	56.0	12.4	- 31.0	- 25.4	- 17.8	5.1	4.4	Bâtiments et travaux publics
Wholesale & retail trade, restaurants, hotels	6.0	0.7	0.6	3.3	8.0	- 1.1	- 4.8	5.1	4.4	Commerce de gros et de détail, restaurants et hôtels
Finance, insurance, real estate, etc.	5.6	- 1.5	20.9	14.7	- 4.4	11.4	18.9	5.1	4.4	Banques, assurances, affaires immobilières
Transport and communications	7.3	18.0	- 0.5	5.5	9.1	13.0	- 2.2	5.1	4.4	Transport(s) et communications
Public administration and defense	- 5.4	15.6	40.1	14.4	10.4	4.1	30.3	5.1	4.4	Administrations publiques et défense
Education	23.0	36.7	1.0	- 8.7	4.0	15.2	- 10.4	5.1	4.4	Education
Health And Social Work	- 10.5	- 4.8	- 6.9	- 2.4	27.8	12.4	- 3.0	5.1	4.4	Santé et Actions Sociales
Other services	- 3.2	2.2	37.3	15.1	7.6	- 1.2	15.2	5.1	4.4	Autres services
Less Imputed Service Charges	19.2	15.0	51.1	14.3	0.1	23.5	20.7	5.1	4.4	Moins Services d'intermédiation financière
Gross domestic product at factor cost / basic prices	4.9	5.8	7.7	6.0	4.9	5.7	3.9	5.1	4.4	Produit intérieur brut aux couts des facteurs / prix de base
Plus: Indirect Taxes / taxes on products, less subsidies	46.1	8.7	- 3.0	10.9	15.5	7.6	18.3	5.1	4.4	Plus taxes indirectes/impôts sur les produits, moins les subventions
Gross domestic product at market prices	5.5	6.1	6.4	6.5	6.1	5.9	5.7	5.1	4.4	Produit intérieur brut aux prix du marché
EXPENDITURE ON GROSS DOMESTIC PRODUCT AT CONSTANT PURCHASERS' VALUES *ANNUAL GROWTH RATES (%)*										**EMPLOIS DU PRODUIT INTÉRIEUR BRUT AUX PRIX CONSTANTS D'ACQUISITION** *TAUX DE CROISSANCE ANNUEL (%)*
Government final consumption	0.2	25.4	39.2	- 2.0	5.7	15.0	17.9	5.1	4.4	Consommation finale des administrations publiques
Private final consumption	3.2	3.8	2.7	1.5	5.5	4.9	4.4	5.1	4.4	Consommation finale privée
Gross fixed capital formation	16.5	9.7	35.1	- 0.5	13.4	13.7	14.0	5.1	4.4	Formation brute de capital fixe
Exports of goods and services	10.7	9.9	21.3	9.7	7.5	- 8.0	- 1.8	5.1	4.4	Exportations de biens et services
Less imports of goods and services	6.5	10.0	27.0	- 3.6	18.1	- 5.3	12.2	5.1	4.4	Moins importations de biens et services

III INFLATION

Annual growth rates (%)	2009	2010	2011	2012	2013	2014	2015	2016	2017	Taux de croissance annuel (%)
All item	3.7	1.5	3.6	2.6	1.8	0.2	1.8	0.9	- 0.7	Ensemble
of which:										dont:
Food and non-alcoholic beverages	9.5	- 0.3	1.2	3.4	0.6	- 4.3	5.9	3.1	- 4.2	Alimentation et boissons non alcoolisés
Alcoholic beverages, tobacco and narcotics	5.4	4.1	- 2.3	0.5	1.7	0.4	1.0	2.0	- 3.0	Boissons alcoolisées et tabacs
Clothing and footwear	- 1.2	1.2	1.6	0.9	1.6	0.5	1.0	3.0	0.8	Habillement et chaussures
Housing, water, electricity, gas and other fuels	1.4	1.4	5.8	6.0	2.0	2.8	1.1	0.4	0.6	Logement, eau, électricité, gaz et autres combustibles
Furnishings, household equipment and routine household maintenance	0.5	1.3	5.1	1.2	1.7	1.6	0.7	0.6	1.0	Meubles, articles de ménage et entretien courant
Health	1.6	0.7	3.5	- 1.6	- 1.6	- 0.2	1.0	- 0.3	0.9	Santé
Transport	1.4	6.2	5.2	4.9	- 0.6	4.2	- 2.7	- 5.6	1.3	Transport
Communication	- 0.5	- 0.1	3.6	- 4.6	3.1	- 0.8	- 0.1	- 2.2	- 1.6	Communication
Recreation and culture	- 1.7	0.8	2.8	0.2	- 1.9	- 0.8	- 0.5	0.3	- 1.4	Loisirs et culture
Education	3.7	- 0.1	1.0	2.4	4.1	2.6	1.6	0.3	1.3	Enseignement
Restaurants and hotels	3.7	3.2	5.8	1.3	5.2	2.6	0.9	2.3	1.0	Restaurants et hôtels
Miscellaneous goods and services	0.9	- 0.9	6.0	4.8	5.0	1.1	1.1	1.0	0.9	Biens et Services divers

IV AGRICULTURAL PRODUCTION - PRODUCTION AGRICOLE

TONNES (THOUSAND)	2009	2010	2011	2012	2013	2014	2015	2016	2017	Tonnes (milliers)
Cassava	896	909	999	960	903	1 153	1 039	1 027	...	Manioc
Maize	652	638	651	826	693	833	795	827	...	Maïs
Yams	704	710	728	864	661	786	781	814	...	Ignames
Sorghum	238	245	243	221	285	293	271	273	...	Sorgho
Rice, paddy	121	110	112	161	165	148	...	...	...	Riz, Paddy

V MINING PRODUCTION - PRODUCTION MINIERE

	2009	2010	2011	2012	2013	2014	2015	2016	2017	
Gypsum; anhydrite; limestone and other calcareous stone - Production, metric tons (thousands)	2	2	2	1	1	1	1	1	...	"Gypse; anhydrite; pierres à chaux ou à ciment - Production, tonnes métriques (milliers)"
	...	...	...	...	...	...	...	...		
Gold including gold plated with platinum - Production (Kilograms)	10	16	16	18	21	21	16	...	...	Or (y compris l'or platiné) - Production (Kilogrammes)

VI ENERGY - ENERGIE

	2009	2010	2011	2012	2013	2014	2015	2016	2017	
Total electricity generation (GWh)	126	132	139	202	208	336	600	...	...	Production électrique totale (GWh)
of which										dont
Production of electricity from fossil fuels (GWh)	31	32	34	111	111	171	434	...	...	Production d'électricité à partir de combustibles fossiles (GWh)
Production of hydro electricity (GWh)	93	98	103	89	95	136	136	...	...	Production d'électricité d'origine hydraulique (GWh)
Production of electricity from solar, wind, tide, wave and other sources (GWh)	...	...	...	...	...	23	24	...	...	Production d'électricité d'origine solaire, éolienne, marée motrice et autres (GWh)

VII TOURISM AND INFRASTRUCTURE - TOURISME ET INFRASTUCTURE

VII-1 Tourism	2009	2010	2011	2012	2013	2014	2015	2016	2017	VII-1 Tourisme
International tourist arrivals (thousands)	150	202	300	235	327	282	273	287	345	Arrivées de touristes internationaux (milliers)
Rooms in hotels and similar establishments (thousands)	...	4	4	5	6	8	8	13	13	Chambres d'hôtels et établissements assimilés (milliers)
Overnight stays (thousands)	318	421	673	515	795	660	644	707	847	Nuitées (milliers)
Tourism receipts (US$ thousand)	67 700	64 900	96 300	109 900	124 300	124 100	112 700	115 768	127 950	Recettes touristiques (milliers de $ EU)
Total contribution to GDP (%)	5.2	6.3	7.8	7.9	9.3	8.7	8.7	8.6	8.6	Contribution totale au PIB (%)
Total contribution to Employment (%)	4.2	5.1	6.4	7.0	7.5	7.2	7.4	7.4	7.4	Contribution totale à l'emploi (%)
VII-2 Infrastructure										**VII-2 Infrastructure**
Paved road (% of total)	...	...	...	...	...	...	...	...	...	Routes asphaltées (% du total)
Total network (Railways-km)	...	...	...	...	...	...	...	...	...	Réseau total voies ferrées-Km
Main telephone lines (per 100 inhabitants)	2.9	1.0	0.9	0.9	0.9	0.8	0.7	...	...	Lignes téléphoniques fixes (pour 100 habitants)
Mobile cellular subscribers (per 100 inhabitants)	35.6	41.3	41.6	49.9	62.5	64.6	67.7	74.9	...	Abonnés aux téléphones mobiles (pour 100 habitants)
Internet users per 100 inhabitants	2.6	3.0	3.5	4.0	4.5	5.7	7.1	11.3	...	Utilisateurs Internet par 100 Habitants
Fixed (wired)-broadband subscriptions per 100 inhabitants	...	...	0.5	0.6	...	...	0.9	0.6	...	Abonnements à l'Internet fixe (filaire) à large bande pour 100 habitants, par débit

VIII EXTERNAL TRADE - COMMERCE EXTERIEUR

US$ (MILLIONS) EXPORTS, FOB	2009	2010	2011	2012	2013	2014	2015	2016	2017	$ E.U (MILLIONS) EXPORTATIONS, FÀB
Exports - Total	903	976	1 179	1 314	1 519	1 324	1 010	1 293	...	Exportations - Total
Exports to Africa	546	339	603	636	764	682	487	690	...	Exportations vers l'Afrique
Main products										**Principaux produits**
Crude fertilizers (excluding those of division 56)	91	91	108	140	115	111	77	74	...	Engrais bruts (à l'exclusion de ceux de la division 56)
Gold, non-monetary (excluding gold ores and concentrates)	27	74	78	293	362	292	177	256	...	Or, non monétaire (à l'exclusion des minerais d'or et des concentrés)
Lime, cement, fabrica. constr. mat. (excludingglass, clay)	159	163	166	140	166	94	43	69	...	Chaux, ciment, tissu. constr. tapis. (sauf verre, argile)
Perfumery, cosmetics or toilet prepar. (excluding soaps)	27	26	31	21	39	47	59	103	...	Parfumerie, cosmétique ou préparation de toilette. (sauf savons)
Petroleum oils or bituminous minerals > 70 % oil	28	65	45	120	130	176	104	43	...	Huiles de pétrole ou de minéraux bitumineux> 70% d'huile
Main destinations										**Principales destinations**
Benin	119	87	149	122	164	133	108	150	...	Bénin
Burkina Faso	77	53	87	113	145	192	71	102	...	Burkina Faso
India	81	48	70	76	76	109	112	89	...	Inde
Nigeria	86	4	66	83	106	79	74	99	...	Nigéria
Switzerland	4	1	12	231	264	103	25	1	...	Suisse
IMPORTS, CIF										
Imports - Total	1 509	1 683	2 187	2 380	2 764	2 526	2 335	2 387	...	Importations - Total (millions)
Imports from Africa	164	207	977	299	169	131	175	243	...	Importations en provenance de l'Afrique
Main products										**Principaux produits**
Cotton fabrics, woven	125	180	148	172	158	137	108	115	...	Tissus de coton, tissés
Fabrics, woven, of man-made fabrics	49	52	49	60	34	32	34	41	...	Tissus tissés en tissus synthétiques ou artificiels
Motorcycles & cycles	51	66	64	52	69	51	65	82	...	Motos et cycles
Petroleum oils or bituminous minerals > 70 % oil	152	116	210	787	1 237	1 315	1 076	959	...	Huiles de pétrole ou de minéraux bitumineux> 70% d'huile
Residual petroleum products, n.e.s., related mater.	15	20	35	43	60	44	34	28	...	Produits pétroliers résiduels, n.d.a.
Main origin										**Principales provenances**
Belgium	35	56	65	135	456	486	400	310	...	Belgique
China	457	530	396	713	614	483	508	621	...	Chine
France	133	139	97	124	153	197	159	123	...	France
Netherlands	102	79	56	188	256	226	235	245	...	Pays-Bas
United States	50	68	45	101	249	187	63	70	...	États-Unis

TOGO

	2009	2010	2011	2012	2013	2014	2015	2016	2017	
IX-1 MONETARY STATISTICS *CFA FRANC (MILLIONS)*										**IX-1 STATISTIQUES MONÉTAIRES** *FRANC CFA (MILLIONS)*
Money supply (M1)	616 690	717 031	831 304	905 579	999 015	1 096 948	1 319 048	1 489 368	1 676 226	Masse monétaire (M1)
Quasi-money	243 774	297 660	330 972	378 952	452 597	507 730	599 059	668 612	731 689	Quasi-monnaie
of which demand deposit	...	...	...	...	...	...	...	...	...	dont Monnaie scripturale
Net foreign assets	246 367	265 228	290 234	276 770	316 576	6 623	- 31 648	33 682	5 315	Avoirs extérieurs nets
Domestic credit	407 248	497 536	604 966	731 245	771 171	898 318	1 015 564	1 114 969	1 227 111	Crédit intérieur
of which claims on private sector	112 238	138 779	98 939	129 445	80 555	82 906	60 948	32 212	166 452	dont créances sur le secteur privé
of which claims on government sector, net	295 010	358 757	506 027	601 800	690 616	758 177	889 264	1 025 014	983 491	dont créances nettes sur le gouvernement
International reserves (millions US$)	705	716	842	430	485	562	587	452	546	Réserves internationales (millions $EU)
Average exchange rate (National currency per US$)	472	495	472	511	494	494	591	593	582	Taux de change (moyen) (monnaie nationale par $ EU)
IX-2 PUBLIC FINANCE *CFA FRANC (MILLIONS)*										**IX-2 FINANCES PUBLIQUES** *FRANC CFA (MILLIONS)*
Total Revenues and Grants	317 264	359 143	401 144	419 584	522 112	551 175	628 194	695 017	...	Recettes totales et dons
Direct taxes (on income, profits)	56 935	51 352	59 584	63 470	89 373	109 601	109 680	151 299	...	Taxes directes
Domestic indirect taxes revenues	27 365	39 374	44 571	58 215	46 820	67 409	75 195	78 736	...	Taxes Indirectes
Trade taxes	139 814	150 551	180 113	199 356	258 583	272 120	323 190	334 037	...	Taxes sur le commerce extérieur
Other taxes	4 975	5 396	7 143	6 655	8 741	9 093	8 211	4 414	...	Autres taxes
Other revenues	23 296	50 213	25 128	43 872	46 859	47 190	54 681	50 930	...	Autres recettes
Grants	64 879	62 257	84 603	48 015	71 736	45 762	57 238	75 601	...	Dons
Total Expenditures and Net Lending	326 297	354 473	420 750	534 978	614 392	626 443	780 551	912 744	...	Dépenses totales et prêts nets
Current expenditure	221 335	215 849	264 604	341 049	414 003	390 458	456 060	517 559	...	Dépenses courantes
Wages and Salaries	94 334	82 622	104 682	120 409	130 633	143 441	171 656	182 686	...	Rémunérations et salaires
Other purchases of goods and services	40 378	48 421	45 544	50 344	62 675	54 872	51 520	69 972	...	Achat de biens et services
Other current expenditure	62 760	56 927	48 906	77 337	122 784	112 371	153 092	183 863	...	Autres dépenses courantes
Current transfers	23 862	27 879	65 473	92 959	97 911	79 774	79 791	81 038	...	Transferts courants
Interest payments	12 795	15 056	11 508	18 588	22 498	28 292	45 402	62 912	...	Intérêts
Capital expenditure	92 169	123 558	144 250	175 067	177 221	207 318	277 714	332 377	...	Dépenses d'équipement
Net lending	- 2	10	388	274	670	374	1 375	- 105	...	Prêts nets
Fiscal balance	- 9 033	4 670	- 19 607	- 115 393	- 92 280	- 75 268	- 152 357	- 217 727	...	Solde global y compris les dons
IX-3 BALANCE OF PAYMENTS *CFA FRANC (MILLIONS)*										**IX-3 BALANCE DES PAIEMENTS** *FRANC CFA (MILLIONS)*
Trade balance	- 194 607	- 222 001	- 396 841	- 284 859	- 430 047	- 438 394	- 610 801	- 571 673	- 560 245	Balance commerciale
Services Balance	- 38 326	- 41 475	16 617	8 000	7 232	31 067	67 824	84 696	86 293	Balance des services
Net primary income	- 8 991	- 11 624	110 202	3 051	12 474	22 791	83 149	25 841	45 038	Revenus primaires nets
Compensation of employees	15 409	13 238	9 702	11 166	11 080	13 737	15 130	...	...	Rémunération des salariés
Investment income	- 24 400	- 24 862	92 274	- 11 415	- 1 887	3 182	62 234	...	...	Revenus des investissements
Net secondary income	158 503	176 189	127 657	123 643	129 600	158 163	187 264	202 388	205 996	Revenus secondaires nets
Net official transfers	38 335	49 805	41 088	42 640	42 535	41 868	44 640	...	...	Transferts officiels nets
Workers' remittances	108 543	122 373	61 973	86 601	97 325	121 487	147 046	...	...	Envois de fonds des travailleurs
Other private transfers	11 625	4 011	24 596	- 5 598	- 10 260	- 5 191	- 4 422	...	...	Autres transferts privés
Current account balance	- 83 421	- 98 911	- 142 366	- 150 164	- 280 741	- 226 373	- 272 563	- 258 747	- 222 918	Solde du compte courant
Capital and financial account	85 863	130 020	177 724	129 944	319 818	147 693	384 865	323 356	186 226	Comptes de capital et financier
Capital account	63 821	687 480	130 461	146 151	155 608	157 538	159 393	163 551	166 840	Compte de capital
Financial account	- 22 042	557 460	- 47 263	16 207	- 164 210	9 845	- 225 472	159 805	19 385	Compte financier
Errors and omissions	2 602	5 394	- 1 942	2 895	2 492	2 190	2 694	2 541	...	Erreurs et omissions
Overall balance	5 044	36 503	33 416	- 17 325	41 570	- 76 490	114 995	67 150	- 36 693	Balance générale

TOGO

X DEBT AND FINANCIAL FLOWS - DETTE ET FLUX FINANCIERS

	2009	2010	2011	2012	2013	2014	2015	2016	2017	
X-1 DEBT *US $ (MILLIONS)*										**X-1 DETTE EXTÉRIEURE** *$ E.U (MILLIONS)*
Total external debt	1 668	574	486	520	619	790	878	875	999	Dette extérieure totale
Private	...	...	...	...	...	...	...	...	...	Privée
Public	1 668	574	486	520	619	790	878	875	...	Publique
Total external debt service	54	54	17	35	49	53	47	62	...	Service de la dette extérieure
Present value of external debt	25	25	25	25	25	25	...	706	...	Valeur actuelle de la dette extérieure
Total government domestic debt, National currency (millions)	...	467	592	629	687			...	...	Dette publique intérieure
X-2 FINANCIAL FLOWS *US $ (MILLIONS)*										**X-2 FLUX FINANCIERS** *$ E.U (MILLIONS)*
Net Foreign Direct Investment Inflows	49	86	711	122	184	54	258	255	...	Investissements étranger direct (flux nets entrants)
Main origin of FDI inflows										**Principales origines de l'IDE entrant:**
Sweden	9	12	14	13	...	...	...	...	...	Suède
...	...	...	...	...	...	...	...	...	...	...
...	...	...	...	...	...	...	...	...	...	...
Italy	- 1	...	...	...	...	...	...	...	...	Italie
...	...	...	...	...	...	...	...	...	...	...
African countries	...	...	...	...	...	...	...	...	...	Pays africains
Net total official development assistance	495	403	542	245	226	211	200	165	...	Aide publique au développement (nette totale)
Main origin of net ODA										**Principales origines de l'APD nette**
International Development Association [IDA]	6	8	56	37	31	40	26	23	...	International Development Association
...	...	...	...	...	...	...	...	...	...	...
...	...	...	...	...	...	...	...	...	...	...
...	...	...	...	...	...	...	...	...	...	...
...	...	...	...	...	...	...	...	...	...	...

SOURCES AND NOTES - SOURCES ET NOTES

External trade - Total exports, fob: UNCTAD	Commerce exterieur - Exportation, fab: CNUCED
External trade - Total import, cif: UNCTAD	Commerce exterieur - Imporations, caf: CNUCED
ODA: OECD	APD: OCDE
Monetary statistics: IMF	Statistiques monétaires: FMI
National Accounts: 2014-2015 : Revised; 2016-2017Projection	Comptes nationaux: 2014-2015: Révisées;2016-2017:Projections
Poverty: World Bank	Pauvreté: Banque mondiale

	AREA (km2)		163 610		SUPERFICIE (KM2)
	CAPITAL CITY	Tunis		Tunis	CAPITALE
	CURRENCY	Tunisian Dinar		Dinar Tunisien	MONNAIE

I SOCIAL AND DEMOGRAPHIC INDICATORS — INDICATEURS DEMOGRAPHIQUES ET SOCIAUX

	Year Année	Value Valeur	Charts Graphiques	
Population				**Population**
Population ('000)	2016	11 304.5		Population ('000)
Female (%)	2016	50.3		Féminine (%)
Urban (%)	2016	67.9		Urbaine (%)
Average annual growth rate	2016	1.3		Taux de croissance annuel
Active population ('000)	2017	4 084.2		Population active ('000)
Population by age group ('000)				Population par groupe d'âge ('000)
0-14 years	2016	2 756.7		0-14 ans
15-64 years	2016	7 158.7		15-64 ans
65+ years	2016	1 389.0		65+ ans
Economically active population in agriculture (%)	2015	14.8		Participation de la population active agricole (%)
Crude birth rate	2016	19.4		Taux brut de natalité
Crude death rate	2016	5.5		Taux brut de mortalité
Total fertility rate	2016	2.3		Indice synthétique de fécondité
Life expectancy at birth - Total (years)	2015	75.1		Espérance de vie à la naissance - Totale (années)
Dependency ratio - Total (%)	2016	57.9		Taux de dépendance - Total (%)
Health				**Santé**
Percentage of children under-five and underweight	2012	2.3		% d'enfants de moins de cinq ans avec insuffisance pondérale
Prevalence of undernourishment	2015	5.0		Prévalence de la malnutrition
Under five mortality rate (per 1 000 live births)	2015	14.0		Taux de mortalité de moins de 5 ans (les deux sexes, pour 1000)
Infant mortality rate (per 1 000 live births)	2015	15.3		Taux de mortalité infantile (les deux sexes) par 1000
Neonatal mortality rate (per 1 000 live births)	2015	10.2		Le taux de mortalité néonatale (pour 1000 naissances vivantes)
Percentage of children provided the vaccines :				Pourcentage d'enfants vaccinés :
BCG	2014	95.0		BCG
DPT3	2014	98.0		DTC3
Polio	2011	98.0		polio
Measles	2014	98.0		rougeole
Percentage of mothers provided at least one antenatal care (%)	2008	96.0		Pourcentage de mères ayant au moins reçu un soin prénatal (%)
Percentage of deliveries attended by skilled health personnel	2015	92.0		% d'accouchements assistés par un personnel de santé qualifié
Number of doctors (per 10,000 population)	2016	12.0		Nombre de médecins (pour 10.000 habitants)
Number of nurses (per 10,000 population)	2016	25.0		Nombre d'infirmiers (pour 10.000 habitants)
Hospital beds - Total (per 10,000 population)	2017	18.0		Nombre de lits d'hôpitaux - Total (pour 10 000)
Births registered (per 1,000)	2015	22.3		Naissances enregistrées (pour 1000)
Deaths registered (per 1,000)	2015	6.6		Décès enregistrés (pour 1000)
Budget allocation to health (%)	2013	13.3		Dépenses publiques consacrées à la santé (% du budget)
Education				**Education**
Enrolment in primary education (000)	2017	1 100.8		Scolarisation dans le primaire (000)
Female	2017	529.9		Féminine
Enrolment in secondary education (000)	2017	894.3		Scolarisation dans le secondaire (000)
Female	2017	481.0		Féminine
Enrolment in tertiary education (000)	2017	282.2		Scolarisation dans le tertiaire (000)
Female	2017	178.4		Féminine
Literacy rate	2015	82.0		Taux d'alphabétisation (deux sexes)
Male	...	...		Masculin
Female	...	...		Féminin
Pupil teacher ratio - primary	2017	17.2		Ratio élève-enseignant
Budget allocation to education (%)	2017	15.1		Dépenses publiques consacrées à l'enseignement (% du budget)
Poverty				**Pauvreté**
GNI per capita, PPP (current int. $)	2016	11150.0		RNB par habitant, ($ PPA inter. courants)
Human Poverty Index (HPI-1) Value (%)	2007	15.6		Valeur de l'Indice de pauvreté (IPH-1) (%)
Population below Inter. poverty line ($2/ day) (%)	2010	2.0		Population sous le seuil inter. de pauvreté (2$/Jour) (%)
Share of income held by richest 10%	2010	27.0		% de revenu des 10% plus riches
Share of income held by poorest 10%	2010	2.6		% de revenu des 10% plus pauvres
GINI index	2010	35.8		Indice de GINI

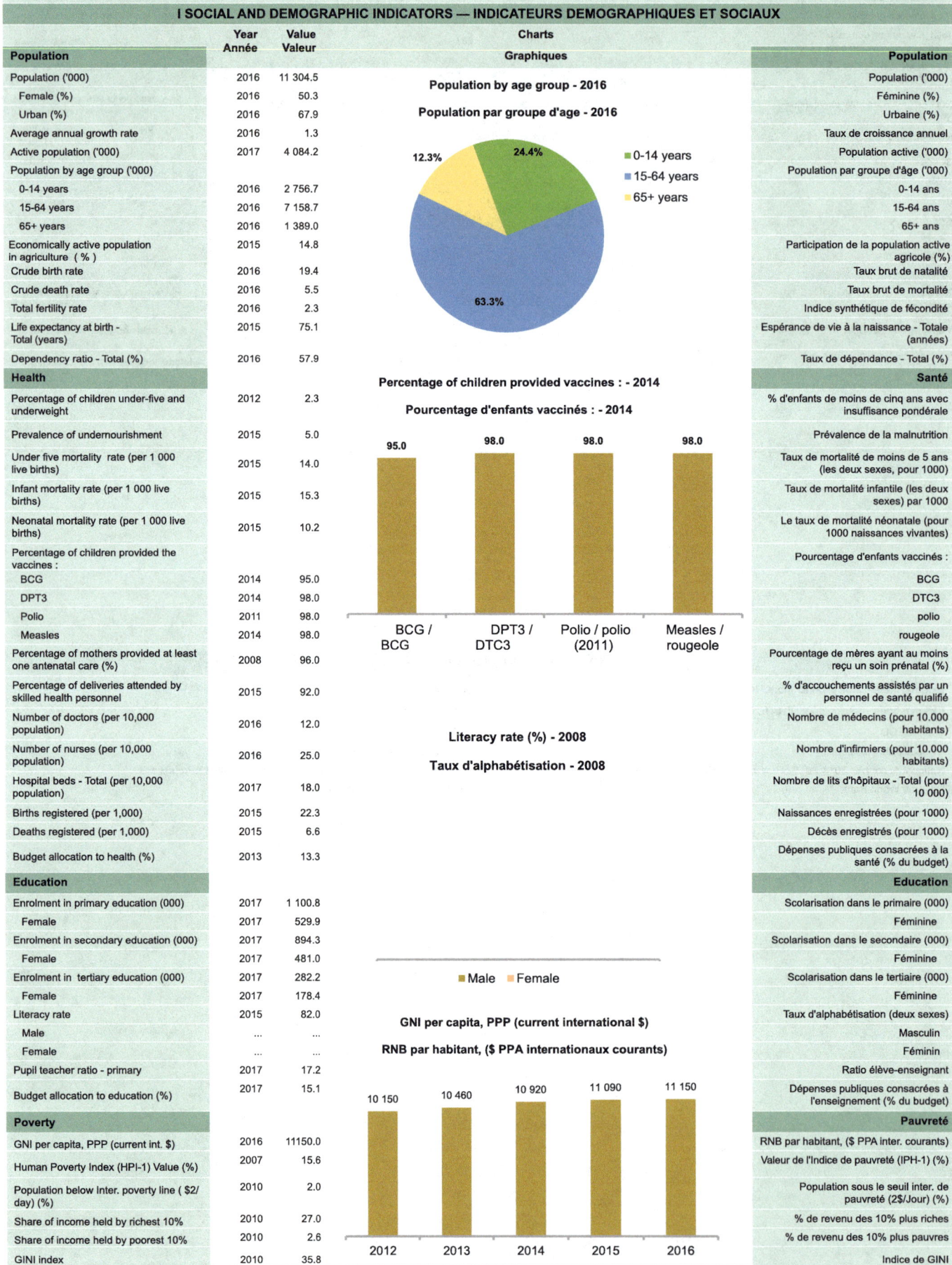

Population by age group - 2016
Population par groupe d'age - 2016

- 0-14 years: 24.4%
- 15-64 years: 63.3%
- 65+ years: 12.3%

Percentage of children provided vaccines : - 2014
Pourcentage d'enfants vaccinés : - 2014

BCG / BCG	DPT3 / DTC3	Polio / polio (2011)	Measles / rougeole
95.0	98.0	98.0	98.0

Literacy rate (%) - 2008
Taux d'alphabétisation - 2008

■ Male ■ Female

GNI per capita, PPP (current international $)
RNB par habitant, ($ PPA internationaux courants)

2012	2013	2014	2015	2016
10 150	10 460	10 920	11 090	11 150

TUNISIA

	2009	2010	2011	2012	2013	2014	2015	2016	2017	
GROSS DOMESTIC PRODUCT BY KIND OF ECONOMIC ACTIVITY AT CURRENT PRICES *TUNISIAN DINAR (MILLIONS)*										**PRODUIT INTÉRIEUR BRUT PAR BRANCHE D'ACTIVITÉ ÉCONOMIQUE AUX PRIX COURANTS** *DINAR TUNISIEN (MILLIONS)*
Agriculture, hunting , forestry and Fishing	4 962	4 751	5 504	6 391	6 681	7 402	8 708	8 494	...	Agriculture, chasse sylviculture et Pêche
Mining and quarrying	3 274	4 304	4 751	5 351	5 205	4 476	3 354	2 949	...	Industries extractives
Manufacturing	9 938	10 422	10 708	11 429	11 984	12 584	12 935	13 394	...	Industries manufacturières
Electricity, gas & water	719	818	857	971	1 139	1 146	1 174	1 410	...	Electricité, gaz et eau
Construction	2 523	2 728	2 908	3 103	3 292	3 532	3 654	3 796	...	Bâtiments et travaux publics
Wholesale & retail trade, restaurants, hotels	7 680	8 157	8 237	9 214	10 097	10 827	11 506	12 183	...	Commerce de gros et de détail, restaurants et hôtels
Finance, insurance, real estate, etc.	9 673	9 465	10 079	10 807	11 735	12 438	13 336	14 248	...	Banques, assurances, affaires immobilières
Transport and communications	7 327	8 295	7 913	8 595	8 878	9 285	9 209	9 733	...	Transport(s) et communications
Public administration and defense	4 370	4 584	5 222	5 960	7 573	8 229	8 852	9 735	...	Administrations publiques et défense
Education	2 672	3 373	3 700	3 910	3 990	4 332	4 718	5 400	...	Education
Health And Social Work	896	1 602	1 786	2 036	1 458	1 567	1 731	1 895	...	Santé et Actions Sociales
Other services	245	264	288	316	339	360	386	411	...	Autres services
Less Imputed Service Charges	- 762	- 822	- 875	- 1 042	- 1 078	- 1 112	- 1 158	- 1 276	...	Moins Services d'intermédiation financière
Gross domestic product at factor cost / basic prices	53 517	57 940	61 077	67 041	71 293	75 068	78 406	82 371	...	Produit intérieur brut aux couts des facteurs / prix de base
Plus: Indirect Taxes / taxes on products, less subsidies	5 160	5 114	3 415	3 313	3 851	5 798	6 243	7 433	...	Plus taxes indirectes/impôts sur les produits, moins les subventions
EXPENDITURE ON GROSS DOMESTIC PRODUCT AT CURRENT PURCHASER'S VALUES *TUNISIAN DINAR (MILLIONS)*										**EMPLOI DU PRODUIT INTÉRIEUR BRUT AUX PRIX COURANTS D'ACQUISITION** *DINAR TUNISIEN (MILLIONS)*
Government final consumption	9 759	10 478	11 609	12 818	14 012	15 117	16 551	18 400	...	Consommation finale des administrations publiques
Private final consumption	36 390	39 665	42 804	46 979	51 199	55 890	60 403	64 485	...	Consommation finale privée
Gross fixed capital formation	14 278	15 502	14 096	15 824	16 466	16 435	16 811	17 336	...	Formation brute de capital fixe
Change in inventories	- 26	659	798	1 373	619	2 301	82	- 775	...	Variation des stocks
Exports of goods and services	26 428	31 210	31 299	34 154	35 293	36 328	33 940	35 927	...	Exportations de biens et services
Less imports of goods and services	28 152	34 460	36 114	40 795	42 444	45 205	43 139	45 569	...	Moins importations de biens et services
GDP at purchasers' values	58 677	63 055	64 492	70 354	75 144	80 866	84 648	89 804	...	PIB aux prix d'acquisition
GROSS DOMESTIC PRODUCT BY KIND OF ECONOMIC ACTIVITY AT CONSTANT PRICES *ANNUAL GROWTH RATES (%)*										**PRODUIT INTÉRIEUR BRUT PAR BRANCHE D'ACTIVITÉ ECONOMIQUE AUX PRIX CONSTANTS** *TAUX DE CROISSANCE ANNUEL (%)*
Agriculture, hunting , forestry and Fishing	9.2	- 9.1	10.3	5.8	- 3.6	4.8	12.3	- 8.5	2.6	Agriculture, chasse sylviculture et Pêche
Mining and quarrying	-	1.1	- 17.3	- 2.8	- 10.3	- 8.6	- 6.9	- 5.3	-11.1	Industries extractives
Manufacturing	- 1.4	3.0	- 2.7	2.1	1.7	1.1	0.2	0.5	0.8	Industries manufacturières
Electricity, gas & water	- 2.8	15.1	1.8	6.1	2.6	3.4	3.4	1.5	3.9	Electricité, gaz et eau
Construction	3.7	3.5	- 1.3	1.6	3.1	3.6	- 3.1	1.0	-1.8	Bâtiments et travaux publics
Wholesale & retail trade, restaurants, hotels	2.2	3.1	- 7.1	5.4	3.0	2.1	- 3.1	2.3	2.3	Commerce de gros et de détail, restaurants et hôtels
Finance, insurance, real estate, etc.	6.9	- 5.6	0.9	2.1	4.8	3.2	2.4	3.4	5.6	Banques, assurances, affaires immobilières
Transport and communications	5.5	9.0	- 5.6	7.2	6.2	3.3	- 1.1	4.3	4.1	Transport(s) et communications
Public administration and defense	3.0	2.5	12.1	7.9	21.2	3.4	2.6	1.3	0.3	Administrations publiques et défense
Education	1.0	20.9	3.8	0.7	- 2.6	3.3	3.9	5.4	...	Education
Health And Social Work	2.7	70.4	1.7	11.2	- 31.1	2.3	5.4	0.8	...	Santé et Actions Sociales
Other services	2.9	2.1	4.7	3.5	4.6	4.4	4.1	4.2	4.0	Autres services
Less Imputed Service Charges	6.2	4.8	12.0	6.1	6.8	3.6	6.5	7.8	10.0	Moins Services d'intermédiation financière
Gross domestic product at factor cost / basic prices	3.1	3.2	- 1.6	3.8	2.0	2.0	1.1	0.8	1.8	Produit intérieur brut aux couts des facteurs / prix de base
Plus: Indirect Taxes / taxes on products, less subsidies	3.9	0.6	- 6.1	5.3	8.8	9.5	2.3	3.8	4.0	Plus taxes indirectes/impôts sur les produits, moins les subventions
Gross domestic product at market prices	3.1	3.0	- 1.9	3.9	2.3	2.4	1.2	1.0	1.9	Produit intérieur brut aux prix du marché
EXPENDITURE ON GROSS DOMESTIC PRODUCT AT CONSTANT PURCHASERS' VALUES *ANNUAL GROWTH RATES (%)*										**EMPLOIS DU PRODUIT INTÉRIEUR BRUT AUX PRIX CONSTANTS D'ACQUISITION** *TAUX DE CROISSANCE ANNUEL (%)*
Government final consumption	5.8	3.7	6.1	5.2	4.3	2.7	4.4	2.5	...	Consommation finale des administrations publiques
Private final consumption	3.6	4.3	4.1	4.4	3.0	4.1	3.2	3.1	...	Consommation finale privée
Gross fixed capital formation	3.5	4.3	- 12.7	6.1	0.2	- 2.9	- 0.5	1.0	...	Formation brute de capital fixe
Exports of goods and services	- 7.0	10.6	- 4.3	4.3	1.9	- 1.5	- 5.3	0.2	...	Exportations de biens et services
Less imports of goods and services	- 8.2	15.3	- 2.4	5.4	- 1.8	0.9	- 2.6	2.8	...	Moins importations de biens et services

III INFLATION

	2009	2010	2011	2012	2013	2014	2015	2016	2017	
Annual growth rates (%)										**Taux de croissance annuel (%)**
All item	3.5	4.2	3.5	5.1	5.8	4.9	4.9	3.7	5.3	Ensemble
of which:										dont:
Food and non-alcoholic beverages	4.4	6.8	5.1	7.5	8.0	5.4	5.2	2.6	5.6	Alimentation et boissons non alcoolisés
Alcoholic beverages, tobacco and narcotics	9.1	5.2	2.8	9.5	5.0	5.4	6.5	- 0.7	4.8	Boissons alcoolisées et tabacs
Clothing and footwear	2.3	3.6	4.0	7.5	7.2	7.5	6.8	7.1	7.9	Habillement et chaussures
Housing, water, electricity, gas and other fuels	2.8	3.0	3.2	3.0	4.0	5.3	5.2	5.4	5.0	Logement, eau, électricité, gaz et autres combustibles
Furnishings, household equipment and routine household maintenance	3.7	2.1	3.1	6.0	6.3	5.4	5.6	4.6	4.8	Meubles, articles de ménage et entretien courant
Health	2.7	1.4	1.9	2.1	2.1	2.7	3.4	2.7	3.6	Santé
Transport	3.0	3.4	2.9	2.6	6.3	3.6	2.4	2.2	5.9	Transport
Communication	0.5	- 0.4	1.5	0.4	1.0	- 0.3	- 2.8	- 0.8	1.7	Communication
Recreation and culture	0.5	1.1	- 0.3	1.9	3.2	3.5	3.1	1.9	2.5	Loisirs et culture
Education	1.4	10.8	3.0	4.9	3.1	2.7	5.7	9.3	5.3	Enseignement
Restaurants and hotels	6.0	4.5	4.8	7.8	7.3	6.7	9.8	4.5	6.2	Restaurants et hôtels
Miscellaneous goods and services	3.6	3.1	2.9	5.1	5.2	5.9	6.5	6.1	4.7	Biens et Services divers

TUNISIE

IV AGRICULTURAL PRODUCTION - PRODUCTION AGRICOLE

TONNES (THOUSAND)	2009	2010	2011	2012	2013	2014	2015	2016	2017	Tonnes (milliers)
Tomatoes	1 135	1 296	1 284	1 375	1 013	1 288	1 600	1 330	...	Tomates
Olives	800	750	600	900	1 100	400	1 700	700	...	Olives
Wheat	1 654	822	1 606	1 523	975	1 513	912	927	...	Blé
Potatoes	324	370	360	350	385	390	400	440	...	Pommes de terre
Chillies and peppers, dry	281	304	268	315	384	380	511	455	...	Piments forts, piment doux, secs

V MINING PRODUCTION - PRODUCTION MINIERE

	2009	2010	2011	2012	2013	2014	2015	2016	2017	
Natural phosphates, P2O5 content - Production, metric tons (thousands)	7 216	8 132	2 509	2 605	3 284	3 784	3 240	3 664	4 422	Phosphates naturels, teneur en P2O5 - Production, tonnes métriques (milliers)
Iron ores and concentrates - Production, metric tons (thousands)	150	172	172	215	245	250	...	...	...	"Minerais de fer et leurs concentrés - Production, tonnes métriques (milliers)"
	...	...	...	...	...	...	...	...	...	

VI ENERGY - ENERGIE

	2009	2010	2011	2012	2013	2014	2015	2016	2017	
Total electricity generation (GWh)	15 251	16 521	17 909	18 056	18 369	16 079	17 847	19 568	...	Production électrique totale (GWh)
of which										dont
Production of electricity from fossil fuels (GWh)	15 075	15 907	16 332	17 746	17 944	15 813	17 325	18 988	...	Production d'électricité à partir de combustibles fossiles (GWh)
Production of hydro electricity (GWh)	79	50	54	196	60	54	54	66	...	Production d'électricité d'origine hydraulique (GWh)
Production of electricity from solar, wind, tide, wave and other sources (GWh)	97	139	109	113	365	212	468	513	...	Production d'électricité d'origine solaire, éolienne, marée motrice et autres (GWh)

VII TOURISM AND INFRASTRUCTURE - TOURISME ET INFRASTUCTURE

	2009	2010	2011	2012	2013	2014	2015	2016	2017	
VII-1 Tourism										**VII-1 Tourisme**
International tourist arrivals (thousands)	6 901	6 903	4 785	5 990	6 269	6 069	4 202	4 526	5 743	Arrivées de touristes internationaux (milliers)
Rooms in hotels and similar establishments (thousands)	120	121	121	121	120	120	120	118	117	Chambres d'hôtels et établissements assimilés (milliers)
Overnight stays (thousands)	34 624	35 565	20 635	30 035	30 001	29 108	16 178	17 880	22 043	Nuitées (milliers)
Tourism receipts (US$ thousand)	3 471 900	3 522 500	2 364 500	3 175 300	3 221 400	3 625 600	2 414 700	2 317 400	2 793 500	Recettes touristiques (milliers de $ EU)
Total contribution to GDP (%)	20.4	20.0	16.1	17.4	16.7	17.2	13.8	13.7	14.2	Contribution totale au PIB (%)
Total contribution to Employment (%)	18.5	18.1	14.9	15.8	14.9	15.6	12.6	12.5	13.0	Contribution totale à l'emploi (%)
VII-2 Infrastructure										**VII-2 Infrastructure**
Paved road (% of total)	75.2	76.0	76.3	...	...	...	...	...	...	Routes asphaltées (% du total)
Total network (Railways-km)	1 991	...	2 165	2 165	2 165	3 835	...	...	...	Réseau total voies ferrées-Km
Main telephone lines (per 100 inhabitants)	12.2	12.1	11.3	10.1	9.3	8.5	8.4	8.6	...	Lignes téléphoniques fixes (pour 100 habitants)
Mobile cellular subscribers (per 100 inhabitants)	93.2	104.5	115.2	118.1	115.6	128.5	129.9	125.8	...	Abonnés aux téléphones mobiles (pour 100 habitants)
Internet users per 100 inhabitants	34.1	36.8	39.1	41.4	43.8	46.2	46.5	49.6	...	Utilisateurs Internet par 100 Habitants
Fixed (wired)-broadband subscriptions per 100 inhabitants	3.5	4.5	5.2	4.8	4.7	4.5	5.1	5.6	...	Abonnements à l'Internet fixe (filaire) à large bande pour 100 habitants, par débit

VIII EXTERNAL TRADE - COMMERCE EXTERIEUR

US$ (MILLIONS) EXPORTS, FOB	2009	2010	2011	2012	2013	2014	2015	2016	2017	$ E.U (MILLIONS) EXPORTATIONS, FÀB
Exports - Total	14 445	16 427	17 847	17 007	17 060	16 760	14 073	13 575	...	Exportations - Total
Exports to Africa	1 894	1 926	2 022	2 026	2 041	1 971	1 712	1 655	...	Exportations vers l'Afrique
Main products										**Principaux produits**
Apparatus for electrical circuits; board, panels	752	756	762	630	741	821	720	779		Appareils pour circuits électriques; panneau, panneaux
Articles of apparel, of textile fabrics, n.e.s.	1 606	1 709	1 715	1 445	1 471	1 470	1 184	1 129		Vêtements, en tissus, n.d.a.
Equipment for distributing electricity, n.e.s.	1 010	1 299	1 757	1 639	1 684	1 829	1 632	1 565		Matériel de distribution d'électricité, n.d.a.
Men's clothing of textile fabrics, not knitted	761	723	881	700	744	694	517	570		Vêtements pour hommes en matières textiles, non tricotés
Petroleum oils, oils from bitumin. materials, crude	1 553	2 081	2 289	1 876	1 748	1 435	633	564		Huiles de pétrole, huiles de bitume. matériaux bruts
Main destinations										**Principales destinations**
France	4 283	4 717	5 477	4 587	4 503	4 753	4 127	4 342	...	France
Germany	1 270	1 388	1 616	1 398	1 533	1 710	1 477	1 431	...	Allemagne
Italy	3 038	3 265	3 864	3 212	3 151	3 205	2 597	2 364	...	Italie
Libya	832	732	785	828	869	668	540	443	...	Libye
Spain	487	637	768	737	803	593	700	475	...	Espagne
IMPORTS, CIF										
Imports - Total	19 096	22 215	23 952	24 471	24 266	24 793	20 223	19 487	...	Importations - Total (millions)
Imports from Africa	1 376	1 269	1 008	1 778	2 017	2 124	1 216	1 142	...	Importations en provenance de l'Afrique
Main products										**Principaux produits**
Apparatus for electrical circuits; board, panels	705	913	993	838	906	982	835	826		Appareils pour circuits électriques; panneau, panneaux
Motor vehicles for the transport of persons	652	779	623	801	820	809	776	748		Véhicules à moteur pour le transport de personnes
Petroleum gases, other gaseous hydrocarbons, n.e.s.	345	364	510	924	1 030	1 343	692	634		Gaz de pétrole, autres hydrocarbures gazeux, n.d.a.
Petroleum oils or bituminous minerals > 70 % oil	1 107	1 884	2 342	2 008	1 917	1 836	1 533	964		Huiles de pétrole ou de minéraux bitumineux> 70% d'huile
Petroleum oils, oils from bitumin. materials, crude	502	162	274	860	957	895	333	299		Huiles de pétrole, huiles de bitume. matériaux bruts
Main origin										**Principales provenances**
Algeria	501	621	637	983	1 185	1 572	801	713	...	Algérie
China	957	1 344	1 456	1 686	1 533	1 783	1 692	1 820	...	Chine
France	3 832	4 203	4 381	4 017	4 437	4 045	3 598	3 010	...	France
Germany	1 673	1 697	1 768	1 684	1 740	1 740	1 479	1 505	...	Allemagne
Italy	3 109	3 907	3 790	3 467	3 522	3 635	3 014	2 829	...	Italie

	2009	2010	2011	2012	2013	2014	2015	2016	2017	
IX-1 MONETARY STATISTICS *TUNISIAN DINAR (MILLIONS)*										**IX-1 STATISTIQUES MONÉTAIRES** *DINAR TUNISIEN (MILLIONS)*
Money supply (M1)	38 591	43 267	47 203	51 168	54 549	58 802	61 899	66 883	73 571	Masse monétaire (M1)
Quasi-money	21 427	23 961	24 524	26 838	29 124	31 322	32 240	34 782	37 258	Quasi-monnaie
of which demand deposit	...	...	...	...	...	...	...	...	...	dont Monnaie scripturale
Net foreign assets	9 785	9 230	6 131	7 648	4 458	2 512	2 018	- 842	- 1 344	Avoirs extérieurs nets
Domestic credit	38 413	44 615	51 261	55 985	60 839	66 665	72 600	79 942	89 901	Crédit intérieur
of which claims on private sector	3 608	3 157	4 304	5 009	5 882	6 735	8 956	10 330	11 039	dont créances sur le secteur privé
of which claims on government sector, net	34 805	41 459	46 958	50 976	54 957	59 930	63 643	69 613	78 861	dont créances nettes sur le gouvernement
International reserves (millions US$)	10 587	9 509	7 525	8 655	7 689	7 660	7 401	5 941	7 239	Réserves internationales (millions $EU)
Average exchange rate (National currency per US$)	1	1	1	2	2	2	2	2	2	Taux de change (moyen) (monnaie nationale par $ EU)
IX-2 PUBLIC FINANCE *TUNISIAN DINAR (MILLIONS)*										**IX-2 FINANCES PUBLIQUES** *DINAR TUNISIEN (MILLIONS)*
Total Revenues and Grants	13 762	14 823	16 413	17 189	18 443	20 264	20 116	20 718	...	Recettes totales et dons
Direct taxes (on income, profits)	4 645	5 033	5 914	6 089	7 118	8 169	7 822	7 577	...	Taxes directes
Domestic indirect taxes revenues	3 400	3 750	3 848	4 376	4 452	5 107	5 058	5 138	...	Taxes Indirectes
Trade taxes	520	564	561	716	729	825	833	640	...	Taxes sur le commerce extérieur
Other taxes	3 120	3 352	3 306	3 684	4 023	4 572	4 833	5 348	...	Autres taxes
Other revenues	1 899	2 071	2 576	1 692	1 897	1 221	1 278	1 887	...	Autres recettes
Grants	178	54	207	633	225	370	292	130	...	Dons
Total Expenditures and Net Lending	15 355	15 420	18 333	20 410	23 426	23 968	23 893	26 099	...	Dépenses totales et prêts nets
Current expenditure	9 365	10 001	12 503	14 636	17 448	17 285	17 228	18 420	...	Dépenses courantes
Wages and Salaries	6 299	6 785	7 679	8 656	9 608	10 541	11 581	13 164	...	Rémunérations et salaires
Other purchases of goods and services	833	841	892	983	970	943	1 046	1 078	...	Achat de biens et services
Other current expenditure	...	...	...	...	...	...	...	...	...	Autres dépenses courantes
Current transfers	2 234	2 375	3 931	4 997	6 870	5 801	4 600	4 179	...	Transferts courants
Interest payments	1 180	1 152	1 190	1 268	1 414	1 516	1 644	1 986	...	Intérêts
Capital expenditure	4 014	4 302	4 729	4 766	4 393	4 792	4 799	5 422	...	Dépenses d'équipement
Net lending	796	- 36	- 89	- 260	171	376	222	271	...	Prêts nets
Fiscal balance	- 1 593	- 596	- 1 920	- 3 220	- 4 983	- 3 705	- 3 777	- 5 381	...	Solde global y compris les dons
IX-3 BALANCE OF PAYMENTS *TUNISIAN DINAR (MILLIONS)*										**IX-3 BALANCE DES PAIEMENTS** *DINAR TUNISIEN (MILLIONS)*
Trade balance	- 4 994	- 6 548	- 6 756	- 9 535	- 9 635	- 11 324	- 9 867	- 10 305	- 12 841	Balance commerciale
Services Balance	3 409	3 521	2 102	3 053	2 634	2 448	594	669	869	Balance des services
Net primary income	- 393	- 296	- 468	282	125	875	1 133	1 219	1 393	Revenus primaires nets
Compensation of employees	313	475	478	540	607	635	601	669	696	Rémunération des salariés
Investment income	- 2 190	- 2 432	- 2 460	- 2 434	- 2 869	- 2 324	- 1 850	- 1 683	- 1 772	Revenus des investissements
Net secondary income	312	310	356	387	574	632	588	482	492	Revenus secondaires nets
Net official transfers	...	...	...	...	...	...	...	...	...	Transferts officiels nets
Workers' remittances	2 322	2 459	2 318	2 970	3 082	3 301	3 214	3 185	3 735	Envois de fonds des travailleurs
Other private transfers	...	...	...	...	...	...	...	...	...	Autres transferts privés
Current account balance	- 1 666	- 3 012	- 4 766	- 5 812	- 6 302	- 7 369	- 7 552	- 7 935	- 10 087	Solde du compte courant
Capital and financial account	3 781	2 633	2 280	7 830	5 002	8 739	8 132	6 329	10 085	Comptes de capital et financier
Capital account	222	118	259	701	186	510	441	204	341	Compte de capital
Financial account	3 559	2 515	2 021	7 128	4 815	8 229	7 691	6 125	9 744	Compte financier
Errors and omissions	89	106	96	151	205	225	203	465	...	Erreurs et omissions
Overall balance	2 204	- 274	- 2 391	2 168	- 1 095	1 595	783	- 1 142	- 2	Balance générale

TUNISIE

X DEBT AND FINANCIAL FLOWS - DETTE ET FLUX FINANCIERS

	2009	2010	2011	2012	2013	2014	2015	2016	2017	
X-1 DEBT US $ (MILLIONS)										**X-1 DETTE EXTÉRIEURE** $ E.U (MILLIONS)
Total external debt	21 516	21 369	22 051	24 030	26 000	26 649	27 049	27 043	30 008	Dette extérieure totale
Private	4 832	4 968	5 108	6 191	6 572	6 846	6 565	5 909	...	Privée
Public	15 062	14 798	15 227	16 240	17 721	18 197	18 939	19 561	...	Publique
Total external debt service	2 371	2 347	2 725	2 682	2 092	1 829	1 766	2 032	...	Service de la dette extérieure
Present value of external debt	2 313	2 434	2 893	3 201	2 503	2 114	...	18 862	...	Valeur actuelle de la dette extérieure
Total government domestic debt, National currency (millions)	1 434	1 567	1 013	1 606	2 177	3 227	2 790	...	...	Dette publique intérieure
X-2 FINANCIAL FLOWS US $ (MILLIONS)										**X-2 FLUX FINANCIERS** $ E.U (MILLIONS)
Net Foreign Direct Investment Inflows	1 688	1 513	1 148	1 603	1 117	1 064	1 002	958	...	Investissements étranger direct (flux nets entrants)
Main origin of FDI inflows										**Principales origines de l'IDE entrant:**
Italy	432	227	196	156	...	...	...	...	...	Italie
Germany	46	10	26	65	...	...	...	...	...	Allemagne
Sweden	59	30	60	3	...	...	...	...	...	Suède
Turkey	1	1	...	...	...	...	...	...	...	Turquie
...	...	...	...	...	...	...	...	...	...	...
African countries	31	65	9	...	...	...	...	...	...	Pays africains
Net total official development assistance	494	550	925	1 022	715	923	475	627	...	Aide publique au développement (nette totale)
Main origin of net ODA										**Principales origines de l'APD nette**
France	170	127	304	242	67	66	22	68	...	France
...	...	...	...	...	...	...	...	...	...	...
...	...	...	...	...	...	...	...	...	...	...
Germany	31	24	31	43	68	53	89	126	...	Allemagne
...	...	...	...	...	...	...	...	...	...	...

SOURCES AND NOTES - SOURCES ET NOTES

External trade - Total exports, fob: UNCTAD	Commerce exterieur - Exportation, fab: CNUCED
External trade - Total import, cif: UNCTAD	Commerce exterieur - Imporations, caf: CNUCED
ODA: OECD	APD: OCDE
Monetary statistics: IMF	Statistiques monétaires: FMI
National Accounts: NA: 2016 Semi-Final-2017 provisional.	Comptes nationaux: 2016 Semi-Définitive-2017:provisoire
National Accounts : The annual Growth Rates for 2017 are previsions based on the sum of four quarters of 2017.	Comptes Nationaux: Les croissances annuelles de L'année 2017 sont estimées à partir des comptes trimestriels
Poverty: World Bank	Pauvreté: Banque mondiale

AREA (km2)		241 550		**SUPERFICIE (KM2)**
CAPITAL CITY	Kampala		Kampala	**CAPITALE**
CURRENCY	Uganda Shilling		Shilling Ugandais	**MONNAIE**

I SOCIAL AND DEMOGRAPHIC INDICATORS — INDICATEURS DEMOGRAPHIQUES ET SOCIAUX

Population	Year Année	Value Valeur	Charts Graphiques	Population
Population ('000)	2017	37 673.8		Population ('000)
Female (%)	2017	19.2		Féminine (%)
Urban (%)	...	...		Urbaine (%)
Average annual growth rate	...	...		Taux de croissance annuel
Active population ('000)	2017	19 103.9		Population active ('000)
Population by age group ('000)				Population par groupe d'âge ('000)
0-14 years	2017	17 596.0		0-14 ans
15-64 years	2017	19 132.7		15-64 ans
65+ years	2017	945.1		65+ ans
Economically active population in agriculture (%)	2011	12.0		Participation de la population active agricole (%)
Crude birth rate	2016	38.7		Taux brut de natalité
Crude death rate	...	...		Taux brut de mortalité
Total fertility rate	2016	5.4		Indice synthétique de fécondité
Life expectancy at birth - Total (years)	2016	59.2		Espérance de vie à la naissance - Totale (années)
Dependency ratio - Total (%)	2017	96.9		Taux de dépendance - Total (%)
Health				**Santé**
Percentage of children under-five and underweight	2016	11.0		% d'enfants de moins de cinq ans avec insuffisance pondérale
Prevalence of undernourishment	2015	25.5		Prévalence de la malnutrition
Under five mortality rate (per 1 000 live births)	2016	64.0		Taux de mortalité de moins de 5 ans (les deux sexes, pour 1000)
Infant mortality rate (per 1 000 live births)	2016	43.0		Taux de mortalité infantile (les deux sexes) par 1000
Neonatal mortality rate (per 1 000 live births)	2016	22.0		Le taux de mortalité néonatale (pour 1000 naissances vivantes)
Percentage of children provided the vaccines :				Pourcentage d'enfants vaccinés :
BCG	2016	96.0		BCG
DPT3	2016	95.0		DTC3
Polio	2016	60.0		polio
Measles	2016	87.0		rougeole
Percentage of mothers provided at least one antenatal care (%)	2016	97.3		Pourcentage de mères ayant au moins reçu un soin prénatal (%)
Percentage of deliveries attended by skilled health personnel	2016	74.2		% d'accouchements assistés par un personnel de santé qualifié
Number of doctors (per 10,000 population)	2005	1.2		Nombre de médecins (pour 10.000 habitants)
Number of nurses (per 10,000 population)	2005	13.1		Nombre d'infirmiers (pour 10.000 habitants)
Hospital beds - Total (per 10,000 population)	2011	5.0		Nombre de lits d'hôpitaux - Total (pour 10 000)
Births registered (per 1,000)	2016	42.0		Naissances enregistrées (pour 1000)
Deaths registered (per 1,000)	2016	9.3		Décès enregistrés (pour 1000)
Budget allocation to health (%)	2016	18.0		Dépenses publiques consacrées à la santé (% du budget)
Education				**Education**
Enrolment in primary education (000)	2015	8 264.0		Scolarisation dans le primaire (000)
Female	2015	4 141.7		Féminine
Enrolment in secondary education (000)	2015	1 284.0		Scolarisation dans le secondaire (000)
Female	2015	608.8		Féminine
Enrolment in tertiary education (000)	2015	250.6		Scolarisation dans le tertiaire (000)
Female	2015	110.9		Féminine
Literacy rate	2014	72.2		Taux d'alphabétisation (deux sexes)
Male	2014	77.4		Masculin
Female	2014	67.6		Féminin
Pupil teacher ratio - primary	2015	22.0		Ratio élève-enseignant
Budget allocation to education (%)	2014	6.8		Dépenses publiques consacrées à l'enseignement (% du budget)
Poverty				**Pauvreté**
GNI per capita, PPP (current int. $)	2016	1790.0		RNB par habitant, ($ PPA inter. courants)
Human Poverty Index (HPI-1) Value (%)	2007	28.8		Valeur de l'Indice de pauvreté (IPH-1) (%)
Population below Inter. poverty line ($2/day) (%)	2012	33.2		Population sous le seuil inter. de pauvreté (2$/Jour) (%)
Share of income held by richest 10%	2012	33.9		% de revenu des 10% plus riches
Share of income held by poorest 10%	2012	2.4		% de revenu des 10% plus pauvres
GINI index	2012	42.4		Indice de GINI

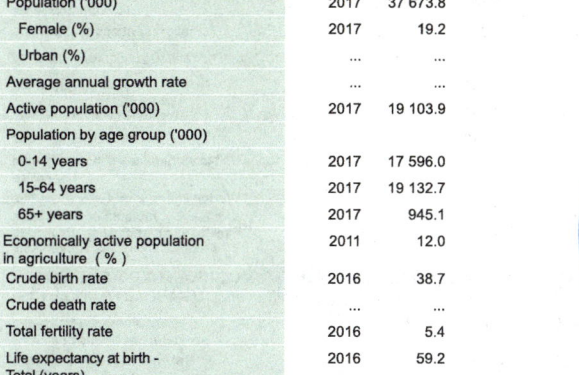

Population by age group - 2017

Population par groupe d'age - 2017

- 0-14 years: 46.7%
- 15-64 years: 50.8%
- 65+ years: 2.5%

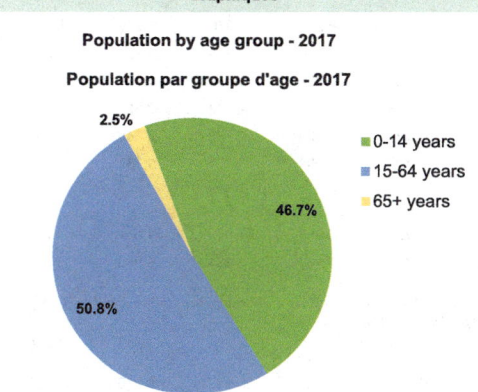

Percentage of children provided vaccines : - 2016

Pourcentage d'enfants vaccinés : - 2016

- BCG / BCG: 96.0
- DPT3 / DTC3: 95.0
- Polio / polio: 60.0
- Measles / rougeole: 87.0

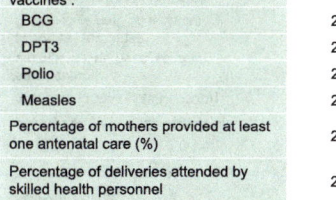

Literacy rate (%) - 2014

Taux d'alphabétisation - 2014

- Male: 77.4
- Female: 67.6

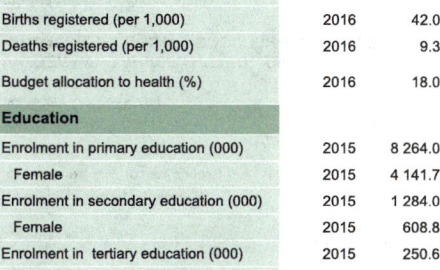

GNI per capita, PPP (current international $)

RNB par habitant, ($ PPA internationaux courants)

2012	2013	2014	2015	2016
1 600	1 630	1 690	1 740	1 790

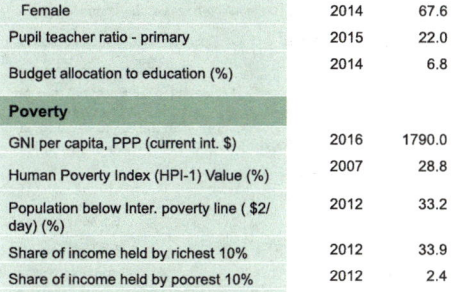

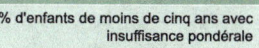
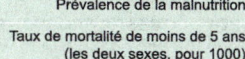

II NATIONAL ACCOUNTS — COMPTES NATIONAUX

	2009	2010	2011	2012	2013	2014	2015	2016	2017	
GROSS DOMESTIC PRODUCT BY KIND OF ECONOMIC ACTIVITY AT CURRENT PRICES *UGANDAN SHILLING (BILLIONS)*										**PRODUIT INTÉRIEUR BRUT PAR BRANCHE D'ACTIVITÉ ÉCONOMIQUE AUX PRIX COURANTS** *SHILLING OUGANDAIS (MILLIARDS)*
Agriculture, hunting , forestry and Fishing	10 754	10 452	14 176	16 073	16 662	18 069	19 321	20 358	...	Agriculture, chasse sylviculture et Pêche
Mining and quarrying	486	401	430	580	535	514	534	605	...	Industries extractives
Manufacturing	2 989	4 048	5 822	5 843	6 046	6 028	7 339	7 780	...	Industries manufacturières
Electricity, gas & water	1 532	1 200	1 377	1 855	2 161	2 453	2 753	3 226	...	Electricité, gaz et eau
Construction	2 143	2 493	3 951	4 289	4 976	5 527	5 960	6 542	...	Bâtiments et travaux publics
Wholesale & retail trade, restaurants, hotels	5 900	6 677	9 410	10 240	10 840	11 122	13 054	13 466	...	Commerce de gros et de détail, restaurants et hôtels
Finance, insurance, real estate, etc.	4 328	5 359	6 207	6 976	7 240	8 315	9 443	10 226	...	Banques, assurances, affaires immobilières
Transport and communications	3 032	3 447	2 759	3 515	4 182	4 664	5 200	4 665	...	Transport(s) et communications
Public administration and defense	1 061	1 380	1 626	1 801	1 904	1 977	1 909	1 964	...	Administrations publiques et défense
Education	1 864	2 225	2 405	2 928	3 689	4 377	5 139	6 563	...	Education
Health And Social Work	1 166	1 289	1 426	1 799	2 140	2 366	2 553	2 768	...	Santé et Actions Sociales
Other services	662	756	904	1 103	1 241	1 361	1 518	1 704	...	Autres services
Less Imputed Service Charges	...	...	...	...	...	...	...	...	...	Moins Services d'intermédiation financière
Gross domestic product at factor cost / basic prices	35 916	39 727	50 493	57 002	61 617	66 772	74 724	79 867	...	Produit intérieur brut aux couts des facteurs / prix de base
Plus: Indirect Taxes / taxes on products, less subsidies	2 779	3 134	3 702	4 224	4 900	5 578	6 505	6 889	...	Plus taxes indirectes/impôts sur les produits, moins les subventions
EXPENDITURE ON GROSS DOMESTIC PRODUCT AT CURRENT PURCHASER'S VALUES *UGANDAN SHILLING (BILLIONS)*										**EMPLOI DU PRODUIT INTÉRIEUR BRUT AUX PRIX COURANTS D'ACQUISITION** *SHILLING OUGANDAIS (MILLIARDS)*
Government final consumption	3 325	4 968	5 717	4 973	5 373	6 485	6 845	6 914	...	Consommation finale des administrations publiques
Private final consumption	29 208	32 865	41 222	45 867	49 216	55 096	63 330	65 055	...	Consommation finale privée
Gross fixed capital formation	9 756	10 815	14 955	17 212	18 011	18 375	19 829	20 854	...	Formation brute de capital fixe
Change in inventories	208	134	197	235	306	332	381	459	...	Variation des stocks
Exports of goods and services	6 790	7 556	10 871	12 315	13 374	12 352	15 659	15 394	...	Exportations de biens et services
Less imports of goods and services	10 592	13 476	18 767	19 376	19 762	20 289	24 814	21 919	...	Moins importations de biens et services
GDP at purchasers' values	38 695	42 861	54 195	61 226	66 517	72 351	81 229	86 756	...	PIB aux prix d'acquisition
GROSS DOMESTIC PRODUCT BY KIND OF ECONOMIC ACTIVITY AT CONSTANT PRICES *ANNUAL GROWTH RATES (%)*										**PRODUIT INTÉRIEUR BRUT PAR BRANCHE D'ACTIVITÉ ECONOMIQUE AUX PRIX CONSTANTS** *TAUX DE CROISSANCE ANNUEL (%)*
Agriculture, hunting , forestry and Fishing	5.6	2.6	1.9	0.4	2.7	2.7	3.8	-	...	Agriculture, chasse sylviculture et Pêche
Mining and quarrying	-0.5	19.2	12.6	6.7	2.5	12.9	19.0	- 1.8	...	Industries extractives
Manufacturing	4.8	5.8	6.1	- 1.1	0.6	4.5	10.2	- 0.1	...	Industries manufacturières
Electricity, gas & water	10.0	7.9	5.3	10.1	4.0	6.0	5.5	6.2	...	Electricité, gaz et eau
Construction	11.7	5.3	19.0	- 0.7	9.7	8.1	4.1	6.4	...	Bâtiments et travaux publics
Wholesale & retail trade, restaurants, hotels	5.2	6.8	5.4	0.8	2.0	2.2	4.1	1.7	...	Commerce de gros et de détail, restaurants et hôtels
Finance, insurance, real estate, etc.	4.1	6.0	4.4	3.0	5.4	13.1	6.6	4.4	...	Banques, assurances, affaires immobilières
Transport and communications	19.0	28.6	5.1	19.0	16.3	- 0.1	11.0	11.7	...	Transport(s) et communications
Public administration and defense	5.7	20.3	2.3	- 2.0	0.7	10.6	- 15.0	- 3.6	...	Administrations publiques et défense
Education	2.1	6.2	8.2	8.9	7.5	3.6	3.6	2.4	...	Education
Health And Social Work	3.3	5.2	4.5	3.8	5.4	5.0	4.5	4.1	...	Santé et Actions Sociales
Other services	7.6	18.5	6.3	- 3.4	- 1.0	8.2	1.7	- 2.6	...	Autres services
Less Imputed Service Charges	...	...	...	...	...	...	...	...	...	Moins Services d'intermédiation financière
Gross domestic product at factor cost / basic prices	6.6	8.4	5.4	2.8	4.7	4.6	5.0	2.7	...	Produit intérieur brut aux couts des facteurs / prix de base
Plus: Indirect Taxes / taxes on products, less subsidies	10.8	5.5	12.0	8.0	5.2	3.7	12.2	0.4	...	Plus taxes indirectes/impôts sur les produits, moins les subventions
Gross domestic product at market prices	6.9	8.2	5.9	3.2	4.7	4.5	5.6	2.5	...	Produit intérieur brut aux prix du marché
EXPENDITURE ON GROSS DOMESTIC PRODUCT AT CONSTANT PURCHASERS' VALUES *ANNUAL GROWTH RATES (%)*										**EMPLOIS DU PRODUIT INTÉRIEUR BRUT AUX PRIX CONSTANTS D'ACQUISITION** *TAUX DE CROISSANCE ANNUEL (%)*
Government final consumption	6.5	47.2	6.8	- 19.3	2.7	12.8	8.3	- 11.1	...	Consommation finale des administrations publiques
Private final consumption	7.3	8.1	4.8	1.6	4.0	7.5	5.8	- 3.9	...	Consommation finale privée
Gross fixed capital formation	10.2	5.2	14.7	5.4	2.2	1.3	6.5	1.9	...	Formation brute de capital fixe
Exports of goods and services	-10.3	6.6	4.0	12.7	10.2	- 16.5	16.1	- 7.2	...	Exportations de biens et services
Less imports of goods and services	-0.8	15.2	9.8	- 2.1	3.7	- 2.7	13.9	- 25.1	...	Moins importations de biens et services

III INFLATION

	2009	2010	2011	2012	2013	2014	2015	2016	2017	
Annual growth rates (%)										**Taux de croissance annuel (%)**
All item	17.9	4.9	16.2	12.7	4.9	3.1	5.6	5.7	5.2	Ensemble
of which:										dont:
Food and non-alcoholic beverages	22.4	3.5	25.7	12.8	2.3	3.5	7.3	5.6	10.1	Alimentation et boissons non alcoolisés
Alcoholic beverages, tobacco and narcotics	17.2	7.2	11.6	11.5	11.2	1.0	1.5	5.4	0.3	Boissons alcoolisées et tabacs
Clothing and footwear	23.3	3.4	25.9	18.3	5.0	4.7	6.5	7.8	1.7	Habillement et chaussures
Housing, water, electricity, gas and other fuels	11.6	6.3	17.4	20.8	6.9	2.9	5.9	5.2	3.9	Logement, eau, électricité, gaz et autres combustibles
Furnishings, household equipment and routine household maintenance	1.9	5.5	22.6	14.0	5.9	3.6	4.1	4.5	4.7	Meubles, articles de ménage et entretien courant
Health	37.5	10.9	6.5	19.3	8.5	5.2	2.4	3.1	- 0.4	Santé
Transport	5.6	1.8	14.3	6.9	3.9	0.3	2.4	4.4	1.0	Transport
Communication	0.1	- 2.3	- 10.2	4.2	1.5	4.0	14.0	- 3.6	- 2.8	Communication
Recreation and culture	15.2	1.8	7.7	5.6	3.2	2.0	1.6	2.2	6.2	Loisirs et culture
Education	43.9	4.6	3.1	11.4	14.5	9.3	6.4	14.8	9.2	Enseignement
Restaurants and hotels	15.8	9.2	12.3	12.4	6.5	1.2	3.8	6.2	5.4	Restaurants et hôtels
Miscellaneous goods and services	12.2	8.1	15.3	13.0	5.0	1.8	4.5	6.6	2.7	Biens et Services divers

IV AGRICULTURAL PRODUCTION - PRODUCTION AGRICOLE

TONNES (THOUSAND)	2009	2010	2011	2012	2013	2014	2015	2016	2017	Tonnes (milliers)
Plantains	9 512	4 694	4 699	4 503	4 375	4 578	4 623	3 396	...	Bananes plantains
Cassava	5 179	3 017	2 712	2 807	2 980	2 813	2 727	2 729	...	Manioc
Maize	2 355	2 374	2 551	2 734	2 748	2 868	2 813	2 483	...	Maïs
Sweet potatoes	2 766	1 987	1 798	1 852	1 811	1 818	2 045	1 911	...	Patates douces

V MINING PRODUCTION - PRODUCTION MINIERE

	2009	2010	2011	2012	2013	2014	2015	2016	2017	
Gold ores and concentrates - Production (Kilograms)	...	...	...	4	5	24	13	11	...	Minerais d'or et leurs concentrés - Production (Kilogrammes)
Salt and pure sodium chloride - Production (metric tons)	15 000	15 000	15 000	...	...	...	...	...	...	Sel et chlorure de sodium pur - Production (tonnes métriques)
	...	...	...	...	...	...	...	...	...	

VI ENERGY - ENERGIE

	2009	2010	2011	2012	2013	2014	2015	2016	2017	
Total electricity generation (GWh)	2 189	2 406	2 222	2 224	3 203	3 207	3 207	...	...	Production électrique totale (GWh)
of which										dont
Production of electricity from fossil fuels (GWh)	703	821	547	547	613	613	613	...	...	Production d'électricité à partir de combustibles fossiles (GWh)
Production of hydro electricity (GWh)	1 396	1 485	1 514	1 514	2 393	2 393	2 393	...	...	Production d'électricité d'origine hydraulique (GWh)
Production of electricity from solar, wind, tide, wave and other sources (GWh)	...	...	18	19	21	...	...	...	...	Production d'électricité d'origine solaire, éolienne, marée motrice et autres (GWh)

VII TOURISM AND INFRASTRUCTURE - TOURISME ET INFRASTUCTURE

	2009	2010	2011	2012	2013	2014	2015	2016	2017	
VII-1 Tourism										**VII-1 Tourisme**
International tourist arrivals (thousands)	807	946	1 151	1 197	1 206	1 266	1 303	1 323	1 449	Arrivées de touristes internationaux (milliers)
Rooms in hotels and similar establishments (thousands)	...	...	...	...	261	329	...	...	...	Chambres d'hôtels et établissements assimilés (milliers)
Overnight stays (thousands)	3 230	3 537	4 744	4 401	4 518	4 866	4 741	4 952	5 495	Nuitées (milliers)
Tourism receipts (US$ thousand)	636 700	747 000	926 300	1 106 400	1 307 400	763 300	1 152 400	747 000	843 993	Recettes touristiques (milliers de $ EU)
Total contribution to GDP (%)	7.2	7.6	8.2	8.7	9.3	6.7	8.9	7.1	7.3	Contribution totale au PIB (%)
Total contribution to Employment (%)	6.5	6.8	6.9	6.7	8.1	5.8	7.8	6.2	6.3	Contribution totale à l'emploi (%)
VII-2 Infrastructure										**VII-2 Infrastructure**
Paved road (% of total)	...	...	16.3	...	...	...	...	20.2	20.7	Routes asphaltées (% du total)
Total network (Railways-km)	...	...	...	...	...	...	...	...	...	Réseau total voies ferrées-Km
Main telephone lines (per 100 inhabitants)	0.7	1.0	1.3	0.9	0.7	0.8	0.8	0.9	...	Lignes téléphoniques fixes (pour 100 habitants)
Mobile cellular subscribers (per 100 inhabitants)	28.6	37.7	47.5	45.0	48.1	52.4	50.4	55.1	...	Abonnés aux téléphones mobiles (pour 100 habitants)
Internet users per 100 inhabitants	9.8	12.5	13.0	14.1	15.5	16.9	17.8	21.9	...	Utilisateurs Internet par 100 Habitants
Fixed (wired)-broadband subscriptions per 100 inhabitants	...	...	...	...	...	...	...	...	...	Abonnements à l'Internet fixe (filaire) à large bande pour 100 habitants, par débit

VIII EXTERNAL TRADE - COMMERCE EXTERIEUR

US$ (MILLIONS) EXPORTS, FOB	2009	2010	2011	2012	2013	2014	2015	2016	2017	$ E.U (MILLIONS) EXPORTATIONS, FÀB
Exports - Total	1 568	1 619	2 159	2 357	2 408	2 262	2 267	2 543	...	Exportations - Total
Exports to Africa	723	771	1 005	1 295	1 367	1 255	1 271	1 297	...	Exportations vers l'Afrique
Main products										**Principaux produits**
Coffee and coffee substitutes	352	308	490	401	466	447	425	409	...	Café et succédanés du café
Fish, fresh (live or dead), chilled or frozen	126	125	120	88	117	107	89	144	...	Poissons frais (vivants ou morts), réfrigérés ou congelés
Lime, cement, fabrica. constr. mat. (excludingglass, clay)	81	75	100	115	121	101	91	93	...	Chaux, ciment, tissu. constr. tapis. (sauf verre, argile)
Tea and mate	40	44	78	86	64	86	72	131	...	Thé et maté
Tobacco, unmanufactured; tobacco refuse	88	97	76	89	147	100	98	156	...	Tabac, non manufacturé; déchets de tabac
Main destinations										**Principales destinations**
Democratic Republic of Congo	182	199	208	276	297	194	162	208	...	République Démocratique du Congo
Kenya	131	162	211	257	271	276	395	517	...	Kenya
Rwanda	158	174	229	271	247	268	244	226	...	Rwanda
South Sudan	...	...	...	20	191	294	275	87	...	Soudan du sud
United Arab Emirates	79	125	145	143	79	45	98	359	...	Emirates Arabes
IMPORTS, CIF										
Imports - Total	4 247	4 664	5 631	6 044	5 818	6 074	5 528	5 099	...	Importations - Total (millions)
Imports from Africa	1 058	1 171	1 353	1 402	1 291	1 339	1 188	883	...	Importations en provenance de l'Afrique
Main products										**Principaux produits**
Medicaments (incl. veterinary medicaments)	212	202	252	274	354	354	330	253	...	Médicaments (y compris les médicaments vétérinaires)
Motor vehic. for transport of goods, special purpo.	104	125	152	178	152	171	180	165	...	Véhicule à moteur pour le transport de marchandises, spécial.
Motor vehicles for the transport of persons	129	172	172	187	178	194	157	150	...	Véhicules à moteur pour le transport de personnes
Petroleum oils or bituminous minerals > 70 % oil	573	723	963	963	858	982	706	627	...	Huiles de pétrole ou de minéraux bitumineux> 70 % d'huile
Telecommunication equipment, n.e.s.; & parts, n.e.s.	243	234	364	286	237	166	208	169	...	Matériel de télécommunication, n.es .; & parties, n.e.s.
Main origin										**Principales provenances**
China	373	411	523	725	655	761	880	932	...	Chine
India	451	570	804	1 057	1 280	1 265	1 061	878	...	Inde
Japan	243	296	293	294	303	336	314	258	...	Japon
Kenya	667	707	843	805	774	766	715	483	...	Kenya
United Arab Emirates	388	369	341	440	381	410	382	436	...	Emirates Arabes

UGANDA

	2009	2010	2011	2012	2013	2014	2015	2016	2017	
IX-1 MONETARY STATISTICS *UGANDAN SHILLING (MILLIONS)*										**IX-1 STATISTIQUES MONÉTAIRES** *SHILLING OUGANDAIS (MILLIONS)*
Money supply (M1)	6 745 061	9 544 423	10 550 477	12 123 126	13 270 542	15 286 509	17 069 551	18 971 871	21 699 268	Masse monétaire (M1)
Quasi-money	2 396 744	3 456 282	4 203 461	4 775 472	5 305 310	6 130 563	6 877 191	7 446 001	8 387 941	Quasi-monnaie
of which demand deposit	1 925 606	2 611 458	2 468 300	3 162 491	...	...	...	...	...	dont Monnaie scripturale
Net foreign assets	5 216 106	6 171 302	6 312 456	8 454 662	8 510 372	8 620 158	10 255 825	12 118 962	13 829 250	Avoirs extérieurs nets
Domestic credit	3 551 577	5 968 455	7 588 848	8 170 322	9 057 951	11 508 854	13 327 180	14 401 337	15 605 792	Crédit intérieur
of which claims on private sector	- 567 572	436 860	239 382	- 28 987	346 004	1 584 225	1 891 324	2 258 625	2 775 570	dont créances sur le secteur privé
of which claims on government sector, net	3 995 283	5 464 063	7 269 283	8 127 792	8 628 587	9 843 695	11 353 132	12 058 475	12 762 489	dont créances nettes sur le gouvernement
International reserves (millions US$)	2 506	2 417	2 362	2 910	3 103	3 219	2 890	3 016	3 228	Réserves internationales (millions $EU)
Average exchange rate (National currency per US$)	2 030	2 178	2 523	2 505	2 587	2 600	3 241	3 420	3 611	Taux de change (moyen) (monnaie nationale par $ EU)
IX-2 PUBLIC FINANCE *UGANDAN SHILLING (MILLIONS)*										**IX-2 FINANCES PUBLIQUES** *SHILLING OUGANDAIS (MILLIONS)*
Total Revenues and Grants	4 671	5 183	7 292	7 763	8 277	8 870	11 045	12 095	15 718 310	Recettes totales et dons
Direct taxes (on income, profits)	1 028	1 301	2 853	2 379	2 426	2 613	3 355	3 460	4 736 598	Taxes directes
Domestic indirect taxes revenues	2 191	2 458	2 882	3 493	3 959	4 496	5 428	5 989	3 298 331	Taxes Indirectes
Trade taxes	426	421	540	623	753	882	1 062	1 320	5 283 957	Taxes sur le commerce extérieur
Other taxes	18	25	32	33	12	40	49	62	119 864	Autres taxes
Other revenues	124	114	95	106	191	137	221	318	787 924	Autres recettes
Grants	885	864	891	1 129	936	702	931	946	1 491 637	Dons
Total Expenditures and Net Lending	5 175	6 831	8 972	9 273	10 521	11 682	14 379	16 168	19 012 375	Dépenses totales et prêts nets
Current expenditure	3 217	4 004	5 728	5 107	4 986	5 756	6 701	7 628	8 769 424	Dépenses courantes
Wages and Salaries	1 184	1 308	1 659	1 832	2 160	2 385	2 759	3 075	3 389 751	Rémunérations et salaires
Other purchases of goods and services	1 302	1 874	2 716	2 001	1 709	2 160	2 506	3 396	3 412 000	Achat de biens et services
Other current expenditure	448	740	1 159	985	1 053	1 191	1 211	1 038	1 852 673	Autres dépenses courantes
Current transfers	283	82	194	289	63	20	225	119	115 000	Transferts courants
Interest payments	358	385	424	603	890	970	1 213	1 682	1 611 000	Intérêts
Capital expenditure	1 657	2 478	2 851	3 603	4 237	4 937	5 230	5 326	7 399 462	Dépenses d'équipement
Net lending	- 57	- 37	- 30	- 39	409	19	1 235	1 532	1 232 490	Prêts nets
Fiscal balance	- 504	- 1 648	- 1 680	- 1 510	- 2 245	- 2 812	- 3 334	- 4 073	-3 294 065	Solde global y compris les dons
IX-3 BALANCE OF PAYMENTS *US$ (MILLIONS)*										**IX-3 BALANCE DES PAIEMENTS** *$ E.U (MILLIONS)*
Trade balance	- 1 509	- 2 212	- 2 478	- 2 451	- 2 145	- 2 375	- 2 245	- 1 503	...	Balance commerciale
Services Balance	- 366	- 499	- 684	- 361	- 276	- 700	- 528	- 111	...	Balance des services
Net primary income	- 376	- 276	- 418	- 465	- 639	- 573	- 935	- 625	...	Revenus primaires nets
Compensation of employees	- 88	- 79	- 103	- 178	- 154	- 109	- 160	- 138	...	Rémunération des salariés
Investment income	- 288	- 197	- 315	- 287	- 485	- 465	- 775	- 486	...	Revenus des investissements
Net secondary income	1 192	1 362	1 475	1 612	1 257	1 267	1 442	1 484	...	Revenus secondaires nets
Net official transfers	...	...	...	...	...	...	...	1 146	...	Transferts officiels nets
Workers' remittances	...	...	...	...	...	...	...	...	...	Envois de fonds des travailleurs
Other private transfers	...	...	...	...	...	...	...	44	...	Autres transferts privés
Current account balance	- 1 058	- 1 624	- 2 104	- 1 666	- 1 804	- 2 381	- 2 266	- 754	...	Solde du compte courant
Capital and financial account	- 1 490	- 1 068	- 1 495	- 1 597	- 1 282	- 2 027	- 1 378	- 899	...	Comptes de capital et financier
Capital account	...	...	12	22	80	95	108	139	...	Compte de capital
Financial account	- 1 490	- 1 068	- 1 507	- 1 619	- 1 362	- 2 122	- 1 486	- 1 038	...	Compte financier
Errors and omissions	- 235	514	504	560	592	659	285	- 104	...	Erreurs et omissions
Overall balance	- 197	42	81	- 534	- 230	- 494	387	- 319	...	Balance générale

X DEBT AND FINANCIAL FLOWS - DETTE ET FLUX FINANCIERS

	2009	2010	2011	2012	2013	2014	2015	2016	2017	
X-1 DEBT US $ (MILLIONS)										**X-1 DETTE EXTÉRIEURE** $ E.U (MILLIONS)
Total external debt	3 956	5 105	5 782	6 909	7 945	8 299	9 153	9 721	11 041	Dette extérieure totale
Private	...	...	...	...	...	...	...	...	...	Privée
Public	2 274	2 705	2 990	3 594	4 177	4 247	4 913	5 392	...	Publique
Total external debt service	175	156	183	239	290	321	417	576	...	Service de la dette extérieure
Present value of external debt	...	...	...	...	...	...	...	3 939	...	Valeur actuelle de la dette extérieure
Total government domestic debt, National currency (millions)	...	...	...	...	...	...	...	...	...	Dette publique intérieure
X-2 FINANCIAL FLOWS US $ (MILLIONS)										**X-2 FLUX FINANCIERS** $ E.U (MILLIONS)
Net Foreign Direct Investment Inflows	842	544	894	1 205	1 096	1 059	538	541	...	Investissements étranger direct (flux nets entrants)
Main origin of FDI inflows										**Principales origines de l'IDE entrant:**
Belgium	29	- 43	- 61	- 24	...	...	...	...	...	Belgique
France	3	5	- 3	- 2	...	...	...	...	...	France
Netherlands	16	125	164	611	...	...	...	...	...	Pays-Bas
...	...	...	...	...	...	...	...	...	...	...
United Kingdom	228	130	116	117	...	...	...	...	...	Royaume-Uni
African countries	199	199	291	131	...	...	...	...	...	Pays africains
Net total official development assistance	1 786	1 690	1 573	1 643	1 697	1 634	1 628	1 757	...	Aide publique au développement (nette totale)
Main origin of net ODA										**Principales origines de l'APD nette**
...	...	...	...	...	...	...	...	...	...	...
...	...	...	...	...	...	...	...	...	...	...
...	...	...	...	...	...	...	...	...	...	...
...	...	...	...	...	...	...	...	...	...	...
...	...	...	...	...	...	...	...	...	...	...

OUGANDA

SOURCES AND NOTES - SOURCES ET NOTES

External trade - Total exports, fob: UNCTAD

External trade - Total import, cif: UNCTAD

ODA: OECD

Monetary statistics: IMF

National Accounts: 2016 data is Provisional

National Account :The Annual accounts are based on new prices of 2009/2010 from 2008

Poverty: World Bank

Commerce exterieur - Exportation, fab: CNUCED

Commerce exterieur - Imporations, caf: CNUCED

APD: OCDE

Statistiques monétaires: FMI

Comptes nationaux: Les donées de l'année 2016 sont provisoires

Comptes Nationaux : Les Comptes Nationaux : Les comptes annuels sont élaborés selon la nouvelle base des prix 2009/2010 à partir de 2008

Pauvreté: Banque mondiale

			SUPERFICIE (KM2)
AREA (km2)		752 610	
CAPITAL CITY	Lusaka	Lusaka	CAPITALE
CURRENCY	Zambian Kwacha	Kwacha zambien	MONNAIE

I SOCIAL AND DEMOGRAPHIC INDICATORS — INDICATEURS DEMOGRAPHIQUES ET SOCIAUX

Population	Year Année	Value Valeur	Charts / Graphiques	Population
Population ('000)	2017	16 405.2		Population ('000)
Female (%)	2017	50.5		Féminine (%)
Urban (%)	2017	42.5		Urbaine (%)
Average annual growth rate	2017	2.9		Taux de croissance annuel
Active population ('000)	2015	5 899.1		Population active ('000)
Population by age group ('000)				Population par groupe d'âge ('000)
0-14 years	2017	7 529.5		0-14 ans
15-64 years	2017	8 445.7		15-64 ans
65+ years	2017	430.1		65+ ans
Economically active population in agriculture (%)	2015	62.5		Participation de la population active agricole (%)
Crude birth rate	2017	41.6		Taux brut de natalité
Crude death rate	2017	12.6		Taux brut de mortalité
Total fertility rate	2017	5.5		Indice synthétique de fécondité
Life expectancy at birth - Total (years)	2015	60.8		Espérance de vie à la naissance - Totale (années)
Dependency ratio - Total (%)	2017	94.2		Taux de dépendance - Total (%)
Health				**Santé**
Percentage of children under-five and underweight	2017	0.9		% d'enfants de moins de cinq ans avec insuffisance pondérale
Prevalence of undernourishment	2015	47.8		Prévalence de la malnutrition
Under five mortality rate (per 1 000 live births)	2017	10.7		Taux de mortalité de moins de 5 ans (les deux sexes, pour 1000)
Infant mortality rate (per 1 000 live births)	2017	3.4		Taux de mortalité infantile (les deux sexes) par 1000
Neonatal mortality rate (per 1 000 live births)	2017	5.3		Le taux de mortalité néonatale (pour 1000 naissances vivantes)
Percentage of children provided the vaccines :				Pourcentage d'enfants vaccinés :
BCG	2017	104.0		BCG
DPT3	2017	94.0		DTC3
Polio	2017	90.9		polio
Measles	2017	96.0		rougeole
Percentage of mothers provided at least one antenatal care (%)	2017	77.0		Pourcentage de mères ayant au moins reçu un soin prénatal (%)
Percentage of deliveries attended by skilled health personnel	2017	60.0		% d'accouchements assistés par un personnel de santé qualifié
Number of doctors (per 10,000 population)	2017	1.1		Nombre de médecins (pour 10.000 habitants)
Number of nurses (per 10,000 population)	2017	8.9		Nombre d'infirmiers (pour 10.000 habitants)
Hospital beds - Total (per 10,000 population)	2017	12.1		Nombre de lits d'hôpitaux - Total (pour 10 000)
Births registered (per 1,000)	2017	555.0		Naissances enregistrées (pour 1000)
Deaths registered (per 1,000)	2017	0.8		Décès enregistrés (pour 1000)
Budget allocation to health (%)	2013	12.6		Dépenses publiques consacrées à la santé (% du budget)
Education				**Education**
Enrolment in primary education (000)	2015	3 215.7		Scolarisation dans le primaire (000)
Female	2015	1 601.5		Féminine
Enrolment in secondary education (000)	2015	802.3		Scolarisation dans le secondaire (000)
Female	...	...		Féminine
Enrolment in tertiary education (000)	2013	91.3		Scolarisation dans le tertiaire (000)
Female	...	...		Féminine
Literacy rate	2007	61.4		Taux d'alphabétisation (deux sexes)
Male	2007	71.9		Masculin
Female	2007	51.8		Féminin
Pupil teacher ratio - primary	2015	42.7		Ratio élève-enseignant
Budget allocation to education (%)	2008	5.7		Dépenses publiques consacrées à l'enseignement (% du budget)
Poverty				**Pauvreté**
GNI per capita, PPP (current int. $)	2016	3850.0		RNB par habitant, ($ PPA inter. courants)
Human Poverty Index (HPI-1) Value (%)	2007	35.5		Valeur de l'Indice de pauvreté (IPH-1) (%)
Population below Inter. poverty line ($2/day) (%)	2010	64.4		Population sous le seuil inter. de pauvreté (2$/Jour) (%)
Share of income held by richest 10%	2010	45.2		% de revenu des 10% plus riches
Share of income held by poorest 10%	2010	1.5		% de revenu des 10% plus pauvres
GINI index	2010	55.6		Indice de GINI

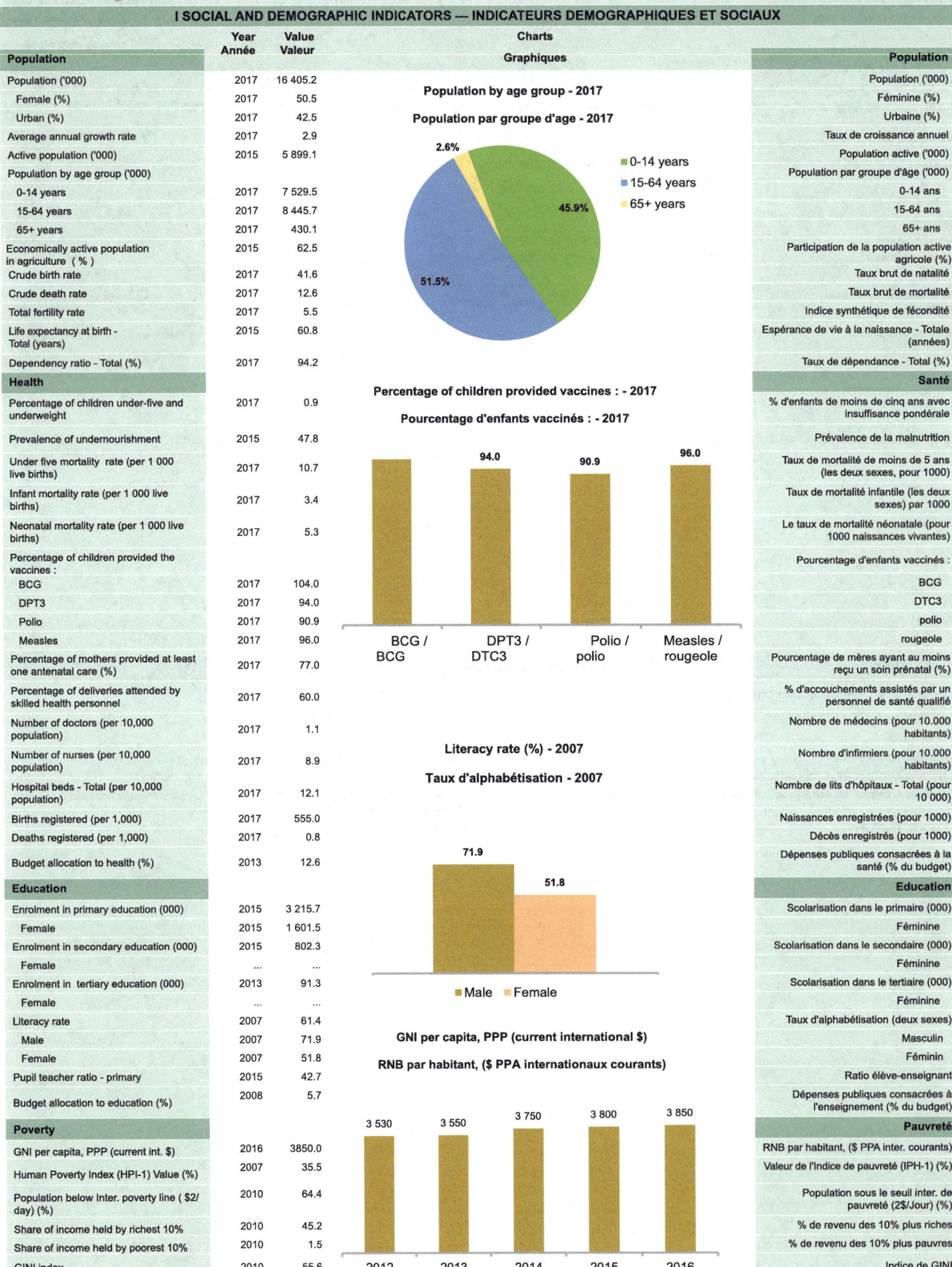

Population by age group - 2017
Population par groupe d'age - 2017

0-14 years — 45.9%
15-64 years — 51.5%
65+ years — 2.6%

Percentage of children provided vaccines : - 2017
Pourcentage d'enfants vaccinés : - 2017

BCG / BCG ; DPT3 / DTC3 94.0 ; Polio / polio 90.9 ; Measles / rougeole 96.0

Literacy rate (%) - 2007
Taux d'alphabétisation - 2007

Male 71.9 ; Female 51.8

GNI per capita, PPP (current international $)
RNB par habitant, ($ PPA internationaux courants)

2012: 3 530 ; 2013: 3 550 ; 2014: 3 750 ; 2015: 3 800 ; 2016: 3 850

II NATIONAL ACCOUNTS — COMPTES NATIONAUX

	2009	2010	2011	2012	2013	2014	2015	2016	2017	
GROSS DOMESTIC PRODUCT BY KIND OF ECONOMIC ACTIVITY AT CURRENT PRICES *ZAMBIAN KWACHA (MILLIONS)*										**PRODUIT INTÉRIEUR BRUT PAR BRANCHE D'ACTIVITÉ ÉCONOMIQUE AUX PRIX COURANTS** *KWACHA ZAMBIEN (MILLIONS)*
Agriculture, hunting , forestry and Fishing	8 936	9 159	11 002	12 237	12 449	11 326	9 134	13 460	17 602	Agriculture, chasse sylviculture et Pêche
Mining and quarrying	6 678	12 429	17 515	19 057	25 687	24 450	23 244	28 494	36 275	Industries extractives
Manufacturing	6 718	7 367	8 571	9 289	9 363	11 393	13 795	16 610	18 598	Industries manufacturières
Electricity, gas & water	1 515	1 784	2 783	2 710	2 702	4 293	6 038	8 033	7 645	Electricité, gaz et eau
Construction	8 468	9 761	10 408	10 965	11 588	14 899	18 353	22 232	25 210	Bâtiments et travaux publics
Wholesale & retail trade, restaurants, hotels	16 422	19 190	24 135	28 276	35 822	39 170	44 205	48 682	50 446	Commerce de gros et de détail, restaurants et hôtels
Finance, insurance, real estate, etc.	13 628	11 073	10 903	12 600	14 003	16 273	20 219	24 463	26 074	Banques, assurances, affaires immobilières
Transport and communications	5 254	7 293	8 281	9 810	9 206	9 834	12 620	14 512	21 908	Transport(s) et communications
Public administration and defense	1 647	3 905	3 481	6 484	7 034	7 352	8 103	9 295	9 647	Administrations publiques et défense
Education	3 891	6 819	7 687	9 265	11 008	13 086	14 383	15 800	16 652	Education
Health And Social Work	691	1 900	1 842	2 226	1 801	2 175	2 404	2 611	3 135	Santé et Actions Sociales
Other services	420	1 156	1 128	1 168	1 467	1 505	1 455	1 725	1 725	Autres services
Less Imputed Service Charges	- 2 076	...	...	...	...	...	...	...	...	Moins Services d'intermédiation financière
Gross domestic product at factor cost / basic prices	72 191	91 836	107 736	124 088	142 130	155 754	173 953	205 916	234 917	Produit intérieur brut aux couts des facteurs / prix de base
Plus: Indirect Taxes / taxes on products, less subsidies	5 158	5 380	6 297	7 186	9 201	11 299	9 428	10 182	10 769	Plus taxes indirectes/impôts sur les produits, moins les subventions
EXPENDITURE ON GROSS DOMESTIC PRODUCT AT CURRENT PURCHASER'S VALUES *ZAMBIAN KWACHA (MILLIONS)*										**EMPLOI DU PRODUIT INTÉRIEUR BRUT AUX PRIX COURANTS D'ACQUISITION** *KWACHA ZAMBIEN (MILLIONS)*
Government final consumption	12 898	9 119	11 683	15 618	18 439	24 263	27 105	...	...	Consommation finale des administrations publiques
Private final consumption	40 293	53 072	58 594	72 572	86 877	89 961	96 209	...	...	Consommation finale privée
Gross fixed capital formation	21 303	25 174	32 761	31 656	39 400	51 805	70 491	...	...	Formation brute de capital fixe
Change in inventories	2 945	3 872	5 604	10 029	12 110	5 064	7 981	...	...	Variation des stocks
Exports of goods and services	22 592	35 995	46 149	52 618	61 263	64 854	68 107	...	...	Exportations de biens et services
Less imports of goods and services	22 683	30 015	40 758	51 219	66 759	68 894	86 512	...	...	Moins importations de biens et services
GDP at purchasers' values	77 348	97 216	114 033	131 274	151 331	167 053	183 381	216 098	245 686	PIB aux prix d'acquisition
GROSS DOMESTIC PRODUCT BY KIND OF ECONOMIC ACTIVITY AT CONSTANT PRICES *ANNUAL GROWTH RATES (%)*										**PRODUIT INTÉRIEUR BRUT PAR BRANCHE D'ACTIVITÉ ECONOMIQUE AUX PRIX CONSTANTS** *TAUX DE CROISSANCE ANNUEL (%)*
Agriculture, hunting , forestry and Fishing	0.6	- 6.0	7.8	3.4	- 3.8	1.1	- 7.7	3.7	16.5	Agriculture, chasse sylviculture et Pêche
Mining and quarrying	33.2	27.1	0.1	0.8	3.6	- 2.3	0.2	7.3	3.0	Industries extractives
Manufacturing	3.6	1.5	10.6	4.8	6.2	6.5	5.4	1.9	4.4	Industries manufacturières
Electricity, gas & water	4.4	2.2	18.5	4.8	11.0	0.3	- 2.3	- 12.2	15.1	Electricité, gaz et eau
Construction	4.2	- 6.2	2.1	0.6	- 3.5	10.6	18.0	10.2	6.4	Bâtiments et travaux publics
Wholesale & retail trade, restaurants, hotels	4.8	7.7	18.1	10.2	18.4	3.5	1.3	-	1.1	Commerce de gros et de détail, restaurants et hôtels
Finance, insurance, real estate, etc.	4.3	0.9	- 6.1	8.2	- 1.6	6.1	6.1	1.8	3.1	Banques, assurances, affaires immobilières
Transport and communications	15.9	22.1	11.8	12.3	- 12.6	7.1	1.5	7.6	- 3.6	Transport(s) et communications
Public administration and defense	15.1	3.7	- 16.2	38.6	27.8	4.5	2.0	9.7	2.8	Administrations publiques et défense
Education	15.2	11.8	4.4	10.4	6.0	10.9	0.5	4.7	6.7	Education
Health And Social Work	7.7	7.2	- 10.9	12.6	- 23.4	10.9	2.9	1.6	17.4	Santé et Actions Sociales
Other services	- 15.8	46.7	- 4.4	- 1.0	23.1	6.7	3.3	2.3	0.5	Autres services
Less Imputed Service Charges	- 1.9	...	...	...	...	...	...	...	...	Moins Services d'intermédiation financière
Gross domestic product at factor cost / basic prices	9.1	10.1	5.6	7.6	5.1	4.7	2.8	3.8	4.2	Produit intérieur brut aux couts des facteurs / prix de base
Plus: Indirect Taxes / taxes on products, less subsidies	12.2	14.0	5.6	7.6	5.1	5.1	5.4	3.5	1.3	Plus taxes indirectes/impôts sur les produits, moins les subventions
Gross domestic product at market prices	9.2	10.3	5.6	7.6	5.1	4.7	2.9	3.8	4.1	Produit intérieur brut aux prix du marché
EXPENDITURE ON GROSS DOMESTIC PRODUCT AT CONSTANT PURCHASERS' VALUES *ANNUAL GROWTH RATES (%)*										**EMPLOIS DU PRODUIT INTÉRIEUR BRUT AUX PRIX CONSTANTS D'ACQUISITION** *TAUX DE CROISSANCE ANNUEL (%)*
Government final consumption	...	...	...	...	-	- 200.0	100.0	2 035.2	...	Consommation finale des administrations publiques
Private final consumption	...	...	...	...	...	...	...	...	...	Consommation finale privée
Gross fixed capital formation	...	...	...	...	...	...	...	...	...	Formation brute de capital fixe
Exports of goods and services	...	...	...	...	...	...	...	...	...	Exportations de biens et services
Less imports of goods and services	...	...	...	...	...	...	...	...	...	Moins importations de biens et services

III INFLATION

	2009	2010	2011	2012	2013	2014	2015	2016	2017	
Annual growth rates (%)										**Taux de croissance annuel (%)**
All item	13.4	8.5	6.4	6.6	7.0	7.8	10.0	18.2	6.6	Ensemble
of which:										dont:
Food and non-alcoholic beverages	14.4	5.6	4.8	7.0	6.5	7.2	11.0	21.8	5.8	Alimentation et boissons non alcoolisés
Alcoholic beverages, tobacco and narcotics	...	...	3.5	4.1	6.3	13.4	7.1	18.3	5.3	Boissons alcoolisées et tabacs
Clothing and footwear	...	...	8.5	6.4	7.9	7.0	10.6	17.1	8.3	Habillement et chaussures
Housing, water, electricity, gas and other fuels	11.4	20.8	12.7	5.2	8.4	9.7	7.7	5.4	10.9	Logement, eau, électricité, gaz et autres combustibles
Furnishings, household equipment and routine household maintenance	...	...	7.4	7.3	5.2	7.4	12.4	21.4	4.5	Meubles, articles de ménage et entretien courant
Health	15.9	8.3	6.0	6.3	4.8	5.9	9.4	14.6	5.4	Santé
Transport	- 3.4	14.0	6.4	6.2	8.0	10.7	9.1	17.6	8.5	Transport
Communication	...	...	0.3	1.5	2.7	3.4	2.4	8.9	3.3	Communication
Recreation and culture	...	...	5.6	6.3	4.3	7.3	11.1	18.6	4.7	Loisirs et culture
Education	...	...	8.2	9.0	12.5	1.0	5.2	16.8	7.3	Enseignement
Restaurants and hotels	...	...	7.2	3.9	7.0	7.7	7.4	11.1	3.5	Restaurants et hôtels
Miscellaneous goods and services	...	...	5.3	6.1	7.4	5.8	8.4	16.1	5.2	Biens et Services divers

ZAMBIE

IV AGRICULTURAL PRODUCTION - PRODUCTION AGRICOLE

	2009	2010	2011	2012	2013	2014	2015	2016	2017	
TONNES (THOUSAND)										**Tonnes (milliers)**
Sugar cane	3 200	3 500	3 500	3 900	4 000	4 015	...	4 085	...	Canne à sucre
Maize	1 887	2 795	3 020	2 853	2 533	3 350	3 519	2 873	...	Maïs
Cassava	1 161	1 152	1 087	1 062	1 070	919	953	854	...	Manioc
Wheat	195	172	237	254	274	202	239	160	...	Blé
Soybeans	119	112	117	203	261	214	208	267	...	Soja

V MINING PRODUCTION - PRODUCTION MINIERE

	2009	2010	2011	2012	2013	2014	2015	2016	2017	
Copper ores and concentrates - Production, metric tons (thousands)	698 646	767 008	739 759	699 020	763 805	708 259	710 860	770 598	578 352	Minerais de cuivre et leurs concentrés - Production, tonnes métriques (milliers)
Cobalt - Production, Tonnes (thousands)	3 660	2 128	2 137	771	5 000	...	...	...	...	Cobalt - Production, tonnes (milliers)
	...	...	...	...						

VI ENERGY - ENERGIE

	2009	2010	2011	2012	2013	2014	2015	2016	2017	
Total electricity generation (GWh)	10 308	11 304	11 916	11 916	11 917	11 918	11 919	...	...	Production électrique totale (GWh)
of which										dont
Production of electricity from fossil fuels (GWh)	32	31	781	781	781	781	781	...	...	Production d'électricité à partir de combustibles fossiles (GWh)
Production of hydro electricity (GWh)	10 276	11 273	11 134	11 134	11 134	11 134	11 134	...	...	Production d'électricité d'origine hydraulique (GWh)
Production of electricity from solar, wind, tide, wave and other sources (GWh)	...	...	2	2	3	3	4	...	...	Production d'électricité d'origine solaire, éolienne, marée motrice et autres (GWh)

VII TOURISM AND INFRASTRUCTURE - TOURISME ET INFRASTUCTURE

	2009	2010	2011	2012	2013	2014	2015	2016	2017	
VII-1 Tourism										**VII-1 Tourisme**
International tourist arrivals (thousands)	710	815	920	859	915	947	932	934	969	Arrivées de touristes internationaux (milliers)
Rooms in hotels and similar establishments (thousands)	...	...	...	35	42	43	43	32		Chambres d'hôtels et établissements assimilés (milliers)
Overnight stays (thousands)	4 972	5 601	6 669	4 975	5 396	5 981	5 953	5 796	5 936	Nuitées (milliers)
Tourism receipts (US$ thousand)	474 300	491 700	555 000	518 100	551 500	641 500	660 200	682 600	727 079	Recettes touristiques (milliers de $ EU)
Total contribution to GDP (%)	7.7	6.8	6.2	5.2	5.2	5.8	7.6	7.7	7.3	Contribution totale au PIB (%)
Total contribution to Employment (%)	4.8	4.6	4.6	4.0	3.6	4.0	5.3	5.5	5.3	Contribution totale à l'emploi (%)
VII-2 Infrastructure										**VII-2 Infrastructure**
Paved road (% of total)	...	...	...	...	...	...	...	...		Routes asphaltées (% du total)
Total network (Railways-km)	...	...	...	...	...	...	...	...		Réseau total voies ferrées-Km
Main telephone lines (per 100 inhabitants)	0.7	0.9	0.6	0.6	0.8	0.8	0.7	0.6		Lignes téléphoniques fixes (pour 100 habitants)
Mobile cellular subscribers (per 100 inhabitants)	34.4	41.2	59.9	74.8	71.5	67.3	74.5	74.9		Abonnés aux téléphones mobiles (pour 100 habitants)
Internet users per 100 inhabitants	6.3	10.0	11.5	13.5	15.4	19.0	21.0	25.5		Utilisateurs Internet par 100 Habitants
Fixed (wired)-broadband subscriptions per 100 inhabitants	...	...	...	...	...	...	...	...		Abonnements à l'Internet fixe (filaire) à large bande pour 100 habitants, par débit

VIII EXTERNAL TRADE - COMMERCE EXTERIEUR

	2009	2010	2011	2012	2013	2014	2015	2016	2017	
US$ (MILLIONS) **EXPORTS, FOB**										**$ E.U (MILLIONS)** **EXPORTATIONS, FÀB**
Exports - Total	4 312	7 200	9 001	9 365	10 594	9 688	6 983	5 804	...	Exportations - Total
Exports to Africa	1 259	1 695	2 298	2 744	3 315	2 434	1 895	1 275	...	Exportations vers l'Afrique
Main products										**Principaux produits**
Copper	2 573	4 946	6 447	6 290	6 750	6 628	4 699	3 960	...	Cuivre
Inorganic chemical elements, oxides & halogen salts	32	56	77	140	441	311	80	97	...	Eléments chimiques inorganiques, oxydes et sels halogénés
Maize (not including sweet corn), unmilled	38	60	264	450	173	92	339	114	...	Maïs (à l'exclusion du maïs sucré), non moulu
Sugar, molasses and honey	95	165	170	146	188	182	129	113	...	Sucre, mélasse et miel
Tobacco, unmanufactured; tobacco refuse	186	258	207	263	281	276	206	163	...	Tabac, non manufacturé; déchets de tabac
Main destinations										**Principales destinations**
China	864	2 090	2 223	2 307	2 856	2 413	1 432	1 079	...	Chine
Democratic Republic of Congo	304	354	489	761	1 328	901	543	383	...	République Démocratique du Congo
South Africa	295	497	640	651	798	561	377	342	...	Afrique du Sud
Switzerland	1 001	1 910	2 323	2 038	2 086	2 383	1 578	2 304	...	Suisse
United Arab Emirates	165	401	612	893	1 003	795	410	324	...	Emirates Arabes
IMPORTS, CIF										
Imports - Total	3 793	5 321	7 178	8 805	10 162	9 539	8 420	7 014	...	Importations - Total (millions)
Imports from Africa	2 438	3 482	4 455	5 200	6 433	6 051	5 204	4 156	...	Importations en provenance de l'Afrique
Main products										**Principaux produits**
Civil engineering & contractors' plant & equipment	140	260	411	477	473	425	301	252	...	Génie civil et installations et équipements des entrepreneurs
Copper ores and concentrates; copper mattes, cemen	285	627	852	925	1 565	1 357	463	657	...	Minerais et concentrés de cuivre; mattes de cuivre, cemen
Fertilizers (other than those of group 272)	138	147	256	249	326	246	325	286	...	Engrais (autres que ceux du groupe 272)
Motor vehic. for transport of goods, special purpo.	114	199	337	411	382	330	228	205	...	Véhicule à moteur pour le transport de marchandises, spécial.
Petroleum oils or bituminous minerals > 70 % oil	104	89	144	232	684	676	764	534	...	Huiles de pétrole ou de minéraux bitumineux> 70% d'huile
Main origin										**Principales provenances**
China	172	312	701	862	797	915	762	572	...	Chine
Democratic Republic of Congo	544	1 282	1 382	1 384	2 080	1 628	1 184	1 011	...	République Démocratique du Congo
India	110	121	230	294	434	460	436	289	...	Inde
Kuwait	384	550	364	612	236	139	132	579	...	Koweit
South Africa	1 541	1 862	2 623	3 131	3 389	3 368	3 006	2 366	...	Afrique du Sud

IX FINANCIAL AND MONETARY STATISTICS - FINANCES ET STATISTIQUES MONETAIRES

	2009	2010	2011	2012	2013	2014	2015	2016	2017	
IX-1 MONETARY STATISTICS *ZAMBIAN KWACHA (MILLIONS)*										**IX-1 STATISTIQUES MONÉTAIRES** *KWACHA ZAMBIEN (MILLIONS)*
Money supply (M1)	13 797	17 917	21 805	25 699	31 042	34 959	47 262	44 567	50 813	Masse monétaire (M1)
Quasi-money	4 700	5 647	7 479	9 432	11 913	13 562	18 554	15 275	20 022	Quasi-monnaie
of which demand deposit	...	...	...	...	...	...	...	...	...	dont Monnaie scripturale
Net foreign assets	4 913	6 690	9 393	12 014	11 663	15 306	29 575	21 881	21 985	Avoirs extérieurs nets
Domestic credit	11 976	14 689	16 850	19 739	28 404	31 987	40 428	41 339	53 577	Crédit intérieur
of which claims on private sector	3 963	5 548	5 200	3 242	10 335	9 182	10 933	14 606	25 315	dont créances sur le secteur privé
of which claims on government sector, net	7 741	8 942	11 454	15 707	17 675	22 335	28 884	26 152	27 524	dont créances nettes sur le gouvernement
International reserves (millions US$)	1 753	1 896	2 169	2 455	2 251	2 530	2 230	1 897	1 711	Réserves internationales (millions $EU)
Average exchange rate (National currency per US$)	5	5	5	5	5	6	9	10	10	Taux de change (moyen) (monnaie nationale par $ EU)
IX-2 PUBLIC FINANCE *ZAMBIAN KWACHA (MILLIONS)*										**IX-2 FINANCES PUBLIQUES** *KWACHA ZAMBIEN (MILLIONS)*
Total Revenues and Grants	12 182	15 198	20 233	24 541	26 678	31 564	34 421	39 410	42 058	Recettes totales et dons
Direct taxes (on income, profits)	4 838	6 914	10 655	10 275	9 814	11 499	12 888	14 927	16 844	Taxes directes
Domestic indirect taxes revenues	3 499	4 536	5 638	6 945	9 685	12 366	11 619	11 148	13 740	Taxes Indirectes
Trade taxes	1 089	1 250	1 725	2 041	1 808	1 972	1 929	1 953	2 912	Taxes sur le commerce extérieur
Other taxes	...	...	...	...	...	...	...	...	...	Autres taxes
Other revenues	889	1 109	1 501	3 042	3 175	4 460	7 615	10 856	6 753	Autres recettes
Grants	1 867	1 389	714	2 238	2 196	1 267	369	525	1 810	Dons
Total Expenditures and Net Lending	13 773	17 563	22 267	28 258	35 987	41 094	51 545	51 945	61 449	Dépenses totales et prêts nets
Current expenditure	10 524	13 681	17 282	18 589	24 615	28 513	34 128	36 340	39 814	Dépenses courantes
Wages and Salaries	5 274	6 325	7 402	9 393	11 897	15 750	16 091	18 807	21 070	Rémunérations et salaires
Other purchases of goods and services	2 881	3 250	4 480	4 640	4 799	5 062	5 519	4 897	5 587	Achat de biens et services
Other current expenditure	105	917	195	571	118	1 032	1 456	835	765	Autres dépenses courantes
Current transfers	2 264	3 189	5 205	3 985	7 801	6 668	11 062	11 801	12 391	Transferts courants
Interest payments	1 033	1 370	1 082	1 737	2 231	3 711	5 224	7 448	8 812	Intérêts
Capital expenditure	2 217	2 512	3 902	7 932	9 141	8 870	12 193	8 157	12 823	Dépenses d'équipement
Net lending	...	...	...	...	...	...	...	...	...	Prêts nets
Fiscal balance	- 1 591	- 2 364	- 2 034	- 3 717	- 9 309	- 9 530	- 17 124	- 12 535	- 19 392	Solde global y compris les dons
IX-3 BALANCE OF PAYMENTS *ZAMBIAN KWACHA (MILLIONS)*										**IX-3 BALANCE DES PAIEMENTS** *KWACHA ZAMBIEN (MILLIONS)*
Trade balance	958	2 774	2 299	1 595	1 648	1 625	- 74	- 4	364	Balance commerciale
Services Balance	- 143	- 317	- 428	- 344	- 1 058	- 794	- 571	- 508	- 660	Balance des services
Net primary income	- 419	- 1 363	- 1 157	- 333	- 1 153	- 552	- 412	- 654	- 804	Revenus primaires nets
Compensation of employees	...	...	...	...	...	...	...	...	...	Rémunération des salariés
Investment income	...	...	...	...	...	...	...	...	...	Revenus des investissements
Net secondary income	318	283	244	330	345	301	227	212	359	Revenus secondaires nets
Net official transfers	...	...	...	...	...	...	...	...	...	Transferts officiels nets
Workers' remittances	...	...	...	...	...	...	...	...	...	Envois de fonds des travailleurs
Other private transfers	...	...	...	...	...	...	...	...	...	Autres transferts privés
Current account balance	714	1 377	958	1 248	- 218	581	- 831	- 954	- 741	Solde du compte courant
Capital and financial account	839	1 714	1 121	1 491	555	665	- 272	- 728	- 698	Comptes de capital et financier
Capital account	237	150	151	223	278	202	81	55	58	Compte de capital
Financial account	601	1 564	970	1 268	277	463	- 353	- 783	- 756	Compte financier
Errors and omissions	- 8	- 27	- 30	- 32	- 30	1	- 24	7	...	Erreurs et omissions
Overall balance	- 342	65	- 109	- 171	247	- 322	432	188	...	Balance générale

ZAMBIE

X DEBT AND FINANCIAL FLOWS - DETTE ET FLUX FINANCIERS

	2009	2010	2011	2012	2013	2014	2015	2016	2017	
X-1 DEBT US $ (MILLIONS)										**X-1 DETTE EXTÉRIEURE** $ E.U (MILLIONS)
Total external debt	3 638	3 202	3 544	4 412	5 640	7 449	15 274	17 202	17 984	Dette extérieure totale
Private	2 250	1 721	1 676	921	1 839	2 186	8 082	9 209	...	Privée
Public	1 387	1 481	1 868	3 491	3 801	5 263	7 193	7 993	...	Publique
Total external debt service	626	299	188	552	325	724	662	733	...	Service de la dette extérieure
Present value of external debt	...	...	...	...	...	...	...	7 315	...	Valeur actuelle de la dette extérieure
Total government domestic debt, National currency (millions)	10	10	12	12	...	...	...	...	...	Dette publique intérieure
X-2 FINANCIAL FLOWS US $ (MILLIONS)										**X-2 FLUX FINANCIERS** $ E.U (MILLIONS)
Net Foreign Direct Investment Inflows	426	634	1 110	1 732	2 100	1 489	1 583	469	...	Investissements étranger direct (flux nets entrants)
Main origin of FDI inflows										**Principales origines de l'IDE entrant:**
United States	17	10	6	15	9	25	...	...	...	États-Unis
Germany	...	...	4	- 2	- 19	-	...	...	...	Allemagne
Luxembourg	3	- 3	- 17	5	10	- 6	...	...	...	Luxembourg
...	...	...	...	...	...	...	...	...	...	...
United Kingdom	- 98	251	112	227	509	551	...	...	...	Royaume-Uni
African countries	13	127	- 73	620	345	278	...	...	...	Pays africains
Net total official development assistance	1 271	919	1 033	957	1 145	998	797	963	...	Aide publique au développement (nette totale)
Main origin of net ODA										**Principales origines de l'APD nette**
United States	232	228	275	303	313	321	267	368	...	États-Unis
International Development Association [IDA]	43	33	72	79	71	79	61	86	...	International Development Association
United Kingdom	74	79	93	84	94	150	77	78	...	Royaume-Uni
Germany	56	33	40	34	36	38	32	27	...	Allemagne
Japan	37	46	46	48	67	50	24	39	...	Japon

SOURCES AND NOTES - SOURCES ET NOTES

External trade - Total exports, fob: UNCTAD

External trade - Total import, cif: UNCTAD

ODA: OECD

Monetary statistics: IMF

National Accounts: 2017:Estimates are provisional

National Account :The Accounts are calculated using the new base year 2010

Poverty: World Bank

Commerce exterieur - Exportation, fab: CNUCED

Commerce exterieur - Imporations, caf: CNUCED

APD: OCDE

Statistiques monétaires: FMI

Comptes nationaux: 2017:Les estimations sont provisoires

Comptes Nationaux : Les Comptes Nationaux Les comptes Annuels sont élaborés selon la nouvelle année de base 2010

Pauvreté: Banque mondiale

	AREA (km2)		390 757		SUPERFICIE (KM2)
	CAPITAL CITY	Harare		Harare	CAPITALE
	CURRENCY	US Dollars		Dollars E.U.	MONNAIE

I SOCIAL AND DEMOGRAPHIC INDICATORS — INDICATEURS DEMOGRAPHIQUES ET SOCIAUX

Population	Year Année	Value Valeur	Charts Graphiques	Population
Population ('000)	2015	10 879.8		Population ('000)
Female (%)	2015	50.1		Féminine (%)
Urban (%)	2015	44.0		Urbaine (%)
Average annual growth rate	2015	2.6		Taux de croissance annuel
Active population ('000)	2015	4 461.5		Population active ('000)
Population by age group ('000)				Population par groupe d'âge ('000)
0-14 years	2016	5 529.8		0-14 ans
15-64 years	2016	8 169.4		15-64 ans
65+ years	2016	540.9		65+ ans
Economically active population in agriculture (%)	2015	37.4		Participation de la population active agricole (%)
Crude birth rate	2015	35.6		Taux brut de natalité
Crude death rate	2015	9.2		Taux brut de mortalité
Total fertility rate	2015	4.7		Indice synthétique de fécondité
Life expectancy at birth - Total (years)	2015	59.8		Espérance de vie à la naissance - Totale (années)
Dependency ratio - Total (%)	2016	74.3		Taux de dépendance - Total (%)
Health				**Santé**
Percentage of children under-five and underweight	2017	10.0		% d'enfants de moins de cinq ans avec insuffisance pondérale
Prevalence of undernourishment	2015	7.5		Prévalence de la malnutrition
Under five mortality rate (per 1 000 live births)	2017	69.0		Taux de mortalité de moins de 5 ans (les deux sexes, pour 1000)
Infant mortality rate (per 1 000 live births)	2017	50.0		Taux de mortalité infantile (les deux sexes) par 1000
Neonatal mortality rate (per 1 000 live births)	2017	29.0		Le taux de mortalité néonatale (pour 1000 naissances vivantes)
Percentage of children provided the vaccines :				Pourcentage d'enfants vaccinés :
BCG	2017	90.0		BCG
DPT3	2017	83.0		DTC3
Polio	2017	82.0		polio
Measles	2017	82.0		rougeole
Percentage of mothers provided at least one antenatal care	2017	93.0		Pourcentage de mères ayant au moins reçu un soin prénatal (%)
Percentage of deliveries attended by skilled health personnel	2017	78.0		% d'accouchements assistés par un personnel de santé qualifié
Number of doctors (per 10,000 population)	2015	1.0		Nombre de médecins (pour 10.000 habitants)
Number of nurses (per 10,000 population)	2015	13.0		Nombre d'infirmiers (pour 10.000 habitants)
Hospital beds - Total (per 10,000 population)	2016	16.0		Nombre de lits d'hôpitaux - Total (pour 10 000)
Births registered (per 1,000)	2017	32.0		Naissances enregistrées (pour 1000)
Deaths registered (per 1,000)	2015	9.2		Décès enregistrés (pour 1000)
Budget allocation to health (%)	2017	8.0		Dépenses publiques consacrées à la santé (% du budget)
Education				**Education**
Enrolment in primary education (000)	2015	2 133.3		Scolarisation dans le primaire (000)
Female	2015	1 010.0		Féminine
Enrolment in secondary education (000)	2015	896.8		Scolarisation dans le secondaire (000)
Female	2015	360.8		Féminine
Enrolment in tertiary education (000)	2014	145.5		Scolarisation dans le tertiaire (000)
Female	2014	39.7		Féminine
Literacy rate	...	...		Taux d'alphabétisation (deux sexes)
Male	...	...		Masculin
Female	...	...		Féminin
Pupil teacher ratio - primary	2013	44.0		Ratio élève-enseignant
Budget allocation to education (%)	2015	22.2		Dépenses publiques consacrées à l'enseignement (% du budget)
Poverty				**Pauvreté**
GNI per capita, PPP (current int. $)	2016	1810.0		RNB par habitant, ($ PPA inter. courants)
Human Poverty Index (HPI-1) Value (%)	2007	34.0		Valeur de l'Indice de pauvreté (IPH-1) (%)
Population below Inter. poverty line ($2/day) (%)	...	...		Population sous le seuil inter. de pauvreté (2$/Jour) (%)
Share of income held by richest 10%	...	...		% de revenu des 10% plus riches
Share of income held by poorest 10%	...	...		% de revenu des 10% plus pauvres
GINI index	...	...		Indice de GINI

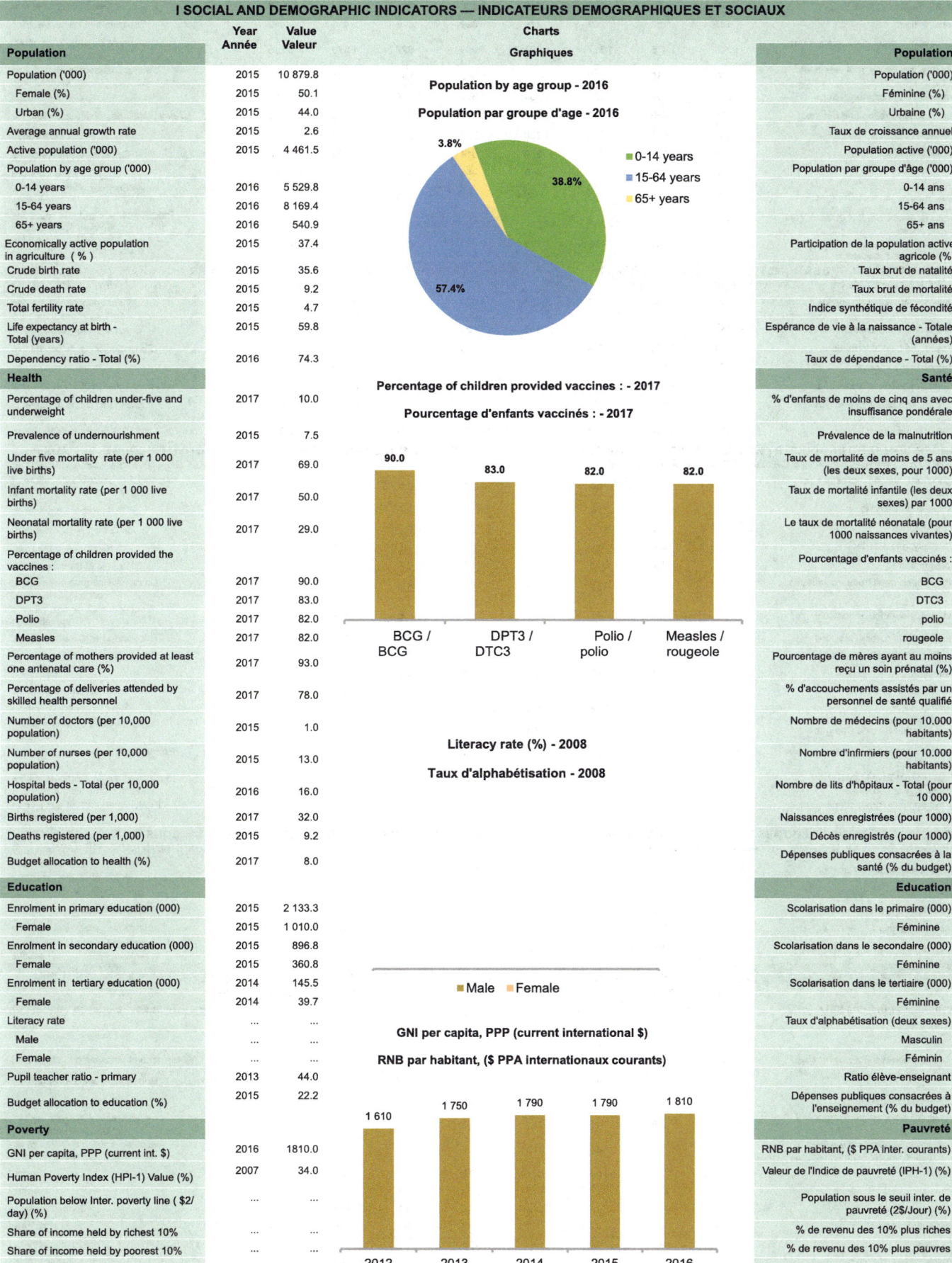

Population by age group - 2016
Population par groupe d'age - 2016

- 0-14 years 38.8%
- 15-64 years 57.4%
- 65+ years 3.8%

Percentage of children provided vaccines : - 2017
Pourcentage d'enfants vaccinés : - 2017

BCG / BCG 90.0 — DPT3 / DTC3 83.0 — Polio / polio 82.0 — Measles / rougeole 82.0

Literacy rate (%) - 2008
Taux d'alphabétisation - 2008

■ Male ■ Female

GNI per capita, PPP (current international $)
RNB par habitant, ($ PPA internationaux courants)

2012 1 610 — 2013 1 750 — 2014 1 790 — 2015 1 790 — 2016 1 810

II NATIONAL ACCOUNTS — COMPTES NATIONAUX

	2009	2010	2011	2012	2013	2014	2015	2016	2017	
GROSS DOMESTIC PRODUCT BY KIND OF ECONOMIC ACTIVITY AT CURRENT PRICES *US DOLLARS (MILLIONS)*										**PRODUIT INTÉRIEUR BRUT PAR BRANCHE D'ACTIVITÉ ÉCONOMIQUE AUX PRIX COURANTS** *DOLLARS E.U. (MILLIONS)*
Agriculture, hunting , forestry and Fishing	1 038	1 157	1 222	1 377	1 364	1 705	1 654	1 618	...	Agriculture, chasse sylviculture et Pêche
Mining and quarrying	561	802	1 006	1 064	1 187	1 157	1 089	1 219	...	Industries extractives
Manufacturing	1 066	1 109	1 293	1 420	1 457	1 450	1 402	1 408	...	Industries manufacturières
Electricity, gas & water	279	359	436	448	492	546	533	287	...	Electricité, gaz et eau
Construction	137	182	289	376	399	426	426	442	...	Bâtiments et travaux publics
Wholesale & retail trade, restaurants, hotels	1 207	1 376	1 397	1 601	1 909	1 927	1 979	2 216	...	Commerce de gros et de détail, restaurants et hôtels
Finance, insurance, real estate, etc.	936	835	923	1 430	1 642	1 335	1 401	1 502	...	Banques, assurances, affaires immobilières
Transport and communications	1 080	1 137	1 320	1 334	1 374	1 478	1 498	1 509	...	Transport(s) et communications
Public administration and defense	324	540	910	1 272	1 301	1 447	1 496	1 613	...	Administrations publiques et défense
Education	301	657	948	1 326	1 524	1 684	1 834	1 890	...	Education
Health And Social Work	69	130	206	279	314	348	395	418	...	Santé et Actions Sociales
Other services	378	428	494	456	443	449	460	528	...	Autres services
Less Imputed Service Charges	- 22	- 36	- 50	- 67	- 77	- 86	- 93	- 102	...	Moins Services d'intermédiation financière
Gross domestic product at factor cost / basic prices	7 354	8 678	10 396	12 317	13 327	13 866	14 074	14 547	...	Produit intérieur brut aux couts des facteurs / prix de base
Plus: Indirect Taxes / taxes on products, less subsidies	1 268	1 464	1 702	1 926	2 125	2 025	2 230	2 073	...	Plus taxes indirectes/impôts sur les produits, moins les subventions
EXPENDITURE ON GROSS DOMESTIC PRODUCT AT CURRENT PURCHASER'S VALUES *US Dollars (Millions)*										**EMPLOI DU PRODUIT INTÉRIEUR BRUT AUX PRIX COURANTS D'ACQUISITION** *DOLLARS E.U. (MILLIONS)*
Government final consumption	913	1 844	2 647	3 424	3 520	3 813	3 769	4 131	...	Consommation finale des administrations publiques
Private final consumption	8 045	7 911	9 983	11 837	13 121	12 788	12 981	12 792	...	Consommation finale privée
Gross fixed capital formation	960	2 048	2 064	2 079	1 753	1 873	1 995	2 015	...	Formation brute de capital fixe
Change in inventories	272	211	390	- 392	5	6	8	11	...	Variation des stocks
Exports of goods and services	1 645	3 290	4 576	4 004	3 862	3 717	3 614	4 098	...	Exportations de biens et services
Less imports of goods and services	3 213	5 162	7 562	6 710	6 809	6 306	6 062	6 427	...	Moins importations de biens et services
GDP at purchasers' values	8 622	10 142	12 098	14 242	15 452	15 891	16 305	16 620	...	PIB aux prix d'acquisition
GROSS DOMESTIC PRODUCT BY KIND OF ECONOMIC ACTIVITY AT CONSTANT PRICES *ANNUAL GROWTH RATES (%)*										**PRODUIT INTÉRIEUR BRUT PAR BRANCHE D'ACTIVITÉ ECONOMIQUE AUX PRIX CONSTANTS** *TAUX DE CROISSANCE ANNUEL (%)*
Agriculture, hunting , forestry and Fishing	...	7.2	1.4	7.8	- 2.5	23.0	- 5.2	- 3.6	...	Agriculture, chasse sylviculture et Pêche
Mining and quarrying	...	37.3	24.4	7.9	11.8	- 3.5	0.4	8.2	...	Industries extractives
Manufacturing	...	2.0	13.9	5.3	- 0.6	- 5.1	0.2	- 4.0	...	Industries manufacturières
Electricity, gas & water	...	19.4	6.3	0.3	5.1	5.4	- 5.6	- 23.5	...	Electricité, gaz et eau
Construction	...	13.9	65.4	23.3	4.1	6.6	4.0	4.9	...	Bâtiments et travaux publics
Wholesale & retail trade, restaurants, hotels	...	8.9	4.3	4.3	3.9	2.5	3.8	7.7	...	Commerce de gros et de détail, restaurants et hôtels
Finance, insurance, real estate, etc.	...	-16.5	3.7	51.3	11.2	- 16.6	6.9	8.4	...	Banques, assurances, affaires immobilières
Transport and communications	...	4.6	18.3	10.9	7.3	3.0	6.2	- 1.3	...	Transport(s) et communications
Public administration and defense	...	38.9	82.9	39.7	0.6	9.1	1.3	7.4	...	Administrations publiques et défense
Education	...	108.0	45.7	33.1	13.8	5.3	- 5.6	0.9	...	Education
Health And Social Work	...	88.4	57.7	33.9	9.2	11.0	11.8	5.9	...	Santé et Actions Sociales
Other services	...	14.3	10.2	- 9.9	- 4.0	- 2.7	- 4.0	13.0	...	Autres services
Less Imputed Service Charges	...	31.8	41.4	9.8	11.1	4.0	11.5	10.3	...	Moins Services d'intermédiation financière
Gross domestic product at factor cost / basic prices	...	12.8	16.0	15.5	5.1	2.0	0.6	2.3	...	Produit intérieur brut aux couts des facteurs / prix de base
Plus: Indirect Taxes / taxes on products, less subsidies	...	11.4	11.9	10.6	8.2	2.9	8.2	- 9.0	...	Plus taxes indirectes/impôts sur les produits, moins les subventions
Gross domestic product at market prices	...	12.6	15.4	14.8	5.5	2.1	1.7	0.6	...	Produit intérieur brut aux prix du marché
EXPENDITURE ON GROSS DOMESTIC PRODUCT AT CONSTANT PURCHASERS' VALUES *ANNUAL GROWTH RATES (%)*										**EMPLOIS DU PRODUIT INTÉRIEUR BRUT AUX PRIX CONSTANTS D'ACQUISITION** *TAUX DE CROISSANCE ANNUEL (%)*
Government final consumption	...	59.1	43.5	2.8	18.8	19.6	13.1	11.4	...	Consommation finale des administrations publiques
Private final consumption	...	4.3	7.2	38.7	- 11.4	- 5.7	7.7	- 12.5	...	Consommation finale privée
Gross fixed capital formation	...	84.3	- 5.7	- 22.2	22.4	12.7	5.6	0.5	...	Formation brute de capital fixe
Exports of goods and services	...	83.9	32.9	- 15.4	- 4.1	- 2.6	- 4.0	8.8	...	Exportations de biens et services
Less imports of goods and services	...	52.8	15.7	4.9	- 17.9	- 5.8	16.9	- 13.0	...	Moins importations de biens et services

III INFLATION

	2009	2010	2011	2012	2013	2014	2015	2016	2017	
Annual growth rates (%)										**Taux de croissance annuel (%)**
All item	11.5	3.0	3.5	3.7	1.6	- 0.2	- 2.4	- 1.6	0.9	Ensemble
of which:										dont:
Food and non-alcoholic beverages	10.6	3.8	4.0	4.6	1.7	- 3.1	- 3.3	- 3.3	2.5	Alimentation et boissons non alcoolisés
Alcoholic beverages, tobacco and narcotics	...	10.6	4.9	6.3	5.2	1.9	0.3	- 1.2	0.3	Boissons alcoolisées et tabacs
Clothing and footwear	3.0	- 6.6	1.6	0.8	- 0.2	- 0.4	- 1.4	- 1.7	- 0.1	Habillement et chaussures
Housing, water, electricity, gas and other fuels	1.8	8.0	4.5	11.8	4.5	0.9	- 2.6	- 2.4	- 1.4	Logement, eau, électricité, gaz et autres combustibles
Furnishings, household equipment and routine household maintenance	3.4	- 5.6	0.9	1.2	...	- 2.1	- 2.2	- 2.9	3.5	Meubles, articles de ménage et entretien courant
Health	4.7	0.5	- 0.3	1.6	2.8	0.7	0.7	- 0.1	0.2	Santé
Transport	1.9	4.7	7.5	1.9	5.3	0.7	- 1.5	- 2.3	- 0.7	Transport
Communication	- 0.1	- 4.7	1.6	7.8	- 10.2	- 4.1	- 13.9	- 1.7	- 0.2	Communication
Recreation and culture	3.5	- 2.0	0.2	0.6	- 0.5	- 0.8	- 0.9	- 0.8	1.8	Loisirs et culture
Education	3.5	4.9	4.0	9.3	10.3	16.0	0.2	10.4	- 0.6	Enseignement
Restaurants and hotels	8.4	9.6	5.0	6.1	1.6	0.8	- 1.0	-	1.4	Restaurants et hôtels
Miscellaneous goods and services	9.4	- 0.8	4.5	2.8	0.8	- 2.0	- 1.0	- 1.8	2.3	Biens et Services divers

IV AGRICULTURAL PRODUCTION - PRODUCTION AGRICOLE

	2009	2010	2011	2012	2013	2014	2015	2016	2017	
TONNES (THOUSAND)										**Tonnes (milliers)**
Sugar cane	2 338	2 692	3 058	3 929	3 960	3 856	3 348	3 483	...	Canne à sucre
Maize	700	1 192	1 010	1 096	939	975	643	853	...	Maïs
	...	...	...	...	...	...	...	...	...	
Cottonseed	236	150	140	248	141	75	43	110	...	Graines de coton
Groundnuts, with shell	137	98	72	68	57	52	...	...	...	Arachides (en coques)

V MINING PRODUCTION - PRODUCTION MINIERE

	2009	2010	2011	2012	2013	2014	2015	2016	2017	
Hard Coal - Production, metric tons (thousands)	5	10	13	15	14	15	20	23	26	Houille - Production, tonnes métriques (milliers)
	...	...	...	...	...	...	...	...	...	
	...	...	...	...	...	...	...	...	...	

VI ENERGY - ENERGIE

	2009	2010	2011	2012	2013	2014	2015	2016	2017	
Total electricity generation (GWh)	6 646	8 473	9 019	8 963	9 315	9 783	9 482	...	...	Production électrique totale (GWh)
of which										dont
Production of electricity from fossil fuels (GWh)	1 569	2 710	3 817	3 575	4 333	4 381	4 529	...	...	Production d'électricité à partir de combustibles fossiles (GWh)
Production of hydro electricity (GWh)	5 077	5 763	5 202	5 387	4 982	5 402	4 939	...	...	Production d'électricité d'origine hydraulique (GWh)
Production of electricity from solar, wind, tide, wave and other sources (GWh)	...	...	4	4	4	5	14	...	...	Production d'électricité d'origine solaire, éolienne, marée motrice et autres (GWh)

VII TOURISM AND INFRASTRUCTURE - TOURISME ET INFRASTUCTURE

	2009	2010	2011	2012	2013	2014	2015	2016	2017	
VII-1 Tourism										**VII-1 Tourisme**
International tourist arrivals (thousands)	1 881	2 089	2 260	1 673	1 728	1 890	2 052	2 163	2 294	Arrivées de touristes internationaux (milliers)
Rooms in hotels and similar establishments (thousands)	5	8	6	6	6	6	6	6	...	Chambres d'hôtels et établissements assimilés (milliers)
Overnight stays (thousands)	301	288	325	352	281	258	360	308	319	Nuitées (milliers)
Tourism receipts (US$ thousand)	116 088	121 301	150 115	159 884	168 741	170 897	173 154	175 630	194 141	Recettes touristiques (milliers de $ EU)
Total contribution to GDP (%)	9.4	6.8	7.3	6.9	7.2	7.0	7.2	7.3	7.1	Contribution totale au PIB (%)
Total contribution to Employment (%)	7.9	5.5	5.8	5.4	5.4	4.9	4.8	4.7	4.4	Contribution totale à l'emploi (%)
VII-2 Infrastructure										**VII-2 Infrastructure**
Paved road (% of total)	...	...	...	...	...	...	...	...	...	Routes asphaltées (% du total)
Total network (Railways-km)	351	351	351	351	...	...	...	...	...	Réseau total voies ferrées-Km
Main telephone lines (per 100 inhabitants)	3.0	2.9	2.7	2.2	2.1	2.3	2.2	2.0	...	Lignes téléphoniques fixes (pour 100 habitants)
Mobile cellular subscribers (per 100 inhabitants)	31.0	58.9	68.9	91.9	96.3	80.8	84.8	83.2	...	Abonnés aux téléphones mobiles (pour 100 habitants)
Internet users per 100 inhabitants	4.0	6.4	8.4	12.0	15.5	16.4	22.7	23.1	...	Utilisateurs Internet par 100 Habitants
Fixed (wired)-broadband subscriptions per 100 inhabitants	...	...	...	0.5	0.7	1.0	1.1	1.1	...	Abonnements à l'Internet fixe (filaire) à large bande pour 100 habitants, par débit

VIII EXTERNAL TRADE - COMMERCE EXTERIEUR

	2009	2010	2011	2012	2013	2014	2015	2016	2017	
US$ (MILLIONS) **EXPORTS, FOB**										**$ E.U (MILLIONS)** **EXPORTATIONS, FÀB**
Exports - Total	2 269	3 199	3 512	3 882	3 507	3 064	2 704	2 832	...	Exportations - Total
Exports to Africa	1 201	1 589	1 782	1 978	1 875	1 474	1 439	1 609	...	Exportations vers l'Afrique
Main products										**Principaux produits**
Gold, non-monetary (excluding gold ores and concentrates)	100	425	251	437	236	316	363	506	...	Or, non monétaire (à l'exclusion des minerais d'or et des concentrés)
Nickel ores & concentrates; nickel mattes, etc.	198	266	460	244	289	166	233	357	...	Minerais de nickel et concentrés; mattes de nickel, etc.
Pearls, precious & semi-precious stones	28	150	305	374	298	301	100	93	...	Perles, pierres précieuses et semi-précieuses
Pig iron & spiegeleisen, sponge iron, powder & granu	118	283	235	231	195	298	219	144	...	Fonte de fer et spiegeleisen, fer d'éponge, poudre et granu
Tobacco, unmanufactured; tobacco refuse	328	488	708	783	991	917	888	939	...	Tabac, non manufacturé; déchets de tabac
Main destinations										**Principales destinations**
China	150	349	421	471	491	552	501	511	...	Chine
Mozambique	72	68	87	183	231	301	257	169	...	Mozambique
South Africa	807	1 135	1 374	1 498	1 344	934	954	1 233	...	Afrique du Sud
United Arab Emirates	25	287	366	612	362	246	189	168	...	Emirates Arabes
Zambia	100	106	104	116	137	111	101	82	...	Zambie
IMPORTS, CIF										
Imports - Total	2 900	3 800	4 400	4 400	4 300	4 200	4 000	3 700	...	Importations - Total (millions)
Imports from Africa	2 309	2 825	3 190	3 170	3 097	2 988	2 722	2 703	...	Importations en provenance de l'Afrique
Main products										**Principaux produits**
Fertilizers (other than those of group 272)	61	106	340	103	253	123	122	70	...	Engrais (autres que ceux du groupe 272)
Maize (not including sweet corn), unmilled	108	75	242	326	165	131	316	344	...	Maïs (à l'exclusion du maïs sucré), non moulu
Motor vehic. for transport of goods, special purpo.	157	142	149	164	142	151	138	98	...	Véhicule à moteur pour le transport de marchandises, spécial.
Petroleum oils or bituminous minerals > 70 % oil	261	392	358	312	291	282	264	248	...	Huiles de pétrole ou de minéraux bitumineux> 70 % d'huile
Telecommunication equipment, n.e.s.; & parts, n.e.s.	74	114	106	137	89	99	131	88	...	Matériel de télécommunication, n.e.s .; & parties, n.e.s.
Main origin										**Principales provenances**
China	113	225	280	295	289	289	394	286	...	Chine
India	29	61	110	102	139	152	188	96	...	Inde
South Africa	1 577	1 988	2 264	2 184	2 196	2 124	1 834	1 893	...	Afrique du Sud
United Kingdom	36	55	98	155	147	79	67	43	...	Royaume-Uni
Zambia	396	427	484	593	530	472	544	459	...	Zambie

ZIMBABWE

ZIMBABWE

IX FINANCIAL AND MONETARY STATISTICS - FINANCES ET STATISTIQUES MONETAIRES

	2009	2010	2011	2012	2013	2014	2015	2016	2017	
IX-1 MONETARY STATISTICS *US DOLLARS (MILLIONS)*										**IX-1 STATISTIQUES MONÉTAIRES** *DOLLARS E.U. (MILLIONS)*
Money supply (M1)	1 381	2 329	3 100	3 719	3 888	4 377	4 736	5 637	6 230	Masse monétaire (M1)
Quasi-money	...	...	...	...	...	...	...	...	...	Quasi-monnaie
of which demand deposit	...	...	...	...	...	...	...	...	...	dont Monnaie scripturale
Net foreign assets	...	...	...	...	...	...	...	...	...	Avoirs extérieurs nets
Domestic credit	...	...	...	...	...	...	...	...	...	Crédit intérieur
of which claims on private sector	...	...	...	...	...	...	...	...	...	dont créances sur le secteur privé
of which claims on government sector, net	...	...	...	...	...	...	...	...	...	dont créances nettes sur le gouvernement
International reserves (millions US$)	437	453	366	398	284	303	339	310	221	Réserves internationales (millions $EU)
Average exchange rate (National currency per US$)	1	1	1	1	1	1	1	1	1	Taux de change (moyen) (monnaie nationale par $ EU)
IX-2 PUBLIC FINANCE *US DOLLARS (MILLIONS)*										**IX-2 FINANCES PUBLIQUES** *DOLLARS E.U. (MILLIONS)*
Total Revenues and Grants	975	2 199	2 921	3 496	3 741	3 770	3 900	3 502	3 714	Recettes totales et dons
Direct taxes (on income, profits)	200	684	884	1 105	1 149	1 265	1 234	1 074	1 111	Taxes directes
Domestic indirect taxes revenues	435	854	1 218	1 480	1 579	1 490	1 673	1 605	1 753	Taxes Indirectes
Trade taxes	212	340	333	354	361	351	391	273	280	Taxes sur le commerce extérieur
Other taxes	35	196	225	340	326	413	449	285	294	Autres taxes
Other revenues	51	124	261	217	327	251	154	265	275	Autres recettes
Grants	41	1	...	...	...	...	...	...	...	Dons
Total Expenditures and Net Lending	1 144	2 132	2 987	3 492	3 994	3 988	4 059	4 863	4 595	Dépenses totales et prêts nets
Current expenditure	901	1 603	2 516	3 186	3 466	3 518	3 579	3 877	3 822	Dépenses courantes
Wages and Salaries	409	758	1 269	1 732	1 926	2 106	2 300	2 278	2 231	Rémunérations et salaires
Other purchases of goods and services	260	362	504	505	359	322	305	370	446	Achat de biens et services
Other current expenditure	133	295	468	548	763	613	496	751	667	Autres dépenses courantes
Current transfers	98	188	275	402	418	477	478	478	478	Transferts courants
Interest payments	198	113	39	40	116	136	165	127	191	Intérêts
Capital expenditure	45	415	431	266	411	333	315	859	582	Dépenses d'équipement
Net lending	...	...	...	...	...	...	...	...	...	Prêts nets
Fiscal balance	- 169	67	- 66	4	- 253	- 218	- 158	- 1 361	- 881	Solde global y compris les dons
IX-3 BALANCE OF PAYMENTS *US DOLLARS (MILLIONS)*										**IX-3 BALANCE DES PAIEMENTS** *DOLLARS E.U. (MILLIONS)*
Trade balance	- 2 206	- 2 871	- 4 365	- 4 050	- 4 403	- 4 107	- 3 503	- 2 329	...	Balance commerciale
Services Balance	- 687	- 1 071	- 1 477	- 1 435	- 1 541	- 1 590	- 1 137	- 867	...	Balance des services
Net primary income	- 284	- 547	- 901	- 963	- 1 034	- 888	- 639	...	...	Revenus primaires nets
Compensation of employees	...	...	...	...	...	...	...	...	...	Rémunération des salariés
Investment income	...	...	...	...	...	...	...	...	...	Revenus des investissements
Net secondary income	926	1 194	1 538	1 679	1 635	1 663	1 828	...	...	Revenus secondaires nets
Net official transfers	...	...	...	...	...	...	...	...	...	Transferts officiels nets
Workers' remittances	555	662	1 029	1 164	1 104	1 166	1 253	1 103	...	Envois de fonds des travailleurs
Other private transfers	...	...	...	...	...	...	...	...	...	Autres transferts privés
Current account balance	941	- 1 444	- 2 432	- 1 836	- 2 526	- 2 254	- 1 521	- 553	...	Solde du compte courant
Capital and financial account	31	- 238	- 415	- 271	- 1 104	- 1 431	- 616	- 302	...	Comptes de capital et financier
Capital account	391	231	346	738	251	369	398	242	...	Compte de capital
Financial account	- 360	- 469	- 761	- 1 008	- 1 355	- 1 800	- 1 014	- 545	...	Compte financier
Errors and omissions	- 190	- 743	- 1 326	- 90	- 920	- 85	- 108	234	...	Erreurs et omissions
Overall balance	- 1 867	- 408	- 783	- 435	- 195	- 40	- 142	...	...	Balance générale

X DEBT AND FINANCIAL FLOWS - DETTE ET FLUX FINANCIERS										
	2009	2010	2011	2012	2013	2014	2015	2016	2017	
X-1 DEBT *US $ (MILLIONS)*										**X-1 DETTE EXTÉRIEURE** *$ E.U (MILLIONS)*
Total external debt	7 616	7 122	7 532	8 226	9 228	10 148	10 917	10 760	9 461	Dette extérieure totale
Private	...	...	...	...	...	...	...	...	...	Privée
Public	5 422	5 880	5 713	6 033	6 274	6 263	6 530	6 788	...	Publique
Total external debt service	...	...	...	...	...	...	...	...	...	Service de la dette extérieure
Present value of external debt	...	...	...	...	...	...	...	4 962	...	Valeur actuelle de la dette extérieure
Total government domestic debt, National currency (millions)	...	...	...	...	...	...	...	...	...	Dette publique intérieure
X-2 FINANCIAL FLOWS *US $ (MILLIONS)*										**X-2 FLUX FINANCIERS** *$ E.U (MILLIONS)*
Net Foreign Direct Investment Inflows	105	166	387	400	400	545	421	319	...	Investissements étranger direct (flux nets entrants)
Main origin of FDI inflows										**Principales origines de l'IDE entrant:**
...	...	...	...	...	...	...	...	...	...	...
Italy	10	8	14	- 22	...	...	...	...	...	Italie
...	...	...	...	...	...	...	...	...	...	...
Germany	1	...	...	...	...	...	...	...	...	Allemagne
Germany	1	...	...	...	...	...	...	...	...	Allemagne
African countries	...	...	...	...	...	...	...	...	...	Pays africains
Net total official development assistance	737	713	723	1 002	828	761	788	655	...	Aide publique au développement (nette totale)
Main origin of net ODA										**Principales origines de l'APD nette**
United States	250	155	187	172	169	178	154	217	...	États-Unis
United Kingdom	110	108	78	220	147	171	142	135	...	Royaume-Uni
Germany	35	33	59	57	32	36	28	36	...	Allemagne
Sweden	29	30	39	40	37	35	29	29	...	Suède
Japan	12	19	18	22	12	5	7	15	...	Japon

ZIMBABWE

SOURCES AND NOTES - SOURCES ET NOTES

External trade - Total exports, fob: UNCTAD

External trade - Total import, cif: UNCTAD

ODA: OECD

Monetary statistics: IMF

National Accounts: 2016 Projection

National Accounts:All figures in monetary values are in Zimbabwean Dollars (Z$) for the period 2000 - 2008. For 2009 and beyond, monetary values are in United States Dollars (US$).

Poverty: World Bank

Commerce exterieur - Exportation, fab: CNUCED

Commerce exterieur - Imporations, caf: CNUCED

APD: OCDE

Statistiques monétaires: FMI

Comptes nationaux: 2016 Projection

Comptes Nationaux : Les données sont exprimées en $ EU à partir de 2009

Pauvreté: Banque mondiale